W9-BHT-583

ASP.NET AJAX Programmer's Reference with ASP.NET 2.0 or ASP.NET 3.5

Acknowledgments xi

Introduction xxix

Chapter 1: AJAX Technologies 1

Chapter 2: JavaScript Base Type Extensions. 27

Chapter 3: Built-In and Custom Exception Types. 53

Chapter 4: JavaScript Object-Oriented Programming and
Type Reflection Extensions 77

Chapter 5: Event Programming Extensions 131

Chapter 6: DOM Extensions 161

Chapter 7: Component Development Infrastructure. 219

Chapter 8: Developing Client Controls 281

Chapter 9: Event Bubbling and Button Client Control 323

Chapter 10: Type Description Extensions 349

Chapter 11: Data Classes 407

Chapter 12: Client-Server Communications. 457

Chapter 13: Consuming Web Services Via Soap Messages 511

Chapter 14: Consuming Web Services Via JSON Messages 535

Chapter 15: Proxy Classes. 597

Chapter 16: Behaviors. 659

Chapter 17: Script and Extender Server Controls 707

Chapter 18: Web Services Bridges and Transformers 773

Chapter 19: UpdatePanel and ScriptManager 857

Chapter 20: Using UpdatePanel in User Controls and Custom Controls . . . 911

Chapter 21: Page Life Cycle and Asynchronous Partial Page Rendering. . . 965

Chapter 22: ASP.NET AJAX Client-Side PageRequestManager 1033

Continues

Chapter 23: Asynchronous Partial Page Rendering:
Server Side Processing **1105**

Chapter 24: Asynchronous Partial Page Rendering:
Client-Side Processing **1179**

Appendix A: XML Script **1275**

Appendix B: Binding **1325**

Appendix C: Actions **1341**

Appendix D: Data Control **1357**

Appendix E: Templated Controls **1381**

Appendix F: ListView **1409**

Index **1481**

ASP.NET AJAX Programmer's Reference with ASP.NET 2.0 or ASP.NET 3.5

ASP.NET AJAX Programmer's Reference with ASP.NET 2.0 or ASP.NET 3.5

Dr. Shahram Khosravi

Wiley Publishing, Inc.

ASP.NET AJAX Programmer's Reference with ASP.NET 2.0 or ASP.NET 3.5

Published by
Wiley Publishing, Inc.
10475 Crosspoint Boulevard
Indianapolis, IN 46256
www.wiley.com

Published simultaneously in Canada

ISBN: 978-0-470-10998-4

Manufactured in the United States of America

10 9 8 7 6 5 4 3 2 1

For general information on our other products and services or to obtain technical support, please contact our Customer Care Department within the U.S. at (800) 762-2974, outside the U.S. at (317) 572-3993 or fax (317) 572-4002.

Library of Congress Cataloging-in-Publication Data:

Khosravi, Shahram, 1963-
    ASP.NET Ajax programmer's reference / Shahram Khosravi.
        p. cm.
    Includes index.
    ISBN 978-0-470-10998-4 (paper/website)
 1. Active server pages. 2. Internet programming. 3. Web site development.
4. Ajax (Web site development technology) 5. Microsoft .NET. I. Title.
    TK5105.8885.A26K538 2007

 005.2'76--dc22

                                                                2007024239

About the Author

Shahram Khosravi, Ph.D., is a senior software engineer, consultant, author, and instructor specializing in ASP.NET, Windows Communications Foundation (WCF), ASP.NET AJAX, Windows Workflow Foundation (WF), IIS7 and ASP.NET Integrated Programming, ADO.NET, Web services, .NET, and XML technologies such as XSD, XSLT, XPath, SOAP, and WSDL. He also has years of experience in object-oriented analysis, design, and programming, architectural and design patterns, service-oriented analysis, design, and programming, 3D computer graphics programming, user interface design, and usability.

Shahram is the author of the following four books: *Professional ASP.NET 3.5 and .NET 3.5 Programming (ASP.NET Internals plus ASP.NET AJAX, IIS 7.0, Enterprise Library Application Blocks, Windows Workflow Foundation, and Windows Communication Foundation), ASP.NET AJAX Programmer's Reference with ASP. NET 2.0 or ASP.NET 3.5, Professional IIS7 and ASP.NET Integrated Programming*, and *Professional ASP.NET Server Control and Component Development*. He has written articles on the ASP.NET, ADO.NET, .NET, and XML technologies for the industry's leading magazines, such as *Dr. Dobb's Journal, asp.netPRO* magazine, and *Microsoft MSDN Online*.

Credits

Senior Acquisitions Editor
Jim Minatel

Development Editor
Brian MacDonald

Technical Editors
Alexei Gorkov
Darren J. Kindberg
Sam Judson
Dan Maharry
Cody Reichenau

Production Editor
Eric Charbonneau

Copy Editors
Kathryn Duggan
S. B. Kleinman

Editorial Manager
Mary Beth Wakefield

Production Manager
Tim Tate

Vice President and Executive Group Publisher
Richard Swadley

Vice President and Executive Publisher
Joseph B. Wikert

Project Coordinator, Cover
Adrienne Martinez

Proofreader
Ian Golder

Indexer
Jack Lewis

Anniversary Logo Design
Richard Pacifico

Acknowledgments

First and foremost, I would like to greatly thank Jim Minatel, the senior acquisitions editor on the book, for giving me the opportunity to work on this exciting project and for all his support and guidance throughout the process. Huge thanks go to Brian MacDonald, the book's development editor. I greatly appreciate all your input, comments, and advice. Thanks, Brian, for everything! Special thanks go to the book's technical editors; Alexei Gorkov, Darren J. Kindberg, Sam Judson, Dan Maharry and Cody Reichenau. Thank you gentlemen, for all your input and comments.

Additional thanks go to Eric Charbonneau, the book's production editor. Thanks also go to Kathi Duggan and S.B. Kleinman, the copy editors; as well as Ian Golder, the proofreader.

Contents

Acknowledgments   **xi**

Introduction   **xxix**

Chapter 1: AJAX Technologies   1

Google Suggest   **1**

XMLHttpRequest   **4**

XML   **16**

JSON   **20**

object   20

array   20

string   20

number   21

null, true, and false   21

ASP.NET AJAX   **24**

Installing the ASP.NET AJAX Extensions and ASP.NET Futures   **25**

Summary   **25**

Chapter 2: JavaScript Base Type Extensions   27

ASP.NET AJAX Array Type Extensions   **28**

add   28

addRange   29

clear   29

clone   30

contains   30

enqueue and dequeue   31

forEach   33

indexOf   34

insert   35

parse   36

remove   36

removeAt   37

ASP.NET AJAX Boolean Type Extensions   **37**

ASP.NET AJAX Date Type Extensions   **38**

ASP.NET AJAX Object Type Extensions   **38**

Contents

ASP.NET AJAX String Type Extensions   **39**

     endsWith   39

     startsWith   40

     trim   40

     Formatting   41

ASP.NET AJAX Error Type Extensions   **41**

     create   41

     popStackFrame   45

     Under the Hood of popStackFrame   48

Summary   **52**

Chapter 3: Built-In and Custom Exception Types   **53**

ASP.NET AJAX Built-In Exception Types   **53**

     ArgumentException   53

     ArgumentNullException   56

     ArgumentOutOfRangeException   58

     ArgumentTypeException   60

     ArgumentUndefinedException   64

     InvalidOperationException   66

     NotImplementedException   66

     ParameterCountException   68

Implementing Custom Exception Types   **70**

     Recipe for Implementing Custom Exception Types   70

     Using the Recipe   71

Summary   **76**

Chapter 4: JavaScript Object-Oriented Programming and Type Reflection Extensions   **77**

JavaScript Functions   **78**

JavaScript Classes   **79**

Type   **80**

registerClass   **81**

getName   **83**

isClass   **84**

registerNamespace   **85**

isNamespace   **88**

registerInterface   **89**

getInterfaces   **92**

isInterface   **95**

Inheritance   **96**

getBaseType	**100**
initializeBase	**102**
resolveInheritance	**103**
callBaseMethod	**104**
getBaseMethod	**110**
implementsInterface	**113**
inheritsFrom	**118**
isImplementedBy	**121**
getRootNamespaces	**123**
parse	**125**
registerEnum	**127**
isEnum	**129**
isFlags	**129**
Summary	**130**
Chapter 5: Event Programming Extensions	**131**
Event Programming	**131**
Sys.EventArgs	132
Sys.CancelEventArgs	132
EventHandlerList	133
Using Event Programming	**138**
Base Classes	138
Events	144
Summary	**159**
Chapter 6: DOM Extensions	**161**
DomElement	**161**
getElementById	161
addCssClass	166
containsCssClass	167
removeCssClass	167
toggleCssClass	169
getLocation	171
setLocation	172
getBounds	175
MouseButton	**176**
Key	**176**
Delegates	**177**
Namespace	183
Mover	184

Contents

TextProvider 184

ImageProvider 185

DomEvent **185**

Constructor **186**

Static Methods 189

Instance Methods 198

Using the DomEvent Class **203**

Mover 209

TableProvider 216

Summary **217**

Chapter 7: Component Development Infrastructure 219

Interfaces **220**

IDisposable 220

INotifyDisposing 224

INotifyPropertyChanged 228

Component **235**

IContainer **238**

Application **239**

addComponent 240

removeComponent 241

getComponents 242

findComponent 242

Application Lifecycle **243**

Component **248**

Continuing the Application Journey **253**

endCreateComponents 253

raiseLoad 256

Summary of the Application Lifecycle 257

Application Level Events **258**

init 258

load 259

unload 260

Disposable Objects **260**

Using the Application Object and Component Base Class **263**

dispose 264

initialize 267

id 269

raisePropertyChanged 270

get_events 271

INotifyPropertyChange   272
INotifyDisposing   272
Summary   **280**

Chapter 8: Developing Client Controls   **281**

Control   **281**
Definition   281
get_element   283
get_id   283
set_id   284
set_parent   284
get_parent   285
get_visibilityMode   286
get_visible   286
set_visibilityMode   286
set_visible   287
addCssClass   288
removeCssClass   288
toggleCssClass   288
dispose   288
onBubbleEvent   289
raiseBubbleEvent   290
Developing Custom Client Controls   **290**
Label Client Control   **291**
Constructor   291
htmlEncode   291
text   292
prototype   294
descriptor   294
Using Label Client Control   **295**
Image Client Control   **297**
Constructor   298
prototype   298
imageURI   299
width   299
height   299
alternateText   300
Using the Image Client Control   **300**
Extending Image Client Control   **302**
Constructor   306
prototype   307

Contents

imageURL 307

mouseOverImageURL 308

mouseOverCallback 308

mouseOutCallback 309

Duration 309

transition 310

Transition Enumeration 310

initialize 311

dispose 312

Using Image2 Client Control **312**

HyperLink Client Control **314**

Constructor 314

prototype 315

navigateURL 315

initialize 315

add_click 316

remove_click 317

_onClick 317

dispose 318

descriptor 318

Using the HyperLink Client Control **319**

Summary **321**

Chapter 9: Event Bubbling and Button Client Control **323**

CommandEventArgs **323**

Button Client Control **325**

Constructor 325

prototype 325

argument 326

command 326

initialize 327

add_click 328

_onClick 328

dispose 329

descriptor 330

Using Button Client Control **330**

Catching a Bubbled Event 330

Bubbling an Event 337

Summary **348**

Chapter 10: Type Description Extensions   349

TypeDescriptor   350
Constructor   350
getTypeDescriptor   369
getProperty   374
getAttribute   376
setProperty   377
invokeMethod   382
getPropertyType   384
Using the ASP.NET AJAX Type Description Capabilities   385
StringBuilder   385
CustomTable   389
Dynamic Injection of Metadata Information   399
addProperty   400
addMethod   401
addEvent   402
addAttribute   403
ICustomTypeDescriptor   403
Summary   405

Chapter 11: Data Classes   407

IData   407
DataColumn   409
DataRow   412
Constructor   412
descriptor   413
ICustomTypeDescriptor   414
Owner   419
INotifyPropertyChange   420
DataTable   422
Constructor   422
IData   424
Descriptor   432
INotifyPropertyChange   434
INotifyCollectionChanged   436
createRow   439
getChanges   441
getColumn   442
raiseRowChanged   443
parseFromJson   443

Contents

Using DataColumn, DataRow, and DataTable	**446**
Summary	**456**

Chapter 12: Client-Server Communications	**457**

WebRequest	**457**
Constructor	457
Target URL	458
HTTP Verb	458
Body	459
Timeout	459
Web Request Executor	460
Headers	460
Completed Event	461
Invoking a Web Request	462
WebRequestExecutor	**463**
Constructor	463
WebRequest	463
get_started	464
get_responseAvailable	464
get_timedOut	465
get_aborted	465
get_responseData	465
get_statusCode	466
get_statusText	466
get_xml	466
get_object	466
executeRequest	467
abort	467
getResponseHeader	467
getAllResponseHeaders	468
WebRequestManager	**468**
Constructor	468
Default Timeout	469
Default Executor Type	469
Events	470
Executing a Web Request	471
NetworkRequestEventArgs	473
XMLHttpRequest	**474**
XMLDOM	**474**
XMLHttpExecutor	**475**
Constructor	475
get_timedOut	479

get_started 479

get_responseAvailable 479

get_aborted 479

Executing the Request 480

getResponseHeader 482

getAllResponseHeaders 483

get_responseData 484

get_statusCode 484

get_statusText 484

get_xml 485

abort 486

Using WebRequest, WebRequestManager, and XMLHttpExecutor **487**

Summary **510**

Chapter 13: Consuming Web Services Via Soap Messages **511**

Building the Web Service **511**

WSDL Documents **512**

Argument Names, Types, and Order 514

Return Value Types and Order 515

Describing the Method 515

Describing the Communication Protocol for Accessing the Method 516

Specifying the Site for Method Access 517

Specifying the Method Class 518

SOAP Messages **518**

Summary **533**

Chapter 14: Consuming Web Services Via JSON Messages **535**

WebServiceProxy **535**

Timeout 535

Default Succeeded Callback 536

Default Failed Callback 536

Path 537

Invoking a Web Method 537

Using WebServiceProxy **549**

WebServiceError **553**

Using WebServiceError **557**

Calling Page Methods **561**

Calling Custom Methods **564**

Under the Hood **570**

ScriptHandlerFactory 571

RestHandlerFactory 574

Contents

RestHandler   577
HandlerWrapper   582
Page Methods Demystified   583
Web Services Bridges Demystified   590
Using the Replicas   593
Summary   **595**

Chapter 15: Proxy Classes   **597**

What's a Proxy, Anyway?   **597**
Proxy Class   **599**
Proxy Classes Associated with Web Services   600
Proxy Classes Associated with Page Methods   605
Proxy Classes Associated with Custom Classes   608
Automatic Proxy Class Generation   **608**
Declarative Approach   608
Imperative Approach   618
Parent/Child Pages   621
Under the Hood   **623**
ScriptManager   624
ServiceReference   627
ClientProxyGenerator   630
RestClientProxyHandler   648
Using the Replicas   **650**
Summary   **658**

Chapter 16: Behaviors   **659**

What is a Behavior, Anyway?   **659**
The Behavior Class   **661**
Properties   668
Instance Methods   672
Static Methods   674
ClickBehavior   **675**
descriptor   676
The click Event   677
initialize   677
Using the ClickBehavior   678
The ASP.NET AJAX Control Toolkit   **680**
BehaviorBase   681
The TextBoxWatermarkBehavior   687
Summary   **706**

Chapter 17: Script and Extender Server Controls   707

Why You Need Script and Extender Server Controls	**707**
Extender Server Controls	**709**
IExtenderControl	709
ExtenderControl	710
Script Server Controls	**713**
IScriptControl	713
ScriptControl	714
ScriptDescriptor	**716**
ScriptComponentDescriptor	717
ScriptControlDescriptor	730
ScriptBehaviorDescriptor	731
ScriptReference	**733**
ScriptReferenceCollection	**735**
ScriptManager	**735**
Scripts	741
LoadScriptsBeforeUI	741
ScriptControls	741
RegisterScriptControl	741
ExtenderControls	742
RegisterExtenderControl	742
GetCurrent	742
OnInit	742
Page_PreRenderComplete	743
CollectScripts	744
AddScriptReferencesForScriptControls	745
RegisterScriptDescriptors For Extender Controls	746
ResolveScriptReference Event	**747**
Putting it All Together	**750**
Developing a Custom Extender Server Control	**751**
WatermarkText	755
WatermarkCssClass	755
ClientState	755
ClientStateFieldID	756
CreateClientStateField	756
BehaviorID	756
GetScriptReferences	756
GetScriptDescriptors	756
OnInit	758
Page_PreLoad	759
OnLoad	759

Contents

OnPreRender   761
Render   763
Using the Extender Server Control   763
Developing a Script Control   **764**
PreRender   768
Render   769
Using the Script Server Control   769
Script Server Controls versus Extender Server Controls   **770**
Summary   **771**

Chapter 18: Web Services Bridges and Transformers   **773**

Amazon Web Services   **773**
ItemSearch   774
Developing Web Services Bridge-Enabled Script Server Controls   **781**
AspNetAjaxAmazonSearch   781
AmazonSearchScriptControl   789
HtmlGenerator   798
HtmlGeneratorScriptControl   803
Using the Components   811
Transformers   **813**
Using Transformers   **823**
XmlBridgeTransformer   823
XsltBridgeTransformer   848
Summary   **855**

Chapter 19: UpdatePanel and ScriptManager   **857**

Enabling Asynchronous Partial Page Rendering   **857**
Conditional Updates   **860**
Children as Triggers   863
Inclusion of One UpdatePanel in another UpdatePanel   864
Using Triggers   877
Imperative Update   878
Developing Partial-Rendering Enabled Custom Composite Server Controls   **881**
BaseMasterDetailControl   882
BaseMasterDetailControl2   906
Summary   **910**

Chapter 20: Using UpdatePanel in User Controls and Custom Controls   911

MasterDetailControl   **911**
CreateBaseDataBoundControlMaster   913
RegisterMasterEventHandlers   914
Properties   916
Using MasterDetailControl in a Web Page   **916**
MasterDetailControl2   **921**
CreateBaseDataBoundControlMaster   923
RegisterMasterEventHandlers   923
Master_SelectedIndexChanged   923
Master_DataBound   923
Properties   924
Using MasterDetailControl2   **924**
MasterDetailControl3   **927**
Using MasterDetailControl3   **928**
MasterDetailControl4   **930**
Developing Partial-Rendering-Enabled Data Control Fields   **931**
Extending BoundField   932
Overriding InitializeDataCell   937
Handling the DataBound Event   938
Extracting Values from Cells   939
Appearance Properties   939
Using MasterDetailField   940
Developing Partial-Rendering-Enabled User Controls   **945**
Displaying all Messages   957
Displaying the Details of a Message   958
Deleting a Message   959
Updating a Message   960
Replying to a Message   961
Starting a New Thread   963
Summary   **964**

Chapter 21: Page Life Cycle and Asynchronous Partial Page Rendering   965

Processing a Request   **966**
The Page Life Cycle   **969**
The First Visit to a Partial-Page-Rendering-Enabled Web Page   **971**
InitRecursive   **971**
The OnInit Method of ScriptManager   972
The OnInit Method of UpdatePanel   980
Templated Controls   987

Contents

LoadRecursive **995**
The Initialize Method of the UpdatePanel 998
Rendering **1019**
The Render Method of ScriptManager 1020
The Render Method of the UpdatePanel 1028
Summary **1029**

Chapter 22: ASP.NET AJAX Client-Side PageRequestManager 1033

Instantiating and Initializing the Client-Side PageRequestManager **1034**
The getInstance Method of the Client-Side PageRequestManager 1036
The Constructor of the Client-Side PageRequestManager Class 1037
The _initializeInternal Method of the Client-Side PageRequestManager 1040
_updateControls **1046**
The _pageLoadedInitialLoad Method of the Client-Side PageRequestManager **1050**
The _pageLoaded Method of the Client-Side PageRequestManager 1050
The pageLoaded Event **1052**
Using the pageLoaded Event 1055
Making an Asynchronous Page Postback **1071**
Helper Methods 1071
_doPostBack 1077
_onFormSubmit 1081
The initializeRequest Event **1090**
Using the initializeRequest Event 1092
The beginRequest Event **1099**
Using the beginRequest Event 1101
Summary **1104**

Chapter 23: Asynchronous Partial Page Rendering: Server Side Processing 1105

RetrievePostData **1105**
LoadScrollPosition **1109**
InitRecursive **1111**
The IsAsyncPostBackRequest Method of the PageRequestManager 1111
The OnInit Method of PageRequestManager 1112
Load Post Data **1113**
UpdatePanel 1117
ScriptManager **1117**
The LoadPostData Method of PageRequestManager **1118**
The Raise Post Data Changed Event **1120**

Contents

PreRender   **1121**
The OnPreRender Method of PageRequestManager   1121
Rendering   **1122**
The Encode Method of PageRequestManager   1123
The RenderPageCallback Method of PageRequestManager   1124
Server Response   **1162**
Summary   **1178**

Chapter 24: Asynchronous Partial Page Rendering: Client-Side Processing   **1179**

Arrival of the Server Response Text   **1179**
The _updatePanel Method of PageRequestManager   **1207**
The registerDisposeScript Method of PageRequestManager   **1209**
_destroyTree   **1209**
_ScriptLoader   **1210**
readLoadedScripts   1210
getInstance   1211
queueScriptBlock   1212
queueCustomScriptTag   1212
isScriptLoaded   1212
_getLoadedScript   1213
queueScriptReference   1213
loadScripts   1213
_loadScriptsInternal   1215
_createScriptElement   1217
The Constructor of the _ScriptLoader Class   1218
_scriptLoaderHandler   1218
_ScriptLoaderTask   **1219**
The Constructor of the_ScriptLoaderTask Class   1219
execute   1220
_scriptLoadHandler   1221
_scriptsLoadComplete   **1221**
_pageLoaded   1223
_endPostBack   **1224**
pageLoading   **1231**
Using the pageLoading Event   1242
pageLoaded   **1253**
endRequest   **1255**
Using the endRequest Event   1257
Summary   **1273**

Contents

Appendix A: XML Script   **1275**

Appendix B: Binding   **1325**

Appendix C: Actions   **1341**

Appendix D: Data Control   **1357**

Appendix E: Templated Controls   **1381**

Appendix F: ListView   **1409**

Index   **1481**

Introduction

Welcome to *ASP.NET AJAX Programmer's Reference with ASP.NET 2.0 or ASP.NET 3.5*. The ASP.NET AJAX framework consists of two frameworks: the ASP.NET AJAX client-side framework and the ASP.NET AJAX server-side framework.

It's a well-known fact that client-side programming is very different from server-side programming. The main difference lies in the fact that client-side programming lacks a feature-rich programming framework like the ASP.NET/.NET framework. Wouldn't be great if you could write your client-side code in a framework with programming styles and capabilities like those of the ASP.NET/.NET framework? Enter the ASP.NET AJAX client-side framework. It simulates the rich programming features of the ASP.NET/ .NET framework on the client side as much as possible. The capabilities of these simulations are only limited by the fundamental limitations of client-side technologies such as JavaScript.

The ASP.NET AJAX server-side framework extends the ASP.NET Framework to provide server-side support for Ajax-enabled Web applications. The ASP.NET AJAX client-side and server-side frameworks work hand in hand to meet both the client-side and server-side needs of your Ajax-enabled applications. That said, the ASP.NET AJAX client-side framework can also work alongside server technologies other than the ASP.NET Framework.

This book uses a unique approach characterized by the following attributes to provide you with an in-depth coverage of both the ASP.NET AJAX client-side and server-side frameworks:

❑ **Practical real-world examples:** The discussions in this book are presented in the context of numerous practical real-world examples that you can use in your own ASP.NET AJAX applications.

❑ **Under-the-hood looks:** This book takes you under the hood of both ASP.NET AJAX client-side and server-side frameworks, where you can see for yourself how they work from the inside out and how you can extend them to meet your application requirements.

❑ **Code walkthroughs:** I'll use numerous code walkthroughs to help you gain the skills, experience, and knowledge you need to implement similar features in your own ASP.NET AJAX applications.

Who This Book Is For

This book is aimed at the ASP.NET developer who wants to learn ASP.NET AJAX for the first time. No knowledge of ASP.NET AJAX is assumed.

What This Book Covers

This book is divided into 24 chapters and six appendices, as follows:

❑ **Chapter 1, "Ajax Technologies,"** provides an overview of the main technologies used in Ajax-enabled Web applications, such as XMLHttpRequest, XML, and JSON, in the context of examples.

❑ **Chapter 2, "JavaScript Base Type Extensions,"** explains the JavaScript base type extensions. You'll learn how these extensions enhance the JavaScript base types such as Array, Boolean, Date, Error, Object, and String to enable you to experience these types — as much as possible — as you would their .NET counterparts.

❑ **Chapter 3, "Built-In and Custom Exception Types,"** first covers the ASP.NET AJAX built-in exception types, including ArgumentException, ArgumentNullException, ArgumentOutOfRangeException, ArgumentTypeException, ArgumentUndefinedException, InvalidOperationException, NotImplementedException, and ParameterCountException, in depth. Then it provides you with a recipe for developing custom exception types, uses this recipe to implement a custom exception type named DuplicateItemException, and implements a page that uses this custom exception type.

❑ **Chapter 4, "JavaScript Object-Oriented Programming and Type Reflection Extensions,"** first examines those JavaScript technologies that the ASP.NET AJAX object-oriented programming (OOP) and type reflection extensions use under the hood to extend JavaScript to add OOP and type reflection support. Then it provides a comprehensive coverage of the Type and its methods, where you'll learn through numerous examples how to define namespaces, interfaces, classes, and enumeration types, how to implement classes that implement one or more interfaces, and how to implement classes that derives from other classes.

❑ **Chapter 5, "Event Programming Extensions,"** provides you with a detailed step-by-step recipe for implementing and adding events to your custom ASP.NET AJAX client classes to enable the clients of your classes to extend their functionality to execute application-specific logic. It then presents and discusses a practical example that uses this recipe. This chapter also describes the EventArgs, CancelEventArgs, and EventHandlerList classes and their methods and properties in detail.

❑ **Chapter 6, "DOM Extensions,"** shows you how the ASP.NET AJAX DOM extensions extend traditional DOM programming to add support for .NET-like methods and properties, and how to use these extensions in your own DOM programming. It covers the ASP.NET AJAX delegates and the DomElement and DomEvent client classes and their methods and properties.

❑ **Chapter 7, "Component Development Infrastructure,"** covers the ASP.NET AJAX component development infrastructure and its main constituent interfaces, including IDisposable, INotifyDisposing, INotifyPropertyChanged, and IContainer and its main constituent classes, including Component and Application. You'll also learn through numerous examples how to implement these interfaces and how to implement a custom component that derives from the Component base class. This chapter also covers the application and component life cycles and application level events in detail.

❑ **Chapter 8, "Developing Client Controls,"** describes the Control, Label, Image, and HyperLink client controls and their methods and properties, and presents examples that use these client controls. This chapter also presents and discusses the implementation of a custom Image client control that extends the functionality of the ASP.NET AJAX Image client control.

❑ **Chapter 9, "Event Bubbling and Button Client Control,"** first covers the `CommandEventArgs` event data class and the `Button` client control. Then it discusses ASP.NET AJAX event bubbling and shows you how to implement custom controls that bubble their events up to their parents, and how to implement custom controls that capture events bubbled up by their children. This chapter implements a client control named `GridView`, which uses ASP.NET AJAX event bubbling.

❑ **Chapter 10, "Type Description Extensions,"** provides comprehensive coverage of the `TypeDescriptor` class and `ICustomTypeDescriptor` interface, from which you'll learn how to take advantage of the ASP.NET type description capabilities in your own applications in order to isolate your client code from the specifics of the types of the objects that your client code deals with. This will allow your code to interact with different types of objects without code change. This chapter implements three Web pages that you can use to generically inspect the properties, events, and methods of any ASP.NET AJAX type. This chapter also implements a custom client control named `CustomTable` that uses the ASP.NET AJAX type description capabilities to display any type of data records. Finally, this chapter shows you how to dynamically inject metadata information.

❑ **Chapter 11, "Data Classes,"** first discusses the `IData` interface and then dives into the ASP.NET AJAX `DataColumn`, `DataRow`, and `DataTable` data classes. It also implements a custom client control that can display data from any data source, such as `DataTable`, and that implements the `IData` interface.

❑ **Chapter 12, "Client-Server Communications,"** covers the client-server communications layer of the ASP.NET AJAX framework and its constituent classes, including detailed discussions of `WebRequest`, `WebRequestExecutor`, `WebRequestManager`, `NetworkRequestEventArgs`, and `XMLHttpExecutor`, and presents several examples that show you how to use these classes in your own ASP.NET AJAX applications.

❑ **Chapter 13, "Consuming Web Services Via SOAP Messages,"** first discusses WSDL documents and SOAP messages in detail and then presents an example that uses the classes in the client-server communications layer of the ASP.NET AJAX framework to exchange SOAP messages with a Web service.

❑ **Chapter 14, "Consuming Web Services Via JSON Messages,"** provides in-depth coverage of the `WebServiceProxy` and `WebServiceError` classes and teaches you three different ways to invoke server-side methods from your client code: calling page methods, Web service methods, and Web services bridges. It also covers `.asbx` files in detail. This chapter then presents and implements fully functional replicas of the main components of the ASP.NET AJAX REST method call-request-processing infrastructure, including the `ScriptHandlerFactory`, `RestHandlerFactory`, `RestHandler`, `HandlerWrapper`, and `ScriptModule` classes, and implements an example in which these replicas are used. This chapter also uses these replicas to demystify page method calls and Web services bridges.

❑ **Chapter 15, "Proxy Classes,"** first covers proxy classes associated with page methods, Web services bridges, and Web services methods in detail. Next, it discusses `ScriptManager` and `ScriptManagerProxy` server controls and the role of `ScriptManagerProxy` server controls in parent/child page scenarios. This chapter then implements fully functional replicas of the main components of the ASP.NET AJAX automatic proxy-class-generation infrastructure, such as `ScriptManager`, `ServiceReferenceCollection`, `ServiceReference`, `ClientProxyGenerator`, and `RestClientProxyHandler`, and you'll see for yourself how this infrastructure generates the proxy classes associated with page methods, Web services bridges, and Web services methods. This chapter then implements an example that uses these replicas.

Introduction

- ❑ **Chapter 16, "Behaviors,"** begins by providing in-depth coverage of the `Behavior` base class and its methods and properties, and shows you how to derive from this base class to implement your own custom behaviors. It then discusses the ASP.NET AJAX control toolkit behavior base class named `BehaviorBase`, and shows you how to derive from the `BehaviorBase` class to implement your own custom toolkit behavior.

- ❑ **Chapter 17, "Script and Extender Server Controls,"** implements fully functional replicas of those components of the ASP.NET AJAX server-side framework that are deeply involved in the internal functioning of two important types of server controls, known as script controls and extender controls, to help you gain a solid understanding of these server controls, how they interact with their associated client-side components, how they differ from one another, and how to implement your own custom script controls and extender controls. The components of the ASP.NET AJAX server-side framework whose replicas these chapter implements include `IExtenderControl`, `ExtenderControl`, `IScriptControl`, `ScriptControl`, `ScriptDescriptor`, `ScriptComponentDescriptor`, `ScriptBehaviorDescriptor`, `ScriptControlDescriptor`, `ScriptReference`, `ResolveScriptReference`, `ScriptReferenceCollection`, and `ScriptManager`. This chapter then implements custom script and extender server controls, and you'll gain the skills you need to develop your own custom script and extender server controls.

- ❑ **Chapter 18, "Web Services Bridges and Transformers,"** first walks you through the implementation of a Web services bridge–enabled script server control that uses the Amazon Web services. Then it discusses ASP.NET AJAX transformers in detail, including `XmlBridgeTransformer` and `XsltBridgeTransformer`, and uses them to enhance the Web services bridge–enabled script server control. This chapter also shows you how to implement your own custom transformers.

- ❑ **Chapter 19, "UpdatePanel and ScriptManager,"** uses numerous examples in which you learn how to enable asynchronous partial page rendering, how to use triggers, and several different ways to conditionally update an `UpdatePanel` server control, including by setting its `ChildrenAsTrigger` property, by directly adding it to another `UpdatePanel` server control, by indirectly adding it to another `UpdatePanel` server control via a user control, by indirectly adding it to another `UpdatePanel` server control via a content page, and by explicitly calling its `Update` method from your code. This chapter then implements two base custom partial-page-rendering-enabled server controls named `BaseMasterDetailControl` and `BaseMasterDetailControl2`.

- ❑ **Chapter 20, "Using UpdatePanel in User Controls and Custom Controls,"** implements three custom partial-page-rendering-enabled server controls named `MasterDetailControl`, `MasterDetailControl2`, and `MasterDetailControl3`, a custom partial-page-rendering-enabled data control field named `MasterDetailField`, and a partial-page-rendering-enabled threaded discussion forum user control. This chapter also implements pages that use these partial-page-rendering-enabled custom server controls, data control field, and user control.

- ❑ **Chapter 21, "Page Life Cycle and Asynchronous Partial Page Rendering,"** follows the `Page` object through its life cycle phases to process the first request to a partial-page-rendering-enabled Web page to help you gain a solid understanding of the ASP.NET AJAX asynchronous partial-page-rendering infrastructure and its main components, such as the `ScriptManager` and server-side `PageRequestManager`, `UpdatePanel`, `UpdatePanelTrigger`, `UpdatePanelControlTrigger`, and `AsyncPostBackTrigger` classes. This chapter also implements a custom `UpdatePanel` server control named `CustomUpdatePanel` and a custom trigger named `AsyncMultiPostBackTrigger`.

❑ **Chapter 22, "ASP.NET AJAX Client-Side PageRequestManager,"** first provides a comprehensive coverage of the instantiation and initialization process of the current client-side `PageRequestManager` instance, where you also learn about this instance's `pageLoaded` event and its associated `PageLoadedEventArgs` event data class. It also shows an example in which this event is used. This chapter then dives into the process through which the current client-side `PageRequestManager` instance makes an asynchronous page postback request to the server, and you also learn about this instance's `initializeRequest` and `beginRequest` events. It also shows examples in which you'll learn how to use these events in your own ASP.NET AJAX applications.

❑ **Chapter 23, "Asynchronous Partial Page Rendering: Server-Side Processing,"** follows the `Page` object through its life cycle phases to process an asynchronous page postback request where you'll learn about the role of the server-side `PageRequestManager`, `RetrievePostData`, `ScriptManager`, `UpdatePanel`, `ScriptRegisterationManager`, and triggers in generating the final response text. This chapter also implements a page that enables you to inspect the server response text.

❑ **Chapter 24, "Asynchronous Partial Page Rendering: Client-Side Processing,"** follows the client-side `PageRequestManager` instance through its life cycle phases to process the server response to an asynchronous page postback request where you'll see for yourself how the current client-side `PageRequestManager` manages to parse the server response text, download the required scripts, and update the required `UpdatePanel` server controls on the client side. You'll also learn about the `pageLoading` and `endRequest` events of the current client-side `PageRequestManager` instance and their associated `PageLoadingEventArgs` and `EndRequestEventArgs` event data classes. This chapter shows examples in which these events and their associated event data classes are used. It also covers the `PageRequestManagerTimeoutException`, `PageRequestManagerServerErrorException`, `PageRequestManagerParserErrorException`, and `InvalidOperationException` exceptions that the current client-side `PageRequestManager` instance raises. Finally, it implements a custom error handler and a page that uses this error handler.

❑ **Appendix A, "XML Script,"** provides comprehensive coverage of the ASP.NET AJAX xml-script, which enables you to program declaratively with little or no imperative or procedural JavaScript code. This appendix covers the main components of the ASP.NET AJAX xml-script parsing infrastructure, such as `MarkupContext` and `MarkupParser`, and you'll learn through numerous examples how to enable the clients of your client classes to declaratively instantiate and initialize instances of your classes in xml-script without writing any procedural JavaScript code. You'll also learn how to extend the ASP.NET AJAX xml-script parsing infrastructure to add support for custom parsing of your own client classes.

❑ **Appendix B, "Binding,"** covers ASP.NET AJAX binding in detail. The `BindingBase` client class, built-in and custom transformers, and the `Binding` client class are discussed in depth.

❑ **Appendix C, "Actions,"** discusses the ASP.NET AJAX actions including the `IAction` client interface, the `Action` base class, actions in xml-script, and built-in actions such as `InvokeMethodAction`, `SetPropertyAction`, and `PostBackAction` in detail.

❑ **Appendix D, "Data Control,"** first provides a comprehensive coverage of the ASP.NET AJAX `DataControl` base class and its methods, properties, and events. Then it implements a custom data control named `CustomTable` that derives from the `DataControl` base class, and uses the ASP.NET AJAX type description capabilities to display any type of data records.

❑ **Appendix E, "Templated Controls,"** first covers the `ITemplate` client interface, `TemplateInstance` client class, and `Template` client class in detail. Then it develops a custom template named `TemplateField` that derives from the `Template` class and supports its own `parseFromMarkup` static method, which tells the ASP.NET AJAX xml-script parsing infrastructure how to parse an instance of the `TemplateField` class declared in xml-script. Finally, it develops a custom templated data control that enables its clients to use `TemplateField` instances in xml-script to specify different types of HTML markup texts for rendering different types of database fields.

❑ **Appendix F, "ListView,"** begins by providing an overview of the ASP.NET AJAX `ListView` client control and its methods, properties, and events, and goes on to present examples in which this client control is used to display data records downloaded from a backend Web service. Then it dives into the internals of the `ListView` client control and its methods, properties, events, and surrounding classes and interfaces such as `ITask`, `_TaskManager`, and `ListViewRenderTask`. You'll learn the skills you need to develop a custom templated data control as complex as the `ListView` client control.

What You Need To Use This Book

You'll need the following items to run the code samples in this book:

❑ ASP.NET AJAX Extensions 1.0

❑ ASP.NET Futures

❑ Windows Server 2003, Windows 2000, Windows XP, or Windows Vista

❑ Visual Studio 2005, Visual Studio 2005 Express Edition, Visual Studio 2008, or Visual Studio 2008 Express Edition

❑ SQL Server 2005 or SQL Server 2005 Express Edition

You can download free copies of Visual Studio 2005 Express Edition or Visual Studio 2008 Express Edition and SQL Server 2005 Express Edition from `http://msdn.microsoft.com/vstudio/express/` and ASP.NET AJAX Extensions 1.0 and ASP.NET Futures from `http://ajax.asp.net/downloads/`.

Conventions

To help you get the most from the text and keep track of what's happening, we've used a number of conventions throughout the book.

> **Boxes like this one hold important, not-to-be forgotten information that is directly relevant to the surrounding text.**

Tips, hints, tricks, and asides to the current discussion are offset and placed in italics like this.

As for styles in the text:

- ❑ We *highlight* new terms and important words when we introduce them.
- ❑ We show keyboard strokes like this: Ctrl+A.
- ❑ We show file names, URLs, and code within the text like so: `persistence.properties`.
- ❑ We present code in two different ways:

```
In code examples we highlight new and important code with a gray background.
```

```
The gray highlighting is not used for code that's less important in the present
context, or that has been shown before.
```

Source Code

As you work through the examples in this book, you may choose either to type in all the code manually or to use the source code files that accompany the book. All the source code used in this book is available for download at `http://www.wrox.com`. Once at the site, simply locate the book's title (either by using the Search box or by using one of the title lists) and click the Download Code link on the book's detail page to obtain all the source code for the book.

> *Because many books have similar titles, you may find it easiest to search by ISBN; this book's ISBN is 978-0-470-10998-4.*

Once you download the code, just decompress it with your favorite compression tool. Alternately, you can go to the main Wrox code download page at `http://www.wrox.com/dynamic/books/download.aspx` to see the code available for this book and all other Wrox books.

Errata

We make every effort to ensure that there are no errors in the text or in the code. However, no one is perfect, and mistakes do occur. If you find an error in one of our books, like a spelling mistake or faulty piece of code, we would be very grateful for your feedback. By sending in errata you may save another reader hours of frustration and at the same time you will be helping us provide even higher-quality information.

To find the errata page for this book, go to `http://www.wrox.com` and locate the title using the Search box or one of the title lists. Then, on the book details page, click the Book Errata link. On this page you can view all errata that have been submitted for this book and posted by Wrox editors. A complete book list including links to each's book's errata is also available at `www.wrox.com/misc-pages/booklist.shtml`.

If you don't spot "your" error on the Book Errata page, go to `www.wrox.com/contact/techsupport.shtml` and complete the form there to send us the error you have found. We'll check the information and, if appropriate, post a message to the book's errata page and fix the problem in subsequent editions of the book.

P2P.WROX.COM

For author and peer discussion, join the P2P forums at p2p.wrox.com. The forums are a Web-based system for you to post messages relating to Wrox books and related technologies and interact with other readers and technology users. The forums offer a subscription feature to e-mail you topics of interest of your choosing when new posts are made to the forums. Wrox authors, editors, other industry experts, and your fellow readers are present on these forums.

At http://p2p.wrox.com you will find a number of different forums that will help you not only as you read this book, but also as you develop your own applications. To join the forums, just follow these steps:

1. Go to p2p.wrox.com and click the Register link.

2. Read the terms of use and click Agree.

3. Complete the required information to join, as well as any optional information you wish to provide, and click Submit.

4. You will receive an e-mail with information describing how to verify your account and complete the joining process.

You can read messages in the forums without joining P2P, but in order to post your own messages you must join.

Once you join, you can post new messages and respond to messages other users post. You can read messages at any time on the Web. If you would like to have new messages from a particular forum e-mailed to you, click the Subscribe to this Forum icon by the forum name in the forum listing.

For more information about how to use the Wrox P2P, be sure to read the P2P FAQs for answers to questions about how the forum software works as well as many common questions specific to P2P and Wrox books. To read the FAQs, click the FAQ link on any P2P page.

AJAX Technologies

Traditional Web pages use server-side technologies and resources to operate and deliver their features and services to end users. These Web pages require end users to perform full-page postbacks to the server, where these pages can run the required server-side code to deliver the requested service or feature. In other words, these Web pages use the click-and-wait, user-unfriendly interaction pattern, which is characterized by waiting periods that disrupt user workflow and degrade the user experience. This click-and-wait user interaction pattern is what makes the traditional Web applications act and feel very different from their desktop counterparts.

Asynchronous JavaScript And XML (abbreviated *AJAX*) is a popular Web application development approach that uses client-side technologies such as HTML, XHTML, CSS, DOM, XML, XSLT, Javascript, and asynchronous client-callback techniques such as XMLHttp requests and hidden-frame techniques to develop more sophisticated and responsive Web applications that break free from the click-and-wait pattern and, consequently, act and feel more like a desktop application. In other words, AJAX is closing the gap between Web applications and their desktop counterparts.

This chapter begins by discussing the main characteristics of AJAX-enabled Web pages in the context of an example.

Google Suggest

The Google Suggest Web page (www.google.com/webhp?complete=1) contains an AJAX-enabled search box that completes your search items as you type them in, as shown in Figure 1-1. Under the hood, this AJAX-enabled search box uses AJAX techniques to asynchronously download the required data from the Web server and to display them to the end user without interrupting the user's interaction with the page. All the client-server communications are performed in the background as the end user types into the search box.

An AJAX-enabled component such as the Google Suggest search box exhibits the following four important characteristics:

❑ It uses HTML, XHTML, CSS, DOM, and JavaScript client-side technologies to implement most of its functionalities where the code runs locally on the client machine to achieve the

Figure 1-1

same response time as its desktop counterpart. This allows an AJAX-enabled component to break free from the click-and-wait user-interaction pattern.

❑ It uses asynchronous client-callback techniques such as XMLHttpRequest to communicate with the server. The main goal of this asynchronous communication model is to ensure that the communication with the server doesn't interrupt what the user is doing. This asynchronous communication model is another step that allows an AJAX-enabled component to break free from the click-and-wait pattern.

❑ AJAX-enabled components normally send data to and receive data from the server in either XML or JSON format (discussed in detail later in this chapter). This characteristic enables the client-side code to exchange data with any type of server-side code, and vice versa, because almost all platforms have built-in support for reading, writing, and manipulating XML or JSON data.

❑ The asynchronous communication between the client-side code and the server-side code are normally governed by AJAX communication patterns. These patterns enable AJAX components to take full advantage of the asynchronous nature of the communication between the client-side code and the server-side code to determine the best time for uploading the data to or downloading the data from the server so the data exchange with the server won't interrupt the user workflow and degrade the user experience.

In a traditional Web page, the end users trigger synchronous communications with the Web server, and they then have to wait until the required data is downloaded from the server and the entire page is rendered all over again to display the new information. AJAX changes all that. As you can see in Figure 1-2, the Ajax engine takes complete control over the client-server communications and the rendering of the new information to ensure that these communications and renderings do not interrupt the user interactions.

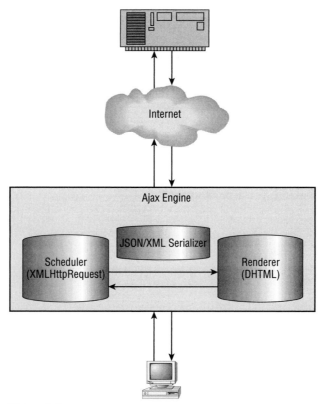

Figure 1-2

As this figure shows, the AJAX engine consists of the following three main components:

❑ **Scheduler:** The scheduler uses AJAX technologies such as XMLHttpRequest to send data to and receive data from the server in an asynchronous fashion. As the name suggests, the scheduler schedules and makes the client requests to the server.

❑ **Renderer:** The renderer component of the AJAX engine uses DHTML to dynamically update only those portions of the current page that need refreshing without re-rendering or re-loading the entire page.

❑ **JSON/XML Serializer:** The client and server exchange data in JSON or XML format. The JSON/XML serializer has two main responsibilities:

   ❑ Serialize the client data, which are JavaScript objects, into their JSON or XML representations before these objects are sent to the server

   ❑ Deserialize JavaScript objects from the JSON or XML data received from the server

This chapter provides an overview of the following client-side technologies that form the foundations of the above three main AJAX engine components in the context of an example:

❑ XMLHttpRequest

❑ DHTML

❑ XML

❑ JSON

XMLHttpRequest

XMLHttpRequest is one of the main AJAX technologies that the scheduler component of an AJAX engine uses to make asynchronous requests to the server. The instantiation process of the XMLHttpRequest object is browser-dependent. Listing 1-1 encapsulates the browser-dependent nature of this instantiation process in a class named XMLHttpRequest.

Listing 1-1: Instantiating XMLHttpRequest

```
if (!window.XMLHttpRequest)
{
  window.XMLHttpRequest = function window$XMLHttpRequest()
  {
    var progIDs = [ 'Msxml2.XMLHTTP', 'Microsoft.XMLHTTP' ];
    for (var i = 0; i < progIDs.length; i++)
    {
      try
      {
        var xmlHttp = new ActiveXObject(progIDs[i]);
        return xmlHttp;
      }
      catch (ex) {}
    }
    return null;
  }
}
```

This script first checks whether the window object already contains a definition for this class. If not, it defines the constructor of the class. The constructor contains the following array of program ids:

```
var progIDs = [ 'Msxml2.XMLHTTP', 'Microsoft.XMLHTTP' ];
```

This array covers all the possible instantiation scenarios on Internet Explorer. The constructor iterates through the program ids array and takes the following steps for each enumerated program id:

1. It instantiates an ActiveXObject, passing in the enumerated program id.

2. If the instantiation succeeds, it returns this ActiveXObject instance.

3. If the instantiation fails, the try block throws an exception, which the catch block catches and forces the loop to move to the next iteration, where the next program id is used.

The `XMLHttpRequest` object exposes the following methods and properties:

❑ open: This method takes up to five parameters, but only the first two parameters are required. The first required parameter is a string that contains the HTTP verb (`POST` or `GET`) being used to make the request to the server. The second required parameter is a string that contains the target URL, which is the URL of the resource for which the request is made. The third optional parameter is a Boolean value that specifies whether the request is asynchronous. If you don't specify a value for this parameter, it defaults to `true`. The fourth and fifth optional parameters specify the requester's credentials — the username and password.

❑ readyState: The `XMLHttpRequest` exposes an integer property named `readyState` with possible values of 0, 1, 2, 3, or 4. The `XMLHttpRequest` goes through different states during its lifecycle, and each state is associated with one of these five possible values.

❑ onreadystatechange: You must assign a reference to a JavaScript function to this property. The `XMLHttpRequest` invokes this JavaScript function every time its state changes, which is every time its `readyState` property changes value. Every time your JavaScript function is invoked, it must check the value of the `XMLHttpRequest`'s `readyState` property to determine the state of the `XMLHttpRequest`. The current request is completed only when `XMLHttpRequest` enters the state associated with the `readyState` property value of 4. As a result, the typical implementation of the JavaScript function assigned to the `onreadystatechange` property is as follows:

```
function readyStateChangeCallback()
{
  if (request.readyState == 4 && request.status == 200)
  {
    // Process the server response here
  }
}
```

The global variable named `request` in this code fragment references the `XMLHttpRequest` object. This JavaScript function checks whether the `readyState` property of the `XMLHttpRequest` is 4, meaning the request is completed. If so, it processes the server response. If not, it simply returns.

❑ status: This property contains the HTTP status code of the server response. The JavaScript function that you assign to the `onreadystatechange` property must also check whether the status property of the `XMLHttpRequest` is 200, as shown in the boldface portion of the following code fragment. If the status code is a not 200, this is an indication that a server-side error has occurred.

```
function readyStateChangeCallback()
{
  if (request.readyState == 4 && request.status == 200)
  {
    // Process the server response here
  }
}
```

Strictly speaking, any status code within the 200–299 range is considered a success. However, a status code of 200 is good enough in this case.

❑ `statusText`: This property contains the HTTP status text of the server response. The text describes the HTTP status code. For example, the status text for status code `200` is `OK`.

❑ `setRequestHeader`: This method sets a specified HTTP request header to a specified value. As such, this method takes two parameters: the first parameter is a string that contains the name of the HTTP request header whose value is being set, and the second parameter is a string that contains the value of this HTTP request header.

❑ `send`: This is the method that actually sends the request to the server. It takes a string parameter that contains the request body. If you're making a `GET` HTTP request, pass `null` as the value of this parameter. If you're making a `POST` HTTP request, generate a string that contains the body of the request and pass this string into the `send` method.

❑ `responseText`: This property contains the server response in text format.

❑ `responseXML`: This property contains the server response in XML format (an XML `Document` to be exact). This property is set only when the `Content-Type` response header is set to the value `text/xml`. If the server-side code does not set the response header to this value, the `response-XML` property will be `null` even when the actual data is in XML format. In such cases, you must load the content of the `responseText` property into an XML document before you can use the client-side XML API to read the XML data.

The `overrideMimeType` property of `XMLHttpRequest` in Mozilla browsers enables you to override the MIME type of the server response. However, this is a browser-specific issue that the current discussion does not need to address.

❑ `getResponseHeader`: This method returns the value of a response header with a specified name. As such, it takes the name of the response header as its only argument.

❑ `getAllResponseHeaders`: This method returns the names and values of all response headers.

❑ `abort`: Use this method to abort a request.

Listing 1-2 presents an example that uses `XMLHttpRequest` to make an asynchronous request to the server. If you access this page, you see the result shown in Figure 1-3. This page consists of a simple user interface with two text boxes and a button. If you enter the text "**username**" in the top text box and the text "**password**" in the bottom text box and then click the button, you get the result shown in Figure 1-4.

Listing 1-2: A page that uses XMLHttpRequest

```
<%@ Page Language="C#" %>
<!DOCTYPE html PUBLIC "-//W3C//DTD XHTML 1.0 Transitional//EN"
"http://www.w3.org/TR/xhtml11/DTD/xhtml11-transitional.dtd">
<script runat="server">
  void Page_Load(object sender, EventArgs e)
  {
    if (Request.Headers["MyCustomHeader"] != null)
    {
      if (Request.Form["passwordtbx"] == "password" &&
          Request.Form["usernametbx"] == "username")
      {
        Response.Write("Shahram|Khosravi|22223333|Some Department|");
        Response.End();
      }
      else
```

```
                throw new Exception("Wrong credentials");
        }
    }
</script>
<html xmlns="http://www.w3.org/1999/xhtml">
<head id="Head1" runat="server">
  <title>Untitled Page</title>
  <script type="text/javascript" language="javascript">
  var request;

  if (!window.XMLHttpRequest)
  {
    window.XMLHttpRequest = function window$XMLHttpRequest()
    {
      var progIDs = [ 'Msxml2.XMLHTTP', 'Microsoft.XMLHTTP' ];

      for (var i = 0; i < progIDs.length; i++)
      {
        try
        {
          var xmlHttp = new ActiveXObject(progIDs[i]);
          return xmlHttp;
        }
        catch (ex) {}
      }

      return null;
    }
  }

  window.employee = function window$employee(firstname, lastname,
                                             employeeid, departmentname)
  {
    this.firstname = firstname;
    this.lastname = lastname;
    this.employeeid = employeeid;
    this.departmentname = departmentname
  }

  function deserialize()
  {
    var delimiter="|";
    var responseIndex = 0;
    var delimiterIndex;
    var response = request.responseText;

    delimiterIndex = response.indexOf(delimiter, responseIndex);
    var firstname = response.substring(responseIndex, delimiterIndex);
    responseIndex = delimiterIndex + 1;
    delimiterIndex = response.indexOf(delimiter, responseIndex);
    var lastname = response.substring(responseIndex, delimiterIndex);
    responseIndex = delimiterIndex + 1;

    delimiterIndex = response.indexOf(delimiter, responseIndex);
```

(continued)

Listing 1-2 *(continued)*

```
      var employeeid = response.substring(responseIndex, delimiterIndex);
      responseIndex = delimiterIndex + 1;

      delimiterIndex = response.indexOf(delimiter, responseIndex);
      var departmentname = response.substring(responseIndex, delimiterIndex);

      return new employee(firstname, lastname, employeeid, departmentname);
}

function readyStateChangeCallback()
{
   if (request.readyState == 4 && request.status == 200)
   {
      var credentials = document.getElementById("credentials");
      credentials.style.display="none";
      var employeeinfotable = document.getElementById("employeeinfo");
      employeeinfotable.style.display="block";

      var employee = deserialize();

      var firstnamespan = document.getElementById("firstname");
      firstnamespan.innerText = employee.firstname;
      var lastnamespan = document.getElementById("lastname");
      lastnamespan.innerText = employee.lastname;

      var employeeidspan = document.getElementById("employeeid");
      employeeidspan.innerText = employee.employeeid;

      var departmentnamespan = document.getElementById("departmentname");
      departmentnamespan.innerText = employee.departmentname;
   }
}

window.credentials = function window$credentials(username, password)
{
   this.username = username;
   this.password = password;
}

function serialize(credentials)
{
   var requestBody="";
   requestBody += "usernametbx";
   requestBody += "=";
   requestBody += encodeURIComponent(credentials.username);
   requestBody += "&";
   requestBody += "passwordtbx";
   requestBody += "=";
   requestBody += encodeURIComponent(credentials.password);
   return requestBody;
}

function submitCallback()
```

```
      {
        var usernametbx = document.getElementById("usernametbx");
        var passwordtbx = document.getElementById("passwordtbx");
        var credentials1= new credentials(usernametbx.value, passwordtbx.value);
        var body = serialize(credentials1);

        request = new XMLHttpRequest();
        request.open("POST", document.form1.action);
        request.onreadystatechange = readyStateChangeCallback;
        request.setRequestHeader("MyCustomHeader", "true");
        request.setRequestHeader('Content-Type', 'application/x-www-form-urlencoded');
        request.send(body);
      }
    </script>
</head>
<body>
  <form id="form1" runat="server">
    <table id="credentials">
      <tr>
        <td align="right" style="font-weight: bold">
          Username:
        </td>
        <td align="left">
          <asp:TextBox runat="server" ID="usernametbx" /></td>
      </tr>
      <tr>
        <td align="right" style="font-weight: bold">
          Password:
        </td>
        <td align="left">
          <asp:TextBox runat="server" ID="passwordtbx"
          TextMode="Password" />
        </td>
      </tr>
      <tr>
        <td align="center" colspan="2">
          <button id="Button1" type="button"
          onclick="submitCallback()">Submit</button>
        </td>
      </tr>
    </table>
    <table id="employeeinfo"
    style="background-color: LightGoldenrodYellow;
          border-color: Tan; border-width: 1px;
          color: Black; display: none" cellpadding="2">
      <tr style="background-color: Tan; font-weight: bold">
        <th colspan="2">
          Your Information</th>
      </tr>
      <tr>
        <td style="font-weight: bold">
          First Name</td>
        <td>
          <span id="firstname" />
        </td>
```

(continued)

Listing 1-2 *(continued)*

```
        </tr>
        <tr style="background-color: PaleGoldenrod">
          <td style="font-weight: bold">
            Last Name</td>
          <td>
            <span id="lastname" />
          </td>
        </tr>
        <tr>
          <td style="font-weight: bold">
            Employee ID</td>
          <td>
            <span id="employeeid" />
          </td>
        </tr>
        <tr style="background-color: PaleGoldenrod">
          <td style="font-weight: bold">
            Department
          </td>
          <td>
            <span id="departmentname" />
          </td>
        </tr>
      </table>
    </form>
  </body>
</html>
```

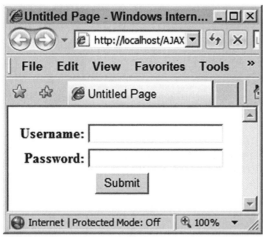

Figure 1-3

Figure 1-4

Note that Listing 1-2 registers a JavaScript function named `submitCallback` as an event handler for the `click` event of the button. This function encapsulates the logic that schedules and makes the asynchronous request to the server. This logic is what is referred to as the Scheduler in Figure 1-2.

Now let's walk through the `submitCallback` function in the listing. First, `submitCallback` calls the `getElementbyId` method on the `document` object to return a reference to the username text box DOM element:

```
var usernametbx = document.getElementById("usernametbx");
```

Next, it calls the `getElementById` method again to return a reference to the password text box DOM element:

```
var passwordtbx = document.getElementById("passwordtbx");
```

Next, it creates an instance of a class named `credentials`:

```
var credentials1 = new credentials(usernametbx.value, passwordtbx.value);
```

Listing 1-2 defines the `credentials` class as follows:

```
window.credentials = function window$credentials(username, password)
{
  this.username = username;
  this.password = password;
}
```

The next order of business is to serialize this `credentials` object into a format that the server-side code understands. This is exactly what the following JavaScript function named `serialize` does:

```
var body = serialize(credentials1);
```

This function basically contains the logic referred to as the Serializer in Figure 1-2. The `serialize` function is discussed in more detail shortly, but for now it suffices to say that this function serializes the specified `credentials` object into a string with a specific format.

Next, the `submitCallback` function creates an instance of the `XMLHttpRequest` class previously defined in Listing 1-1:

```
request = new XMLHttpRequest();
```

As previously discussed, this class encapsulates the browser-dependent logic that instantiates the appropriate object.

Then, the `submitCallback` function invokes the `open` method on this `XMLHttpRequest` object, passing in two parameters. The first parameter is the string "POST" because the function is making a POST HTTP request to the server. The second parameter is the value of the `action` property of the `form` element. The `action` property contains the URL of the current page. The page is basically posting back to itself in asynchronous fashion.

```
request.open("POST", document.form1.action);
```

Next, `submitCallback` assigns a reference, which references a JavaScript function named `readyStateChangeCallback`, to the `onreadystatechange` property of the `XMLHttpRequest` object:

```
request.onreadystatechange = readyStateChangeCallback;
```

Then, it invokes the `setRequestHeader` method on the `XMLHttpRequest` object to add a custom header named `MyCustomHeader` with the value `true`:

```
request.setRequestHeader("MyCustomHeader", "true");
```

As you'll see later, when the page finally posts back to itself, the server-side code uses this header to distinguish between ansynchronous and normal synchronous postback requests.

Next, the `submitCallback` function invokes the `setRequestHeader` method again, this time to set the value of the `Content-Type` header request to `application/x-www-form-urlencoded`:

```
request.setRequestHeader('Content-Type', 'application/x-www-form-urlencoded');
```

As you'll see later, this will allow you to use the `Request` object to access the posted data.

Finally, `submitCallback` invokes the `send` method on the `XMLHttpRequest` object, passing in the string that contains the post data to make an HTTP `POST` request to the server:

```
request.send(body);
```

As previously discussed, this string is the return value of the `serialize` method.

Now let's walk through the implementation of the `serialize` function:

```
function serialize(credentials)
{
  var requestBody="";
  requestBody += "usernametbx";
  requestBody += "=";
  requestBody += encodeURIComponent(credentials.username);
  requestBody += "&";
  requestBody += "passwordtbx";
  requestBody += "=";
  requestBody += encodeURIComponent(credentials.password);
  return requestBody;
}
```

The `serialize` function generates a string that consists of two substrings separated by the `&` character. The first substring itself consists of two substrings separated by the equal sign (=), where the first substring contains the `name` HTML attribute value of the username text box DOM element and the second substring contains the value that the end user has entered into this text box:

```
var requestBody = "";
requestBody += "usernametbx";
requestBody += "=";
requestBody += usernametbx.value;
```

The second substring itself consists of two substrings separated by the equal sign (=), where the first substring contains the name HTML attribute value of the password text box DOM element and the second substring contains the value that the end user has entered into this text box:

```
requestBody += "passwordtbx";
requestBody += "=";
requestBody += passwordtbx.value;
```

When this HTTP POST request arrives at the server, ASP.NET automatically loads the body of the request into the Request object's Form collection property because the Content-Type request header is set to the value application/x-www-form-urlencoded. When the Page_Load method shown in Listing 1-2 is finally invoked, it first checks whether the current request contains an HTTP header named MyCustomHeader:

```
if (Request.Headers["MyCustomHeader"] != null)
```

If so, this is an indication that the current page postback is an asynchronous page postback and, consequently, the Page_Load method first validates the user's credentials. To keep the current discussion focused, this method hardcodes the valid credentials as shown here:

```
if (Request.Form["passwordtbx"] == "password" &&
    Request.Form["usernametbx"] == "username")
```

If the validation succeeds, Page_Load generates a string that contains the server data (which is again hardcoded to keep this discussion focused), invokes the Write method on the Response object to write this string into the response output stream, and invokes the End method on the Response object to end the current response and, consequently, to send the server response to the client:

```
Response.Write("Shahram|Khosravi|22223333|Some Department|");
Response.End();
```

Ending the current response ensures that the current page will not go through its normal rendering routine where it renders the entire page all over again. That is the reason behind adding the custom HTTP request header "MyCustomHeader".

The arrival of the server response changes the state of the XMLHttpRequest object to the completed state, which in turn changes the value of the readyState property of the object to 4. This change in value automatically invokes the readyStateChangeCallback JavaScript function assigned to the onreadystatechange property of the object.

The readyStateChangeCallback JavaScript function encapsulates the logic that uses DHTML to dynamically update those portions of the page that need refreshing without re-rendering and reloading the entire page all over again. This logic is what is referred to as the Renderer in Figure 1-2.

The readyStateChangeCallback JavaScript function first checks whether the readyState and status properties of the XMLHttpRequest object are set to 4 and 200, respectively. If so, it invokes the getElementById method on the document object to return a reference to the table DOM element that displays the login dialog box, and sets the `display` property of this DOM element's `style` property to `none` to hide the dialog box:

```
var credentials = document.getElementById("credentials");
credentials.style.display="none";
```

Next, `readyStateChangeCallback` invokes the `getElementById` method again, this time to return a reference to the table DOM element that displays the server data, and sets the `display` property of this DOM element's `style` property to `block` to show this DOM element:

```
var employeeinfotable = document.getElementById("employeeinfo");
employeeinfotable.style.display="block";
```

Then, it invokes the `responseText` property on the `XMLHttpRequest` object to return a string that contains the server data:

```
var response = request.responseText;
```

Keep in mind that the server data is in the following format:

```
Shahram|Khosravi|22223333|Some Department|
```

The next order of business is to deserialize an `employee` object from the server data. The following excerpt from Listing 1-2 defines the `employee` class:

```
window.employee = function window$employee(firstname, lastname,
                                           employeeid, departmentname)
{
   this.firstname = firstname;
   this.lastname = lastname;
   this.employeeid = employeeid;
   this.departmentname = departmentname
}
```

As you can see in the following excerpt from Listing 1-2, the `readyStateChangeCallback` function invokes a JavaScript function named `deserialize`:

```
var employee = deserialize();
```

This `deserialize` JavaScript function encapsulates the logic that deserializes an `employee` object from the server data (described in more detail later). This logic is what is referred to as the Serializer in Figure 1-2.

Next, the `readyStateChangeCallback` function uses DHTML to update the relevant parts of the page with employee information in the `employee` object. First, it calls the `getElementyById` method on the `document` object to return a reference to the `<span>` DOM element with the id HTML attribute of `firstname`, and assigns the `firstname` property of the employee object to the `innerText` property of this DOM element to display the first name of the employee:

```
var firstnamespan = document.getElementById("firstname");
firstnamespan.innerText = employee.firstname;
```

Next, it calls the `getElementyById` method again, this time to return a reference to the `<span>` DOM element with the id HTML attribute of `lastname`, and assigns the `lastname` property of the employee object to the `innerText` property of this DOM element to display the last name of the employee:

```
var lastnamespan = document.getElementById("lastname");
lastnamespan.innerText = employee.lastname;
```

It then repeats the same process to display the employee's id and department name:

```
var employeeidspan = document.getElementById("employeeid");
employeeidspan.innerText = employee.employeeid;

var departmentnamespan = document.getElementById("departmentname");
departmentnamespan.innerText = employee.departmentname;
```

As mentioned, the `deserialize` JavaScript function deserializes an employee object from the server data:

```
function deserialize(response)
{
  var delimiter="|";
  var responseIndex = 0;
  var delimiterIndex;

  delimiterIndex = response.indexOf(delimiter, responseIndex);
  var firstname = response.substring(responseIndex, delimiterIndex);
  responseIndex = delimiterIndex + 1;
  delimiterIndex = response.indexOf(delimiter, responseIndex);
  var lastname = response.substring(responseIndex, delimiterIndex);
  responseIndex = delimiterIndex + 1;

  delimiterIndex = response.indexOf(delimiter, responseIndex);
  var employeeid = response.substring(responseIndex, delimiterIndex);
  responseIndex = delimiterIndex + 1;

  delimiterIndex = response.indexOf(delimiter, responseIndex);
  var departmentname = response.substring(responseIndex, delimiterIndex);

  return new employee(firstname, lastname, employeeid, departmentname);
}
```

The `deserialize` function basically contains the logic that knows how to parse a string with the following format into an `employee` object:

```
Shahram|Khosravi|22223333|Some Department|
```

XML

As you saw earlier, Listing 1-2 contains a JavaScript function named `serialize` that serializes a given credentials object into a string with the following format before this object is sent over the wire to the server:

```
usernametbx=username&passwordtbx=password
```

Listing 1-2 also contains a JavaScript function named `deserialize` that deserializes an `employee` object from a string with the following format:

```
Shahram|Khosravi|22223333|Some Department|
```

The `serialize` and `deserialize` methods encapsulate the logic that was referred to as the Serializer in Figure 1-2.

The great thing about the XML format is that the server- and client-side technologies provide built-in support for serializing objects into XML and deserializing objects from XML. Listing 1-3 presents a new version of Listing 1-2 where the `Page_Load` server-side method serializes the server data into XML, which is then sent over the wire to the client, where the `deserialize` JavaScript function deserializes an `employee` object from the XML.

Listing 1-3: A version of Listing 1-2 that uses XML format

```
<%@ Page Language="C#" %>
<%@ Import Namespace="System.Xml" %>
<%@ Import Namespace="System.IO" %>
<!DOCTYPE html PUBLIC "-//W3C//DTD XHTML 1.0 Transitional//EN"
"http://www.w3.org/TR/xhtml1/DTD/xhtml1-transitional.dtd">
<script runat="server">
  void Page_Load(object sender, EventArgs e)
  {
    if (Request.Headers["MyCustomHeader"] != null)
    {
      if (Request.Form["passwordtbx"] == "password" &&
          Request.Form["usernametbx"] == "username")
      {
        string xml="";
        using (StringWriter sw = new StringWriter())
        {
          XmlWriterSettings settings = new XmlWriterSettings();
          settings.Indent = true;
          settings.OmitXmlDeclaration = true;
          using (XmlWriter xw = XmlWriter.Create(sw, settings))
          {
            xw.WriteStartDocument();
            xw.WriteStartElement("employeeInfo");
            xw.WriteElementString("firstName", "Shahram");
            xw.WriteElementString("lastName", "Khosravi");
            xw.WriteElementString("employeeId", "22223333");
            xw.WriteElementString("departmentName", "Some Department");
            xw.WriteEndElement();
```

```
            xw.WriteEndDocument();
          }
          xml = sw.ToString();
        }
        Response.ContentType = "text/xml";
        Response.Write(xml);
        Response.End();
      }
      else
      throw new Exception("Wrong credentials");
    }
  }
</script>
<html xmlns="http://www.w3.org/1999/xhtml">
<head id="Head1" runat="server">
  <title>Untitled Page</title>
  <script type="text/javascript" language="javascript">
  var request;

  if (!window.XMLHttpRequest)
  {
    // Same as Listing 2
  }

  window.employee = function window$employee(firstname, lastname,
                                     employeeid, departmentname)
  {
    // Same as Listing 2
  }

  function deserialize()
  {
    var response = request.responseXML;
    var employeeInfo = response.documentElement;
    var firstNameElement = employeeInfo.childNodes[0];
    var firstname = firstNameElement.firstChild.nodeValue;

    var lastNameElement = employeeInfo.childNodes[1];
    var lastname = lastNameElement.firstChild.nodeValue;

    var employeeIdElement = employeeInfo.childNodes[2];
    var employeeid = employeeIdElement.firstChild.nodeValue;

    var departmentNameElement = employeeInfo.childNodes[3];
    var departmentname = departmentNameElement.firstChild.nodeValue;

    return new employee(firstname, lastname, employeeid, departmentname);
  }

  function readyStateChangeCallback()
  {
    // Same as Listing 2
  }

  window.credentials = function window$credentials(username, password)
```

(continued)

Listing 1-3 *(continued)*

```
    {
       // Same as Listing 2
    }

    function serialize(credentials)
    {
       // Same as Listing 2
    }

    function submitCallback()
    {
       // Same as Listing 2
    }
    </script>
  </head>
  <body>
    <form id="form1" runat="server">
      <!- Same as Listing 2 ->
    </form>
  </body>
</html>
```

Now let's walk through the implementations of the `Page_Load` server-side method and the `deserialize` JavaScript function in this listing, starting with the `Page_Load` method.

The `Page_Load` method begins by instantiating a `StringWriter` into which the XML data will be written:

```
string xml = "";
using (StringWriter sw = new StringWriter())
```

Then it instantiates an `XmlWriterSettings` object that specifies the settings for the XML document. In this case, the XML document will be indented and it will not contain the XML declaration:

```
XmlWriterSettings settings = new XmlWriterSettings();
settings.Indent = true;
settings.OmitXmlDeclaration = true;
```

Next, it instantiates an `XmlWriter` object with the specified settings and wraps the `StringWriter`. In other words, this `XmlWriter` will write the XML into the `StringWriter`:

```
using (XmlWriter xw = XmlWriter.Create(sw, settings))
```

Then, it invokes the `WriteStartDocument` method on the `XmlWriter` to mark the beginning of the XML document:

```
xw.WriteStartDocument();
```

Next, it invokes the `WriteStartElement` method on the `XmlWriter` to write a new element named `employeeInfo` into the `XmlWriter`, which in turn writes this element into the `StringWriter`:

```
xw.WriteStartElement("employeeInfo");
```

This element will act as the document element of the XML document. Every XML document must have a single element known as the *document element* that encapsulates the rest of the XML document.

`Page_Load` then invokes the `WriteElementString` method four times to write three elements named `firstName`, `lastName`, `employeeId`, and `departmentName` with the specified values into the `XmlWriter`, which in turn writes these elements into the `StringWriter`:

```
xw.WriteElementString("firstName", "Shahram");
xw.WriteElementString("lastName", "Khosravi");
xw.WriteElementString("employeeId", "22223333");
xw.WriteElementString("departmentName", "Some Department");
```

Next, `Page_Load` invokes the `ToString` method on the `StringWriter` to return a string that contains the entire XML document:

```
xml = sw.ToString();
```

Then, it sets the `Content-Type` HTTP response header to the value `text/xml` to signal the client code that the server response contains XML data:

```
Response.ContentType="text/xml";
```

Next, it writes the string that contains the XML data into the server response output stream:

```
Response.Write(xml);
```

Finally, it invokes the `End` method on the `Response` object to end the response right away and, consequently, to send the XML document to the client, bypassing the normal rendering routine of the current page:

```
Response.End();
```

Now let's walk through the implementation of the `deserialize` JavaScript function in Listing 1-3. This function invokes the `responseXML` property on the `XMLHttpRequest` object to return the XML document:

```
var response = request.responseXML;
var employeeInfo = response.documentElement;
```

Then, it uses the XML API to extract the employee's `firstname`, `lastname`, `employeeid`, and `departmentname` from the XML document:

```
var firstNameElement = employeeInfo.childNodes[0];
var firstname = firstNameElement.firstChild.nodeValue;

var lastNameElement = employeeInfo.childNodes[1];
var lastname = lastNameElement.firstChild.nodeValue;

var employeeIdElement = employeeInfo.childNodes[2];
var employeeid = employeeIdElement.firstChild.nodeValue;

var departmentNameElement = employeeInfo.childNodes[3];
var departmentname = departmentNameElement.firstChild.nodeValue;
```

Finally, it instantiates and returns an `employee` object with the returned `firstname`, `lastname`, `employeeid`, and `departmentname`:

```
return new employee(firstname, lastname, employeeid, departmentname);
```

JSON

One of the main tasks in an AJAX-enabled application is to serialize client/server-side objects into the *appropriate* format before data is sent over the wire and to deserialize client/server-side objects from an *appropriate* format after data is received over the wire. In general there are two common data-interchange formats: XML and JSON. XML format was discussed in the previous section. Now let's move on to the second common data-interchange format: JSON.

JavaScript Object Notation (JSON) is a data-interchange format based on a subset of the JavaScript language. The following sections present the fundamental JSON concepts and terms.

object

A JSON object is an unordered, comma-separated list of name/value pairs enclosed within a pair of braces. The name and value parts of each name/value pair are separated by a colon (`:`). The name part of each name/value pair is a string; and the value part is an array, another object, a string, a number, `true`, `false`, or `null`.

array

A JSON array is an ordered, comma-separated list of values enclosed within a pair of square brackets (`[ ]`). Each value is an array, another object, a string, a number, `true`, `false`, or `null`.

string

A JSON string is a collection of zero or more Unicode characters enclosed within double quotes (`" "`). You must use a JSON string to represent a single character, and the character must be in double quotes. You must use the backslash character (`\`) to escape the following characters:

❑ Quotation mark (`\"`)

❑ Solidus (`\/`)

- ❏ Reverse solidus (\\)
- ❏ Backspace (\b)
- ❏ Formfeed (\f)
- ❏ Newline (\n)
- ❏ Carriage return (\r)
- ❏ Horizontal tab (\t)

number

A JSON number is very similar to a C# number with one major exception: JSON does not support octal and hexadecimal formats.

null, true, and false

JSON supports `null`, `true`, and `false` as valid values.

JSON is a simple-yet-powerful, data-interchange format. It has the same hierarchical nature as XML, without the extra angle brackets, as shown in the following example:

```
{
  "departments":[
            {"departmentName":"department1",
             "departementManager":{"name":"someName1",
                                   "employeeID":1,
                                   "managesMultipleDepts":true
                                   },
             "sections":[
                       {"sectionName":"section1",
                        "sectionManager":{"name":"someName2",
                                          "employeeID":2
                                          },
                        "employees":[
                                    {"name":"someName3",
                                     "employeeID":3
                                     },
                                    {"name":"someName4",
                                     "employeeID":4
                                     }
                                    ]
                        },
                       {"sectionName":"section2",
                        "sectionManager":{"name":"someName5",
                                          "employeeID":5
                                          },
                        "employees":[
                                    {"name":"someName6",
                                     "employeeID":6
                                     },
```

(continued)

```
                                    {"name":"someName7",
                                     "employeeID":7
                                    }
                                ]
                            }
                        ]
                    }
                ]
            }
        ]
    }
```

One of the great things about JSON is that JavaScript provides easy, built-in support for parsing a JSON representation, as shown in Listing 1-4. This example is a version of Listing 1-2 that uses JSON.

Listing 1-4: A version of Listing 1-2 that uses JSON

```
<%@ Page Language="C#" %>
<%@ Import Namespace="System.Xml" %>
<%@ Import Namespace="System.IO" %>
<!DOCTYPE html PUBLIC "-//W3C//DTD XHTML 1.0 Transitional//EN"
"http://www.w3.org/TR/xhtml1/DTD/xhtml1-transitional.dtd">
<script runat="server">
  void Page_Load(object sender, EventArgs e)
  {
    if (Request.Headers["MyCustomHeader"] != null)
    {
      if (Request.Form["passwordtbx"] == "password" &&
          Request.Form["usernametbx"] == "username")
      {
        string json="{\"firstname\": \"Shahram\",";
        json += "\"lastname\": \"Khosravi\",";
        json += "\"employeeid\": 22223333,";
        json += "\"departmentname\": \"Some Department\"}";
        Response.Write(json);
        Response.End();
      }
      else
        throw new Exception("Wrong credentials");
    }
  }
</script>
<html xmlns="http://www.w3.org/1999/xhtml">
<head id="Head1" runat="server">
  <title>Untitled Page</title>
  <script type="text/javascript" language="javascript">
  var request;

  if (!window.XMLHttpRequest)
  {
    // Same as Listing 2
  }

  function readyStateChangeCallback()
  {
    if (request.readyState == 4 && request.status == 200)
    {
```

```
            var credentials = document.getElementById("credentials");
            credentials.style.display="none";
            var employeeinfotable = document.getElementById("employeeinfo");
            employeeinfotable.style.display="block";

            var response = request.responseText;
            eval("var employee = " + response + ";");

            var firstnamespan = document.getElementById("firstname");
            firstnamespan.innerText = employee.firstname;
            var lastnamespan = document.getElementById("lastname");
            lastnamespan.innerText = employee.lastname;

            var employeeidspan = document.getElementById("employeeid");
            employeeidspan.innerText = employee.employeeid;

            var departmentnamespan = document.getElementById("departmentname");
            departmentnamespan.innerText = employee.departmentname;
        }
    }

    window.credentials = function window$credentials(username, password)
    {
        // Same as Listing 2
    }

    function serialize(credentials)
    {
        // Same as Listing 2
    }

    function submitCallback()
    {
        // Same as Listing 2
    }
    </script>
</head>
<body>
    <form id="form1" runat="server">
        // Same as Listing 2
    </form>
</body>
</html>
```

In this listing, the Page_Load method generates a string that contains the JSON representation of the employee object. This method writes the JSON representation into the response output stream and ends the response as usual:

```
        string json="{\"firstname\": \"Shahram\",";
        json += "\"lastname\": \"Khosravi\",";
        json += "\"employeeid\": 22223333,";
        json += "\"departmentname\": \"Some Department\"}";

        Response.Write(json);
        Response.End();
```

Things are pretty simple on the client side, as you can see in the following code fragment from Listing 1-4:

```
var response = request.responseText;
eval("var employee=" + response + ";");
```

This simply calls the eval JavaScript function to deserialize an employee object in the JSON string received from the server. As you can see, the messy XML deserialization code presented in Listing 1-3 is all gone and replaced with a simple call into the eval JavaScript function. However, this simplicity comes with a price. Because the eval JavaScript function basically trusts the scripts that it runs, it introduces serious security issues. This is not a problem in this example because the JSON representation is coming from a trusted server. However, in general, you must be very careful about what gets passed into eval.

ASP.NET AJAX

The ASP.NET AJAX framework brings to the world of AJAX-enabled Web application development what ASP.NET and the .NET Framework brought to the world of server-side Web application development over the past few years. The biggest advantage of ASP.NET over the earlier server-side Web development technologies such as the classic ASP is that you get to program in the .NET Framework, which provides the following benefits among many others:

❑ The .NET Framework is a full-fledged, object-oriented framework that enables you to take full advantage of all the well-known benefits of object-oriented programming such as classes, interfaces, namespaces, polymorphism, inheritance, and the like.

❑ The .NET Framework comes with a large set of managed classes with convenient methods, properties, and events that save you from having to write lots of infrastructure and generic code that have nothing to do with the specifics of your application.

❑ The .NET Framework includes a full-fledged typing and type-reflection system that enables you to perform runtime type inspections, discoveries, instantiations, invocations, and the like.

❑ The .NET Framework provides you with groundbreaking facilities and capabilities such as the following:

   ❑ *Application lifecycle and its events:* The HttpApplication object that represents an ASP.NET application goes through a set of steps or phases collectively known as the application lifecycle. This object raises events before and/or after each lifecycle phase to allow you to customize the application lifecycle.

   ❑ *Page lifecycle and its events:* Every ASP.NET page goes through a set of steps or phases collectively known as the page lifecycle. The Page object that represents the ASP.NET page raises events before and/or after each lifecycle phase to allow you to customize the page lifecycle.

   ❑ *Server controls:* Server controls enable you to program against the underlying markup using the .NET Framework and its rich, object-oriented class library. This gives you the same programming experience as these server controls desktop counterparts provide.

❑ *Control architecture:* Every server control goes through a set of steps or phases collectively known as the control lifecycle, and raises events before and/or after each lifecycle phase to allow you to customize the control lifecycle.

❑ *Declarative programming:* The ASP.NET declarative programming enables you to program declaratively without writing a single line of imperative code. The ASP.NET runtime automatically parses the declarative code, dynamically generates the associated imperative code, dynamically compiles the imperative code, caches the compiled imperative code for future use, and instantiates and initializes the associated compiled .NET types.

Thanks to ASP.NET and the .NET Framework, the server-side Web application development world can take full advantage of these important programming benefits to enormously boost productivity and to write more reliable and architecturally sound programs.

As you'll see throughout this book, the ASP.NET AJAX framework provides similar programming benefits to developers of AJAX-enabled Web applications. The ASP.NET AJAX Framework consists of two frameworks: the ASP.NET AJAX client-side framework and the ASP.NET AJAX server-side framework. The ASP.NET AJAX server-side framework is an extension of the ASP.NET Framework, which provides all the server-side support that an AJAX-enabled Web application needs.

Installing the ASP.NET AJAX Extensions and ASP.NET Futures

Make sure both the ASP.NET AJAX Extensions and ASP.NET Futures are installed on your computer. You can download free copies of the ASP.NET AJAX Extensions and ASP.NET Futures from the official Microsoft ASP.NET AJAX site at

Summary

This chapter first discussed the main AJAX technologies. Then it provided a brief description of the ASP.NET AJAX framework. As mentioned, the ASP.NET AJAX framework consists of two main frameworks: the ASP.NET AJAX client-side framework and ASP.NET AJAX server-side framework.

The next chapter begins your journey of the ASP.NET AJAX client-side framework, where you'll learn a great deal about the ASP.NET AJAX JavaScript base type extensions.

JavaScript Base Type Extensions

The main goal of the ASP.NET AJAX client-side framework is to emulate the ASP.NET and .NET Framework *as much as possible* to bring similar .NET-style programming to your client-side scripting. The ASP.NET AJAX JavaScript base type extensions are the first step toward achieving this goal.

These extensions extend the functionality of the JavaScript base types such as `Array`, `Boolean`, `Date`, `Error`, `Number`, `Object`, and `String` to add support for .NET-like methods and properties. As such, the ASP.NET AJAX JavaScript base type extensions make client-side programming against these JavaScript base types more like server-side programming against their .NET counterparts *as much as possible*.

The code samples presented in this chapter use a new JavaScript function named `pageLoad` and a new server control named `ScriptManager` as shown in the boldfaced portion of Listing 2-1.

Listing 2-1: The ASP.NET Page Used by the Examples

```
<%@ Page Language = "C#" %>
<html xmlns = "http://www.w3.org/1999/xhtml">
<head runat = "server">
  <title>Untitled Page</title>
  <script language = "JavaScript" type = "text/javascript">
    function pageLoad() {
    . . .
    }
  </script>
</head>
<body>
  <form id = "form1" runat = "server">
    <asp:ScriptManager ID = "ScriptManager1" runat = "server" />
  </form>
</body>
</html>
```

I'll discuss the `pageLoad` JavaScript function and `ScriptManager` server control in detail in future chapters. For now, here are two key concepts:

❑ One of the responsibilities of the `ScriptManager` server control is to download the ASP.NET AJAX client-side framework to the requesting browser to make it available to the browser's JavaScript engine.

❑ The ASP.NET AJAX client-side framework automatically calls the `pageLoad` JavaScript function after the page and the related client-side scripts are completely loaded.

ASP.NET AJAX Array Type Extensions

The .NET `Array` type features methods such as `Clone`, `Add`, `Clear`, `Contains`, `IndexOf`, `Insert`, `Remove`, and `RemoveAt`. The ASP.NET AJAX client-side framework extends the JavaScript `Array` type to add support for similar methods. These extensions allow the JavaScript `Array` type to emulate its .NET counterpart as much as possible to make you feel like you're programming against the .NET `Array` type.

Keep in mind that these new methods are static methods, which means that you must call these methods directly on the `Array` class itself.

add

The `add` method takes two arguments of type `Array` and `Object`, respectively and adds the `Object` to the end of the `Array` as shown in the following code. Because the second argument is of type `Object`, you can add any type of object to the specified array.

```
<%@ Page Language = "C#" %>
<html xmlns = "http://www.w3.org/1999/xhtml">
<head runat = "server">
  <title>Untitled Page</title>
  <script language = "JavaScript" type = "text/javascript">

    function pageLoad() {
      var a = ['m1','m2'];
      Array.add(a, 'm3');
      for (var i = 0; i<a.length; i++)
        alert(a[i]);
    }
  </script>
</head>
<body>
  <form id = "form1" runat = "server">
    <asp:ScriptManager ID = "ScriptManager1" runat = "server" />
  </form>
</body>
</html>
```

addRange

The `addRange` method takes two arguments of type `Array` and adds the contents of the second `Array` object to the end of the first `Array` object, as shown in the following code:

```
<%@ Page Language = "C#" %>
<html xmlns = "http://www.w3.org/1999/xhtml">
<head runat = "server">
  <title>Untitled Page</title>
  <script language = "JavaScript" type = "text/javascript">

    function pageLoad() {
      var a1 = ['m1','m2'];
      var a2 = ['m3','m4','m5'];
      Array.addRange(a1, a2);
      for (var i = 0; i<a1.length; i++)
        alert(a1[i]);
    }
  </script>
</head>
<body>
  <form id = "form1" runat = "server">
    <asp:ScriptManager ID = "ScriptManager1" runat = "server" />
  </form>
</body>
</html>
```

clear

The `clear` method clears the specified `Array` object and sets its `length` property to zero, as shown in the following code fragment:

```
<%@ Page Language = "C#" %>
<html xmlns = "http://www.w3.org/1999/xhtml">
<head runat = "server">
  <title>Untitled Page</title>
  <script language = "JavaScript" type = "text/javascript">

    function pageLoad() {
      var a1 = ['m1','m2'];
      alert(a1.length);
      Array.clear(a1);
      alert(a1.length);
    }
  </script>
</head>
<body>
  <form id = "form1" runat = "server">
    <asp:ScriptManager ID = "ScriptManager1" runat = "server" />
  </form>
</body>
</html>
```

clone

The `clone` method clones the specified `Array` object. This cloning operation is a *shallow copy*, which means that the object referenced in the `Array` object and its clone reference the same objects. That is, the references are copied, but the objects being referenced are not copied, as shown in the following code:

```
<%@ Page Language = "C#" %>
<html xmlns = "http://www.w3.org/1999/xhtml">
<head runat = "server">
  <title>Untitled Page</title>
  <script language = "JavaScript" type = "text/javascript">

    function pageLoad() {
      var a1 = ['m1','m2'];
      var a2 = Array.clone(a1);
      alert("a1[0] = " + a1[0] + "\n" + "a2[0] = " + a2[0]);
      alert("a1[1] = " + a1[1] + "\n" + "a2[1] = " + a2[1]);
    }
  </script>
</head>
<body>
  <form id = "form1" runat = "server">
    <asp:ScriptManager ID = "ScriptManager1" runat = "server" />
  </form>
</body>
</html>
```

contains

The `contains` method returns a Boolean value that indicates whether the specified `Array` object contains the specified element. For example:

```
<%@ Page Language = "C#" %>
<html xmlns = "http://www.w3.org/1999/xhtml">
<head runat = "server">
  <title>Untitled Page</title>
  <script language = "JavaScript" type = "text/javascript">

    function pageLoad() {
      var a1 = ['m1','m2'];
      alert(Array.contains(a1,'m2'));
      alert(Array.contains(a1,'m4'));
    }
  </script>
</head>
<body>
  <form id = "form1" runat = "server">
    <asp:ScriptManager ID = "ScriptManager1" runat = "server" />
  </form>
</body>
</html>
```

enqueue and dequeue

The JavaScript `Array` type can be used as a stack. The standard JavaScript `Array` type exposes two methods named `push` and `pop`. The `push` method pushes a specified item onto the top of the stack, and the `pop` method pops up the item at the top of the stack. Here is an example:

```
<%@ Page Language = "C#" %>
<html xmlns = "http://www.w3.org/1999/xhtml">
<head runat = "server">
  <title>Untitled Page</title>
  <script language = "JavaScript" type = "text/javascript">

    function pageLoad() {
      var a = [];
      a.push('m1');
      a.push('m2');
      a.push('m3');
      alert(a.pop());
    }
  </script>
</head>
<body>
  <form id = "form1" runat = "server">
    <asp:ScriptManager ID = "ScriptManager1" runat = "server" />
  </form>
</body>
</html>
```

This example respectively pushes the `m1`, `m2`, and `m3` items onto the top of the stack. Note that the last pushed item—that is, `m3`—sits on the top of the stack. The call into the `pop` method pops up the topmost item—that is, `m3`. Figure 2-1 presents the stack before and after the call into the `pop` method.

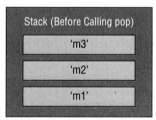
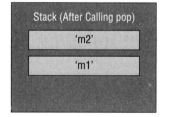

Figure 2-1

The JavaScript `Array` type can also be used as a queue. A queue is the opposite of a stack. A queue uses a FIFO (first in, first out) algorithm where the first item added to the queue is the first item to be served. The JavaScript `Array` type includes a method named `shift` that allows you to access the first item added to the list. Here is an example of a queue in JavaScript:

```
<%@ Page Language = "C#" %>
<html xmlns = "http://www.w3.org/1999/xhtml">
<head runat = "server">
  <title>Untitled Page</title>
  <script language = "JavaScript" type = "text/javascript">

    function pageLoad() {
      var a = [];
      a[0] = 'm1';
      a[1] = 'm2';
      a[2] = 'm3';
      alert(a.shift());
    }
  </script>
</head>
<body>
  <form id = "form1" runat = "server">
    <asp:ScriptManager ID = "ScriptManager1" runat = "server" />
  </form>
</body>
</html>
```

As you can see, JavaScript already supports the concept of queueing. However, the way this is done in JavaScript is quite different from the way it's done in the .NET Framework. The main problem is that JavaScript uses an unintuitive approach to implement a queue. The ASP.NET AJAX client-side framework extends the functionality of the JavaScript `Array` type to add support for two convenient .NET-like methods named `enqueue` and `dequeue`, as shown here:

```
<%@ Page Language = "C#" %>
<html xmlns = "http://www.w3.org/1999/xhtml">
<head runat = "server">
  <title>Untitled Page</title>
  <script language = "JavaScript" type = "text/javascript">

    function pageLoad() {
      var a = [];
      Array.enqueue(a,'m1');
      Array.enqueue(a,'m2');
      Array.enqueue(a,'m3');
      alert(Array.dequeue(a));
    }
  </script>
</head>
<body>
  <form id = "form1" runat = "server">
    <asp:ScriptManager ID = "ScriptManager1" runat = "server" />
  </form>
</body>
</html>
```

Figure 2-2 presents the queue before and after the call into the `dequeue` method.

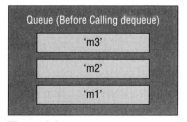
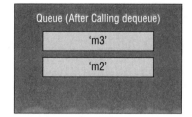

Figure 2-2

forEach

The ASP.NET AJAX client-side framework extends the functionality of the JavaScript `Array` type to add support for a method named `forEach`. The best way to understand what this method does is to look at the internal implementation of this method as shown in Listing 2-2.

Listing 2-2: The Internal Implementation of the forEach Method

```
Array.forEach = function(b, e, d)
{
  for(var a = 0, f = b.length; a < f; a ++ )
  {
    var c = b[a];
    if(typeof c !== "undefined")
      e.call(d, c, a, b);
  }
}
```

The `forEach` method takes the following three parameters:

- ❑ b: This parameter references a JavaScript `Array` object.
- ❑ e: This parameter references a JavaScript function that takes three parameters, which will be discussed shortly.
- ❑ d: This parameter references a JavaScript object.

As Listing 2-2 shows, the `forEach` function iterates through the elements of the `Array` object (b), calls the JavaScript function (e) once for each enumerated element, and passes the following parameters into the `call` method of this JavaScript function (e):

- ❑ The JavaScript object (d)
- ❑ The value of the enumerated element (c)
- ❑ The index of the enumerated element (a)
- ❑ The JavaScript `Array` itself (b)

It's completely up to the implementation of the JavaScript function (e) and the JavaScript object (d) what to do with the enumerated element of the specified `array` object (b) when the JavaScript function (e) is called. Listing 2-3 shows an example.

33

Listing 2-3: Demonstration of the forEach Method

```
<%@ Page Language = "C#" %>
<html xmlns = "http://www.w3.org/1999/xhtml">
<head runat = "server">
  <title>Untitled Page</title>
  <script language = "JavaScript" type = "text/javascript">
    function multiply(val,index,ar)
    {
      ar[index] = val * this.get_c();
    }

    function myClass(c)
    {
      this.c = c;
      this.get_c = function ()
      {
        return this.c;
      };
    }

    function pageLoad() {
      var a = [1, 2, 3, 4];
      var myObj = new myClass(6);
      Array.forEach(a, multiply, myObj);
      for (var j = 0; j<a.length; j++)
        alert(a[j]);
    }
  </script>
</head>
<body>
  <form id = "form1" runat = "server">
    <asp:ScriptManager ID = "ScriptManager1" runat = "server" />
  </form>
</body>
</html>
```

In this case, the forEach function calls the multiply JavaScript function once for each element of the Array (a). Note that Listing 2-3 also defines a class named myClass with a simple field and a getter method that returns the value of this field. In this case, the forEach function simply multiplies the value of each element of the array by the number 6.

indexOf

The ASP.NET AJAX client-side framework extends the functionality of the JavaScript Array type to add support for a method named indexOf. As the name implies, this method returns the index of a specified element of a specified array. As such, it takes the following three parameters:

❑   The JavaScript array to be searched

❑   The array element to search for

❑   The index at which to start searching the array

Here is an example:

```
<%@ Page Language = "C#" %>
<html xmlns = "http://www.w3.org/1999/xhtml">
<head runat = "server">
  <title>Untitled Page</title>
  <script language = "JavaScript" type = "text/javascript">

    function pageLoad() {
      var a = [1, 2, 3, 4];
      alert (Array.indexOf(a, 3, 1));
    }
  </script>
</head>
<body>
  <form id = "form1" runat = "server">
    <asp:ScriptManager ID = "ScriptManager1" runat = "server" />
  </form>
</body>
</html>
```

insert

The ASP.NET AJAX client-side framework extends the JavaScript `Array` type to add support for a method named `insert`, which inserts a specified object into a specified array at the specified index. The following code fragment inserts the number 5 into the specified array at position 1, which means that after the insertion, the array will contain these elements: 1, 5, 2, 3, and 4.

```
<%@ Page Language = "C#" %>
<html xmlns = "http://www.w3.org/1999/xhtml">
<head runat = "server">
  <title>Untitled Page</title>
  <script language = "JavaScript" type = "text/javascript">

    function pageLoad() {
      var a = [1, 2, 3, 4];
      Array.insert(a, 1, 5);
      for (var i = 0; i<a.length; i++)
        alert(a[i]);
    }
  </script>
</head>
<body>
  <form id = "form1" runat = "server">
    <asp:ScriptManager ID = "ScriptManager1" runat = "server" />
  </form>
</body>
</html>
```

parse

The `parse` extension method allows you to parse the content of a string into an array. The string must follow this format: `"[m1, m2, m3, m4, m5]"`. Here is an example:

```
<%@ Page Language = "C#" %>
<html xmlns = "http://www.w3.org/1999/xhtml">
<head runat = "server">
  <title>Untitled Page</title>
  <script language = "JavaScript" type = "text/javascript">

    function pageLoad() {
      var str = "[1, 2, 3, 4]";
      var a = Array.parse(str);
      for (var i = 0; i<a.length; i++)
        alert(a[i]);
    }
  </script>
</head>
<body>
  <form id = "form1" runat = "server">
    <asp:ScriptManager ID = "ScriptManager1" runat = "server" />
  </form>
</body>
</html>
```

remove

The `remove` extension method allows you to remove a specified item from a specified array. The following code fragment removes the number 3 from the specified array:

```
<%@ Page Language = "C#" %>
<html xmlns = "http://www.w3.org/1999/xhtml">
<head runat = "server">
  <title>Untitled Page</title>
  <script language = "JavaScript" type = "text/javascript">

    function pageLoad() {
      var a = [1, 2, 3, 4];
      Array.remove(a,3);
      for (var i = 0; i<a.length; i++)
        alert(a[i]);
    }
  </script>
</head>
<body>
  <form id = "form1" runat = "server">
    <asp:ScriptManager ID = "ScriptManager1" runat = "server" />
  </form>
</body>
</html>
```

removeAt

The removeAt method removes an item with the specified index from the specified array. The following code listing removes the item with an index of 2 (that is, the number 3) from the specified array:

```
<%@ Page Language = "C#" %>
<html xmlns = "http://www.w3.org/1999/xhtml">
<head runat = "server">
  <title>Untitled Page</title>
  <script language = "JavaScript" type = "text/javascript">

    function pageLoad() {
      var a = [1, 2, 3, 4];
      Array.removeAt(a,2);
      for (var i = 0; i<a.length; i++)
        alert(a[i]);
    }
  </script>
</head>
<body>
  <form id = "form1" runat = "server">
    <asp:ScriptManager ID = "ScriptManager1" runat = "server" />
  </form>
</body>
</html>
```

ASP.NET AJAX Boolean Type Extensions

The ASP.NET AJAX client-side framework extends the JavaScript Boolean type to add support for a new .NET-like method named parse that parses the string values of "true" and "false" into a valid JavaScript Boolean value. Here's an example:

```
<%@ Page Language = "C#" %>
<html xmlns = "http://www.w3.org/1999/xhtml">
<head runat = "server">
  <title>Untitled Page</title>
  <script language = "JavaScript" type = "text/javascript">

    function pageLoad() {
      var b = Boolean.parse("false");
      alert(b);
    }
  </script>
</head>
<body>
  <form id = "form1" runat = "server">
    <asp:ScriptManager ID = "ScriptManager1" runat = "server" />
  </form>
</body>
</html>
```

ASP.NET AJAX Date Type Extensions

The ASP.NET AJAX `Date` type extensions extend the JavaScript `Date` type to add support for two new methods named `format` and `localeFormat`, which format a date using the invariant and current cultures, respectively. Here is an example of both methods:

```
<%@ Page Language = "C#" %>
<html xmlns = "http://www.w3.org/1999/xhtml">
<head runat = "server">
  <title>Untitled Page</title>
  <script language = "JavaScript" type = "text/javascript">

    function pageLoad() {
      var d = new Date();
      var f1 = d.format("hh:mm:ss");
      alert(f1);
      var f2 = d.localeFormat("d");
      alert(f2);
    }
  </script>
</head>
<body>
  <form id = "form1" runat = "server">
    <asp:ScriptManager ID = "ScriptManager1" runat = "server" />
  </form>
</body>
</html>
```

ASP.NET AJAX Object Type Extensions

The .NET `Object` class exposes a method named `GetType` that you can call on an object to query its type at runtime. The ASP.NET AJAX client-side framework extends the JavaScript `Object` type to add support for two .NET-like methods named `getType` and `getTypeName`, which return the type of the object and the fully qualified name of the type, respectively. Here's an example:

```
<%@ Page Language = "C#" %>
<html xmlns = "http://www.w3.org/1999/xhtml">
<head runat = "server">
  <title>Untitled Page</title>
  <script language = "JavaScript" type = "text/javascript">
    function Person (firstName, lastName)
    {
      this.firstName = firstName;
      this.lastName = lastName;
    }

    function pageLoad() {
      var p = new Person("Shahram", "Khosravi");
      var b = Object.getType(p);
      var name = Object.getTypeName(b);
      alert(name);
    }
```

```
      </script>
    </head>
    <body>
      <form id = "form1" runat = "server">
        <asp:ScriptManager ID = "ScriptManager1" runat = "server" />
      </form>
    </body>
  </html>
```

This code fragment first defines a new class named `Person` and instantiates an instance of this class. Next, it calls the `getType` method of the `Object` class, passing in the new `Person` instance to return a reference to the type of the instance; that is, the constructor of the `Person` class. Then, it calls the `getTypeName` method of the `Object` class to return the name of the instance type.

ASP.NET AJAX String Type Extensions

The ASP.NET AJAX client-side framework extends the functionality of the JavaScript `String` type to add support for the .NET-like methods discussed in the following sections. These extensions make programming against the JavaScript String type more like programming against the .NET `String` type. This is yet another attempt on the part of the ASP.NET AJAX framework to make client-side programming feel more like server-side .NET programming.

endsWith

The `endsWith` .NET-like extension method returns a Boolean value that specifies whether a specified string ends with the specified substring. Note that any leading or trailing white space of the substring is considered part of the substring itself. In other words, the `endsWith` method does not trim the substring. For example, the second call to the `endsWith` method in the following code fragment returns `false`, because the string passed into the method contains a trailing white space:

```
<%@ Page Language = "C#" %>
<html xmlns = "http://www.w3.org/1999/xhtml">
<head runat = "server">
  <title>Untitled Page</title>
  <script language = "JavaScript" type = "text/javascript">

    function pageLoad() {
      var str = "Programming ASP.NET";
      alert(str.endsWith(".NET 3.0"));
      alert(str.endsWith(".NET 3.0 "));
    }
  </script>
</head>
<body>
  <form id = "form1" runat = "server">
    <asp:ScriptManager ID = "ScriptManager1" runat = "server" />
  </form>
</body>
</html>
```

startsWith

The `startsWith` method returns a Boolean value that specifies whether a specified string starts with the specified substring. Again, leading or trailing white space of the substring is considered part of the substring itself. In this example, just like the previous one, the second call to `startsWith` returns `false` because the string passed into the method contains extra leading white space:

```
<%@ Page Language = "C#" %>
<html xmlns = "http://www.w3.org/1999/xhtml">
<head runat = "server">
  <title>Untitled Page</title>
  <script language = "JavaScript" type = "text/javascript">

    function pageLoad() {
      var str = "Programming ASP.NET";
      alert(str.startsWith("Programming "));
      alert(str.startsWith(" Programming "));
    }
  </script>
</head>
<body>
  <form id = "form1" runat = "server">
    <asp:ScriptManager ID = "ScriptManager1" runat = "server" />
  </form>
</body>
</html>
```

trim

The `trim` method trims the specified string — that is, it removes the leading and trailing white space. For example, the following code fragment returns `true` in both cases even though the second case contains trailing white space because the call to `trim` removes this white space:

```
<%@ Page Language = "C#" %>
<html xmlns = "http://www.w3.org/1999/xhtml">
<head runat = "server">
  <title>Untitled Page</title>
  <script language = "JavaScript" type = "text/javascript">

    function pageLoad() {
      var str = "Programming ASP.NET";
      alert(str.startsWith("Programming "));
      alert(str.startsWith(" Programming ".trim()));
    }
  </script>
</head>
<body>
  <form id = "form1" runat = "server">
    <asp:ScriptManager ID = "ScriptManager1" runat = "server" />
  </form>
</body>
</html>
```

The ASP.NET AJAX client-side framework also adds two new methods named `trimEnd` and `trimStart` that respectively remove only the trailing and leading white space from the specified string.

Formatting

The ASP.NET AJAX client-side framework extends the `String` JavaScript type to add support for two formatting methods named `format` and `localeFormat`, which use the invariant and current culture to format the specified string, respectively. The first argument of these two methods contains the formatting string, very similar to the .NET formatting strings. Here is an example of both methods:

```
<%@ Page Language = "C#" %>
<html xmlns = "http://www.w3.org/1999/xhtml">
<head runat = "server">
  <title>Untitled Page</title>
  <script language = "JavaScript" type = "text/javascript">

    function pageLoad() {
      var a = 5, b = 8;
      var str = String.format("a = {0}\nb = {1}", a, b);
      alert(str);
    }
  </script>
</head>
<body>
  <form id = "form1" runat = "server">
    <asp:ScriptManager ID = "ScriptManager1" runat = "server" />
  </form>
</body>
</html>
```

ASP.NET AJAX Error Type Extensions

One of the highly recommended programming practices is to wrap critical parts of the code in a `try-catch-finally` block to trap and handle runtime exceptions. The .NET Framework includes a set of convenient exception classes such as `ArgumentException`, `ArgumentNullException`, and `ArgumentOutOfRangeException` for server-side exception programming. The ASP.NET AJAX `Error` type extensions extend the functionality of the JavaScript `Error` type to add support for similar .NET-like exception programming facilities on the client side.

create

The `create` function is a new static function of the JavaScript `Error` type that allows you to create a new `Error` object with additional error information. This function takes two arguments. The first argument is the error message. The second argument is an optional object with properties that provide more information about the error. This object must contain a property named `name` that uniquely identifies the error type. The rest of the properties can have any name and values that make sense to your application. For example, you may want to assign a unique integer number to each error type.

The following page code presents an example where the `create` function is used:

```
<%@ Page Language = "C#" %>
<!DOCTYPE html PUBLIC "-//W3C//DTD XHTML 1.0 Transitional//EN"
"http://www.w3.org/TR/xhtml1/DTD/xhtml1-transitional.dtd">
<html xmlns = "http://www.w3.org/1999/xhtml">
<head runat = "server">
  <title>Untitled Page</title>
  <script language = "javascript" type = "text/javascript">
    function validateInput(input)
    {
      var reg = new RegExp("(\\d\\d)[-/](\\d\\d)[-/](\\d\\d(?:\\d\\d)?)");
      var date = reg.exec(input);
      if (date == null)
      {
          var err = Error.create("Please enter a valid date!",
                                 {name : "MyError", errorNumber : 234});
          throw err;
      }
    }

    function clickCallback()
    {
      var date = document.getElementById("date");
      try
      {
        validateInput(date.value);
      }
      catch (e)
      {
        alert("Error Message: " + e.message +
              "\nError Number: " + e.errorNumber);
        date.value = "";
      }
    }

  </script>
</head>
<body>
  <form id = "form1" runat = "server">
    <asp:ScriptManager runat = "server" ID = "ScriptManager1" />
    Enter date: <input type = "text" id = "date" /> 
    <input type = "button" value = "Validate" onclick = "clickCallback()" />
  </form>
</body>
</html>
```

Figure 2-3 shows what you'll see in your browser when you access this page.

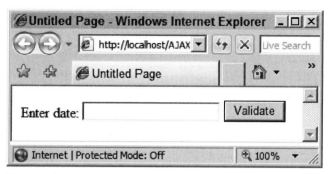

Figure 2-3

As you can see, this is a simple page that consists of a text box and a button. When you enter a date in the text box and click the button, the `clickCallback` function is invoked as follows:

```
function clickCallback()
{
  var date = document.getElementById("date");
  try
  {
    validateInput(date.value);
  }

  catch (e)
  {
    alert("Error Message: " + e.message +
          "\nError Number: " + e.errorNumber);
    date.value = "";
  }
}
```

This function first accesses the text box element, like this:

```
var date = document.getElementById("date");
```

Notice that the `clickCallback` function wraps the call to a function named `validateInput` in a `try` block and catches the exceptions that the `validateInput` function raises in the associated `catch` block. As the name implies, the `validateInput` function validates the value you entered in the textbox. For example:

```
function validateInput(input)
{
  var reg = new RegExp("(\\d\\d)[-/](\\d\\d)[-/](\\d\\d(?:\\d\\d)?)");
  var date = reg.exec(input);
  if (date == null)
  {
    var err = Error.create("Please enter a valid date!",
                           {name : "MyError", errorNumber : 234});
    throw err;
  }
}
```

This function first creates a RegExp JavaScript object, passing in the regular expression pattern that specifies the valid date formats:

```
var reg = new RegExp("(\\d\\d)[-/](\\d\\d)[-/](\\d\\d(?:\\d\\d)?)");
```

The validateInput function then calls the exec method on the RegExp object to execute the regular expression passing in the date you entered in the text box:

```
var date = reg.exec(input);
```

If the entered value does not match a valid date format specified in the regular expression pattern, the exec function returns null, and consequently the validateInput function calls the create static method of the Error class to create a new Error object:

```
var err = Error.create("Please enter a valid date!",
                   {name : "MyError", errorNumber : 234});
```

Finally, the validateInput function throws the exception:

```
throw err;
```

As discussed earlier, the clickCallback function catches this error in its catch block and calls the alert function to display the values of the message and errorNumber properties of the error object, as shown in the following code. Recall that the errorNumber property was defined in the validateInput function when the create function was called.

```
catch (e)
{
  alert("Error Message: " + e.message +
        "\nError Number: " + e.errorNumber);
  date.value = "";
}
```

Now take a look at the internal implementation of the create function as shown in the following code fragment:

```
Error.create = function(d, b)
{
  var a = new Error(d);
  a.message = d;
  if(b)
    for(var c in b)
      a[c] = b[c];
  a.popStackFrame();
  return a
};
```

As this code shows, the create function creates a new Error object, passing in its first argument:

```
var a = new Error(d);
```

Next, it assigns the properties of the object or array passed in as its second argument to the newly created `Error` object:

```
for(var c in b)
    a[c] = b[c];
```

Finally, it calls the `popStackFrame` function, which will be thoroughly discussed in the next section.

popStackFrame

The JavaScript `Error` type features two properties named `fileName` and `lineNumber`. Some browsers set the values of these properties to respectively specify the URL of the document and the line number in the document where the error occurred.

These two properties provide great debugging information for developers. Some browsers set these properties to the URL of the document and the line number in the document where the error was created as opposed to the URL of the document and the line number in the document where the error occurred. To help you understand the difference between these two scenarios, let's revisit the previous example. In the previous example, the error is created in the `validateInput` function, but it occurs in the `clickCallback` function at the point where the `validateInput` function is invoked. To see how this works, first you need to modify the `clickCallback` method to add the highlighted code shown in the following code fragment. The highlighted code simply displays the values of the `fileName` and `lineNumber` properties.

```
function clickCallback()
{
    var date = document.getElementById("date");
    try
    {
      validateInput(date.value);
    }
    catch (e)
    {
      alert("Error Message: " + e.message +
            "\nError Number: " + e.errorNumber +

            "\nDocument: " + e.fileName +
            "\nLine Number: " + e.lineNumber);

      date.value = "";
    }
}
```

As mentioned in the previous section, the `Error.create` method contains a call into the `popStack-Frame` method. You want to see the effect of the `popStackFrame` method, so you also need to comment out the line of code in the `Error.create` method that calls the `popStackFrame` method. This means that you need to use the following implementation instead of the standard implementation.

To distinguish between the `Error.create` standard method and the following version, give your version a different name, `MyErrorCreate`:

```
Function MyErrorCreate(d, b)
{
  var a = new Error(d);
  a.message = d;
  if(b)
    for(var c in b)
      a[c] = b[c];
  //a.popStackFrame();
  return a
};
```

The following code presents a new version of the previous example, which uses your own `MyErrorCreate` method:

```
<%@ Page Language = "C#" %>
<!DOCTYPE html PUBLIC "-//W3C//DTD XHTML 1.0 Transitional//EN"
"http://www.w3.org/TR/xhtml1/DTD/xhtml1-transitional.dtd">
<html xmlns = "http://www.w3.org/1999/xhtml">
<head id = "Head1" runat = "server">
  <title>Untitled Page</title>
  <script language = "javascript" type = "text/javascript">
    function MyErrorCreate(d, b)
    {
      var a = new Error(d);
      a.message = d;
      if(b)
      for(var c in b)
      a[c] = b[c];
      //a.popStackFrame();
      return a
    };

    function validateInput(input)
    {
      var reg = new RegExp("(\\d\\d)[-/](\\d\\d)[-/](\\d\\d(?:\\d\\d)?)");
      var date = reg.exec(input);
      if (date == null)
      {
        var err = MyErrorCreate("Please enter a valid date!",
                          {name : "MyError", errorNumber : 234});
        throw err;
      }
    }

    function clickCallback()
    {
      var date = document.getElementById("date");
      try
      {
        validateInput(date.value);
```

```
        }
        catch (e)
        {
         alert("Error Message: " + e.message +
               "\nError Number: " + e.errorNumber +
               "\nDocument: " + e.fileName +
               "\nLine Number: " + e.lineNumber);
          date.value = "";
        }
      }

  </script>
</head>
<body>
  <form id = "form1" runat = "server">
    <asp:ScriptManager runat = "server" ID = "ScriptManager1" />
    Enter date: <input type = "text" id = "date" /> 
    <input type = "button" value = "Validate" onclick = "clickCallback()" />
  </form>
</body>
</html>
```

Next, you need to run this example in a browser such as Mozilla Firefox that supports the `fileName` and `lineNumber` properties. If you run this example in Mozilla Firefox and enter an invalid value in the text box, you'll get the pop-up message shown in Figure 2-4.

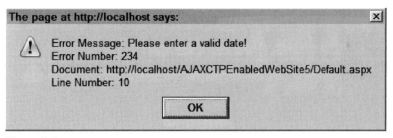

Figure 2-4

According to this message, the error occurred in line number 10. Select the Page Source option from the browser's View menu to view the page source. As the page source shows, the line number 10 is the code line highlighted in the following code fragment:

```
function MyErrorCreate(d, b)
{
  var a = new Error(d);
  a.message = d;
  if(b)
  for(var c in b)
  a[c] = b[c];
  //a.popStackFrame();
  return a
};
```

In other words, according the pop-up message shown in Figure 2-4, the error occurred where the `Error` object was created. This isn't right because the error occurred where the `MyErrorCreate` function was actually called, as shown in the highlighted portion of the following code:

```
function validateInput(input)
{
  var reg = new RegExp("(\\d\\d)[-/](\\d\\d)[-/](\\d\\d(?:\\d\\d)?)");
  var date = reg.exec(input);
  if (date == null)
  {
    var err = MyErrorCreate("Please enter a valid date!",
                           {name : "MyError", errorNumber : 234});
    throw err;
  }
}
```

As this example shows, browsers such as Mozilla Firefox set the `fileName` and `lineNumber` properties of the `Error` object to the URL of the document and the line in the document where the `Error` object was created.

To correct this misbehavior of browsers such as Mozilla Firefox, the ASP.NET AJAX client-side framework extends the functionality of the JavaScript `Error` type to add support for a function named `popStackFrame`. To illustrate how this function works, uncomment the line of code in `MyErrorCreate` that invokes `popStackFrame`. Now if you run the example again, you'll get the pop-up message shown in Figure 2-5.

Figure 2-5

According to this message, the error occurred at line 26. Now if you view the page source again, you'll notice that line 26 contains the highlighted code shown in the previous code listing. In other words, thanks to the `popStackFrame` function, the pop-up message reports that the error occurred where the `MyCreateError` method (which is the `Error.create` method) was actually called.

Under the Hood of popStackFrame

You may be wondering how the `popStackFrame` function manages to fix this problem. To answer this question, first you need to understand an important property of the JavaScript `Error` object named `stack`, which is a string that contains a list of substrings separated by `"\n"`, where each substring contains the information about a particular stack frame. Each stack frame corresponds to a particular function call. To help you understand what an error stack and a stack frame are, run the page shown in Listing 2-4.

Listing 2-4: A Web Page that Displays an Error Stack

```
<%@ Page Language = "C#" %>

<!DOCTYPE html PUBLIC
"-//W3C//DTD XHTML 1.0 Transitional//EN"
"http://www.w3.org/TR/xhtml1/DTD/xhtml1-transitional.dtd">
<html xmlns = "http://www.w3.org/1999/xhtml">
<head runat = "server">
  <title>Untitled Page</title>
  <script language = "javascript" type = "text/javascript">
    function getStack(err)
    {
      var a = err.stack.split("\n");
      Array.forEach(a, function(item, i, array)
      {
        array[i] = String.format("a[{0}] = {1}", i, item);
      });
      alert(a.join("\n"));
    }

    function validateInput(input)
    {
      var reg = new RegExp("(\\d\\d)[-/](\\d\\d)[-/](\\d\\d(?:\\d\\d)?)");
      var date = reg.exec(input);
      if (date == null)
      {
        var err = Error.create("Please enter a valid date!",
                          {name : "MyError", errorNumber : 234});
        getStack(e);
        err.popStackFrame();
        throw err;
      }
    }

    function clickCallback()
    {
      var date = document.getElementById("date");
      try
      {
        validateInput(date.value);
      }
      catch (e)
      {
        getStack(err);
        date.value = "";
      }
    }

  </script>
</head>
```

(continued)

Listing 2-4 *(continued)*

```
<body>
  <form id = "form1" runat = "server">
    <asp:ScriptManager runat = "server" ID = "ScriptManager1" />
    Enter date: <input type = "text" id = "date" />  <input type = "button"
    value = "Validate" onclick = "clickCallback()" />
    <br /><span id = "span1"></span>
  </form>
</body>
</html>
```

As the first boldfaced portion of Listing 2-4 shows, this page takes these steps:

1. It splits the `stack` string into its constituent substrings, where each substring represents a stack frame:

```
var a = err.stack.split("\n");
```

2. It iterates through the substrings, or stack frames, to display each stack frame on a single line in the pop-up message shown in Figure 2-6.

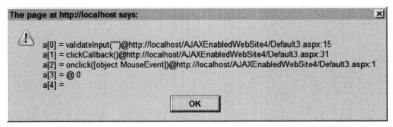

Figure 2-6

As Figure 2-6 shows, this error stack consists of three main stack frames, where each frame represents a particular function call. For example, the first stack frame represents the call to the `validateInput` function. Also note that each stack frame consists of two main parts, separated by the @ character, where the first part is the function call. The second part itself consists of two parts separated by a colon (:), where the first part is the URL of the document that contains the function and the second part is the line number in the document.

Figure 2-6 displays the contents of the stack before the call into the `popStackFrame` function. The second boldfaced portion of Listing 2-4 displays the contents of the stack after the call into the `popStackFrame` function, as shown in Figure 2-7. Comparing Figures 2-6 and 2-7 clearly shows that the `popStackFrame` function removes the stack frame that represents the call into the `validateInput` function. In other words, the new stack now reports line 31 of the `clickCallback` function as the place where the error occurred as opposed to the line 15 of the `validateInput` function where the error object was created.

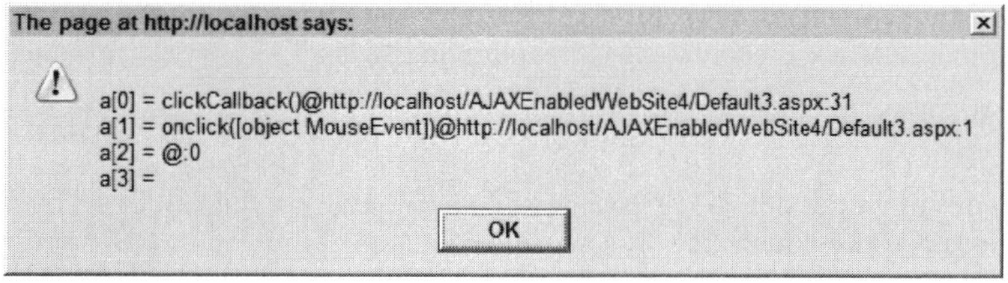

The page at http://localhost says:

⚠ a[0] = clickCallback()@http://localhost/AJAXEnabledWebSite4/Default3.aspx:31
a[1] = onclick([object MouseEvent])@http://localhost/AJAXEnabledWebSite4/Default3.aspx:1
a[2] = @:0
a[3] =

OK

Figure 2-7

Now let's look at the internal implementation of the `popStackFrame` function to see how this function removes the previously mentioned stack frame. Listing 2-5 presents the internal implementation of the `popStackFrame` function.

Listing 2-5: The Internal Implementation of the popStackFrame Function

```
Error.prototype.popStackFrame = function()
{
  if(typeof this.stack === "undefined" || this.stack === null ||
     typeof this.fileName === "undefined" || this.fileName === null ||
     typeof this.lineNumber === "undefined" || this.lineNumber === null)
    return;
  var a = this.stack.split("\n"),
      c = a[0],
      e = this.fileName + ":" + this.lineNumber;
  while(typeof c !== "undefined" && c !== null && c.indexOf(e) === - 1)
  {
    a.shift();
    c = a[0]
  }
  var d = a[1];
  if(typeof d === "undefined" || d === null)
    return;
  var b = d.match(/@(.*):(\d+)$/);
  if(typeof b === "undefined" || b === null)
    return;
  this.fileName = b[1];
  this.lineNumber = parseInt(b[2]);
  a.shift();
  this.stack = a.join("\n")
};
```

The `popStackFrame` function first splits the stack string into its constituent substrings as expected (remember that each substring represents a stack frame):

```
var a = this.stack.split("\n")
```

In the case of Listing 2-5, the array that the `split` function returns contains the elements shown in Figure 2-6. `popStackFrame` then evaluates the following string:

```
e = this.fileName + ":" + this.lineNumber;
```

Note that the current values of the `fileName` and `lineNumber` are the values set by the Mozilla Firefox browser. As discussed previously, the browser sets the value of the `lineNumber` property to a line number at which the `Error` object was created. In the case of Listing 2-3, this value is 15 (see Figure 2-6). The correct value should be 31. To fix this problem, you need to first locate the stack frames that contain the wrong line number and remove them from the stack. This is exactly what the `popStackFrame` does:

```
while(typeof c !== "undefined" && c !== null && c.indexOf(e) === - 1)
{
  a.shift();
  c = a[0]
}
```

In the case of Figure 2-6, this removes the top stack frame — that is, the one that represents the call to the `validateInput` function. After removing this stack frame, you have to access the stack frame that represents the `clickCallback` function:

```
var d = a[1];
if(typeof d === "undefined" || d === null)
   return;
var b = d.match(/@(.*):(\d+)$/);
if(typeof b === "undefined" || b === null)
   return;
```

You can now retrieve the correct line number from this stack frame and assign it the `lineNumber` property of the `Error` object, as follows:

```
this.fileName = b[1];
this.lineNumber = parseInt(b[2]);
```

Summary

In this chapter, you learned a great deal about the ASP.NET AJAX JavaScript base type extensions, which make programming against these JavaScript base types more like programming against their .NET counterparts. In the next chapter, you learn how the ASP.NET AJAX client-side framework uses the `create` and `popStackFrame` JavaScript extension functions of the JavaScript `Error` type to add support for .NET-like exception types. You also learn how to use these two JavaScript extension functions to build your own custom exception types.

Built-In and Custom Exception Types

The previous chapter discussed two important ASP.NET AJAX JavaScript `Error` type extension functions named `create` and `popStackFrame`. This chapter shows you how the ASP.NET AJAX client-side script framework uses these two JavaScript functions to provide you with a set of .NET-like exception types. The chapter then presents you with a recipe for developing your own custom exception types in the ASP.NET AJAX client-side framework, and shows you how to use the recipe to implement a custom exception type.

ASP.NET AJAX Built-In Exception Types

One of the great things about the .NET Framework is that it comes with a rich set of exception types that address different programming scenarios. For example, you can use the `ArgumentNullException` type in your method to raise an exception to inform the callers if your method does not accept `null` values for a particular parameter. Exception programming is one of the fundamental aspects of any modern programming framework.

The ASP.NET AJAX client-side framework presents a rich set of exception types that emulate many of the .NET exception types to make client-side exception programming more like server-side .NET exception programming. This section provides in-depth coverage of the ASP.NET AJAX client-side framework's built-in exception types.

ArgumentException

The .NET Framework comes with an exception type named `ArgumentException`. This exception is raised when a method is invoked and one of the parameters passed into the method does not meet the requirements that the method expects of the parameter. The .NET `ArgumentException` exposes a read-only property named `ParamName` that specifies the name of the parameter that caused the exception to occur.

The ASP.NET AJAX client-side framework extends JavaScript to add support for a similar exception type named `ArgumentException`, which belongs to a namespace called `Sys`. (I discuss namespaces in future chapters.) This JavaScript `ArgumentException` exposes two properties named `paramName` and `name`. The `name` property, like the `name` property of any JavaScript exception, contains the string that uniquely identifies the exception type. The `paramName` property is the equivalent of the .NET `ArgumentException` type's `ParamName` property.

The ASP.NET AJAX client-side framework also extends the functionality of the JavaScript `Error` type to add support for a static method named `argument` that automatically creates an instance of the `Sys.ArgumentException` exception and returns the instance to its caller. The best way to understand what this function does is to take a look at its internal implementation:

```
Error.argument = function(a, c)
{
   var b = "Sys.ArgumentException: " +
              (c ? c : Sys.Res.argument);
   if(a)
      b += "\n" + String.format(Sys.Res.paramName, a);
   var d = Error.create(b,
                           { name : "Sys.ArgumentException",
                             paramName : a});
   d.popStackFrame();
   return d;
};
```

Notice that the `argument` static method takes two arguments. The first argument is a string that contains the name of the parameter that caused the exception to occur. The second argument is a string that contains the error message. The argument function internally calls the `create` static method discussed in Chapter 2:

```
var d = Error.create(b,
                        { name : "Sys.ArgumentException",
                          paramName : a});
```

The `create` static method takes an object as its second parameter. This object provides extra information about the `Error` object being created. Note that the `argument` method passes an object literal as the second parameter of the `create` method. This object literal specifies the string that uniquely identifies the exception and the parameter that caused the exception.

The `Sys.ArgumentException` does not come with a constructor function, so you cannot instantiate it using the `new` operator. Instead, you must use the `argument` static function of the JavaScript `Error` object to instantiate an instance of this exception.

The `validateInput` function in the following page code raises a `Sys.ArgumentException` exception if the parameter passed into it does not meet the requirement specified in the regular expression. The `clickCallback` function catches this exception in its `catch` block and displays the value of the exception object's `message` property.

```
<%@ Page Language="C#" %>

<!DOCTYPE html PUBLIC
"-//W3C//DTD XHTML 1.0 Transitional//EN"
"http://www.w3.org/TR/xhtml1/DTD/xhtml1-transitional.dtd">
<html xmlns="http://www.w3.org/1999/xhtml">
<head id="Head1" runat="server">
  <title>Untitled Page</title>
  <script language="javascript" type="text/javascript">
    function validateInput(input)
    {
      var reg = new RegExp("(\\d\\d)[-/](\\d\\d)[-/](\\d\\d(?:\\d\\d)?)");
      var date = reg.exec(input);
      if (date == null)
      {
        var err = Error.argument("input", "Invalid date!");
        throw err;
      }
    }

    function clickCallback()
    {
      var date = document.getElementById("date");
      try
      {
        validateInput(date.value);
      }
      catch (e)
      {
        alert(e.message);
        date.value="";
      }
    }

  </script>
</head>
<body>
  <form id="form1" runat="server">
    <asp:ScriptManager runat="server"
    ID="ScriptManager1" />
    Enter date: <input type="text" id="date" /> 
    <input type="button" value="Validate"
    onclick="clickCallback()" />
  </form>
</body>
</html>
```

As Figure 3-1 shows, the message property displays the type of the exception (which in this case is Sys.ArgumentException), the exception message, and the name of the parameter that caused the exception to occur.

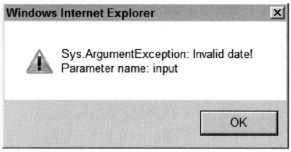

Figure 3-1

ArgumentNullException

The .NET Framework includes an exception type named `ArgumentNullException`. This exception is raised when a method is invoked and one of the parameters passed into it is `null`. As you can see, `ArgumentNullException` is more specific than `ArgumentException`.

The ASP.NET AJAX client-side framework follows this .NET pattern and introduces an exception type named `Sys.ArgumentNullException`, which is more specific than `Sys.ArgumentException`. Just like its .NET counterpart, `Sys.ArgumentNullException` is raised only when one of the parameters passed into a JavaScript function is `null`.

The ASP.NET AJAX client-side framework also extends the JavaScript `Error` type to add support for a new static method named `argumentNull`, which hides the instantiation of the `Sys.ArgumentNull Exception` object from its callers. As the following code shows, the internal implementation of the `argumentNull` method is the same as the `argument` method:

```
Error.argumentNull = function(a, c)
{
  var b = "Sys.ArgumentNullException: " +
          (c ? c : Sys.Res.argumentNull);
  if(a)
    b += "\n" + String.format(Sys.Res.paramName, a);
  var d = Error.create(b,
                       { name : "Sys.ArgumentNullException",
                         paramName : a });
  d.popStackFrame();
  return d;
};
```

As you can see, the `argumentNull` static method takes the same arguments as the `argument` static method discussed in the previous section. The only difference between the two methods is the value part of the first name/value pair of the object literal passed into the `Error` type's `create` static method. This value is a string that uniquely identifies an exception type for other exception types.

The `validateInput` function in the following code uses the `argumentNull` static method of the `Error` object to create and raise a `Sys.ArgumentNullException` when the user does not enter a date into the text box. The `clickCallback` function catches this exception in its `catch` block and displays the value of the exception object's `message` property.

```
<%@ Page Language="C#" %>

<!DOCTYPE html PUBLIC
"-//W3C//DTD XHTML 1.0 Transitional//EN"
"http://www.w3.org/TR/xhtml1/DTD/xhtml1-transitional.dtd">
<html xmlns="http://www.w3.org/1999/xhtml">
<head id="Head1" runat="server">
  <title>Untitled Page</title>
  <script language="javascript" type="text/javascript">
    function validateInput(input)
    {
      if (input == null || input.trim() == "")
      {
        var er = Error.argumentNull("input","Date cannot be null!");
        throw er;
      }
      var reg = new RegExp("(\\d\\d)[-/](\\d\\d)[-/](\\d\\d(?:\\d\\d)?)");
      var date = reg.exec(input);
      if (date == null)
      {
        var err = Error.argument("input","Invalid date!");
        throw err;
      }
    }

    function clickCallback()
    {
      var date = document.getElementById("date");
      try
      {
        validateInput(date.value);
      }
      catch (e)
      {
        alert(e.message);
        date.value="";
      }
    }

  </script>
</head>
<body>
  <form id="form1" runat="server">
    <asp:ScriptManager runat="server"
    ID="ScriptManager1" />
    Enter date: <input type="text" id="date" /> 
    <input type="button" value="Validate"
    onclick="clickCallback()" />
  </form>
</body>
</html>
```

As Figure 3-2 shows, the message property contains the exception type (Sys.ArgumentNullException), the exception message passed into the argumentNull function, and the name of the parameter that caused the exception to occur.

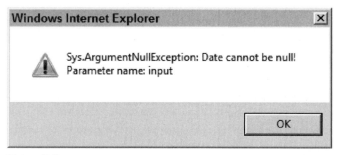

Figure 3-2

ArgumentOutOfRangeException

The .NET Framework includes an exception of type ArgumentOutOfRangeException. This exception is raised when a method is invoked and one of the parameters passed into it is out of the range of valid values. ArgumentOutOfRangeException features two important properties named ParamName and ActualValue, which contain the name and value of the parameter that caused the exception to occur, respectively.

Following the same .NET pattern, the ASP.NET AJAX client-side script framework includes an exception of type Sys.ArgumentOutOfRangeException, which exposes the same two paramName and actual-Value properties. In addition, the ASP.NET AJAX client-side framework extends the JavaScript Error type to add support for a new static method named argumentOutOfRange that hides the instantiation of the Sys.ArgumentOutOfRangeException. The following code presents the internal implementation of this static method:

```
Error.argumentOutOfRange = function(c, a, d)
{
  var b="Sys.ArgumentOutOfRangeException: " +
         (d ? d : Sys.Res.argumentOutOfRange);
  if(c)
    b += "\n" + String.format(Sys.Res.paramName, c);
  if(typeof a !== "undefined" && a !== null)
    b += "\n" + String.format(Sys.Res.actualValue, a);

  var e = Error.create(b,
                  {name : "Sys.ArgumentOutOfRangeException",
                   paramName : c, actualValue : a});
  e.popStackFrame();
  return e;
};
```

The argumentOutOfRange method takes three arguments. The first and second arguments are the name and value of the parameter that caused the exception to occur. The third argument is the exception message that provides more information about the exception. The `argumentOutOfRange` method first creates a string that contains the values of the three arguments:

```
var b="Sys.ArgumentOutOfRangeException: " +
        (d ? d : Sys.Res.argumentOutOfRange);
if(c)
    b += "\n" + String.format(Sys.Res.paramName, c);
if(typeof a !== "undefined" && a !== null)
    b += "\n" + String.format(Sys.Res.actualValue, a);
```

Then, it calls the `create` static method of the JavaScript `Error` type, passing in two parameters to create the associated `Error` object. The first parameter is the previously mentioned string. The second parameter is a JavaScript object literal that contains information about the `Sys.ArgumentOutOfRangeException` exception. Finally, the `argumentOutOfRange` function calls the `popStackFrame` function to reset the values of the `Error` object's `fileName` and `lineNumber` properties (discussed in Chapter 2).

As the boldfaced portion of the following code shows, if the date entered in the text box is not in the specified range, the `validateInput` function invokes the `argumentOutOfRange` function to create a `Sys.ArgumentOutOfRangeException`. The `clickCallback` function catches this exception in its `catch` block and displays the pop-up message shown in Figure 3-3. The message property of the `Error` object displays the exception type (`Sys.ArgumentOutOfRangeException`), the exception message passed into the `argumentOutOfRange` function, and the name and value of the parameter that caused the exception to occur.

```
<%@ Page Language="C#" %>

<!DOCTYPE html PUBLIC
"-//W3C//DTD XHTML 1.0 Transitional//EN"
"http://www.w3.org/TR/xhtml1/DTD/xhtml1-transitional.dtd">
<html xmlns="http://www.w3.org/1999/xhtml">
<head id="Head1" runat="server">
  <title>Untitled Page</title>
  <script language="javascript" type="text/javascript">
    function validateInput(input)
    {
      if (input == null || input.trim() == "")
      {
        var er = Error.argumentNull("input","Date cannot be null!");
        throw er;
      }
      var reg = new RegExp("(\\d\\d)[-](\\d\\d)[-](\\d\\d\\d\\d)");
      var date = reg.exec(input);
      if (date == null)
      {
        var err = Error.argument("input","Invalid date!");
        throw err;
      }

      var ar = input.split("-");

      if (ar[2] < 1900 || ar[2] > 2008)
```

(continued)

```
    {
        var err2=Error.argumentOutOfRange("input",input);
        throw err2;
    }
}

function clickCallback()
{
    var date = document.getElementById("date");
    try
    {
        validateInput(date.value);
    }
    catch (e)
    {
        alert(e.message);
        date.value="";
    }
}
</script>
</head>
<body>
    <form id="form1" runat="server">
        <asp:ScriptManager runat="server" ID="ScriptManager1"/>
        Enter date: <input type="text" id="date" /> 
        <input type="button" value="Validate"
        onclick="clickCallback()" />
    </form>
</body>
</html>
```

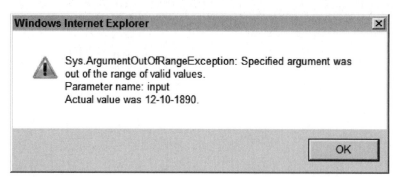

Figure 3-3

ArgumentTypeException

When you implement a method in the .NET Framework with a given set of parameters of specific types, you can rest assured that the Framework will ensure that users call your method with only the types of parameters that your method expects.

The ASP.NET AJAX client-side framework includes an exception type named `Sys.ArgumentTypeEx ception` that you can call from within your JavaScript functions to make programming against your functions more like programming against .NET methods.

The `Sys.ArgumentTypeException` exception is raised when a method is invoked and one of the parameters passed into it is not of the type that the method expects. This exception, just like all other exceptions in the ASP.NET AJAX client-side framework, does not come with a constructor function. This means that you cannot use the `new` operator to instantiate it. Instead, the ASP.NET AJAX client-side framework includes a new static method named `argumentType` to the JavaScript `Error` type that automatically instantiates this exception under the hood.

This method takes four arguments. The first, second, and third arguments contain the name, actual type, and expected type of the parameter that caused the exception to occur. The last argument is the exception message that provides more information about the exception.

The `validateInput` function in the following code throws a `Sys.ArgumentTypeException` exception when the input is not a valid date value. The `clickCallback` function then catches this exception in its `catch` block and displays the message shown in Figure 3-4. Note that the `catch` block uses the value of the exception object's `name` property to determine the type of the exception.

```
<%@ Page Language="C#" %>

<!DOCTYPE html PUBLIC
"-//W3C//DTD XHTML 1.0 Transitional//EN"
"http://www.w3.org/TR/xhtml1/DTD/xhtml1-transitional.dtd">
<html xmlns="http://www.w3.org/1999/xhtml">
<head id="Head1" runat="server">
  <title>Untitled Page</title>
  <script language="javascript" type="text/javascript">
    function validateInput(input)
    {
      if (input == null || input.trim() == "")
      {
        var er = Error.argumentNull("input","Date cannot be null!");
        throw er;
      }
      var reg = new RegExp("(\\d\\d)[-/](\\d\\d)[-/](\\d\\d(?:\\d\\d)?)");
      var date = reg.exec(input);
      if (date == null)
      {
        var err = Error.argumentType("input", null, Date, "Invalid type!");
        throw err;
      }

      var ar = input.split("-");

      if (ar[2] < 1900 || ar[2] > 2008)
      {
```

(continued)

```
            var err2=Error.argumentOutOfRange("input",input);
            throw err2;
        }
    }

    function clickCallback()
    {
        var date = document.getElementById("date");
        try
        {
            validateInput(date.value);
        }
        catch (e)
        {
            if (e.name == "Sys.ArgumentTypeException")
                alert(e.message + "\nExpected Type : " +
                    e.expectedType.getName());
            else
                alert(e.message);
            date.value="";
        }
    }

    </script>
</head>
<body>
    <form id="form1" runat="server">
        <asp:ScriptManager runat="server" ID="ScriptManager1"/>
        Enter date: <input type="text" id="date" /> 
        <input type="button" value="Validate"
        onclick="clickCallback()" />
    </form>
</body>
</html>
```

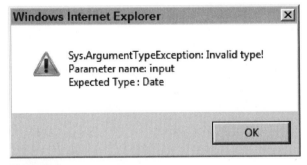

Figure 3-4

Now take a look at the internal implementation of the `argumentType` function in the following code:

```
Error.argumentType = function(d, c, b, e)
{
  var a = "Sys.ArgumentTypeException: " +
          (e ? e : "");
  if(c && b)
    a += String.format(Sys.Res.argumentTypeWithTypes, c.getName(), b.getName());
  else
    a += Sys.Res.argumentType;
  if(d)
    a += "\n" + String.format(Sys.Res.paramName, d);
  var f = Error.create(a,
                  {name : "Sys.ArgumentTypeException",
                   paramName : d, actualType : c,
                   expectedType : b});
  f.popStackFrame();
  return f
};
```

The `argumentType` method first builds a string that contains the following:

❑   The error message:

```
var a="Sys.ArgumentTypeException: " + (e ? e : "");
```

❑   The names of the actual and expected types (if any):

```
if(c && b)
   a += String.format(Sys.Res.argumentTypeWithTypes,
                      c.getName(), b.getName());
```

It then calls the `create` static function of the `Error` type, passing the following parameters to create the `Error` object:

❑   The string built in the first step

❑   An object literal that provides more information about the exception. Note that this object contains the following properties: `name`, `paramName`, `actualType`, and `expectedType`:

```
var f = Error.create(a,
                  {name : "Sys.ArgumentTypeException",
                   paramName : d, actualType : c,
                   expectedType : b});
```

Finally, the exception calls the `popStackFrame` function on the `Error` object to reset the values of the `fileName` and `lineNumber` properties (discussed previously).

ArgumentUndefinedException

The ASP.NET AJAX client-side framework includes an exception type named `Sys.ArgumentUndefined-Exception`. This exception is raised when a function is invoked and one of the parameters passed into it is undefined. This exception, like all other exceptions in the ASP.NET AJAX client-side framework, does not come with a constructor function and therefore cannot be instantiated using the `new` operator. The ASP.NET AJAX client-side framework includes a static method on the `Error` type named `argumentUndefined` that instantiates this exception for you. This method takes two arguments. The first argument is the name of the parameter that caused the exception. The second argument is an exception message that provides more information about the exception. The internal implementation of the `argumentUndefined` static method follows the same implementation pattern as any other static method of the ASP.NET AJAX Framework's `Error` type that instantiates an exception object.

The method first builds a string that contains the exception message and the name of the parameter that caused the exception, as follows:

```
var b = "Sys.ArgumentUndefinedException: " +
        (c ? c : Sys.Res.argumentUndefined);
if(a)
    b += "\n" + String.format(Sys.Res.paramName, a);
```

It then calls the `Error` object's `create` static method, passing in two arguments, as shown in the following code. The first argument is the string built in the first step. The second argument is the JavaScript object literal that provides more information about the `Sys.ArgumentUndefinedException` exception.

```
var d = Error.create(b,
                {name : "Sys.ArgumentUndefinedException",
                 paramName : a});
```

Next, it calls the `popStackFrame` JavaScript function to reset the values of the `fileName` and `lineNumber` properties of the `Error` object:

```
d.popStackFrame();
```

Finally, it returns the exception object to its caller:

```
Error.argumentUndefined = function(a, c)
{
    var b="Sys.ArgumentUndefinedException: " +
            (c ? c : Sys.Res.argumentUndefined);
    if(a)
        b += "\n" + String.format(Sys.Res.paramName, a);
    var d = Error.create(b,
                    {name : "Sys.ArgumentUndefinedException",
                     paramName : a});
    d.popStackFrame();
    return d;
};
```

The `validateInput` function in the following example calls the `argumentUndefined` static method on the `Error` type to raise a `Sys.ArgumentUndefinedException` exception when the end user enters an undefined value into the text box. The `clickCallback` function then catches this exception and displays the pop-up message shown in Figure 3-5.

```
<%@ Page Language="C#" %>

<!DOCTYPE html PUBLIC
"-//W3C//DTD XHTML 1.0 Transitional//EN"
"http://www.w3.org/TR/xhtml1/DTD/xhtml1-transitional.dtd">
<html xmlns="http://www.w3.org/1999/xhtml">
<head id="Head1" runat="server">
  <title>Untitled Page</title>
  <script language="javascript" type="text/javascript">
    function validateInput(input)
    {
      if (input == null || input.trim() == "")
      {
        var er = Error.argumentNull("input","Date cannot be null!");
        throw er;
      }
      var reg = new RegExp("(\\d\\d)[-](\\d\\d)[-](\\d\\d\\d\\d)");
      var date = reg.exec(input);
      if (date == null)
      {
        var err = Error.argumentUndefined("input", "Undefined value!");
        throw err;
      }

      var ar = input.split("-");

      if (ar[2] < 1900 || ar[2] > 2008)
      {
        var err2=Error.argumentOutOfRange("input",input);
        throw err2;
      }
    }

    function clickCallback()
    {
      var date = document.getElementById("date");
      try
      {
        validateInput(date.value);
      }
      catch (e)
      {
        alert(e.message);
        date.value="";
      }
    }
```

(continued)

```
    </script>
  </head>
  <body>
    <form id="form1" runat="server">
      <asp:ScriptManager runat="server" ID="ScriptManager1"/>
      Enter date: <input type="text" id="date" /> 
      <input type="button" value="Validate"
      onclick="clickCallback()" />
    </form>
  </body>
</html>
```

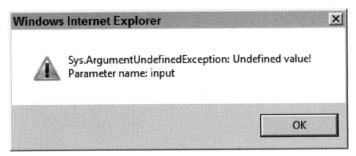

Figure 3-5

InvalidOperationException

Sys.InvalidOperationException is raised when a method call fails due to reasons other than the argument problems discussed in the previous sections. This exception object, like any other exception in the ASP.NET AJAX client-side script framework, features a property called name whose value uniquely identifies the exception type. The JavaScript Error object's invalidOperation static method encapsulates the logic that instantiates a Sys.InvalidOperationException. This function takes a single argument that contains the exception message. Here is the internal implementation of this function:

```
Error.invalidOperation = function(a)
{
  var c = "Sys.InvalidOperationException: " +
          (a ? a : Sys.Res.invalidOperation),
      b = Error.create(c,
                {name : "Sys.InvalidOperationException"});
  b.popStackFrame();
  return b;
};
```

NotImplementedException

When you're implementing a base class in the .NET Framework, you have two options when it comes to the implementation of a virtual method or property of your base class. You can either provide a default implementation for the method or property, or raise a .NET exception named NotImplementedException. The ASP.NET AJAX client-side script framework provides you with the same type of exception, which is called Sys.NotImplementedException and exposes a single name property.

It shouldn't come as a surprise that the ASP.NET AJAX client-side framework also extends the
`Error` object to add a static method named `notImplemented` to instantiate and return an instance
of the `Sys.NotImplementedException` exception. This method takes a single argument, which contains the exception message. As the following code shows, the internal implementation of this method
has the same implementation pattern as the internal implementation of any other ASP.NET AJAX
method on the `Error` type that instantiates an exception:

```
Error.notImplemented = function(a)
{
  var c = "Sys.NotImplementedException: " +
          (a ? a : Sys.Res.notImplemented),
      b = Error.create(c,
                    {name : "Sys.NotImplementedException"});
  b.popStackFrame();
  return b;
};
```

The following example defines a JavaScript class named `Validator`, which exposes a method named
`validateInput`. Note that the `Validator` class's implementation of the `validateInput` function
simply raises a `Sys.NotImplementedException` exception to inform its caller that this class does not
implement this method. In subsequent chapters, you learn how to use a subclass of this class that
implements this method.

```
<%@ Page Language="C#" %>

<!DOCTYPE html PUBLIC
"-//W3C//DTD XHTML 1.0 Transitional//EN"
"http://www.w3.org/TR/xhtml1/DTD/xhtml1-transitional.dtd">
<html xmlns="http://www.w3.org/1999/xhtml">
<head id="Head1" runat="server">
  <title>Untitled Page</title>
  <script language="javascript" type="text/javascript">
    function Validator (name)
    {
      var _name = name;
      this.getName = function() {return _name;};
    }

    Validator.prototype.validateInput = function(input)
    {
      var err = Error.notImplemented("Input validation is not supported!");
      throw err;
    };

    function clickCallback()
    {
      var date = document.getElementById("date");
      try
      {
        var v = new Validator("MyValidator");
        v.validateInput(date.value);
```

(continued)

```
        }
        catch (e)
        {
          alert(e.message);
          date.value="";
        }
      }
    </script>
  </head>
  <body>
    <form id="form1" runat="server">
      <asp:ScriptManager runat="server" ID="ScriptManager1"/>
      Enter date: <input type="text" id="date" /> 
      <input type="button" value="Validate"
      onclick="clickCallback()" />
    </form>
  </body>
</html>
```

ParameterCountException

When you write a method in the .NET Framework that takes a specific number of parameters of specific types, you can rest assured that the Framework will not allow anyone to call your method with fewer parameters than your method expects. That's why your method does not need to check whether the required number of parameters is passed into it.

JavaScript functions, on the other hand, allow their callers to call them with fewer parameters or no parameters at all. To make programming against JavaScript functions more like programming against .NET methods, the ASP.NET AJAX client-side Framework features an exception of type Sys.ParameterCountException that you can raise from within the body of your JavaScript functions to ensure that no one can call your function with fewer parameters than expected. This exception features a single name property that contains the name of the exception type — Sys.ParameterCountException.

The ASP.NET AJAX client-side Framework also extends the JavaScript Error type to add a new member static method named parameterCount that encapsulates the logic that instantiates the Sys.ParameterCountException exception. This method takes a single argument, which contains the exception message. As the following code shows, the internal implementation of this exception has the same implementation pattern as other exception-generating methods on the Error type:

```
Error.parameterCount = function(a)
{
  var c="Sys.ParameterCountException: " +
        (a ? a : Sys.Res.parameterCount),
    b = Error.create(c,
                {name : "Sys.ParameterCountException"});
  b.popStackFrame();
  return b;
};
```

The validateInput function in the following page code throws a Sys.ParameterCountException exception if the number of parameters passed into the function is not equal to the number of parameters that the function expects. The `clickCallback` function catches this exception and displays the value of the `Error` object's `message` property in the pop-up message box shown in Figure 3-6.

```
<%@ Page Language="C#" %>

<!DOCTYPE html PUBLIC
"-//W3C//DTD XHTML 1.0 Transitional//EN"
"http://www.w3.org/TR/xhtml1/DTD/xhtml1-transitional.dtd">
<html xmlns="http://www.w3.org/1999/xhtml">
<head id="Head1" runat="server">
  <title>Untitled Page</title>
  <script language="javascript" type="text/javascript">
    function validateInput(input)
    {
      if (arguments.length != arguments.callee.length)
      {
        var err3=Error.parameterCount("Invalid argument count!");
        throw err3;
      }

      if (input == null || input.trim() == "")
      {
        var er = Error.argumentNull("input", "Date cannot be null!");
        throw er;
      }
      var reg = new RegExp("(\\d\\d)[-](\\d\\d)[-](\\d\\d\\d\\d)");
      var date = reg.exec(input);
      if (date == null)
      {
        var err = Error.argumentUndefined("input", "Undefined value!");
        throw err;
      }

      var ar = input.split("-");

      if (ar[2] < 1900 || ar[2] > 2008)
      {
        var err2=Error.argumentOutOfRange("input",input);
        throw err2;
      }
    }

    function clickCallback()
    {
      var date = document.getElementById("date");
      try
      {
        validateInput(date.value, 3);
      }
```

(continued)

```
        catch (e)
        {
          alert(e.message);
          date.value="";
        }
      }

    </script>
  </head>
  <body>
    <form id="form1" runat="server">
      <asp:ScriptManager runat="server" ID="ScriptManager1"/>
      Enter date: <input type="text" id="date" /> 
      <input type="button" value="Validate"
      onclick="clickCallback()" />
    </form>
  </body>
</html>
```

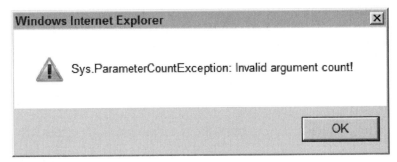

Figure 3-6

Implementing Custom Exception Types

The previous section walked you through the internal implementation of the built-in exception types of the ASP.NET AJAX client-side framework. This section builds on the skills you learned in the previous section to show you how to implement your own custom exception types.

Recipe for Implementing Custom Exception Types

To implement your own custom exception type in the ASP.NET AJAX client-side script framework, the first thing you need to do is choose an appropriate name for your custom exception type. This name must be unique. Make sure you don't use the exception type names of the ASP.NET AJAX built-in exception types. Also make sure you use Pascal casing and end the type name with the word Exception.

Next, decide how many and what types of properties you want your exception type to support. Choose appropriate names for these properties. Your exception type must expose a name property. This is the only required property.

Next, extend the functionality of the JavaScript `Error` type to add support for a static JavaScript method that encapsulates the logic that instantiates your custom exception type. Follow these steps to implement this static method:

1. Choose an appropriate name for the method. Use the same name as the name of your exception type except for two differences: use camel casing instead of Pascal casing, and drop the word `Exception` from the end of the name.

2. Decide on how many and what types of parameters you want this method to support. This normally consists of two sets of parameters. The first set consists of a single string parameter that contains the error message. The second set contains one parameter for each property of your custom exception type. In other words, the second set must provide the values for the properties of your custom exception type.

3. Build a string that contains the values of all the parameters passed into the method.

4. Call the `create` static function on the JavaScript `Error` type, passing in two arguments to create an `Error` object. The first argument must contain the string you built in step 3. The second argument must be a container of the properties that describe your custom exception. This container is normally an object literal.

5. Call the `popStackFrame` method on the `Error` object you created in step 4 to reset the values of the `fileName` and `lineNumber` properties of the `Error` object.

6. Return the `Error` object to the caller of the function.

Using the Recipe

In this section, you use the recipe to develop a custom ASP.NET AJAX exception type. This exception type is raised when a duplicate item is added to a collection. First you need to pick a name for your custom exception type that meets the requirements specified in step 1 of the recipe. I think you'll agree with me that `DuplicateItemException` is an appropriate name for this custom exception type. Following step 1 of the recipe, this name uses Pascal casing and ends with the word `Exception`. Next, you need to decide on how many and what types of properties you want the `DuplicateItemException` exception to support. Every exception type in the ASP.NET AJAX client-side framework must expose a `name` property; therefore, one of the properties of your custom exception must be the `name` property. It's also a good idea to present the `catch` block that will catch your exception with more information about the duplicated item. So, your exception type should also support a second property named `item` that references the duplicated item. You're done with the second step of the recipe.

Next you need to extend the JavaScript `Error` type to add support for a static method that encapsulates the logic that instantiates the `DuplicateItemException` exception type. According to the recipe, the name of this method must be the camel-casing version of the exception name. You must also drop the keyword `Exception` from the end of the method name. So, the name of your exception-generating method should be `duplicateItem`.

Following the recipe, the `duplicateItem` static method must take two arguments. The first argument contains the optional exception message. The second argument references the duplicated item. Now, let's get down to the implementation of the `duplicateItem` static method:

```
Error.duplicateItem = function(e, myitem)
{
  var a="Sys.DuplicateItemException: " +
          (e ? e : "Duplicate item!") + "\n";
  if (myitem)
    for (var c in myitem)
      a += (c + ": " + myitem[c] + "\n");
  var f = Error.create(a,
                      {name: "Sys.DuplicateItemException",
                       item: myitem});
  f.popStackFrame();
  return f;
};
```

Following the recipe, the `duplicateItem` method first builds a string that contains the string representation of all the parameters passed into the method. The first parameter is the optional string that
contains the error message:

```
var a="Sys.DuplicateItemException: " +
        (e ? e : "Duplicate item!") + "\n";
```

The second parameter is an object that references the duplicated item. The `duplicateItem` method iterates through the properties of this object and adds the name and value of each enumerated property to
the string being built:

```
if (myitem)
  for (var c in myitem)
    a += (c + ": " + myitem[c] + "\n");
```

Next, the `duplicateItem` calls the `create` static method on the JavaScript `Error` type and passes the
two arguments into it to create a new `Error` object. The first argument is the string you just built. The
second argument is the object literal that provides more information about your `Sys.DuplicateItem`
`Exception`. Note that this object literal defines two properties for your custom exception as expected:

```
var f = Error.create(a,
                    {name: "Sys.DuplicateItemException",
                     item: myitem});
```

Next, the `duplicateItem` calls the `popStackFrame` function on the newly created `Error` object to reset
the values of the `fileName` and `lineNumber` properties of the object:

```
f.popStackFrame();
```

Now you can use your custom exception in a page as shown in the following code:

```
<%@ Page Language="C#" %>

<!DOCTYPE html PUBLIC
"-//W3C//DTD XHTML 1.0 Transitional//EN"
"http://www.w3.org/TR/xhtml1/DTD/xhtml1-transitional.dtd">
<html xmlns="http://www.w3.org/1999/xhtml">
```

```
<head id="Head1" runat="server">
  <title>Untitled Page</title>
  <script language="javascript" type="text/javascript">
    Error.duplicateItem = function(e,myitem)
    {
      var a="Sys.DuplicateItemException: " + (e ? e : "Duplicate item!") + "\n";
      if (myitem)
        for (var c in myitem)
          a += (c + ": " + myitem[c] + "\n");
      var f = Error.create(a,
                    {name: "Sys.DuplicateItemException", item: myitem});
      f.popStackFrame();
      return f;
    };

    var products = {};
    function validateInput(pname, pcategory, pdistributor)
    {
      if (products[pname])
      {
        var err = Error.duplicateItem("Duplicate item!",
                          {name: pname,
                           category: pcategory,
                           distributor: pdistributor});
        throw err;
      }
    }

    function clickCallback()
    {
      var name = document.getElementById("name");
      var category = document.getElementById("category");
      var distributor = document.getElementById("distributor");
      try
      {
        validateInput(name.value, category.value,
                  distributor.value);
        products[name.value] = {name: name.value,
                          category: category.value,
                          distributor: distributor.value};
      }
      catch (e)
      {
        alert(e.message);
      }
    }

  </script>
</head>
<body>
  <form id="form1" runat="server">
    <asp:ScriptManager runat="server" ID="ScriptManager1"/>
    <table style="background-color:LightGoldenrodYellow;
                border-color:Tan; border-width:1px;
                color:Black;" cellpadding="2">
```

(continued)

```
    <tr style="background-color:Tan; font-weight:bold">
      <th colspan="2">Product Description</th>
    </tr>
    <tr>
      <td align="right">Name:</td>
      <td align="left">
        <input type="text" id="name" />
      </td>
    </tr>
     <tr>
      <td align="right">Category:</td>
      <td align="left">
        <input type="text" id="category" />
      </td>
    </tr>
     <tr>
      <td align="right">Distributor:</td>
      <td align="left">
        <input type="text" id="distributor" />
      </td>
    </tr>
     <tr style="background-color:PaleGoldenrod">
      <td align="center" colspan="2">
        <input type="button" value="Add Product"
        onclick="clickCallback()" />
      </td>
    </tr>
  </table>
 </form>
</body>
</html>
```

Figure 3-7 shows what you'll see in your browser when you access this page. Note that the page consists of three simple text boxes and a button. This page allows you to add a product with a specified name, category, and distributor to an internal collection.

Figure 3-7

If you attempt to add a product with the same name as an existing product, the pop-up message shown in Figure 3-8 is displayed to warn you that the specified item already exists in the collection. As Figure 3-8 shows, the warning message also displays the names and values of the duplicate item. The item features three properties: name, category, and distributor.

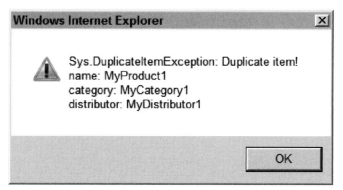

Figure 3-8

Now, let's walk through the previous code listing.

clickCallback

When the end user clicks the Add Product button, the clickCallback JavaScript function is invoked as follows:

```
function clickCallback()
{
  var name = document.getElementById("name");
  var category = document.getElementById("category");
  var distributor = document.getElementById("distributor");
  try
  {
    validateInput(name.value, category.value, distributor.value);
    products[name.value] =
            {name: name.value,
              category: category.value,
              distributor: distributor.value};
  }
  catch (e)
  {
    alert(e.message);
  }
}
```

This function first retrieves the values that the end user has entered for the name, category, and distributor of the product being added, and then passes these values to the validateInput JavaScript function to ensure that the product with the same name does not already exist in the internal collection:

```
validateInput(name.value, category.value,
          distributor.value);
```

Note that the `clickCallback` function wraps the calls into the `validateInput` function in a `try` block because the `validateInput` function could raise an exception.

If the validation succeeds, the `clickCallback` function uses the JavaScript object literal representation to instantiate a new product and adds the product to the internal collection:

```
products[name.value] = {name: name.value,
                        category: category.value,
                        distributor: distributor.value};
```

If the validation fails, the `validateInput` function raises a `DuplicateItemException` exception, which is then caught by the `clickCallback` function in the `catch` block.

validateInput

The `validateInput` function takes the name, category, and distributor of the new product as its arguments as shown in the following code:

```
function validateInput(pname, pcategory, pdistributor)
{
  if (products[pname])
  {
    var err = Error.duplicateItem("Duplicate item!",
              {name: pname, category: pcategory,
               distributor: pdistributor});
    throw err;
  }
}
```

The `validateInput` function calls the `duplicateItem` static method on the `Error` object, passing in the following parameters to create a new `Error` object if the `products` object already contains an object with the specified name:

❑   The "Duplicate item!" error message.

❑   The object literal representation of the duplicate product. Notice that this representation exposes three properties: `name`, `category`, and `distributor`.

Summary

This chapter provided you with an in-depth coverage of the ASP.NET AJAX built-in exception types. It then gave you a recipe for building your own custom exception types and showed you how to use the recipe to implement a custom exception type named `DuplicateItemException`.

The ASP.NET AJAX JavaScript base type extensions and exception types are only part of the ASP.NET AJAX client-side framework. The next chapter discusses two other important parts of this framework: ASP.NET AJAX JavaScript object-oriented programming (OOP) and type reflection extensions.

JavaScript Object-Oriented Programming and Type Reflection Extensions

The .NET Framework comes with the following two important programming capabilities:

❑ Fully fledged typing and type reflection capabilities, allowing you to perform runtime-type inspections, discoveries, invocations, instantiations, and the like

❑ Fully fledged object-oriented capabilities, allowing you to take full advantage of all the well-known benefits of object-oriented programming (OOP) such as classes, interfaces, inheritance, and the like

Because the main goal of the ASP.NET AJAX client-side framework is to emulate the ASP.NET and .NET Frameworks as much as possible, the ASP.NET AJAX client-side framework comes with a set of extensions — known as the ASP.NET AJAX OOP and type reflection extensions — that add .NET-like OOP and type reflection capabilities to JavaScript as much as possible.

You've already seen some reflection capabilities in Chapter 2 where the ASP.NET AJAX client-side Framework extends the JavaScript Object type to add support for the getType and getTypeName methods.

The .NET Framework comes with an important class named Type that provides most of the reflection capabilities of the Framework. Following the same pattern, the ASP.NET AJAX client-side framework introduces a type named Type, which provides both OOP and type reflection capabilities, which I'll discuss in this chapter.

First, I'll examine the JavaScript technologies that the ASP.NET AJAX OOP and type reflection extensions use under the hood to extend JavaScript to add OOP and type reflection support. This examination will put you in a much better position to understand and to use the ASP.NET AJAX client-side framework.

JavaScript Functions

Every JavaScript function is an instance of a JavaScript type named `Function` and supports the following properties:

- `arguments`: This property contains the parameters of a JavaScript function, which also includes the parameters that the original definition of the function does not contain. You can use this property to access the parameters of a function within the body of the function. As the following code shows, you can even define a function without any parameters and use the `arguments` property to access the parameters. However, this is not a recommended practice.

```
function MyFunction()
{
  for (var i = 0; i<arguments.length; i++)
    alert (arguments[i]);
}

window.onload = function()
{
  MyFunction('info1');
  MyFunction('info1','info2');
}
```

- `constructor`: The constructor property references the function or constructor that was invoked to create an object. For example, if you run the following code, the alert will show *function Function() { [native code] }*:

```
<%@ Page Language="C#" %>
<html xmlns="http://www.w3.org/1999/xhtml">
<head runat="server">
  <title>Untitled Page</title>
  <script language="JavaScript" type="text/javascript">
    function MyFunction()
    {
      // Body of the function goes here
    }

    window.onload = function() {
      alert(MyFunction.constructor);
    }
  </script>
</head>
<body>
  <form id="form1" runat="server">
  </form>
</body>
</html>
```

- `prototype`: The `prototype` property allows you to extend the functionality of a type to add support for new instance properties and methods. JavaScript guarantees that all instances of the type will automatically inherit these new properties and methods. As you'll see later, the ASP.NET AJAX client-side framework makes extensive use of this property to add OOP support to JavaScript.

Every JavaScript function also supports two methods, `call` and `apply`, that you can use to invoke a function object. Using these methods to invoke a function may sound redundant because you can invoke a function by simply naming it. For example, you can invoke the `MyFunction` JavaScript function defined in the previous code fragment by simply calling `MyFunction();`. Why would anyone then call `MyFunction.call()` to invoke the function when you can directly call the function itself?

The `call` and `apply` methods enable you to specify the `this` value used inside a JavaScript function. As you can see, JavaScript enables you to specify not only the parameters passed into a JavaScript function but also the `this` value. As such, the first parameter of the call and apply methods references a JavaScript object, which is used to set this value. Note that this JavaScript object does note have to own the JavaScript function on which the call or apply method is invoked. As you'll see later, the ASP.NET AJAX client-side framework uses this feature when it's adding OOP support to JavaScript.

Based on the fact that both the `call` and `apply` methods do the same thing — that is, invoke their associated method — you may be wondering why there are two methods. The main difference between these two methods is in how the parameters of their associated JavaScript functions are passed into these two methods. If your parameters are already loaded into an array, you can call the `apply` method and pass the array directly to this method. Otherwise, you can call the `call` method, passing the parameters as a list of comma-separated items.

JavaScript Classes

JavaScript is inherently an object-based programming language, *not* an object-oriented programming language. As such, it has limited OOP support, which is discussed in this section. There is no JavaScript keyword equivalent to the C# or VB.NET `class` keyword. The constructor of a JavaScript class also defines the class itself. Listing 4-1 presents an example of a JavaScript class named `Employee`.

Listing 4-1: A JavaScript Class

```
<%@ Page Language="C#" %>
<html xmlns="http://www.w3.org/1999/xhtml">
<head runat="server">
  <title>Untitled Page</title>

  <script language="JavaScript" type="text/javascript">
    function Employee (firstName, lastName)
    {
      this._firstName = firstName;
      this._lastName = lastName;
    }

    Employee.prototype =
    {
      get_firstName : function () {return this._firstName;},
      set_firstName : function (value) {this._firstName = value;},
      get_lastName : function() {return this._lastName;},
      set_lastName : function (value) {this._lastName = value;}
    }
```

(continued)

Listing 4-1: *(continued)*

```
     window.onload = function()
     {
       var e = new Employee ("Shahram", "Khosravi");
       alert(e.get_firstName());
       e.set_firstName("Shahram1");
       alert(e.get_firstName());
     }
   </script>
 </head>
 <body>
   <form id="form1" runat="server">
   </form>
 </body>
 </html>
```

Type

As mentioned earlier, the ASP.NET AJAX client-side framework introduces a new type or class named Type. Let's take a look under the hood to see what the Type class is:

```
window.Type = Function;
```

As you can see, Type is basically a new alias for the Function class. This aliasing is done because "Type" makes more sense in the context of the .NET Framework. Keep in mind that the main goal of ASP.NET AJAX is to make the client-side framework act like the .NET Framework as much as possible. Aliasing Function to Type is just a simple first step toward this goal. The next step is to extend the Type (formerly known as Function) class to add support for new methods and properties that will help make the client-side programming more like server-side .NET programming.

As discussed previously, Type (or Function) features a property named prototype. The JavaScript engine guarantees that every instance of Type automatically inherits every method and property assigned to the prototype property. This means that every JavaScript function will automatically inherit or pick up every method and property assigned to the prototype property of the Type or Function class. Because the constructor of every JavaScript class, including your own custom classes such as Employee, is nothing but a JavaScript function, this also means that every JavaScript class, including your own custom classes, will automatically inherit every method and property assigned to the prototype property of the Type or Function class.

Next, you'll learn how the ASP.NET AJAX client-side framework takes full advantage of this powerful feature of JavaScript to extend Type to add support for common OOP features such as namespaces, classes, inheritance, interfaces, and the like. Each of the following sections covers one of the new methods or properties that the ASP.NET AJAX client-side framework has added to Type (or Function). Each section consists of three parts. The first part describes what the method does. The second part presents an example where the method is used. The third part looks under the hood to show you how the method is implemented internally. Knowing the internals of these methods and properties will put you in a much better position to understand and to extend the ASP.NET AJAX client-side framework.

registerClass

The ASP.NET AJAX client-side framework extends the functionality of `Type` to add support for a new method named `registerClass`. As the name implies, this method registers a specified class with the ASP.NET AJAX client-side framework.

To add a new class to the ASP.NET AJAX client-side framework, you first need to implement the class. For example, the following code implements a class named `Employee`:

```
Employee = function (firstName, lastName)
{
  this_firstName = firstName;
  this_lastName = lastName;


}

Employee.prototype =
{
  get_firstName : function () {return this._firstName;},
  set_firstName : function (value) {this._firstName = value;},
  get_lastName : function() {return this._lastName;},
  set_lastName : function (value) {this._lastName = value;}
}
```

Then, call the `registerClass` function of the `Employee` class to register your new class with the ASP.NET AJAX client-side framework, as follows:

```
Employee.registerClass("Employee");
```

Listing 4-2 presents a page that defines, registers, and uses the new `Employee` class.

Listing 4-2: Registering the Employee Class

```
<%@ Page Language="C#" %>
<html xmlns="http://www.w3.org/1999/xhtml">
<head id="Head1" runat="server">
  <title>Untitled Page</title>
</head>
<body>
  <form id="form1" runat="server">
   <asp:ScriptManager runat="server" ID="ScriptManager1" />

    <script language="JavaScript" type="text/javascript">
      Employee = function (firstName, lastName)
      {
          this._firstName = firstName;
          this._lastName = lastName;
      }
```

(continued)

Listing 4-2 *(continued)*

```
Employee.prototype =
{
    get_firstName : function () {return this._firstName;},
    set_firstName : function (value) {this._firstName = value;},
    get_lastName : function() {return this._lastName;},
    set_lastName : function (value) {this._lastName = value;}
}

Employee.registerClass("Employee");

var e = new Employee ("Shahram", "Khosravi");
alert(e.get_firstName());
e.set_firstName("Shahram1");
alert(e.get_firstName());
        </script>
    </form>
</body>
</html>
```

The following line of code seems to suggest that the Employee class has a method named registerClass:

```
Employee.registerClass("Employee");
```

However, as Listing 4-2 shows, the Employee class does not contain this method. To understand how this is possible, you need to look at the internal implementation of the registerClass method shown in Listing 4-3. As this code listing shows, the registerClass is assigned to the prototype property of the Type or Function class. As discussed before, every JavaScript class, including your own custom classes, automatically inherits any method or property assigned to the prototype property of Type.

Listing 4-3: The Portion of the Internal Implementation of the registerClass Function

```
Type.prototype.registerClass = function(c, b, d)
{
    . . .
    this.prototype.constructor = this;
    this.__typeName = c;
    this.__class = true;
    . . .
    if(!window.__classes)
        window.__classes = {};

    window.__classes[c.toUpperCase()] = this;
    . . .
    return this;
};
```

Note that Listing 4-3 presents a portion of the internal implementation of the registerClass function. You'll see the rest of the implementation of this function in the following sections. Also notice that `registerClass` takes three arguments. The second and third arguments are discussed later. As Listing 4-3 shows, the `registerClass` method takes these actions:

1. It assigns its first parameter to an internal field named `__typeName`:

```
this.__typeName = c;
```

As Listing 4-2 shows, this parameter contains the name of the class being registered — for example, `"Employee"`.

2. It sets an internal Boolean field named `__class` to `true` to specify that the entity being registered is a class:

```
this.__class = true;
```

3. It instantiates a global object named `_classes`, if it hasn't already been instantiated:

```
if(!window.__classes)
    window.__classes = {};
```

4. It uses the name of the class as an index to store the current class in the `_classes` object:

```
window.__classes[c.toUpperCase()] = this;
```

This means that the ASP.NET AJAX client-side framework maintains an internal object that contains all the classes registered with the framework. This allows you to perform runtime class reflection queries, similar to .NET class reflection queries.

This also means that every class registered with the ASP.NET AJAX client-side framework maintains metadata information, such as the type name, in its internal fields, such as `_typeName`. This enables you to perform runtime object reflections similar to .NET object reflections on registered classes. You'll see an example of this reflection in the next section.

getName

The `getName` method returns the name of the specified type, as shown in the following example. This is a simple example of the reflection capabilities of the ASP.NET AJAX client-side framework.

```
<%@ Page Language="C#" %>
<html xmlns="http://www.w3.org/1999/xhtml">
<head id="Head1" runat="server">
  <title>Untitled Page</title>
</head>
<body>
  <form id="form1" runat="server">
   <asp:ScriptManager runat="server" ID="ScriptManager1" />

     <script language="JavaScript" type="text/javascript">
```

(continued)

```
            Employee = function (firstName, lastName)
            {
              this_firstName = firstName;
              this._lastName = lastName;
            }

            Employee.prototype =
            {
              get_firstName : function () {return this._firstName;},
              set_firstName : function (value) {this._firstName = value;},
              get_lastName : function() {return this._lastName;},
              set_lastName : function (value) {this._lastName = value;}
            }

            Employee.registerClass("Employee");
            alert(Employee.getName());
          </script>
        </form>
      </body>
    </html>
```

Once again, note that the getName method is called directly on the Employee class, implying that this class contains this method. As the following code shows, this is possible because the getName method is assigned to the prototype property of Type:

```
Type.prototype.getName = function()
{
    return typeof this.__typeName === "undefined" ? "" : this.__typeName;
};
```

Notice that the getName function simply returns the value of the __typeName field discussed previously.

isClass

The isClass method is a static method of the Type class, which means that you must call this method directly on the Type itself. This method returns a Boolean value that specifies whether the parameter passed into it is a class. For example, the call into the isClass function in the boldfaced portion of the following code listing returns true, because Employee is registered as a class:

```
<%@ Page Language="C#" %>
<html xmlns="http://www.w3.org/1999/xhtml">
<head id="Head1" runat="server">
  <title>Untitled Page</title>
</head>
<body>
  <form id="form1" runat="server">
    <asp:ScriptManager runat="server" ID="ScriptManager1" />
      <script language="JavaScript" type="text/javascript">
```

```
          Employee = function (firstName, lastName)
          {
            this._firstName = firstName;
            this._lastName = lastName;
          }

          Employee.prototype =
          {
            get_firstName : function () {return this._firstName;},
            set_firstName : function (value) {this._firstName = value;},
            get_lastName : function() {return this._lastName;},
            set_lastName : function (value) {this._lastName = value;}
          }

          Employee.registerClass("Employee");
          alert(Type.isClass(Employee));
        </script>
      </form>
    </body>
  </html>
```

As the following code shows, the `isClass` method is a static method because it's not defined on the `prototype` property. Note that this method simply returns the value of the `_class` private field discussed in Listing 4-3. The `isClass` method is yet another example of the ASP.NET AJAX client-side framework's type reflection capabilities.

```
Type.isClass = function(a)
{
  if(typeof a === "undefined" || a === null)
    return false;
  return !!a.__class;
};
```

registerNamespace

The idea of a namespace is one of the fundamental OOP concepts, but JavaScript does not support namespaces. The ASP.NET AJAX client-side framework extends the functionality of `Type` to add support for a static method named `registerNamespace` that makes it possible to define namespaces in JavaScript. Because this method is static, you must call it directly on the `Type` itself. Here is an example:

```
<%@ Page Language="C#" %>

<html xmlns="http://www.w3.org/1999/xhtml">
<head id="Head1" runat="server">
  <title>Untitled Page</title>
</head>
<body>
  <form id="form1" runat="server">
    <asp:ScriptManager runat="server" ID="ScriptManager1" />
      <script language="JavaScript" type="text/javascript">
        Type.registerNamespace("MyNamespace");
```

(continued)

```
                    MyNamespace.Employee = function (firstName, lastName)
                    {
                      this._firstName = firstName;
                      this._lastName = lastName;
                    }

                    MyNamespace.Employee.prototype =
                    {
                      get_firstName : function () {return this._firstName;},
                      set_firstName : function (value) {this._firstName = value;},
                      get_lastName : function() {return this._lastName;},
                      set_lastName : function (value) {this._lastName = value;}
                    }

                    MyNamespace.Employee.registerClass("MyNamespace.Employee");
                    alert(Type.isClass(MyNamespace.Employee));
                </script>
            </form>
        </body>
    </html>
```

This example first registers a namespace named `MyNamespace`:

```
Type.registerNamespace ("MyNamespace");
```

Then it defines a class named `Employee` that belongs to this namespace:

```
                    MyNamespace.Employee = function (firstName, lastName)
                    {
                      this._firstName = firstName;
                      this._lastName = lastName;
                    }

                    MyNamespace.Employee.prototype =
                    {
                      get_firstName : function () {return this._firstName;},
                      set_firstName : function (value) {this._firstName = value;},
                      get_lastName : function() {return this._lastName;},
                      set_lastName : function (value) {this._lastName = value;}
                    }
```

Finally, it registers the class with the ASP.NET AJAX client-side framework:

```
MyNamespace.Employee.registerClass("MyNamespace.Employee");
```

Note that the namespace of a class is part of the name of the class.

Listing 4-4 presents the internal implementation of the `registerNamespace` method. As the first line of code shows, the ASP.NET AJAX client-side framework adds a new global array named `_rootNamespaces` to the window object. As you'll see shortly, the `registerNamespace` method adds the global namespace being registered to this global array. In other words, this global array contains all the global namespaces registered with the ASP.NET AJAX client-side framework.

Listing 4-4: The Internal Implementation of the registerNamespace Function

```
window.__rootNamespaces = [];

Type.registerNamespace = function(f)
{
  var d = window, c = f.split(".");
  for(var b = 0; b < c.length; b ++ )
  {
    var e = c[b], a = d[e];
    if( ! a)
    {
      a = d[e] = {};
      if(b === 0)
      window.__rootNamespaces[window.__rootNamespaces.length] = a;

      a.__namespace = true;
      a.__typeName = c.slice(0, b + 1).join(".");
      a.getName = function()
      {
        return this.__typeName;
      };
    }
    d = a;
  }
}
```

Now, I'll walk through the code shown in Listing 4-4 to examine how the ASP.NET AJAX client-side framework manages to add a namespace capability to JavaScript. In general, there are two types of namespaces: global and local. A local namespace is one that is a subset of another namespace. A global namespace is a namespace that does not belong to any other namespace. For example, you could have a global namespace named `Department`, which in turn may contain one or more local namespaces, such as `Section`, as in `Department.Section`. The `Section` sub-namespace in turn may contain one or more namespaces, such as `SubSection`, as in `Department.Section.SubSection`.

As Listing 4-4 shows, the ASP.NET AJAX client-side framework maintains all global namespaces in the `_rootNamespaces` array. In the following section of the listing, the object that represents a namespace features a Boolean field named `_namespace` that specifies that this object is a namespace, a string field named `_typeName` that contains the fully qualified name of the namespace such as `Department .Section`, and a getter method named `getName` that returns the fully qualified name of the namespace:

```
a.__namespace = true;
a.__typeName = c.slice(0, b + 1).join(".");
a.getName = function()
{
  return this.__typeName
}
```

The object that represents a namespace, such as `Department`, also acts as a container (hash) for the objects that represent its sub-namespaces, such as `Section`.

isNamespace

The isNamespace method is a static method of the Type class. This method returns a Boolean value that specifies whether the specified object is a namespace. For example, the call into the isNamespace function in the boldfaced portion of the following code returns true because MyNamespace is registered as a namespace:

```
<%@ Page Language="C#" %>
<html xmlns="http://www.w3.org/1999/xhtml">
<head id="Head1" runat="server">
  <title>Untitled Page</title>
</head>
<body>
  <form id="form1" runat="server">
   <asp:ScriptManager runat="server" ID="ScriptManager1" />

     <script language="JavaScript" type="text/javascript">
      Type.registerNamespace("MyNamespace");
      MyNamespace.Employee = function (firstName, lastName)
      {
         this._firstName = firstName;
         this._lastName = lastName;
      }

      MyNamespace.Employee.prototype =
      {
         get_firstName : function () {return this._firstName;},
         set_firstName : function (value) {this._firstName = value;},
         get_lastName : function() {return this._lastName;},
         set_lastName : function (value) {this._lastName = value;}
      }

      MyNamespace.Employee.registerClass("MyNamespace.Employee");
      alert(Type.isNamespace(MyNamespace));
    </script>
  </form>
</body>
</html>
```

Listing 4-5 presents the internal implementation of the isNamespace method. This method simply returns the value of the _namespace field of the object. As you may recall from Listing 4-4, the registerNamespace method sets the _namespace field of the object that represents the namespace to true to signal that the object is a namespace. This is yet another example of the type reflection capabilities of the ASP.NET AJAX client-side framework.

Listing 4-5: The Internal Implementation of isNamespace

```
Type.isNamespace = function(a)
{
  if(typeof a === "undefined" || a === null)
    return false;
  return ! ! a.__namespace;
};
```

registerInterface

The ASP.NET AJAX client-side framework extends Type to add support for a new method named registerInterface, which enables you to register an interface with the framework. The best way to understand this is to walk through the example shown in Listing 4-6.

Listing 4-6: An Example that uses the registerInterface

```
<%@ Page Language="C#" %>
<html xmlns="http://www.w3.org/1999/xhtml">
<head id="Head1" runat="server">
  <title>Untitled Page</title>
</head>
<body>
  <form id="form1" runat="server">
   <asp:ScriptManager runat="server" ID="ScriptManager1" />

    <script language="JavaScript" type="text/javascript">
    Type.registerNamespace("Department");
    Department.IEmployee = function Department$IEmployee()
    {
      throw Error.notImplemented();
    };

    function Department$IEmployee$get_employeeID ()
    {
      throw Error.notImplemented();
    };

    function Department$IEmployee$set_employeeID ()
    {
      throw Error.notImplemented();
    };

    Department.IEmployee.prototype =
    {
      get_employeeID : Department$IEmployee$get_employeeID,
      set_employeeID: Department$IEmployee$set_employeeID
    }

    Department.IEmployee.registerInterface("Department.IEmployee");

    Department.Employee = function (firstName, lastName)
    {
      this._firstName = firstName;
      this._lastName = lastName;
    }

    Department.Employee.prototype =
    {
      get_firstName : function () {return this._firstName;},
```

(continued)

Listing 4-6 *(continued)*

```
            set_firstName : function (value) {this._firstName = value;},
            get_lastName : function() {return this._lastName;},
            set_lastName : function (value) {this._lastName = value;},
            get_employeeID : function () {return this._employeeID;},
            set_employeeID : function (value) {this._employeeID = value;}
        }

        Department.Employee.registerClass("Department.Employee", null,
                                Department.IEmployee);
    </script>
  </form>
 </body>
</html>
```

Obviously, you have to first define the interface before you can register it. Defining an interface is pretty much like defining a class, with one big difference: The constructors, methods, and properties raise exceptions.

Next, you need to register the interface, as follows:

```
Department.IEmployee.registerInterface("Department.IEmployee");
```

Listing 4-6 shows you how to write a class that implements the interface. First you need to define the class. As the boldfaced portion of the following code shows, the Employee class implements the get_employeeID and set_employeeID methods of the IEmployee interface:

```
        Department.Employee = function (firstName, lastName)
        {
          this._firstName = firstName;
          this._lastName = lastName;
        }

        Department.Employee.prototype =
        {
          get_firstName : function () {return this._firstName;},
          set_firstName : function (value) {this._firstName = value;},
          get_lastName : function() {return this._lastName;},
          set_lastName : function (value) {this._lastName = value;},
          get_employeeID : function () {return this._employeeID;},
          set_employeeID : function (value) {this._employeeID = value;}
        }
```

Next, you need to register your class, like this:

```
Department.Employee.registerClass("Department.Employee", null, Department .IEmployee);
```

Note that the registerClass method takes a third parameter, which references the interface. Passing this parameter into the registerClass tells the ASP.NET AJAX client-side framework that the class being registered implements the specified interface, as you can see here:

```
Department.Employee.prototype.getEmployeeID = function ()
{
  return this._employeeID;
};

Department.Employee.prototype.setEmployeeID = function (value)
{
  this._employeeID = value;
};
```

Listing 4-7 presents the internal implementation of the registerInterface method. This method simply sets the _typeName string field to the name of the interface being registered and the _interface Boolean field to true to specify that the current object is an interface. As you can see, the registration simply creates the metadata necessary for .NET-like reflection.

Listing 4-7: The Internal Implementation of registerInterface

```
Type.prototype.registerInterface = function(a)
{
  this.prototype.constructor = this;
  this.__typeName = a;
  this.__interface = true;
  window.__registeredTypes[a] = true;
  return this;
};
```

Listing 4-3 presented a portion of the implementation of the registerClass function. The first parameter of the registerClass method contains the fully qualified name of the class being registered, including its namespace hierarchy — for example, Department.Employee. The second parameter is discussed in later sections of this chapter. The third optional parameter of registerClass contains the interfaces that the class being registered implements. The highlighted portion of Listing 4-8 shows the internal implementation of the registerClass method that handles the third parameter.

Listing 4-8: The Portion of the Internal Implementation of the registerClass Function

```
Type.prototype.registerClass = function(c, b, d)
{
  this.prototype.constructor = this;
  this.__typeName = c;
  this.__class = true;
  . . .
  if(!window.__classes)
    window.__classes = [];

  window.__classes[c.toUpperCase()] = this;

  if(d)
  {
    this.__interfaces = [];
    for(var a = 2; a<arguments.length; a ++ )
```

(continued)

Listing 4-8 *(continued)*

```
        {
          var e = arguments[a];
          this.resolveInheritance();
          for (var methodName in interfaceType.prototype)
          {
            var method = interfaceType.prototype[methodName];
            if (!this.prototype[methodName])
            {
              this.prototype[methodName] = method;
            }
          }
          this.__interfaces.push(e)
        }
      }
      return this
    };
```

The highlighted portion of Listing 4-8 takes these steps:

1. It defines and instantiates a new array field named _interfaces. As you'll see shortly, the registerClass method uses this array field as a stack, which JavaScript implements as an array.

```
      this.__interfaces = [];
```

2. It iterates through the interfaces that the third parameter of registerClass contains and pushes each enumerated interface onto the top of the stack:

```
var e = arguments[a];
this.__interfaces.push(e)
```

As these steps show, each class maintains an internal stack that contains the interfaces that the class implements. As you'll see in the next sections, this internal stack enables you to perform .NET-like interface-related reflections on a given type or class. This stack is an example of .NET-like metadata.

getInterfaces

The getInterfaces method enables you to query a type for all the interfaces that the type and its ancestor types implement. The boldfaced portion of the following code first calls the getInterfaces function on the Department.Employee type to return an array that contains all the interfaces that this type and its ancestor types implement, and then iterates through these interfaces and displays their names:

```
<%@ Page Language="C#" %>
<html xmlns="http://www.w3.org/1999/xhtml">
<head id="Head1" runat="server">
  <title>Untitled Page</title>
</head>
```

```
<body>
  <form id="form1" runat="server">
    <asp:ScriptManager runat="server" ID="ScriptManager1" />

    <script language="JavaScript" type="text/javascript">
      Type.registerNamespace("Department");
      Department.IEmployee = function Department$IEmployee()
      {
        throw Error.notImplemented();
      };

      function Department$IEmployee$get_employeeID ()
      {
        throw Error.notImplemented();
      };

      function Department$IEmployee$set_employeeID ()
      {
        throw Error.notImplemented();
      };

      Department.IEmployee.prototype =
      {
        get_employeeID : Department$IEmployee$get_employeeID,
        set_employeeID: Department$IEmployee$set_employeeID
      }

      Department.IEmployee.registerInterface("Department.IEmployee");

      Department.Employee = function (firstName, lastName)
      {
        this._firstName = firstName;
        this._lastName = lastName;
      }

      Department.Employee.prototype =
      {
        get_firstName : function () {return this._firstName;},
        set_firstName : function (value) {this._firstName = value;},
        get_lastName : function() {return this._lastName;},
        set_lastName : function (value) {this._lastName = value;},
        get_employeeID : function () {return this._employeeID;},
        set_employeeID : function (value) {this._employeeID = value;}
      }

      Department.Employee.registerClass("Department.Employee", null,
                                        Department.IEmployee);

      var interfaces = Department.Employee.getInterfaces();
      for (var i = 0; i<interfaces.length; i++)
       alert(interfaces[i].getName());
    </script>
    </form>
</body>
</html>
```

Listing 4-9 presents the internal implementation of the getInterfaces function.

Listing 4-9: The Internal Implementation of the getInterfaces Method

```
Type.prototype.getInterfaces = function()
{
  var a = [], b = this;
  while(b)
  {
    var c = b.__interfaces;
    if(c)
    {
      for(var d = 0, f = c.length; d < f; d ++ )
      {
        var e = c[d];
        if(!Array.contains(a, e))
          a[a.length] = e;
      }
    }
    b = b.__baseType;
  }
  return a;
};
```

As you can see in this listing, the getInterfaces function takes the following steps:

1. It defines and instantiates a local JavaScript array:

```
var a = []
```

2. It assigns the current type to a local variable:

```
b = this;
```

3. It accesses the interfaces that the current type implements: As you saw in Listing 4-7, every type maintains the list of the interfaces that it implements in an internal array named _interfaces:

```
var c = b.__interfaces;
```

4. It iterates through the interfaces that the current type implements and adds each enumerated interface to the local JavaScript array defined in step 1:

```
a[a.length] = e
```

5. It assigns the base type of the current type to the local variable defined in step 2, which means that the base type is now the current type:

```
b = b.__baseType
```

6. It repeats steps 3, 4, and 5.

As these steps show, the getInterfaces method returns all the interfaces that the type and all its ancestor types implement.

isInterface

You can use the isInterface function to determine whether a specified object is an interface. Note that this method is static, which means that you must call this method directly on the Type itself. The boldfaced portion of the following code calls the isInterface function to determine whether Department.IEmployee is an interface:

```
<%@ Page Language="C#" %>
<html xmlns="http://www.w3.org/1999/xhtml">
<head id="Head1" runat="server">
  <title>Untitled Page</title>
</head>
<body>
  <form id="form1" runat="server">
   <asp:ScriptManager runat="server" ID="ScriptManager1" />

    <script language="JavaScript" type="text/javascript">
    Type.registerNamespace("Department");
    Department.IEmployee = function Department$IEmployee()
    {
       throw Error.notImplemented();
    };

    function Department$IEmployee$get_employeeID ()
    {
       throw Error.notImplemented();
    };

    function Department$IEmployee$set_employeeID ()
    {
       throw Error.notImplemented();
    };

    Department.IEmployee.prototype =
    {
       get_employeeID : Department$IEmployee$get_employeeID,
       set_employeeID: Department$IEmployee$set_employeeID
    }

    Department.IEmployee.registerInterface("Department.IEmployee");

    Department.Employee = function (firstName, lastName)
    {
       this._firstName = firstName;
       this._lastName = lastName;
    }

    Department.Employee.prototype =
    {
       get_firstName : function () {return this._firstName;},
       set_firstName : function (value) {this._firstName = value;},
       get_lastName : function() {return this._lastName;},
       set_lastName : function (value) {this._lastName = value;},
```

(continued)

```
                get_employeeID : function () {return this._employeeID;},
                set_employeeID : function (value) {this._employeeID = value;}
         }

Department.Employee.registerClass("Department.Employee", null,
                                  Department.IEmployee);
         var isInterface = Type.isInterface(Department.IEmployee);
         alert(isInterface);
      </script>
      </form>
   </body>
   </html>
```

Listing 4-10 contains the internal implementation of `isInterface`. `isInterface` simply returns the value of the `_interface` Boolean field discussed earlier. This is yet another example of the .NET-like type reflection capabilities of the ASP.NET AJAX client-side framework.

Listing 4-10: The Internal Implementation of isInterface

```
Type.isInterface = function(a)
{
  if(typeof a === "undefined" || a === null)
    return false;
  return ! ! a.__interface;
};
```

Inheritance

One of the main characteristics of any OOP language is support for the class inheritance. The ASP.NET AJAX client-side framework extends JavaScript to add support for this all-important feature. As an example, Listing 4-11 implements a new class named `Department.Manager` that inherits the `Department.Employee` class.

Listing 4-11: A Page that uses Inheritance

```
<%@ Page Language="C#" %>
<html xmlns="http://www.w3.org/1999/xhtml">
<head id="Head1" runat="server">
  <title>Untitled Page</title>
</head>
<body>
  <form id="form1" runat="server">
    <asp:ScriptManager runat="server" ID="ScriptManager1" />

    <script language="JavaScript" type="text/javascript">
      Type.registerNamespace("Department");
      Department.IEmployee = function Department$IEmployee()
      {
        throw Error.notImplemented();
      };
```

```
function Department$IEmployee$get_employeeID ()
{
  throw Error.notImplemented();
};

function Department$IEmployee$set_employeeID ()
{
  throw Error.notImplemented();
};

Department.IEmployee.prototype =
{
  get_employeeID : Department$IEmployee$get_employeeID,
  set_employeeID: Department$IEmployee$set_employeeID
}

Department.IEmployee.registerInterface("Department.IEmployee");

Department.Employee = function (firstName, lastName)
{
  this._firstName = firstName;
  this._lastName = lastName;
}

Department.Employee.prototype =
{
  get_firstName : function () {return this._firstName;},
  set_firstName : function (value) {this._firstName = value;},
  get_lastName : function() {return this._lastName;},
  set_lastName : function (value) {this._lastName = value;},
  get_employeeID : function () {return this._employeeID;},
  set_employeeID : function (value) {this._employeeID = value;}
}

Department.Employee.registerClass("Department.Employee", null,
                      Department.IEmployee);

Department.Manager = function (firstName, lastName, department)
{
  Department.Manager.initializeBase(this,[firstName,lastName]);
  this._department = department;
};

Department.Manager.prototype =
{
  get_department : function () {return this._department;},
  set_department : function (value) {this._department = value;}
};

Department.Manager.registerClass("Department.Manager", Department.Employee);

var mgr = new Department.Manager("SomeFirstName", "SomeLastName",
                      "SomeDepartment");
var str = "First Name: " + mgr.get_firstName() + "\n";
```

(continued)

Listing 4-11 *(continued)*

```
      str += ("Last Name: " + mgr.get_lastName() + "\n");
      str += ("Department: " + mgr.get_department() + "\n");
      alert(str);
    </script>
  </form>
</body>
</html>
```

The first order of business is to define the new `Manager` class or the new `Manager` constructor as shown in Listing 4-12.

Listing 4-12: The Manager Constructor in JavaScript

```
Department.Manager = function (firstName, lastName, department)
{
  Department.Manager.initializeBase(this,[firstName,lastName]);
  this._department = department;
};
```

Note that the `Manager` constructor first calls a method named `initializeBase`. To understand the role of this method, take a look at the `Manager` constructor in an OOP language such as C#, as shown in Listing 4-13.

Listing 4-13: The Manager Constructor in C#

```
public Manager(string firstName, string lastName:base(firstName, lastName),
               string department)
{
   this._department = department;
}
```

The `Manager` constructor uses the boldfaced syntax shown in Listing 4-13 to call the constructor of its base class — that is, the `Employee` class. The `Manager` constructor in the ASP.NET AJAX client-side framework, on the other hand, uses the boldfaced syntax shown in Listing 4-12 to achieve the same goal — that is, to call the constructor of the base class. Therefore, calling the `initializeBase` method is equivalent to calling the `base` syntax shown in Listing 4-13. I'll discuss the internal implementation of the `initializeBase` method later in this chapter. For now, suffice it to say that the constructor of a base class must first call the `initializeBase` method.

As mentioned, the first order of business in subclassing an existing class such as the `Department` `.Employee` class is to define the constructor of the subclass (see Listing 4-12). The next order of business is to register the subclass with the ASP.NET AJAX client-side framework, like this:

```
Department.Manager.registerClass("Department.Manager", Department.Employee);
```

Note that you must pass the base class itself as the second parameter of the `registerClass` method. This tells the ASP.NET AJAX client-side framework that the class being registered is a subclass of the specified class.

Because the `Department.Manager` class derives from the `Department.Employee` class, it inherits the `get_firstName`, `set_firstName`, `get_lastName`, and `set_lastName` methods from its base class. You can now instantiate an instance of the `Department.Manager` class and call these four methods on the instance even though the class itself does not directly contain these four methods:

```
var mgr = new Department.Manager("SomeFirstName", "SomeLastName",
                                 "SomeDepartment");
var str = "First Name: " + mgr.get_firstName() + "\n";
str += ("Last Name: " + mgr.get_lastName() + "\n");
str += ("Department: " + mgr.get_department() + "\n");
alert(str);
```

Listings 4-3 and 4-8 presented portions of the internal implementation of the `registerClass` method. Listing 4-14 presents the complete code for this method.

Listing 4-14: A Portion of the Internal Implementation of the registerClass Function

```
Type.prototype.registerClass = function(c, b, d)
{
  this.prototype.constructor = this;
  this.__typeName = c;
  this.__class = true;

  if(b)
  {
    this.__baseType = b;
    this.__basePrototypePending = true;
  }

  if(!window.__classes)
    window.__classes = [];

  window.__classes[c.toUpperCase()] = this;

  if(d)
  {
    this.__interfaces = [];
    for(var a = 2; a < arguments.length; a ++ )
    {
      var e = arguments[a];
      this.resolveInheritance();
      for (var methodName in interfaceType.prototype)
      {
        var method = interfaceType.prototype[methodName];
        if (!this.prototype[methodName])
        {
          this.prototype[methodName] = method;
        }
      }
      this.__interfaces.push(e);
    }
  }
  window.__registeredTypes[c] = true;
  return this;
};
```

The highlighted portion of this code takes the following steps:

1. It assigns the base class to a field named _baseType. Think of this field as .NET-like metadata, which allows you to query a type for its base type.

```
this.__baseType = b;
```

2. It sets a Boolean field named _basePrototypePending to true. I'll discuss the significance of this field in the next section.

getBaseType

The getBaseType method enables you to access the _baseType metadata of a specified type. This metadata references the base type of the type. Listing 4-15 presents a page that uses the getBaseType method.

Listing 4-15: A Page that uses the getBaseType Method

```
<%@ Page Language="C#" %>
<html xmlns="http://www.w3.org/1999/xhtml">
<head id="Head1" runat="server">
  <title>Untitled Page</title>
</head>
<body>
  <form id="form1" runat="server">
    <asp:ScriptManager ID="ScriptManager1" runat="server" />

    <script language="JavaScript" type="text/javascript">
      Type.registerNamespace("Department");
      Department.IEmployee = function Department$IEmployee()
      {
        throw Error.notImplemented();
      };

      function Department$IEmployee$get_employeeID ()
      {
        throw Error.notImplemented();
      };

      function Department$IEmployee$set_employeeID ()
      {
        throw Error.notImplemented();
      };

      Department.IEmployee.prototype =
      {
        get_employeeID : Department$IEmployee$get_employeeID,
```

```
    set_employeeID: Department$IEmployee$set_employeeID
}

Department.IEmployee.registerInterface("Department.IEmployee");

Department.Employee = function (firstName, lastName)
{
  this._firstName = firstName;
  this._lastName = lastName;
}

Department.Employee.prototype =
{
  get_firstName : function () {return this._firstName;},
  set_firstName : function (value) {this._firstName = value;},
  get_lastName : function() {return this._lastName;},
  set_lastName : function (value) {this._lastName = value;},
  get_employeeID : function () {return this._employeeID;},
  set_employeeID : function (value) {this._employeeID = value;}
}

Department.Employee.registerClass("Department.Employee", null,
                        Department.IEmployee);

Department.Manager = function (firstName, lastName, department)
{
  Department.Manager.initializeBase(this,[firstName,lastName]);
  this._department = department;
};

Department.Manager.prototype =
{
  get_department : function () {return this._department;},
  set_department : function (value) {this._department = value;}
};

Department.Manager.registerClass("Department.Manager", Department.Employee);
alert(Department.Manager.getBaseType());
        </script>
      </form>
    </body>
  </html>
```

Note that the line of code in the pageLoad method calls the alert method to display the result of the call into the getBaseType method of the Manager class:

```
alert(Department.Manager.getBaseType());
```

If you run this code, you'll get the pop-up message shown in Figure 4-1.

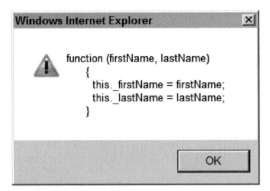

Figure 4-1

Note that this pop-up message shows the following code:

```
Department.Employee = function (firstName, lastName)
{
   var _firstName = firstName;
   var _lastName = lastName;
}
```

This is the boldfaced code shown in Listing 4-15 — that is, the definition of the constructor of the `Department.Employee` class. As this example shows, the `getBaseType` method returns a reference to the actual `Department.Employee` class.

Listing 4-16 presents the internal implementation of the `getBaseType` method. This method simply returns the value of the _baseType metadata as expected. This is yet another example of the runtime type reflection capabilities of the ASP.NET AJAX client-side framework.

Listing 4-16: The getBaseType Method

```
Type.prototype.getBaseType = function()
{
   return typeof this.__baseType === "undefined" ? null : this.__baseType;
};
```

initializeBase

As you saw in Listing 4-12, the constructor of every subclass must first call the `initializeBase` method. As discussed earlier, this method is the ASP.NET AJAX equivalent of the `base` syntax in C# (see Listings 4-12 and 4-13). As such, the main responsibility of the `initializeBase` method is to invoke the constructor of the base class. Before diving into the internal implementation of this method, let's revisit Listing 4-12:

```
Department.Manager = function (firstName, lastName, department)
{
   Department.Manager.initializeBase(this, [firstName, lastName]);

   this._department = department;
};
```

As the highlighted portion of this code shows, the `initializeBase` method takes two parameters. The first parameter references the instance of the subclass that is calling the method. The subclass in this case is the `Department.Manager` class. The second parameter — which is optional — is a JavaScript array that contains the parameters that must be passed into the constructor of the base class.

Listing 4-17 presents the internal implementation of the `initializeBase` method.

Listing 4-17: The Internal Implementation of initializeBase

```
Type.prototype.initializeBase = function(a, b)
{
  this.resolveInheritance();
  if(this.__baseType)
  {
    if(!b)
      this.__baseType.apply(a);
    else
      this.__baseType.apply(a, b);
  }
  return a;
};
```

This method takes the following steps:

1. It calls a method named `resolveInheritance` (discussed in more detail in the next section):

```
this.resolveInheritance();
```

2. If the current class is indeed a subclass of another class — that is, if `_baseType` is not null — the `initializeBase` method calls the `apply` method on the constructor of the base class, passing in the JavaScript array that contains the parameters of this constructor:

```
this.__baseType.apply(a, b);
```

resolveInheritance

The best way to understand what the `resolveInheritance` method does is to study its internal implementation as presented in Listing 4-18.

Listing 4-18: The resolveInheritance Method

```
Type.prototype.resolveInheritance = function()
{
  if(this.__basePrototypePending)
  {
    var b = this.__baseType;
    b.resolveInheritance();
    for(var a in b.prototype)
```

(continued)

Listing 4-18 *(continued)*

```
    {
      var c = b.prototype[a];
      if( ! this.prototype[a])
        this.prototype[a] = c
    }
    delete this.__basePrototypePending;
  }
}
```

This method first checks whether the _basePrototypePending field has been defined for the current type. The registerClass method is the only place where this field is defined (see Listing 4-14). The registerClass method defines this field to tell the resolveInheritance method that it must execute the boldfaced code shown in Listing 4-18. Note that the resolveInheritance method deletes the _basePrototypePending field after it executes this boldfaced portion to ensure that this code is not executed more than once when the resolveInheritance method is called multiple times.

Now, let's study the boldfaced code. Note that the resolveInheritance is a recursive function because it is recursively called for each ancestor type of a specified type. For example, when the resolveInheritance method of the Department.Manager class is called, the resolveInheritance method of the Department.Employee base class is automatically called as well.

As Listing 4-18 shows, when the resolveInheritance method of a class is called, the method first accesses the base class of the class:

```
      var b = this.__baseType;
```

It then iterates through the members (methods or properties) assigned to the prototype property of the base class and assigns each enumerated member (method or property) to the prototype property of the class on which the resolveInheritance method was called.

Therefore, the end result of calling the resolveInheritance method on a given type is that all the members assigned to the prototype properties of all its ancestor types are assigned to the prototype property of the type.

This is how the ASP.NET AJAX client-side framework manages to emulate the inheritance object-oriented feature in JavaScript to make client-side programming more like server-side .NET programming.

callBaseMethod

To understand the role of the callBaseMethod method, consider a similar situation in an OOP language such as C#. A C# class exposes virtual methods to allow its subclasses to override the implementations of these methods. This is how a subclass extends the functionality of its base class. Most of the time, the subclass's implementation of a virtual method calls its base class's implementation in addition to providing its own implementation. In other words, the subclass's implementation complements the base class's implementation.

The `callBaseMethod` method in the ASP.NET AJAX client-side framework allows a subclass's implementation of a method to call its base class's implementation. This is yet another step that the ASP.NET AJAX client-side framework takes to emulate the .NET Framework. To help you understand how this works in the ASP.NET AJAX client-side framework, I'll walk through the example shown in Listing 4-19.

Listing 4-19: An ASP.NET Page that Sets the Stage for using callBaseMethod

```
<%@ Page Language="C#" %>
<html xmlns="http://www.w3.org/1999/xhtml">
<head id="Head1" runat="server">
  <title>Untitled Page</title>
</head>
<body>
  <form id="form1" runat="server">
    <asp:ScriptManager ID="ScriptManager1" runat="server" />

    <script language="JavaScript" type="text/javascript">
      Type.registerNamespace("Department");
      Department.IEmployee = function Department$IEmployee()
      {
        throw Error.notImplemented();
      };

      function Department$IEmployee$get_employeeID ()
      {
        throw Error.notImplemented();
      };

      function Department$IEmployee$set_employeeID ()
      {
        throw Error.notImplemented();
      };

      Department.IEmployee.prototype =
      {
        get_employeeID : Department$IEmployee$get_employeeID,
        set_employeeID: Department$IEmployee$set_employeeID
      }

      Department.IEmployee.registerInterface("Department.IEmployee");

      Department.Employee = function (firstName, lastName)
      {
        this._firstName = firstName;
        this._lastName = lastName;
      }

      Department.Employee.prototype =
      {
        get_firstName : function () {return this._firstName;},
        set_firstName : function (value) {this._firstName = value;},
```

(continued)

Listing 4-19 *(continued)*

```
        get_lastName : function() {return this._lastName;},
        set_lastName : function (value) {this._lastName = value;},
        get_employeeID : function () {return this._employeeID;},
        set_employeeID : function (value) {this._employeeID = value;},
        getEmployeeInfo : function ()
        {
            var info = "First Name: " + this.get_firstName() + "\n";
            info += ("Last Name: " + this.get_lastName() + "\n");
            if (this._employeeID)
              info += ("Employee ID: " + this._employeeID + "\n");
            return info;
        }
    }

    Department.Employee.registerClass("Department.Employee", null,
                            Department.IEmployee);

    Department.Manager = function (firstName, lastName, department)
    {
      Department.Manager.initializeBase(this,[firstName,lastName]);
      this._department = department;
    };

    Department.Manager.prototype =
    {
      get_department : function () {return this._department;},
      set_department : function (value) {this._department = value;}
    };

    Department.Manager.registerClass("Department.Manager", Department.Employee);

    var mgr = new Department.Manager("SomeFirstName", "SomeLastName",
                            "SomeDepartment");
    mgr.set_employeeID(324);
    alert (mgr.getEmployeeInfo());
  </script>
 </form>
</body>
</html>
```

As the first boldfaced portion of Listing 4-19 shows, a new function named `getEmployeeInfo` is added to the `prototype` property of the `Department.Employee` class.

This function simply displays the first name, last name, and employee ID of the current employee object. Because the `Department.Manager` class derives from the `Department.Employee` class, it automatically inherits the `getEmployeeInfo` method from its base class. That is why you can create an instance of the `Department.Manager` class and call this function on it as shown in the second boldfaced portion of Listing 4-19.

If you run Listing 4-19, you get the pop-up message shown in Figure 4-2. Notice that this message displays the first name, last name, and employee ID, but it does not display the manager's department. This

```
Department.IEmployee.prototype =
{
  get_employeeID : Department$IEmployee$get_employeeID,
  set_employeeID: Department$IEmployee$set_employeeID
}

Department.IEmployee.registerInterface("Department.IEmployee");

Department.Employee = function (firstName, lastName)
{
  this._firstName = firstName;
  this._lastName = lastName;
}

Department.Employee.prototype =
{
  get_firstName : function () {return this._firstName;},
  set_firstName : function (value) {this._firstName = value;},
  get_lastName : function() {return this._lastName;},
  set_lastName : function (value) {this._lastName = value;},
  get_employeeID : function () {return this._employeeID;},
  set_employeeID : function (value) {this._employeeID = value;},
  getEmployeeInfo : function ()
  {
    var info = "First Name: " + this.get_firstName() + "\n";
    info += ("Last Name: " + this.get_lastName() + "\n");
    if (this._employeeID)
      info += ("Employee ID: " + this._employeeID + "\n");
    return info;
  }
}

Department.Employee.registerClass("Department.Employee", null,
                                  Department.IEmployee);

Department.Manager = function (firstName, lastName, department)
{
  Department.Manager.initializeBase(this,[firstName,lastName]);
  this._department = department;
};

Department.Manager.prototype =
{
  get_department : function () {return this._department;},
  set_department : function (value) {this._department = value;},
  getEmployeeInfo : function()
  {
    var info = Department.Manager.callBaseMethod(this, "getEmployeeInfo",
                                      null);
    info += ("Department: " + this._department + "\n");
    return info;
  }
};
```

(continued)

Listing 4-22 *(continued)*

```
        Department.Manager.registerClass("Department.Manager", Department.Employee);

        var mgr = new Department.Manager("SomeFirstName", "SomeLastName",
                                    "SomeDepartment");
        var ref1 = Department.Manager.getBaseMethod(mgr, "getEmployeeInfo");
        alert (ref1);
      </script>
    </form>
  </body>
</html>
```

The second boldfaced portion of Listing 4-22 calls the getBaseMethod function on the Department
.Manager class, passing in a reference to the class itself and the string that contains the name of the
getEmployeeInfo function. If you run this code, you get the pop-up message shown in Figure 4-4.
Compare the content of this message and the first bold portion of Listing 4-22. As you can see, the
getBaseMethod function returns the getEmployeeInfo function of the base class — that is, the
Department.Employee class.

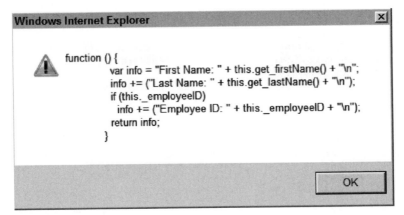

Figure 4-4

Listing 4-23 presents the internal implementation of the function.

Listing 4-23: The getBaseMethod Method

```
Type.prototype.getBaseMethod = function(d, c)
{
  var b = this.getBaseType();
  if(b)
  {
    var a = b.prototype[c];
    return a instanceof Function ? a : null;
  }
  return null;
};
```

This function calls the getBaseType method to access the object that represents the base type of the current class:

```
var b = this.getBaseType();
```

getBaseMethod then uses the name of the function as an index into the prototype collection property of the object that represents the base type to access and returns the Function object that represents the function with the specified name:

```
var a = b.prototype[c];
return a instanceof Function ? a : null
```

implementsInterface

The implementsInterface function takes an interface as its argument and returns a Boolean value that specifies whether the type on which the function is called implements the specified interface. Here's an example:

```
<%@ Page Language="C#" %>
<html xmlns="http://www.w3.org/1999/xhtml">
<head id="Head1" runat="server">
  <title>Untitled Page</title>
</head>
<body>
  <form id="form1" runat="server">
    <asp:ScriptManager ID="ScriptManager1" runat="server" />

    <script language="JavaScript" type="text/javascript">
      function getEmployeeID(obj)
      {
        var objType = Object.getType(obj);
        alert(objType);
        var flag = objType.implementsInterface(Department.IEmployee);
        alert(flag);
        if (!flag)
          throw Error.argument(
                  "Must implement the Department.IEmployee interface");
        return obj.getemployeeID();
      }

      Type.registerNamespace("Department");
      Department.IEmployee = function Department$IEmployee()
      {
        throw Error.notImplemented();
      };

      function Department$IEmployee$get_employeeID ()
      {
        throw Error.notImplemented();
      };
```

(continued)

113

```javascript
function Department$IEmployee$set_employeeID ()
{
  throw Error.notImplemented();
};

Department.IEmployee.prototype =
{
  get_employeeID : Department$IEmployee$get_employeeID,
  set_employeeID: Department$IEmployee$set_employeeID
}

Department.IEmployee.registerInterface("Department.IEmployee");

Department.Employee = function (firstName, lastName)
{
  this._firstName = firstName;
  this._lastName = lastName;
}

Department.Employee.prototype =
{
  get_firstName : function () {return this._firstName;},
  set_firstName : function (value) {this._firstName = value;},
  get_lastName : function() {return this._lastName;},
  set_lastName : function (value) {this._lastName = value;},
  get_employeeID : function () {return this._employeeID;},
  set_employeeID : function (value) {this._employeeID = value;},
  getEmployeeInfo : function () {
      var info="First Name: " + this.get_firstName() + "\n";
      info += ("Last Name: " + this.get_lastName() + "\n");
      if (this._employeeID)
        info += ("Employee ID: " + this._employeeID + "\n");
      return info;
    }
}

Department.Employee.registerClass("Department.Employee", null,
                          Department.IEmployee);

Department.Manager = function (firstName, lastName, department)
{
  Department.Manager.initializeBase(this,[firstName, lastName]);
  this._department = department;
};

Department.Manager.prototype =
{
  get_department : function () {return this._department;},
  set_department : function (value) {this._department = value;},
  getEmployeeInfo : function() {
      var info = Department.Manager.callBaseMethod(this, "getEmployeeInfo",
                                          null);
      info += ("Department: " + this._department + "\n");
```

```
                   return info;
            }
     };

     Department.Manager.registerClass("Department.Manager", Department.Employee);


     var mgr = new Department.Manager("SomeFirstName", "SomeLastName",
                             "SomeDepartment");
     mgr.set_employeeID(234);
     var employeeID = getEmployeeID(mgr);
     alert (employeeID);
    </script>
  </form>
</body>
</html>
```

As the second boldfaced portion of this code listing shows, the Department.Employee class directly implements the Department.IEmployee interface. As you'll see shortly, even though the Department.Manager class does not directly implement this interface, the call into the implementsInterface function returns true because this class derives from the Department.Employee class.

The third boldfaced portion of this code listing first instantiates an instance of the Department.Manager class:

```
var mgr = new Department.Manager("SomeFirstName", "SomeLastName", "SomeDepartment");
```

It then calls a JavaScript function named getEmployeeID, passing in the Department.Manager object to return the employee ID of the object:

```
var employeeID = getEmployeeID(mgr);
```

Finally, it displays the employee ID:

```
alert (employeeID);
```

The first boldfaced portion of this code listing presents the implementation of the getEmployeeID JavaScript function. This function takes an object as its argument and performs the following tasks:

1. It calls the getType function of the JavaScript Object, passing in the object that was passed into it:

```
var objType = Object.getType(obj);
```

As previously discussed, the getType function returns an object that references the type of a specified object. In this case, the Department.Manager object is passed into the getType function, which means that this function returns the Function object that represents the Department.Manager class.

2. It calls the alert function to display the return value of the getType function:

```
alert(objType);
```

As Figure 4-5 shows, in this case the getType function returns the Function object that represents the constructor of the Department.Manager class.

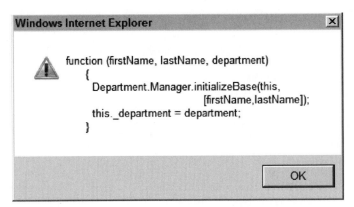

Figure 4-5

3. It calls the implementsInterface function on the return value of the getType function, passing in the Department.IEmployee interface:

    ```
    var flag = objType.implementsInterface(Department.IEmployee);
    ```

    The implementsInterface function determines whether the type on which the function is called (and its ascendant types) implements the specified interface. In this case, the Department.Manager type does not directly implement the Department.IEmployee interface. However, its parent class, Department.Employee, does implement this interface. That is why the implementsInterface function returns true.

4. It throws a Sys.ArgumentException exception if the specified type does not implement the specified interface:

    ```
    if (!flag)
        throw Error.argument("Must implement the Department.IEmployee interface");
    ```

5. It calls the getemployeeID function on the specified object if the specified type does indeed implement the specified interface:

    ```
    return obj.getemployeeID();
    ```

In this case, the Department.Manager class inherits the getEmployeeID function from its base class, Department.Employee.

Listing 4-24 presents the internal implementation of the implementsInterface function.

Listing 4-24: The Internal Implementation of implementsInterface

```
Type.prototype.implementsInterface = function(d)
{
  this.resolveInheritance();
  var c = d.getName(), a = this.__interfaceCache;
  if(a)
  {
    var e = a[c];
    if(typeof e !== "undefined")
      return e;
  }
  else
    a = this.__interfaceCache = {};
  var b = this;
  while(b)
  {
    var f = b.__interfaces;
    if(f)
      if(Array.indexOf(f, d) !== - 1)
        return a[c] = true;
    b = b.__baseType;
  }
  return a[c] = false;
};
```

This function first calls the `resolveInheritance` function:

```
this.resolveInheritance();
```

This is a recursive function. It copies all members of the `prototype` collection properties of the current type's ancestor types into the `prototype` collection property of the current type. Therefore, after this call, the current type contains all members that it inherits from its ancestor types. This is how the ASP.NET AJAX client-side framework emulates inheritance, as discussed previously. This step is important because there are cases such as `Department.Manager` where the current type itself does not implement a given interface, but one of its ancestor types does. The `resolveInheritance` method copies the interface-related members such as `getEmployeeID` to the `prototype` collection property of the current type.

The `implementsInterface` function then calls the `getName` function on the interface passed into it to access the fully qualified name of the interface:

```
var c = d.getName();
```

The function then accesses an internal collection named `_interfaceCache`:

```
var a = this.__interfaceCache;
```

As you'll see shortly, this collection caches the fully qualified names of all interfaces that the current type and its ancestor types implement. This cache is added to improve performance.

If the cache contains an entry for the specified interface, the function retrieves the interface directly from the cache and returns it:

```
if(a)
{
  var e = a[c];
  if(typeof e !== "undefined")
    return e;
}
```

If the cache hasn't been created yet, it instantiates the cache:

```
else
    a = this.__interfaceCache = {};
```

Finally, the function iterates through the current type and all its ancestor types to determine whether the _interfaces collection of any of these types contains an entry for the specified interface. If so, it adds an entry for the interface to the cache and returns the interface:

```
var b = this;
while(b)
{
  var f = b.__interfaces;
  if(f)
    if(Array.indexOf(f, d) !== - 1)
      return a[c] = true;
  b = b.__baseType
}
return a[c] = false
```

Caching allows you to avoid going through this logic the next time.

inheritsFrom

The inheritsFrom function returns a Boolean value that specifies whether the type on which the inheritsFrom is called inherits from the type passed into it as its argument. The following code presents an example where the inheritsFrom function is called on the Department.Manager type to determine whether this type inherits from the Department.Employee type:

```
<%@ Page Language="C#" %>
<html xmlns="http://www.w3.org/1999/xhtml">
<head id="Head1" runat="server">
  <title>Untitled Page</title>
</head>
<body>
  <form id="form1" runat="server">
    <asp:ScriptManager ID="ScriptManager1" runat="server" />

    <script language="JavaScript" type="text/javascript">
      Type.registerNamespace("Department");
```

```
Department.IEmployee = function Department$IEmployee()
{
  throw Error.notImplemented();
};

function Department$IEmployee$get_employeeID ()
{
  throw Error.notImplemented();
};

function Department$IEmployee$set_employeeID ()
{
  throw Error.notImplemented();
};

Department.IEmployee.prototype =
{
  get_employeeID : Department$IEmployee$get_employeeID,
  set_employeeID: Department$IEmployee$set_employeeID
}

Department.IEmployee.registerInterface("Department.IEmployee");

Department.Employee = function (firstName, lastName)
{
  this._firstName = firstName;
  this._lastName = lastName;
}

Department.Employee.prototype =
{
  get_firstName : function () {return this._firstName;},
  set_firstName : function (value) {this._firstName = value;},
  get_lastName : function() {return this._lastName;},
  set_lastName : function (value) {this._lastName = value;},
  get_employeeID : function () {return this._employeeID;},
  set_employeeID : function (value) {this._employeeID = value;},
  getEmployeeInfo : function () {
    var info="First Name: " + this.get_firstName() + "\n";
    info += ("Last Name: " + this.get_lastName() + "\n");
    if (this._employeeID)
      info += ("Employee ID: " + this._employeeID + "\n");
    return info;
  }
}

Department.Employee.registerClass("Department.Employee", null,
                                  Department.IEmployee);

Department.Manager = function (firstName, lastName, department)
{
  Department.Manager.initializeBase(this,
                                    [firstName,lastName]);
  this._department = department;
};
```

(continued)

```
        Department.Manager.prototype =
        {
          get_department : function () {return this._department;},
          set_department : function (value) {this._department = value;},
          getEmployeeInfo : function()
          {
                var info = Department.Manager.callBaseMethod(this, "getEmployeeInfo",
                                                    null);
                info += ("Department: " + this._department + "\n");
                return info;
          }
        };

        Department.Manager.registerClass("Department.Manager", Department.Employee);

        var flag = Department.Manager.inheritsFrom(Department.Employee);
        alert (flag);
      </script>
    </form>
  </body>
</html>
```

Listing 4-25 contains the internal implementation of the `inheritsFrom` function.

Listing 4-25: The Internal Implementation of inheritsFrom

```
Type.prototype.inheritsFrom = function(b)
{
  this.resolveInheritance();
  var a = this.__baseType;
  while(a)
  {
    if(a === b)
      return true;
    a = a.__baseType
  }
  return false
};
```

This function first calls the `resolveInheritance` function as usual:

```
      this.resolveInheritance();
```

Then it searches through the ancestor types of the current type for the specified type, with each type identifying its base type through its _baseType field:

```
      var a = this.__baseType;
      while(a)
      {
        if(a === b)
          return true;
        a = a.__baseType;
      }
      return false;
```

isImplementedBy

The `isImplementedBy` function returns a Boolean value that specifies whether the object passed into it implements the interface type on which the function is called. The boldfaced portion of the following code first instantiates instances of the `Department.Employee` and `Department.Manager` types. Then, it calls the `isImplementedBy` function on the `Department.IEmployee` interface type twice, each time passing in one of these two instances. Notice that in both cases the function returns `true`.

```
<%@ Page Language="C#" %>
<html xmlns="http://www.w3.org/1999/xhtml">
<head id="Head1" runat="server">
  <title>Untitled Page</title>
</head>
<body>
  <form id="form1" runat="server">
    <asp:ScriptManager ID="ScriptManager1" runat="server" />

    <script language="JavaScript" type="text/javascript">
      Type.registerNamespace("Department");
      Department.IEmployee = function Department$IEmployee()
      {
        throw Error.notImplemented();
      };

      function Department$IEmployee$get_employeeID ()
      {
        throw Error.notImplemented();
      };

      function Department$IEmployee$set_employeeID ()
      {
        throw Error.notImplemented();
      };

      Department.IEmployee.prototype =
      {
        get_employeeID : Department$IEmployee$get_employeeID,
        set_employeeID: Department$IEmployee$set_employeeID
      }

      Department.IEmployee.registerInterface("Department.IEmployee");

      Department.Employee = function (firstName, lastName)
      {
        this._firstName = firstName;
        this._lastName = lastName;
      }
```

(continued)

```
      Department.Employee.prototype =
      {
        get_firstName : function () {return this._firstName;},
        set_firstName : function (value) {this._firstName = value;},
        get_lastName : function() {return this._lastName;},
        set_lastName : function (value) {this._lastName = value;},
        get_employeeID : function () {return this._employeeID;},
        set_employeeID : function (value) {this._employeeID = value;},
        getEmployeeInfo : function () {
              var info="First Name: " + this.get_firstName() + "\n";
              info += ("Last Name: " + this.get_lastName() + "\n");
              if (this._employeeID)
                info += ("Employee ID: " + this._employeeID + "\n");
              return info;
          }
      }

      Department.Employee.registerClass("Department.Employee", null,
                              Department.IEmployee);

      Department.Manager = function (firstName, lastName, department)
      {
        Department.Manager.initializeBase(this,
                                    [firstName,lastName]);
        this._department = department;
      };

      Department.Manager.prototype =
      {
        get_department : function () {return this._department;},
        set_department : function (value) {this._department = value;},
        getEmployeeInfo : function()
        {
              var info = Department.Manager.callBaseMethod(this, "getEmployeeInfo",
                                                    null);
              info += ("Department: " + this._department + "\n");
              return info;
          }
      };

      Department.Manager.registerClass("Department.Manager", Department.Employee);

      var employee = new Department.Employee("SomeFirstName", "SomeLastName");
      var flag = Department.IEmployee.isImplementedBy(employee);
      alert (flag);
      var mgr = new Department.Manager("SomeFirstName", "SomeLastName",
                                    "SomeDepartment");
      flag = Department.IEmployee.isImplementedBy(mgr);
      alert (flag);
    </script>
  </form>
</body>
</html>
```

Listing 4-26 contains the code for the internal implementation of the isImplementedBy function.

Listing 4-26: The Internal Implementation of isImplementedBy

```
Type.prototype.isImplementedBy = function(a)
{
  if(typeof a === "undefined" || a === null)
    return false;
  var b = Object.getType(a);
  return !!(b.implementsInterface && b.implementsInterface(this));
};
```

The function calls the getType function on the JavaScript Object type, passing in the object passed into the isImplementedBy function:

```
var b = Object.getType(a);
```

The getType function returns the type of the specified object.

The function then calls the implementsInterface function on the type returned from the getType function, passing in the interface type:

```
return !!(b.implementsInterface && b.implementsInterface(this));
```

This function returns a Boolean that specifies whether the type on which this function is called implements the specified interface type.

getRootNamespaces

As discussed earlier, in general there are two types of namespaces: local and global (or root). A local namespace is a namespace that belongs to another namespace. A global namespace, on the other hand, does not belong to any other namespace. The getRootNamespaces JavaScript function returns an array that contains all the namespaces registered at the global level. Here's an example:

```
<%@ Page Language="C#" %>
<html xmlns="http://www.w3.org/1999/xhtml">
<head id="Head1" runat="server">
  <title>Untitled Page</title>
</head>
<body>
  <form id="form1" runat="server">
    <asp:ScriptManager runat="server" ID="ScriptManager1" />
    <script language="JavaScript" type="text/javascript">
      Type.registerNamespace("Department");
      Type.registerNamespace("MyNamespace");
      Type.registerNamespace("Department.Section");
      var ar = Type.getRootNamespaces();
      var str = "";
      for (var i = 0; i<ar.length; i++)
        str += (ar[i].getName() + "\n");
      alert(str);
    </script>
  </form>
</body>
</html>
```

This code first registers two global namespaces, `Department` and `MyNamespace`, and a local namespace, `Department.Section`:

```
Type.registerNamespace("Department");
Type.registerNamespace("MyNamespace");
Type.registerNamespace("Department.Section");
```

Next, it calls the `getRootNamespace` static function of the `Type` to return the array that contains all the root namespaces:

```
var ar = Type.getRootNamespaces();
```

Then, it iterates through the namespaces in the array, calls the `getName` function on each enumerated namespace to return the fully qualified name of the namespace, and appends this name to the specified string:

```
var str="";
for (var i = 0; i<ar.length; i++)
    str += (ar[i].getName() + "\n");
```

Finally, it displays the string shown in Figure 4-6.

Figure 4-6

As this figure shows, the collection that the `getRootNamespaces` function returns does not contain the `Department.Section` local namespace. However, the collection does contain a root namespace, `Sys` (discussed in detail in subsequent chapters).

Listing 4-27 presents the internal implementation of the `getRootNamespaces` function. This function simply clones the content of the `_rootNamespaces` collection, which contains all the global namespaces.

Listing 4-27: The Internal Implementation of getRootNamespaces

```
Type.getRootNamespaces = function()
{
    return Array.clone(window.__rootNamespaces);
};
```

parse

The `parse` static method of the `Type` class returns the `Function` object that represents the type with the specified name. This method takes two parameters where the second parameter is optional. The first parameter must be a string that contains the following:

❑ The fully qualified name of the type, including its namespace containment hierarchy if the second parameter is not specified

❑ The name of the type without its namespace containment hierarchy if the second parameter is specified

The second parameter must reference the actual namespace that contains the type being parsed.

The following example defines a class named `Department.Employee` and registers it with the ASP.NET AJAX client-side framework. It then calls the `parse` static method on the `Type`, passing the fully qualified name of the class.

```
<%@ Page Language"C#" %>
<html xmlns="http://www.w3.org/1999/xhtml">
<head id="Head1" runat="server">
  <title>Untitled Page</title>
</head>
<body>
  <form id="form1" runat="server">
    <asp:ScriptManager ID="ScriptManager1" runat="server" />

    <script language="JavaScript" type="text/javascript">
      Type.registerNamespace("Department");
      Department.Employee = function (firstName, lastName)
      {
        this._firstName = firstName;
        this._lastName = lastName;
      }

      Department.Employee.prototype =
      {
        get_firstName : function () {return this._firstName;},
        set_firstName : function (value) {this._firstName = value;},
        get_lastName : function() {return this._lastName;},
        set_lastName : function (value) {this._lastName = value;}
      }

      Department.Employee.registerClass("Department.Employee");

      alert (Type.parse("Department.Employee"));
    </script>
  </form>
</body>
</html>
```

Figure 4-7 shows what you get when you run this code. Compare this to the boldfaced portion of the code. As you can see, the `parse` function returns a `Function` object that represents the constructor of the `Department.Employee` class.

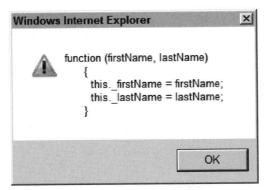

Figure 4-7

The following code is a version of the previous code that passes the name of the Employee class without its namespace as the first parameter of the parse method and the reference to the actual Department namespace that contains the Employee class. If you run this code, you get the same result as shown in Figure 4-7. Note that the second parameter is *not* a string that contains the name of the Department namespace. Instead, it is a reference to the actual namespace.

```
<%@ Page Language"C#" %>
<html xmlns="http://www.w3.org/1999/xhtml">
<head id="Head1" runat="server">
  <title>Untitled Page</title>
</head>
<body>
  <form id="form1" runat="server">
    <asp:ScriptManager ID="ScriptManager1" runat="server" />

    <script language="JavaScript" type="text/javascript">
      Type.registerNamespace("Department");
      Department.Employee = function (firstName, lastName)
      {
        this._firstName = firstName;
        this._lastName = lastName;
      }

      Department.Employee.prototype =
      {
        get_firstName : function () {return this._firstName;},
        set_firstName : function (value) {this._firstName = value;},
        get_lastName : function() {return this._lastName;},
        set_lastName : function (value) {this._lastName = value;}
      }

      Department.Employee.registerClass("Department.Employee");

      alert (Type.parse("Employee", Department));
    </script>
  </form>
</body>
</html>
```

Listing 4-28 shows the internal implementation of the `parse` static method of the `Type` class. The main responsibility of this function is to return the type with the specified name and namespace. To do so, this function uses the `eval` JavaScript function. To improve performance, the evaluated type is stored in a local cache named `_htClasses` for future reference. In other words, future calls for the same type name will be served from the cache instead of calling the `eval` method.

Listing 4-28: The Internal Implementation of parse

```
Type.parse = function(typeName, ns)
{
  var fn;
  if (ns)
  {
    if (!window.__classes)
      return null;

    fn = window.__classes[ns.getName().toUpperCase() + '.' +
        typeName.toUpperCase()];
    return fn || null;
  }
  if( ! typeName)
    return null;

  if( ! Type.__htClasses)
    Type.__htClasses = {};

  fn = Type.__htClasses[typeName];
  if(!fn)
  {
    fn = eval(typeName);
    Type.__htClasses[typeName] = fn;
  }
  return fn;
};
```

registerEnum

The `registerEnum` method enables you to register an enumeration with the ASP.NET AJAX client-side framework. Here's an example:

```
<%@ Page Language="C#" %>

<!DOCTYPE html PUBLIC "-//W3C//DTD XHTML 1.0 Transitional//EN"
"http://www.w3.org/TR/xhtml1/DTD/xhtml1-transitional.dtd">
<html xmlns="http://www.w3.org/1999/xhtml">
<head id="Head1" runat="server">
  <title>Untitled Page</title>
</head>
<body>
  <form id="form1" runat="server">
    <asp:ScriptManager ID="ScriptManager1" runat="server" />
```

(continued)

```
<script language="javascript" type="text/javascript">
  Type.registerNamespace("MyNamespace");
  MyNamespace.State = function ()
  {
     throw Error.notImplemented();
  }

  MyNamespace.State.prototype =
  {
     State1 : 1,
     State2 : 2,
     State3 : 4
  }
  MyNamespace.State.registerEnum("MyNamespace.State");
  alert(MyNamespace.State.State1);
  alert(MyNamespace.State.State2);
  alert(MyNamespace.State.State3);
</script>
</form>
</body>
</html>
```

This code first defines an enumeration named `MyNamespace.State`. Defining an enumeration involves
two tasks. First, you need to define a constructor that raises an exception, which ensures that no one else
can create an instance of your enumeration:

```
MyNamespace.State = function ()
{
   throw Error.notImplemented();
}
```

Next, you need to assign a JavaScript object literal to the prototype property of the newly created enumeration. This JavaScript object literal must expose one name/value pair for each enumeration value:

```
MyNamespace.State.prototype = {
   State1 : 1,
   State2 : 2,
   State3 : 3
}
```

Finally, you need to register your enumeration with the ASP.NET AJAX client-side framework:

```
MyNamespace.State.registerEnum("MyNamespace.State");
```

The `registerEnum` method takes a second argument of type Boolean. Pass `true` for this argument to tell
the ASP.NET AJAX client-side framework that your enumeration supports bitwise operations. This
allows the clients of your enumeration to use the bitwise OR operation to combine two or more of the
enumeration values of your enumeration:

```
MyNamespace.State.registerEnum("MyNamespace.State", true);
```

isEnum

The isEnum static method of the Type class enables you to determine whether a specified object is an enumeration. This is yet another example of the type reflection capabilities of the ASP.NET AJAX client-side framework. The following code shows an example where this method is used:

```
<%@ Page Language="C#" %>

<!DOCTYPE html PUBLIC "-//W3C//DTD XHTML 1.0 Transitional//EN"
"http://www.w3.org/TR/xhtml1/DTD/xhtml1-transitional.dtd">
<html xmlns="http://www.w3.org/1999/xhtml">
<head id="Head1" runat="server">
  <title>Untitled Page</title>
</head>
<body>
  <form id="form1" runat="server">
    <asp:ScriptManager ID="ScriptManager1" runat="server" />
    <script language="javascript" type="text/javascript">
    Type.registerNamespace("MyNamespace");
    MyNamespace.State = function ()
    {
      throw Error.notImplemented();
    }

    MyNamespace.State.prototype = {
      State1 : 1,
      State2 : 2,
      State3 : 4
    }
    MyNamespace.State.registerEnum("MyNamespace.State");
    alert(Type.isEnum(MyNamespace.State));
  </script>
  </form>
</body>
</html>
```

isFlags

The isFlags static method of the Type class returns a Boolean value that specifies whether a specified enumeration allows bitwise operations between its values. The following code shows an example that uses the isFlags method. Note that this code passes true as the second argument of the registerEnum method to tell the ASP.NET AJAX client-side framework that the enumeration being registered supports bitwise operations.

```
<%@ Page Language="C#" %>

<!DOCTYPE html PUBLIC "-//W3C//DTD XHTML 1.0 Transitional//EN"
"http://www.w3.org/TR/xhtml1/DTD/xhtml1-transitional.dtd">
<html xmlns="http://www.w3.org/1999/xhtml">
```

(continued)

129

```
<head id="Head1" runat="server">
  <title>Untitled Page</title>
</head>
<body>
  <form id="form1" runat="server">
    <asp:ScriptManager ID="ScriptManager1" runat="server" />
    <script language="javascript" type="text/javascript">
      Type.registerNamespace("MyNamespace");
      MyNamespace.State = function ()
      {
        throw Error.notImplemented();
      }

      MyNamespace.State.prototype = {
        State1 : 1,
        State2 : 2,
        State3 : 4
      }
      MyNamespace.State.registerEnum("MyNamespace.State", true);
      alert(Type.isFlags(MyNamespace.State));
  </script>
  </form>
</body>
</html>
```

Summary

This chapter presented in-depth coverage of the ASP.NET AJAX OOP and type reflection capabilities. The next chapter discusses another important part of the ASP.NET AJAX client-side framework: the ASP.NET AJAX event programming extensions.

Event Programming Extensions

One of the great advantages of the .NET Framework is its event-programming facilities. The ASP.NET AJAX client-side framework provides you with similar facilities to make client-side JavaScript event programming more like server-side .NET event programming as much as possible. This chapter provides you with in-depth coverage of the ASP.NET AJAX event-programming extensions and examples that use these extensions.

Event Programming

The .NET Framework provides you with the following three classes to facilitate event programming in the .NET Framework:

❑ System.EventArgs: This is the base class from which all event data classes derive, directly or indirectly. This class exposes a single read-only property of type EventArgs named Empty, which simply instantiates and returns an instance of the class.

❑ System.ComponentModel.CancelEventArgs: This is the base class from which all event data classes associated with cancelable events derive, directly or indirectly. This class exposes a single read/write Boolean property named Cancel.

❑ System.ComponentModel.EventHandlerList: This class is a linked list, where each list entry contains the event handlers for an event type with a specified key. This class exposes the following three important methods:

    ❑ AddHandler: This method adds a specified event handler to the list entry associated with an event type with a specified key.

    ❑ RemoveHandler: This method removes a specified event handler from the list entry associated with an event type with a specified key.

    ❑ AddHandlers: This method adds the content of a specified EventHandlerList — that is, a link list of list entries — to the EventHandlerList on which the method is called.

The ASP.NET AJAX client-side framework comes with three classes named `Sys.EventArgs`, `Sys.CancelEventArgs`, and `Sys.EventHandlerList` that respectively emulate the .NET `System.EventArgs`, `System.ComponentModel.CancelEventArgs`, and `System.ComponentModel.EventHandlerList` classes as discussed in the following sections.

Before diving into the implementation of these classes, here's a basic description of what an event data class is and what role it plays in server-side .NET or client-side ASP.NET AJAX event programming. An instance of a class raises an event to inform interested clients that something of interest to the clients has occurred. The clients of certain types of events may need more information to process the event. This information is known as event data. The event data class is a class whose instances contain the event data associated with a particular type of event. An event data class normally exposes properties that contain the event data. As you'll see later, it is the responsibility of the instance that raises the event to instantiate an instance of the appropriate event data class, to initialize the properties of this event data class instance with the appropriate event data, and to pass this event data class instance into the event handlers registered for the specified event when it invokes these event handlers.

Sys.EventArgs

The ASP.NET AJAX client-side framework contains a base event data class that emulates the .NET `System.EventArgs` base event data class, as shown in Listing 5-1.

Listing 5-1: The Sys.EventArgs Base Event Data Class

```
Sys.EventArgs = function Sys$EventArgs() { }
Sys.EventArgs.registerClass('Sys.EventArgs');
```

The `Sys.EventArgs` base event data class of the ASP.NET AJAX client-side framework, just like the `System.EventArgs` base event data class of the .NET Framework, features a static property named `Empty`. Here's how it works:

```
Sys.EventArgs.Empty = new Sys.EventArgs();
```

Sys.CancelEventArgs

The ASP.NET AJAX client-side framework also includes an event data class named `Sys.CancelEventArgs` that emulates the .NET `System.ComponentModel.CancelEventArgs` event data class, as defined in Listing 5-2. The `Sys.CancelEventArgs` class inherits from the `Sys.EventArgs` base class and extends its functionality to add support for a new read/write Boolean property named `cancel`. The `Sys.CancelEventArgs` class, just like its .NET counterpart, is the base class for the event data classes of all cancelable events in the ASP.NET AJAX client-side framework.

Listing 5-2: The Sys.CancelEventArgs Event Data Class

```
Sys.CancelEventArgs = function Sys$CancelEventArgs() {
  Sys.CancelEventArgs.initializeBase(this);
  this._cancel = false;
}
```

(continued)

```
function Sys$CancelEventArgs$get_cancel() {
  return this._cancel;
}

function Sys$CancelEventArgs$set_cancel(value) {
  this._cancel = value;
}

Sys.CancelEventArgs.prototype = {
  get_cancel: Sys$CancelEventArgs$get_cancel,
  set_cancel: Sys$CancelEventArgs$set_cancel
}

Sys.CancelEventArgs.registerClass('Sys.CancelEventArgs', Sys.EventArgs);
```

EventHandlerList

Listing 5-3 presents the definition of the Sys.EventHandlerList class.

Listing 5-3: The Sys.EventHandlerList Class

```
Sys.EventHandlerList = function Sys$EventHandlerList() {
  this._list = {};
}

Sys.EventHandlerList.prototype = {
  addHandler: Sys$EventHandlerList$addHandler,
  removeHandler: Sys$EventHandlerList$removeHandler,
  getHandler: Sys$EventHandlerList$getHandler,

  _getEvent: Sys$EventHandlerList$_getEvent
}

Sys.EventHandlerList.registerClass('Sys.EventHandlerList');
```

As you can see, the constructor of this class simply instantiates an internal object named _list:

```
this._list = {};
```

Also note that this class features four methods: addHandler, removeHandler, getHandler, and _getEvent. The definitions of these methods are presented in the following sections.

_getEvent

The Sys.EventHandlerList class contains an internal method named _getEvent as defined in Listing 5-4. As mentioned, this method is used internally by other methods of the class, which means that you should not directly use this method in your JavaScript code. Instead, you should use the other methods of the class. However, understanding the internal implementation of this method helps you get a better understanding of the other methods of the class.

Listing 5-4: The _getEvent Method

```
function Sys$EventHandlerList$_getEvent(id, create) {
  if (!this._list[id]) {
    if (!create)
      return null;
    this._list[id] = [];
  }
  return this._list[id];
}
```

As you can see, the _getEvent method takes two arguments. The first argument is used as an index into the _list. The second argument is a Boolean value that specifies whether the method should instantiate a subarray associated with the specified index if the _list does not already contain the subarray. In summary, the _getEvent method uses its first argument as an index into the _list to return the subarray associated with the index.

addHandler

This method adds a specified event handler to the subarray of the _list with the specified index. This subarray contains the event handlers for the event type associated with the specified index. As such, this method takes two arguments. The first argument is used as an index into the _list to access the associated subarray. The second argument references the event handler being added. As Listing 5-5 shows, addHandler first calls the _getEvent method to return the subarray associated with the specified index, and then calls the add method on the Array class to add the specified event handler to this subarray.

Listing 5-5: The addHandler Method

```
function Sys$EventHandlerList$addHandler(id, handler) {
  Array.add(this._getEvent(id, true), handler);
}
```

removeHandler

This method removes a specified event handler from the subarray of the _list with the specified index. This subarray contains the event handlers for the event type associated with the specified index. As such, this method takes two arguments, as shown in Listing 5-6. The first argument is used as an index into the _list to access the associated subarray. The second argument references the event handler being removed.

Listing 5-6: The removeHandler Method

```
function Sys$EventHandlerList$removeHandler(id, handler) {
  var evt = this._getEvent(id);
  if (!evt)
    return;
  Array.remove(evt, handler);
}
```

As you can see, removeHandler first calls the _getEvent method to access the subarray associated with the specified index and then calls the remove method on the Array class to remove the specified event handler from the subarray.

getHandler

This method returns a reference to a JavaScript function whose invocation automatically invokes all the event handlers for an event type with a specified index. See Listing 5-7 for the implementation of this method.

Listing 5-7: The getHandler Class

```
function Sys$EventHandlerList$getHandler(id) {
  var evt = this._getEvent(id);
  if (!evt || (evt.length === 0))
    return null;
  evt = Array.clone(evt);
  if (!evt._handler) {
    evt._handler = function(source, args) {
      for (var i = 0, l = evt.length; i < l; i++) {
        evt[i](source, args);
      }
    };
  }
  return evt._handler;
}
```

As you can see, getHandler first calls the _getEvent method to access the subarray of the _list with the specified index:

```
var evt = this._getEvent(id);
```

Then it defines a function that iterates through the event handlers in this subarray and invokes each enumerated event handler:

```
evt._handler = function(source, args) {
  for (var i = 0, l = evt.length; i < l; i++) {
    evt[i](source, args);
  }
};
```

One of the great features of the ASP.NET Framework is its convenient event programming pattern for implementing a new event. That is, adding a new event to a class involves the following steps:

1. Add a property of type EventHandlerList to your class if your class does not already contain this property.

2. Choose an appropriate name for your event.

3. Choose an appropriate key for your event. The key is normally an instance of the `System.Object` class.

4. Determine whether your class must pass data to the event subscribers when it raises the event. If so, proceed to step 5. If not, use the `EventArgs` and `EventHandler` base classes as your event data class and event delegate, and proceed to step 9 (skipping steps 5 through 8).

5. Determine whether the .NET Framework or your own custom library already comes with an event data class and event delegate that you can use directly. If so, skip steps 6, 7, and 8 and go directly to step 9. Otherwise, proceed to the next step.

6. Determine which event data class of the .NET Framework or your own custom library is the most appropriate base class.

7. Implement an event data class that derives from the base class chosen in step 6.

8. Define an event delegate that takes two arguments where the first argument is of type `System.Object` and the second argument is of the same type as your event data class.

9. Declare an event with the same type as your event delegate as the member of your class. The `add` and `remove` event accessors must add and remove the specified event handler for the event type with the specified key to the `EventHandlerList` property of your class.

10. Add a method to your class that raises the event. This method must first access the list entry in the `EventHandlerList` link list that contains the event handlers for the event type with the specified key. This list entry exposes a delegate property whose invocation automatically invokes the event handlers that the list entry contains in the order in which they were added to the list entry.

Following the ASP.NET Framework, the ASP.NET AJAX client-side framework offers this similar event programming pattern:

1. Add a method named `get_events` to your class if your class does not already contain this method. The method must return an instance of the `EventHandlerList` type. This instance is where your class must store all the event handlers registered for its events. A typical implementation of this method is as follows:

```
function get_events()
{
  if (!this.events)
    this.events = new Sys.EventHandlerList();

  return this.events;
}
```

2. Choose an appropriate name for your event.

3. Determine whether your class must pass data to the event subscribers when it raises the event. If so, proceed to step 4. If not, use the `EventArgs` base class as your event data class, skip steps 4 through 6, and go directly to Step 7.

4. Determine whether the ASP.NET AJAX client-side framework or your own custom library already comes with an event data class that you can directly use. If so, skip steps 5 and 6 and go directly to step 7. Otherwise, proceed to step 5.

5. Determine which event data class of the ASP.NET AJAX client-side framework or your own custom library is the most appropriate base class.

6. Implement an event data class that derives from the base class chosen in step 5.

7. Implement a method named `add_EventName` where the `EventName` is the placeholder for the name of the event. The clients of your class will use this method to register event handlers for the event with the specified name. A typical implementation of this method is as follows:

```
function add_EventName(handler)
{
  var eventHandlerList = this.get_events();
  eventHandlerList.addHandler("EventName", handler);
}
```

This method must take a single argument that references a JavaScript function and perform the following tasks:

1. It must invoke the `get_events` method to return a reference to the `EventHandlerList` object where the class stores all the event handlers registered for its events.

2. It must invoke the `addHandler` method on this `EventHandlerList` object to add the specified event handler to the list of event handlers registered for the event with the specified name.

8. Implement a method named `remove_EventName` where the `EventName` is the placeholder for the name of the event. The clients of your class will use this method to remove event handlers from the list of event handlers registered for the event with the specified name. A typical implementation of this method is as follows:

```
function remove_EventName(handler)
{
  var eventHandlerList = this.get_events();
  eventHandlerList.removeHandler("EventName", handler);
}
```

This method must take a single argument that references a JavaScript function and perform the following tasks:

1. It must invoke the `get_events` method to return a reference to the `EventHandlerList` object where the class stores all the event handlers registered for its events.

2. It must invoke the `removeHandler` method on this `EventHandlerList` object to remove the specified event handler from the list of event handlers registered for the event with a specified name.

9. Implement a method named `onEventName` where the `EventName` is the placeholder for the name of the event. Your class must use this method to raise the event and consequently to invoke the event handlers registered for the event with the specified name. A typical implementation of this method is as follows:

```
function onEventName(e)
{
  var eventHandlerList = this.get_events();
  var handler = eventHandlerList.getHandler("EventName");
  if (handler)
    handler(this, e);
}
```

This method must take a single argument that references the event data class instance that contains the event data and perform the following tasks:

1. It must invoke the `get_events` method to return a reference to the `EventHandlerList` object where the class stores all the event handlers registered for its events.

2. It must invoke the `getHandler` method on this `EventHandlerList` object, passing in the name of the event. This method returns a reference to a JavaScript function. This function automatically invokes all the event handlers registered for the event with the specified name.

10. Implement a method that includes the logic that instantiates the event data class instance, initializes the properties of this instance with the event data, and invokes the `onEventName` method, passing in the event data class instance. You'll see an example of this later in the chapter.

Using Event Programming

This section shows you how to use the previously mentioned event programming pattern to add new events to your client-side classes. The example used in this section is a shopping cart application. First, the basic classes of the application are presented, and then the application is enhanced with events.

Base Classes

Listing 5-8 presents the content of a JavaScript file named `ShoppingCart.js` that contains the implementation of the base classes. As you can see, the example shopping cart application consists of two base classes:

❑ `ShoppingCartItem`: As the name suggests, the instances of this class represent the shopping cart items that the end user adds to the shopping cart.

❑ `ShoppingCart`: As the name implies, the instances of this class represent the user's shopping carts.

Listing 5-8: The Content of the ShoppingCart.js JavaScript File

```
Type.registerNamespace("Shopping");

Shopping.ShoppingCartItem = function Shopping$ShoppingCartItem(id, name, price)
{
  this.id = id;
  this.name = name;
  this.price = price;
}

function Shopping$ShoppingCartItem$get_id()
{
  return this.id;
}

function Shopping$ShoppingCartItem$get_name()
{
  return this.name;
}
```

```
function Shopping$ShoppingCartItem$get_price()
{
  return this.price;
}

Shopping.ShoppingCartItem.prototype =
{
  get_id : Shopping$ShoppingCartItem$get_id,
  get_name : Shopping$ShoppingCartItem$get_name,
  get_price : Shopping$ShoppingCartItem$get_price
};

Shopping.ShoppingCartItem.registerClass("Shopping.ShoppingCartItem");

Shopping.ShoppingCart = function() {
}

function Shopping$ShoppingCart$initialize()
{
  this.shoppingCartItems = {};
}

function Shopping$ShoppingCart$get_shoppingCartItems()
{
  return this.shoppingCartItems;
}

function Shopping$ShoppingCart$addShoppingCartItem(shoppingCartItem)
{
  var cartItems = this.get_shoppingCartItems();
  var cartItemId = shoppingCartItem.get_id();

  if (cartItems[cartItemId])
  {
    var exception = Error.duplicateItem("Duplicate Shopping Cart Item!",
                                        {name: shoppingCartItem.get_name()});
    throw exception;
  }

  else
    this.shoppingCartItems[cartItemId] = shoppingCartItem;
}

Shopping.ShoppingCart.prototype = {
  addShoppingCartItem : Shopping$ShoppingCart$addShoppingCartItem,
  initialize : Shopping$ShoppingCart$initialize,
  get_shoppingCartItems : Shopping$ShoppingCart$get_shoppingCartItems
};

Shopping.ShoppingCart.registerClass("Shopping.ShoppingCart");

if(typeof(Sys)!=='undefined')
  Sys.Application.notifyScriptLoaded();
```

Listing 5-9 presents an ASP.NET page that uses these base classes, which are discussed in more detail later.

Listing 5-9: A Page that uses the Base Classes

```
<%@ Page Language="C#" %>

<!DOCTYPE html PUBLIC "-//W3C//DTD XHTML 1.0 Transitional//EN"
"http://www.w3.org/TR/xhtml1/DTD/xhtml1-transitional.dtd">

<html xmlns="http://www.w3.org/1999/xhtml">
<head runat="server">
  <title>Untitled Page</title>
  <script type="text/javascript" language="javascript"
    src="ShoppingCartApp1.js">
  </script>
  <script type="text/javascript" language="javascript">
    function pageLoad()
    {
      var shoppingCart = new Shopping.ShoppingCart();
      shoppingCart.initialize();
      var shoppingCartItem = new Shopping.ShoppingCartItem(1, "item1", 23);
      shoppingCart.addShoppingCartItem(shoppingCartItem);
      var shoppingCartItems = shoppingCart.get_shoppingCartItems();
      for (var id in shoppingCartItems)
      {
        alert(shoppingCartItems[id].get_name());
      }
    }
  </script>
</head>
<body>
  <form id="form1" runat="server">
    <asp:ScriptManager runat="server" ID="ScripManager1">
      <Scripts>
        <asp:ScriptReference Path="ShoppingCart.js" />
      </Scripts>
    </asp:ScriptManager>
  </form>
</body>
</html>
```

As you can see from Listing 5-9, the `pageLoad` method first instantiates a `ShoppingCart` object to represent the current user's shopping cart:

```
var shoppingCart = new Shopping.ShoppingCart();
```

Next, it calls the `initialize` method (discussed in more detail later) on the newly instantiated `ShoppingCart` object to initialize the object:

```
shoppingCart.initialize();
```

Then, it instantiates a `ShoppingCartItem` object to represent the item that the current user wants to add to her shopping cart:

```
var shoppingCartItem = new Shopping.ShoppingCartItem(1, "item1", 23);
```

To keep this discussion focused, I've skipped the user interface that presents the current user with the list of available items to choose from and hard-coded the item being added.

Next, the `pageLoad` method adds the newly instantiated `ShoppingCartItem` object to the current user's shopping cart:

```
shoppingCart.addShoppingCartItem(shoppingCartItem);
```

Finally, it pops up a message that displays the name of the item just added to the shopping cart:

```
alert(shoppingCart.get_shoppingCartItems()[0].get_name());
```

Namespace

The `ShoppingCart.js` JavaScript file defines a namespace named `Shopping` that will contain all the other classes of the shopping cart application, as follows:

```
Type.registerNamespace("Shopping");
```

ShoppingCartItem

The `ShoppingCart.js` JavaScript file defines a class named `ShoppingCartItem`, as shown in Listing 5-10.

Listing 5-10: The ShoppingCartItem Class

```
Shopping.ShoppingCartItem = function Shopping$ShoppingCartItem(id, name, price)
{
  this.id = id;
  this.name = name;
  this.price = price;
}

Shopping.ShoppingCartItem.prototype =
{
  get_id : Shopping$ShoppingCartItem$get_id,
  get_name : Shopping$ShoppingCartItem$get_name,
  get_price : Shopping$ShoppingCartItem$get_price
};

Shopping.ShoppingCartItem.registerClass("Shopping.ShoppingCartItem");
```

As you can see, the `ShoppingCartItem` class exposes three properties named `id`, `name`, and `price`. The `id` property of a `ShoppingCartItem` object uniquely identifies the object among other

ShoppingCartItem objects. Notice that Listing 5-10 assigns the following object to the `prototype` property of the `ShoppingCartItem` class:

```
{
    get_id : Shopping$ShoppingCartItem$get_id,
    get_name : Shopping$ShoppingCartItem$get_name,
    get_price : Shopping$ShoppingCartItem$get_price
};
```

The object shown in this code fragment exposes three methods named get_id, get_name, and get_price, which respectively reference three JavaScript functions named Shopping$ShoppingCartItem$get_id, Shopping$ShoppingCartItem$get_name, and Shopping$ShoppingCartItem$get_price.

This ensures that all instances of the `ShoppingCartItem` class share the same copy of the get_id, get_name, and get_price methods. If you were to directly define these three methods inside the constructor of the `ShoppingCartItem` class, each instance of the class would have its own copy of these methods. This would waste a lot of resources.

As Listing 5-11 shows, the Shopping$ShoppingCartItem$get_id, Shopping$ShoppingCartItem$get_name, and Shopping$ShoppingCartItem$get_price methods respectively return the id, name, and price of the associated `ShoppingCartItem` object.

Listing 5-11: The Referenced JavaScript Functions

```
function Shopping$ShoppingCartItem$get_id()
{
  return this.id;
}

function Shopping$ShoppingCartItem$get_name()
{
  return this.name;
}

function Shopping$ShoppingCartItem$get_price()
{
  return this.price;
}
```

ShoppingCart

Listing 5-12 shows the implementation of the `ShoppingCart` class.

Listing 5-12: The ShoppingCart Class

```
    Shopping.ShoppingCart = function() {
    }

    Shopping.ShoppingCart.prototype = {
      addShoppingCartItem : Shopping$ShoppingCart$addShoppingCartItem,
```

(continued)

```
    initialize : Shopping$ShoppingCart$initialize,
    get_shoppingCartItems : Shopping$ShoppingCart$get_shoppingCartItems
};

Shopping.ShoppingCart.registerClass("Shopping.ShoppingCart");
```

In this listing, the following object is added to the `prototype` property of the `ShoppingCart` class:

```
{
    addShoppingCartItem : Shopping$ShoppingCart$addShoppingCartItem,
    initialize : Shopping$ShoppingCart$initialize,
    get_shoppingCartItems : Shopping$ShoppingCart$get_shoppingCartItems
};
```

This object features three methods named `addShoppingCartItem`, `initialize`, and `get_shopping-CartItems`, which respectively reference the `Shopping$ShoppingCart$addShoppingCartItem`, `Shopping$ShoppingCart$initialize`, and `Shopping$ShoppingCart$get_shoppingCartItems` JavaScript functions, as discussed in the following sections.

initialize

As you can see in Listing 5-13, the `initialize` JavaScript function instantiates an internal object named `shoppingCartItems` that will contain the `ShoppingCartItems` added to the current user's shopping cart.

Listing 5-13: The initialize JavaScript Function

```
function Shopping$ShoppingCart$initialize()
{
    this.shoppingCartItems = {};
}
```

get_shoppingCartItems

As Listing 5-14 shows, this JavaScript function returns a reference to the `shoppingCartItems` internal array that contains the `ShoppingCartItem` objects added to the current user's shopping cart.

Listing 5-14: The get_shoppingCartItems JavaScript Function

```
function Shopping$ShoppingCart$get_shoppingCartItems()
{
    return this.shoppingCartItems;
}
```

addShoppingCartItem

As you can see in Listing 5-15, this method takes several steps to add the specified `ShoppingCartItem` object to the `shoppingCartItems` collection. First, it checks whether the `shoppingCartItems` collection contains an object with the same `id` as the object being added. If so, it throws a `DuplicateItemException` (discussed in previous chapters). If not, it adds the specified `ShoppingCartItem` to the `shoppingCartItems` collection.

Listing 5-15: The Shopping$ShoppingCart$addShoppingCartItem JavaScript Functions

```
function Shopping$ShoppingCart$addShoppingCartItem(shoppingCartItem)
{
  var cartItems = this.get_shoppingCartItems();
  var cartItemId = shoppingCartItem.get_id();

  if (cartItems[cartItemId])
  {
    var exception = Error.duplicateItem("Duplicate Shopping Cart Item!",
                                        {name: shoppingCartItem.get_name()});
    throw exception;
  }

  else
    this.shoppingCartItems[cartItemId] = shoppingCartItem;
}
```

Events

In this section, the functionality of the ShoppingCart class developed in the previous section is extended to add support for events. You may be wondering why you need to enhance a class with events. When you're implementing a class, you do your best to ensure that your class provides its clients with the necessary functionality. However, you cannot add application-specific functionality to your class if you want different applications to use your class. This means that your class will not meet the application-specific requirements of its clients.

Let's take a look at some of the application-specific requirements that the version of the ShoppingCart class discussed in the previous section does not meet.

In Listing 5-13, the initialize method of the ShoppingCart class performed a single task — that is, it instantiated the shoppingCartItems collection that will contain the ShoppingCartItem objects added to the current user's shopping cart. There are several application-specific requirements that the current implementation of the initialize method does not meet, such as the following:

❑ As part of the initialization process, a typical shopping cart application also needs to populate the shoppingCartItems collection with the items that the current user selected in the previous session. To do so, the application needs to run some application-specific code to retrieve the previous session's items from the underlying data store.

❑ As part of the initialization process, a shopping cart application may also need to run some application-specific code to perform certain filtering on the items that the current user selected in the previous session.

As you'll see later in this section, the ShoppingCart class can be enhanced with an event named ShoppingCartInitialized, which the initialize method can raise to allow the clients of the class to execute application-specific initialization code.

In Listing 5-15, the addShoppingCartItem method of the ShoppingCart class added the specified ShoppingCartItem object to the shoppingCartItems collection. Before adding the object to the collection, the shopping cart application may need to run some code that contains some application-specific logic to determine whether the addition of the specified object would violate some application-specific rules.

As you'll see later in this section, the ShoppingCart class can be enhanced with a cancelable event named ShoppingCartItemAdding, which the addShoppingCartItem method can raise to allow the clients of the class to cancel the add operation if it violates application-specific rules.

In Listing 5-15, the addShoppingCartItem method raised a DuplicateItemException exception if the shoppingCartItems already contains a ShoppingCartItem object with the same id value as the one being added. Many applications prefer to use application-specific exception-handling mechanisms to handle exceptions.

As you'll see later, the ShoppingCart class can be enhanced with an event named ShoppingCart-ItemAdded, which the addShoppingCartItem method can raise to allow the clients of the class to use application-specific exception-handling logic to handle the exception.

This event is useful even when no exception is raised because it allows the application to run application-specific code after an item is added. For example, the application may want to display information about a special promotion for the newly added item.

As you can see, enhancing your classes with events enables the clients of your classes to extend the functionality of your classes to incorporate application-specific logic.

Listing 5-16 presents the new version of the ShoppingCart.js JavaScript file that contains the implementation of all the classes of the shopping cart application. These classes are discussed in detail later in this chapter.

Listing 5-16: The New Version of the ShoppingCart.js File

```
Type.registerNamespace("Shopping");

Shopping.ShoppingCartItem = function Shopping$ShoppingCartItem(id, name, price)
{
  this.id = id;
  this.name = name;
  this.price = price;
}

function Shopping$ShoppingCartItem$get_id()
{
  return this.id;
}

function Shopping$ShoppingCartItem$get_name()
{
  return this.name;
}
```

(continued)

Listing 5-16 *(continued)*

```
function Shopping$ShoppingCartItem$get_price()
{
  return this.price;
}

Shopping.ShoppingCartItem.prototype = {
  get_id : Shopping$ShoppingCartItem$get_id,
  get_name : Shopping$ShoppingCartItem$get_name,
  get_price : Shopping$ShoppingCartItem$get_price
};

Shopping.ShoppingCartItem.registerClass("Shopping.ShoppingCartITem");

Shopping.ShoppingCart = function() { }

function Shopping$ShoppingCart$get_events() {
  if (!this.events)
    this.events = new Sys.EventHandlerList();

  return this.events;
}

function Shopping$ShoppingCart$initialize()
{
  this.shoppingCartItems = {};
  this.onShoppingCartInitialized(Sys.EventArgs.Empty);
}

function Shopping$ShoppingCart$onShoppingCartInitialized(e)
{
  var handler = this.get_events().getHandler("shoppingCartInitialized");
  if (handler)
    handler(this, e);
}

function Shopping$ShoppingCart$addShoppingCartItem(shoppingCartItem)
{
  var e1 = new Shopping.ShoppingCartItemAddingEventArgs(shoppingCartItem);
  this.onShoppingCartItemAdding(e1);

  if (!e1.get_cancel())
  {
    var exception = null;
    var cartItems = this.get_shoppingCartItems();
    var cartItemId = shoppingCartItem.get_id();

    if (cartItems[cartItemId])
      exception = Error.duplicateItem("Duplicate Shopping Cart Item!",
                             {name: shoppingCartItem.get_name()});
    else
      this.shoppingCartItems[cartItemId] = shoppingCartItem;
```

```
      var e2 =
          new Shopping.ShoppingCartItemAddedEventArgs(shoppingCartItem, exception);
      this.onShoppingCartItemAdded(e2);

      if (!e2.get_exceptionHandled())
        throw exception;
    }
}

function Shopping$ShoppingCart$onShoppingCartItemAdding(e)
{
  var handler = this.get_events().getHandler("shoppingCartItemAdding");
  if (handler)
    handler(this, e);                      ·
}

function Shopping$ShoppingCart$onShoppingCartItemAdded(e)
{
  var handler = this.get_events().getHandler("shoppingCartItemAdded");
  if (handler)
    handler(this, e);
}

function Shopping$ShoppingCart$add_shoppingCartInitialized(handler)
{
  this.get_events().addHandler("shoppingCartInitialized", handler);
}

function Shopping$ShoppingCart$add_shoppingCartItemAdding(handler)
{
  this.get_events().addHandler("shoppingCartItemAdding", handler);
}

function Shopping$ShoppingCart$add_shoppingCartItemAdded(handler)
{
  this.get_events().addHandler("shoppingCartItemAdded", handler);
}

function Shopping$ShoppingCart$remove_shoppingCartInitialized(handler)
{
  this.get_events().removeHandler("shoppingCartInitialized", handler);
}

function Shopping$ShoppingCart$remove_shoppingCartItemAdding(handler)
{
  this.get_events().removeHandler("shoppingCartItemAdding", handler);
}

function Shopping$ShoppingCart$remove_shoppingCartItemAdded(handler)
{
  this.get_events().removeHandler("shoppingCartItemAdded", handler);
}
```

(continued)

Listing 5-16 *(continued)*

```
function Shopping$ShoppingCart$get_shoppingCartItems()
{
  return this.shoppingCartItems;
}

Shopping.ShoppingCart.prototype = {
  addShoppingCartItem : Shopping$ShoppingCart$addShoppingCartItem,
  initialize : Shopping$ShoppingCart$initialize,
  get_shoppingCartItems : Shopping$ShoppingCart$get_shoppingCartItems,

  get_events : Shopping$ShoppingCart$get_events,

  add_shoppingCartInitialized :
                   Shopping$ShoppingCart$add_shoppingCartInitialized,
  remove_shoppingCartInitialized :
                Shopping$ShoppingCart$remove_shoppingCartInitialized,
  onShoppingCartInitialized : Shopping$ShoppingCart$onShoppingCartInitialized,

  add_shoppingCartItemAdding : Shopping$ShoppingCart$add_shoppingCartItemAdding,
  remove_shoppingCartItemAdding:
                Shopping$ShoppingCart$remove_shoppingCartItemAdding,
  onShoppingCartItemAdding : Shopping$ShoppingCart$onShoppingCartItemAdding,

  add_shoppingCartItemAdded : Shopping$ShoppingCart$add_shoppingCartItemAdded,
  remove_shoppingCartItemAdded:
                Shopping$ShoppingCart$remove_shoppingCartItemAdded,
  onShoppingCartItemAdded : Shopping$ShoppingCart$onShoppingCartItemAdded
};

Shopping.ShoppingCart.registerClass("Shopping.ShoppingCart");

Shopping.ShoppingCartItemAddingEventArgs =
function Shopping$ShoppingCartItemAddingEventArgs (shoppingCartItem)
{
  Shopping.ShoppingCartItemAddingEventArgs.initializeBase(this);
  this.shoppingCartItem = shoppingCartItem;
}

function Shopping$ShoppingCartItemAddingEventArgs$get_shoppingCartItem()
{
  return this.shoppingCartItem;
}

Shopping.ShoppingCartItemAddingEventArgs.prototype = {
  get_shoppingCartItem :
      Shopping$ShoppingCartItemAddingEventArgs$get_shoppingCartItem
};
```

```
Shopping.ShoppingCartItemAddingEventArgs.registerClass(
        "Shopping.ShoppingCartItemAddingEventArgs", Sys.CancelEventArgs);

Shopping.ShoppingCartItemAddedEventArgs =
function Shopping$ShoppingCartItemAddedEventArgs (shoppingCartItem, exception)
{
  Shopping.ShoppingCartItemAddedEventArgs.initializeBase(this);
  this.shoppingCartItem = shoppingCartItem;
  this.exception = exception;
  this.exceptionHandled = false;
}

function Shopping$ShoppingCartItemAddedEventArgs$get_shoppingCartItem()
{
  return this.shoppingCartItem;
}

function Shopping$ShoppingCartItemAddedEventArgs$get_exception()
{
  return this.exception;
}

function Shopping$ShoppingCartItemAddedEventArgs$get_exceptionHandled()
{
  return !this.exception || this.exceptionHandled;
}

function Shopping$ShoppingCartItemAddedEventArgs$set_exceptionHandled(value)
{
  this.exceptionHandled = value;
}

Shopping.ShoppingCartItemAddedEventArgs.prototype = {
  get_shoppingCartItem :
        Shopping$ShoppingCartItemAddedEventArgs$get_shoppingCartItem,
  get_exception : Shopping$ShoppingCartItemAddedEventArgs$get_exception,
  get_exceptionHandled :
        Shopping$ShoppingCartItemAddedEventArgs$get_exceptionHandled,
  set_exceptionHandled :
        Shopping$ShoppingCartItemAddedEventArgs$set_exceptionHandled
};

Shopping.ShoppingCartItemAddedEventArgs.registerClass(
        "Shopping.ShoppingCartItemAddedEventArgs", Sys.EventArgs);

if(typeof(Sys)!=='undefined')
  Sys.Application.notifyScriptLoaded();
```

Listing 5-17 presents a page containing the new version of the shopping cart class that uses events.

Listing 5-17: A Page that uses the New Version of the Shopping Cart Class

```
<%@ Page Language="C#" %>

<!DOCTYPE html PUBLIC "-//W3C//DTD XHTML 1.0 Transitional//EN"
"http://www.w3.org/TR/xhtml1/DTD/xhtml1-transitional.dtd">

<html xmlns="http://www.w3.org/1999/xhtml">
<head id="Head1" runat="server">
  <title>Untitled Page</title>
  <script type="text/javascript" language="javascript">
    function shoppingCartInitializedCallback(sender, e)
    {
      alert("Shopping cart is initialized!");
    }

    function shoppingCartItemAddingCallback(sender, e)
    {
      e.set_cancel(false);
      alert("Adding " + e.get_shoppingCartItem().get_name());
    }

    function shoppingCartItemAddedCallback(sender, e)
    {
      alert("Added " + e.get_shoppingCartItem().get_name());
      if (e.get_exception())
        alert(e.get_exception());
    }

    function pageLoad()
    {
      var shoppingCart = new Shopping.ShoppingCart();
      shoppingCart.add_shoppingCartInitialized(shoppingCartInitializedCallback);
      shoppingCart.add_shoppingCartItemAdding(shoppingCartItemAddingCallback);
      shoppingCart.add_shoppingCartItemAdded(shoppingCartItemAddedCallback);
      shoppingCart.initialize();
      var shoppingCartItem = new Shopping.ShoppingCartItem(1, "item1", 23);
      shoppingCart.addShoppingCartItem(shoppingCartItem);
      shoppingCart.remove_shoppingCartInitialized(shoppingCartInitializedCallback);
      shoppingCart.remove_shoppingCartItemAdding(shoppingCartItemAddingCallback);
      shoppingCart.remove_shoppingCartItemAdded(shoppingCartItemAddedCallback);
    }
  </script>
</head>
```

```
<body>
  <form id="form1" runat="server">
    <asp:ScriptManager runat="server" ID="ScripManager1">
      <Scripts>
        <asp:ScriptReference Path="ShoppingCart.js" />
      </Scripts>
    </asp:ScriptManager>
  </form>
</body>
</html>
```

As you can see, the `pageLoad` method instantiates a `ShoppingCart` object to represent the current user's shopping cart:

```
var shoppingCart = new Shopping.ShoppingCart();
```

Next, it calls the `add_shoppingCartInitialized` method on the `ShoppingCart` object to register a JavaScript function named `shoppingCartInitializedCallback` as an event handler for the `ShoppingCartInitialized` event of the `ShoppingCart` object:

```
shoppingCart.add_shoppingCartInitialized(shoppingCartInitializedCallback);
```

The `pageLoad` method then calls the `add_shoppingCartItemAdding` method on the `ShoppingCart` object to register a JavaScript function named `shoppingCartItemAddingCallback` as the event handler for the `ShoppingCartItemAdding` event of the `ShoppingCart` object:

```
shoppingCart.add_shoppingCartItemAdding(shoppingCartItemAddingCallback);
```

Next, it calls the `add_shoppingCartItemAdded` method on the `ShoppingCart` object to register a JavaScript function named `shoppingCartItemAddedCallback` as the event handler for the `ShoppingCartItemAdded` event of the `ShoppingCart` object:

```
shoppingCart.add_shoppingCartItemAdded(shoppingCartItemAddedCallback);
```

Then, it calls the `initialize` method on the `ShoppingCart` object to initialize the object:

```
shoppingCart.initialize();
```

Next, it instantiates a `ShoppingCartItem` object with the specified `id`, `name`, and `price`, and calls the `addShoppingCartItem` method on the `ShoppingCart` object, passing in the `ShoppingCartItem` object to add the object to `shoppingCartItems`:

```
var shoppingCartItem = new Shopping.ShoppingCartItem(1, "item1", 23);
shoppingCart.addShoppingCartItem(shoppingCartItem);
```

Finally, it calls the associated `remove` methods on the `ShoppingCard` object to remove the JavaScript functions that were previously registered:

```
shoppingCart.remove_shoppingCartInitialized(shoppingCartInitializedCallback);
shoppingCart.remove_shoppingCartItemAdding(shoppingCartItemAddingCallback);
shoppingCart.remove_shoppingCartItemAdded(shoppingCartItemAddedCallback);
```

You'll understand the implementation of the `shoppingCartInitializedCallback`, `shoppingCartItemAddingCallback`, and `shoppingCartItemAddedCallback` event handlers better when the events of the `ShoppingCart` class are discussed later in this chapter.

ShoppingCartItemAddingEventArgs

This class is the event data class for the `ShoppingCartItemAdding` event. As you can see in Listing 5-18, this class exposes a getter method named `get_shoppingCartItem` that returns a reference to the `ShoppingCartItem` object being added.

Note that the `ShoppingCartItemAddingEventArgs` event data class derives from the `Sys.CancelEventArgs` class, which is the base event data class for all cancelable events. As discussed earlier, the `Sys.CancelEventArgs` class features two important methods named `get_cancel` and `set_cancel` that allow an event handler for a cancelable event to cancel the event.

As such, the `ShoppingCartItemAddingEventArgs` event data class inherits the `get_cancel` and `set_cancel` methods from its base class.

Listing 5-18: The ShoppingCartItemAddingEventArgs Event Data Class

```
Shopping.ShoppingCartItemAddingEventArgs =
function Shopping$ShoppingCartItemAddingEventArgs (shoppingCartItem)
{
  Shopping.ShoppingCartItemAddingEventArgs.initializeBase(this);
  this.shoppingCartItem = shoppingCartItem;
}

function Shopping$ShoppingCartItemAddingEventArgs$get_shoppingCartItem()
{
  return this.shoppingCartItem;
}

Shopping.ShoppingCartItemAddingEventArgs.prototype = {
  get_shoppingCartItem :
       Shopping$ShoppingCartItemAddingEventArgs$get_shoppingCartItem
};

Shopping.ShoppingCartItemAddingEventArgs.registerClass(
       "Shopping.ShoppingCartItemAddingEventArgs", Sys.CancelEventArgs);
```

ShoppingCartItemAddedEventArgs

This class acts as the event data class for the ShoppingCartItemAdded event as shown in Listing 5-19.

Listing 5-19: The ShoppingCartItemAddedEventArgs Event Data Class

```
Shopping.ShoppingCartItemAddedEventArgs =
function Shopping$ShoppingCartItemAddedEventArgs (shoppingCartItem, exception)
{
  Shopping.ShoppingCartItemAddedEventArgs.initializeBase(this);
  this.shoppingCartItem = shoppingCartItem;
  this.exception = exception;
  this.exceptionHandled = false;
}

function Shopping$ShoppingCartItemAddedEventArgs$get_shoppingCartItem()
{
  return this.shoppingCartItem;
}

function Shopping$ShoppingCartItemAddedEventArgs$get_exception()
{
  return this.exception;
}

function Shopping$ShoppingCartItemAddedEventArgs$get_exceptionHandled()
{
  return !this.exception || this.exceptionHandled;
}

function Shopping$ShoppingCartItemAddedEventArgs$set_exceptionHandled(value)
{
  this.exceptionHandled = value;
}

Shopping.ShoppingCartItemAddedEventArgs.prototype = {
  get_shoppingCartItem :
      Shopping$ShoppingCartItemAddedEventArgs$get_shoppingCartItem,
  get_exception : Shopping$ShoppingCartItemAddedEventArgs$get_exception,
  get_exceptionHandled :
      Shopping$ShoppingCartItemAddedEventArgs$get_exceptionHandled,
  set_exceptionHandled :
      Shopping$ShoppingCartItemAddedEventArgs$set_exceptionHandled
};

Shopping.ShoppingCartItemAddedEventArgs.registerClass(
              "Shopping.ShoppingCartItemAddedEventArgs", Sys.EventArgs);
```

As you can see in this listing, the `ShoppingCartItemAddedEventArgs` class exposes the following four methods:

❑ `get_shoppingCartItem`: This getter returns a reference to the `ShoppingCartItem` object that was added to the `shoppingCartItems` of the `ShoppingCart` object that represents the current user's shopping cart.

❑ `get_exception`: This getter returns a reference to the `Exception` object raised during the execution of the `addShoppingCartItem` method of the `ShoppingCart` object. An event handler can call this getter to access the `Exception` object and use application-specific exception-handling logic to handle the exception.

❑ `set_exceptionHandled`: This setter allows an event handler to inform the `addShoppingCart-Item` method of the `ShoppingCart` object to bypass the default exception-handling logic because the exception has already been handled by application-specific exception-handling logic.

❑ `get_exceptionHandled`: The `addShoppingCartItem` method calls this getter to find out if the event handler has already handled the exception.

ShoppingCart

As you can see in Listing 5-20, the `ShoppingCart.js` JavaScript file defines the `ShoppingCart` class whose instances represent user shopping carts. The methods of this class are discussed in the following sections.

Listing 5-20: The ShoppingCart.js JavaScript File

```
Shopping.ShoppingCart = function() { }

Shopping.ShoppingCart.prototype = {
  addShoppingCartItem : Shopping$ShoppingCart$addShoppingCartItem,
  initialize : Shopping$ShoppingCart$initialize,
  get_shoppingCartItems : Shopping$ShoppingCart$get_shoppingCartItems,

  get_events : Shopping$ShoppingCart$get_events,

  add_shoppingCartInitialized :
            Shopping$ShoppingCart$add_shoppingCartInitialized,
  remove_shoppingCartInitialized :
            Shopping$ShoppingCart$remove_shoppingCartInitialized,
  onShoppingCartInitialized : Shopping$ShoppingCart$onShoppingCartInitialized,

  add_shoppingCartItemAdding : Shopping$ShoppingCart$add_shoppingCartItemAdding,
  remove_shoppingCartItemAdding:
            Shopping$ShoppingCart$remove_shoppingCartItemAdding,
  onShoppingCartItemAdding : Shopping$ShoppingCart$onShoppingCartItemAdding,

  add_shoppingCartItemAdded : Shopping$ShoppingCart$add_shoppingCartItemAdded,
```

```
        remove_shoppingCartItemAdded:
                    Shopping$ShoppingCart$remove_shoppingCartItemAdded,
        onShoppingCartItemAdded : Shopping$ShoppingCart$onShoppingCartItemAdded
    };

    Shopping.ShoppingCart.registerClass("Shopping.ShoppingCart");
```

get_events

As discussed earlier, the ASP.NET AJAX client-side framework exposes a class named Sys.EventHandlerList that emulates the .NET System.ComponentModel.EventHandlerList class. As you can see in Listing 5-21, the ShoppingCart class exposes a getter named get_events whose main responsibility is to instantiate the Sys.EventHandlerList class if it hasn't already been instantiated and to return the instance to its caller.

Listing 5-21: The get_events Method of the ShoppingCart Class

```
function Shopping$ShoppingCart$get_events() {
  if (!this.events)
    this.events = new Sys.EventHandlerList();

  return this.events;
}
```

initialize

Listing 5-22 contains the code for the initialize method of the ShoppingCart class.

Listing 5-22: The initialize Method of the ShoppingCart Class

```
function Shopping$ShoppingCart$initialize()
{
  this.shoppingCartItems = {};
  this.onShoppingCartInitialized(Sys.EventArgs.Empty);
}
```

As you can see in this listing, the initialize method of the ShoppingCart class performs two important tasks. First, it instantiates the shoppingCartItems where the ShoppingCartItem objects will be stored. Second, it calls the onShoppingCartInitialized method of the ShoppingCart object, passing in the Sys.EventArgs.Empty parameter to raise the ShoppingCartInitialized event. This event does not involve any event data, so it uses the Sys.EventArgs base class as its event data class. This is very similar to .NET, where the System.EventArgs base class is used as the event data class for events that do not involve any event data. The Sys.EventArgs.Empty provides the same programming convenience as its .NET counterpart — that is, the System.EventArgs.Empty.

onShoppingCartInitialized

Listing 5-23 presents the implementation of the onShoppingCartInitialized method of the ShoppingCart class.

Listing 5-23: The onShoppingCartInitialized Method of the ShoppingCart Class

```
function Shopping$ShoppingCart$onShoppingCartInitialized(e)
{
  var handler = this.get_events().getHandler("shoppingCartInitialized");
  if (handler)
    handler(this, e);
}
```

This method calls the `getHandler` method of the `EventHandlerList` object, passing in the name of the event — which is `shoppingCartInitialized` in this case. As discussed earlier, the `getHandler` method returns a JavaScript function that iterates through the event handlers registered for the event with the specified name and calls each enumerated event handler.

addShoppingCartItem

The main responsibility of the `addShoppingCartItem` method of the `ShoppingCart` class is to add the specified `ShoppingCartItem` object to the `shoppingCartItems` collection, as shown in Listing 5-24.

Listing 5-24: The addShoppingCartItem Method of the ShoppingCart Class

```
function Shopping$ShoppingCart$addShoppingCartItem(shoppingCartItem)
{
  var e1 = new Shopping.ShoppingCartItemAddingEventArgs(shoppingCartItem);
  this.onShoppingCartItemAdding(e1);

  if (!e1.get_cancel())
  {
    var exception = null;
    var cartItems = this.get_shoppingCartItems();
    var cartItemId = shoppingCartItem.get_id();

    if (cartItems[cartItemId])
      exception = Error.duplicateItem("Duplicate Shopping Cart Item!",
                {name: shoppingCartItem.get_name()});
    else
      this.shoppingCartItems[cartItemId] = shoppingCartItem;

    var e2 =
          new Shopping.ShoppingCartItemAddedEventArgs(shoppingCartItem, exception);
    this.onShoppingCartItemAdded(e2);

    if (!e2.get_exceptionHandled())
      throw exception;
  }
}
```

This method takes the following steps:

1. It instantiates a `ShoppingCartItemAddingEventArgs` object, passing in the `ShoppingCartItem` object being added:

```
var e1 = new Shopping.ShoppingCartItemAddingEventArgs(shoppingCartItem);
```

2. It calls the `onShoppingCartItemAdding` method (discussed in the next section), passing the `ShoppingCartItemAddingEventArgs` object:

```
this.onShoppingCartItemAdding(e1);
```

As you'll see in the next section, the `onShoppingCartItemAdding` method invokes the event handlers for the `ShoppingCartItemAdding` event, passing each event handler the `ShoppingCartItemAdding-EventArgs` object. It's the responsibility of each event handler to use application-specific logic to determine whether adding the specified `ShoppingCartItem` object to the `shoppingCartItems` collection will violate application-specific business rules. If so, the event handler must use the `set_cancel` method of the `ShoppingCartItemAddingEventArgs` object to set the `_cancel` field of the object to `true`.

As Listing 5-24 shows, the `addShoppingCartItem` method uses the `ShoppingCartItemAddingEventArgs` object's `get_cancel` method to access the `_cancel` field value in order to determine whether the event handler has decided that the addition of the specified `ShoppingCartItem` object to the `shoppingCartItems` collection should proceed. If so, the `addShoppingCartItem` method first determines whether the `shoppingCartItems` collection already contains a `ShoppingCartItem` object with the same `id` as the `ShoppingCartItem` object being added. If so, it creates a `DuplicateItemException` object:

```
exception = Error.duplicateItem("Duplicate Shopping Cart Item!",
                                {name: shoppingCartItem.get_name()});
```

If not, it adds the `ShoppingCartItem` object to the `shoppingCartItems` collection:

```
this.shoppingCartItems[cartItemId] = shoppingCartItem;
```

Next, `addShoppingCartItem` creates a `ShoppingCartItemAddedEventArgs` object, passing in the `ShoppingCartItem` being added and the `Exception` object (if any):

```
var e2 = new Shopping.ShoppingCartItemAddedEventArgs(shoppingCartItem, exception);
```

Then, it calls the `onShoppingCartItemAdded` method, passing in the `ShoppingCartItemAddedEventArgs` object to raise the `ShoppingCartItemAdded` event:

```
this.onShoppingCartItemAdded(e2);
```

As you'll see in the next section, the `onShoppingCartItemAdded` method invokes all the event handlers registered for the `ShoppingCartItemAdded` event, passing the `ShoppingCartItemAddedEventArgs` object. It's the responsibility of each event handler to call the `get_exception` method of the `ShoppingCartItemAddedEventArgs` object to access the `Exception` object (if any), to use application-specific exception-handling logic to handle the exception, and to call the `set_exceptionHandled` method on the `ShoppingCartItemAddedEventArgs` object to set its `exceptionHandled` Boolean field to `true`. As Listing 5-24 shows, `addShoppingCartItem` calls the `get_exceptionHandled` method on the `ShoppingCartItemAddedEventArgs` object to access the value of the `_exceptionHandled` Boolean field. `addShoppingCartItem` throws the exception (if any) only if this field has been set to `true`:

```
if (!e2.get_exceptionHandled())
  throw exception;
```

onShoppingCartItemAdding

Listing 5-25 shows the implementation of the onShoppingCartItemAdding method of the ShoppingCart class.

Listing 5-25: The onShoppingCartItemAdding Method of the ShoppingCart Class

```
function Shopping$ShoppingCart$onShoppingCartItemAdding(e)
{
  var handler = this.get_events().getHandler("shoppingCartItemAdding");
  if (handler)
    handler(this, e);
}
```

As you can see, this method calls the getHandler method on the EventHandlerList collection, passing in the name of the event — shoppingCartItemAdding in this case. As discussed earlier, the get_handler method returns a JavaScript function that iterates through all the event handlers registered for the event with the specified name and calls each enumerated event handler, passing in the ShoppingCardItemAdding object passed into the onShoppingCartItemAdding method.

onShoppingCartItemAdded

Listing 5-26 shows the code for the onShoppingCartItemAdded method of the ShoppingCart class.

Listing 5-26: The onShoppingCartItemAdded Method of the ShoppingCart Class

```
function Shopping$ShoppingCart$onShoppingCartItemAdded(e)
{
  var handler = this.get_events().getHandler("shoppingCartItemAdded");
  if (handler)
    handler(this, e);
}
```

This method takes a single argument of type ShoppingCartItemAddedEventArgs. The method calls the getHandler method on this collection, passing in the name of the event — that is, shoppingCartItemAdded. It then calls the JavaScript function that the getHandler method returns, passing in the ShoppingCartItemAddedEventArgs object.

Adding an Event Handler

As Listing 5-27 shows, the ShoppingCart class provides you with three methods named add_shoppingCartInitialized, add_shoppingCartItemAdding, and add_shoppingCartItemAdded, which allow you to add event handlers for the ShoppingCartInitialized, ShoppingCartItemAdding, and ShoppingCartItemAdded events, respectively. Notice that each add method delegates to the addHandler method of the internal EventHandlerList object.

Listing 5-27: The Methods of the ShoppingCart Class that Add Event Handlers

```
function Shopping$ShoppingCart$add_shoppingCartInitialized(handler)
{
  this.get_events().addHandler("shoppingCartInitialized", handler);
}

function Shopping$ShoppingCart$add_shoppingCartItemAdding(handler)
{
  this.get_events().addHandler("shoppingCartItemAdding", handler);
}

function Shopping$ShoppingCart$add_shoppingCartItemAdded(handler)
{
  this.get_events().addHandler("shoppingCartItemAdded", handler);
}
```

Removing an Event Handler

As Listing 5-28 shows, the `ShoppingCart` class also presents three methods named `remove_shopping-CartInitialized`, `remove_shoppingCartItemAdding`, and `remove_shoppingCartItemAdded`, which you can use to remove a specified event handler registered for the `ShoppingCartInitialized`, `ShoppingCartItemAdding`, and `ShoppingCartItemAdded` events, respectively. Notice that each `remove` method delegates to the `removeHandler` method of the internal `EventHandlerList` object.

Listing 5-28: The Methods of the ShoppingCart Class that Remove Event Handlers

```
function Shopping$ShoppingCart$remove_shoppingCartInitialized(handler)
{
  this.get_events().removeHandler("shoppingCartInitialized", handler);
}

function Shopping$ShoppingCart$remove_shoppingCartItemAdding(handler)
{
  this.get_events().removeHandler("shoppingCartItemAdding", handler);
}

function Shopping$ShoppingCart$remove_shoppingCartItemAdded(handler)
{
  this.get_events().removeHandler("shoppingCartItemAdded", handler);
}
```

Summary

The ASP.NET AJAX event-programming extensions emulate the .NET event-programming paradigm. This enables you to use a programming model very similar to the .NET event-programming model to add events to your JavaScript classes. The next chapter discusses Document Object Model (DOM) event programming — a common client-side event programming practice.

6

DOM Extensions

Document Object Model (DOM) programming is one of the most common client-side programming tasks in the world of Web development. The ASP.NET AJAX DOM extensions extend traditional DOM programming to add support for .NET-like methods and properties. This chapter provides in-depth coverage of these extensions. As you'll see in subsequent chapters, this convenient set of classes and enumerations are used extensively in the ASP.NET AJAX client-side framework.

DomElement

As Listing 6-1 shows, the ASP.NET AJAX DOM extensions define a new JavaScript class named DomElement. As you'll see in the following sections, this class exposes static methods and properties that introduce .NET-like programming convenience into your client-side DOM scripting. Because all these methods and properties are static, you must call them directly on the DomElement class itself. Note that the DomElement class belongs to the Sys.UI namespace. Also note that you should not directly instantiate an instance of this class because all members of the class are static.

Listing 6-1: The DomElement Class

```
Sys.UI.DomElement = function Sys$UI$DomElement() { }
Sys.UI.DomElement.registerClass('Sys.UI.DomElement');
```

getElementById

This static method of the DomElement class takes up to two parameters. The first parameter contains the value of the id HTML attribute of a DOM element. The second parameter, which is optional, references the parent DOM element of the DOM element whose id HTML attribute's value is given by the first parameter. The main responsibility of the getElementById method is to return a reference to the JavaScript object that represents the DOM element whose id HTML attribute is given by the first parameter.

To see how the getElementById method returns this reference, let's take a look at the internal implementation of this method as shown in Listing 6-2.

Listing 6-2: The Internal Implementation of the getElementById Method of the DomElement Class

```
var $get = Sys.UI.DomElement.getElementById = function(f, e)
{
  if(!e)
    return document.getElementById(f);

  if(e.getElementById)
    return e.getElementById(f);

  var c = [], d = e.childNodes;
  for(var b = 0; b < d.length; b ++ )
  {
    var a = d[b];
    if(a.nodeType == 1)
      c[c.length] = a;
  }
  while(c.length)
  {
    a = c.shift();
    if(a.id == f)
      return a;
    d = a.childNodes;
    for(b = 0; b < d.length; b ++ )
    {
      a = d[b];
      if(a.nodeType == 1)
        c[c.length] = a;
    }
  }
  return null;
}
```

The getElementById method first checks whether its second parameter has been specified. If not, it simply delegates to the getElementById method of the current document JavaScript object. In other words, by default, the getElementById method uses the current document object as the parent of the DOM element with the id HTML attribute given by the first parameter:

```
if(!e)
    return document.getElementById(f);
```

If the second argument of the method has indeed been specified, the method checks whether the parent DOM element that the second argument references supports a method named getElementById. If so, it simply delegates to the getElementById method of the parent element. For example, if your page uses a frameset consisting of two frames, and you want to access a child element of one of these frames from the other frame, you can pass the document DOM object of the other frame as the second argument of the getElementById method:

```
if(e.getElementById)
    return e.getElementById(f);
```

This tells the getElementById method to call the getElementById method of the document element of the other frame as opposed to the document element of the current frame. You'll see an example of this scenario shortly.

If the second argument of the getElementById method of the DomElement class has indeed been specified but it does not support the getElementById method, the getElementById method of the DomElement class simply searches through the descendants of the parent element for the element with the specified id attribute value:

```
var c = [], d = e.childNodes;
for(var b = 0; b < d.length; b ++ )
{
  var a = d[b];
  if(a.nodeType == 1)
    c[c.length] = a
}
while(c.length)
{
  a = c.shift();
  if(a.id == f)
    return a;
  d = a.childNodes;
  for(b = 0; b < d.length; b ++ )
  {
    a = d[b];
    if(a.nodeType == 1)
      c[c.length] = a
  }
}
return null
```

This is great for situations where you want to limit the search to the descendant of a particular DOM element. You'll see an example of this scenario shortly.

As the internal implementation of the getElementById method of the DomElement class shows, this method handles the following three scenarios:

❑ The default scenario where the search for the DOM element with the specified id HTML attribute is limited to the descendant DOM elements of the current document object

❑ The scenario where the search for the DOM element with the specified id HTML attribute is limited to the descendant DOM elements of the specified document object, which may or may not be the current document object

❑ The scenario where the search for the DOM element with the specified id HTML attribute is limited to the descendant DOM elements of the specified DOM element

The following code presents an example of the first scenario. As the boldfaced portion of this code shows, the getElementById method of the DomElement class is called without specifying the second argument. This instructs the getElementById method to search through the descendant DOM elements of the current document.

```
<%@ Page Language="C#" %>
<!DOCTYPE html PUBLIC "-//W3C//DTD XHTML 1.0 Transitional//EN"
"http://www.w3.org/TR/xhtml11/DTD/xhtml11-transitional.dtd">
<html xmlns="http://www.w3.org/1999/xhtml">
<head runat="server">
  <title>Untitled Page</title>
  <script language="javascript" type="text/javascript">
    function frame1ClickCallback()
    {
       var frame1TextBox = Sys.UI.DomElement.getElementById("frame1TextBox");
       alert(frame1TextBox.value);
    }
  </script>
</head>
<body>
  <form id="form1" runat="server">
    <asp:ScriptManager runat="server" ID="ScriptManager1" />
    <input type="text" id="frame1TextBox" /> 
    <input type="button" onclick="frame1ClickCallback()"
    value="Send" />
  </form>
</body>
</html>
```

Now, let's take look at the example of the second scenario shown in the following code. The boldfaced portion of this code passes the document.form1 element as the second argument of the getElementById method. As you can see, document.form1 is the parent of the frame1TextBox element. This limits the search to the child elements of the document.form1 element.

```
<%@ Page Language="C#" %>
<!DOCTYPE html PUBLIC "-//W3C//DTD XHTML 1.0 Transitional//EN"
"http://www.w3.org/TR/xhtml11/DTD/xhtml11-transitional.dtd">
<html xmlns="http://www.w3.org/1999/xhtml">
<head runat="server">
  <title>Untitled Page</title>
  <script language="javascript" type="text/javascript">
    function frame1ClickCallback()
    {
       var frame1TextBox = Sys.UI.DomElement.getElementById("frame1TextBox",
                                                 document.form1);
       alert(frame1TextBox.value);
    }
  </script>
</head>
<body>
  <form id="form1" runat="server">
    <asp:ScriptManager runat="server" ID="ScriptManager1" />
    <input type="text" id="frame1TextBox" /> 
    <input type="button" onclick="frame1ClickCallback()"
    value="Send" />
  </form>
</body>
</html>
```

Now, let's take a look at an example of the third scenario. This example consists of three ASP.NET pages. The first page uses a frameset as shown in Listing 6-3. The frameset consists of two frames named `frame1` and `frame2` that respectively display the contents of the `frame1.aspx` and `frame2.aspx` pages.

Listing 6-3: The page that uses the frameset

```
<%@ Page Language="C#" %>
<!DOCTYPE html PUBLIC "-//W3C//DTD XHTML 1.0 Transitional//EN"
"http://www.w3.org/TR/xhtml1/DTD/xhtml1-transitional.dtd">
<html xmlns="http://www.w3.org/1999/xhtml">
<head runat="server">
  <title>Untitled Page</title>
</head>
  <frameset cols="60%,40%">
    <frame src="frame1.aspx" name="frame1"/>
    <frame src="frame2.aspx" name="frame2"/>
  </frameset>
</html>
```

Listing 6-4 presents the `frame2.aspx` page. As you can see, this page is very simple. It consists of a single text box element.

Listing 6-4: The frame2.aspx Page

```
<%@ Page Language="C#" %>
<!DOCTYPE html PUBLIC "-//W3C//DTD XHTML 1.0 Transitional//EN"
"http://www.w3.org/TR/xhtml1/DTD/xhtml1-transitional.dtd">
<html xmlns="http://www.w3.org/1999/xhtml">
<head runat="server">
  <title>Untitled Page</title>
</head>
<body>
  <form id="form1" runat="server">
    <input type="text" id="frame2TextBox" />
  </form>
</body>
</html>
```

Listing 6-5 presents the `frame1.aspx` page.

Listing 6-5: The frame1.aspx Page

```
<%@ Page Language="C#" %>
<!DOCTYPE html PUBLIC "-//W3C//DTD XHTML 1.0 Transitional//EN"
"http://www.w3.org/TR/xhtml1/DTD/xhtml1-transitional.dtd">
<html xmlns="http://www.w3.org/1999/xhtml">
<head runat="server">
  <title>Untitled Page</title>
  <script language="javascript" type="text/javascript">
```

(continued)

Listing 6-5 (continued)

```
        function frame1ClickCallback()
        {
            var frame1TextBox = Sys.UI.DomElement.getElementById("frame1TextBox");
            var frame2TextBox = Sys.UI.DomElement.getElementById("frame2TextBox",
                                                      parent.frame2.document);

            frame2TextBox.value = frame1TextBox.value;
        }
    </script>
</head>
<body>
    <form id="form1" runat="server">
      <asp:ScriptManager runat="server" ID="ScriptManager1" />
      <input type="text" id="frame1TextBox" /> 
      <input type="button" onclick="frame1ClickCallback()"
      value="Send" />
    </form>
</body>
</html>
```

This page consists of a text box and a button. When you enter a value into the text box and click the button, the `frame1ClickCallback` JavaScript function is called. As the boldfaced portion of Listing 6-5 shows, this JavaScript function takes the following actions:

1. It calls the `getElementById` method of the `DomElement` class to return a reference to the text box displayed in the `frame1.aspx` — that is, the current document.

   ```
   var frame1TextBox = Sys.UI.DomElement.getElementById("frame1TextBox");
   ```

2. It calls the `getElementById` method of the `DomElement` class to return a reference to the text box displayed in the other frame — that is, `frame2.aspx`. Note that the `frame1ClickCallback` method passes the document object of the other frame as the second argument to the `getElementById` method to instruct this method to search through the child DOM elements of the other frame for the specified text box.

   ```
   var frame2TextBox = Sys.UI.DomElement.getElementById("frame2TextBox",
                                            parent.frame2.document);
   ```

3. It assigns the value of the text box of `frame1.aspx` to the text box of `frame2.aspx`.

   ```
   frame2TextBox.value = frame1TextBox.value;
   ```

addCssClass

The `addCssClass` static method of the `DomElement` class adds a new CSS class name to the specified DOM element, if it hasn't been already added. Listing 6-6 presents the internal implementation of this method. Note that this method first calls the `containsCssClass` static method of the `DomElement` class to check whether the DOM object already contains the specified CSS class name. If not, it simply appends the new CSS class name to the `className` property of the DOM object.

Listing 6-6: The Internal Implementation of the addCssClass Method

```
Sys.UI.DomElement.addCssClass = function(a, b)
{
  if(!Sys.UI.DomElement.containsCssClass(a, b))
  {
    if(a.className === "")
      a.className = b;
    else
      a.className += " " + b;
  }
}
```

containsCssClass

The containsCssClass static method of the DomElement class returns a Boolean value that specifies whether a specified DOM object contains the specified CSS class name. Listing 6-7 presents the internal implementation of this method. Note that this method simply delegates to the contains static method of the Array class. The ASP.NET AJAX client-side script framework extends the Array class to add support for the contains static method, as discussed in chapter 2.

Listing 6-7: The Internal Implementation of the containsCssClass Method

```
Sys.UI.DomElement.containsCssClass = function(b, a)
{
  return Array.contains(b.className.split(" "), a)
}
```

removeCssClass

The removeCssClass static method of the DomElement class removes a specified CSS class name from the specified DOM object. Listing 6-8 contains the code for the internal implementation of this method. As you can see, this method uses a simple string manipulation to remove the specified CSS class name.

Listing 6-8: The Internal Implementation of the removeCssClass Method

```
Sys.UI.DomElement.removeCssClass = function(d, c)
{
  var a =" " + d.className + " ",
      b = a.indexOf(" " + c + " ");

  if(b >= 0)
    d.className =
        (a.substring(0, b) + " " + a.substring(b + c.length + 1,
        a.length)).trim();
}
```

Take a look at the example in Listing 6-9, which uses the addCssClass and removeCssClass methods of the DomElement class.

Listing 6-9: A page that uses the addCssClass and removeCssClass Methods

```
<%@ Page Language="C#" %>

<!DOCTYPE html PUBLIC "-//W3C//DTD XHTML 1.0 Transitional//EN"
"http://www.w3.org/TR/xhtml1/DTD/xhtml1-transitional.dtd">
<html xmlns="http://www.w3.org/1999/xhtml">
<head runat="server">
  <title>Untitled Page</title>
  <style type="text/css">
    .CssClass1 {
      background-color: Blue;
      color: Yellow;
      font-weight: bold;
    }
    .CssClass2 {
      background-color: Yellow;
      color: Blue;
      font-weight: bold;
    }
  </style>
  <script language="javascript" type="text/javascript">
    var myLinkDomElementObj;
    var myList;

    function addCallback()
    {
      var myCssClass = myList.options[myList.selectedIndex].value;
      Sys.UI.DomElement.addCssClass(myLinkDomElementObj, myCssClass);
    }

    function removeCallback()
    {
      var myCssClass = myList.options[myList.selectedIndex].value;
      Sys.UI.DomElement.removeCssClass(myLinkDomElementObj, myCssClass);
    }

    function pageLoad()
    {
      myLinkDomElementObj = Sys.UI.DomElement.getElementById("myLink");
      myList = document.getElementById("myList");
    }
  </script>
</head>
<body>
  <form id="form1" runat="server">
    <asp:ScriptManager runat="server" ID="ScriptManager1" />
    <a href="http://www.wrox.com" id="myLink">
      Wrox Web Site</a>  
    <select id="myList">
      <option value="CssClass1">CSS Class 1</option>
      <option value="CssClass2">CSS Class 2</option>
    </select>  
```

```
        <input type="button" value="Add" onclick="addCallback()" /> 
        <input type="button" value="Remove" onclick="removeCallback()" />
      </form>
    </body>
  </html>
```

Figure 6-1 shows what you'll see when you access this page. Run the program, select a CSS class name from the list, and click the Add button. You should see the effects of the selected CSS class. Now click the Remove button. The link should go back to its default format.

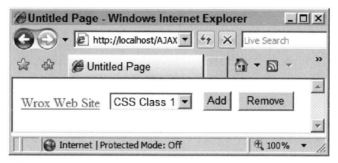

Figure 6-1

toggleCssClass

The `toggleCssClass` static method of the `DomElement` class toggles a specified CSS class name on or off on a specified DOM object. The best way to understand what this method does is to use it in an example. Listing 6-10 presents a page that uses this method.

Listing 6-10: A page that uses the toggleCssClass Method

```
<%@ Page Language="C#" %>

<!DOCTYPE html PUBLIC "-//W3C//DTD XHTML 1.0 Transitional//EN"
"http://www.w3.org/TR/xhtml1/DTD/xhtml1-transitional.dtd">
<html xmlns="http://www.w3.org/1999/xhtml">
<head runat="server">
  <title>Untitled Page</title>
  <style type="text/css">
    .CssClass1 {
      background-color: Blue;
      color: Yellow;
      font-size: 40px;
    }
  </style>
  <script language="javascript" type="text/javascript">
    function toggleCssClass(myLink)
    {
      Sys.UI.DomElement.toggleCssClass(myLink, "CssClass1");
    }
  </script>
```

(continued)

Listing 6-10 *(continued)*

```
  </head>
  <body>
    <form id="form1" runat="server">
      <asp:ScriptManager runat="server" ID="ScriptManager1" />
      <a href="http://www.wrox.com"
      onmouseover="toggleCssClass(this)"
      onmouseout="toggleCssClass(this)">Wrox Web Site</a>
    </form>
  </body>
</html>
```

If you run this code, you'll see the result shown in Figure 6-2, which is a very simple page that contains a single hyperlink. Now if you move the mouse over the link, you'll get the result shown in Figure 6-3. If you move the mouse away from the link, you'll get the result shown in Figure 6-2 again. Therefore, moving the mouse over and out of the link switches the style of the class between what you see in the two figures.

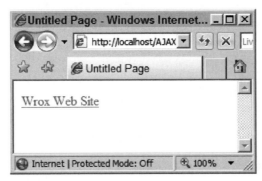

Figure 6-2

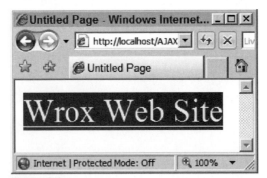

Figure 6-3

Listing 6-11 shows the internal implementation of the `toggleCssClass` method. This method first calls the `containsCssClass` method to check whether the specified DOM object already contains the specified CSS class name. If so, it calls the `removeCssClass` method to remove the CSS class name. If not, it calls the `addCssClass` method to add the CSS class name.

Listing 6-11: The Internal Implementation of the toggleCssClass Method

```
Sys.UI.DomElement.toggleCssClass = function(b, a)
{
  if(Sys.UI.DomElement.containsCssClass(b, a))
    Sys.UI.DomElement.removeCssClass(b, a);
  else
    Sys.UI.DomElement.addCssClass(b, a);
}
```

getLocation

Listing 6-12 presents the simplified version of the internal implementation of the DomElement class's getLocation static method.

Listing 6-12: The Simplified Version of the Internal Implementation of the getLocation Method

```
Sys.UI.DomElement.getLocation = function(d)
{
  var b = 0, c = 0, a;
  for(a = d; a; a = a.offsetParent)
  {
    if(a.offsetLeft)
      b += a.offsetLeft;

    if(a.offsetTop)
      c += a.offsetTop
  }
  return { x : b, y : c }
}
```

This method returns a JavaScript object literal that contains the *x* and *y* coordinates of the specified DOM element with respect to the top-left corner of the browser window. Note that the internal implementation of the getLocation method uses the following three important properties of DOM elements:

❑   offsetParent: Returns a reference to the first positioned DOM element in the containment hierarchy of the current DOM element.

❑   offsetLeft: Returns the number of pixels that the current DOM element is offset to the left within its offsetParent DOM element.

❑   offsetTop: Returns the number of pixels that the current DOM element is offset from the top within its offsetParent DOM element.

As Listing 6-12 shows, the getLocation method iterates through the DOM elements in the containment hierarchy of the specified DOM element and accumulates the values of the offsetLeft and offsetTop properties of these enumerated DOM elements. Therefore, the two accumulated values at the end specify the number of pixels that the specified DOM element is offset to the left and to the top within the browser window.

Listing 6-13 shows an example that uses the getLocation method.

Listing 6-13: A page that uses the getLocation Method

```
<%@ Page Language="C#" %>

<!DOCTYPE html PUBLIC "-//W3C//DTD XHTML 1.0 Transitional//EN"
"http://www.w3.org/TR/xhtml1/DTD/xhtml1-transitional.dtd">
<html xmlns="http://www.w3.org/1999/xhtml">
<head runat="server">
  <title>Untitled Page</title>
  <script language="javascript" type="text/javascript">
    function clickCallback(myspan)
    {
      var obj = Sys.UI.DomElement.getLocation(myspan);
      alert("x=" + obj.x + "\n" + "y=" + obj.y);
    }
  </script>
</head>
<body>
  <form id="form1" runat="server">
    <asp:ScriptManager runat="server" />
    <span id="myspan" onclick="clickCallback(this)">Click here!</span>
  </form>
</body>
</html>
```

If you run this program and click the Click here! link, you should get a pop-up message the displays the *x* and *y* coordinates of the label.

setLocation

The setLocation static method of the DomElement class sets the *x* and *y* coordinates of a specified DOM element to specified values. As such, it takes the following three arguments:

❏   b: References the DOM element whose *x* and *y* coordinates are being set.

❏   c: Specifies the new value in pixels of the *x* coordinate.

❏   d: Specifies the new value in pixels of the *y* coordinate.

As Listing 6-14 shows, the setLocation method also sets the position style property to absolute. In other words, this method absolutely positions the specified DOM element.

Listing 6-14: The Internal Implementation of the setLocation Method

```
Sys.UI.DomElement.setLocation = function(b, c, d)
{
  var a = b.style;
  a.position="absolute";
  a.left = c + "px";
  a.top = d + "px";
}
```

Listing 6-15 shows an example of how the `getLocation` and `setLocation` methods are used.

Listing 6-15: An ASP.NET page that uses the getLocation and setLocation Methods

```
<%@ Page Language="C#" %>

<!DOCTYPE html PUBLIC "-//W3C//DTD XHTML 1.0 Transitional//EN"
"http://www.w3.org/TR/xhtml1/DTD/xhtml1-transitional.dtd">

<html xmlns="http://www.w3.org/1999/xhtml">
<head id="Head1" runat="server">
  <title>Untitled Page</title>
  <script language="javascript" type="text/javascript">
    function mousedowncb(event)
    {
      event = event || window.event;
      document.oldClientX = event.clientX;
      document.oldClientY = event.clientY;
      document.onmousemove = mousemovecb;
      document.onmouseup = mouseupcb;
      return false;
    }

    function mouseupcb(event)
    {
      event = event || window.event;
      document.onmousemove = null;
      document.onmouseup = null;
      return false;
    }

    function mousemovecb(event)
    {
      event = event || window.event;
      var deltaClientX = event.clientX - document.oldClientX;
      var deltaClientY = event.clientY - document.oldClientY;

      var sender = $get("mydiv");
      var senderLocation = Sys.UI.DomElement.getLocation(sender);
      Sys.UI.DomElement.setLocation(sender, senderLocation.x+deltaClientX,
                                    senderLocation.y+deltaClientY);

      document.oldClientX = event.clientX;
      document.oldClientY = event.clientY;

      return false;
    }

  </script>
</head>
```

(continued)

Listing 6-15 *(continued)*

```
<body>
  <div id="mydiv" style="position: absolute; left: 0px; top: 0px"
          onmousedown="mousedowncb(event)">
    <a href="javascript:void(0)" id="myspan"
            style="font-weight: bold">Wrox Web Site</a>
  </div>
  <form id="form1" runat="server">
    <asp:ScriptManager ID="ScriptManager1" runat="server" />
  </form>
</body>
</html>
```

This page simply renders the "Wrox Web Site" text and allows you to move this text by clicking the text and holding the mouse button down while moving the mouse around. Note that this page registers the mousedowncb method as an event handler for the mousedown event of the div HTML element with the id HTML attribute value of mydiv as shown in the following code:

```
function mousedowncb(event)
{
    event = event || window.event;
   document.oldClientX = event.clientX;
   document.oldClientY = event.clientY;
   document.onmousemove = mousemovecb;
   document.onmouseup = mouseupcb;
   return false;
}
```

This method takes two steps. First, it accesses and stores the mouse position's *x* and *y* coordinates from the event object's clientX and clientY properties. Next, it registers the mousemovecb and mouseupcb methods as callbacks for the document object's mousemove and mouseup events.

As Listing 6-15 shows, the mousemovecb method first accesses the current *x* and *y* coordinates of the mouse position from the clientX and clientY properties of the event object and the old *x* and *y* coordinates of the mouse. Next, it evaluates the number of pixels the mouse has moved:

```
var deltaClientX = event.clientX - document.oldClientX;
var deltaClientY = event.clientY - document.oldClientY;
```

The method then uses $get syntax to access a reference to the mydiv DOM element:

```
var sender = $get("mydiv");
```

Next, it calls the getLocation method, passing in the above reference to return the JavaScript object literal that contains the current *x* and *y* coordinates of the mydiv DOM element:

```
var senderLocation = Sys.UI.DomElement.getLocation(sender);
```

Then, it calls the `setLocation` method to set the `mydiv` DOM element's *x* and *y* coordinates to new values. These new values basically increment the current values by the number of pixels that the mouse has moved:

```
Sys.UI.DomElement.setLocation(sender, senderLocation.x+deltaClientX,
                              senderLocation.y+deltaClientY);
```

getBounds

Because the `getBounds` method returns an object of type `Bounds`, first we need to study `Bounds`. Listing 6-16 presents the internal implementation of the `Bounds` type. As this code listing shows, `Bounds` is a class with four properties: x, y, `height`, and `width`. These properties contain the *x* and *y* coordinates and the height and width of a specified DOM element.

Listing 6-16: The Bounds Type

```
Sys.UI.Bounds = function Sys$UI$Bounds(x, y, width, height) {
    this.x = x;
    this.y = y;
    this.height = height;
    this.width = width;
}
Sys.UI.Bounds.registerClass('Sys.UI.Bounds');
```

As you can see, there is no sign of the DOM element in the definition of the `Bounds` type. This is where the `getBounds` method comes into play. As Listing 6-17 shows, this method returns a `Bounds` object that contains the *x* and *y* coordinates and the width and height of the specified DOM element.

Listing 6-17: The Internal Implementation of the getBounds Method

```
Sys.UI.DomElement.getBounds = function Sys$UI$DomElement$getBounds(element) {
    var offset = Sys.UI.DomElement.getLocation(element);

    return new Sys.UI.Bounds(offset.x, offset.y,
                             element.offsetWidth || 0,
                             element.offsetHeight || 0);
}
```

The ASP.NET page shown in Listing 6-18 uses the `getBounds` method to access the width of the span DOM element called `myspan`.

Listing 6-18: An ASP.NET page that uses the getBounds Method

```
<%@ Page Language="C#" %>

<!DOCTYPE html PUBLIC "-//W3C//DTD XHTML 1.0 Transitional//EN"
"http://www.w3.org/TR/xhtml1/DTD/xhtml1-transitional.dtd">

<html xmlns="http://www.w3.org/1999/xhtml">
 <head id="Head1" runat="server">
  <title>Untitled Page</title>
  <script language="javascript" type="text/javascript">
    function pageLoad()
    {
      var bounds = Sys.UI.DomElement.getBounds($get("myspan"));
      alert(bounds.width);
    }
  </script>
</head>
<body>
<span id="myspan" style="font-weight:bold;">Wrox Web Site</span>
  <form id="form1" runat="server">
    <asp:ScriptManager ID="ScriptManager1" runat="server" />
  </form>
</body>
</html>
```

MouseButton

One of the most common event sources is the mouse. The ASP.NET AJAX DOM extensions define an enumeration named `MouseButton` whose values represent different buttons of the mouse, as shown in Listing 6-19. As you can see, this enumeration has three enumeration values: `leftButton`, `middleButton`, and `rightButton`.

Listing 6-19: The MouseButton Enumeration

```
Sys.UI.MouseButton = function Sys$UI$MouseButton() {}

Sys.UI.MouseButton.prototype = {
  leftButton: 0,
  middleButton: 1,
  rightButton: 2
}
Sys.UI.MouseButton.registerEnum("Sys.UI.MouseButton");
```

Key

Another very common source of events is the keyboard. The ASP.NET AJAX DOM extensions define an enumeration named `Key` that features one enumeration value for each key, as shown in Listing 6-20.

Listing 6-20: The Key Enumeration

```
Sys.UI.Key = function Sys$UI$Key() { }

Sys.UI.Key.prototype = {
  backspace: 8,
  tab: 9,
  enter: 13,
  esc: 27,
  space: 32,
  pageUp: 33,
  pageDown: 34,
  end: 35,
  home: 36,
  left: 37,
  up: 38,
  right: 39,
  down: 40,
  del: 127
}
Sys.UI.Key.registerEnum("Sys.UI.Key");
```

Delegates

A method of a .NET class is characterized by the following:

- ❑ The name of the method
- ❑ The class to which the method belongs
- ❑ The number of its arguments
- ❑ The order of its arguments
- ❑ The types of its arguments
- ❑ The type of the value the method returns
- ❑ The body of the method — that is, its implementation

For the most part, the callers of a method are only interested in knowing what they need to pass into the method and what the method returns. In other words, they're only interested in the method's argument count, order, and types, and type of the value it returns. They don't care what the name of the method is, which class owns the method, or how the method is implemented (the body of the method).

As far as the callers are concerned, methods of different names and implementations belonging to different classes are the same as long as they all have the same argument count, order, and types, and return the same type. You can think of the argument count, order, and types and the return type of a method as the type of the method.

Each method has the following two characteristics:

- ❑ Its type, which consists of its argument count, order, and types and return type
- ❑ Its method-specific aspects, which consists of its name, class, and body

When the callers of a method call the method directly, they unnecessarily get coupled to its method-specific aspects — that is, its name, class, and body. This will not allow these callers to invoke other methods of the same type with different names and implementations belonging to different classes. Therefore, you need a mechanism that will allow the caller of a method to indirectly call the method without using its method-specific aspects (its name, class, and body). This will ensure that the caller of a method is coupled only to its type, not its method-specific aspects.

The .NET Framework offers two approaches to decouple the callers of a method from its method-specific aspects. The first approach requires the classes owning the methods to implement an interface that exposes a method with the same argument count, order, and types and return value type. In other words, the interface hides the method-specific aspects of a method — its class and body.

The second approach requires you to define a delegate with the same argument count, order, and types and return value type. A delegate is an object that encapsulates and hides the name, class, and body of the method that it represents. In other words, a delegate is just like an interface, but it exposes the method's argument count, order, and types and return-value type.

You may be wondering which approach is better because it seems that they both do the same thing — they both hide the method-specific aspects of the method. The answer is, "It depends." Because a delegate represents a single type of method, it provides more granularity than an interface, which could contain more than one type of method. As such, if you just want to hide the method-specific aspects of a single method, you're better off using a delegate, which only targets a single type of method.

There are two ways to define a .NET delegate. The most common approach is to use the `delegate` keyword to declare the delegate without actually implementing it. The `delegate` keyword instructs the compiler to generate the necessary code for the declared delegate at compile time. This saves you from having to implement the delegate yourself. Another approach to defining a .NET delegate is to use the `CreateDelegate` static method of the `Delegate` class. This method allows you to create a delegate to represent a specified method of a specified .NET class.

The ASP.NET AJAX client-side framework extends the functionality of the JavaScript `Function` type to add support for a new static method named `createDelegate` that emulates the `CreateDelegate` method of the .NET `Delegate` class. It allows you to create a delegate to represent a specified method of a specified JavaScript object. Listing 6-21 presents the internal implementation of the `createDelegate` method. Because the `createDelegate` method is a static method, you must call it directly on the `Function` class itself.

Listing 6-21: The createDelegate Method of the JavaScript Function Type

```
Function.createDelegate =
function Function$createDelegate(instance, method) {
  return function() {
    return method.apply(instance, arguments);
  }
}
```

The `createDelegate` method takes two parameters. The first parameter references the JavaScript object owning the method that the delegate represents. The second parameter references the `Function` object that represents the method the delegate represents. As you can see, the `createDelegate` method defines and returns a new JavaScript function that calls the `apply` method on the `Function` object, passing in the reference to the JavaScript object and the array that contains the values of the parameters of the method that the `Function` object represents.

Strictly speaking, since the createDelegate method internally used the apply method, the JavaScript function passed into the createDelegate method as its second argument doesn't need to be a method of the JavaScript object passed into the createDelegate method as its first argument. When the apply method is invoked on the JavaScript function passed in the createDelegate method as its second argument, the JavaScript keyword within the scope of the body of the JavaScript function is automatically set to reference the JavaScript object passed into the createDelegate method as its first argument. This allows the JavaScript function to use the JavaScript keyword within the body of the function to access the JavaScript object passed into the createDelegate method as its first argument. The same argument applies to all cases in this book where the apply or call methods are used internally to implement those cases.

Listing 6-22 shows an example that uses the `createDelegate` method. This example defines a new ASP .NET AJAX client class named `Mover` that belongs to a namespace named `Delegates`. This class encapsulates the logic that allows the end user to move a specified object (such as text or an image) around. Each type of movable object comes with its own provider. A provider is an ASP.NET AJAX client class that exposes a method that populates a specified container HTML element with the movable content. For example, as you'll see shortly, the `TextProvider` client class is the provider associated with a text. This client class exposes a method named `addText` that populates the specified container HTML element with the specified text.

Listing 6-22: An example that uses the createDelegate method

```
<%@ Page Language="C#" %>

<!DOCTYPE html PUBLIC "-//W3C//DTD XHTML 1.0 Transitional//EN"
"http://www.w3.org/TR/xhtml1/DTD/xhtml1-transitional.dtd">

<html xmlns="http://www.w3.org/1999/xhtml">
<head runat="server">
  <title>Untitled Page</title>
  <script type="text/javascript" language="javascript">
    function pageLoad()
    {
      var mover = new Delegates.Mover();
      var textProvider = new Delegates.TextProvider("Wrox Web Site");
      var addTextDelegate = Function.createDelegate(textProvider,
                                          textProvider.addText);
      mover.invokeAddContentDelegate (addTextDelegate);
    }
  </script>
</head>
<body>

  <form id="form1" runat="server">
    <asp:ScriptManager runat="server" ID="ScriptManager1">
      <Scripts>
        <asp:ScriptReference Path="Delegate.js" />
      </Scripts>
    </asp:ScriptManager>
  </form>
</body>
</html>
```

As you can see in this listing, the `pageLoad` method takes the following actions:

❏ It instantiates the `Mover` object:

```
var mover = new Delegates.Mover();
```

❏ It instantiates the `TextProvider` object, passing in the movable text:

```
var textProvider = new Delegates.TextProvider("Wrox Web Site");
```

❏ It calls the `createDelegate` method on the `Function` class to instantiate a delegate that represents the `addText` method of the `TextProvider` object. The `addText` method is responsible for providing the text that the end user can move.

```
var addTextDelegate = Function.createDelegate(textProvider, textProvider.addText);
```

❏ It calls the `invokeAddContentDelegate` method on the `Mover` object, passing in the delegate. This method invokes the delegate to add the text that the end user can move around.

```
mover.invokeAddContentDelegate (addTextDelegate);
```

The delegate isolates the `Mover` from what the `Mover` is moving — that is, the movable content. `Mover` has no idea that it is moving text. The sole responsibility of the `Mover` is to enable the end user to move the displayed content. The `Mover` is not responsible for displaying and determining the movable content, whether it's text, an image, or something else. This responsibility is delegated to another object. In the example in Listing 6-22, this object is the `TextProvider` object. Listing 6-22 wraps the `addText` method of this `TextProvider` object in a delegate and passes the delegate into the `invokeAddContentDelegate` method of the `Mover` object. As you'll see shortly, the `invokeAddContentDelegate` method invokes the delegate, which in turn invokes the `addText` method of the `TextProvider` object. In other words, the invocation of the `addText` method of the `TextProvider` object has been assigned to the delegate.

Thanks to the delegate, the `Mover` can indirectly invoke the `addText` method of the `TextProvider` object without knowing the method-specific characteristics of the method. In addition, the `Mover` can execute any method of any class as long as the method takes a single argument and returns no value. This means that you can replace the `TextProvider` with another class to provide different type of movable content. For example, Listing 6-23 uses an instance of a class named `ImageProvider` to provide an image as the movable content. Notice that in this case the `Mover` executes a method with a different name (`addImage` instead of `addText`) and a different implementation that belongs to a different class (`ImageProvider` instead of `TextProvider`).

Listing 6-23: A page that uses different movable content

```
<%@ Page Language="C#" %>

<!DOCTYPE html PUBLIC "-//W3C//DTD XHTML 1.0 Transitional//EN"
"http://www.w3.org/TR/xhtml1/DTD/xhtml1-transitional.dtd">

<html xmlns="http://www.w3.org/1999/xhtml">
<head runat="server">
  <title>Untitled Page</title>
  <script type="text/javascript" language="javascript">
```

```
      function pageLoad()
      {
        var mover = new Delegates.Mover();
        var imageProvider = new Delegates.ImageProvider("images.jpg");
        var addImageDelegate = Function.createDelegate(imageProvider,
                                        imageProvider.addImage);
        mover.invokeAddContentDelegate(addImageDelegate);
      }
    </script>
  </head>
  <body>

    <form id="form1" runat="server">
      <asp:ScriptManager runat="server" ID="ScriptManager1">
        <scripts>
          <asp:ScriptReference Path="Delegate.js" />
        </scripts>
      </asp:ScriptManager>
    </form>
  </body>
</html>
```

Notice that Listings 6-22 and 6-23 use a <asp:ScriptReference> element to register the Delegate.js JavaScript file. This file contains the entire application logic.

```
<asp:ScriptReference Path="Delegate.js" />
```

The ScriptReference *class is discussed later in this book. For now suffice it to say that the* ScriptManager *server control exposes a collection property named* Scripts *that contains zero or more instances of a class named* ScriptReference, *where each instance registers a particular JavaScript file. Notice that the* ScriptReference *class exposes a property named* Path. *You must set this to the path of the JavaScript file being registered.*

Listing 6-24 presents the content of the Delegate.js JavaScript file. As you can see, this file contains the implementation of the Mover, TextProvider, and ImageProvider ASP.NET AJAX client classes.

Listing 6-24: The Delegate.js JavaScript File

```
Type.registerNamespace("Delegates");

function Delegates$Mover$invokeAddContentDelegate(addContentDelegate)
{
  addContentDelegate("container1");
}

function mousedowncb(event)
{
  event = event || window.event;
  document.oldClientX = event.clientX;
  document.oldClientY = event.clientY;
```

(continued)

Listing 6-24 *(continued)*

```
    document.onmousemove = mousemovecb;
    document.onmouseup = mouseupcb;
    return false;
}

function mouseupcb(event)
{
  event = event || window.event;
  document.onmousemove = null;
  document.onmouseup = null;
  return false;
}

function mousemovecb(event)
{
  event = event || window.event;
  var deltaClientX = event.clientX - document.oldClientX;
  var deltaClientY = event.clientY - document.oldClientY;

  var container = document.getElementById("container1");

  var containerLocation = Sys.UI.DomElement.getLocation(container);
  Sys.UI.DomElement.setLocation(container,
                                containerLocation.x + deltaClientX,
                                containerLocation.y + deltaClientY);

  document.oldClientX = event.clientX;
  document.oldClientY = event.clientY;

  return false;
}

function Delegates$TextProvider$addText(containerId)
{
  var container = document.getElementById(containerId);
  container.innerHTML =
      '<a href="javascript:void(0)" id="myspan"' +
      ' style="font-weight: bold">' + this.text + '</a>';
}

function Delegates$ImageProvider$addImage(containerId)
{
  var container = document.getElementById(containerId);
  container.innerHTML = "<img src='" + this.imagePath + "' alt='img' />";
}

Delegates.TextProvider = function (text) {
  this.text = text;
}
```

```
Delegates.TextProvider.prototype = {
  addText : Delegates$TextProvider$addText
}

Delegates.TextProvider.registerClass("Delegates.TextProvider");

Delegates.ImageProvider = function (imagePath) {
  this.imagePath = imagePath;
}

Delegates.ImageProvider.prototype = {
  addImage : Delegates$ImageProvider$addImage
}

Delegates.ImageProvider.registerClass("Delegates.ImageProvider");

Delegates.Mover = function () {
  var container = document.getElementById("container1");
  if (!container)
  {
    container = document.createElement("div");
    container.id = "container1";
    container.style.position = "absolute";
    document.body.insertBefore(container, document.forms[0]);
    container.onmousedown = mousedowncb;
  }
}

Delegates.Mover.prototype = {
  invokeAddContentDelegate : Delegates$Mover$invokeAddContentDelegate
}

Delegates.Mover.registerClass("Delegates.Mover");
```

The following sections walk you through this listing and describe the implementation of the Delegates namespace and Mover, TextProvider, and ImageProvider client classes.

Namespace

The Delegates.js file defines and registers a namespace named Delegates, which contains all the classes defined for this application:

```
Type.registerNamespace("Delegates");
```

Mover

The Delegates.js file defines and registers the Mover class. Note that the constructor of this class first checks whether the <body> HTML element of the current document contains a <div> HTML element with an id HTML attribute value of container1. If not, it takes the following steps to create the element and initialize its properties:

1. It calls the createElement method on the current document to create the container <div> HTML element. This element will be used as a container for the movable content.

```
container = document.createElement("div");
```

2. It initializes the properties of the newly instantiated container <div> HTML element:

```
container.id = "container1";
container.style.position = "absolute";
```

3. It adds the container element before the <form> HTML element:

```
document.body.insertBefore(container, document.forms[0]);
```

4. It registers the mousedowncb global JavaScript function as the event handler for the mousedown event of the container element. The implementation of this function is discussed later in this chapter.

```
container.onmousedown = mousedowncb;
```

Note that the Mover is not responsible for specifying the content of the container <div> HTML element. This responsibility is delegated to another class such as TextProvider or ImageProvider. As you'll see in subsequent sections, the TextProvider and ImageProvider classes populate the container <div> HTML element with a text and an image.

The Mover class exposes a method named invokeAddContentDelegate that takes a delegate as its argument and invokes that delegate, passing in the value of the id HTML attribute of the container <div> HTML element, container1:

```
function Delegates$Mover$invokeAddContentDelegate(addContentDelegate)
{
    addContentDelegate("container1");
}
```

TextProvider

The Delegates.js file defines and registers the TextProvider class. The constructor of this class takes some text and stores it in an internal field for future reference:

```
Delegates.TextProvider = function (text) {
    this.text = text;
}
```

Note that the `TextProvider` class exposes a method named `addText` that takes the value of the `id` HTML attribute of the container `<div>` HTML element as its argument:

```
function Delegates$TextProvider$addText(containerId)
{
  var container = document.getElementById(containerId);
  container.innerHTML = '<a href="javascript:void(0);" id="myspan"' +
                        'style="font-weight: bold">' + this.text + '</a>';
}
```

The `addText` method first calls the `getElementById` method on the document object to access a reference to the container `<div>` HTML element:

```
var container = document.getElementById(containerId);
```

Next, it renders the specified text as a hyperlink within the opening and closing tags of the container `<div>` HTML element:

```
container.innerHTML = '<a href="javascript:void(0);" id="myspan"' +
                      'style="font-weight:bold">' + this.text + '</a>';
```

ImageProvider

The `Delegates.js` file defines the `ImageProvider` class. The constructor of this class takes a single parameter, which contains the path to a specified image, and stores the image path in an internal field for future reference:

```
Delegates.ImageProvider = function (imagePath) {
    this.imagePath = imagePath;
}
```

Note that the `ImageProvider` class features a single method named `addImage` that takes the value of the `id` HTML attribute of the container `<div>` HTML element as its argument:

```
function Delegates$ImageProvider$addImage(containerId)
{
  var container = document.getElementById(containerId);
  container.innerHTML = "<img src='" + this.imagePath + "' alt='img' />";
}
```

This method first accesses the container `<div>` HTML element and then renders an `<img>` HTML element with the specified `src` HTML attribute value as the content of the container `<div>` HTML element.

DomEvent

DOM event programming is a complex task, mainly because different types of browsers use different types of event models. As such, programmers spend most of their time adding custom code to make up for the differences between these event models. The ASP.NET AJAX client-side framework comes with a class named `DomEvent` that encapsulates all the logic that deals with event modeling differences among browsers, and provides you with a convenient API to interact with all these browsers as if they were of the same type. This enables you to write one set of code that works with all types of browsers. The following sections discuss the members of the `DomEvent` class in detail.

Constructor

As Listing 6-25 shows, the constructor of the `DomEvent` class takes a single parameter that references the event object. Every time an event occurs, the browser automatically creates an event object, which exposes properties that provide more information about the event, such as whether the ALT key was pressed when the event occurred, which mouse button was pressed when the event occurred, and so on.

The event object of different types of browsers exposes different properties. These browser inconsistencies make client-side event programming a daunting task. As you can see in Listing 6-25, the `DomEvent` constructor maps the event object's browser-dependent, inconsistent properties into a consistent set of properties that enable you to write one set of code that runs on all types of browsers.

Listing 6-25: The Constructor of the DomEvent Class

```
Sys.UI.DomEvent = function Sys$UI$DomEvent(eventObject)
{
  var e = eventObject;
  this.rawEvent = e;
  this.altKey = e.altKey;

  if (typeof(e.button) !== 'undefined')
    this.button = (typeof(e.which) !== 'undefined') ? e.button :
                  (e.button === 4) ? Sys.UI.MouseButton.middleButton :
                  (e.button === 2) ? Sys.UI.MouseButton.rightButton :
                  Sys.UI.MouseButton.leftButton;

  if (e.type === 'keypress')
    this.charCode = e.charCode || e.keyCode;

  else if (e.keyCode && (e.keyCode === 46))
    this.keyCode = 127;

  else
    this.keyCode = e.keyCode;

  this.clientX = e.clientX;
  this.clientY = e.clientY;
  this.ctrlKey = e.ctrlKey;
  this.target = e.target ? e.target : e.srcElement;

  if (this.target) {
    var loc = Sys.UI.DomElement.getLocation(this.target);
    this.offsetX = (typeof(e.offsetX) !== 'undefined') ? e.offsetX :
                   window.pageXOffset + (e.clientX || 0) - loc.x;
    this.offsetY = (typeof(e.offsetY) !== 'undefined') ? e.offsetY :
                   window.pageYOffset + (e.clientY || 0) - loc.y;
  }
```

```
        this.screenX = e.screenX;
        this.screenY = e.screenY;
        this.shiftKey = e.shiftKey;
        this.type = e.type;
    }

    Sys.UI.DomEvent.registerClass('Sys.UI.DomEvent');
```

The DomEvent class has the following properties:

❑ rawEvent: Gets a reference to the event object, as follows:

```
        this.rawEvent = e;
```

❑ altKey: Gets a Boolean value that specifies whether the ALT key was pressed when the event occurred. This property simply reflects the value of the altKey property of the event object, as follows:

```
    this.altKey = e.altKey;
```

❑ button: Gets a Sys.UI.MouseButton enumeration value that specifies which mouse button was pressed when the event occurred. This property maps the value of the event object's button property to a more programmer-friendly Sys.UI.MouseButton enumeration value:

```
    if (typeof(e.button) !== 'undefined')
        this.button = (typeof(e.which) !== 'undefined') ? e.button :
                        (e.button === 4) ? Sys.UI.MouseButton.middleButton :
                        (e.button === 2) ? Sys.UI.MouseButton.rightButton :
                        Sys.UI.MouseButton.leftButton;
```

❑ charCode: Gets an integer value that specifies the character code of the key that raised the event. This property presents the value of the event object's charCode property if the event object exposes this property; otherwise, it presents the value of the keyCode property of the event object:

```
    if (e.type === 'keypress')
        this.charCode = e.charCode || e.keyCode;
```

❑ clientX: Gets an integer value that specifies the horizontal offset (in pixels) between the mouse position and the left side of the browser window's client area when the event occurred. This property simply returns the value of the event object's clientX property, as follows:

```
    this.clientX = e.clientX;
```

❑ clientY: Gets an integer value that specifies the vertical offset (in pixels) between the mouse position and the top of the browser window's client area when the event occurred. This property simply returns the value of the event object's clientY property, as follows:

```
    this.clientY = e.clientY;
```

❑   ctrlKey: Gets a Boolean value that specifies whether the CTRL key was pressed when the event occurred, as follows:

```
this.ctrlKey = e.ctrlKey;
```

❑   target: Gets a reference to the object that raised the event. This property returns the value of the event object's target property if the event object exposes this property; otherwise it returns the value of the srcElement property. Internet Explorer (IE) exposes the event target through the srcElement property, whereas other browsers such as Mozilla expose the event target through the target property.

```
this.target = e.target ? e.target : e.srcElement;
```

❑   offsetX: Gets an integer value that specifies the horizontal offset (in pixels) between the mouse position and the left side of the event target when the event occurred. This property returns the value of the event object's offsetX property if the event object contains this property; otherwise, it evaluates the value as follows:

```
var loc = Sys.UI.DomElement.getLocation(this.target);
this.offsetX = (typeof(e.offsetX) !== 'undefined') ? e.offsetX :
               window.pageXOffset + (e.clientX || 0) - loc.x;
```

❑   offsetY: Gets an integer value that specifies the vertical offset (in pixels) between the mouse position and the top of the event target when the event occurred. This property returns the value of the event object's offsetY property if the event object contains this property; otherwise, it evaluates the value as follows:

```
this.offsetY = (typeof(e.offsetY) !== 'undefined') ? e.offsetY :
               window.pageYOffset + (e.clientY || 0) - loc.y;
```

❑   screenX: Gets an integer value that specifies the horizontal offset (in pixels) between the mouse position and the left side of the user's screen when the event occurred. This property simply returns the value of the event object's screenX property, as follows:

```
this.screenX = e.screenX;
```

❑   screenY: Gets an integer value that specifies the vertical offset (in pixels) between the mouse position and the top of the user's screen when the event occurred. This property simply returns the value of the event object's screenY property, as follows:

```
this.screenY = e.screenY;
```

❑   shiftKey: Gets a Boolean value that specifies whether the SHIFT key was pressed when the event occurred. This property simply returns the value of the shiftKey property of the event object, as follows:

```
this.shiftKey = e.shiftKey;
```

❑ type: Gets a string value that contains the name of the event. The name of the event is the same as the event handler's name, without the on prefix. For example, the event associated with the onclick event handler is named click. This enables you to write a single JavaScript function that uses the type property's value in a switch statement in order to determine the type of the event and consequently to determine which event handler must be called.

```
this.type = e.type;
```

The DomEvent object acts as a wrapper around the event object that the browser generates to represent the event when an event occurs. The ASP.NET AJAX DOM extensions contain the infrastructure that provides event handlers (registered for an event) with the DomEvent object that encapsulates the event object the browser generates. This ensures that the event handlers use the DomEvent object instead of the event object. This infrastructure consists of several methods, which are discussed in the following sections.

Static Methods

The DomEvent class exposes two sets of methods: static and instance. The static methods are methods that are defined directly on the DomEvent class. As such they must be invoked on the class itself. They cannot be invoked on an instance of the class. These static methods are addHandler, removeHandler, addHandlers, and clearHandlers. The following sections discuss these methods.

addHandler

The DomEvent class exposes a static method named addHandler that you can use to register an event handler for a specified event.

The addHandler method takes three parameters. The first parameter references the DOM element that raised the event. The second parameter is a string that contains the name of the event, excluding the on prefix. The third parameter references the event handler being added. Listing 6-26 contains an example the uses the addHandler method.

Listing 6-26: An example that uses the addHandler method

```
<%@ Page Language="C#" %>

<!DOCTYPE html PUBLIC "-//W3C//DTD XHTML 1.0 Transitional//EN"
"http://www.w3.org/TR/xhtml1/DTD/xhtml1-transitional.dtd">

<html xmlns="http://www.w3.org/1999/xhtml">
<head id="Head1" runat="server">
  <title>Untitled Page</title>
  <script type="text/javascript" language="javascript">
    function clickcb(domEvent)
    {
      var msg = "altKey    ----> " + domEvent.altKey;
      msg += ("\nbutton   ----> " + domEvent.button);
      msg += ("\ntype     ----> " + domEvent.type);
```

(continued)

Listing 6-26 *(continued)*

```
            msg += ("\nctrlKey   ----> " + domEvent.ctrlKey);
            msg += ("\ntarget    ----> " + domEvent.target);
            msg += ("\noffsetX   ----> " + domEvent.offsetX);
            msg += ("\noffsetY   ----> " + domEvent.offsetY);
            msg += ("\nclientX   ----> " + domEvent.clientX);
            msg += ("\nclientY   ----> " + domEvent.clientY);
            msg += ("\nscreenX   ----> " + domEvent.screenX);
            msg += ("\nscreenY   ----> " + domEvent.screenY);
            msg += ("\nshiftKey  ----> " + domEvent.shiftKey);
            alert (msg);
        }

        function pageLoad()
        {
            var mybtn = $get("mybtn");
            $addHandler (mybtn, "click", clickcb);
        }
    </script>
</head>
<body>
    <form id="form1" runat="server">
        <asp:ScriptManager runat="server" ID="ScriptManager1" />
        <button id="mybtn" type="button">Click Here</button>
    </form>
</body>
</html>
```

This example renders a simple <button> HTML element. As this example shows, adding an event handler for an event involves the following steps:

1. Access a reference to the DOM element that will raise the event:

```
        var mybtn = $get("mybtn");
```

2. Call the addHandler method, passing in the reference to the DOM element, the name of the event, and the reference to the event handler:

```
        $addHandler (mybtn, "click", clickcb);
```

The clickcb event handler simply pops up an alert that displays the property values of the DomEvent object that represents the click event, as shown in Figure 6-4. As you can see, the ASP.NET AJAX DOM extensions automatically instantiate a DomEvent object under the hood and pass it into the clickcb event handler.

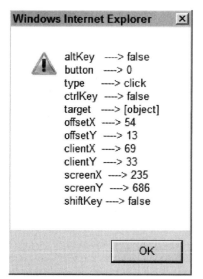

Figure 6-4

Listing 6-27: The addHandler Method

```
var $addHandler = Sys.UI.DomEvent.addHandler =
function Sys$UI$DomEvent$addHandler(element, eventName, handler)
{
  if (!element._events)
    element._events = {};

  var eventCache = element._events[eventName];
  if (!eventCache)
    element._events[eventName] = eventCache = [];

  var browserHandler;
  if (element.addEventListener) {
    browserHandler = function(e) {
      return handler.call(element, new Sys.UI.DomEvent(e));
    }
    element.addEventListener(eventName, browserHandler, false);
  }

  else if (element.attachEvent) {
    browserHandler = function() {
      return handler.call(element, new Sys.UI.DomEvent(window.event));
    }
    element.attachEvent('on' + eventName, browserHandler);
  }
  eventCache[eventCache.length] =
                {handler: handler, browserHandler: browserHandler};
}
```

Now, let's walk through the implementation of the `addHandler` method shown in Listing 6-27. This method first checks whether the DOM element that will raise the event contains an object named `_events`. If not, it instantiates and adds this object to the DOM element:

```
if (!element._events)
  element._events = {};
```

Next, `addHandler` uses the event name as an index into the `_events` to access the subarray associated with the specified event name. If `_events` does not contain a subarray for the specified event name, `addHandlers` instantiates and adds this subarray to `_events`:

```
var eventCache = element._events[eventName];
if (!eventCache)
  element._events[eventName] = eventCache = [];
```

Then, `addHandler` checks whether the DOM element that will raise the event supports a method named `addEventListener`. The DOM elements of browsers such as Mozilla support this method. If the DOM element supports this method, `addHandler` takes the following steps:

1. It defines a JavaScript function that contains two statements. The first statement instantiates a `DomEvent`, passing in the event object to represent the event. The second statement invokes the `call` method on the event handler being registered, passing in the reference to the DOM element that will raise the event and the `DomEvent` object that represents the event. JavaScript sets the value of the JavaScript keyword within the scope of the event handler being registered to reference the DOM element passed into the call method. This means that you can use the JavaScript keyword within the body of this event handler to access the DOM element that raised the event.

2. It invokes the `addEventListener` method on the DOM element that will raise the event, passing in the event name and the JavaScript function defined previously to register the JavaScript function as the event handler for the event with the specified name.

In other words, `addHandler` wraps the call into the event handler being added in a new event handler and registers this new event handler for the event. Therefore, when the specified DOM element finally raises the event, it calls the new event handler, which in turn instantiates the `DomEvent` object and calls the event handler being added, passing in the `DomEvent` object:

```
var browserHandler;
if (element.addEventListener) {
  browserHandler = function(e) {
    var domEvent = new Sys.UI.DomEvent(e);
    return handler.call(element, domEvent);
  }
  element.addEventListener(eventName, browserHandler, false);
}
```

If the DOM element that will raise the event does not support the `addEventListener` method, `addHandler` checks whether it supports the `attachEvent` method. The DOM elements of IE browsers support this method. If the DOM element supports this method, `addHandler` first defines a JavaScript function that consists of two statements. The first statement instantiates a `DomEvent` object that encapsulates the `window.event` event object. The second statement invokes the `call` method on the event handler being added, passing in the reference to the DOM element and the `DomEvent` object. Next, addHandler calls the attachEvent method on the DOM element, passing in the on-prefixed name of the event and the JavaScript function just defined:

```
else if (element.attachEvent) {
   browserHandler = function() {
      var domEvent = new Sys.UI.DomEvent(window.event);
      return handler.call(element, domEvent);
   }
   element.attachEvent('on' + eventName, browserHandler);
}
```

Finally, addHandler stores an object with two properties in the subarray associated with the event. The first property, handler, references the event handler being added; and the second property, browserHandler, references the JavaScript function defined previously:

```
eventCache[eventCache.length] =
                {handler: handler, browserHandler: browserHandler};
```

removeHandler

The DomEvent class exposes a method named removeHandler that removes a specified event handler. As Listing 6-28 shows, the removeHandler is defined on the DomEvent class itself. As such, it is a static method that must be called on the class itself.

As you can see, the removeHandler method takes three parameters. The first parameter references the DOM element that exposes the event with the specified name. The second parameter is a string that contains the name of the event. The third parameter references the event handler method being removed.

Listing 6-28: The removeHandler Method of the DomEvent Class

```
var $removeHandler = Sys.UI.DomEvent.removeHandler =
function Sys$UI$DomEvent$removeHandler(element, eventName, handler)
{
   var cache = element._events[eventName];
   var browserHandler = null;
   for (var i = 0, l = cache.length; i < l; i++)
   {
      if (cache[i].handler === handler)
      {
         browserHandler = cache[i].browserHandler;
         break;
      }
   }

   if (element.removeEventListener)
      element.removeEventListener(eventName, browserHandler, false);

   else if (element.detachEvent)
      element.detachEvent('on' + eventName, browserHandler);

   cache.splice(i, 1);
}
```

Now, let's walk through the implementation of the `removeHandler` method. This method first uses the event name as an index into the `_events` object of the DOM element that exposes the event with the specified name, and returns a reference to the array that contains all the event handlers for the event with the specified name:

```
var cache = element._events[eventName];
```

Next, it iterates through the event handlers of the array to locate the event handler to be removed:

```
for (var i = 0, l = cache.length; i < l; i++) {
  if (cache[i].handler === handler) {
    browserHandler = cache[i].browserHandler;
    break;
  }
}
```

Then, it checks whether the DOM element that exposes the event supports the `removeEventListener` method. The DOM elements of browsers such as Mozilla support this method. If the DOM element supports the method, `removeHandler` simply calls the `removeEventListener` method on the DOM element to remove the specified event handler:

```
element.removeEventListener(eventName, browserHandler, false);
```

If the DOM element does not support the `removeEventListener` method, `removeHandler` checks whether it supports the `detachEvent` method. The DOM elements of browsers such as IE support this method. If the DOM element supports the method, `removeHandler` calls the method to remove the specified event handler:

```
element.detachEvent('on' + eventName, browserHandler);
```

Finally, `removeHandler` removes the event handler from the array:

```
cache.splice(i, 1);
```

As you can see, thanks to the `removeHandler` method of the `DomEvent` class, you don't have to worry about the discrepancies among the browsers. It's all taken care of under the hood. The `DomEvent` class also takes care of the bookkeeping logic required to store and remove event handlers — storing and removing event handlers from the associated arrays of `_events`. Later in this chapter, you'll see an example where you need to call the `removeHandler` method to remove a specified event handler.

addHandlers

The `DomEvent` class exposes a method named `addHandlers` that allows you to register event handlers for different events of a specified DOM element. As Listing 6-29 shows, this method takes three arguments. The first argument references the DOM element that will raise the specified events. The second argument is a collection that contains the event names and the handlers being registered for these events. The third argument references the object that is the context for the delegates that the `addHandlers` method creates internally to represent the event handlers (discussed in detail later in this chapter).

Listing 6-29: The Internal Implementation of the addHandlers Method

```
var $addHandlers = Sys.UI.DomEvent.addHandlers =
function Sys$UI$DomEvent$addHandlers(element, events, handlerOwner)
{
  for (var name in events) {
    var handler = events[name];

    if (handlerOwner)
      handler = Function.createDelegate(handlerOwner, handler);

    $addHandler(element, name, handler);
  }
}
```

Now let's walk through this listing. Here's what's going on:

1. The `addHandlers` method is defined on the `DomEvent` class itself instead of its `prototype` property. This means that this method is a static method and must be invoked on the class itself.

2. The ASP.NET AJAX DOM extensions define a shortcut method named `$addHandlers` that allows you to use the following short syntax to invoke the `addHandler` method:

```
$addHandlers(element, events, handlerOwner);
```

`addHandlers` iterates through the event handlers that the events dictionary contains and takes the following actions for each enumerated event handler:

❏ It uses the event name as an index into the events dictionary to access the enumerated event handler:

```
var handler = events[name];
```

❏ It checks whether the caller has passed a value for the third argument. If so, `addHandlers` invokes the `createDelegate` method on the `Function` type, passing in the third argument and the event handler itself:

```
    if (handlerOwner)
      handler = Function.createDelegate(handlerOwner, handler);
```

As discussed earlier in this chapter, the `createDelegate` method creates a delegate that encapsulates and represents the event handler associated with the specified object.

❏ It calls the `addHandler` method of the `DomEvent` class, passing in three arguments. The first argument references the DOM element that will raise the event; the second argument is a string value that contains the event name; and the third argument references the event handler being added:

```
    $addHandler(element, name, handler);
```

Listing 6-30 shows an example that uses the `addHandlers` method.

Listing 6-30: An example that uses the addHandlers method

```
<%@ Page Language="C#" %>

<!DOCTYPE html PUBLIC "-//W3C//DTD XHTML 1.0 Transitional//EN"
"http://www.w3.org/TR/xhtml1/DTD/xhtml1-transitional.dtd">

<html xmlns="http://www.w3.org/1999/xhtml">
<head id="Head1" runat="server">
  <title>Untitled Page</title>
  <script type="text/javascript" language="javascript">
    function blurcb(domEvent)
    {
      alert("blurcb was invoked!");
    }

    function mousedowncb(domEvent)
    {
      alert("mousedowncb was invoked!");
    }

    function pageLoad()
    {
      var mybtn = $get("mybtn");
      var events = {blur:blurcb, mousedown:mousedowncb};
      $addHandlers(mybtn, events);
    }
  </script>
</head>
<body>
  <form id="form1" runat="server">
    <asp:ScriptManager runat="server" ID="ScriptManager1" />
    <button id="mybtn" type="button">Click Here</button>
  </form>
</body>
</html>
```

As you can see, the pageLoad method first creates a JavaScript object literal that contains two name/value pairs where the name part of each pair contains the event name and the value part contains the event handler. Then it calls the addHandlers method of the DomEvent class, passing in the reference to the <button> HTML element and this JavaScript object literal.

In this case, you could also call the addHandler method twice to achieve the same effect, as shown in the boldfaced portion of Listing 6-31. If you don't specify the third argument of the addHandlers method, the method is equivalent to multiple calls into the addHandler method. However, as you'll see later in this chapter, if you do specify the third argument of the addHandlers method, the method does more than just make multiple calls into the addHandler methods.

Listing 6-31: A version of Listing 6-30 that uses the addHandler method

```
<%@ Page Language="C#" %>

<!DOCTYPE html PUBLIC "-//W3C//DTD XHTML 1.0 Transitional//EN"
"http://www.w3.org/TR/xhtml1/DTD/xhtml1-transitional.dtd">

<html xmlns="http://www.w3.org/1999/xhtml">
<head id="Head1" runat="server">
  <title>Untitled Page</title>
  <script type="text/javascript" language="javascript">
    function blurcb(domEvent)
    {
      alert("blurcb was invoked!");
    }

    function mousedowncb(domEvent)
    {
      alert("mousedowncb was invoked!");
    }

    function pageLoad()
    {
      var mybtn = $get("mybtn");

      $addHandler (mybtn, "blur", blurcb);
      $addHandler (mybtn, "mousedown", mousedowncb);
    }
  </script>
</head>
<body>
  <form id="form1" runat="server">
    <asp:ScriptManager runat="server" ID="ScriptManager1" />
    <button id="mybtn" type="button">Click Here</button>
  </form>
</body>
</html>
```

clearHandlers

The DomEvent class exposes a method named clearHandlers that allows you to clear all event handlers registered for all the events of a specified DOM element. In Listing 6-32, the DomEvent class does the following:

1.   It defines the clearHandlers method on the DomEvent class itself. As such, this method is a static method that must be directly called on the class itself.

2.   It defines a shortcut method named $clearHandlers that allows you to use the following notation to invoke the clearHandlers method:

```
$clearHandlers(element);
```

Listing 6-32: The clearHandlers Method of the DomEvent Class

```
var $clearHandlers = Sys.UI.DomEvent.clearHandlers =
function Sys$UI$DomEvent$clearHandlers(element)
{
  if (element._events) {
    var cache = element._events;
    for (var name in cache) {
      var handlers = cache[name];
      for (var i = handlers.length - 1; i >= 0; i--)
        $removeHandler(element, name, handlers[i].handler);
    }
    element._events = null;
  }
}
```

In its internal implementation, the clearHandlers method simply iterates through the event handlers in the _events dictionary of the specified DOM element and takes the following steps for each enumerated event type:

1. It uses the event name as an index into the _events dictionary to access the array that contains the event handlers for the event with the specified name:

```
var handlers = cache[name];
```

2. It iterates through the event handlers in the array and calls the removeHandler method once for each enumerated event handler to remove the handler:

```
for (var i = handlers.length - 1; i >= 0; i--)
  $removeHandler(element, name, handlers[i].handler);
```

Again thanks to the DomEvent class, you can remove all the event handlers registered for all the events of a specified DOM element by one simple call into the clearHandler method. All the associated book-keeping work is managed under the hood for you.

Instance Methods

As mentioned previously, the DomEvent class exposes two sets of methods: static and instance. The static methods were discussed in the previous section. This section discusses the instance methods of the DomEvent class. The instance methods are defined directly on the prototype property of the DomEvent class. As such, they must be invoked on an instance of the class. They cannot be invoked on the class itself. These instance methods are preventDefault and stopPropagation.

preventDefault

As discussed earlier, when an event occurs, the browser instantiates an event object and populates its properties with specific information about the event. Each event normally has a default behavior. For example, the click event of <input type="submit"> posts the form data back to the server. Most applications nowadays need to validate the form data on the client-side and cancel the postback operation altogether if the validation fails. Obviously the cancellation must be performed inside the event handler method that handles the click event. The event object associated with the event exposes a member that allows these applications to cancel the default action of the event. The event object created by browsers such as Mozilla exposes a method named preventDefault that can be invoked on the event object to cancel the default action. The event object created by some other browsers such as IE, on the other hand, exposes a Boolean property named returnValue that can be set to cancel the default action.

The DomEvent class exposes an instance method named preventDefault that encapsulates this browser-dependent event cancellation logic, enabling you to cancel the event with a single method call that works on all types of browsers. Listing 6-33 presents the internal implementation of the preventDefault method.

Listing 6-33: The preventDefault Instance Method of the DomEvent Class

```
function Sys$UI$DomEvent$preventDefault() {
  if (this.rawEvent.preventDefault)
    this.rawEvent.preventDefault();

  else if (window.event)
    window.event.returnValue = false;
}
```

Listing 6-34 contains a page the uses the preventDefault instance method of the DomEvent class.

Listing 6-34: A page that uses the preventDefault method

```
<%@ Page Language="C#" %>

<!DOCTYPE html PUBLIC "-//W3C//DTD XHTML 1.0 Transitional//EN"
"http://www.w3.org/TR/xhtml1/DTD/xhtml1-transitional.dtd">
<script runat="server">
  void Page_Load(object sender, EventArgs e)
  {
    if (IsPostBack)
      info.Text="You entered: " + date.Value;
  }
</script>
<html xmlns="http://www.w3.org/1999/xhtml">
<head id="Head1" runat="server">
  <title>Untitled Page</title>
  <script language="javascript" type="text/javascript">
    function validateInput(input)
    {
      if (arguments.length != arguments.callee.length)
      {
        var err3=Error.parameterCount("Invalid argument count!");
        throw err3;
      }
```

(continued)

Listing 6-34 *(continued)*

```
      if (input == null || input.trim() == "")
      {
        var er = Error.argumentNull("input", "Date cannot be null!");
        throw er;
      }
      var reg = new RegExp("(\\d\\d)[-](\\d\\d)[-](\\d\\d\\d\\d)");
      var date = reg.exec(input);
      if (date == null)
      {
        var err = Error.argumentUndefined("input", "Undefined value!");
        throw err;
      }

      var ar = input.split("-");

      if (ar[2] < 1900 || ar[2] > 2008)
      {
        var err2=Error.argumentOutOfRange("input", input);
        throw err2;
      }
    }

    function clickCallback(domEvent)
    {
      var date = $get("date");
      var info = $get("info");
      info.innerHTML="";
      try
      {
        validateInput(date.value);
      }
      catch (e)
      {
        alert(e.message);
        date.value="";
        domEvent.preventDefault();
      }
    }

    function pageLoad()
    {
      var submitbtn = $get("submitbtn");
      $addHandler(submitbtn, "click", clickCallback);
    }

  </script>
</head>
```

```
<body>
  <form id="form1" runat="server">
    <asp:ScriptManager runat="server" ID="ScriptManager1" />
    Enter date: <input type="text" id="date" runat="server"/> 
    <button type="submit" id="submitbtn">Submit</button><br /><br />
    <asp:Label ID="info" runat="server" />
  </form>
</body>
</html>
```

This page covers a very common scenario in Web applications: the validation of the data that the end user enters into a text box before submitting the form to the server. As you can see, this page contains a text box and a Submit button that submits the value of the text box to the server. The pageLoad JavaScript function uses the addHandler method of the DomEvent class to register the clickCallback JavaScript function as the event handler for the click event of the Submit button:

```
function pageLoad()
{
  var submitbtn = $get("submitbtn");
  $addHandler(submitbtn, "click", clickCallback);
}
```

The clickCallback event handler first calls the validateInput JavaScript function to validate the date that the end user entered in the text box. The validateInput JavaScript function performs the validations discussed in Chapter 3, and raises an exception if the validation fails.

The catch block of the clickCallback event handler catches this exception and calls the preventDefault method of the DomEvent object to cancel the form submission to the server.

stopPropagation

Event propagation is one of the important aspects of client-side event programming. To understand event propagation, first you need to understand the concept of containment hierarchy. The containment hierarchy of a specified DOM element such as the Submit button in Listing 6-34 is a tree, or hierarchy, of DOM elements that contains all the ancestor DOM elements of the specified DOM element in addition to the DOM element itself. The root DOM element of a containment hierarchy is the window object.

For example, the containment hierarchy of the Submit button in Listing 6-34 contains these DOM elements: window, document, HTML, body, form, and button. Prior to modern browsers, when the end user clicked the Submit button, the button would raise the click event, which had to be handled at the Submit button level. In other words, you had to register an event handler for the click event of the Submit button to handle the event. If there were no event handlers registered for the click event of the Submit button, the event would be lost forever. You had to handle the event at the event target itself.

That's all in the past. Modern browsers propagate the event that a DOM element raises all the way through the containment hierarchy of the element. For example, in the case of the Submit button in Listing 6-34, when the end user clicks the button and raises the click event, the event object associated with this event is passed to the ancestor DOM elements (document, HTML, and so on) for the Submit button. This has two important benefits:

❑ You can now register an event handler with a higher-level DOM element, such as the document element, to handle the event that a lower-level DOM element, such as the Submit button, raises.

❑ You can handle the same event multiple times at multiple hierarchy levels. For example, you can handle the event that the Submit button raises at the document and body levels in addition to the Submit-button level.

In general, there are three event propagation models:

❑ **Netscape Navigator 4–only event propagation model:** Netscape Navigator 4 is the only browser that supports this event propagation model. As more people are moving from Netscape Navigator 4 to more modern browsers, this event propagation model is used less often. In this event propagation model, when a DOM element such as the Submit button in Listing 6-34 raises an event, the event propagates from the top of the DOM element's containment hierarchy (the window object) all the way down to the event target (the DOM element itself). The Netscape Navigator 4 event propagation model is also known as event capture. By default, Netscape Navigator 4 event propagation is turned off.

❑ **Internet Explorer 4 and higher event propagation model:** In this event propagation model, when a DOM element such as the Submit button in Listing 6-34 raises an event, the event propagates from the bottom of the DOM element's containment hierarchy (the DOM element itself) all the way up to the top of the containment hierarchy (the window object). In other words, the Internet Explorer 4 and higher propagation model is the opposite of the Netscape Navigator 4 event propagation model. The Internet Explorer 4 and higher propagation model is known as event bubbling. Internet Explorer 4 and higher event bubbling is very similar to the ASP.NET Framework's event bubbling. By default, Internet Explorer 4 and higher event propagation is turned on.

❑ **W3C event propagation model:** In this event propagation model, when a DOM element such as the Submit button in Listing 6-34 raises an event, the event propagates from the top of the DOM element's containment hierarchy (the window object) all the way down to the event target and then bubbles from there all the way back up to the top of the containment hierarchy. The W3C event propagation model accommodates both Netscape Navigator 4 and Internet Explorer 4 and higher event propagation models. Unfortunately, because the other two propagation models are still in use, the W3C event propagation model had to introduce a new syntax to avoid conflicts. By default, only the event bubbling portion of the W3C event propagation is turned on.

By default, event capture is turned off no matter which event propagation model is used. There are times when an application needs to stop the default behavior of event bubbling at a particular level of a containment hierarchy. For example, in the case of Listing 6-34, you may not want the click event to propagate to the document level because it would interfere with some other events that your application handles at that level. Both the Internet Explorer 4 and higher and W3C propagation models allow you to stop the event bubbling at a desired level of a containment hierarchy. However, these models require you to invoke different members of the event object to achieve this. In the case of the W3C event propagation model, you must call the stopPropagation method on the event object to stop the event bubbling at a specified hierarchy level. In the case of the Internet Explorer 4 and higher event propagation model, you must set the cancelBubble property of the event object to true to stop the event bubbling at a specified hierarchy level.

The DomEvent class exposes an instance method named stopPropagation that encapsulates this browser-dependent code, allowing you to stop the event bubbling at a desired level by making a single method call that works with all types of browsers.

Listing 6-35 presents the internal implementation of the stopPropagation method of the DomEvent class.

Listing 6-35: The stopPropagation Instance Method of the DomEvent Class

```
function Sys$UI$DomEvent$stopPropagation() {
  if (this.rawEvent.stopPropagation)
    this.rawEvent.stopPropagation();

  else if (window.event)
    window.event.cancelBubble = true;
}
```

As you can see in this listing, the stopPropagation method first checks whether the event object supports a method named stopPropagation. If so, this indicates that the browser is using the W3C event propagation model, and the stopPropagation method of the event object is called to stop the event bubbling. The constructor of the DomEvent class assigns the event object to the rawEvent property of the DomEvent object:

```
this.rawEvent.stopPropagation();
```

If the event object does not support the stopPropagation method, Listing 6-35 checks whether the window object supports a property named event. If so, this indicates that the browser is using the Internet Explorer 4 and higher event propagation model, and the cancelBubble property of the event object is set to true to stop the event bubbling.

Using the DomEvent Class

Listing 6-36 presents an example that uses the methods of the DomEvent class. This example is a new version of the example discussed earlier in the chapter (see Listing 6-22 through 6-24). Recall that the previous version did the following:

❑   It loaded and displayed a single movable object such as text.

❑   It instantiated a single mover that enables the end user to move the movable object.

As you can see, the previous version of the example supports loading, displaying, and moving a single movable object. The new version of the example supports loading, displaying, and moving multiple movable objects simultaneously. The new version allows you to attach a separate mover object to each movable object so you can move them independently. The new version also adds support for a new type of movable object that displays a table of data. As Listing 6-36 shows, this page displays three movable objects simultaneously, allowing you to move them independently. These movable objects are text, an image, and a table of data as shown in Figure 6-5.

Listing 6-36: A page that uses the DomEvent Class

```
<%@ Page Language="C#" %>

<!DOCTYPE html PUBLIC "-//W3C//DTD XHTML 1.0 Transitional//EN"
"http://www.w3.org/TR/xhtml1/DTD/xhtml1-transitional.dtd">

<html xmlns="http://www.w3.org/1999/xhtml">
<head runat="server">
  <title>Untitled Page</title>
  <style type="text/css">
    .myTable {
        background-color: LightGoldenrodYellow;
        border-color:Tan;
        border-width:1px;
        color:Black;
    }

    .myTable th, .myTable td
    {
        padding: 2px 5px;
    }

    .header {
        background-color:Tan;
        font-weight:bold
    }

    .odd {
        background-color:PaleGoldenrod;
    }

  </style>
  <script type="text/javascript" language="javascript">
    function pageLoad()
    {
      var imageMover = new Delegates.Mover("container1");
      var imageProvider = new Delegates.ImageProvider("images.jpg");
      var addImageDelegate = Function.createDelegate(imageProvider,
                                          imageProvider.addImage);
      imageMover.addContent(addImageDelegate);

      var textMover = new Delegates.Mover("container2");
      var textProvider = new Delegates.TextProvider("Wrox Web Site");
      var addTextDelegate = Function.createDelegate(textProvider,
                                          textProvider.addText);
      textMover.addContent(addTextDelegate);

      var headers = ["Product", "Distributor", "Producer"];
      var rows = [];
```

```
        for (var i=0; i<10; i++)
        {
          rows[i] = ["Product"+i, "Distributor"+i, "Producer"+i];
        }

        var tableMover = new Delegates.Mover("container3");
        var tableProvider = new Delegates.TableProvider(headers, rows);
        var addTableDelegate =
              Function.createDelegate(tableProvider,
              tableProvider.addTable);
        tableMover.addContent(addTableDelegate);
      }
  </script>
</head>
<body>

  <form id="form1" runat="server">
    <asp:ScriptManager runat="server" ID="ScriptManager1">
      <Scripts>
        <asp:ScriptReference Path="Delegate.js" />
      </Scripts>
    </asp:ScriptManager>
  </form>
</body>
</html>
```

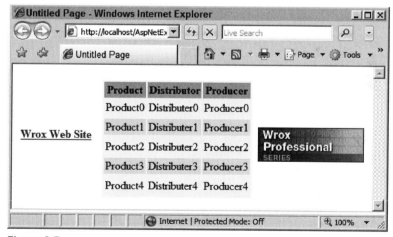

Figure 6-5

Adding a new type of movable object requires you to write a new provider class. As such, this example implements a new class named TableProvider that renders a table of data. The data could be coming from any type of source, such as SQL Server, XML documents, or a Web service. To keep the discussion focused, in this case I hardcoded the required data. As you can see in Listing 6-36, the constructor of the `TableProvider` class takes two arguments. The first argument is an array that contains the header texts of the table; the second argument is an array of subarrays, where each subarray contains the field values for a data record or row:

```
var headers = ["Product", "Distributor", "Producer"];
var rows = [];
for (var i=0; i<10; i++)
{
   rows[i] = ["Product"+i, "Distributor"+i, "Producer"+i];
}

var tableProvider = new Delegates.TableProvider(headers, rows);
```

Notice that Listing 6-36 uses the following script reference:

```
<asp:ScriptReference Path="Delegate.js" />
```

This script reference references the `Delegate.js` script file that contains the entire application logic. Listing 6-37 presents the content of this file. I'll discuss the JavaScript functions defined in this code listing in the following sections.

Lisitng 6-37: The Content of Delegate.js Script File

```
Type.registerNamespace("Delegates");

Delegates.Mover = function (containerId)
{
  var container = $get(containerId);
  Delegates.Mover.incrementMoversCount();
  if (!container)
  {
    container = document.createElement("div");

    this.containerId = container.id = containerId;
    container.style.position = "absolute";
    document.body.insertBefore(container, document.forms[0]);

    $addHandlers(container, { mousedown: this.mousedowncb }, this);
  }
}

Delegates.Mover.prototype =
{
  addContent : Delegates$Mover$invokeAddContentDelegate,
  mousedowncb : Delegates$Mover$mousedowncb,
  mouseupcb : Delegates$Mover$mouseupcb,
  mousemovecb : Delegates$Mover$mousemovecb
}
```

```
Delegates.Mover.incrementMoversCount = function()
{
  if (typeof(this.moversCount) == "undefined")
    this.moversCount = 0;

  this.moversCount++;
}

Delegates.Mover.get_moversCount = function()
{
  return this.moversCount;
}

function Delegates$Mover$invokeAddContentDelegate(addContentDelegate)
{
  addContentDelegate(this.containerId);
}

function Delegates$Mover$mousedowncb(domEvent)
{
  var container = $get(this.containerId);
  this.oldClientX = domEvent.clientX;
  this.oldClientY = domEvent.clientY;
  var events = {mousemove: this.mousemovecb, mouseup: this.mouseupcb}
  $addHandlers(document, events, this);
  container.style.zIndex += Delegates.Mover.get_moversCount();
  domEvent.preventDefault();
}

function Delegates$Mover$mouseupcb(domEvent)
{
  var container = $get(this.containerId);
  $clearHandlers(document);
  container.style.zIndex -= Delegates.Mover.get_moversCount();
  domEvent.preventDefault();
}

function Delegates$Mover$mousemovecb(domEvent)
{
  var container = $get(this.containerId);
  var deltaClientX = domEvent.clientX - this.oldClientX;
  var deltaClientY = domEvent.clientY - this.oldClientY;

  var containerLocation = Sys.UI.DomElement.getLocation(container);
  Sys.UI.DomElement.setLocation(container, containerLocation.x+deltaClientX,
                                containerLocation.y+deltaClientY);

  this.oldClientX = domEvent.clientX;
  this.oldClientY = domEvent.clientY;

  domEvent.preventDefault();
}
```

(continued)

Lisitng 6-37 *(continued)*

```
Delegates.TableProvider = function (headers, rows)
{
  this.headers = headers;
  this.rows = rows;
}

Delegates.TableProvider.prototype =
{
  addTable : Delegates$TableProvider$addTable
}

function Delegates$TableProvider$addTable(containerId)
{
  var container = $get(containerId);
  var table = document.createElement("table");
  Sys.UI.DomElement.addCssClass(table, "myTable");
  var headerRow = table.insertRow(0);
  Sys.UI.DomElement.addCssClass(headerRow, "header");

  function renderHeaderCell(dataFieldName, cellIndex, dataFieldNames)
  {
    var headerCell = document.createElement("th");
    headerCell.appendChild(document.createTextNode(dataFieldName));
    headerRow.appendChild(headerCell);
  };

  function renderDataCell(dataFieldValue, index, dataFieldValues)
  {
    var dataCell = row.insertCell(row.cells.length);
    dataCell.appendChild(document.createTextNode(dataFieldValue));
  };

  Array.forEach(this.headers, renderHeaderCell);

  for (var rowIndex in this.rows)
  {
    var row = table.insertRow(table.rows.length);
    if (rowIndex % 2 == 1)
      Sys.UI.DomElement.addCssClass(row, "odd");

    Array.forEach(this.rows[rowIndex], renderDataCell);
  }
  container.appendChild(table);
}

Delegates.TextProvider = function (text)
{
  this.text = text;
}
```

```
Delegates.TextProvider.prototype =
{
  addText : Delegates$TextProvider$addText
}


Delegates.ImageProvider = function (imagePath)
{
  this.imagePath = imagePath;
}


Delegates.ImageProvider.prototype =
{
  addImage : Delegates$ImageProvider$addImage
}


function Delegates$TextProvider$addText(containerId)
{
  var container = $get(containerId);
  container.innerHTML = '<a href="javascript:void(0);" id="myspan"' +
                        ' style="font-weight:bold">' +
                        this.text + '</a>';
}


function Delegates$ImageProvider$addImage(containerId)
{
  var container = $get(containerId);
  container.innerHTML = "<img src='" + this.imagePath + "' alt='img' />";
}


Delegates.Mover.registerClass("Delegates.Mover");
Delegates.TextProvider.registerClass("Delegates.TextProvider");
Delegates.ImageProvider.registerClass("Delegates.ImageProvider");
Delegates.TableProvider.registerClass("Delegates.TableProvider");

if (typeof(Sys) !== 'undefined') Sys.Application.notifyScriptLoaded();
```

Mover

Listing 6-38 presents the implementation of the Mover class. The new version of the Mover class features the following enhancements:

❑ The constructor of the new version takes a string argument that contains the id HTML attribute value of the container <div> HTML element. This is an improvement over the previous version where this value was hardcoded. This improvement allows you to instantiate multiple Mover objects and to attach each one to a separate movable object so you can move each object independently from the others.

❑ The new version stores the id of the container <div> HTML element in an internal field named containerId, as follows:

```
this.containerId = containerId;
```

209

Listing 6-38: The Mover Class

```
Delegates.Mover = function (outerDivId)
{
  var container = $get(containerId);
  Delegates.Mover.incrementMoversCount();
  if (!container)
  {
    container = document.createElement("div");

    this.containerId = containerId;

    container.id = outerDivId;
    container.style.position="absolute";
    document.body.insertBefore(container, document.forms[0]);

    var events = {mousedown:this.mousedowncb};
    $addHandlers(container, events, this);
  }
}

Delegates.Mover.prototype = {
  addContent : Delegates$Mover$invokeAddContentDelegate,
  mousedowncb : Delegates$Mover$mousedowncb,
  mouseupcb : Delegates$Mover$mouseupcb,
  mousemovecb : Delegates$Mover$mousemovecb
}

Delegates.Mover.incrementMoversCount = function() {
  if (typeof(this.moversCount) == "undefined")
    this.moversCount = 0;
  this.moversCount++;
}

Delegates.Mover.get_moversCount = function() {
  return this.moversCount;
}

Delegates.Mover.registerClass("Delegates.Mover");
```

Note that the new version of the Mover class constructor uses the DomEvent class's addHandlers method to register the mousedowncb method as the event handler for the mousedown event of the container <div> HTML element. Also note that the mousedowncb method is now an instance method of the Mover class.

```
var events = {mousedown:this.mousedowncb};
$addHandlers(container, events, this);
```

This is a great improvement over the previous version where mousedowncb was a global JavaScript function and was directly assigned to the onmousedown member of the container <div> HTML element, as shown in the following code fragment:

```
container.mousedown = mousedowncb;
```

In such a direct assignment of the event handler method, the method is directly invoked on the HTML element that raises the event, which in this case is the container <div> HTML element. This means that if the this keyword is used inside the mousedowncb method, it will reference the container JavaScript object.

The addHandlers method of the DomEvent class does not directly register the mousedowncb method with the HTML element that raises the event. Instead, it defines a new JavaScript function that wraps a call into the mousedowncb method and directly registers this new JavaScript function as the event handler for the mousedown event of the container <div> HTML element. This means that the keyword used inside the mousedowncb method will reference the Mover object instead of the container object.

Now let's see the proof for these arguments. As shown in the highlighted portion of the following code snippet taken from Listing 6-29, the addHandlers method of the DomEvent class calls the createDelegate method on the Function class. Note that the addHandlers method passes two parameters into the createDelegate method. The first parameter specifies the JavaScript object to which the this pointer from the event handler (that is, mousedowncb) will refer — the Mover object in this case. The second parameter references the event handler being registered — the mousedowncb method in this case.

```
var $addHandlers = Sys.UI.DomEvent.addHandlers =
function Sys$UI$DomEvent$addHandlers(element, events, handlerOwner)
{
  for (var name in events) {
    var handler = events[name];

    if (handlerOwner)
      handler = Function.createDelegate(handlerOwner, handler);

    $addHandler(element, name, handler);
  }
}
```

The createDelegate method of the Function class defines a new JavaScript function that calls the apply method on the second argument passed into the createDelegate method, as shown in the following code. The second argument in this case references the mousedowncb method. Note that the createDelegate method passes its first parameter into the apply method. The first parameter in this case references the Mover object. This means that the pointer used inside the mousedowncb method points to the Mover object.

```
Function.createDelegate =
function Function$createDelegate(instance, method) {
  return function() {
    return method.apply(instance, arguments);
  }
}
```

The addHandlers method calls the addHandler method of the DomEvent class to register the new event handler (that is, the one that wraps a call into the mousedowncb method of the Mover object) as the callback for the mousedown event of the container <div> HTML element, as shown in the highlighted portion of the following code snippet taken from Listing 6-29:

```
var $addHandlers = Sys.UI.DomEvent.addHandlers =
function Sys$UI$DomEvent$addHandlers(element, events, handlerOwner)
{
  for (var name in events) {
    var handler = events[name];

    if (handlerOwner)
      handler = Function.createDelegate(handlerOwner, handler);

    $addHandler(element, name, handler);

  }
}
```

Note that the Mover class exposes six methods: addContent, mousedowncb, mouseupcb, mousemovecb, incrementMoversCount, and get_moversCount. Because the first four methods are defined on the prototype property of the Mover class instead of the class itself, they are considered instance methods; therefore, they must be invoked on an instance of the Mover class, not directly on the class itself.

Because the incrementMoversCount and get_moversCount methods are defined on the Mover class itself, they are considered static methods and must be invoked on the Mover class itself instead of an instance of the class. As shown in the following code snippet taken from Listing 6-38, the constructor of the Mover class invokes the incrementMoversCount static method on the Mover class to increment the moversCount field by one:

```
Delegates.Mover.incrementMoversCount();
```

As you'll see later, the get_moversCount static method of the Mover class will be invoked to retrieve the total number of the Mover objects in the application.

The following sections discuss the implementation of the Mover class instance methods.

addContent

The addContent method takes a delegate as an argument and invokes the delegate, passing in the id HTML attribute value of the container <div> HTML element, as shown in Listing 6-39. It's the responsibility of the delegate to populate the container <div> HTML element with the appropriate content. This content could be as simple as a text and as complex as an interface that consists of many GUI elements such as buttons, pictures, and drop-down lists.

Listing 6-39: The addContent Method of the Mover Class

```
function Delegates$Mover$invokeAddContentDelegate(addContentDelegate)
{
   addContentDelegate(this.containerId);
}
```

mousedowncb

Listing 6-40 shows the mousedowncb method of the Mover class.

Listing 6-40: The mousedowncb Method of the Mover Class

```
function Delegates$Mover$mousedowncb(domEvent)
{
   this.oldClientX = domEvent.clientX;
   this.oldClientY = domEvent.clientY;
   var events = {mousemove:this.mousemovecb, mouseup:this.mouseupcb};
   $addHandlers(document, events, this);
   var container = $get(this.containerId);
   container.style.zIndex += Delegates.Mover.get_moversCount();
   domEvent.preventDefault();
}
```

As you can see in this listing, the mousedowncb method of the Mover class takes the following actions:

❑ It instantiates a JavaScript object literal with two name/value pairs, where the name part of each pair contains an event name and the value part references the event handler being registered for the event with the specified name:

```
var events = {mousemove:this.mousemovecb, mouseup:this.mouseupecb};
```

❑ It calls the addHandlers method of the DomEvent class, passing three parameters. The first parameter is the reference to the DOM element that raises the events, which is the document element in this case. The second parameter is the JavaScript object literal that contains the event handlers being registered, which is the events object in this case. The third parameter is the reference to the JavaScript object to which the pointers used inside the event handler being registered will refer, which is the Mover object in this case.

```
$addHandlers(document, events, this);
```

As discussed earlier and shown in Listing 6-40, you can use the this keyword inside the mousedowncb method to reference the Mover object and consequently to reference the other properties and methods of the Mover object as follows:

❏ You can use the this keyword to directly access the oldClientX and oldClientY properties of the Mover object from within the mousedowncb method to store the values of the DomEvent object's clientX and clientY properties for future reference. This allows each Mover object to do its own bookkeeping. This is important in this case because you want to attach a separate Mover object to each movable object so you can move the movable objects independently.

❏ You can use the this keyword to directly access the Mover object's mousemovecb and mouseupcb methods.

❏ You can use the this keyword to directly access the Mover object's containerId property from within the mousedowncb to increment the value of its zIndex property. This will ensure that when the user selects a moveable object partially covered by other objects, the selected object moves to the front.

Note that the zIndex value is incremented by the number returned from the get_moversCount static method of the Mover class. This method returns the total number of Mover objects in the current application.

mouseupcb

Listing 6-41 contains the code for the mouseupcb method of the Mover class.

Listing 6-41: The mouseupcb Method of the Mover Class

```
function Delegates$Mover$mouseupcb(domEvent)
{
  $clearHandlers(document);
  var container = $get(this.containerId);
  container.style.zIndex -= Delegates.Mover.get_moversCount();
  domEvent.preventDefault();
}
```

As you can see in this listing, the mouseupcb method calls the clearHandlers static method of the DomEvent class, passing in the document object to clear all event handlers registered for the events that the document element exposes. The method then decrements the zIndex value of the container <div> HTML element:

```
container.style.zIndex -= Delegates.Mover.get_moversCount();
```

mousemovecb

Listing 6-42 shows the mousemovecb method of the Mover class.

Listing 6-42: The mousemovecb Method of the Mover Class

```
function Delegates$Mover$mousemovecb(domEvent)
{
  var deltaClientX = domEvent.clientX - this.oldClientX;
  var deltaClientY = domEvent.clientY - this.oldClientY;

  var container = $get(this.containerId);
  var containerLocation = Sys.UI.DomElement.getLocation(container);
  Sys.UI.DomElement.setLocation(container, containerLocation.x + deltaClientX,
                      containerLocation.y + deltaClientY);

  this.oldClientX = domEvent.clientX;
  this.oldClientY = domEvent.clientY;

  domEvent.preventDefault();
}
```

As you can see in this listing, the mousemovecb method first determines how many pixels the mouse pointer has moved horizontally and vertically:

```
var deltaClientX = domEvent.clientX - this.oldClientX;
var deltaClientY = domEvent.clientY - this.oldClientY;
```

Next, it calls the getLocation static method of the DomElement class to return the JavaScript object literal that contains the current x and y coordinates of the container <div> HTML element:

```
var outerDivLocation = Sys.UI.DomElement.getLocation(container);
```

Then, it then calls the setLocation static method of the DomElement class to increment the current x and y coordinates of the container <div> HTML element by the number of pixels the mouse pointer has moved horizontally and vertically:

```
Sys.UI.DomElement.setLocation(container, containerLocation.x + deltaClientX,
                    containerLocation.y + deltaClientY);
```

Finally, it stores the current x and y coordinates of the mouse pointer in the oldClientX and oldClientY properties of the Mover object. As you can see, each Mover object keeps track of the x and y coordinates of its associated container <div> HTML element. This enables you to have more than one Mover object in the application, each keeping track of the x and y coordinates of its associated container <div> HTML element.

TableProvider

Listing 6-43 presents the implementation of the `TableProvider` class. As you can see, the constructor of this class takes two arguments. The first argument is an array that contains the header text. The second argument is an array of subarrays, where each subarray contains the field values for a particular data row.

Listing 6-43: The TableProvider Class

```
Delegates.TableProvider = function (headers, rows) {
  this.headers = headers;
  this.rows = rows;
}

Delegates.TableProvider.prototype = {
  addTable : Delegates$TableProvider$addTable
}

Delegates.TableProvider.registerClass("Delegates.TableProvider");
```

Note that the `TableProvider` class exposes a method named `addTable`. Because this method is directly defined on the `prototype` property of the class, it must be invoked on an instance of the class. Listing 6-44 contains the code for the `addTable` method, which iterates through the header text in the `headers` array and renders each enumerated header text in a `<th>` HTML element. Then, it iterates through the subarrays in the `rows` array and renders each enumerated subarray in a `<tr>` HTML element.

Listing 6-44: The addTable Method of the TableProvider Class

```
function Delegates$TableProvider$addTable(containerId)
{
  var container = $get(containerId);
  var table = document.createElement("table");
  Sys.UI.DomElement.addCssClass(table, "myTable");
  var headerRow = table.insertRow(0);
  Sys.UI.DomElement.addCssClass(headerRow, "header");

  function renderHeaderCell(dataFieldName, cellIndex, dataFieldNames)
  {
    var headerCell = document.createElement("th");
    headerCell.appendChild(document.createTextNode(dataFieldName));
    headerRow.appendChild(headerCell);
  };

  function renderDataCell(dataFieldValue, index, dataFieldValues)
  {
    var dataCell = row.insertCell(row.cells.length);
    dataCell.appendChild(document.createTextNode(dataFieldValue));
  };

  Array.forEach(this.headers, renderHeaderCell);
```

```
    for (var rowIndex in this.rows)
    {
      var row = table.insertRow(table.rows.length);
      if (rowIndex % 2 == 1)
         Sys.UI.DomElement.addCssClass(row, "odd");

      Array.forEach(this.rows[rowIndex], renderDataCell);
    }
    container.appendChild(table);
}
```

Summary

This chapter provided in-depth coverage of several classes and enumerations of the ASP.NET AJAX DOM extensions. It also provided in-depth coverage of the DomEvent class and showed how you can use the methods and properties of this class in your client-side event programming tasks. As you'll see in subsequent chapters, the ASP.NET AJAX client-side framework uses the DomEvent class and its methods extensively.

Component Development Infrastructure

The ASP.NET and .NET Frameworks provide server-side programmers with the necessary infrastructure for component development. You can think of a component as a unit of functionality that implements a well-known API. A component may or may not have a visual presence in the user interface of an application. For example, a timer is a component that does not render visual markup in an ASP.NET page. A `GridView`, on the other hand, is a component that does render visual markup in a page. Thanks to the ASP.NET and .NET component development infrastructure, you can develop components such as `GridView` with minimal time and effort.

The ASP.NET AJAX client-side framework provides client-side programmers with a component-development infrastructure that emulates its ASP.NET and .NET counterparts to enable you to develop client-side components with minimal time and effort. The ASP.NET AJAX component-development infrastructure consists of a set of well-defined interfaces and classes as discussed in this chapter.

First, this chapter presents the main interfaces that make up the ASP.NET AJAX component-development infrastructure. Then the chapter introduces two main classes of this infrastructure: `Component` and `_Application`.

Every ASP.NET AJAX component (including your own custom components) directly or indirectly derives from the `Component` base class. This base class defines the lifecycle that every component application must go through. A component lifecycle consists of well-defined phases, as discussed in this chapter. Therefore, deriving your custom component classes from the `Component` base class automatically enables your component to participate in a typical component lifecycle.

Every ASP.NET AJAX application is represented by an instance of the `_Application` class. This instance is created by the ASP.NET AJAX framework and exposed through the `Sys.Application` variable. The `_Application` class defines the lifecycle that every ASP.NET AJAX application must go through. An application lifecycle consists of well-defined phases, as discussed in this chapter.

Interfaces

The ASP.NET AJAX client-side framework extends the core functionality of JavaScript to add support for object-oriented features such as classes, inheritance, enumerations, interfaces, and so on. Interfaces are at the heart of every object-oriented framework. They act as contracts between the classes that implement them and the clients of these classes. This allows you to replace the existing classes with new ones without affecting the client code as long as the new classes honor the established contract by implementing the required interfaces.

The ASP.NET and .NET Frameworks come with well-known sets of interfaces that are used throughout these frameworks and the ASP.NET and .NET applications. The ASP.NET AJAX client-side framework includes a set of interfaces that emulate their ASP.NET and .NET counterparts. These interfaces are used throughout the ASP.NET AJAX client-side framework and the ASP.NET AJAX applications. The following sections cover some of these interfaces.

IDisposable

The .NET Framework defines an interface named `IDisposable` that exposes a single method named `Dispose`. Every .NET class that holds valuable resources must implement this interface, and the class's implementation of the `Dispose` method must release the resources that it holds. The `Dispose` method of a .NET class instance is invoked right before the instance is disposed of.

The ASP.NET AJAX client-side framework includes an interface named `IDisposable` that emulates the .NET `IDisposable` interface as shown in Listing 7-1. The ASP.NET AJAX `IDisposable` interface, just like its .NET counterpart, exposes a single method named `dispose`. Note that this interface belongs to the `Sys` namespace.

Listing 7-1: The IDisposable Interface

```
Sys.IDisposable = function Sys$IDisposable() {
  throw Error.notImplemented();
}

function Sys$IDisposable$dispose() {
  throw Error.notImplemented();
}

Sys.IDisposable.prototype = {
  dispose: Sys$IDisposable$dispose
}

Sys.IDisposable.registerInterface('Sys.IDisposable');
```

Listing 7-2 references a JavaScript file named `Monitor.js` that contains the code for a class that implements the `IDisposable` interface. This file defines a class named `Monitor` whose main purpose is to monitor mouse movement and display the *x* and *y* coordinates of the mouse pointer as it is moving.

Listing 7-2: A Class that Implements the IDisposable Interface

```
<%@ Page Language="C#" %>

<!DOCTYPE html PUBLIC "-//W3C//DTD XHTML 1.0 Transitional//EN"
"http://www.w3.org/TR/xhtml1/DTD/xhtml1-transitional.dtd">

<html xmlns="http://www.w3.org/1999/xhtml">
<head runat="server">
  <title>Untitled Page</title>
  <script type="text/javascript" language="javascript">
    function pageLoad()
    {
      var monitor = new Disposables.Monitor();
      var btn = $get("btn");
      var disposeDelegate = Function.createDelegate(monitor, monitor.dispose);
      $addHandler(btn, "click", disposeDelegate);
    }
  </script>
</head>
<body>
  <form id="form1" runat="server">
    <asp:ScriptManager ID="ScriptManager1" runat="server" >
      <Scripts>
        <asp:ScriptReference Path="Monitor.js" />
      </Scripts>
    </asp:ScriptManager>

    <button id="btn" type="button">Dispose Monitor</button>
    <div>
    </div>
  </form>
</body>
</html>
```

Listing 7-3 presents the contents of the `Monitor.js` JavaScript file.

Listing 7-3: The Monitor.js JavaScript File

```
Type.registerNamespace("Disposables");

Disposables.Monitor = function() {
  this.div = document.createElement("div");
  document.body.insertBefore(this.div,document.forms[0]);
  this.registerMonitor();
}
```

(continued)

Listing 7-3 (continued)

```
Disposables.Monitor.prototype =
{
  registerMonitor : function() {
    this.delegate = Function.createDelegate(this, this.print);
    $addHandler(document, "mousemove", this.delegate);
  },

  print : function(domEvent) {
    this.div.innerHTML = "X-Coordinate: " + domEvent.clientX + "<br/>" +
                         "Y-Coordinate: " + domEvent.clientY;
  },

  dispose : function() {
    $removeHandler(document, "mousemove", this.delegate);
  }
}

Disposables.Monitor.registerClass("Disposables.Monitor", null,
                                  Sys.IDisposable);

if(typeof(Sys)!=='undefined')
  Sys.Application.notifyScriptLoaded();
```

The `Monitor.js` first defines a namespace named `Disposables`:

```
Type.registerNamespace("Disposables");
```

Next, it defines the constructor of the `Monitor` class. Note that the `Monitor` class belongs to the `Disposables` namespace. This constructor first creates the `<div>` HTML element that will display the *x* and *y* coordinates of the mouse pointer:

```
this.div = document.createElement("div");
```

Next, it inserts this `<div>` HTML element before the `<form>` HTML element:

```
document.body.insertBefore(this.div, document.forms[0]);
```

Finally, the constructor calls the `registerMonitor` method of the `Monitor` class:

```
this.registerMonitor();
```

The `Monitor.js` file then defines the instance methods of the `Monitor` class. The first instance method is the `registerMonitor` method. The `registerMonitor` method first calls the `createDelegate` static method on the `Function` class to create a delegate that represents the `Monitor` object's `print` method:

```
this.delegate = Function.createDelegate(this, this.print);
```

Next, the `registerMonitor` method calls the `addHandler` static method on the `DomEvent` class to register the delegate as the event handler for the `document` object's `mousedown` event:

```
$addHandler(document, "mousemove", this.delegate);
```

Next, the `Monitor.js` file defines the `print` instance method of the `Monitor` class. The `print` method takes an argument of type `DomEvent` that represents the event object. The `print` method prints the values of the `clientX` and `clientY` properties of the `DomEvent` object within the opening and closing tags of the `<div>` HTML element:

```
this.div.innerHTML = "X-Coordinate: " + domEvent.clientX + "<br/>" +
                     "Y-Coordinate: " + domEvent.clientY;
```

The `Monitor.js` file then defines the `dispose` method of the `Monitor` class. As discussed earlier, the `dispose` method of a class instance is where the class instance must do the final cleanup before the instance is disposed of. In this case, the `Monitor` object removes the event handler that it registered for the `document` object's `mousemove` event:

```
dispose : function() {
        $removeHandler(document, "mousemove", this.delegate);
    }
```

Next, the `Monitor.js` file registers the `Monitor` class with the ASP.NET AJAX client-side framework. Note that it passes `Sys.IDisposable` as the third argument to the `registerClass` method to inform the framework that the class being registered (the `Monitor` class) implements the `Sys.IDisposable` interface:

```
Disposables.Monitor.registerClass("Disposables.Monitor", null, Sys.IDisposable);
```

As you can see in the following excerpt from Listing 7-2, the `pageLoad` method first creates an instance of the `Monitor` class:

```
var monitor = new Disposables.Monitor();
```

Next, the `pageLoad` method calls the `createDelegate` method on the `Function` class to create a delegate that represents the `dispose` method of the newly created `Monitor` object:

```
var disposeDelegate = Function.createDelegate(monitor, monitor.dispose);
```

Finally, the `pageLoad` method calls the `addHandler` static method on the `DomEvent` class to register the delegate as the event handler for the `click` event of the specified `<button>` DOM element:

```
var btn = $get("btn");
$addHandler(btn, "click", disposeDelegate);
```

When you click the `<button>` HTML element shown in Figure 7-1, the `disposeDelegate` delegate is automatically invoked. The delegate then calls the `dispose` method of the `Monitor` object, which in turn removes the event handler that the `Monitor` object had registered for the `document` object's `mousemove` event. Therefore, after clicking the `<button>` HTML element, the monitor will no longer keep track of the mouse movement.

Figure 7-1

This example explicitly calls the dispose method. This was done for educational purposes. As you'll see later, the ASP.NET AJAX client-side framework provides you with an infrastructure that automatically calls the dispose method of a component when the component is about to be disposed of.

INotifyDisposing

As discussed in the previous section, your ASP.NET AJAX client classes must implement the IDisposable interface to perform final cleanup such as releasing the resources they're holding before they're disposed of. There are times when the client of an instance of an ASP.NET AJAX client class needs to be notified when the instance is about to be disposed of — that is, when the dispose method of the instance is invoked. To address these cases, your ASP.NET AJAX client classes must also implement the INotifyDisposing interface as defined in Listing 7-4. This interface exposes the following two methods:

❑ add_disposing: Your ASP.NET AJAX client class's implementation of this method must register the specified event handler as the callback for the disposing event. Your class must raise this event when its dispose method is invoked.

❑ remove_disposing: Your ASP.NET AJAX client class's implementation of this method must remove the specified event handler from the list of event handlers registered for the disposing event.

Listing 7-4: The INotifyDisposing Interface

```
Sys.INotifyDisposing = function Sys$INotifyDisposing() {
  throw Error.notImplemented();
}

function Sys$INotifyDisposing$add_disposing(handler) {
  throw Error.notImplemented();
}
```

```
function Sys$INotifyDisposing$remove_disposing(handler) {
  throw Error.notImplemented();
}

Sys.INotifyDisposing.prototype = {
  add_disposing: Sys$INotifyDisposing$add_disposing,
  remove_disposing: Sys$INotifyDisposing$remove_disposing
}

Sys.INotifyDisposing.registerInterface("Sys.INotifyDisposing");
```

Listing 7-5 presents the content of the new version of the Monitor.js JavaScript file for the new version of the Monitor class that implements the INotifyDisposing interface.

Listing 7-5: The new version of the Monitor.js JavaScript file

```
Type.registerNamespace("Disposables");

Disposables.Monitor = function() {
  this.div = document.createElement("div");
  document.body.insertBefore(this.div,document.forms[0]);
  this.registerMonitor();
}

Disposables.Monitor.prototype =
{
  registerMonitor : function() {
    this.delegate = Function.createDelegate(this, this.print);
    $addHandler(document, "mousemove", this.delegate);
  },

  print : function(domEvent) {
    this.div.innerHTML = "X-Coordinate: " + domEvent.clientX + "<br/>" +
                         "Y-Coordinate: " + domEvent.clientY;
  },

  dispose : function() {
    if (this.events) {
      var handler = this.events.getHandler("disposing");
      if (handler)
        handler(this, Sys.EventArgs.Empty);
    }

    delete this.events;
    $removeHandler(document, "mousemove", this.delegate);
  },
```

(continued)

Listing 7-5 *(continued)*

```
get_events : function() {
  if (!this.events)
    this.events = new Sys.EventHandlerList();
  return this.events;
},

add_disposing : function(handler) {
  this.get_events().addHandler("disposing", handler);
},

remove_disposing : function(handler) {
  this.get_events().removeHandler("disposing", handler);
}
}

Disposables.Monitor.registerClass("Disposables.Monitor", null,
                                  Sys.IDisposable,
                                  Sys.INotifyDisposing);
if(typeof(Sys)!=='undefined')
  Sys.Application.notifyScriptLoaded();
```

As you can see in this listing, the new version of the Monitor class implements the following three new methods:

❑ get_events: This method returns a reference to an EventHandlerList object. This object will be used to store the JavaScript functions that the Monitor object's clients register as event handlers for the events the Monitor class exposes. Currently the Monitor class exposes a single event: disposing.

```
get_events : function() {
  if (!this.events)
    this.events = new Sys.EventHandlerList();
  return this.events;
}
```

❑ add_disposing: This method provides the Monitor class's implementation of the add_disposing method of the INotifyDisposing interface. This method calls the addHandler method on the EventHandlerList object (this.events) to register the specified handler for the disposing event:

```
add_disposing : function(handler) {
  this.get_events().addHandler("disposing", handler);
}
```

❑ remove_disposing: This method provides the Monitor class's implementation of the remove_disposing method of the INotifyDisposing interface. This method calls the removeHandler method on the EventHandlerList object to remove the specified handler:

```
remove_disposing : function(handler) {
  this.get_events().removeHandler("disposing", handler);
}
```

Listing 7-6 presents a page that uses the new version of the Monitor class. Note that the pageLoad method calls the Monitor object's add_disposing method to register the disposingcb JavaScript function as the event handler for the object's disposing event:

```
monitor.add_disposing(disposingcb);
```

When you click the Dispose Monitor button to call the Monitor object's dispose method, it automatically invokes the disposingcb JavaScript function.

Listing 7-6: A Page that Uses the New Version of the Monitor Class

```
<%@ Page Language="C#" %>

<!DOCTYPE html PUBLIC "-//W3C//DTD XHTML 1.0 Transitional//EN"
"http://www.w3.org/TR/xhtml1/DTD/xhtml1-transitional.dtd">

<html xmlns="http://www.w3.org/1999/xhtml">
<head runat="server">
  <title>Untitled Page</title>
  <script type="text/javascript" language="javascript">
    function disposingcb()
    {
      alert("The Disposing event was raised!");
    }

    function pageLoad()
    {
      var monitor = new Disposables.Monitor();
      monitor.add_disposing(disposingcb);
      var btn = $get("btn");
      var disposeDelegate = Function.createDelegate(monitor, monitor.dispose);
      $addHandler(btn, "click", disposeDelegate);
    }
  </script>
</head>
<body>
  <form id="form1" runat="server">
    <asp:ScriptManager ID="ScriptManager1" runat="server">
```

(continued)

Listing 7-6 *(continued)*

```
    <Scripts>
      <asp:ScriptReference Path="Monitor.js" />
    </Scripts>
  </asp:ScriptManager>

  <button id="btn" type="button">Dispose Monitor</button>
  <div>
  </div>
 </form>
</body>
</html>
```

INotifyPropertyChanged

If the clients of an instance of your ASP.NET AJAX client class need to be notified when one or more of the properties of the instance change value, your class must implement the INotifyPropertyChange interface as defined in Listing 7-7.

Listing 7-7: The INotifyPropertyChanged Interface

```
Sys.INotifyPropertyChange = function Sys$INotifyPropertyChange() {
  throw Error.notImplemented();
}

function Sys$INotifyPropertyChange$add_propertyChanged(handler) {
  throw Error.notImplemented();
}

function Sys$INotifyPropertyChange$remove_propertyChanged(handler) {
  throw Error.notImplemented();
}

Sys.INotifyPropertyChange.prototype = {
  add_propertyChanged: Sys$INotifyPropertyChange$add_propertyChanged,
  remove_propertyChanged: Sys$INotifyPropertyChange$remove_propertyChanged
}

Sys.INotifyPropertyChange.registerInterface('Sys.INotifyPropertyChange');
```

As you can see, the INotifyPropertyChange interface exposes the following two methods:

❏ add_propertyChanged: Your ASP.NET AJAX client class's implementation of this method must register the specified handler as the event handler for the propertyChanged event. Your class must raise this event when one of its properties changes value.

❑   remove_propertyChanged: Your ASP.NET AJAX client class's implementation of this method must remove the specified handler from the list of handlers registered for the propertyChanged event.

Listing 7-8 presents the new version of the Monitor.js JavaScript file that contains a new version of the Monitor class. This class implements the INotifyPropertyChange interface to allow its client to register callbacks for its propertyChanged event.

Listing 7-8: A New Version of the Monitor.js File

```
Type.registerNamespace("Disposables");

Disposables.Monitor = function() {
  this.id="Monitor1";
  this.div = document.createElement("div");
  document.body.insertBefore(this.div,document.forms[0]);
  this.registerMonitor();
}

Disposables.Monitor.prototype =
{
  registerMonitor : function() {
    this.delegate = Function.createDelegate(this, this.print);
    $addHandler(document, "mousemove", this.delegate);
  },

  print : function(domEvent) {
    this.div.innerHTML = "Monitor id: " + this.get_id() + "<br/>" +
                         "X-Coordinate: " + domEvent.clientX + "<br/>" +
                         "Y-Coordinate: " + domEvent.clientY;
  },

  dispose : function()
  {
    if (this.events) {
      var handler = this.events.getHandler("disposing");
      if (handler)
        handler(this, Sys.EventArgs.Empty);
    }

    delete this.events;
    $removeHandler(document, "mousemove", this.delegate);
  },
```

(continued)

Listing 7-8 *(continued)*

```
  get_events : function() {
    if (!this.events)
      this.events = new Sys.EventHandlerList();
    return this.events;
  },

  add_disposing : function(handler) {
    this.get_events().addHandler("disposing", handler);
  },

  remove_disposing : function(handler) {
    this.get_events().removeHandler("disposing", handler);
  },

  add_propertyChanged : function(handler) {
    this.get_events().addHandler("propertyChanged", handler);
  },

  remove_propertyChanged : function(handler) {
    this.get_events().removeHandler("propertyChanged", handler);
  },

  raisePropertyChanged : function (propertyName) {
    if (!this.events)
      return;

    var handler = this.events.getHandler("propertyChanged");
    if (handler)
      handler(this, new Sys.PropertyChangedEventArgs(propertyName));
  },

  get_id : function() {
    return this.id;
  },

  set_id : function(value) {
    this.id = value;
    this.raisePropertyChanged("id");
  }
}

Disposables.Monitor.registerClass("Disposables.Monitor", null,
                                  Sys.IDisposable,
                                  Sys.INotifyDisposing,
                                  Sys.INotifyPropertyChange);

if(typeof(Sys)!=='undefined')
  Sys.Application.notifyScriptLoaded();
```

Listing 7-9 presents a page that uses the new version of the Monitor class. Figure 7-2 shows what you'll see in your browser when you access this page. Notice that the page now contains a new text box where you can enter a new value for id property of the Monitor object. Enter a new value and click the Change Property button to change the value of the id property. You should see a pop-up message shown in Figure 7-3, which informs you that the value of the id property has changed.

Listing 7-9: A page that uses new version of the Monitor class that implements the INotifyPropertyChanged interface

```
<%@ Page Language="C#" %>

<!DOCTYPE html PUBLIC "-//W3C//DTD XHTML 1.0 Transitional//EN"
"http://www.w3.org/TR/xhtml1/DTD/xhtml1-transitional.dtd">

<html xmlns="http://www.w3.org/1999/xhtml">
<head runat="server">
  <title>Untitled Page</title>
  <script type="text/javascript" language="javascript">
    var monitor;

    function disposingcb()
    {
      alert("The Disposing event was raised!");
    }

    function propertyChangedcb(sender,e)
    {
      alert(e.get_propertyName() + " property changed!");
    }

    function changeProperty(domEvent)
    {
      var id = $get("id");
      monitor.set_id(id.value);
    }

    function pageLoad()
    {
      monitor = new Disposables.Monitor();
      monitor.add_disposing(disposingcb);
      monitor.add_propertyChanged(propertyChangedcb);
      var disposebtn = $get("disposebtn");
      var disposeDelegate = Function.createDelegate(monitor, monitor.dispose);
      $addHandler(disposebtn, "click", disposeDelegate);
      var changePropertybtn = $get("changePropertybtn");
      $addHandler(changePropertybtn, "click", changeProperty);
    }
  </script>
</head>
<body>
  <form id="form1" runat="server">
    <asp:ScriptManager ID="ScriptManager1" runat="server">
```

(continued)

Listing 7-9 *(continued)*

```
        <Scripts>
          <asp:ScriptReference Path="Monitor.js" />
        </Scripts>
      </asp:ScriptManager>
      Enter new Monitor id: <input type="text" id="id" /> 
      <button id="changePropertybtn" type="button">
        Change Property
      </button><br /><br />
      <button id="disposebtn" type="button">Dispose Monitor</button>
    </form>
  </body>
</html>
```

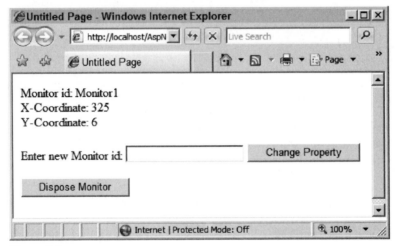

Figure 7-2

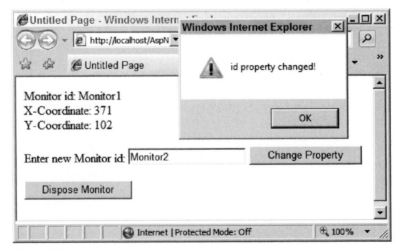

Figure 7-3

The new version of the Monitor class exposes the following five new methods (as shown in Listing 7-8):

❑ add_propertyChanged: This method provides the Monitor class's implementation of the add_propertyChanged method of the INotifyPropertyChange interface. This method calls the addHandler method on the EventHandlerList to register the specified callback as the event handler for the propertyChanged event:

```
add_propertyChanged : function(handler) {
  this.get_events().addHandler("propertyChanged", handler);
},
```

❑ remove_propertyChanged: This method provides the Monitor class's implementation of the remove_propertyChanged method of the INotifyPropertyChange interface. This method calls the removeHandler method on the EventHandlerList to remove the specified handler from the list of handlers registered for the propertyChanged event:

```
remove_propertyChanged : function(handler) {
  this.get_events().removeHandler("propertyChanged", handler);
},
```

❑ raisePropertyChanged: As the name implies, the main responsibility of this method is to raise the propertyChanged event to invoke all event handlers registered for the propertyChanged event. This method instantiates an instance of a class named PropertyChangedEventArgs, passing in the name of the property whose value has changed and passing the instance into the event handler when it invokes the event handler. The PropertyChangedEventArgs class is discussed in more detail later in this section. For now suffice it to say that this class is the event data class for the propertyChanged event.

```
raisePropertyChanged : function (propertyName) {
  if (!this.events)
     return;

  var handler = this.events.getHandler("propertyChanged");
  if (handler)
     handler(this, new Sys.PropertyChangedEventArgs(propertyName));
},
```

❑ get_id: This getter simply returns the value of the id property of the Monitor object:

```
get_id : function() {
  return this.id;
},
```

❑ set_id: This setter takes two steps. First, it assigns the new value to the id property of the Monitor object. Then, it calls the raisePropertyChanged method, passing in the name of the property whose value has changed (which is the id property in this case) to raise the propertyChanged event.

```
        set_id : function(value) {
          this.id = value;
          this.raisePropertyChanged("id");
        }
```

Note that the `pageLoad` method in Listing 7-9 adds the `propertyChangedcb` JavaScript function as the event handler for the `propertyChanged` event of the `Monitor` object:

```
monitor.add_propertyChanged(propertyChangedcb);
```

As the following code snippet shows, the `propertyChangedcb` function simply displays the pop-up message shown previously in Figure 7-3, informing you that the value of the `id` property has changed:

```
function propertyChangedcb(sender,e)
{
  alert(e.get_propertyName() + " property changed!");
}
```

As this code shows, when the `Monitor` object calls the `propertyChangedcb` function, it passes two parameters into it. The first parameter references the `Monitor` object itself, which means that the code inside the `propertyChangedcb` function has complete access to the public methods and properties of the `Monitor` object that raised the event. The second parameter references the `PropertyChangedEventArgs` object that contains the name of the property whose value has changed. As you'll see shortly, the `PropertyChangedEventArgs` class exposes a getter named `get_propertyName` that returns the name of the property whose value has changed.

As the following code snippet from Listing 7-9 shows, the `pageLoad` method adds the `changeProperty` JavaScript function as the event handler for the Change Property button's `click` event:

```
    var changePropertybtn = $get("changePropertybtn");
    $addHandler(changePropertybtn, "click", changeProperty);
```

The `changeProperty` function first retrieves the new value that the end user has entered into the text box and then calls the `set_id` setter method of the `Monitor` object to set the value of the `id` property to the new value:

```
function changeProperty(domEvent)
{
  var id = $get("id");
  monitor.set_id(id.value);
}
```

As discussed earlier, the `set_id` setter calls the `raisePropertyChanged` method to raise the `propertyChanged` event.

Listing 7-10 presents the internal implementation of the `PropertyChangedEventArgs` event data class. As you can see, this class, like any other ASP.NET AJAX event data class, derives from the `EventArgs` base class. It exposes a single method, \ get_propertyName, which returns the name of the property whose value has changed.

Listing 7-10: The Internal Implementation of the PropertyChangedEventArgs Class

```
Sys.PropertyChangedEventArgs =
function Sys$PropertyChangedEventArgs(propertyName)
{
  Sys.PropertyChangedEventArgs.initializeBase(this);
  this._propertyName = propertyName;
}

function Sys$PropertyChangedEventArgs$get_propertyName() {
  return this._propertyName;
}

Sys.PropertyChangedEventArgs.prototype = {
  get_propertyName: Sys$PropertyChangedEventArgs$get_propertyName
}

Sys.PropertyChangedEventArgs.registerClass('Sys.PropertyChangedEventArgs',
                                           Sys.EventArgs);
```

Component

An ASP.NET AJAX client class, such as the Monitor class, implements the IDisposable, INotifyDisposing, and INotifyPropertyChange interfaces to offer the following features:

- ❑ Sys.IDisposable: Implementing this interface enables an instance of the class to perform final cleanup, such as releasing resources that the instance is holding before the instance is disposed of.

- ❑ Sys.INotifyDisposing: Implementing this interface enables an instance of the class to inform its clients when it is about to be disposed of.

- ❑ Sys.INotifyPropertyChange: Implementing this interface enables an instance of the class to inform its clients when a property of the instance changes value.

Because many ASP.NET AJAX client classes need to offer these three features, the ASP.NET AJAX client-side framework includes a base class named Component that implements these three interfaces. Therefore, any ASP.NET AJAX client class that derives from the Component class automatically offers these three features without having to re-implement them.

As Listing 7-11 shows, the Component class implements the IDisposable, INotifyDisposing, and INotifyPropertyChange interfaces. This class simply encapsulates the logic that other ASP.NET AJAX client classes such as Monitor would have to re-implement otherwise.

Listing 7-11: The Component Class

```
Sys.Component = function Sys$Component() {

  // More code to come

}

function Sys$Component$get_events() {
  if (!this._events)
    this._events = new Sys.EventHandlerList();

  return this._events;
}

function Sys$Component$get_id() {
  return this._id;
}

function Sys$Component$set_id(value) {

  // More code to come

  this._id = value;
}

function Sys$Component$add_disposing(handler) {
  this.get_events().addHandler("disposing", handler);
}

function Sys$Component$remove_disposing(handler) {
  this.get_events().removeHandler("disposing", handler);
}

function Sys$Component$add_propertyChanged(handler) {
  this.get_events().addHandler("propertyChanged", handler);
}

function Sys$Component$remove_propertyChanged(handler) {
  this.get_events().removeHandler("propertyChanged", handler);
}

function Sys$Component$dispose() {
  if (this._events) {
    var handler = this._events.getHandler("disposing");
    if (handler)
      handler(this, Sys.EventArgs.Empty);
  }
```

```
    delete this._events;

    // More code to come
}

function Sys$Component$raisePropertyChanged(propertyName) {
    if (!this._events)
        return;

    var handler = this._events.getHandler("propertyChanged");
    if (handler)
        handler(this, new Sys.PropertyChangedEventArgs(propertyName));
}

Sys.Component.prototype = {
    get_events: Sys$Component$get_events,
    get_id: Sys$Component$get_id,
    set_id: Sys$Component$set_id,
    add_disposing: Sys$Component$add_disposing,
    remove_disposing: Sys$Component$remove_disposing,
    add_propertyChanged: Sys$Component$add_propertyChanged,
    remove_propertyChanged: Sys$Component$remove_propertyChanged,
    dispose: Sys$Component$dispose,
    raisePropertyChanged: Sys$Component$raisePropertyChanged,

    // More methods to come
}

Sys.Component.registerClass('Sys.Component', null,
                            Sys.IDisposable,
                            Sys.INotifyPropertyChange,
                            Sys.INotifyDisposing);
```

The Component base class does much more than just implementing the IDisposable, INotifyDisposing, and INotifyPropertyChange interfaces, as you'll see later in this chapter. To help you understand the significance of the Component class, let's revisit a similar situation in the .NET Framework.

All MarshallByRef components in the .NET Framework derive from the .NET Component base class, either directly or indirectly. As a matter of fact, directly or indirectly inheriting this base class is what makes a .NET component a component. In the .NET Framework's jargon, a component is a class that directly or indirectly inherits the .NET Component base class.

The ASP.NET AJAX Component base class plays a similar role in the ASP.NET AJAX client-side framework. An ASP.NET AJAX component is an ASP.NET AJAX client class that directly or indirectly derives from the ASP.NET AJAX Component base class; and deriving directly or indirectly from this base class is what makes an ASP.NET AJAX component a component.

IContainer

All components in the .NET Framework can be contained in a container. Keep in mind that this containment does not have to be a visual containment; it could be a logical containment. The .NET containers that logically or visually contain .NET components implement an interface named IContainer. You can think of this interface as a contract between the .NET components and their containers. This allows the .NET components to be contained in any container as long as the container implements the IContainer interface.

The ASP.NET AJAX client-side framework includes an interface named IContainer that emulates the .NET IContainer interface. ASP.NET AJAX components can be contained in any ASP.NET AJAX container as long as the container implements the ASP.NET AJAX IContainer interface. Keep in mind that this container may or may not be a visual container.

Listing 7-12 presents the definition of the ASP.NET AJAX IContainer interface. This interface exposes the following methods:

❑ addComponent: Adds the specified Component object to the current IContainer object.

❑ removeComponent: Removes the specified Component object from the current IContainer object.

❑ findComponent: Returns a reference to the Component object with the specified id. Keep in mind that each Component object is uniquely identified by its id, which is a string.

❑ getComponents: Returns an array that contains references to all Component objects that the current IContainer object contains.

Listing 7-12: The ASP.NET AJAX IContainer Interface

```
Sys.IContainer = function Sys$IContainer() {
  throw Error.notImplemented();
}

function Sys$IContainer$addComponent(component) {
  throw Error.notImplemented();
}

function Sys$IContainer$removeComponent(component) {
  throw Error.notImplemented();
}

function Sys$IContainer$findComponent(id) {
  throw Error.notImplemented();
}

function Sys$IContainer$getComponents() {
  throw Error.notImplemented();
}
```

```
Sys.IContainer.prototype =
{
    addComponent: Sys$IContainer$addComponent,
    removeComponent: Sys$IContainer$removeComponent,
    findComponent: Sys$IContainer$findComponent,
    getComponents: Sys$IContainer$getComponents
}

Sys.IContainer.registerInterface("Sys.IContainer");
```

Application

The ASP.NET AJAX client-side framework includes an implementation of the IContainer interface named _Application, as shown in Listing 7-13. The name of this class has been prefixed with an underscore to emphasize that the ASP.NET AJAX applications are not allowed to instantiate this class. The ASP.NET AJAX client-side framework automatically instantiates a single instance of the _Application class when an ASP.NET AJAX application is loaded. The framework defines a variable named Sys.Application that references this singular instance of the _Application class:

```
Sys.Application = new Sys._Application();
```

You can use this variable to access this singular instance of the _Application class from within your JavaScript code. As you'll see in next few chapters, this singular instance represents your ASP.NET AJAX application in the ASP.NET AJAX client-side framework.

As you can see in Listing 7-13, The constructor of the _Application class defines and instantiates a dictionary named _components. This is where all the Component objects added to the application will be stored. Note that the _Application class derives from the Component class:

```
Sys._Application.registerClass('Sys._Application', Sys.Component, Sys.IContainer);
```

In other words, the _Application class is a component that acts as a container for other components. This also means that the _Application class inherits the get_events, add_disposing, remove_disposing, add_propertyChanged, remove_propertyChanged, dispose, and raisePropertyChanged methods from the Component base class.

Listing 7-13: The _Application Class

```
Sys._Application = function Sys$_Application() {
    Sys._Application.initializeBase(this);

    this._components = {};

    // More code to come
}

function Sys$_Application$addComponent(component)
{
    // More code to come
}
```

(continued)

Listing 7-13 *(continued)*

```
function Sys$_Application$findComponent(id, parent)
{
  // More code to come
}

function Sys$_Application$getComponents()
{
  // More code to come
}

function Sys$_Application$removeComponent(component)
{
  // More code to come
}

Sys._Application.prototype = {
  addComponent: Sys$_Application$addComponent,
  findComponent: Sys$_Application$findComponent,
  getComponents: Sys$_Application$getComponents,
  removeComponent: Sys$_Application$removeComponent

  // More to class members to come
}

Sys._Application.registerClass('Sys._Application', Sys.Component, Sys.IContainer);
```

As this code listing shows, the `Sys._Application` class implements the `addComponent`, `findComponent`, `getComponents`, and `removeComponent` methods of the `IContainer` interface. The following sections discuss these methods.

addComponent

Listing 7-14 presents the internal implementation of the `addComponent` method of the `_Application` class.

Listing 7-14: The addComponent Method of the _Application Class

```
function Sys$_Application$addComponent(component) {
  var id = component.get_id();
  if (!id)
    throw Error.invalidOperation(Sys.Res.cantAddWithoutId);

  if (typeof(this._components[id]) !== 'undefined')
    throw Error.invalidOperation(String.format(Sys.Res.appDuplicateComponent, id));

  this._components[id] = component;
}
```

This method first calls the `get_id` method on the `Component` object being added to access its `id`:

```
var id = component.get_id();
```

If the `id` of the `Component` object being added has not been specified, the `addComponent` method does not add the `Component` object to the `_components` internal collection; instead, it raises an `InvalidOperation` exception. This means that you must specify the `id` of your component before you attempt to add it to the `_Application`:

```
if (!id)
  throw Error.invalidOperation(Sys.Res.cantAddWithoutId);
```

Next, the `addComponent` method checks whether the `_component` internal dictionary already contains a `Component` object with the specified `id`. If so, it raises an `InvalidOperation` exception, which ensures that all the `Component` objects in the `_Application` have unique `id`s:

```
if (typeof(this._components[id]) !== 'undefined')
  throw Error.invalidOperation(String.format(Sys.Res.appDuplicateComponent, id));
```

Finally, the `addComponent` method uses the `id` of the `Component` object as an index into the `_components` internal dictionary to add the `Component` object to the dictionary:

```
this._components[id] = component;
```

removeComponent

Listing 7-15 contains the code for the `removeComponent` method of the `_Application` class.

Listing 7-15: The removeComponent Method of the _Application Class

```
function Sys$_Application$removeComponent(component) {
  var id = component.get_id();
  if (id)
    delete this._components[id];
}
```

This method first calls the `get_id` method on the `Component` object to access the `id` of the Component object being removed:

```
var id = component.get_id();
```

Next, it uses this id as an index into the `_components` dictionary to return a reference to the `Component` object with the specified id, which is subsequently deleted:

```
delete this._components[id];
```

getComponents

As you can see in Listing 7-16, the getComponents method of the _Application class first creates a local array. Then, it iterates through the Component objects in the _components dictionary and adds each enumerated Component object to this local array, which is then returned to its caller.

Listing 7-16: The getComponents Method of the Application Class

```
function Sys$_Application$getComponents() {
  var res = [];
  var components = this._components;
  for (var name in components)
    res[res.length] = components[name];

  return res;
}
```

findComponent

Listing 7-17 contains the code for the findComponent method of the _Application class. This method takes two arguments. The first argument contains the id of the Component object being searched for. The second argument references the parent of the Component object being searched for.

Listing 7-17: The findComponent Method of the Application Class

```
function Sys$_Application$findComponent(id, parent)
{
 return
    parent ? ( Sys.IContainer.isInstanceOfType(parent) ?
             parent.findComponent(id) : parent[id] || null) :
        Sys.Application._components[id] || null;
}
```

As you can see in this listing, the second argument — the parent — determines where to look for the Component object with the specified id. If the parent hasn't been specified, the findComponent method uses the value of the first argument — the id of the Component object being searched for — as an index into the _components dictionary to return a reference to the Component object with the specified id, as shown in the boldfaced portion of the following code snippet:

```
return
   parent ? ( Sys.IContainer.isInstanceOfType(parent) ?
            parent.findComponent(id) : parent[id] || null) :
        Sys.Application._components[id] || null;
```

If the parent has been specified and the parent itself is a container (that is, the parent implements the IContainer interface), the findComponent method delegates to the findComponent method of the parent as shown in the boldfaced portion of the following code snippet:

```
return
   parent ? ( Sys.IContainer.isInstanceOfType(parent) ?
            parent.findComponent(id) : parent[id] || null) :
        Sys.Application._components[id] || null;
```

If the parent has been specified, but it doesn't implement the `IContainer` interface, the `findComponent` method first assumes that the parent is a DOM element and the `Component` object being searched is its DOM child element. Consequently, it uses the `id` as an index into the parent to return a reference to the `Component` object with the specified `id`:

```
return
    parent ? ( Sys.IContainer.isInstanceOfType(parent) ?
            parent.findComponent(id) : parent[id] || null) :
        Sys.Application._components[id] || null;
```

If the parent is not a DOM element, the `findComponent` method returns `null`.

When you need to call the `findComponent` method to return a reference to a `Component` object with a specified id, you have three options:

❑   If you know for a fact that the component you're looking for is a top-level component (it is directly added to the `Application` object itself), call the `findComponent` method with a single argument that contains the `id` of the component being search for. This will limit the search to the `_components` collection of the `Application` object.

❑   If you know for a fact that the component that you're looking for is not a top-level component (it is not directly added to the `Application` object itself), and if you know which component contains the component that you are searching for, call the `findComponent` method with two arguments. The first argument must contain the `id` of the component being searched for. The second argument must contain a reference to the `Component` object that contains the component being searched for. This will limit the search to the components contained in the specified `Component` object.

❑   If you know for a fact that the component that you're looking for is a child component of a DOM element, call the `findComponent` method with two arguments. The first argument must contain the `id` of the component you're searching for. The second argument must contain a reference to the DOM element that contains the component. This will limit the search to the components contained in the specified DOM element.

Application Lifecycle

The application lifecycle begins when the `Application` object representing the application springs into life and ends when this object is finally disposed of. To help you identify the constituent phases of the application lifecycle, this section follows the `Application` object from the time it is instantiated to the time it is disposed of.

The instance of the `_Application` class, like the instance of any other class, is created when the constructor of the class is invoked. This happens when the `MicrosoftAjax.js` JavaScript file is loaded into the memory of the browser. This file includes the following statement, which invokes the constructor of the `_Application` class:

```
Sys.Application = new Sys._Application();
```

Listing 7-18 presents the internal implementation of the _Application class constructor.

Listing 7-18: The Constructor of the _Application Class

```
Sys._Application = function Sys$_Application() {
  Sys._Application.initializeBase(this);

  this._disposableObjects = [];
  this._components = {};
  this._createdComponents = [];
  this._secondPassComponents = [];

  this._unloadHandlerDelegate = Function.createDelegate(this, this._unloadHandler);
  this._loadHandlerDelegate = Function.createDelegate(this, this._loadHandler);

  Sys.UI.DomEvent.addHandler(window, "unload", this._unloadHandlerDelegate);
  Sys.UI.DomEvent.addHandler(window, "load", this._loadHandlerDelegate);
}
```

This constructor takes the following actions:

1. It calls the initializeBase method, passing in the reference to the Application object to initialize the Component class, which is the base class of the _Application class:.

```
Sys._Application.initializeBase(this);
```

2. It defines and instantiates an internal array named _disposableObjects:

```
this._disposableObjects = [];
```

As the name implies, this collection contains disposable objects of an ASP.NET AJAX application. A disposable object is an object whose type implements the IDisposable interface. As you'll see later, when the Application object is about to be disposed of, it automatically calls the dispose methods of these disposable objects to allow them to release the resources they're holding. Therefore, if you have a disposable object, you must add your object to the _disposableObjects collection to have the Application object call its dispose method before the object is disposed of.

3. It defines and instantiates an internal dictionary named _components:

```
this._components = {};
```

As discussed earlier in this chapter, the _components dictionary contains all the components of an ASP.NET AJAX application.

4. It defines and instantiates an internal array named _createdComponents (discussed in more detail later in this chapter):

```
this._createdComponents = [];
```

5. It defines and instantiates an internal array named _secondPassComponents (discussed in more detail later in this chapter):

```
this._secondPassComponents = [];
```

6. It calls the createDelegate method on the Function class to create a delegate named _unloadHandlerDelegate that represents the Application object's _unloadHandler method:

```
this._unloadHandlerDelegate = Function.createDelegate(this, this._unloadHandler);
```

7. It registers the _unloadHandlerDelegate delegate as an event handler for the window object's unload event:

```
Sys.UI.DomEvent.addHandler(window, "unload", this._unloadHandlerDelegate);
```

This means that when the current window unloads, it automatically calls the _unloadHandlerDelegate delegate, which in turn calls the Application object's _unloadHandler method to allow the application to unload itself. (The _unloadHandler method is discussed in more detail later in this chapter.)

8. It calls the createDelegate method on the Function class to create a delegate named _loadHandlerDelegate that represents the Application object's _loadHandler method:

```
this._loadHandlerDelegate = Function.createDelegate(this, this._loadHandler);
```

9. It registers the _loadHandlerDelegate delegate as an event handler for the window object's load event:

```
Sys.UI.DomEvent.addHandler(window, "load", this._loadHandlerDelegate);
```

This means that when the window object's load event is raised, the _loadHandlerDelegate delegate is automatically invoked. This delegate in turn automatically invokes the Application object's _loadHandler method to allow the application to load itself. (The _loadHandler method is discussed in more detail later in this section.)

As you can see, the Application object gets instantiated when the MicrosoftAjax.js JavaScript file gets loaded. However, it doesn't get initialized until the window raises the load event and, consequently, the _loadHandler method of the Application object is invoked.

Listing 7-19 presents the implementation of the Application object's _loadHandler method.

Listing 7-19: The _loadHandler Method of the Application Object

```
function Sys$_Application$_loadHandler() {
  if(this._loadHandlerDelegate) {
    Sys.UI.DomEvent.removeHandler(window, "load", this._loadHandlerDelegate);
    this._loadHandlerDelegate = null;
  }
  this.initialize();
}
```

This _loadHandler method calls the Application object's initialize method to initialize the application as shown in Listing 7-20.

Listing 7-20: The initialize Method of the Application Object

```
function Sys$_Application$initialize() {
  if (!this._initialized && !this._initializing) {
    this._initializing = true;
    window.setTimeout(Function.createDelegate(this, this._doInitialize), 0);
  }
}
```

The initialize method first checks whether the current Application object has already been initialized. If so, it simply returns. You may be wondering how the current Application object could be initialized before the window object raises its load event and consequently invokes the _loadHandler method, which in turn invokes the initialize method to initialize the Application. The answer lies in the fact that the _loadHandler method is not the only mechanism that triggers the invocation of the initialize method. As you'll see later in this book, the current ScriptManager server control explicitly renders the following script block into the current page right before the closing tag of the form HTML DOM element (with the runat = server attribute):

```
<script type="text/javascript">
<!--
Sys.Application.initialize();
// -->
</script>
```

As you can see, this script block contains a call into the initialize method of the current Application object. Therefore, there are two initialization mechanisms for the current Application object. As Listing 7-20 shows, the Application object exposes a private Boolean field named _initializing, ensuring that the current Application object does not get initialized twice. Whichever mechanism gets to call the initialize method first gets to initialize the current Application object. In other words, the first caller wins.

Next, the initialize method sets the _initializing field to true to signal that the application is being initialized. Then it calls the setTimeout method on the window object to register the Application object's _doInitialize method to be invoked after a delay of 0 milliseconds. This doesn't mean that the _doInitialize method is invoked right away. The delay of 0 milliseconds is a common trick used in the scripting world to ensure that the execution of the specified method — _doInitialize — is deferred until the document is done with other tasks and ready to execute the method.

Listing 7-21 presents the internal code for the Application object's _doInitialize method.

Listing 7-21: The _doInitialize Method of the Application Object

```
function Sys$_Application$_doInitialize() {
  Sys._Application.callBaseMethod(this, 'initialize');

  var handler = this.get_events().getHandler("init");
  if (handler) {
    this.beginCreateComponents();
    handler(this, Sys.EventArgs.Empty);
    this.endCreateComponents();
  }
  this.raiseLoad();
  this._initializing = false;
}
```

The _doInitialize method first calls `callBaseMethod` to invoke the `initialize` method of the base class, which is the `Component` class:

```
Sys._Application.callBaseMethod(this, 'initialize');
```

Next, the _doInitialize method calls the `get_events` method to access the `EventHandlerList` object that contains all the event handlers registered for the events that the `Application` object exposes. The `_Application` class inherits the `get_events` method from the `Component` class (see Listing 7-13). The _doInitialize method then calls the `getHandler` method on the `EventHandlerList` object, passing the string `"init"` to return a reference to the JavaScript function whose invocation automatically invokes all the event handlers registered for the `Application` object's `init` event:

```
var handler = this.get_events().getHandler("init");
```

The `getHandler` method of the `EventHandlerList` class defines and returns a JavaScript function that iterates through the event handlers registered for a particular type of event and invokes each enumerated event handler, as shown in the highlighted portion of the following code excerpt from Listing 5-7:

```
function Sys$EventHandlerList$getHandler(id) {
  var evt = this._getEvent(id);
  if (!evt || (evt.length === 0))
    return null;
  evt = Array.clone(evt);
  if (!evt._handler) {
    evt._handler = function(source, args) {
      for (var i = 0, l = evt.length; i < l; i++) {
        evt[i](source, args);
      }
    };
  }
  return evt._handler;
}
```

Now back to the implementation of the _doInitialize method in Listing 7-21. If the EventHandlerList object contains event handlers for the init event of the Application object, the _doInitialize method takes the following steps:

1. It calls the beginCreateComponents method of the Application object:

```
this.beginCreateComponents();
```

As the following code snippet shows, the beginCreateComponent method simply sets an internal flag named _creatingComponents to true, to signal that the application has now entered the phase where components of the application are created:

```
function Sys$_Application$beginCreateComponents() {
  this._creatingComponents = true;
}
```

2. It invokes the JavaScript function returned from the EventHandlerList object's getHandler method. As discussed earlier, the invocation of this function automatically invokes all the event handlers registered for the init event of the Application object:

```
handler(this, Sys.EventArgs.Empty);
```

3. It calls the endCreateComponents method. The main responsibility of this method is to set the values of the properties of the components that reference other components (described in more detail later).

```
this.endCreateComponents();
```

As you can see, the Application object raises the init event before the cross references among the components of the application are resolved. As such, the event handler that you register for the init event of the Application object must not attempt to access other components.

4. It calls the raiseLoad method of the Application object to raise the Load event and sets the _initializing flag to false to signal the end of the application initialization process:

```
this.raiseLoad();
this._initializing = false;
```

Component

At this point on the journey through the Application object's life-cycle phases, the endCreateComponents and raiseLoad methods of the Application object have just been invoked. To continue the journey, we need to go inside these two methods. However, understanding the internal implementation of the Application object's endCreateComponents and raiseLoad methods requires a solid understanding of the typical lifecycle of an ASP.NET AJAX application's constituent components. In other words, the journey has reached the point where the application lifecycle overlaps the lifecycles of the constituent components of the application. Therefore, we need to accompany these constituent components on their journey through their life-cycle phases. The Component base class defines the typical lifecycle of an ASP.NET AJAX application's component.

The lifecycle of a component begins when the `create` method of the `Component` base class is invoked to instantiate the component, as shown in Listing 7-22. The main responsibility of the `create` method is to create, initialize, and add a new `Component` object with the specified characteristics to the current ASP.NET AJAX application. An example of a `Component` object is the `Monitor` object discussed earlier in this chapter. As you can see, you must not use the `new` operator directly to create a `Component` object. Instead, you must use the `create` method of the `Component` base class to create the object. This method takes the following parameters:

❏ `type`: Contains a reference to the constructor of the component class whose instance is being created. For example, in the case of the `Monitor` class, you must pass `Delegates.Monitor` as the value of the `type` parameter.

❏ `properties`: References a JavaScript object literal containing name/value pairs. Each of these pairs must specify the name and value of a particular property of the `Component` object being created.

❏ `events`: References a JavaScript object literal containing name/value pairs. Each of these pairs must specify the name and event handlers of a particular event of the `Component` object being created.

❏ `references`: References a JavaScript object literal containing name/value pairs. Each of these pairs must specify the name of the property of the `Component` object being created and the `id` property value of the `Component` object that the property references.

❏ `element`: References the DOM element with which the `Component` object being created is associated. A `Component` object may or may not be associated with a DOM element, as discussed later in this chapter.

Listing 7-22: The create Method of the Component Class

```
var $create = Sys.Component.create =
function Sys$Component$create(type, properties, events, references, element)
{
  var component = (element ? new type(element): new type());

  component.beginUpdate();
  if (properties)
    Sys$Component$_setProperties(component, properties);

  if (events) {
    for (var name in events) {
      var eventHandlers = events[name];
      var addEventHandlerMethodName = "add_" + name;
      var addEventHandlerMethod = component[addEventHandlerMethodName];
      addEventHandlerMethod(eventHandlers);
    }
  }
```

(continued)

Listing 7-22 *(continued)*

```
var createdComLen = Sys.Application._createdComponents.length;      var
elong to differenct object. I add a bit of text to clarify
this.
  Sys.Application._createdComponents[createdComLen] = component;

  if (component.get_id())
    Sys.Application.addComponent(component);

  if (Sys.Application.get_isCreatingComponents()) {
    if (references)
      Sys.Application._addComponentToSecondPass(component, references);

    else
      component.endUpdate();
  }

  else
  {
    if (references)
      Sys$Component$_setReferences(component, references);

    component.endUpdate();
  }

  return component;
}
```

As Listing 7-22 shows, the `create` method of the `Component` class first invokes the `new` operator on its first argument to instantiate the new `Component` object. The instantiation is the first life-cycle phase of the newly created `Component` object. The first argument of the `create` method references the constructor of the component class whose instance is being created. For example, in the case of the `Monitor` class, this argument will reference the constructor of the `Monitor` class. Note that if the `Component` object is associated with a DOM element, the reference to the DOM element is passed into the constructor:

```
var component = (element ? new type(element): new type());
```

Next, the `create` method calls the `beginUpdate` method on the newly created `Component` object:

```
component.beginUpdate();
```

As Listing 7-23 shows, the `beginUpdate` method of the `Component` class sets an internal flag named `_updating` to `true` to mark the beginning of the newly created `Component` object's updating life-cycle phase.

Listing 7-23: The beginUpdate Method of the Component Class

```
function Sys$Component$beginUpdate() {
  this._updating = true;
}
```

Returning to Listing 7-22, the `create` method then calls the `_setProperties` static method on the `Component` base class, passing in two parameters. The first parameter is the reference to the newly created `Component` object. The second parameter is the JavaScript object literal containing the name/value pairs that specify the names and values of the newly created `Component` object properties.

```
if (properties)
   Sys$Component$_setProperties(component, properties);
```

As you'll see later, the main responsibility of the `_setProperties` method is to iterate through the name/value pairs of the object literal and assign the value portion of each pair to the property of the newly created `Component` object with the same name as the name portion of the pair.

Next, the `create` method iterates through the name/value pairs of the object literal and performs the following tasks for each enumerated pair:

1. It uses the event name as an index into the object literal to return all the event handlers for the event with specified name:

```
var eventHandlers = events[name];
```

2. It appends the event name to the string `"add_"` to form a string that contains the name of the newly created `Component` object's method that registers event handlers for the specified event:

```
var addEventHandlerMethodName="add_" + name;
```

For example, the `Monitor` class exposes an event named `disposing`. If you append this event name to the string `"add_"`, you'll end up with a string called `"add_disposing"`, which is the name of the `Monitor` class's `add_disposing` method. This method takes an event handler as its argument and registers the handler as the callback for the `Monitor` class's `disposing` event.

3. It uses the event-handler method name as an index into the newly created `Component` object to access a reference to the method itself:

```
var addEventHandlerMethod = component[addEventHandlerMethodName];
```

In the case of the `Monitor` example, this will return a reference to the `add_disposing` method.

4. It invokes the event-handler method, passing in the event handlers to register them as callbacks for the specified event:

```
addEventHandlerMethod(eventHandlers);
```

As Listing 7-22 shows, the `create` method then adds the newly created `Component` object to the `_createdComponents` collection of the `Application` object:

```
var createdComLen = Sys.Application._createdComponents.length;    var
elong to differenct object. I add a bit of text to clarify
this.
Sys.Application._createdComponents[createdComLen] = component;
```

This collection temporarily contains all the newly created `Component` objects. As you'll see later, when the application enters the `Load` phase of its lifecycle, it raises the `load` event and consequently invokes

251

all event handlers registered for this event, passing the _createdComponents collection. This allows the event handlers to customize the newly created Component objects. This is very similar to the ItemCreated event of the GridView control, where the event handlers for this event can update the newly created GridViewRow object.

The create method then calls the Application object's addComponent method to add the newly created component to the Application object's _components collection, where the component is permanently stored until it is explicitly disposed of:

```
if (component.get_id())
    Sys.Application.addComponent(component);
```

Next, the create method calls the get_isCreatingComponents method on the Application object to access the value of its _creatingComponents field: The Application object sets this field to true to mark the beginning of the Component Creation phase of the current ASP.NET AJAX application.

If the application has already entered the Component Creation phase of its lifecycle, and the JavaScript object literal passed in as the fourth argument of the create method is not null, the create method calls the _addComponentToSecondPass method on the Application object, passing in the reference to the newly created Component object and the reference to the object literal:

```
Sys.Application._addComponentToSecondPass(component, references);
```

As Listing 7-24 shows, the _addComponentToSecondPass method of the _Application class simply creates a new object literal that contains two name/value pairs. The first name/value pair contains the name "component" and the value referencing the newly created Component object. The second name/value pair contains the name "references" and the value referencing the object literal passed in as the second argument of the _addComponentToSecondPass method. Each name/value pair of this object literal contains the name of a property of the newly created Component object and the value of the id property of another Component object that the property references.

Listing 7-24: The _addComponentToSecondPass method of the Application object

```
function Sys$_Application$_addComponentToSecondPass(component, references) {
    this._secondPassComponents[this._secondPassComponents.length] =
                        {component: component, references: references};
}
```

As this listing shows, the _addComponentToSecondPass method then adds the new object literal to the _secondPassComponents collection of the Application object to be processed later. As you'll see later, the endCreateComponents method of the Application object will process the contents of the _secondPassComponents collection.

Now back to the implementation of the create method in Listing 7-22. As this code listing shows, if the Application is in the Component Creation phase, but the object passed into the create method as the fourth argument is null, the create method calls the endUpdate method on the newly created Component object:

```
component.endUpdate();
```

Listing 7-25 shows the Component class's endUpdate method. This method first sets an internal flag named _updating to false to mark the end of the newly created Component object's updating life-cycle phase, and then calls the updated method of the object.

Listing 7-25: The endUpdate Method of the Component Class

```
function Sys$Component$endUpdate() {
  this._updating = false;
  if (!this._initialized)
    this.initialize();

  this.updated();
}
```

As Listing 7-26 shows, the updated method of the Component class doesn't do anything. However, your custom component can override this method to perform post-update tasks.

Listing 7-26: The updated Method of the Component Class

```
function Sys$Component$updated() { }
```

Returning to Listing 7-22, if the Application is not in its Component Creation life-cycle phase, and the object passed into the create method as its fourth argument is not null (that is, if the newly created Component object contains properties that reference other components of the application), the create method calls the _setReferences static method, passing in the reference to the newly created Component object and the fourth parameter:

```
Sys$Component$_setReferences(component, references);
```

As you'll see later, the main responsibility of the _setReferences method is to access references to the referenced Component objects and assign them to the associated properties of the newly created Component object.

Finally, the create method calls the endUpdate method on the newly created Component object:

```
component.endUpdate();
```

Continuing the Application Journey

Now that you have a solid understanding of the typical lifecycle of an ASP.NET AJAX component, let's go back to the endCreateComponents and raiseLoad methods of the Application object to finish the journey with Application.

endCreateComponents

Listing 7-27 presents the internal implementation of the endCreateComponents method of the Application object.

Listing 7-27: The endCreateComponents Method of the Application Object

```
function Sys$_Application$endCreateComponents() {
    var components = this._secondPassComponents;
    for (var i = 0, l = components.length; i < l; i++) {
        var component = components[i].component;
        var references = components[i].references;
        Sys$Component$_setReferences(component, references);
        component.endUpdate();
    }
    this._secondPassComponents = [];
    this._creatingComponents = false;
}
```

As you saw previously in Listing 7-18, the constructor of the _Application class instantiates an internal array named _secondPassComponents:

```
this._secondPassComponents = [];
```

This array contains all the Component objects that meet the following two requirements:

❏ They were created before the endCreateComponents method of the Application object was invoked.

❏ They contain properties that reference other Component objects in the application.

As discussed in the previous section, the Component base class exposes a method named create that allows you to create, initialize, and add a new Component object to your ASP.NET AJAX application. If you call this method within an event handler registered for the init event of the Application object, and if the newly created Component object references other Component objects, the create method automatically adds the newly created Component object to the _secondPassComponents array of the Application object because the newly created Component object meets both of the previously mentioned requirements:

❏ It was created before the calls into the endCreateComponents method because the init event occurs before the endCreateComponents method is invoked (as previously shown in Listing 7-21).

❏ It contains properties that reference other Component objects.

The create method of the Component class calls the _addComponentToSecondPass method on the Application object to add the newly created component to the _secondPassComponents array (as previously shown in Listing 7-22). The _addComponentToSecondPass method of the _Application class simply creates a new object literal that contains two name/value pairs (as previously shown in Listing 7-24). The first name/value pair contains the name "component" and the value referencing the newly created Component object. The second name/value pair contains the name "references" and the value referencing the object passed in as the second argument of the _addComponentToSecondPass method. The _addComponentToSecondPass method then adds the new object literal to the _secondPassComponents collection of the Application object:

```
function Sys$_Application$_addComponentToSecondPass(component, references) {
    this._secondPassComponents[this._secondPassComponents.length] =
                    {component: component, references: references};
}
```

Therefore, the _secondPassComponents array contains a bunch of object literals with two name/value pairs as just described.

Now back to Listing 7-27. As this code listing shows, the endCreateComponents method iterates through the objects in the _secondPassComponents array and takes the following steps for each enumerated object literal:

1. It accesses the value portion of the first name/value pair of the enumerated object. This value references the newly created Component object as follows:

```
var component = components[i].component;
```

2. It accesses the value portion of the second name/value pair of the enumerated object. This value portion references the object literal that contains a name/value pair for each property of the newly created Component object and the id of another Component object that the property references:

```
var references = components[i].references;
```

3. It calls the _setReferences static method on the Component base class, passing in two arguments. The first argument references the newly created Component object, and the second argument references the object literal just discussed:

```
Sys$Component$_setReferences(component, references);
```

The main responsibility of the _setReferences method is to iterate through the name/value pairs of the object literal, find a reference to the Component object whose id is given by the value portion of the enumerated name/value pair, and assign this reference to the property whose name is given by the name portion of the enumerated name/value pair.

4. It calls the endUpdate method on the newly-created Component object:

```
component.endUpdate();
```

Finally, the endCreateComponents method first resets the _secondPassComponents array and then sets the _creatingComponents flag to false to mark the end of the application's Component Creation lifecycle phase:

```
this._secondPassComponents = [];
this._creatingComponents = false;
```

raiseLoad

The call into the raiseLoad method of the Application object is the last phase in its initialization process. Listing 7-28 shows this method.

Listing 7-28: The raiseLoad Method of the Application Object

```
function Sys$_Application$raiseLoad() {
  var h = this.get_events().getHandler("load");
  var args = new Sys.ApplicationLoadEventArgs(Array.clone(this._createdComponents),
                                              !this._initializing);

  if (h)
    h(this, args);

  if (window.pageLoad)
    window.pageLoad(this, args);

  this._createdComponents = [];
}
```

As this listing shows, the raiseLoad method calls the get_events method to access a reference to the EventHandlerList that contains all the event handlers registered for the events that the Application object exposes. Then, it calls the getHandler method on the EventHandlerList, passing in the string "load" to access the JavaScript function whose invocation automatically invokes all the event handlers registered for the load event of the Application object:

```
var h = this.get_events().getHandler("load");
```

The raiseLoad method then instantiates an instance of a class named ApplicationLoadEventArgs, passing in the contents of an internal array named _createdComponents that contains all the newly created Component objects:

```
var args = new Sys.ApplicationLoadEventArgs(Array.clone(this._createdComponents),
                                            !this._initializing);
```

As you saw in the previous sections, the create method of the Component class adds the newly created Component object to the _createdComponents array.

Next, the raiseLoad method invokes the JavaScript function returned from the getHandler method:

```
if (h)
  h(this, args);
```

If your event handler for the Application object's init event registers an event handler for that object's load event, the event handler will be invoked automatically at this phase, which means that your event handler will have access to the contents of the _createdComponents array. This enables you to access the newly created Component objects inside your event handler for the load event and customize the component. This is similar to the OnItemCreated event of the GridView and DetailsView controls.

The `raiseLoad` method then invokes the `pageLoad` method on the `window` object:

```
if (window.pageLoad)
   window.pageLoad(this, args);
```

Finally, the `raiseLoad` method resets the `_createdComponents` array:

```
this._createdComponents = [];
```

Summary of the Application Lifecycle

As the discussions in the previous sections show, an ASP.NET AJAX application goes through the following life-cycle phases:

1. **Instantiation Phase:** This is the first phase of an ASP.NET AJAX application lifecycle. This is the phase where the constructor of the `_Application` class is invoked to do the following:

    1. Instantiate the `Application` object that represents the ASP.NET AJAX application.

    2. Instantiate the `_disposableObjects` array that will contain the disposable objects of the application.

    3. Instantiate the `_components` collection that will contain the components of the application.

    4. Register the `_loadHandler` method as the event handler for the `load` event of the `window` object.

    5. Register the `_unloadHandler` method as the event handler for the `unload` event of the `window` object.

2. **Beginning of the Initialization Phase:** This phase occurs after the instantiation phase when either the `window` object raises the `load` event and consequently calls the `_loadHandler` method or the following script block gets executed:

```
<script type="text/javascript">
<!--
Sys.Application.initialize();
// -->
</script>
```

   Here is what happens in this phase:

    1. An internal flag named `_initializing` is set to `true` to mark the beginning of the initialization phase of the application.

    2. The `_doInitialize` method is queued for execution.

3. **Beginning of the Component Creation phase:** This is the phase where the `beginCreateComponents` method of the `Application` object is invoked. As discussed earlier, this method simply sets an internal flag named `_creatingComponents` to `true` to mark the beginning of the Component Creation lifecycle phase.

4. **Raising the Init Event:** This phase occurs immediately after the application enters the Component Creation phase. This is the phase where the application raises the `init` event and consequently invokes all the event handlers registered for this event. Because the application

has just entered the component creation phase, the cross references among the components of the application have not been resolved yet. As such, the event handlers that you register for the init event of the Application object must not access other components of the application.

5. **End of the Component Creation Phase:** This phase occurs right after all the event handlers for the init event of the Application have been invoked. This is the phase where the endCreateComponents method of the Application object is invoked to resolve the cross references among the constituent components of an ASP.NET AJAX application.

6. **Load Phase:** This phase occurs after all the cross references among the constituent components of an ASP.NET AJAX application have been resolved. This is the phase where the raiseLoad method of the Application object is invoked. Here is what happens in this phase:

   1. The application raises the load event and consequently invokes all the event handlers registered for the load event. The Application object passes an ApplicationLoadEventArgs object into each event handler. This object contains the contents of the Application object's _createdComponents array. The create static method of the Component base class adds the newly created Component object to this array, which means that you can access the newly created Component objects from within your load event handler to customize them. This is very similar to the ItemCreated event of the GridView, which allows you to customize the GridViewRow objects right after they're created.

      Because the load event is raised after all the cross references among the constituent components of an application are resolved, you can safely access any component of the application from within your load event handler.

   2. If a page contains the pageLoad method, this method is invoked right after the load event is raised.

   3. The _createdComponents array is reset.

Application Level Events

The Application object that represents an ASP.NET AJAX application exposes three important events, as discussed in the following sections.

init

The Application object features a method named add_init that allows you to register a specified event handler for the init event of the Application object as shown in Listing 7-29.

Listing 7-29: The add_init Method of the Application Object

```
function Sys$_Application$add_init(handler) {
  if (this._initialized)
    handler(this, Sys.EventArgs.Empty);

  else
    this.get_events().addHandler("init", handler);
}
```

As you can see in this code listing, the `add_init` method first checks whether the `Application` object has already raised the `init` event. The `init` event is raised only once in the lifetime of an ASP.NET AJAX application, as discussed earlier. If the `init` event has already been raised, the `add_init` method does not add the event handler being registered to the internal `EventHandlerList`. This is because when an event handler is added to the `EventHandlerList`, it will not be invoked until the associated event is raised. In this case, because the `init` event has already been raised, the event handler will remain in the `EventHandlerList` forever without ever being invoked. That is why the `add_init` method invokes the event handler being registered synchronously:

```
if (this._initialized)
   handler(this, Sys.EventArgs.Empty);
```

However, if the event handler is added before the `Application` raises the `init` event, the `add_init` method first calls the `get_events` method to return a reference to the internal `EventHandlerList` and then calls the `addHandler` method on the `EventHandlerList` to register the event handler for the `init` event of the `Application` object:

```
else
   this.get_events().addHandler("init", handler);
```

The `Application` object also exposes a method named `remove_init`, shown in Listing 7-30, that allows you to remove a specified event handler from the list of event handlers registered for the `Application` object's `init` event.

Listing 7-30: The remove_init Method of the Application Object

```
function Sys$_Application$remove_init(handler) {
   this.get_events().removeHandler("init", handler);
}
```

load

You can use the `add_load` and `remove_load` methods of the `Application` object to add a specified event handler to and remove a specified event handler from the list of event handlers registered for the `Application` object's `load` event, as shown in Listing 7-31.

Listing 7-31: The add_load and remove_load Methods of the Application Object

```
function Sys$_Application$add_load(handler) {
   this.get_events().addHandler("load", handler);
}

function Sys$_Application$remove_load(handler) {
   this.get_events().removeHandler("load", handler);
}
```

unload

The `Application` object's `add_unload` and `remove_unload` methods allow you to add a specified event handler to and remove a specified event handler from the list of event handlers registered for the `Application` object's `unload` event of, as shown in Listing 7-32.

Listing 7-32: The add_unload and remove_unload Methods of the Application Object

```
function Sys$_Application$add_unload(handler) {
  this.get_events().addHandler("unload", handler);
}

function Sys$_Application$remove_unload(handler) {
  this.get_events().removeHandler("unload", handler);
}
```

Disposable Objects

As shown in the following code snippet from Listing 7-18, the constructor of the `_Application` class defines and instantiates an array named `_disposableObjects`:

```
this._disposableObjects = [];
```

A disposable object is an instance of a class that implements the `IDisposable` interface. Recall that the `IDisposable` interface exposes a single method named `dispose` that must be implemented by classes that derive from this interface. A class's implementation of the `dispose` method must release the resources that the instance of the class is holding before the instance is disposed of. The `Application` object that represents an ASP.NET AJAX application guarantees to call the `dispose` method of your disposable objects before these objects are disposed of if you call the `registerDisposableObject` method on the `Application` object to register your disposable object.

As you can see in Listing 7-33, the `registerDisposableObject` method adds the disposable object to the internal `_disposableObjects` array.

Listing 7-33: The registerDisposableObject Method of the Application Object

```
function Sys$_Application$registerDisposableObject(object) {
  if (!this._disposing)
    this._disposableObjects[this._disposableObjects.length] = object;
}
```

As shown in the following code snippet from Listing 7-18, the constructor of the `_Application` class calls the `createDelegate` method on the `Function` class to create a delegate that represents the `Application` object's `_unloadHandler` method and registers this delegate as the event handler for the `window` object's `unload` event:

```
this._unloadHandlerDelegate = Function.createDelegate(this, this._unloadHandler);
Sys.UI.DomEvent.addHandler(window, "unload", this._unloadHandlerDelegate);
```

When the `window` object finally raises the `unload` event, it automatically calls the `_unloadHandlerDelegate` delegate, which in turn calls the `Application` object's `_unloadHandler` method.

Listing 7-34 presents the implementation of the `_unloadHandler` method.

Listing 7-34: The _unloadHandler Method of the Application Object

```
function Sys$_Application$_unloadHandler(event) {
  this.dispose();
}
```

As you can see, the `_unloadHandler` method calls the `dispose` method on the `Application` object to dispose of the object. Listing 7-35 presents the implementation of the `Application` object's `dispose` method.

Listing 7-35: The dispose Method of the Application Object

```
function Sys$_Application$dispose()
{
  if (!this._disposing)
  {
    this._disposing = true;

    if (window.pageUnload)
      window.pageUnload(this, Sys.EventArgs.Empty);

    var unloadHandler = this.get_events().getHandler("unload");
    if (unloadHandler)
      unloadHandler(this, Sys.EventArgs.Empty);

    var disposableObjects = Array.clone(this._disposableObjects);
    for (var i = 0, l = disposableObjects.length; i < l; i++)
      disposableObjects[i].dispose();

    Array.clear(this._disposableObjects);

    Sys.UI.DomEvent.removeHandler(window, "unload", this._unloadHandlerDelegate);
    if(this._loadHandlerDelegate)
    {
      Sys.UI.DomEvent.removeHandler(window, "load", this._loadHandlerDelegate);
      this._loadHandlerDelegate = null;
    }

    var sl = Sys._ScriptLoader.getInstance();
    if(sl)
      sl.dispose();

    Sys._Application.callBaseMethod(this, 'dispose');
  }
}
```

The `dispose` method first sets an internal flag named `_disposing` to `true` to ensure that the `dispose` method is not called more than once during the lifetime of the current ASP.NET AJAX application:

```
this._disposing = true;
```

Next, it checks whether the `window` object contains a method named `pageUnload`. If so, it invokes this method:

```
if (window.pageUnload)
    window.pageUnload(this, Sys.EventArgs.Empty);
```

Next, it calls the `get_events` method on the `Application` object to return a reference to the internal `EventHandlerList` that contains all the event handlers registered for the events of the `Application` object. It then calls the `getHandler` method on the `EventHandlerList` object, passing in the string "unload" to return a reference to the JavaScript function whose invocation automatically invokes all the event handlers registered for the `unload` event of the `Application` object:

```
var unloadHandler = this.get_events().getHandler("unload");
```

Next, it invokes this JavaScript function to invoke the associated event handlers:

```
if (unloadHandler)
    unloadHandler(this, Sys.EventArgs.Empty);
```

As you can see, you have two options when it comes to handling the `unload` event of the `Application` object. One option is to implement a JavaScript function named `pageUnload`. When the `dispose` method of the `Application` object invokes the `pageUnload` method, it passes a reference to the `Application` object raising the event, which means that you can use this reference to access the methods and properties of the `Application` object that represents the current ASP.NET AJAX application. Another option is to call the `add_unload` method on the `Application` object to register an event handler for the `unload` event.

As the following code snippet from Listing 7-35 shows, the `dispose` method then iterates through the disposable objects in the `_disposableObjects` collection and invokes the `dispose` method on each enumerated disposable object. The `dispose` method of a disposable object must perform final cleanup and release all the resources the object is holding.

```
var disposableObjects = Array.clone(this._disposableObjects);
for (var i = 0, l = disposableObjects.length; i < l; i++)
    disposableObjects[i].dispose();
```

Next, it calls the `clear` static method on the `Array` class to clear the `_disposableObjects` collection and consequently dispose these objects:

```
Array.clear(this._disposableObjects);
```

As you can see, the `Application` object disposes the disposable objects only after it invokes their `dispose` method — that is, only after these objects get the chance to perform their final cleanup and to release the resources they're holding.

The `dispose` method then performs its final cleanup and releases the resources that the application is holding. In this case, it unregisters the `_unloadHandlerDelegate` and `_loadHandlerDelgate` event handlers (which the constructor of the `_Application` class previously registered for the `unload` and `load` events of the `window` object):

```
Sys.UI.DomEvent.removeHandler(window, "unload", this._unloadHandlerDelegate);
if(this._loadHandlerDelegate)
{
  Sys.UI.DomEvent.removeHandler(window, "load", this._loadHandlerDelegate);
  this._loadHandlerDelegate = null;
}
```

Next, the `dispose` method of Application calls the `dispose` method of the `_ScriptLoader` object to allow this object to release the resources it is holding:

```
var sl = Sys._ScriptLoader.getInstance();
if(sl)
  sl.dispose();
```

Finally, the `dispose` method of Application invokes the `dispose` method of its base class, which in this case is the `Component` class. Your custom class's implementation of the `dispose` method must always invoke the `dispose` method of its base class before it returns to allow the base class to perform its final cleanup and to release the resources it is holding. You must call the following method at the end of the `dispose` method of your class — that is, after your class releases the resources it is holding:

```
Sys._Application.callBaseMethod(this, 'dispose');
```

There are times when you may decide to unregister your disposable object. This is where the `Application` object's `unregisterDisposableObject` method comes into play, as shown in Listing 7-36.

Listing 7-36: The unregisterDisposableObject Method of the Application Object

```
function Sys$_Application$unregisterDisposableObject(object) {
  if (!this._disposing)
    Array.remove(this._disposableObjects, object);
}
```

Using the Application Object and Component Base Class

The previous sections of this chapter provided you with in-depth coverage of the important methods and events of the `Application` object and `Component` base class. This section shows you how to use the `Application` object and `Component` base class and their methods and events in your own ASP.NET AJAX applications. The example presented in this section is a new version of the `Monitor` class discussed earlier in this chapter. The following sections go over the old version of this class to point out the differences between the old and new versions and the logic behind these differences.

dispose

Listing 7-26 took extra steps to emulate a `disposing` event, as shown in the highlighted portions of the following code:

```
<%@ Page Language="C#" %>

<!DOCTYPE html PUBLIC "-//W3C//DTD XHTML 1.0 Transitional//EN"
"http://www.w3.org/TR/xhtml1/DTD/xhtml1-transitional.dtd">

<html xmlns="http://www.w3.org/1999/xhtml">
<head runat="server">
  <title>Untitled Page</title>
  <script type="text/javascript" language="javascript">
    var monitor;

      function disposingcb()
      {
        alert("The Disposing event was raised!");
      }


      . . .
      function pageLoad()
      {
        monitor = new Disposables.Monitor();
        monitor.add_disposing(disposingcb);

        var disposebtn = $get("disposebtn");
        var disposeDelegate = Function.createDelegate(monitor, monitor.dispose);
        $addHandler(disposebtn, "click", disposeDelegate);


        . . .
      }
  </script>
</head>
<body>
  <form id="form1" runat="server">
    <asp:ScriptManager ID="ScriptManager1" runat="server">
      . . .
    </asp:ScriptManager>
    Enter new Monitor id: <input type="text" id="id" /> 
    <button id="changePropertybtn" type="button">Change Property</button><br/><br/>

      <button id="disposebtn" type="button">Dispose Monitor</button>

    <div>
    </div>
  </form>
</body>
</html>
```

The highlighted portions of code do the following:

- ❑ Add a button named Dispose Monitor:

```
<button id="disposebtn" type="button">Dispose Monitor</button>
```

- ❑ Call the `createDelegate` method on the `Function` class to create a delegate that represents the `dispose` method of the `Monitor` class:

```
var disposeDelegate = Function.createDelegate(monitor, monitor.dispose);
```

- ❑ Call the `addHandler` method on the `DomEvent` class to register this delegate as an event handler for the `click` event of the Dispose Monitor button:

```
$addHandler(disposebtn, "click", disposeDelegate);
```

When the end user clicks this button, the delegate is automatically called, which in turn calls the `dispose` method of the `Monitor` class.

As mentioned before, this was done for educational purposes. In a real-life project, the `Monitor` object must be registered as a disposable object with the `Application` object to have the `Application` object automatically call its `dispose` method before it is disposed of. As the following code shows, the constructor of the `Component` base class automatically registers the component as a disposable object with the `Application` object:

```
Sys.Component = function Sys$Component() {
  if (Sys.Application)
    Sys.Application.registerDisposableObject(this);
}
```

Therefore, if you inherit the `Monitor` class from the `Component` base class and have the constructor of the `Monitor` class invoke the constructor of the base class as shown in the boldfaced portion of the following code, every `Monitor` object is guaranteed to be registered as a disposable object with the `Application` object:

```
Type.registerNamespace("CustomComponents");

CustomComponents.Monitor = function() {
  CustomComponents.Monitor.initializeBase(this);
  . . .
}
CustomComponents.Monitor.registerClass("CustomComponents.Monitor", Sys.Component);
```

Because the `Monitor` class is now an ASP.NET AJAX component (meaning it derives from the `Component` base class), it makes more sense to define a more appropriate namespace such as `CustomComponents`.

As the highlighted portion of the following code snippet from Listing 7-8 shows, the dispose method of the Monitor class implements the logic that raises disposing event and consequently invokes the event handlers registered for this event:

```
dispose : function() {
    if (this.events)    {
       var handler = this.events.getHandler("disposing");
       if (handler)
          handler(this, Sys.EventArgs.Empty);
    }

    delete this.events;

    $removeHandler(document, "mousemove", this.delegate);
},
```

As you can see in the following code snippet from Listing 7-11, the dispose method of the Component base class includes the highlighted code from the previous code fragment:

```
function Sys$Component$dispose() {

    if (this._events) {
       var handler = this._events.getHandler("disposing");
       if (handler)
          handler(this, Sys.EventArgs.Empty);
    }

    delete this._events;


    . . .

}
```

Therefore, you can simplify the implementation of the dispose method of the Monitor class if you inherit the Monitor class from the Component base class and invoke the callBaseMethod method from the dispose method of the Monitor class, as shown in the following code fragment:

```
dispose : function() {
    $removeHandler(document, "mousemove", this.delegate);
    CustomComponents.Monitor.callBaseMethod(this, "dispose");
},
```

The callBaseMethod method invokes the dispose method of the Component base class.

If you derive a custom component from the Component base class and if your custom component needs to override the dispose method, your custom component's implementation of this method must use the callBaseMethod method to invoke the dispose method of the Component base class. Otherwise, the disposing event of your custom component will not be raised and, consequently, the event handlers registered for this event will not be invoked.

initialize

The `create` static method of the `Component` base class invokes the `endUpdate` method when it is done with updating the newly instantiated component, as shown in the highlighted portions of the following code snippet from Listing 7-5:

```
var $create = Sys.Component.create =
        function Sys$Component$create(type, properties, events, references, element)
{
  var component = (element ? new type(element): new type());

  component.beginUpdate();
  . . .
  if (Sys.Application.get_isCreatingComponents()) {
    if (references)
      Sys.Application._addComponentToSecondPass(component, references);

    else

      component.endUpdate();

  }

  else {
    if (references)
      Sys$Component$_setReferences(component, references);

    component.endUpdate();

  }

  return component;
}
```

The `endUpdate` method invokes the `initialize` method if this method has not been already explicitly invoked, as shown in the highlighted portion of the following code snippet from Listing 7-8. The `Component` base class guarantees that the `initialize` method will be automatically invoked if it is not explicitly invoked.

```
function Sys$Component$endUpdate() {
  this._updating = false;
  if (!this._initialized)
    this.initialize();

  this.updated();

}
```

As you can see in the following code fragment, the `initialize` method of the `Component` base class doesn't do much. It simply sets the `_initialized` flag to `true` to ensure that the `initialize` method is not twice:

```
function Sys$Component$initialize() {
  this._initialized = true;
}
```

Because the `Component` base class guarantees the one-time automatic invocation of the `initialize` method, this method is the best place for your custom component to initialize itself. The `Monitor` class initializes itself partly inside its constructor and partly inside the `registerMonitor` method, as shown in the highlighted portions of the following code snippet from Listing 7-8:

```
CustomComponents.Monitor = function() {
  CustomComponents.Monitor.initializeBase(this);

  this.id = "Monitor1";
  this.div = document.createElement("div");
  document.body.insertBefore(this.div,document.forms[0]);
  this.registerMonitor();

}

CustomComponents.Monitor.prototype =
{
  registerMonitor : function() {

    this.delegate = Function.createDelegate(this, this.print);
    $addHandler(document, "mousemove", this.delegate);

  },
  . . .
}
```

The new version of the `Monitor` class overrides the `initialize` method that it inherits from the `Component` base class and moves all its initialization logic from its constructor and the `registerMonitor` method into the `initialize` method, as shown in the following code fragment:

```
CustomComponents.Monitor.prototype =
{
  initialize : function() {
    CustomComponents.Monitor.callBaseMethod(this, "initialize");
    this.printFormat = "Monitor id: {0} <br />X-Coordinate: {1}" +
                       "<br />Y-Coordinate: {2}";
    this.div = document.createElement("div");
    document.body.insertBefore(this.div,document.forms[0]);
    this.delegate = Function.createDelegate(this, this.print);
    $addHandler(document, "mousemove", this.delegate);
  }
}
```

Note that the `Monitor` class's implementation of the `initialize` method uses the `callBaseMethod` method to invoke the `initialize` method of its `Component` base class.

When you inherit a custom component from the `Component` *base class, your custom component's implementation of the initialize method must use the* `callBaseMethod` *method to invoke the* `Component` *base class's* `initialize` *method. This enables the base class to set the* _initialized *internal flag, which ensures that your custom component is not initialized twice.*

id

The `Monitor` class implements a getter named `get_id` and a setter named `set_id` to allow its clients to get and to set the id of a `Monitor` object, as shown in the following code snippet from Listing 7-8:

```
get_id : function() {
  return this.id;
},

set_id : function(value) {
  this.id = value;
  this.raisePropertyChanged("id");
},
```

Because the new version of the `Monitor` class derives from the `Component` base class, it automatically inherits the `get_id` and `set_id` methods from its base class and, consequently, there is no need to implement these two methods. The following code fragment shows the `set_id` method of the `Component` base class:

```
function Sys$Component$set_id(value) {
  if (this._idSet)
    throw Error.invalidOperation(Sys.Res.componentCantSetIdTwice);

  this._idSet = true;
  var oldId = this.get_id();
  if (oldId && Sys.Application.findComponent(oldId))
    throw Error.invalidOperation(Sys.Res.componentCantSetIdAfterAddedToApp);
  this._id = value;
}
```

As this code shows, the `set_id` method performs the following two tasks before it sets the id of the component:

1. It raises an exception if the `set_id` method has already been invoked to ensure that the id of a component is not set twice:

```
if (this._idSet)
    throw Error.invalidOperation(Sys.Res.componentCantSetIdTwice);
```

2. It invokes the `findComponent` method on the current `Application` object to determine whether the current application already contains a component with the specified id, and if so, it raises an exception to ensure that the id of the component is not set after the component is added to the application:

```
if (oldId && Sys.Application.findComponent(oldId))
    throw Error.invalidOperation(Sys.Res.componentCantSetIdAfterAddedToApp);
```

These two checks are necessary because the id of the component uniquely identifies the component among other components in the current ASP.NET AJAX application.

If you implement a custom component that derives from the `Component` *base class, and your custom component needs to override the* `set_id` *method to run some custom code, your custom component's implementation of this method must use the* `callBaseMethod` *method to invoke the* `set_id` *method of its base class. Otherwise, the two checks will not be performed.*

raisePropertyChanged

The `Monitor` class implements a method named `raisePropertyChanged` that raises the `propertyChanged` event and, consequently, invokes the event handlers registered for this event, as shown in the following code fragment from Listing 7-8:

```
raisePropertyChanged : function (propertyName) {
    if (!this.events)
        return;

    var handler = this.events.getHandler("propertyChanged");
    if (handler)
        handler(this, new Sys.PropertyChangedEventArgs(propertyName));
},
```

As you can see in the following code listing, the `Component` base class exposes the same method, which contains the same logic:

```
function Sys$Component$raisePropertyChanged(propertyName) {
    if (!this._events)
        return;

    var handler = this._events.getHandler("propertyChanged");
    if (handler)
        handler(this, new Sys.PropertyChangedEventArgs(propertyName));
}
```

Because the new implementation of the `Monitor` class inherits the `Component` base class, it automatically inherits the `raisePropertyChanged` method from its base class and, therefore, there is no need to implement this method.

If you implement a custom component that derives from the Component *base class, and your custom component needs to override the* raisePropertyChanged *method to run some custom code, your custom component's implementation of the* raisePropertyChanged *method must use the* callBaseMethod *method to invoke the* raisePropertyChanged *method of the base class. Otherwise the* propertyChanged *event of your custom component will be not raised and, consequently, the event handlers registered for this event will not be invoked.*

get_events

Classes such as Monitor that expose events must perform the following tasks:

1. Support a method such as get_events that returns a reference to the EventHandlerList object where the class stores all the event handlers registered for the events of the class. The following code presents a typical implementation of this method:

```
get_events : function() {
  if (!this.events)
    this.events = new Sys.EventHandlerList();
  return this.events;
},
```

2. Support a method named add_*EventName* where the *EventName* is the placeholder for the name of the event. This method normally takes a single argument that references a JavaScript function and registers this function as the event handler for the specified event. The following code fragment presents a typical implementation of this method. As you can see, this method first invokes the method in step 1 to return a reference to the EventHandlerList object and then invokes the addHandler method on this object to register the specified handler for the event with the specified name.

```
add_EventName : function (handler) {
  var eventHandlerList = this.get_events();
  eventHandlerList.addHandler("EventName", handler);
}
```

3. Support a method named remove_*EventName* where the *EventName* is the place holder for the name of the event. This method normally takes a single argument that references a JavaScript function and registers this function as the event handler for the specified event. The following code fragment presents a typical implementation of this method. As you can see, this method first invokes the method in step 1 to return a reference to the EventHandlerList object and then invokes the removeHandler method on this object to remove the specified handler from the list of event handlers registered for the event with the specified name.

```
remove_EventName : function (handler) {
  var eventHandlerList = this.get_events();
  eventHandlerList.removeHandler("EventName", handler);
}
```

Because the `Component` base class implements the `get_events` method, any class that derives from the `Component` base class automatically inherits this method and, consequently, does not need to re-implement this method. The class only needs to implement the `add_EventName` and `remove_EventName` methods. Therefore, the new version of the `Monitor` class does not need to implement the `get_events` method.

INotifyPropertyChange

As discussed earlier and shown in the following code fragment, the `Component` base class implements the `INotifyPropertyChange` interface and its `add_propertyChanged` and `remove_propertyChanged` methods:

```
function Sys$Component$add_propertyChanged(handler) {
  this.get_events().addHandler("propertyChanged", handler);
}

function Sys$Component$remove_propertyChanged(handler) {
  this.get_events().removeHandler("propertyChanged", handler);
}
```

Because the new version of the `Monitor` class derives from the `Component` base class, it automatically inherits these two methods from the base class and, consequently, does not need to implement these two methods.

If you derive a custom component from the `Component` base class, and if your custom component needs to override the `add_propertyChanged` or `remove_propertyChanged` method to run some custom code, your custom component's implementation of these two methods must use the `callBaseMethod` method to invoke the `add_propertyChanged` or `remove_propertyChanged` method of the `Component` base class. Otherwise, the clients of your custom component will not be able to register or unregister event handlers for the `propertyChanged` event of your component.

INotifyDisposing

As discussed earlier and shown in the following code fragment, the `Component` base class implements the `INotifyDisposing` interface and its `add_disposing` and `remove_disposing` methods:

```
function Sys$Component$add_disposing(handler) {
  this.get_events().addHandler("disposing", handler);
}

function Sys$Component$remove_disposing(handler) {
  this.get_events().removeHandler("disposing", handler);
}
```

Because the new version of the `Monitor` class derives from the `Component` base class, it automatically inherits these two methods from the base class and, consequently, does not need to implement these two methods.

If you derive a custom component from the `Component` base class, and if your custom component needs to override the `add_disposing` or `remove_disposing` method to run some custom code, your custom component's implementation of these two methods must use the `callBaseMethod` method to invoke the `add_disposing` or `remove_disposing` method of the `Component` base class. Otherwise, the clients of your custom component will not be able to register or un-register event handlers for the disposing event of your component.

Listing 7-37 presents the content of the `Monitor.js` JavaScript file that contains the implementation of the new version of the `Monitor` class.

Listing 7-37: The Content of the Monitor.js JavaScript File that Contains the New Version of the Monitor Class

```
Type.registerNamespace("CustomComponents");

CustomComponents.Monitor = function() {
  CustomComponents.Monitor.initializeBase(this);
}

CustomComponents.Monitor.prototype =
{
  print : function(domEvent) {
     this.div.innerHTML = String.format(this.printFormat, this.get_id(),
                                   domEvent.clientX, domEvent.clientY)
  },

  dispose : function() {
     $removeHandler(document, "mousemove", this.delegate);
     CustomComponents.Monitor.callBaseMethod(this, "dispose");
  },

  set_fontSize : function(value) {
    if (value != this.fontSize)
    {
      this.raisePropertyChanged("fontSize");
      this.fontSize = value;
      this.div.style.fontSize = this.fontSize + "px";
    }
  },

  get_fontSize : function() {
    return this.fontSize;
  },
```

(continued)

Listing 7-37 (continued)

```
  initialize : function() {
    CustomComponents.Monitor.callBaseMethod(this, "initialize");
    this.printFormat = "Monitor id: {0} <br />X-Coordinate: {1}" +
                       "<br />Y-Coordinate: {2}";
    this.div = document.createElement("div");
    document.body.insertBefore(this.div,document.forms[0]);
    this.delegate = Function.createDelegate(this, this.print);
    $addHandler(document, "mousemove", this.delegate);
  }
}

CustomComponents.Monitor.registerClass("CustomComponents.Monitor", Sys.Component);

if(typeof(Sys)!=='undefined')
  Sys.Application.notifyScriptLoaded();
```

As this listing shows, the `Monitor` class exposes two new methods named `get_fontSize` and `set_fontSize` that allow you to change the font size for the text that displays the current *x* and *y* coordinates of the mouse pointer:

```
        set_fontSize : function(value) {
          if (value != this.fontSize)
          {
              this.raisePropertyChanged("fontSize");
              this.fontSize = value;
              this.div.style.fontSize = this.fontSize + "px";
          }
        },

        get_fontSize : function()
        {
            return this.fontSize;
        },
```

Note that the `set_fontSize` method calls the `raisePropertyChanged` method of the `Component` base class, passing in the name of the property — that is, the string value "`fontSize`" — to raise the `propertyChanged` event.

Next, the `print` method is modified to use the font size:

```
print : function(domEvent) {
   this.div.innerHTML = String.format(this.printFormat, this.get_id(),
                                      domEvent.clientX, domEvent.clientY)
},
```

Finally, the end of the JavaScript file shown in Listing 7-37 contains the following script:

```
if(typeof(Sys)!=='undefined')
  Sys.Application.notifyScriptLoaded();
```

You must always include this script at the end of JavaScript files that contain the required scripts for your ASP.NET AJAX application. As you can see, this script invokes the `notifyScriptLoaded` method on the current `Application` object to notify the object that the loading of the current JavaScript file is completed.

Listing 7-38 presents a page that uses the new version of the `Monitor` class.

Listing 7-38: A Page that Uses the New Version of the Monitor Class

```
<%@ Page Language="C#" %>

<!DOCTYPE html PUBLIC "-//W3C//DTD XHTML 1.0 Transitional//EN"
"http://www.w3.org/TR/xhtml1/DTD/xhtml1-transitional.dtd">

<html xmlns="http://www.w3.org/1999/xhtml">
<head id="Head1" runat="server">
  <title>Untitled Page</title>
  <script type="text/javascript" language="javascript">
    var monitor;

    function disposingcb()
    {
      alert("The Disposing event was raised!");
    }

    function propertyChangedcb(sender,e)
    {
      alert(e.get_propertyName() + " property changed!");
    }

    function changeFontSize(domEvent)
    {
      var fontSizetxt = $get("fontSizetxt");
      monitor.set_fontSize(fontSizetxt.value);
    }

    function changeId(domEvent)
    {
      var id = $get("id");
      try
      {
        monitor.set_id(id.value);
      }
      catch (ex)
      {
        alert(ex.message);
      }
    }
```

(continued)

Listing 7-38 *(continued)*

```
function pageLoad()
{
  var type = CustomComponents.Monitor;
  var properties = {id : "Monitor1"};
  var events = {disposing : disposingcb, propertyChanged : propertyChangedcb};
  var references = null;
  var element = null;

  monitor = $create(type, properties, events, references, element);
  var changeIdbtn = $get("changeIdbtn");
  $addHandler(changeIdbtn, "click", changeId);
  var changeFontSizebtn = $get("changeFontSizebtn");
  $addHandler(changeFontSizebtn, "click", changeFontSize);
}
    </script>
  </head>
<body>
  <form id="form1" runat="server">
    <asp:ScriptManager ID="ScriptManager1" runat="server">
      <Scripts>
        <asp:ScriptReference Path="Monitor.js" />
      </Scripts>
    </asp:ScriptManager>
    Enter new Monitor id: <input type="text" id="id" /> 
    <button id="changeIdbtn" type="button">Change Id</button>
    <br /><br />
    Enter new font size: <input type="text" id="fontSizetxt" /> 
    <button id="changeFontSizebtn" type="button">
    Change Font Size</button>
    <div>
    </div>
  </form>
</body>
</html>
```

As you can see, this pageLoad method invokes the create static method on the Component base class (recall that $create is shortcut for the create static method), passing in the following five parameters to instantiate and initialize a Monitor object and to add this object to the current ASP.NET AJAX application:

❏ type: This parameter references the constructor of the Monitor class — CustomComponents .Monitor. The type information must also contain the complete namespace containment hierarchy of the class being instantiated.

```
var type = CustomComponents.Monitor;
```

The create static method invokes the new operator on this constructor to instantiate the component.

❏ properties: This parameter is an object whose property values are used to initialize the properties of the component that have the same names as the properties of the object. Typically, this object is a JavaScript object literal that contains one name/value pair for each property being initialized:

```
var properties = {id : "Monitor1"};
```

In this case, you're only initializing the id property of the Monitor class. The Monitor class inherits this property from the Component base class.

❑ events: This parameter is an object whose property values are registered as event handlers for the events of the component that have the same names as the properties of the object. Typically, this object is a JavaScript object literal that contains one name/value pair for each event of interest:

```
var events = {disposing : disposingcb, propertyChanged : propertyChangedcb};
```

In this case, the object literal consists of two name/value pairs:

❑ The name part of the first name/value pair contains the word disposing, which is the name of the Monitor class's disposing event, and the value part of this pair references the disposingcb JavaScript function. This instructs the create static method to register the disposingcb function as the event handler for the disposing event.

❑ The name part of the second name/value pair contains the word propertyChanged, which is the name of the Monitor class's propertyChanged event, and the value part of this pair references the propertyChangedcb JavaScript function. This instructs the create static method to register the propertyChangedcb function as the event handler for the propertyChanged event of the newly instantiated Monitor object.

❑ references: This parameter is an object whose property values are used to initialize the properties of the component that have the same names as the properties of the object and reference other components in the current application. Typically, this object is a JavaScript object literal that contains one name/value pair for each property being initialized. In this case, the Monitor class does not expose any properties that reference other components in the current application. Therefore, you pass null as the value of this parameter:

```
var references = null;
```

❑ element: This parameter references the DOM element associated with the component being initialized. In this case, the Monitor class is not associated with any DOM elements on the current page, so you pass null as the value of this parameter:

```
var element = null;
```

As you can see, the pageLoad method invokes the create static method and passes the five parameters into it. The create method instantiates and initializes a Monitor object, adds the object to the current application, and returns a reference to this object. The pageLoad method stores this reference in a variable named monitor for future reference:

```
monitor = $create(type, properties, events, references, element);
```

The pageLoad method then registers the changeId JavaScript function as the event handler for the click event of the changeIdbtn HTML button:

```
var changeIdbtn = $get("changeIdbtn");
$addHandler(changeIdbtn, "click", changeId);
```

Finally, the pageLoad method registers the changeFontSizebtn JavaScript function as the event handler for the click event of the changeFontSizebtn HTML button:

```
var changeFontSizebtn = $get("changeFontSizebtn");
$addHandler(changeFontSizebtn, "click", changeFontSize);
```

If you run this page, you should see the result shown in Figure 7-4. As you can see, the page consists of two text boxes and their associated buttons.

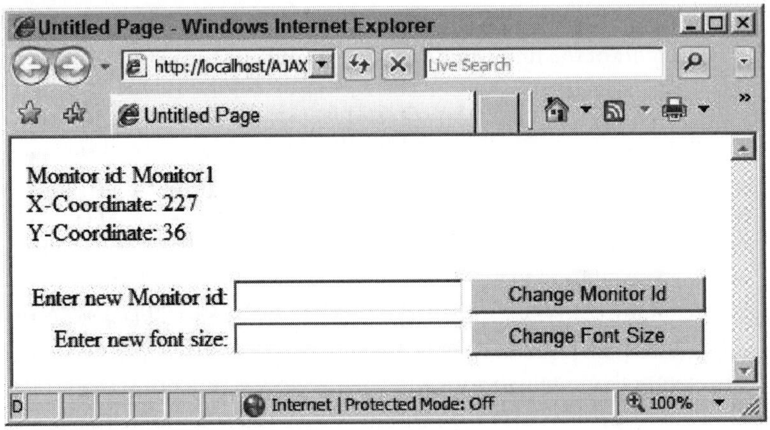

Figure 7-4

Enter a new value for the font size and click the Change Font Size button. You should see the pop-up message shown in Figure 7-5.

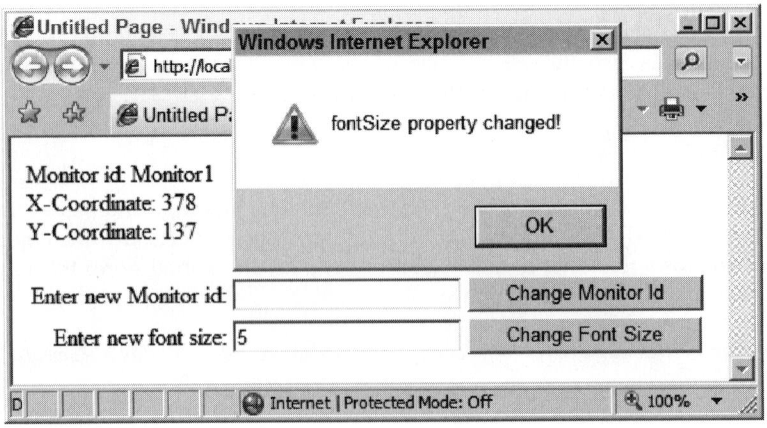

Figure 7-5

278

Next, enter a new URL in the address bar of your browser and press Enter to load the new page. The browser displays the pop-up message shown in Figure 7-6 before it loads the new page. This message indicates that the Application object automatically invoked the dispose method on the Monitor object before disposing of the object.

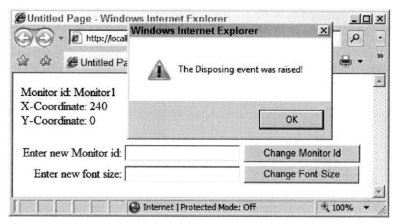

Figure 7-6

The changeId JavaScript function wraps the call into the set_id method of the Monitor object in a try block and catches the associated exception in the catch block, as shown in the following code excerpt from Listing 7-38:

```
function changeId(domEvent)
{
  var id = $get("id");
  try
  {
    monitor.set_id(id.value);
  }
  catch (ex)
  {
    alert(ex.message);
  }
}
```

As discussed earlier and shown again in highlighted portion of the following code fragment, the set_id method raises an exception if the value of the id is being set twice:

```
function Sys$Component$set_id(value) {
  if (this._idSet)

    throw Error.invalidOperation(Sys.Res.componentCantSetIdTwice);

  this._idSet = true;
  var oldId = this.get_id();
  if (oldId && Sys.Application.findComponent(oldId))
    throw Error.invalidOperation(Sys.Res.componentCantSetIdAfterAddedToApp);
  this._id = value;
}
```

The `create` static method of the `Component` base class sets the specified properties of the component to the specified values (previously shown in Listing 7-5). Because Listing 7-39 invokes the `set_id` method after the call into the `create` method — that is, after `id` property value is set — the `set_id` method invoked within the `changeId` JavaScript function shown in Listing 7-39 is bound to raise an exception. To see this in action, run the application again. Enter a new id for the `Monitor` and click the Change Monitor Id button. This should pop up the alert shown in Figure 7-7.

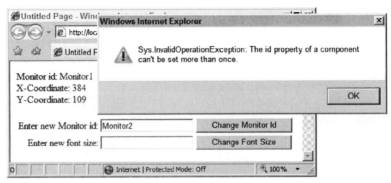

Figure 7-7

Summary

This chapter presented some of the important classes and interfaces that make up the ASP.NET AJAX component-development framework. This chapter also provided in-depth coverage of the two main classes of the ASP.NET AJAX component-development infrastructure: the `_Application` and `Component` classes. The next chapter presents a breed of components named client controls.

8

Developing Client Controls

As discussed in the previous chapter, the `Component` class is the base class for all ASP.NET AJAX components. The ASP.NET AJAX client-side framework includes two important subclasses of the `Component` base class: `Sys.UI.Control` and `Sys.UI.Behavior`. Therefore, when it comes to choosing a base class from which to derive your component class, you have three options: `Component`, `Control`, and `Behavior`. The previous chapter showed you how to implement an ASP.NET AJAX component that derives from the `Component` base class. This chapter first provides you with in-depth coverage of the `Control` class and its methods, properties, and events. Then it provides you with a recipe for developing ASP.NET AJAX components that derive from the `Control` class. Finally, it uses this recipe to implement a custom control class.

Control

This section discusses the methods and properties of the `Control` base class. Because your custom controls must override the members of the `Control` class, you need to have a good understanding of what each member does and how you should override them to provide your own implementation for these members.

Definition

Listing 8-1 presents the definition of the `Control` class. Note that this code listing registers the `Control` class as the subclass of the `Component` base class:

```
Sys.UI.Control.registerClass('Sys.UI.Control', Sys.Component);
```

The `Control` class exposes several methods and properties, which are discussed in the following sections. This section discusses the constructor of the class.

Listing 8-1: The Definition of the Control Class

```
Sys.UI.Control = function Sys$UI$Control(element) {
  if (typeof(element.control) != 'undefined')
    throw Error.invalidOperation(Sys.Res.controlAlreadyDefined);

  Sys.UI.Control.initializeBase(this);
  this._element = element;
  element.control = this;
  this._oldDisplayMode = this._element.style.display;
  if (!this._oldDisplayMode || (this._oldDisplayMode == 'none'))
    this._oldDisplayMode='';
}

Sys.UI.Control.prototype={
  _parent: null,
  _visibilityMode: Sys.UI.VisibilityMode.hide,
  get_element: Sys$UI$Control$get_element,
  get_id: Sys$UI$Control$get_id,
  set_id: Sys$UI$Control$set_id,
  get_parent: Sys$UI$Control$get_parent,
  set_parent: Sys$UI$Control$set_parent,
  get_visibilityMode: Sys$UI$Control$get_visibilityMode,
  set_visibilityMode: Sys$UI$Control$set_visibilityMode,
  get_visible: Sys$UI$Control$get_visible,
  set_visible: Sys$UI$Control$set_visible,
  addCssClass: Sys$UI$Control$addCssClass,
  dispose: Sys$UI$Control$dispose,
  initialize: Sys$UI$Control$initialize,
  onBubbleEvent: Sys$UI$Control$onBubbleEvent,
  raiseBubbleEvent: Sys$UI$Control$raiseBubbleEvent,
  removeCssClass: Sys$UI$Control$removeCssClass,
  toggleCssClass: Sys$UI$Control$toggleCssClass
}

Sys.UI.Control.registerClass('Sys.UI.Control', Sys.Component);
```

As you can see, the constructor of the Control class takes a single argument that references the DOM element that the Control instance being instantiated will represent. You can think of the Control instance as the ASP.NET AJAX representation of the DOM element. Consequently, the DOM element that the Control instance is supposed to represent must already exist in the document where the Control instance is instantiated.

Notice that the constructor assigns the newly instantiated Control instance to the control property of the DOM element, signifying that the DOM element knows which ASP.NET AJAX Control object represents it:

```
element.control = this;
```

As a result, every DOM element can be represented by only one `Control` object. To enforce this requirement, the constructor first checks whether the `control` property of the specified DOM element already references an object. If so, the constructor raises an exception:

```
if (typeof(element.control) != 'undefined')
  throw Error.invalidOperation(Sys.Res.controlAlreadyDefined);
```

Note that the constructor calls the `initializeBase` method, passing in the reference to the `Control` instance being instantiated to invoke the constructor of its base class, which is the `Component` base class:

```
Sys.UI.Control.initializeBase(this);
```

The constructor stores the DOM element passed into it in a field named `_element`:

```
this._element = element;
```

The constructor then stores the value of the `display` property of the style property of the DOM element in another field named `_oldDisplayMode`:

```
this._oldDisplayMode = this._element.style.display;
if (!this._oldDisplayMode || (this._oldDisplayMode == 'none'))
  this._oldDisplayMode='';
```

get_element

The `get_element` method of the `Control` class returns a reference to the DOM element that the `Control` represents, as shown in Listing 8-2.

Listing 8-2: The get_element Method of the Control Class

```
function Sys$UI$Control$get_element() {
  return this._element;
}
```

get_id

As discussed in the previous chapter, the `Component` base class exposes a property named `id` whose value uniquely identifies a component among other components stored in the `Application` object's `_components` collection. Because the `Control` class derives from the `Component` base class, every `Control` object is also a `Component` object and consequently is added to the `_components` collection of the `Application` object. This means that every `Control` object must have a unique `id` value.

Because a `Control` object is an ASP.NET AJAX representation of a DOM element in an ASP.NET AJAX application, it makes lot of sense to use the value of the DOM element's `id` HTML attribute as the `id` of the `Control` object that represents the DOM element. Therefore, the `Control` class overrides the `get_id` method that it inherits from its base class (the `Component` class) to return the value of the `id` attribute of the DOM element that the `Control` represents, as shown in Listing 8-3.

Listing 8-3: The get_id Method of the Control Class

```
function Sys$UI$Control$get_id() {
  if (!this._element)
    return '';
  return this._element.id;
}
```

set_id

Because the value of a Control object's id property is the same as the value of the id HTML attribute of the DOM element that the Control object represents, the id property of the Control object cannot be set. Therefore, the Control class overrides the set_id method that it inherits from the Component base class to raise an InvalidOperation exception. This exception informs the client of a Control object that calls this method that setting the value of the id property of the Control object is an invalid operation, as shown in Listing 8-4.

Listing 8-4: The set_id Method of the Control Class

```
function Sys$UI$Control$set_id(value) {
  throw Error.invalidOperation(Sys.Res.cantSetId);
}
```

set_parent

The Control class exposes a property named parent that references the parent Control object of a Control object. The Control class features a method named set_parent that allows you to specify another Control object as the parent of the Control object on which this method is invoked, as shown in Listing 8-5.

Listing 8-5: The set_parent Method of the Control Class

```
function Sys$UI$Control$set_parent(value) {
  var parents = [this];
  var current = value;
  while (current) {
    if (Array.contains(parents, current))
      throw Error.invalidOperation(Sys.Res.circularParentChain);

    parents[parents.length] = current;
    current = current.get_parent();
  }
  this._parent = value;
}
```

get_parent

The Control class exposes a method named get_parent that returns the parent Control object of a Control object on which this method is invoked, as shown in Listing 8-6.

Listing 8-6: The get_parent Method of the Control Class

```
function Sys$UI$Control$get_parent() {
  if (this._parent)
    return this._parent;

  else
  {
    var parentElement = this._element.parentNode;
    while (parentElement)
    {
      if (parentElement.control)
        return parentElement.control;

      parentElement = parentElement.parentNode;
    }
    return null;
  }
}
```

As you can see in this listing, the get_parent method returns the value of the _parent property of the Control object on which the method is invoked if the value of this property has been set:

```
if (this._parent)
  return this._parent;
```

However, if the value of the _parent property of the Control object has not been specified, the get_parent method searches upward through the containment hierarchy of the DOM element that the Control object represents for the first DOM element whose control property has been specified and returns the value of this control property as the parent Control object. As previously shown in Listing 8-2, the value of a control property of a DOM element references the Control object that represents the DOM element.

Therefore, if the value of the parent property of the Control object that represents a DOM element is not explicitly specified, the Control object that represents the first parent DOM element in the containment hierarchy of the DOM element will be used as the parent Control object of the DOM element.

As Listing 8-6 shows, if the parent property of the Control object that represents a DOM element is not specified, and no parent DOM element in the containment hierarchy of the DOM element is represented by a Control object, the get_parent method returns null. This means that it is possible to have a Control object without a parent.

get_visibilityMode

The `Control` class exposes a property of type `VisibilityMode` named `visibilityMode`. Listing 8-7 presents the definition of the `VisibilityMode` type. As you can see, the `VisibilityMode` is an enumeration with two possible values: `hide` and `collapse`.

Listing 8-7: The VisibilityMode Type

```
Sys.UI.VisibilityMode = function Sys$UI$VisibilityMode() {
  throw Error.notImplemented();
}

Sys.UI.VisibilityMode.prototype = {
  hide: 0,
  collapse: 1
}

Sys.UI.VisibilityMode.registerEnum("Sys.UI.VisibilityMode");
```

The `get_visibilityMode` method of the `Control` class returns the value of the `visibilityMode` property of the `Control`, as shown in Listing 8-8.

Listing 8-8: The get_visibilityMode Method of the Control Class

```
function Sys$UI$Control$get_visibilityMode() {
  return this._visibilityMode;
}
```

get_visible

The `Control` class contains a method named `get_visible` that returns the visibility status of the DOM element that the current `Control` object represents, as shown in Listing 8-9. In other words, the visibility status of a `Control` object is same as the visibility status of the DOM element that the `Control` object represents.

Listing 8-9: The get_visible Method of the Control Class

```
function Sys$UI$Control$get_visible() {
  return (this._element.style.visibility != 'hidden');
}
```

set_visibilityMode

The `set_visibilityMode` method of the `Control` class enables you to set the value of the `visibilityMode` property of the `Control` object on which this method is invoked, as shown in Listing 8-10. Due to the fact that a `Control` object is an ASP.NET AJAX representation of a DOM element, setting its properties affects the DOM element that it represents. In this case, setting the `visibilityMode` property of a

Control object changes the value of the display property of the DOM element's style property if the DOM element is invisible. More specifically, if the visibilityMode property is set to the enumeration value VisibilityMode.hide, the display property reverts to its original value. The constructor of the Control class stores the original value of the display property of the DOM element's style property in a field named _oldDisplayMode. If the visibilityMode property is set to the enumeration value VisibilityMode.collapse, the display property of the DOM element's style property is set to none.

Listing 8-10: The set_visibilityMode Method of the Control Class

```
function Sys$UI$Control$set_visibilityMode(value)
{
  if (this._visibilityMode !== value)
  {
    this._visibilityMode = value;
    if (this.get_visible() === false)
    {
      if (this._visibilityMode === Sys.UI.VisibilityMode.hide)
        this._element.style.display = this._oldDisplayMode;

      else
        this._element.style.display = 'none';
    }
  }
  this._visibilityMode = value;
}
```

set_visible

Listing 8-11 presents the internal implementation of the set_visible method of the Control class. As you can see, the visible property of a Control object basically reflects the visibility property of the style property of the DOM element that the Control object represents. In other words, the visible property of a Control object allows you to treat the visibility of the underlying DOM element as a Boolean value as opposed to a string value such as visible or hidden.

Listing 8-11: The set_visible Method of the Control Class

```
function Sys$UI$Control$set_visible(value) {
  if (value != this.get_visible())
  {
    this._element.style.visibility = value ? 'visible' : 'hidden';
    if (value || (this._visibilityMode === Sys.UI.VisibilityMode.hide))
      this._element.style.display = this._oldDisplayMode;

    else
      this._element.style.display='none';
  }
}
```

addCssClass

When this method is invoked on a `Control` object, it calls the `addCssClass` static method on the `DomElement` class to add the specified CSS class to the DOM element that the `Control` object represents, as shown in Listing 8-12.

Listing 8-12: The addCssClass Method of the Control Class

```
function Sys$UI$Control$addCssClass(className) {
  Sys.UI.DomElement.addCssClass(this._element, className);
}
```

removeCssClass

When this method is invoked on a `Control` object, it calls the `removeCssClass` static method on the `DomElement` class to remove the specified CSS class from the DOM element that the `Control` object represents, as shown in Listing 8-13.

Listing 8-13: The removeCssClass Method of the Control Class

```
function Sys$UI$Control$removeCssClass(className) {
  Sys.UI.DomElement.removeCssClass(this._element, className);
}
```

toggleCssClass

When this method is called on a `Control` object, it calls the `toggleCssClass` static method on the `DomElement` class to toggle the specified CSS class of the DOM element that the `Control` object represents, as shown in Listing 8-14. What this means is that if the DOM element already contains the specified CSS class, the `toggleCssClass` method removes the CSS class. Otherwise, the method adds the CSS class to the DOM element.

Listing 8-14: The toggleCssClass Method of the Control Class

```
function Sys$UI$Control$toggleCssClass(className) {
  Sys.UI.DomElement.toggleCssClass(this._element, className);
}
```

dispose

The `Control` class overrides the `dispose` method that it inherits from the `Component` base class, as shown in Listing 8-15. This method calls the `delete` method on the `element` property that references the DOM element that the current `Control` object represents.

Listing 8-15: The dispose Method of the Control Class

```
function Sys$UI$Control$dispose() {
  Sys.UI.Control.callBaseMethod(this, 'dispose');
  if (this._element)
  {
    this._element.control = undefined;
    delete this._element;
  }
}
```

onBubbleEvent

The `Control` base class in the ASP.NET Framework exposes a method named `OnBubbleEvent` that its subclasses can override to catch the events that their child controls bubble up. For example, the `GridViewRow` class overrides the `OnBubbleEvent` method to catch the `Command` events that its child Image, Button, or Link controls bubble up.

The ASP.NET AJAX `Control` base class exposes a method named `onBubbleEvent` that emulates the `OnBubbleEvent` method of the ASP.NET `Control` base class. This means that your custom client control can override this method to catch the events that its child `Control` objects bubble up, as shown in Listing 8-16.

Listing 8-16: The onBubbleEvent Method of the Control Class

```
function Sys$UI$Control$onBubbleEvent(source, args) {
  return false;
}
```

As the listing shows, the `onBubbleEvent` method takes two arguments and returns a Boolean value. The first argument references the child `Control` object that bubbled up the event. The second argument is of type `EventArgs`. As mentioned, the `OnBubbleEvent` method allows your custom client control to catch the events that its child controls bubble up. What your custom client control does with the events that it catches is up to your custom control. Normally, your custom client control is only interested in certain types of events. It's the responsibility of your custom client control's implementation of the `onBubbleEvent` method to use the second argument of the method to determine the type of the event. If the event is not of the type that your custom control is interested in, your custom control's implementation of the method must return `false` to allow the event to bubble further up in the containment hierarchy of your control. However, if the event is indeed of the type that your custom control is interested in, your custom control must return `true` to stop the event from bubbling further up the containment hierarchy (as shown later in this chapter).

In Listing 8-16, the `onBubbleEvent` method of the `Control` base class returns `false` to allow the event to bubble further up in the containment hierarchy.

raiseBubbleEvent

The ASP.NET `Control` base class exposes a method named `RaiseBubbleEvent` that its subclasses can invoke to bubble up their events. For example, the `GridViewRow` control calls this method to bubble its events up to the containing `GridView` control, where the `GridView` control catches these events in its `OnBubbleEvent` method.

The ASP.NET AJAX `Control` base class exposes a method named `raiseBubbleEvent` that emulates the `RaiseBubbleEvent` method of the ASP.NET `Control` base class. Your custom client control can call this method to bubble its events up to its containing controls. You'll see an example of this later in this chapter.

Now let's take a look at the internal implementation of the `Control` base class's `raiseBubbleEvent` method, which is shown in Listing 8-17.

Listing 8-17: The raiseBubbleEvent Method of the Control Class

```
function Sys$UI$Control$raiseBubbleEvent(source, args) {
  var currentTarget = this.get_parent();
  while (currentTarget) {
    if (currentTarget.onBubbleEvent(source, args))
      return;

    currentTarget = currentTarget.get_parent();
  }
}
```

As you can see, this method marches upward through the containment hierarchy of the control that invokes the `raiseBubbleEvent` and keeps calling the `onBubbleEvent` method on each node of the hierarchy until it reaches the node whose `onBubbleEvent` method returns `true`. The `onBubbleEvent` method of a client control returns `true` when it catches an event that it can handle.

Developing Custom Client Controls

An ASP.NET AJAX client control is an ASP.NET AJAX client component that directly or indirectly derives from the `Control` base class. You can think of an ASP.NET AJAX client control as an ASP.NET AJAX representation of a specific DOM element on a page.

The ASP.NET AJAX client controls essentially emulate their corresponding ASP.NET server controls. Most basic ASP.NET server controls, such as `Label` and `Image`, are ASP.NET representations of DOM elements. These representations enable you to program against the underlying DOM elements using the ASP.NET/.NET Framework. In other words, these representations enable you to treat DOM elements as .NET objects.

The ASP.NET AJAX client controls play a similar role in the client-side programming. These controls are the ASP.NET AJAX representations of DOM elements, allowing you to program against these elements using the ASP.NET AJAX Framework. In other words, these representations enable you to treat DOM elements as ASP.NET AJAX objects.

Every ASP.NET AJAX client control emulates its corresponding ASP.NET server control as much as possible. As such, they expose similar methods and properties as their server counterparts.

The ASP.NET AJAX client-side framework includes with a `Sys.Preview` namespace defined as follows:

```
Type.registerNamespace('Sys.Preview');
```

The `Sys.Preview` namespace contains a `UI` namespace defined as follows:

```
Type.registerNamespace('Sys.Preview.UI');
```

The `Sys.Preview.UI` namespace contains several client controls that directly or indirectly derive from the ASP.NET AJAX `Control` base class. The following sections walk you through the code for these client controls to help you gain the skills you need to develop your own custom client controls. You'll also take a look at the code for Web pages that use these client controls.

Label Client Control

The ASP.NET AJAX `Label` client control is the ASP.NET AJAX representation of the `<span>` HTML element. The `Label` client control derives from the `Control` base class and extends its functionality to add support for two new properties named `htmlEncode` and `text`. The following sections discuss the members of the `Label` client control.

Constructor

Listing 8-18 presents the implementation of the constructor of the `Label` client control. Note that this constructor takes a single argument, which references the DOM span element that the `Label` control represents.

Listing 8-18: The Constructor of the Label Client Control

```
Sys.Preview.UI.Label = function Sys$Preview$UI$Label(associatedElement)
{
  Sys.Preview.UI.Label.initializeBase(this, [associatedElement]);
}

Sys.Preview.UI.Label.registerClass('Sys.Preview.UI.Label',Sys.UI.Control);
```

This constructor calls the `initializeBase` method to invoke the constructor of its base class—`Control`—passing in the reference to the DOM element that the `Label` control represents.

htmlEncode

The `Label` client control exposes a getter method named `get_htmlEncode` and a setter method named `set_htmlEncode` that respectively get and set the value of the `htmlEncode` Boolean property of the control, as shown in Listing 8-19.

Listing 8-19: The Getter and Setter Methods of the htmlEncode Property

```
function Sys$Preview$UI$Label$get_htmlEncode()
{
  return this._htmlEncode;
}

function Sys$Preview$UI$Label$set_htmlEncode(value)
{
  this._htmlEncode = value;
}
```

text

Listing 8-20 presents the implementation of the Label control's get_text getter method, which returns the value of the text property of the control.

Listing 8-20: The get_text Getter Method of the Label Control

```
function Sys$Preview$UI$Label$get_text()
{
  var element = this.get_element();

  if (this._htmlEncode)
    return element.innerText;
  else
    return element.innerHTML;
}
```

This method first calls the get_element method to return a reference to the DOM element that the Label control represents:

```
var element = this.get_element();
```

The Label control inherits the get_element method from its base class—Control.

Next, the get_text method checks whether the value of the htmlEncode property is set to true. If so, it returns the value of the innerText property of the DOM element that the Label control represents:

```
if (this._htmlEncode)
    return element.innerText;
```

If not, it returns the value of the innerHTML property of the DOM element that the Label control represents:

```
else
    return element.innerHTML;
```

Listing 8-21 presents the implementation of the set_text method of the Label control.

Listing 8-21: The set_text Method of the Label Control

```
function Sys$Preview$UI$Label$set_text(value)
{
  if (!value)
    value="";

  var element = this.get_element();
  if (this._htmlEncode)
  {
    if (element.innerText !== value)
    {
      element.innerText = value;
      this.raisePropertyChanged('text');
    }
  }

  else
  {
    if (element.innerHTML !== value)
    {
      element.innerHTML = value;
      this.raisePropertyChanged('text');
    }
  }
}
```

This method first calls the `get_element` method of its base class to return a reference to the DOM element that the `Label` control represents:

```
var element = this.get_element();
```

Next, it checks whether the value of the `Label` control's `htmlEncode` property has been set to `true`. If so, it assigns the new value to the `innerText` property of the DOM element and calls the `raisePropertyChanged` method to raise the `propertyChanged` event:

```
element.innerText = value;
this.raisePropertyChanged('text');
```

The `Label` control inherits the `raisePropertyChanged` method from the `Component` base class.

If the `htmlEncode` property has been set to false, `get_text` assigns the new value to the `innerHTML` property of the DOM element and calls the `raisePropertyChanged` method to raise the `propertyChanged` event.

The `get_text` and `set_text` methods of the `Label` control constitute convenient wrappers around the `innerText` and `innerHTML` properties of the DOM element that the control represents.

If you're wondering how the `get_text` and `set_text` methods work in a browser such as Firefox that does not support the `innerText` property, the answer lies in the Mozilla compatibility layer of the ASP. NET AJAX client-side framework, which includes the logic that adds the support for this property. Refer to the `PreviewScripts.js` JavaScript file for more information on the Mozilla compatibility layer.

prototype

As Listing 8-22 shows, the `get_htmlEncode`, `set_htmlEncode`, `get_text`, and `set_text` methods of the `Label` client control are directly defined on the `prototype` property of the control. This means that these methods are instance methods and must be invoked on the instances of the `Label` control class, not the class itself.

Listing 8-22: The prototype Property of the Label Control

```
Sys.Preview.UI.Label.prototype =
{
  _htmlEncode: false,
  get_htmlEncode: Sys$Preview$UI$Label$get_htmlEncode,
  set_htmlEncode: Sys$Preview$UI$Label$set_htmlEncode,
  get_text: Sys$Preview$UI$Label$get_text,
  set_text: Sys$Preview$UI$Label$set_text
}
```

descriptor

Every component, including the `Label` control, must expose a property named `descriptor` that references an object literal describing the members of the component. The ASP.NET AJAX client-side framework includes a class named `TypeDescriptor` that uses the `descriptor` property of a component to discover its members. In other words, the `descriptor` property of a component contains metadata about the type of the component and its members. As such, the `descriptor` property of a component must always be defined directly on the component class itself.

The `descriptor` property of a component references an object literal that contains one or more name/value pairs, where each name/value pair describes a specific group of members. The name part of the name/value pair that describes the properties of a component contains the word `properties`, and the value part is an array of object literals where each object literal describes a particular property. In the case of the `Label` control, this array contains two object literals, where the first object literal describes the `htmlEncode` property and the second object literal describes the `text` property (see Listing 8-23). Each object literal contains two name/value pairs. The name part of the first name/value pair is the word `name`, and the value part is the string that contains the name of the property being described. The name part of the second name/value pair is the word `type`, and the value part references the constructor of the type of the property being described.

Listing 8-23: The descriptor Property of the Label Control

```
Sys.Preview.UI.Label.descriptor =
{
  properties: [ { name: 'htmlEncode', type: Boolean },
                { name: 'text', type: String } ]
}
```

Using Label Client Control

Listing 8-24 presents a page that uses the Label client control.

Listing 8-24: A Page that Uses the Label Client Control

```
<%@ Page Language="C#" %>
<!DOCTYPE html PUBLIC "-//W3C//DTD XHTML 1.0 Transitional//EN"
"http://www.w3.org/TR/xhtml1/DTD/xhtml1-transitional.dtd">
<html xmlns="http://www.w3.org/1999/xhtml">
<head runat="server">
  <title>Untitled Page</title>
  <script type="text/javascript" language="javascript">
    var label;

    function clickcb(domEvent)
    {
      var chkbx = $get("chkbx");
      label.set_htmlEncode($get("chkbx").checked);
      var txtbx = $get("txtbx");
      label.set_text(txtbx.value);
    }

    function pageLoad()
    {
      var btn = $get("btn");
      $addHandler(btn, "click", clickcb);
      label = $create(Sys.Preview.UI.Label, null, null, null, $get("myspan"));
    }
  </script>
</head>
<body>
  <form id="form1" runat="server">
    <asp:ScriptManager ID="ScriptManager1" runat="server">
      <Scripts>
        <asp:ScriptReference Assembly="Microsoft.Web.Preview"
        Name="PreviewScript.js" />
      </Scripts>
    </asp:ScriptManager>
    <input type="checkbox" id="chkbx"/>
    <label for="chkbx">Enable HTML encoding</label>
    <br /><br />
    Enter text: <input type="text" id="txtbx" />
    <button id="btn" type="button">Submit</button><br /><br />
    <span id="myspan"></span>
    <div>
    </div>
  </form>
</body>
</html>
```

Figure 8-1 shows what you'll see in your browser when you access this page:

❑ A check box that allows you to toggle HTML encoding on or off

❑ A text box where you can enter text

❑ A Submit button

❑ A `<span>` HTML element

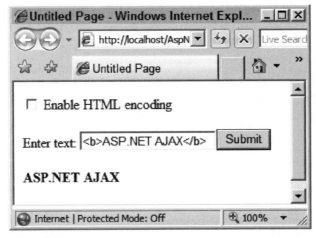

Figure 8-1

When you enter a text into the text box and click the Submit button, the callback for the button retrieves the text and displays it inside the `<span>` HTML element. Figure 8-2 presents a different scenario from what's shown in Figure 8-1. The text "`<b>ASP.NET AJAX</b>`" is entered in both cases, containing the opening and closing tags of the `<b>` HTML element. In Figure 8-1, however, the HTML encoding is off. In this case, the opening and closing tags of the `<b>` HTML element are not HTML-encoded and consequently the `<span>` HTML element shows the text in bold. In Figure 8-2, on the other hand, the HTML encoding is on. In this case, the opening and closing tags of the `<b>` element are HTML encoded and consequently the `<span>` element displays these tags as if they were normal non-HTML characters.

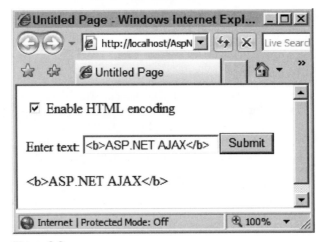

Figure 8-2

Note that the page shown in Listing 8-24 contains the following reference:

```
<asp:ScriptReference Assembly="Microsoft.Web.Preview"
Path="PrevewScript.js" />
```

This script references a JavaScript file named `PreviewScripts.js` that contains the definition of the `Label` client control. This JavaScript file is embedded in the `Microsoft.Web.Preview.dll` assembly. You need to add this assembly to the `bin` directory of your application. When you install the Microsoft ASP.NET Futures, it automatically adds the necessary template to the Visual Studio. Therefore, if you use this template when you're creating a new Web site, the `Microsoft.Web.Preview.dll` assembly will be automatically added to the `bin` directory of your Web site.

As Listing 8-24 shows, `pageLoad` calls the `addHandler` static method on the `DomEvent` class to register the `clickcb` JavaScript function as the event handler for the `click` event of the Submit button:

```
var btn = $get("btn");
$addHandler(btn, "click", clickcb);
```

Then `pageLoad` instantiates an instance of the `Label` client control to represent the `<span>` HTML element:

```
label = $create(Sys.Preview.UI.Label, null, null, null, $get("myspan"));
```

Now let's walk through the code for the `clickcb` JavaScript function. This function first uses the `$get` global JavaScript function to return a reference to the check box element:

```
var chkbx = $get("chkbx");
```

It then passes the check box status into the `set_htmlEncode` method of the `Label` client control:

```
label.set_htmlEncode($get("chkbx").checked);
```

Finally, it calls the `set_text` method on the `Label` client control that represents the `<span>` element to display the value entered into the text box:

```
var txtbx = $get("txtbx");
label.set_text(txtbx.value);
```

Image Client Control

The ASP.NET `Image` server control is the ASP.NET representation of an `image` DOM element. As such, it exposes the `width`, `height`, `src`, and `alt` properties of this DOM element as the `Width`, `Height`, `ImageURL`, and `AlternateText` properties on the `Image` server control itself. This allows you to treat these DOM properties as properties on the `Image` server-control.NET object.

The ASP.NET AJAX `Image` client control plays the same role in the ASP.NET AJAX client-side framework. It is the ASP.NET AJAX representation of an image DOM element. As such, it exposes the DOM `width`, `height`, `src`, and `alt` properties of this DOM element as the `width`, `height`, `imageURL`, and alterateText properties on the Image client control itself. This allows you to treat these DOM properties as properties on an ASP.NET AJAX Image client control object. The following sections discuss the implementation of the Image client control members.

Constructor

As Listing 8-25 shows, the constructor of the Image client control takes a single argument, which references the <img> HTML element the Image client control will represent. This constructor simply calls the initializeBase method to invoke the constructor of its Control base class, passing in the reference to the <img> element. The registerClass method is then called to register the Image class as the subclass of the Control base class.

Listing 8-25: The Constructor of the Image Client Control

```
Sys.Preview.UI.Image =
function Sys$Preview$UI$Image(associatedElement)
{
    Sys.Preview.UI.Image.initializeBase(this, [associatedElement]);
}
Sys.Preview.UI.Image.registerClass('Sys.Preview.UI.Image', Sys.UI.Control);
```

prototype

Listing 8-26 presents the implementation of the prototype property of the Image client control. In this implementation, an object literal describing all the instance methods of the control has been assigned to the prototype property. As discussed in the previous chapter, an instance method of a class is a method that is directly defined on the prototype property of the class, as opposed to the class itself. An instance method must always be invoked on an instance of a class, not the class itself.

Listing 8-26: The prototype Property of the Image Client Control

```
Sys.Preview.UI.Image.prototype =
{
    get_alternateText: Sys$Preview$UI$Image$get_alternateText,
    set_alternateText: Sys$Preview$UI$Image$set_alternateText,
    get_height: Sys$Preview$UI$Image$get_height,
    set_height: Sys$Preview$UI$Image$set_height,
    get_imageURL: Sys$Preview$UI$Image$get_imageURL,
    set_imageURL: Sys$Preview$UI$Image$set_imageURL,
    get_width: Sys$Preview$UI$Image$get_width,
    set_width: Sys$Preview$UI$Image$set_width
}
```

As you can see in this listing, the Image client control exposes four pairs of instance methods. Each pair allows you to set and get the value of a particular property of the Image class. For example, the set_height and get_height instance methods allow you to set and get the value of the height property of the Image client control.

The four properties that the Image client control exposes — width, height, imageURL, and alternateText — are given the same names as the corresponding properties of its Image server control counterpart to make client-side programming feel more like server-side ASP.NET programming.

imageURI

The Image client control exposes two methods named `get_imageURL` and `set_imageURL` that allow you to get and set the value of the `src` property of the underling DOM element, as shown in Listing 8-27. As you can see from this code listing, both methods first call the `get_element` method to return a reference to the `<img>` element that the Image client control represents. The Image client control inherits this method from its `Control` base class.

Listing 8-27: The set_imageURL and get_imageURL Methods of the Image Client Control

```
function Sys$Preview$UI$Image$get_imageURL()
{
  return this.get_element().src;
}

function Sys$Preview$UI$Image$set_imageURL(value)
{
  this.get_element().src = value;
}
```

width

The Image client control exposes two methods named `get_width` and `set_width` that allow you to get and set the value of the `width` property of the image DOM element that the control represents. As you can see in Listing 8-28, these methods are just wrappers around the `width` property of the DOM element, which means you can treat this the same way as a property on an ASP.NET AJAX object.

Listing 8-28: The set_width and get_width Methods of the Image Client Control

```
function Sys$Preview$UI$Image$get_width()
{
  return this.get_element().width;
}

function Sys$Preview$UI$Image$set_width(value)
{
  this.get_element().width = value;
}
```

height

As you can see in Listing 8-29, the `set_height` and `get_height` methods act as wrappers around the `height` property of the underlying image DOM element. This enables you to treat this as a property on an ASP.NET AJAX object, which is the Image client control in this case.

Listing 8-29: The set_height and get_height Methods of the Image Client Control

```
function Sys$Preview$UI$Image$get_height()
{
  return this.get_element().height;
```

(continued)

Listing 8-29 *(continued)*

```
    }
      function Sys$Preview$UI$Image$set_height(value)
    {
      this.get_element().height = value;
    }
```

alternateText

The `get_alternateText` and `set_alternateText` methods allow you to get and set the value of the `alt` property of the image DOM element using the ASP.NET AJAX client-side framework in the same way as you would to get and set the value of this property using the ASP.NET Framework (see Listing 8-30).

Listing 8-30: The set_alternateText and get_alternateText Methods of the Image Client Control

```
    function Sys$Preview$UI$Image$get_alternateText()
    {
      return this.get_element().alt;
    }

    function Sys$Preview$UI$Image$set_alternateText(value)
    {
      this.get_element().alt = value;
    }
```

Using the Image Client Control

Listing 8-31 presents a page that uses the `Image` client control. Previously, we implemented a similar page that showed how to use the `Label` client control where the page used the following script reference to reference the `PreviewScript.js` JavaScript file embedded in the `Microsoft.Web.PreviewScript.dll` assembly:

```
<asp:ScriptReference Assembly="Microsoft.Web.Preview" Name="PreviewScript.js" />
```

As you can see, Listing 8-31 uses the same script reference because the same JavaScript file also contains the definition of the `Image` client control.

Listing 8-31: A Page that uses the Image client control

```
<%@ Page Language="C#" %>
<!DOCTYPE html PUBLIC "-//W3C//DTD XHTML 1.0 Transitional//EN"

"http://www.w3.org/TR/xhtml1/DTD/xhtml1-transitional.dtd">
<html xmlns="http://www.w3.org/1999/xhtml">
<head runat="server">
  <title>Untitled Page</title>
  <script type="text/javascript" language="javascript">
```

```
      function pageLoad()
      {
        var type = Sys.Preview.UI.Image;
        var properties = { imageURL: "wroxProgrammerSmall.jpg",
                  alternateText : "Wrox Programmer's Reference Series",
                  width: 155, height: 58 };
        var events = null;
        var references = null;
        var element = $get("myImage");
        $create(type, properties, events, references, element);
      }
    </script>
  </head>
  <body>
    <form id="form1" runat="server">
      <asp:ScriptManager ID="ScriptManager1" runat="server">
        <Scripts>
          <asp:ScriptReference Assembly="Microsoft.Web.Preview"
          Name="PreviewScript.js" />
        </Scripts>
      </asp:ScriptManager>
      <img id="myImage" />
    </form>
  </body>
</html>
```

The pageLoad method uses the $create shortcut method (the shortcut for the create static method of the Component base class) to instantiate and initialize an Image client control and to add the control to the _components collection of the Application object that represents the current ASP.NET AJAX application. pageLoad passes the following parameters into the create method:

❑ type: This parameter references the constructor of the component being created, which is the Sys.Preview.UI.Image constructor in this case.

❑ properties: This parameter references an object (normally an object literal) that contains the names and values of the properties of the component being created that you want to initialize. The create method internally assigns these values to the properties with the specified names. In this case, the object literal contains four name/value pairs where the name and value parts of each pair respectively contain the name and value of a particular property of the Image client control being created:

```
      var properties = { imageURL: "wroxProgrammerSmall.jpg",
                  alternateText : "Wrox Programmer's Reference Series",
                  width: 155, height: 58 };
```

❑ events: This parameter references an object (normally an object literal) that specifies the event handlers that you want to register for events with the specified names. In this case, the events object is null so any event handlers will be registered.

❑ references: This parameter references an object (normally an object literal) that specifies the values of the properties of the component being created that reference other components in the _components collection of the current Application object. In this case, this object is null because the `Image` client control does not expose any properties that reference other components of the application.

❑ `element`: This parameter references the DOM element on the current page that the newly created `Image` client control will represent. In this case, this parameter references the `<img>` HTML element with `id` HTML attribute value of `"myImage"`:

```
var element = $get("myImage");
```

The `pageLoad` method then invokes the `create` method, passing in the five parameters to create the `Image` client control:

```
$create(type, properties, events, references, element);
```

Extending Image Client Control

In this section, we'll implement a client control named `Image2` that extends the functionality of the `Image` client control to add support for a DHTML feature known as *transition*. The `Image2` client control will use the transition feature to provide an animated effect when the user moves the mouse pointer over and out of the DOM `image` element that the control represents. Because this feature is only supported on Internet Explorer version 4 (IE4) or higher, we need a way to ensure that the `Image2` client control is used in only IE4 or higher.

The ASP.NET AJAX client-side framework defines an object named `browser`, as presented in Listing 8-32, which emulates the `HttpBrowserCapabilities` class in the ASP.NET Framework.

Listing 8-32: The browser Object

```
Sys.Browser = {};
Sys.Browser.InternetExplorer = {};
Sys.Browser.Firefox = {};
Sys.Browser.Safari = {};
Sys.Browser.Opera = {};
Sys.Browser.agent = null;
Sys.Browser.hasDebuggerStatement = false;
Sys.Browser.name = navigator.appName;
Sys.Browser.version = parseFloat(navigator.appVersion);
if (navigator.userAgent.indexOf(' MSIE ') > -1)
{
   Sys.Browser.agent = Sys.Browser.InternetExplorer;
   Sys.Browser.version =
         parseFloat(navigator.userAgent.match(/MSIE (\d+\.\d+)/)[1]);
   Sys.Browser.hasDebuggerStatement = true;
}

else if (navigator.userAgent.indexOf(' Firefox/') > -1)
{
   Sys.Browser.agent = Sys.Browser.Firefox;
   Sys.Browser.version =
      parseFloat(navigator.userAgent.match(/ Firefox\/(\d+\.\d+)/)[1]);
```

```
        Sys.Browser.name = 'Firefox';
        Sys.Browser.hasDebuggerStatement = true;
    }

    else if (navigator.userAgent.indexOf(' Safari/') > -1)
    {
        Sys.Browser.agent = Sys.Browser.Safari;
        Sys.Browser.version =
            parseFloat(navigator.userAgent.match(/ Safari\/(\d+\.\d+)/)[1]);
        Sys.Browser.name = 'Safari';
    }

    else if (navigator.userAgent.indexOf('Opera/') > -1)
    {
        Sys.Browser.agent = Sys.Browser.Opera;
    }
```

As you can see in this listing, the ASP.NET AJAX client-side framework automatically populates the browser object with the information about the current browser when the ASP.NET AJAX scripts are downloaded. The browser object exposes two important properties named agent and version that specify the type and version of the current browser. The possible values of the agent property are Sys.Browser.InternetExplorer, Sys.Browser.Firefox, Sys.Browser.Safari, and Sys.Browser.Opera.

Now back to the original goal, which is implementing the Image2 client control that supports the transition DHTML feature. Listing 8-33 presents the Image2.js JavaScript file that defines the Image2 client control. The following sections discuss all the members of this control.

Listing 8-33: The Content of the Image2.js File

```
Type.registerNamespace("CustomComponents");
CustomComponents.Image2 =
function CustomComponents$Image2(associatedElement)
{
    if (Sys.Browser.agent != Sys.Browser.InternetExplorer ||
        Sys.Browser.version < 4)
        throw Error.invalidOperation;

    CustomComponents.Image2.initializeBase(this, [associatedElement]);
    associatedElement.style.filter = "revealTrans(duration=0.4, transition=1)";
}

function CustomComponents$Image2$set_imageURL(value)
{
    this.mouseOutImageURL = value;
    CustomComponents.Image2.callBaseMethod(this, "set_imageURL", [value]);
}

function CustomComponents$Image2$get_mouseOverImageURL()
{
    return this.mouseOverImageURL;
}
```

(continued)

Listing 8-33 (continued)

```
function CustomComponents$Image2$set_mouseOverImageURL(value)
{
  this.mouseOverImageURL = value;
}

function CustomComponents$Image2$mouseOverCallback ()
{
  this.get_element().filters["revealTrans"].apply();
  this.get_element().src = this.mouseOverImageURL;
  this.get_element().filters["revealTrans"].play();
}

function CustomComponents$Image2$mouseOutCallback ()
{
  this.get_element().filters["revealTrans"].apply();
  this.get_element().src = this.mouseOutImageURL;
  this.get_element().filters["revealTrans"].play();
}

function CustomComponents$Image2$get_duration()
{
  return this.get_element().filters["revealTrans"].duration;
}

function CustomComponents$Image2$set_duration(value)
{
  this.get_element().filters["revealTrans"].duration = value;
  this.get_element().filters["revealTrans"].apply();
}

function CustomComponents$Image2$get_transition()
{
  return this.get_element().filters["revealTrans"].transition;
}

function CustomComponents$Image2$set_transition(value)
{
  this.get_element().filters["revealTrans"].transition = value;
  this.get_element().filters["revealTrans"].apply();
}

function CustomComponents$Image2$initialize()
{
  CustomComponents.Image2.callBaseMethod(this, "initialize");
  this.mouseOverDelegate = Function.createDelegate(this,
                                        this.mouseOverCallback);
  this.mouseOutDelegate = Function.createDelegate(this,
                                        this.mouseOutCallback);
  $addHandler(this.get_element(), "mouseover", this.mouseOverDelegate);
  $addHandler(this.get_element(), "mouseout", this.mouseOutDelegate);
}
```

```
function CustomComponents$Image2$dispose()
{
  $removeHandler(this.get_element(), "mouseover", this.mouseoverDelegate);
  $removeHandler(this.get_element(), "mouseout", this.mouseOutDelegate);
  CustomComponents.Image2.callBaseMethod(this, "dispose");
}

CustomComponents.Image2.prototype =
{
  set_imageURL: CustomComponents$Image2$set_imageURL,
  get_mouseOverImageURL : CustomComponents$Image2$get_mouseOverImageURL,
  set_mouseOverImageURL : CustomComponents$Image2$set_mouseOverImageURL,
  get_duration : CustomComponents$Image2$get_duration,
  set_duration : CustomComponents$Image2$set_duration,
  get_transition : CustomComponents$Image2$get_transition,
  set_transition : CustomComponents$Image2$set_transition,
  mouseOverCallback : CustomComponents$Image2$mouseOverCallback,
  mouseOutCallback : CustomComponents$Image2$mouseOutCallback,
  initialize : CustomComponents$Image2$initialize
}

CustomComponents.Image2.registerClass('CustomComponents.Image2',
                                      Sys.Preview.UI.Image);

CustomComponents.Transition = function CustomComponents$Transition()
{
  throw Error.notImplemented();
}

CustomComponents.Transition.prototype =
{
  boxIn : 0,
  boxOut : 1,
  circleIn : 2,
  circleOut : 3,
  wipeUp : 4,
  wipeDown : 5,
  wipeRight : 6,
  wipeLeft : 7,
  verticalBlinds : 8,
  horizontalBlinds : 9,
  checkerboardAcross : 10,
  checkerboardDown : 11,
  randomDissolve : 12,
  splitVerticalIn : 13,
  splitVerticalOut : 14,
  splitHorizontalIn : 15,
  splitHorizontalOut : 16,
```

(continued)

Listing 8-33 (continued)

```
    stripsLeftDown : 17,
    stripsLeftUp : 18,
    stripsRightDown : 19,
    stripsRightUp : 20,
    randomBarsHorizontal : 22,
    randomBarsVertical : 23,
    randomTransition : 24
}

CustomComponents.Transition.registerEnum("CustomComponents.Transition");

if(typeof(Sys)!=='undefined')
  Sys.Application.notifyScriptLoaded();
```

Constructor

Listing 8-34 presents the implementation of the Image2 client control's constructor.

Listing 8-34: The Constructor of the Image2 Client Control

```
CustomComponents.Image2 =
function CustomComponents$Image2(associatedElement)
{
  if (Sys.Browser.agent != Sys.Browser.InternetExplorer ||
      Sys.Browser.version < 4)
    throw Error.invalidOperation;

  CustomComponents.Image2.initializeBase(this, [associatedElement]);
  associatedElement.style.filter = "revealTrans(duration=0.4, transition=1)";
}

CustomComponents.Image2.registerClass('CustomComponents.Image2',
                                      Sys.Preview.UI.Image);
```

The constructor takes a single argument that references the image DOM element that the Image2 client control represents. The constructor first uses the values of the agent and version properties of the Sys.Browser object to determine whether the current browser is IE4 or higher. If not, it raises an exception, which ensures that the Image2 client control is used only on IE4 or later browsers:

```
    if (Sys.Browser.agent != Sys.Browser.InternetExplorer ||
        Sys.Browser.version < 4)
      throw Error.invalidOperation;
```

Next, the constructor calls the initializeBase method to invoke the constructor of its base class — that is, the Image client control:

```
  CustomComponents.Image2.initializeBase(this, [associatedElement]);
```

The constructor then adds the revealTrans filter to the image DOM element that the Image2 client control represents:

```
associatedElement.style.filter = "revealTrans(duration=0.4, transition=1)";
```

Note that Listing 8-33 registers the Image2 class as the subclass of the Image class:

```
CustomComponents.Image2.registerClass('Sys.Preview.UI.Image2',
                                      Sys.Preview.UI.Image);
```

prototype

Listing 8-35 presents the code for the prototype property of the Image2 client control. This code listing assigns an object literal to the prototype property. Each name/value pair of this object literal describes a method of the Image2 client control. These methods are discussed in the following sections.

Listing 8-35: The prototype Property of the Image2 Client Control

```
CustomComponents.Image2.prototype =
{
  set_imageURL: CustomComponents$Image2$set_imageURL,
  get_mouseOverImageURL : CustomComponents$Image2$get_mouseOverImageURL,
  set_mouseOverImageURL : CustomComponents$Image2$set_mouseOverImageURL,
  get_duration : CustomComponents$Image2$get_duration,
  set_duration : CustomComponents$Image2$set_duration,
  get_transition : CustomComponents$Image2$get_transition,
  set_transition : CustomComponents$Image2$set_transition,
  mouseOverCallback : CustomComponents$Image2$mouseOverCallback,
  mouseOutCallback : CustomComponents$Image2$mouseOutCallback,
  initialize : CustomComponents$Image2$initialize
}
```

imageURL

The Image2 client control overrides the set_imageURL method that it inherits from the Image client control and stores the value assigned to the src property of the underlying DOM element in a new field named mouseOutImageURL, as shown in Listing 8-36.

Listing 8-36: The set_imageURL Method of the Image2 Client Control

```
function CustomComponents$Image2$set_imageURL(value)
{
  this.mouseOutImageURL = value;
  CustomComponents.Image2.callBaseMethod(this, "set_imageURL", [value]);
}
```

Note that this code calls the callBaseMethod to invoke the set_imageURL method of the base class — the Image client control. As discussed in the previous sections, the set_imageURL method of the base class simply assigns the specified value to the src property of the underlying DOM element.

As the name implies, the image whose path is given by the `mouseOutImageURL` field will be displayed when the mouse moves out of the `image` DOM element.

mouseOverImageURL

As Listing 8-37 shows, the `Image2` client control exposes a property named `mouseOverImageURL` and two methods named `get_mouseOverImageURL` and `set_mouseOverImageURL` to get and set the value of this property. The value of this property must be set to the URL of the image that the `Image2` client control will display when the end user moves the mouse pointer over the `image` DOM element that the control represents.

Listing 8-37: The set_mouseOverImageURL and get_mouseOverImageURL Methods

```
function CustomComponents$Image2$get_mouseOverImageURL()
{
  return this.mouseOverImageURL;
}

function CustomComponents$Image2$set_mouseOverImageURL(value)
{
  this.mouseOverImageURL = value;
}
```

mouseOverCallback

When the end user moves the mouse pointer over the image DOM element that the `Image2` client control represents, the `mouseOverCallback` method shown in Listing 8-38 is automatically invoked.

Listing 8-38: The mouseOverCallback Method

```
function CustomComponents$Image2$mouseOverCallback ()
{
  this.get_element().filters["revealTrans"].apply();
  this.get_element().src = this.mouseOverImageURL;
  this.get_element().filters["revealTrans"].play();
}
```

This method first calls the `apply` method on the `revealTrans` filter of the image DOM element to capture the snapshot of the element:

```
this.get_element().filters["revealTrans"].apply();
```

It then assigns the value of the `mouseOverImageURL` property to the `src` property of the DOM element:

```
this.get_element().src = this.mouseOverImageURL;
```

Finally, it calls the `play` method on the `revealTrans` filter of the DOM element to display the image whose URL is given by the `mouseOverImageURL` property in animated fashion:

```
this.get_element().filters["revealTrans"].play();
```

mouseOutCallback

When the end user moves the mouse pointer out of the image DOM element that the Image2 client control represents, the mouseOutCallback method shown in Listing 8-39 is automatically invoked.

Listing 8-39: The mouseOutCallback Method

```
function CustomComponents$Image2$mouseOutCallback ()
{
  this.get_element().filters["revealTrans"].apply();
  this.get_element().src = this.mouseOutImageURL;
  this.get_element().filters["revealTrans"].play();
}
```

This method first calls the apply method on the revealTrans filter of the image DOM element to capture the snapshot of the element:

```
this.get_element().filters["revealTrans"].apply();
```

It then assigns the value of the mouseOutImageURL property to the src property of the DOM element:

```
this.get_element().src = this.mouseOutImageURL;
```

Finally, it calls the play method on the revealTrans filter of the DOM element to display the image whose URL is given by the mouseOutImageURL property in animated fashion:

```
this.get_element().filters["revealTrans"].play();
```

Duration

The revealTrans filter exposes a property named duration. As the name implies, the duration property is a float value that determines the duration of the animation. As you can see in Listing 8-40, the Image2 client control exposes two methods named get_duration and set_duration that get and set the value of the duration property of the revealTrans filter. Note that after setting the value of the property, the set_duration method calls the apply method on the revealTrans filter to take a new snapshot.

Listing 8-40: The get_duration and set_duration Methods

```
function CustomComponents$Image2$get_duration()
{
  return this.get_element().filters["revealTrans"].duration;
}

function CustomComponents$Image2$set_duration(value)
{
  this.get_element().filters["revealTrans"].duration = value;
  this.get_element().filters["revealTrans"].apply();
}
```

transition

The `revealTrans` filter exposes a property named `transition` that determines the animation flavor. The `Image2` client control features two methods named `get_transition` and `set_transition` that allow you to get and set the value of the transition property of the `revealTrans` filter, as shown in Listing 8-41.

Listing 8-41: The get_transition and set_transition Methods

```
function CustomComponents$Image2$get_transition()
{
  return this.get_element().filters["revealTrans"].transition;
}

function CustomComponents$Image2$set_transition(value)
{
  this.get_element().filters["revealTrans"].transition = value;
  this.get_element().filters["revealTrans"].apply();
}
```

Transition Enumeration

The transition property of the `revealTrans` filter takes one of the predefined possible values. As such, it makes lot of sense to define an enumeration type named `Transition` as shown in Listing 8-42. This ensures that only valid values are used for the `transition` property.

Listing 8-42: The Transition Enumeration

```
CustomComponents.Transition = function CustomComponents$Transition()
{
  throw Error.notImplemented();
}

CustomComponents.Transition.prototype =
{
  boxIn : 0,
  boxOut : 1,
  circleIn : 2,
  circleOut : 3,
  wipeUp : 4,
  wipeDown : 5,
  wipeRight : 6,
  wipeLeft : 7,
  verticalBlinds : 8,
  horizontalBlinds : 9,
  checkerboardAcross : 10,
  checkerboardDown : 11,
  randomDissolve : 12,
  splitVerticalIn : 13,
  splitVerticalOut : 14,
  splitHorizontalIn : 15,
  splitHorizontalOut : 16,
  stripsLeftDown : 17,
```

```
    stripsLeftUp : 18,
    stripsRightDown : 19,
    stripsRightUp : 20,
    randomBarsHorizontal : 22,
    randomBarsVertical : 23,
    randomTransition : 24
}

CustomComponents.Transition.registerEnum("CustomComponents.Transition");
```

initialize

The `Image2` control overrides the initialize method that it inherits from its base class, as shown in Listing 8-43.

Listing 8-43: The initialize Method

```
function CustomComponents$Image2$initialize()
{
  CustomComponents.Image2.callBaseMethod(this, "initialize");
  this.mouseOverDelegate = Function.createDelegate(this, this.mouseOverCallback);
  this.mouseOutDelegate = Function.createDelegate(this, this.mouseOutCallback);
  $addHandler(this.get_element(), "mouseover", this.mouseOverDelegate);
  $addHandler(this.get_element(), "mouseout", this.mouseOutDelegate);
}
```

This method begins by invoking the `initialize` method of its base class:

```
CustomComponents.Image2.callBaseMethod(this, "initialize");
```

Next, it creates a delegate that represents the `mouseOverCallback` method of the `Image2` control and stores this delegate in a private field named `mouseOverDelegate` for future reference:

```
this.mouseOverDelegate = Function.createDelegate(this, this.mouseOverCallback);
```

Then, it creates another delegate to represent the `mouseOutCallback` method of the `Image2` control and stores this delegate in a private field named `mouseOutDelegate` for future reference:

```
this.mouseOutDelegate = Function.createDelegate(this, this.mouseOutCallback);
```

Next, it registers the `mouseOverDelegate` delegate as the event handler for the `mouseover` event of the `Image2` control's associated element. This means that when the end user moves the mouse over this element, the element will automatically invoke the `mouseOverDelegate` delegate, which in turn will invoke the `mouseOverCallback` method:

```
$addHandler(this.get_element(), "mouseover", this.mouseOverDelegate);
```

Finally, it registers the `mouseOutDelegate` delegate as the event handler for the `mouseout` event of the `Image2` control's associated element. This means that when the end user moves the mouse out of this element, the element will automatically invoke the `mouseOutDelegate` delegate, which in turn will invoke the `mouseOutCallback` method:

```
$addHandler(this.get_element(), "mouseout", this.mouseOutDelegate);
```

dispose

The Image2 control overrides the `dispose` method that it inherits from its base class, as shown in Listing 8-44. The current `Application` object automatically calls this method to allow the `Image2` control to perform its final cleanup before the control is disposed of.

Listing 8-44: The dispose Method

```
function CustomComponents$Image2$dispose()
{
    $removeHandler(this.get_element(), "mouseover", this.mouseoverDelegate);
    $removeHandler(this.get_element(), "mouseout", this.mouseOutDelegate);
    CustomComponents.Image2.callBaseMethod(this, "dispose");
}
```

As you saw previously in Listing 8-43, the `initialize` method registered the `mouseOverDelegate` and `mouseOutDelegate` delegates as event handlers for the `mouseover` and `mouseout` events of the associated elements of the `Image2` control. The `dispose` method simply removes these two delegates from the list of event handlers registered for the `mouseover` and `mouseout` events. Note that the method finally uses the `callBaseMethod` method to invoke the `dispose` method of its base class. Your custom component's implementation of the `dispose` method must always invoke the `dispose` method of its base class to allow the base class to perform its final cleanup, raise the disposing event, and invoke the event handlers registered for this event.

Using Image2 Client Control

Listing 8-45 shows a page where the `Image2` client control is used.

Listing 8-45: A Page that Uses the Image2 Client Control

```
<%@ Page Language="C#" %>
<!DOCTYPE html PUBLIC "-//W3C//DTD XHTML 1.0 Transitional//EN"
"http://www.w3.org/TR/xhtml1/DTD/xhtml1-transitional.dtd">
<html xmlns="http://www.w3.org/1999/xhtml">
<head id="Head1" runat="server">
  <title>Untitled Page</title>
  <script type="text/javascript" language="javascript">
    function pageLoad()
    {
      var type = CustomComponents.Image2;
      var properties = {imageURL : "wroxProgrammerSmall.jpg",
                alternateText : "Wrox Programmer's Reference Series",
                width : 155, height : 58,
```

```
                        mouseOverImageURL : "wroxProfessionalSmall.jpg", duration : 0.4,
                        transition : CustomComponents.Transition.circleIn};
        var events = null;
        var references = null;
        var element = $get("myImage");

        $create(type, properties, events, references, element);
    }
  </script>
</head>
<body>
  <form id="form1" runat="server">
    <asp:ScriptManager ID="ScriptManager1" runat="server">
      <Scripts>
        <asp:ScriptReference Assembly="Microsoft.Web.Preview"
        Name="PreviewScript.js" />
        <asp:ScriptReference Path="Image2.js" />
      </Scripts>
    </asp:ScriptManager>
    <img id="myImage" />
  </form>
</body>
</html>
```

The page shown in this listing uses the `<asp:ScriptManager>` to register the `PreviewScript.js` and `Image2.js` JavaScript files:

```
<asp:ScriptManager ID="ScriptManager1" runat="server">
  <Scripts>
    <asp:ScriptReference Assembly="Microsoft.Web.Preview"
    Name="PreviewScript.js" />
    <asp:ScriptReference Path="Image2.js" />
  </Scripts>
</asp:ScriptManager>
```

The `pageLoad` method passes the following five parameters into the `create` static method of the `Component` base class, using `$create` as a shortcut for this method:

❑ type: This parameter references the constructor of the `Image2` client control, with the `create` method internally applying the `new` operator on this constructor to instantiate the client control:

```
var type = CustomComponents.Image2;
```

❑ properties. This parameter is an object literal that contains one name/value pair for each property of the `Image2` control to be initialized — which in this case are the property values of `imageURL`, `alternateText`, `width`, `height`, `mouseOverImageURL`, `duration`, and `transition`. The `create` method internally iterates through these name/value pairs and assigns the value part of each name/value pair to the property of the `Image2` control with the same name as the name part of the pair.

```
var properties = {imageURL : "wroxProgrammerSmall.jpg",
                   alternateText : "Wrox Programmer's Reference Series",
                   width : 155,
                   height : 58,
                   mouseOverImageURL : "wroxProfessionalSmall.jpg",
                   duration : 0.4,
                   transition : CustomComponents.Transition.circleIn};
```

❑ events: Because no event handlers are being registered in this case, this parameter is null:

```
var events = null;
```

❑ references: Because no property that references other components in the current application is being initialized in this case, this parameter is null:

```
var references = null;
```

❑ element: This parameter references the DOM element that the Image2 control will represent:

```
var element = $get("myImage");
```

The pageLoad method invokes the create method and passes the five parameters into it:

```
$create(type, properties, events, references, element);
```

HyperLink Client Control

The ASP.NET AJAX HyperLink client control derives from the Label client control and extends its functionality to enable you to program against the hyperlink DOM element (<a>) using an ASP.NET-like programming style.

Constructor

Listing 8-46 presents the constructor of the HyperLink client control. At the end of this listing, the registerClass method is called to register the HyperLink class as the subclass of the Label class.

Listing 8-46: The Definition of the HyperLink Client Control

```
Sys.Preview.UI.HyperLink =
function Sys$Preview$UI$HyperLink(associatedElement)
{
  Sys.Preview.UI.HyperLink.initializeBase(this, [associatedElement]);
}

Sys.Preview.UI.HyperLink.registerClass('Sys.Preview.UI.HyperLink',
                                       Sys.Preview.UI.Label);
```

prototype

As you can see in Listing 8-47, an object literal has been assigned to the prototype property of the HyperLink client control. Note that each name/value pair of this object describes a member of the HyperLink class.

Listing 8-47: The prototype Property of the HyperLink Client Control

```
Sys.Preview.UI.HyperLink.prototype =
{
  _clickHandler: null,
  get_navigateURL: Sys$Preview$UI$HyperLink$get_navigateURL,
  set_navigateURL: Sys$Preview$UI$HyperLink$set_navigateURL,
  initialize: Sys$Preview$UI$HyperLink$initialize,
  dispose: Sys$Preview$UI$HyperLink$dispose,
  add_click: Sys$Preview$UI$HyperLink$add_click,
  remove_click: Sys$Preview$UI$HyperLink$remove_click,
  _onClick: Sys$Preview$UI$HyperLink$_onClick
}
```

navigateURL

The ASP.NET AJAX HyperLink client control is just like its server counterpart — that is, the ASP.NET HyperLink server control exposes a property named navigateURL. As Listing 8-48 shows, the setter and getter of this property — set_navigateURL and get_navigateURL — simply delegate to the href property of the DOM element that the HyperLink client control represents. These two .NET-like methods enable you to program against the href property using a .NET-like programming style.

Listing 8-48: The set_navigateURL and get_navigateURL Methods of the HyperLink Client Control

```
function Sys$Preview$UI$HyperLink$get_navigateURL()
{
  return this.get_element().href;
}

function Sys$Preview$UI$HyperLink$set_navigateURL(value)
{
  this.get_element().href = value ? value : "";
}
```

initialize

As you can see in Listing 8-49, the HyperLink client control overrides the initialize method that it inherits from its Label base class.

Listing 8-49: The initialize Method of the HyperLink Client Control

```
function Sys$Preview$UI$HyperLink$initialize()
{
  Sys.Preview.UI.HyperLink.callBaseMethod(this, 'initialize');
  this._clickHandler = Function.createDelegate(this, this._onClick);
  $addHandler(this.get_element(), "click", this._clickHandler);
}
```

First, the HyperLink client control calls the callBaseMethod method to invoke the initialize method of its base class:

```
Sys.Preview.UI.HyperLink.callBaseMethod(this, 'initialize');
```

In general, every time you override the initialize method, you must use the callBaseMethod method from within your implementation of the initialize method to call the base class's initialize method to allow the base class to initialize itself.

The initialize method then calls the createDelegate method on the Function class to create a delegate that represents the _onClick method of the HyperLink client control. This delegate is stored in a field named _clickHandler for future reference:

```
this._clickHandler = Function.createDelegate(this, this._onClick);
```

The initialize method then calls the addHandler static method on the DomEvent class to register the delegate as the event handler for the click event of the DOM element that the HyperLink client control represents:

```
$addHandler(this.get_element(), "click", this._clickHandler);
```

Therefore, when the DOM element is clicked, it automatically invokes the _clickHandler delegate, which in turn invokes the _onClick method on the HyperLink client control that represents the DOM element.

add_click

Listing 8-50 presents the implementation of the add_click method of the HyperLink client control.

Listing 8-50: The add_click Method of the HyperLink Client Control

```
function Sys$Preview$UI$HyperLink$add_click(handler)
{
  this.get_events().addHandler("click", handler);
}
```

This method enables you to register an event hander for the click event of the HyperLink client control — *not* the click event of the DOM element that the HyperLink client control represents. Keep in mind that the HyperLink client control is a wrapper around the DOM element. What the users actually interacts with is the DOM element, not the HyperLink client control. In other words, when the user clicks the DOM element, it is the DOM element that raises the click event, not the HyperLink client control.

You may be wondering what the connection is between the `click` event of the `HyperLink` client control and the `click` event of the DOM element that the control represents. You'll learn the answer to this question shortly. For now, keep in mind that the `add_click` method of the `HyperLink` client control enables you to register an event handler for the `click` event of the `HyperLink` client control itself.

remove_click

As you can see in Listing 8-51, the `remove_click` method of the `HyperLink` client control is the opposite of the `add_click` method. It removes a specified event handler from the list of event handlers registered for the `click` event of the `HyperLink` client control.

Listing 8-51: The remove_click Method of the HyperLink Client Control

```
function Sys$Preview$UI$HyperLink$remove_click(handler)
{
  this.get_events().removeHandler("click", handler);
}
```

_onClick

Listing 8-52 shows the code for the `_onClick` method of the `HyperLink` client control.

Listing 8-52: The_onClick Method of the HyperLink Client Control

```
function Sys$Preview$UI$HyperLink$_onClick()
{
  var handler = this.get_events().getHandler("click");
  if (handler)
    handler(this, Sys.EventArgs.Empty);
}
```

This method first calls the `get_events` method to return a reference to the `EventHandlerList` that contains all the event handlers for the `HyperLink` client control events. The `HyperLink` client control inherits the `get_events` method from the `Component` base class. The `_onClick` method then invokes the `getHandler` method on the `EventHandlerList` to return a reference to the JavaScript function whose invocation automatically invokes all the event handlers registered for the `HyperLink` client control's `click` event:

```
var handler = this.get_events().getHandler("click");
```

Finally, the `_onClick` method invokes the JavaScript function, which in turn invokes all the event handlers registered for the `HyperLink` control's `click` event.

Now let's put it altogether :

❑   The `initialize` method of the `HyperLink` client control registers the `_onClick` method as the event handler for the `click` event of the DOM element that the control represents (shown in Listing 8-49). This means that when the end user clicks the DOM element, the `_onClick` method of the `HyperLink` client control is automatically invoked.

317

❑   The add_click method of the HyperLink client control adds a specified handler as the event handler for the click event of the HyperLink client control (shown in Listing 8-50).

❑   The _onClick method of the HyperLink client control calls all the event handlers registered for the click event of the HyperLink control (shown in Listing 8-52).

dispose

The HyperLink client control overrides the dispose method that it inherits from its base class, as shown in Listing 8-53.

Listing 8-53: The dispose Method of the HyperLink Client Control

```
function Sys$Preview$UI$HyperLink$dispose()
{
  if (this._clickHandler)
    $removeHandler(this.get_element(), "click", this._clickHandler);

  Sys.Preview.UI.HyperLink.callBaseMethod(this, 'dispose');
}
```

The dispose method calls the removeHandler static method on the DomEvent class using $removeHandler as a shortcut) to remove the _clickHandler delegate from the list of event handlers registered for the HyperLink client control's click event. As previously shown in Listing 8-49, the _clickHandler delegate represents the _onClick method of the HyperLink client control.

descriptor

The HyperLink client control, like any other client component, exposes a property named descriptor, as shown in Listing 8-54.

Listing 8-54: The descriptor Property of the HyperLink Client Control

```
Sys.Preview.UI.HyperLink.descriptor ={
  properties: [ { name: 'navigateURL', type: String } ],
  events: [ { name: 'click' } ]
}
```

This code listing assigns an object literal to the descriptor property. This object contains two name/value pairs. The first name/value pair describes the name and types of the properties of the HyperLink client control. As discussed, this control exposes a single property of type string named navigateURL:

```
properties: [ { name: 'navigateURL', type: String } ],
```

The second name/value pair describes the events that the control exposes. As discussed, the HyperLink client control exposes a single event named click:

```
events: [ { name: 'click' } ]
```

Using the HyperLink Client Control

Listing 8-55 shows a page where the HyperLink client control is used.

Listing 8-55: A Page that Uses the HyperLink Client Control

```
<%@ Page Language="C#" %>
<!DOCTYPE html PUBLIC "-//W3C//DTD XHTML 1.0 Transitional//EN"
"http://www.w3.org/TR/xhtml1/DTD/xhtml1-transitional.dtd">
<html xmlns="http://www.w3.org/1999/xhtml">
<head runat="server">
  <title>Untitled Page</title>
  <script type="text/javascript" language="javascript">
    function pageLoad()
    {
      var type = Sys.Preview.UI.HyperLink;
      var properties = { navigateURL: "http://www.wrox.com",
                         text: "<b>Wrox Web Site</b>",
                         htmlEncode: false  };
      var events = null;
      var references = null;
      var element = $get("myHyperLink");
      $create(type, properties, events, references, element);
    }
  </script>
</head>
<body>
  <form id="form1" runat="server">
    <asp:ScriptManager ID="ScriptManager1" runat="server">
    <Scripts>
      <asp:ScriptReference Assembly="Microsoft.Web.Preview"
       Name="PreviewScript.js" />
    </Scripts>
    </asp:ScriptManager>
    <a id="myHyperLink" />
  </form>
</body>
</html>
```

The pageLoad JavaScript function invokes the create static method on the Component base class to instantiate and initialize an instance of the HyperLink client control to represent the specified <a> HTML element. pageLoad passes the following object literal into the create method to initialize the navigateURL, text, and htmlEncode properties of the HyperLink client control being created.

```
var properties = { navigateURL: "http://www.wrox.com",
                   text: "<b>Wrox Web Site</b>",
                   htmlEncode: false  };
```

As discussed earlier, the HyperLink client control inherits the text and htmlEncode methods from the Label client control.

Listing 8-56 shows an example that uses the click event of the HyperLink control.

Listing 8-56: A Page that Uses the Click Event of the HyperLink Client Control

```
<%@ Page Language="C#" %>
<!DOCTYPE html PUBLIC "-//W3C//DTD XHTML 1.0 Transitional//EN"
"http://www.w3.org/TR/xhtml1/DTD/xhtml1-transitional.dtd">
<html xmlns="http://www.w3.org/1999/xhtml">
<head runat="server">
  <title>Untitled Page</title>
  <script type="text/javascript" language="javascript">
    function clickCallback(domEvent)
    {
      alert("Click event was raised!");
    }

    function pageLoad()
    {
      var type = Sys.Preview.UI.HyperLink;
      var properties = { text: "<b>Click here!</b>", htmlEncode: false };
      var events = { click: clickCallback };
      var references = null;
      var element = $get("myHyperLink");
      $create(type, properties, events, references, element);
    }
  </script>
</head>
<body>
  <form id="form1" runat="server">
    <asp:ScriptManager ID="ScriptManager1" runat="server">
      <Scripts>
        <asp:ScriptReference Assembly="Microsoft.Web.Preview"
        Name="PreviewScript.js" />
      </Scripts>
    </asp:ScriptManager>
    <a id="myHyperLink" />
  </form>
</body>
</html>
```

The `pageLoad` method in this code listing invokes the `create` static method on the `Component` base class to instantiate and initialize an instance of the `HyperLink` control. It passes the following parameters into the `create` method:

❑ `type`: This parameter references the constructor of the `HyperLink` client control. Keep in mind that the value of this parameter must contain the complete namespace containment hierarchy of the client component being instantiated.

```
var type = Sys.Preview.UI.HyperLink;
```

❑ `properties`. This parameter is an object literal that specifies the values of the `text` and `htmlEncode` properties of the `HyperLink` client control being instantiated.

```
var properties = { text: "<b>Click here!</b>", htmlEncode: false };
```

❑   events: This parameter is an object literal that specifies the clickCallback JavaScript function as the function to be registered as event handler for the click event of the HyperLink client control being instantiated.

```
var events = { click: clickCallback };
```

❑   references. This parameter is null because no properties are being initialized that reference other components of the current application.

```
var references = null;
```

❑   element: This parameter references the <a> DOM element with the id HTML attribute value of "myHyperLink".

```
var element = $get("myHyperLink");
```

Summary

This chapter first dove into the Control base class and its members. Then it provided you with in-depth coverage of several standard ASP.NET AJAX client controls. Finally, it showed you how to develop your own custom client controls. The next chapter moves on to the Button client control and event bubbling.

9

Event Bubbling and Button Client Control

This chapter discusses the implementation of the ASP.NET AJAX Button client control and Web pages that use this control. You'll also learn how to implement custom client controls that bubble their events up to their parent client controls, and how to implement custom client controls that catch the events that their child controls bubble up.

CommandEventArgs

As you'll see later in this chapter, the Button client control raises an event named command when the user clicks the button. The ASP.NET AJAX CommandEventArgs class is the event data class for the command event, as defined in Listing 9-1.

Listing 9-1: The CommandEventArgs Class

```
Sys.Preview.UI.CommandEventArgs =
function Sys$Preview$UI$CommandEventArgs(commandName, argument)
{
  Sys.Preview.UI.CommandEventArgs.initializeBase(this);
  this._commandName = commandName;
  this._argument = argument;
}

function Sys$Preview$UI$CommandEventArgs$get_argument()
{
  return this._argument;
}

function Sys$Preview$UI$CommandEventArgs$get_commandName()
{
  return this._commandName;
}
```

(continued)

Listing 9-1 *(continued)*

```
Sys.Preview.UI.CommandEventArgs.prototype =
{
    get_argument: Sys$Preview$UI$CommandEventArgs$get_argument,
    get_commandName: Sys$Preview$UI$CommandEventArgs$get_commandName
}

Sys.Preview.UI.CommandEventArgs.descriptor =
{
    properties: [   {name: 'argument', type: String, readOnly: true},
                    {name: 'commandName', type: String, readOnly: true} ]
}
Sys.Preview.UI.CommandEventArgs.registerClass('Sys.Preview.UI.CommandEventArgs',
                                    Sys.EventArgs);
```

The `CommandEventArgs` class exposes two read-only properties of type `string` named `commandName` and `argument`. The constructor of this class takes two string parameters and assigns them to these two properties:

```
Sys.Preview.UI.CommandEventArgs =
function Sys$Preview$UI$CommandEventArgs(commandName, argument)
{
    Sys.Preview.UI.CommandEventArgs.initializeBase(this);
    this._commandName = commandName;
    this._argument = argument;
}
```

The constructor of this class is the only way to set the values of the `commandName` and `argument` properties. The `CommandEventArgs` class comes with two methods named `get_commandName` and `get_argument` that respectively return the values of the `commandName` and `argument` properties of the `CommandEventArgs`.

The `get_commandName` and `get_argument` methods are defined on the `prototype` property of the `CommandEventArgs` class. As such, they are considered instance methods and must be invoked on a class instance.

The `CommandEventArgs` class, like any other ASP.NET AJAX class, exposes a property named `descriptor` that describes the members of the class. An object literal with a single name/value pair is assigned to the prototype property. This name/value pair describes the `commandName` and `argument` properties of the `CommandEventArgs` class.

Every ASP.NET AJAX event data class must directly or indirectly inherit from the `EventArgs` base class. The `CommandEventArgs` class is no exception:

```
Sys.Preview.UI.CommandEventArgs.registerClass('Sys.Preview.UI.CommandEventArgs',
                                    Sys.EventArgs);
```

Button Client Control

The ASP.NET Button server control exposes the following important features:

❑ An event named Command: When the end user clicks a Button server control, the control raises two events, Click and Command. The event data class associated with the Command event is an ASP.NET class named CommandEventArgs. When the Button server control invokes an event handler registered for its Command event, it passes an instance of the CommandEventArgs event data class into it.

❑ A property named CommandName: The Button server control assigns the value of its Command-Name property to the CommandName property of the CommandEventArgs object that it passes into the event handlers registered for its Command event.

❑ A property named CommandArgument: The Button server control optionally assigns the value of its CommandArgument property to the CommandArgument property of the CommandEventArgs object that it passes into the event handlers registered for its Command event.

The ASP.NET AJAX Button client control emulates the ASP.NET Button server control to offer these three features on the client side, as discussed in the following sections.

Constructor

As you can see in Listing 9-2, the constructor of the Button client control takes a single argument that references the DOM element that the control represents. The constructor calls the initializeBase method to invoke the constructor of its base class, passing in the reference to the DOM element. The Button client control is then registered as the subclass of the Control base class.

Listing 9-2: The Constructor of the Button Client Control

```
Sys.Preview.UI.Button = function Sys$Preview$UI$Button(associatedElement)
{
    Sys.Preview.UI.Button.initializeBase(this, [associatedElement]);
}

Sys.Preview.UI.Button.registerClass('Sys.Preview.UI.Button', Sys.UI.Control)
```

prototype

As Listing 9-3 shows, the Button client control exposes nine instance methods. They are instance methods because they're directly defined on the prototype property of the class. As such, you must invoke these methods on a class instance.

Listing 9-3: The prototype Property of the Button Client Control

```
Sys.Preview.UI.Button.prototype =
{
  _command: null,
  _arg: null,
  _clickHandler: null,
  get_argument: Sys$Preview$UI$Button$get_argument,
  set_argument: Sys$Preview$UI$Button$set_argument,
  get_command: Sys$Preview$UI$Button$get_command,
  set_command: Sys$Preview$UI$Button$set_command,
  initialize: Sys$Preview$UI$Button$initialize,
  dispose: Sys$Preview$UI$Button$dispose,
  add_click: Sys$Preview$UI$Button$add_click,
  remove_click: Sys$Preview$UI$Button$remove_click,
  _onClick: Sys$Preview$UI$Button$_onClick
  }
```

argument

The `Button` client control exposes a property named `argument`, which emulates the `CommandArgument` property of the `Button` server control. As Listing 9-4 shows, the `get_argument` and `set_argument` methods of the `Button` client control emulate the getter and setter of the `Button` server control's `CommandArgument` property.

Note that the `set_argument` method calls the `raisePropertyChanged` method to raise the `propertyChanged` event. The `Button` client control inherits this method from its base class.

Listing 9-4: The get_argument and set_argument Methods of the Button Client Control

```
function Sys$Preview$UI$Button$get_argument()
{
  return this._arg;
}

function Sys$Preview$UI$Button$set_argument(value)
{
  if (this._arg !== value)
  {
    this._arg = value;
    this.raisePropertyChanged('argument');
  }
}
```

command

As Listing 9-5 shows, the `Button` client control exposes a property named `command` and two methods named `get_command` and `set_command` that emulate the `CommandName` property of the `Button` server control and its associated getter and setter methods. Again, note that the `set_command` method invokes the `raisePropertyChanged` method to raise the `propertyChanged` event and, consequently, to invoke all the event handlers registered for this event.

Listing 9-5: The get_command and set_command Methods of the Button Client Control

```
function Sys$Preview$UI$Button$get_command()
{
  return this._command;
}

function Sys$Preview$UI$Button$set_command(value)
{
  if (this._command !== value)
  {
    this._command = value;
    this.raisePropertyChanged('command');
  }
}
```

initialize

The `Button` client control overrides the `initialize` method that it inherits from its base class, as shown in Listing 9-6.

Listing 9-6: The initialize Method of the Button Client Control

```
function Sys$Preview$UI$Button$initialize()
{
  Sys.Preview.UI.Button.callBaseMethod(this, 'initialize');
  this._clickHandler = Function.createDelegate(this, this._onClick);
  $addHandler(this.get_element(), "click", this._clickHandler);
}
```

The `Button` client control's implementation of this method follows the same implementation pattern as the `initialize` method of the `HyperLink` client control discussed in the previous chapter. First, it calls the `callBaseMethod` method to invoke the `initialize` method of its base class. Every time you implement a client component that overrides the `initialize` method, your component's implementation must always call the `callBaseMethod` method to invoke the `initialize` method of its base class to allow the base class to `initialize` itself:

```
Sys.Preview.UI.Button.callBaseMethod(this, 'initialize');
```

Next, the `initialize` method of the `Button` client control calls the `createDelegate` method on the `Function` class to create a delegate that represents the `_onClick` method of the `Button` control:

```
this._clickHandler = Function.createDelegate(this, this._onClick);
```

Finally, it calls the `addHandler` static method on the `DomEvent` class to register this delegate as an event handler for the `click` event of the DOM element that the `Button` client control represents. This means that when the end user clicks the DOM element and raises its `click` event, it automatically invokes this delegate, which in turn invokes the method that it represents — the `_onClick` method.

add_click

Following the same implementation pattern as the HyperLink client control, the Button client control exposes two methods named add_click and remove_click that allow you to add a specified handler to and remove a specified handler from the list of handlers registered for the click event of the Button client control, as shown in Listing 9-7.

Listing 9-7: The add_click Method of the Button Client Control

```
function Sys$Preview$UI$Button$add_click(handler)
{
  this.get_events().addHandler("click", handler);
}

function Sys$Preview$UI$Button$remove_click(handler) {
  this.get_events().removeHandler("click", handler);
}
```

_onClick

One of the great things about the ASP.NET Button server control is that it bubbles its Command event up to its parent server controls. This plays a significant role in composite controls such as GridView and DetailsView. Thanks to event bubbling, these composite controls can catch the events raised by their child controls, such as a Button server control, and expose them as top-level events. This allows these composite controls to hide their child controls from their clients and consequently act as a single entity.

The _onClick method of the Button client control emulates the same feature in client-side programming, as shown in Listing 9-8.

Listing 9-8: The _onClick Method of the Button Client Control

```
function Sys$Preview$UI$Button$_onClick()
{
  var handler = this.get_events().getHandler("click");
  if (handler)
    handler(this, Sys.EventArgs.Empty);

  if (this._command)
  {
    var e = new Sys.Preview.UI.CommandEventArgs(this._command, this._arg);
    this.raiseBubbleEvent(this, e);
  }
}
```

This method first calls the get_events method to return a reference to the EventHandlerList that contains all the event handlers registered for the events that the Button client control exposes. The Button client control inherits the get_events method from its base class. Next, the _onClick method calls the getHandler method on the EventHandlerList to return a JavaScript function whose invocation automatically invokes all the event handlers registered for the click event of the Button control:

```
var handler = this.get_events().getHandler("click");
```

Next, the _onClick method calls this JavaScript function to invoke all the event handlers registered for the click event:

```
handler(this, Sys.EventArgs.Empty);
```

So far, there was nothing special about the _onClick method. What makes the _onClick method of the Button client control very different from the _onClick method of client controls such as the HyperLink control is that the _onClick method creates an instance of the CommandEventArgs event data class (discussed in the previous section), passing in the values of the command and argument properties of the Button client control:

```
var e = new Sys.Preview.UI.CommandEventArgs(this._command, this._arg);
```

Finally, the _onClick method calls the raiseBubbleEvent method, passing in the CommandEventArgs event data object to bubble the Button control's command event up to its parent client control:

```
this.raiseBubbleEvent(this, e);
```

Keep in mind that every client control inherits the raiseBubbleEvent method from the Control class. This method provides you with a very nice mechanism to bubble the events of your custom controls to their parent controls to allow the event handlers of the parent controls to handle these events. This enables the parent of a child control to catch the events raised by its child controls and expose them as its own events. This way, the clients of the parent control do not have to deal with the child controls. Instead, they register their event handlers for the events that the parent control exposes. You'll see an example of this later.

dispose

As you can see in Listing 9-9, the Button client control overrides the dispose method of its base class to remove all the event handlers registered for its click event. Note that the Button control's implementation of this method calls the callBaseMethod method to invoke the dispose method of its base class to allow its base class to do its final cleanup before it is disposed of. Your custom client control's implementation of the dispose method must always invoke the dispose method of its base class.

Listing 9-9: The dispose Method of the Button Client Control

```
function Sys$Preview$UI$Button$dispose()
{
  if (this._clickHandler)
    $removeHandler(this.get_element(), "click", this._clickHandler);

  Sys.Preview.UI.Button.callBaseMethod(this, 'dispose');
}
```

descriptor

The `Button` client control, like any ASP.NET AJAX client class, exposes a property named `descriptor` that describes the members of the `Button` control. The value of this property is always an object literal. As Listing 9-10 shows, this object contains two name/value pairs, where the first name/value pair describes the properties of the `Button` control, and the second name/value pair describes the events that the control exposes. The `Button` control exposes the `command` and `argument` properties and the `click` event.

Listing 9-10: The descriptor Property of the Button Client Control

```
Sys.Preview.UI.Button.descriptor =
{
  properties: [ { name: 'command', type: String },
                { name: 'argument', type: String } ],
  events: [ { name: 'click' } ]
}
```

Using Button Client Control

This section uses a couple of examples to show you the significance of the `Button` client control's event-bubbling capability. Event bubbling involves two important methods of the `Control` base class: `onBubbleEvent` and `raiseBubbleEvent`. It is the responsibility of a child client control to invoke the `raiseBubbleEvent` method to bubble its events to its parent client controls. It is the responsibility of the parent client control to override the `onBubbleEvent` method to catch and to optionally handle the event bubbled up by its child client control.

Catching a Bubbled Event

The `_onClick` method of the `Button` client control calls the `raiseBubbleEvent` method to bubble its `command` event up to its parent client controls. The first example shows you a parent client control named `GridView` that overrides the `onBubbleEvent` method to catch the command event that its child `Button` client controls bubble up.

Listing 9-11 presents the `GridView.js` JavaScript file that contains the implementation of the `GridView` client control.

Listing 9-11: The GridView.js JavaScript File Containing the GridView Client Control Implementation

```
Type.registerNamespace("CustomComponents");

CustomComponents.GridView = function CustomComponents$GridView(associatedElement)
{
  CustomComponents.GridView.initializeBase(this, [associatedElement]);
}

function CustomComponents$GridView$onBubbleEvent(source, args)
{
```

```
    var handled = false;
    if (args instanceof Sys.Preview.UI.CommandEventArgs)
    {
      switch (args.get_commandName())
      {
        case "Select":
          alert(args.get_argument() + " is selected!");
          handled = true;
          break;
        case "Delete":
          alert(args.get_argument() + " is deleted!");
          handled = true;
          break;
      }
    }
    return handled;
}

CustomComponents.GridView.prototype =
{
  onBubbleEvent : CustomComponents$GridView$onBubbleEvent
}

CustomComponents.GridView.registerClass("CustomComponents.GridView",
                               Sys.UI.Control);

if(typeof(Sys)!=='undefined')
  Sys.Application.notifyScriptLoaded();
```

As you can see, the GridView client control exposes a constructor and a method named onBubbleEvent that override the onBubbleEvent method of the Control base class.

Constructor

Listing 9-12 shows the constructor of the GridView client control.

Listing 9-12: The Constructor of the GridView Client Control

```
CustomComponents.GridView = function CustomComponents$GridView(associatedElement)
{
  CustomComponents.GridView.initializeBase(this, [associatedElement]);
}

CustomComponents.GridView.registerClass("CustomComponents.GridView",
                               Sys.UI.Control);
```

As with any other ASP.NET AJAX client control, this constructor takes an argument that references the DOM element that the control represents. It then calls the initializeBase method to invoke the constructor of its base class, passing in the reference to the DOM element.

At the end of this listing, the GridView client control is registered as the subclass of the Control base class:

```
CustomComponents.GridView.registerClass("CustomComponents.GridView",
                               Sys.UI.Control);
```

onBubbleEvent

The `GridView` client control overrides the `onBubbleEvent` method of its `Control` base class, as shown in Listing 9-13. Pay close attention to the implementation pattern used to implement the `onBubbleEvent` method, because the same pattern is used to implement the `onBubbleEvent` method of all parent client controls that need to catch the events raised by their child client controls.

Listing 9-13: The onBubbleEvent Method of the GridView Client Control

```
function CustomComponents$GridView$onBubbleEvent(source, args)
{
  var handled = false;
  if (args instanceof Sys.Preview.UI.CommandEventArgs)
  {
    switch (args.get_commandName())
    {
      case "Select":
        alert(args.get_argument() + " is selected!");
        handled = true;
        break;
      case "Delete":
        alert(args.get_argument() + " is deleted!");
        handled = true;
        break;
    }
  }
  return handled;
}
```

As shown in this listing, you take the following steps to implement the `onBubbleEvent` method of a parent client control:

1. Declare a local variable named `handled` and initialize its value to `false`:

```
var handled = false;
```

2. Use the `instanceof` operator to determine whether the event is of the type that the parent client control handles. In this case, the `GridView` client control handles only `command` events:

```
if (args instanceof Sys.Preview.UI.CommandEventArgs)
```

3. Call the `get_commandName` method on the second parameter passed into the `onBubbleEvent` method to access the command name:

```
var commandName = args.get_commandName();
```

4. Use a `switch` statement that contains one branch for each command name that the parent client control handles. In this case the `GridView` client control handles only the `Select` and `Delete` commands.

5. Handle the event within each branch and set the value of the `handled` variable to `true`. The logic that handles the event can call the `get_argument` method on the second parameter passed into the `onBubbleEvent` method to access the command argument. In this case, the

GridView client control's handling of the Select and Delete events is pretty simple — the control simply calls the alert method to display a message that contains the value returned from the get_argument method.

6. Return the value of the handled variable to the caller of the onBubbleEvent.

The caller of the onBubbleEvent method of a parent client control is the raiseBubbleEvent method of the child client control as shown in the following code snippet from Listing 8-17. The child client control calls the raiseBubbleEvent method to bubble its event up to its parent.

```
function Sys$UI$Control$raiseBubbleEvent(source, args)
{
  var currentTarget = this.get_parent();
  while (currentTarget) {
    if (currentTarget.onBubbleEvent(source, args))
      return;

    currentTarget = currentTarget.get_parent();
  }
}
```

The raiseBubbleEvent method marches upward through the containment hierarchy of the control that invokes the raiseBubbleEvent and keeps calling the onBubbleEvent method on each node of the hierarchy until it reaches the node whose onBubbleEvent method returns true. In this case, the onBubbleEvent method of the GridView client control returns true after handling the Select and Delete events.

Listing 9-14 contains a Web page that demonstrates the GridView and Button client controls' event-bubbling capabilities. Figure 9-1 shows what you'll see when you access this page.

Listing 9-14: A Page Showing the GridView and Button Client Controls' Event-Bubbling Capabilities

```
<%@ Page Language="C#" %>
<!DOCTYPE html PUBLIC "-//W3C//DTD XHTML 1.0 Transitional//EN"
"http://www.w3.org/TR/xhtml1/DTD/xhtml1-transitional.dtd">

<html xmlns="http://www.w3.org/1999/xhtml">
<head id="Head1" runat="server">
  <title>Untitled Page</title>
  <script type="text/javascript" language="javascript">
    function pageLoad()
    {
      $create(CustomComponents.GridView, null, null, null, $get("products"));

      $create(Sys.Preview.UI.Button,
              { command: "Select", argument: "Product1" },
              null,
              { parent: "products"},
              $get("product1Selectbtn1"));
```

(continued)

Listing 9-14 *(continued)*

```
        $create(Sys.Preview.UI.Button,
               { command: "Delete", argument: "Product1" },
               null,
               { parent: "products"},
               $get("product1Deletebtn1"));

        $create(Sys.Preview.UI.Button,
               { command: "Select", argument: "Product2" },
               null, { parent: "products"}, $get("product2Selectbtn1"));

        $create(Sys.Preview.UI.Button,
               { command: "Delete", argument: "Product2" },
               null,
               { parent: "products"},
               $get("product2Deletebtn1"));
    }
  </script>
</head>
<body>
  <form id="form1" runat="server">
    <asp:ScriptManager ID="ScriptManager1" runat="server">
      <Scripts>
        <asp:ScriptReference Assembly="Microsoft.Web.Preview"
        Name="PreviewScript.js" />
        <asp:ScriptReference Path="GridView.js" />
      </Scripts>
    </asp:ScriptManager>
        <table id="products" style="background-color:LightGoldenrodYellow;
               border-color:Tan; border-width:1px; color:Black" cellpadding="0">
        <tr style="background-color:Tan; font-weight:bold">
          <th>Product Name</th>
          <th>Unit Price</th>
        </tr>
        <tr id="row1">
          <td>Product1</td>
          <td>$100</td>
          <td><button id="product1Selectbtn1" type="button">Select</button></td>
          <td><button id="product1Deletebtn1" type="button">Delete</button></td>
        </tr>
        <tr id="row2" style="background-color:PaleGoldenrod">
          <td>Product2</td>
          <td>$200</td>
          <td><button id="product2Selectbtn1" type="button">Select</button></td>
          <td><button id="product2Deletebtn1" type="button">Delete</button></td>
        </tr>
      </table>
  </form>
</body>
</html>
```

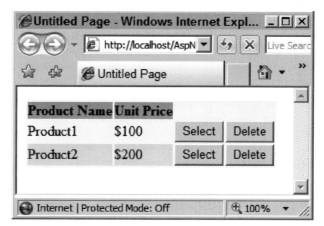

Figure 9-1

This page renders a table with the id HTML attribute value of "products" that contains two table rows. Each table row contains two table cells, and each table cell contains a <button> HTML element. Therefore, altogether you're looking at four <button> HTML elements with id HTML attribute values of product1Selectbtn1, product1Deletebtn1, product2Selectbtn1, and product2Deletebtn1. Notice that each <button> HTML element displays either the Select or the Delete text.

As you can see, we've basically hard-coded a table of rows where each row displays one product and two buttons. One button allows you to select the row and the other button allows you to delete the row. To keep this discussion focused, the onBubbleEvent method of the GridView client control does not contain the logic that actually selects or deletes a row. Instead, this method simply calls the alert method to inform the user that a specified product is selected or deleted (see Listing 9-13).

```
<table id="products" style="background-color:LightGoldenrodYellow;
        border-color:Tan; border-width:1px; color:Black" cellpadding="0">
  <tr style="background-color:Tan; font-weight:bold">
    <th>Product Name</th>
    <th>Unit Price</th>
  </tr>
  <tr id="row1">
    <td>Product1</td>
    <td>$100</td>
    <td><button id="product1Selectbtn1" type="button">Select</button></td>
    <td><button id="product1Deletebtn1" type="button">Delete</button></td>
  </tr>
  <tr id="row2" style="background-color:PaleGoldenrod">
    <td>Product2</td>
    <td>$200</td>
    <td><button id="product2Selectbtn1" type="button">Select</button></td>
    <td><button id="product2Deletebtn1" type="button">Delete</button></td>
  </tr>
</table>
```

Now, lets walk though the implementation of the `pageLoad` method shown in Listing 9-14. This method first instantiates an instance of the `GridView` client control to represent the table DOM element with id HTML attribute value of "products":

```
$create(Sys.Preview.UI.GridView, null, null, null, $get("products"));
```

Then, the method instantiates a `Button` client control to represent the `button` DOM element with the id HTML attribute value of `product1Selectbtn1`. This button DOM element allows the user to select the first row:

```
$create(Sys.Preview.UI.Button,
        { command: "Select", argument: "Product1" },
        null,
        { parent: "products"},
        $get("product1Selectbtn1"));
```

The following object literal is passed as the third argument into the `create` static method:

```
{ parent: "products"}
```

The third argument of the `create` method specifies the values of the properties of the component that reference other components in the current application. As discussed in Chapter 8, the `Control` base class exposes a property name `parent` that references the parent client control of the current control. In this case, the `{parent: "products"}` object literal is passed as the third parameter of the `create` method that creates the `product1Selectbtn1` client control to tell the `create` method that the client control with an id property value of `"products"` is the parent control of the `product1Selectbtn1` client control. The `create` method internally locates this parent control in the `_components` collection of the current `Application` object and assigns it to the `parent` property of the `product1Selectbtn1` client control.

The `pageLoad` method passes the `{command: "Select", argument: "Product1"}` object literal as the second parameter of the `create` method that creates the `product1Selectbtn1` client control. As you can see, this object literal specifies the string `"Product1"` as the value of the argument property of this client control. As you saw previously in Listing 9-13, this allows the `onBubbleEvent` method of the `GridView` client control to use the `get_argument` method to access the argument value and consequently the name of the product being selected:

The `pageLoad` method follows similar steps to instantiate and initialize the `Button` client controls that represent the `<button>` HTML elements with id HTML attribute values of `product1Deletebtn1`, `product2Selectbtn1`, and `product2Deletebtn1`.

Finally, this page registers the `PreviewScript.js` and `GridView.js` JavaScript files with the `ScriptManager`:

```
<asp:ScriptManager ID="ScriptManager1" runat="server">
  <Scripts>
    <asp:ScriptReference Assembly="Microsoft.Web.Preview"
    Name="PreviewScript.js" />
    <asp:ScriptReference Path="GridView.js" />
  </Scripts>
</asp:ScriptManager>
```

Run the page and click the Delete button that deletes the second row. This should pop up the message shown in Figure 9-2. This message contains the name of the product being deleted.

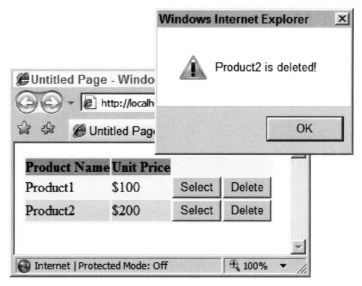

Figure 9-2

Bubbling an Event

The next example shows you how to use the `raiseBubbleEvent` method in your own custom client control to bubble the events that your control exposes. This example involves three ASP.NET AJAX classes: a new version of the `GridView` client control, a new client control named `GridViewRow`, and a new event data class named `GridViewCommandEventArgs`.

GridViewRow

Listing 9-15 presents a JavaScript file named `GridViewRow.js`. This file contains the implementation of a new client control named `GridViewRow` that represents a table row in the `GridView` client control.

Listing 9-15: The GridViewRow.js JavaScript file Containing the GridViewRow Client Control Implementation

```
Type.registerNamespace("CustomComponents");

CustomComponents.GridViewRow =
function CustomComponents$GridViewRow(associatedElement)
{
  CustomComponents.GridViewRow.initializeBase(this, [associatedElement]);
}
```

(continued)

Listing 9-15 *(continued)*

```
function CustomComponents$GridViewRow$set_rowIndex(value)
{
  if (this._rowIndexSet)
    throw Error.invalidOperation("rowIndex property cannot be set twice!");
  this._rowIndexSet = true;
  this._rowIndex = value;
}

function CustomComponents$GridViewRow$get_rowIndex()
{
  return this._rowIndex;
}

function CustomComponents$GridViewRow$onBubbleEvent(source, args)
{
  var handled = false;

  if (args instanceof Sys.Preview.UI.CommandEventArgs)
  {
    var args2=new CustomComponents.GridViewCommandEventArgs(this, source, args);
    this.raiseBubbleEvent(this, args2);
    handled = true;
  }

  return handled;
}

CustomComponents.GridViewRow.prototype =
{
  get_rowIndex : CustomComponents$GridViewRow$get_rowIndex,
  set_rowIndex : CustomComponents$GridViewRow$set_rowIndex,
  onBubbleEvent : CustomComponents$GridViewRow$onBubbleEvent
}

CustomComponents.GridViewRow.descriptor =
{
  properties : [{name : 'rowIndex', type : Number}]
};

CustomComponents.GridViewRow.registerClass( "CustomComponents.GridViewRow",
                                 Sys.UI.Control);

if(typeof(Sys)!=='undefined')
  Sys.Application.notifyScriptLoaded();
```

The following sections discuss the implementation of the members of the `GridViewRow` client control.

Constructor

Listing 9-16 shows the constructor of the `GridViewRow` client control. This constructor takes an argument that references the table row DOM element the control represents. At the end of the listing, the `GridViewRow` class is registered as the subclass of the `Control` base class.

Listing 9-16: The Constructor of the GridViewRow Client Control

```
CustomComponents.GridViewRow =
function CustomComponents$GridViewRow(associatedElement)
{
    CustomComponents.GridViewRow.initializeBase(this, [associatedElement]);

}
CustomComponents.GridViewRow.registerClass("CustomComponents.GridViewRow",
                                           Sys.UI.Control);
```

rowIndex

The `GridViewRow` client control exposes a property of type `integer` named `rowIndex` that specifies the index of the table row DOM element that the control represents. The `get_rowIndex` method of the control, shown in Listing 9-17, returns the value of the `rowIndex` property. As you'll see later, you use the `set_rowIndex` method to set the value of this property when you create the `GridViewRow` client control. This property value can be set only once, which ensures that the value cannot be overridden.

Listing 9-17: The get_rowIndex and set_rowIndex Methods of the GridViewRow Client Control

```
function CustomComponents$GridViewRow$set_rowIndex(value)
{
    if (this._rowIndexSet)
        throw Error.invalidOperation("rowIndex property cannot be set twice!");

    this._rowIndexSet = true;
    this._rowIndex = value;
}

function CustomComponents$GridViewRow$get_rowIndex()
{
    return this._rowIndex;
}
```

onBubbleEvent

As you can see in Listing 9-18, the `GridViewRow` client control overrides the `onBubbleEvent` method of its base class to catch the events that its child client controls fire. In this case, the table row DOM element that the `GridViewRow` client control represents contains two `Button` client controls that allow the end user to select and delete the table row. Therefore, the `onBubbleEvent` method of the `GridViewRow` control catches the `command` events that these `Button` client controls raise. As such, the first parameter of the `onBubbleEvent` method references the `Button` client control that raised the `command` event, and the second parameter of the method references the `CommandEventArgs` event data object that the `_onClick` method of the `Button` client control passed into the `raiseBubbleEvent` method (shown previously in Listing 9-8).

Listing 9-18: The onBubbleEvent Method of the GridViewRow Client Control

```
function CustomComponents$GridViewRow$onBubbleEvent(source, args)
{
  var handled = false;

  if (args instanceof Sys.Preview.UI.CommandEventArgs)
  {
    var args2=new CustomComponents.GridViewCommandEventArgs(this,source, args);
    this.raiseBubbleEvent(this, args2);
    handled = true;
  }

  return handled;
}
```

This method first checks whether the event that it just caught is a `command` event. The easiest way to do this is to check whether the event data object passed into the `onBubbleEvent` method as its second argument is of type `CommandEventArgs`:

```
if (args instanceof Sys.Preview.UI.CommandEventArgs)
```

As previously shown in Listing 9-8, only `command` events use this type as their event data class.

Next, the `onBubbleEvent` method creates an instance of the `GridViewCommandEventArgs` class. As you'll see in the next section, this class is the event data class associated with an event named `GridViewCommand`. The constructor of this event data class takes three arguments. The first argument references the `GridViewRow` client control; the second argument references the `Button` client control that raised the `Command` event; and the third argument references the `CommandEventArgs` object passed into the `onBubbleEvent`:

```
var args2=new CustomComponents.GridViewCommandEventArgs(this, source, args);
```

Next, the `onBubbleEvent` method calls the `raiseBubbleEvent` method, passing in two parameters. The first parameter references the `GridViewRow` client control; and the second parameter references the `GridViewCommandEventArgs` object:

```
this.raiseBubbleEvent(this, args2);
```

Therefore, the `onBubbleEvent` method catches the command event that its `Button` child controls raise and raises a `GridViewCommand` event instead. In this case, it returns `true` to stop its `Button` child control's `command` event from bubbling to the parent of the `GridViewRow` control, which is the `GridView` client control. In other words, the `GridView` client control never gets to handle the original `command` event raised by the `Button` child control. Instead, it receives and handles the `GridViewCommand` event that the `GridViewRow` client control raises.

descriptor

The `GridViewRow` client control, like any other ASP.NET AJAX class, implements a property named `descriptor`. You must always define the `descriptor` property of your ASP.NET AJAX class on the class itself, not on the `prototype` property of your class. In other words, the `descriptor` property must be a static property. This is because the `descriptor` property describes the members of the class using metadata that is shared by all instances of the class.

Listing 9-19 assigns an object literal to the `descriptor` property. In this case, the object contains a single name/value pair that describes the properties of the `GridViewRow` client control. Because this control contains a single property named `rowIndex`, the value portion of this name/value pair is an array that contains a single object literal. This object consists of three name/value pairs. The first name/value pair specifies the name of the property: `rowIndex`. The second name/value pair specifies the type of the property: `Number`.

Listing 9-19: The descriptor Property of the GridViewRow Client Control

```
CustomComponents.GridViewRow.descriptor =
{
  properties : [{name : 'rowIndex', type : Number}]
};
```

GridViewCommandEventArgs

As discussed in the previous section, the `GridViewRow` client control raises an event named `GridViewCommand` that uses a new event data class named `GridViewCommandEventArgs`. Listing 9-20 presents a JavaScript file named `GridViewCommandEventArgs.js` that contains the implementation of the `GridViewCommandEventArgs` class.

Listing 9-20: The GridViewCommandEventArgs.js File Containing GridViewCommandEventArgs Event Data Class Implementation

```
Type.registerNamespace("CustomComponents");

CustomComponents.GridViewCommandEventArgs =
function CustomComponents$GridViewCommandEventArgs (row, source, args)
{
  CustomComponents.GridViewCommandEventArgs.initializeBase(this,
                                    [args.get_commandName(), args.get_argument()]);
  this._commandSource = source;
  this._row = row;
}

function CustomComponents$GridViewCommandEventArgs$get_commandSource()
{
  return this._commandSource;
}
```

(continued)

Listing 9-20 *(continued)*

```
function CustomComponents$GridViewCommandEventArgs$get_row()
 {
  return this._row;
}

CustomComponents.GridViewCommandEventArgs.prototype =
{
  get_commandSource : CustomComponents$GridViewCommandEventArgs$get_commandSource,
  get_row : CustomComponents$GridViewCommandEventArgs$get_row
};

CustomComponents.GridViewCommandEventArgs.descriptor =
{
  properties: [{name:'commandSource', type:Sys.Preview.UI.Control, readOnly:true},
               {name : 'row', type : CustomComponents.GridViewRow, readOnly: true}]
}

CustomComponents.GridViewCommandEventArgs.registerClass(
                     "CustomComponents.GridViewCommandEventArgs",
                     Sys.Preview.UI.CommandEventArgs);

if(typeof(Sys)!=='undefined')
  Sys.Application.notifyScriptLoaded();
```

The following sections walk you through the implementation of the `GridViewCommandEventArgs` event data class.

Constructor

Listing 9-21 shows the constructor of the `GridViewCommandEventArgs` event data class. This constructor takes three parameters. The first parameter references the `GridViewRow` client control that bubbles the event up to the `GridView` control (shown previously in Listing 9-18). The second parameter references the `Button` child client control that raised the original command event (shown previously in Listing 9-8). The third parameter references the `CommandEventArgs` event data object that the `Button` child client's `_onClick` method instantiated (shown previously in Listing 9-8).

Listing 9-21: The Constructor of the GridViewCommandEventArgs Event Data Class

```
CustomComponents.GridViewCommandEventArgs =
function CustomComponents$GridViewCommandEventArgs (row, source, args)
{
  CustomComponents.GridViewCommandEventArgs.initializeBase(this,
                               [args.get_commandName(), args.get_argument()]);
  this._commandSource = source;
  this._row = row;
}

CustomComponents.GridViewCommandEventArgs.registerClass(
                               "CustomComponents.GridViewCommandEventArgs",
                               Sys.Preview.UI.CommandEventArgs);
```

The constructor first calls the initializeBase method to invoke the constructor of its CommandEvent-Args base class. An array of two items is passed to the constructor of the CommandEventArgs class. These items contain the command name and argument, respectively.

The GridViewCommandEventArgs constructor stores the references to the GridViewRow and Button client controls in internal fields named _commandSource and _row. Listing 9-21 registers the GridViewCommandEventArgs class as the subclass of the CommandEventArgs class:

```
CustomComponents.GridViewCommandEventArgs.registerClass(
                         "CustomComponents.GridViewCommandEventArgs",
                         Sys.Preview.UI.CommandEventArgs);
```

get_commandSource

As you can see in Listing 9-22, the get_commandSource method returns a reference to the Button child control that raised the original command event.

Listing 9-22: The get_commandSource Method of the GridViewCommandEventArgs Class

```
function CustomComponents$GridViewCommandEventArgs$get_commandSource()
{
  return this._commandSource;
}
```

get_row

As you can see in Listing 9-23, the get_row method returns a reference to the GridViewRow client control that raised the GridViewCommand event.

Listing 9-23: The get_row Method of the GridViewCommandEventArgs Class

```
function CustomComponents$GridViewCommandEventArgs$get_row()
{
  return this._row;
}
```

descriptor

The GridViewCommandEventArgs class defines a property named descriptor that returns an object literal describing the members of the class, as shown in Listing 9-24. In this case, the object contains a single name/value pair that describes the properties of the class. The value part of the name/value pair contains an array of two object literals that describe the commandSource and row properties of the class. Each object literal contains three name/value pairs. The first two pairs describe the name and type of the property. The last pair specifies that the property is read-only.

Listing 9-24: The descriptor Property of the GridViewCommandEventArgs Class

```
CustomComponents.GridViewCommandEventArgs.descriptor =
{
  properties: [{name:'commandSource', type:Sys.Preview.UI.Control, readOnly:true},
               {name : 'row', type : CustomComponents.GridViewRow, readOnly: true}]
}
```

GridView

Listing 9-25 presents a new version of the `GridView.js` JavaScript file that contains the implementation of a new version of the `GridView` client control.

Listing 9-25: The Content of a New Version of the GridView.js File that Contains the Implementation of a New Version of the GridView Client Control

```
Type.registerNamespace("CustomComponents");

CustomComponents.GridView = function Sys$Preview$UI$GridView(associatedElement)
{
  CustomComponents.GridView.initializeBase(this, [associatedElement]);
}

function CustomComponents$GridView$onBubbleEvent(source, args)
{
  var handled = false;
  if (args instanceof CustomComponents.GridViewCommandEventArgs)
  {
    switch (args.get_commandName())
    {
      case "Select":
        alert(args.get_argument() + " from row number " +
                             args.get_row().get_rowIndex() + " is selected!");
        handled = true;
        break;
      case "Delete":
        alert(args.get_argument() + " from row number " +
                             args.get_row().get_rowIndex() + " is deleted!");
        handled = true;
        break;
    }
  }
  return handled;
}

CustomComponents.GridView.prototype =
{
  onBubbleEvent : CustomComponents$GridView$onBubbleEvent
}
```

```
CustomComponents.GridView.registerClass("CustomComponents.GridView",
                                Sys.UI.Control);
if(typeof(Sys)!=='undefined')
  Sys.Application.notifyScriptLoaded();
```

This GridView client control overrides the onBubbleEvent method of its base class to catch the events that its GridViewRow child client controls raise. As previously shown in Listing 9-18, the GridViewRow client control raises and bubbles up the GridViewCommand event. Because the GridView client control handles only GridViewCommand events, onBubbleEvent first checks whether the event just caught is of type GridViewCommand. The standard way to do this is to check the type of the second parameter passed into the onBubbleEvent. This parameter references an event data object. As you can see from the following code snippet, if this parameter is of type GridViewCommandEventArgs, you can rest assured that the event just caught is of type GridViewCommand because only this type of event uses the GridViewCommandEventArgs class as its event data class.

```
if (args instanceof CustomComponents.GridViewCommandEventArgs)
```

Next, the onBubbleEvent method does what the earlier version of the GridView client control did. The main difference here is that the messages that the alert methods pop up now contain the index of the table row that raised the GridViewCommand event (see Figure 9-3).

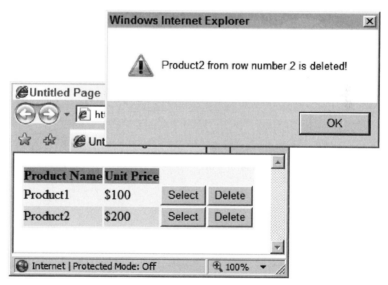

Figure 9-3

Listing 9-26 shows a page that uses the new version of the `GridView` client control.

Listing 9-26: A Page that Uses the GridView Control

```
<%@ Page Language="C#" %>

<!DOCTYPE html PUBLIC "-//W3C//DTD XHTML 1.0 Transitional//EN"
"http://www.w3.org/TR/xhtml1/DTD/xhtml1-transitional.dtd">
<html xmlns="http://www.w3.org/1999/xhtml">
<head runat="server">
  <title>Untitled Page</title>
  <script type="text/javascript" language="javascript">
    function pageLoad()
    {
      $create(CustomComponents.GridView, null, null, null, $get("products"));

      $create(CustomComponents.GridViewRow,
              {rowIndex: 1}, null, {parent: "products"}, $get("row1"));

      $create(Sys.Preview.UI.Button,
              { command: "Select", argument: "Product1" }, null,
              { parent: "row1"},
              $get("product1Selectbtn1"));

      $create(Sys.Preview.UI.Button,
              { command: "Delete", argument: "Product1" },
              null,
              { parent: "row1"},
              $get("product1Deletebtn1"));

      $create(CustomComponents.GridViewRow,
              {rowIndex: 2}, null, {parent: "products"}, $get("row2"));

      $create(Sys.Preview.UI.Button,
              { command: "Select", argument: "Product2" }, null,
              { parent: "row2"},
              $get("product2Selectbtn1"));

      $create(Sys.Preview.UI.Button,
              { command: "Delete", argument: "Product2" }, null,
              { parent: "row2"},
              $get("product2Deletebtn1"));
    }
  </script>
</head>
<body>
  <form id="form1" runat="server">
    <asp:ScriptManager ID="ScriptManager1" runat="server">
      <Scripts>
        <asp:ScriptReference Assembly="Microsoft.Web.Preview"
        Name="PreviewScript.js" />
        <asp:ScriptReference Path="GridViewCommandEventArgs.js" />
        <asp:ScriptReference Path="GridViewRow.js" />
        <asp:ScriptReference Path="GridView.js" />
      </Scripts>
    </asp:ScriptManager>
```

```
        <table id="products" style="background-color:LightGoldenrodYellow;
                 border-color:Tan; border-width:1px; color:Black" cellpadding="0">
          <tr style="background-color:Tan; font-weight:bold">
            <th>Product Name</th>
            <th>Unit Price</th>
          </tr>
          <tr id="row1">
            <td>Product1</td>
            <td>$100</td>
            <td><button id="product1Selectbtn1" type="button">Select</button></td>
            <td><button id="product1Deletebtn1" type="button">Delete</button></td>
          </tr>
          <tr id="row2" style="background-color:PaleGoldenrod">
            <td>Product2</td>
            <td>$200</td>
            <td><button id="product2Selectbtn1" type="button">Select</button></td>
            <td><button id="product2Deletebtn1" type="button">Delete</button></td>
          </tr>
        </table>
      </form>
    </body>
  </html>
```

Let's walk through the implementation of the `pageLoad` method shown in the listing. This method first instantiates an instance of the `GridView` client control to represent the table with an `id` HTML attribute value of `products`:

```
$create(CustomComponents.GridView, null, null, null, $get("products"));
```

Then, the method instantiates an instance of the `GridViewRow` client control to represent the first row of the table:

```
$create(CustomComponents.GridViewRow,
        {rowIndex: 1},
        null,
        {parent: "products"},
        $get("row1"));
```

As this code fragment shows, the `pageLoad` method passes the `{parent: "products"}` object literal as the third argument into the `create` method to specify the `GridView` client control with `id` property value of `"products"` as the parent of the `GridViewRow` client control being instantiated. As you saw previously in Listing 9-18, the `GridViewRow` client control's `onBubbleEvent` method calls the `raiseBubbleEvent` method to bubble the `GridViewCommand` event to its parent client control. Therefore, you must specify the `GridView` client control as the parent control of the `GridViewRow` control if you want the `onBubbleEvent` method of the `GridView` client control to catch the `GridViewCommand` event. Also note that the `pageLoad` method passes the `{rowIndex: 1}` object literal as the second argument into the `create` method to initialize the `rowIndex` property of the `GridViewRow` client control being instantiated to 1.

Then, the `pageLoad` method takes the same steps that the `pageLoad` method previously shown in Listing 9-14 took. The main difference is that Listing 9-26 specifies the `GridViewRow` client control as the parent control of the `Button` client controls as opposed to the `GridView` control itself, as shown in the boldfaced portions of the following code:

```
$create(Sys.Preview.UI.Button,
        { command: "Select", argument: "Product1" },
        null,
        { parent: "row1"},
        $get("product1Selectbtn1"));

$create(Sys.Preview.UI.Button,
        { command: "Delete", argument: "Product1" },
        null,
        { parent: "row1"},
        $get("product1Deletebtn1"));
```

The `pageLoad` method then repeats the previous steps to create the second `GridViewRow` client control and its two `Button` child client controls.

At the end of Listing 9-26, two new JavaScript files named `GridViewCommandEventArgs.js` and `GridViewRow.js` are registered with the `ScriptManager`:

```
<asp:ScriptManager ID="ScriptManager1" runat="server">
  <Scripts>
    <asp:ScriptReference Assembly="Microsoft.Web.Preview"
    Name="PreviewScript.js" />
    <asp:ScriptReference Path="GridViewCommandEventArgs.js" />
    <asp:ScriptReference Path="GridViewRow.js" />
    <asp:ScriptReference Path="GridView.js" />
  </Scripts>
</asp:ScriptManager>
```

The `GridViewCommandEventArgs.js` file contains the code that defines and registers the `GridViewCommandEventArgs` class (shown previously in Listing 9-20). The `GridViewRow.js` file contains the code that defines and registers the `GridViewRow` client control (shown previously in Listing 9-25).

Summary

This chapter showed you how to implement client controls that bubble their events up to their parent client controls and how to implement client controls that catch the events that their child controls bubble up. The next chapter moves on to another important topic in the ASP.NET AJAX client-side framework: the type description extensions.

10

Type Description Extensions

The ASP.NET Framework provides you with two ways to inspect the metadata associated with a given type: reflection and `TypeDescriptor`. Metadata inspection plays a central role in the ASP.NET Framework. For example, metadata inspection is an integral part of the ASP.NET server controls such as `GridView`, where data records come from many different data sources. It is a well-known fact that different types of data stores expose different types of data records. For example, data records stored into or retrieved from a relational database via the ADO.NET layer normally are of type `DataRow` or `DataRowView`. Data records stored into or retrieved from an XML document via the .NET XML layer are of type `XmlNode`.

If an ASP.NET server control such as `GridView` were to know about the actual type of the data records being retrieved or stored, it would be tied to a particular type of data record, and, consequently, a particular type of data store. For example, if an ASP.NET server control were to directly interact with the `DataRow` or `DataRowView` objects returned from the ADO.NET layer, it would not be able to interact with `XmlNode` objects returned from the .NET XML layer. In other words, the server control would only be able to retrieve data from and store data into a relational database via the ADO.NET layer and would not be able to retrieve data from and store data into an XML document via the .NET XML layer.

The metadata inspection capabilities of the .NET Framework allows a server control such as `GridView` to interact with the data records in generic fashion without knowing their actual types. This allows the same server control to retrieve and store any type of data records.

The ASP.NET AJAX client-side framework introduces two metadata inspection facilities that emulate their .NET counterparts, reflection and `TypeDescriptor`. Previous chapters covered the reflection capabilities of the ASP.NET AJAX client-side framework. This chapter discusses the ASP.NET AJAX type description capabilities, which emulate the .NET type description capabilities. As you'll see later, the ASP.NET AJAX type descriptions provide the client controls with the same capabilities as their server counterparts. These capabilities enable the client controls to deal with data records in a generic fashion without having to know their actual types.

The ASP.NET AJAX type description infrastructure consists of the following main components:

- ❑   `TypeDescriptor`
- ❑   `ICustomTypeDescriptor`

TypeDescriptor

The ASP.NET AJAX client-side framework includes a client class named TypeDescriptor that emulates the ASP.NET server-side TypeDescriptor class. The following sections discuss the members of this client class.

Constructor

Listing 10-1 presents the implementation of the TypeDescriptor client class's constructor. As the name suggests, a TypeDescriptor object describes a type. A type exposes up to three different kinds of members: properties, methods, and events. Every type can also be annotated with zero or more metadata attributes that provide more information about the type.

A type also inherits the properties, methods, events, and attributes of its base types. Therefore, a complete description of a type must include the type's and its ancestor type's properties, methods, events, and attributes. That is why the TypeDescriptor client class in Listing 10-1 exposes four properties named properties, methods, events, and attributes.

As the listing shows, the TypeDescriptor class also exposes four getter methods named _get _properties, _get_methods, _get_events, and _get_attributes that provide access to these four properties. The following sections discuss these properties.

Listing 10-1: The Constructor of the TypeDescriptor Client Class

```
Sys.Preview.TypeDescriptor = function Sys$Preview$TypeDescriptor()
{
    var _properties = { };
    var _events = { };
    var _methods = { };
    var _attributes = { };

    this._getAttributes = function this$_getAttributes()
    {
        return _attributes;
    }

    this._getEvents = function this$_getEvents()
    {
        return _events;
    }

    this._getMethods = function this$_getMethods()
    {
        return _methods;
    }

    this._getProperties = function this$_getProperties()
    {
        return _properties;
    }
}

Sys.Preview.TypeDescriptor.registerClass('Sys.Preview.TypeDescriptor');
```

_properties

This property references a JavaScript object literal that contains one name/value pair for each property of the type (or its base type) that the `TypeDescriptor` object describes. The name part of each name/value contains the name of the property associated with the pair. The value part of each name/value pair is a JavaScript object literal that describes the property associated with the pair. This JavaScript object literal contains up to five name/value pairs, where each pair provides a piece of metadata information about the property that the object literal describes, as follows:

- ❑ The first name/value pair specifies the name of the property. The name part of this name/value pair is `name`, and the value part is a string that contains the name of the property.

- ❑ The second name/value pair describes the type of the property. The name part of this name/value pair is `type`, and the value part references the constructor of the property type.

- ❑ The third name/value pair specifies whether the property is read-only. The name part of this name/value pair is `readOnly`, and the value part is a Boolean value.

- ❑ The fourth name/value pair describes the metadata attributes that annotate the type of the property. The name part of this name/value pair is `attributes`, and the value part is an object that contains the attributes.

- ❑ The fifth name/value pair specifies whether the property references a DOM element. The name part of this name/value pair is `isDomElement`, and the value part is a Boolean value.

For example, the `Component` base class exposes the properties shown in the following table.

Property Name	Property Type	Read Only
dataContext	Object	False
id	String	False
isInitialized	Boolean	True
isUpdating	Boolean	True

Based on this table, the `_properties` property of the `TypeDescriptor` object that describes the `Component` base class references the JavaScript object literal shown in Listing 10-2.

Listing 10-2: The JavaScript Object Literal Referenced by the _properties of the TypeDescriptor Object that Describes the Component Base Class

```
{
  'dataContext': {name: 'dataContext', type: Object, readOnly: false},
  'id': {name: 'id', type: String, readOnly: false},
  'isInitialized': {name: 'isInitialized', type: Boolean, readOnly: true},
  'isUpdating': {name: 'isUpdating', type: Boolean, readOnly: true}
}
```

This object literal contains five name/value pairs. The name part of each of these name/value pairs contains the name of a property — `dataContext`, `id`, `isInitialized`, and `isUpdating`. The value part of each of these name/value pairs contains the JavaScript object literal that describes the corresponding property of the Component base class:

- ❑ {name: 'dataContext', type: Object, readOnly: false}

- ❑ {name: 'id', type: String, readOnly: false}

- ❑ {name: 'isInitialized', type: Boolean, readOnly: true}

- ❑ {name: 'isUpdating', type: Boolean, readOnly: true}

Now, let's take a look at the content of the TypeDescriptor object's _properties property. Because the Control class derives from the Component base class, it inherits all the properties of its base class. The following table presents all the properties of the Control base class, including those that it inherits from its base class.

Property Name	Property Type	Read Only
dataContext	Object	false
Id	String	false
isInitialized	Boolean	true
isUpdating	Boolean	true
Element	Object	true
Role	String	true
Parent	Object	false
Visible	Boolean	false
visibilityMode	Sys.UI.VisibilityMode	false

Based on this table, the _properties property of the TypeDescriptor object that describes the Control base class references the JavaScript object literal shown in Listing 10-3.

Listing 10-3: The JavaScript Object Literal Referenced by the _properties of the TypeDescriptor Object that Describes the Control Base Class

```
{
  'dataContext': {name: 'dataContext', type: Object, readOnly: false},
  'id': {name: 'id', type: String, readOnly: false},
  'isInitialized': {name: 'isInitialized', type: Boolean, readOnly: true},
  'isUpdating': {name: 'isUpdating', type: Boolean, readOnly: true},
  'element': {name: 'element', type: Object, readOnly: true},
  'role': {name: 'role', type: String, readOnly: true},
  'parent': {name: 'parent', type: Object, readOnly: false},
  'visible': {name: 'visible', type: Boolean},
  'visibilityMode': {name:'visibilityMode', type: Sys.UI.VisibilityMode,
                     readOnly:false}
}
```

Listing 10-4 shows a page that enables you to display the _properties property of the TypeDescriptor object associated with any ASP.NET AJAX client class, including your own custom classes.

Listing 10-4: A Page that Displays the _properties of the TypeDescriptor Object Associated with an ASP.NET AJAX Client Class

```
<%@ Page Language="C#" %>

<!DOCTYPE html PUBLIC "-//W3C//DTD XHTML 1.0 Transitional//EN"
"http://www.w3.org/TR/xhtml1/DTD/xhtml1-transitional.dtd">

<html xmlns="http://www.w3.org/1999/xhtml">
<head id="Head1" runat="server">
  <title>Untitled Page</title>
    <style type="text/css">
      .properties
      {
        background-color: LightGoldenrodYellow;
        color: black;
        border-collapse: collapse;
      }

      .properties td, .properties th
      {
        border: 1px solid Tan;
        padding: 5px;
      }

      .header { background-color: Tan; }

      .odd { background-color: PaleGoldenrod; }
  </style>
  <script type="text/javascript" language="javascript">
    function displayProperties(instance)
    {
      var td = Sys.Preview.TypeDescriptor.getTypeDescriptor(instance);
      var properties = td._getProperties();

      var columns = ["Property Name", "Property Type", "ReadOnly",
                     "Property Attributes (Name/Value)"];

      var table = document.createElement("table");
      Sys.UI.DomElement.addCssClass(table, "properties");
      var headerRow = table.insertRow(0);
      Sys.UI.DomElement.addCssClass(headerRow, "header");

      var headerCell = null;
      for (var i=0, length = columns.length; i<length; i++)
      {
        headerCell = document.createElement("th");
        headerCell.appendChild(document.createTextNode(columns[i]));
        headerRow.appendChild(headerCell);
      }

      for (var property in properties)
      {
        insertRow(table, properties[property]);
      }
```

(continued)

Listing 10-4 *(continued)*

```
      var container = $get("myDiv");
      container.innerHTML="";
      container.appendChild(table);
    }

    function insertRow(table, property)
    {
      var rowIndex = table.rows.length;
      var row = table.insertRow(rowIndex);
      if (rowIndex % 2 == 1)
        Sys.UI.DomElement.addCssClass(row, "odd");

      insertCell(row, property["name"]);
      insertCell(row, property["type"]);
      insertCell(row, property["readOnly"]);

      var attributesText="No attributes are defined!";
      if (property["attributes"])
      {
        var attributes = property["attributes"];
        var attrBuffer = [];
        for(var attribute in attributes)
        {
          attrBuffer.push(String.format("{0}={1}", attribute,
                                      attributes[attribute]));
        }
        attributesText = attrBuffer.join();
      }
      insertCell(row, attributesText);
    }

    function insertCell(row, value)
    {
      var cell = row.insertCell(row.cells.length);
      cell.appendChild(document.createTextNode(value));
    }

    function pageLoad()
    {
      var instance = new Sys.UI.Control($get("forControl"));
      displayProperties(instance);
    }
  </script>
</head>
<body>
  <form id="form1" runat="server">
    <asp:ScriptManager runat="server" ID="ScriptManager1">
      <Scripts>
        <asp:ScriptReference Assembly="Microsoft.Web.Preview"
        Name="PreviewScript.js" />
      </Scripts>
```

(continued)

Listing 10-4 *(continued)*

```
    </asp:ScriptManager>
    <div id="myDiv"></div>
    <div id="forControl"></div>
  </form>
</body>
</html>
```

For example, if you run this page to view the _properties property of the TypeDescriptor object that describes the Control base class, you'll get the result shown in Figure 10-1.

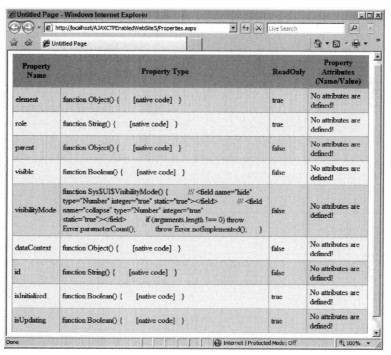

Figure 10-1

Now take a look at the implementation of the pageLoad and displayProperties JavaScript functions shown in Listing 10-4. The pageLoad method instantiates an instance of the Control base class and invokes the displayProperties JavaScript function, passing in the instance as its argument:

```
function pageLoad()
{
  var instance = new Sys.UI.Control($get("forControl"));
  displayProperties(instance);
}
```

The displayProperties method has no knowledge of what the real type of the instance is. All it knows is that the parameter passed into it is an instance of an ASP.NET AJAX client class.

The displayProperties function displays information about the properties of the instance passed into it as its arguments. Thanks to the TypeDescriptor class, the logic that the displayProperties uses to inspect the properties of an ASP.NET AJAX client class instance is type-agnostic, meaning it can be used to inspect the properties of any ASP.NET AJAX client type. This logic is highlighted in the following code:

```
function displayProperties(instance)
{

    var td = Sys.Preview.TypeDescriptor.getTypeDescriptor(instance);
    var properties = td._getProperties();


    ...


    for (var property in properties)
    {
        insertRow(table, properties[property]);
    }


    var container = $get("myDiv");
    container.innerHTML="";
    container.appendChild(table);
}

function insertRow(table, property)

{
    var rowIndex = table.rows.length;
    var row = table.insertRow(rowIndex);
    if (rowIndex % 2 == 1)
        Sys.UI.DomElement.addCssClass(row, "odd");

    insertCell(row, property["name"]);
    insertCell(row, property["type"]);
    insertCell(row, property["readOnly"]);

    var attributesText = "No attributes are defined!";

    if (property["attributes"])

    {

        var attributes = property["attributes"];

        var attrBuffer = [];

        for(var attribute in attributes)
        {
            attrBuffer.push(String.format("{0}={1}", attribute,
                                    attributes[attribute]));
        }

        attributesText = attrBuffer.join();
    }
    insertCell(row, attributesText);
}
```

Here's how this logic works. The `displayProperties` function first needs to access the `TypeDescriptor` object that describes the type of the specified ASP.NET AJAX class instance in a generic fashion. You cannot use the `new` operator to create an instance of the `TypeDescriptor` class directly. Instead, you must call the `getTypeDescriptor` static method on the `TypeDescriptor` method. This static method is discussed in detail later in the chapter, but for now it suffices to say that this method takes an instance of an ASP.NET AJAX type as its argument, and instantiates and returns a `TypeDescriptor` object that describes the type:

```
var td = Sys.Preview.TypeDescriptor.getTypeDescriptor(instance);
```

The `displayProperties` function then calls the `_getProperties` method on the `TypeDescriptor` object to return a reference to its `_properties` property. As discussed previously, this property references a single object literal that contains one name/value pair for each property of the type that the `TypeDescriptor` object describes:

```
var properties = td._getProperties();
```

The `displayProperties` function then iterates through the name/value pairs of this object literal:

```
for (var property in properties)
```

The function invokes the following method for each enumerated name/value pair:

```
insertRow(table, properties[property]);
```

The `insertRow` method inserts a new table row that displays information about the enumerated property or name/value pair. As discussed earlier, the name part of the enumerated name/value pair is a string that contains the name of the associated property. The `displayProperties` function uses this string as an index into the `_properties` property of the `TypeDescriptor` object to access the value part of the enumerated name/value pair. It then passes this value as the second argument into the `insertRow` method.

As discussed earlier, the value part of an enumerated name/value pair references the object literal that describes the property associated with that name/value pair. This object literal contains five name/value pairs. The first name/value pair specifies the name of the property that the object literal describes. The name part of this name/value pair contains `name`, and the value part is a string that contains the name of the property. The `insertRow` method uses `name` as an index into this object literal to access the name of the property, which is then passed into the `insertCell` method to display it within the opening and closing tags of a `<td>` HTML element:

```
insertCell(row, property["name"]);
```

The second name/value pair of this object literal specifies the type of the property that the object literal describes. As discussed earlier, the name part of this name/value pair contains `type`, and the value part references the constructor of the type of the property. The `insertRow` method uses `type` as an index into this object literal to access the reference to this constructor, which is then passed into the `insertCell` method to display it within the opening and closing tags of a `<td>` HTML element:

```
insertCell(row, property["type"]);
```

The `property["type"]` returns a reference to the actual constructor of the property type, which means that you can directly call the `new` operator on this reference to create a new instance of the property type.

357

As discussed earlier, the third name/value pair of this object literal specifies whether the property that the object literal describes is read-only. The name part of this name/value pair is a string that contains `readOnly`, and the value part is a Boolean value. The `insertRow` method uses the string `readOnly` as an index into the object literal to access this Boolean value, which is then passed into the `insertCell` method to display it within the opening and closing tags of a `td` HTML element:

```
insertCell(row, property["readOnly"]);
```

The fourth name/value pair of this object literal describes the attributes that annotate the type of the property that the object literal describes. As discussed previously, the name part of this name/value pair contains `attributes`, and the value part references an object that contains the attributes. The `insertRow` uses `attributes` as an index into the object literal to access this value, iterates through the attributes that this value contains, and displays the value of each attribute within the opening and closing tags of a `<td>` HTML element:

```
var attributesText = "No attributes are defined!";
if (property["attributes"])
{
    var attributes = property["attributes"];
    var attrBuffer = [];
    for(var attribute in attributes)
    {
       attrBuffer.push(String.format("{0}={1}", attribute,
                                  attributes[attribute]));
    }
    attributesText = attrBuffer.join();
}
insertCell(row, attributesText);
```

_methods

This property references an object literal that contains one name/value pair for each method of the type (or base type) that the `TypeDescriptor` object describes. The name part of each name/value is a string that contains the name of the associated method. The value part of each name/value pair is an object literal that describes the associated method. This object literal contains two name/value pairs, and each pair provides a piece of metadata information about the method that the object literal describes, as follows:

❑   The first name/value pair specifies the name of the method. The name part of this name/value pair is `name`, and the value part is a string that contains the name of the method.

❑   The second name/value pair describes the parameters of the method. The name part of this name/value pair is `parameters`, and the value part is an array of object literals. Each object literal in the array describes a parameter of the method and contains two name/value pairs, as follows:

❑   The first name/value pair specifies the name of the parameter. The name part of this name/value pair is `name`, and the value part is a string that contains the name of the parameter.

❑   The second name/value pair describes the type of the parameter. The name part of this name/value pair is `type`, and the value part references the constructor of the type of the property.

For example, the `Control` base class exposes the methods shown in the following table.

Method Name	Parameter Name	Parameter Type
addCssClass	className	String
removeCssClass	className	String
toggleCssClass	className	String

Based on this table, the _methods property of the `TypeDescriptor` object that describes the `Control` base class references the object literal shown in Listing 10-5.

Listing 10-5: The Object Literal Referenced by the _methods Property of the TypeDescriptor Object that Describes Control Base Class References

```
{
  'addCssClass': {name: 'addCssClass',
                  parameters: [{name: 'className', type: String]},
  'removeCssClass': {name: 'removeCssClass',
                     parameters: [{name: 'className', type: String]},
  'toggleCssClass': {name: 'toggleCssClass',
                     parameters: [{name: 'className', type: String]}
}
```

This object literal contains three name/value pairs. The name part of each name/value pair contains the name of a method: `'addCssClass'`, `'removeCssClass'`, and `'toggleCssClass'`. The value part of each name/value pair contains the object literal that describes the corresponding method of the `Control` base class, as follows:

❑ `{name: 'addCssClass', parameters: [{name: 'className', type: String]}`

❑ `{name: 'removeCssClass', parameters: [{name: 'className', type: String]}`

❑ `{name: 'toggleCssClass', parameters: [{name: 'className', type: String]}`

Listing 10-6 shows a page that enables you to display _methods property of the TypeDescriptor object associated with any ASP.NET AJAX client class, including your own custom classes. Figure 10-2 shows what you'll see in your browser when you access this page.

Listing 10-6: A Page that Displays the _methods Property of the TypeDescriptor Object Associated with an ASP.NET AJAX Client Class

```
<%@ Page Language="C#" %>

<!DOCTYPE html PUBLIC "-//W3C//DTD XHTML 1.0 Transitional//EN"
"http://www.w3.org/TR/xhtml1/DTD/xhtml1-transitional.dtd">

<html xmlns="http://www.w3.org/1999/xhtml">
<head id="Head1" runat="server">
  <title>Untitled Page</title>
    <style type="text/css">
```

(continued)

Listing 10-6 *(continued)*

```
    .properties
    {
      background-color: LightGoldenrodYellow;
      color: black;
      border-collapse: collapse;
    }

    .properties td, .properties th
    {
      border: 1px solid Tan;
      padding: 5px;
    }

    .header { background-color: Tan; }

    .odd { background-color: PaleGoldenrod; }
</style>
<script type="text/javascript" language="javascript">
  function displayMethods(instance)
  {
    var td = Sys.Preview.TypeDescriptor.getTypeDescriptor(instance);
    var methods = td._getMethods();

    var columns = ["Method Name", "Parameter (Name/Type)"];

    var table = document.createElement("table");
    Sys.UI.DomElement.addCssClass(table, "properties");
    var headerRow = table.insertRow(0);
    Sys.UI.DomElement.addCssClass(headerRow, "header");

    var headerCell = null;
    for (var i=0, length = columns.length; i<length; i++)
    {
      headerCell = document.createElement("th");
      headerCell.appendChild(document.createTextNode(columns[i]));
      headerRow.appendChild(headerCell);
    }

    for (var m in methods)
    {
      insertRow(table, methods[m]);
    }

    var container = $get("myDiv");
    container.innerHTML = "";
    container.appendChild(table);
  }
```

(continued)

Listing 10-6 *(continued)*

```
  function insertRow(table, method)
  {
    var rowIndex = table.rows.length;
    var row = table.insertRow(rowIndex);
    if (rowIndex % 2 == 1)
      Sys.UI.DomElement.addCssClass(row, "odd");

    insertCell(row, method["name"]);

    var parametersText = "No parameters are defined!";
    if (method["parameters"])
    {
      var parameters = method["parameters"];
      var paramBuffer = [];
      for(var parameter in parameters)
      {
        paramBuffer.push(String.format("({0} / {1})",
            parameters[parameter].name, parameters[parameter].type.getName()));
      }
      parametersText = paramBuffer.join();
    }
    insertCell(row, parametersText);
  }

  function insertCell(row, value)
  {
    var cell = row.insertCell(row.cells.length);
    cell.appendChild(document.createTextNode(value));
  }

  function pageLoad()
  {
    var instance = new Sys.UI.Control($get("forControl"));
    displayMethods(instance);
  }
  </script>
</head>
<body>
  <form id="form1" runat="server">
    <asp:ScriptManager runat="server" ID="ScriptManager1">
      <Scripts>
        <asp:ScriptReference Assembly="Microsoft.Web.Preview"
        Name="PreviewScript.js" />
      </Scripts>
    </asp:ScriptManager>
    <div id="myDiv"></div>
    <div id="forControl"></div>
  </form>
</body>
</html>
```

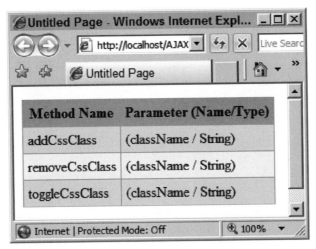

Figure 10-2

As you can see in Listing 10-6, the `pageLoad` method instantiates an instance of the `Control` base class and invokes the `displayMethods` JavaScript function, passing in the instance as its argument:

```
function pageLoad()
{
  var instance = new Sys.UI.Control($get("forControl"));
  displayMethods(instance);
}
```

The `displayMethods` function has no knowledge of what the real type of the instance is. All it knows is that the parameter passed into it is an instance of an ASP.NET AJAX client class.

The `displayMethods` function displays information about the methods of the instance passed into it as its arguments. Thanks to the `TypeDescriptor` class, the logic that `displayMethods` uses to inspect the methods of an ASP.NET AJAX client class instance is type-agnostic, which means it can be used to inspect the methods of any ASP.NET AJAX client type. This logic is highlighted in the following code:

```
function displayMethods(instance)
{

  var td = Sys.Preview.TypeDescriptor.getTypeDescriptor(instance);
  var methods = td._getMethods();

  ...

  for (var m in methods)
  {
    insertRow(table, methods[m]);
  }

  var container = $get("myDiv");
  container.innerHTML = "";
  container.appendChild(table);
}
```

(continued)

(continued)

```
function insertRow(table, method)
{
  var rowIndex = table.rows.length;
  var row = table.insertRow(rowIndex);
  if (rowIndex % 2 == 1)
    Sys.UI.DomElement.addCssClass(row, "odd");

  insertCell(row, method["name"]);

  var parametersText = "No parameters are defined!";

  if (method["parameters"])
  {
    var parameters = method["parameters"];
    var paramBuffer = [];

    for(var parameter in parameters)
    {
      paramBuffer.push(String.format("({0} / {1})",
          parameters[parameter].name, parameters[parameter].type.getName()));
    }

    parametersText = paramBuffer.join();
  }
  insertCell(row, parametersText);
}
```

The `displayMethods` function first accesses the `TypeDescriptor` object:

```
var td = Sys.Preview.TypeDescriptor.getTypeDescriptor(instance);
```

The `displayMethods` function then calls the `_getMethods` method on the `TypeDescriptor` object to return a reference to its `_methods` property. This property references a single object literal that contains one name/value pair for each method of the type that the `TypeDescriptor` object describes:

```
var methods = td._getMethods();
```

The `displayMethods` function then iterates through the name/value pairs of this object literal:

```
for (var m in methods)
```

As discussed earlier, the name part of the enumerated name/value pair is a string that contains the name of the associated method. The `displayMethods` function uses this string as an index into the `_methods` property of the `TypeDescriptor` object to access the value part of the enumerated name/value pair. The value part references the object literal that describes the method associated with the name/value pair. The `displayMethods` then passes this object literal into the `insertRow` method:

```
insertRow(table, methods[m]);
```

This object literal contains two name/value pairs. The first name/value pair specifies the name of the method that the object literal describes. The name part of this name/value pair contains name, and the value part is a string that contains the name of the method. insertRow uses name as an index into this object literal to access the name of the method, which is then passed into the insertCell method to display it within the opening and closing tags of a <td> HTML element:

```
insertCell(row, method["name"]);
```

The second name/value pair of this object literal describes the parameters of the method that the object literal describes. The name part of this name/value pair contains parameters, and the value part references an array that contains one object for each parameter of the associated method. Each of these objects in turn contains two name/value pairs that describe the name and type of the parameter.

insertRow iterates through these objects and displays the name and type of each parameter:

```
for(var parameter in parameters)
{
  paramBuffer.push(String.format("({0} / {1})",
      parameters[parameter].name, parameters[parameter].type.getName()));
}
parametersText = paramBuffer.join();

insertCell(row, parametersText);
```

_events

This property references an object literal that contains one name/value pair for each event of the type (or base type) that the TypeDescriptor object describes. The name part of each name/value is a string that contains the name of the event associated with the pair. The value part of each name/value pair is an object literal that describes the event associated with the pair. This object literal contains a single name/value pair that specifies the name of the event. The name part of this name/value pair is name, and the value part is a string that contains the name of the event.

For example, the Control base class exposes a single event named propertyChanged. Therefore, the _events property of the TypeDescriptor object that describes the Control base class references the object literal shown in Listing 10-7.

Listing 10-7: The Object Literal Referenced by the _events Property of the TypeDescriptor Object that Describes Control Base Class References

```
{
  'propertyChanged': {name: 'propertyChanged'}
}
```

This object literal contains a single name/value pair. The name part of this name/value pair is a string that contains the name of the event: 'propertyChanged'. The value part of this name/value pair contains the object literal that describes the event of the Control base class: {name: 'propertyChanged'}.

Now, let's take a look at the _events property of the TypeDescriptor object that describes the Button client control. Because the Button control derives from the Control class, it inherits the propertyChanged event from its base class. The Button control also exposes an event of its own named click. Listing 10-8 shows the object literal that the _events property of the TypeDescriptor object references.

Listing 10-8: The Object Literal Referenced by the _events Property of the TypeDescriptor Object that Describes Button Base Class References

```
{
  'click': {name: 'click'},
  'propertyChanged': {name: 'propertyChanged'}
}
```

Listing 10-9 shows a page that displays the _events property of the TypeDescriptor object associated with any ASP.NET AJAX client class, including custom classes. Figure 10-3 shows what the browser displays when you access this page.

Listing 10-9: A Page that Displays the _events Property of the TypeDescriptor Object Associated with an ASP.NET AJAX Client Class

```
<%@ Page Language="C#" %>

<!DOCTYPE html PUBLIC "-//W3C//DTD XHTML 1.0 Transitional//EN"
"http://www.w3.org/TR/xhtml1/DTD/xhtml1-transitional.dtd">

<html xmlns="http://www.w3.org/1999/xhtml">
<head id="Head1" runat="server">
  <title>Untitled Page</title>
    <style type="text/css">
      .properties
      {
        background-color: LightGoldenrodYellow;
        color: black;
        border-collapse: collapse;
      }

      .properties td, .properties th
      {
        border: 1px solid Tan;
        padding: 5px;
      }

      .header { background-color: Tan; }

      .odd { background-color: PaleGoldenrod; }
    </style>
    <script type="text/javascript" language="javascript">
      function displayEvents(instance)
      {
        var td = Sys.Preview.TypeDescriptor.getTypeDescriptor(instance);
        var events = td._getEvents();

        var columns = ["Event Name"];

        var table = document.createElement("table");
        Sys.UI.DomElement.addCssClass(table, "properties");
        var headerRow = table.insertRow(0);
        Sys.UI.DomElement.addCssClass(headerRow, "header");
```

(continued)

Listing 10-9 *(continued)*

```
      var headerCell = null;
      for (var i=0, length = columns.length; i<length; i++)
      {
        headerCell = document.createElement("th");
        headerCell.appendChild(document.createTextNode(columns[i]));
        headerRow.appendChild(headerCell);
      }

      for (var e in events)
      {
        insertRow(table, events[e]);
      }

      var container = $get("myDiv");
      container.innerHTML = "";
      container.appendChild(table);
    }

    function insertRow(table, event)
    {
      var rowIndex = table.rows.length;
      var row = table.insertRow(rowIndex);
      if (rowIndex % 2 == 1)
        Sys.UI.DomElement.addCssClass(row, "odd");

      insertCell(row, event["name"]);
    }

    function insertCell(row, value)
    {
      var cell = row.insertCell(row.cells.length);
      cell.appendChild(document.createTextNode(value));
    }

    function pageLoad()
    {
      var instance = new Sys.Preview.UI.Button($get("forControl"));
      displayEvents(instance);
    }
  </script>
</head>
<body>
  <form id="form1" runat="server">
    <asp:ScriptManager runat="server" ID="ScriptManager1">
      <Scripts>
        <asp:ScriptReference Assembly="Microsoft.Web.Preview"
Name="PreviewScript.js" />
      </Scripts>
    </asp:ScriptManager>
    <center><div id="myDiv"></div></center>
    <div id="forControl"></div>
  </form>
</body>
</html>
```

Figure 10-3

If you run the page shown in Listing 10-9 for the Button control, you should see the result shown in Figure 10-4.

Figure 10-4

Now, let's take a look at the implementation of the pageLoad method and displayEvents function shown in Listing 10-9. The pageLoad method instantiates an instance of the Control base class as usual and invokes the displayEvents JavaScript function, passing in the instance as its argument:

```
function pageLoad()
{
  var instance = new Sys.UI.Control($get("forControl"));
  displayEvents (instance);
}
```

displayEvents has no knowledge of what the real type of the instance is. All it knows is that the parameter passed into it is an instance of an ASP.NET AJAX client class.

The displayEvents function displays information about the events of the instance passed into it as its arguments. Thanks to the TypeDescriptor class, the logic that displayEvents uses to inspect the events of an ASP.NET AJAX client class instance is type-agnostic, which means you can use it to inspect

367

the events of any ASP.NET AJAX client type. This logic is highlighted in the following code:

```
function displayEvents(instance)
{
    var td = Sys.Preview.TypeDescriptor.getTypeDescriptor(instance);
    var events = td._getEvents();

    ...

    for (var e in events)
    {
        insertRow(table, events[e]);
    }

    var container = $get("myDiv");
    container.innerHTML="";
    container.appendChild(table);
}

function insertRow(table, event)

{
    var rowIndex = table.rows.length;
    var row = table.insertRow(rowIndex);
    if (rowIndex % 2 == 1)
        Sys.UI.DomElement.addCssClass(row, "odd");

    insertCell(row, event["name"]);

}
```

Here's how this logic works. The `displayEvents` function first calls the `getTypeDescriptor` static method on the `TypeDescriptor` class, passing in the instance to access the `TypeDescriptor` object that describes the type of the instance in a generic fashion:

```
var td = Sys.Preview.TypeDescriptor.getTypeDescriptor(instance);
```

The `displayEvents` function then calls the `_getEvents` method on the `TypeDescriptor` object to return a reference to its `_events` property. This property references a single object literal that contains one name/value pair for each event of the type that the `TypeDescriptor` object describes:

```
var properties = td._getEvents();
```

The `displayEvents` function then iterates through the name/value pairs of this object literal:

```
for (var e in events)
```

The name part of the enumerated name/value pair is a string that contains the name of the associated event. The `displayEvents` function uses this string as an index into the `_events` property of the `TypeDescriptor` object to access the value part of the enumerated name/value pair. The value part references the object literal that describes the event associated with the name/value pair. The `displayEvents` function then passes this object literal into the `insertRow` method:

```
insertRow(table, events[e]);
```

This object literal contains a single name/value pair. The name part of the pair is `name`, and the value part is a string that contains the name of the event. The `insertRow` function invokes the `insertCell` method to display this value:

```
insertCell(row, event["name"]);
```

getTypeDescriptor

The previous sections provided several examples of how you can use the `getTypeDescriptor` method in your own applications. This section walks you through the internal implementation of this method to introduce its extensibility points, setting the stage for later discussions of why, when, and how to extend the `getTypeDescriptor` method.

The `getTypeDescriptor` method takes an instance of a type as its argument and returns a `TypeDescriptor` object that describes the type, as shown in Listing 10-10.

Listing 10-10 : The getTypeDescriptor Static Method of the TypeDescriptor Class

```
Sys.Preview.TypeDescriptor.getTypeDescriptor =
function Sys$Preview$TypeDescriptor$getTypeDescriptor(instance)
{
  var type = Object.getType(instance);
  var td = type._descriptor;
  if (!td && !type._descriptorChecked)
  {
    if (Sys.Preview.ITypeDescriptorProvider.isImplementedBy(instance))
      td = instance.getDescriptor();

    else
      td = Sys.Preview.TypeDescriptor.generateDescriptor(type);

    type._descriptor = td;
    type._descriptorChecked = true;
  }
  return td;
}
```

The `getTypeDescriptor` method first calls the `getType` static method on the `Object` class, passing in the type instance to return a reference to the type itself:

```
var type = Object.getType(instance);
```

Next, it checks whether the type instance implements an interface named `ITypeDescriptorProvider`. If so, it delegates the responsibility of creating and initializing the `TypeDescriptor` object that represents the type to the `getDescriptor` method of the type itself. If not, it calls the `generateDescriptor` static method on the `TypeDescriptor` class to create and initialize a `TypeDescriptor` object that describes the type. In either case, the `TypeDescriptor` object is cached in an internal field named `_descriptor` for future access. Subsequent calls to the `getTypeDescriptor` method will be serviced from the cache to improve performance.

You can extend the functionality of the `TypeDescriptor` class by having your type implement the `ITypeDescriptorProvider` interface. This interface exposes a single method named `getDescriptor`.

369

Your type's implementation of this method must use whatever logic is necessary to create and initialize an `ICustomTypeDescriptor` object and return the object to its caller.

generateDescriptor

This section presents the internal implementation of the `TypeDescriptor` class's `generateDescriptor` static method to help you understand the significant role that the `descriptor` property of a type plays in enabling others to inspect its members, and why it is important to implement the `descriptor` property of your ASP.NET AJAX client classes.

Listing 10-11 contains the internal code for the `generateDescriptor` static method of the `TypeDescriptor` class. This method takes a reference to a type and returns a `TypeDescriptor` object that describes the type.

Listing 10-11 : The generateDescriptor Static Method of the TypeDescriptor Class

```
Sys.Preview.TypeDescriptor.generateDescriptor =
function Sys$Preview$TypeDescriptor$generateDescriptor(type)
{
  var td = null;
  var current = type;
  while(current)
  {
    if(current.descriptor)
    {
      if(!td)
        td = new Sys.Preview.TypeDescriptor();

      Sys.Preview.TypeDescriptor.append(td, current.descriptor);
    }
    current = current.getBaseType();
  }
  return td;
}
```

The `generateDescriptor` method first instantiates an instance of the `TypeDescriptor` class:

```
td = new Sys.Preview.TypeDescriptor();
```

Then, starting with the type itself, the `generateDescriptor` method marches upward through the ancestor types, calling the `append` static method on the `TypeDescriptor` class to append each type's `descriptor` property to the newly instantiated `TypeDescriptor` object.

The default implementation of the `getTypeDescriptor` method (the method that calls the `generateDescriptor` method) assumes that your ASP.NET AJAX type and its ancestor ASP.NET AJAX types expose metadata information about their properties, methods, events, and attributes through a static property named `descriptor`. If your ASP.NET AJAX client type does not implement the `descriptor` property, the clients of your type will not be able to use the `TypeDescriptor` class to inspect its members. If one of the ancestor ASP.NET AJAX client types of your ASP.NET AJAX client type does not implement the `descriptor` property, the clients of your type will not be able to inspect the members that your type inherits from that ancestor type.

Your type can override this default implementation by implementing the ITypeDescriptorProvider interface, as you'll see later.

append

This section walks you through the internal implementation of the TypeDescriptor class's append static method to help you understand the following:

❑ The significant role that the descriptor static property of a type plays in the ASP.NET AJAX type description capabilities

❑ How to implement the descriptor property of your own ASP.NET AJAX client types

❑ The four different kinds of metadata information that the descriptor static property of your ASP.NET AJAX class can expose to its clients

A descriptor static property of a type references an object literal that contains up to five name/value pairs, as follows:

❑ The first name/value pair describes the properties of the type. The name part of this name/value pair contains properties, and the value part references an array of object literals. Each object literal in this array describes a property of the type and contains up to four name/value pairs, as follows:

　❑ The first name/value pair specifies the name of the property. The name part of this name/value pair is name, and the value part is a string that contains the name of the property.

　❑ The second name/value pair specifies the type of the property. The name part of this name/value pair is type, and the value part references the actual type of the property.

　❑ The third name/value pair specifies whether the property is read-only. The name part of this name/value pair is the 'readOnly' string, and value part is a Boolean.

　❑ The fourth name/value pair specifies the attributes of the property.

　❑ The fifth name/value pair specifies whether the property references a DOM element. The name part of this name/value pair is isDomElement, and the value part is a Boolean value.

❑ The second name/value pair describes the methods of the type. The name part of the pair is methods, and the value part is an array of object literals. Each object literal in this array describes a method of the type and contains two name/value pairs, as follows:

　❑ The first name/value pair specifies the name of the method. The name part of the pair is name, and the value part is a string that contains the name of the method.

　❑ The second name/value pair describes the parameters of the method. The name part of the pair is parameters, and the value part is an array of object literals. Each object literal in this array describes a parameter of the method and contains two name/value pairs. The first name/value pair specifies the name of the parameter where the name part of the pair is name, and the value part is a string that contains the name of the parameter. The second name/value pair specifies the type of the parameter where the name part of the pair is type, and the value part references the actual type of the parameter.

❑ The third name/value pair describes the events of the type. The name part of the pair is events, and the value part is an array of object literals. Each object literal in this array describes an event of the type and contains a single name/value pair where the name part of the pair is `name`, and the value part is a string that contains the name of the event.

❏ The fourth name/value pair describes the attributes of the type. The name part of the pair is `attributes`, and the value part is an array of object literals. Each object literal in this array describes an attribute and contains two name/value pairs, as follows:

❏ The first name/value pair specifies the name of the attribute. The name part of the pair is `name`, and the value part is a string that contains the name of the attribute.

❏ The second name/value pair specifies the value of the attribute The name part of the pair is `value`, and the value part is the actual value of the attribute.

Listing 10-12 shows the `append` static method of the `TypeDescriptor` class.

Listing 10-12: The append Static Method of the TypeDescriptor Class

```
Sys.Preview.TypeDescriptor.append =
function Sys$Preview$TypeDescriptor$append(td, descriptor)
{
  if (descriptor.properties)
  {
    var length = descriptor.properties.length;
    for (var i = 0; i < length; i++)
    {
      var property = descriptor.properties[i];
      var propertyName = property.name;
      var associatedAttributes = property.attributes;
      var readOnly = property.readOnly? property.readOnly : false;
      var isDomElement = !!(property.isDomElement);
      var isInteger = !!(property.isInteger);

      if (! td._getProperties()[propertyName])
      {
        var args = [propertyName, property.type, readOnly, isDomElement];
        if(typeof(associatedAttributes) === 'array')
        {
          for(var j = 0, l = associatedAttributes.length; j < l; j++)
          {
            var attrib = associatedAttributes[j];
            args[args.length] = attrib.name;
            args[args.length] = attrib.value;
          }
        }

        var propInfo = td.addProperty.apply(td, args);
        propInfo.isInteger = isInteger;
      }
    }
  }
}
```

(continued)

Listing 10-12 *(continued)*

```javascript
  if (descriptor.events)
  {
    var length = descriptor.events.length;
    for (var i = 0; i < length; i++)
    {
      var eventName = descriptor.events[i].name
      if (! td._getEvents()[eventName])
        td.addEvent(eventName);
    }
  }

  if (descriptor.methods)
  {
    var length = descriptor.methods.length;
    for (var i = 0; i < length; i++)
    {
      var methodName = descriptor.methods[i].name;
      if (! td._getMethods()[methodName])
      {
        var params = descriptor.methods[i].params;
        if(!params)
          params = descriptor.methods[i].parameters;
        if (params)
          td.addMethod(methodName, params);

        else
          td.addMethod(methodName);
      }
    }
  }

  if (descriptor.attributes)
  {
    var length = descriptor.attributes.length;
    for (var i = 0; i < length; i++)
    {
      var attributeName = descriptor.attributes[i].name
      if (! td._getAttributes()[attributeName])
        td.addAttribute(attributeName, descriptor.attributes[i].value);
    }
  }
}
```

The append static method takes two arguments. The first argument references the TypeDescriptor object that describes a type, and the second argument references the descriptor property of another type. The main goal of the append method is to copy the contents of the descriptor property of the latter type into the TypeDescriptor object that describes the former type.

The descriptor property contains up to four name/value pairs. The name parts of these four pairs are properties, events, methods, and attributes. The value parts of these four pairs are arrays of object literals, where each object literal describes a property, event, method, or attribute of the type. That is why the append static method consists of four major sections — each section copies the contents of the associated array into the specified TypeDescriptor object.

After the completion of the call into the `append` method, the `TypeDescriptor` object contains the contents of the `descriptor` property of the other type in addition to its original content. As previously discussed, the `generateDescriptor` method calls the `append` method to append the contents of the `descriptor` properties of all the ancestor types of a given type into the `TypeDescriptor` object that represents the type. Therefore, the `_getProperties`, `_getMethods`, `_getEvents`, and `_getAttributes` methods of the `TypeDescriptor` object return all the properties, methods, events, and attributes of the ancestor types of the type, in addition to the properties, methods, events, and attributes of the type itself.

getProperty

The `TypeDescriptor` class includes a static method named `getProperty` that takes up to three parameters. The first parameter references an instance of a type whose property value is being queried. The second parameter is a string that contains the name of a property whose value is being queried. The last parameter is optional. The main responsibility of the `getProperty` method is to return the value of the specified property of the specified instance of the type.

This section walks you through the internal implementation of the `getProperty` method to help you understand the following:

❑ The extensibility points of this method, which sets the stage for later discussions of why, when, and how to extend the `getProperty` method of the `TypeDescriptor` class

❑ The role that the last argument of the `getProperty` method plays, and why and when you should specify this argument

Listing 10-13 shows the `getProperty` static method.

Listing 10-13: The getProperty Static Method of the TypeDescriptor Class

```
Sys.Preview.TypeDescriptor.getProperty =
function Sys$Preview$TypeDescriptor$getProperty(instance, propertyName, key)
{
  if (Sys.Preview.ICustomTypeDescriptor.isImplementedBy(instance))
    return instance.getProperty(propertyName, key);

  var td = Sys.Preview.TypeDescriptor.getTypeDescriptor(instance);
  ...

  var propertyInfo = td._getProperties()[propertyName];
  var getter = instance['get_' + propertyInfo.name];
  var object = getter.call(instance);
  if (key)
    object = key.indexOf('.') === -1 ? (object[key]) :
             (Sys.Preview.TypeDescriptor._evaluatePath(object, key));

  return object;
}
```

The `getProperty` method first checks whether the instance implements the `ICustomTypeDescriptor` interface. If so, the method delegates the responsibility of retrieving the property value to the `getProperty` method of the instance itself. Note that the method simply returns the value returned from the `getProperty` method of the instance:

```
if (Sys.Preview.ICustomTypeDescriptor.isImplementedBy(instance))
    return instance.getProperty(propertyName, key);
```

Therefore, you can customize the functionality of the getProperty method by having your type implement the ICustomTypeDescriptor interface. As you'll see later, your type's implementation of the getProperty method of this interface must use whatever logic necessary to retrieve the value of the property with the specified name.

If the instance does not implement the ICustomTypeDescriptor interface, the getProperty method takes the following actions:

❑ It calls the getTypeDescriptor static method on the TypeDescriptor class, passing in the instance to return a reference to the TypeDescriptor object that describes the type of the instance in a generic fashion:

```
var td = Sys.Preview.TypeDescriptor.getTypeDescriptor(instance);
```

This is the first step you must take every time you need to use the ASP.NET AJAX type inspection capabilities. (This was also the first step taken in Listings 10-4, 10-6, and 10-9.)

❑ It calls the _getProperties method on the TypeDescriptor object to return a reference to the _properties array property of the object. It uses the property name as an index into this array to return the object literal that describes the property with the specified name:

```
var propertyInfo = td._getProperties()[propertyName];
```

As discussed earlier, this object literal contains up to four name/value pairs where each pair provides a piece of metadata information about the property. The first name/value pair specifies the name of the property where the name part of the pair is name, and the value part is a string that contains the name of the property. The getProperty method uses name to access the value part (the string containing the name of the property) and appends this string to the string "get_" to arrive at the name of the getter method that gets the value of the property.

❑ It uses the name of the getter method as an index into the instance to return a reference to the getter method itself:

```
var getter = instance['get_' + propertyInfo.name];
```

❑ It invokes the call method on the getter method, passing in the instance to return the value of the property:

```
var object = getter.call(instance);
```

The third optional parameter of the getProperty method is named key. The meaning of key depends on the implementation of the getProperty method. The default implementation (which is what's shown in Listing 10-13) interprets the key as the name of a descendant subproperty of the specified property. The descendant subproperties of a property include the subproperties of the property, the subproperties of the subproperties of the property, the subproperties of the subproperties of the subproperties of the property, and so on. Therefore, if you call the getProperty method with the third argument, the method assumes that you're asking for the value of a descendant subproperty whose name is given by the key parameter.

If the `key` does not contain the character dot (.), the `getProperty` method assumes that you're asking for the value of the immediate subproperty, as shown in boldfaced portion of the following code fragment:

```
object = key.indexOf('.') === -1 ? (object[key]) :
              (Sys.Preview.TypeDescriptor._evaluatePath(object, key));
```

Otherwise, the method calls the `_evaluatePath` method, where it iterates through the descendant subproperties of the specified property to find the subproperty whose name is given by the `key`, as shown in Listing 10-14.

Listing 10-14: The _evaluatePath Static Method of the TypeDescriptor Class

```
Sys.Preview.TypeDescriptor._evaluatePath =
function Sys$Preview$TypeDescriptor$_evaluatePath(instance, path)
{
  var part;
  var parts = path.split('.');
  var current = instance;
  for(var i = 0; i < parts.length; i++)
  {
    part = parts[i];
    current = current[part];
    if(typeof(current) === 'undefined' || current === null)
      return null;
  }
  return current;
}
```

The great thing about the `getProperty` method is that it enables you to access the value of the property of an ASP.NET AJAX type instance without having to know the real type of the instance. This enables you to access the values of the properties of ASP.NET AJAX objects in type-agnostic fashion, which means that you can write one set of JavaScript code to query the property values of any ASP.NET AJAX object of any type.

getAttribute

The `TypeDescriptor` class features a static method named `getAttribute` that takes two parameters. The first parameter references an instance of an ASP.NET AJAX type. The second parameter is a string that contains the name of an attribute of the type. The main goal of the `getAttribute` method is to retrieve and return the value of the specified attribute of a specified instance. Listing 10-15 shows this method.

Listing 10-15: The getAttribute Static Method of the TypeDescriptor Class

```
Sys.Preview.TypeDescriptor.getAttribute =
function Sys$Preview$TypeDescriptor$getAttribute(instance, attributeName)
{
  var td = Sys.Preview.TypeDescriptor.getTypeDescriptor(instance);
  return td._getAttributes()[attributeName];
}
```

The `getAttribute` method first invokes the `getTypeDescriptor` static method on the `TypeDescriptor` class, passing in the instance to return a reference to the `TypeDescriptor` object that describes the type of the instance in a generic fashion:

```
var td = Sys.Preview.TypeDescriptor.getTypeDescriptor(instance);
```

Next, it invokes the `_getAttributes` method on the `TypeDescriptor` object to return a reference to the object's `_attributes` collection, and uses the attribute name as an index into this collection to return the attribute's value:

```
return td._getAttributes()[attributeName];
```

setProperty

The `setProperty` method of the `TypeDescriptor` class takes up to four parameters. The first parameter references an instance of an ASP.NET AJAX type. The second parameter is a string that contains the name of a property of the type. The third parameter contains the value of the property. The fourth parameter is optional. The main goal of the `setProperty` method is to set the specified property of the specified instance to a specified value.

This section walks you through the internal implementation of the `setProperty` method to help you understand the following:

❑ The extensibility points of this method

❑ The role the last argument of the `setProperty` method plays, and why and when you should specify this argument

Listing 10-16 shows this method.

Listing 10-16: The setProperty Static Method of the TypeDescriptor Class

```
Sys.Preview.TypeDescriptor.setProperty =
function Sys$Preview$TypeDescriptor$setProperty(instance, propertyName, value, key)
{
  if (Sys.Preview.ICustomTypeDescriptor.isImplementedBy(instance))
  {
    instance.setProperty(propertyName, value, key);
    return;
  }

  var td = Sys.Preview.TypeDescriptor.getTypeDescriptor(instance);
  ...
  var propertyInfo = td._getProperties()[propertyName]; if (key)
  {
    var getter = instance['get_' + propertyInfo.name];
    var object = getter.call(instance);
    if(key.indexOf('.') === -1)
      object[key] = value;
```

(continued)

Listing 10-16 (continued)

```
    else
       Sys.Preview.TypeDescriptor._setPath(object, key, value);
    }

    else
    {
      var setter = instance['set_' + propertyInfo.name];
      value = Sys.Preview.TypeDescriptor._evaluateValue( propertyInfo.type,
                                                         propertyInfo.isDomElement,
                                                         propertyInfo.isInteger,
                                                         value);

      setter.call(instance, value);
    }
}
```

The setProperty method first checks whether the instance implements the ICustomTypeDescriptor interface. If so, it delegates the responsibility of setting the value of the property to the setProperty method of the instance itself:

```
if (Sys.Preview.ICustomTypeDescriptor.isImplementedBy(instance))
{
  instance.setProperty(propertyName, value, key);
  return;
}
```

You can customize the setProperty method by having your type implement the ICustomTypeDescriptor interface. The setProperty method of this interface must use the appropriate logic to set the specified property to the specified value.

If the instance does not implement the ICustomTypeDescriptor interface, the setProperty method takes these actions to set the value of the property. First, it invokes the getTypeDescriptor static method on the TypeDescriptor class, passing in the instance to return a reference to the TypeDescriptor object that describes the type of the instance in generic fashion:

```
var td = Sys.Preview.TypeDescriptor.getTypeDescriptor(instance);
```

This is always the first step whenever you need to use the type description capabilities of the ASP.NET AJAX client-side framework.

Next, the method invokes the _getProperties method on the TypeDescriptor object to return a reference to the _properties object that contains one object literal for each property of the type, and uses the property name as an index into this object to return a reference to the object literal associated with the property with the specified name:

```
var propertyInfo = td._getProperties()[propertyName];
```

What the setProperty method does next depends on whether you have invoked the method with the fourth argument — the key value.

If you did not specify a key, the setProperty method assumes that you're trying to set the value of the property itself, not one of its subproperties. As such, the method appends the name of the property to the string "set_" to arrive at the name of the setter method that sets the value of the property:

```
var setter = instance['set_' + propertyInfo.name];
```

Next, the method invokes the _evaluateValue static method on the TypeDescriptor class:

```
value = Sys.Preview.TypeDescriptor._evaluateValue( propertyInfo.type,
                                                   propertyInfo.isDomElement,
                                                   propertyInfo.isInteger,
                                                   value);
```

As you'll see shortly, this method converts the specified value to the type that the property expects if the value is not of the same type as the property type:

Then, the setProperty method invokes the call method on the setter method to set the value of the specified property to the specified value:

```
setter.call(instance, value);
```

If you specified a key, the setProperty method assumes that you're not trying to set the value of the property with the specified name. Instead, you want to set the value of the descendant subproperty whose fully qualified name, including its complete containment hierarchy, is given by the key parameter. As such, the setProperty method first appends the name of the property to the string "get_" to arrive at the name of the getter method for the property with the specified name:

```
var getter = instance['get_' + propertyInfo.name];
```

It then invokes the call method on the getter method, passing in the instance to return the value of the specified property:

```
var object = getter.call(instance);
```

Next, it checks whether key contains the dot (.) character. If not, it assumes that you're trying to set the value of the immediate subproperty whose name is given by key:

```
if(key.indexOf('.') === -1) object[key] = value;
```

If the key contains the dot (.) character, it calls the _setPath method on the TypeDescriptor class, as shown in Listing 10-17.

Listing 10-17: The _setPath Static Method of the TypeDescriptor Class

```
Sys.Preview.TypeDescriptor._setPath =
function Sys$Preview$TypeDescriptor$_setPath(instance, path, value)
{
  var current = instance;
  var parts = path.split('.');
  var part;
```

(continued)

379

Listing 10-17 *(continued)*

```
    for(var i = 0; i < parts.length-1; i++)
    {
      part = parts[i];
      current = current[part];
      if(!current) break;
    }

    if(current)
      current[parts[parts.length-1]] = value;
}
```

The _setPath method searches through the descendant subproperties of the specified property to find the subproperty whose fully qualified name (including its complete containment hierarchy) is given by key, and then sets its value:

```
    else
      Sys.Preview.TypeDescriptor._setPath(object, key, value);
```

Now let's move on to the internal implementation of the _evaluateValue method of the TypeDescriptor class. It is important that you understand what kinds of type conversions this method supports because if you call the setProperties method to set the value of a property to a value whose type the _evaluateValue method cannot convert, the call will fail.

Listing 10-18 shows the _evaluateValue method.

Listing 10-18: The _evaluateValue Static Method of the TypeDescriptor Class

```
Sys.Preview.TypeDescriptor._evaluateValue =
function Sys$Preview$TypeDescriptor$_evaluateValue(targetType, isDomElement,
                                                   isInteger, value)
{
  var valueType = typeof(value);
  if(isDomElement)
  {
    if(valueType === "string")
      value = $get(value);
  }

  else if(targetType === Object || targetType === Sys.Component ||
          targetType.inheritsFrom(Sys.Component))
  {
    if(valueType === "string")
      value = $find(value);
  }

  else
  {
    if(targetType !== String && valueType === "string")
    {
      if(Type.isEnum(targetType))
        value = targetType.parse(value, true);
      else
```

(continued)

Listing 10-18 *(continued)*

```
      {
        value = targetType.parse(value);
        if (targetType === Number && isInteger)
          value = Math.floor(value);
      }
    }

    else if(targetType === String && valueType !== "string")
      value = value.toString();

    else if(targetType === Number && isInteger)
      value = Math.floor(value);
  }

  return value;
}
```

The _evaluateValue static method of the TypeDescriptor class takes four parameters. The first parameter references the type of the property. The second parameter is a Boolean value that specifies whether the property references a DOM element. The third parameter is a Boolean value that specifies whether the property is an integer. The fourth parameter is the value to be assigned to the property. The _evaluateValue method supports the following three important type conversion scenarios:

❑ If the property references a DOM element and the value to be assigned to the property is a string, the _evaluateValue assumes that the string contains the value of the DOM element's id HTML attribute and, consequently, calls the $get global JavaScript function to return a reference to the associated DOM element. In a way, the _evaluateValue method converts the string into a DOM element, which can then be assigned to the property as its value:

```
if(isDomElement)
{
  if(valueType === "string")
    value = $get(value);
}
```

❑ If the property references an ASP.NET AJAX component, and the value to be assigned to the property is a string, the _evaluateValue method assumes that the string contains the value of the id property of a component and, consequently, uses the $find global JavaScript function to return a reference to the associated component, which can then been assigned to the property. In a way, the _evaluateValue method converts this string into an ASP.NET AJAX component:

```
else if(targetType === Object || targetType === Sys.Component ||
        targetType.inheritsFrom(Sys.Component))
{
  if(valueType === "string") value = $find(value);
}
```

❑ If the property is of type enumeration, and the value to be assigned to the property is a string, the _evaluateValue method calls the parse method on the type to convert the string into the type of the property, which can then be assigned to the property:

```
value = targetType.parse(value, true);
```

❑ If the property is not of type `string`, but the value to be assigned to the property is a string, the `_evaluateValue` method calls the `parse` or `parseInvariant` method on the type to convert the string into the type of the property, which can then be assigned to the property:

```
value = (targetType.parseInvariant || targetType.parse)(value);
```

❑ If the property is of type `string`, but the value to be assigned to the property is not a string, the `_evaluateValue` method calls the `toString` method on the value to convert the value into a string, which can then be assigned to the property:

```
else if(targetType === String && valueType !== "string")
  value = value.toString();
```

❑ If the property is of type `integer`, the `_evaluateValue` method passes the value to be assigned to the property into the `floor` static method of the `Math` class. The return value of this static method can then be assigned to the property:

```
else if(targetType === Number && isInteger)
  value = Math.floor(value);
```

❑ In all other cases, no conversion is done, and the value is used as is.

invokeMethod

The `TypeDescriptor` class exposes a static method named `InvokeMethod` that takes three parameters. The first parameter references the type instance on which the specified method must be invoked. The second parameter is a string that contains the name of the method to be invoked. The third parameter is an object literal that contains one name/value pair for each parameter of the method where the name part of each pair is a string that contains the name of the associated parameter and the value part contains the value of the parameter.

This section discusses the internal implementation of the `invokeMethod` static method to introduce the extensibility points of the method. Listing 10-19 shows this method.

Listing 10-19: The invokeMethod Static Method of the TypeDescriptor Class

```
Sys.Preview.TypeDescriptor.invokeMethod =
function Sys$Preview$TypeDescriptor$invokeMethod(instance, methodName, parameters)
{
  if (Sys.Preview.ICustomTypeDescriptor.isImplementedBy(instance))
    return instance.invokeMethod(methodName, parameters);

  var td = Sys.Preview.TypeDescriptor.getTypeDescriptor(instance);
  ...

  var methodInfo = td._getMethods()[methodName];
  var method = instance[methodInfo.name];
```

(continued)

Listing 10-19 *(continued)*

```
if (!parameters || !methodInfo.parameters ||!methodInfo.parameters.length)
  return method.call(instance);

else
{
  var arguments = [];
  for (var i = 0; i < methodInfo.parameters.length; i++)
  {
    var parameterInfo = methodInfo.parameters[i];
    var value = parameters[parameterInfo.name];
    value = Sys.Preview.TypeDescriptor._evaluateValue(
                              parameterInfo.type,
                              parameterInfo.isDomElement,
                              parameterInfo.isInteger,
                              value);
    arguments[i] = value;
  }

  return method.apply(instance, arguments);
}
}
```

The `InvokeMethod` first checks whether the instance implements the `ICustomTypeDescriptor` interface. If so, it delegates the responsibility of invoking the specified method to the `invokeMethod` of the instance itself:

```
if (Sys.Preview.ICustomTypeDescriptor.isImplementedBy(instance))
    return instance.invokeMethod(methodName, parameters);
```

You can customize the `invokeMethod` method by having your type implement the `ICustomTypeDescriptor` interface. Your type's implementation of the `invokeMethod` method of the interface must use whatever logic is deemed appropriate to invoke the specified method and to return the value of the method.

If the instance does not implement the `ICustomTypeDescriptor` interface, the `invokeMethod` method takes the following actions:

❑   It invokes the `getTypeDescriptor` static method on the `TypeDescriptor` class, passing in the instance to return a reference to the `TypeDescriptor` object that describes the type of the instance as usual:

```
var td = Sys.Preview.TypeDescriptor.getTypeDescriptor(instance);
```

❑   It invokes the `_getMethods` method on the `TypeDescriptor` object to return a reference to the `_methods` object, which contains one object literal for each method of the type and uses the name of the method as an index into this object to return a reference to the object literal associated with the method with the specified name:

```
var methodInfo = td._getMethods()[methodName];
```

❑   It uses the name of the method as an index into the instance to return a reference to the method itself:

```
var method = instance[methodInfo.name];
```

❑ It iterates through the parameters of the method and calls the _evaluateValue method for each enumerated parameter to convert the specified value to the type that the parameter expects, which is then passed as the value of the parameter when the method is invoked:

```
return method.apply(instance, arguments);
```

getPropertyType

This section discusses the implementation of the getPropertyType method to help you understand the following:

❑ The extensibility points of this method

❑ The role that the last argument of the getPropertyType method plays, and why and when you should specify this argument

The getPropertyType static method of the TypeDescriptor class takes three parameters, as shown in Listing 10-20. The first parameter references the instance that owns the property whose type is being queried. The second parameter is a string that contains the name of the property. The third parameter is optional. The main responsibility of this method is to return a reference to the type of the property with the specified name or a reference to the type of the descendant subproperty whose fully qualified name, including its complete containment hierarchy, is given by the key parameter.

Listing 10-20: The getPropertyType Static Method of the TypeDescriptor Class

```
Sys.Preview.TypeDescriptor.getPropertyType =
function Sys$Preview$TypeDescriptor$getPropertyType(instance, propertyName, key)
{
  if (Sys.Preview.ICustomTypeDescriptor.isImplementedBy(instance))
    return Object;

  if (key)
    return Object;

  var td = Sys.Preview.TypeDescriptor.getTypeDescriptor(instance);
  if(!td)
    return Object;

  var propertyInfo = td._getProperties()[propertyName];
  return propertyInfo.type || null;
}
```

The getPropertyType static method first checks whether the instance implements the ICustomTypeDescriptor interface, and if so, it returns Object as the type of the specified property:

```
if (Sys.Preview.ICustomTypeDescriptor.isImplementedBy(instance))
  return Object;
```

If the instance does not implement the `ICustomTypeDescriptor` interface, the `getPropertyType` method checks whether the caller has specified a value for the key parameter, and if so, it returns `Object` as the type:

```
if (key)
    return Object;
```

If the caller has not specified the key parameter value, the `getPropertyType` method first calls the `getTypeDescriptor` method as usual to return a reference to the `TypeDescriptor` object that describes the type of the instance:

```
var td = Sys.Preview.TypeDescriptor.getTypeDescriptor(instance);
```

Next, it invokes the `_getProperties` method on the `TypeDescriptor` object, passing in the instance to return a reference to the `_properties` object of the `TypeDescriptor` object and uses the property name as an index into this object to return a reference to the object literal associated with the property:

```
var propertyInfo = td._getProperties()[propertyName];
```

Finally, the `getPropertyType` method simply returns the value part of the name/value pair of the object literal that specifies the type of the property:

```
return propertyInfo.type || null;
```

This object literal contains several name/value pairs, where each name/value pair provides specific metadata information about the property that the object literal represents.

Using the ASP.NET AJAX Type Description Capabilities

This section presents an example that shows you how to use the methods of the `TypeDescriptor` class discussed in this chapter. The example implements a custom client control named `CustomTable` that can display any type of data records. It is a well-known fact that different types of data sources support different types of data records. If the `CustomTable` control were aware of the actual type of data records being displayed, it would be tied to a particular type of data source and would not be able to display data records from other types of data sources. This is where the ASP.NET AJAX type description capabilities come into play. As you'll see in this section, these capabilities enable the `CustomTable` client control to display data records of any type.

Because the implementation of this control makes use of an ASP.NET AJAX class named `StringBuilder`, the next section covers this class before diving into the implementation of the `CustomTable` control.

StringBuilder

Listing 10-21 presents the internal implementation of the `StringBuilder` ASP.NET AJAX class. As the name suggests, you can use an instance of this class to build a string from its constituent substrings. Every `StringBuilder` object maintains two internal collections named `_parts` and `_value`, where the former is used to collect the constituent substrings of the final string and the latter is used to store different versions of the final string. The only difference between these versions is the substring that is used as the separator between the constituent substrings of the final string.

Listing 10-21: The StringBuilder ASP.NET AJAX Class

```
Sys.StringBuilder = function Sys$StringBuilder(initialText)
{
   this._parts = (typeof(initialText) !== 'undefined' &&
                 initialText !== null && initialText !== '') ?
                   [initialText.toString()] : [];
   this._value = {};
   this._len = 0;
}

function Sys$StringBuilder$append(text)
{
   this._parts[this._parts.length] = text;
}

function Sys$StringBuilder$appendLine(text)
{
   this._parts[this._parts.length] =
            ((typeof(text) === 'undefined') || (text === null) ||
             (text === '')) ? '\r\n' : text + '\r\n';
}

function Sys$StringBuilder$clear()
{
   this._parts = {};
   this._value = {};
   this._len = 0;
}

function Sys$StringBuilder$isEmpty()
{
   if (this._parts.length === 0)
     return true;
   return this.toString() === '';
}

function Sys$StringBuilder$toString(separator)
{
   separator = separator || '';
   if (typeof(this._value[separator]) === 'undefined')
     this._value[separator] = this._parts.join(separator);

   return this._value[separator];
}
```

(continued)

Listing 10-21 *(continued)*

```
Sys.StringBuilder.prototype =
{
  append: Sys$StringBuilder$append,
  appendLine: Sys$StringBuilder$appendLine,
  clear: Sys$StringBuilder$clear,
  isEmpty: Sys$StringBuilder$isEmpty,
  toString: Sys$StringBuilder$toString
}

Sys.StringBuilder.registerClass('Sys.StringBuilder');
```

The following sections discuss the constructor and methods of the `StringBuilder` class.

Constructor

As you can see from Listing 10-21, the constructor of the `StringBuilder` class takes a single optional argument. The constructor does not make any assumptions about the type of the object passed into it as its first argument as long as this object exposes a method named `toString`, which returns the string representation of the object. As the following code snippet taken from Listing 10-21 shows, the constructor simply stores the string representation of this object into the internal `_parts` collection and instantiates the internal `_value` dictionary. In other words, after calling the constructor, the internal `_parts` array contains a single substring while the internal `_value` dictionary is empty.

```
this._parts = (typeof(initialText) !== 'undefined' &&
              initialText !== null && initialText !== '') ?
              [initialText.toString()] : [];
this._value = {};
```

append

As you can see in the following code fragment from Listing 10-21, the `append` method of the `StringBuilder` class takes a single argument and adds it to the `_parts` array:

```
this._parts[this._parts.length] = text;
```

appendLine

As the following code fragment from Listing 10-21 shows, the `appendLine` method does what the `append` method does plus one more thing: it also adds a new line, hence the name `appendLine`.

```
this._parts[this._parts.length] =
        ((typeof(text) === 'undefined') || (text === null) || (text === '')) ?
        '\r\n' : text + '\r\n';
```

clear

As the following code fragment from Listing 10-21 shows, the `clear` method does exactly what its name says it does — it clears both the `_parts` and `_value` collections.

```
this._parts = [];
this._value = {};
this._len = 0;
```

isEmpty

As the name suggests, the isEmpty method returns a Boolean value that specifies whether the _parts array is empty:

```
if (this._parts.length === 0)
  return true;
return this.toString() === '';
```

toString

Listing 10-21 presents a simplified version of the internal implementation of the toString method. As you can see in the following code fragment, this method takes a string as its argument and calls the join method on the _parts array, passing in this string to return a string that contains the strings stored in the _parts array, separated by the string passed into the toString method. Note that the toString method uses the string passed into it as an index into the _value dictionary to store the string returned from the join method.

```
function Sys$StringBuilder$toString(separator)
{
  separator = separator || '';
  if (typeof(this._value[separator]) === 'undefined')
    this._value[separator] = this._parts.join(separator);

  return this._value[separator];
}
```

As you can see, the _value dictionary stores different concatenations of the strings stored in the _parts array. The only difference between these concatenations is the string used as the separator between the concatenated strings.

Listing 10-22 presents a page that uses the StringBuilder class. If you run this page, you should see the pop-up message shown in Figure 10-5. Note that this message displays two strings that contain the same substrings. The only difference between the two is the separator strings. One uses the string " , " as the separator, and the other uses the string " | | " as the separator.

Listing 10-22: A Page that uses the StringBuilder Class

```
<%@ Page Language="C#" %>

<!DOCTYPE html PUBLIC "-//W3C//DTD XHTML 1.0 Transitional//EN"
"http://www.w3.org/TR/xhtml1/DTD/xhtml1-transitional.dtd">

<html xmlns="http://www.w3.org/1999/xhtml">
<head runat="server">
  <title>Untitled Page</title>
  <script type="text/javascript" language="javascript">
    function pageLoad()
    {
      var sb = new Sys.StringBuilder();
      sb.append("s1");
      sb.append("s2");
      sb.append("s3");
      sb.append("s4");
```

(continued)

Listing 10-22 *(continued)*

```
        alert(sb.toString(",") + "\n\n" + sb.toString("||"));
    }
  </script>
</head>
<body>
  <form id="form1" runat="server">
    <asp:ScriptManager ID="ScriptManager1" runat="server" />
  </form>
</body>
</html>
```

Figure 10-5

CustomTable

Listing 10-23 presents the contents of a JavaScript file named `CustomTable.js`, which contains the implementation of the `CustomTable` client control. This client control exposes a property named `dataSource` and a method named `dataBind`. The control also exposes a getter and a setter method named `get_dataSource` and `set_dataSource`, which allow you to get and set the value of the `dataSource` property. As you'll see later, you must assign the collection containing the data records to be displayed to the `dataSource` property, and call the `dataBind` method to have the control display the records in a table. The `CustomTable` client control derives from the `Control` base class, like any other client control:

```
CustomComponents.CustomTable.registerClass("CustomComponents.CustomTable",
                                            Sys.UI.Control);
```

Listing 10-23: The CustomTable.js File

```
Type.registerNamespace("CustomComponents");

CustomComponents.CustomTable =
function CustomComponents$CustomTable(associatedElement)
{
  CustomComponents.CustomTable.initializeBase(this, [associatedElement]);
}

 function CustomComponents$CustomTable$get_dataSource()
{
  return this._dataSource;
}
```

(continued)

Listing 10-23 *(continued)*

```
function CustomComponents$CustomTable$set_dataSource(value)
{
  this._dataSource = value;
}

function CustomComponents$CustomTable$dataBind()
{
  var sb = new Sys.StringBuilder('<table align="center" id="products" ');
  sb.append('style="background-color:LightGoldenrodYellow;');
  sb.append('border-color:Tan;border-width:1px; color:Black"');
  sb.append(' cellpadding="5">');
  var propertyNames = [];
  for (var i=0; i<this._dataSource.length; i++)
  {
    var dataItem = this._dataSource[i];

    if (i == 0)
    {
      var td = Sys.Preview.TypeDescriptor.getTypeDescriptor(dataItem);

      var properties = td._getProperties();

      sb.append('<tr style="background-color:Tan; font-weight:bold">');
      for (var c in properties)
      {
        var propertyObj = properties[c];
        var propertyName = propertyObj.name;
        propertyNames[propertyNames.length] = propertyName;
        sb.append('<td>');
        sb.append(propertyName);
        sb.append('</td>');
      }
      sb.append('</tr>');
    }

    if (i % 2 == 1)
      sb.append('<tr style="background-color:PaleGoldenrod">');
    else
      sb.append('<tr>');

    for (var j in propertyNames)
    {
      var propertyName = propertyNames[j];

      var propertyValue = Sys.Preview.TypeDescriptor.getProperty(dataItem,
                                                    propertyName, null);

      var typeName = Object.getTypeName(propertyValue);
```

(continued)

Listing 10-23 *(continued)*

```
        if (typeName !== 'String' && typeName !== 'Number' && typeName !== 'Boolean')
        {
          var convertToStringMethodName = Sys.Preview.TypeDescriptor.getAttribute(
                                 propertyValue, "convertToStringMethodName");

          if (convertToStringMethodName)
            propertyValue = Sys.Preview.TypeDescriptor.invokeMethod(propertyValue,
                                 convertToStringMethodName, null);
        }

        sb.append('<td>')
        sb.append(propertyValue);
        sb.append('</td>');
      }

      sb.append('</tr>');
    }

    sb.append('</table>');
    this.get_element().innerHTML = sb.toString();
}

CustomComponents.CustomTable.prototype =
{
  get_dataSource : CustomComponents$CustomTable$get_dataSource,
  set_dataSource : CustomComponents$CustomTable$set_dataSource,
  dataBind : CustomComponents$CustomTable$dataBind
}

CustomComponents.CustomTable.registerClass("CustomComponents.CustomTable",
                                 Sys.UI.Control);

if(typeof(Sys)!=='undefined')
  Sys.Application.notifyScriptLoaded();
```

Now, let's walk through the implementation of the `dataBind` method of the `CustomTable` control. This method first instantiates a `StringBuilder` object and calls the `append` method a couple of times, passing in strings that contain the opening tag of the table HTML element and its associated HTML attributes:

```
var sb = new Sys.StringBuilder('<table align="center" id="products" ');
sb.append('style="background-color:LightGoldenrodYellow;'); ('border-color:Tan;
border-width:1px; color:Black"');
sb.append(' cellpadding="5">');
```

Next, the method iterates through the data records in the `dataSource` collection property and performs these tasks. First, it accesses a reference to the enumerated data record:

```
var dataItem = this._dataSource[i];
```

Next, it checks whether the enumerated data record is the first record of the collection:

```
if (i == 0)
```

If so, it calls the `getTypeDescriptor` static method on the `TypeDescriptor` class, passing in the reference to the data record to return a reference to the `TypeDescriptor` object that describes the type of the data record:

```
var td = Sys.Preview.TypeDescriptor.getTypeDescriptor(dataItem);
```

Note that the `CustomTable` control has no idea what the type of the data record is. The control only has access to the `TypeDescriptor` object that describes the type of the data record.

Next, the `dataBind` method calls the `_getProperties` instance method on the `TypeDescriptor` object that describes the enumerated data record to return a reference to the `_properties` dictionary of the `TypeDescriptor` object:

```
var properties = td._getProperties();
```

As previously discussed, the `TypeDescriptor` object exposes an internal dictionary named `_properties` that contains one object literal for each property of the type that the `TypeDescriptor` object describes. The `CustomTable` control has no idea what the names and types of these properties are — it only has access to the object literal associated with the property.

Next, the `dataBind` method calls the `append` method on the `StringBuilder` object to add a string that contains the opening tag of a `<tr>` HTML element with its associated attributes:

```
sb.append('<tr style="background-color:Tan; font-weight:bold">');
```

As you'll see shortly, this `<tr>` HTML element will display the header texts of the table.

Next, the `dataBind` method iterates through the object literals returned from the call into the `_getProperties` method of the `TypeDescriptor` object and performs these tasks for each enumerated object literals. Recall that each object literal is associated with a particular property of the type that the `TypeDescriptor` object represents:

```
var propertyObj = properties[c];
```

The `dataBind` method then calls the `name` property on the enumerated object literal to access the name of the associated property, and stores the property in a local array:

```
var propertyName = propertyObj.name;
propertyNames[propertyNames.length] = propertyName;
```

Next, it calls the append method on the StringBuilder object to append a string that contains a <td> HTML element that displays the name of the property, which acts as the header text:

```
sb.append('<td>');
sb.append(propertyName);
sb.append('</td>');
```

After adding all the substrings that display the header texts of the table to the StringBuilder object, the dataBind method adds a string containing the opening tag of the <tr> HTML element that will display the field values of the current data record:

```
if (i % 2 == 1)
   sb.append('<tr style="background-color:PaleGoldenrod">');
else
   sb.append('<tr>');
```

Next, the dataBind method iterates through all the property names stored in the local array:

```
var propertyName = propertyNames[j];
```

First, it calls the getProperty static method on the TypeDescriptor class, passing in two arguments. The first argument references the current data record, and the second argument contains the property name:

```
var propertyValue = Sys.Preview.TypeDescriptor.getProperty(dataItem,
                                               propertyName, null);
```

As discussed earlier, the getProperty method returns the value of the property with the specified name.

Next, the dataBind method calls the getTypeName static method on the Object class, passing in the value of the property with the specified name:

```
var typeName = Object.getTypeName(propertyValue);
```

This returns a string that contains the fully qualified name of the type of the value, including its namespace hierarchy.

Next, the dataBind method checks whether the type of the value is of the primitive types, such as String, Number, and Boolean. If not, it has the type convert the value to a string so it can be displayed in the table. (The current implementation of the CustomTable control displays only string values.) To accomplish this, the dataBind method calls the getAttribute static method on the TypeDescriptor class, passing in two parameters. The first parameter contains the value of the property, and the second parameter is the string "convertToStringMethodName":

```
var convertToStringMethodName = Sys.Preview.TypeDescriptor.getAttribute(
                             propertyValue, "convertToStringMethodName");
```

As discussed earlier, the `getAttribute` method returns the value of the attribute with the specified name. In this case, the method returns the value of an attribute named "convertToStringMethodName". As its name suggests, the value of this attribute contains the name of the method that can convert the property value to a string. The `CustomTable` control assumes the following:

❑ Each property value is either a primitive type (such as `String`, `Number`, or `Boolean`) or a type that exposes a method that can convert the value into string.

❑ The type is annotated with an attribute named `"convertToStringMethodName"` whose value specifies the name of the method that can covert the value into string.

The `dataBind` method then calls the `invokeMethod` static method on the `TypeDescriptor` class, passing in two parameters. The first parameter contains the value, and the second parameter contains the name of the method to be invoked:

```
if (convertToStringMethodName)
    propertyValue = Sys.Preview.TypeDescriptor.invokeMethod(propertyValue,
                                    convertToStringMethodName, null);
```

As discussed earlier, the `invokeMethod` method invokes the method with the specified name on the specified object and returns the return value of the method. In this case, the return value is the string representation of the value. Thanks to the ASP.NET AJAX type description capabilities, the `CustomTable` control is able to convert a value to its string representation without knowing the actual type of the value.

Next, the `dataBind` method calls the `append` method on the `StringBuilder` object to append a string that contains a `<td>` HTML element that displays the property value:

```
sb.append('<td>')
sb.append(propertyValue);
sb.append('</td>');
```

Finally, the `dataBind` method calls the `get_element` method to return a reference to the DOM element that the `CustomTable` element represents, and assigns the return value of the call into the `toString` method of the `StringBuilder` object to the `innerHTML` property of the DOM element:

```
this.get_element().innerHTML = sb.toString();
```

Thanks to the ASP.NET AJAX type description capabilities, the `CustomTable` control can now display records of any type. To see this in action, let's define a new record type named `Product` and check whether the `CustomTable` control can indeed display data records of type `Product`.

Listing 10-24 presents a JavaScript file named `Product.js`, that contains the code for the `Product` type. An instance of the `Product` type represents a product. As such, the `Product` type exposes three properties named `productName`, `distributorName`, and `distributorAddress`, along with three getter methods named `get_productName`, `get_distributorName`, and `get_distributorAddress` that enable you to access the values of these properties.

Listing 10-24: The Product.js File

```
Type.registerNamespace("CustomComponents");

CustomComponents.Product =
function CustomComponents$Product(productName, distributorName, distributorAddress)
{
  this._productName = productName;
  this._distributorName = distributorName;
  this._distributorAddress = distributorAddress;
}

function CustomComponents$Product$get_productName()
{
  return this._productName;
}

function CustomComponents$Product$get_distributorName()
{
  return this._distributorName;
}

function CustomComponents$Product$get_distributorAddress()
{
  return this._distributorAddress;
}

CustomComponents.Product.prototype =
{
  get_productName : CustomComponents$Product$get_productName,
  get_distributorName : CustomComponents$Product$get_distributorName,
  get_distributorAddress : CustomComponents$Product$get_distributorAddress
}

CustomComponents.Product.descriptor =
{
  properties : [{name : 'productName', type : String, readOnly : true},
                {name : 'distributorName', type : String, readOnly : true},
                {name : 'distributorAddress', type : CustomComponents.Address,
                 readOnly : true}]
}

CustomComponents.Product.registerClass("CustomComponents.Product");

if(typeof(Sys)!=='undefined')
  Sys.Application.notifyScriptLoaded();
```

To enable the clients of the Product type (such as the CustomTable control) to use the ASP.NET AJAX type description capabilities to inspect it, the type also exposes a static property named descriptor whose value is set to an object literal containing a single name/value pair that describes the properties of the type:

```
CustomComponents.Product.descriptor =
{
  properties : [{name : 'productName', type : String, readOnly : true},
                {name : 'distributorName', type : String, readOnly : true},
                {name : 'distributorAddress', type : CustomComponents.Address,
                readOnly : true}]
}
```

The name part of this name/value pair is the keyword `properties`, and the value part is an array that contains one object literal for each property of the type. In turn, each object literal contains three name/value pairs. The first name/value pair of the object literal specifies the name of the property, the second name/value pair specifies the type of the property, and the third name/value pair specifies whether the property is read only.

Notice that the second name/value pair of the third object literal (the one associated with the `distributorAddress` property) specifies `CustomComponents.Address` as the type of this property:

```
{name : 'distributorAddress', type : Sys.Preview.UI.Address, readOnly : true}
```

In other words, the `distributorAddress` property is not of a primitive type such as `String`, `Number`, or `Boolean`. The `CustomTable` control expects a non-primitive type to do the following:

❑ Expose a method that knows how to convert a given value of the type to string

❑ Expose an attribute that specifies the name of the method

Listing 10-25 presents a JavaScript file named `Address.js` that contains the implementation of the `CustomComponents.Address` type.

Listing 10-25: The Content of the Address.js File

```
Type.registerNamespace("CustomComponents");

CustomComponents.Address =
function CustomComponents$Address(street, city, state, zip)
{
  this._street = street;
  this._city = city;
  this._state = state;
  this._zip = zip;
}

function CustomComponents$Address$convertToString()
{
  return this._street + ", " + this._city + ", " + this._state + " " + this._zip;
}
```

(continued)

Listing 10-25 *(continued)*

```
CustomComponents.Address.prototype =
{
  convertToString : CustomComponents$Address$convertToString
}

CustomComponents.Address.descriptor =
{
  methods : [{name: 'convertToString'}],
  attributes : [{name: 'convertToStringMethodName', value: 'convertToString'}]
}

CustomComponents.Address.registerClass("CustomComponents.Address");

if(typeof(Sys)!=='undefined')
  Sys.Application.notifyScriptLoaded();
```

The constructor of the `CustomComponents.Address` type takes four parameters that make up an address and stores them in its associated fields. Note that the `Address` type exposes a method named `convertToString` that returns a string representation of an address:

```
function CustomComponents$Address$convertToString()
{
  return this._street + ", " + this._city + ", " + this._state + " " + this._zip;
}
```

The clients of the `Address` type (such as `CustomTable`) have no way of knowing that the name of this method is `convertToString`. Therefore, the `Address` type method exposes an attribute that specifies the name of the method:

```
CustomComponents.Address.descriptor =
{
  methods : [{name: 'convertToString'}],
  attributes : [{name: 'convertToStringMethodName', value: 'convertToString'}]
}
```

Now, let's see if the `CustomTable` control can indeed display records of type `Product`. Listing 10-26 contains a page that uses the `CustomTable` control to display records of type `Product`.

Listing 10-26: A Page that Uses the CustomTable Control to Display Product Records

```
<%@ Page Language="C#" %>
<!DOCTYPE html PUBLIC "-//W3C//DTD XHTML 1.0 Transitional//EN"

"http://www.w3.org/TR/xhtml1/DTD/xhtml1-transitional.dtd">
<html xmlns="http://www.w3.org/1999/xhtml">
<head runat="server">
  <title>Untitled Page</title>
  <script type="text/javascript" language="javascript">
    function pageLoad()
```

(continued)

Listing 10-26 *(continued)*

```
      {
        var products = [];
        var product;
        var distributoraddress;
        for (var i=0; i<4; i++)
        {
          distributoraddress =
              new CustomComponents.Address("street"+i, "city"+i, "state"+i, "zip"+i);

          product = new CustomComponents.Product("Product"+i, "Distributor"+i,
                                      distributoraddress);

          products[i] = product;
        }

        var customTable = $create(CustomComponents.CustomTable,
                            {dataSource : products}, null, null,
                            $get("myDiv"));
        customTable.dataBind();
      }
    </script>
  </head>
  <body>
    <form id="form1" runat="server">
      <asp:ScriptManager runat="server" ID="ScriptManager1">
        <Scripts>
          <asp:ScriptReference Assembly="Microsoft.Web.Preview"
          Name="PreviewScript.js" />
          <asp:ScriptReference Path="CustomTable.js" />
          <asp:ScriptReference Path="Address.js" />
          <asp:ScriptReference Path="Product.js" />
        </Scripts>
      </asp:ScriptManager>
      <div id="myDiv">
      </div>
    </form>
  </body>
</html>
```

Now, let's walk through the implementation of the `pageLoad` method. This method first creates several `Product` objects and stores them in a local array named `products`. Because the constructor of the `Product` type requires an `Address` object as its third argument, the `pageLoad` method creates an `Address` object:

```
distributoraddress =
            new CustomComponents.Address("street"+i, "city"+i, "state"+i, "zip"+i);
```

Then, it creates the associated `Product` object, passing in the `Address` object:

```
product = new CustomComponents.Product("Product"+i, "Distributor"+i,
                                  distributoraddress);
```

After creating the `Product` objects and storing them in the `products` array, the `pageLoad` method invokes the `$create` shortcut method to create and initialize an instance of the `CustomTable` control and add this instance to the _components collection of the current Application object. Note that the pageLoad method passes an object literal with a single name/value pair into the create method to have the method assign the products array to the dataSource property of the CustomTable control:

```
var customTable = $create(CustomComponents.CustomTable,
                        {dataSource : products}, null, null, $get("myDiv"));
```

Finally, the pageLoad method calls the dataBind method on the CustomTable control to have the control display the specified products:

```
customTable.dataBind();
```

If you run the page shown in Listing 10-26, you should get the result shown in Figure 10-6. As you can see, the CustomTable control is capable of displaying data records of type Product. Thanks to the ASP.NET AJAX type inspection capabilities, the CustomTable control is able to invoke the convertToString method of the Address type to convert the Address objects into their string representations.

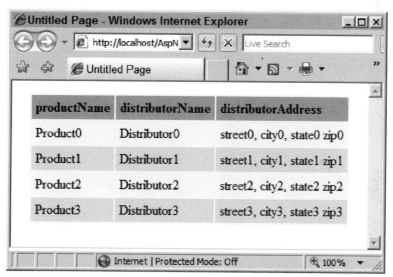

Figure 10-6

Dynamic Injection of Metadata Information

The main idea behind the metadata inspection capabilities of the ASP.NET AJAX client-side framework is to allow a given ASP.NET AJAX type to dynamically discover the complete information about the properties, methods, events, and attributes of another type at runtime.

As discussed earlier, the descriptor static property of an ASP.NET AJAX type references an object literal that contains up to four name/value pairs. These name/value pairs provide metadata information about the properties, methods, events, and attributes of the type. The default implementation of the TypeDescriptor class's getTypeDescriptor method uses the descriptor property of a type as the source for the metadata information about its properties, methods, events, and attributes (shown previously in Listings 10-25 and 10-26). Therefore, this default implementation assumes that the type statically contains this metadata information.

There are runtime circumstances where a type that does not statically contain the required metadata information may need to provide this information to operate properly. The TypeDescriptor class exposes four methods named addProperty, addMethod, addEvent, and addAttribute that allow you to dynamically inject the required metadata information into the TypeDescriptor object that describes the type. As discussed earlier, other types do not directly inspect the metadata information of a type. Instead, they call the getTypeDescriptor static method on the TypeDescriptor object to instantiate and return the TypeDescriptor object that describes the type. They then use this TypeDescriptor object to inspect the metadata information. Therefore, the dynamic injection of metadata information into the TypeDescriptor object will give other types the illusion that the type itself contains the metadata.

The following sections discuss the addProperty, addMethod, addEvent, and addAttribute methods. Keep in mind that all four of these methods are instance methods. As such, they must be invoked on an instance of the TypeDescriptor class, not the class itself.

addProperty

The addProperty instance method of the TypeDescriptor class enables you to inject metadata information about a particular property. As Listing 10-27 shows, the addProperty instance takes five parameters. The first parameter is a string that contains the name of the property. The second parameter references the type of the property. The third parameter is a Boolean that specifies whether the property is read only. The fourth parameter is a Boolean that specifies whether the property references a DOM element. The fifth parameter is an array that contains the attributes of the property.

Listing 10-27: The addProperty Instance Method of the TypeDescriptor Class

```
Sys.Preview.TypeDescriptor.prototype.addProperty =
function Sys$Preview$TypeDescriptor$addProperty(propertyName, propertyType,
                                                readOnly, isDomElement,
                                                associatedAttributes)
{
  if (!readOnly)
    readOnly = false;

  var attribs;
  if (associatedAttributes)
  {
    attribs = { };
    for (var i = 4; i < arguments.length; i += 2)
    {
      var attribute = arguments[i];
      var value = arguments[i + 1];
      attribs[attribute] = value;
    }
  }
  return this._getProperties()[propertyName] =
                          { name: propertyName,
                            type: propertyType,
                            'readOnly': readOnly,
                            'isDomElement': isDomElement,
                            attributes: attribs };
}
```

The boldface portion of the following code fragment from Listing 10-27 shows that the `addProperty` method creates an object literal with five name/value pairs. The first name/value pair specifies the name of the property. The second name/value pair specifies the type of the property. The third name/value pair specifies whether the property is read only. The fourth name/value pair specifies whether the property references a DOM element. The fifth name/value pair specifies the attributes of the property.

```
this._getProperties()[propertyName] =
                            { name: propertyName,
                              type: propertyType,
                              'readOnly': readOnly,
                              'isDomElement': isDomElement,
                              attributes: attribs };
```

As the boldface portion of the following code fragment shows, the `addProperty` method calls the `_getProperties` method to return a reference to the `_properties` dictionary of the `TypeDescriptor` object. It then uses the property name as an index into this dictionary to store the object literal into the dictionary.

```
return this._getProperties()[propertyName] =
                            { name: propertyName,
                              type: propertyType,
                              'readOnly': readOnly,
                              'isDomElement': isDomElement,
                              attributes: attribs };
```

addMethod

The `addMethod` instance method of the `TypeDescriptor` class enables you to dynamically inject metadata information about a specific method into the `TypeDescriptor` object that represents an ASP.NET AJAX type. As Listing 10-28 shows, this method takes two arguments. The first argument is a string that contains the name of the method. The second argument is an array of object literals, where each object literal describes a parameter of the method.

Listing 10-28: The addMethod Instance Method of the TypeDescriptor Class

```
Sys.Preview.TypeDescriptor.prototype.addMethod =
function Sys$Preview$TypeDescriptor$addMethod(methodName,
                                              associatedParameters,
                                              isDomElement)
{
  return this._getMethods()[methodName] =
                        { name: methodName, parameters: associatedParameters };
}
```

The `addMethod` method creates an object literal with two name/value pairs to describe the specified method. The first name/value pair specifies the name of the method, and the second name/value pair specifies the parameters of the method, as shown in the boldface portion of the following code fragment:

```
this._getMethods()[methodName] =
                        { name: methodName, parameters: associatedParameters };
```

The addMethod method then calls the _getMethods method on the TypeDescriptor object to return a reference to the _methods dictionary. It then uses the method name as an index into this dictionary to store the object literal into the dictionary, as shown in the boldface portion of the following code fragment:

```
return this._getMethods()[methodName] =
                        { name: methodName, parameters: associatedParameters };
```

When you call addMethod, you must pass an array of object literals into the method. The TypeDescriptor class includes a convenient method named createParameter that you can use to create the object literal that describes a given parameter as shown in Listing 10-29. This method takes four arguments. The first argument is a string that contains the name of the parameter. The second argument references the type of the parameter. The third argument is a Boolean that specifies whether the parameter references a DOM element. The fourth argument is a Boolean that specifies whether the parameter is an integer. As you can see, this method simply creates and returns an object literal. Note that this method is a static method and must be called on the TypeDescriptor class itself.

Listing 10-29: The createParameter Static Method of the TypeDescriptor Class

```
Sys.Preview.TypeDescriptor.createParameter =
function Sys$Preview$TypeDescriptor$createParameter(parameterName, parameterType,
                                                    isDomElement, isInteger)
{
  return { name: parameterName, type: parameterType,
           'isDomElement': isDomElement, 'isInteger': !!isInteger  };
}
```

addEvent

The addEvent method of the TypeDescriptor class allows you to dynamically inject metadata information about a given event into the TypeDescriptor object that describes a given ASP.NET AJAX type. The addEvent method takes a single argument, which is a string that contains the name of the event. Listing 10-30 shows this method.

Listing 10-30: The addEvent Instance Method of the TypeDescriptor Class

```
Sys.Preview.TypeDescriptor.prototype.addEvent =
function Sys$Preview$TypeDescriptor$addEvent(eventName)
{
  return this._getEvents()[eventName] = { name: eventName };
}
```

The addEvent method creates an object literal with a single name/value pair that specifies the name of the event, as shown in the boldface portion of the following code fragment from Listing 10-30:

```
this._getEvents()[eventName] = { name: eventName };
```

The method then calls the _getEvents method to return a reference to the _events dictionary. It uses the name of the event as an index into this dictionary to store the object literal, as shown in the boldface portion of the following code fragment:

```
return this._getEvents()[eventName] = { name: eventName };
```

addAttribute

The addAttribute method of the TypeDescriptor class enables you to dynamically inject metadata information about a given attribute into the TypeDescriptor object that describes a given ASP.NET AJAX type. The addAttribute method takes two arguments. The first argument is a string that contains the name of the attribute, and the second argument contains the value of the attribute. Listing 10-31 shows this method.

Listing 10-31: The addAttribute Instance Method of the TypeDescriptor Class

```
Sys.Preview.TypeDescriptor.prototype.addAttribute =
function Sys$Preview$TypeDescriptor$addAttribute(attributeName, attributeValue)
{
    this._getAttributes()[attributeName] = attributeValue;
}
```

The addAttribute method calls the _getAttributes method to return a reference to the _attributes dictionary, and uses the name of the attribute as an index into this dictionary to store the value of the attribute.

ICustomTypeDescriptor

As Listing 10-32 shows, the ICustomTypeDescriptor interface exposes three instance methods named getProperty, setProperty, and invokeMethod.

Listing 10-32: The ICustomTypeDescriptor Interface

```
Sys.Preview.ICustomTypeDescriptor = function Sys$Preview$ICustomTypeDescriptor()
{
    throw Error.notImplemented();
}

function Sys$Preview$ICustomTypeDescriptor$getProperty()
{
    throw Error.notImplemented();
}

function Sys$Preview$ICustomTypeDescriptor$setProperty()
{
    throw Error.notImplemented();
}
```

(continued)

Listing 10-32 (continued)

```
function Sys$Preview$ICustomTypeDescriptor$invokeMethod()
{
  throw Error.notImplemented();
}

Sys.Preview.ICustomTypeDescriptor.prototype =
{
  getProperty: Sys$Preview$ICustomTypeDescriptor$getProperty,
  setProperty: Sys$Preview$ICustomTypeDescriptor$setProperty,
  invokeMethod: Sys$Preview$ICustomTypeDescriptor$invokeMethod
}

Sys.Preview.ICustomTypeDescriptor.registerInterface(
                                  'Sys.Preview.ICustomTypeDescriptor');
```

As discussed earlier, you can customize the getProperty, setProperty, and invokeMethod methods of the TypeDescriptor class by having your type implement the ICustomTypeDescriptor interface.

You may be wondering why and when you should have your type implement this interface to customize the previously mentioned methods of the TypeDescriptor class. As discussed earlier in this chapter, the default implementation of these TypeDescriptor class methods use the descriptor static property of a type to retrieve the required information about the properties, events, methods, and attributes of the type. And there may be times when a type must expose some information to the outside world as if it were the value of one of its properties.

As an example, consider the ASP.NET AJAX DataRow type shown in Listing 10-33. As the name suggests, instances of the DataRow type are used to represent tabular data records, where each record consists of one or more data fields (such as database records). A DataRow object takes an object literal that describes the data fields of a record and presents the properties of this object literal as if they were its own properties.

Listing 10-33: A Page that Uses the DataRow Type

```
<%@ Page Language="C#" %>

<!DOCTYPE html PUBLIC "-//W3C//DTD XHTML 1.0 Transitional//EN"
"http://www.w3.org/TR/xhtml1/DTD/xhtml1-transitional.dtd">

<html xmlns="http://www.w3.org/1999/xhtml">
<head runat="server">
  <title>Untitled Page</title>
  <script type="text/javascript" language="javascript">
    function pageLoad()
    {
      var dataRow = new Sys.Preview.Data.DataRow(
              {productName: 'p1', unitPrice: 30, distributor: 'd1'});

      alert ("Product Name: " + dataRow.getProperty("productName") +
             "\nUnit Price: " + dataRow.getProperty("unitPrice") +
             "\nDistributor: " + dataRow.getProperty("distributor"));
    }
  </script>
</head>
```

(continued)

Listing 10-33 *(continued)*

```
<body>
  <form id="form1" runat="server">
    <asp:ScriptManager ID="ScriptManager1" runat="Server">
      <Scripts>
        <asp:ScriptReference Path="PreviewScriptjs" />
      </Scripts>
    </asp:ScriptManager>
  </form>
</body>
</html>
```

This page creates a `DataRow` object, passing the following object literal:

```
{productName: 'p1', unitPrice: 30, distributor: 'd1'}
```

This object exposes three properties named `productName`, `unitPrice`, and `distributor`. The following code fragment from Listing 10-33 calls the `getProperty` method directly on the `DataRow` object instead of the object literal, passing in the names of the properties of the object to access the values of these properties as if they were the properties of the `DataRow` object itself:

```
alert ("Product Name: " + dataRow.getProperty("productName") +
       "\nUnit Price: " + dataRow.getProperty("unitPrice") +
       "\nDistributor: " + dataRow.getProperty("distributor"));
```

If you run the page shown in Listing 10-33, you should see the result shown in Figure 10-7.

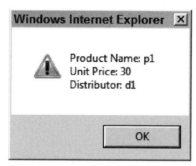

Figure 10-7

Summary

This chapter walked you through some of the important type description capabilities of the ASP.NET AJAX client-side framework. As you saw in this chapter, the `DataRow` class implements the `ICustomTypeDescriptor` interface to expose its data fields as if they were its own properties. This enables the clients of the `DataRow` class to call the `getProperty` method on the `DataRow` object itself to access the values of its data fields. The `DataRow` class is part of a rich set of ASP.NET AJAX types that fall under the category of data sources, which are covered in the next two chapters.

11

Data Classes

Tabular data, such as relational data, plays a central role in today's data-driven Web applications. The .NET Framework comes with three rich classes named `DataColumn`, `DataRow`, and `DataTable` that you can use in your .NET code to represent and to program against tabular data.

The ASP.NET AJAX client-side framework comes with the same set of data classes — `DataColumn`, `DataRow`, and `DataTable` — that emulate their .NET countparts. You can use these data classes in your client-side code to represent and program against tabular data such as relational data. This chapter discusses these three ASP.NET AJAX data classes. All these classes belong to a namespace named `Sys.Preview.Data`:

```
Type.registerNamespace('Sys.Preview.Data');
```

The ASP.NET AJAX `DataTable` class implements an interface named `IData`. The chapter begins with this interface.

IData

Most ASP.NET AJAX client data classes, such as `DataTable`, implement an ASP.NET AJAX interface named `IData`, either directly or indirectly. As a matter of fact, if none of the existing data classes meet your requirements, you can write a new data class that implements this interface. Implementing this interface enables your custom data class to seamlessly integrate into the ASP.NET AJAX client-side framework. For example, the ASP.NET AJAX `Selector` client control can bind to any data class that implements the `IData` interface (as discussed in more detail later).

Listing 11-1 contains the definition of this interface. As you can see, the `IData` interface exposes the following five methods:

❑ `add`: Your custom data class's implementation of this method must add the specified data row to the internal collection where data rows are stored.

❑   `clear`: Your custom data class's implementation of this method must clear the internal collection where data rows are stored.

❑   `get_length`: Your custom data class's implementation of this method must return an integer that specifies the total number of data rows in the internal collection where data rows are stored.

❑   `getRow`: Your custom data class's implementation of this method must return a reference to the specified data row.

❑   `remove`: Your custom data class's implementation of this method must remove the specified data row from the internal collection where data rows are stored.

Listing 11-1: The Definition of the IData Interface

```
Sys.Preview.Data.IData = function Sys$Preview$Data$IData()
{
  throw Error.notImplemented();
}

function Sys$Preview$Data$IData$add()
{
  throw Error.notImplemented();
}

function Sys$Preview$Data$IData$clear()
{
  throw Error.notImplemented();
}

function Sys$Preview$Data$IData$get_length()
{
  throw Error.notImplemented();
}

function Sys$Preview$Data$IData$getRow()
{
  throw Error.notImplemented();
}

function Sys$Preview$Data$IData$remove()
{
  throw Error.notImplemented();
}

Sys.Preview.Data.IData.prototype =
{
  add: Sys$Preview$Data$IData$add,
  clear: Sys$Preview$Data$IData$clear,
  get_length: Sys$Preview$Data$IData$get_length,
  getRow: Sys$Preview$Data$IData$getRow,
  remove: Sys$Preview$Data$IData$remove
}

Sys.Preview.Data.IData.registerInterface('Sys.Preview.Data.IData');
```

DataColumn

The instances of the .NET DataColumn class are used to represent the columns of a data table. For example, each column of a relational database table is represented by a DataColumn instance. The ASP.NET AJAX client-side framework exposes an ASP.NET AJAX class named DataColumn, which emulates the .NET DataColumn. Listing 11-2 presents the internal implementation of this client class.

Listing 11-2: The ASP.NET AJAX DataColumn Client Class

```
Sys.Preview.Data.DataColumn =
function Sys$Preview$Data$DataColumn(columnName, dataType, defaultValue,
                                     isKey, isReadOnly)
{
  this._columnName = columnName;
  this._dataType = dataType;
  this._defaultValue = defaultValue;
  this._readOnly = isReadOnly;
  this._key = isKey;
}

function Sys$Preview$Data$DataColumn$get_columnName()
{
  return this._columnName;
}

function Sys$Preview$Data$DataColumn$get_dataType()
{
  return this._dataType;
}

function Sys$Preview$Data$DataColumn$get_defaultValue()
{
  return this._defaultValue;
}

function Sys$Preview$Data$DataColumn$get_isKey()
{
  return this._key;
}

function Sys$Preview$Data$DataColumn$get_readOnly()
{
  return !!this._readOnly;
}

function Sys$Preview$Data$DataColumn$dispose()
{
  this._columnName = null;
  this._dataType = null;
  this._defaultValue = null;
}
```

(continued)

Listing 11-2 *(continued)*

```
Sys.Preview.Data.DataColumn.prototype =
{
  get_columnName: Sys$Preview$Data$DataColumn$get_columnName,
  get_dataType: Sys$Preview$Data$DataColumn$get_dataType,
  get_defaultValue: Sys$Preview$Data$DataColumn$get_defaultValue,
  get_isKey: Sys$Preview$Data$DataColumn$get_isKey,
  get_readOnly: Sys$Preview$Data$DataColumn$get_readOnly,
  dispose: Sys$Preview$Data$DataColumn$dispose
}

Sys.Preview.Data.DataColumn.parseFromJson =
function Sys$Preview$Data$DataColumn$parseFromJson(json)
{
  return new Sys.Preview.Data.DataColumn(json.name,
         typeof(json.dataType === 'string') ? eval(json.dataType) : json.dataType,
         json.defaultValue, json.isKey, json.readOnly);
}

Sys.Preview.Data.DataColumn.descriptor =
{
  properties: [ { name: 'columnName', type: String, readOnly: true },
                { name: 'dataType', type: Sys.Type, readOnly: true },
                { name: 'defaultValue', readOnly: true },
                { name: 'isKey', type: Boolean, readOnly: true },
                { name: 'readOnly', type: Boolean, readOnly: true } ]
}

Sys.Preview.Data.DataColumn.registerClass('Sys.Preview.Data.DataColumn', null,
                             Sys.IDisposable);
```

The constructor of the `DataColumn` class takes the following five parameters:

❑ `columnName`: This parameter is a string that contains the name of the data field that the `DataColumn` object represents. For example, if you want to create a `DataColumn` object to represent the `ProductName` database field of the `Products` database table, you must pass the string value `"ProductName"` into the constructor of the `DataColumn` class as the first parameter.

❑ `dataType`: This parameter references the data type of the data field that the `DataColumn` object represents. For example, if you want to create a `DataColumn` object to represent the `UnitPrice` database field of the `Products` database table, you must pass `Number` into the constructor of the `DataColumn` class as the second argument.

❑ `defaultValue`: This parameter contains the default value for the data field that the `DataColumn` object represents. The type of this parameter depends on the type of data field.

❑ `isKey`: This parameter is a Boolean value that specifies whether the data field that the `DataColumn` represents is a primary key field. For example, if you want to create a `DataColumn` object to represent the `ProductID` primary key field of the `Products` database table, you must pass `true` into the constructor of the `DataColumn` class as the fourth argument.

❑ `isReadOnly`: This parameter is a Boolean value that specifies whether the data field that the `DataColumn` represents is editable.

As Listing 11-2 shows, the `DataColumn` client class exposes five properties with the same names as these parameters: `columnName`, `dataType`, `defaultValue`, `isKey`, and `isReadOnly`. Like any other ASP.NET AJAX client class, this class exposes a static property named `descriptor`. The `descriptor` property is set to an object literal that contains a single name/value pair describing the properties of the `DataColumn` class:

```
Sys.Preview.Data.DataColumn.descriptor =
{
    properties: [ { name: 'columnName', type: String, readOnly: true },
                  { name: 'dataType', type: Sys.Type, readOnly: true },
                  { name: 'defaultValue', readOnly: true },
                  { name: 'isKey', type: Boolean, readOnly: true },
                  { name: 'readOnly', type: Boolean, readOnly: true } ]
}
```

The `DataColumn` client class exposes five getter methods named `get_columnName`, `get_dataType`, `get_defaultValue`, `get_isKey`, and `get_isReadOnly` that return the values of the `columnName`, `dataType`, `defaultValue`, `isKey`, and `isReadOnly` properties of the class. The `DataColumn` class does not expose any setter methods for these properties. You must set the values of these properties through the constructor of the class when you're instantiating the class. This fact has also been reflected in the `descriptor` static property of the class, where all object literals describing the properties of the class contain the `readOnly: true` name/value pair.

In general, there are two ways to create a `DataColumn` object to represent the data field of a given data table. One approach is to use the constructor of the `DataColumn` class directly as discussed earlier. Another approach is to invoke the `parseFromJson` method on the `DataColumn` class. As Listing 11-2 shows, the `DataColumn` class exposes this method as a static method, which means that you must call this method on the class itself:

```
Sys.Preview.Data.DataColumn.parseFromJson =
function Sys$Preview$Data$DataColumn$parseFromJson(json)
{
    return new Sys.Preview.Data.DataColumn(json.columnName,
            typeof(json.dataType) === 'string') ? eval(json.dataType) : json.dataType,
            json.defaultValue, json.isKey, json.readOnly);
}
```

This approach enables you to pass an object that contains the required information about a data field into the `parseFromJson` static method, and have this method instantiate and return the associated `DataColumn` object. For example, the following code fragment presents the object literal representation of the `Products` database table's `UnitPrice` data field:

```
{
    columnName: 'UnitPrice', dataType: Number, defaultValue: 100,
    isKey: false, isReadOnly: true
}
```

As you can see, the object literal that represents a data field contains five name/value pairs that specify the data field name, type, and default value; whether the data field is a primary key; and whether the data field is editable.

Now you can call the `parseFromJson` static method on the `DataColumn` class, passing in the object literal representation of the data field to instantiate and return the `DataColumn` object that represents the data field:

```
var dataColumn = Sys.Preview.Data.DataColumn.parseFromJson (
                {
                    columnName: 'UnitPrice', dataType: Number,
                    defaultValue: 100, isKey: false,
                    isReadOnly: true
                } );
```

DataRow

In .NET, every data row is represented by an instance of a .NET class named `DataRow`. The ASP.NET AJAX client-side framework includes a client class named `DataRow` that emulates its .NET counterpart. The following sections discuss the members of this client class.

Constructor

Listing 11-3 shows the constructor of the `DataRow` client class.

Listing 11-3: The DataRow Client Class

```
Sys.Preview.Data.DataRow =
function Sys$Preview$Data$DataRow(objectDataRow, dataTableOwner, index)
{
  this._owner = dataTableOwner;
  this._row = objectDataRow;
  this._index = index;
}
```

`DataRow` takes the following three parameters:

❑ `objectDataRow`: This parameter references a JavaScript object that contains the data field names and values of the data row that the `DataRow` object being instantiated will represent. An example of such an object is a JavaScript object literal that contains one name/value pair for each data field, where the name part of the pair is the name of the data field, and the value part is the value of the data field. For example, the following JavaScript object literal represents a data row in the `Products` database table:

```
{productName: 'p1', unitPrice: 30, distributor: 'd1'}
```

❑ `dataTableOwner`: This parameter references the `Sys.Preview.Data.DataTable` object that owns the `DataRow` object being instantiated. This `DataTable` object represents the data table that owns the data row the `DataRow` object represents. (`DataTable` is discussed in more detail later.)

❑   index: This parameter is an integer that specifies the index of the DataRow object being instantiated in the collection that contains all DataRow objects for a particular DataTable object. This collection is maintained by the DataTable object. (DataTable is discussed in more detail later.)

The constructor of the DataRow client class respectively stores the values of the objectDataRow, dataTableOwner, and index parameters in three internal fields named _row, _owner, and _index for future reference. In other words, every DataRow object maintains a reference to the DataTable object that owns it and knows its index in the underlying collection.

descriptor

As Listing 11-4 shows, the DataRow client class exposes a static property named descriptor that describes the members of the class.

Listing 11-4: The descriptor Property of the DataRow Class

```
Sys.Preview.Data.DataRow.descriptor =
{
  properties: [ { name: '$isDirty', type: Boolean, readOnly: true },
                { name: '$index', type: Number, readOnly: true },
                { name: '$selected', type: Boolean } ],
  events: [ { name: 'propertyChanged', readOnly: true } ]
}
```

The DataRow class exposes three properties and a single event as follows:

❑ $isDirty: This read-only property returns a Boolean value that specifies whether any of the data field values of the DataRow object has changed value. Note that the name of this property begins with the dollar sign character. As you'll see later, when the ASP.NET AJAX JavaScriptSerializer class is serializing an object, it skips the properties with names that begin with a dollar sign.

❑ $index: This read-only property returns an integer that specifies the index of the DataRow object in the underlying collection where the DataRow objects belonging to the same DataTable object are stored. As mentioned earlier, this collection is maintained internally by the DataTable object itself.

❑ $selected: This read/write property returns a Boolean value that specifies whether the current DataRow has been selected.

❑   propertyChanged: The DataRow object raises this event when it's selected or deselected and when its _row field or isDirty property changes value.

The DataRow class exposes the get_isDirty, get_index, and get_selected getter methods to allow its clients to access the values of these three properties. Because the $selected property is writable, the class also exposes a setter method named set_selected to allow its clients to set the value of this property. This setter method calls an internal method named _onPropertyChanged to raise the propertyChanged event.

```
function Sys$Preview$Data$DataRow$get_isDirty()
{
  return typeof(this._row._original) === "object";
}

function Sys$Preview$Data$DataRow$get_index()
{
  return this._index;
}

function Sys$Preview$Data$DataRow$get_selected()
{
  return this._selected;
}

function Sys$Preview$Data$DataRow$set_selected(value)
{
  if (this._selected !== value)
  {
    this._selected = value;
    this._onPropertyChanged("$selected");
  }
}
```

ICustomTypeDescriptor

The `DataRow` class implements the `ICustomTypeDescriptor` interface as shown in the boldfaced portion of the following code fragment:

```
Sys.Preview.Data.DataRow.registerClass('Sys.Preview.Data.DataRow', null,
                          Sys.Preview.ICustomTypeDescriptor,
                          Sys.INotifyPropertyChange, Sys.IDisposable);
```

An ASP.NET AJAX client class normally implements the `ICustomTypeDescriptor` to expose information that is not directly exposed through its properties, as if they were the values of its own properties. This allows the clients of the class to access this information as if they were accessing the values of class properties.

A `DataRow` object represents a data row from a data table. As such, it contains the names and values of the data fields of its associated data row. What if the `DataRow` class could somehow expose the names and values of its constituent data fields as if they were the names and values of its own properties? For example, consider the following data row from the `Products` database table:

ProductName	UnitPrice	Distributor
Product1	100	Distributor1

Now, let's instantiate a `DataRow` object to represent this data row as follows:

```
var dataRow = new Sys.Preview.Data.DataRow(
        {productName: 'product1', unitPrice: 100, distributor: 'Distributor1'});
```

Wouldn't it be great if the clients of this `DataRow` object could treat the `productName`, `unitPrice`, and `distributor` data fields as if they were the properties of the `DataRow` class itself? This would allow the clients to access the values of these data fields as if they were accessing the values of properties with the same names, which means that these clients could call the `getProperty` method directly on the `DataRow` object itself to access the value of a specified data field, like this:

```
var productName = dataRow.getProperty("productName");
var unitPrice = dataRow.getProperty("unitPrice");
var distributor = dataRow.getProperty("distributor");
```

The `DataRow` class implements the `ICustomTypeDescriptor` interface to achieve this goal. In the previous chapter, you learned that this interface exposes three methods named `getProperty`, `setProperty`, and `invokeMethod`. The following sections walk you through the `DataRow` class's implementation of these methods to help you gain the experience you'll need to implement the `ICustomTypeDescriptor` interface.

getProperty

Listing 11-5 presents the `DataRow` class's implementation of the `ICustomTypeDescriptor` interface's `getProperty` method.

Listing 11-5: The getProperty Method

```
function Sys$Preview$Data$DataRow$getProperty(name, key)
{
  if (!name)
    return typeof(this._row._rowObject) !== "undefined" ?
                this._row._rowObject : this._row;

  switch(name)
  {
    case "$isDirty":
      return this.get_isDirty();

    case "$index":
      return this._index;

    case "$selected":
      return this.get_selected();
  }

  return Sys.Preview.TypeDescriptor.getProperty(this._row, name, key);
}
```

This method first checks whether the property whose value is being queried is one of the `DataRow` class's own properties: `$isDirty`, `$index`, or `$selected`. If so, it returns the value of the associated property.

Your custom type's implementation of the ICustomTypeDescriptor interface's getProperty methodmust do the same — it must first check whether the property whose value is being queried is one of its own properties. If so, it must return the value of the property. Otherwise, the clients of your custom type would not be able to access the values of your type properties in a generic fashion via the getProperty method.

As Listing 11-5 shows, if the property whose value is being queried is not one of the DataRow class's own properties, the DataRow class's implementation of the getProperty method delegates the responsibility of returning the value of the specified property to the type of the _row field. The constructor of the DataRow class stores the value of its first parameter in the _row field (as previously shown in Listing 11-3). This parameter references a JavaScript object that contains the names and values of the data fields of the data row that the DataRow object represents.

This means that the type of the JavaScript object that you pass into the constructor of the DataRow class as its first parameter must treat the names and values of its constituent data fields as its own properties. For example, an object literal that contains one name/value pair for each data field is an example of a JavaScript object that exposes the names and values of its constituent data fields as its own properties.

setProperty

Listing 11-6 presents the DataRow class's implementation of the ICustomTypeDescriptor interface's setProperty method . As discussed earlier, the DataRow class exposes three properties named $isDirty, $index, and $selected. The $selected property is the only property that the clients of the DataRow object can set. As far as the clients of the class are concerned, the other two properties are read-only.

Listing 11-6: The DataRowState Enumeration

```
Sys.Preview.Data.DataRowState = function Sys$Preview$Data$DataRowState()
{
  throw Error.invalidOperation();
}

Sys.Preview.Data.DataRowState.prototype =
{
  Unchanged: 0,
  Added: 1,
  Deleted: 2,
  Detached: 3,
  Modified: 4
}

Sys.Preview.Data.DataRowState.registerEnum('Sys.Preview.Data.DataRowState');
```

The setProperty method first checks whether the property whose value is being set is the $selected property. If so, it simply calls the set_selected setter method to set the property value and returns, as follows:

```
if (name === "$selected")
{
  this.set_selected(value);
  return;
}
```

Your custom type's implementation of the ICustomTypeDescriptor interface's setProperty method must do the same — it must check whether the property whose value is being set is one of its own properties. If so, it must set the value of the property and return.

If the property whose value is being set is not the $selected property, the DataRow object simply delegates the responsibility of setting the value of the property to the setProperty method of its _row field. This field references a JavaScript object that contains the names and values of the data fields in the data row that the DataRow object represents, as follows:

```
Sys.Preview.TypeDescriptor.setProperty(this._row, name, value, key);
```

This normally happens when you call the setProperty method on the DataRow object to set the value of a specified data field. In other words, you're setting the value of a data field as if the DataRow object exposed a property with the same name as the data field and you're setting the value of this property.

As Listing 11-6 shows, the setProperty method of the DataRow class takes a few other steps before calling the setProperty method of its _row field. This is because the DataRow object needs to mark itself as dirty even though it delegates the responsibility of setting the value of the property (or data field) to its _row field. Here are the steps that the setProperty method of the DataRow class takes before invoking the setProperty method of the _row field:

1. It iterates through the data fields that the _row field contains and copies these data field names and values into a local object named original:

```
var original = {};
for (var columnName in this._row)
{
  if ((columnName.charAt(0) !== '_') &&
      (typeof(this._row[columnName]) !== "function"))
    original[columnName] = this._row[columnName];
}
```

2. It stores this local object into a field named _original, on the _row field:

```
this._row._original = original;
```

3. It calls an internal setter method named _set_state to change the state of the DataRow object to Modified:

```
this._set_state(Sys.Preview.Data.DataRowState.Modified);
```

The implementation of the _set_state method is as follows:

```
function Sys$Preview$Data$DataRow$_set_state(value)
{
  this._state = value;
}
```

Note that the _set_state method is an internal method and must not be directly called from your code. This allows the DataRow class to have complete control over when it should be marked as dirty.

417

The DataRow class exposes a getter method named get_state that you can call to query the state of the DataRow object, as follows:

```
function Sys$Preview$Data$DataRow$get_state()
{
  return this._state;
}
```

A DataRow object could be in one of the states defined by the DataRowState enumeration presented in Listing 11-7.

Listing 11-7: The setProperty Method of the DataRow Class

```
function Sys$Preview$Data$DataRow$setProperty(name, value, key)
{
  if (name === "$selected")
  {
    this.set_selected(value);
    return;
  }

  if (this._row[name] === value)
    return;

  var isDirty = this.get_isDirty();
  if (!isDirty && this._owner &&
      (this.get_state() === Sys.Preview.Data.DataRowState.Unchanged))
  {
    var original = {};
    for (var columnName in this._row)
    {
      if ((columnName.charAt(0) !== '_') &&
          (typeof(this._row[columnName]) !== "function"))
        original[columnName] = this._row[columnName];
    }
    this._row._original = original;
    this._set_state(Sys.Preview.Data.DataRowState.Modified);
  }

  Sys.Preview.TypeDescriptor.setProperty(this._row, name, value, key);

  this._onPropertyChanged(name);

  if (!isDirty)
    this._onPropertyChanged("$isDirty");

  this._owner.raiseRowChanged(this._row);
}
```

When the get_isDirty getter method is invoked, this method checks whether the _original field value of the _row field has been set. If so, it returns true to inform its caller that the DataRow object has been modified:

```
function Sys$Preview$Data$DataRow$get_isDirty()
{
  return typeof(this._row._original) === "object";
}
```

The `setProperty` method finally calls the `_onPropertyChanged` method to raise the `propertyChanged` event:

```
this._onPropertyChanged(name);

if (!isDirty)
  this._onPropertyChanged("$isDirty");
```

It also calls the `raiseRowChanged` method on the `_owner` field. This field references the `DataTable` object that owns the `DataRow` object (as shown previously in Listing 11-3). The `DataTable` class and its `raiseRowChanged` method are discussed later in this chapter, but for now suffice it to say that the owner `DataTable` object is notified every time one of its constituent `DataRow` objects changes:

```
this._owner.raiseRowChanged(this._row);
```

invokeMethod

As Listing 11-8 shows, the `DataRow` class's implementation of the `ICustomTypeDescriptor` interface's `invokeMethod` method does not do anything. In general, your custom type's implementation of any interface must implement all the members of the interface. Even if there is a member that you're not interested in, you must still provide an implementation that does nothing.

Listing 11-8: The invokeMethod Method

```
function Sys$Preview$Data$DataRow$invokeMethod(methodName, parameters)
{
}
```

Owner

As Listing 11-9 shows, the `DataRow` class exposes a getter method named `get_table` that you can call on a `DataRow` object to return a reference to the `DataTable` object that owns the `DataRow`.

Listing 11-9: The get_table Getter Method

```
function Sys$Preview$Data$DataRow$get_table()
{
  return this._owner;
}
```

Note that the `DataRow` object exposes an internal setter method named `_set_table` that specifies a given `DataTable` object as the owner of the `DataRow` object:

```
function Sys$Preview$Data$DataRow$_set_table(value)
{
  this._owner = value;
}
```

This setter method is for internal use, and you must never call it from your code. The only way to specify the `DataTable` object that owns a `DataRow` object is when you're calling the constructor of the `DataRow` class (as previously shown in Listing 11-3) to instantiate the `DataRow` object. You cannot change the `DataTable` object that owns a given `DataRow` object after you create the `DataRow` object.

INotifyPropertyChange

As the boldface portion of the following code fragment shows, the `DataRow` class implements the `INotifyPropertyChange` interface discussed in the previous chapters:

```
Sys.Preview.Data.DataRow.registerClass('Sys.Preview.Data.DataRow', null,
                                Sys.Preview.ICustomTypeDescriptor,
                                Sys.INotifyPropertyChange, Sys.IDisposable);
```

Implementing this interface allows a type such as `DataRow` to raise the `propertyChanged` event.

The `DataRow` class follows the ASP.NET AJAX event implementation pattern discussed in the previous chapters to implement the `propertyChanged` event. This pattern requires an ASP.NET AJAX type to take the following steps:

1. Expose a private field named _events, which references an `EventHandlerList` object where the event handlers registered for the events of the type will be stored.

2. Expose a getter method named `get_events` or `get_eventHandlerList` that returns a reference to this `EventHandlerList` object.

3. Expose a method named add_*EventName* where *EventName* stands for the name of the event, which is `propertyChanged` in the case of the `DataRow` type. This method must call the `addHandler` method on the `EventHandlerList` to add the specified JavaScript function as an event handler for the event with the specifed name.

4. Expose a method named remove_*EventName* where *EventName* stands for the name of the event, which is `propertyChanged` in the case of the `DataRow` type. This method must call the `removeHandler` method on the `EventHandlerList` object to remove the specified JavaScript function from the list of event handlers registered for the event with the specified name.

5. Expose a method named on*EventName* where *EventName* stands for the name of the event. This method must call the `getHandler` method on the `EventHandlerList` object to return a reference to a JavaScript function whose invocation automatically invokes all event handlers registered for the event with the specified name. Next, it must instantiate an instance of the event data class associated with the event with the specified name. Finally, it must call the JavaScript function returned from the `getHandler` method passing in the event data class instance. Calling this function automatically calls all event handlers registered for the specified event, passing in the event data class instance.

Following this standard ASP.NET AJAX event implementation pattern, the `DataRow` class first exposes the `get_events` method shown in Listing 11-10.

Listing 11-10: The get_events Method

```
function Sys$Preview$Data$DataRow$get_events()
{
  if (!this._events)
    this._events = new Sys.EventHandlerList();

  return this._events;
}
```

Next, it implements two methods named `add_propertyChanged` and `remove_propertyChanged` as shown in Listing 11-11. Notice that the names of these two methods follow the naming convension specified in the ASP.NET AJAX event implementation pattern. These two methods are also the methods of the `INotifyPropertyChange` interface that the `DataRow` class must implement.

Listing 11-11: The add_propertyChanged and remove_propertyChanged Methods

```
function Sys$Preview$Data$DataRow$add_propertyChanged(handler)
{
  this.get_events().addHandler("propertyChanged", handler);
}

function Sys$Preview$Data$DataRow$remove_propertyChanged(handler)
{
  this.get_events().removeHandler("propertyChanged", handler);
}
```

Following the ASP.NET AJAX event implementation pattern, the `DataRow` class exposes a method named `_onPropertyChanged` that raises the `propertyChanged` event. As you saw before, a `DataRow` object calls the `_onPropertyChanged` method every time either of the following occurs:

❑ Its `$selected` property changes value, which occurs when the `DataRow` object is selected or deselected.

❑ Its `$isDirty` property changes value, which occurs when the constituent data fields of the `DataRow` object change value.

You can use the `add_propertyChanged` method to register a callback as an event handler for the `DataRow` object's `propertyChanged` event.

Listing 11-12 shows the `_onPropertyChanged` method.

Listing 11-12: The _onPropertyChanged Method

```
function Sys$Preview$Data$DataRow$_onPropertyChanged(propertyName)
{
  var handler = this.get_events().getHandler("propertyChanged");
  if (handler)
    handler(this, new Sys.PropertyChangedEventArgs(propertyName));
}
```

When the _onPropertyChanged method is invoked, it first calls the get_events method to return a reference to the internal EventHandlerList object that contains all event handlers registered for the DataRow object's events. Then it calls the getHandler method on this EventHandlerList object to return a reference to a JavaScript function whose invocation automatically invokes all event handlers registered for the the DataRow object's propertyChanged event.

```
var handler = this.get_events().getHandler("propertyChanged");
```

Finally, the _onPropertyChange method invokes this JavaScript function:

```
handler(this, new Sys.PropertyChangedEventArgs(propertyName));
```

Note that the method passes a Sys.PropertyChangedEventArgs object that encapsulates the name of the property whose value has changed into the event handler.

DataTable

The .NET DataTable class is a powerful data class that is used to represent a data table such as a relational database table. The ASP.NET AJAX client-side framework includes a powerful client data class named DataTable that emulates the .NET DataTable class and provides client-side programmers with features that are similar to what its .NET counterpart offers. The following sections discuss the members of the DataTable client data class.

Constructor

As Listing 11-13 shows, the constructor of the DataTable class takes two parameters. The first parameter is an array of DataColumn objects, where each DataColumn object represents a particular data column of the data table that the DataTable object being instantiated will represent. The second parameter, which is optional, is an array of JavaScript objects, where each JavaScript object contains the data field names and values of a particular data row of the data table that the DataTable object being instantiated will represent.

Listing 11-13: The Constructor of the DataTable Class

```
Sys.Preview.Data.DataTable =
function Sys$Preview$Data$DataTable(columns, tableArray)
{
  this._array = Array.isInstanceOfType(tableArray) ? tableArray : [];
  this._columns = Array.isInstanceOfType(columns) ? columns : [];
  this._rows = [];
  this._deletedRows = [];
  this._newRows = [];
  this._updatedRows = [];
  this._columnDictionary = {};
  this._keys = null;
  this._events = null;
}
```

The `DataTable` class exposes the following internal fields:

❑ `_array`: This field is an array that contains one JavaScript object for each data row of the data table that the `DataTable` object represents. Each JavaScript object contains the data field names and values of its associated data row. This JavaScript object is known as a `row` object.

❑ `_columns`: This field is an array that contains one `DataColumn` object for each data column of the data table that the `DataTable` object represents. Each `DataColumn` object specifies the following information about its associated data column:

   ❑ Its column name, type, and default value

   ❑ Whether it is a primary key field

   ❑ Whether it is editable

❑ `_rows`: This field is an array that contains one `DataRow` object for each data row of the data table that the `DataTable` object represents. Each `DataRow` object provides the following information about its associated data row:

   ❑ A JavaScript object (via the `get_rowObject` getter method) that contains the data field names and values of the associated data row. The `DataRow` class exposes a getter method named `get_rowObject` that returns a reference to this JavaScript object:

```
function Sys$Preview$Data$DataRow$get_rowObject()
{
  return typeof(this._row._rowObject) !== "undefined" ?
             this._row._rowObject : this._row;
}
```

   ❑ The `_row` field references the object that is passed into the constructor of the `DataRow` class as its first argument (as shown previously in Listing 11-3). If this object references an existing `DataRow` object, the `get_rowObject` method returns a reference to the `_rowObject` field of this `DataRow` object (which is the object used to instantiate this `DataRow` object in the first place). Otherwise, it just returns a reference to the `_row` field itself (which is the object used to instantiate the current `DataRow` object).

   ❑ A Boolean value (via the `get_selected` getter method) that specifies whether the associated data row has been selected.

   ❑ A `DataRowState` enumeration value (via the `get_state` getter method) that specifies the state of the associated data row.

   ❑ A Boolean value (via the `get_isDirty` getter method) that specifies whether the associated data row is dirty. (A data row is considered dirty when one of its constituent data fields changes value.)

❑ `_deletedRows`: This field is an array that contains references to row objects associated with the `DataRow` objects that represent the *to-be deleted* data rows of the data table that the `DataTable` object represents.

Here's what "*to-be deleted* data rows" means. The `DataTable` class works in what is known as disconnected mode, which means that the `DataTable` object is not connected to the data table that it represents. The `DataTable` object is an in-memory representation of its associated data table, which could be sitting in some relational database in some remote server. Therefore, changes made to this in-memory representation do not automatically propagate to the underlying data table, which means that deleting a `DataRow` object from the `_rows` array does not automatically delete the associated data row in the underlying data table. You have to explicitly propagate the changes to the underlying data table. This propagation can be done either immediately after a `DataRow` object is removed from the `_rows` array, or you can accumulate the row objects associated with the deleted `DataRow` objects in the `_deletedRows` array and commit the changes in one shot to improve the performance of your application.

❑ `_newRows`: This field is an array that contains references to row objects associated with the `DataRow` objects that represent the *to-be added* data rows of the data table that the `DataTable` object represents.

Because the `DataTable` object is an in-memory representation of its associated data table, changes made to this in-memory representation do not automatically propagate to the underlying data table, which means that adding a new `DataRow` object to the `_rows` array does not automatically add a new data row to the underlying data table. You have to explicitly propagate the changes to the underlying data table. This propagation can be done either immediately after a `DataRow` object is added to the `_rows` array, or you can accumulate the row objects associated with the new `DataRow` objects in the `_newRows` array and commit the changes in one shot to improve the performance of your application.

❑ `_updatedRows`: This field is an array that contains references to row objects associated with the `DataRow` objects that represent the *to-be updated* data rows of the data table that the `DataTable` object represents.

Because the `DataTable` object is an in-memory representation of its associated data table, changes made to this in-memory representation do not automatically propagate to the underlying data table. You can propagate the changes either immediately after a `DataRow` object in the `_rows` array is updated, or you can accumulate the row objects associated with the updated `DataRow` objects in the `_updatedRows` array and commit the changes in one shot.

❑ `_columnDictionary`: This field is a dictionary of `DataColumn` objects, where each `DataColumn` object represents a data column of the data table associated with the `DataTable` object.

The `_columns` field also stores the same set of `DataColumn` objects. You can think of the `_columnDictionary` field as a cache to improve performance. As you'll see later, every time you access a `DataColumn` object from the `_columns` array, it gets cached in the `_columnDictionary` field, which means that the next request for the same `DataColumn` object is serviced from the cache.

❑ `_keys`: This field is an array that contains all `DataColumn` objects associated with the primary key data fields of the data table that the `DataTable` object represents.

❑ `_events`: This field references the `EventHandlerList` object that contains all event handlers registered for the events of the `DataTable` object. As you'll see later, the `DataTable` class exposes two events named `propertyChanged` and `collectionChanged`.

IData

As you can see in the boldface portion of the following code fragment, the `DataTable` class implements the `IData` interface:

```
Sys.Preview.Data.DataTable.registerClass('Sys.Preview.Data.DataTable', null,
                               Sys.Preview.Data.IData,
                               Sys.INotifyPropertyChange,
                               Sys.Preview.INotifyCollectionChanged,
                               Sys.IDisposable);
```

The IData interface exposes five methods named add, clear, get_length, getRow, and remove (as previously shown in Listing 11-3). The following sections discuss the DataTable class's implementation of these five methods to help you gain the skills you need to provide your own custom implementation for this interface. Keep in mind that implementing this interface allows a data class such as DataTable to seamlessly integrate into the ASP.NET AJAX client-side framework, where the data class can be bound to client controls such as Selector. You'll see an example of such a data binding scenario later in this chapter.

add

The main responsibility of the add method is to add a new DataRow object to the list of existing DataRow objects of the DataTable object on which the method is invoked. Listing 11-14 shows this method.

Listing 11-14: The add Method

```
function Sys$Preview$Data$DataTable$add(rowObject)
{
  var row;
  if (Sys.Preview.Data.DataRow.isInstanceOfType(rowObject))
  {
    row = rowObject;
    row._set_table(this);
    rowObject = rowObject.get_rowObject();
  }

  else
    row = new Sys.Preview.Data.DataRow(rowObject, this);

  var index = this._array.length;
  row._set_index(index);
  var columns = this.get_columns();
  if (columns)
  {
    for(var i = columns.length - 1; i >= 0; i--)
    {
      var column = columns[i];
      if (typeof(rowObject[column.get_columnName()]) === "undefined")
        rowObject[column.get_columnName()] = column.get_defaultValue();
    }
  }

  var oldIsDirty = this.get_isDirty();
  this._array[index] = rowObject;
  this._rows[index] = row;
  Array.add(this._newRows, rowObject);
  row._set_state(Sys.Preview.Data.DataRowState.Added);
```

(continued)

Listing 11-14 *(continued)*

```
      this._onCollectionChanged(Sys.Preview.NotifyCollectionChangedAction.Add, row);
      this._onPropertyChanged("length");
      if (!oldIsDirty)
        this._onPropertyChanged("isDirty");

      return row;
  }
```

The `add` method of the `DataTable` class takes a single argument, which can be of one of the following types:

❑   `Sys.Preview.Data.DataRow`: In this case, you're adding an already instantiated `DataRow` object into the list of `DataRow` objects of the `DataTable` object. The `add` method calls the `set_table` method on this `DataRow` object, passing in a reference to the `DataTable` object to specify the `DataTable` object as its owner:

```
    row = rowObject;
    row._set_table(this);
```

The `add` method then calls the `get_rowObject` method to return a reference to the `row` object associated with the `DataRow` object. Every `DataRow` object is associated with an object known as a row object, which contains the names and values of all data fields of the `DataRow` object. The `DataRow` object exposes a method named `get_rowObject` that returns a reference to its associated row object:

```
    rowObject = rowObject.get_rowObject();
```

❑   A JavaScript object such as an object literal: In this case, the `add` method calls the constructor of the `DataRow` class, passing in the row object to instantiate a new `DataRow` object:

```
  row = new Sys.Preview.Data.DataRow(rowObject, this);
```

In either case, the `add` method accesses the length of the `_array` collection that contains the row objects and assigns it as the index of the new `DataRow` object:

```
    var index = this._array.length;
    row._set_index(index);
```

Next, the `add` method calls the `get_columns` method to return an array that contains the `DataColumn` objects:

```
    var columns = this.get_columns();
```

It then iterates through these objects and takes the following steps for each enumerated `DataColumn` object:

1.   It calls the `get_columnName` method on the enumerated `DataColumn` object to access the name of the column, and uses this name as an index into the row object to determine whether the row object contains a value for the data column with the specified name:

```
        var column = columns[i];
        if (typeof(rowObject[column.get_columnName()]) === "undefined")
```

2. If the row object does not contain a value for the specified data column, the add method calls the get_defaultValue method on the enumerated DataColumn object to return the default value for the specified data column and assigns the value to the associated data field of the row object:

```
        rowObject[column.get_columnName()] = column.get_defaultValue();
```

3. It stores the current value of the isDirty property of the DataTable object in a local variable:

```
    var oldIsDirty = this.get_isDirty();
```

4. It stores the new row object in the _array collection (which contains all row objects associated with the DataRow objects in the _rows array):

```
    this._array[index] = rowObject;
```

5. It stores the new DataRow object in the _rows collection (which contains all DataRow objects that belong to the same DataTable object):

```
    this._rows[index] = row;
```

6. It stores the new row object in the _newRows collection (which contains the row objects associated with the newly-added DataRow objects):

```
    Array.add(this._newRows, rowObject);
```

7. It calls the _set_state method on the new DataRow object to set its state to Added to indicate that the DataRow object has been added to its owner DataTable object:

```
    row._set_state(Sys.Preview.Data.DataRowState.Added);
```

8. It invokes the _onCollectionChanged method to raise the collectionChanged event (discussed in more detail later in this section):

```
    this._onCollectionChanged(Sys.Preview.NotifyCollectionChangedAction.Add, row);
```

9. It calls the _onPropertyChanged method to raise the propertyChanged event because the value of the length property of the DataTable has changed due to the addition of the new DataRow object:

```
    this._onPropertyChanged("length");
```

If the DataTable wasn't marked as dirty to begin with, the add method calls the _onPropertyChanged method to signal that the value of the isDirty property has changed due to the addition of the new data row:

```
    if (!oldIsDirty)
      this._onPropertyChanged("isDirty");
```

clear

The main responsibility of the `clear` method is to clear the current `DataTable` object. Listing 11-15 presents the internal implementation of the `clear` method of the `DataTable` class.

Listing 11-15: The clear Method

```
function Sys$Preview$Data$DataTable$clear()
{
  if (this.get_length() > 0)
  {
    var oldIsDirty = this.get_isDirty();
    for (var i = this._array.length - 1; i >= 0; i--)
    {
      var row = this._array[i];
      if (row && !Array.contains(this._newRows, row))
      {
        Array.add(this._deletedRows, row);
                this._rows[i]._set_state(Sys.Preview.Data.DataRowState.Deleted);
      }
    }
    this._rows = [];
    this._array = [];
    this._newRows = [];
    this._updatedRows = [];
    this._onCollectionChanged
                        (Sys.Preview.NotifyCollectionChangedAction.Reset, null);
    this._onPropertyChanged("length");
    if (!oldIsDirty)
      this._onPropertyChanged("isDirty");
  }
}
```

The `clear` method first calls the `get_isDirty` method to return the Boolean value that specifies whether the `DataTable` object is currently dirty:

```
var oldIsDirty = this.get_isDirty();
```

Next, it iterates through the row objects stored in the `_array` collection and takes the following steps for each enumerated row object:

1. It checks whether the `_newRows` collection contains the enumerated row object. As discussed previously, the `_newRows` collection contains the row objects associated with newly-added `DataRow` objects. If this collection does not contain the enumerated row object, the `clear` method does the following:

    a. It adds the row object to the `_deletedRows` array (which contains the deleted row objects associated with the deleted `DataRow` objects):

    ```
    Array.add(this._deletedRows, row);
    ```

    b. It calls the `_set_state` method on the `DataRow` object associated with the enumerated row object to set its state to `Deleted`:

```
            this._rows[i]._set_state(Sys.Preview.Data.DataRowState.Deleted);
```

2. It clears the _rows, _array, _newRows, and _updatedRows collections:

```
        this._rows = [];
        this._array = [];
        this._newRows = [];
        this._updatedRows = [];
```

3. It calls the _onCollectionChanged method to raise the collectionChanged event:

```
    this._onCollectionChanged(Sys.Preview.NotifyCollectionChangedAction.Reset, null);
```

4. It calls the _onPropertyChanged method to raise the propertyChanged event for the length property:

```
        this._onPropertyChanged("length");
```

If the DataTable wasn't dirty to begin with, the clear method calls the _onPropertyChanged method to raise the propertyChanged event for the isDirty property:

```
        if (!oldIsDirty)
          this._onPropertyChanged("isDirty");
```

get_length

As Listing 11-16 shows, the get_length method of the DataTable class returns the length of the _array array. This array contains the row objects associated with all DataRow objects in the _rows array.

Listing 11-16: The get_length Method

```
function Sys$Preview$Data$DataTable$get_length()
{
  return this._array.length;
}
```

getRow

As you can see in Listing 11-17, the getRow method returns the DataRow object in the _rows array with the specified index.

Listing 11-17: The getRow Method

```
function Sys$Preview$Data$DataTable$getRow(index)
{
  var row = this._rows[index];
  if (!row)
  {
    var rowObject = this._array[index];
    if (rowObject)
```

(continued)

Listing 11-17 (continued)

```
    {
      row = Sys.Preview.Data.DataRow.isInstanceOfType(rowObject) ? rowObject :
          new Sys.Preview.Data.DataRow(rowObject, this, index);
      this._rows[index] = row;
    }
  }
  return row;
}
```

The DataTable also exposes a method named getItem that simply delegates to the getRow method, as shown in Listing 11-18.

Listing 11-18: The getItem Method

```
function Sys$Preview$Data$DataTable$getItem(index)
{
  return this.getRow(index);
}
```

Remove

Listing 11-19 shows the DataTable class's Remove method.

Listing 11-19: The Remove Method of the DataTable Class

```
function Sys$Preview$Data$DataTable$remove(rowObject)
{
  if (Sys.Preview.Data.DataRow.isInstanceOfType(rowObject))
    rowObject = rowObject.get_rowObject();

  var oldIsDirty = this.get_isDirty();
  var index = Array.indexOf(this._array, rowObject);
  var row = this.getItem(index);
  if(typeof(this._array.removeAt) === "function")
    this._array.removeAt(index);

  else
    Array.removeAt(this._array, index);

  Array.removeAt(this._rows, index);
  index = Array.indexOf(this._newRows, rowObject);
  if (index !== -1)
    Array.removeAt(this._newRows, index);

  else
    Array.add(this._deletedRows, rowObject);

  row._set_state(Sys.Preview.Data.DataRowState.Deleted);
```

```
      this._onCollectionChanged(Sys.Preview.NotifyCollectionChangedAction.Remove, row);
      this._onPropertyChanged("length");
      if (oldIsDirty !== this.get_isDirty())
        this._onPropertyChanged("isDirty");
   }
```

The Remove method takes a JavaScript object as its argument. The object can be a DataRow or a row object. Remove first checks whether this object is a DataRow. If so, it calls the get_rowObject method on the DataRow object to return a reference to its associated row object:

```
      if (Sys.Preview.Data.DataRow.isInstanceOfType(rowObject))
        rowObject = rowObject.get_rowObject();
```

Next, the Remove method calls the get_isDirty method to return and store the current value of the isDirty property in a local variable named oldIsDirty for future reference:

```
      var oldIsDirty = this.get_isDirty();
```

This is done because the code following this line of code could change the current value of this property:

The Remove method then determines the index of the row object in the _array array, which contains all row objects associated with the DataRows object of the current DataTable object:

```
      var index = Array.indexOf(this._array, rowObject);
```

Next, the Remove method calls the getItem method, passing in the index of the row object to return a reference to DataRow object associated with the row object:

```
      var row = this.getItem(index);
```

It then calls the removeAt method to remove the row object from the _array array:

```
      if(typeof(this._array.removeAt) === "function")
        this._array.removeAt(index);

      else
        Array.removeAt(this._array, index);
```

Next, it invokes the removeAt static method on the Array class to remove the DataRow object from the _rows array, which contains all the DataRow objects that the current DataTable owns:

```
      Array.removeAt(this._rows, index);
```

It then checks whether the _newRows array contains the row object; and if so, it removes the row object from this array as well:

```
      index = Array.indexOf(this._newRows, rowObject);
      if (index !== -1)
        Array.removeAt(this._newRows, index);

      else
        Array.add(this._deletedRows, rowObject);
```

Next, it calls the internal _set_state method on the DataRow object to change its state to Deleted:

```
row._set_state(Sys.Preview.Data.DataRowState.Deleted);
```

As you can see, _set_state is an internal method and you should not directly use this method in your own code.

Then, the Remove method calls the _onCollectionChanged method to raise the collectionChanged event:

```
this._onCollectionChanged(Sys.Preview.NotifyCollectionChangedAction.Remove, row);
```

This is expected because the Remove method is removing a row object from the _array collection.

Next, the Remove method calls the _onPropertyChanged method to raise the propertyChanged event for the length property of the DataTable object:

```
this._onPropertyChanged("length");
```

Again this is expected because the Remove method is removing a row object from the _array collection and, consequently, changing the length of the collection.

Finally, the Remove method calls the get_isDirty method to access the current value of the isDirty property of the DataTable object and compares this value with the old value. If they are different, it calls the _onPropertyChanged method to raise the propertyChanged event for the isDirty property:

```
if (oldIsDirty !== this.get_isDirty())
    this._onPropertyChanged("isDirty");
```

Descriptor

As Listing 11-20 shows, the DataTable class exposes a static property named descriptor, which enables its clients to use the ASP.NET AJAX type inspection capabilities to inspect its members at runtime.

Listing 11-20: The descriptor Property of the DataTable Class

```
Sys.Preview.Data.DataTable.descriptor =
{
  properties: [ { name: 'columns', type: Array, readOnly: true },
                { name: 'keyNames', type: Array, readOnly: true },
                { name: 'length', type: Number, readOnly: true },
                { name: 'isDirty', type: Boolean, readOnly: true } ],
  methods: [ { name: 'add' },
             { name: 'clear' },
             { name: 'remove' } ],
  events: [ { name: 'collectionChanged', readOnly: true },
            { name: 'propertyChanged', readOnly: true } ]
}
```

The descriptor property of the DataTable class is set to an object literal that contains the following three name/value pairs:

❑ The first name/value pair describes the properties of the DataTable class. The name part of the name/value pair is properties, and the value part is an array of four object literals that describe the columns, keyNames, length, and isDirty properties of the DataTable class. Each object literal itself contains three name/value pairs, where the first pair specifies the name of the property, the second pair describes the type of the property, and the last pair specifies whether the property is editable.

```
properties: [ { name: 'columns', type: Array, readOnly: true },
               { name: 'keyNames', type: Array, readOnly: true },
               { name: 'length', type: Number, readOnly: true },
               { name: 'isDirty', type: Boolean, readOnly: true } ]
```

❑ The second name/value pair describes the methods of the DataTable class. The name of the pair is methods, and the value is an array of three object literals that describe the add, clear, and remove methods of the DataTable class:

```
methods: [ { name: 'add' },
           { name: 'clear' },
           { name: 'remove' } ],
```

❑ The third name/value pair describes the events of the DataTable class. The name part of the pair is the keyword events, and the value part is an array of two object literals that describe the collectionChanged and propertyChanged events of the DataTable class:

```
events: [ { name: 'collectionChanged', readOnly: true },
          { name: 'propertyChanged', readOnly: true } ]
```

As Listing 11-21 shows, the DataTable class exposes three getter methods named get_columns, get_keyNames, and get_isDirty that you can invoke to access the values of the columns, keyNames, and isDirty properties of a given DataTable object.

Listing 11-21: The get_columns, get_keyNames, and get_isDirty Getter Methods

```
function Sys$Preview$Data$DataTable$get_columns()
{
  return this._columns;
}

function Sys$Preview$Data$DataTable$get_keyNames()
{
  if (!this._keys)
  {
    this._keys = [];
    var len = this._columns.length;
    for (var i = 0; i < len; i++)
    {
      var col = this._columns[i];
      if (col.get_isKey())
        Array.add(this._keys, col.get_columnName());
    }
```

(continued)

Listing 11-21 (continued)

```
  }
  return this._keys;
}

function Sys$Preview$Data$DataTable$get_isDirty()
{
  return (this._deletedRows.length !== 0) ||
         (this._newRows.length !== 0) ||
         (this._updatedRows.length !== 0);
}
```

The DataTable object properties that the getter methods expose include the following:

❑   The columns property is an array that contains all the DataColumn objects that the DataTable owns.

❑   The keyNames property is an array that contains the column names of all DataColumn objects that represent the primary key data fields of the data table that the DataTable represents.

❑   The isDirty property is a Boolean value that specifies whether the DataTable object is dirty. A DataTable object is considered dirty when one or more of the following arrays contains one or more row objects:

   ❑   _deletedRows: This array contains the row objects associated with the deleted DataRow objects of the DataTable object.

   ❑   _newRows: This array contains the row objects associated with the newly added DataRow objects.

   ❑   _updatedRows: This array contains the row objects associated with the updated DataRow objects.

```
return (this._deletedRows.length !== 0) ||
       (this._newRows.length !== 0) ||
       (this._updatedRows.length !== 0);
```

INotifyPropertyChange

The boldface portion of the following code fragment shows how the DataTable class implements the INotifyPropertyChange interface discussed in the previous chapters:

```
Sys.Preview.Data.DataTable.registerClass('Sys.Preview.Data.DataTable', null,
                                          Sys.Preview.Data.IData,
                                          Sys.INotifyPropertyChange,
                                          Sys.Preview.INotifyCollectionChanged,
                                          Sys.IDisposable);
```

Listing 11-22 presents the DataTable class's implementation of the members of the INotifyPropertyChange interface. This interface exposes the following two methods:

❑ add_propertyChanged: This method adds the specified method as an event handler for the propertyChanged event.

❑ remove_propertyChanged: This method removes the specified method from the list of event handlers registered for the propertyChanged event.

Listing 11-22: The DataTable Class's Implementation of the INotifyPropertyChange Interface

```
function Sys$Preview$Data$DataTable$get_events()
{
  if (!this._events)
    this._events = new Sys.EventHandlerList();

  return this._events;
}

function Sys$Preview$Data$DataTable$add_propertyChanged(handler)
{
  this.get_events().addHandler("propertyChanged", handler);
}

function Sys$Preview$Data$DataTable$remove_propertyChanged(handler)
{
  this.get_events().removeHandler("propertyChanged", handler);
}

function Sys$Preview$Data$DataTable$_onPropertyChanged(propertyName)
{
  var handler = this.get_events().getHandler("propertyChanged");
  if (handler)
    handler(this, new Sys.PropertyChangedEventArgs(propertyName));
}
```

The DataTable class's implementation of the propertyChanged event follows the event implementation pattern discussed in the previous chapters. As previously discussed, implementing an event requires an ASP.NET AJAX class to support a private field of type EventHandlerList named _events where the event handlers registered for the events of the class will be stored. The class must also expose a getter method named get_events that returns a reference to this EventHandlerList object:

```
function Sys$Preview$Data$DataTable$get_events()
{
  if (!this._events)
    this._events = new Sys.EventHandlerList();

  return this._events;
}
```

The DataTable class's implementation of the add_propertyChanged method of the INotifyPropertyChange interface first calls the get_events method to return a reference to the EventHandlerList object that maintains all the event handlers registered for the events of the

435

DataTable class, and then calls the addHandler method on this EventHandlerList object to add the specified method as the event handler for the propertyChanged event:

```
this.get_events().addHandler("propertyChanged", handler);
```

The DataTable class's implementation of the INotifyPropertyChange interface's remove_propertyChanged method works the same as the add_propertyChanged method, with one difference. Instead of invoking the addHandler method, it invokes the removeHandler method to remove the specified handler from the list of handlers registered for the propertyChanged event of the DataTable class:

```
this.get_events().removeHandler("propertyChanged", handler);
```

Following the event implementation pattern discussed in the previous chapters, the DataTable class exposes a method named _onPropertyChanged that raises the propertyChanged event:

```
function Sys$Preview$Data$DataTable$_onPropertyChanged(propertyName)
{
  var handler = this.get_events().getHandler("propertyChanged");
  if (handler)
    handler(this, new Sys.PropertyChangedEventArgs(propertyName));
}
```

The _onPropertyChanged method first calls the get_events method to return a reference to the EventHandlerList that maintains all the event handlers registered for the events of the DataTable class. Then it calls the getHandler method on the EventHandlerList object. This method returns a JavaScript function whose invocation automatically invokes all event handlers registered for the propertyChanged event of the DataTable class. Finally, the _onPropertyChanged method instantiates a PropertyChangedEventArgs object that encapsulates the name of the property whose value has changed. This instance is finally passed into the event handlers registered for the propertyChanged event. This enables the event handlers to determine the value of which property has changed.

INotifyCollectionChanged

The boldface portion of the following code fragment shows how the DataTable class implements an interface named INotifyCollectionChanged:

```
Sys.Preview.Data.DataTable.registerClass('Sys.Preview.Data.DataTable', null,
                            Sys.Preview.Data.IData,
                            Sys.INotifyPropertyChange,
                            Sys.Preview.INotifyCollectionChanged,
                            Sys.IDisposable);
```

Implementing this interface enables an ASP.NET AJAX class to raise an event named collectionChanged. This event is useful in ASP.NET AJAX classes that contain one or more collections and want to inform their clients when the contents of these collections change. For example, the DataTable class contains the _array collection where all the row objects associated with the DataRow objects of the current DataTable object are stored. Implementing the INofiyCollectionChanged interface enables the DataTable class to raise the collectionChanged event when any of the following occurs:

❑　A new row object is added to the _array collection.

❑　A row object is removed from the _array collection.

❑　A row object in the _array collection is updated. Because a row object contains the names and values of the data fields of its associated DataRow object, updating a row object means updating the values of these data fields.

As Listing 11-23 shows, this interface exposes two methods named add_collectionChanged and remove_collectionChanged. Your custom ASP.NET AJAX type's implementation of these two methods must add the specified event handler to and remove the specified event handler from the internal collection where your type maintains the event handlers registered for its events. This collection is an object of type EventHandlerList as discussed earlier.

Listing 11-23: The INotifyCollectionChanged Interface

```
Sys.Preview.INotifyCollectionChanged =
function Sys$Preview$INotifyCollectionChanged()
{
    throw Error.notImplemented();
}


function Sys$Preview$INotifyCollectionChanged$add_collectionChanged()
{
    throw Error.notImplemented();
}


function Sys$Preview$INotifyCollectionChanged$remove_collectionChanged()
{
    throw Error.notImplemented();
}


Sys.Preview.INotifyCollectionChanged.prototype =
{
    add_collectionChanged:
                    Sys$Preview$INotifyCollectionChanged$add_collectionChanged,
    remove_collectionChanged:
                    Sys$Preview$INotifyCollectionChanged$remove_collectionChanged
}


Sys.Preview.INotifyCollectionChanged.registerInterface(
                                    'Sys.Preview.INotifyCollectionChanged');
```

As you can see in Listing 11-24, the DataTable class follows the same event implementation pattern discussed earlier to implement the collectionChanged event.

Listing 11-24: The DataTable Class's Implementation of the INotifyCollectionChanged Interface

```
function Sys$Preview$Data$DataTable$add_collectionChanged(handler)
{
  this.get_events().addHandler("collectionChanged", handler);
}

function Sys$Preview$Data$DataTable$remove_collectionChanged(handler)
{
  this.get_events().removeHandler("collectionChanged", handler);
}

function Sys$Preview$Data$DataTable$_onCollectionChanged(action, changedItem)
{
  var handler = this.get_events().getHandler("collectionChanged");
  if (handler)
    handler(this, new Sys.Preview.CollectionChangedEventArgs(action, changedItem));
}
```

Note that the `DataTable` class exposes a method named `_onCollectionChanged` that raise the `collectionChanged` event. This method passes an instance of an event data class named `CollectionChangedEventArgs` into the event handlers registered for the `collectionChanged` event when it calls these handlers. Listing 11-25 presents the implementation of the `CollectionChangedEventArgs` event data class.

Listing 11-25: The CollectionChangedEventArgs Event Data Class

```
Sys.Preview.CollectionChangedEventArgs =
function Sys$Preview$CollectionChangedEventArgs(action, changedItem)
{
  Sys.Preview.CollectionChangedEventArgs.initializeBase(this);
  this._action = action;
  this._changedItem = changedItem;
}

function Sys$Preview$CollectionChangedEventArgs$get_action()
{
  return this._action;
}

function Sys$Preview$CollectionChangedEventArgs$get_changedItem()
{
  return this._changedItem;
}

Sys.Preview.CollectionChangedEventArgs.prototype =
{
  get_action: Sys$Preview$CollectionChangedEventArgs$get_action,
  get_changedItem: Sys$Preview$CollectionChangedEventArgs$get_changedItem
}
```

```
Sys.Preview.CollectionChangedEventArgs.descriptor =
{
  properties: [
    {name: 'action',type: Sys.Preview.NotifyCollectionChangedAction,readOnly: true},
    {name: 'changedItem', type: Object, readOnly: true} ]
}

Sys.Preview.CollectionChangedEventArgs.registerClass(
                                        'Sys.Preview.CollectionChangedEventArgs',
                                        Sys.EventArgs);
```

The constructor of the CollectionChangedEventArgs event data class takes two arguments. The first argument is an enumeration of type NotifyCollectionChangedAction, and the second argument references an object. As Listing 11-26 shows, the NofityCollectionChangedAction enumeration has the following three values:

❑ Add: This enumeration value specifies that the JavaScript object passed into the CollectionChangedEventArgs constructor as its second argument has been added to the collection. In the case of the DataTable class, this JavaScript object is a row object associated with a new DataRow object being added to the DataTable object.

❑ Remove: This enumeration value specifies that the object passed into the CollectionChangedEventArgs constructor as its second argument has been removed from the collection. In the case of the DataTable class, this object is a row object associated with a DataRow object being removed from the DataTable object.

❑ Reset: This enumeration value specifies that the collection has been cleared.

Listing 11-26: The NotifyCollectionChangedAction Enumeration

```
Sys.Preview.NotifyCollectionChangedAction =
function Sys$Preview$NotifyCollectionChangedAction()
{
  throw Error.invalidOperation();
}

Sys.Preview.NotifyCollectionChangedAction.prototype =
{
  Add: 0,
  Remove: 1,
  Reset: 2
}

Sys.Preview.NotifyCollectionChangedAction.registerEnum(
                                        'Sys.Preview.NotifyCollectionChangedAction');
```

createRow

The DataTable class comes with a method named createRow that you can use to create and optionally initialize a new DataRow object. You must call this method to create a new DataRow object instead of using the new operator directly. Listing 11-27 contains the code for the createRow method. As you can see, this method takes an optional parameter that provides initial values for the data fields of the newly created DataRow object.

Listing 11-27: The createRow Method

```
function Sys$Preview$Data$DataTable$createRow(initialData)
{
  var obj = {};
  var undef = {};
  for (var i = this._columns.length - 1; i >= 0; i--)
  {
    var column = this._columns[i];
    var columnName = column.get_columnName();
    var val = undef;
    if (initialData)
      val = Sys.Preview.TypeDescriptor.getProperty(initialData, columnName);

    if ((val === undef) || (typeof(val) === "undefined"))
      val = column.get_defaultValue();

    obj[columnName] = val;
  }
  var row = new Sys.Preview.Data.DataRow(obj, this, -1);
  row._set_state(Sys.Preview.Data.DataRowState.Detached);
  return row;
}
```

Now, let's walk through this listing. As previously discussed, the DataTable class contains an array named _columns that contains all the DataColumn objects of the DataTable object. The createRow method iterates through the DataColumn objects in this array and takes the following steps for each enumerated object:

1. It calls the get_columnName method on the enumerated DataColumn object to access the name of the column:

```
var columnName = column.get_columnName();
```

2. It calls the getProperty static method on the TypeDescriptor class, passing in the optional object passed into the createRow method to return the value of the data field with the specified name:

```
var val = undef;
if (initialData)
  val = Sys.Preview.TypeDescriptor.getProperty(initialData, columnName);
```

The object that you pass into the createRow method must return the value of a data field as if it were returning the value of a property with the same name as the data field.

If the object passed into the createRow method does not contain a property with the same name as the data field, the method calls the get_defaultValue method on the enumerated DataColumn object to return the default value of the associated data field and uses this value as the value of the data field:

```
if ((val === undef) || (typeof(val) === "undefined"))
  val = column.get_defaultValue();
```

3. It stores the data field name and value into a local object:

```
    obj[columnName] = val;
}
```

As you'll see shortly, this local object will be used as the row object for the new DataRow object.

The createRow method then calls the constructor of the Data, Row class, passing in the local object just created and a reference to the current DataTable object to instantiate the new DataRow object. Note that the createRow method passes -1 as the third argument of the constructor. This argument specifies the index of the DataRow object in the _rows collection of the DataTable object. Because the DataRow object has not yet been added to the _rows collection of the DataTable object, it has no index:

```
    var row = new Sys.Preview.Data.DataRow(obj, this, -1);
```

Next, the createRow method calls the internal _set_state method to set the state of the newly created DataRow object to Detached to signal that the DataRow object is still detached from its DataTable object:

```
    row._set_state(Sys.Preview.Data.DataRowState.Detached);
```

As you'll see later, the state of the DataRow object will be changed to Added when it is actually added to the _rows collection of the DataTable object.

getChanges

The DataTable class exposes a method named getChanges, as shown in Listing 11-28.

Listing 11-28: The getChanges Method

```
function Sys$Preview$Data$DataTable$getChanges()
{
  return {updated : this._updatedRows, inserted : this._newRows,
          deleted : this._deletedRows};
}
```

This method returns an object literal that contains the following three name/value pairs:

❑ The first name/value pair describes the collection that contains the updated row objects. The name part of this pair is the keyword updated, and the value part references the _updatedRows array that contains the updated row objects. Therefore, you can use the following code fragment to get a reference to the _updatedRows array:

```
var dt;
. . .
var jsonObj = dt.getChanges();
var updatedRows = jsonObj.updated;
for (var rowObject in updatedRows)
{
  // Do something with the updated row object
}
```

❑ The second name/value pair describes the collection that contains the new row objects. The name part of this pair is the keyword inserted, and the value part references the _newRows array that contains the new row objects. Therefore, you can use the following code fragment to get a reference to the _ newRows array:

```
var dt;
. . .
var jsonObj = dt.getChanges();
var newRows = jsonObj.inserted;
for (var rowObject in newRows)
{
  // Do something with the new row object
}
```

❑ The third name/value pair describes the collection that contains the deleted row objects. The name part of this pair is the keyword deleted, and the value part references the _deletedRows array that contains the deleted row objects. Therefore, you can use the following code fragment to get a reference to the _deletedRows array:

```
var dt;
. . .
var jsonObj = dt.getChanges();
var deletedRows = jsonObj. deleted;
for (var rowObject in deletedRows)
{
  // Do something with the deleted row object
}
```

getColumn

As previously discussed, the DataTable class stores all its constituent DataColumn objects in an internal array named _columns. As you can see in Listing 19-29, the getColumn method returns a reference to the DataColumn with the specified column name. This method caches each requested DataColumn object in an internal cache named _columnDictionary to improve performance. Subsequent requests for the same DataColumn objects are serviced from this cache.

Listing 11-29: The getColumn Method

```
function Sys$Preview$Data$DataTable$getColumn(name)
{
  var col = this._columnDictionary[name];
  if (col)
    return col;

  for (var c = this._columns.length - 1; c >= 0; c--)
  {
    var column = this._columns[c];
    if (column.get_columnName() === name)
    {
```

```
        this._columnDictionary[name] = column;
        return column;
      }
    }
  }
  return null;
}
```

raiseRowChanged

The setProperty method of a DataRow object calls the raiseRowChanged method on the DataTable object that owns the DataRow object, passing in the updated row object (as previously shown in Listing 11-7).

Listing 11-30 shows the raiseRowChanged method. This method adds the updated row object to the _updatedRows array of the DataTable object and calls the _onPropertyChanged method to raise the propertyChanged event for the isDirty property.

Listing 11-30: The raiseRowChanged Method

```
function Sys$Preview$Data$DataTable$raiseRowChanged(changedItem)
{
  if ((Array.indexOf(this._updatedRows, changedItem) === -1) &&
      (Array.indexOf(this._newRows, changedItem) === -1))
  {
    var oldIsDirty = this.get_isDirty();
    Array.add(this._updatedRows, changedItem);
    if (!oldIsDirty)
      this._onPropertyChanged("isDirty");
  }
}
```

parseFromJson

The DataTable class exposes a static method named parseFromJson that creates a DataTable object from a JavaScript object, which is normally an object literal. This object must contain the following two name/value pairs:

- ❑ The first name/value pair must describe the columns of the data table. The name part of the pair must be the keyword columns, and the value part must be an array of object literals where each object literal describes a column. In turn, each object literal must expose the following five name/value pairs:

  - ❑ The first name/value pair must describe the column name. The name part must be name, and the value part must be a string that contains the column name.

  - ❑ The second name/value pair must describe the data type of the column. The name part must be dataType, and the value part must reference the actual data type.

  - ❑ The third name/value pair must describe the default value. The name part must be defaultValue, and the value part must reference the actual default value.

❑ The fourth name/value pair must describe whether the column is a primary key column. The name part of the pair must be isKey, and the value part must be a Boolean value.

❑ The fifth name/value pair must describe whether the column is editable. The name part must be readOnly, and the value part must be a Boolean value.

For example, the following three object literals describe the ProductId, ProductName, and UnitPrice columns of the Products data table:

```
{name: 'ProductId', dataType: Number, defaultValue: 1,
isKey: true, readOnly: true}

{name: 'ProductName', dataType: String, defaultValue: 'Unknown',
isKey: false, readOnly: true}

{name: 'UnitPrice', dataType: Number, defaultValue: 50,
isKey: false, readOnly: false}
```

Note that the value part of the fourth name/value pair of the object literal that describes the ProductId column has been set to true to signal that this column is a primary key column. If the primary key of a data table consists of multiple columns, you must set the value of the fourth name/value pair of *all* the object literals that describe the constituent columns of the primary key to true.

❑ The second name/value pair must describe the data rows of the data table. The name part of the pair must be rows, and the value part must be an array of object literals where each object literal describes a data row. In turn, each object literal must contain one name/value pair for each data field of the data row. The name part of each pair must be a string that contains the name of the data field, and the value part must reference the actual value of the data field. For example, the following three object literals describe three data rows of the Products data table:

```
{'ProductId': 1, 'ProductName': 'Product1', 'UnitPrice': 100}
{'ProductId': 2, 'ProductName': 'Product2', 'UnitPrice': 50}
{'ProductId': 3, 'ProductName': 'Product3', 'UnitPrice': 80}
```

Here is an example of an object literal that can be passed into the parseFromJson static method of the DataTable class:

```
{
    columns:    [ {name: 'ProductId', dataType: Number, defaultValue: 1,
                  isKey: true, readOnly: true},

                  {name: 'ProductName', dataType: String, defaultValue: 'Unknown',
                  isKey: false, readOnly: true},

                  {name: 'UnitPrice', dataType: Number, defaultValue: 50,
                  isKey: false, readOnly: false} ],

    rows:     [ {'ProductId': 1, 'ProductName': 'Product1', 'UnitPrice': 100},
                {'ProductId': 2, 'ProductName': 'Product2', 'UnitPrice': 50},
                {'ProductId': 3, 'ProductName': 'Product3', 'UnitPrice': 80} ]
}
```

ProductID	ProductName	UnitPrice
1	Product1	100
2	Product2	50
3	Product3	80

This object literal describes the `Products` data table with three columns named `ProductId`, `ProductName`, and `UnitPrice` and three data rows, as shown in the following table.

Listing 11-31 shows the `parseFromJson` method.

Listing 11-31: The parseFromJson Method

```
Sys.Preview.Data.DataTable.parseFromJson =
function Sys$Preview$Data$DataTable$parseFromJson(json)
{
  var columnArray = null;
  if(json.columns)
  {
    columnArray = [];
    for(var i=0; i < json.columns.length; i++)
      Array.add(columnArray,
                    Sys.Preview.Data.DataColumn.parseFromJson(json.columns[i]));
  }
    return new Sys.Preview.Data.DataTable(columnArray, json.rows);
}
```

As discussed earlier, the object literal passed into the `parseFromJson` method contains two name/value pairs whose name parts are `columns` and `rows`. The method uses `columns` to access its associated value part, which is an array of object literals where each object literal describes a column of the data table. The method iterates through these object literals and passes each enumerated object literal into the `parseFromJson` static method of the `DataColumn` class:

```
    for(var i=0; i < json.columns.length; i++)
      Array.add(columnArray,
                    Sys.Preview.Data.DataColumn.parseFromJson(json.columns[i]));
```

The `parseFromJson` static method of the `DataColumn` class creates a `DataColumn` object from the specified object literal representation. Note that Listing 11-31 stores all these `DataColumn` objects into a local array.

The `parseFromJson` method of the `DataTable` class then uses the `rows` on the object literal to access its associated value part, which is an array of object literals where each object literal describes a data row. The method then passes this array and the local array that contains the `DataColumn` objects into the `DataTable` constructor to instantiate the `DataTable` object.

Using DataColumn, DataRow, and DataTable

This section provides an example of how you can use the `DataColumn`, `DataRow`, and `DataTable` client classes in your own client-side code. In Chapter 10, we implemented a custom client control named `CustomTable` that uses the ASP.NET AJAX type inspection capabilities to display data records of any type. This custom client control exposes a method named `dataBind` that iterates through the data records to display them, as shown in Listing 11-32.

Listing 11-32: The dataBind Method of the CustomTable Client Control

```
function CustomComponents$CustomTable$dataBind()
{
  var sb = new Sys.StringBuilder('<table align="center" id="products" ');
  sb.append('style="background-color:LightGoldenrodYellow; border-color:Tan;
             border-width:1px; color:Black"');
  sb.append(' cellpadding="5">');
  var propertyNames = [];
  for (var i=0; i<this._dataSource.length; i++)
  {
    var dataItem = this._dataSource[i];

    if (i == 0)
    {
      var td = Sys.Preview.TypeDescriptor.getTypeDescriptor(dataItem);

      var properties = td._getProperties();

      sb.append('<tr style="background-color:Tan; font-weight:bold">');
      for (var c in properties)
      {
        var propertyJsonObj = properties[c];
        var propertyName = propertyJsonObj.name;
        propertyNames[propertyNames.length] = propertyName;
        sb.append('<td>');
        sb.append(propertyName);
        sb.append('</td>');
      }
      sb.append('</tr>');
    }

    if (i % 2 == 1)
      sb.append('<tr style="background-color:PaleGoldenrod">');
    else
      sb.append('<tr>');

    for (var j in propertyNames)
    {
      var propertyName = propertyNames[j];

      var propertyValue = Sys.Preview.TypeDescriptor.getProperty(dataItem,
                                                    propertyName, null);

      var typeName = Object.getTypeName(propertyValue);
```

```
    if (typeName !== 'String' && typeName !== 'Number' && typeName !== 'Boolean')
    {
      var convertToStringMethodName = Sys.Preview.TypeDescriptor.getAttribute(
                          propertyValue, "convertToStringMethodName");

      if (convertToStringMethodName)
        propertyValue = Sys.Preview.TypeDescriptor.invokeMethod(propertyValue,
                                          convertToStringMethodName);
    }

    sb.append('<td>')
    sb.append(propertyValue);
    sb.append('</td>');
  }

  sb.append('</tr>');
}

sb.append('</table>');
this.get_element().innerHTML = sb.toString();
}
```

As the boldface portions of this code listing show, the current implementation of the dataBind method assumes that the data source is an array because of the following:

❑ It relies on the length property, which is only supported on arrays:

```
for (var i=0; i<this._dataSource.length; i++)
```

❑ It relies on indexing into the data source to access the current data row:

```
var dataItem = this._dataSource[i];
```

This means that the current implementation of the CustomTable client control would not allow the control to work with other types of data sources such as DataTable. To fix this problem, you need to add support for any data source that implements the IData interface — which is the DataTable in this case.

Another problem with the current implementation of the CustomTable client control is that it does not provide its clients with a mechanism to specify the values of the data-source data fields that should be displayed.

Listing 11-33 presents a new implementation of the dataBind method that supports both arrays and IData type data sources.

Listing 11-33: The Content of the New Version of CustomTable.js File that Contains the New Version of the CustomTable Control

```
Type.registerNamespace("CustomComponents");

CustomComponents.CustomTable =
function CustomComponents$CustomTable(associatedElement)
{
  CustomComponents.CustomTable.initializeBase(this, [associatedElement]);
}

function CustomComponents$CustomTable$get_dataSource()
{
  return this._dataSource;
}

function CustomComponents$CustomTable$set_dataSource(value)
{
  this._dataSource = value;
}

function CustomComponents$CustomTable$set_dataFieldNames(value)
{
 this._dataFieldNames = value;
}

function CustomComponents$CustomTable$get_dataFieldNames()
{
 return this._dataFieldNames;
}

function CustomComponents$CustomTable$dataBind()
{
 var isArray = true;

 if (this._dataSource && Sys.Preview.Data.IData.isImplementedBy(this._dataSource))
   isArray = false;

 else if (Array.isInstanceOfType(this._dataSource))
  throw Error.createError('Unknown data source type!');

  var sb = new Sys.StringBuilder('<table align="center" id="products" ');
  sb.append('style="background-color:LightGoldenrodYellow;');
  sb.append('border-color:Tan;border-width:1px; color:Black"');
  sb.append(' cellpadding="5">');
  var propertyNames = [];

  var length = isArray ? this._dataSource.length : this._dataSource.get_length();

  for (var i=0; i<length; i++)
   {
     var dataItem = isArray ? this._dataSource[i] : this._dataSource.getRow(i);
```

```
      if (i == 0)
      {
        sb.append('<tr style="background-color:Tan; font-weight:bold">');
        for (var c in this._dataFieldNames)
        {
          sb.append('<td>');
          sb.append(this._dataFieldNames[c]);
          sb.append('</td>');
        }
        sb.append('</tr>');
      }

      if (i % 2 == 1)
        sb.append('<tr style="background-color:PaleGoldenrod">');
      else
        sb.append('<tr>');

      for (var j in this._dataFieldNames)
      {
        var dataFieldName = this._dataFieldNames[j];

        var dataFieldValue = Sys.Preview.TypeDescriptor.getProperty(dataItem,
                                            dataFieldName, null);
        var typeName = Object.getTypeName(dataFieldValue);

        if (typeName !== 'String' && typeName !== 'Number' && typeName !== 'Boolean')
        {
          var convertToStringMethodName =
              Sys.Preview.TypeDescriptor.getAttribute(dataFieldValue,
                                          "convertToStringMethodName");

          if (convertToStringMethodName)
            dataFieldValue =
              Sys.Preview.TypeDescriptor.invokeMethod(dataFieldValue,
                                          convertToStringMethodName);
        }

        sb.append('<td>')
        sb.append(dataFieldValue);
        sb.append('</td>');
      }

      sb.append('</tr>');
    }

  sb.append('</table>');
  this.get_element().innerHTML = sb.toString();
}

CustomComponents.CustomTable.prototype =
{
```

(continued)

Listing 11-33 *(continued)*

```
    get_dataSource : CustomComponents$CustomTable$get_dataSource,
    set_dataSource : CustomComponents$CustomTable$set_dataSource,
    get_dataFieldNames : CustomComponents$CustomTable$get_dataFieldNames,
    set_dataFieldNames : CustomComponents$CustomTable$set_dataFieldNames,
    dataBind : CustomComponents$CustomTable$dataBind
}


CustomComponents.CustomTable.registerClass("CustomComponents.CustomTable",
                                   Sys.UI.Control);


if(typeof(Sys)!=='undefined')
  Sys.Application.notifyScriptLoaded();
```

As the boldface portion of this code listing shows, the new implementation of the `CustomTable` control exposes the following:

- ❑ A new property of a type array named `dataFieldNames`

- ❑ A new setter method named `set_dataFieldNames` that enables you to specify the names of those data fields whose values should be displayed in the `CustomTable` client control:

```
function CustomComponents$CustomTable$set_dataFieldNames(value)
{
   this._dataFieldNames = value;
}
```

- ❑ A new getter method named `get_dataFieldNames` that returns a reference to the array containing the names of the data fields whose values should be displayed in the `CustomTable` client control:

```
function CustomComponents$CustomTable$get_dataFieldNames()
{
   return this._dataFieldNames;
}
```

Next, let's take a look at the `dataBind` method of the `CustomTable` control. As previously discussed, the main responsibility of this method is to iterate through the data records and display the data field values of each record.

The new implementation of this method begins with the following code fragment from Listing 11-33:

```
    var isArray = true;

    if (this._dataSource && Sys.Preview.Data.IData.isImplementedBy(this._dataSource))
       isArray = false;

    else if (Array.isInstanceOfType(this._dataSource))
       throw Error.create('Unknown data source type!');
```

This code first checks whether the specified data source implements the `IData` interface. If so, it sets a local Boolean variable named `isArray` to `false` to signal that the data source is not an array. Next, the code raises an exception if the data source is neither of type `Array` nor of type `IData`.

Notice how the `dataBind` method determines the total number of data records in the specified data source:

```
var length = isArray ? this._dataSource.length : this._dataSource.get_length();
```

If `isArray` is set to `true`, it means the data source is of type `Array` and, consequently, it calls the `length` property on the data source to access the total data record count. If `isArray` is set to `false`, it means the data source is of type `IData` and, consequently, it calls the `get_length` method on the data source to return the total data record count. As previously discussed, the `IData` interface exposes a method named `get_length`.

Also note how the `dataBind` method gets the reference to the current data row of the specified data source:

```
for (var i=0; i<length; i++)
{
  var dataItem = isArray ? this._dataSource[i] : this._dataSource.getRow(i);
```

If `isArray` is set to `true`, it means the data source is of type `Array` and, consequently, it uses a typical array indexing to return the reference to the current data row. If `isArray` is set to `false`, it means the data source is of type `IData` and, consequently, it uses the `getRow` method to return the reference to the current data row. As discussed previously, the `IData` interface exposes a method named `getRow`.

As the following code fragment from Listing 11-33 shows, the `dataBind` method only displays the header text for data fields whose names are included in the `dataFieldNames` property:

```
if (i == 0)
{
  sb.append('<tr style="background-color:Tan; font-weight:bold">');
  for (var c in this._dataFieldNames)
  {
    sb.append('<td>');
    sb.append(this._dataFieldNames[c]);
    sb.append('</td>');
  }
  sb.append('</tr>');
}
```

As the following code fragment from Listing 11-33 shows, the `dataBind` method iterates through only the data fields whose names are included in the `dataFieldNames` array:

```
for (var j in this._dataFieldNames)
{
  var dataFieldName = this._dataFieldNames[j];
  var dataFieldValue = Sys.Preview.TypeDescriptor.getProperty(dataItem,
                                                    dataFieldName, null);

  . . .

  sb.append('<td>')
  sb.append(dataFieldValue);
  sb.append('</td>');
}
```

Note that the method invokes the `getProperty` static method on the `TypeDescriptor` class, passing in the reference to the current data row to return the value of the data field with the specified field name. As you can see, the `getProperty` method allows the `CustomTable` client control to access the value of a data field, with the specified name, of the current data row as if it were accessing the value of a property, with the same name as the data field, of the current data row. This is possible only if one of the following conditions are met:

❑ The data fields themselves are the properties of the data row. This is the case when the data row is an object literal that contains one name/value pair for each data field, where the name part of the pair contains the name of the data field and the value part contains the value of the data field. Here is an example:

```
{'ProductName': 'Product1'}
```

❑ The data row implements the `ICustomTypeDescriptor` interface where its implementation of the `getProperty` method of this interface returns the value of the specified data field. As discussed earlier, the `DataRow` class is one of the ASP.NET AJAX classes that implement this interface. As such, if you bind a `DataTable` object to the `CustomTable` client control, the following code will be able to extract the value of each data field.

Listing 11-34 contains a page that binds a `DataTable` to the `CustomTable` client control. If you run this page, you should see the result shown in Figure 11-1.

Listing 11-34: A Page that Uses the New Implementation of the CustomTable Control

```
<%@ Page Language="C#" %>

<!DOCTYPE html PUBLIC "-//W3C//DTD XHTML 1.0 Transitional//EN"
"http://www.w3.org/TR/xhtml1/DTD/xhtml11-transitional.dtd">
<html xmlns="http://www.w3.org/1999/xhtml">
<head runat="server">
  <title>Untitled Page</title>
  <script type="text/javascript" language="javascript">
    function pageLoad()
    {
      var dataColumns = [];
      dataColumns[dataColumns.length] =
              new Sys.Preview.Data.DataColumn('ProductId', Number, 1, true, true);
      dataColumns[dataColumns.length] =
              new Sys.Preview.Data.DataColumn('ProductName', String, 'Unknown',
                                      true, false);
      dataColumns[dataColumns.length] =
              new Sys.Preview.Data.DataColumn('UnitPrice', Number, 50, true,
                                      false);

      var dataTable = new Sys.Preview.Data.DataTable(dataColumns);
      var rowObject = {'ProductId': 1, 'ProductName': 'Product1', 'UnitPrice': 60};
      var dataRow = dataTable.createRow(rowObject);
      dataTable.add(dataRow);

      rowObject = {'ProductId': 2, 'ProductName': 'Product2', 'UnitPrice': 40};
      dataRow = dataTable.createRow(rowObject);
```

```
            dataTable.add(dataRow);

            rowObject = {'ProductId': 3, 'ProductName': 'Product3', 'UnitPrice': 20};
            dataRow = dataTable.createRow(rowObject);
            dataTable.add(dataRow);

            var customTable = new CustomComponents.CustomTable($get("myDiv"));
            var dataFieldNames = ['ProductName', 'UnitPrice'];
            customTable.set_dataFieldNames(dataFieldNames);
            customTable.set_dataSource(dataTable);
            customTable.dataBind();
        }
    </script>
</head>
<body>
    <form id="form1" runat="server">
        <asp:ScriptManager runat="server" ID="ScriptManager1">
            <Scripts>
                <asp:ScriptReference Assembly="Microsoft.Web.Preview"
                Name="PreviewScript.js" />
                <asp:ScriptReference Path="CustomTable.js" />
            </Scripts>
        </asp:ScriptManager>
        <div id="myDiv">
        </div>
    </form>
</body>
</html>
```

Now, let's walk through the implementation of the pageLoad method shown in Listing 11-34. This method first creates three DataColumn objects to represent the ProductId, ProductName, and UnitPrice columns of the Products table. The method passes four parameters into the constructor of

Figure 11-1

the `DataColumn` class. The first parameter is a string that contains the name of the column (for example, `'ProductId'`); the second parameter references the actual data type of the column (for example, `Number`); the third parameter contains the default value of the column (for example, 1); the fourth parameter is a Boolean value that specifies whether the column is read-only; and the fifth parameter is a Boolean value that specifies whether the column is a primary key:

```
var dataColumns = [];
dataColumns[dataColumns.length] =
        new Sys.Preview.Data.DataColumn('ProductId', Number, 1, true, true);
dataColumns[dataColumns.length] =
        new Sys.Preview.Data.DataColumn('ProductName', String, 'Unknown',
                                    true, false);
dataColumns[dataColumns.length] =
        new Sys.Preview.Data.DataColumn('UnitPrice', Number, 50, true,
                                    false);
```

Next, the `pageLoad` method calls the constructor of the `DataTable` class, passing in the array that contains the three `DataColumn` objects to create a `DataTable` object that represents the `Products` table:

```
var dataTable = new Sys.Preview.Data.DataTable(dataColumns);
```

Then, the `pageLoad` method repeats the following steps three times to create and add three `DataRow` objects to the `DataTable` object:

1. It creates an object literal that contains three name/value pairs where each name/value pair describes a particular data field of the `DataRow` object being added:

```
var rowObject = {'ProductId': 1, 'ProductName': 'Product1', 'UnitPrice': 60};
```

This object literal will be used as the row object of the `DataRow` object being added.

2. It calls the `createRow` instance method on the `DataTable` object, passing in the row object from step 1 to instantiate the `DataRow` object associated with the row object:

```
var dataRow = dataTable.createRow(rowObject);
```

As discussed earlier, the `createRow` method uses the name/value pairs of this row object to initialize the data fields of the newly instantiated `DataRow` object.

3. It calls the `add` instance method on the `DataTable` object, passing in the newly instantiated `DataRow` object to add the `DataRow` object to the `DataTable` object:

```
dataTable.add(dataRow);
```

Keep in mind that the `createRow` method creates the `DataRow` object, but does not add it to the `DataTable` object.

The `pageLoad` method then instantiates the `CustomTable` client control:

```
var customTable = new CustomComponents.CustomTable($get("myDiv"));
```

Next, it calls the `set_dataFieldNames` method on the client control, passing in an array that contains the names of the data fields that you want the control to display:

```
var dataFieldNames = ['ProductName', 'UnitPrice'];
customTable.set_dataFieldNames(dataFieldNames);
```

It then calls the `set_dataSource` method, passing in the `DataTable` object to specify this object as the data source of the `CustomTable` control:

```
customTable.set_dataSource(dataTable);
```

Finally, it calls the `dataBind` method on the `CustomTable` control to have the control display the specified data fields of the data rows that the `DataTable` contains:

```
customTable.dataBind();
```

Listing 11-34 explicitly created the required `DataColumn` and `DataRow` objects. Listing 11-35 uses a different approach where you do not need to explicitly create these objects. As the boldface portion of this code listing shows, you can form an object literal that contains information about all the columns and rows of the `Products` table, and pass this object literal into the `parseFromJson` static method of the `DataTable` class to instantiate and initialize the `DataTable` object.

Listing 11-35: A Page that Uses a DataTable Control without Explicitly Instantantiating the Required DataColumn and DataRow Objects

```
<%@ Page Language="C#" %>

<!DOCTYPE html PUBLIC "-//W3C//DTD XHTML 1.0 Transitional//EN"
"http://www.w3.org/TR/xhtml1/DTD/xhtml1-transitional.dtd">
<html xmlns="http://www.w3.org/1999/xhtml">
<head runat="server">
  <title>Untitled Page</title>
  <script type="text/javascript" language="javascript">
    function pageLoad()
    {
      var jsonObj =
      {
          columns: [ {name: 'ProductId', dataType: Number, defaultValue: 1,
                      isKey: true, readOnly: true},

                     {name: 'ProductName', dataType: String, defaultValue: 'Unknown',
                      isKey: false, readOnly: true},

                     {name: 'UnitPrice', dataType: Number, defaultValue: 50,
                      isKey: false, readOnly: false} ],

          rows:    [ {'ProductId': 1, 'ProductName': 'Product1', 'UnitPrice': 60},
                     {'ProductId': 2, 'ProductName': 'Product2', 'UnitPrice': 40},
                     {'ProductId': 3, 'ProductName': 'Product3', 'UnitPrice': 20} ]
      };

      var dataTable = Sys.Preview.Data.DataTable.parseFromJson(jsonObj);

      var customTable = new CustomComponents.CustomTable($get("myDiv"));
      var dataFieldNames = ['ProductName', 'UnitPrice'];
```

(continued)

455

Listing 11-35 *(continued)*

```
        customTable.set_dataFieldNames(dataFieldNames);
        customTable.set_dataSource(dataTable);
        customTable.dataBind();
    }
  </script>
</head>
<body>
  <form id="form1" runat="server">
    <asp:ScriptManager runat="server" ID="ScriptManager1">
      <Scripts>
        <asp:ScriptReference Assembly="Microsoft.Web.Preview"
        Name="PreviewScript.js" />
        <asp:ScriptReference Path="CustomTable.js" />
        <asp:ScriptReference Path="Address.js" />
        <asp:ScriptReference Path="Product.js" />
      </Scripts>
    </asp:ScriptManager>
    <div id="myDiv">
    </div>
  </form>
</body>
</html>
```

Summary

This chapter provided in-depth coverage of three important ASP.NET AJAX data classes: `DataColumn`, `DataRow`, and `DataTable`. It then implemented a custom client control that can display data from data sources such as `DataTable` that implement the `IData` interface.

The page shown in Listing 11-35 manually created and populated the `DataTable` object that binds to the `CustomTable` client control. In data-driven Web applications, data normally comes from a server. This means that ASP.NET AJAX applications need to communicate with the server. This is where the client-server communication layer of the ASP.NET AJAX client-side framework comes into play. The next chapter discusses this layer and its constituent ASP.NET AJAX types.

Client-Server Communications

The ASP.NET AJAX client-server communication layer consists of several important types that are discussed in this chapter. These types emulate their ASP.NET/.NET counterparts, which enables you to use similar server-side network programming techniques in your client-side network programming. The types in the ASP.NET AJAX client-server communication layer belong to the following namespace:

```
Type.registerNamespace('Sys.Net');
```

WebRequest

The ASP.NET AJAX WebRequest client class represents a Web request that the client-side code makes to the server. The following sections discuss the important members of this class.

Constructor

As you can see in Listing 12-1, the WebRequest constructor defines the following fields:

- ❑ _url: A string that contains the target URL for the request.
- ❑ _headers: A dictionary that contains the names and values of the request headers.
- ❑ _body: A string that contains the body of the request.
- ❑ _userContext: Contains a JavaScript object that provides application-specific contextual information.
- ❑ _httpVerb: A string that contains the HTTP verb being used to make the request.
- ❑ _executor: A field of type WebRequestExecutor that references the WebRequestExecutor object responsible for executing the request. The WebRequestExecutor base class and its subclasses are discussed later, but for now suffice it to say that every WebRequest object is associated with a WebRequestExecutor object whose main responsibility is to execute or make the request.

❏ _invokeCalled: A Boolean value that ensures that the request is executed or made only once.

❏ _timeout: The field that specifies the request timeout. The request automatically gets canceled if the server response does not arrive within the time interval specified by this field.

Listing 12-1: The Constructor of the WebRequest Class

```
Sys.Net.WebRequest = function Sys$Net$WebRequest()
{
  this._url = "";
  this._headers = { };
  this._body = null;
  this._userContext = null;
  this._httpVerb = null;
  this._executor = null;
  this._invokeCalled = false;
  this._timeout = 0;
}
```

Target URL

As Listing 12-2 shows, the WebRequest class exposes a getter named get_url and a setter named set_url that you can use to get and set the target URL of the Web request.

Listing 12-2: Getting and Setting the Target URL

```
function Sys$Net$WebRequest$get_url()
{
  return this._url;
}

function Sys$Net$WebRequest$set_url(value)
{
  this._url = value;
}
```

HTTP Verb

As Listing 12-3 shows, the WebRequest class exposes a getter named get_httpVerb and a setter named set_httpVerb that you can use to get and set the HTTP verb being used to send the Web request. If neither the HTTP verb nor the body of the Web request is specified, the GET HTTP verb will be used by default.

Listing 12-3: Getting and Setting the HTTP Verb

```
function Sys$Net$WebRequest$get_httpVerb()
{
  if (this._httpVerb === null)
  {
    if (this._body === null)
      return "GET";

    return "POST";
```

```
    }
    return this._httpVerb;
}

function Sys$Net$WebRequest$set_httpVerb(value)
{
    this._httpVerb = value;
}
```

Body

You invoke the get_body and set_body instance methods on the WebRequest object to get and set the body of the request, as shown in Listing 12-4. Keep in mind that the body of a request is of type string.

Listing 12-4: Getting and Setting the Body of the Web Request

```
function Sys$Net$WebRequest$get_body()
{
    return this._body;
}

function Sys$Net$WebRequest$set_body(value)
{
    this._body = value;
}
```

Timeout

You invoke the get_timeout and set_timeout instance methods on the WebRequest object to get and set the Web request timeout, as shown in Listing 12-5. Note that the get_timeout method calls the get_defaultTimeout static method on an ASP.NET AJAX class named _WebRequestManager to return the default timeout if the timeout has been set to 0. The _WebRequestManager class and its methods are discussed later, but for now suffice it to say that when you load your ASP.NET AJAX application, the ASP.NET AJAX client-side framework automatically creates an instance of the _WebRequestManager class. The main job of this instance is to manage all Web requests made to the server. Every ASP.NET AJAX application can have only one instance of the _WebRequestManager class.

Listing 12-5: Getting and Setting the Web Request Timeout

```
function Sys$Net$WebRequest$get_timeout()
{
    if (this._timeout === 0)
        return Sys.Net.WebRequestManager.get_defaultTimeout();

    return this._timeout;
}

function Sys$Net$WebRequest$set_timeout(value)
{
    this._timeout = value;
}
```

Web Request Executor

The ASP.NET AJAX client-side framework includes a client class named `WebRequestExecutor`. The main job of a `WebRequestExecutor` object is to execute or make a specified Web request. You call the `get_executor` and `set_executor` methods on the `WebRequest` object to get and set the `WebRequestExecutor` object responsible for executing the Web request, as shown in Listing 12-6.

Listing 12-6: Getting and Setting the Web Request Executor

```
function Sys$Net$WebRequest$get_executor()
{
  return this._executor;
}

function Sys$Net$WebRequest$set_executor(value)
{
  if (this._executor !== null && this._executor.get_started())
    throw Error.invalidOperation(Sys.Res.setExecutorAfterActive);

  this._executor = value;
  this._executor._set_webRequest(this);
}
```

Note that the `set_executor` method invokes an internal method named `_set_webRequest` on the `WebRequestExecutor` object to specify the current `WebRequest` object as the `WebRequest` object that the `WebRequestExecutor` object must execute.

> *Keep in mind that, by convention, any member of an ASP.NET AJAX class whose name begins with the underscore character (_) is considered an internal method. Consequently, you cannot call these methods from your client-side code.*

The `set_executor` setter method raises an exception if you attempt to set the executor of a `WebRequest` object after the request has been sent to the server. As you'll see later, the `WebRequestExecutor` base class exposes a method named `get_started` that returns a Boolean value specifying whether the request has already been sent to the server.

Headers

Call the `get_headers` method shown in Listing 12-7 on the `WebRequest` object to get a reference to the `_headers` dictionary, which contains the names and values of the request headers.

Listing 12-7: Getting the Web Request Headers

```
function Sys$Net$WebRequest$get_headers()
{
  return this._headers;
}
```

Completed Event

The WebRequest class exposes an event named completed, which is raised when the Web request has been completed. The WebRequest class follows the event implementation pattern discussed in the previous chapters to implement the completed event as follows:

1. It exposes a field of type EventHandlerList named _events that references an EventHandlerList object where all the event handlers registered for the events of the WebRequest class will be stored.

2. It exposes a getter method named get_eventHandlerList that returns a reference to this EventHandlerList object, as shown in Listing 12-8.

Listing 12-8: The get_events Method

```
function Sys$Net$WebRequest$_get_eventHandlerList()
{
  if (!this._events)
    this._events = new Sys.EventHandlerList();

  return this._events;
}
```

3. It implements a method named add_completed that calls the addHandler method on the EventHandlerList to add the specified function as an event handler for the completed event of the WebRequest object, as shown in Listing 12-9.

Listing 12-9: The add_completed Method

```
function Sys$Net$WebRequest$add_completed(handler)
{
  this._get_eventHandlerList().addHandler("completed", handler);
}
```

4. It implements a method named remove_completed that calls the removeHandler method on the EventHandlerList to remove the specified event handler from the list of the event handlers registered for the completed event, as shown in Listing 12-10.

Listing 12-10: The remove_completed Method

```
function Sys$Net$WebRequest$remove_completed(handler)
{
  this._get_eventHandlerList().removeHandler("completed", handler);
}
```

5. It implements a method named completed that raises the completed event, as shown in Listing 12-11.

Listing 12-11: The completed Method

```
function Sys$Net$WebRequest$completed(eventArgs) {
  var handler = Sys.Net.WebRequestManager._get_eventHandlerList().getHandler(
                                              "completedRequest");
  if (handler)
    handler(this._executor, eventArgs);

  handler = this._get_eventHandlerList().getHandler("completed");
  if (handler)
    handler(this._executor, eventArgs);
}
```

This method calls the `getHandler` method on the `EventHandlerList` object. As discussed in the previous chapters, the `getHandler` method returns a reference to a JavaScript function whose invocation automatically invokes all event handlers registered for a specified event, which is the `completed` event in this case:

```
handler = this._get_eventHandlerList().getHandler("completed");
if (handler)
  handler(this._executor, eventArgs);
```

As you'll see later, the `_WebRequestManager` class exposes an event named `completedRequest`, which maps to the `completed` event of the `WebRequest` object being executed. In other words, the `_WebRequestManager` class must raise its `completedRequest` event when the `WebRequest` object raises its `completed` event. The `_WebRequestManager` class also uses the same event implementation pattern to implement the `completedRequest` event, which means that this class also exposes an `_events` field of type `EventHandlerList` that references an `EventHandlerList` object containing all event handlers registered for the events of the `WebRequestManager` object.

As Listing 12-11 shows, the `completed` method of the `WebRequest` object calls the `getHandler` method on the `EventHandlerList` object that contains the event handlers registered for the events of the `WebRequestManager` object to return a reference to the JavaScript function whose invocation automatically invokes all the event handlers registered for the `completedRequest` event. The `completed` method then invokes this JavaScript function, passing in a reference to the `WebRequestExecutor` object. This tricks the event handlers registered for the `completedRequest` event of the `WebRequestManager` object into thinking that the `WebRequestExecutor` object itself raised the event and called these handlers.

Invoking a Web Request

You call the `invoke` instance method on the `WebRequest` object that represents a Web request to make the request to the server. As Listing 12-12 shows, this method delegates the responsibility of executing the request to the `executeRequest` method of the current `WebRequestManager` instance. (The `_WebRequestManager` class and its methods are discussed later in this chapter.) Note that the `WebRequest` object uses an internal Boolean flag named `_invokeCalled` to ensure that the same request is not executed more than once.

Listing 12-12: Invoking a Web Request

```
function Sys$Net$WebRequest$invoke()
{
  if (this._invokeCalled)
    throw Error.invalidOperation(Sys.Res.invokeCalledTwice);

  Sys.Net.WebRequestManager.executeRequest(this);
  this._invokeCalled = true;
}
```

WebRequestExecutor

As discussed in the previous section, every ASP.NET AJAX Web request is represented by an instance of the WebRequest class. The ASP.NET AJAX client-side framework includes a class named WebRequestExecutor whose sole responsibility is to execute a given Web request represented by a given WebRequest object. The following sections discuss the main members of the WebRequestExecutor class.

Constructor

As you can see in Listing 12-13, the WebRequestExecutor constructor defines the following two fields:

❑ _webRequest: This field references the WebRequest object that the WebRequestExecutor object executes.

❑ _resultObject: This field references the JSON object that contains the data received from the server. For example, this can be the JSON representation of a DataTable object and, consequently, can be passed into the parseFromJson static method of the DataTable class to deserialize the DataTable object.

Listing 12-13: The Constructor of the WebRequestExecutor Class

```
Sys.Net.WebRequestExecutor = function Sys$Net$WebRequestExecutor()
{
  this._webRequest = null;
  this._resultObject = null;
}
```

WebRequest

You invoke the get_webRequest instance method on the WebRequestExecutor object responsible for executing a given request to get a reference to the WebRequest object that represents the request, as shown in Listing 12-14.

Listing 12-14: Getting and Setting the WebRequest Object

```
function Sys$Net$WebRequestExecutor$get_webRequest()
{
  return this._webRequest;
}

function Sys$Net$WebRequestExecutor$_set_webRequest(value)
{
  if (this.get_started())
    throw Error.invalidOperation(String.format(Sys.Res.cannotCallOnceStarted,
                                 'set_webRequest'));

  this._webRequest = value;
}
```

As this code listing shows, the WebRequestExecutor class contains an *internal* setter method named _set_webRequest that specifies the WebRequest object that the current WebRequestExecutor must execute. You should never call this method to set the WebRequest object for a WebRequestExecutor object. Instead, you must call the set_executor instance method on the WebRequest object to specify its associated WebRequestExecutor object. As previously shown in Listing 12-6, the set_executor method of the WebRequest object calls the _set_webRequest internal method under the hood to register itself with the specified WebRequestExecutor.

The _set_webRequest internal method first calls the get_started method to return a Boolean value that specifies whether the request has already been made. If the request has already been made, it raises an exception.

get_started

The WebRequestExecutor exposes a method named get_started that you can call on the WebRequestExecutor object to check whether the request has already been sent to the server. As Listing 12-15 shows, the WebRequestExecutor base class does not implement this method. Instead, the subclasses of the WebRequestExecutor base class must implement this method to include the logic necessary to determine whether the request has already been made.

Listing 12-15: The get_started Method

```
function Sys$Net$WebRequestExecutor$get_started()
{
  throw Error.notImplemented();
}
```

get_responseAvailable

You can call the get_responseAvailable method on a WebRequestExecutor object to return a Boolean value that specifies whether the response from the server has arrived, as shown in Listing 12-16. It is the responsibility of the subclasses of the WebRequestExecutor base class must implement this method to incorporate the necessary logic.

Listing 12-16: The get_responseAvailable Method

```
function Sys$Net$WebRequestExecutor$get_responseAvailable()
{
  throw Error.notImplemented();
}
```

get_timedOut

You can call the get_timedOut method on a WebRequestExecutor object to return a Boolean value that specifies whether the specified request has timed out, as shown in Listing 12-17. Again it is the responsibility of the subclasses of the WebRequestExecutor base class to implement this method.

Listing 12-17: The get_timedOut Method

```
function Sys$Net$WebRequestExecutor$get_timedOut()
{
  throw Error.notImplemented();
}
```

get_aborted

You can invoke this method on a WebRequestExecutor object to return a Boolean value that specifies whether the Web request has aborted, as shown in Listing 12-18. Once again it is the responsibility of the subclasses of the WebRequestExecutor base class to implement this method.

Listing 12-18: The get_aborted Method

```
function Sys$Net$WebRequestExecutor$get_aborted()
{
  throw Error.notImplemented();
}
```

get_responseData

You can invoke this method on a WebRequestExecutor object to return a string that contains the data received from the server as shown in Listing 12-19. The subclasses of the WebRequestExecutor base class must implement this method as well.

Listing 12-19: The get_responseData Method

```
function Sys$Net$WebRequestExecutor$get_responseData()
{
  throw Error.notImplemented();
}
```

get_statusCode

You can invoke this method on a `WebRequestExecutor` object to return an integer that specifies the status code of the server response as shown in Listing 12-20. The subclasses of the `WebRequestExecutor` base class must implement this method.

Listing 12-20: The get_statusCode Method

```
function Sys$Net$WebRequestExecutor$get_statusCode()
{
    throw Error.notImplemented();
}
```

get_statusText

You can invoke this method on a `WebRequestExecutor` object to return a string that contains the status text of the server response as shown in Listing 12-21. The subclasses of the `WebRequestExecutor` base class must implement this method.

Listing 12-21: The get_statusText Method

```
function Sys$Net$WebRequestExecutor$get_statusText()
{
    throw Error.notImplemented();
}
```

get_xml

You can invoke this method on a `WebRequestExecutor` object to return an XML document that contains the data received from the server as shown in Listing 12-22. The subclasses of the `WebRequestExecutor` base class must implement this method.

Listing 12-22: The get_xml Method

```
function Sys$Net$WebRequestExecutor$get_xml()
{
    throw Error.notImplemented();
}
```

get_object

You can invoke this method on a `WebRequestExecutor` object to return a JavaScript object that contains the data received from the server as shown in Listing 12-23.

Listing 12-23: The get_object Method

```
function Sys$Net$WebRequestExecutor$get_object()
{
  if (!this._resultObject)
    this._resultObject = Sys.Serialization.JavaScriptSerializer.deserialize(
                                            this.get_responseData());

  return this._resultObject;
}
```

As this code listing shows, the `get_object` method calls the `deserialize` static method on the `JavaScriptSerializer` class to deserialize a JavaScript object from the string that contains the JSON representation of the object. For example, you can use this method to deserialize a `DataTable` object from its JSON representation.

executeRequest

You can call this method on a `WebRequestExecutor` object to execute its associated `WebRequest` object, that is, to make the specified request as shown in Listing 12-24. The subclasses of the `WebRequestExecutor` base class must implement this method.

Listing 12-24: The executeRequest Method

```
function Sys$Net$WebRequestExecutor$executeRequest()
{
  throw Error.notImplemented();
}
```

abort

You can invoke this method on a `WebRequestExecutor` object as shown in Listing 12-25. This method aborts the associated `WebRequest` object. The subclasses of the `WebRequestExecutor` base class must implement this method.

Listing 12-25: The abort Method

```
function Sys$Net$WebRequestExecutor$abort()
{
  throw Error.notImplemented();
}
```

getResponseHeader

You can invoke this method on a `WebRequestExecutor` object to return the value of the response header with the specified name as shown in Listing 12-26. The subclasses of the `WebRequestExecutor` base class must implement this method.

Listing 12-26: The getResponseHeader Method

```
function Sys$Net$WebRequestExecutor$getResponseHeader(header)
{
  throw Error.notImplemented();
}
```

getAllResponseHeaders

You can invoke this method on a `WebRequestExecutor` object to return all response headers as shown in Listing 12-27. The subclasses of the `WebRequestExecutor` base class must implement this method.

Listing 12-27: The getAllResponseHeaders Method

```
function Sys$Net$WebRequestExecutor$getAllResponseHeaders()
{
  throw Error.notImplemented();
}
```

WebRequestManager

When an ASP.NET AJAX application is loading, the ASP.NET AJAX client-side framework instantiates a single instance of an ASP.NET AJAX client class named `_WebRequestManager` and assigns the instance to a global variable named `Sys.Net.WebRequestManager`. You cannot create a new instance of this class. Instead, you use the `WebRequestManager` to get a reference to the instance that the ASP.NET AJAX client-side framework has created for your application. This sole instance of the `_WebRequestManager` class is responsible for managing all the Web requests made in the current application. As such, any settings that you specify on this instance will be applied to all Web requests made in the application. The following sections discuss the main methods of the `_WebRequestManager` class.

Constructor

As Listing 12-28 shows, the constructor of this class is an internal method, which means you cannot call it from within your client code.

Listing 12-28: The _WebRequestManager Constructor

```
Sys.Net._WebRequestManager = function Sys$Net$_WebRequestManager()
{
  this._this = this;
  this._defaultTimeout = 0;
  this._defaultExecutorType = "Sys.Net.XMLHttpExecutor";
}
```

This constructor defines the following three fields:

❑   _this: This field references the instance of the class that the ASP.NET AJAX client-side framework creates for the current application.

❑ _defaultTimeout: This field specifies the default timeout for all the Web requests made in the current application. If you do not explicitly specify the timeout for a given WebRequest object, this default value will be used. As Listing 12-28 shows, the constructor of the _WebRequestManager class assigns a value of 0 to this field. However, as you'll see later, you can specify a different default timeout value.

❑ _defaultExecutorType: This field is a string that contains the fully qualified name of the subtype of the WebRequestExecutor type that will be used as the default executor type. If you do not explicitly specify a WebRequestExecutor object for a given WebRequest object, an instance of this default subtype will be used. As Listing 12-28 shows, the constructor of the _WebRequestManager class assigns the string value "Sys.Net.XMLHttpExecutor" to this field. However, as you'll see later, you can specify a different subtype of the WebRequestExecutor base class as the default executor type.

Default Timeout

As stated in the previous section, the default timeout is 0 by default. However, the _WebRequestManager class exposes a setter named set_defaultTimout that you can invoke on the WebRequestManager object to specify a different value as the default timeout, as shown in Listing 12-29.

Listing 12-29: Getting and Setting the Default Timeout

```
function Sys$Net$_WebRequestManager$get_defaultTimeout()
{
  return this._defaultTimeout;
}

function Sys$Net$_WebRequestManager$set_defaultTimeout(value)
{
  this._defaultTimeout = value;
}
```

Default Executor Type

As stated earlier, the default executor type is XMLHttpExecutor by default. However, the _WebRequestManager class exposes a setter named set_defaultExecutorType that you can invoke on the WebRequestManager object to specify a different type of executor as the default executor type, as shown in Listing 12-30.

Listing 12-30: Getting and Setting the Default Executor Type

```
function Sys$Net$_WebRequestManager$get_defaultExecutorType()
{
  return this._defaultExecutorType;
}
function Sys$Net$_WebRequestManager$set_defaultExecutorType(value)
{
  this._defaultExecutorType = value;
}
```

Events

The _WebRequestManager class exposes the following two events:

☐ invokingRequest: The WebRequestManager object fires this event when it's about to invoke or execute a Web request. If you need to run some application-specific logic before a Web request is executed, implement a JavaScript function that encapsulates this logic, and register the function as the event handler for the invokingRequest event.

☐ completedRequest: The WebRequestManager object fires this event when the execution of a request is completed.

The _WebRequestManager class follows the typical ASP.NET AJAX event implementation pattern to implement these events as follows:

1. It defines a new field named _events that references an EventHandlerList object where the event handlers registered for the events of the _WebRequestManager class will be stored. Then it defines a new getter method named _get_eventHandlerList that returns a reference to this EventHandlerList object, as shown in Listing 12-31. Note that this getter method is internal, so you cannot call it from within your client code.

Listing 12-31: The _get_eventHandlerList Method

```
function Sys$Net$_WebRequestManager$_get_eventHandlerList()
{
  if (!this._events)
    this._events = new Sys.EventHandlerList();

  return this._events;
}
```

2. It defines an add_invokingRequest method that calls the addHandler method on the EventHandlerList object to add the specified function as the event handler for the invokingRequest event, as shown in Listing 12-32.

Listing 12-32: The add_invokingRequest Method

```
function Sys$Net$_WebRequestManager$add_invokingRequest(handler)
{
  this._get_eventHandlerList().addHandler("invokingRequest", handler);
}
```

If you need to run some application-specific code before a Web request is executed, wrap your code in a JavaScript function. Then invoke the add_invokingRequest method on the Sys.Net.WebRequestManager object, passing in a reference to the wrapping JavaScript function. (The Sys.Net.WebRequestManager object is the sole instance of the _WebRequestManager class in a given ASP.NET AJAX application.)

3. It implements a method named remove_invokingRequest that invokes the removeHandler method on the EventHandlerList object to remove the specified handler from the list of event handlers registered for the invokingRequest event, as shown in Listing 12-33.

Listing 12-33: The remove_invokingRequest Method

```
function Sys$Net$_WebRequestManager$remove_invokingRequest(handler)
{
  this._get_eventHandlerList().removeHandler("invokingRequest", handler);
}
```

4. It repeats steps 2 and 3 to implement similar methods named `add_completedRequest` and `remove_completedRequest` for the `completedRequest` event, as shown in Listings Listing 12-34 and Listing 12-35.

Listing 12-34: The add_completedRequest Method

```
function Sys$Net$_WebRequestManager$add_completedRequest(handler)
{
  this._get_eventHandlerList().addHandler("completedRequest", handler);
}
```

Listing 12-35: The remove_completedRequest method

```
function Sys$Net$_WebRequestManager$remove_completedRequest(handler) {
  this._get_eventHandlerList().removeHandler("completedRequest", handler);
}
```

Any settings you specify on the `WebRequestManager` object will be applied to all Web requests made in the application. Therefore, any event handler that you register through the `add_invokingRequest` and `add_completedRequest` methods of the `WebRequestManager` object will be called for every Web request made in the application.

Executing a Web Request

The `_WebRequestManager` class exposes an instance method named `executeRequest`. This method takes a single argument that references a `WebRequest` object and executes the Web request, as shown in Listing 12-36.

Listing 12-36: The executeRequest method

```
function Sys$Net$_WebRequestManager$executeRequest(webRequest)
{
  var executor = webRequest.get_executor();
  if (!executor)
  {
    var failed = false;
    try
    {
      var executorType = eval(this._defaultExecutorType);
      executor = new executorType();
    }
```

(continued)

Listing 12-36 *(continued)*

```
    catch (e)
    {
      failed = true;
    }

    if (failed  ||  !Sys.Net.WebRequestExecutor.isInstanceOfType(executor) ||
        !executor)
      throw Error.argument("defaultExecutorType",
                           String.format(Sys.Res.invalidExecutorType,
                           this._defaultExecutorType));
    webRequest.set_executor(executor);
  }

  if (executor.get_aborted())
    return;

  var evArgs = new Sys.Net.NetworkRequestEventArgs(webRequest);
  var handler = this._get_eventHandlerList().getHandler("invokingRequest");
  if (handler)
    handler(this, evArgs);

  if (!evArgs.get_cancel())
    executor.executeRequest();
}
```

The executeRequest method calls the get_executor method on the WebRequest object to return a reference to the WebRequestExecutor object responsible for executing the Web request:

```
var executor = webRequest.get_executor();
```

If no WebRequestExecutor object has been specified for the WebRequest object, it uses the default executor type. The _WebRequestManager contains a field named _defaultExecutorType whose value is a string containing the fully qualified name of a subtype of the WebRequestExecutor type. The executeRequest method passes this string into the JavaScript eval method to return a reference to the actual type:

```
var executorType = eval(this._defaultExecutorType);
```

Next, executeRequest uses the JavaScript new operator to instantiate an instance of this type:

```
executor = new executorType();
```

Then it calls the set_executor method on the WebRequest object to register the executor object as its executor:

```
webRequest.set_executor(executor);
```

Next, executeRequest instantiates an instance of an ASP.NET AJAX event data class named NetworkRequestEventArgs, passing in a reference to the WebRequest object:

```
var evArgs = new Sys.Net.NetworkRequestEventArgs(webRequest);
```

Then it calls the getHandler method on the EventHandlerList object that contains all event handlers registered for the invokingRequest event of the WebRequestManager object:

```
var handler = this._get_eventHandlerList().getHandler("invokingRequest");
```

This method returns a JavaScript function whose invocation automatically invokes all these event handlers:

Next, executeRequest invokes the JavaScript function and, consequently, all event handlers registered for the invokingRequest event:

```
if (handler)
   handler(this, evArgs);
```

The NetworkRequestEventArgs object gets passed into the event handlers; therefore, if you registered an event handler for the invokingRequest event of the WebRequestManager object, you can access the NetworkRequestEventArgs object from within your handler. As you'll see later, this object provides access to the WebRequest object that represents the current Web request. This enables you to use application-specific business rules to determine whether the WebRequestManager object may proceed with the execution of the specified request. If the execution of the current Web request does indeed break your business rules, you can set the cancel property of the NetworkRequestEventArgs object to true to instruct the WebRequestManager object to abort the execution of the current Web request.

As Listing 12-36 shows, the executeRequest method calls the get_cancel method on the NetworkRequestEventArgs object to determine whether your event handler has set the cancel property of this object to true. If not, it invokes the executeRequest method on the executor associated with the current Web request to execute the request:

```
if (!evArgs.get_cancel())
   executor.executeRequest();
```

NetworkRequestEventArgs

Event handlers registered for the invokingRequest event of the WebRequestManager object receive an object of type NetworkRequestEventArgs. As Listing 12-37 shows, this type derives from the CancelEventArgs base class.

Listing 12-37: The NetworkRequestEventArgs Event Data Class

```
Sys.Net.NetworkRequestEventArgs = function
Sys$Net$NetworkRequestEventArgs(webRequest)
{
  Sys.Net.NetworkRequestEventArgs.initializeBase(this);
  this._webRequest = webRequest;
}

function Sys$Net$NetworkRequestEventArgs$get_webRequest()
{
  return this._webRequest;
}
```

(continued)

Listing 12-37 (continued)

```
Sys.Net.NetworkRequestEventArgs.prototype =
{
    get_webRequest: Sys$Net$NetworkRequestEventArgs$get_webRequest
}

Sys.Net.NetworkRequestEventArgs.registerClass('Sys.Net.NetworkRequestEventArgs',
                                    Sys.CancelEventArgs);
```

The `CancelEventArgs` base class exposes two methods named `get_cancel` and `set_cancel`. An event handler can call the `set_cancel` method to set the value of the `cancel` property to `true`. This tells the `WebRequestManager` object that it must abort the execution of the current Web request.

The `NetworkRequestEventArgs` class also exposes a getter method named `get_webRequest` that an event handler can invoke to get a reference to the current `WebRequest` object, which contains the complete information about the current Web request. An event handler can use this information to check whether the execution of the current request would break any application-specific business rules. If so, it can call the `set_cancel` method on the `NetworkRequestEventArgs` object to tell the `WebRequestManager` object to abort the execution of the current request.

XMLHttpRequest

The `XMLHttpRequest` is a wrapper around the browser-specific logic that instantiates the `XMLHttpRequest` object, as shown in Listing 12-38.

Listing 12-38: The XMLHttpRequest Class

```
if (!window.XMLHttpRequest)
{
    window.XMLHttpRequest = function window$XMLHttpRequest()
    {
        var progIDs = [ 'Msxml2.XMLHTTP', 'Microsoft.XMLHTTP' ];

        for (var i = 0; i < progIDs.length; i++)
        {
            var xmlHttp = new ActiveXObject(progIDs[i]);
            return xmlHttp;
        }

        return null;
    }
}
```

XMLDOM

The `XMLDOM` encapsulates the browser-specific logic that creates an XML document. As Listing 12-39 shows, the constructor of this class takes a string that contains the XML data and returns a reference to an `XMLDOM` document that contains the data.

Listing 12-39: The XMLDOM Class

```javascript
window.XMLDOM = function window$XMLDOM(markup)
{
  if (!window.DOMParser)
  {
    var progIDs = [ 'Msxml2.DOMDocument.3.0', 'Msxml2.DOMDocument' ];
    for (var i = 0; i < progIDs.length; i++)
    {
      var xmlDOM = new ActiveXObject(progIDs[i]);

      xmlDOM.async = false;
      xmlDOM.loadXML(markup);
      xmlDOM.setProperty('SelectionLanguage', 'XPath');
      return xmlDOM;
    }
    return null;
  }

  else
  {
    var domParser = new window.DOMParser();
    return domParser.parseFromString(markup, 'text/xml');
  }
  return null;
}
```

XMLHttpExecutor

The members of the `WebRequestExecutor` base class define the API that every Web request executor must implement. The ASP.NET AJAX client-side framework includes an implementation of this API named `XMLHttpExecutor`:

```javascript
Sys.Net.XMLHttpExecutor.registerClass('Sys.Net.XMLHttpExecutor',
                                      Sys.Net.WebRequestExecutor);
```

This implementation uses the `XMLHttpRequest` class discussed in the previous section to make Web requests to the server. As such, most of the members of `XMLHttpExecutor` class, one way or another, map to settings on the `XMLHttpRequest` class.

Constructor

As Listing 12-40 shows, the constructor of the `XMLHttpExecutor` class defines the following fields and methods:

- ❑ `_xmlHttpRequest`: This field references the `XMLHttpRequest` object that the `XMLHttpExecutor` object uses to make the current Web request to the server.

- ❑ `_webRequest`: This field references the `WebRequest` object that represents the current Web request and contains the complete information about the request.

❑ _responseAvailable: This Boolean field specifies whether the server response has arrived.

❑ _timedOut: This Boolean field specifies whether the current request has timed out.

❑ _aborted: This Boolean field specifies whether the current request has aborted.

❑ _started: This Boolean field specifies whether the execution of the current request has startedand has been sent to the server.

❑ _onReadyStateChange: The XMLHttpExecutor class registers this internal method as an event handler for the onreadystatechange event of the XMLHttpRequest object being used to make the current request to the server.

❑ _clearTimer: This internal method clears the timer.

❑ _onTimeout: This internal method is invoked when the current request times out.

Listing 12-40: The Constructor of the XMLHttpExecutor Class

```
Sys.Net.XMLHttpExecutor = function Sys$Net$XMLHttpExecutor()
{
  Sys.Net.XMLHttpExecutor.initializeBase(this);

  var _this = this;
  this._xmlHttpRequest = null;
  this._webRequest = null;
  this._responseAvailable = false;
  this._timedOut = false;
  this._timer = null;
  this._aborted = false;
  this._started = false;

  this._onReadyStateChange = function () { . . . }

  this._clearTimer = function this$_clearTimer() { . . . }

  this._onTimeout = function this$_onTimeout() { . . . }
}
```

The following sections walk you through the implementation of the _onReadyStateChange, _clearTimer, and _onTimeout internal methods.

_onReadyStateChange

The XMLHttpExecutor registers the _onReadyStateChange method as an event handler for the onreadystatechange event of the XMLHttpRequest object, as shown in Listing 12-41.

Listing 12-41: The _onReadyStateChange Method

```
this._onReadyStateChange = function ()
{
  if (_this._xmlHttpRequest.readyState === 4 /*complete*/)
  {
    _this._clearTimer();
    _this._responseAvailable = true;
    _this._webRequest.completed(Sys.EventArgs.Empty);
```

```
          if (_this._xmlHttpRequest != null)
          {
            _this._xmlHttpRequest.onreadystatechange = Function.emptyMethod;
            _this._xmlHttpRequest = null;
          }
        }
    }
```

This method checks the value of the readyState property of the XMLHttpRequest object. If the value is set to 4, meaning the request is completed and the response has arrived, the method takes the following steps:

1. It clears the timer:

```
    _this._clearTimer();
```

As you'll see later, this timer is what makes a request time out after a specified period of time.

2. It sets the _responseAvailable field to true to signal that the server response has arrived:

```
    _this._responseAvailable = true;
```

3. It invokes the completed method on the WebRequest object to inform the object that the request is completed and the response has arrived:

```
    _this._webRequest.completed(Sys.EventArgs.Empty);
```

As shown previously in Listing 12-11, the completed method invokes all event handlers registered for the completedRequest event of the WebRequestManager and the completed event of the WebRequest.

_clearTimer

As Listing 12-42 shows, the _clearTimer method simply calls the clearTimeout method on the window object. As mentioned, a timer causes a request to time out after a specified period of time.

Listing 12-42: The _clearTimer Method

```
    this._clearTimer = function this$_clearTimer()
    {
      if (_this._timer != null)
      {
        window.clearTimeout(_this._timer);
        _this._timer = null;
      }
    }
```

_onTimeout

The XMLHttpExecutor object calls the _onTimeout method when the request times out, as shown in Listing 12-43.

477

Listing 12-43: The _onTimeout Method

```
this._onTimeout = function this$_onTimeout()
{
  if (!_this._responseAvailable)
  {
    _this._clearTimer();
    _this._timedOut = true;
    _this._xmlHttpRequest.onreadystatechange = Function.emptyMethod;
    _this._xmlHttpRequest.abort();
    _this._webRequest.completed(Sys.EventArgs.Empty);
    _this._xmlHttpRequest = null;
  }
}
```

This method first checks whether the server response has arrived. If not, it clears the timer:

```
_this._clearTimer();
```

Then, it sets the _timedOut field to true to signal that the request has timed out:

```
_this._timedOut = true;
```

Next, it unregisters the _onReadyStateChange method (which was previously registered by XMLHttpExecutor as an event handler for the XMLHttpRequest object's onreadystatechange):

```
_this._xmlHttpRequest.onreadystatechange = Function.emptyMethod;
```

Then, it calls the abort method on the XMLHttpRequest object to abort the current request:

```
_this._xmlHttpRequest.abort();
```

Next, it calls the completed method on the WebRequest object that represents the current request to inform the object that the current request has completed:

```
_this._webRequest.completed(Sys.EventArgs.Empty);
```

As previously shown in Listing 12-11, the completed method invokes all event handlers registered for the completedRequest event of the WebRequestManager and the completed event of the WebRequest. However, the completion of a request does *not* mean that the server response has arrived. Therefore, when your completedRequest or completed event's event handler is invoked, you should not make the assumption that everything went fine and the server response has arrived.

Finally, the _onTimeout method discards the current XMLHttpRequest, because every request must use a new XMLHttpRequest object:

```
_this._xmlHttpRequest = null;
```

get_timedOut

You can call the get_timedOut method on the XMLHttpExecutor object responsible for executing a WebRequest object to access the value of the _timedOut Boolean field (see Listing 12-44). This field specifies whether the current request has timed out.

Listing 12-44: The get_timedOut Method

```
function Sys$Net$XMLHttpExecutor$get_timedOut()
{
  /// <value type="Boolean"></value>
  return this._timedOut;
}
```

get_started

You can call the get_started method on the XMLHttpExecutor object responsible for executing a WebRequest object to access the value of the _started Boolean field (see Listing 12-45). This field specifies whether the execution of the current request has started and the current request has been sent to the server.

Listing 12-45: The get_started Method

```
function Sys$Net$XMLHttpExecutor$get_started()
{
  /// <value type="Boolean"></value>
  return this._started;
}
```

get_responseAvailable

You can call the get_ responseAvailable method on the XMLHttpExecutor object responsible for executing a WebRequest object to access the value of the _responseAvailable Boolean field (see Listing 12-46). This field specifies whether the server response has arrived.

Listing 12-46: The get_responseAvailable Method

```
function Sys$Net$XMLHttpExecutor$get_responseAvailable()
{
  /// <value type="Boolean"></value>
  return this._responseAvailable;
}
```

get_aborted

You can call the get_aborted method on the XMLHttpExecutor object responsible for executing a WebRequest object to access the value of the _aborted Boolean field (see Listing 12-47). This field specifies whether the current request has been aborted.

Listing 12-47: The get_aborted Method

Listing 12-47: The get_aborted Method

```
function Sys$Net$XMLHttpExecutor$get_aborted()
{
  /// <value type="Boolean"></value>
  return this._aborted;
}
```

Executing the Request

The executeRequest method is at the heart of the XMLHttpExecutor class. The main job of this method is to execute the current request, as shown in Listing 12-48.

Listing 12-48: The executeRequest Method

```
function Sys$Net$XMLHttpExecutor$executeRequest()
{
  this._webRequest = this.get_webRequest();

  if (this._started)
    throw Error.invalidOperation(String.format(Sys.Res.cannotCallOnceStarted,
                                               'executeRequest'));

  if (this._webRequest === null)
    throw Error.invalidOperation(Sys.Res.nullWebRequest);

  var body = this._webRequest.get_body();
  var headers = this._webRequest.get_headers();
  this._xmlHttpRequest = new XMLHttpRequest();
  this._xmlHttpRequest.onreadystatechange = this._onReadyStateChange;
  var verb = this._webRequest.get_httpVerb();
  this._xmlHttpRequest.open(verb, this._webRequest.getResolvedUrl(),
                            true /*async*/);
  if (headers)
  {
    for (var header in headers)
    {
      var val = headers[header];
      if (typeof(val) !== "function")
        this._xmlHttpRequest.setRequestHeader(header, val);
    }
  }

  if (verb.toLowerCase() === "post")
  {
    // If it's a POST but no Content-Type was specified, default to
    // application/x-www-form-urlencoded
    if ((headers === null) || !headers['Content-Type'])
      this._xmlHttpRequest.setRequestHeader('Content-Type',
                                            'application/x-www-form-urlencoded');

    // If POST with no body, default to "" (FireFox needs this)
    if (!body)
      body = "";
```

```
        }

    var timeout = this._webRequest.get_timeout();
    if (timeout > 0)
        this._timer = window.setTimeout(Function.createDelegate(this, this._onTimeout),
                                        timeout);

    this._xmlHttpRequest.send(body);
    this._started = true;
}
```

As this listing shows, the executeRequest method first calls the get_webRequest method to return a reference to the WebRequest object that represents the request being executed, and then assigns this reference to the _webRequest field for future reference:

```
this._webRequest = this.get_webRequest();
```

Next, it calls the get_body method on the WebRequest object to return a string that contains the body of the Web request:

```
var body = this._webRequest.get_body();
```

Then, it calls the get_headers method on the WebRequest object to return a dictionary that contains the names and values of all request headers:

```
var headers = this._webRequest.get_headers();
```

Then, it creates an XMLHttpRequest object, which will be used to make the request to the server:

```
this._xmlHttpRequest = new XMLHttpRequest();
```

Next, it registers the _onReadyStateChange method as the event handler for the onreadystatechange event of the XMLHttpRequest object:

```
this._xmlHttpRequest.onreadystatechange = this._onReadyStateChange;
```

Then, it calls the get_httpVerb method on the WebRequest object to return a string that contains the HTTP verb to be used to make the request:

```
var verb = this._webRequest.get_httpVerb();
```

Next, it calls the open method on the XMLHttpRequest object, passing three parameters. The first parameter is the string that contains the HTTP verb; the second parameter is the string that contains the target URL; and third parameter is the Boolean value true, which tells the XMLHttpRequest object to make an asynchronous request to the server:

```
this._xmlHttpRequest.open(verb, this._webRequest.getResolvedUrl(),
                          true /*async*/);
```

All requests made using the XMLHttpExecutor are asynchronous, because the last parameter passed into the open method of the XMLHttpRequest object is hardcoded to true.

Next, `executeRequest` iterates through the items of the dictionary that contains the names and values of all request headers, and then calls the `setRequestHeader` method on the `XMLHttpRequest` object for each enumerated item to set the value of the specified header:

```
for (var header in headers)
{
  var val = headers[header];
  if (typeof(val) !== "function")
    this._xmlHttpRequest.setRequestHeader(header, val);
}
```

If the HTTP verb is `POST` and the `Content-Type` header has not been specified, `executeRequest` calls the `setRequestHeader` method on the `XMLHttpRequest` object to use `application/x-www-form-urlencoded` as the value of the `Content-Type` header:

```
if ((headers === null) || !headers['Content-Type'])
    this._xmlHttpRequest.setRequestHeader('Content-Type',
                                'application/x-www-form-urlencoded');
```

Next, `executeRequest` calls the `get_timeout` method on the `WebRequest` object to access the current Web request timeout:

```
var timeout = this._webRequest.get_timeout();
```

Then, it calls the `createDelegate` static method on the `Function` class to create a delegate that represents the `_onTimeout` method:

```
var delegate = Function.createDelegate(this, this._onTimeout);
```

Next, it invokes the `setTimeout` method on the window object to have the delegate called after the amount of time specified by the timeout value. When this delegate is finally invoked, the delegate internally invokes the `_onTimeout` method on the `XMLHttpExecutor` method:

```
this._timer = window.setTimeout(delegate, timeout);
```

Then, `executeRequest` invokes the `send` method on the `XMLHttpRequest` object, passing in the body of the request to make the request to the server:

```
this._xmlHttpRequest.send(body);
```

Finally, it sets the `_started` Boolean field to `true` to signal that the request has already been made:

```
this._started = true;
```

getResponseHeader

When the server response arrives, you can call the `getResponseHeader` method on the `XMLHttpExecutor` object, passing in the name of the response header to access the value of the header. As Listing 12-49 shows, this method simply calls the `getResponseHeader` method on the `XMLHttpRequest` object. However, before you can call this method, you must first call the get_responseAvailable method on the XMLHttpExecutor object to make sure that the server response has arrived; otherwise, getResponseHeader raises an exception if it is called before the server response arrives.

Listing 12-49: The getResponseHeader Method

```
function Sys$Net$XMLHttpExecutor$getResponseHeader(header)
{
  /// <param name="header" type="String"></param>
  /// <returns type="String"></returns>
  if (!this._responseAvailable)
    throw Error.invalidOperation(String.format(Sys.Res.cannotCallBeforeResponse,
                                               'getResponseHeader'));

  if (!this._xmlHttpRequest)
    throw Error.invalidOperation(String.format(Sys.Res.cannotCallOutsideHandler,
                                               'getResponseHeader'));

  var result = this._xmlHttpRequest.getResponseHeader(header);

  if (!result)
    result = "";

  return result;
}
```

getAllResponseHeaders

After the server response arrives, you can call the getAllResponseHeaders method on the XMLHttpExecutor object to return a dictionary that contains the names and values of all the response headers. As Listing 12-50 shows, this method simply calls the getAllResponseHeaders method on the XMLHttpRequest object. However, before you can call this method, you must first call the get_responseAvailable method on the XMLHttpExecutor object to make sure that the server response has arrived; otherwise, getAllResponseHeaders raises an exception if it is called before the server response arrives.

Listing 12-50: The getAllResponseHeaders Method

```
function Sys$Net$XMLHttpExecutor$getAllResponseHeaders()
{
  /// <returns type="String"></returns>
  if (!this._responseAvailable)
    throw Error.invalidOperation(
        String.format (Sys.Res.cannotCallBeforeResponse, 'getAllResponseHeaders'));
  if (!this._xmlHttpRequest)
    throw Error.invalidOperation(
        String.format(Sys.Res.cannotCallOutsideHandler, 'getAllResponseHeaders'));
  return this._xmlHttpRequest.getAllResponseHeaders();
}
```

get_responseData

After the arrival of the server response, call this method on the XMLHttpExecutor object to return a string that contains the server data. As you can see in Listing 12-51, this method simply returns the value of the responseText property of the XMLHttpRequest object used to make the request. If this method is invoked before the response arrives, it will raise an exception.

Listing 12-51: The get_responseData Method

```
function Sys$Net$XMLHttpExecutor$get_responseData()
{
  /// <value type="String"></value>
  if (!this._responseAvailable)
    throw Error.invalidOperation(
        String.format(Sys.Res.cannotCallBeforeResponse, 'get_responseData'));
  if (!this._xmlHttpRequest)
    throw Error.invalidOperation(
        String.format(Sys.Res.cannotCallOutsideHandler, 'get_responseData'));
  return this._xmlHttpRequest.responseText;
}
```

get_statusCode

You can call this method on the XMLHttpExecutor object to access the HTTP status code of the server response. As Listing 12-52 shows, this method simply returns the value of the status property of the XMLHttpRequest object used to make the request. Before calling this method, you must call the get_responseAvailable method on the XMLHttpExecutor object to ensure that the server response has arrived and avoid getting an exception.

Listing 12-52: The get_statusCode Method

```
function Sys$Net$XMLHttpExecutor$get_statusCode()
{
  /// <value type="Number"></value>
  if (!this._responseAvailable)
    throw Error.invalidOperation(
                String.format(Sys.Res.cannotCallBeforeResponse, 'get_statusCode'));

  if (!this._xmlHttpRequest)
    throw Error.invalidOperation(
                String.format(Sys.Res.cannotCallOutsideHandler, 'get_statusCode'));
  return this._xmlHttpRequest.status;
}
```

get_statusText

You can call this method on the XMLHttpExecutor object to return a string that contains the HTTP status text of the server response. This method returns the value of the statusText property of the XMLHttpRequest object used to make the request, as shown in Listing 12-53. Like the previous methods, this method raises an exception if it is called before the response arrives.

Listing 12-53: The get_statusText Method

```
function Sys$Net$XMLHttpExecutor$get_statusText()
{
  /// <value type="String"></value>
  if (!this._responseAvailable)
    throw Error.invalidOperation (
                String.format(Sys.Res.cannotCallBeforeResponse, 'get_statusText'));

  if (!this._xmlHttpRequest)
    throw Error.invalidOperation (
                String.format(Sys.Res.cannotCallOutsideHandler, 'get_statusText'));
  return this._xmlHttpRequest.statusText;
}
```

get_xml

Invoke this method on the XMLHttpExecutor object to return an XML document that contains the server data. As you can see in Listing 12-54, this method returns the responseXML property value of the XMLHttpRequest object used to make the request. This method encapsulates the logic that you would have to implement otherwise. For example, the server may not set the Content-Type header to text/xml to signal the client that the response contains XML data, which means that the responseXML property of the XMLHttpRequest method will return null. The get_xml method calls the XMLDOM constructor, passing in the XMLHttpRequest method's responseText property value to load the content of this property into an XML document.

Listing 12-54: The get_xml Method

```
function Sys$Net$XMLHttpExecutor$get_xml()
{
  /// <value></value>
  if (!this._responseAvailable)
    throw Error.invalidOperation (
                    String.format(Sys.Res.cannotCallBeforeResponse, 'get_xml'));

  if (!this._xmlHttpRequest)
    throw Error.invalidOperation(
                    String.format(Sys.Res.cannotCallOutsideHandler, 'get_xml'));
  var xml = this._xmlHttpRequest.responseXML;
  if (!xml || !xml.documentElement)
  {
    // This happens if the server doesn't set the content type to text/xml.
    xml = new XMLDOM(this._xmlHttpRequest.responseText);

    // If we still couldn't get an XML DOM, the data is probably not XML
    if (!xml || !xml.documentElement)
      return null;
  }
  // REVIEW: todo this used to use Sys.Runtime get_hostType
  else if (navigator.userAgent.indexOf('MSIE') !== -1)
    xml.setProperty('SelectionLanguage', 'XPath');
```

(continued)

Listing 12-54 *(continued)*

```
    // For Firefox parser errors have document elements of parser error
    if (xml.documentElement.namespaceURI ===
       "http://www.mozilla.org/newlayout/xml/parsererror.xml" &&
                         xml.documentElement.tagName === "parsererror")
      return null;

    // For Safari, parser errors are always the first child of the root
    if (xml.documentElement.firstChild &&
         xml.documentElement.firstChild.tagName === "parsererror")
      return null;

    return xml;
}
```

abort

You can call this method on the XMLHttpExecutor object to abort the execution of a request, as shown in Listing 12-55.

Listing 12-55: The abort Method

```
function Sys$Net$XMLHttpExecutor$abort()
{
  if (!this._started)
    throw Error.invalidOperation(Sys.Res.cannotAbortBeforeStart);

  // aborts are no ops if we are done, timedout, or aborted already
  if (this._aborted || this._responseAvailable || this._timedOut)
    return;

  this._aborted = true;
  this._clearTimer();

  if (this._xmlHttpRequest && !this._responseAvailable)
  {
    // Remove the onreadystatechange first otherwise abort would
    // trigger readyState to become 4
    this._xmlHttpRequest.onreadystatechange = Function.emptyMethod;
    this._xmlHttpRequest.abort();

    this._xmlHttpRequest = null;
    var handler = this._webRequest._get_eventHandlerList().getHandler("completed");
    if (handler)
      handler(this, Sys.EventArgs.Empty);
  }
}
```

The abort method first sets the _aborted Boolean field to true to signal that the request is aborted:

```
    this._aborted = true;
```

Next, it clears the timer:

```
        this._clearTimer();
```

Then, it unregisters the `_onReadyStateChange` event handler:

```
        this._xmlHttpRequest.onreadystatechange = Function.emptyMethod;
```

Next, it calls the `abort` method on the `XMLHttpRequest` object used to make the request:

```
        this._xmlHttpRequest.abort();
```

Next, it discards the `XMLHttpRequest` object to ensure that the next request is made using a new `XMLHttpRequest` object:

```
        this._xmlHttpRequest = null;
```

Then, it calls the `getHandler` method on the `EventHandlerList` object that contains all event handlers registered for the `XMLHttpExecutor` object's events:

```
        var handler = this._webRequest._get_eventHandlerList().getHandler("completed");
```

This returns a reference to a JavaScript function whose invocation automatically invokes all event handlers registered for the `XMLHttpExecutor` object's completed event.

The `abort` method invokes this JavaScript function and, consequently, all event handlers registered for the completed event, passing in a reference to the `XMLHttpExecutor` object.

```
        handler(this, Sys.EventArgs.Empty);
```

Using WebRequest, WebRequestManager, and XMLHttpExecutor

The page shown in Listing 12-56 uses `WebRequest` to make an asynchronous postback request to the server. If you run this page, you should see the result shown in Figure 12-1.

Listing 12-56: A Page that Uses the WebRequest

```
<%@ Page Language="C#" %>

<!DOCTYPE html PUBLIC "-//W3C//DTD XHTML 1.0 Transitional//EN"
"http://www.w3.org/TR/xhtml1/DTD/xhtml1-transitional.dtd">

<script runat="server">
  void Page_Load(object sender, EventArgs e)
  {
    if (Request.Headers["CustomClientClasses_AsyncPostBack"] != null)
    {
      if (Request["passwordtbx"] == "password" &&
          Request["usernametbx"] == "username")
```

(continued)

Listing 12-56 *(continued)*

```
      {
        Response.Write("Shahram|Khosravi|22223333|Some Department|");
        Response.End();
      }

      else
        throw new Exception("Wrong credentials");
    }
  }
</script>

<html xmlns="http://www.w3.org/1999/xhtml">
<head runat="server">
  <title>Untitled Page</title>
  <script type="text/javascript" language="javascript">
    function completedCallback(sender, eventArgs)
    {
      if (sender.get_timedOut())
      {
        alert("Request timed out!");
        return;
      }
      if (sender.get_aborted())
      {
        alert("Request aborted!");
        return;
      }

      if (sender.get_statusCode() !== 200)
      {
        alert("Error occured!");
        return;
      }

      var reply = sender.get_responseData();
      var delimiter = "|";
      var replyIndex = 0;
      var delimiterIndex;

      var employeeinfotable = $get("employeeinfo");
      employeeinfotable.style.visibility = "visible";

      delimiterIndex = reply.indexOf(delimiter, replyIndex);
      var firstname = reply.substring(replyIndex, delimiterIndex);
      var firstnamespan = $get("firstname");
      firstnamespan.innerText = firstname;
      replyIndex = delimiterIndex + 1;

      delimiterIndex = reply.indexOf(delimiter, replyIndex);
      var lastname = reply.substring(replyIndex, delimiterIndex);
      var lastnamespan = $get("lastname");
      lastnamespan.innerText = lastname;
      replyIndex = delimiterIndex + 1;
```

```
          delimiterIndex = reply.indexOf(delimiter, replyIndex);
          var employeeid = reply.substring(replyIndex, delimiterIndex);
          var employeeidspan = $get("employeeid");
          employeeidspan.innerText = employeeid;
          replyIndex = delimiterIndex + 1;

          delimiterIndex = reply.indexOf(delimiter, replyIndex);
          var departmentname = reply.substring(replyIndex, delimiterIndex);
          var departmentnamespan = $get("departmentname");
          departmentnamespan.innerText = departmentname;
        }

      function submitCallback(evt)
      {
        var usernametbx = $get("usernametbx");
        var passwordtbx = $get("passwordtbx");
        var requestBody = new Sys.StringBuilder();
        requestBody.append("usernametbx");
        requestBody.append('=');
        requestBody.append(encodeURIComponent(usernametbx.value));
        requestBody.append('&');
        requestBody.append("passwordtbx");
        requestBody.append('=');
        requestBody.append(encodeURIComponent(passwordtbx.value));

        var request = new Sys.Net.WebRequest();
        request.set_url(document.form1.action);
        request.get_headers()['CustomClientClasses_AsyncPostBack'] = 'true';
        request.get_headers()['Cache-Control'] = 'no-cache';
        request.set_timeout(90000);
        request.add_completed(completedCallback);
        request.set_body(requestBody.toString());
        request.invoke();
      }

      function pageLoad()
      {
        var submitbtn = $get("submitbtn");
        $addHandler(submitbtn, "click", submitCallback);
      }
    </script>
  </head>
<body>
  <form id="form1" runat="server">
    <asp:ScriptManager ID="ScriptManager1" runat="server">
      <Scripts>
        <asp:ScriptReference Assembly="Microsoft.Web.Preview"
        Name="PreviewScript.js" />
      </Scripts>
    </asp:ScriptManager>
    <strong>Username: </strong><asp:TextBox runat="server" ID="usernametbx" />
    <br />
    <strong>Password:  </strong><asp:TextBox runat="server" ID="passwordtbx"
                                TextMode="Password" />
    <br />
```

(continued)

Listing 12-56 *(continued)*

```html
<button id="submitbtn" type="button">Submit</button><br /><br />

<table id="employeeinfo" style="background-color:LightGoldenrodYellow;
                                border-color:Tan; border-width:1px;
                                color:Black; visibility:hidden"
   cellpadding="2">
  <tr style="background-color:Tan; font-weight:bold">
    <th colspan="2">Your Information</th>
  </tr>
  <tr>
    <td style=" font-weight:bold">First Name</td>
    <td><span id="firstname" /></td>
  </tr>

  <tr style="background-color:PaleGoldenrod">
    <td style=" font-weight:bold">Last Name</td>
    <td><span id="lastname" /></td>
  </tr>

  <tr>
    <td style=" font-weight:bold">Employee ID</td>
    <td><span id="employeeid" /></td>
  </tr>

  <tr style="background-color:PaleGoldenrod">
    <td style=" font-weight:bold">Department</td>
    <td><span id="departmentname" /></td>
  </tr>
</table>

</form>
</body>
</html>
```

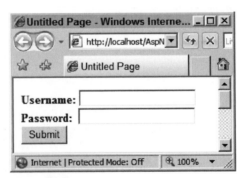

Figure 12-1

As this figure shows, the page consists of two text fields, where the end user can enter his or her username and password. When this page is loaded and the `pageLoad` method is invoked, it registers the `submitCallback` method as an event handler for the `click` event of the Submit button:

```
function pageLoad()
{
  var submitbtn = $get("submitbtn");
  $addHandler(submitbtn, "click", submitCallback);
}
```

When the user clicks the Submit button, the button raises the `click` event and, consequently, calls the `submitCallback` JavaScript function:

```
function submitCallback(evt)
{
  var usernametbx = $get("usernametbx");
  var passwordtbx = $get("passwordtbx");
  var requestBody = new Sys.StringBuilder();
  requestBody.append("usernametbx");
  requestBody.append('=');
  requestBody.append(usernametbx.value);
  requestBody.append('&');
  requestBody.append("passwordtbx");
  requestBody.append('=');
  requestBody.append(passwordtbx.value);

  var request = new Sys.Net.WebRequest();
  request.set_url(document.form1.action);
  request.get_headers()['CustomClientClasses_AsyncPostBack'] = 'true';
  request.get_headers()['Cache-Control'] = 'no-cache';
  request.set_timeout(90000);
  request.add_completed(completedCallback);
  request.set_body(requestBody.toString());
  request.invoke();
}
```

The `submitCallback` function first calls the `$get` global JavaScript function twice to return references to the username and password text fields:

```
var usernametbx = $get("usernametbx");
var passwordtbx = $get("passwordtbx");
```

Next, `submitCallback` instantiates a `StringBuilder` that will accumulate the data that makes up the body of the request:

```
var requestBody = new Sys.StringBuilder();
```

Then, it appends a string that consists of two substrings separated by the equal sign (=), where the first substring contains the value of the `UniqueID` property of the username `TextBox` server control, and the second substring contains the value that the end user entered into this server control:

```
requestBody.append("usernametbx");
requestBody.append('=');
requestBody.append(encodeURIComponent(usernametbx.value));
```

Keep in mind that every server control renders its `UniqueID` property value as the `name` attribute on the server control element on the current page.

The name = value *format is used to send the value of the username text field to the server in order to do what the browser does when it's posting the form data back to the server, but in asynchronous fashion. Browsers follow the* name = value *format to submit the value of a form element such as a text field to the server, where the* name *part of this format is a string that contains the value of the* name *HTML attribute of the form element, and the* value *part is a string that contains the value of the form element.*

Next, it appends the string `"&"`:

```
requestBody.append('&');
```

Then, `submitCallback` appends a string that consists of two substrings separated by the equal sign (=), where the first substring contains the value of the `UniqueID` property of the password `TextBox` server control, and the second substring contains the value that the end user entered into this server control:

```
requestBody.append("passwordtbx");
requestBody.append('=');
requestBody.append(encodeURIComponent(passwordtbx.value));
```

The string `'&'` *is used as a separator between the* name = value *strings because the browser uses the same string as a separator. The body of the request is a string that consists of one or more substrings separated by the string* `'&'`, *where each substring uses the* name = value *format to store the value of the form element with the specified* name *HTML attribute value.*

Next, `submitCallback` instantiates a `WebRequest` object to represent the current request. As you'll see shortly, this object will contain the complete information about the current request:

```
var request = new Sys.Net.WebRequest();
```

Then, it calls the `set_url` method on the `WebRequest` object to set the target URL for the current request. The value of the form DOM element's `action` property is used as the target URL so the page will not be posted back to itself (which is what the browser would do):

```
request.set_url(document.form1.action);
```

Next, `submitCallback` calls the `get_headers` method on the `WebRequest` object to return a dictionary that contains the names and values of the request headers:

```
var requestHeaders = request.get_headers();
```

Then, it adds a custom header named `'CustomClientClasses_AsyncPostBack'` to the header dictionary, and sets its value to `true` to signal the server that the current request is an asynchronous postback:

```
requestHeaders['CustomClientClasses_AsyncPostBack'] = 'true';
```

Next, it calls the `set_timeout` method on the `WebRequest` object to set the timeout for the current request so it will automatically time out if the server response does not arrive within the specified time:

```
request.set_timeout(90000);
```

Because this is an asynchronous request, you must register a callback for the `completed` event of the `WebRequest` object so you will be informed when the server response arrives. The `submitCallback` function calls the add_completed method on the WebRequest object to register the completedCallback JavaScript function as an event handler for the completed event of the object:

```
request.add_completed(completedCallback);
```

Next, the submitCallback method calls the set_body method on the WebRequest object to specify the contents of the StringBuilder as the body of the request:

```
request.set_body(requestBody.toString());
```

Finally, submitCallback calls the invoke method on the WebRequest object to sent the request to the server:

```
request.invoke();
```

The WebRequestExecutor object that executes the current request raises the requestCompleted event and, consequently, calls the completedCallback JavaScript function when the request is completed:

```
function completedCallback(sender, eventArgs)
{
  if (sender.get_timedOut())
  {
    alert("Request timed out!");
    return;
  }

  if (sender.get_aborted())
  {
    alert("Request aborted!");
    return;
  }

  if (sender.get_statusCode() !== 200)
  {
    alert("Error occured!");
    return;
  }

  var reply = sender.get_responseData();
  var delimiter = "|";
  var replyIndex = 0;
  var delimiterIndex;

  var employeeinfotable = $get("employeeinfo");
  employeeinfotable.style.visibility = "visible";

  delimiterIndex = reply.indexOf(delimiter, replyIndex);
  var firstname = reply.substring(replyIndex, delimiterIndex);
  var firstnamespan = $get("firstname");
  firstnamespan.innerText = firstname;
  replyIndex = delimiterIndex + 1;

  delimiterIndex = reply.indexOf(delimiter, replyIndex);
  var lastname = reply.substring(replyIndex, delimiterIndex);
```

(continued)

```
    var lastnamespan = $get("lastname");
    lastnamespan.innerText = lastname;
    replyIndex = delimiterIndex + 1;

    delimiterIndex = reply.indexOf(delimiter, replyIndex);
    var employeeid = reply.substring(replyIndex, delimiterIndex);
    var employeeidspan = $get("employeeid");
    employeeidspan.innerText = employeeid;
    replyIndex = delimiterIndex + 1;

    delimiterIndex = reply.indexOf(delimiter, replyIndex);
    var departmentname = reply.substring(replyIndex, delimiterIndex);
    var departmentnamespan = $get("departmentname");
    departmentnamespan.innerText = departmentname;
}
```

A request is considered completed when one of the following occurs:

❏ The request times out because the server response did not arrive on time.

❏ The request is aborted because some code called the `abort` method to explicitly abort the request. (You'll see an example of this in the following chapters.)

❏ A server error occurs, such as when the server code raises an exception.

❏ Everything proceeds as planned, and the server response arrives.

As you can see, the completion of a request does not necessarily mean that everything went fine and the server response has arrived. That's why the `completedCallback` JavaScript function first calls the `get_timedOut` method on the `WebRequestExecutor` object to check whether the current request has timed out:

```
    if (sender.get_timedOut())
    {
      alert("Request timed out!");
      return;
    }
```

Next, it calls the `get_aborted` method on the `WebRequestExecutor` object to check whether the current request was aborted:

```
    if (sender.get_aborted())
    {
      alert("Request aborted!");
      return;
    }
```

Then, it calls the `get_statusCode` method on the `WebRequestExecutor` object to check whether the status code of the response is something other than 200, meaning a server error has occurred:

```
    if (sender.get_statusCode() !== 200)
    {
      alert("Error occured!");
      return;
    }
```

If the request neither timed out nor was aborted, and if there was no server error, this indicates that the server response has arrived and, consequently, the `completed` event was raised. As such, the `completedCallback` JavaScript function calls the `get_responseData` method on the `WebRequestExecutor` object to return the string that contains the response data:

```
var reply = sender.get_responseData();
```

Next, the `completedCallback` function calls the `$get` global JavaScript function to return a reference to the table that will be used to display the employee's information, and sets its visibility to `visible`:

```
var employeeinfotable = $get("employeeinfo");
employeeinfotable.style.visibility = "visible";
```

As you'll see later, the server uses the `firstname|lastname|employeeID|departmentName|` format to serialize the information about the current employee. The `completedCallback` function takes the following steps to parse the string that contains the server data:

1. It accesses the index of the first delimiter (`|`) character and uses that to extract the first name of the employee:

```
delimiterIndex = reply.indexOf(delimiter, replyIndex);
var firstname = reply.substring(replyIndex, delimiterIndex);
```

2. It uses the `$get` global JavaScript function to return a reference to the `<span>` HTML element responsible for displaying the first name of the employee, and sets its `innerText` property to the first name of the employee:

```
var firstnamespan = $get("firstname");
firstnamespan.innerText = firstname;
```

3. It repeats steps 1 and 2 to extract the last name, employee id, and department name from the string that contains the server data, and displays them in their associated `<span>` HTML elements:

```
replyIndex = delimiterIndex + 1;

delimiterIndex = reply.indexOf(delimiter, replyIndex);
var lastname = reply.substring(replyIndex, delimiterIndex);
var lastnamespan = $get("lastname");
lastnamespan.innerText = lastname;
replyIndex = delimiterIndex + 1;

delimiterIndex = reply.indexOf(delimiter, replyIndex);
var employeeid = reply.substring(replyIndex, delimiterIndex);
var employeeidspan = $get("employeeid");
employeeidspan.innerText = employeeid;
replyIndex = delimiterIndex + 1;

delimiterIndex = reply.indexOf(delimiter, replyIndex);
var departmentname = reply.substring(replyIndex, delimiterIndex);
var departmentnamespan = $get("departmentname");
departmentnamespan.innerText = departmentname;
```

Now let's look at what happens on the server side when the asynchronous postback request arrives. As shown in the following excerpt from Listing 12-56, the `Page_Load` method is where all the action on the server side occurs:

```
void Page_Load(object sender, EventArgs e)
{
    if (Request.Headers["CustomClientClasses_AsyncPostBack"] != null)
    {
        if (Request["passwordtbx"] == "password" &&
            Request["usernametbx"] == "username")
        {
            Response.Write("Shahram|Khosravi|22223333|Some Department|");
            Response.Flush();
            Response.End();
        }

        else
            throw new Exception("Wrong credentials");
    }
}
```

This `Page_Load` method first checks whether the current request contains a custom header named `CustomClientClasses_AsyncPostBack`, which indicates that the current request is an asynchronous page postback:

```
if (Request.Headers["CustomClientClasses_AsyncPostBack"] != null)
```

Next, it validates the user's credentials. To keep this discussion focused, Listing 12-56 uses a very simple validation logic. This logic expects the username and password to be the strings `password` and `username`. If the validation succeeds, the `Page_Load` method takes the following steps:

1. It creates a string that contains four substrings separated by the | character containing the first name, last name, employee `id`, and department name of the employee whose credentials were just validated. It then calls the `Write` method on the ASP.NET `Response` object to write this string into the response output stream:

   ```
   Response.Write("Shahram|Khosravi|22223333|Some Department|");
   ```

2. It calls the `End` method on the `Response` object:

   ```
   Response.End();
   ```

Figure 12-2 shows the results after the end user clicks the Submit button. Note that the page renders the employee information in a table.

The `WebRequestExecutor` defines the API that must be implemented by its subclasses in order to execute a `WebRequest` object. However, as you may have noticed, there is no sign of the `WebRequestExecutor` in Listing 12-56. This is because when you don't explicitly specify a `WebRequestExecutor` for a `WebRequest` object, it uses `XMLHttpExecutor` by default. `XMLHttpExecutor` is a subclass of the `WebRequestExecutor` base class that provides an implementation of the API that uses the `XMLHttpRequest`. If, for whatever reason, you're not happy with this implementation of the API, you can provide your own API implementation and use your own custom `WebRequestExecutor` to execute requests for your applications.

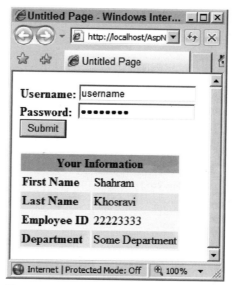

Figure 12-2

Listing 12-57 shows a version of the Listing 12-56 where the XMLHttpExecutor is explicitly specified and used. The boldface portion is the only difference between these two code listings.

Listing 12-57: A Page that Explicitly Uses a WebRequestExecutor

```
<%@ Page Language="C#" %>

<!DOCTYPE html PUBLIC "-//W3C//DTD XHTML 1.0 Transitional//EN"
"http://www.w3.org/TR/xhtml11/DTD/xhtml11-transitional.dtd">

<script runat="server">
  void Page_Load(object sender, EventArgs e)
  {
    //Same as Listing 12-56
  }
</script>

<html xmlns="http://www.w3.org/1999/xhtml">
<head runat="server">
  <title>Untitled Page</title>
  <script type="text/javascript" language="javascript">
    function completedCallback(sender, eventArgs)
    {
      //Same as Listing 12-56
    }
    function submitCallback(evt)
    {
      var usernametbx = $get("usernametbx");
      var passwordtbx = $get("passwordtbx");
      var requestBody = new Sys.StringBuilder();
```

(continued)

Listing 12-57 *(continued)*

```
            requestBody.append("usernametbx");
            requestBody.append('=');
            requestBody.append(usernametbx.value);
            requestBody.append('&');
            requestBody.append("passwordtbx");
            requestBody.append('=');
            requestBody.append(passwordtbx.value);

            var request = new Sys.Net.WebRequest();
            var executor = new Sys.Net.XMLHttpExecutor();
            request.set_executor(executor);
            request.set_url(document.form1.action);
            request.get_headers()['CustomClientClasses_AsyncPostBack'] = 'true';
            request.get_headers()['Cache-Control'] = 'no-cache';
            request.set_timeout(90000);
            request.add_completed(completedCallback);
            request.set_body(requestBody.toString());
            executor.executeRequest();
        }

        function pageLoad()
        {
            //Same as Listing 12-56
        }
    </script>
</head>
<body>
  <form id="form1" runat="server">
    <!-- Same as Listing 12-56 -->
  </form>
</body>
</html>
```

The `submitCallback` function in this listing first instantiates an instance of the
`XMLHttpExecutor` class:

```
var executor = new Sys.Net.XMLHttpExecutor();
```

Then it calls the `set_executor` method on the `WebRequest` object to set the newly-instantiated
`XMLHttpExecutor` object as the executor for the `WebRequest` object:

```
request.set_executor(executor);
```

Finally, `submitCallback` calls the `executeRequest` method on the newly instantiated `XMLHttpExecutor`
object to execute the request:

```
executor.executeRequest();
```

However, you don't have to call this method to execute the request — you can call the `invoke` method to
do so instead.

498

As discussed earlier, every ASP.NET AJAX page can have only one instance of the _WebRequestManager class. The ASP.NET AJAX client-side framework automatically creates this instance and assigns it to a global variable named Sys.Net.WebRequestManager when the page is loaded for the first time. You cannot instantiate a new instance of this class. Instead, you must use the Sys.Net.WebRequestManager global variable to access the current _WebRequestManager instance.

The current _WebRequestManager instance manages all the requests the current page makes to the server. As such, the settings specified for the current _WebRequestManager are applied to all requests. Listing 12-58 presents a new version of Listing 12-56 that makes explicit use of the WebRequestManager.

Listing 12-58: A Page that Makes Explicit Use of the WebRequestManager

```
<%@ Page Language="C#" %>

<!DOCTYPE html PUBLIC "-//W3C//DTD XHTML 1.0 Transitional//EN"
"http://www.w3.org/TR/xhtml1/DTD/xhtml1-transitional.dtd">

<script runat="server">
  void Page_Load(object sender, EventArgs e)
  {
    if (Request.Headers["CustomClientClasses_AsyncPostBack"] != null)
    {
      if (Request["passwordtbx"] == "password" &&
          Request["usernametbx"] == "username")
      {
        Response.Write("Shahram|Khosravi|22223333|Some Department|");
        Response.End();
      }

      else
        throw new Exception("Wrong credentials");
    }
  }
</script>

<html xmlns="http://www.w3.org/1999/xhtml">
<head runat="server">
  <title>Untitled Page</title>
  <script type="text/javascript" language="javascript">
    function invokingRequestCallback(sender, args)
    {
      var request = args.get_webRequest();
      var builder = new Sys.StringBuilder();
      builder.append("Default request timeout: ");
      builder.append(sender.get_defaultTimeout());
      builder.append("\r\n\r\nDefault executor type: ");
      builder.append(sender.get_defaultExecutorType());
      builder.append("\r\n\r\nTarget URL: ");
      builder.append(request.get_url());
      builder.append("\r\n\r\nHTTP verb: ");
      builder.append(request.get_httpVerb());
      builder.append("\r\n\r\nRequest body: ");
      builder.append(request.get_body());
```

(continued)

Listing 12-58 *(continued)*

```
      builder.append("\r\n\r\nRequest timeout: ");
      builder.append(request.get_timeout());
      builder.append("\r\n\r\nRequest headers: ");
      var headers = request.get_headers();
      for(var header in headers)
      {
        builder.append("\r\n\t");
        builder.append(header);
        builder.append(": ");
        builder.append(headers[header]);
      }
      builder.append("\r\n\r\nClick the Cancel button to cancel the request");
      builder.append(" or OK button to submit the request.");

      var result = Sys.Preview.UI.Window.messageBox(builder.toString(),
                                    Sys.Preview.UI.MessageBoxStyle.OKCancel);

      if (result == Sys.Preview.UI.DialogResult.Cancel)
        args.set_cancel(true);
    }

    function completedCallback(sender, eventArgs)
    {
      if (sender.get_timedOut())
      {
        alert("Request timed out!");
        return;
      }

      if (sender.get_aborted())
      {
        alert("Request aborted!");
        return;
      }

      if (sender.get_statusCode() !== 200)
      {
        alert("Error occured!");
        return;
      }

      var reply = sender.get_responseData();
      var delimiter = "|";
      var replyIndex = 0;
      var delimiterIndex;

      var employeeinfotable = $get("employeeinfo");
      employeeinfotable.style.visibility = "visible";

      delimiterIndex = reply.indexOf(delimiter, replyIndex);
      var firstname = reply.substring(replyIndex, delimiterIndex);
      var firstnamespan = $get("firstname");
      firstnamespan.innerText = firstname;
      replyIndex = delimiterIndex + 1;
```

```
            delimiterIndex = reply.indexOf(delimiter, replyIndex);
            var lastname = reply.substring(replyIndex, delimiterIndex);
            var lastnamespan = $get("lastname");
            lastnamespan.innerText = lastname;
            replyIndex = delimiterIndex + 1;

            delimiterIndex = reply.indexOf(delimiter, replyIndex);
            var employeeid = reply.substring(replyIndex, delimiterIndex);
            var employeeidspan = $get("employeeid");
            employeeidspan.innerText = employeeid;
            replyIndex = delimiterIndex + 1;

            delimiterIndex = reply.indexOf(delimiter, replyIndex);
            var departmentname = reply.substring(replyIndex, delimiterIndex);
            var departmentnamespan = $get("departmentname");
            departmentnamespan.innerText = departmentname;
        }

    function submitCallback(evt)
    {
        var usernametbx = $get("usernametbx");
        var passwordtbx = $get("passwordtbx");
        var requestBody = new Sys.StringBuilder();
        requestBody.append("usernametbx");
        requestBody.append('=');
        requestBody.append(usernametbx.value);
        requestBody.append('&');
        requestBody.append("passwordtbx");
        requestBody.append('=');
        requestBody.append(passwordtbx.value);

        var request = new Sys.Net.WebRequest();
        request.set_timeout(70000);
        request.set_url(document.form1.action);
        request.get_headers()['CustomClientClasses_AsyncPostBack'] = 'true';
        request.get_headers()['Cache-Control'] = 'no-cache';
        request.set_body(requestBody.toString());
        request.invoke();
    }

    function pageLoad()
    {
        var submitbtn = $get("submitbtn");
        $addHandler(submitbtn, "click", submitCallback);
        Sys.Net.WebRequestManager.set_defaultTimeout(90000);
        Sys.Net.WebRequestManager.set_defaultExecutorType("Sys.Net.XMLHttpExecutor");
        Sys.Net.WebRequestManager.add_invokingRequest(invokingRequestCallback);
        Sys.Net.WebRequestManager.add_completedRequest(completedCallback);

    }
  </script>
</head>
<body>
  <form id="form1" runat="server">
```

(continued)

501

Listing 12-58 (continued)

```
    <asp:ScriptManager ID="ScriptManager1" runat="server">
      <Scripts>
        <asp:ScriptReference Assembly="Microsoft.Web.Preview"
        Name="PreviewScript.js" />
      </Scripts>
    </asp:ScriptManager>
    <strong>Username: </strong><asp:TextBox runat="server" ID="usernametbx" />
    <br />
    <strong>Password:  </strong><asp:TextBox runat="server" ID="passwordtbx"
                            TextMode="Password" /><br />
    <button id="submitbtn"type="button">Submit</button><br /><br />
    <table id="employeeinfo" style="background-color:LightGoldenrodYellow; border-
color:Tan; border-width:1px; color:Black; visibility:hidden" cellpadding="2">
        <tr style="background-color:Tan; font-weight:bold">
          <th colspan="2">Your Information</th>
        </tr>
        <tr>
          <td style=" font-weight:bold">First Name</td>
          <td><span id="firstname" /></td>
        </tr>

        <tr style="background-color:PaleGoldenrod">
          <td style=" font-weight:bold">Last Name</td>
          <td><span id="lastname" /></td>
        </tr>

        <tr>
          <td style=" font-weight:bold">Employee ID</td>
          <td><span id="employeeid" /></td>
        </tr>

        <tr style="background-color:PaleGoldenrod">
          <td style=" font-weight:bold">Department</td>
          <td><span id="departmentname" /></td>
        </tr>
      </table>

    </form>
  </body>
</html>
```

First, let's walk through the implementation of the pageLoad method, as shown in the following excerpt from Listing 12-58:

```
function pageLoad()
{
  var submitbtn = $get("submitbtn");
  $addHandler(submitbtn, "click", submitCallback);
  Sys.Net.WebRequestManager.set_defaultTimeout(90000);
  Sys.Net.WebRequestManager.set_defaultExecutorType("Sys.Net.XMLHttpExecutor");
  Sys.Net.WebRequestManager.add_invokingRequest(invokingRequestCallback);
  Sys.Net.WebRequestManager.add_completedRequest(completedCallback);
}
```

As the boldface portion of this code shows, the `pageLoad` method first calls the `set_defaultTimeout` method on the current `WebRequestManager` instance to set the default timeout for all the requests:

```
Sys.Net.WebRequestManager.set_defaultTimeout(90000);
```

This means that all requests will use the specified timeout value unless you explicitly call the `set_timout` method on a particular `WebRequest` to specify a different timeout value (see Listing 12-58).

Next, `pageLoad` calls the `set_defaultExecutorType` method on the current `WebRequestManager` instance to specify the `XMLHttpExecutor` as the default executor type for all requests:

```
Sys.Net.WebRequestManager.set_defaultExecutorType("Sys.Net.XMLHttpExecutor");
```

Strictly speaking, this call does not make a difference, because the `WebRequestManager` instance uses this executor by default anyway:

Next, `pageLoad` calls the `add_invokingRequest` method on the current `WebRequestManager` instance to register the `invokingRequestCallback` JavaScript function as an event handler for the `invokingRequest` event of the `WebRequestManager` instance:

```
Sys.Net.WebRequestManager.add_invokingRequest(invokingRequestCallback);
```

The `WebRequestManager` instance will call this JavaScript function for every asynchronous request that the current page makes before the request is actually made:

Next, `pageLoad` calls the `add_completedRequest` method on the current `WebRequestManager` instance to register the `completedCallback` JavaScript function as an event handler for the `completedRequest` event of the `WebRequestManager` instance:

```
Sys.Net.WebRequestManager.add_completedRequest(completedCallback);
```

The `WebRequestManager` instance will call this JavaScript function for every single asynchronous request that the current page makes when the request is finally completed. As discussed earlier, the completion of a request does not necessarily mean that everything went fine and the server response has arrived.

Next, let's walk through the implementation of the `invokingRequestCallback` JavaScript function, as shown in the following excerpt from Listing 12-58:

```
function invokingRequestCallback(sender, args)
{
    var request = args.get_webRequest();
    var builder = new Sys.StringBuilder();
    builder.append("Default request timeout: ");
    builder.append(sender.get_defaultTimeout());
    builder.append("\r\n\r\nDefault executor type: ");
    builder.append(sender.get_defaultExecutorType());
    builder.append("\r\n\r\nTarget URL: ");
    builder.append(request.get_url());
    builder.append("\r\n\r\nHTTP verb: ");
    builder.append(request.get_httpVerb());
```

(continued)

(continued)

```
          builder.append("\r\n\r\nRequest body: ");
          builder.append(request.get_body());
          builder.append("\r\n\r\nRequest timeout: ");
          builder.append(request.get_timeout());
          builder.append("\r\n\r\nRequest headers: ");
          var headers = request.get_headers();
          for(var header in headers)
          {
            builder.append("\r\n\t");
            builder.append(header);
            builder.append(": ");
            builder.append(headers[header]);
          }
          builder.append("\r\n\r\nDo want to cancel this request?");

          var result = Sys.Preview.UI.Window.messageBox(builder.toString(),
                                        Sys.Preview.UI.MessageBoxStyle.OKCancel);

          if (result == Sys.Preview.UI.DialogResult.Cancel)
            args.set_cancel(true);
      }
```

This function takes two arguments. The first argument references the current `WebRequestManager` instance. The second argument references the `NetworkRequestEventArgs` object that contains the event data for the `invokingRequest` event of the current `WebRequestManager` instance.

The `invokingRequestCallback` function first calls the `get_webRequest` method on the `NetworkRequestEventArgs` object to return a reference to the `WebRequest` object that represents the current request:

```
      var request = args.get_webRequest();
```

Next, it creates a `StringBuilder`, which will be used to accumulate the complete information about the current request:

```
      var builder = new Sys.StringBuilder();
```

Next, it calls the `get_defaultTimeout` method on the current `WebRequestManager` instance to return the default timeout, and appends this value to the `StringBuilder`:

```
      builder.append("Default request timeout: ");
      builder.append(sender.get_defaultTimeout());
```

Then, it calls the `get_defaultExecutorType` method on the current `WebRequestManager` instance to return the string that contains the fully qualified name of the type of the default executor, including its namespace hierarchy, and appends this information to the `StringBuilder`:

```
      builder.append("\r\n\r\nDefault executor type: ");
      builder.append(sender.get_defaultExecutorType());
```

Next, it calls the `get_url` method on the `WebRequest` object that represents the current request to return a string that contains the target URL, and appends this string to the `StringBuilder`:

```
builder.append("\r\n\r\nTarget URL: ");
builder.append(request.get_url());
```

Then, it calls the `get_httpVerb` method on the `WebRequest` object to return a string that contains the HTTP verb being used to make the current request, and appends this information to the `StringBuilder`:

```
builder.append("\r\n\r\nHTTP verb: ");
builder.append(request.get_httpVerb());
```

Next, it calls the `get_body` method on the `WebRequest` object to return a string that contains the body of the current request, and appends this string to the `StringBuilder`:

```
builder.append("\r\n\r\nRequest body: ");
builder.append(request.get_body());
```

Then, it calls the `get_timeout` method on the `WebRequest` object to return a string that contains the timeout value for the current request, and appends this string to the `StringBuilder`:

```
builder.append("\r\n\r\nRequest timeout: ");
builder.append(request.get_timeout());
```

Note that this value may be different from the value returned from the call into the `get_defaultTimeout` method on the current `WebRequestManager` instance.

Next, `invokingRequestCallback` calls the `get_headers` method on the `WebRequest` object to return the dictionary that contains the names and values of the request headers:

```
builder.append("\r\n\r\nRequest headers: ");
var headers = request.get_headers();
```

Then it iterates through these headers and appends their names and values to the `StringBuilder`:

```
for(var header in headers)
{
  builder.append("\r\n\t");
  builder.append(header);
  builder.append(": ");
  builder.append(headers[header]);
}
builder.append("\r\n\r\nDo want to cancel this request?");
```

Next, it launches the ASP.NET AJAX `messageBox` to display the content of the `StringBuilder`:

```
var result = Sys.Preview.UI.Window.messageBox(builder.toString(),
                          Sys.Preview.UI.MessageBoxStyle.OKCancel);
```

This content contains the complete information about the current request. Note that this `messageBox` contains both the OK and Cancel buttons.

Finally, `invokingRequestCallback` checks whether the end user has clicked the Cancel button. If so, it calls the `set_cancel` method on the `NetworkRequestEventArgs` object to request the current `WebRequestManager` instance to cancel the current request:

```
if (result == Sys.Preview.UI.DialogResult.Cancel)
    args.set_cancel(true);
```

If you run Listing 12-58, enter the string `"username"` for the username and the string `"password"` for the password, and click the Submit button, you should see the pop-up box shown in Figure 12-3.

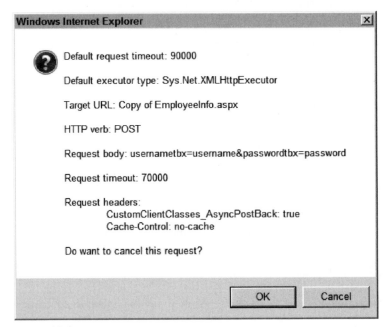

Windows Internet Explorer ☒

? Default request timeout: 90000

Default executor type: Sys.Net.XMLHttpExecutor

Target URL: Copy of EmployeeInfo.aspx

HTTP verb: POST

Request body: usernametbx=username&passwordtbx=password

Request timeout: 70000

Request headers:
    CustomClientClasses_AsyncPostBack: true
    Cache-Control: no-cache

Do want to cancel this request?

[OK]   [Cancel]

Figure 12-3

If you click the OK button on this pop-up box, the request will be made and the result will be displayed as expected. If you click the Cancel button, the current `WebRequestManager` instance will automatically cancel the request as specified in Listing 12-36.

Canceling a request is different from aborting the request. To abort a request, the abort method must be explicitly called on the `WebRequestExecutor` object responsible for executing the request. As shown in the following excerpt from Listing 12-36, the `executeRequest` method of the `WebRequestManager` does not call the `abort` method when it is canceling a request:

```
function Sys$Net$_WebRequestManager$executeRequest(webRequest)
{
  var executor = webRequest.get_executor();
```

```
if (!executor)
{
  var failed = false;
  try
  {
    var executorType = eval(this._defaultExecutorType);
    executor = new executorType();
  }

  catch (e)
  {
    failed = true;
  }

  if (failed  || !Sys.Net.WebRequestExecutor.isInstanceOfType(executor) ||
      !executor)
    throw Error.argument("defaultExecutorType",
                         String.format(Sys.Res.invalidExecutorType,
                         this._defaultExecutorType));

  webRequest.set_executor(executor);
}

if (executor.get_aborted())
  return;

var evArgs = new Sys.Net.NetworkRequestEventArgs(webRequest);
var handler = this._get_eventHandlerList().getHandler("invokingRequest");
if (handler)
  handler(this, evArgs);

if (!evArgs.get_cancel())
  executor.executeRequest();
}
```

As the boldface portion of this code excerpt shows, canceling a request simply means not calling the executeRequest method on the WebRequestExecutor object. Therefore, if you click the Cancel button on the pop-up box shown in Figure 12-3, the completedCallback method and, consequently, the boldface portion shown in the following code never gets called:

```
function completedCallback(sender, eventArgs)
{
  if (sender.get_timedOut())
  {
    alert("Request timed out!");
    return;
  }

  if (sender.get_aborted())
  {
    alert("Request aborted!");
    return;
  }
```

(continued)

```
      if (sender.get_statusCode() !== 200)
      {
        alert("Error occured!");
        return;
      }

      var reply = sender.get_responseData();
      ...
    }
```

Listing 12-59 presents the definition of the two ASP.NET AJAX enumerators used in Listing 12-58: `DialogResult` and `MessageBoxStyle`.

Listing 12-59: The DialogResult and MessageBoxStyle Enumerators

```
Sys.Preview.UI.DialogResult = function Sys$Preview$UI$DialogResult()
{
    throw Error.invalidOperation();
}

Sys.Preview.UI.DialogResult.prototype =
{
    OK: 0,
    Cancel: 1
}
Sys.Preview.UI.DialogResult.registerEnum('Sys.Preview.UI.DialogResult');

Sys.Preview.UI.MessageBoxStyle = function Sys$Preview$UI$MessageBoxStyle()
{
    throw Error.invalidOperation();
}

Sys.Preview.UI.MessageBoxStyle.prototype =
{
    OK: 0,
    OKCancel: 1
}

Sys.Preview.UI.MessageBoxStyle.registerEnum('Sys.Preview.UI.MessageBoxStyle');
```

The `DialogResult` enumerator represents the result of an ASP.NET AJAX pop-up dialog box that contains up to two buttons: OK and/or Cancel. The value of `OK` specifies that the OK button was clicked, and the value of `Cancel` specifies that the Cancel button was clicked. Listing 12-58 used the `DialogResult` enumerator to determine whether to cancel the current request.

The `MessageBoxStyle` enumerator specifies the style of an ASP.NET AJAX message box. This enumerator takes two values: `OK` and `OKCancel`. The `OK` value instructs the message box to display only the OK button, and the `OKCancel` value instructs it to display both the OK and Cancel buttons.

Listing 12-60 presents the implementation of the `Window` class. This class is a wrapper around the `alert`, `confirm`, and `prompt` methods of the `window` object.

Listing 12-60: The Window Class

```
Sys.Preview.UI.Window = function Sys$Preview$UI$Window()
{
  throw Error.invalidOperation();
}

Sys.Preview.UI.Window.messageBox =
function Sys$Preview$UI$Window$messageBox(text, style)
{
  if (!style)
    style = Sys.Preview.UI.MessageBoxStyle.OK;

  var result = Sys.Preview.UI.DialogResult.OK;
  switch (style)
  {
    case Sys.Preview.UI.MessageBoxStyle.OK:
      window.alert(text);
      break;
    case Sys.Preview.UI.MessageBoxStyle.OKCancel:
      if (window.confirm(text) === false)
        result = Sys.Preview.UI.DialogResult.Cancel;
      break;
  }

  return result;
}

Sys.Preview.UI.Window.inputBox =
function Sys$Preview$UI$Window$inputBox(promptText, defaultValue)
{
  if (!defaultValue)
    defaultValue = '';

  return window.prompt(promptText, defaultValue);
}
```

The `Window` class exposes two static methods named `messageBox` and `inputBox`. Because these two methods are static, they must be invoked directly on the `Window` class itself. You should never instantiate an instance of the `Window` class. As the following excerpt from Listing 12-60 shows, the constructor of this class raises an `invalideOperation` exception if you try to instantiate the class:

```
Sys.Preview.UI.Window = function Sys$Preview$UI$Window()
{
  throw Error.invalidOperation();
}
```

The `messageBox` static method of the `Window` class takes two parameters. The first parameter is a string that contains the message being displayed. The second parameter is a `MessageBoxSyle` enumerator value that specifies whether the message box must contain only the OK button or both the OK and Cancel buttons. If the second parameter is not provided, the message box defaults to displaying only the OK button.

The messageBox method checks the value of its second parameter. If it is set to OK, messageBox calls the alert method on the window object to display the alert pop-up box, which contains only the OK button:

```
case Sys.Preview.UI.MessageBoxStyle.OK:
    window.alert(text);
    break;
```

If the second parameter is set to OKCancel, the messageBox method calls the confirm method on the window object to launch the confirmation pop-up box, which contains both the OK and Cancel buttons:

```
case Sys.Preview.UI.MessageBoxStyle.OKCancel:
    if (window.confirm(text) === false)
        result = Sys.Preview.UI.DialogResult.Cancel;
    break;
```

Note that if the confirm method returns false, the messageBox method returns the enumerator value of DialogResult.Cancel to its caller.

Finally, the messageBox static method returns a DialogResult enumerator value that specifies whether the end user clicked the OK or Cancel button.

The inputBox static method of the Window class takes two parameters. The first parameter is a string that contains the prompt text. The second parameter is a string that contains the default value for the text field on the inputBox. The inputBox method delegates to the prompt method of the window object, which means that the return value of the inputBox method is the same as the return value of the prompt method:

```
Sys.Preview.UI.Window.inputBox =
function Sys$Preview$UI$Window$inputBox(promptText, defaultValue)
{
    if (!defaultValue)
        defaultValue = '';

    return window.prompt(promptText, defaultValue);
}
```

Summary

This chapter provided in-depth coverage of the ASP.NET AJAX client-server communication layer and its constituent WebRequest, WebRequestExecutor, XMLHttpExecutor, and WebRequestManager components. It then used examples to show you how to use these components in your own applications.

The next chapter shows you how to use these components in your ASP.NET AJAX applications to exchange SOAP messages with XML Web services.

Consuming Web Services Via Soap Messages

The previous chapter discussed the ASP.NET AJAX client-server communication layer and its constituent components. You learned how to use `WebRequest`, `WebRequestManager`, and `WebRequestExecutor` to make asynchronous requests to the server right from within your client-side code. This chapter builds on what you learned in the previous chapter to show you how to consume Web services in your ASP.NET AJAX applications. The chapter begins by implementing an ASP.NET Web service. It then shows you how to use the techniques that you learned in the previous chapter to consume this Web service in an ASP.NET AJAX application.

Building the Web Service

In the previous chapter, a Web page was implemented that uses the `WebRequest`, `WebRequestExecutor`, and `WebRequestManager` ASP.NET AJAX client classes to make an asynchronous page post back to the server to retrieve detailed information about a given employee. In Listing 12-58, the `Page_Load` method is the server-side method responsible for validating an employee's credentials and returning the detailed employee information back to the requesting browser.

This section implements a Web service that does exactly what the `Page_Load` method does — it validates user credentials and returns the detailed employee information to the requesting browser. In other words, instead of asynchronously posting back to itself to validate user credentials and retrieve the employee information, the page makes an asynchronous call into this Web service. Although the end result is the same — both approaches validate user credentials and retrieve the employee information — the mechanisms are quite different. Whereas one uses page post back, the other calls into a Web service.

Listing 13-1 presents the implementation of this Web service called `EmployeeInfo`. It exposes a single Web-callable method named `GetEmployeeInfo` that takes the username and password as its argument, validates user credentials, and returns the employee information. As you can see, the `GetEmployeeInfo` method does exactly what the `Page_Load` method did in the previous chapter.

Listing 13-1: The EmployeeInfo Web Service

```
using System;
using System.Web;
using System.Web.Services;
using System.Web.Services.Protocols;

[WebService(Namespace = "http://www.employees/")]
[WebServiceBinding(ConformsTo = WsiProfiles.BasicProfile1_1)]
public class EmployeeInfo : System.Web.Services.WebService
{
  [WebMethod]
  public string GetEmployeeInfo(string username, string password)
  {
    if (password == "password" && username == "username")
      return "Shahram|Khosravi|22223333|Some Department|";

    return "Validation failed";
  }
}
```

If you run `EmployeeInfo` in Visual Studio, you should see the page shown in Figure 13-1.

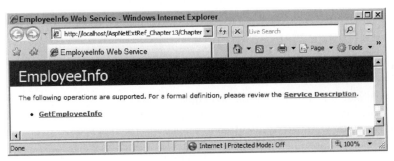

Figure 13-1

If you click the `Service Description` link shown in Figure 13-1, it takes you to a page that is known as the Web Service Description Language (WSDL; pronounced *whiz-dull*) document. The next section describes this document.

If you click the `GetEmployeeInfo` link shown in Figure 13-1, it takes you to a page that displays HTTP request and response messages, known as SOAP messages. These messages are described in subsequent sections.

WSDL Documents

The WSDL document of an XML Web service provides you with the following information about the method of the XML Web service that you want to invoke:

❑   The names, types, and order of the arguments of the method

❑   The types and order of the return values of the method

❑   The name of the method

❑   The communication protocol through which the method must be accessed

❑   The URL of the site from which the method must be accessed

❑   The name of the class to which the method belongs

The WSDL document uses the XML constructs of the WSDL markup language to provide all this information about a given method of the XML Web service. Listing 13-2 shows the WSDL document that describes the `EmployeeInfo` XML Web service. The following sections discuss different parts of this WSDL document in detail.

Listing 13-2: The WSDL Document that Describes the EmployeeInfo XML Web Service

```
<?xml version="1.0" encoding="utf-8" ?>
<wsdl:definitions xmlns:soap="http://schemas.xmlsoap.org/wsdl/soap/"
xmlns:tm="http://microsoft.com/wsdl/mime/textMatching/"
xmlns:soapenc="http://schemas.xmlsoap.org/soap/encoding/"
xmlns:mime="http://schemas.xmlsoap.org/wsdl/mime/"
xmlns:tns="http://www.employees/" xmlns:s="http://www.w3.org/2001/XMLSchema"
xmlns:soap12="http://schemas.xmlsoap.org/wsdl/soap12/"
xmlns:http="http://schemas.xmlsoap.org/wsdl/http/"
targetNamespace="http://www.employees/" xmlns="http://schemas.xmlsoap.org/wsdl/">

  <types>
    <s:schema elementFormDefault="qualified"
    targetNamespace="http://www.employees/">

      <s:element name="GetEmployeeInfo">
        <s:complexType>
          <s:sequence>
            <s:element minOccurs="0" maxOccurs="1" name="username"
            type="s:string" />
            <s:element minOccurs="0" maxOccurs="1" name="password"
            type="s:string" />
          </s:sequence>
        </s:complexType>
      </s:element>

      <s:element name="GetEmployeeInfoResponse">
        <s:complexType>
          <s:sequence>
            <s:element minOccurs="0" maxOccurs="1" name="GetEmployeeInfoResult"
            type="s:string" />
          </s:sequence>
        </s:complexType>
      </s:element>

    </s:schema>
  </types>
```

(continued)

Listing 13-2 *(continued)*

```xml
<message name="GetEmployeeInfoSoapIn">
  <part name="parameters" element="tns:GetEmployeeInfo" />
</message>
<message name="GetEmployeeInfoSoapOut">
  <part name="parameters" element="tns:GetEmployeeInfoResponse" />
</message>

<portType name="EmployeeInfoSoap">
  <operation name="GetEmployeeInfo">
    <input message="tns:GetEmployeeInfoSoapIn" />
    <output message="tns:GetEmployeeInfoSoapOut" />
  </operation>
</portType>

<binding name="EmployeeInfoSoap12" type="tns:EmployeeInfoSoap">
  <soap12:binding transport="http://schemas.xmlsoap.org/soap/http" />
  <operation name="GetEmployeeInfo">
    <soap12:operation soapAction="http://www.employees/GetEmployeeInfo"
     style="document" />
    <input>
      <soap12:body use="literal" />
    </input>
    <output>
      <soap12:body use="literal" />
    </output>
  </operation>
</binding>

<service name="EmployeeInfo">
  <port name="EmployeeInfoSoap12" binding="tns:EmployeeInfoSoap12">
    <soap12:address
    location="http://localhost/WebServicesViaSoap/EmployeeInfo.asmx" />
  </port>
</service>

</definitions>
```

A WSDL document, like all XML documents, has a single outermost element called the document element. The document element of a WSDL document is named `<definitions>`. This element contains the following child elements: `<types>`, `<message>`, `<portType>`, `<binding>`, and `<service>`. These child elements are discussed in the following sections.

Complete coverage of the WSDL markup language and WSDL documents is beyond the scope of this book. This chapter covers only the aspects of WSDL markup language and WSDL documents that relate specifically to the chapter topic.

Argument Names, Types, and Order

The `<types>` section of the WSDL document shown in the following excerpt from Listing 13-2 uses an XML schema `<element>` element with the `name` attribute value of `GetEmployeeInfo` to describe the names, types, and order of the arguments of the XML Web service's `GetEmployeeInfo` method:

```
    <s:element name="GetEmployeeInfo">
      <s:complexType>
        <s:sequence>
          <s:element minOccurs="0" maxOccurs="1" name="username"
          type="s:string" />
          <s:element minOccurs="0" maxOccurs="1" name="password"
          type="s:string" />
        </s:sequence>
      </s:complexType>
    </s:element>
```

This `<element>` element contains a `<sequence>` element, which in turn contains two `<element>` elements. The `<sequence>` element is used to specify the order of the arguments of the method, and the two `<element>` elements are used to specify the names and types of the arguments. The order of the two `<element>` elements within the `<sequence>` element determines the order of the method's arguments. The `name` and `type` attributes of each `<element>` element determine the name and type of the respective argument of the method.

Return Value Types and Order

The `<types>` section of the WSDL document shown in the following excerpt from Listing 13-2 uses an `<element>` element with the `name` attribute value of `GetEmployeeInfoResponse` to describe the names, types, and order of the return values of the XML Web service's `GetEmployeeInfo` method:

```
    <s:element name="GetEmployeeInfoResponse">
      <s:complexType>
        <s:sequence>
          <s:element minOccurs="0" maxOccurs="1" name="GetEmployeeInfoResult"
          type="s:string" />
        </s:sequence>
      </s:complexType>
    </s:element>
```

This `<element>` element contains a `<sequence>` element, which in turn contains an `<element>` element. The `<sequence>` element specifies the order of the return values of the method. Because the `GetEmployeeInfo` method returns a single value, the order is not an issue. The `type` attribute of the `<element>` element specifies the `GetEmployeeInfo` method's return value type.

Describing the Method

In a non-distributed environment, invoking the `GetEmployeeInfo` method is considered a single action, where the caller passes two string values as the arguments of the method and receives a string value as the return value. However, in a distributed environment, invoking the `GetEmployeeInfo` method is simulated through the exchange of two messages: a request message and a response message. The request message contains the two input string values, and the response message is the return string value.

The WSDL document shown in Listing 13-2 uses a `<message>` element with the `name` attribute value of `GetEmployeeInfoSoapIn` to represent the request message, and a `<part>` element to represent the content of the message. As previously discussed, the content of the request message is just the two input string values, and the WSDL document's `<types>` section uses an `<element>` element with the `name` attribute value of `GetEmployeeInfo` to describe the names, types, and order of the `GetEmployeeInfo` method's arguments.Therefore, the `<part>` element simply references this `<element>` element of the `<types>` section. This reference is assigned to the element attribute of the `<part>` element as follows:

```
<message name="GetEmployeeInfoSoapIn">
  <part name="parameters" element="tns:GetEmployeeInfo" />
</message>
```

The WSDL document uses a `<message>` element with the name attribute value of GetEmployeeInfoSoapOut to represent the response message, and a `<part>` element to represent the content of the message. As previously discussed, the response message is the return value of the GetEmployeeInfo method, and the `<types>` section uses an `<element>` element with the name attribute value of GetEmployeeInfoResponse to describe the GetEmployeeInfo method's return value type. Therefore, the `<part>` element simply references this `<element>` element of the `<types>` section, as follows:

```
<message name="GetEmployeeInfoSoapOut">
  <part name="parameters" element="tns:GetEmployeeInfoResponse" />
</message>
```

These two `<message>` elements define the two messages that simulate the GetEmployeeInfo method. The WSDL document shown in Listing 13-2 uses an `<operation>` element with the name attribute value of GetEmployeeInfo to represent the GetEmployeeInfo method itself, and the `<input>` and `<output>` elements to represent the contents of the GetEmployeeInfo method. Because the content of the GetEmployeeInfo method is just the request and response messages that simulate the method, the `<input>` and `<output>` elements simply refer to the respective request and response messages as follows:

```
<portType name="EmployeeInfoSoap">
  <operation name="GetEmployeeInfo">
    <input message="tns:GetEmployeeInfoSoapIn" />
    <output message="tns:GetEmployeeInfoSoapOut" />
  </operation>
</portType>
```

Notice that the `<operation>` element is the child element of the `<portType>` element. The `<portType>` element is used to group different methods of the XML Web service when the XML Web service exposes numerous methods. This doesn't apply to this example because the XML Web service exposes a single method.

Describing the Communication Protocol for Accessing the Method

The WSDL document uses the `<binding>` element to describe the communication protocol and message format that clients must use to access the GetEmployeeInfo method, as shown in the following excerpt from Listing 13-2:

```
<binding name="EmployeeInfoSoap12" type="tns:EmployeeInfoSoap">
  <soap12:binding transport="http://schemas.xmlsoap.org/soap/http" />
  <operation name="GetEmployeeInfo">
    <soap12:operation soapAction="http://www.employees/GetEmployeeInfo"
      style="document" />
    <input>
      <soap12:body use="literal" />
    </input>
```

```
      <output>
        <soap12:body use="literal" />
      </output>
    </operation>
  </binding>
```

The WSDL document uses the `<portType>` element to group the related methods of the XML Web service. Grouping is very useful when it comes to defining the communication protocol. It wouldn't make sense to force the clients of the XML Web service to use different communication protocols to access different methods of the same group. That's why the WSDL document defines a single communication protocol to access all methods in the same `portType`. The `type` attribute of the `<binding>` element refers to the `<portType>` element for which the communication protocol is defined.

The WSDL document uses the `<soap12:binding>` element to specify that its clients must use SOAP 1.2 messages to access the methods of the respective `portType`. The `transport` attribute of the `<soap12:binding>` element specifies that SOAP messages must be exchanged via HTTP protocol. The `style` attribute of the `<soap12:binding>` element specifies that SOAP messages must use document style instead of RPC style.

The `<soap12:binding>` element specifies the settings that apply to all methods of the respective `portType`. However, there are some settings that are method-specific. For example, XML Web services assign a unique string `id` to each method for identification purposes. The `SOAPAction` header of the respective HTTP message is normally set to the unique string id of the respective method.

The WSDL document uses an `<operation>` element to represent a method. The operation element that represents the `GetEmployeeInfo` method is reused in the `<binding>` element to set the appropriate parameters of the method.

The `<soap12:operation>` element is used to set the parameters of a given method of the XML Web service. The `soapAction` attribute of the `<soap12:operation>` element is set to the unique string id that uniquely identifies the method among other methods of the XML Web service. The `style` attribute overrides the `style` setting of the `<soap12:binding>` element.

The `<soap12:operation>` element specifies the settings that apply to the entire method. However, the `GetEmployeeInfo` method consists of two messages. The `<soap12:body>` element allows you to set the parameters that apply to individual messages. The WSDL document uses a `<part>` element to specify the content of a message. The `use` attribute of the `<soap12:body>` element is set to `"literal"` to signal that the content of the message is literally the content of the `<part>` element, and there is no need for further encoding.

Specifying the Site for Method Access

The WSDL document uses the `<port>` element to specify the URL of the site where clients access the method, as shown in the following excerpt from Listing 13-2:

```
<port name="EmployeeInfoSoap12" binding="tns:EmployeeInfoSoap12">
  <soap12:address
  location="http://localhost/WebServicesViaSoap/EmployeeInfo.asmx" />
</port>
```

The `binding` attribute of the `<port>` element refers to the `<binding>` element that describes the communication protocol clients must use to access the method. Because the `<binding>` element defines the communication protocol for a `portType` (a group of methods), the `<port>` element specifies the URL of the site from which all the methods of a given `portType` can be accessed. It would not make much sense to force users to access different methods of the same group from different sites. The `location` attribute of the `<soap12:address>` element determines the URL of the site where the clients can access the method. The same `<port>` element may contain more than one `<soap12:address>` element. This means that the same method may be accessed from different sites.

Specifying the Method Class

The WSDL document uses the `name` attribute of the `<service>` element to specify the name of the class (from the client perspective to be exact) that the method belongs to, as shown in the following excerpt from Listing 13-2:

```
<service name="EmployeeInfo">
  <port name="EmployeeInfoSoap12" binding="tns:EmployeeInfoSoap12">
    <soap12:address
location="http://localhost/WebServicesViaSoap/EmployeeInfo.asmx" />
  </port>
</service>
```

SOAP Messages

XML Web services and their clients exchange data through messages known as SOAP messages. A SOAP message is an XML document that uses the SOAP XML markup language to describe the data being exchanged. A SOAP message, like any other XML document, has a single element known as the document element. The document element in a SOAP message is an XML element named `<Envelope>`. This document element contains an optional child element named `<Header>` and a mandatory child element named `<Body>`. The `<Envelope>`, `<Header>`, and `<Body>` elements belong to the `http://schemas.xmlsoap.org/soap/envelope/` namespace.

If you click the `GetEmployeeInfo` link previously shown in Figure 13-1, it takes you to a page that contains Listings 13-3 and 13-4. Listing 13-3 shows the HTTP request message, which is the HTTP message that the client of the `EmployeeInfo` Web service must send to the Web service to invoke its `GetEmployeeInfo` method. Listing 13-4 shows the HTTP response message, which is the HTTP message that the Web service sends to clients in response to the HTTP request message.

Listing 13-3: The HTTP Request Message

```
POST /WebServicesViaSoap/EmployeeInfo.asmx HTTP/1.1
Host: localhost
Content-Type: application/soap+xml; charset=utf-8
Content-Length: length

<?xml version="1.0" encoding="utf-8"?>
<soap12:Envelope xmlns:xsi="http://www.w3.org/2001/XMLSchema-instance"
xmlns:xsd="http://www.w3.org/2001/XMLSchema"
xmlns:soap12="http://www.w3.org/2003/05/soap-envelope">
```

```
    <soap12:Body>
      <GetEmployeeInfo xmlns="http://www.employees/">
        <username>
          String
        </username>
        <password>
          String
        </password>
      </GetEmployeeInfo>
    </soap12:Body>
</soap12:Envelope>
```

Listing 13-4: The HTTP Response Message

```
HTTP/1.1 200 OK
Content-Type: application/soap+xml; charset=utf-8
Content-Length: length

<?xml version="1.0" encoding="utf-8"?>
<soap12:Envelope xmlns:xsi="http://www.w3.org/2001/XMLSchema-instance"
xmlns:xsd="http://www.w3.org/2001/XMLSchema"
xmlns:soap12="http://www.w3.org/2003/05/soap-envelope">
  <soap12:Body>
    <GetEmployeeInfoResponse xmlns="http://www.employees/">
      <GetEmployeeInfoResult>string</GetEmployeeInfoResult>
    </GetEmployeeInfoResponse>
  </soap12:Body>
</soap12:Envelope>
```

Here is a question for you: What is the relationship between the WSDL document shown previously in Listing 13-2 and the HTTP request and response messages shown in Listings 13-3 and 13-4? Here is another related question: Does this mean that every time you want to know what type of HTTP request message a Web service expects to receive from its clients and what type of HTTP response message the clients of a Web service should expect to receive from the Web service, you have to run the Web service in Visual Studio as you did for the `EmployeeInfo` Web service to access a page similar to the page shown in Figure 13-1, and from there go to the page that contains the HTTP request and response messages? When you click the `GetEmployeeInfo` link shown in Figure 13-1 to go to the page that displays the formats of the HTTP request and response messages, how does this page figure out what these formats are? And how did this page know that the client and Web service must use the HTTP protocol to communicate with one another?

The answer to all these questions is the WSDL document. The page parses the WSDL document to find out what communication protocol must be used and what the format of the request and response message should be. Here's how it works. The `transport` attribute of the `<binding>` element's `<soap12:binding>` child element tells you that the client and Web service must use SOAP over HTTP to communicate with one another, as shown in the boldface portion of the following excerpt from Listing 13-2:

```
<binding name="EmployeeInfoSoap12" type="tns:EmployeeInfoSoap">
  <soap12:binding transport="http://schemas.xmlsoap.org/soap/http" />
  <operation name="GetEmployeeInfo">
    <soap12:operation soapAction="http://www.employees/GetEmployeeInfo"
      style="document" />
```

(continued)

(continued)

```
        <input>
          <soap12:body use="literal" />
        </input>
        <output>
          <soap12:body use="literal" />
        </output>
      </operation>
    </binding>
```

Next, let's discuss the HTTP request message shown in Listing 13-3. This HTTP request message, like any other HTTP message, has two main parts: header and body. The header of the message consists of the following four lines:

❑   The first line specifies the virtual path of the Web service on the server:

```
POST /WebServicesViaSoap/EmployeeInfo.asmx HTTP/1.1
```

This virtual path information comes from the WSDL document. First, you search the WSDL document for the `<service>` element with the same `name` attribute value as the Web service itself, which is `EmployeeInfo`, as shown in the following excerpt from Listing 13-2:

```
<service name="EmployeeInfo">
      <port name="EmployeeInfoSoap12" binding="tns:EmployeeInfoSoap12">
        <soap12:address
location="http://localhost/WebServicesViaSoap/EmployeeInfo.asmx" />
      </port>
  </service>
```

The `location` attribute of the `<soap12:address>` child element specifies the virtual path of the Web service on the server as you can see in the boldface portion of the code excerpt.

❑   The second line specifies the hostname or host IP address of the server where the Web service is located:

```
Host: localhost
```

This hostname information comes from the WSDL document. First, you search the WSDL document for the `<service>` element with the same `name` attribute value as the Web service itself, which is `EmployeeInfo`, as shown in the following excerpt from Listing 13-2:

```
<service name="EmployeeInfo">
      <port name="EmployeeInfoSoap12" binding="tns:EmployeeInfoSoap12">
        <soap12:address
location="http://localhost/WebServicesViaSoap/EmployeeInfo.asmx" />
      </port>
  </service>
```

The `location` attribute of the `<soap12:address>` child element specifies the server hostname as you can see in the lower boldface portion of the code excerpt.

❑   The third line specifies the content type of the HTTP message body. Because the body of this message contains a SOAP message, the content type is set to `application/soap+xml`:

```
Content-Type: application/soap+xml; charset=utf-8
```

❏ The fourth line specifies the length (in bytes) of the message body:

```
Content-Length: length
```

The body of the HTTP request message shown in Listing 13-3 contains a SOAP message. This SOAP message is an XML document with the `<Envelope>` document element that contains a `<Body>` child element. Note that the `<Body>` child element contains the following XML fragment:

```
<GetEmployeeInfo xmlns="http://www.employees/">
  <username>string</username>
  <password>string</password>
</GetEmployeeInfo>
```

The outermost XML element of this XML fragment has the same name as the Web method being invoked, which is the `GetEmployeeInfo` method. The body of the `<GetEmployeeInfo>` element contains two elements with the same names as the parameters of the method being invoked: `username` and `password`. The string within the opening and closing tags of the `<username>` and `<password>` elements specify the values being passed into the `GetEmployeeInfo` method.

Listing 13-4 contains the HTTP response message that the `EmployeeInfo` Web service sends back to the client in response to the HTTP request message shown in Listing 13-3. The HTTP response message has two parts: header and body. The header consists of the following three lines:

❏ The first line consists of three parts:

  ❏ The first part specifies the version of the HTTP protocol that the server supports, which is version 1.1 in this case.

  ❏ The second part specifies the HTTP response status code, which is `200` in this case. A status code value of `200` signals that no error occurred on the server side.

  ❏ The third part specifies the HTTP response status text, which is `OK` in this case.

❏ The second line specifies the content type of the response message body. Because the body of the response message is a SOAP message, the content type is set to `application/soap+xml`:

```
Content-Type: application/soap+xml; charset=utf-8
```

❏ The third line specifies the length (in bytes) of the response message body.

The body of the HTTP response message shown in Listing 13-4 contains a SOAP message. Note that the `<Body>` of this SOAP message contains the following XML fragment:

```
<GetEmployeeInfoResponse xmlns="http://www.employees/">
  <GetEmployeeInfoResult>string</GetEmployeeInfoResult>
</GetEmployeeInfoResponse>
```

This XML fragment contains a child XML element named `<GetEmployeeInfoResult>` that encapsulates the return value of the `GetEmployeeInfo` method of the Web service.

All the information about the method, its parameters, and return value also comes from the WSDL document. First, you search the WSDL document shown in Listing 13-2 for the `<service>` element with the same name attribute value as the Web service itself, which is EmployeeInfo:

```
<service name="EmployeeInfo">

    . . .
</service>
```

Next, you retrieve the binding attribute value of the `<service>` element's `<port>` child element:

```
<service name="EmployeeInfo">

    <port binding="tns:EmployeeInfoSoap12"

        name="EmployeeInfoSoap12">
            <soap12:address
location="http://localhost/WebServicesViaSoap/EmployeeInfo.asmx" />
        </port>
    </service>
```

Then, you search the WSDL document for the `<binding>` element whose name is given by the binding attribute value of the `<port>` child element:

```
<binding name="EmployeeInfoSoap12"

    type="tns:EmployeeInfoSoap">
    . . .
</binding>
```

Next, you retrieve type attribute value of the `<binding>` element and the name attribute value of its child `<operation>` element:

```
<binding name="EmployeeInfoSoap12"

    type="tns:EmployeeInfoSoap">

    <soap12:binding transport="http://schemas.xmlsoap.org/soap/http" />

    <operation name="GetEmployeeInfo">

        . . .
    </operation>
</binding>
```

As you can see, the name attribute value of this child `<operation>` element is just the name of the Web method, GetEmployeeInfo.

Now that you know the name of the method, you need to get information about this method's parameters. For that, you first search the WSDL document for the `<portType>` whose name attribute value is given by the type attribute value of the `<binding>` element, and then you search for the `<operation>`

child element of this `<portType>` whose name attribute value is given by the name attribute value of the `<binding>` element's `<operation>` child element:

```
<portType name="EmployeeInfoSoap">
  <operation name="GetEmployeeInfo">

    . . .
  </operation>
</portType>
```

Next, you retrieve the values of the message attributes of the `<input>` and `<output>` child elements of the `<operation>` element:

```
<portType name="EmployeeInfoSoap">
  <operation name="GetEmployeeInfo">

    <input message="tns:GetEmployeeInfoSoapIn" />
    <output message="tns:GetEmployeeInfoSoapOut" />

  </operation>
</portType>
```

Next, you search the WSDL document for the `<message>` elements whose name attribute values are given by the values of the message attributes of the `<input>` and `<output>` child elements:

```
<message name="GetEmployeeInfoSoapIn">

  . . .
</message>
```

```
<message name="GetEmployeeInfoSoapOut">

  . . .
</message>
```

Then, you retrieve the values of the element attributes of the `<part>` child elements of the two `<message>` elements:

```
<message name="GetEmployeeInfoSoapIn">

  <part element="tns:GetEmployeeInfo"

  name="parameters" />
</message>
<message name="GetEmployeeInfoSoapOut">

  <part element="tns:GetEmployeeInfoResponse"

  name="parameters" />
</message>
```

Next, you search the `<types>` section of the WSDL document for `<element>` elements with same `name` attribute values as the `element` attribute values of the two `<part>` child elements:

```
<s:element name="GetEmployeeInfo">
  <s:complexType>
    <s:sequence>
      <s:element minOccurs="0" maxOccurs="1" name="username"
       type="s:string" />
      <s:element minOccurs="0" maxOccurs="1" name="password"
       type="s:string" />
    </s:sequence>
  </s:complexType>
</s:element>

<s:element name="GetEmployeeInfoResponse">
  <s:complexType>
    <s:sequence>
      <s:element minOccurs="0" maxOccurs="1" name="GetEmployeeInfoResult"
       type="s:string" />
    </s:sequence>
  </s:complexType>
</s:element>
```

The two `<element>` elements define the schemas of the XML fragment enclosed within the opening and closing tags of the `<Body>` element of the request and response SOAP messages:

```
<GetEmployeeInfo xmlns="http://www.employees/">
  <username>string</username>
  <password>string</password>
</GetEmployeeInfo>

<GetEmployeeInfoResponse xmlns="http://www.employees/">
  <GetEmployeeInfoResult>string</GetEmployeeInfoResult>
</GetEmployeeInfoResponse>
```

As you can see, you can write client-side code that does the following:

1. It uses `WebRequest`, `WebRequestExecutor`, and `WebRequestManager` to download the WSDL document from the server and load it into an XMLDOM document.

2. It uses the methods and properties of the `XMLDOM` class to search the WSDL document as just discussed to determine the format of the SOAP request and response messages.

3. It uses `WebRequest`, `WebRequestExecutor`, and `WebRequestManager` to send the HTTP request to the server and receive the HTTP response from the server.

To keep this discussion focused, let's skip the implementation of the first two steps and use Listings 13-3 and 13-4 to implement the third step. In this step, `WebRequest`, `WebRequestExecutor`, and `WebRequestManager` are used to send a SOAP request message over HTTP to the server and receive a SOAP response message over HTTP from the server, as shown in Listing 13-5.

Listing 13-5: A Page that Exchanges SOAP Messages with the Web Service

```
<%@ Page Language="C#" %>

<!DOCTYPE html PUBLIC "-//W3C//DTD XHTML 1.0 Transitional//EN"
"http://www.w3.org/TR/xhtml1/DTD/xhtml1-transitional.dtd">

<html xmlns="http://www.w3.org/1999/xhtml">
<head id="Head1" runat="server">
  <title>Untitled Page</title>
  <script type="text/javascript" language="javascript">
    function invokingRequestCallback(sender, args)
    {
      var request = args.get_webRequest();
      var builder = new Sys.StringBuilder();
      builder.append("Default request timeout: ");
      builder.append(sender.get_defaultTimeout());
      builder.append("\r\n\r\nDefault executor type: ");
      builder.append(sender.get_defaultExecutorType());
      builder.append("\r\n\r\nTarget URL: ");
      builder.append(request.get_url());
      builder.append("\r\n\r\nHTTP verb: ");
      builder.append(request.get_httpVerb());
      builder.append("\r\n\r\nRequest body: ");
      builder.append(request.get_body());
      builder.append("\r\n\r\nRequest timeout: ");
      builder.append(request.get_timeout());
      builder.append("\r\n\r\nRequest headers: ");
      var headers = request.get_headers();
      for(var header in headers)
      {
        builder.append("\r\n\t");
        builder.append(header);
        builder.append(": ");
        builder.append(headers[header]);
      }
      builder.append("\r\n\r\nClick the Cancel button to cancel the request or OK
                    button to submit the request.");

      var result = Sys.Preview.UI.Window.messageBox(builder.toString(),
                                     Sys.Preview.UI.MessageBoxStyle.OKCancel);

      if (result == Sys.Preview.UI.DialogResult.Cancel)
        args.set_cancel(true);
    }

    function completedCallback(sender, eventArgs)
    {
      if (sender.get_timedOut())
      {
        alert("Request timed out!");
        return;
      }
```

(continued)

Listing 13-5 *(continued)*

```javascript
        if (sender.get_aborted())
        {
          alert("Request aborted!");
          return;
        }

        if (sender.get_statusCode() !== 200)
        {
          alert("Error occured!");
          return;
        }

        var reply2 = sender.get_xml();
        var nodes = reply2.getElementsByTagName("GetEmployeeInfoResult");
        var reply = nodes[0].firstChild.nodeValue ;

        var delimiter = "|";
        var replyIndex = 0;
        var delimiterIndex;

        var employeeinfotable = $get("employeeinfo");
        employeeinfotable.style.visibility = "visible";

        delimiterIndex = reply.indexOf(delimiter, replyIndex);
        var firstname = reply.substring(replyIndex, delimiterIndex);
        var firstnamespan = $get("firstname");
        firstnamespan.innerText = firstname;
        replyIndex = delimiterIndex + 1;

        delimiterIndex = reply.indexOf(delimiter, replyIndex);
        var lastname = reply.substring(replyIndex, delimiterIndex);
        var lastnamespan = $get("lastname");
        lastnamespan.innerText = lastname;
        replyIndex = delimiterIndex + 1;

        delimiterIndex = reply.indexOf(delimiter, replyIndex);
        var employeeid = reply.substring(replyIndex, delimiterIndex);
        var employeeidspan = $get("employeeid");
        employeeidspan.innerText = employeeid;
        replyIndex = delimiterIndex + 1;

        delimiterIndex = reply.indexOf(delimiter, replyIndex);
        var departmentname = reply.substring(replyIndex, delimiterIndex);
        var departmentnamespan = $get("departmentname");
        departmentnamespan.innerText = departmentname;
      }

      function submitCallback(evt)
      {
        var usernametbx = $get("usernametbx");
        var passwordtbx = $get("passwordtbx");
```

```
        var requestBodyBuilder = new Sys.StringBuilder();

        requestBodyBuilder.append('<?xml version="1.0" encoding="utf-8"?>');
        requestBodyBuilder.append('<soap12:Envelope ');
        requestBodyBuilder.append(
                        'xmlns:xsi="http://www.w3.org/2001/XMLSchema-instance" ');
        requestBodyBuilder.append('xmlns:xsd="http://www.w3.org/2001/XMLSchema" ');
        requestBodyBuilder.append(
                        'xmlns:soap12="http://www.w3.org/2003/05/soap-envelope">');
        requestBodyBuilder.append('<soap12:Body>');
        requestBodyBuilder.append('<GetEmployeeInfo xmlns="http://www.employees/">');
        requestBodyBuilder.append('<username>');
        requestBodyBuilder.append(usernametbx.value);
        requestBodyBuilder.append('</username>');
        requestBodyBuilder.append('<password>');
        requestBodyBuilder.append(passwordtbx.value);
        requestBodyBuilder.append('</password>');
        requestBodyBuilder.append('</GetEmployeeInfo>');
        requestBodyBuilder.append('</soap12:Body>');
        requestBodyBuilder.append('</soap12:Envelope>');

        var requestBody = requestBodyBuilder.toString();
        var request = new Sys.Net.WebRequest();
        request.set_timeout(70000);
        request.set_httpVerb("POST");
        request.set_url("EmployeeInfo.asmx");
        request.get_headers()['Content-Type'] =
                'application/soap+xml; charset=utf-8';
        request.get_headers()['Content-Length'] = requestBody.length;
        request.set_body(requestBody);
        request.invoke();
    }

    function pageLoad()
    {
        var submitbtn = $get("submitbtn");
        $addHandler(submitbtn, "click", submitCallback);
        Sys.Net.WebRequestManager.set_defaultTimeout(90000);
        Sys.Net.WebRequestManager.set_defaultExecutorType("Sys.Net.XMLHttpExecutor");
        Sys.Net.WebRequestManager.add_invokingRequest(invokingRequestCallback);
        Sys.Net.WebRequestManager.add_completedRequest(completedCallback);
    }
  </script>
</head>
<body>
  <form id="form1" runat="server">
    <asp:ScriptManager ID="ScriptManager1" runat="server">
    <Scripts>
      <asp:ScriptReference Assembly="Microsoft.Web.Preview"
      Name="PreviewScript.js" />
    </Scripts>
```

(continued)

Listing 13-5 (continued)

```
    </asp:ScriptManager>
    <strong>Username: </strong><asp:TextBox runat="server" ID="usernametbx" />
    <br />
    <strong>Password:  </strong><asp:TextBox runat="server" ID="passwordtbx"
                                TextMode="Password" />
     <br />
    <button id="submitbtn" type="button">Submit</button><br /><br />
    <table id="employeeinfo" style="background-color:LightGoldenrodYellow;
                                border-color:Tan; border-width:1px;
                                color:Black; visibility:hidden"
                                cellpadding="2">
      <tr style="background-color:Tan; font-weight:bold">
        <th colspan="2">Your Information</th>
      </tr>
      <tr>
        <td style=" font-weight:bold">First Name</td>
        <td><span id="firstname" /></td>
      </tr>

       <tr style="background-color:PaleGoldenrod">
        <td style=" font-weight:bold">Last Name</td>
        <td><span id="lastname" /></td>
      </tr>

      <tr>
        <td style=" font-weight:bold">Employee ID</td>
        <td><span id="employeeid" /></td>
      </tr>

      <tr style="background-color:PaleGoldenrod">
        <td style=" font-weight:bold">Department</td>
        <td><span id="departmentname" /></td>
      </tr>
    </table>

  </form>
</body>
</html>
```

First, let's walk through the implementation of the `submitCallback` JavaScript function. The page shown in Listing 13-5 registers this JavaScript function as an event handler for the `click` event of the Submit button.

The `submitCallback` function first instantiates a `StringBuilder` that will be used to create the string that contains the body of the HTTP request message:

```
    var requestBodyBuilder = new Sys.StringBuilder();
```

As you can see in the following excerpt from Listing 13-3, the body of the request begins with the xml declaration:

```
<?xml version="1.0" encoding="utf-8"?>
```

As such, this xml declaration is the first line that submitCallback adds to the StringBuilder:

```
requestBodyBuilder.append('<?xml version="1.0" encoding="utf-8"?>');
```

The second line in Listing 13-3 (shown again in the following excerpt) is the opening tag of the Envelope XML element and its attributes:

```
<soap12:Envelope xmlns:xsi="http://www.w3.org/2001/XMLSchema-instance"
xmlns:xsd="http://www.w3.org/2001/XMLSchema"
xmlns:soap12="http://www.w3.org/2003/05/soap-envelope">
```

This element is the outermost element in a SOAP message, and as such, it's the next thing that submitCallback adds to the StringBuilder:

```
requestBodyBuilder.append('<soap12:Envelope ');
requestBodyBuilder.append(
                    'xmlns:xsi="http://www.w3.org/2001/XMLSchema-instance" ');
requestBodyBuilder.append('xmlns:xsd="http://www.w3.org/2001/XMLSchema" ');
requestBodyBuilder.append(
                    'xmlns:soap12="http://www.w3.org/2003/05/soap-envelope">');
```

The next line in Listing 13-3 (shown again in the following excerpt) is the opening tag of the SOAP request message's Body XML element:

```
<soap12:Body>
```

This element contains the body of the SOAP message. Therefore, it's the next line that submitCallback adds to the StringBuilder:

```
requestBodyBuilder.append('<soap12:Body>');
```

The next line in Listing 13-3 (shown again in the following excerpt) is the opening tag of the XML element that represents the Web method being invoked, which is the GetEmployeeInfo method in this case:

```
<GetEmployeeInfo xmlns="http://www.employees/">
```

As such, this is the next line that submitCallback adds to the StringBuilder:

```
requestBodyBuilder.append('<GetEmployeeInfo xmlns="http://www.employees/">');
```

The next line in Listing 13-3 (shown again in the following excerpt) is the opening tag of the XML element that represents the first parameter of the Web method being invoked, which is the username parameter in this case:

```
<username>
```

Therefore, this is the next line that `submitCallback` adds to the `StringBuilder`:

```
requestBodyBuilder.append('<username>');
```

The next line in Listing 13-3 is the string that contains the value of the `username` parameter of the `GetEmployeeInfo` Web method. Therefore, the `submitCallback` method first calls the `$get` JavaScript function to return a reference to the `username` text field and then calls the `value` property on this text field to access the value that the end user entered into the text field. The method then adds this value to the `StringBuilder`:

```
var usernametbx = $get("usernametbx");
requestBodyBuilder.append(usernametbx.value);
```

The next line in Listing 13-3 (shown again in the following excerpt) is the closing tag of the XML element that represents the first parameter of the Web method being invoked, which is the `username` parameter in this case:

```
</username>
```

As such, this is the next line that `submitCallback` adds to the `StringBuilder`:

```
requestBodyBuilder.append('</username>');
```

The next line in Listing 13-3 (shown again in the following excerpt) is the opening tag of the XML element that represents the second parameter of the Web method being invoked, which is the `password` parameter in this case:

```
<password>
```

Therefore, this is the next line that `submitCallback` adds to the `StringBuilder`:

```
requestBodyBuilder.append('<password>');
```

The next line in Listing 13-3 is the string that contains the value of the `GetEmployeeInfo` Web method's `password` parameter. Therefore, the `submitCallback` method first calls the `$get` JavaScript function to return a reference to the `password` text field, and then calls the `value` property on the text field to access the value that the end user entered into the text field. The method then adds this value to the `StringBuilder`:

```
var passwordtbx = $get("passwordtbx");
requestBodyBuilder.append(passwordtbx.value);
```

Next, `submitCallback` adds the closing tag of the XML element that represents the second parameter, the closing tag of the XML element that represents the `GetEmployeeInfo` Web method, the closing tags of the `Body` element, and finally the closing tag of the `Envelope` element, as shown in the following excerpt from Listing 13-3:

```
requestBodyBuilder.append('</password>');
requestBodyBuilder.append('</GetEmployeeInfo>');
requestBodyBuilder.append('</soap12:Body>');
requestBodyBuilder.append('</soap12:Envelope>');
```

Next, the submitCallback method stores the contents of the StringBuilder (which contains the body of the request being made to the server) into a local variable named requestBody StringBuilder:

```
var requestBody = requestBodyBuilder.toString();
```

Then, submitCallback instantiates a WebRequest object to represent the current request:

```
var request = new Sys.Net.WebRequest();
```

Next, submitCallback calls the set_timeout method on the WebRequest object to set the request timeout:

```
request.set_timeout(70000);
```

The header of the HTTP request message begins with the following line when the HTTP verb POST is used to submit the request to the server:

```
POST /WebServicesViaSoap/EmployeeInfo.asmx HTTP/1.1
```

Therefore, the submitCallback method calls the set_httpVerb method on the WebRequest object to specify that the HTTP verb POST must be used to submit the request to the server:

```
request.set_httpVerb("POST");
```

The first two header lines of the HTTP request message specify the virtual path of the Web service on the server and the hostname or IP address of the server, as shown in the following excerpt from Listing 13-3:

```
POST /WebServicesViaSoap/EmployeeInfo.asmx HTTP/1.1
Host: localhost
```

Therefore, the submitCallback method calls the set_url method on the WebRequest object to specify the hostname and the virtual path of the Web service on the host:

```
request.set_url("EmployeeInfo.asmx");
```

The third header line of the HTTP request message (shown in the following excerpt from Listing 13-3) specifies application/soap+xml as the content type for the body of the request because the body contains a SOAP message:

```
Content-Type: application/soap+xml; charset=utf-8
```

Therefore, the submitCallback method first calls the get_headers method on the WebRequest object to return a reference to the dictionary that contains the names and values of the request headers, and then assigns application/soap+xml as the value of the Content_Type header:

```
request.get_headers()['Content-Type'] = 'application/soap+xml; charset=utf-8';
```

The fourth header line of the HTTP request message in Listing 13-3 specifies the value of the Content-Length header. This header specifies the length (in bytes) of the body of the message.

The submitCallback method first calls the get_headers method again on the WebRequest object to return the dictionary that contains the names and values of the request headers, and then assigns the value of the length property of the requestBody local variable (which contains the entire SOAP message being sent to the server) as the Content-Length request header value:

```
request.get_headers()['Content-Length'] = requestBody.length;
```

Next, submitCallback calls the set_body method on the WebRequest object to specify the contents of the requestBody local variable as the body of the HTTP request being sent to the server:

```
request.set_body(requestBody);
```

Finally, the submitCallback method calls the invoke method on the WebRequest object to send the request to the server:

```
request.invoke();
```

When the server response finally arrives, the WebRequest object automatically invokes the completedCallback JavaScript function. The pageLoad method registers this function as an event handler for the requestCompleted event of the current WebRequestManager instance. This method begins by ensuring that the request hasn't timed out or aborted and no server error has occurred:

```
if (sender.get_timedOut())
{
  alert("Request timed out!");
  return;
}

if (sender.get_aborted())
{
  alert("Request aborted!");
  return;
}

if (sender.get_statusCode() !== 200)
{
  alert("Error occured!");
  return;
}
```

Next, the completedCallback method calls the get_xml method on the WebRequestExecutor object to return the XMLDOM document that contains the server response (shown previously in its entirety in Listing 13-4):

```
var reply2 = sender.get_xml();
```

As the following excerpt from Listing 13-4 shows, the return value of the `GetEmployeeInfo` method is encapsulated in an element named `<GetEmployeeInforResult>`:

```
<?xml version="1.0" encoding="utf-8"?>
<soap12:Envelope xmlns:xsi="http://www.w3.org/2001/XMLSchema-instance"
xmlns:xsd="http://www.w3.org/2001/XMLSchema"
xmlns:soap12="http://www.w3.org/2003/05/soap-envelope">
  <soap12:Body>
    <GetEmployeeInfoResponse xmlns="http://www.employees/">

      <GetEmployeeInfoResult>string</GetEmployeeInfoResult>

    </GetEmployeeInfoResponse>
  </soap12:Body>
</soap12:Envelope>
```

Therefore, the `completedCallback` method calls the `getElementsByTagName` method on this XMLDOM document to return a reference to the `<GetEmployeeInfoResult>` element:

```
var nodes = reply2.getElementsByTagName("GetEmployeeInfoResult");
```

Next, the `completedCallback` method accesses the reply string that the first child element of this element encapsulates:

```
var reply = nodes[0].firstChild.nodeValue ;
```

The rest of the implementation of the `completedCallback` method is just like the previous version of the `completedCallback` method.

The example used in this section assumed that you know the formats of the request and response messages. As discussed earlier, the WSDL document can be used to determine the formats of these messages. As a matter of fact, you can think of the WSDL document as a receipt for building SOAP messages that the Web service expects to receive from the client and that the client must expect to receive from the Web service. As thoroughly discussed earlier, you must parse the WSDL document to determine the formats of these messages.

Summary

This chapter showed you how to use the `WebRequest`, `WebRequestExecutor`, and `WebRequestManager` ASP.NET AJAX client classes to exchange SOAP messages with XML Web services. SOAP messages are not the only means of communication between Web services and their clients. Another very common client-server communication method uses JSON messages, which are discussed in the next chapter.

Consuming Web Services Via JSON Messages

As you saw in the previous chapter, you can use the XMLHttpExecutor, WebRequestManager, and WebRequest classes to make requests to the server. However, this approach requires you to write lot of code to make a request. The ASP.NET AJAX client-side framework includes a class named WebServiceProxy that encapsulates all the logic that uses the XMLHttpExecutor, WebRequestManager, and WebRequest classes to make a request to the server. This enables you to make a request with minimal time and effort. The downside of the WebServiceProxy approach is that it supports only JSON messages. If you need to use normal SOAP messages to communicate with a Web service, you have to use the techniques discussed in the previous chapter. This chapter begins by discussing the important members of the WebServiceProxy class.

WebServiceProxy

As you can see in Listing 14-1, the constructor of the WebServiceProxy class doesn't do anything.

Listing 14-1: The Constructor of the WebServiceProxy Class

```
Sys.Net.WebServiceProxy = function Sys$Net$WebServiceProxy() { }
Sys.Net.WebServiceProxy.registerClass('Sys.Net.WebServiceProxy');
```

Timeout

The WebServiceProxy class exposes a getter named get_timeout and a setter named set_timeout that enable you to get and set the request timeout, as shown in Listing 14-2.

Listing 14-2: Getting and Setting the Request Timeout

```
function Sys$Net$WebServiceProxy$set_timeout(value)
{
  this._timeout = value;
}

function Sys$Net$WebServiceProxy$get_timeout()
{
  return this._timeout;
}
```

Default Succeeded Callback

You call the set_defaultSucceededCallback method on the WebServiceProxy object to specify a JavaScript function as the default succeeded callback for Web requests (see Listing 14-3). As the name implies, this JavaScript function is automatically invoked when a request is completed successfully. You call the get_defaultSucceededCallback method on the WebServiceProxy object to return a reference to the JavaScript function registered as the default succeeded callback (see Listing 14-3).

Listing 14-3: Getting and Setting the Default Succeeded Callback

```
function Sys$Net$WebServiceProxy$set_defaultSucceededCallback(value)
{
  this._succeeded = value;
}

function Sys$Net$WebServiceProxy$get_defaultSucceededCallback()
{
  return this._succeeded;
}
```

Default Failed Callback

You can call the set_ defaultFailedCallback method on the WebServiceProxy object to specify a JavaScript function as the default failed callback for Web requests (see Listing 14-4). As the name suggests, this JavaScript function is automatically invoked when a request fails. Call the get_defaultFailedCallback method on the WebServiceProxy object to return a reference to the JavaScript function registered as the default failed callback (see Listing 14-4).

Listing 14-4: Getting and Setting the Default Failed Callback

```
function Sys$Net$WebServiceProxy$set_defaultFailedCallback(value)
{
  this._failed = value;
}

function Sys$Net$WebServiceProxy$get_defaultFailedCallback()
{
  return this._failed;
}
```

Path

Call the `set_path` method on the `WebServiceProxy` object to specify a URL as the target URL for Web requests (see Listing 14-5). Call the `get_path` method on the `WebServiceProxy` object to return the target URL (see Listing 14-5).

Listing 14-5: Getting and Setting the Path

```
function Sys$Net$WebServiceProxy$set_path(value)
{
  this._path = value;
}

function Sys$Net$WebServiceProxy$get_path()
{
  return this._path;
}
```

Invoking a Web Method

Invoking a Web method is at the heart of the `WebServiceProxy` class. The main responsibility of the `_invoke` method is to invoke the Web method with a specified name and parameter names and values that belong to a Web service with a specified URL. As you can see in Listing 14-6, the `_invoke` method takes the following parameters:

❑ `servicePath`: This parameter specifies the target URL for the Web service. For example, if you have a Web service named `Service.asmx` running locally on your machine, its service path is as follows:

```
http://localhost/Service.asmx
```

❑ `methodName`: This parameter is a string that contains the name of the Web method being invoked.

❑ `useGet`: This parameter is a Boolean value that specifies whether the request must be made using the GET HTTP verb.

❑ `params`: This parameter is a dictionary that contains the names and values of the parameters of the Web method being invoked.

❑ `onSuccess`: This optional parameter references a JavaScript function that will be called when the request completes successfully.

❑ `onFailure`: This optional parameter references a JavaScript function that will be called when the request fails.

❑ `userContext`: This optional parameter references a JavaScript object that will be passed into the JavaScript functions referenced by the `onSuccess` and `onFailure` parameters when they're invoked. This enables you to pass arbitrary information into the `_invoke` method for retrieval when these JavaScript functions are called. The type of this information depends on the specifics of your application. The `WebServiceProxy` class does not do anything with the user context. It simply keeps it somewhere and passes it into the JavaScript functions referenced by the `onSuccess` and `onFailure` parameters when they're invoked.

Listing 14-6: The _invoke Method

```
function Sys$Net$WebServiceProxy$_invoke(servicePath, methodName, useGet,
                                          params, onSuccess, onFailure, userContext)
{
  if (onSuccess === null || typeof onSuccess === 'undefined')
    onSuccess = this.get_defaultSucceededCallback();

  if (onFailure === null || typeof onFailure === 'undefined')
    onFailure = this.get_defaultFailedCallback();

  if (userContext === null || typeof userContext === 'undefined')
    userContext = this.get_defaultUserContext();

  return Sys.Net.WebServiceProxy.invoke(servicePath, methodName, useGet, params,
                              onSuccess, onFailure, userContext, this.get_timeout());
}
```

Note that the _invoke method returns a reference to the WebRequest object that represents the request made to the Web service.

Now, let's walk through the implementation of the _invoke method. If no JavaScript function has been assigned to the onSuccess parameter as a succeeded callback, the _invoke method calls the get_defaultSucceededCallback method to return and use the JavaScript function registered as the default succeeded callback:

```
  if (onSuccess === null || typeof onSuccess === 'undefined')
    onSuccess = this.get_defaultSucceededCallback();
```

If no JavaScript function has been assigned to the onFailure parameter as a failed callback, the _invoke method calls the get_defaultFailedCallback method to return and use the JavaScript function registered as the default failed callback:

```
  if (onFailure === null || typeof onFailure === 'undefined')
    onFailure = this.get_defaultFailedCallback();
```

If no JavaScript object has been assigned to the userContext parameter, the _invoke method calls the get_defaultUserContext method to return and use the JavaScript object registered as the default user context:

```
  if (userContext === null || typeof userContext === 'undefined')
    userContext = this.get_defaultUserContext();
```

Finally, the _invoke method delegates the responsibility of invoking the Web method with a specified name and parameter names and values to the invoke static method of the WebServiceProxy class:

```
  return Sys.Net.WebServiceProxy.invoke(servicePath, methodName, useGet, params,
                              onSuccess, onFailure, userContext, this.get_timeout());
```

Note that the _invoke method passes the return value of the get_timeout method as the last parameter into the invoke method. This return value specifies the request timeout.

invoke

Listing 14-7 presents the internal implementation of the `WebServiceProxy` class's `invoke` static method.

Listing 14-7: The invoke Static Method of the WebServiceProxy Class

```
Sys.Net.WebServiceProxy.invoke =
function Sys$Net$WebServiceProxy$invoke(servicePath, methodName, useGet, params,
                                        onSuccess, onFailure, userContext, timeout)
{
  var request = new Sys.Net.WebRequest();

  request.get_headers()['Content-Type'] = 'application/json; charset=utf-8';
  if (!params)
    params = {};

  var urlParams = params;
  if (!useGet || !urlParams)
    urlParams = {};

  request.set_url(Sys.Net.WebRequest._createUrl(servicePath+"/"+methodName,
                                                urlParams));
  var body = null;
  if (!useGet)
  {
    body = Sys.Serialization.JavaScriptSerializer.serialize(params);

    if (body === "{}")
      body = "";
  }

  request.set_body(body);
  request.add_completed(onComplete);
  if (timeout && timeout > 0)
    request.set_timeout(timeout);

  request.invoke();

  function onComplete(response, eventArgs)
  {
    if (response.get_responseAvailable())
    {
      var statusCode = response.get_statusCode();
      var result = null;

      try
      {
        var contentType = response.getResponseHeader("Content-Type");
        if (contentType.startsWith("application/json"))
          result = response.get_object();

        else if (contentType.startsWith("text/xml"))
          result = response.get_xml();

        else
          result = response.get_responseData();
      }
```

(continued)

Listing 14-7 *(continued)*

```
    catch (ex)
    {
    }

    var error = response.getResponseHeader("jsonerror");
    var errorObj = (error === "true");
    if (errorObj)
      result = new Sys.Net.WebServiceError(false, result.Message,
                                           result.StackTrace,
                                           result.ExceptionType);

    if (((statusCode < 200) || (statusCode >= 300)) || errorObj)
    {
      if (onFailure)
      {
        if (!result || !errorObj)
          result = new Sys.Net.WebServiceError(false /*timedout*/,
              String.format(Sys.Res.webServiceFailedNoMsg, methodName), "", "");

        result._statusCode = statusCode;
        onFailure(result, userContext, methodName);
      }

      else
      {
        var error;
        if (result && errorObj)
          error = result.get_exceptionType() + "-- " + result.get_message();

        else
          error = response.get_responseData();

        alert(String.format(Sys.Res.webServiceFailed, methodName, error));
      }
    }

    else if (onSuccess)
      onSuccess(result, userContext, methodName);
  }

  else
  {
    var msg;
    if (response.get_timedOut())
      msg = String.format(Sys.Res.webServiceTimedOut, methodName);

    else
      msg = String.format(Sys.Res.webServiceFailedNoMsg, methodName)

    if (onFailure)
      onFailure(
              new Sys.Net.WebServiceError(response.get_timedOut(), msg, "", ""),
              userContext, methodName);
```

```
        else
           alert(msg);
      }
   }

   return request;
}
```

This method first instantiates a `WebRequest` object to represent the current Web request:

```
var request = new Sys.Net.WebRequest();
```

Next, it calls the `get_headers` method to return a reference to the dictionary that contains the names and values of the request headers, and assigns the string `'application/json; charset=utf-8'` as the value of the `Content-Type` request header:

```
request.get_headers()['Content-Type'] = 'application/json; charset=utf-8';
```

This value instructs the server that the body of the message contains a JSON object. As you'll see later, the server-side code uses a serializer to deserialize a .NET object from this JSON representation.

Next, it checks whether at least one of the following conditions are met:

❑   You're making a GET HTTP request to the server. As previously discussed, the third parameter passed into the invoke method is a Boolean that specifies whether the GET HTTP verb must be used.

❑   The Web method being invoked does not take any arguments.

If at least one of these conditions is met, the `invoke` method passes the dictionary that contains the names and values of the arguments of the Web method being invoked as the second argument to a method named `_createUrl`. If neither of the conditions is met, the `invoke` method passes an empty dictionary as the second argument.

The main responsibility of the `_createUrl` method is to create a URL that consists of the following two main parts:

❑   The URL part, which itself consists of two parts separated by the forward slash character (/), where the first part contains the service path (the target URL) of the Web service, and the second part contains the name of the Web method being invoked. As you can see in the following code excerpt from Listing 14-7, the Web method name is passed to the server as part of the URL.

❑   The query string part, which consists of query string parameters and their associated values, where each parameter and its associated value respectively contain the name and value of an argument of the Web method being invoked. As you can see in the following code excerpt from Listing 14-7, the names and values of the arguments of the Web method are passed to the server as a query string if at least one of the previously mentioned conditions is met.

```
var urlParams = params;
if (!useGet || !urlParams)
  urlParams = {};

var url = Sys.Net.WebRequest._createUrl(servicePath+"/"+methodName, urlParams);
```

Next, the `invoke` static method calls the `set_url` getter on the `WebRequest` object that represents the current request to specify the URL returned from the `_createUrl` method as the target URL of the request:

```
request.set_url(url);
```

Then, the `invoke` method checks the value of its third parameter to determine whether it must make a POST HTTP request to the server. If so, it invokes a static method named `serialize` on an ASP.NET AJAX class named `JavaScriptSerializer`, passing in the dictionary that contains the names and values of the arguments of the Web method being invoked to serialize this dictionary into a JSON object. It assigns this JSON object to a local variable named `body`, which contains the body of the POST HTTP request being made to the server.

```
var body = null;
if (!useGet)
{
  body = Sys.Serialization.JavaScriptSerializer.serialize(params);

  if (body === "{}")
    body = "";
}
```

Next, the `invoke` static method calls the `set_body` method on the `WebRequest` object that represents the current request, passing in the `body` local variable to set the body of the request:

```
request.set_body(body);
```

If the request is a GET HTTP request, the body is `null`. If the request is a POST HTTP request, the body contains the JSON representation of the names and values of the parameters of the Web method being invoked. In other words, the names and values of the parameters are passed as part of query string if the request is a GET HTTP request, and as part of the body of the request if the request is a POST HTTP request.

Next, the `invoke` static method calls the `add_completed` method on the `WebRequest` object that represents the current GET or POST HTTP request, to register a private JavaScript function named `onComplete` as an event handler for the completed event of the `WebRequest` object:

```
request.add_completed(onComplete);
```

This object raises its `completed` event when the request finally completes.

The `onComplete` function is private to the `invoke` static method and cannot be accessed from outside this method (discussed in more detail later in this chapter).

Next, the `invoke` static method calls the `set_timeout` method on the `WebRequest` object that represents the current GET or POST HTTP request to set the request timeout:

```
if (timeout && timeout > 0)
    request.set_timeout(timeout);
```

Finally, it calls the invoke method on the `WebRequest` object to make the request to the Web service:

```
request.invoke();
```

_createUrl

As Listing 14-8 shows the `_createUrl` static method of the `WebRequest` class takes the following two parameters:

❑ url: This parameter is a string that contains the target URL.

❑ queryString: This parameter is a dictionary that contains the names and values of parameters being sent to the server as a query string. For example, in the case of Listing 14-7, these parameters are the parameters of the Web method being invoked.

Listing 14-8 : The _createUrl Static Method of the WebRequest Class

```
Sys.Net.WebRequest._createUrl =
function Sys$Net$WebRequest$_createUrl(url, queryString)
{
  if (!queryString)
    return url;

  var qs = Sys.Net.WebRequest._createQueryString(queryString);
  if (qs.length > 0)
  {
    var sep = '?';
    if (url && url.indexOf('?') !== -1)
      sep = '&';
    return url + sep + qs;
  }

  else
    return url;
}
```

The `_createUrl` static method first calls the `_createQueryString` static method on the `WebRequest` class, passing in the dictionary that contains the names and values of the parameters being sent to the server as a query string:

```
var qs = Sys.Net.WebRequest._createQueryString(queryString);
```

As you'll see shortly, this static method builds and returns a valid query string out of the items in this dictionary.

Next, the `_createUrl` method checks whether the URL contains the required ? separator character, which separates a query string from its associated URL. If it does not contain this character, the `_createUrl` method adds it between the URL and the query string:

```
    var sep = '?';
    if (url && url.indexOf('?') !== -1)
      sep = '&';
    return url + sep + qs;
```

_createQueryString

Listing 14-9 presents the internal implementation of the `WebRequest` class's `_createQueryString` static method. As you can see, this method takes the following two parameters:

❑ `queryString`: This parameter references a dictionary that contains the names and values of the parameters to be embedded in the query string. In the case of Listing 14-7, this dictionary contains the names and values of the parameters of the Web method being invoked.

❑ `encodeMethod`: This parameter references a JavaScript function that takes a string as its parameter and encodes certain characters in the string.

Listing 14-9 : The _createQueryString Method of the WebRequest Class

```
Sys.Net.WebRequest._createQueryString =
function Sys$Net$WebRequest$_createQueryString(queryString, encodeMethod)
{
  if (!encodeMethod)
    encodeMethod = encodeURIComponent;

  var sb = new Sys.StringBuilder();

  var i = 0;
  for (var arg in queryString)
  {
    var obj = queryString[arg];
    if (typeof(obj) === "function")
      continue;

    var val = Sys.Serialization.JavaScriptSerializer.serialize(obj);
    if (i !== 0)
      sb.append('&');

    sb.append(arg);
    sb.append('=');
    sb.append(encodeMethod(val));

    i++;
  }

  return sb.toString();
}
```

The `_createQueryString` method first checks whether the caller has specified a value for the `encodeMethod` parameter. If not, it uses the JavaScript `encodeURIComponent` function as the encoding method:

```
  if (!encodeMethod)
    encodeMethod = encodeURIComponent;
```

The `encodeURIComponent` function takes a string as its parameter and replaces certain characters in the string with their UTF-8 encoding representations.

Next, the `_createQueryString` method creates a `StringBuilder` object:

```
var sb = new Sys.StringBuilder();
```

Then, it iterates through the items in the dictionary passed into it as its first argument and takes the following steps for each enumerated item (in the case of Listing 14-7, each enumerated item contains the name and value of a parameter of the Web method being invoked):

1. It uses the name of the enumerated item as an index into the dictionary to access the associated value of the parameter:

```
var obj = queryString[arg];
```

2. It calls the `serialize` static method of an ASP.NET AJAX class named `JavaScriptSerializer`, passing in the value of the parameter to serialize this value into its JSON representation:

```
var val = Sys.Serialization.JavaScriptSerializer.serialize(obj);
```

3. It calls the `append` method on the `StringBuilder` object to append the name of the parameter:

```
sb.append(arg);
```

4. It calls the `append` method on the `StringBuilder` object to append the = character:

```
sb.append('=');
```

5. It calls the `append` method again, this time to append the JSON representation of the value of the parameter:

```
sb.append(encodeMethod(val));
```

Finally, the `_createQueryString` method returns the content of the `StringBuilder` object to its caller:

```
return sb.toString();
```

In the case of Listing 14-7, the `_createQueryString` method creates a query string that contains the names and JSON representations of the values of the parameters of the Web method being invoked.

Regardless of whether the current request is a GET or POST HTTP request, the Web service must expect to receive the JSON representations of the parameter values of the Web method being invoked. It must also be able to deserialize these JSON representations into the objects of the types that the Web method expects before it passes these parameter values into the method. This requires some changes in the normal ASP.NET Web service–handling infrastructure to enable it to process requests coming from the ASP.NET AJAX applications, because the normal ASP.NET Web service handler expects to receive the names and values of the parameters of the Web method being invoked as part of the body of the SOAP message. They also expect to receive the SOAP representations of the values of these parameters, not their JSON representations. This is discussed in more detail later in this chapter.

onComplete

As you saw in Listing 14-7, the invoke static method of the `WebServiceProxy` class registers the `onComplete` private JavaScript function as the event handler for the `completed` event of the `WebRequest` object that represents the current request. Listing 14-10 shows the internal implementation of this function.

Listing 14-10: The onComplete Private JavaScript Function

```
function onComplete(response, eventArgs)
{
  if (response.get_responseAvailable())
  {
    var result = null;

    try
    {
      var contentType = response.getResponseHeader("Content-Type");
      if (contentType.startsWith("application/json"))
        result = response.get_object();

      else if (contentType.startsWith("text/xml"))
        result = response.get_xml();

      else
        result = response.get_responseData();
    }
    catch (ex) { }

    var error = response.getResponseHeader("jsonerror");
    var errorObj = (error === "true");
    if (errorObj)
      result = new Sys.Net.WebServiceError(false, result.Message,
                                           result.StackTrace,
                                           result.ExceptionType);

    var statusCode = response.get_statusCode();

    if (((statusCode < 200) || (statusCode >= 300)) || errorObj)
    {
      if (onFailure)
      {
        if (!result || !errorObj)
          result = new Sys.Net.WebServiceError(false /*timedout*/,
                String.format(Sys.Res.webServiceFailedNoMsg, methodName), "", "");

        result._statusCode = statusCode;
        onFailure(result, userContext, methodName);
      }

      else
      {
        var error;
        if (result && errorObj)
```

```
                    error = result.get_exceptionType() + "-- " + result.get_message();

                else
                    error = response.get_responseData();

                alert(String.format(Sys.Res.webServiceFailed, methodName, error));
            }
        }

        else if (onSuccess)
            onSuccess(result, userContext, methodName);
    }

    else
    {
        var msg;
        if (response.get_timedOut())
            msg = String.format(Sys.Res.webServiceTimedOut, methodName);

        else
            msg = String.format(Sys.Res.webServiceFailedNoMsg, methodName)

        if (onFailure)
            onFailure(
                    new Sys.Net.WebServiceError(response.get_timedOut(), msg, "", ""),
                    userContext, methodName);

        else
            alert(msg);
    }
}
```

When this function is invoked, two parameters are passed into it. The first parameter references the `WebRequestExecutor` object responsible for executing the current request. As discussed in the previous chapters, the completion of a request does not automatically mean that everything went fine and the server response has successfully arrived. Because the `completed` event could be raised for a number of reasons, the `onComplete` method must first determine what caused the `completed` event to fire (as does any method registered for a `WebRequest` object's `completed` event). The boldface portions of Listing 14-10 contain the code that makes this determination.

As you can see in the following excerpt from Listing 14-10, if the request has completed because something went wrong (for example, because the request timed out), the `onComplete` function invokes the `failure` JavaScript function if such a function has been specified. Otherwise, it simply calls the `alert` function to display the error massage in a pop-up box.

```
var msg;
if (response.get_timedOut())
 msg = String.format(Sys.Res.webServiceTimedOut, methodName);

else
  msg = String.format(Sys.Res.webServiceFailedNoMsg, methodName)
```

(continued)

```
    if (onFailure)
      onFailure(
              new Sys.Net.WebServiceError(response.get_timedOut(), msg, "", ""),
              userContext, methodName);

    else
      alert(msg);
```

If the request has completed because the server response has successfully arrived, the `onComplete`
function performs the following tasks:

1. It invokes the `getResponseHeader` method on the `WebRequestExecutor` object responsible for
executing the current request to return the value of the response header named `Content-Type`:

```
    var contentType = response.getResponseHeader("Content-Type");
```

2. If the value of the `Content-Type` response header starts with the string `"application/json"`,
the response contains a JSON object and, consequently, the `onComplete` method invokes the
`get_object` method on the `WebRequestExecutor` object to access this JSON object, and stores
the object in a local variable named `result`:

```
    if (contentType.startsWith("application/json"))
        result = response.get_object();
```

3. If the value of the `Content-Type` response header starts with the string `"text/xml"`, the
response contains an XML document and, consequently, the `onComplete` method calls the
`get_xml` method on the `WebRequestExecutor` object to access this XML document, and stores
this document in the `result` local variable:

```
      else if (contentType.startsWith("text/xml"))
          result = response.get_xml();
```

4. If the value of the `Content-Type` response header does not start with either the
`"application/json"` string or the `"text/xml"` string, the `onComplete` method calls the
`get_responseData` method on the `WebRequestExecutor` object to access the server response,
and stores it in the `result` local variable:

```
      else
          result = response.get_responseData();
```

Next, the `onComplete` method calls the `getResponseHeader` method on the `WebRequestExecutor`
object to return the value of a response header named `jsonerror`:

```
    var error = response.getResponseHeader("jsonerror");
```

If the server response contains this response header, and if the value of this header is the string
`"true"`, the response contains information about an error that occurred when the server was processing
the current request. The server response is stored in the `result` local variable, and the server uses the
`jsonerror` custom HTTP header to signal the `onComplete` method that the response contains
information about an error. This information includes the error message, stack trace, and exception type.
As the following excerpt from Listing 14-10 shows, the `onComplete` method creates an instance of a
class named `Sys.Net.WebServiceError`, passing in the error message, stack trace, and exception type,
and stores this instance in the `result` local variable:

548

```
var errorObj = (error === "true");
if (errorObj)
  result = new Sys.Net.WebServiceError(false, result.Message,
                                       result.StackTrace,
                                       result.ExceptionType);
```

Next, the invoke method calls the get_statusCode method on the WebRequestExecutor object to return the HTTP status code of the server response:

```
var statusCode = response.get_statusCode();
```

The method then checks whether at least one of the following conditions is met:

❏ The HTTP status code is less than 200, or greater than or equal to 300, which indicates that a server error has occurred.

❏ The server response contains a response header named jsonerror with a value of true.

Either of these conditions indicates a server error and, consequently, the invoke method takes the following steps to report the error:

1. If the onFailure parameter is not null, it means the caller of the invoke method has specified a JavaScript function as the value of this parameter. Consequently, the invoke method sets the _statusCode property of the result local variable to the server response's HTTP status code, and invokes the JavaScript function referenced by the onFailure parameter, passing in three parameters. The first parameter references the result local variable, the second parameter references the user context object, and the third parameter references the name of the Web method that was invoked:

```
result._statusCode = statusCode;
onFailure(result, userContext, methodName);
```

2. If the caller of the invoke method has not specified a value for the onFailure parameter, the method invokes the alert function to display the error message in a pop-up box:

```
alert(String.format(Sys.Res.webServiceFailed, methodName, error));
```

3. If the server response HTTP status code is a number equal to or greater than 200 but less than 300, this indicates that everything has gone fine on the server side and, consequently, the invoke method invokes the JavaScript function referenced by the onSuccess parameter (if any), passing in three parameters. The first parameter references the result local variable, the second parameter references the user context, and the third parameter contains the name of the Web method invoked:

```
else if (onSuccess)
  onSuccess(result, userContext, methodName);
```

Using WebServiceProxy

Listing 14-11 presents a page that uses the WebServiceProxy class. If you run this page, you'll get the result shown in Figure 14-1.

Listing 14-11: A Page that Uses the WebServiceProxy Class

```
<%@ Page Language="C#" %>

<!DOCTYPE html PUBLIC "-//W3C//DTD XHTML 1.0 Transitional//EN"
"http://www.w3.org/TR/xhtml1/DTD/xhtml1-transitional.dtd">
<html xmlns="http://www.w3.org/1999/xhtml">
<head runat="server">
  <title>Untitled Page</title>

  <script type="text/javascript" language="javascript">
    var request;

    function onSuccess(result, userContext, methodName)
    {
      userContext.innerHTML = "<b><u>" + result + "</b></u>";
    }

    function onFailure(result, userContext, methodName) { }

    function add()
    {
      var servicePath = "http://localhost/WebServicesViaJSON/Math.asmx";
      var methodName = "Add";
      var useGet = false;
      var xValue = $get("firstNumber").value;
      var yValue = $get("secondNumber").value;
      var params = {x : xValue, y : yValue};

      var userContext = $get("result");
      var webServiceProxy = new Sys.Net.WebServiceProxy();
      webServiceProxy.set_timeout(0);
      request = webServiceProxy._invoke(servicePath, methodName, useGet, params,
                                       onSuccess, onFailure, userContext);
    }
  </script>

</head>
<body>
  <form id="form1" runat="server">
    <asp:ScriptManager runat="server" ID="ScriptManager1" />
    <table>
      <tr>
        <td style="font-weight: bold" align="right">
          First Number:
        </td>
        <td align="left">
          <input type="text" id="firstNumber" /></td>
      </tr>
      <tr>
        <td style="font-weight: bold" align="right">
          Second Number:
        </td>
        <td align="left">
          <input type="text" id="secondNumber" /></td>
      </tr>
```

```
          <tr>
            <td colspan="2" align="center">
              <button onclick="add()">
                Add</button></td>
          </tr>
          <tr>
            <td style="font-weight: bold" align="right">
              Result:
            </td>
            <td align="left">
              <span id="result" />
            </td>
          </tr>
        </table>
      </form>
    </body>
  </html>
```

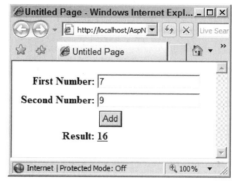

Figure 14-1

This page consists of two text boxes where the end user enters two numbers. When the user clicks the Add button, the page connects to the Web service shown in Listing 14-12 in asynchronous fashion, invokes its Add method, and uses DHTML to display the result of this method. The Web service is marked with the ScriptService metadata attribute, which enables it to process JSON messages from the client code. Without this metadata attribute, the Web service will act like a normal Web service, which responds only to SOAP messages.

Listing 14-12: The Web Service Used by Listing 14-11

```
<%@ WebService Language="C#" Class="MyNamespace.Math" %>

using System;
using System.Web;
using System.Web.Services;
using System.Web.Services.Protocols;
using System.Web.Script.Services;
```

(continued)

Listing 14-12 *(continued)*

```
namespace MyNamespace
{
  [WebService(Namespace = "http://tempuri.org/")]
  [WebServiceBinding(ConformsTo = WsiProfiles.BasicProfile1_1)]
  [ScriptService]
  public class Math
  {
    [WebMethod]
    public double Add(double x, double y)
    {
      return x + y;
    }
  }
}
```

Now let's walk through the implementation of the add JavaScript function. Note that Listing 14-11 registers this function as the event handler for the click event of the Add button.

The add function begins by instantiating an instance of the WebServiceProxy class:

```
var webServiceProxy = new Sys.Net.WebServiceProxy();
```

Next, it sets the request timeout:

```
webServiceProxy.set_timeout(0);
```

You must call set_timeout *to set the request timeout. Otherwise you'll get an error.*

Next, the add function specifies the parameters that you need to pass into the _invoke method of the WebServiceProxy instance. The first parameter is the service path, which is the URL where the Web service is located:

```
var servicePath = "http://localhost/WebServicesViaJSON/WebService.asmx";
```

The second parameter is the name of the Web method being invoked, which is the Add method in this case:

```
var methodName = "Add";
```

The third parameter is a Boolean value that specifies whether the WebServiceProxy instance must make a GET or POST HTTP request to the Web service. In this case, you set the Boolean parameter to false because you want the WebServiceProxy instance to make a POST HTTP request to the Web service:

```
var useGet = false;
```

The fourth parameter must specify the names and values of the parameters of the Web method being invoked. As Listing 14-12 shows, the Add Web method takes two parameters named x and y. The add function retrieves the values of these two parameters from the user-entry text boxes:

```
var xValue = $get("firstNumber").value;
var yValue = $get("secondNumber").value;
var params = {x : xValue, y : yValue};
```

The fifth parameter is a reference to a JavaScript function that the WebServiceProxy instance will automatically invoke when everything goes fine and the server response arrives. In this case, this is a JavaScript function named onSuccess, which simply displays the return value of the Add Web method:

```
function onSuccess(result, userContext, methodName)
{
    userContext.innerHTML = "<b><u>" + result + "</b></u>";
}
```

The sixth parameter is a reference to a JavaScript function that the WebServiceProxy instance will automatically invoke when something goes wrong. In this case, this JavaScript function is named onFailure, which will be discussed shortly.

The seventh (and final) parameter is a reference to the user context. In this case, the user context references a <span> HTML element with the id value of "result", where the onSuccess and onFailure JavaScript functions display the result:

```
var userContext = $get("result");
```

As you can see in the following excerpt from Listing 14-11, the add function calls the _invoke method on the WebServiceProxy instance, passing in the seven parameters to invoke the Add Web method:

```
request = webServiceProxy._invoke(servicePath, methodName, useGet, params,
                                  onSuccess, onFailure, userContext);
```

The _invoke method returns a reference to the WebRequest object that represents the current request, and provides you with complete information about the current request.

WebServiceError

As shown previously in Listing 14-7, the invoke static method of the WebServiceProxy class registers the onComplete method as an event handler for the completed event of the WebRequest object that represents the request made to the Web service. Listing 14-10 contained the implementation of the onComplete method. This implementation is shown again in Listing 14-13, with highlighted portions showing how the onComplete method invokes the onFailure JavaScript function when an error occurs. This function takes three parameters. The first parameter references a Sys.Net.WebServiceError object that contains the complete information about the error, the second parameter references the user context, and the third parameter is a string that contains the name of the Web method.

Listing 14-13: The onComplete Method

```
function onComplete(response, eventArgs)
{
    if (response.get_responseAvailable())
    {
        . . .

        var error = response.getResponseHeader("jsonerror");
        var errorObj = (error === "true");
```

(continued)

Listing 14-13 *(continued)*

```
        if (errorObj)
          result = new Sys.Net.WebServiceError(false, result.Message,
                                       result.StackTrace,
                                       result.ExceptionType);


        var statusCode = response.get_statusCode();

        if (((statusCode < 200) || (statusCode >= 300)) || errorObj)
        {
          if (onFailure)
          {
            if (!result || !errorObj)
              result = new Sys.Net.WebServiceError(false /*timedout*/,
                  String.format(Sys.Res.webServiceFailedNoMsg, methodName), "", "");

            result._statusCode = statusCode;
            onFailure(result, userContext, methodName);

          }
          . . .
        }
        . . .
      }

      else
      {

        var msg;
        if (response.get_timedOut())
          msg = String.format(Sys.Res.webServiceTimedOut, methodName);

        else
          msg = String.format(Sys.Res.webServiceFailedNoMsg, methodName)

        if (onFailure)
          onFailure(
                  new Sys.Net.WebServiceError(response.get_timedOut(), msg, "", ""),
                  userContext, methodName);

        . . .
      }
    }
```

As you can see, the constructor of the Sys.Net.WebServiceError class takes four parameters:

```
        result = new Sys.Net.WebServiceError(false, result.Message,
                                       result.StackTrace,
                                       result.ExceptionType);
```

Listing 14-14 presents the definition of the WebServiceError class.

Listing 14-14: The WebServiceError Class

```
Sys.Net.WebServiceError =
function Sys$Net$WebServiceError(timedOut, message, stackTrace, exceptionType)
{
  this._timedOut = timedOut;
  this._message = message;
  this._stackTrace = stackTrace;
  this._exceptionType = exceptionType;
  this._statusCode = -1;
}

Sys.Net.WebServiceError.prototype =
{
  get_timedOut: Sys$Net$WebServiceError$get_timedOut,
  get_statusCode: Sys$Net$WebServiceError$get_statusCode,
  get_message: Sys$Net$WebServiceError$get_message,
  get_stackTrace: Sys$Net$WebServiceError$get_stackTrace,
  get_exceptionType: Sys$Net$WebServiceError$get_exceptionType
}

Sys.Net.WebServiceError.registerClass('Sys.Net.WebServiceError');
```

The constructor of this class takes the following four parameters:

❑   timedOut: This Boolean parameter specifies whether the WebServiceError error was raised because of a request timeout. As Listing 14-14 demonstrates, the WebServiceError constructor assigns the value of this parameter to a private field named _timedOut. The WebServiceError class exposes a public getter named get_timedOut that you can call from your client code to access the value of this private field:

```
function Sys$Net$WebServiceError$get_timedOut()
{
  return this._timedOut;
}
```

For example, the last highlighted portion of Listing 14-13 (as shown again in the following code fragment) invokes the get_timedOut method on the WebRequestExecutor object responsible for executing the current request to return a Boolean value that specifies whether the request has timed out. Note that the return value of the get_timedOut method is passed into the constructor of the WebServiceError class as its first argument:

```
var msg;
if (response.get_timedOut())
  msg = String.format(Sys.Res.webServiceTimedOut, methodName);

else
  msg = String.format(Sys.Res.webServiceFailedNoMsg, methodName)

if (onFailure)
  onFailure(
          new Sys.Net.WebServiceError(response.get_timedOut(), msg, "", ""),
          userContext, methodName);
```

❑ message: This parameter is a string that contains the error message. As you can see in Listing 14-14, the WebServiceError constructor assigns the value of this parameter to a private field named _message. The WebServiceError class exposes a public getter named get_message that you can call from your client code to access the value of this private field:

```
function Sys$Net$WebServiceError$get_message()
{
  return this._message;
}
```

❑ stackTrace: This parameter is a string that contains the stack trace. As you can see in Listing 14-14, the WebServiceError constructor assigns the value of this parameter to a private field named _stackTrace. The WebServiceError class exposes a public getter named get_stackTrace that you can call from your client code to access the value of this private field:

```
function Sys$Net$WebServiceError$get_stackTrace()
{
  return this._stackTrace;
}
```

❑ exceptionType: This parameter is a string that contains the fully qualified name of the type of the exception that the server side code raised (if any). As you can see in Listing 14-14, the WebServiceError constructor assigns the value of this parameter to a private field named _exceptionType. The WebServiceError class exposes a public getter named get_exceptionType that you can call from your client code to access the value of this private field:

```
function Sys$Net$WebServiceError$get_exceptionType()
{
  return this._exceptionType;
}
```

Note that the WebServiceError also features a private field named _statusCode whose value is set outside the constructor, as you can see in the boldfaced part of the following excerpt from Listing 14-13:

```
    if (!result || !errorObj)
        result = new Sys.Net.WebServiceError(false /*timedout*/,
            String.format(Sys.Res.webServiceFailedNoMsg, methodName), "", "");

    result._statusCode = statusCode;
    onFailure(result, userContext, methodName);
```

As a matter of fact, the WebServiceError class exposes a public property named get_statusCode that you can call from your client code to access the value of the _statusCode private field:

```
function Sys$Net$WebServiceError$get_statusCode()
{
  return this._statusCode;
}
```

Using WebServiceError

Listing 14-15 presents a page that uses the `WebServiceError` class to get more information about an error. This page invokes the `Divide` Web method of the Web service shown in Listing 14-16. This Web method takes two parameters, divides the first parameter by the second parameter, and returns the result. Note that this Web method raises a `System.DivideByZeroException` exception if its second parameter is 0.

Listing 14-15: A Page that Uses the WebServiceError Class

```
<%@ Page Language="C#" %>

<!DOCTYPE html PUBLIC "-//W3C//DTD XHTML 1.0 Transitional//EN"
"http://www.w3.org/TR/xhtml1/DTD/xhtml1-transitional.dtd">
<html xmlns="http://www.w3.org/1999/xhtml">
<head runat="server">
  <title>Untitled Page</title>

  <script type="text/javascript" language="javascript">
    var request;

    function onSuccess(result, userContext, methodName)
    {
       userContext.innerHTML = "<b><u>" + result + "</b></u>";
    }

    function onFailure(result, userContext, methodName)
    {
      var builder = new Sys.StringBuilder();
      builder.append("timedOut: ");
      builder.append(result.get_timedOut());
      builder.appendLine();
      builder.appendLine();
      builder.append("message: ");
      builder.append(result.get_message());
      builder.appendLine();
      builder.appendLine();
      builder.append("stackTrace: ");
      builder.appendLine();
      builder.append(result.get_stackTrace());
      builder.appendLine();
      builder.appendLine();
      builder.append("exceptionType: ");
      builder.append(result.get_exceptionType());
      builder.appendLine();
      builder.appendLine();
      builder.append("statusCode: ");
      builder.append(result.get_statusCode());
      builder.appendLine();
      builder.appendLine();
      builder.append("methodName: ");
      builder.append(methodName);

      alert(builder.toString());
    }
```

(continued)

Listing 14-15 *(continued)*

```
    function divide()
    {
      var servicePath = "http://localhost/WebServicesViaJSON/Math.asmx";
      var methodName = "Divide";
      var useGet = false;
      var xValue = $get("firstNumber").value;
      var yValue = $get("secondNumber").value;
      var params = {x : xValue, y : yValue};

      var userContext = $get("result");
      var webServiceProxy = new Sys.Net.WebServiceProxy();
      webServiceProxy.set_timeout(0);
      request = webServiceProxy._invoke(servicePath, methodName, useGet, params,
                                       onSuccess, onFailure, userContext);

    }
  </script>

</head>
<body>
  <form id="form1" runat="server">
    <asp:ScriptManager runat="server" ID="ScriptManager1" />
    <table>
      <tr>
        <td style="font-weight: bold" align="right">
          First Number:
        </td>
        <td align="left">
          <input type="text" id="firstNumber" /></td>
      </tr>
      <tr>
        <td style="font-weight: bold" align="right">
          Second Number:
        </td>
        <td align="left">
          <input type="text" id="secondNumber" /></td>
      </tr>
      <tr>
        <td colspan="2" align="center">
          <button onclick="divide()">
            Divide</button></td>
      </tr>
      <tr>
        <td style="font-weight: bold" align="right">
          Result:
        </td>
        <td align="left">
          <span id="result" />
        </td>
      </tr>
    </table>
  </form>
</body>
</html>
```

Listing 14-16: The Web Service

```csharp
<%@ WebService Language="C#" Class="MyNamespace.Math" %>

using System;
using System.Web;
using System.Web.Services;
using System.Web.Services.Protocols;
using System.Web.Script.Services;

namespace MyNamespace
{
  [WebService(Namespace = "http://tempuri.org/")]
  [WebServiceBinding(ConformsTo = WsiProfiles.BasicProfile1_1)]
  [ScriptService]
  public class Math
  {
    [WebMethod]
    public double Divide(double x, double y)
    {
      if (y == 0)
        throw new DivideByZeroException();
      return x / y;
    }
  }
}
```

Let's walk through the implementation of the onFailure method. The WebServiceProxy automatically invokes this method when something goes wrong. The onFailure method takes three parameters: the first parameter references the WebServiceError object that provides complete information about the error, the second parameter references the user context object, and the third parameter is a string that contains the name of the Web method invoked.

The onFailure method method instantiates a StringBuilder and populates it with the complete information about the error. First, it calls the get_timedOut method on the WebServiceError object to return a Boolean value that specifies whether the request has timed out, and appends this Boolean value to the StringBuilder:

```javascript
var builder = new Sys.StringBuilder();
builder.append("timedOut: ");
builder.append(result.get_timedOut());
builder.appendLine();
builder.appendLine();
```

Next, it calls the get_message method on the WebServiceError object to return a string that contains the error message, and appends this string to the StringBuilder:

```javascript
builder.append("message: ");
builder.append(result.get_message());
builder.appendLine();
builder.appendLine();
```

Then, it calls the `get_stackTrace` method on the `WebServiceError` object to return a string that contains the stack trace, and appends this string to the `StringBuilder`:

```
builder.append("stackTrace: ");
builder.appendLine();
builder.append(result.get_stackTrace());
builder.appendLine();
builder.appendLine();
```

Next, it calls the `get_exceptionType` method on the `WebServiceError` object to return a string that contains the fully qualified name of the type of the exception, and appends this string to the `StringBuilder`. In this case, the string is `"System.DivideByZeroException"` because this is the exception that the `Divide` Web service method raises:

```
builder.append("exceptionType: ");
builder.append(result.get_exceptionType());
builder.appendLine();
builder.appendLine();
```

Next, it calls the `get_statusCode` method on the `WebServiceError` object to return the server response status code and appends it to the `StringBuilder`. In this case, this status code will be 500 when the `Divide` method raises its `System.DivideByZeroException`:

```
builder.append("statusCode: ");
builder.append(result.get_statusCode());
builder.appendLine();
builder.appendLine();
```

Then, it appends the method name to the `StringBuilder`:

```
builder.append("methodName: ");
builder.append(methodName);
```

Finally, it invokes the `alert` function to display the content of the `StringBuilder` in a pop-up box:

```
alert(builder.toString());
```

If you run the page shown in Listing 14-16 and enter **0** for the second number, you'll get the pop-up box shown in Figure 14-2, which displays the contents of the previously mentioned `StringBuilder`.

Figure 14-2

Calling Page Methods

As you saw in the previous section, if you have some server-side logic that you need to execute from your client code, you can create a Web service with a Web method that encapsulates this logic and invoke this method from your client code. The downside of this approach is that it requires you to move this logic to a separate file with the extension .asmx. There are times when you need to keep this logic in your Web page together with the rest of the page.

The ASP.NET AJAX framework enables you to encapsulate this logic in a method in your Web page and invoke this method from your client code, provided that this method meets the following requirements:

- ❏ It must be public.
- ❏ It must be static.
- ❏ It must be annotated with the WebMethodAttribute metadata attribute.

Listing 14-17 presents a version of Listing 14-16 where the division logic is encapsulated in a public static method named Divide on the .aspx page (the first boldface portion of the listing) instead of a Web service in a separate .asmx file. The service path is set to the URL of the current page, as shown in the bottom boldface portion of the listing and again here:

```
var servicePath = "/AJAXFuturesEnabledWebSite2/PageMethods.aspx";
```

Listing 14-17: A Page that Allows You to Invoke its Methods from Your Client Code

```
<%@ Page Language="C#" %>

<%@ Import Namespace="System.Web.Services" %>
<!DOCTYPE html PUBLIC "-//W3C//DTD XHTML 1.0 Transitional//EN"
"http://www.w3.org/TR/xhtml1/DTD/xhtml1-transitional.dtd">

<script runat="server">
  [WebMethod]
  public static double Divide(double x, double y)
  {
    if (y == 0)
      throw new DivideByZeroException();

    return x / y;
  }
</script>

<html xmlns="http://www.w3.org/1999/xhtml">
<head id="Head1" runat="server">
  <title>Untitled Page</title>

  <script type="text/javascript" language="javascript">
    var request;

    function onSuccess(result, userContext, methodName)
    {
      userContext.innerHTML = "<b><u>" + result + "</b></u>";
    }

    function onFailure(result, userContext, methodName)
    {
      var builder = new Sys.StringBuilder();
      builder.append("timedOut: ");
      builder.append(result.get_timedOut());
      builder.appendLine();
      builder.appendLine();
      builder.append("message: ");
      builder.append(result.get_message());
      builder.appendLine();
      builder.appendLine();
      builder.append("stackTrace: ");
      builder.appendLine();
      builder.append(result.get_stackTrace());
      builder.appendLine();
      builder.appendLine();
      builder.append("exceptionType: ");
      builder.append(result.get_exceptionType());
      builder.appendLine();
      builder.appendLine();
      builder.append("statusCode: ");
      builder.append(result.get_statusCode());
      builder.appendLine();
      builder.appendLine();
      builder.append("methodName: ");
      builder.append(methodName);
```

```
            alert(builder.toString());
        }

        function divide()
        {
          var servicePath = "/WebServicesViaJSON/PageMethods.aspx";
          var methodName = "Divide";
          var useGet = false;
          var xValue = $get("firstNumber").value;
          var yValue = $get("secondNumber").value;
          var params = {x : xValue, y : yValue};

          var userContext = $get("result");
          var webServiceProxy = new Sys.Net.WebServiceProxy();
          webServiceProxy.set_timeout(0);
          request = webServiceProxy._invoke(servicePath, methodName, useGet, params,
                                            onSuccess, onFailure, userContext);
        }
    </script>

</head>
<body>
    <form id="form1" runat="server">
      <asp:ScriptManager runat="server" ID="ScriptManager1" />
      <table>
        <tr>
          <td style="font-weight: bold" align="right">
            First Number:
          </td>
          <td align="left">
            <input type="text" id="firstNumber" /></td>
        </tr>
        <tr>
          <td style="font-weight: bold" align="right">
            Second Number:
          </td>
          <td align="left">
            <input type="text" id="secondNumber" /></td>
        </tr>
        <tr>
          <td colspan="2" align="center">
            <button onclick="divide()">
              Divide</button></td>
        </tr>
        <tr>
          <td style="font-weight: bold" align="right">
            Result:
          </td>
          <td align="left">
            <span id="result" />
          </td>
        </tr>
      </table>
    </form>
</body>
</html>
```

Calling Custom Methods

If you have some application logic that you need to execute from your client script, you can encapsulate it in a method, and invoke this method from your client script in asynchronous fashion. The fundamental question is where this method should go. Two options have been discussed thus far:

❑ You can turn this method into a Web method, which is part of a Web service in a separate file with extension .asmx.

❑ You can add this method directly to your Web page.

There may be times when neither of these two solutions meets your requirements because this method must be part of a custom class that is neither part of a Web service nor a Web page. The most common application of this scenario is what is known as a *Web services bridge*.

As you saw in previous chapters, the ASP.NET AJAX network programming infrastructure uses XMLHttpRequest to communicate with the server. Due to security considerations, XMLHttpRequest cannot be used to make requests to resources that reside on a site other than the site from which the current page was downloaded in the first place.

Therefore, if your client code needs to communicate with a Web service that does not reside on the same site from which your client code was downloaded, it has no choice but to do this indirectly through its downloading site. This means that you need to encapsulate or wrap the logic that invokes the Web method of the remote Web service in a method on your site, and have your client side invoke this method instead of directly invoking the remote Web method.

This raises the following question: Where should this wrapper method go? The ASP.NET AJAX framework provides you with three choices:

❑ Make this wrapper method a Web method that belongs to a Web service on your site. This Web service acts as an intermediary between your client side code and the remote Web service, as discussed earlier in this chapter.

❑ Make this wrapper method a public static page method that belongs to a Web page on your site. This public static page method acts as an intermediary between your client side code and the remote Web service, as discussed earlier in this chapter.

❑ Make this wrapper method a public method that belongs to a custom class on your site. This custom class acts as an intermediary between your client side code and the remote Web service. This option is called a Web services bridge and is discussed in this section.

To use a Web services bridge, you must take the following steps:

1. Add your custom class to the App_Code directory of your application. This saves you from having to manually compile your class. Another option is to compile your custom class into an assembly and reference the assembly from your application.

2. Create a file with extension .asbx that describes your custom class, and add the file to the root directory of your application.

3. Instruct the IIS Web server to hand over to the ASP.NET framework all resource requests with extension .asbx.

The best way to understand these three steps is to look at an example that uses them.

Listing 14-18 presents a new version of the Divide method shown in Listing 14-17. As you can see, the new version is now an instance method of a custom class named Math.

Listing 14-18: The Math Custom Class

```
using System;

namespace CustomComponents
{
  public class Math
  {
    public double Divide(double x, double y)
    {
      if (y == 0)
        throw new DivideByZeroException();

      return x / y;
    }
  }
}
```

The second step of the previously mentioned three-step procedure requires you to create a new file with extension .asbx that describes the Math custom class defined in Listing 14-18. Listing 14-19 presents the contents of the Math.asbx file. As you can see, an .asbx file is just an XML file.

Listing 14-19: The.asbx File that Describes the Math Custom Class

```
<?xml version="1.0" encoding="utf-8" ?>
<bridge namespace="MyNamespace" className="MyMath">
  <proxy type="CustomComponents.Math, App_Code"/>
  <method name="Divide">
    <input>
      <parameter name="x" />
      <parameter name="y" />
    </input>
  </method>
</bridge>
```

This XML file, like any other XML file, contains a single element known as the document element. In the case of the .asbx file, this element is named bridge and exposes two attributes named namespace and className. You can set the values of these two attributes to anything, as long as the attribute values do not violate the standard XML rules.

The bridge document element contains a child element named proxy that exposes an attribute named type. You must set the value of the type attribute to the fully qualified name of your custom class, including its complete namespace containment hierarchy, plus its location. In this case, the fully qualified name of the custom class is CustomComponents.Math, which is located in the App_Code directory of the application.

The proxy element basically describes your custom class. As Listing 14-19 shows this element contains a child element named method that exposes an attribute named name. You must set this name attribute to the name of the method being described, which in this case is the Divide method of your custom class.

The `method` element also contains a child element named `input` that describes the input parameters of the method. The `input` child element contains one `parameter` element for each input parameter of the method. In this case, the `Divide` method takes two parameters named x and y, and consequently the `input` element contains two `parameter` child elements. You must set the `name` attribute of each `parameter` child element to the name of the parameter of the method that the child element describes.

Listing 14-20 presents a new version of the page shown in Listing 14-17. This version uses the bridge approach to enable the client code to invoke the `Math` custom class's `Divide` method.

Listing 14-20: A Page that Uses the Bridge Approach

```
<%@ Page Language="C#" %>
<%@ Import Namespace="System.Web.Services" %>

<!DOCTYPE html PUBLIC "-//W3C//DTD XHTML 1.0 Transitional//EN"
"http://www.w3.org/TR/xhtml1/DTD/xhtml1-transitional.dtd">

<html xmlns="http://www.w3.org/1999/xhtml">
<head id="Head1" runat="server">
  <title>Untitled Page</title>

  <script type="text/javascript" language="javascript">
    var request;

    function onSuccess(result, userContext, methodName)
    {
      userContext.innerHTML = "<b><u>" + result + "</b></u>";
    }

    function onFailure(result, userContext, methodName)
    {
      var builder = new Sys.StringBuilder();
      builder.append("timedOut: ");
      builder.append(result.get_timedOut());
      builder.appendLine();
      builder.appendLine();
      builder.append("message: ");
      builder.append(result.get_message());
      builder.appendLine();
      builder.appendLine();
      builder.append("stackTrace: ");
      builder.appendLine();
      builder.append(result.get_stackTrace());
      builder.appendLine();
      builder.appendLine();
      builder.append("exceptionType: ");
      builder.append(result.get_exceptionType());
      builder.appendLine();
      builder.appendLine();
      builder.append("statusCode: ");
      builder.append(result.get_statusCode());
      builder.appendLine();
      builder.appendLine();
      builder.append("methodName: ");
      builder.append(methodName);
```

```
        alert(builder.toString());
    }

    function divide()
    {
        var servicePath = "/WebServicesViaJSON/Math.asbx";
        var methodName = "Divide";
        var useGet = false;
        var xValue = $get("firstNumber").value;
        var yValue = $get("secondNumber").value;
        var params = {x : xValue, y : yValue};

        var userContext = $get("result");
        var webServiceProxy = new Sys.Net.WebServiceProxy();
        webServiceProxy.set_timeout(0);
        request = webServiceProxy._invoke(servicePath, methodName, useGet,
                                        {args : params},
                                        onSuccess, onFailure, userContext);
    }
  </script>
</head>
<body>
  <form id="form1" runat="server">
    <asp:ScriptManager runat="server" ID="ScriptManager1"/>
    <table>
      <tr>
        <td style="font-weight: bold" align="right">
          First Number:
        </td>
        <td align="left">
          <input type="text" id="firstNumber" /></td>
      </tr>
      <tr>
        <td style="font-weight: bold" align="right">
          Second Number:
        </td>
        <td align="left">
          <input type="text" id="secondNumber" /></td>
      </tr>
      <tr>
        <td colspan="2" align="center">
          <button onclick="divide()">
            Divide</button></td>
      </tr>
      <tr>
        <td style="font-weight: bold" align="right">
          Result:
        </td>
        <td align="left">
          <span id="result" />
        </td>
      </tr>
    </table>
  </form>
</body>
</html>
```

As the following excerpt from this code listing shows, the service path is set to the URL of the `.asbx` file that describes the `Math` custom class:

```
var servicePath = "/AJAXFuturesEnabledWebSite2/Math.asbx";
```

The other major difference is how you pass the parameters of the method being invoked. As the boldface portions of Listing 14-20 show, you must create an object literal that contains a single name/value pair, where the name part of the pair contains `args` and the value part contains the object literal that contains one name/value pair for each parameter of the method being invoked. In this case, the `Divide` method takes two parameters named `x` and `y`, and consequently, this object literal contains two name/value pairs:

```
var params = {x : xValue, y : yValue};

var userContext = $get("result");
var webServiceProxy = new Sys.Net.WebServiceProxy();
webServiceProxy.set_timeout(0);
request = webServiceProxy._invoke(servicePath, methodName, useGet,
                            {args : params}, onSuccess, onFailure, userContext);
```

There are two more things you must do before you can run the page shown in Listing 14-20. As previously mentioned, the service path is set to the URL of the `.asbx` file. Therefore, the request is made for this `.asbx` file. When this request arrives at the server, the IIS Web server picks up the request. What happens next depends on the version of IIS that you're using:

❑   If you're using IIS 5.1 (the version of IIS running on the Windows XP operating system) or IIS 6.0 (the version of IIS running on Windows 2003 Server), IIS searches its metabase for an ISAPI extension that is registered for handling requests for the `.asbx` extension. If it finds such an ISAPI extension, it hands the request over to this extension. If it doesn't find such an extension, it rejects the request because no one can handle it. You must ensure that the `aspnet_isapi` extension has been registered with the IIS metabase to handle requests for `.asbx` extensions. The `aspnet_isapi` extension acts as an intermediary between IIS and ASP.NET, where it receives requests from IIS and hands them over to ASP.NET for processing. You must use the IIS Manager to register the `aspnet_isapi` extension to handle requests for the `.asbx` extensions, and you must have administrative privileges to do this.

Your installation of ASP.NET AJAX must automatically take care of the next step for you. If not, you need to do it yourself. The next step requires you to register a managed HTTP handler factory named `ScriptHandlerFactory` for handling requests for `.asbx` extensions. As previously mentioned, the IIS hands the request over to the `aspnet_isapi` extension, which in turn hands it over to ASP.NET, which in turn hands it over to the `ScriptHandlerFactory`. To register this handler factory, you need to add the following XML fragment to the `web.config` file in your application:

```
<configuration>
  <system.web>
    <httpHandlers>
      <add verb="GET, HEAD, POST" path="*.asbx"
        type="System.Web.Script.Services.ScriptHandlerFactory,
              System.Web.Extensions, Version=1.0.61025.0, Culture=neutral,
              PublicKeyToken=31bf3856ad364e35"
        validate="false" />
    </httpHandlers>
  </system.web>
</configuration>
```

❑   If you're using IIS7 (the version of IIS running on Windows Vista) in ISAPI mode, you must follow the same procedure as the IIS 5.1 or IIS 6.0 to register the aspnet_isapi extension and ScriptHandlerFactory. However, if you're using IIS7 in the new integrated mode, the aspnet_isapi extension drops out of the picture, because IIS7 in integrated mode does not use ISAPI extensions. This means that you don't need to register the aspnet_isapi extension. The IIS7 (in integrated mode) directly passes the request for extension .asbx to the ScriptHandlerFactory, which means that you have to use the IIS7 Manager to register this handler factory with IIS7. This registration automatically adds the following XML fragment to the web.config file of your application:

```
<configuration>
  <system.webServer>
    <handlers>
      <add name="ASBXHandler" verb="GET,HEAD,POST" path="*.asbx"
        preCondition="integratedMode"
        type="System.Web.Script.Services.ScriptHandlerFactory,
              System.Web.Extensions, Version=1.0.61025.0, Culture=neutral,
              PublicKeyToken=31bf3856ad364e35"/>
    </handlers>
  </system.webServer>
</configuration>
```

The last thing that you need to do before you can run the page shown in Listing 14-20 is add the following XML fragment to the web.config file of your application if your installation of the ASP.NET AJAX doesn't automatically do it for you:

```
<configuration>
  <system.web>
    <compilation>
      <buildProviders>
        <add extension=".asbx"
          type="Microsoft.Web.Preview.Services.BridgeBuildProvider" />
      </buildProviders>
    </compilation>
  </system.web>
</configuration>
```

This XML fragment registers a managed class named BridgeBuildProvider with the ASP.NET compilation infrastructure. As you'll see later, the BridgeBuildProvider parses the content of the .asbx file into a dynamically generated class with the name specified in the `className` attribute of the `<bridge>` document element. The document element also belongs to a namespace with the name specified in the `namespace` attribute of this document element.

In summary, the main application of the Web services bridge is to enable the client code to invoke a Web method that belongs to a Web service that does not reside on the same site from which the client code was downloaded. The ASP.NET AJAX Web services bridge allows you to do the following:

❑   Write a custom wrapper class (such as the `Math` class shown in Listing 14-19) that exposes a method (such as the `Divide` method shown in Listing 14-19) that wraps the logic to invoke the remote Web method. In the case of Listing 14-19, the `Divide` wrapper class does not wrap any such logic. Instead, it performs the division operation locally on the server. An example is given later in this book where the wrapper method contains the logic that invokes a remote Web method.

❑   Have the client side invoke this wrapper method instead of directly invoking the remote Web method.

Under the Hood

The previous sections showed you three different ways to enable client-side code to invoke a server side method in asynchronous fashion:

❑   Turn the method into a Web method that belongs to a Web service that resides on the same site from which the client-side code was downloaded in the first place.

❑   Move the method into a Web page that belongs to a Web application that resides on the same site from which the client-side code was downloaded in the first place.

❑   Move the method into a custom class that resides on the same site from which the client-side code was downloaded in the first place, and add an `.asbx` file that describes this custom class and the method.

This section takes you under the hood, where you'll see that all these three approaches are handled by the same underlying logic. The main goal of this section is to demystify this underlying logic and set the stage for the next chapter, where you'll learn how to customize this logic to meet your application requirements. The best way to understand this underlying logic is to build a functional replica of its main components. These components include the following:

❑   `ScriptHandlerFactory`

❑   `RestHandlerFactory`

❑   `RestHandler`

❑   `HandlerWrapper`

❑   `ScriptModule`

To keep the discussion focused, this section leaves out the dirty little details of these components and concentrates on how they pertain to the topics in this and the next chapter.

ScriptHandlerFactory

As discussed earlier, when a request for a resource with the extension `.asbx` or `.asmx` arrives at the Web server, the request is handed over to a managed component named `ScriptHandlerFactory`. This component is part of a group of ASP.NET components known as *HTTP handler factories*. Each HTTP handler factory is specifically designed to handle requests for a particular set of file extensions. For example, the `PageHandlerFactory` HTTP handler factory is specifically designed to handle requests for extension `.aspx`. The `ScriptHandlerFactory` component is specifically designed to handle requests for `.asbx` and `.asmx`.

Every HTTP handler factory implements an interface named `IHttpHandlerFactory`, as defined in Listing 14-21.

Listing 14-21: The IHttpHandlerFactory Interface

```
public interface IHttpHandlerFactory
{
    IHttpHandler GetHandler(HttpContext context, string requestType,
                            string url, string pathTranslated);
    void ReleaseHandler(IHttpHandler handler);
}
```

This interface exposes the following two methods:

- ❏ `GetHandler`: This method takes the following four arguments:

  - ❏ `context`: This argument references the current HTTP context instance. You can think of this instance as the ASP.NET representation of the current HTTP request/response. As such, it contains the complete information about the current HTTP request and response.

  - ❏ `requestType`: This argument is a string that contains the HTTP verb (for example, GET or POST) used to make the current request.

  - ❏ `url`: This argument is a string that contains the virtual path of the requested resource. For example, if the request is made for an `.asbx` file, this argument contains the URL of this file. If the request is made for an `.asmx` file (a Web service), this argument contains the URL of this file.

  - ❏ `pathTranslated`: This argument is a string that contains the physical path of the requested resource on the server.

  The main responsibility of the `GetHandler` method is to instantiate, initialize, and return the HTTP handler component that knows how to handle the request for the specified extension. The HTTP handler factory does not actually process the request passed into it. Instead, it instantiates an HTTP handler and hands the request over to this component for processing. Every HTTP handler implements an interface named `IHttpHandler`; therefore, the return type of the `GetHandler` method is `IHttpHandler`.

- ❏ `ReleaseHandler`: This method takes the HTTP handler instance that the `GetHandler` method creates as its argument, and releases all resources that the `GetHandler` method had to allocate when it created the handler.

Listing 14-22 presents the implementation of a fully functional replica `ScriptHandlerFactory`.

Listing 14-22: The ScriptHandlerFactory Class

```csharp
using System;
using System.Data;
using System.Configuration;
using System.Web;
using System.Reflection;
using System.Web.Compilation;
using System.ComponentModel;
using System.Web.Services;
using System.Web.Script.Serialization;
using System.Collections.Generic;
using System.Collections;
using System.Web.Services.Protocols;
using System.IO;

namespace CustomComponents
{
  public class ScriptHandlerFactory : IHttpHandlerFactory
  {
    private IHttpHandlerFactory _restHandlerFactory;
    private IHttpHandlerFactory _webServiceHandlerFactory;

    public ScriptHandlerFactory()
    {
      this._restHandlerFactory = new RestHandlerFactory();
      this._webServiceHandlerFactory = new WebServiceHandlerFactory();
    }

    public virtual IHttpHandler GetHandler(HttpContext context, string requestType,
                                string url, string pathTranslated)
    {
      IHttpHandlerFactory handlerFactory;
      if (RestHandlerFactory.IsRestRequest(context))
        handlerFactory = this._restHandlerFactory;

      else
        handlerFactory = this._webServiceHandlerFactory;

      IHttpHandler handler = handlerFactory.GetHandler(context, requestType,
                                      url, pathTranslated);
      return new HandlerWrapper(handler, handlerFactory);
    }

    public virtual void ReleaseHandler(IHttpHandler handler)
    {
      ((HandlerWrapper)handler).ReleaseHandler();
    }
  }
}
```

Note that the constructor of this replica, just like the actual `ScriptHandlerFactory`, instantiates instances of two other HTTP handler factories named `RestHandlerFactory` and `WebServiceHandlerFactory`:

```
this._restHandlerFactory = new RestHandlerFactory();
this._webServiceHandlerFactory = new WebServiceHandlerFactory();
```

The implementation of the replica `RestHandlerFactory` is discussed later in this chapter. The `WebServiceHandlerFactory` is the standard ASP.NET HTTP handler factory that handles SOAP requests made to a Web service. This book does not discuss this handler factory because the ASP.NET AJAX framework uses REST messages as opposed to SOAP messages to interact with the backend Web method.

Now let's walk through the implementation of the `GetHandler` method of the replica `ScriptHandlerFactory`. This method first invokes the `IsRestRequest` static method on the `RestHandlerFactory` to determine whether the current request is a REST (JSON) request. If so, it invokes the `GetHandler` method of the `RestHandlerFactory` to instantiate, initialize, and return an HTTP handler that knows how to process REST (JSON) requests. If not, it assumes that the request is a SOAP request and invokes the `GetHandler` method of the `WebServiceHandlerFactory` to instantiate, initialize, and return an HTTP handler that knows how to process SOAP requests.

```
IHttpHandlerFactory handlerFactory;
if (RestHandlerFactory.IsRestRequest(context))
  handlerFactory = this._restHandlerFactory;

else
  handlerFactory = this._webServiceHandlerFactory;
IHttpHandler handler = handlerFactory.GetHandler(context, requestType,
                                                 url, pathTranslated);
```

Finally, the `GetHandler` method instantiates an instance of an HTTP handler named `HandlerWrapper` that wraps the HTTP handler returned from the calls into the `GetHandler` method of `RestHandlerFactory` or `WebServiceHandlerFactory`:

```
return new HandlerWrapper(handler, handlerFactory);
```

This wrapper, like any other wrapper, hides the actual type of the HTTP handler from the caller of the `GetHandler` method of the `ScriptHandlerFactory`. As previously mentioned, the actual HTTP handler type depends on whether the `GetHandler` method of the `RestHandlerFactory` or the `GetHandler` method of the `WebServiceHandlerFactory` is invoked — in other words, whether the current request is a REST or SOAP request.

If you check out the `web.config` file of your ASP.NET AJAX application, you'll see the XML fragment shown in Listing 14-23. Note that the boldface portion of this listing will only show up if you are running IIS7.

Listing 14-23: The web.config File

```
<configuration>
  <system.web>
    <httpHandlers>
      <remove verb="*" path="*.asmx" />

      <add verb="*" path="*.asmx" validate="false"
        type="System.Web.Script.Services.ScriptHandlerFactory,
              System.Web.Extensions, Version=1.0.61025.0, Culture=neutral,
              PublicKeyToken=31bf3856ad364e35"/>
```

(continued)

Listing 14-23 *(continued)*

```
        <add verb="GET,HEAD,POST" path="*.asbx" validate="false"
          type="System.Web.Script.Services.ScriptHandlerFactory,
              System.Web.Extensions, Version=1.0.61025.0, Culture=neutral,
              PublicKeyToken=31bf3856ad364e35" />
      </httpHandlers>
    </system.web>

    <system.webServer>
      <handlers>
        <remove name="WebServiceHandlerFactory-Integrated" />

        <add name="ScriptHandlerFactory" verb="*" path="*.asmx"
          preCondition="integratedMode"
          type="System.Web.Script.Services.ScriptHandlerFactory,
              System.Web.Extensions, Version=1.0.61025.0, Culture=neutral,
              PublicKeyToken=31bf3856ad364e35" />

        <add name="ASBXHandler" verb="GET,HEAD,POST" path="*.asbx"
          preCondition="integratedMode"
          type="System.Web.Script.Services.ScriptHandlerFactory,
              System.Web.Extensions, Version=1.0.61025.0, Culture=neutral,
              PublicKeyToken=31bf3856ad364e35" />
      </handlers>
    </system.webServer>
  </configuration>
```

Both the boldface and non-boldfaced portions of this code listing begin by removing the HTTP handler factory registered for handling the extension `.asmx`. The non-boldface portion uses the following XML line to remove this handler:

```
<remove verb="*" path="*.asmx" />
```

The boldface portion uses the following XML line to remove this handler:

```
<remove name="WebServiceHandlerFactory-Integrated" />
```

The removed HTTP handler factory in both cases is `WebServiceHandlerFactory`. Both cases then register the `ScriptHandlerFactory` for handling the requests for extensions `.asmx` and `.asbx`. In other words, requests for these two extensions are now handled by the same HTTP handler factory. As discussed earlier, the `GetHandler` method of `ScriptHandlerFactory` then uses the `IsRestRequest` static method of the `RestHandlerFactory` to determine whether the current request is a REST or SOAP request. If the current request is a normal SOAP request, the request is handed back to the originally removed HTTP handler factory: `WebServiceHandlerFactory`. This enables `ScriptHandlerFactory` to hand all REST requests over to `RestHandlerFactory`, including the REST requests for extension `.asmx` and the REST requests for extension `.asbx`.

RestHandlerFactory

As discussed earlier, the `ScriptHandlerFactory` hands the REST requests for both the `.asmx` and `.asbx` extensions to the `RestHandlerFactory` for processing. Listing 14-24 presents the implementation of a fully functional `RestHandlerFactory` replica.

Listing 14-24: The RestHandlerFactory

```
using System;
using System.Data;
using System.Configuration;
using System.Web;
using System.Reflection;
using System.Web.Compilation;
using System.ComponentModel;
using System.Web.Services;
using System.Web.Script.Serialization;
using System.Collections.Generic;
using System.Collections;
using System.Web.Services.Protocols;
using System.IO;

namespace CustomComponents
{
  internal class RestHandlerFactory : IHttpHandlerFactory
  {
    public virtual IHttpHandler GetHandler(HttpContext context, string requestType,
                                        string url, string pathTranslated)
    {
      if (IsClientProxyRequest(context.Request.PathInfo))
        return new RestClientProxyHandler();

      return RestHandler.CreateHandler(context);
    }

    internal static bool IsRestRequest(HttpContext context)
    {
      if (!IsRestMethodCall(context.Request))
        return IsClientProxyRequest(context.Request.PathInfo);

      return true;
    }

    internal static bool IsRestMethodCall(HttpRequest request)
    {
      if (string.IsNullOrEmpty(request.PathInfo))
        return false;

      if (!request.ContentType.StartsWith("application/json;",
                                     StringComparison.OrdinalIgnoreCase))
        return string.Equals(request.ContentType, "application/json",
                                     StringComparison.OrdinalIgnoreCase);

      return true;
    }

    internal static bool IsClientProxyRequest(string pathInfo)
    {
      return string.Equals(pathInfo, "/js", StringComparison.OrdinalIgnoreCase);
    }
```

(continued)

Listing 14-24 *(continued)*

```
        public virtual void ReleaseHandler(IHttpHandler handler) { }
    }
}
```

First, let's walk through the implementation of the `IsRestRequest` static method. As previously discussed, the `ScriptHandlerFactory` invokes this method to determine whether the current request is a REST request. In general, the ASP.NET AJAX framework supports the following two types of REST requests:

❑ REST method call: The client code makes this type of REST request to invoke a server-side method. You saw several examples of this earlier in this chapter.

❑ Client proxy request: The client code makes this type of REST request to download the script that defines the proxy class. The next chatper discusses this proxy class.

As Listing 14-24 shows, the `IsRestRequest` static method first invokes a method named `IsRestMethodCall` to determine whether the currest request is a REST method call request. If not, the `IsRestRequest` method invokes the `IsClientProxyRequest` method to determine whether the current request is a client proxy request.

Now let's walk through the implementation of the `IsRestMethodCall` method. As you can see in the following excerpt from Listing 14-24, this method first calls the `PathInfo` property on the ASP.NET `Request` object to determine whether the request URL contains a path information trailer. The client code adds a trailer to the request URL that contains information such as the name of the server method being invoked. Therefore, the absence of a path information trailer by itself indicates that the current request cannot be a REST method call.

```
    internal static bool IsRestMethodCall(HttpRequest request)
    {
        if (string.IsNullOrEmpty(request.PathInfo))
            return false;
```

If the request URL contains a path information trailer, the `IsRestMethodCall` method checks whether the `Content-Type` HTTP request header contains the string `"application/json"`. The client code adds this value to the `Content-Type` HTTP header to inform the `RestHttpHandler` that the current request is a REST method call, which means that the client is trying to invoke a server method:

```
        if (!request.ContentType.StartsWith("application/json;",
                                    StringComparison.OrdinalIgnoreCase))
            return string.Equals(request.ContentType, "application/json",
                            StringComparison.OrdinalIgnoreCase);

        return true;
    }
```

As discussed earlier, the `IsRestRequest` method invokes the `IsClientProxyRequest` method to determine whether the current request is a client proxy request. This method simply checks whether the path information trailer is the `js` or `jsdebug` string. The client code adds the `js` path information trailer to the request URL to inform `RestHandlerFactory` that it needs to download the release version of the script that contains the proxy class. The client code adds the `jsdebug` path information trailer to the request URL to inform `RestHandlerFactory` that it needs to download the debug version of the script that contains the proxy class. As you can see, the presence of this path information trailer by itself signals that the client code has made the current request to download the script that contains the proxy class. In other words, the current request is *not* a REST method call request. To keep this discussion focused, the replica only considers the requests made for downloading the release version. The next chapter discusses the proxy class and the script code that contains the definition of the proxy class in the next chapter.

The `RestHandlerFactory`, like any other HTTP handler factory, implements the `GetHandler` method of the `IHttpHandlerFactory`. As you can see in Listing 14-24, this method first invokes the `IsClientProxyRequest` method to determine whether the client code has made the current request to download the script that contains the proxy class. If so, it instantiates and returns an instance of an HTTP handler named `RestClientProxyHandler`. If not, it invokes the `CreateHandler` static method on an ASP.NET class named `RestHandler` to instantiate and to return an instance of the `RestHandler` HTTP handler. The next chapter discusses the `RestClientProxyHandler` as part of its coverage of the proxy class and the script that defines it. For now, suffice it to say that the `RestClientProxyHandler` and `RestHandler` know how to handle REST client proxy and REST method call requests, respectively.

RestHandler

Listing 14-25 presents the implementation of the replica `RestHandler` HTTP handler. As previously shown in Listing 14-24, the `GetHandler` method of `RestHandlerFactory` invokes the `CreateHandler` static method on the `RestHandler` class to instantiate an instance of this class.

Listing 14-25: The RestHandler HTTP Handler

```
using System;
using System.Data;
using System.Configuration;
using System.Web;
using System.Web.UI;
using System.Reflection;
using System.Web.Compilation;
using System.ComponentModel;
using System.Web.Services;
using System.Web.Script.Serialization;
using System.Collections.Generic;
using System.Collections;
using System.Web.Services.Protocols;
using System.IO;

namespace CustomComponents
{
    internal class RestHandler : IHttpHandler
    {
        private MethodInfo _methodInfo;

        internal static IHttpHandler CreateHandler(HttpContext context)
        {
            string servicePath = context.Request.FilePath;

            Type serviceType = BuildManager.GetCompiledType(servicePath);
            if (serviceType == null)
```

(continued)

Listing 14-25 (continued)

```
    {
      object obj = BuildManager.CreateInstanceFromVirtualPath(servicePath,
                                                        typeof(Page));
      serviceType = obj.GetType();
    }

    string methodName = context.Request.PathInfo.Substring(1);
    MethodInfo[] infoArray = serviceType.GetMethods();
    MethodInfo minfo = null;
    foreach (MethodInfo info in infoArray)
    {
      object[] objArray = info.GetCustomAttributes(typeof(WebMethodAttribute),
                                                  true);
      if (objArray.Length != 0 && info.Name == methodName)
      {
        minfo = info;
        break;
      }
    }

    RestHandler handler = new RestHandler();
    handler._methodInfo = minfo;
    return handler;
  }

  public void ProcessRequest(HttpContext context)
  {
    string text = new StreamReader(context.Request.InputStream).ReadToEnd();
    IDictionary<string, object> rawParams;
    JavaScriptSerializer serializer = new JavaScriptSerializer();

    if (string.IsNullOrEmpty(text))
      rawParams = new Dictionary<string, object>();

    else
      rawParams = serializer.Deserialize<IDictionary<string, object>>(text);

    ArrayList parameters = new ArrayList();
    ParameterInfo[] infos = _methodInfo.GetParameters();
    TypeConverter converter;
    foreach (KeyValuePair<string, object> entry in rawParams)
    {
      IDictionary<string, object> dictionary =
                                  entry.Value as IDictionary<string, object>;
      if (dictionary != null)
        parameters.Add(dictionary);

      else
      {
        for (int i = 0; i < infos.Length; i++)
        {
          if (entry.Key == infos[i].Name)
          {
            converter = TypeDescriptor.GetConverter(infos[i].ParameterType);
```

```
              if (converter.CanConvertFrom(entry.Value.GetType()))
                  parameters.Add(converter.ConvertFrom(entry.Value));
            }
          }
        }
      }

      object[] methodParameters = new object[parameters.Count];
      parameters.CopyTo(methodParameters);
      object target = Activator.CreateInstance(_methodInfo.DeclaringType);

      object obj3 = _methodInfo.Invoke(target, methodParameters);

      string s = serializer.Serialize(obj3);
      context.Response.ContentType = "application/json";
      if (s != null)
        context.Response.Write(s);
    }

    public bool IsReusable
    {
      get { return false; }
    }
  }
}
```

The CreateHandler method begins by calling the FilePath property on the ASP.NET Request object to access the virtual path of the requested file:

```
string servicePath = context.Request.FilePath;
```

For example, if the request is made for an .asbx file, the FilePath returns the virtual path of this .asbx file. If the request is made for a Web service (an .asmx file), the FilePath returns the URL of the Web service.

Next, the CreateHandler method invokes a static method named GetCompiledType on an ASP.NET class named BuildManager, passing in the virtual path of the requested file:

```
Type serviceType = BuildManager.GetCompiledType(servicePath);
```

This static method parses and compiles the file with the specified virtual path into a dynamically generated .NET type or class and returns a Type object that represents this class. For example, consider the request made for the .asbx file shown in the following excerpt from Listing 14-19:

```
<?xml version="1.0" encoding="utf-8" ?>
<bridge namespace="MyNamespace" className="MyMath">
  <proxy type="CustomComponents.Math, App_Code"/>
  <method name="Divide">
    <input>
      <parameter name="x" />
      <parameter name="y" />
    </input>
  </method>
</bridge>
```

In this case, the GetCompiledType static method will dynamically create a class with the name specified in the className attribute on the bridge document element. This element also belongs to a namespace with the name specified in the namespace attribute on this element. That is, the GetCompiledType method will create a class named MyMath that belongs to a namespace named MyNamespace. The method will then dynamically compile this class into an assembly, load this assembly into the application domain where the current application is running, and return a Type object that represents the MyMath class.

Next, the CreateHandler method extracts a substring of the PathInfo property of the ASP.NET Request object whose starting index is 1:

```
string methodName = context.Request.PathInfo.Substring(1);
```

The PathInfo property contains the data that comes after the virtual path of a file, and the substring contains the name of the server method being invoked.

The CreateHandler method then invokes the GetMethods method on the Type object that represents the dynamically generated class to return an array of MethodInfo objects, where each object represents a method of this class:

```
MethodInfo[] infoArray = serviceType.GetMethods();
```

Next, the CreateHandler method searches this array for a MethodInfo object that represents a method with the name specified in the first substring of the PathInfo trailer and annotated with the WebMethodAttribute metadata attribute:

```
MethodInfo minfo = null;
foreach (MethodInfo info in infoArray)
{
  object[] objArray = info.GetCustomAttributes(typeof(WebMethodAttribute),
                                               true);
  if (objArray.Length != 0 && info.Name == methodName)
  {
    minfo = info;
    break;
  }
}
```

The CreateHandler method then instantiates a RestHandler HTTP handler and assigns the MethodInfo object to its _methodInfo private field:

```
RestHandler handler = new RestHandler();
handler._methodInfo = minfo;
return handler;
```

As you can see in Listing 14-25, the RestHandler HTTP handler, like any other HTTP handler, implements a method named ProcessRequest. This method is responsible for processing the current REST request. It begins by loading the request stream into a StreamReader and then invoking the ReadToEnd method on this StreamReader to load the content of the StreamReader and, consequently, the entire client request into a string. Because the current request is a REST (JSON) request, this string contains a JSON object that consists of name/value pairs:

```
string text = new StreamReader(context.Request.InputStream).ReadToEnd();
```

Next, `ProcessRequest` instantiates a `JavaScriptSerializer` and invokes its `Deserialize` method to deserialize an `IDictionary` object from the JSON object. `IDictionary` is a collection of `KeyValuePair` objects. In this case, each `KeyValuePair` object represents a name/value pair of the JSON object:

```
IDictionary<string, object> rawParams;
JavaScriptSerializer serializer = new JavaScriptSerializer();

rawParams = serializer.Deserialize<IDictionary<string, object>>(text);
```

Next, the `ProcessRequest` method invokes the `GetParameters` method on the `MethodInfo` object that represents the method being invoked to return an array of `ParameterInfo` objects, where each `ParameterInfo` object represents a parameter of the method being invoked:

```
ParameterInfo[] infos = _methodInfo.GetParameters();
```

Then, it iterates through the `KeyValuePair` objects in the `IDictionary` collection and uses the type converter associated with each value part of each `KeyValuePair` object to convert the value into its associated .NET type if the value part is not of type `IDictionary`. Otherwise, it uses the value part as is.

Keep in mind that the value part of the `KeyValuePair` contains the value part of the name/value pair of the original JSON object, and each name/value pair in the original JSON object represents a parameter of the method being invoked. To keep this discussion focused, the following code uses a simple conversion mechanism:

```
TypeConverter converter;
ArrayList parameters = new ArrayList();

foreach (KeyValuePair<string, object> entry in rawParams)
{
  IDictionary<string, object> dictionary =
                        entry.Value as IDictionary<string, object>;
  if (dictionary != null)
    parameters.Add(dictionary);

  else
  {
    for (int i = 0; i < infos.Length; i++)
    {
      if (entry.Key == infos[i].Name)
      {
        converter = TypeDescriptor.GetConverter(infos[i].ParameterType);
        if (converter.CanConvertFrom(entry.Value.GetType()))
          parameters.Add(converter.ConvertFrom(entry.Value));
      }
    }
  }
}
```

Next, the `ProcessRequest` method calls the `CreateInstance` static method on the `Activator` class to dynamically instantiate an instance of the class that contains the method being invoked:

```
            object[] methodParameters = new object[parameters.Count];
            parameters.CopyTo(methodParameters);
            object target = Activator.CreateInstance(_methodInfo.DeclaringType);
```

Then the `ProcessRequest` method calls the `Invoke` method on the `MethodInfo` object that represents the method being invoked to invoke the method in a generic fashion:

```
            object obj3 = _methodInfo.Invoke(target, methodParameters);
```

Next, the `ProcessRequest` method calls the `Serialize` method on the `JavaScriptSerializer` object to serialize the return value of the method into its JSON representation:

```
            string s = serializer.Serialize(obj3);
```

Next, it sets the `Content-Type` response HTTP header to the string `"application/json"` to inform the client code that the response contains a JSON string:

```
            context.Response.ContentType = "application/json";
```

Finally, it invokes the `Write` method on the ASP.NET `Response` object to write the JSON string representation of the return value of the method into the response output stream, which is then sent back to the client:

```
            if (s != null)
                context.Response.Write(s);
```

HandlerWrapper

As previously shown in Listing 14-22, the `GetHandler` method of the `ScriptHandlerFactory` calls the `GetHandler` method of the `RestHandlerFactory` if the current request is a SOAP request, or the `GetHandler` method of the `WebServiceHandlerFactory` if the current request is a REST (JSON) request. It then hides the return value of the `GetHandler` method of `RestHandlerFactory` or `WebServiceHandlerFactory` in a wrapper HTTP handler named `HandlerWrapper`, as defined in Listing 14-26.

Listing 14-26: The HandlerWrapper HTTP Handler

```
using System;
using System.Data;
using System.Configuration;
using System.Web;
using System.Reflection;
using System.Web.Compilation;
using System.ComponentModel;
using System.Web.Services;
using System.Web.Script.Serialization;
using System.Collections.Generic;
using System.Collections;
using System.Web.Services.Protocols;
using System.IO;

namespace CustomComponents
{
```

```
internal class HandlerWrapper : IHttpHandler
{
  private IHttpHandlerFactory _handlerFactory;
  protected IHttpHandler _handler;

  internal HandlerWrapper(IHttpHandler handler,
                          IHttpHandlerFactory handlerFactory)
  {
    this._handlerFactory = handlerFactory;
    this._handler = handler;
  }

  public void ProcessRequest(HttpContext context)
  {
    this._handler.ProcessRequest(context);
  }

  internal void ReleaseHandler()
  {
    this._handlerFactory.ReleaseHandler(this._handler);
  }

  public bool IsReusable
  {
    get
    {
      return this._handler.IsReusable;
    }
  }

}
}
```

Page Methods Demystified

As discussed earlier, the ASP.NET AJAX framework provides you with three different approaches to enable your client-side code to invoke a server-side method in asynchronous fashion. Again, the options are as follows:

- ❑ Have your client-side code make a request for an .asbx file that describes the server-side method.

- ❑ Have your client-side code make a request for an .asmx file that contains the server-side method as a Web method of a Web service.

- ❑ Have your client-side code make a request for an .aspx file that contains the server-side method as a page method annotated with the WebMethod metadata attribute.

The web.config file of your ASP.NET AJAX application directly registers the ScriptHandlerFactory as the handler for requests for resources with file extensions .asbx and .asmx. This registration covers only the first two approaches. How about the third approach, where the server side method is a method that resides in an .aspx file instead of .asbx or .asmx? The web.config file does not directly register the ScriptHandlerFactory as the handler for the requests for resources with the file extension .aspx because .aspx files must be handled by PageHandlerFactory. Therefore, you need a way to make a distinction between the following two types of requests made for a resource with the file extension .aspx:

❑ A normal ASP.NET request for an .aspx file

❑ A REST request when the client is trying to invoke a particular server-side method that happens to reside on the .aspx file

This is where the ScriptModule comes into play. If you check out the web.config file of your ASP.NET AJAX application, you'll see the XML fragment shown in Listing 14-27. Note that the boldface portion of this listing will only show up if you're running IIS7. Both the boldface and non-boldface portions of this listing register the ScriptModule with the ASP.NET request processing pipeline. Every ASP.NET request is guaranteed to go through this pipeline, and every module in this pipeline registers one or more event handlers for one or more events of the HttpApplication object that represents the current ASP.NET application. The HttpApplication object raises its request level events for every single ASP.NET request.

Listing 14-27: The web.config File

```xml
<configuration>
  <system.web>
    <httpModules>
      <add name="ScriptModule"
        type="System.Web.Handlers.ScriptModule, System.Web.Extensions,
            Version=1.0.61025.0, Culture=neutral, PublicKeyToken=31bf3856ad364e35"/>
    </httpModules>
  </system.web>

  <system.webServer>
    <modules>
      <add name="ScriptModule" preCondition="integratedMode"
        type="System.Web.Handlers.ScriptModule, System.Web.Extensions,
            Version=1.0.61025.0, Culture=neutral, PublicKeyToken=31bf3856ad364e35"/>
    </modules>
  </system.webServer>
</configuration>
```

The modules that make up the ASP.NET request processing pipeline are known as *HTTP modules*. All HTTP modules implement an ASP.NET interface named IHttpModule, as defined in Listing 14-28. This interface exposes the following two methods:

❑ Init: Every HTTP module must implement this method to register one or more event handlers for one or more events of the HttpApplication object that represents the current ASP.NET application. ASP.NET automatically passes a reference to the current HttpApplication object into this method.

❑ Dispose: Every HTTP module must implement this method to perform its final cleanup before it is disposed of.

Listing 14-28: The IHttpModule Interface

```
public interface IHttpModule
{
  void Dispose();
  void Init(HttpApplication context);
}
```

Listing 14-29 presents the implementation of the replica ScriptModule. Like all HTTP modules, ScriptModule implements the IHttpModule interface.

Listing 14-29: ScriptModule

```
using System;
using System.Data;
using System.Configuration;
using System.Web;
using System.Web.UI;
using System.Reflection;
using System.Web.Compilation;
using System.ComponentModel;
using System.Web.Services;
using System.Web.Script.Serialization;
using System.Collections.Generic;
using System.Collections;
using System.Web.Services.Protocols;
using System.IO;

namespace CustomComponents
{
  public class ScriptModule : IHttpModule
  {
    protected virtual void Dispose() { }
    protected virtual void Init(HttpApplication context)
    {
      context.PostAcquireRequestState +=
        new EventHandler(this.OnPostAcquireRequestState);
    }

    private void OnPostAcquireRequestState(object sender, EventArgs eventArgs)
    {
      HttpApplication application = (HttpApplication)sender;
      HttpRequest request = application.Context.Request;
      if ((application.Context.Handler is Page) &&
          RestHandlerFactory.IsRestMethodCall(request))
      {
        IHttpHandler restHandler = RestHandler.CreateHandler(application.Context);
        restHandler.ProcessRequest(application.Context);
        application.CompleteRequest();
      }
    }
  }
```

(continued)

585

Listing 14-29 *(continued)*

```
      void IHttpModule.Dispose()
      {
        this.Dispose();
      }

      void IHttpModule.Init(HttpApplication context)
      {
        this.Init(context);
      }
    }
  }
```

As the following excerpt from Listing 14-29 shows, the Init method of ScriptModule registers its OnPostAcquireRequestState method as an event handler for the PostAcquireRequestState event of the current HttpApplication object:

```
context.PostAcquireRequestState +=
                        new EventHandler(this.OnPostAcquireRequestState);
```

The HttpApplication object fires PostAcquireRequestState after the current request acquires its state from the underlying data store. This state includes the session state if the session state is enabled for the current page.

Now let's walk through the implementation of the OnPostAcquireRequestState method. When the current HttpApplication object finally raises its PostAcquireRequestState event and, consequently, invokes the OnPostAcquireRequestState method, it passes a reference to itself into this method as its first argument:

```
      HttpApplication application = (HttpApplication)sender;
      HttpRequest request = application.Context.Request;
```

The OnPostAcquireRequestState method, like the Init method of any other HTTP module, uses this reference to access the current HTTP context object. This object contains the context in which the current request is running. As such, it includes the complete information about the current request and response.

Next, the OnPostAcquireRequestState method checks whether the following two conditions are met:

❑ The HTTP handler responsible for handling the current request is of type Page. If so, this indicates that the current request has been made for a resource with the file extension .aspx.

❑ The Init method then invokes the IsRestMethodCall static method on the RestHandler-Factory to determine whether the current request is a REST method call. As previously discussed, a REST method call request is a request that the client code makes to the server to invoke a server method.

```
      if ((application.Context.Handler is Page) &&
          RestHandlerFactory.IsRestMethodCall(request))
      {
```

If both of the conditions are met, this indicates that the client has made the current request to invoke a server method that resides on an .aspx file, and consequently, the Init method takes the following steps:

1. It invokes the CreateHandler static method on the RestHandler to create a RestHandler HTTP handler:

```
IHttpHandler restHandler = RestHandler.CreateHandler(application.Context);
```

As previously discussed, the RestHandler HTTP handler knows how to process REST method call requests.

2. It calls the ProcessRequest method on this RestHandler HTTP handler to process the current REST method call request:

```
restHandler.ProcessRequest(application.Context);
```

As discussed earlier, this method invokes the server method.

3. It calls the CompleteRequest method on the current HttpApplication object to complete and shortcut the request, and return the response to the client:

```
    application.CompleteRequest();
}
```

As you can see, the current request does not go any further down the ASP.NET request processing pipeline. To understand the significance of this shortcut, you need to take a look at a normal ASP.NET request processing pipeline where a normal ASP.NET request goes all the way down this pipeline, which consists of the following steps:

1. BeginRequest: The current HttpApplication object raises the BeginRequest event when it begins processing the current request. An HTTP module can register an event handler for this event to perform tasks that must be performed at the beginning of the request. For example, this is a good place for an HTTP module to perform URL rewriting.

2. AuthenticateRequest: The current HttpApplication object raises the AuthenticateRequest event to enable interested HTTP modules and application code to authenticate the current request.

3. PostAuthenticateRequest: The current HttpApplication object fires the PostAuthenticateRequest event after the request is authenticated. An HTTP module can register an event handler for this event to perform tasks that must be performed after the current request is authenticated.

4. AuthorizeRequest: The current HttpApplication object fires the AuthorizeRequest event to enable interested HTTP modules and application code to authorize the current request.

5. PostAuthorizeRequest: The current HttpApplication object fires the PostAuthorizeRequest event after the request is authorized. An HTTP module can register an event handler for this event to perform tasks that must be performed after the current request is authorized.

6. ResolveRequestCache: The current HttpApplication object fires the ResolveRequestCache event to enable interested HTTP modules and application code to service the current request from the cache, bypassing the rest of the request processing pipeline to improve the performance of the application.

7. `PostResolveRequestCache`: If the response for the current request has not been cached (because the current request is the first request to the specified resource for example), the current `HttpApplication` object fires the `PostResolveRequestCache` event. An HTTP module can register an event handler for this event to perform tasks that must be performed after the search in the cache fails.

8. `PostMapRequestHandler`: The current `HttpApplication` object fires the `PostMapRequestHandler` event after it has been detemined what type of HTTP handler must handle the current request. An HTTP module can register an event handler for this event to perform tasks that must be performed after the type of HTTP handler is specified.

9. `AcquireRequestState`: The current `HttpApplication` object fires the `AcquireRequestState` event to enable interested HTTP modules and application code to acquire the request state from the underlying data store.

10. `PostAcquireRequestState`: The current `HttpApplication` object fires the `PostAcquireRequestState` event after the request state is acquired to enable interested HTTP modules and application code to perform tasks that must be performed after the request state is acquired.

11. `PreRequestHandlerExecute`: The current `HttpApplication` object fires the `PreReqeustHandlerExecute` event before executing the HTTP handler responsible for handling the current request. An HTTP module can register an event handler for this event to perform tasks that must be performed right before the `ProcessRequest` method of the HTTP handler is invoked to execute the handler.

12. `PostRequestHandlerExecute`: The current `HttpApplication` object fires the `PostRequestHandlerExecute` event after the `ProcessRequest` method of the HTTP handler returns, signifying that the HTTP handler responsible for handling the current request has been executed.

13. `ReleaseRequestState`: The current `HttpApplication` object fires the `ReleaseRequestState` event to enable interested HTTP modules to release or store the request state into the underlying data store.

14. `PostReleaseRequestState`: The current `HttpApplication` object fires the `PostReleaseRequestState` event right after the request state is stored into the underlying data store to enable the interested HTTP modules and application code to run logic that must be run after the request state is saved.

15. `UpdateRequestCache`: The current `HttpApplication` object fires the `UpdateRequestCache` event to enable interested HTTP modules to cache the current response in the ASP.NET cache.

16. `PostUpdateRequestCache`: The current `HttpApplication` object fires the `PostUpdateRequestCache` event after the current response is cached in the ASP.NET `Cache` object.

17. `EndRequest`: The current `HttpApplication` object fires the `EndRequest` event after the current response is sent to the client to mark the end of processing the current request.

As discussed earlier, the `ScriptModule` kicks in when the current `HttpApplication` fires its `PostAcquireRequestState` event. As you can see in Listing 14-29, the `ScriptModule`'s event handler for this event invokes the `CompleteRequest` method on the current `HttpApplication` object to force this object to bypass the rest of the events and directly raise the last event: `EndRequest`.

To see this in action, follow these steps:

1. Create an AJAX-enabled Web site in Visual Studio.

2. Add a `Global.asax` file to the root directory of this Web site.

3. Add the code shown in Listing 14-30 to the `Global.asax` file.

4. Add a breakpoint to each method in the `Global.asax` file.

5. Add a Web form (`.aspx` file) to this Web site.

6. Add the code previously shown in Listing 14-17 to the `.aspx` file created in step 5.

7. Press F5 to run the Web site in debug mode.

    The debugger stops at every breakpoint in the `Global.asax` file, in top-to-bottom order. This signifies two things. First, the first request goes through the entire ASP.NET request processing pipeline. Second, the current `HttpApplication` raises its events in the order discussed earlier.

8. When the Web page appears, enter two numbers in the specified text boxes and press F5 to run the Web site in debug mode again.

    The debugger jumps from the breakpoint in the `Application_AcquireRequestState` method directly to the breakpoint in the `Application_EndRequest` method. This clearly shows that the current request goes through only the first 10 steps of the pipeline, skipping the last eight steps.

Listing 14-30: The Global.asax File

```
<%@ Application Language="C#" %>

<script RunAt="server">
  void Application_BeginRequest(object sender, EventArgs e) { }
  void Application_AuthenticateRequest(object sender, EventArgs e) { }
  void Application_PostAuthenticateRequest(object sender, EventArgs e){ }
  void Application_AuthorizeRequest(object sender, EventArgs e) { }
  void Application_PostAuthorizeRequest(object sender, EventArgs e) { }
  void Application_ResolveRequestCache(object sender, EventArgs e) { }
  void Application_PostResolveRequestCache(object sender, EventArgs e) { }
  void Application_PostMapRequestHandler(object sender, EventArgs e) { }
  void Application_AcquireRequestState(object sender, EventArgs e) { }
  void Application_PostAcquireRequestState(object sender, EventArgs e) { }
  void Application_PreRequestHandlerExecute(object sender, EventArgs e) { }
  void Application_PostRequestHandlerExecute(object sender, EventArgs e) { }
  void Application_ReleaseRequestState(object sender, EventArgs e) { }
  void Application_PostReleaseRequestState(object sender, EventArgs e) { }
  void Application_UpdateRequestCache(object sender, EventArgs e) { }
  void Application_PostUpdateRequestCache(object sender, EventArgs e) { }
  void Application_EndRequest(object sender, EventArgs e) { }
</script>
```

If you decide to allow your client-side code to asynchronously invoke a server-side method that belongs to a Web page in your application, you must keep the following in mind:

❑   None of the event handlers registered for `PostAcquireRequestState`,
`PreRequestHandlerExecute`, `ReleaseRequestState`, `PostReleaseRequestState`,
`UpdateRequestCache`, and `PostUpdateRequestCache` will be invoked.

❑   The request state, such as `Session` data, will not be stored in the underlying data store
because the request skips the `ReleaseRequestState` step during which the request state is
stored in the data store. This means that none of the changes made to the session data will
be stored in the data store, and therefore, they will be lost at the end of the current request.

❑   The server response will not be cached in the ASP.NET `Cache` object because the current request
skips the `UpdateRequestCache` step.

Due to these fundamental limitations, the ASP.NET AJAX framework requires the server-side method to
be static.

As previously shown in Listing 14-29, the `ScriptModule` hands the request over to the `RestHandler`
HTTP handler if the current request is a REST request. In other words, after the `ScriptModule` kicks in,
the `Page` is no longer the HTTP handler responsible for processing the current request. The `ScriptModule`
delegates this responsibility from `Page` to the `RestHandler` HTTP handler, and consequently, the
`ProcessRequest` method of the `RestHandler` HTTP handler (not `Page`) is invoked. This has significant
consequences. The `ProcessRequest` method of the `Page` class starts what is known as the `Page` lifecycle.
This means that the `Page` does not go through its lifecycle phases when the current request is a REST
method call request. Therefore, you cannot access any of the server controls on the current page. This is yet
another reason why the server-side method must be static.

Web Services Bridges Demystified

As the implementation of the `RestHandler` class's `CreateHandler` static method clearly shows, this
method assumes that the method being invoked is annotated with the `WebMethodAttribute` metadata
attribute. In other words, the `RestHandler` HTTP handler assumes that the method being invoked is
always a Web method.

How does the `RestHandler` HTTP handler process requests for an `.asbx` file given the fact that this file
has nothing to do with Web services? To find the answer to this question, you need to revisit the implementation of the `CreateHandler` static method, which is shown again in Listing 14-31. As the highlighted portion of this listing shows, the `CreateHandler` method invokes the `GetCompiledType` static
method on the `BuildManager` class. This method parses and compiles the file with the specified virtual
path into a dynamically generated class.

Listing 14-31: The CreateHandler Static Method Revisited

```
internal static IHttpHandler CreateHandler(HttpContext context)
{
    string servicePath = context.Request.FilePath;

    Type serviceType = BuildManager.GetCompiledType(servicePath);

    . . .
}
```

Now the question is: What type of class does the `GetCompiledType` method generate for an `.asbx` file?
To find the answer to this question, run Listing 14-20 in debug mode. The client code contained in this

listing makes a REST request to the server to invoke the `Divide` method of the `Math` class. This request is made for a file with extension `.asbx` that describes the class and method.

After running Listing 14-20, go to the following directory on your machine (or, if you have installed .NET framework in a different directory than the following standard directory, go to that directory):

```
%windir%\Microsoft.NET\Framework\v2.0.50727\Temporary ASP.NET Files
```

In this directory, search for the directory with the same name as your application. Then go down to a different directory, and search for a source file with a name that has the following format:

```
App_Web_math.asbx.23fc0e6b.kgwm5mhb.0.cs
```

Note that the name of this source file begins with `App_Web_`, followed by the name of the `.asbx` file (which is `math.asbx` in this case), followed by some randomly generated hash values to ensure the uniqueness of the file name.

If you open this file in your favorite editor, you should see the code shown in Listing 14-32 (which has been cleaned up for presentation purposes).

Listing 14-32: The Dynamically Generated Code for the Web Service that Wraps a Custom Class

```
namespace MyNamespace
{
  using System;
  using System.Net;
  using System.Web.Services;
  using System.Collections;
  using System.Xml.Serialization;
  using Microsoft.Web.Preview.Services;
  using System.Web.Script.Services;
  using System.Collections.Generic;

  [ScriptService()]
  [WebService(Name = "http://tempuri.org/")]
  [WebServiceBinding(ConformsTo = WsiProfiles.BasicProfile1_1)]
  public partial class MyMath : BridgeHandler
  {
    public MyMath()
    {
      this.VirtualPath = "/AJAXFuturesEnabledWebSite2/NewFolder1/Math.asbx";

      this.BridgeXml = @"<?xml version=""1.0"" encoding=""utf-8"" ?>
                       <bridge namespace=""MyNamespace"" className=""MyMath"">
                         <proxy type=""CustomComponents.Math, App_Code""/>
                           <method name=""Divide"">
                             <input>
                               <parameter name=""x"" />
                               <parameter name=""y"" />
                             </input>
                           </method>
                         </bridge>";
    }
```

(continued)

Listing 14-32 *(continued)*

```
[WebMethodAttribute()]
[ScriptMethodAttribute(UseHttpGet = false,
                       ResponseFormat = ResponseFormat.Json)]
public virtual object Divide(System.Collections.IDictionary args)
{
  BridgeRequest brequest = new BridgeRequest("Divide", args);
  return this.Invoke(brequest);
}

public override object CallServiceClassMethod(string method,
                                     Dictionary<string, object> args,
                                     ICredentials credentials,
                                     string url)
{
  if ("Divide".Equals(method))
  {
    Math proxy = new Math();
    object obj;
    if (args.TryGetValue("x", out obj)) { }

    else
       throw new ArgumentException("Argument not found: x");

    double arg0 = ((double)(BridgeHandler.ConvertToType(obj, typeof(double))));

    if (args.TryGetValue("y", out obj)) { }

    else
       throw new ArgumentException("Argument not found: y");

    double arg1 = ((double)(BridgeHandler.ConvertToType(obj, typeof(double))));
    return proxy.Divide(arg0, arg1);
  }
  throw new ArgumentException("CallServiceClassMethod: Unknown method");
}

[WebMethodAttribute()]
[ScriptMethodAttribute(UseHttpGet = false,
                       ResponseFormat = ResponseFormat.Json)]
public virtual object @__invokeBridge(string method, IDictionary args)
{
  BridgeRequest brequest = new BridgeRequest(method, args);
  return this.Invoke(brequest);
}
  }
}
```

This code defines a class with the name specified in the `className` attribute on the `bridge` document element. The document element also belongs to a namespace with the name specified in the `namespace` attribute on this element. Note that this class exposes a string property named `BridgeXml` that contains the contents of the `.asbx` file.

As you can see in the code listing, this class is annotated with the WebServiceAttribute metadata attribute, which means that this class is a Web service. Therefore, the call into the BuildManager class's GetCompiledType static method that was previously highlighted in Listing 14-31 creates a Web service under the hood with the name specified in the className attribute on the bridge document element. This exposes a Web method with the name specified in the name attribute on the <method> element of the .asbx file. The ASP.NET AJAX Web services bridge simply creates a Web service wrapper around your custom class and exposes its methods as Web methods.

Considering the fact that the GetCompiledType static method of the BuildManager class takes only the virtual path of the file being compiled, and has no knowledge of the type of file it is dealing with, how does this method know what type of class to generate? The answer is it doesn't. Under the hood, the GetCompiledType method delegates the responsibility of parsing the file and generating the code for the class that represents the file to another component known as a *build provider*. Each type of build provider is specifically designed to parse and generate code for a file with specific extension. The following table presents a few examples of build providers and the file extension for which each build provider generates code.

Build Provider	File Type
PageBuildProvider	.aspx
UserControlBuildProvider	.ascx
WsdlBuildProvider	.wsdl
XsdBuildProvider	.xsd
MasterPageBuildProvider	.master
WebServiceBuildProvider	.asmx
BridgeBuildProvider	.asbx

As shown in this table, the ASP.NET framework includes a build provider named BridgeBuildProvider, which is specifically designed to parse and generate code for files with extension .asbx. This build provider is the one that generates the code for the Web service wrapper shown in Listing 14-32. If you check out the web.config file in your AJAX-enabled Web site, you'll see the following code, which registers the BridgeBuildProvider with the ASP.NET compilation infrastructure:

```
<compilation debug="true">
  <buildProviders>
    <add extension=".asbx"
      type="Microsoft.Web.Preview.Services.BridgeBuildProvider" />
  </buildProviders>
</compilation>
```

Using the Replicas

The previous sections provided you with the complete replica implementations of the following main components of the ASP.NET AJAX REST method call request processing infrastructure:

❑ ScriptHandlerFactory

❑ RestHandlerFactory

❑   RestHandler

❑   HandlerWrapper

❑   ScriptModule

As mentioned earlier, these replicas are fully functional. Follow these steps to see the replicas in action:

1.   Create an AJAX-enabled Web site in Visual Studio.

2.   Add an App_Code directory in this Web site.

3.   Add a new source file named ScriptHandlerFactory.cs to the App_Code directory, and then add the code shown in Listing 14-22 to this source file.

4.   Add a new source file named RestHandlerFactory.cs to the App_Code directory, and then add the code shown in Listing 14-24 to this source file. Comment out the following two lines of code from this source file to remove the reference to the RestClientProxyHandler (which hasn't been covered yet):

```
//if (IsClientProxyRequest(context.Request.PathInfo))
//   return new RestClientProxyHandler();
```

5.   Add a new source file named RestHandler.cs to the App_Code directory, and then add the code shown in Listing 14-25 to this source file.

6.   Add a new source file named HandlerWrapper.cs to the App_Code directory, and then add the code shown in Listing 14-26 to this source file.

7.   Add a new source file named ScriptModule.cs to the App_Code directory, and then add the code shown in Listing 14-29 to this source file.

8.   Add a new Web form (.aspx file) named PageMethods.aspx, and then add the code shown in Listing 14-17 to this .aspx file.

9.   Add a new Web form (.aspx file) named Math.aspx to the root directory of this Web site, and then add the code shown in Listing 14-18 to this .aspx file.

10. Add a new XML file named Math.asbx to the root directory of this Web site, and then add the XML document shown in Listing 14-19.

11. Add a new source file named Math.cs to the App_Code directory, and then add the code shown in Listing 14-18 to this source file.

12. Add a new Web form (.aspx file) named Math2.aspx to the root directory of this Web site, and then add the code shown in Listing 14-15 to this .aspx file.

13. Add a new Web service (.asmx) named Math.asmx to the root directory of this Web site, and then add the code shown in Listing 14-16 to this .asmx file.

14. In the web.config file, comment out the italicized lines shown in the following code, and add the boldface portion of the code (which is basically replacing the standard ASP.NET ScriptHandlerFactory and ScriptModule with the replica ScriptHandlerFactory and ScriptModule):

```
<httpHandlers>
  <remove verb="*" path="*.asmx" />
  <!--
      <add verb="*" path="*.asmx" validate="false"
        type="System.Web.Script.Services.ScriptHandlerFactory,
              System.Web.Extensions, Version=1.0.61025.0, Culture=neutral,
              PublicKeyToken=31bf3856ad364e35" />
      <add verb="*" path="*_AppService.axd" validate="false"
        type="System.Web.Script.Services.ScriptHandlerFactory,
              System.Web.Extensions, Version=1.0.61025.0, Culture=neutral,
              PublicKeyToken=31bf3856ad364e35" />
      <add verb="GET,HEAD,POST" path="*.asbx"
        type="System.Web.Script.Services.ScriptHandlerFactory,
              System.Web.Extensions, Version=1.0.61025.0, Culture=neutral,
              PublicKeyToken=31bf3856ad364e35" validate="false" />
  -->

  <add verb="*" path="*.asmx" validate="false"
    type="CustomComponents.ScriptHandlerFactory" />
  <add verb="GET,HEAD,POST" path="*.asbx"
    type="CustomComponents.ScriptHandlerFactory" />
    . . .
</httpHandlers>

<httpModules>
  <!--
      <add name="ScriptModule" type="System.Web.Handlers.ScriptModule,
        System.Web.Extensions, Version=1.0.61025.0, Culture=neutral,
        PublicKeyToken=31bf3856ad364e35" />
  -->

  <add name="ScriptModule" type="CustomComponents.ScriptModule" />
    . . .
</httpModules>
```

Now if you run the `PageMethods.aspx`, `Math.aspx`, and `Math2.aspx` pages, you should be able to see the same results you saw when you ran these pages with the standard ASP.NET `ScriptHandlerFactory` and `ScriptModule`. Feel free to play with the code to get a better understanding of the processing infrastructure of the ASP.NET AJAX REST method call request.

Summary

This chapter provided you with in-depth coverage of the ASP.NET AJAX REST method call request's processing infrastructure. It introduced Web services bridges, which are covered in more detail in Chapter 19, where you'll learn how to develop a custom script server control that uses a bridge to enable the client code to interact with Amazon Web services.

The next chapter builds on what you learned in this chapter to show you how this infrastructure manages to hide its complexity behind proxy classes.

15

Proxy Classes

The previous chapter provided you with in-depth coverage of the ASP.NET AJAX REST method call request processing infrastructure. This chapter shows you how this infrastructure hides its complexity behind proxy classes to enable you to program against a remote object as you would against a local object.

What's a Proxy, Anyway?

Let's revisit the `add` JavaScript function shown in Listing 14-14 of Chapter 14, and shown again here in Listing 15-1. This JavaScript function was registered as the event handler for the Add button's `click` event of in Listing 14-14.

Listing 15-1: The add Method

```
function add()
{
    var servicePath = " http://localhost/AJAXEnabledFuturesWebSite2/Math.asmx";
    var methodName = "Add";
    var useGet = false;
    var xValue = $get("firstNumber").value;
    var yValue = $get("secondNumber").value;
    var params = {x : xValue, y : yValue};

    var userContext = $get("result");
    var webServiceProxy = new Sys.Net.WebServiceProxy();
    webServiceProxy.set_timeout(0);
     request = webServiceProxy._invoke(servicePath, methodName, useGet, params,
                                      onSuccess, onFailure, userContext);
}
```

Now here is a question for you: How would you code this `add` method if the `Math` class (see Listing 14-15) were a local class in your client-side code, such as the local class shown in Listing 15-2?

Listing 15-2: A Local Class with the Same Name and Methods as the Remote Web Service

```
Type.registerNamespace("MyNamespace");

MyNamespace.Math = function ()
{
}

MyNamespace.Math.prototype =
{
   Add : function (x, y) { return x + y; }
}

MyNamespace.Math.registerClass("MyNamespace.Math");
```

Wouldn't your implementation of the add method be something like the one shown in Listing 15-3?

Listing 15-3: Implementation of add Method if the Web Service Class Were a Local Class

```
function add()
{
   var math = new MyNamespace.Math();
   var xValue = $get("firstNumber").value;
   var yValue = $get("secondNumber").value;
   var z = math.Add(Number.parseInvariant(xValue),
                     Number.parseInvariant(yValue));
   $get("result").innerText = z;
}
```

As you can see in this listing, if the Math object were a local object, you would directly invoke the Add method on the object and directly pass the x and y values into the Add method itself.

However, when the Math object becomes a Web service, it is a remote object, so you cannot directly invoke the Add method on it, nor can you directly pass the x and y values into it. When you're calling the Add method on the remote Math object:

❑   You have to worry about the service path where the remote Math object is located:

```
var servicePath = "http://localhost/AJAXEnabledFuturesWebSite2/Math.asmx";
```

You don't have to worry about the location of a local Math object, because it always resides in the same address space as the rest of your program and, consequently, you have direct access to the object.

❑   You have to pass the name of the method as a *string* into the _invoke method of the WebServiceProxy object:

```
var methodName = "Add";
request = webServiceProxy._invoke(servicePath, methodName, useGet, params,
                                  onSuccess, onFailure, userContext);
```

This is obviously very different from a local method invocation where you directly invoke the method on the object instead of passing a string around.

❑ You have to pass the names and values of the parameters of the method as a *dictionary* into the `_invoke` method of the `WebServiceProxy` object.

```
var params = {x : xValue, y : yValue};
request = webServiceProxy._invoke(servicePath, methodName, useGet, params,
                                  onSuccess, onFailure, userContext);
```

This is obviously very different from a local method invocation where you directly pass these parameters into the method itself instead of passing a dictionary around.

❑ You're trying to call a method named `Add`, which takes two parameters of type double and returns a value of type `double`, on an object of type `Math`, but you have to call a method with a different name (`_invoke`), with completely different parameters (`servicePath`, `methodName`, `useGet`, `params`, `onSucess`, `onFailure`, and `userContext`), and with a completely different return type (`WebRequest`), on a completely different object (the `WebServiceProxy` object):

```
request = webServiceProxy._invoke(servicePath, methodName, useGet, params,
                                  onSuccess, onFailure, userContext);
```

This is obviously very different from a local method invocation where you directly invoke the `Add` method on the `Math` object.

As you can see, invoking the `Add` method on the remote `Math` object doesn't look anything like invoking the `Add` method on a local `Math` object.

Proxy Class

The ASP.NET AJAX framework provides you with a local object that has the following characteristics:

❑ It has the same name as the remote object. For example, in the case of the `Math` Web service, the AJAX framework provides you with a local object named `Math`.

❑ It exposes methods with the same names as the methods of the remote object. For example, the local `Math` object associated with the remote `Math` Web service object exposes a method named `Add`.

❑ Its methods take parameters with the same names as the associated methods of the remote object. For example, the `Add` method of the local `Math` object associated with the remote `Math` Web service object also takes two parameters with the same names as the parameters of the `Add` method of the remote `Math` Web service object: x and y.

❑ Its methods take parameters of the same types as the associated methods of the remote object. For example, the `Add` method of the local `Math` object associated with the remote `Math` Web service object also takes two parameters of the same types as the parameters of the `Add` method of the remote `Math` Web service object: `double`.

❑ Its methods return values of the same types as the associated methods of the remote object. For example, the `Add` method of the local `Math` object associated with the remote `Math` Web service object returns a value of the same type as the return value of the `Add` method of the remote `Math` Web service object: `double`.

This enables you to program against the local object, instead of the `WebServiceProxy` object as you did in the last chapter, and consequently, makes programming against remote objects more like programming against local objects. Because this local object makes it feel like you're directly interacting with the remote object, it is known as a *proxy object*. In other words, this local object acts as a *proxy* for the remote object.

Let's begin by discussing the implementation of the proxy class and object that the ASP.NET AJAX framework automatically generates for you. (The mechanism that actually generates this proxy class and object is discussed later in the chapter.)

As you learned in the previous chapter, there are three types of remote method invocations:

❑ Invoking a Web method that is part of a Web service

❑ Invoking a page method that is part of an ASP.NET page

❑ Invoking a method that is part of a custom class

Therefore, there are three types of proxy classes:

❑ Proxy classes associated with Web services

❑ Proxy classes associated with page methods

❑ Proxy classes associated with custom classes

Proxy Classes Associated with Web Services

Listing 15-4 presents the implementation of the local `Math` proxy class associated with the remote `Math` Web service class.

Listing 15-4: The Local Math Proxy Class Associated with the Remote Math Web Service Class

```
Type.registerNamespace('MyNamespace');

MyNamespace.Math = function()
{
  MyNamespace.Math.initializeBase(this);
  this._timeout = 0;
  this._userContext = null;
  this._succeeded = null;
  this._failed = null;
}

MyNamespace.Math.prototype =
{
    Add : function(x, y, succeededCallback, failedCallback, userContext)
        {
            var servicePath = MyNamespace.Math.get_path();
            var methodName = 'Add';
            var useGet = false;
            var params = {x : x, y : y};
            var onSuccess = succeededCallback;
```

```
                    var onFailure = failedCallback;

              return this._invoke(servicePath, methodName, useGet, params,
                                   onSuccess,onFailure, userContext);
          }
}

MyNamespace.Math.registerClass('MyNamespace.Math', Sys.Net.WebServiceProxy);

MyNamespace.Math._staticInstance = new MyNamespace.Math();
MyNamespace.Math.set_path = function(value)
{
  MyNamespace.Math._staticInstance._path = value;
}

MyNamespace.Math.get_path = function()
{
  return MyNamespace.Math._staticInstance._path;
}

MyNamespace.Math.set_timeout = function(value)
{
  MyNamespace.Math._staticInstance._timeout = value;
}

MyNamespace.Math.get_timeout = function()
{
  return MyNamespace.Math._staticInstance._timeout;
}

MyNamespace.Math.set_defaultUserContext = function(value)
{
  MyNamespace.Math._staticInstance._userContext = value;
}

MyNamespace.Math.get_defaultUserContext = function()
{
  return MyNamespace.Math._staticInstance._userContext;
}

MyNamespace.Math.set_defaultSucceededCallback = function(value)
{
  MyNamespace.Math._staticInstance._succeeded = value;
}
MyNamespace.Math.get_defaultSucceededCallback = function()
{
  return MyNamespace.Math._staticInstance._succeeded;
}

MyNamespace.Math.set_defaultFailedCallback = function(value)
{
  MyNamespace.Math._staticInstance._failed = value;
}
```

(continued)

Listing 15-4 *(continued)*

```
MyNamespace.Math.get_defaultFailedCallback = function()
{
  return MyNamespace.Math._staticInstance._failed;
}

MyNamespace.Math.set_path("/AJAXFuturesEnabledWebSite2/Math.asmx");

MyNamespace.Math.Add = function(x, y, onSuccess, onFailed, userContext)
{
  MyNamespace.Math._staticInstance.Add(x, y, onSuccess, onFailed, userContext);
}
```

This code listing defines a namespace with the same name as the namespace of the remote `Math` Web service class:

```
Type.registerNamespace('MyNamespace');
```

The local `Math` proxy class derives from the `WebServiceProxy` class:

```
MyNamespace.Math.registerClass('MyNamespace.Math', Sys.Net.WebServiceProxy);
```

All ASP.NET AJAX proxy classes directly or indirectly derive from the `Sys.Net.WebServiceProxy` *class.*

As you can see from in the following excerpt from Listing 15-4, this local `Math` proxy class exposes a method with the same name as the remote Web service class — `Add`. This method takes parameters with the same names and types as the remote Web service class's `Add` method parameters, and returns a value of the same type as the remote Web service class's `Add` method return value:

```
MyNamespace.Math.prototype =
{
    Add : function(x, y, succeededCallback, failedCallback, userContext)
        {
            var servicePath = MyNamespace.Math.get_path();
            var methodName = 'Add';
            var useGet = false;
            var params = {x : x, y : y};
            var onSuccess = succeededCallback;
            var onFailure = failedCallback;

            return this._invoke(servicePath, methodName, useGet, params,
                                onSuccess,onFailure, userContext);
        }
}
```

The `Add` method of this local `Math` proxy class encapsulates the code that you would otherwise have to write to interact with the `WebServiceProxy` object as you did in the previous chapter. Note that Listing 15-4 instantiates an instance of this local `Math` proxy class and assigns the instance to a private static field on this class named `_staticInstance`:

```
MyNamespace.Math._staticInstance = new MyNamespace.Math();
```

The code then defines static getters and setters that delegate to the associated getters and setters of this static Math proxy instance. Also note that the code exposes a static method named Add on this local Math proxy class, which delegates to the Add method of the static Math proxy instance:

```
MyNamespace.Math.Add = function(x, y, onSuccess, onFailed, userContext)
{
  MyNamespace.Math._staticInstance.Add(x, y, onSuccess, onFailed, userContext);
}
```

Finally, the code invokes the set_path static method on this local Math proxy class to set the service path for the static Math proxy instance:

```
MyNamespace.Math.set_path("/AJAXFuturesEnabledWebSite2/Math.asmx");
```

Listing 15-5 presents a page that uses the Math proxy class. As you'll see later in this chapter, the ASP.NET AJAX framework automatically generates the code for the proxy class such as the Math proxy class shown in this listing. For now, assume that you generated this code yourself and treat it like any other client code. As such, the content of Listing 15-4 is stored in a JavaScript file named MathWebServiceProxy.js, and Listing 15-5 adds a reference to this JavaScript file.

Now let's walk through the implementation of the add JavaScript function shown in the following excerpt from Listing 15-5:

```
function add()
{
  var userContext = $get("result");
  var xValue = $get("firstNumber").value;
  var yValue = $get("secondNumber").value;
  MyNamespace.Math.Add(xValue, yValue, onSuccess, onFailure, userContext);
}
```

Thanks to the Math proxy class, you get to directly invoke the Add method and directly pass the x and y values into this method. Note that there is no sign of the WebServiceProxy and its weird-looking _invoke method. The Math proxy class enables you to program against the remote Math Web service object as if you were programming against a local Math object. In other words, the Math proxy class gives your client code the illusion that it is making a local method call.

Listing 15-5: A Page that Uses the Local Static Math Proxy Instance

```
<%@ Page Language="C#" %>

<!DOCTYPE html PUBLIC "-//W3C//DTD XHTML 1.0 Transitional//EN"
"http://www.w3.org/TR/xhtml1/DTD/xhtml1-transitional.dtd">
<html xmlns="http://www.w3.org/1999/xhtml">
<head runat="server">
  <title>Untitled Page</title>

  <script type="text/javascript" language="javascript">
    var request;

    function onSuccess(result, userContext, methodName)
    {
```

(continued)

Listing 15-5 *(continued)*

```
        userContext.innerHTML = "<b<>u>" + result + "</u></b>";
    }

    function onFailure(result, userContext, methodName)
    {
      var builder = new Sys.StringBuilder();
      builder.append("timedOut: ");
      builder.append(result.get_timedOut());
      builder.appendLine();
      builder.appendLine();
      builder.append("message: ");
      builder.append(result.get_message());
      builder.appendLine();
      builder.appendLine();
      builder.append("stackTrace: ");
      builder.appendLine();
      builder.append(result.get_stackTrace());
      builder.appendLine();
      builder.appendLine();
      builder.append("exceptionType: ");
      builder.append(result.get_exceptionType());
      builder.appendLine();
      builder.appendLine();
      builder.append("statusCode: ");
      builder.append(result.get_statusCode());
      builder.appendLine();
      builder.appendLine();
      builder.append("methodName: ");
      builder.append(methodName);

      alert(builder.toString());
    }

    function add()
    {
      var userContext = $get("result");
      var xValue = $get("firstNumber").value;
      var yValue = $get("secondNumber").value;
      MyNamespace.Math.Add(xValue, yValue, onSuccess, onFailure, userContext);
    }
  </script>

</head>
<body>
  <form id="form1" runat="server">
    <asp:ScriptManager runat="server" ID="ScriptManager1">
      <Scripts>
        <asp:ScriptReference Path="MathWebServiceProxy.js" />
      </Scripts>
    </asp:ScriptManager>
    <table>
      <tr>
        <td style="font-weight: bold" align="right">
```

```
                First Number:
            </td>
            <td align="left">
                <input type="text" id="firstNumber" /></td>
        </tr>
        <tr>
            <td style="font-weight: bold" align="right">
                Second Number:
            </td>
            <td align="left">
                <input type="text" id="secondNumber" /></td>
        </tr>
        <tr>
            <td colspan="2" align="center">
                <button onclick="add()">
                    Add</button></td>
        </tr>
        <tr>
            <td style="font-weight: bold" align="right">
                Result:
            </td>
            <td align="left">
                <span id="result" />
            </td>
        </tr>
    </table>
  </form>
</body>
</html>
```

Proxy Classes Associated with Page Methods

The following code presents a proxy class associated with a page method named Add, which belongs to the PageMethods.aspx page:

```
PageMethods = function()
{
  PageMethods.initializeBase(this);
  this._timeout = 0;
  this._userContext = null;
  this._succeeded = null;
  this._failed = null;
}

PageMethods.prototype =
{
  Add : function(x, y, succeededCallback, failedCallback, userContext) {
    return this._invoke(PageMethods.get_path(), 'Add', false, {x:x, y:y},
                        succeededCallback, failedCallback, userContext);
  }
}

PageMethods.registerClass('PageMethods', Sys.Net.WebServiceProxy);
```

(continued)

(continued)

```
PageMethods._staticInstance = new PageMethods();

PageMethods.set_path = function(value)
{
  PageMethods._staticInstance._path = value;
}

PageMethods.get_path = function()
{
  return PageMethods._staticInstance._path;
}

PageMethods.set_timeout = function(value)
{
  PageMethods._staticInstance._timeout = value;
}

PageMethods.get_timeout = function()
{
  return PageMethods._staticInstance._timeout;
}

PageMethods.set_defaultUserContext = function(value)
{
  PageMethods._staticInstance._userContext = value;
}

PageMethods.get_defaultUserContext = function()
{
  return PageMethods._staticInstance._userContext;
}

PageMethods.set_defaultSucceededCallback = function(value)
{
  PageMethods._staticInstance._succeeded = value;
}

PageMethods.get_defaultSucceededCallback = function()
{
  return PageMethods._staticInstance._succeeded;
}

PageMethods.set_defaultFailedCallback = function(value)
{
  PageMethods._staticInstance._failed = value;
}

PageMethods.get_defaultFailedCallback = function()
{
  return PageMethods._staticInstance._failed;
}

PageMethods.set_path("/AJAXFuturesEnabledWebSite2/PageMethods.aspx");

PageMethods.Add = function(x, y, onSuccess, onFailed, userContext)
{
  PageMethods._staticInstance.Add(x, y, onSuccess, onFailed, userContext);
};
```

Comparing this code with Listing 15-4 clearly shows that a proxy class associated with page methods has a fixed named — `PageMethods` — and does not belong to any namespace. All methods annotated with `WebMethod` metadata attribute on a given page are associated with the same proxy class named `PageMethods` on the client side. As the boldface portion of the code shows, the `set_path` method is invoked on the `PageMethods` proxy object to specify the URL of the `PageMethods.aspx` page as the target URL for the proxy class.

The following code presents a page that uses the `PageMethods` proxy class. As you'll see later in this chapter, the ASP.NET AJAX framework automatically generates the code for the `PageMethods` proxy class and adds this code to the current page. For now, assume that you generated this code yourself and treat it like any other client script. As such, this code is stored in a JavaScript file named `MathPageMethodsProxy.js`, and the following code adds a reference to this file. Note that the following code is the same as Listing 15-5, except for the boldface portion where the `PageMethods` proxy is used to communicate with the underlying page method.

```
<%@ Page Language="C#" %>

<!DOCTYPE html PUBLIC "-//W3C//DTD XHTML 1.0 Transitional//EN"
"http://www.w3.org/TR/xhtml1/DTD/xhtml1-transitional.dtd">
<html xmlns="http://www.w3.org/1999/xhtml">
<head runat="server">
  <title>Untitled Page</title>

  <script type="text/javascript" language="javascript">
    var request;

    function onSuccess(result, userContext, methodName)
    {
      userContext.innerHTML = "<b><u>" + result + "</b></u>";
    }

    function onFailure(result, userContext, methodName)
    {
      //Same as Listing 15-5
    }

    function add()
    {
      var userContext = $get("result");
      var xValue = $get("firstNumber").value;
      var yValue = $get("secondNumber").value;
      PageMethods.Add(xValue, yValue, onSuccess, onFailure, userContext);
    }
  </script>
</head>
<body>
  <form id="form1" runat="server">
    <asp:ScriptManager runat="server" ID="ScriptManager1">
      <Scripts>
        <asp:ScriptReference Path="MathPageMethodsProxy.js" />
      </Scripts>
    </asp:ScriptManager>
    <!-- Same as Listing 15-5 -->
  </form>
</body>
</html>
```

Proxy Classes Associated with Custom Classes

The proxy classes associated with custom classes are very similar to the proxy classes associated with Web services. The main difference is that the target URL of the proxy class associated with a custom class is set to the URL of the .asbx file that describes the custom class.

Automatic Proxy Class Generation

This illusion will work only if someone implements the Math proxy class for you. Otherwise, if you were to implement this class yourself, it would not be much of an illusion. The main challenge with implementing a proxy class is that one proxy class will not work with all types of remote classes. For example, you cannot use the Math proxy class to talk to the Products Web service class because the Products Web service class is a completely different Web service class than the Math Web service class. For one thing, the Products Web service class exposes methods such as GetProducts as opposed to Add. This means that you have to use separate proxy classes to talk to different remote classes.

This is where the ASP.NET AJAX server-side framework comes to the rescue. This framework contains the logic that automatically generates the code for the proxy class for each remote class that your client code needs to interact with. All you have to do is add a ServiceReference object to the Services collection of the current ScriptManager server control to specify which remote class you need to talk to. You can do this either imperatively or declaratively.

Declarative Approach

Listing 15-6 presents a page that that uses the declarative approach to add a ServiceReference object to the Services collection of the current ScriptManager server control.

Listing 15-6: A Page that Uses the Declarative Approach to Add a ScriptReference Object

```
<%@ Page Language="C#" %>

<!DOCTYPE html PUBLIC "-//W3C//DTD XHTML 1.0 Transitional//EN"
"http://www.w3.org/TR/xhtml11/DTD/xhtml11-transitional.dtd">
<html xmlns="http://www.w3.org/1999/xhtml">
<head runat="server">
  <title>Untitled Page</title>

  <script type="text/javascript" language="javascript">
    var request;

    function onSuccess(result, userContext, methodName)
    {
      userContext.innerHTML = "<b><u>" + result + "</b></u>";
    }

    function onFailure(result, userContext, methodName)
    {
      var builder = new Sys.StringBuilder();
      builder.append("timedOut: ");
      builder.append(result.get_timedOut());
      builder.appendLine();
```

```
            builder.appendLine();
            builder.append("message: ");
            builder.append(result.get_message());
            builder.appendLine();
            builder.appendLine();
            builder.append("stackTrace: ");
            builder.appendLine();
            builder.append(result.get_stackTrace());
            builder.appendLine();
            builder.appendLine();
            builder.append("exceptionType: ");
            builder.append(result.get_exceptionType());
            builder.appendLine();
            builder.appendLine();
            builder.append("statusCode: ");
            builder.append(result.get_statusCode());
            builder.appendLine();
            builder.appendLine();
            builder.append("methodName: ");
            builder.append(methodName);

            alert(builder.toString());
        }

        function add()
        {
            var userContext = $get("result");
            var xValue = $get("firstNumber").value;
            var yValue = $get("secondNumber").value;
            MyNamespace.Math.Add(xValue, yValue, onSuccess, onFailure, userContext);
        }
    </script>

</head>
<body>
    <form id="form1" runat="server">
        <asp:ScriptManager runat="server" ID="ScriptManager1">
            <Services>
                <asp:ServiceReference Path = "/AJAXFuturesEnabledWebSite2/Math.asmx"
                InlineScript="true" />
            </Services>
        </asp:ScriptManager>
        <table>
            <tr>
                <td style="font-weight: bold" align="right">
                    First Number:
                </td>
                <td align="left">
                    <input type="text" id="firstNumber" /></td>
            </tr>
            <tr>
                <td style="font-weight: bold" align="right">
                    Second Number:
                </td>
```

(continued)

Listing 15-6 *(continued)*

```
            <td align="left">
              <input type="text" id="secondNumber" /></td>
          </tr>
          <tr>
            <td colspan="2" align="center">
              <button onclick="add()">
                Add</button></td>
          </tr>
          <tr>
            <td style="font-weight: bold" align="right">
              Result:
            </td>
            <td align="left">
              <span id="result" />
            </td>
          </tr>
        </table>
      </form>
    </body>
  </html>
```

As you can see in the boldface portion of this code listing, the page adds an `<asp:ServiceReference>` element to the `<Services>` child element of the `<asp:ScriptManager>` tag that represents the current `ScriptManager` server control on the `.aspx` page. Note that this page sets the `Path` attribute on this `<asp:ServiceReference>` tag to the service path of the `Math` Web service. Also note that the page sets the `InlineScript` attribute on this tag to `true` to tell the ASP.NET AJAX server-side framework to add the definition of the `Math` proxy class to the markup sent to the requesting browser. As a matter of fact, if you run Listing 15-6 and view the source from your browser, you'll see Listing 15-7.

Listing 15-7: The Source for the Page Shown in Listing 15-6

```
<!DOCTYPE html PUBLIC "-//W3C//DTD XHTML 1.0 Transitional//EN"
"http://www.w3.org/TR/xhtml1/DTD/xhtml1-transitional.dtd">
<html xmlns="http://www.w3.org/1999/xhtml">
<head><title>
  Untitled Page
</title>

  <script type="text/javascript" language="javascript">
    var request;

    function onSuccess(result, userContext, methodName)
    {
      userContext.innerHTML = "<b><u>" + result + "</b></u>";
    }

    function onFailure(result, userContext, methodName)
    {
      var builder = new Sys.StringBuilder();
      builder.append("timedOut: ");
      builder.append(result.get_timedOut());
      builder.appendLine();
```

```
            builder.appendLine();
            builder.append("message: ");
            builder.append(result.get_message());
            builder.appendLine();
            builder.appendLine();
            builder.append("stackTrace: ");
            builder.appendLine();
            builder.append(result.get_stackTrace());
            builder.appendLine();
            builder.appendLine();
            builder.append("exceptionType: ");
            builder.append(result.get_exceptionType());
            builder.appendLine();
            builder.appendLine();
            builder.append("statusCode: ");
            builder.append(result.get_statusCode());
            builder.appendLine();
            builder.appendLine();
            builder.append("methodName: ");
            builder.append(methodName);

            alert(builder.toString());
        }

        function add()
        {
          var userContext = $get("result");
          var xValue = $get("firstNumber").value;
          var yValue = $get("secondNumber").value;
          MyNamespace.Math.Add(xValue, yValue, onSuccess, onFailure, userContext);
        }
    </script>

</head>
<body>
    <form name="form1" method="post" action="WebServiceProxy.aspx" id="form1">
<div>
<input type="hidden" name="__EVENTTARGET" id="__EVENTTARGET" value="" />
<input type="hidden" name="__EVENTARGUMENT" id="__EVENTARGUMENT" value="" />
<input type="hidden" name="__VIEWSTATE" id="__VIEWSTATE"
value="/wEPDwULLTEzMTg5MjA5NzVkZDZArSkraR3ukOEGxC944PmDWFHr" />
</div>

<script type="text/javascript">
<!--
var theForm = document.forms['form1'];
if (!theForm)
{
    theForm = document.form1;
}
function __doPostBack(eventTarget, eventArgument)
{
    if (!theForm.onsubmit || (theForm.onsubmit() != false))
    {
        theForm.__EVENTTARGET.value = eventTarget;
```

(continued)

Listing 15-7 *(continued)*

```
        theForm.__EVENTARGUMENT.value = eventArgument;
        theForm.submit();
    }
}
// -->
</script>

<script src="/AJAXFuturesEnabledWebSite2/WebResource.axd?d=yy2blzBZ_gTxI-
oButV_bA2&amp;t=632968856944906146" type="text/javascript"></script>

<script
src="/AJAXFuturesEnabledWebSite2/ScriptResource.axd?d=
                               5dGbo4QMlo4oM6SEPbeJDlgdNKMbymeDj
oOb3MgwqVCNw7gUy_Hwpl05Bo9fKC03KULnWFJDf9ku4Xp9SqPBxdVQWdcxJCyPuljKGvPcGts1&amp;t=6
33052351733295148" type="text/javascript"></script>
<script
src="/AJAXFuturesEnabledWebSite2/ScriptResource.axd?d=
                               5dGbo4QMlo4oM6SEPbeJDlgdNKMbymeDj
oOb3MgwqVCNw7gUy_Hwpl05Bo9fKC03KULnWFJDf9ku4Xp9SqPBxYKjD_ECoU_mRI6NDMsutIxYndjcl69y
5SLyWOqfgiOM0&amp;t=633052351733295148" type="text/javascript"></script>
<script type="text/javascript">
<!--
Type.registerNamespace('MyNamespace');
MyNamespace.Math=function() {
MyNamespace.Math.initializeBase(this);
this._timeout = 0;
this._userContext = null;
this._succeeded = null;
this._failed = null;
}
MyNamespace.Math.prototype = {
Add:function(x,y,succeededCallback, failedCallback, userContext) {
return this._invoke(MyNamespace.Math.get_path(),
'Add',false,{x:x,y:y},succeededCallback,failedCallback,userContext); }}
MyNamespace.Math.registerClass('MyNamespace.Math',Sys.Net.WebServiceProxy);
MyNamespace.Math._staticInstance = new MyNamespace.Math();
MyNamespace.Math.set_path = function(value) {
var e = Function._validateParams(arguments, [{name: 'path', type: String}]); if (e)
throw e; MyNamespace.Math._staticInstance._path = value; }
MyNamespace.Math.get_path = function() { return
MyNamespace.Math._staticInstance._path; }
MyNamespace.Math.set_timeout = function(value) { var e =
Function._validateParams(arguments, [{name: 'timeout', type: Number}]); if (e)
throw e; if (value < 0) { throw Error.argumentOutOfRange('value', value,
Sys.Res.invalidTimeout); }
MyNamespace.Math._staticInstance._timeout = value; }
MyNamespace.Math.get_timeout = function() {
return MyNamespace.Math._staticInstance._timeout; }
MyNamespace.Math.set_defaultUserContext = function(value) {
MyNamespace.Math._staticInstance._userContext = value; }
MyNamespace.Math.get_defaultUserContext = function() {
return MyNamespace.Math._staticInstance._userContext; }
```

```
MyNamespace.Math.set_defaultSucceededCallback = function(value) {
var e = Function._validateParams(arguments, [{name: 'defaultSucceededCallback',
type: Function}]); if (e) throw e; MyNamespace.Math._staticInstance._succeeded =
value; }
MyNamespace.Math.get_defaultSucceededCallback = function() {
return MyNamespace.Math._staticInstance._succeeded; }
MyNamespace.Math.set_defaultFailedCallback = function(value) {
var e = Function._validateParams(arguments, [{name: 'defaultFailedCallback', type:
Function}]); if (e) throw e; MyNamespace.Math._staticInstance._failed = value; }
MyNamespace.Math.get_defaultFailedCallback = function() {
return MyNamespace.Math._staticInstance._failed; }
MyNamespace.Math.set_path("/AJAXFuturesEnabledWebSite2/Math.asmx");
MyNamespace.Math.Add= function(x,y,onSuccess,onFailed,userContext)
{MyNamespace.Math._staticInstance.Add(x,y,onSuccess,onFailed,userContext); }
// -->
</script>

    <script type="text/javascript">
//<![CDATA[
Sys.WebForms.PageRequestManager._initialize('ScriptManager1',
document.getElementById('form1'));
Sys.WebForms.PageRequestManager.getInstance()._updateControls([], [], [], 90);
//]]>
</script>

    <table>
      <tr>
        <td style="font-weight: bold" align="right">
          First Number:
        </td>
        <td align="left">
          <input type="text" id="firstNumber" /></td>
      </tr>
      <tr>
        <td style="font-weight: bold" align="right">
          Second Number:
        </td>
        <td align="left">
          <input type="text" id="secondNumber" /></td>
      </tr>
      <tr>
        <td colspan="2" align="center">
          <button onclick="add()">
            Add</button></td>
      </tr>
      <tr>
        <td style="font-weight: bold" align="right">
          Result:
        </td>
```

(continued)

Listing 15-7 *(continued)*

```
            <td align="left">
               <span id="result" />
            </td>
         </tr>
      </table>


<script type="text/javascript">
<!--
Sys.Application.initialize();
// -->
</script>
</form>
</body>
</html>
```

As you can see, the boldface portion of this listing is just the inline definition of the Math proxy class.

This inline solution has the following drawbacks:

❏ Like any other inline solution, it does not allow the browser to cache the same script used in different pages to improve performance. For example, if you have multiple pages in your application that use the Math proxy class, every single page will include the boldface portion of Listing 15-7. However, if the script that defines the Math proxy class were in a separate file (as shown in the following code snippet), the browser could download and cache this file once.

❏ It increases the size of the page because the definition of the Math proxy class is directly added to the page. As you can see in Listing 15-7, your pages could get quite large, and the bigger a page is, the longer it takes to download. However, if the boldface portion of Listing 15-7 were in a separate file (as shown in the following code snippet), the browser would download this script once and use it across all pages in your application that use the Math proxy class.

```
<asp:ScriptManager runat="server" ID="ScriptManager1">
  <Services>
    <asp:ServiceReference Path="/AJAXFuturesEnabledWebSite2/Math.asmx"
      InlineScript="true" />
  </Services>
</asp:ScriptManager>
```

If you set the InlineScript attribute on the <asp:ScriptReference> to false, run the same page, and view the source from your browser, you'll get Listing 15-8.

Listing 15-8: The Source of the Page Shown in Listing 15-6 with a ScriptMode Value of Debug

```
<!DOCTYPE html PUBLIC "-//W3C//DTD XHTML 1.0 Transitional//EN"
"http://www.w3.org/TR/xhtml1/DTD/xhtml1-transitional.dtd">
<html xmlns="http://www.w3.org/1999/xhtml">
<head><title>
  Untitled Page
</title>

  <script type="text/javascript" language="javascript">
    var request;

    function onSuccess(result, userContext, methodName)
    {
      userContext.innerHTML = "<b><u>" + result + "</b></u>";
    }

    function onFailure(result, userContext, methodName)
    {
      var builder = new Sys.StringBuilder();
      builder.append("timedOut: ");
      builder.append(result.get_timedOut());
      builder.appendLine();
      builder.appendLine();
      builder.append("message: ");
      builder.append(result.get_message());
      builder.appendLine();
      builder.appendLine();
      builder.append("stackTrace: ");
      builder.appendLine();
      builder.append(result.get_stackTrace());
      builder.appendLine();
      builder.appendLine();
      builder.append("exceptionType: ");
      builder.append(result.get_exceptionType());
      builder.appendLine();
      builder.appendLine();
      builder.append("statusCode: ");
      builder.append(result.get_statusCode());
      builder.appendLine();
      builder.appendLine();
      builder.append("methodName: ");
      builder.append(methodName);

      alert(builder.toString());
    }

    function add()
    {
      var userContext = $get("result");
      var xValue = $get("firstNumber").value;
```

(continued)

Listing 15-8 *(continued)*

```
        var yValue = $get("secondNumber").value;
        MyNamespace.Math.Add(xValue, yValue, onSuccess, onFailure, userContext);
    }
  </script>

</head>
<body>
  <form name="form1" method="post" action="WebServiceProxy.aspx" id="form1">
<div>
<input type="hidden" name="__EVENTTARGET" id="__EVENTTARGET" value="" />
<input type="hidden" name="__EVENTARGUMENT" id="__EVENTARGUMENT" value="" />
<input type="hidden" name="__VIEWSTATE" id="__VIEWSTATE"
value="/wEPDwULLTEzMTg5MjA5NzVkZDZArSkraR3ukOEGxC944PmDWFHr" />
</div>

<script type="text/javascript">
<!--
var theForm = document.forms['form1'];
if (!theForm) {
    theForm = document.form1;
}
function __doPostBack(eventTarget, eventArgument)
{
    if (!theForm.onsubmit || (theForm.onsubmit() != false)) {
        theForm.__EVENTTARGET.value = eventTarget;
        theForm.__EVENTARGUMENT.value = eventArgument;
        theForm.submit();
    }
}
// -->
</script>

<script src="/AJAXFuturesEnabledWebSite2/WebResource.axd?d=yy2blzBZ_gTxI-

oButV_bA2&amp;t=632968856944906146" type="text/javascript"></script>

<script
src="/AJAXFuturesEnabledWebSite2/ScriptResource.axd?d=
                                     5dGbo4QMlo4oM6SEPbeJDlgdNKMbymeDj
oOb3MgwqVCNw7gUy_Hwpl05Bo9fKC03KULnWFJDf9ku4Xp9SqPBxdVQWdcxJCyPuljKGvPcGts1&amp;t=6
33052351733295148" type="text/javascript"></script>
<script
src="/AJAXFuturesEnabledWebSite2/ScriptResource.axd?d=
5dGbo4QMlo4oM6SEPbeJDlgdNKMbymeDjoOb3MgwqVCNw7gUy_Hwpl05Bo9fKC03KULnWFJDf9ku4Xp9SqP
BxYKjD_ECoU_mRI6NDMsutIxYndjcl69y5SLyWOqfgiOM0&amp;t=633052351733295148"
type="text/javascript"></script>
```

```
<script src="/AJAXFuturesEnabledWebSite2/Math.asmx/jsdebug"
type="text/javascript"></script>

    <script type="text/javascript">
//<![CDATA[
Sys.WebForms.PageRequestManager._initialize('ScriptManager1',
document.getElementById('form1'));
Sys.WebForms.PageRequestManager.getInstance()._updateControls([], [], [], 90);
//]]>
</script>

    <table>
      <tr>
        <td style="font-weight: bold" align="right">
          First Number:
        </td>
        <td align="left">
          <input type="text" id="firstNumber" /></td>
      </tr>
      <tr>
        <td style="font-weight: bold" align="right">
          Second Number:
        </td>
        <td align="left">
          <input type="text" id="secondNumber" /></td>
      </tr>
      <tr>
        <td colspan="2" align="center">
          <button onclick="add()">
            Add</button></td>
      </tr>
      <tr>
        <td style="font-weight: bold" align="right">
          Result:
        </td>
        <td align="left">
          <span id="result" />
        </td>
      </tr>
    </table>


<script type="text/javascript">
<!--
Sys.Application.initialize();
// -->
</script>
</form>
</body>
</html>
```

Notice that the boldface portion of Listing 15-7 is replaced by the boldface portion of Listing 15-8:

```
<script src="/AJAXFuturesEnabledWebSite2/Math.asmx/jsdebug"
                                 type="text/javascript"></script>
```

This script block sets the `src` to the value `/AJAXFuturesEnabledWebSite2/Math.asmx/jsdebug`. Note that this value consists of two parts: the first part is the URL of the `Math` Web service, and the second part is `jsdebug`. The path trailer `jsdebug` tells the ASP.NET AJAX server-side framework that the client code wants to download the debug version of the script. If you enter this URL in the address bar of your browser, you'll get the JavaScript file that contains the definition of the `Math` proxy class (the boldfacportion of Listing 15-7).

The `ScriptManager` server control exposes an enumerator property of type `ScriptMode` and named `ScriptMode`. This property determines which version of the script to download. The following code presents the definition of the `ScriptMode` enumerator:

```
public enum ScriptMode
{
  Auto = 0,
  Inherit = 1,
  Debug = 2,
  Release = 3,
}
```

For example, if you set the `ScriptMode` attribute on the `<asp:ServiceReference>` child element previously shown in Listing 15-6 to `Release`, run the listing page, and view the page source from your browser, you'll see that the source contains the following script block. As the boldface portion shows, the path trailer is now `js` instead of `jsdebug`, which means that this time around, the release version of the script will be downloaded:

```
<script src="/AJAXFuturesEnabledWebSite2/Math.asmx/js"
                                  type="text/javascript"> </script>
```

Imperative Approach

Listing 15-9 presents a page that uses the imperative approach to add a `ServiceReference` object to the `Services` collection of the current `ScriptManager` server control.

Listing 15-9: A Page that Uses the Imperative Approach to Add a ServiceReference

```
<%@ Page Language="C#" %>

<!DOCTYPE html PUBLIC "-//W3C//DTD XHTML 1.0 Transitional//EN"
"http://www.w3.org/TR/xhtml1/DTD/xhtml1-transitional.dtd">
<script runat="server">
  void Page_Load(object sender, EventArgs e)
  {
    if (!IsPostBack)
    {
      ServiceReference serviceRef = new ServiceReference();
      serviceRef.InlineScript = false;
      serviceRef.Path = "/AJAXCTPEnabledWebSite2/Math.asmx";

      ScriptManager1.Services.Add(serviceRef);
    }
  }
</script>
```

```
<html xmlns="http://www.w3.org/1999/xhtml">
<head runat="server">
  <title>Untitled Page</title>

  <script type="text/javascript" language="javascript">
    var request;

    function onSuccess(result, userContext, methodName)
    {
      userContext.innerHTML = "<b><u>" + result + "</b></u>";
    }

    function onFailure(result, userContext, methodName)
    {
      var builder = new Sys.StringBuilder();
      builder.append("timedOut: ");
      builder.append(result.get_timedOut());
      builder.appendLine();
      builder.appendLine();
      builder.append("message: ");
      builder.append(result.get_message());
      builder.appendLine();
      builder.appendLine();
      builder.append("stackTrace: ");
      builder.appendLine();
      builder.append(result.get_stackTrace());
      builder.appendLine();
      builder.appendLine();
      builder.append("exceptionType: ");
      builder.append(result.get_exceptionType());
      builder.appendLine();
      builder.appendLine();
      builder.append("statusCode: ");
      builder.append(result.get_statusCode());
      builder.appendLine();
      builder.appendLine();
      builder.append("methodName: ");
      builder.append(methodName);

      alert(builder.toString());
    }

    function add()
    {
      var userContext = $get("result");
      var xValue = $get("firstNumber").value;
      var yValue = $get("secondNumber").value;
      MyNamespace.Math.Add(xValue, yValue, onSuccess, onFailure, userContext);
    }
  </script>

</head>
```

(continued)

Listing 15-9 *(continued)*

```
<body>
  <form id="form1" runat="server">
    <asp:ScriptManager runat="server" ID="ScriptManager1"/>
    <table>
      <tr>
        <td style="font-weight: bold" align="right">
          First Number:
        </td>
        <td align="left">
          <input type="text" id="firstNumber" />
        </td>
      </tr>
      <tr>
        <td style="font-weight: bold" align="right">
          Second Number:
        </td>
        <td align="left">
          <input type="text" id="secondNumber" />
        </td>
      </tr>
      <tr>
        <td colspan="2" align="center">
          <button onclick="add()">
            Add</button></td>
      </tr>
      <tr>
        <td style="font-weight: bold" align="right">
          Result:
        </td>
        <td align="left">
          <span id="result" />
        </td>
      </tr>
    </table>
  </form>
</body>
</html>
```

As the boldface portion of this code listing shows, the `Page_Load` method first instantiates a `ServiceReference` instance:

```
ServiceReference serviceRef = new ServiceReference();
```

Next, it sets the `InlineScript` and `Path` properties of this instance:

```
serviceRef.InlineScript = false;
serviceRef.Path = "/AJAXFuturesEnabledWebSite2/Math.asmx";
```

Finally, it adds the instance to the `Services` collection of the current `ScriptManager` server control:

```
ScriptManager1.Services.Add(serviceRef);
```

Parent/Child Pages

As previously discussed, to take advantage of the ASP.NET AJAX server-side framework automatic proxy-code generation, you must imperatively or declaratively add a `ServiceReference` object to the `Services` collection of the `ScriptManager` server control. To do so, you need to have access to this server control. This causes problems in situations involving parent and child pages. Two common scenarios are master/content and host/user control scenarios. In the master/content page scenario, the parent page is the master page and the child page is the content page. In the host/user control scenario, the child page is the user control and the parent page is the page that hosts the user control.

The problem in these parent/child page scenarios is that the parent and child are finally merged and form a single page, which means that you cannot include a separate instance of the `ScriptManager` server control on the parent and child pages. As previously discussed, every page can contain only a single instance of the `ScriptManager` server control.

If you put the `ScriptManager` server control on the parent page, the child page would not be able to add its `ServiceReference` objects to the `Services` collection of the `ScriptManager` server control. If you put the `ScriptManager` server control on the child page, the parent page would not be able to add its `ServiceReference` objects to the `Services` collection of the `ScriptManager` server control.

You would have the same problem with `ScriptReferences`. If you put the `ScriptManager` server control on the parent page, the child page would not be able to add its `ScriptReference` objects to the `Scripts` collection of the `ScriptManager` server control. If you put the `ScriptManager` server control on the child page, the parent page would not be able to add its `ScriptReference` objects to the `Scripts` collection of the `ScriptManager` server control.

To tackle these situations, the ASP.NET AJAX framework includes a new server control named `ScriptManagerProxy`. A child page whose parent page contains an instance of the `ScriptManager` server control, or a parent page whose child page contains an instance of the `ScriptManager` server control, can add its `ServiceReference` and `ScriptReference` objects to the `Services` and `Scripts` collections of the `ScriptManagerProxy` server control and rest assured that the ASP.NET AJAX framework will automatically add these `ServiceReference` and `ScriptReference` objects to the `ScriptManager` server control. Because the `ServiceReference` and `ScriptReference` objects added to the `Services` and `Scripts` collections of the `ScriptManagerProxy` server control are added to the `Services` and `Scripts` collections of the current `ScriptManager` server control, the `ScriptManagerProxy` server control acts as a proxy for the current `ScriptManager` server control.

Listing 15-10 contains a user control that employs the `ScriptManagerProxy` server control.

Listing 15-10: A User Control that Employs the ScriptManagerProxy Server Control

```
<%@ Control Language="C#" ClassName="MathUserControl" %>

<script type="text/javascript" language="javascript">
    var request;

    function onSuccess(result, userContext, methodName)
    {
        userContext.innerHTML = "<b><u>" + result + "</b></u>";
    }
```

(continued)

Listing 15-10 *(continued)*

```
        function onFailure(result, userContext, methodName)
        {
          var builder = new Sys.StringBuilder();
          builder.append("timedOut: ");
          builder.append(result.get_timedOut());
          builder.appendLine();
          builder.appendLine();
          builder.append("message: ");
          builder.append(result.get_message());
          builder.appendLine();
          builder.appendLine();
          builder.append("stackTrace: ");
          builder.appendLine();
          builder.append(result.get_stackTrace());
          builder.appendLine();
          builder.appendLine();
          builder.append("exceptionType: ");
          builder.append(result.get_exceptionType());
          builder.appendLine();
          builder.appendLine();
          builder.append("statusCode: ");
          builder.append(result.get_statusCode());
          builder.appendLine();
          builder.appendLine();
          builder.append("methodName: ");
          builder.append(methodName);

          alert(builder.toString());
        }

        function add()
        {
          var userContext = $get("result");
          var xValue = $get("firstNumber").value;
          var yValue = $get("secondNumber").value;
          MyNamespace.Math.Add(xValue, yValue, onSuccess, onFailure, userContext);
        }
    </script>

    <asp:ScriptManagerProxy runat="server" ID="ScriptManagerProxy1">
      <Services>
        <asp:ServiceReference Path="/AJAXFuturesEnabledWebSite2/Math.asmx" />
      </Services>
    </asp:ScriptManagerProxy>
    <table>
      <tr>
        <td style="font-weight: bold" align="right">
          First Number:
        </td>
        <td align="left">
          <input type="text" id="firstNumber" /></td>
      </tr>
```

```
  <tr>
    <td style="font-weight: bold" align="right">
      Second Number:
    </td>
    <td align="left">
      <input type="text" id="secondNumber" /></td>
  </tr>
  <tr>
    <td colspan="2" align="center">
      <button onclick="add()">
        Add</button></td>
  </tr>
  <tr>
    <td style="font-weight: bold" align="right">
      Result:
    </td>
    <td align="left">
      <span id="result" />
    </td>
  </tr>
</table>
```

Listing 15-11 presents a page that hosts the user control shown in Listing 15-10. As you can see, the host page contains the `ScriptManager` server control, and the child user control contains the `ScriptManagerProxy` server control.

Listing 15-11: A Page that Hosts the User Control shown in Listing 15-10

```
<%@ Page Language="C#" %>
<%@ Register TagPrefix="custom" TagName="MyUserControl"
Src="~/MathUserControl.ascx" %>

<!DOCTYPE html PUBLIC "-//W3C//DTD XHTML 1.0 Transitional//EN"
"http://www.w3.org/TR/xhtml1/DTD/xhtml1-transitional.dtd">
<html xmlns="http://www.w3.org/1999/xhtml">
<head runat="server">
  <title>Untitled Page</title>
</head>
<body>
  <form id="form1" runat="server">
    <asp:ScriptManager runat="server" ID="ScriptManager1"/>
    <custom:MyUserControl runat="server" ID="MyUserControl1" />
  </form>
</body>
</html>
```

Under the Hood

Adding a `ServiceReference` object to the `Services` collection of the current `ScriptManager` server control is all it takes to instruct the ASP.NET AJAX server-side framework to automatically generate a client script that defines, instantiates, and initializes the proxy class. To help you understand how the ASP.NET AJAX server-side framework manages to do this, this section implements fully functional (as far as the discussions in this section are concerned) replicas of the components of the framework that are responsible for generating a client script that defines, instantiates, and initializes the proxy class.

ScriptManager

Listing 15-12 presents the implementation of the replica `ScriptManager` server control.

Listing 15-12: The Replica ScriptManager Server Control

```
using System;
using System.Data;
using System.Configuration;
using System.Web;
using System.Web.UI;
using System.Web.UI.WebControls;
using System.Web.UI.HtmlControls;
using System.Text;
using System.Collections;
using System.Collections.Generic;
using System.Reflection;
using System.Web.Compilation;
using System.ComponentModel;
using System.Web.Services;
using System.Web.Script.Services;
using System.Collections.ObjectModel;

namespace CustomComponents
{
  [ParseChildren(true), DefaultProperty("Scripts"),
  NonVisualControl, PersistChildren(false)]
  public class ScriptManager : Control
  {
    private ServiceReferenceCollection _services;

    [PersistenceMode(PersistenceMode.InnerProperty),
    Editor("System.Web.UI.Design.CollectionEditorBase,
           System.Web.Extensions.Design, Version=1.0.61025.0, Culture=neutral,
           PublicKeyToken=31bf3856ad364e35",
           typeof(System.Drawing.Design.UITypeEditor)),
    DefaultValue((string)null), MergableProperty(false),
    Category("Behavior")]
    public ServiceReferenceCollection Services
    {
      get
      {
        if (this._services == null)
          this._services = new ServiceReferenceCollection();

        return this._services;
      }
    }
```

```
      protected override void OnInit(EventArgs e)
      {
        base.OnInit(e);
        this.Page.PreRenderComplete += new EventHandler(Page_PreRenderComplete);
      }


      void Page_PreRenderComplete(object sender, EventArgs e)
      {
        if (this._services != null)
        {
          foreach (ServiceReference reference in this._services)
          {
            reference.Register(this);
          }
        }

        if (this.EnablePageMethods)
        {
          ClientProxyGenerator generator2 = new ClientProxyGenerator();
          string script =
              generator2.GetClientProxyScript(this.Page.Request.FilePath, true);
          this.Page.ClientScript.RegisterClientScriptBlock(typeof(Page), script,
                                                script, true);
        }
      }

      public bool EnablePageMethods
      {
        get
        {
          return ViewState["EnablePageMethods"] != null ?
                          (bool)ViewState["EnablePageMethods"] : false;
        }
        set
        {
          ViewState["EnablePageMethods"] = value;
        }
      }
    }
  }
```

Services

The replica ScriptManager exposes a collection property of type ServiceReferenceCollection named Services, as defined in the following excerpt from Listing 15-12. Note that this property is annotated with the PersistenceMode(PersistenceMode.InnerProperty) metadata attribute, which enables page developers to declare the property as the child element of the tag that represents the ScriptManager on the .aspx page.

```
      private ServiceReferenceCollection _services;

      [PersistenceMode(PersistenceMode.InnerProperty),
      Editor("System.Web.UI.Design.CollectionEditorBase,
```

(continued)

(continued)

```
            System.Web.Extensions.Design, Version=1.0.61025.0, Culture=neutral,
            PublicKeyToken=31bf3856ad364e35",
            typeof(System.Drawing.Design.UITypeEditor)),
    DefaultValue((string)null), MergableProperty(false),
    Category("Behavior")]
    public ServiceReferenceCollection Services
    {
      get
      {
        if (this._services == null)
          this._services = new ServiceReferenceCollection();

        return this._services;
      }
    }
```

Listing 15-13 presents the implementation of the replica `ServiceReferenceCollection` class. Thanks to the .NET 2.0 generics, implementing a new type-safe collection class is just a matter of deriving from a generic collection class such as `Collection<ServiceReference>`.

Listing 15-13: The ServiceReferenceCollection Class

```
using System.Collections;
using System.Collections.Generic;
using System.Collections.ObjectModel;

namespace CustomComponents
{
  public class ServiceReferenceCollection : Collection<ServiceReference>
  {
  }
}
```

EnablePageMethods

The replica `ScriptManager` server control also exposes a Boolean property named `EnablePageMethods`, as shown in the following excerpt from Listing 15-12. Page developers can set this property to have the control generate a client script that defines, instantiates, and initializes the `PageMethods` client class.

```
    public bool EnablePageMethods
    {
      get
      {
        return ViewState["EnablePageMethods"] != null ?
                        (bool)ViewState["EnablePageMethods"] : false;
      }
      set
      {
        ViewState["EnablePageMethods"] = value;
      }
    }
```

OnInit

As you can see in the following excerpt from Listing 15-12, the replica `ScriptManager` server control overrides the `OnInit` method that it inherits from the `Control` base class to register a method named `Page_RenderComplete` as the event handler for the `Page` object's `PreRenderComplete` event:

```
protected override void OnInit(EventArgs e)
{
  base.OnInit(e);
  this.Page.PreRenderComplete += new EventHandler(Page_PreRenderComplete);
}
```

Page_PreRenderComplete

When the page finally enters its `PreRenderComplete` lifecycle phase, it automatically calls the `Page_PreRenderComplete` method, which in turn performs the following tasks:

1. It iterates through the `ServiceReference` objects in the `Services` collections and invokes their `Register` methods:

```
reference.Register(this);
```

2. It checks whether the `EnablePageMethods` property is set to `true`. If so, it instantiates an instance of a class named `ClientProxyGenerator`:

```
ClientProxyGenerator generator2 = new ClientProxyGenerator();
```

3. It invokes the `GetClientProxyScript` method on this `ClientProxyGenerator` object to generate the client script that defines, instantiates, and initializes the `PageMethods` client class:

```
string script =
        generator2.GetClientProxyScript(this.Page.Request.FilePath, true);
```

4. It invokes the `RegisterClientScriptBlock` method on the `ClientScript` property of the containing page to register this script for rendering:

```
this.Page.ClientScript.RegisterClientScriptBlock(typeof(Page), script,
                                                  script, true);
```

As a result, when the containing page enters its rendering phase, it will automatically render all registered scripts, including the script that defines, instantiates, and initializes the `PageMethods` client class:

ServiceReference

Listing 15-14 presents the implementation of the replica `ServiceReference` class.

Listing 15-14: The ServiceReference Class

```csharp
using System;
using System.Data;
using System.Configuration;
using System.Web;
using System.Web.Security;
using System.Web.UI;
using System.Web.UI.WebControls;
using System.Web.UI.WebControls.WebParts;
using System.Web.UI.HtmlControls;
using System.Text;
using System.Collections;
using System.Collections.Generic;
using System.Reflection;
using System.Web.Compilation;
using System.ComponentModel;
using System.Web.Services;
using System.Web.Script.Services;
using System.Collections.ObjectModel;

namespace CustomComponents
{
  public class ServiceReference
  {
    private bool _inlineScript;
    public bool InlineScript
    {
      get
      {
        return this._inlineScript;
      }
      set
      {
        this._inlineScript = value;
      }
    }

    private string _path;
    public string Path
    {
      get
      {
        if (this._path == null)
          return string.Empty;

        return this._path;
      }
      set
      {
        this._path = value;
      }
    }
```

```
public void Register(Control control)
{
  if (this._inlineScript)
  {
    ClientProxyGenerator generator = new ClientProxyGenerator();
    string inlineScript;
    inlineScript = generator.GetClientProxyScript(this.Path, false);
    control.Page.ClientScript.RegisterClientScriptBlock(typeof(Page),
                                        inlineScript, inlineScript, true);
  }

  else
  {
    string url = this.Path + "/js";
    control.Page.ClientScript.RegisterClientScriptInclude(typeof(Page),
                                                    url, url);
  }
  }
  }
}
```

The Register method in this listing takes the following steps if the page developer has set the InlineScript Boolean property to true:

1. It instantiates a ClientProxyGenerator object:

```
ClientProxyGenerator generator = new ClientProxyGenerator();
```

2. It invokes the GetClientProxyScript method on this ClientProxyGenerator object to generate the client script that defines, instantiates, and initializes the proxy class:

```
inlineScript = generator.GetClientProxyScript(this.Path, false);
```

3. It invokes the RegisterClientScriptBlock method on the Page object's ClientScript property of to register the client script for rendering:

```
control.Page.ClientScript.RegisterClientScriptBlock(typeof(Page),
                                    inlineScript, inlineScript, true);
```

As a result, when the page enters its rendering phase, it automatically renders all registered client scripts, including the client script that defines, instantiates, and initializes the proxy class.

Conversely, if the page developer has not set the InlineScript Boolean property to true, the Register method simply calls the RegisterClientScriptInclude method on the ClientScript property of the Page object to register a script block whose src attribute is set to the service path plus the path trailer /js:

```
else
{
  string url = this.Path + "/js";
  control.Page.ClientScript.RegisterClientScriptInclude(typeof(Page), url,
                                                  url);
}
```

For the purposes of the current discussion, you can ignore the /jsdebug option.

ClientProxyGenerator

Listing 15-15 presents the implementation of the replica `ClientProxyGenerator` class. The following sections discuss the methods and properties of this class.

Listing 15-15: The ClientProxyGenerator Class

```
using System;
using System.Data;
using System.Configuration;
using System.Web;
using System.Web.Security;
using System.Web.UI;
using System.Web.UI.WebControls;
using System.Web.UI.WebControls.WebParts;
using System.Web.UI.HtmlControls;
using System.Text;
using System.Collections;
using System.Collections.Generic;
using System.Reflection;
using System.Web.Compilation;
using System.ComponentModel;
using System.Web.Services;
using System.Web.Script.Services;
using System.Collections.ObjectModel;

namespace CustomComponents
{
  public class ClientProxyGenerator
  {
    private StringBuilder _builder = new StringBuilder();
    private Type _serviceType;
    private string _serviceFullName;
    private string _servicePath;
    private bool _isPageMethod;
    private ArrayList _methodInfos;
    private Dictionary<MethodInfo, ArrayList> _parameterInfos;

    private void PopulateMethodInfos()
    {
      _methodInfos = new ArrayList();
      MethodInfo[] infoArray = _serviceType.GetMethods();
      foreach (MethodInfo info in infoArray)
      {
        object[] objArray = info.GetCustomAttributes(typeof(WebMethodAttribute),
                                                      true);
        if (objArray.Length != 0)
          _methodInfos.Add(info);
      }
    }

    private void PopulateParameterInfos()
    {
      _parameterInfos = new Dictionary<MethodInfo, ArrayList>();
      ParameterInfo[] list;
      ArrayList list2;
```

```
    foreach (MethodInfo info in _methodInfos)
    {
      list = info.GetParameters();
      list2 = new ArrayList();
      list2.AddRange(list);
      _parameterInfos.Add(info, list2);
    }
}

private void DetermineServiceType()
{
  _serviceType = BuildManager.GetCompiledType(this._servicePath);
  if (_serviceType == null)
    _serviceType = BuildManager.CreateInstanceFromVirtualPath(_servicePath,
                                              typeof(Page)).GetType();
}

private void DetermineServiceFullName()
{
  if (this._isPageMethod)
    _serviceFullName = "PageMethods";
  else
    _serviceFullName = _serviceType.FullName;
}

public string GetClientProxyScript(string servicePath, bool isPageMethod)
{
  this._servicePath = servicePath;
  this._isPageMethod = isPageMethod;

  this.DetermineServiceType();
  this.DetermineServiceFullName();
  this.PopulateMethodInfos();
  this.PopulateParameterInfos();

  if (!this._isPageMethod)
    this.GenerateNamespace();

  this.GenerateConstructor();
  this.GeneratePrototype();
  this.GenerateRegisterClass();
  this.GenerateStaticInstance();
  this.GenerateStaticMethods();
  return this._builder.ToString();
}

private void GenerateNamespace()
{
  this._builder.Append("\r\nType.registerNamespace('");
  this._builder.Append(_serviceType.Namespace);
  this._builder.Append("');\r\n\r\n");
}
```

(continued)

Listing 15-15 *(continued)*

```
private void GenerateConstructor()
{
  _builder.Append(_serviceFullName);
  _builder.Append(" = ");
  _builder.Append("function()\r\n{\r\n\t");
  _builder.Append(_serviceFullName);
  _builder.Append(".initializeBase(this);\r\n");
  _builder.Append("\tthis._timeout = 0;\r\n");
  _builder.Append("\tthis._userContext = null;\r\n");
  _builder.Append("\tthis._succeeded = null;\r\n");
  _builder.Append("\tthis._failed = null;\r\n");
  _builder.Append("}\r\n\r\n");
}

private void GenerateWebMethodProxy(MethodInfo methodInfo)
{
  ArrayList parameterList = _parameterInfos[methodInfo];

  _builder.Append(methodInfo.Name);
  _builder.Append(" : ");
  _builder.Append("function(");
  foreach (ParameterInfo pinfo in parameterList)
  {
    _builder.Append(pinfo.Name);
    _builder.Append(", ");
  }
  _builder.Append("succeededCallback, failedCallback, userContext)");
  _builder.Append("\r\n{\r\n");
  _builder.Append("\treturn this._invoke(");
  _builder.Append(_serviceFullName);
  _builder.Append(".get_path(), ");
  _builder.Append("'");
  _builder.Append(methodInfo.Name);
  _builder.Append("', false, ");

  _builder.Append('{');
  int i = 0;
  foreach (ParameterInfo pinfo in parameterList)
  {
    _builder.Append(pinfo.Name);
    _builder.Append(":");
    _builder.Append(pinfo.Name);
    if (i != (parameterList.Count - 1))
      _builder.Append(", ");
    i++;
  }

  _builder.Append("}");

  _builder.Append(", succeededCallback, failedCallback, userContext); " +
                  "\r\n}\r\n");
}
```

```
private void GeneratePrototype()
{
  this._builder.Append(_serviceFullName);
  this._builder.Append(".prototype");
  this._builder.Append(" = ");
  this._builder.Append("\r\n{");

  bool flag1 = true;
  foreach (MethodInfo methodInfo in _methodInfos)
  {
    if (!flag1)
      _builder.Append(",\r\n");

    flag1 = false;
    this.GenerateWebMethodProxy(methodInfo);
  }

  _builder.Append("}\r\n\r\n");
}

protected void GenerateRegisterClass()
{
  this._builder.Append(this._serviceFullName);
  this._builder.Append(".registerClass('");
  this._builder.Append(this._serviceFullName);
  this._builder.Append("', Sys.Net.WebServiceProxy);\r\n");
}

protected void GenerateStaticInstance()
{
  this._builder.Append(this._serviceFullName);
  this._builder.Append("._staticInstance = new ");
  this._builder.Append(this._serviceFullName);
  this._builder.Append("();\r\n");

  this._builder.Append(this._serviceFullName);
  this._builder.Append(".set_path = function(value) { ");
  this._builder.Append(this._serviceFullName);
  this._builder.Append("._staticInstance._path = value; }\r\n");
  this._builder.Append(this._serviceFullName);
  this._builder.Append(".get_path = function() { return ");
  this._builder.Append(this._serviceFullName);
  this._builder.Append("._staticInstance._path; }\r\n");
  this._builder.Append(this._serviceFullName);
  this._builder.Append(".set_timeout = function(value) { ");
  this._builder.Append(this._serviceFullName);
  this._builder.Append("._staticInstance._timeout = value; }\r\n");
  this._builder.Append(this._serviceFullName);
  this._builder.Append(".get_timeout = function() { return ");
  this._builder.Append(this._serviceFullName);
  this._builder.Append("._staticInstance._timeout; }\r\n");
  this._builder.Append(this._serviceFullName);
  this._builder.Append(".set_defaultUserContext = function(value) { ");
  this._builder.Append(this._serviceFullName);
```

(continued)

Listing 15-15 *(continued)*

```
          this._builder.Append("._staticInstance._userContext = value; }\r\n");
          this._builder.Append(this._serviceFullName);
          this._builder.Append(".get_defaultUserContext = function() { return ");
          this._builder.Append(this._serviceFullName);
          this._builder.Append("._staticInstance._userContext; }\r\n");
          this._builder.Append(this._serviceFullName);
          this._builder.Append(".set_defaultSucceededCallback = function(value) { ");
          this._builder.Append(this._serviceFullName);
          this._builder.Append("._staticInstance._succeeded = value; }\r\n");
          this._builder.Append(this._serviceFullName);
          this._builder.Append(".get_defaultSucceededCallback = function() { return ");
          this._builder.Append(this._serviceFullName);
          this._builder.Append("._staticInstance._succeeded; }\r\n");
          this._builder.Append(this._serviceFullName);
          this._builder.Append(".set_defaultFailedCallback = function(value) { ");
          this._builder.Append(this._serviceFullName);
          this._builder.Append("._staticInstance._failed = value; }\r\n");
          this._builder.Append(this._serviceFullName);
          this._builder.Append(".get_defaultFailedCallback = function() { return ");
          this._builder.Append(this._serviceFullName);
          this._builder.Append("._staticInstance._failed; }\r\n");

          this._builder.Append(this._serviceFullName);
          this._builder.Append(".set_path(\"");
          this._builder.Append(this._servicePath);
          this._builder.Append("\");\r\n");
      }

      protected void GenerateStaticMethods()
      {
          ArrayList parameterList;

          foreach (MethodInfo methodInfo in _methodInfos)
          {
              this._builder.Append(this._serviceFullName);
              this._builder.Append(".");
              this._builder.Append(methodInfo.Name);
              this._builder.Append(" = function(");
              parameterList = this._parameterInfos[methodInfo];
              foreach (ParameterInfo pinfo in parameterList)
              {
                  _builder.Append(pinfo.Name);
                  _builder.Append(',');
              }

              _builder.Append("onSuccess, onFailed, userContext) \r\n{\r\n\t");
              this._builder.Append(this._serviceFullName);
              this._builder.Append("._staticInstance.");
              this._builder.Append(methodInfo.Name);
              this._builder.Append("(");
              foreach (ParameterInfo pinfo in parameterList)
              {
```

```
            _builder.Append(pinfo.Name);
            _builder.Append(',');
          }

          _builder.Append("onSuccess, onFailed, userContext); \r\n}");
        }
      }
    }
  }
```

GetClientProxyScript

Listing 15-16 shows the GetClientProxyScript method of the replica ClientProxyGenerator class. The main responsibility of this method is to generate the client script that defines, instantiates, and initializes the proxy class.

Listing 15-16: The GetClientProxyScript Method

```
public string GetClientProxyScript(string servicePath, bool isPageMethod)
{
  this._servicePath = servicePath;
  this._isPageMethod = isPageMethod;

  this.DetermineServiceType();
  this.DetermineServiceFullName();
  this.PopulateMethodInfos();
  this.PopulateParameterInfos();

  if (!this._isPageMethod)
    this.GenerateNamespace();

  this.GenerateConstructor();
  this.GeneratePrototype();
  this.GenerateRegisterClass();
  this.GenerateStaticInstance();
  this.GenerateStaticMethods();
  return this._builder.ToString();
}
```

The GetClientProxyScript method takes two arguments. The first argument is a string that contains the service path, and the second argument is a Boolean that specifies whether the first parameter of the server method contains the path to an .aspx page, which means it is being invoked as a page method.

This method performs the following tasks:

1. It invokes the DetermineServiceType method to determine the Type object that represents the type of the server class that represents the file with the specified service path:

```
this.DetermineServiceType();
```

2. It invokes the `DetermineServiceFullName` method to determine the full name of the server class:

```
this.DetermineServiceFullName();
```

3. It invokes the `PopulateMethodInfos` method to populate an internal collection named `_methodInfos` with `MethodInfo` objects that represent the server class methods:

```
this.PopulateMethodInfos();
```

4. It invokes the `PopulateParameterInfos` method to populate an internal collection named `_parameterInfos` with `ParameterInfo` objects that represent the parameters of the server class methods:

```
this.PopulateParameterInfos();
```

5. It invokes the `GenerateNamespace` method to generate the client script that defines the namespace of the proxy class if the method being invoked is not a page method:

```
if (!this._isPageMethod)
    this.GenerateNamespace();
```

As previously discussed, the proxy class in this example is named `PageMethods` and does not belong to any namespace:

6. It invokes the `GenerateConstructor` method to generate the client script that defines the constructor of the proxy class:

```
this.GenerateConstructor();
```

7. It invokes the `GeneratePrototype` method to generate the client script that defines the `prototype` property of the proxy class:

```
this.GeneratePrototype();
```

8. It invokes the `GenerateRegisterClass` method to generate the client script that registers the proxy class with the ASP.NET AJAX client-side framework:

```
this.GenerateRegisterClass();
```

9. It invokes the `GenerateStaticInstance` method to generate the client script that defines the `_staticInstance` property of the proxy class:

```
this.GenerateStaticInstance();
```

10. It invokes the `GenerateStaticMethods` method to generate the client script that defines the static method of the proxy class:

```
this.GenerateStaticMethods();
```

As you can see, the `GetClientProxyScript` method basically generates a client script such as the one previously shown in Listing 15-4. Keep that listing in mind as the following sections walk you through the implementation of the methods that the `GetClientProxyScript` method invokes.

DetermineServiceType

As you can see in the following excerpt from Listing 15-15, the `DetermineServiceType` method invokes the `GetCompiledType` static method on the `BuildManager` class. The `GetCompiledType` method takes a string parameter that contains the virtual path of a file, uses this virtual path to locate the file on the server, parses the file, uses the content of the file to dynamically generate the code for a .NET class that represents the file, compiles this dynamically generated class into an assembly, loads the assembly into the current application domain, and returns a reference to the `Type` object that represents the compiled class. Note that the `DetermineServiceType` method stores this reference in a private field named `_serviceType`.

```
private void DetermineServiceType()
{
  _serviceType = BuildManager.GetCompiledType(this._servicePath);
  if (_serviceType == null)
    _serviceType = BuildManager.CreateInstanceFromVirtualPath(_servicePath,
                                          typeof(Page)).GetType();
}
```

DetermineServiceFullName

As you can see in the following excerpt from Listing 15-15, the `DetermineServiceFullName` method first checks whether `_isPageMethod` field of the `ScriptManager` server control is set to `true`. If so, it simply uses `PageMethod` as the service's full name. If not, it uses the `FullName` property value of the `Type` object that represents the service as the service's full name. The `FullName` property returns a string that contains the fully qualified name of the service type, including its complete containment namespace hierarchy.

```
private void DetermineServiceFullName()
{
  if (this._isPageMethod)
    _serviceFullName = "PageMethods";
  else
    _serviceFullName = _serviceType.FullName;
}
```

PopulateMethodInfos

The `PopulateMethodInfos` method takes the following steps to populate an internal collection named `_methodInfos`:

1. It invokes the `GetMethods` method on the `Type` object that represents the type of the service to return an array of `MethodInfo` objects, where each object represents a method of the service:

    ```
    MethodInfo[] infoArray = _serviceType.GetMethods();
    ```

2. It searches through the objects in this array for `MethodInfo` objects annotated with the `WebMethodAttribute` metadata attribute and adds them to the `_methodInfos` collection:

```
foreach (MethodInfo info in infoArray)
{
    object[] objArray = info.GetCustomAttributes(typeof(WebMethodAttribute),
                                                  true);

    if (objArray.Length != 0)
      _methodInfos.Add(info);
}
}
```

PopulateParameterInfos

The `PopulateParameterInfos` method iterates through the `MethodInfo` objects in the `_methodInfos` collection and takes the following steps for each object:

1. It invokes the `GetParameters` method on the `MethodInfo` object to return an array of `ParameterInfo` objects, where each object represents a parameter of the method that the `MethodInfo` object represents:

```
list = info.GetParameters();
```

2. It uses the `MethodInfo` object as an index into the `_parameterInfos` collection to add the `ParameterInfo` objects to the collection:

```
list2 = new ArrayList();
list2.AddRange(list);
_parameterInfos.Add(info, list2);
}
}
```

The `_parameterInfos` collection is a collection of collections, where each collection contains the `ParameterInfo` objects of a particular `MethodInfo` object.

GenerateNamespace

As you can see in the following excerpt from Listing 15-15, the `GenerateNamespace` method generates the client script that defines the namespace of the proxy class. Note that this method uses the namespace of the service as the namespace of the proxy class.

```
private void GenerateNamespace()
{
    this._builder.Append("\r\nType.registerNamespace('");
    this._builder.Append(_serviceType.Namespace);
    this._builder.Append("');\r\n\r\n");
}
```

This method basically generates the following portion of the Listing 15-4 script:

```
Type.registerNamespace('MyNamespace');
```

GenerateConstructor

As you can see in the following excerpt from Listing 15-15, the GenerateConstructor method generates the script that defines the constructor of the proxy class. Note that this method uses the fully qualified name of the service as the name of the proxy class.

```
private void GenerateConstructor()
{
  _builder.Append(_serviceFullName);
  _builder.Append(" = ");
  _builder.Append("function()\r\n{\r\n\t");
  _builder.Append(_serviceFullName);
  _builder.Append(".initializeBase(this);\r\n");
  _builder.Append("\tthis._timeout = 0;\r\n");
  _builder.Append("\tthis._userContext = null;\r\n");
  _builder.Append("\tthis._succeeded = null;\r\n");
  _builder.Append("\tthis._failed = null;\r\n");
  _builder.Append("}\r\n\r\n");
}
```

This method basically generates the following portion of the Listing 15-4 script:

```
MyNamespace.Math = function()
{
  MyNamespace.Math.initializeBase(this);
  this._timeout = 0;
  this._userContext = null;
  this._succeeded = null;
  this._failed = null;
}
```

GeneratePrototype

The GeneratePrototype method generates the portion of the script that defines the prototype property of the proxy class. As you can see in the following excerpt from Listing 15-15, this method iterates through the MethodInfo objects in the _methodInfos collection and invokes the GenerateWebMethodProxy method to generate the script that defines the associated method of the proxy class:

```
private void GeneratePrototype()
{
  this._builder.Append(_serviceFullName);
  this._builder.Append(".prototype");
  this._builder.Append(" = ");
  this._builder.Append("\r\n{");

  bool flag1 = true;
  foreach (MethodInfo methodInfo in _methodInfos)
  {
    if (!flag1)
      _builder.Append(",\r\n");

    flag1 = false;
    this.GenerateWebMethodProxy(methodInfo);
  }
  _builder.Append("}\r\n\r\n");
}
```

This method basically generates the following portion of the Listing 15-4 script:

```
MyNamespace.Math.prototype =
{
    Add : function(x, y, succeededCallback, failedCallback, userContext)
    {
        return this._invoke(MyNamespace.Math.get_path(),'Add', false,
                            {x : x, y : y}, succeededCallback, failedCallback,
                            userContext);
    }
}
```

GenerateWebMethodProxy

The GenerateWebMethodProxy method takes a MethodInfo object as its argument and generates the script that defines the method of the proxy class associated with this MethodInfo object, as shown in Listing 15-17 (which is the GenerateWebProxy method portion of Listing 15-15).

Listing 15-17: The GenerateWebMethodProxy Method

```
private void GenerateWebMethodProxy(MethodInfo methodInfo)
{
    ArrayList parameterList = _parameterInfos[methodInfo];
    _builder.Append(methodInfo.Name);
    _builder.Append(" : ");
    _builder.Append("function(");
    foreach (ParameterInfo pinfo in parameterList)
    {
        _builder.Append(pinfo.Name);
        _builder.Append(", ");
    }
    _builder.Append("succeededCallback, failedCallback, userContext)");
    _builder.Append("\r\n{\r\n");
    _builder.Append("\treturn this._invoke(");
    _builder.Append(_serviceFullName);
    _builder.Append(".get_path(), ");
    _builder.Append("'");
    _builder.Append(methodInfo.Name);
    _builder.Append("', false, ");

    _builder.Append('{');
    int i = 0;
    foreach (ParameterInfo pinfo in parameterList)
    {
        _builder.Append(pinfo.Name);
        _builder.Append(":");
        _builder.Append(pinfo.Name);
        if (i != (parameterList.Count - 1))

            _builder.Append(", ");

        i++;
    }
```

```
        _builder.Append("}");
        _builder.Append(", succeededCallback, failedCallback, userContext);" +
                "\r\n}\r\n");
    }
```

For example, this listing generates the local `Math` proxy class associated with the remote `Math` Web service class, as previously shown in Listing 15-4 and again in Listing 15-18.

Listing 15-18: An Example of the Script that Listing 15-17 Generates

```
Add : function(x, y, succeededCallback, failedCallback, userContext)
    {
        return this._invoke(MyNamespace.Math.get_path(),'Add', false,
                    {x : x, y : y}, succeededCallback, failedCallback,
                    userContext);
    }
```

Keeping this listing in mind, let's walk through the implementation of the `GenerateWebMethodProxy` method shown in Listing 15-17.

The `GenerateWebMethodProxy` method uses the name of the server method as the name of the associated proxy method:

```
        _builder.Append(methodInfo.Name);
```

This code basically generates the following portion of the Listing 15-18 script:

```
Add
```

The following lines of code from Listing 15-17:

```
        _builder.Append(" : ");
        _builder.Append("function(");
```

generate the following portion of the Listing 15-18 script:

```
Add : function(
```

Listing 15-17 uses the names of the parameters of the server method as the names of the parameters of the associated proxy method:

```
        foreach (ParameterInfo pinfo in parameterList)
        {
          _builder.Append(pinfo.Name);
          _builder.Append(", ");
        }
```

This code basically generates the following boldface portion of the Listing 15-18 script:

```
Add : function(x, y,
```

The next lines of code in Listing 15-17:

```
        _builder.Append("succeededCallback, failedCallback, userContext)");
        _builder.Append("\r\n{\r\n");
        _builder.Append("\treturn this._invoke(");
```

generate the following boldface portion of the Listing 15-18 script:

```
Add : function(x, y, succeededCallback, failedCallback, userContext)
{
  this._invoke(
```

The next lines of code in Listing 15-17:

```
        _builder.Append(_serviceFullName);
        _builder.Append(".get_path(), ");
```

generate the following boldface portion of the Listing 15-18 script:

```
Add : function(x, y, succeededCallback, failedCallback, userContext)
{
  this._invoke(MyNamespace.Math.get_path(),
```

The next lines of code in Listing 15-17:

```
        _builder.Append("'");
        _builder.Append(methodInfo.Name);
        _builder.Append("', false, ");
```

generate the following boldface portion of the Listing 15-18 script, which specifies the name of the service method and the value `false` to indicate that you want to make the POST HTTP request:

```
Add : function(x, y, succeededCallback, failedCallback, userContext)
{
  this._invoke(MyNamespace.Math.get_path(),'Add', false,
```

Listing 15-17 then iterates through the parameters of the service method as follows:

```
        _builder.Append('{');
        int i = 0;
        foreach (ParameterInfo pinfo in parameterList)
        {
          _builder.Append(pinfo.Name);
          _builder.Append(":");
          _builder.Append(pinfo.Name);
          if (i != (parameterList.Count - 1))
            _builder.Append(", ");
          i++;
        }

        _builder.Append("}");
```

to generate the following boldface portion of the Listing 15-18 script:

```
Add : function(x, y, succeededCallback, failedCallback, userContext)
{
  this._invoke(MyNamespace.Math.get_path(),'Add', false, {x:x, y:y}
```

The last lines of the code in Listing 15-17:

```
_builder.Append(", succeededCallback, failedCallback, userContext);" +
                "\r\n}\r\n");
```

wrap the rendering of the specified method of the proxy class, as shown in the following boldface portion of the Listing 15-18 script:

```
Add : function(x, y, succeededCallback, failedCallback, userContext)
{
  this._invoke(MyNamespace.Math.get_path(),'Add', false, {x:x, y:y},
  succeededCallback, failedCallback, userContext);
}
```

GenerateRegisterClass

As you can see in the following excerpt from Listing 15-15, the GenerateRegisterClass method generates the script that registers the proxy class with the ASP.NET AJAX client-side framework.

```
protected void GenerateRegisterClass()
{
  this._builder.Append(this._serviceFullName);
  this._builder.Append(".registerClass('");
  this._builder.Append(this._serviceFullName);
  this._builder.Append("', Sys.Net.WebServiceProxy);\r\n");
}
```

This method basically generates the following portion of the Listing 15-4 script:

```
MyNamespace.Math.registerClass('MyNamespace.Math', Sys.Net.WebServiceProxy);
```

GenerateStaticInstance

This method generates the script that defines, instantiates, and initializes the _staticInstance property of the proxy class, as shown in the following excerpt from Listing 15-15:

```
protected void GenerateStaticInstance()
{
  this._builder.Append(this._serviceFullName);
  this._builder.Append("._staticInstance = new ");
  this._builder.Append(this._serviceFullName);
  this._builder.Append("();\r\n");

  this._builder.Append(this._serviceFullName);
  this._builder.Append(".set_path = function(value) { ");
  this._builder.Append(this._serviceFullName);
  this._builder.Append("._staticInstance._path = value; }\r\n");
```

(continued)

643

(continued)

```
        this._builder.Append(this._serviceFullName);
        this._builder.Append(".get_path = function() { return ");
        this._builder.Append(this._serviceFullName);
        this._builder.Append("._staticInstance._path; }\r\n");
        this._builder.Append(this._serviceFullName);
        this._builder.Append(".set_timeout = function(value) { ");
        this._builder.Append(this._serviceFullName);
        this._builder.Append("._staticInstance._timeout = value; }\r\n");
        this._builder.Append(this._serviceFullName);
        this._builder.Append(".get_timeout = function() { return ");
        this._builder.Append(this._serviceFullName);
        this._builder.Append("._staticInstance._timeout; }\r\n");
        this._builder.Append(this._serviceFullName);
        this._builder.Append(".set_defaultUserContext = function(value) { ");
        this._builder.Append(this._serviceFullName);
        this._builder.Append("._staticInstance._userContext = value; }\r\n");
        this._builder.Append(this._serviceFullName);
        this._builder.Append(".get_defaultUserContext = function() { return ");
        this._builder.Append(this._serviceFullName);
        this._builder.Append("._staticInstance._userContext; }\r\n");
        this._builder.Append(this._serviceFullName);
        this._builder.Append(".set_defaultSucceededCallback = function(value) { ");
        this._builder.Append(this._serviceFullName);
        this._builder.Append("._staticInstance._succeeded = value; }\r\n");
        this._builder.Append(this._serviceFullName);
        this._builder.Append(".get_defaultSucceededCallback = function() { return ");
        this._builder.Append(this._serviceFullName);
        this._builder.Append("._staticInstance._succeeded; }\r\n");
        this._builder.Append(this._serviceFullName);
        this._builder.Append(".set_defaultFailedCallback = function(value) { ");
        this._builder.Append(this._serviceFullName);
        this._builder.Append("._staticInstance._failed = value; }\r\n");
        this._builder.Append(this._serviceFullName);
        this._builder.Append(".get_defaultFailedCallback = function() { return ");
        this._builder.Append(this._serviceFullName);
        this._builder.Append("._staticInstance._failed; }\r\n");

        this._builder.Append(this._serviceFullName);
        this._builder.Append(".set_path(\"");
        this._builder.Append(this._servicePath);
        this._builder.Append("\");\r\n");
    }
```

This method basically generates the following portion of the Listing 15-4 script:

```
MyNamespace.Math._staticInstance = new MyNamespace.Math();
MyNamespace.Math.set_path = function(value)
{
    MyNamespace.Math._staticInstance._path = value;
}

MyNamespace.Math.get_path = function()
{
```

```
    return MyNamespace.Math._staticInstance._path;
  }

MyNamespace.Math.set_timeout = function(value)
{
  MyNamespace.Math._staticInstance._timeout = value;
}

MyNamespace.Math.get_timeout = function()
{
  return MyNamespace.Math._staticInstance._timeout;
}

MyNamespace.Math.set_defaultUserContext = function(value)
{
  MyNamespace.Math._staticInstance._userContext = value;
}

MyNamespace.Math.get_defaultUserContext = function()
{
  return MyNamespace.Math._staticInstance._userContext;
}

MyNamespace.Math.set_defaultSucceededCallback = function(value)
{
  MyNamespace.Math._staticInstance._succeeded = value;
}

MyNamespace.Math.get_defaultSucceededCallback = function()
{
  return MyNamespace.Math._staticInstance._succeeded;
}

MyNamespace.Math.set_defaultFailedCallback = function(value)
{
  MyNamespace.Math._staticInstance._failed = value;
}

MyNamespace.Math.get_defaultFailedCallback = function()
{
  return MyNamespace.Math._staticInstance._failed;
}

MyNamespace.Math.set_path("/AJAXFuturesEnabledWebSite2/Math.asmx");
```

GenerateStaticMethods

This method generates the script that defines the static methods of the proxy class as shown in Listing 15-19 (which is the GenerateStaticMethods portion of Listing 15-15).

Listing 15-19: The GenerateStaticMethods Method

```
protected void GenerateStaticMethods()
{
  ArrayList parameterList;

  foreach (MethodInfo methodInfo in _methodInfos)
  {
    this._builder.Append(this._serviceFullName);
    this._builder.Append(".");
    this._builder.Append(methodInfo.Name);
    this._builder.Append(" = function(");
    parameterList = this._parameterInfos[methodInfo];
    foreach (ParameterInfo pinfo in parameterList)
    {
      _builder.Append(pinfo.Name);
      _builder.Append(',');
    }

    _builder.Append("onSuccess, onFailed, userContext) \r\n{\r\n\t");
    this._builder.Append(this._serviceFullName);
    this._builder.Append("._staticInstance.");
    this._builder.Append(methodInfo.Name);
    this._builder.Append("(");
    foreach (ParameterInfo pinfo in parameterList)
    {
      _builder.Append(pinfo.Name);
      _builder.Append(',');
    }

    _builder.Append("onSuccess, onFailed, userContext); \r\n};\r\n");
  }
}
```

Listing 15-20 presents an example of the script that Listing 15-19 generates.

Listing 15-20: An Example of the Script that Listing 15-19 Generates

```
MyNamespace.Math.Add = function(x, y, onSuccess, onFailed, userContext)
{
  MyNamespace.Math._staticInstance.Add(x, y, onSuccess, onFailed, userContext);
}
```

Using this listing as an example, let's walk through the GenerateStaticMethods method in Listing 15-19. This method iterates through the MethodInfo objects in the _methodInfos collection and takes the following steps to generate the script that defines the static method associated with each enumerated MethodInfo object:

1. It uses the name of the server method that the MethodInfo object represents as the name of the static method of the proxy class, prefixed by the full name of the service:

```
this._builder.Append(this._serviceFullName);
this._builder.Append(".");
this._builder.Append(methodInfo.Name);
this._builder.Append(" = function(");
```

This generates a script such as the following portion of Listing 15-20:

```
MyNamespace.Math.Add = function(
```

2. It uses the names of the parameters of this server method as the names of the parameters of the associated static method of the proxy class:

```
foreach (ParameterInfo pinfo in parameterList)
{
  _builder.Append(pinfo.Name);
  _builder.Append(',');
}
```

This generates a script such as the following boldface portion of Listing 15-20:

```
MyNamespace.Math.Add = function(x, y,
```

3. It uses the following line of code:

```
_builder.Append("onSuccess, onFailed, userContext) \r\n{\r\n\t");
```

to generate the following boldface portion of the Listing 15-20 script:

```
MyNamespace.Math.Add = function(x, y, onSuccess, onFailed, userContext)
{
```

4. It uses the following lines of code:

```
this._builder.Append(this._serviceFullName);
this._builder.Append("._staticInstance.");
this._builder.Append(methodInfo.Name);
this._builder.Append("(");
```

to generate the following boldface portion of the Listing 15-20 script:

```
MyNamespace.Math.Add = function(x, y, onSuccess, onFailed, userContext)
{
  MyNamespace.Math._staticInstance.Add(
```

5. It then iterates through the parameters of the enumerated method:

```
foreach (ParameterInfo pinfo in parameterList)
{
  _builder.Append(pinfo.Name);
  _builder.Append(',');
}
```

to generate the following boldface portion of the Listing 15-20 script:

```
MyNamespace.Math.Add = function(x, y, onSuccess, onFailed, userContext)
{
    MyNamespace.Math._staticInstance.Add(x, y,
```

6. It uses the following line of code:

```
    _builder.Append("onSuccess, onFailed, userContext); \r\n};\r\n");
```

to complete the Listing 15-20 script generation:

```
MyNamespace.Math.Add = function(x, y, onSuccess, onFailed, userContext)
{
    MyNamespace.Math._staticInstance.Add(x, y, onSuccess, onFailed, userContext);
};
```

RestClientProxyHandler

The previous chapter left out the discussion of the `RestClientProxyHandler` class used in the `GetHandler` method of the `RestHandlerFactory` class. As a matter of fact, the boldface portion of the following code was commented out in all the examples in that chapter:

```
namespace CustomComponents
{
    internal class RestHandlerFactory : IHttpHandlerFactory
    {
        public virtual IHttpHandler GetHandler(HttpContext context, string requestType,
                                               string url, string pathTranslated)
        {
            if (IsClientProxyRequest(context.Request.PathInfo))
                return new RestClientProxyHandler();

            return RestHandler.CreateHandler(context);
        }

        . . .
    }
}
```

This boldfaced portion first invokes the `IsClientProxyRequest` method discussed in the previous chapter to determine whether the current request is a client proxy request. A client proxy request is a request that the client code makes to the server to download the release or debug version of the script that defines, instantiates, and initializes the proxy class.

When and why would the client code make such a request? The answer depends on the value of the `InlineScript` property of the `ServiceReference` object that registers a service with the current `ScriptManager` server control. If you set this property to `true`, the `ScriptManager` server control will ask the current ASP.NET `Page` object to render the script that defines, instantiates, and initializes the proxy class directly into the page itself. In other words, when the requesting browser is downloading the current page for the first time, this script gets downloaded with the page because it is part of the page.

If you set the `InlineScript` property to `false`, the `ScriptManager` server control will ask the current ASP.NET `Page` object to render a script block such as the following into the current page:

```
<script src="/AJAXFuturesEnabledWebSite2/Math.asbx/js"
                                    type="text/javascript"></script>
```

Note that the `src` attribute of this script element is set to a URL with path information trailer `js` or `jsdebug`. This triggers the requesting browser to make another request for the resource with the URL specified in the `src` attribute. When this request arrives in `RestHandlerFactory` and triggers the call into the `GetHandler` method as discussed in the previous chapter, the `GetHandler` method invokes the `IsClientProxyRequest` method, passing in the URL. As discussed in the previous chapter, this method searches the path information for the `js` or `jsdebug` trailer. If `IsClientProxyRequest` finds the trailer, it returns `true` and, consequently, triggers the `GetHandler` method to instantiate and return an instance of an ASP.NET class named `RestClientProxyHandler`. This class is responsible for generating the script that defines, instantiates, and initializes the proxy class, and returning this script to the requesting browser.

Listing 15-21 presents the implementation of this replica `RestClientProxyHandler` class.

Listing 15-21: The RestClientProxyHandler Class

```csharp
using System;
using System.Web;

namespace CustomComponents
{
  internal class RestClientProxyHandler : IHttpHandler
  {
    public void ProcessRequest(HttpContext context)
    {
      ClientProxyGenerator generator = new ClientProxyGenerator();
      string script = generator.GetClientProxyScript(context.Request.FilePath,
                                              false);
      context.Response.ContentType = "application/x-javascript";
      context.Response.Write(script);
    }

    public bool IsReusable
    {
      get { return false; }
    }
  }
}
```

Like any other ASP.NET HTTP handler, the `RestClientProxyHandler` implements the `IHttpHandler` interface. `RestClientProxyHandler` implements this interface's `ProcessRequest` method as follows:

1. It instantiates a `ClientProxyGenerator` instance:

```csharp
ClientProxyGenerator generator = new ClientProxyGenerator();
```

2. It invokes the `GetClientProxyScript` method on this instance to generate the script that defines, instantiates, and initializes the proxy class:

```
string script = generator.GetClientProxyScript(context.Request.FilePath,
                                               false);
```

3. It sets the `Content-Type` HTTP header to `application/x-javascript` to tell the requesting browser that the response contains JavaScript code:

```
context.Response.ContentType = "application/x-javascript";
```

4. It writes the script that defines, instantiates, and initializes the proxy class into the server output stream:

```
context.Response.Write(script);
```

Using the Replicas

Follow these steps to see the replicas in action:

1. Create an AJAX-enabled Web site in Visual Studio.

2. Add an `App_Code` directory to this Web site.

3. Add a new source file named `ScriptHandlerFactory.cs` to the `App_Code` directory, and add the code shown in Listing 14-24 (located in the previous chapter) to this source file.

4. Add a new source file named `RestHandlerFactory.cs` to the `App_Code` directory, and add the code shown in Listing 14-26 (located in the previous chapter) to this source file.

5. Add a new source file named `RestHandler.cs` to the `App_Code` directory, and add the code shown in Listing 14-27 (located in the previous chapter) to this source file.

6. Add a new source file named `HandlerWrapper.cs` to the `App_Code` directory, and add the code shown in Listing 14-28 (located in the previous chapter) to this source file.

7. Add a new source file named `ScriptModule.cs` to the `App_Code` directory, and add the code shown in Listing 14-31 (located in the previous chapter) to this source file.

8. Add a new source file named `ScriptManager.cs` to the `App_Code` directory, and add the code shown in Listing 15-12 (earlier in this chapter) to this source file.

9. Add a new source file named `ServiceReferenceCollection.cs` to the `App_Code` directory, and add the code shown in Listing 15-13 (earlier in this chapter) to this source file.

10. Add a new source file named `ServiceReference.cs` to the `App_Code` directory, and add the code shown in Listing 15-14 (earlier in this chapter) to this source file.

11. Add a new source file named `ClientProxyGenerator.cs` to the `App_Code` directory, and add the code shown in Listing 15-15 (earlier in this chapter) to this source file.

12. Add a new source file named `RestClientProxyHandler.cs` to the `App_Code` directory, and add the code shown in Listing 15-21 (located after this procedure) to this source file.

13. Add a new Web form (`.aspx` file) named `PageMethods.aspx`, and add the code shown in Listing 15-22 (located after this procedure) to this `.aspx` file.

14. Add a new Web form (.aspx file) named `Math.aspx` to the root directory of this Web site, and add the code shown in Listing 15-23 (located after this procedure) to this .aspx file.

15. Add a new XML file named `Math.asbx` to the root directory of this Web site, and add the XML document shown in Listing 14-21 (located in the previous chapter).

16. Add a new source file named `Math.cs` to the `App_Code` directory, and add the code shown in Listing 14-21 (located in the previous chapter) to this source file.

17. Add a new Web form (.aspx file) named `Math2.aspx` to the root directory of this Web site, and add the code shown in Listing 15-24 (located after this procedure) to this .aspx file.

18. Add a new Web service (.asmx) named `Math.asmx` to the root directory of this Web site, and add the code shown in Listing 14-19 (located in the previous chapter) to this .asmx file.

19. In the `web.config` file, comment out the italicized lines shown in the following code, and add the boldface portion of the code (which is basically replacing the standard ASP.NET `ScriptHandlerFactory` and `ScriptModule` with the replica `ScriptHandlerFactory` and `ScriptModule`):

```
<httpHandlers>
  <remove verb="*" path="*.asmx" />
  <!--
      <add verb="*" path="*.asmx" validate="false"
       type="System.Web.Script.Services.ScriptHandlerFactory,
            System.Web.Extensions, Version=1.0.61025.0, Culture=neutral,
            PublicKeyToken=31bf3856ad364e35" />
      <add verb="*" path="*_AppService.axd" validate="false"
       type="System.Web.Script.Services.ScriptHandlerFactory,
            System.Web.Extensions, Version=1.0.61025.0, Culture=neutral,
            PublicKeyToken=31bf3856ad364e35" />
      <add verb="GET,HEAD,POST" path="*.asbx"
       type="System.Web.Script.Services.ScriptHandlerFactory,
            System.Web.Extensions, Version=1.0.61025.0, Culture=neutral,
            PublicKeyToken=31bf3856ad364e35" validate="false" />
  -->

  <add verb="*" path="*.asmx" validate="false"
   type="CustomComponents.ScriptHandlerFactory" />
  <add verb="GET,HEAD,POST" path="*.asbx"
   type="CustomComponents.ScriptHandlerFactory" />
  . . .
</httpHandlers>

<httpModules>
  <!--
      <add name="ScriptModule" type="System.Web.Handlers.ScriptModule,
       System.Web.Extensions, Version=1.0.61025.0, Culture=neutral,
       PublicKeyToken=31bf3856ad364e35" />
  -->

  <add name="ScriptModule" type="CustomComponents.ScriptModule" />
  . . .
</httpModules>
```

20. Run `PageMethods.aspx`, `Math.aspx`, and `Math2.aspx`, and you should see the same results you saw when you ran these pages with the standard ASP.NET `ScriptHandlerFactory` and `ScriptModule`. Feel free to play with the code to get a better understanding of the processing infrastructure of the ASP.NET AJAX REST method call request.

Listing 15-22: The PageMethods.aspx Page

```
<%@ Page Language="C#" %>
<%@ Register TagPrefix="custom" Namespace="CustomComponents" %>
<%@ Import Namespace="System.Web.Services" %>
<!DOCTYPE html PUBLIC "-//W3C//DTD XHTML 1.0 Transitional//EN"
"http://www.w3.org/TR/xhtml1/DTD/xhtml1-transitional.dtd">

<script runat="server">
  [WebMethod]
  public static double Divide(double x, double y)
  {
    if (y == 0)
      throw new DivideByZeroException();

    return x / y;
  }
</script>

<html xmlns="http://www.w3.org/1999/xhtml">
<head id="Head1" runat="server">
  <title>Untitled Page</title>

  <script type="text/javascript" language="javascript">
    var request;

    function onSuccess(result, userContext, methodName)
    {
      userContext.innerHTML = "<b><u>" + result + "</b></u>";
    }

    function onFailure(result, userContext, methodName)
    {
      var builder = new Sys.StringBuilder();
      builder.append("timedOut: ");
      builder.append(result.get_timedOut());
      builder.appendLine();
      builder.appendLine();
      builder.append("message: ");
      builder.append(result.get_message());
      builder.appendLine();
      builder.appendLine();
      builder.append("stackTrace: ");
      builder.appendLine();
      builder.append(result.get_stackTrace());
      builder.appendLine();
      builder.appendLine();
```

```
      builder.append("exceptionType: ");
      builder.append(result.get_exceptionType());
      builder.appendLine();
      builder.appendLine();
      builder.append("statusCode: ");
      builder.append(result.get_statusCode());
      builder.appendLine();
      builder.appendLine();
      builder.append("methodName: ");
      builder.append(methodName);

      alert(builder.toString());
    }

    function divide()
    {
      var xValue = $get("firstNumber").value;
      var yValue = $get("secondNumber").value;
      var userContext = $get("result");
      PageMethods.Divide(xValue, yValue, onSuccess, onFailure, userContext);
    }
  </script>

</head>
<body>
  <form id="form1" runat="server">
    <asp:ScriptManager runat="server" ID="ScriptManager1" />
    <custom:ScriptManager runat="server" ID="CustomScriptManager2"
    EnablePageMethods="true"/>

    <table>
      <tr>
        <td style="font-weight: bold" align="right">
          First Number:
        </td>
        <td align="left">
          <input type="text" id="firstNumber" /></td>
      </tr>
      <tr>
        <td style="font-weight: bold" align="right">
          Second Number:
        </td>
        <td align="left">
          <input type="text" id="secondNumber" /></td>
      </tr>
      <tr>
        <td colspan="2" align="center">
          <button onclick="divide()">
            Divide</button></td>
      </tr>
      <tr>
```

(continued)

653

Listing 15-22 *(continued)*

```
            <td style="font-weight: bold" align="right">
              Result:
            </td>
            <td align="left">
              <span id="result" />
            </td>
          </tr>
        </table>
      </form>
  </body>
</html>
```

Listing 15-23: The Math.aspx Page

```
<%@ Page Language="C#" %>
<%@ Import Namespace="System.Web.Services" %>
<%@ Register TagPrefix="custom" Namespace="CustomComponents" %>

<!DOCTYPE html PUBLIC "-//W3C//DTD XHTML 1.0 Transitional//EN"
"http://www.w3.org/TR/xhtml1/DTD/xhtml1-transitional.dtd">

<html xmlns="http://www.w3.org/1999/xhtml">
<head id="Head1" runat="server">
  <title>Untitled Page</title>

  <script type="text/javascript" language="javascript">
    var request;

    function onSuccess(result, userContext, methodName)
    {
      userContext.innerHTML = "<b><u>" + result + "</b></u>";
    }

    function onFailure(result, userContext, methodName)
    {
      var builder = new Sys.StringBuilder();
      builder.append("timedOut: ");
      builder.append(result.get_timedOut());
      builder.appendLine();
      builder.appendLine();
      builder.append("message: ");
      builder.append(result.get_message());
      builder.appendLine();
      builder.appendLine();
      builder.append("stackTrace: ");
      builder.appendLine();
      builder.append(result.get_stackTrace());
      builder.appendLine();
```

```
        builder.appendLine();
        builder.append("exceptionType: ");
        builder.append(result.get_exceptionType());
        builder.appendLine();
        builder.appendLine();
        builder.append("statusCode: ");
        builder.append(result.get_statusCode());
        builder.appendLine();
        builder.appendLine();
        builder.append("methodName: ");
        builder.append(methodName);

        alert(builder.toString());
    }

    function divide()
    {
      var xValue = $get("firstNumber").value;
      var yValue = $get("secondNumber").value;
      var userContext = $get("result");
      MyNamespace.MyMath.Divide({ "x" : xValue, "y" : yValue}, onSuccess,
                                                onFailure, userContext);

    }
  </script>

</head>
<body>
  <form id="form1" runat="server">
    <asp:ScriptManager runat="server" ID="ScriptManager1"/>
    <custom:ScriptManager runat="server" ID="CustomScriptManager2">
      <Services>
        <custom:ServiceReference InlineScript="true"
        Path="/AJAXFuturesEnabledWebSite2/Math.asbx" />

      </Services>
    </custom:ScriptManager>
    <table>
      <tr>
        <td style="font-weight: bold" align="right">
          First Number:
        </td>
        <td align="left">
          <input type="text" id="firstNumber" /></td>
      </tr>
      <tr>
        <td style="font-weight: bold" align="right">
          Second Number:
        </td>
        <td align="left">
          <input type="text" id="secondNumber" /></td>
      </tr>
```

(continued)

Listing 15-23 *(continued)*

```
      <tr>
        <td colspan="2" align="center">
          <button onclick="divide()">
            Divide</button></td>
      </tr>
      <tr>
        <td style="font-weight: bold" align="right">
          Result:
        </td>
        <td align="left">
          <span id="result" />
        </td>
      </tr>
    </table>
  </form>
</body>
</html>
```

Listing 15-24: The Math2.aspx Page

```
<%@ Page Language="C#" %>
<%@ Import Namespace="System.Web.Services" %>
<%@ Register TagPrefix="custom" Namespace="CustomComponents" %>

<!DOCTYPE html PUBLIC "-//W3C//DTD XHTML 1.0 Transitional//EN"
"http://www.w3.org/TR/xhtml1/DTD/xhtml1-transitional.dtd">

<html xmlns="http://www.w3.org/1999/xhtml">
<head id="Head1" runat="server">
  <title>Untitled Page</title>

  <script type="text/javascript" language="javascript">
    var request;

    function onSuccess(result, userContext, methodName)
    {
      userContext.innerHTML = "<b<<u>" + result + "</b<</u>";
    }

    function onFailure(result, userContext, methodName)
    {
      var builder = new Sys.StringBuilder();
      builder.append("timedOut: ");
      builder.append(result.get_timedOut());
      builder.appendLine();
      builder.appendLine();
      builder.append("message: ");
      builder.append(result.get_message());
      builder.appendLine();
      builder.appendLine();
      builder.append("stackTrace: ");
```

```
           builder.appendLine();
           builder.append(result.get_stackTrace());
           builder.appendLine();
           builder.appendLine();
           builder.append("exceptionType: ");
           builder.append(result.get_exceptionType());
           builder.appendLine();
           builder.appendLine();
           builder.append("statusCode: ");
           builder.append(result.get_statusCode());
           builder.appendLine();
           builder.appendLine();
           builder.append("methodName: ");
           builder.append(methodName);

           alert(builder.toString());
       }

       function divide()
       {
         var xValue = $get("firstNumber").value;
         var yValue = $get("secondNumber").value;
         var userContext = $get("result");
         MyNamespace.Math.Divide(xValue, yValue, onSuccess, onFailure, userContext);
       }
     </script>

</head>
<body>
   <form id="form1" runat="server">
     <asp:ScriptManager runat="server" ID="ScriptManager1"/>
     <custom:ScriptManager runat="server" ID="CustomScriptManager2">
       <Services>
         <custom:ServiceReference InlineScript="true"
                                  Path="/AJAXFuturesEnabledWebSite2/Math.asmx" />
       </Services>
     </custom:ScriptManager>
     <table>
       <tr>
         <td style="font-weight: bold" align="right">
           First Number:
         </td>
         <td align="left">
           <input type="text" id="firstNumber" /></td>
       </tr>
       <tr>
         <td style="font-weight: bold" align="right">
           Second Number:
         </td>
         <td align="left">
           <input type="text" id="secondNumber" /></td>
       </tr>
```

(continued)

Listing 15-24 *(continued)*

```
        <tr>
          <td colspan="2" align="center">
            <button onclick="divide()">
              Divide</button></td>
        </tr>
        <tr>
          <td style="font-weight: bold" align="right">
            Result:
          </td>
          <td align="left">
            <span id="result" />
          </td>
        </tr>
      </table>
    </form>
  </body>
</html>
```

Summary

This chapter showed you how to use the ASP.NET AJAX proxy classes to program against remote objects as you would against local objects. The next chapter covers another important topic in the ASP.NET AJAX framework: behaviors.

Behaviors

A behavior is a piece of functionality that can be attached to a DOM element. Therefore a behavior is a means of extending the functionality of the DOM element to which the behavior is attached. Not every behavior can be attached to every DOM element. This chapter will provide you with in-depth coverage of some of the standard ASP.NET AJAX behaviors and help you gain the skills you need to develop your own custom behaviors.

What is a Behavior, Anyway?

I'll begin our discussions with the simple page shown in Listing 16-1. As you can see, this page contains a <span> HTML element that displays the text "Wrox Web Site." Moving the mouse over this link toggles the CSS class of this <span> element. As the boldface portion of Listing 16-1 shows, the pageLoad method first invokes the $get global JavaScript function to return a reference to the <span> HTML element:

```
var label1 = $get("label1");
```

Next, it invokes the $addHandler global JavaScript function to register a JavaScript function named toggleCssClass as an event handler for the mouseover event of the <span> HTML element:

```
$addHandler(label1, "mouseover", toggleCssClass);
```

Finally, it invokes the $addHandler JavaScript function once more to register the toggleCssClass function as an event handler for the mouseout event of the <span> HTML element:

```
$addHandler(label1, "mouseout", toggleCssClass);
```

As you can see from the boldface portion of Listing 16-1, the toggleCssClass function simply invokes the toggleCssClass static method on the DomElement class, passing in the event target, which simply references the <span> HTML element, and the string that contains the CSS class of interest:

```
function toggleCssClass(domEvent)
{
    Sys.UI.DomElement.toggleCssClass(domEvent.target, "CssClass1");
}
```

Now imagine a situation in which you need to do the same thing with many other span and label HTML elements in your application. You can't reuse the code shown in the boldface portion of Listing 16-1 because it is tied to the specific <span> element on this specific page in your application. Therefore, you would end up recoding the same logic over and over again in different pages of your application. This introduces two fundamental problems:

❑ You are not able to code this logic once and reuse the same code elsewhere in your application.

❑ Since the implementation of this logic is scattered all around your application, every time you need to enhance this logic or fix a bug you have no choice but to make code changes everywhere it is used.

The ASP.NET AJAX client-side framework enables you to capture this logic in a separate component known as a behavior, which can then be attached to any span or label HTML element in your application. This provides the following two important benefits:

❑ It promotes code reusability.

❑ Since the entire code is confined in a single component, you get to make code changes in a single place and rest assured that these changes will be picked up everywhere in your application that this behavior is used.

Listing 16-1: A Page Containing a <span> HTML Element

```
<%@ Page Language="C#" %>
<!DOCTYPE html PUBLIC "-//W3C//DTD XHTML 1.0 Transitional//EN"
"http://www.w3.org/TR/xhtml1/DTD/xhtml1-transitional.dtd">
<html xmlns="http://www.w3.org/1999/xhtml">
<head runat="server">
  <title>Untitled Page</title>
  <style type="text/css">
    .CssClass1
    {
      background-color: Blue;
      color: Yellow;
      font-size: 40px;
    }
  </style>
  <script type="text/javascript" language="javascript">
    function toggleCssClass(domEvent)
    {
      Sys.UI.DomElement.toggleCssClass(domEvent.target, "CssClass1");
    }
```

```
    function pageLoad()
    {
      var label1 = $get("label1");
      $addHandler(label1, "mouseover", toggleCssClass);
      $addHandler(label1, "mouseout", toggleCssClass);
    }
  </script>
</head>
<body>
  <form id="form1" runat="server">
  <asp:ScriptManager runat="server" ID="ScriptManager1" />
  <span id="label1">Wrox Web Site</span>
  </form>
</body>
</html>
```

The Behavior Class

The ASP.NET AJAX client-side framework comes with a base class named `Behavior` whose members define the API that all behaviors must implement in order to act as a behavior in the ASP.NET AJAX applications. Listing 16-2 presents the definition of this base class.

Listing 16-2: The Create Static Method of the Component Base Class

```
var $create = Sys.Component.create =
function Sys$Component$create(type, properties, events, references, element)
{

  var component = (element ? new type(element): new type());

  component.beginUpdate();

  if (properties)

    Sys$Component$_setProperties(component, properties);

  if (events)
  {
    for (var name in events)
    {
      var eventHandlers = events[name];
      var addEventHandlerMethodName = "add_" + name;
      var addEventHandlerMethod = component[addEventHandlerMethodName];
      addEventHandlerMethod(eventHandlers);
    }
  }
```

(continued)

Listing 16-2 *(continued)*

```
Sys.Application._createdComponents[app._createdComponents.length] = component;
    if (component.get_id())

  Sys.Application.addComponent(component);

if (Sys.Application.get_isCreatingComponents())
{
  if (references)

    Sys.Application._addComponentToSecondPass(component, references);

  else

    component.endUpdate();

}

else
{
  if (references)
    Sys$Component$_setReferences(component, references);

  component.endUpdate();
}
return component;
}
```

Note that the `Behavior` base class derives from the ASP.NET AJAX `Component` base class:

```
Sys.UI.Behavior.registerClass('Sys.UI.Behavior', Sys.Component);
```

This means that a behavior, just like any other ASP.NET AJAX component, goes through the typical component life cycle thoroughly discussed in Chapter 7. Recall that a component's life cycle begins when the component springs into life and ends when it is finally disposed of. As you can see from Listing 7-22, the `create` static method of the `Component` base class shows different life cycle phases of a component, which are shown again in Listing 16-2. The main responsibility of the `create` method is to create, initialize, and add a new `Component` object with the specified characteristics to the current ASP.NET AJAX application. This method takes the following parameters:

- ❏ `type`: Contains a reference to the constructor of the component class whose instance is being created. This means that the clients of your behavior will pass a reference to the constructor of your behavior class to this method as its first argument.

- ❏ `properties`: References an object literal, each of whose name/value pairs contains the name and value of a particular property of the `Component` object being created. Therefore, this object sets the values of your behavior's properties.

- ❏ `events`: References an object literal, each of whose name/value pairs contains the name and event handlers of a particular event of the `Component` object being created. In other words, this object registers event handlers for the events of your behavior.

❑ references: References an object literal, each of whose name/value pairs contains the name of a specific property of the Component object being created and the value of the id of the Component object that the property references. This object basically sets the values of those properties of your behavior that reference other ASP.NET AJAX components in the current ASP.NET AJAX application. This means that you can implement custom behaviors containing properties that reference other components.

❑ element: References the DOM element with which the Component object being created is associated. Therefore, this parameter references the DOM element to which your behavior is attached.

The highlighted portions of Listing 16-2 show some of the life cycle phases of your behavior:

❑ Instantiation: This is the phase in which the new operator is invoked on the constructor of your behavior, to instantiate it.

❑ beginUpdate: This is the phase in which the beginUpdate method of your behavior is invoked. As Listing 16-2 shows, this method is invoked immediately after your behavior is instantiated and before the properties of your behavior are set, before any event handlers are registered for the events of your behavior, and before your behavior is added to the current ASP.NET AJAX application. Recall from Listing 7-22 that the Component base class's implementation of the beginUpdate method simply sets an internal flag named _updating to true to mark the beginning of the updating life cycle phase of your behavior, as shown again in the following code listing:

```
function Sys$Component$beginUpdate()
{
  this._updating = true;
}
```

❑ Your behavior can override the beginUpdate method to perform any tasks deemed necessary before its properties are set, before any event handlers are registered for its events, and before your behavior is added to the current ASP.NET AJAX application. Your behavior's implementation of the beginUpdate method must call the beginUpdate method of its base class to allow the base class to mark the beginning of the updating life cycle phase of your behavior, as shown in following code fragment:

```
YourBehavior.prototype.beginUpdate = function ( )
{
    YourBehavior.callBaseMethod(this, 'beginUpdate');
    . . .
}
```

❑ endUpdate: This is the phase in which the endUpdate method of your behavior is invoked. As Listing 16-2 shows, this method is invoked after the properties of your behavior are set, after the client's event handlers are registered for the events of your behavior, and after your behavior is added to the current ASP.NET AJAX application. Recall from Listing 7-22 that the Component base class's implementation of the endUpdate method sets the _updating internal flag to false to mark the end of updating phase of your behavior, calls the initialize method of your behavior, and finally invokes the updated method of your behavior:

```
function Sys$Component$endUpdate()
{
  this._updating = false;
  if (!this._initialized)
    this.initialize();

  this.updated();
}
```

Your behavior can override the endUpdate method to perform those tasks that must be performed before the end of its updating phase is marked and before its initialize method is invoked. However, your behavior's implementation of the initialize method must invoke the endUpdate method of its base class after performing the previously mentioned tasks:

```
YourBehavior.prototype.endUpdate = function()
{
  . . .
  YourBehavior.callBaseMethod(this, 'endUpdate');
}
```

❑ initialize: This is the phase in which the initialize method of your behavior is invoked. As just discussed, this method is invoked after all properties of your behavior are set, after the client's event handlers are registered for the events of your behavior, after your behavior is added to the current ASP.NET AJAX application, and after the end of updating phase of your behavior is marked. The Component base class's implementation of the initialize method simply sets an internal flag named _initialized to mark your behavior as initialized:

```
function Sys$Component$initialize()
{
    this._initialized = true;
}
```

However, your behavior can override this method to perform its behavior-specific initialization tasks. Your behavior's implementation of the initialize method must invoke the initialize method of its base class to allow the base class to initialize itself and to mark your behavior as initialized.

❑ updated: This is the phase in which the updated method of your behavior is invoked. As just discussed, this method is invoked after all properties of your behavior are set, after the client's event handlers are registered for the events of your behavior, after your behavior is added to the current ASP.NET AJAX application, after the end of updating phase of your behavior is marked, and after its initialize method is invoked. Recall from Listing 7-26 that the Component base class's implementation of the updated method does not do anything.

```
function Sys$Component$updated()
{
}
```

However, your behavior can override this method to perform post-update tasks — that is, the tasks that must be performed after all properties of your behavior are set, after the client's event handlers are registered for the events of your behavior, after your behavior is added to the current ASP.NET AJAX application, after the end of the updating phase of your behavior is marked, and after its `initialize` method is invoked.

Your behavior, like any other ASP.NET AJAX component, inherits the following methods from the `Component` base class:

❑ `get_events`: This getter method returns a reference to the `EventHandlerList` object that contains all the event handlers registered for the events of the component. Therefore, if you're writing a custom behavior that needs to expose a new type of event, follow these steps to implement the event:

  ❑ Implement a new method named `add_eventName` (where `eventName` is a placeholder for the name of your event, whatever it may be) as follows to allow the clients of your behavior to register event handlers for this event:

```
function add_eventName (eventHandler)
{
  var events = this.get_events();
  events.addHandler("eventName", eventHandler);
}
```

  As you can see from the preceding code listing, the `add_eventName` method first calls the `get_events` method that your behavior automatically inherits from the `Component` base class to return a reference to the `EventHandlerList` object. Then it invokes the `addHandler` method on this object to register the specified event handler for your event.

  ❑ Implement a new method named `remove_eventName` (where `eventName` is a placeholder for the name of your event) as follows to allow the clients of your behavior to unregister event handlers:

```
function remove_eventName (eventHandler)
{
  var events = this.get_events();
  events.removeHandler("eventName", eventHandler);
}
```

  Again, as you can see from the preceding code listing, the `remove_eventName` method first calls the `get_events` method that your behavior inherits from the `Component` base class to return a reference to the `EventHandlerList` object. Then it invokes the `removeHandler` method on this object to remove the specified event handler from the list of event handlers registered for your event.

  ❑ Implement a new ASP.NET AJAX event data class named `EventNameEventArgs` (where `EventName` is a placeholder for the name of your event) if necessary. As discussed in previous chapters, every event is associated with a class known as an event data class whose instances hold the event data for the event.

❑ Implement a new method named _onEventName (where EventName is a placeholder for the name of your event) that takes a single argument of type EventNameEventArgs, as follows, to raise your event:

```
function _onEventName (eventNameEventArgs)
{
  var events = this.get_events();
  var handler = events.getHandler("eventName");
  if (handler)
    handler(this, eventNameEventArgs)
}
```

❑ Note that this method first calls the get_events method inherited from the Component base class to return a reference to the EventHandlerList object. Then it invokes the getHandler method on this object, passing in the name of your event to return a reference to a JavaScript function whose invocation automatically invokes all the event handlers registered for your event. Next, it invokes this JavaScript function and consequently all the event handlers registered for your event. Note that the _onEventName method passes two parameters to each event handler, the first referencing your behavior and the second the EventNameEventArgs object that contains the event data for your event.

❑ get_id: This getter method allows the clients of your behavior to return its id property value. Recall that the id property value is a string that uniquely identifies your behavior in the current ASP.NET AJAX application.

❑ set_id: This setter method allows the clients of your behavior to set its id property value.

❑ get_isInitialized: This getter method returns a Boolean value that specifies whether your behavior has been initialized. (Your behavior is considered initialized when its initialize method has already been invoked.) Note that this method simply returns the value of the _initialized flag:

```
function Sys$Component$get_isInitialized()
{
  /// <value type="Boolean"></value>
  return this._initialized;
}
```

❑ get_isUpdating: This getter method returns a Boolean value that specifies whether your behavior is being updated. (Note that this method simply returns the value of the _updating flag.)

```
function Sys$Component$get_isUpdating()
{
  /// <value type="Boolean"></value>
  return this._updating;
}
```

❑ add_disposing: This method allows the clients of your behavior to register event handlers for the disposing event of your behavior. As you can see, your behavior automatically inherits this event from the Component base class. Recall that a component raises this event when it is about to be disposed of, to allow its clients to perform final cleanup and to release the resources they're holding.

❑ `remove_disposing`: This method allows the clients of your behavior to remove event handlers from the list of event handlers registered for the disposing event of your behavior.

❑ `add_propertyChanged`: This method allows the clients of your behavior to register event handlers for the `propertyChanged` event of your behavior. As you can see, your behavior automatically inherits this event from the `Component` base class. Recall that a component raises this event when one of its properties changes value.

❑ `remove_propertyChanged`: This method allows the clients of your behavior to remove items from the list of event handlers registered for the `propertyChanged` event of your behavior.

❑ `dispose`: As the following code listing shows, the `Component` base class's implementation of the `dispose` method first raises the `disposing` event of your behavior and consequently invokes the event handlers that the clients of your behavior have registered for the `disposing` event of your behavior, to allow these clients to perform final cleanup and to release the resources they're holding before your behavior is disposed of. Second, the `dispose` method deletes the `EventHandlerList` object that contains the event handlers registered for the events of your behavior before your behavior is disposed of. Third, it calls the `unregisterDisposableObject` method on the `Application` object that represents the current ASP.NET AJAX application, to unregister all the disposable objects registered with the application. (Recall that disposable objects are objects whose types implement the `IDisposable` interface.) If these objects are not unregistered, their `dispose` methods will be automatically invoked when the application is disposed of, even though your behavior has already been disposed of. Fourth, it calls the `removeComponent` method on the `Application` object to remove your behavior from the current ASP.NET AJAX application.

```
function Sys$Component$dispose()
{
  if (this._events)
  {
    var handler = this._events.getHandler("disposing");
    if (handler)
      handler(this, Sys.EventArgs.Empty);
  }
  delete this._events;
  Sys.Application.unregisterDisposableObject(this);
  Sys.Application.removeComponent(this);
}
```

Your behavior can override the `dispose` method to perform final cleanup and to release the resources it is holding when it is about to be disposed of. It is very important that your behavior's implementation of the `dispose` method call the `dispose` method of its base class. Otherwise, none of the previously-mentioned tasks will be performed.

❑ `raisePropertyChanged`: If your behavior exposes properties of its own that can change value, and if you believe that the clients of your behavior should be informed when these properties change value, the setters of these properties must invoke the `raisePropertyChanged` method. As you can see from the following code listing, the `Component` base class's implementation of this method invokes the event handlers registered for the `propertyChanged` event, passing in the `PropertyChangedEventArgs` object that contains the name of the changed property.

This allows those clients of your behavior that have registered event handlers for the `propertyChanged` event of your behavior to be notified when the properties of your behavior change value.

```
function Sys$Component$raisePropertyChanged(propertyName)
{
  /// <param name="propertyName" type="String"></param>
  if (!this._events)
    return;
  var handler = this._events.getHandler("propertyChanged");
  if (handler)
    handler(this, new Sys.PropertyChangedEventArgs(propertyName));
}
```

As you can see from Listing 16-3, the constructor of the `Behavior` base class takes a single parameter that references the DOM element to which a behavior attaches. This constructor assigns this parameter to a private field named `_element`. Note that the constructor adds the behavior to a custom collection property on this DOM element named `_behaviors`. As the name suggests, the `_behaviors` collection of a DOM element contains references to all behaviors attached to the DOM element. As you can see, you can attach more than one behavior to the same DOM element.

Listing 16-3: The ASP.NET AJAX Behavior Base Class

```
Sys.UI.Behavior = function Sys$UI$Behavior(element)
{
  /// <param name="element" domElement="true"></param>
  Sys.UI.Behavior.initializeBase(this);
  this._element = element;
  var behaviors = element._behaviors;
  if (!behaviors)
    element._behaviors = [this];

  else
    behaviors[behaviors.length] = this;
}
Sys.UI.Behavior.prototype =
{
  _name: null,
  get_element: Sys$UI$Behavior$get_element,
  get_id: Sys$UI$Behavior$get_id,
  get_name: Sys$UI$Behavior$get_name,
  set_name: Sys$UI$Behavior$set_name,
  initialize: Sys$UI$Behavior$initialize,
  dispose: Sys$UI$Behavior$dispose
}
Sys.UI.Behavior.registerClass('Sys.UI.Behavior', Sys.Component);
```

Properties

The ASP.NET AJAX Behavior base class exposes the properties discussed in the following sections.

element

The ASP.NET AJAX `Behavior` base class features a getter method named `get_element`, which returns the value of the `_element` field, as shown in Listing 16-4. Recall that this field references the DOM element to which the behavior is attached. Note that the element is a read-only property. That's why the `Behavior` base class does not expose the `set_element` setter. In other words, the `element` property of a behavior can be set only when the behavior is being instantiated.

Listing 16-4: The Element Property of the Behavior Base Class

```
function Sys$UI$Behavior$get_element()
{
  /// <value domElement="true"></value>
  return this._element;
}
```

name

The `Behavior` base class exposes a read/write property named `name`. Listing 16-5 presents the internal implementation of the `set_name` setter method that enables you to set the `name` property. Note that this setter method raises an exception if:

❑ The DOM element to which the behavior is attached already contains a behavior with the same name. This ensures that the name of a behavior uniquely identifies it among other behaviors attached to the DOM element:

```
if (typeof(this._element[value]) !== 'undefined')
    throw Error.invalidOperation(
                           String.format(Sys.Res.behaviorDuplicateName, value));
```

❑ The behavior has already been initialized — that is, its `initialize` method has already been invoked. In other words, you cannot set the name of a behavior after it has been initialized:

```
if (this.get_isInitialized())
    throw Error.invalidOperation(Sys.Res.cantSetNameAfterInit);
```

Listing 16-5: The set_name Method of the Behavior Base Class

```
function Sys$UI$Behavior$set_name(value)
{
  if ((value === '') || (value.charAt(0) === ' ') ||
      (value.charAt(value.length - 1) === ' '))
    throw Error.argument('value', Sys.Res.invalidId);
  if (typeof(this._element[value]) !== 'undefined')
    throw Error.invalidOperation(
                           String.format(Sys.Res.behaviorDuplicateName, value));
  if (this.get_isInitialized())
    throw Error.invalidOperation(Sys.Res.cantSetNameAfterInit);
  this._name = value;
}
```

Listing 16-6 presents the internal implementation of the `get_name` getter method of the `Behavior` base class. Call this method to access the name of a behavior. As you can see, if the value of the _name field has been set through the explicit call into the `set_name` setter method, the `get_name` getter method simply returns the value of this field:

```
if (this._name)
   return this._name;
```

If your application logic expects the behavior to have a specific name, you must explicitly call the `set_name` *method on the behavior to explicitly set the value of the _name field to the desired value before the behavior's* `initialize` *method is invoked.*

If the value of the _name field has not been set through the explicit call into the `set_name` setter method, the `get_name` method takes the following steps to set and to return the value of this field. First, it calls the `getTypeName` static method on the JavaScript `Object` class, passing in a reference to the current behavior to return a string that contains the fully qualified name of the type of the behavior, including its complete namespace hierarchy. For example, if your custom behavior is an ASP.NET AJAX class named `MyBehavior` that belongs to a namespace named `MyNamespace1`, which belongs to another namespace named `MyNamespace2`, the call into the `getTypeName` method will return the string `"MyNamespace2.MyNamespace1.MyBehavior"`.

```
var name = Object.getTypeName(this);
```

Since the string returned from the `getTypeName` method contains the complete namespace hierarchy of the type of behavior, the `get_name` getter method uses the following logic to extract the name of the behavior class, excluding its namespace hierarchy:

```
var i = name.lastIndexOf('.');
if (i != -1)
   name = name.substr(i + 1);
```

Next, the `get_name` getter method checks whether the behavior has already been initialized — that is, whether its initialized method has already been invoked. If not, it assigns the name of the behavior class — excluding its namespace hierarchy — to the _name field:

```
if (!this.get_isInitialized())
   this._name = name;
```

As you can see, if you don't explicitly assign a value to the _name field of a behavior by explicitly calling the `set_name` method, the behavior will automatically use the name of the behavior class, excluding its namespace hierarchy, as the name.

Listing 16-6: The get_name Method of the Behavior Base Class Function

```
Sys$UI$Behavior$get_name()
{
  if (this._name)
    return this._name;

  var name = Object.getTypeName(this);
  var i = name.lastIndexOf('.');
  if (i != -1)
    name = name.substr(i + 1);
  if (!this.get_isInitialized())
    this._name = name;
  return name;
}
```

id

The Behavior base class inherits a method named set_id from its base class. You can call this method to explicitly set the id property value of a behavior. Listing 16-7 presents the Component base class's implementation of this method.

Listing 16-7: The set_id Method

```
function Sys$Component$set_id(value)
{
  if (this._idSet)
    throw Error.invalidOperation(Sys.Res.componentCantSetIdTwice);

  this._idSet = true;
  var oldId = this.get_id();

  if (oldId && Sys.Application.findComponent(oldId))
    throw Error.invalidOperation(Sys.Res.componentCantSetIdAfterAddedToApp);
  this._id = value;
}
```

As you can see from Listing 16-7, the set_id method raises an exception if it is invoked twice. In other words, you cannot set the id property value of a behavior more than once:

```
if (this._idSet)
    throw Error.invalidOperation(Sys.Res.componentCantSetIdTwice);

this._idSet = true;
```

Note that Listing 16-7 invokes the findComponent method on the Application object that represents the current ASP.NET AJAX application, to determine whether the current application already contains a component with the same name. If so, this indicates that the same behavior has already been added to the application, and consequently the set_id method raises an exception.

You cannot set the value of the id *property of a behavior more than once, or after adding the behavior to the application. Recall from Listing 16-2 that a behavior is added to an application when the* addComponent *method is invoked on the* Application *object, passing in a reference to the behavior. In other words, you cannot change the value of the* id *property of a behavior after the call into the* addComponent *method.*

As you can see, the Behavior base class does not override the set_id setter method of its base class. However, it does override the get_id method that it inherits from the Component base class, in which it takes the steps shown in Listing 16-8. First, it invokes the get_id method of its base class to check whether the base class already contains an id for the behavior — that is, whether the set_id method has already been explicitly invoked to set the id property value. If so, it simply returns the return value of the get_id method of the base class:

```
var baseId = Sys.UI.Behavior.callBaseMethod(this, 'get_id');
if (baseId)
  return baseId;
```

If not, it creates a string that contains two substrings separated by the dollar sign ($), the first containing the id property value of the DOM element to which the behavior is attached and the second containing the name of the behavior:

```
return this._element.id + '$' + this.get_name();
```

If your application logic expects the id *property of a behavior to have a specific value, you must explicitly call the* set_id *method to set the value of this property. Otherwise the previously-mentioned auto-generated* id *value will be used.*

Listing 16-8: The id Property of the Behavior Base Class

```
function Sys$UI$Behavior$get_id()
{
  /// <value type="String"></value>
  var baseId = Sys.UI.Behavior.callBaseMethod(this, 'get_id');
  if (baseId)
    return baseId;
  if (!this._element || !this._element.id)
    return '';

  return this._element.id + '$' + this.get_name();
}
```

Instance Methods

The Behavior base exposes the instance methods discussed in the following sections. Recall that an instance method is a method that is defined on the prototype property of a JavaScript class. As the name suggests, an instance method must be invoked on an instance of the class.

initialize

The `Behavior` base class overrides the `initialize` method that it inherits from the `Component` base class, as shown in Listing 16-9. As you can see, this method defines a custom property on the DOM element to which the behavior is attached. Note that the name of the behavior is used as the name of this custom property. Also note that this method assigns a reference to the current behavior as the value of this custom property.

Therefore, if you have access to a reference to a given DOM element, and if you know the name of the behavior you're looking for, you can access a reference to this behavior using the following line of code:

```
var behavior = domElement[behaviorName];
```

Listing 16-9: The initialize Method of the Behavior Base Class

```
function Sys$UI$Behavior$initialize()
{
  Sys.UI.Behavior.callBaseMethod(this, 'initialize');
  var name = this.get_name();
  if (name)
    this._element[name] = this;
}
```

dispose

The `Behavior` base class overrides the `dispose` method that it inherits from the `Component` base class, as shown in Listing 16-10. As you can see, this method first invokes the `dispose` method of the base class:

```
Sys.UI.Behavior.callBaseMethod(this, 'dispose');
```

Your custom behavior class' implementation of the `dispose` *method must do the same — that is, it must call the* `dispose` *method of its base class to allow the base class to raise the disposing event and to perform its final cleanup.*

Next, the `dispose` method sets the value of the custom property that references the current behavior to `null`. This allows the same name to be reused for other behaviors of the same DOM element:

```
var name = this.get_name();
    if (name)
      this._element[name] = null;
```

Next, it removes the current behavior from the `_behaviors` collection property of the DOM element to which the behavior is attached:

```
Array.remove(this._element._behaviors, this);
```

Listing 16-10: The dispose Method of the Behavior Base Class

```
function Sys$UI$Behavior$dispose()
{
  Sys.UI.Behavior.callBaseMethod(this, 'dispose');
  if (this._element)
  {
    var name = this.get_name();
    if (name)
      this._element[name] = null;

    Array.remove(this._element._behaviors, this);
    delete this._element;
  }
}
```

Static Methods

The `Behavior` base class exposes the static methods discussed in the following sections. Recall that a static method of a JavaScript class is a method that is defined on the class itself.

getBehaviorByName

The `getBehaviorByName` static method of the `Behavior` class takes two parameters and returns a reference to the behavior whose name is given by the second parameter, and whose associated DOM element is referenced by the first parameter (see Listing 16-11). Recall that every DOM element contains a custom property for each behavior attached to it for which the name of the property is the name of the behavior and the value of the property references the behavior itself.

Listing 16-11: The getBehaviorByName Method of the Behavior Base Class

```
Sys.UI.Behavior.getBehaviorByName =
function Sys$UI$Behavior$getBehaviorByName(element, name)
{
  /// <param name="element" domElement="true"></param>
  /// <param name="name" type="String"></param>
  /// <returns type="Sys.UI.Behavior" mayBeNull="true"></returns>
  var b = element[name];
  return (b && Sys.UI.Behavior.isInstanceOfType(b)) ? b : null;
}
```

getBehaviors

The `getBehaviors` static method takes a single parameter that references a DOM element and returns a reference to the `_behaviors` collection (if any) of the DOM element (see Listing 16-12). Recall that this collection contains references to all behaviors attached to the DOM element.

Listing 16-12: The getBehaviors Method of the Behavior Base Class

```
Sys.UI.Behavior.getBehaviors = function Sys$UI$Behavior$getBehaviors(element)
{
  /// <param name="element" domElement="true"></param>
  /// <returns type="Array" elementType="Sys.UI.Behavior"></returns>
  if (!element._behaviors)
    return [];
  return Array.clone(element._behaviors);
}
```

getBehaviorsByType

There are times when you need to search the _behaviors collection of a DOM element by the type of behavior. This is where the getBehaviorsByType static method comes in handy. As Listing 16-13 shows, this method takes two parameters: the first references the DOM element and the second references the constructor of the behavior. (Recall that the constructor of a JavaScript class defines its type.) As you can see, this method iterates through the behaviors in the _behaviors collection of the specified DOM element and calls the isInstanceOfType method on the second parameter to determine whether the enumerated behavior is of the desired type.

Listing 16-13: The getBehaviorsByType Method of the Behavior Base Class

```
Sys.UI.Behavior.getBehaviorsByType =
function Sys$UI$Behavior$getBehaviorsByType(element, type)
{
  /// <param name="element" domElement="true"></param>
  /// <param name="type" type="Type"></param>
  /// <returns type="Array" elementType="Sys.UI.Behavior"></returns>
  var behaviors = element._behaviors;
  var results = [];
  if (behaviors)
  {
    for (var i = 0, l = behaviors.length; i < l; i++)
    {
      if (type.isInstanceOfType(behaviors[i]))
        results[results.length] = behaviors[i];
    }
  }
  return results;
}
```

ClickBehavior

As you have seen on several occasions in this and previous chapters, implementing a new event for an ASP.NET AJAX client control requires you to follow the ASP.NET AJAX event-implementation pattern, which involves several steps. One of the most common events is the click event. If you were to implement this event for several ASP.NET AJAX client controls in your application, you'd end up re-implementing the steps of the same ASP.NET AJAX event implementation pattern over and over again. The ClickBehavior encapsulates this logic, enabling you to attach the ClickBehavior to any ASP.NET AJAX client control for which the click event makes sense, thereby enabling that control to support the click event.

Listing 16-14 presents the definition of the ClickBehavior class. As you can see, the constructor of this class, like the constructor of any behavior class, takes a parameter that references the DOM element to which the behavior is attached. Note that the ClickBehavior class inherits from the Behavior base class and extends its functionality to add support for the click event:

```
Sys.Preview.UI.ClickBehavior.registerClass('Sys.Preview.UI.ClickBehavior',
                                           Sys.UI.Behavior);
```

Listing 16-14: The ClickBehavior Class

```
Sys.Preview.UI.ClickBehavior = function Sys$Preview$UI$ClickBehavior(element)
{
   /// <param name="element" domElement="true"></param>
   Sys.Preview.UI.ClickBehavior.initializeBase(this, [element]);
}
Sys.Preview.UI.ClickBehavior.prototype =
{
   _clickHandler: null,
   add_click: Sys$Preview$UI$ClickBehavior$add_click,
   remove_click: Sys$Preview$UI$ClickBehavior$remove_click,
   dispose: Sys$Preview$UI$ClickBehavior$dispose,
   initialize: Sys$Preview$UI$ClickBehavior$initialize,
   _onClick: Sys$Preview$UI$ClickBehavior$_onClick
}
Sys.Preview.UI.ClickBehavior.registerClass('Sys.Preview.UI.ClickBehavior',
                                           Sys.UI.Behavior);
```

descriptor

As you can see from Listing 16-15, the ClickBehavior class exposes a descriptor property to allow its clients to use the ASP.NET AJAX type-inspection capabilities to interact with the class in a generic way without knowing its type — that is, without knowing that the class they are interacting with is the ClickBehavior class. As discussed in the previous chapters, the descriptor property of a class is an object literal, which contains up to four name/value pairs that describe the events, properties, methods, and attributes of the class. In this case, the object exposes a single name/value pair that describes the events of the class. As you can see, the name part of this name/value pair is events, and the value part is an array of object literals in which each object literal describes an event. Since the ClickBehavior exposes only one event, named click, this array contains a single object, which contains a single name/value pair: the name part of the pair is name and the value part is the string 'click'.

Your custom behavior classes must do the same: that is, they must expose a descriptor *property that describes those events, methods, properties, and attributes that you believe the clients of your behavior may want to access in a generic way via the ASP.NET AJAX type-inspection infrastructure.*

Listing 16-15: The descriptor Property of the ClickBehavior

```
Sys.Preview.UI.ClickBehavior.descriptor =
{
  events: [ {name: 'click'} ]
}
```

The click Event

Listing 16-16 encapsulates the typical logic that follows the ASP.NET AJAX event-implementation pattern to implement the `click` event, saving you from having to write this code over again every time you need to add support for the `click` event to an ASP.NET AJAX client control. As the boldface portion of Listing 16-16 shows, the `Cli ckBehavior` implements a method named `_onClick` that raises the `click` event and consequently invokes all the event handlers registered for this event.

Listing 16-16: The click Event

```
function Sys$Preview$UI$ClickBehavior$add_click(handler)
{
  this.get_events().addHandler('click', handler);
}
function Sys$Preview$UI$ClickBehavior$remove_click(handler)
{
  this.get_events().removeHandler('click', handler);
}
function Sys$Preview$UI$ClickBehavior$_onClick()
{
  var handler = this.get_events().getHandler('click');
  if(handler)
    handler(this, Sys.EventArgs.Empty);
}
function Sys$Preview$UI$ClickBehavior$dispose()
{
  if (this._clickHandler)
    $removeHandler(this.get_element(), 'click', this._clickHandler);

  Sys.Preview.UI.ClickBehavior.callBaseMethod(this, 'dispose');
}
```

initialize

The `ClickBehavior` class overrides the `initialize` method that it inherits from the `Component` base class, taking the steps shown in Listing 16-17. First, it invokes the `initialize` method of its base class:

```
Sys.Preview.UI.ClickBehavior.callBaseMethod(this, 'initialize');
```

Your custom behavior's implementation of the `initialize` *method must do the same — that is, it must begin by calling the* `initialize` *method of its base class to allow the base class to initialize itself first.*

Then it invokes the `createDelegate` static method on the `Function` JavaScript class to create a delegate that represents the `_onClick` method of the `ClickBehavior` class, and assigns this delegate to a private field named `_clickHandler`:

```
this._clickHandler = Function.createDelegate(this, this._onClick);
```

Finally, it uses the `$addHandler` global JavaScript function to register the delegate as an event handler for the `click` event of the DOM element to which the behavior is attached. Therefore, when this DOM element raises its `click` event, it'll automatically invoke this delegate and consequently the `_onClick` method of the behavior. As the boldface portion of Listing 16-16 shows, the `_onClick` method in turn invokes all the event handlers registered for the `click` event of the behavior.

```
$addHandler(this.get_element(), 'click', this._clickHandler);
```

Note that the `ClickBehavior` class stores the delegate in a private field. Recall from Listing 16-16 that before the behavior is disposed of, the `dispose` method of the class uses the `$removeHandler` global JavaScript function to remove this delegate from the list of event handlers registered for the `click` event of the DOM element to which the behavior is attached. Your custom behavior must do the same: it must store its delegates in private fields and override the `dispose` method, using the `$removeHandler` function to remove these delegates from the list of event handlers registered for the specified events of the DOM element to which your behavior is attached before your behavior is disposed of. Otherwise these delegates will be called when the DOM element raises its associated events, even after your behavior is long disposed of.

Listing 16-17: The initialize Method of the ClickBehavior

```
function Sys$Preview$UI$ClickBehavior$initialize()
{
  Sys.Preview.UI.ClickBehavior.callBaseMethod(this, 'initialize');
  this._clickHandler = Function.createDelegate(this, this._onClick);
  $addHandler(this.get_element(), 'click', this._clickHandler);
}
```

Using the ClickBehavior

Listing 16-18 presents a page that attaches the `ClickBehavior` to a `<div>` HTML element. As you can see from this code listing, the `pageLoad` method takes these steps to instantiate the `ClickBehavior` and to attach it to the `<div>` HTML element. First, it defines a dictionary named `events` and populates it with the names of the `ClickBehavior` events and their associated event handlers:

```
var events =
{
  disposing : disposingCallback,
  propertyChanged : propertyChangedCallback,
  click : clickCallback
};
```

In this case, we're registering three event handlers named `disposingCallback`, `propertyChangedCallback`, and `clickCallback` for the `disposing`, `propertyChanged`, and `click` events of the `ClickBehavior` instance being instantiated.

Then the `pageLoad` method defines a dictionary named `properties` and populates it with the names of the `ClickBehavior` properties and their associated values:

```
var properties =
{
  name : "MyClickBehaviorName",
  id : "MyClickBehaviorID"
};
```

In this case, we're setting the `name` and `id` properties to the string values `"MyClickBehaviorName"` and `"MyClickBehaviorID"`, respectively.

Finally, the `pageLoad` method invokes the `$create` global JavaScript function to instantiate the `ClickBehavior` instance. As you can see, this function takes five parameters. The first references the constructor of the `ClickBehavior` class, the second is the properties dictionary, the third is the events dictionary, the fourth is `null`, and the fifth is the reference to the `<div>` DOM element to which the `ClickBehavior` will be attached.

```
clickBehavior1 = $create(Sys.Preview.UI.ClickBehavior, properties,
                         events, null, $get("mydiv"));
```

Listing 16-18: A Page that Uses the ClickBehavior

```
<%@ Page Language="C#" %>
<!DOCTYPE html PUBLIC "-//W3C//DTD XHTML 1.0 Transitional//EN"
"http://www.w3.org/TR/xhtml1/DTD/xhtml1-transitional.dtd">
<html xmlns="http://www.w3.org/1999/xhtml">
<head runat="server">
  <title>Untitled Page</title>
  <script type="text/javascript" language="javascript">
    var clickBehavior1;

    function disposingCallback(sender, args)
    {
      alert("disposing event was raised!");
    }

    function propertyChangedCallback(sender, args)
    {
      alert(args.get_propertyName() + " was changed!");
    }

    function clickCallback()
    {
      alert("name = " + clickBehavior1.get_name() + "\n" +
          "id = " + clickBehavior1.get_id());
    }
```

(continued)

Listing 16-18 *(continued)*

```
      function pageLoad()
      {
        var events =
        {
          disposing : disposingCallback,
          propertyChanged : propertyChangedCallback,
          click : clickCallback
        };

        var properties =
        {
          name : "MyClickBehaviorName",
          id : "MyClickBehaviorID"
        };
        clickBehavior1 = $create(Sys.Preview.UI.ClickBehavior, properties,
                                 events, null, $get("mydiv"));
      }
    </script>
  </head>
  <body>
    <form id="form1" runat="server">
      <asp:ScriptManager runat="server" ID="ScriptManager1">
        <Scripts>
          <asp:ScriptReference Assembly="Microsoft.Web.Preview"
          Name="PreviewScript.js" />
        </Scripts>
      </asp:ScriptManager>
      <div id="mydiv">Click Me</div>
    </form>
  </body>
</html>
```

The ASP.NET AJAX Control Toolkit

The ASP.NET AJAX control toolkit is a shared-source community project that you can download from the official Microsoft ASP.NET AJAX site at `http://ajax.asp.net`. This toolkit contains a bunch of ASP.NET AJAX behaviors that you can use as-is in your own Web applications or enhance to meet your application requirements. Such enhancements require a solid understanding of the internal implementation of these behaviors. All the behaviors included in this toolkit directly or indirectly inherit from a base behavior class named `BehaviorBase`, which in turn inherits from the `Behavior` base class. Note that all the behaviors in this toolkit belong to a namespace called `AjaxControlToolkit`, defined as follows:

```
Type.registerNamespace('AjaxControlToolkit');
```

The main goal of this section is twofold. First, it provides in-depth coverage of the `BehaviorBase` class. Second, it shows you how to derive from the `BehaviorBase` class to implement your own custom behaviors. You do not need to install the ASP.NET AJAX Control Toolkit to run the code presented in this chapter because all the code is self-contained.

BehaviorBase

The BehaviorBase class is the base class for all ASP.NET AJAX toolkit behaviors. Listing 16-19 presents the declaration of the members of this class. I'll discuss the implementation of these members in the following sections.

Listing 16-19: The BehaviorBase Class

```
AjaxControlToolkit.BehaviorBase = function(element)
{
    /// <summary>
    /// Base behavior for all extender behaviors
    /// </summary>
    /// <param name="element" type="Sys.UI.DomElement" domElement="true">
    /// Element the behavior is associated with
    /// </param> AjaxControlToolkit.BehaviorBase.initializeBase(this,[element]);

    this._clientStateFieldID = null;
    this._pageRequestManager = null;
    this._partialUpdateBeginRequestHandler = null;
    this._partialUpdateEndRequestHandler = null;
}
AjaxControlToolkit.BehaviorBase.prototype =
{
    initialize : AjaxControlToolkit$BehaviorBase$initialize,
    dispose : AjaxControlToolkit$BehaviorBase$dispose,

    get_ClientStateFieldID : AjaxControlToolkit$BehaviorBase$get_ClientStateFieldID,
    set_ClientStateFieldID : AjaxControlToolkit$BehaviorBase$set_ClientStateFieldID,
    get_ClientState : AjaxControlToolkit$BehaviorBase$get_ClientState,
    set_ClientState : AjaxControlToolkit$BehaviorBase$set_ClientState,
    registerPartialUpdateEvents :
                        AjaxControlToolkit$BehaviorBase$registerPartialUpdateEvents,
    _partialUpdateBeginRequest :
                        AjaxControlToolkit$BehaviorBase$_partialUpdateBeginRequest,
    _partialUpdateEndRequest :
                        AjaxControlToolkit$BehaviorBase$_partialUpdateBeginRequest
}
AjaxControlToolkit.BehaviorBase.registerClass('AjaxControlToolkit.BehaviorBase',
                                    Sys.UI.Behavior);
```

initialize

The BehaviorBase class, like any other ASP.NET AJAX component, inherits the initialize method from the Component base class. As Listing 16-20 shows, the initialize method of the BehaviorBase class simply calls the initialize method of its base class. However, you can implement a custom behavior that derives from the BehaviorBase class and overrides its initialize method to initialize itself.

Listing 16-20: The initialize Method

```
function AjaxControlToolkit$BehaviorBase$initialize ()
{
  /// <summary>
  /// Initialize the behavior
  /// </summary>
  AjaxControlToolkit.BehaviorBase.callBaseMethod(this, 'initialize');
}
```

ClientStateFieldID

The `BehaviorBase` class exposes a property named `ClientStateFieldID` that specifies the id property value of the hidden field that contains the client state of the behavior. The client state means different things in different types of behaviors. It is the responsibility of each subclass of the `BehaviorBase` class to decide for itself what type of information it needs to store in this hidden field.

As you can see from Listing 16-21, the `BehaviorBase` exposes a getter method named `get_ClientStateFieldID` and a setter method named `set_ClientStateFieldID` that you can call from within your client script to get and set the `ClientStateFieldID` property of the behavior.

Listing 16-21: The ClientStateFieldID Property

```
function AjaxControlToolkit$BehaviorBase$get_ClientStateFieldID ()
{
  /// <value type="String">
  /// ID of the hidden field used to store client state
  /// </value>
  return this._clientStateFieldID;
}
function AjaxControlToolkit$BehaviorBase$set_ClientStateFieldID (value)
{
  if (this._clientStateFieldID != value)
  {
    this._clientStateFieldID = value;
    this.raisePropertyChanged('ClientStateFieldID');
  }
}
```

ClientState

The `BehaviorBase` class exposes a string property named `ClientState`, which contains the information that the behavior stores in the hidden field whose name is given by the `ClientStateFieldID` property. As Listing 16-22 shows, these two methods first call the `getElementById` method to return a reference to the hidden field, and then get or set the value of the `value` property of this field.

Listing 16-22: The ClientState Property

```
function AjaxControlToolkit$BehaviorBase$get_ClientState ()
{
  /// <value type="String">
  /// Client state
  /// </value>
  if (this._clientStateFieldID)
  {
    var input = document.getElementById(this._clientStateFieldID);
    if (input)
      return input.value;
  }
  return null;
}
function AjaxControlToolkit$BehaviorBase$set_ClientState (value)
{
  if (this._clientStateFieldID)
  {
    var input = document.getElementById(this._clientStateFieldID);
    if (input)
      input.value = value;
  }
}
```

registerPartialUpdateEvents

The BehaviorBase class exposes a method named registerPartialUpdateEvents that does exactly what its name says it does: it registers event handlers for the partial update events, such as the beginRequest and endRequest events of the current client-side PageRequestManager instance. The current client-side PageRequestManager instance raises the beginRequest event when it is about to make an asynchronous partial page request to the server, and the endRequest event when the request finally completes. I'll discuss the current client-side PageRequestManager instance and its events later in this book.

Those subclasses of the BehaviorBase class that want to respond to the beginRequest and endRequest events of the current client-side PageRequestManager instance must override the initialize method to invoke the registerPartialUpdateEvents method.

As Listing 16-23 shows, the registerPartialUpdateEvents method first invokes the getInstance static method on the client-side PageRequestManager class to return a reference to the current client-side PageRequestManager instance and stores this reference in an internal field named _pageRequestManager:

```
this._pageRequestManager = Sys.WebForms.PageRequestManager.getInstance();
```

Each page can contain only one instance of the PageRequestManager class. You must never use the new operator in your client code to create a new instance of this class. You must always call the getInstance method to return a reference to the existing instance.

Next, it creates a delegate that represents the _partialUpdateBeginRequest method of the BehaviorBase class and store this delegate in an internal field named _partialUpdateBeginRequestHandler:

```
this._partialUpdateBeginRequestHandler =
            Function.createDelegate(this, this._partialUpdateBeginRequest);
```

Then the registerPartialUpdateEvents method invokes the add_beginRequest method on the current client-side PageRequestManager instance to register the delegate as event handler for the beginRequest event of the current PageRequestManager instance:

```
this._pageRequestManager.add_beginRequest(
                            this._partialUpdateBeginRequestHandler);
```

Next, it creates a delegate that represents the _partialUpdateEndRequest method of the BehaviorBase class and store this delegate in an internal field named _partialUpdateEndRequestHandler:

```
this._partialUpdateEndRequestHandler =
            Function.createDelegate(this, this._partialUpdateEndRequest);
```

Then it invokes the add_endRequest method on the current client-side PageRequestManager instance to register the delegate as event handler for the endRequest event of the current PageRequestManager instance:

```
this._pageRequestManager.add_endRequest(
                            this._partialUpdateEndRequestHandler);
```

Listing 16-23: The registerPartialUpdateEvents Method

```
function AjaxControlToolkit$BehaviorBase$registerPartialUpdateEvents ()
{
  /// <summary>
  /// Register for beginRequest and endRequest events on the PageRequestManager,
  /// (which cause _partialUpdateBeginRequest and _partialUpdateEndRequest to be
  /// called when an UpdatePanel refreshes)
  /// </summary>
  if (Sys && Sys.WebForms && Sys.WebForms.PageRequestManager)
  {
    this._pageRequestManager = Sys.WebForms.PageRequestManager.getInstance();
    if (this._pageRequestManager)
    {
      this._partialUpdateBeginRequestHandler =
                  Function.createDelegate(this, this._partialUpdateBeginRequest);
      this._pageRequestManager.add_beginRequest(
                                  this._partialUpdateBeginRequestHandler);

      this._partialUpdateEndRequestHandler =
                  Function.createDelegate(this, this._partialUpdateEndRequest);
      this._pageRequestManager.add_endRequest(
                                  this._partialUpdateEndRequestHandler);
    }
  }
}
```

_partialUpdateBeginRequest

As you saw in Listing 16-23, the registerPartialUpdateEvents method registers the
_partialUpdateBeginRequest method (the delegate that represents this method to be exact) as event
handler for the beginRequest event of the PageRequestManager instance. As you can see from
Listing 16-24, the BehaviorBase class' implementation of this method doesn't do anything.

However, the subclasses of this base class can override this method to run custom logic in response to
the beginRequest event of the current PageRequestManager instance.

Listing 16-24: The _partialUpdateBeginRequest Method

```
function AjaxControlToolkit$BehaviorBase$_partialUpdateBeginRequest(sender,
                                                            beginRequestEventArgs)
{
  /// <summary>
  /// Method that will be called when a partial update (via an UpdatePanel) begins,
  /// if registerPartialUpdateEvents() has been called.
  /// </summary>
  /// <param name="sender" type="Object">
  /// Sender
  /// </param>
  /// <param name="beginRequestEventArgs"
  /// type="Sys.WebForms.BeginRequestEventArgs">
  /// Event arguments
  /// </param>
  // Nothing done here; override this method in a child class
}
```

_partialUpdateEndRequest

Recall from Listing 16-23 that the registerPartialUpdateEvents method registers the
_partialUpdateEndRequest method (the delegate that represents this method to be exact) as
event handler for the endRequest event of the PageRequestManager instance. As you can see from
Listing 16-25, the BehaviorBase class' implementation of this method doesn't do anything.

However, the subclasses of this base class can override this method to run custom logic in response to
the endRequest event of the current PageRequestManager instance.

Listing 16-25: The _partialUpdateEndRequest Method

```
function AjaxControlToolkit$BehaviorBase$_partialUpdateEndRequest(sender,
                                                            endRequestEventArgs)
{
  /// <summary>
  /// Method that will be called when a partial update (via an UpdatePanel)
  /// finishes,
  /// if registerPartialUpdateEvents() has been called.
  /// </summary>
```

(continued)

Listing 16-25 *(continued)*

```
/// <param name="sender" type="Object">
/// Sender
/// </param>
/// <param name="endRequestEventArgs" type="Sys.WebForms.EndRequestEventArgs">
/// Event arguments
/// </param>
// Nothing done here; override this method in a child class
}
```

dispose

The `BehaviorBase` class, like any other ASP.NET AJAX component, inherits the `dispose` method from the `Component` base class. As Listing 16-26 shows, this class' implementation of this method simply removes the delegates registered for the `beginRequest` and `endRequest` events of the current `PageRequestManager` instance from the list of event handlers registered for these events.

The `dispose` *method of your custom behaviors must do the same — that is, they must unregister the delegates that they register for the* `beginRequest` *and* `endRequest` *events. Otherwise, every time the* `PageRequestManager` *instance raises these two events, it will call these delegates even though your custom behaviors are long disposed of.*

Listing 16-26: The dispose Method

```
function AjaxControlToolkit$BehaviorBase$dispose ()
{
  /// <summary>
  /// Dispose the behavior
  /// </summary>
  AjaxControlToolkit.BehaviorBase.callBaseMethod(this, 'dispose');
  if (this._pageRequestManager)
  {
    if (this._partialUpdateBeginRequestHandler)
    {
      this._pageRequestManager.remove_beginRequest(
                                    this._partialUpdateBeginRequestHandler);
      this._partialUpdateBeginRequestHandler = null;
    }

    if (this._partialUpdateEndRequestHandler)
    {
      this._pageRequestManager.remove_endRequest(
                                    this._partialUpdateEndRequestHandler);
      this._partialUpdateEndRequestHandler = null;
    }

    this._pageRequestManager = null;
  }
}
```

The next section will walk through the implementation of one of the behaviors in the toolkit known as `TextBoxWatermarkBehavior` to help you gain the skills, knowledge, and experience that you need to develop behaviors in the ASP.NET AJAX control toolkit.

The TextBoxWatermarkBehavior

The ASP.NET AJAX control toolkit comes with a behavior named `TextBoxWatermarkBehavior` that derives from the `BehaviorBase` class and extends its functionality to apply a watermark to its associated text box DOM element. Listing 16-27 presents the definition of the `TextBoxWatermarkBehavior`.

Listing 16-27: The Definition of TextBoxWatermarkBehavior

```
AjaxControlToolkit.TextBoxWatermarkBehavior = function(element)
{
  /// <summary>
  /// The TextBoxWatermarkBehavior applies a watermark to a textbox
  /// </summary>
  /// <param name="element" type="Sys.UI.DomElement" domElement="true">
  /// Textbox associated with the behavior
  /// </param>
  AjaxControlToolkit.TextBoxWatermarkBehavior.initializeBase(this, [element]);

  // Properties
  this._watermarkText = null;
  this._watermarkCssClass = null;
  // Member variables
  this._watermarked = null;
  this._focusHandler = null;
  this._blurHandler = null;
  this._keyPressHandler = null;
  this._propertyChangedHandler = null;
  this._oldClassName = null;
  this._clearedForSubmit = null;
  this._maxLength = null;
}
AjaxControlToolkit.TextBoxWatermarkBehavior.prototype =
{
  initialize : AjaxControlToolkit$TextBoxWatermarkBehavior$initialize,
  dispose : AjaxControlToolkit$TextBoxWatermarkBehavior$dispose,
  clearText : AjaxControlToolkit$TextBoxWatermarkBehavior$clearText,
  _onFocus : AjaxControlToolkit$TextBoxWatermarkBehavior$_onFocus,
  _onBlur : AjaxControlToolkit$TextBoxWatermarkBehavior$_onBlur,
  _applyWatermark : AjaxControlToolkit$TextBoxWatermarkBehavior$_applyWatermark,
  _onKeyPress : AjaxControlToolkit$TextBoxWatermarkBehavior$_onKeyPress,
  registerPropertyChanged :
          AjaxControlToolkit$TextBoxWatermarkBehavior$registerPropertyChanged,
  _onPropertyChanged :
          AjaxControlToolkit$TextBoxWatermarkBehavior$_onPropertyChanged,
  _onSubmit : AjaxControlToolkit$TextBoxWatermarkBehavior$_onSubmit,
  _partialUpdateEndRequest :
          AjaxControlToolkit$TextBoxWatermarkBehavior$_partialUpdateEndRequest,
```

(continued)

Listing 16-27 *(continued)*

```
    get_WatermarkText :
                AjaxControlToolkit$TextBoxWatermarkBehavior$get_WatermarkText,
    set_WatermarkText :
                AjaxControlToolkit$TextBoxWatermarkBehavior$set_WatermarkText,
    get_WatermarkCssClass :
                AjaxControlToolkit$TextBoxWatermarkBehavior$get_WatermarkCssClass,
    set_WatermarkCssClass :
                AjaxControlToolkit$TextBoxWatermarkBehavior$set_WatermarkCssClass,
    get_Text : AjaxControlToolkit$TextBoxWatermarkBehavior$get_Text,
    set_Text : AjaxControlToolkit$TextBoxWatermarkBehavior$set_Text
  }
AjaxControlToolkit.TextBoxWatermarkBehavior.registerClass(
                                  'AjaxControlToolkit.TextBoxWatermarkBehavior',
                                  AjaxControlToolkit.BehaviorBase);
```

initialize

The `TextBoxWatermarkBehavior` overrides the `initialize` method that it inherits from its base class to initialize itself, as shown in Listing 16-28. As you can see, the `initialize` method of `TextBoxWatermarkBehavior`, like the `initialize` method of any ASP.NET AJAX component, begins by invoking the `initialize` method of its base class to allow the base class to initialize itself:

```
    AjaxControlToolkit.TextBoxWatermarkBehavior.callBaseMethod(this, 'initialize');
```

The `initialize` *method of your own custom behavior classes must do the same: it must begin by invoking the* `initialize` *method of its base class.*

Next, the `initialize` method invokes the `get_element` method to return a reference to its associated text box DOM element — that is, the text box DOM element to which the `TextBoxWatermarkBehavior` is attached. `TextBoxWatermarkBehavior`, like any other ASP.NET AJAX behavior, inherits the `get_element` method from the ASP.NET AJAX `Behavior` base class:

```
    var e = this.get_element();
```

Next, the `initialize` method invokes the `get_ClientState` method of its base class to return a string that contains the client state of the `TextBoxWatermarkBehavior`. Recall from the previous section that all ASP.NET AJAX control toolkit behaviors store their client states in a hidden field; the `get_ClientState` method simply returns the string value stored in this hidden field. What information an ASP.NET AJAX control toolkit behavior stores in the hidden field is completely up to the behavior and its internal logic. `TextBoxWatermarkBehavior` stores the string `"Focused"` in the hidden field to specify that its associated text box DOM element has the mouse focus, and removes this string from the hidden field to specify that this element no longer has the focus.

As you can see from Listing 16-28, the `initialize` method calls the `get_ClientState` method to determine whether its associated text box DOM element currently has the mouse focus. It then invokes the `set_ClientState` method of its base class to set the value stored in the hidden field to `null`.

```
    hasInitialFocus = (clientState == "Focused");
      AjaxControlToolkit.TextBoxWatermarkBehavior.callBaseMethod(this,
                                              'set_ClientState', null);
```

Next, `initialize` stores the current value of the `className` property of the associated text box DOM element as a private file named `_oldClassName`. This will allow the `TextBoxWatermarkBehavior` to switch between the current style and the watermarked style:

```
this._oldClassName = e.className;
```

Then `initialize` creates three delegates that represent the `_onFocus`, `_onBlur`, and `_onKeyPress` methods of `TextBoxWatermarkBehavior`, stores these delegates in private fields named `_focusHandler`, `_blurHandler`, and `_keyPressHandler`, respectively, and uses the `$addHandler` global JavaScript function to register these delegates for the `focus`, `blur`, and `keypress` events, respectively, of the text box DOM element to which the `TextBoxWatermarkBehavior` is attached. As you'll see later, the `dispose` method will access the delegates stored in the `_focusHandler`, `_blurHandler`, and `_keyPressHandler` fields to remove them from the list of event handlers registered for the `focus`, `blur`, and `keypress` events of the associated text box DOM element before the `TextBoxWatermarkBehavior` is disposed of:

```
this._focusHandler = Function.createDelegate(this, this._onFocus);
this._blurHandler = Function.createDelegate(this, this._onBlur);
this._keyPressHandler = Function.createDelegate(this, this._onKeyPress);
$addHandler(e, 'focus', this._focusHandler);
$addHandler(e, 'blur', this._blurHandler);
$addHandler(e, 'keypress', this._keyPressHandler);
```

The `initialize` method of your own custom behavior class must do the same — that is, it must store in private fields the delegates that it registers for the events of its associated DOM element. The `dispose` method of your custom behavior must then access the delegates stored in these private fields and remove them from the list of event handlers registered for the associated events of the associated DOM element.

Next, `initialize` invokes the `registerPropertyChanged` method to register event handlers for the `propertyChanged` event. (This method will be discussed shortly.)

```
this.registerPropertyChanged();
```

Then `initialize` checks whether the `value` property of the associated text box DOM element of the `TextBoxWatermarkBehavior` is set, and sets an internal flag named `_watermarked`. This flag specifies whether the text box should be watermarked:

```
this._watermarked = (e.value == "");
```

Next, `initialize` calls the `_onFocus` method on the `TextBoxWatermarkBehavior` if the associated text box DOM element must initially have the focus:

```
if (hasInitialFocus)
    this._onFocus();
```

Otherwise, it first invokes the `blur` method on the associated text box DOM element and then invokes the `_onBlur` method on the `TextBoxWatermarkBehavior`:

```
else
{
  e.blur();
  this._onBlur();
}
```

Next, it initializes an internal flag named `_clearedForSubmit` to `false` and invokes the `registerPartialUpdateEvents` method on the `TextBoxWatermarkBehavior` to register event handlers for the partial-update-related events:

```
this._clearedForSubmit = false;
this.registerPartialUpdateEvents();
```

Listing 16-28: The initialize Method of the TextBoxWatermarkBehavior

```
function AjaxControlToolkit$TextBoxWatermarkBehavior$initialize()
{
  /// <summary>
  /// Initialize the behavior
  /// </summary>
  AjaxControlToolkit.TextBoxWatermarkBehavior.callBaseMethod(this, 'initialize');
  var e = this.get_element();

  // Determine if this textbox is focused initially
  var hasInitialFocus = false;

  var clientState = AjaxControlToolkit.TextBoxWatermarkBehavior.callBaseMethod(
                                              this, 'get_ClientState');
  if (clientState != null && clientState != "")
  {
    hasInitialFocus = (clientState == "Focused");
    AjaxControlToolkit.TextBoxWatermarkBehavior.callBaseMethod(this,
                                              'set_ClientState', null);

  }
  // Capture the initial style so we can toggle back and forth
  // between this and the watermarked style
  this._oldClassName = e.className;
  // Create delegates
  this._focusHandler = Function.createDelegate(this, this._onFocus);
  this._blurHandler = Function.createDelegate(this, this._onBlur);
  this._keyPressHandler = Function.createDelegate(this, this._onKeyPress);
  // Attach events
  $addHandler(e, 'focus', this._focusHandler);
  $addHandler(e, 'blur', this._blurHandler);
  $addHandler(e, 'keypress', this._keyPressHandler);
  this.registerPropertyChanged();
  // Initialize state and simulate a blur to apply the watermark if appropriate
  // Note: The comparison against _watermarkText is undesirable, but seemingly
  // necessary to support the load->Home->Back scenario in IE
```

```
      var currentValue = e.value;
      this._watermarked = (("" == currentValue) ||
                            (this._watermarkText == currentValue));
      if (hasInitialFocus)
         this._onFocus();

      else
      {
        e.blur();
        this._onBlur();
      }
      this._clearedForSubmit = false;
      this.registerPartialUpdateEvents();
  }
```

_onFocus

As you can see from Listing 16-28, the `initialize` method registers the `_onFocus` method as callback for the `focus` event of the associated text box DOM element of the `TextBoxWatermarkBehavior`. When the associated DOM element grabs the focus, fires its `focus` event, and consequently invokes the `_onFocus` method, an object of type `DomEvent` is passed into this method. Recall that this object represents the current event object and because of this contains the complete information about the current event.

As you can see from Listing 16-29, the `_onFocus` method first invokes the `get_element` method to return a reference to the associated text box DOM element of the `TextBoxWatermarkBehavior`:

```
      var e = this.get_element();
```

If the `TextBoxWatermarkBehavior` is marked as watermarked, `_onFocus` invokes the `clearText` method on the `TextBoxWatermarkBehavior` to clear the watermark, because the associated text box DOM element is about to put the focus where the end user will enter text into the text box:

```
      if(this._watermarked)
      {
        // Clear watermark
        this.clearText(evt ? true : false);
      }
```

Next, `_onFocus` assigns the old CSS class name to the `className` property of the associated text box DOM element to change the style of the text box back to its original unwatermarked style:

```
      e.className = this._oldClassName;
```

Then it sets the `_watermarked` internal flag to `false` to mark that the associated text box DOM element is no longer watermarked:

```
      this._watermarked = false;
```

Finally, it restores the maxLength property of the associated text box DOM element back to its original value:

```
if (this._maxLength > 0)
{
    this.get_element().maxLength = this._maxLength;
    this._maxLength = null;
}
```

Listing 16-29: The _onFocus Method of the TextBoxWatermarkBehavior

```
function AjaxControlToolkit$TextBoxWatermarkBehavior$_onFocus(evt)
{
    /// <summary>
    /// Handler for the textbox's focus event
    /// </summary>
    /// <param name="evt" type="Sys.UI.DomEvent">
    /// Event info
    /// </param>

    var e = this.get_element();
    if(this._watermarked)
    {
        // Clear watermark
        this.clearText(evt ? true : false);
    }
    e.className = this._oldClassName;
    this._watermarked = false;

    // Restore the MaxLength on the TextBox when we edit
    // the non-watermarked text
    if (this._maxLength > 0)
    {
        this.get_element().maxLength = this._maxLength;
        this._maxLength = null;
    }
}
```

clearText

As the name suggests, the clearText method clears the text from the associated text box DOM element of the TextBoxWatermarkBehavior. As you can see from Listing 16-30, this method takes a single Boolean argument that specifies whether the associated text box DOM element is grabbing the focus. As this code listing shows, the clearText method first invokes the get_element method to return a reference to the associated text box DOM element, and then sets its value property to an empty string to clear the text box:

```
this.get_element().value = "";
```

Next, the clearText method checks whether the associated text box DOM element is grabbing the focus. If so, it first calls the setAttribute method on the associated text box DOM element to turn off its autocomplete feature, to avoid a Firefox-specific NS_ERROR_XPC_JS_THREW_STRING error, and then calls the `select` method on the associated text box DOM element to ensure that the blinking cursor is displayed inside the text box on IE browsers:

```
if(focusing)
{
  // Avoid NS_ERROR_XPC_JS_THREW_STRING error in Firefox
  this.get_element().setAttribute("autocomplete","off");
  // This fix displays the blinking cursor in a focused, empty text box in IE
  this.get_element().select();
}
```

Listing 16-30: The clearText Method

```
function AjaxControlToolkit$TextBoxWatermarkBehavior$clearText(focusing)
{
  /// <summary>
  /// Clear the text from the target
  /// </summary>
  /// <param name="focusing" type="Boolean">
  /// Whether or not we are focusing on the textbox
  /// </param>
  this.get_element().value = "";
  if(focusing)
  {
    // Avoid NS_ERROR_XPC_JS_THREW_STRING error in Firefox
    this.get_element().setAttribute("autocomplete","off");
    // This fix displays the blinking cursor in a focused, empty text box in IE
    this.get_element().select();
  }
}
```

_onBlur

Recall from Listing 16-28 that the `initialize` method registers the `_onBlur` method as an event handler for the `blur` event of the associated text box DOM element of the `TextBoxWatermarkBehavior`. This DOM element fires this event and consequently invokes the `_onBlur` method when it loses focus. As you can see from Listing 16-31, this method first checks whether at least one of the following conditions is met:

❑ The `value` property of the associated text box DOM element is set to an empty string, which means that the text box is empty.

❑ The `_watermarked` flag of the `TextBoxWatermarkBehavior` is set to `true` to specify that the associated text box DOM element must be watermarked.

If either of these conditions is met, the `_onBlur` method takes the following actions. First, it checks whether the watermark text is longer than the maximum number of characters the associated text box DOM element can display. If so, it first stores the value of the `maxLength` property of the text box DOM element in a private field named _maxLength, and then assigns the length of the watermark text as the new value of this property. This ensures that the text box will display the entire watermark text:

```
if (this.get_element().maxLength > 0 &&
    this._watermarkText.length > this.get_element().maxLength)
{
    this._maxLength = this.get_element().maxLength;
    this.get_element().maxLength = this._watermarkText.length;
}
```

Finally, the _onBlur method invokes the _applyWatermark method on the TextBoxWatermarkBehavior to apply the watermark to the text box:

```
this._applyWatermark();
```

Listing 16-31: the _onBlur Method

```
function AjaxControlToolkit$TextBoxWatermarkBehavior$_onBlur()
{
    /// <summary>
    /// Handle the textbox's blur event
    /// </summary>
    if(("" == this.get_element().value) || this._watermarked)
    {
        // Enlarge the TextBox's MaxLength if it's not big enough
        // to accomodate the watermark
        if (this.get_element().maxLength > 0 &&
            this._watermarkText.length > this.get_element().maxLength)
        {
            this._maxLength = this.get_element().maxLength;
            this.get_element().maxLength = this._watermarkText.length;
        }

        this._applyWatermark();
    }
}
```

_applyWatermark

The main responsibility of the _applyWatermark method is to display the watermark. As Listing 16-32 shows, this method first assigns the watermark text to the value property of the associated text box DOM element to display the watermark text in the text box:

```
this.get_element().value = this._watermarkText;
```

Next, it assigns the watermark CSS class name to the className property of the associated text box DOM element to apply the watermarked style to the text box:

```
if(this._watermarkCssClass)
    this.get_element().className = this._watermarkCssClass;
```

Finally, it sets the _watermarked flag to true to specify that the associated text box DOM element is watermarked:

```
this._watermarked = true;
```

Listing 16-32: The _applyWatermark Method

```
function AjaxControlToolkit$TextBoxWatermarkBehavior$_applyWatermark()
{
    /// <summary>
    /// Apply the watermark to the textbox
    /// </summary>
    this.get_element().value = this._watermarkText;
    if(this._watermarkCssClass)
      this.get_element().className = this._watermarkCssClass;

    this._watermarked = true;
}
```

_onKeyPress

Recall from Listing 16-28 that the initialize method registers the _onKeyPress method as an event handler for the keypress event of the associated text box DOM element of the TextBoxWatermarkBehavior. This DOM element fires the keypress event when the user presses the key inside the text box. As you can see from Listing 16-33, this method simply sets the _watermarked flag to false to signal that the text box is no longer watermarked. Note that the text box automatically raises the focus event right after the keypress, consequently invoking the _onFocus method, which undisplays the watermark text and reverts the text box back to its unwatermarked style.

Listing 16-33 The _onKeyPress Method

```
function AjaxControlToolkit$TextBoxWatermarkBehavior$_onKeyPress()
{
    /// <summary>
    /// Handle the textbox's keypress event
    /// </summary>
    this._watermarked = false;
}
```

registerPropertyChanged

Recall from Listing 16-28 that the initialize method invokes the registerPropertyChanged method. As you can see from Listing 16-34, this method first invokes the get_element method to return a reference to the associated text box DOM element of the TextBoxWatermarkBehavior:

```
var e = this.get_element();
```

Next, it checks whether both of the following two conditions are met:

❑ The associated text box DOM element supports a property named control. This happens when the text box is associated with a Sys.Preview.UI.TextBox client control.

❑ The _propertyChangedHandler field is null.

If both of these conditions are met, the `registerPropertyChanged` method first creates a delegate that represents the `_onPropertyChanged` method of the `TextBoxWatermarkBehavior`:

```
this._propertyChangedHandler =
                    Function.createDelegate(this, this._onPropertyChanged);
```

Next, it invokes the `add_propertyChanged` method on the `Sys.Preview.UI.TextBox` client control associated with the text box DOM element, to register the delegate as event handler for the `propertyChanged` event of the client control:

```
e.control.add_propertyChanged(this._propertyChangedHandler);
```

Listing 16-34: The registerPropertyChanged Method

```
function AjaxControlToolkit$TextBoxWatermarkBehavior$registerPropertyChanged()
{
  /// <summary>
  /// Method called to hook up to Sys.Preview.UI.TextBox if present
  /// Note: This method must be called manually if the Sys.Preview.UI.TextBox
  ///       is added after the TextBoxWatermarkBehavior is initialized.
  /// </summary>
  var e = this.get_element();
  if(e.control && !this._propertyChangedHandler)
  {
    this._propertyChangedHandler =
                        Function.createDelegate(this, this._onPropertyChanged);
    e.control.add_propertyChanged(this._propertyChangedHandler);
  }
}
```

_onPropertyChanged

When the `Sys.Preview.UI.TextBox` client control associated with the associated text box DOM element of the `TextBoxWatermarkBehavior` raises its `propertyChanged` event, it automatically invokes the `_onPropertyChanged` method on the `TextBoxWatermarkBehavior`, passing in two parameters. The first parameter references the `Sys.Preview.UI.TextBox` client control that raises the `propertyChanged` event, and the second parameter references the `propertyChangedEventArgs` object that contains the event data for the `propertyChanged` event. As you can see from Listing 16-35, the `_onPropertyChanged` method invokes the `get_propertyName` method of the `propertyChangedEventArgs` object to return the name of the property of the `Sys.Preview.UI.TextBox` client control whose value has changed, and then determines whether this property is the `Text` property. If so, it invokes the `set_Text` method on the `TextBoxWatermarkBehavior` to set the value of its `Text` property to the value of the `value` property of its associated text box DOM element. As you can see, the `Text` property of the `TextBoxWatermarkBehavior` maps to the `value` property of its associated text box DOM element:

```
if("text" == propertyChangedEventArgs.get_propertyName())
    this.set_Text(this.get_element().value);
```

Listing 16-35: The _onPropertyChanged Method

```
function AjaxControlToolkit$TextBoxWatermarkBehavior$_onPropertyChanged(sender,
                                                 propertyChangedEventArgs)
{
  /// <summary>
  /// Handler called automatically when a property change event is fired
  /// </summary>
  /// <param name="sender" type="Object">
  /// Sender
  /// </param>
  /// <param name="propertyChangedEventArgs" type="Sys.PropertyChangedEventArgs">
  /// Event arguments
  /// </param>
  if("text" == propertyChangedEventArgs.get_propertyName())
    this.set_Text(this.get_element().value);
}
```

set_Text

As mentioned earlier, the TextBoxWatermarkBehavior class features a property named Text that maps into the value property of its associated text box DOM element. Because of this, the class also exposes a setter named set_Text (see Listing 16-36) and a getter named get_Text (see Listing 16-37) that you can use in your client code to set and get the value of the Text property.

As you can see from Listing 16-36, the set_Text method first checks whether the new value of the Text property is an empty string. If so, it performs the following tasks:

❑ Assigns the empty string as the value of the value property of the associated text box DOM element, which means that the text box now displays nothing:

```
this.get_element().value = "";
```

❑ Invokes the blur method on the associated text box DOM element to cause the text box to lose focus:

```
this.get_element().blur();
```

❑ Invokes the _onBlur method on the TextBoxWatermarkBehavior. This is necessary because calling the blur method on the associated text box DOM element does not cause the text box to fire its blur event, and therefore does not cause the _onBlur method to be automatically invoked:

```
this._onBlur();
```

If the new value of the Text property is not an empty string, the set_Text method performs the following tasks:

❑ Invokes the _onFocus method on the TextBoxWatermarkBehavior:

```
this._onFocus();  // onFocus sets ""
```

❑ Assigns the new value to the `value` property of the associated text box DOM element:

```
this.get_element().value = value;
```

Listing 16-36: The set_Text Method

```
function AjaxControlToolkit$TextBoxWatermarkBehavior$set_Text(value)
{
  if ("" == value)
  {
    this.get_element().value = "";
    this.get_element().blur();
    this._onBlur();  // onBlur needs to see ""
  }

  else
  {
    this._onFocus();  // onFocus sets ""
    this.get_element().value = value;
  }
}
```

Here is the reason the `TextBoxWatermarkBehavior` wraps the value property of its associated text box DOM element in its `Text` property. As Listing 16-37 shows, the `get_Text` getter method returns an empty string if the text box element, rather than the actual value of the element, is watermarked. Recall that when the text box is watermarked, its `value` property contains the watermark text. This ensures that the clients of the `TextBoxWatermarkBehavior` always receive the value that the end user enters into the text box, rather than the watermark text.

Listing 16-37: The get_Text Method

```
function AjaxControlToolkit$TextBoxWatermarkBehavior$get_Text()
{
  /// <value type="String">
  /// Wrapper for the textbox's text that will ignore or create the
  /// watermark as appropriate
  /// </value>
  return (this._watermarked ? "" : this.get_element().value);
}
```

_partialUpdateEndRequest

Recall from Listing 16-28 that the `initialize` method of the `TextBoxWatermarkBehavior` invokes the `registerPartialUpdateEvents` method that it inherits from the `BehaviorBase` base class. Also recall that the `registerPartialUpdateEvents` method registers the `_partialUpdateEndRequest` method as an event handler for the `endRequest` event of the current client-side `PageRequestManager` instance.

As you can see, if a subclass of the `BehaviorBase` *base class needs to run custom code when the current* `PageRequestManager` *instance raises its* `beginRequest` *and* `endRequest` *events, the subclass must takes two actions. First, it must invoke the* `registerPartialUpdateEvents` *method from its* `initialize` *method. Second, it must override the* `_partialUpdateBeginRequest` *and/or* `_partialUpdateEndRequest` *methods to encapsulate the custom code.*

Since the `TextBoxWatermarkBehavior` is interested only in the `endRequest` event of the current client-side `PageRequestManager` instance, it overrides only the `_partialUpdateEndRequest` method that it inherits from the `BehaviorBase` base class, leaving the `_partialUpdateBeginRequest` method intact. Listing 16-38 contains the `TextBoxWatermarkBehavior` class's implementation of the `_partialUpdateEndRequest` method.

When the current client-side `PageRequestManager` instance finally fires its `endRequest` event and consequently invokes the `_partialUpdateEndRequest` method, it passes two parameters into this method. The first references the current client-side `PageRequestManager` instance, and the second references the `EndRequestEventArgs` object that contains the event data for the current `endRequest` event.

As you can see from Listing 16-38, the `_partialUpdateEndRequest` method first invokes the `partialUpdateEndRequest` method of its base class, passing the aforementioned two parameters:

```
AjaxControlToolkit.TextBoxWatermarkBehavior.callBaseMethod(this,
                   '_partialUpdateEndRequest', [sender, endRequestEventArgs]);
```

> *In general, every time your ASP.NET AJAX class overrides the methods it inherits from its base class, its implementation of these methods must invoke the respective methods of the base class unless you have a good reason to stop the base method from running.*

Next, the `_partialUpdateEndRequest` method checks whether an internal flag named `_clearedForSubmit` has been set. As you'll see in next section, the `_onSubmit` method of the `TextBoxWatermarkBehavior` sets this flag to signal the occurrence of a form submission. Since the `_partialUpdateEndRequest` method is invoked in response to the `endRequest` event of the current client-side `PageRequestManager` instance, and since this event is raised after an asynchronous form submission occurs and the server response arrives, it makes lot of sense to apply the watermark to the text box. To do this, the `_partialUpdateEndRequest` method first invokes the `blur` method on text box element, to cause the element to lose focus:

```
this.get_element().blur();
```

Then it invokes the `_onBlur` method on the `TextBoxWatermarkBehavior`. This is necessary because the `blur` method does not raise the `blur` event and consequently does not automatically invoke the `_onBlur` method:

```
this._onBlur();
```

Listing 16-38: The _partialUpdateEndRequest Method

```
function AjaxControlToolkit$TextBoxWatermarkBehavior$_partialUpdateEndRequest(
                                             sender, endRequestEventArgs)
{
  /// <summary>
  /// Handler Called automatically when a partial postback ends
  /// </summary>
  /// <param name="sender" type="Object">
  /// Sender
  /// </param>
```

(continued)

Listing 16-38 (continued)

```
/// <param name="endRequestEventArgs" type="Sys.WebForms.EndRequestEventArgs">
/// Event arguments
/// </param>
AjaxControlToolkit.TextBoxWatermarkBehavior.callBaseMethod(this,
                    '_partialUpdateEndRequest', [sender, endRequestEventArgs]);
if (this.get_element() && this._clearedForSubmit)
{
    // Restore the cleared watermark (useful when the submit was
    // wrapped in an UpdatePanel)
    this.get_element().blur();
    this._onBlur();
    this._clearedForSubmit = false;
}
}
```

_onSubmit

The TextBoxWatermarkBehavior does not invoke its _onSubmit method. It is the responsibility of the client code that uses the TextBoxWatermarkBehavior to ensure that the _onSubmit method is invoked before the form is submitted. As you can see from Listing 16-39, this method checks whether the associated text box DOM element of the TextBoxWatermarkBehavior is watermarked. If so, it invokes the clearText method to clear the text box before the form is submitted. This ensures that the watermark text is not submitted to the server.

Listing 16-39: The _onSubmit Method

```
function AjaxControlToolkit$TextBoxWatermarkBehavior$_onSubmit()
{
    /// <summary>
    /// Handler Called automatically when a submit happens to clear the
    /// watermark before posting back
    /// </summary>
    if(this._watermarked)
    {
        // Clear watermark text before page is submitted
        this.clearText(false);
        this._clearedForSubmit = true;
    }
}
```

dispose

The TextBoxWatermarkBehavior, like any other ASP.NET AJAX component, inherits the dispose method from the Component base class and overrides it to perform its final cleanup before the Application object representing the current ASP.NET AJAX application disposes of it. As you can see from Listing 16-40, the dispose method first invokes the get_element method to return a reference to the DOM element to which the TextBoxWatermarkBehavior is attached. As discussed earlier, this DOM element is a text box. The TextBoxWatermarkBehavior, like any other behavior, inherits the get_element method from the Behavior base class:

```
var e = this.get_element();
```

Next, the `dispose` method checks whether the following two conditions hold:

❑ The associated text box DOM element exposes a property named `control`. This is true if the associated text box DOM element is itself associated with an instance of a `Sys.Preview.UI.TextBox` control. Recall that the `Control` base class under the hood creates a custom property named `control` on the DOM element associated with a client control, and assigns a reference to the client control (in this case the `Sys.Preview.UI.TextBox` control) to this custom `control` property.

❑ The `_propertyChangedHandler` delegate has been defined.

If both of these conditions are met, the `dispose` method invokes the `remove_propertyChangedHandler` method on the custom control property of the associated text box DOM element, to remove the `_propertyChangedHandler` delegate from the list of event handlers registered for the `propertyChanged` event of the `Sys.Preview.UI.TextBox` client control associated with the text box DOM element.

```
if(e.control && this._propertyChangedHandler)
{
  e.control.remove_propertyChanged(this._propertyChangedHandler);
  this._propertyChangedHandler = null;
}
```

Next, it uses the `$removeHandler` global JavaScript function to remove the `_focusHandler`, `_blurHandler`, and `_keyPressHandler` delegates from the list of event handlers registered for `focus`, `blur`, and `keypress` events of the associated text box DOM element.

Then it invokes the `clearText` method on the `TextBoxWatermarkBehavior` to clear the watermark:

```
if(this._watermarked)
  this.clearText(false);
```

Listing 16-40: The dispose Method of the TextBoxWatermarkBehavior

```
function AjaxControlToolkit$TextBoxWatermarkBehavior$dispose()
{
  /// <summary>
  /// Dispose the behavior
  /// </summary>
  var e = this.get_element();
  // Unhook from Sys.Preview.UI.TextBox if present
  if(e.control && this._propertyChangedHandler)
  {
    e.control.remove_propertyChanged(this._propertyChangedHandler);
    this._propertyChangedHandler = null;
  }
  // Detach events
  if (this._focusHandler)
  {
    $removeHandler(e, 'focus', this._focusHandler);
    this._focusHandler = null;
  }
```

(continued)

Listing 16-40 *(continued)*

```
      if (this._blurHandler)
      {
        $removeHandler(e, 'blur', this._blurHandler);
        this._blurHandler = null;
      }
      if (this._keyPressHandler)
      {
        $removeHandler(e, 'keypress', this._keyPressHandler);
        this._keyPressHandler = null;
      }
      // Clear watermark text to avoid confusion during Refresh/Back/Forward
      if(this._watermarked)
        this.clearText(false);
      AjaxControlToolkit.TextBoxWatermarkBehavior.callBaseMethod(this, 'dispose');
   }
```

WatermarkText

The `TextBoxWatermarkBehavior` exposes a getter named `get_WatermarkText` and a setter named `set_WatermarkText` that you can use in your client code to get and set the watermark text, as shown in Listing 16-41.

Listing 16-41: The WatermarkText Property

```
function AjaxControlToolkit$TextBoxWatermarkBehavior$get_WatermarkText()
{
  /// <value type="String">
  /// The text to show when the control has no value
  /// </value>
  return this._watermarkText;
}
function AjaxControlToolkit$TextBoxWatermarkBehavior$set_WatermarkText(value)
{
  if (this._watermarkText != value)
  {
    this._watermarkText = value;
    if (this._watermarked)
      this._applyWatermark();

    this.raisePropertyChanged('WatermarkText');
  }
}
```

WatermarkCssClass

The `TextBoxWatermarkBehavior` exposes a getter named `get_WatermarkCssClass` and a setter named `set_WatermarkCssClass` that you can use in your client code to get and set the watermark style, as shown in Listing 16-42.

Listing 16-42: The WatermarkCssClass Property

```
function AjaxControlToolkit$TextBoxWatermarkBehavior$get_WatermarkCssClass()
{
  /// <value type="String">
  /// The CSS class to apply to the TextBox when it has no value (e.g. the
  /// watermark text is shown).
  /// </value>
  return this._watermarkCssClass;
}
function AjaxControlToolkit$TextBoxWatermarkBehavior$set_WatermarkCssClass(value)
{
  if (this._watermarkCssClass != value)
  {
    this._watermarkCssClass = value;
    if (this._watermarked)
      this._applyWatermark();

    this.raisePropertyChanged('WatermarkCssClass');
  }
}
```

Using the TextBoxWatermarkBehavior

Listing 16-43 contains a page that uses the `TextBoxWatermarkBehavior`. Takes these steps to run this page:

1. Create an Ajax-enable website in Visual Studio

2. Add a JavaScript file named `BehaviorBase.js` to this website and add the code shown in Listings 16-19 through 16-26 to this JavaScript file.

3. Add a JavaScript file named `TextBoxWatermarkBehavior.js` to this website and add the code shown in Listings 16-27 through 16-43 to this JavaScript file

4. Add the following line at the beginning of both JavaScript files:
   `Type.registerNamespace('AjaxControlToolkit');`

5. Add the following line at the end of both JavaScript files: if (typeof(Sys) !== 'undefined')
   `Sys.Application.notifyScriptLoaded();`

6. Add a Web Form named Default.aspx to this website and add the code shown in Listing 16-44 to the `Default.aspx` file

If you access the `Default.aspx` page for your browser, you should see that the associated text box DOM element of the `TextBoxWatermarkBehavior` is watermarked — that is, that it displays the watermark text and is styled with the watermarked style. If you click this text box, it will revert to its unwatermarked style when it grabs the focus, enabling you to enter new text. If you click the Submit button to submit the form, the watermark text disappears from the text box. This ensures that the watermark text is not submitted to the server.

Listing 16-43: A Page that Uses the TextBoxWatermarkBehavior

```
<%@ Page Language="C#" %>
<!DOCTYPE html PUBLIC "-//W3C//DTD XHTML 1.0 Transitional//EN"
"http://www.w3.org/TR/xhtml1/DTD/xhtml1-transitional.dtd">
<script runat="server">
  void ClickCallback(object sender, EventArgs e)
  {
    Info.Text = TextBox1.Text;
  }
</script>
<html xmlns="http://www.w3.org/1999/xhtml">
<head runat="server">
  <title>Untitled Page</title>
  <style type="text/css">
    .WatermarkCssClass
    {
      background-color: #dddddd
    }
  </style>
  <script type="text/javascript" language="javascript">
    var textBoxWatermarkBehavior;

    function submitCallback()
    {
      textBoxWatermarkBehavior._onSubmit();
    }

    function pageLoad()
    {
      var properties = {name : "MyTextBoxWatermarkBehaviorName",
                        id : "MyTextBoxWatermarkBehaviorID",
                        WatermarkText : "Enter text here",
                        WatermarkCssClass : "WatermarkCssClass"};

      var textBox1 = $get("TextBox1");
      textBoxWatermarkBehavior =
              $create(AjaxControlToolkit.TextBoxWatermarkBehavior, properties,
                      null, null, textBox1);
    }
  </script>
</head>
<body>
  <form id="form1" runat="server" onsubmit="submitCallback();return true;">
    <asp:ScriptManager runat="server" ID="ScriptManager1">
      <Scripts>
        <asp:ScriptReference Path="BehaviorBase.js" />
        <asp:ScriptReference Path="TextBoxWatermarkBehavior.js" />
      </Scripts>
    </asp:ScriptManager>
    <asp:TextBox ID="TextBox1" runat="server" />
    <asp:Button ID="Button1" runat="server" OnClick="ClickCallback" Text="Submit"
            /><br /><br />
```

```
        <asp:Label ID="Info" runat="server" />
    </form>
</body>
</html>
```

I'll walk you through the code shown in Listing 16-43. First, notice that this page contains a CSS class named `WatermarkCssClass`, which defines the watermarked style:

```
<style type="text/css">
  .WatermarkCssClass
  {
    background-color: #dddddd
  }
</style>
```

Also note that this page registers references to two JavaScript files named `BehaviorBase.js` and `TextBoxWatermarkBehavior.js`:

```
<asp:ScriptManager runat="server" ID="ScriptManager1">
  <Scripts>
    <asp:ScriptReference Path="BehaviorBase.js" />
    <asp:ScriptReference Path="TextBoxWatermarkBehavior.js" />
  </Scripts>
</asp:ScriptManager>
```

These two JavaScript files contain the implementation of the `BehaviorBase` and `TextBoxWatermarkBehavior` client classes, respectively. (You can find the complete code for these two classes in the sections of this chapter where we discussed their implementation.) Don't forget to include the following definition at the beginning these two files:

```
Type.registerNamespace("AjaxControlToolkit");
```

Also don't forget to include the following script at the event of these two files:

```
if(typeof(Sys)!=='undefined')
  Sys.Application.notifyScriptLoaded();
```

As Listing 16-43 shows, the `pageLoad` method performs the following tasks. First, it instantiates a dictionary named `properties` and populates it with the names and values of the properties of the `TextBoxWatermarkBehavior`:

```
var properties = [];
properties["name"] = "MyTextBoxWatermarkBehaviorName";
properties["id"] = "MyTextBoxWatermarkBehaviorID";
properties["WatermarkText"] = "Enter text here";
properties["WatermarkCssClass"] = "WatermarkCssClass";
```

Next, it uses the `$get` global JavaScript function to return a reference to the text box DOM element to which we want to attach the `TextBoxWatermarkBehavior` we're about to create:

```
var textBox1 = $get("TextBox1");
```

Finally, it invokes the $create global JavaScript function, passing in five parameters. The first parameter references the constructor of the TextBoxWatermarkBehavior, the second references the dictionary that contains the names and values of the properties of the TextBoxWatermarkBehavior object being instantiated, the third and forth are null, and the last references the text box DOM element to which the TextBoxWatermarkBehavior being instantiated attaches. The $create method instantiates the TextBoxWatermarkBehavior, initializes its properties with the values specified in the properties dictionary, invokes its initialize method, and finally adds it to the current ASP.NET AJAX application.

```
textBoxWatermarkBehavior =
            $create(AjaxControlToolkit.TextBoxWatermarkBehavior, properties,
                    null, null, textBox1);
```

As Listing 16-43 shows, the page also registers an event handler named submitCallback for the submit event of the form. As you can see, this event handler invokes the _onSubmit method on the TextBoxWatermarkBehavior to remove the watermark text from the text box before the form is submitted to the server:

```
function submitCallback()
{
  textBoxWatermarkBehavior._onSubmit();
}
```

Summary

This chapter provided you with in-depth coverage of the ASP.NET AJAX behaviors and helped you gain the experience you need to develop your own custom behaviors.

The next chapter will show you how to develop ASP.NET server controls that take full advantage of the ASP.NET AJAX behaviors.

Script and Extender Server Controls

In this chapter, I'll implement fully functional replicas of those components of the ASP.NET AJAX server-side Framework that are deeply involved in the internal functioning of two important types of server controls, known as *script controls* and *extender controls*, to help you gain a solid understanding of these server controls, how they interact with their associated client-side components, how they differ from one another, and how to implement your own custom script controls and extender controls. These components of the ASP.NET AJAX server side Framework include:

- ❏ IExtenderControl
- ❏ ExtenderControl
- ❏ IScriptControl
- ❏ ScriptControl
- ❏ ScriptDescriptor
- ❏ ScriptComponentDescriptor
- ❏ ScriptBehaviorDescriptor
- ❏ ScriptControlDescriptor
- ❏ ScriptReference
- ❏ ScriptReferenceCollection
- ❏ ScriptManager

Why You Need Script and Extender Server Controls

Let us revisit Listing 16-64. Recall that this code listing contains a page that uses the TextBoxWatermarkBehavior. As this code listing demonstrates, page developers must write quite a bit of JavaScript code to use the TextBoxWatermarkBehavior in their applications.

If you could encapsulate the `TextBoxWatermarkBehavior` and the JavaScript code that instantiates and initializes this behavior, attaches this behavior to its associated DOM element, and adds this behavior to the current ASP.NET AJAX application in a server control, you would provide the clients of your server control with the following important benefits:

❑ This server control could be used declaratively without writing a single line of imperative code such as C#, VB.NET, or JavaScript.

❑ It could be added to the Toolbox of the Visual Studio to allow page developers to drag and drop it on the designer surface.

❑ It could be programmed against by means of the ASP.NET Framework. This would allow page developers to take full advantage of the well-known benefits of programming in the .NET environment.

❑ The C#/VB.NET/JavaScript code encapsulated in this server control could be changed to fix a bug, to optimize the code, or to add a new enhancement without breaking the applications that use this server control — as long as these changes do not affect the API through which these applications interact with this server control.

❑ Since the entire logic that defines, instantiates, and initializes the `TextBoxWatermarkBehavior`, attaches it to its associated DOM element, and adds it to the current ASP.NET AJAX application is encapsulated in a single component (that is, the server control), you could perform any required bug fixes, code optimizations, and enhancements in a single component and rest assured that these changes will be automatically picked up by all applications that use this server control.

The ASP.NET AJAX Framework provides you with two different approaches to encapsulating the logic that performs the following tasks in a server control:

❑ Defines an ASP.NET AJAX component such as `TextBoxWatermarkBehavior`.

❑ Instantiates this component.

❑ Initializes this component. (This initialization involves initializing the properties of the component and registering event handlers for its events.)

❑ Attaches this component to a DOM element.

❑ Adds this component to the current ASP.NET AJAX application.

These two approaches are as follows:

❑ **Script Controls**: This approach encapsulates the logic I just mentioned in a server control that represents the associated DOM element of the ASP.NET AJAX component. For example, in the case of Listing 16-64, the associated DOM element of the `TextBoxWatermarkBehavior` is a text box. As you'll see later in this chapter, you'll develop a custom `TextBox` server control named `TextBoxWatermarkScriptControl` that derives from the ASP.NET `TextBox` server control to encapsulate the preceding logic. As you can see, this script server control represents the associated DOM text box element of the `TextBoxWatermarkBehavior`.

❑ **Extender Controls**: This approach encapsulates the logic I just mentioned in a server control that attaches to the server control that represents the associated DOM element of the ASP.NET AJAX component. For example, in the case of Listing 16-64, the associated DOM element of the

`TextBoxWatermarkBehavior` is a text box. Later in this chapter we'll develop an extender server control named `TextBoxWatermarkExtenderControl` to encapsulate this logic. As you can see, this extender server control does *not* represent the associated DOM text box element of the `TextBoxWatermarkBehavior`. Instead it attaches to the server control that represents this associated element — that is, the ASP.NET `TextBox` server control.

In other words, while the `TextBoxWatermarkScriptControl` derives from the ASP.NET `TextBox` server control, the `TextBoxWatermarkExtenderControl` attaches to the ASP.NET `TextBox` server control instead of deriving from it. This will all be made clear later in this chapter.

Extender Server Controls

An extender server control is an ASP.NET server control that allows you to extend the client-side functionality of an existing ASP.NET server control without touching its code! The ASP.NET server control whose client-side functionality is being extended is completely oblivious to the presence of the extender control. This is a great way to enhance the client-side behavior of an existing ASP.NET server control.

IExtenderControl

Every ASP.NET extender server control implements an interface named `IExtenderControl`, defined in Listing 17-1.

Listing 17-1: The IExtenderControl Interface

```
using System;
using System.Web.UI;
using System.Collections.Generic;

namespace CustomComponents3
{
  public interface IExtenderControl
  {
    IEnumerable<ScriptDescriptor> GetScriptDescriptors(Control targetControl);
    IEnumerable<ScriptReference> GetScriptReferences();
  }
}
```

As you can see, the `IExtenderControl` interface exposes the following two methods:

❑   `GetScriptDescriptors`: This method takes a parameter of type `Control` that references the ASP.NET server control whose client-side functionality the current extender server control extends. The main responsibility of this method is to instantiate, initialize, and return an `IEnumerable` collection of the `ScriptDescriptor` objects, where each `ScriptDescriptor` object generates the client script that instantiates and initializes an ASP.NET AJAX component such as the `TextBoxWatermarkBehavior`, attaches it to its associated DOM element, and adds it to the current ASP.NET AJAX application.

❏   GetScriptReferences: The main responsibility of this method is to instantiate, initialize, and return an IEnumerable collection of the ScriptReference objects where each ScriptReference object references a JavaScript file that normally defines an ASP.NET AJAX component such as the TextBoxWatermarkBehavior or any other required JavaScript code.

ExtenderControl

The ASP.NET AJAX Framework comes with an implementation of the IExtenderControl interface named ExtenderControl. Listing 17-2 presents the implementation of the replica ExtenderControl. This base class contains the base functionality that every extender server control must support. Deriving your extender server controls from the ExtenderControl base class will save you from having to implement this base functionality every time you develop a custom extender server control.

Listing 17-2: The ExtenderControl Base Class

```
namespace CustomComponents3
{
  using System;
  using System.Web.UI;
  using System.ComponentModel;
  using System.Collections.Generic;

  [DefaultProperty("TargetControlID"), ParseChildren(true),
  NonVisualControl,
  PersistChildren(false)]
  public abstract class ExtenderControl : Control, IExtenderControl
  {
    private ScriptManager _scriptManager;
    private string _targetControlID;

    protected abstract IEnumerable<ScriptDescriptor> GetScriptDescriptors(
                                              Control targetControl);
    protected abstract IEnumerable<ScriptReference> GetScriptReferences();

    protected override void OnPreRender(EventArgs e)
    {
      base.OnPreRender(e);
      Control control = this.FindControl(this.TargetControlID);
      ScriptManager scriptManager = ScriptManager.GetCurrent(Page);
      scriptManager.RegisterExtenderControl<ExtenderControl>(this, control);
    }

    protected override void Render(HtmlTextWriter writer)
    {
      base.Render(writer);
      if (!base.DesignMode)
      {
        ScriptManager mgr = ScriptManager.GetCurrent(Page);
        mgr.RegisterScriptDescriptors(this);
      }
    }
  }
```

```
IEnumerable<ScriptDescriptor> IExtenderControl.GetScriptDescriptors(
                                              Control targetControl)
{
  return this.GetScriptDescriptors(targetControl);
}


IEnumerable<ScriptReference> IExtenderControl.GetScriptReferences()

{
  return this.GetScriptReferences();
}

[DefaultValue(""),
IDReferenceProperty, Category("Behavior")]
public string TargetControlID
{
  get
  {
    if (this._targetControlID != null)
      return this._targetControlID;

    return string.Empty;
  }
  set { this._targetControlID = value; }
}

[Browsable(false),
DesignerSerializationVisibility(DesignerSerializationVisibility.Hidden),
EditorBrowsable(EditorBrowsableState.Never)]
public override bool Visible
{
  get { return base.Visible; }
  set { throw new NotImplementedException(); }
}
  }
}
```

As Listing 17-2 shows, the ExtenderControl implements the GetScriptDescriptors and
GetScriptReferences methods of the IExtenderControl interface. The implementations of these
two methods simply delegate to two virtual methods with the same names.

> *This is a typical C# interface implementation pattern, where a class's explicit implementation of the
> methods, properties, and events of an interface simply delegates to protected virtual methods, properties,
> and events with the same names as the methods, properties, and events of the interface. This provides
> two important benefits. First, it saves the subclasses of the class from explicitly implementing the inter-
> face. Second, it allows these subclasses to override these protected virtual methods, properties, and
> events to provide their own implementations. This is a great interface implementation pattern that you
> should use in your own custom classes.*

Note that the protected virtual GetScriptDescriptors and GetScriptReferences methods of the
ExtenderControl base class are marked as abstract. This means that all subclasses of this base class
must implement these two methods.

As Listing 17-2 shows, the `ExtenderControl` base class exposes a read/write string property named `TargetControlID` that specifies the `ID` property value of the server control whose client-side functionality the extender control extends. This server control is known as the *target control* of the extender control. For example, in the case of the `TextBoxWatermarkExtenderControl` extender control, which will be implemented later in this chapter, the target server control is the ASP.NET `TextBox` server control whose functionality this extender control extends.

```
[DefaultValue(""),
IDReferenceProperty, Category("Behavior")]
public string TargetControlID
{
  get
  {
    if (this._targetControlID != null)
      return this._targetControlID;

    return string.Empty;
  }
  set { this._targetControlID = value; }
}
```

As you can see from Listing 17-2, the `ExtenderControl` base class derives from the ASP.NET `Control` base class and overrides the `OnPreRender` and `Render` methods that it inherits from the `Control` class. Next, I'll walk you through the `ExtenderControl` base class's implementation of these two methods.

The `OnPreRender` method begins by invoking the `OnPreRender` method of its base class — that is, the `Control` base class. The `OnPreRender` method of the `Control` base class raises the `PreRender` event and consequently invokes all the event handlers registered for this event.

```
base.OnPreRender(e);
```

If you need to run some code when an extender server control such as `TextBoxWatermarkExtenderControl` enters its PreRender lifecycle phase, you must encapsulate this code in a method and register the method as an event handler for the `PreRender` event of the extender server control.

Next, the `OnPreRender` method of the `ExtenderControl` base class invokes the `FindControl` method, passing in the `ID` property value of the target server control (recall that the target server control of an extender control is the server control whose client-side functionality the extender control is extending) to return a reference to this server control.

```
Control control = this.FindControl(this.TargetControlID);
```

Then, the `OnPreRender` method of the `ExtenderControl` base class invokes the `GetCurrent` static method on the replica `ScriptManager` to return a reference to the current replica `ScriptManager` server control:

```
ScriptManager scriptManager = ScriptManager.GetCurrent(Page);
```

Next, the method invokes the `RegisterExtenderControl` method on the current `ScriptManager` server control to register the current extender control as the extender control for the specified target control. As you'll see later, the `RegisterExtenderControl` method adds the specified extender server control to an internal collection.

```
scriptManager.RegisterExtenderControl<ExtenderControl>(this, control);
```

Next, I'll walk you through the `ExtenderControl` base class's implementation of the `Render` method that it inherits from the `Control` base class. This method begins by calling the `Render` method of the base class. The `Render` method of the `Control` base class iterates through the child controls of the extender control and invokes their `RenderControl` method to allow them to render themselves.

```
base.Render(writer);
```

The `Render` method of the `ExtenderControl` base class then calls the `GetCurrent` static method on the replica `ScriptManager` class to return a reference to the current replica `ScriptManager` server control:

```
ScriptManager mgr = ScriptManager.GetCurrent(Page);
```

Next, the method calls the `RegisterScriptDescriptors` method on the current replica `ScriptManager` server control to allow the extender control to register all the required client scripts for rendering.

```
mgr.RegisterScriptDescriptors(this);
```

Script Server Controls

As the name suggests, an extender server control such as `TextBoxWatermarkExtenderControl` extends the client-side functionality of an existing ASP.NET server control such as `TextBox`. A script server control, such as `TextBoxWatermarkScriptControl`, on the other hand, extends the client-side functionality of an exiting ASP.NET server control such as `TextBox` if it derives from that server control. Otherwise a script server control can be a brand-new server control on its own.

IScriptControl

All ASP.NET AJAX script server controls implement an interface named `IScriptControl`, defined in Listing 17-3. As you can see, the `IScriptControl` interface exposes two methods:

❑ `GetScriptDescriptors`: The `GetScriptDescriptors` method of the `IScriptControl` interface plays the same role in a script server control that the `GetScriptDescriptors` method of the `IExtenderControl` plays in an extender server control. Recall that the `GetScriptDescriptors` method of the `IExtenderControl` interface takes a parameter of type `Control` that references the target server control of the extender server control. The target server control is the server control whose client-side functionality the specified extender server control extends. However, as Listing 17-3 shows, the `GetScriptDescriptors` method of the `IScriptControl` interface does not take this parameter. This is because the script server control that extends the client-side functionality of an existing ASP.NET server control directly derives from that server control; consequently there is no need for this parameter because it references the script server control itself. To put it differently, a script server control is its own target server control.

❑   `GetScriptReferences`: The `GetScriptReferences` method of the `IScriptControl` interface plays the same role in a script server control that the `GetScriptReferences` method of the `IExtenderControl` plays in an extender server control. In other words, the `GetScriptReferences` method returns an `IEnumerable` collection of `ScriptReference` objects in which each `ScriptReference` object references a JavaScript file that contains the JavaScript code that supports the client-side functionality of the script server control, such as the definition of an ASP.NET AJAX component associated with the script server control.

Listing 17-3: The IScriptControl

```
using System.Collections.Generic;

namespace CustomComponents3
{
  public interface IScriptControl
  {
    IEnumerable<ScriptDescriptor> GetScriptDescriptors();
    IEnumerable<ScriptReference> GetScriptReferences();
  }
}
```

ScriptControl

As you saw in the previous section, the ASP.NET AJAX Framework comes with an implementation of the `IExtenderControl` interface named `ExtenderControl`. As I mentioned, the `ExtenderControl` base class contains the base functionality that every extender server control must implement. Because of this, you should derive your custom extender server controls from the `ExtenderControl` base class to save yourself from having to implement this base functionality every time you develop an extender server control.

Similarly, the ASP.NET AJAX Framework comes with an implementation of the `IScriptControl` interface, named `ScriptControl`, which contains the base functionality that every script server control must implement. Therefore, deriving your custom script server controls from the `ScriptControl` base class saves you from having to implement this base functionality every time you develop a script server control. That said, there are times when you cannot derive your script server control from the `ScriptControl` base class, and consequently you have to re-implement this base functionality. This happens when you're implementing a custom script server control that is required to derive from an existing ASP.NET server control. For example, as you'll see later, the `TextBoxWatermarkScriptControl` script server control derives from the ASP.NET `TextBox` server control and extends its client-side functionality. In these situations, you cannot derive from the `ScriptControl` server control because the object-oriented programming languages such as C# and VB.NET do not allow multiple inheritances. Therefore, your custom script control has no choice but to explicitly implement the `IScriptControl` interface, where it must basically do the same thing that the `ScriptControl` base class does.

Listing 17-4 presents the implementation of our replica `ScriptControl` base class. Note that this base class follows the typical C# interface implementation pattern to implement the `GetScriptDescriptors` and `GetScriptReferences` methods of the `IScriptControl` base class, where it exposes two protected virtual methods with the same names as the methods of the interface. Note also that the `ScriptControl` base class marks these two protected virtual methods as abstract, to require its subclasses to implement these two methods.

Listing 17-4: The ScriptControl Base Class

```
namespace CustomComponents3
{
  using System;
  using System.Web.UI;
  using System.Collections.Generic;
  using System.Web.UI.WebControls;

  public abstract class ScriptControl : WebControl, IScriptControl
  {
    protected abstract IEnumerable<ScriptDescriptor> GetScriptDescriptors();
    protected abstract IEnumerable<ScriptReference> GetScriptReferences();

    protected override void OnPreRender(EventArgs e)
    {
      base.OnPreRender(e);
      ScriptManager scriptManager = ScriptManager.GetCurrent(Page);
      scriptManager.RegisterScriptControl<ScriptControl>(this);
    }

    protected override void Render(HtmlTextWriter writer)
    {
      base.Render(writer);
      if (!base.DesignMode)
      {
        ScriptManager scriptManager = ScriptManager.GetCurrent(Page);
        scriptManager.RegisterScriptDescriptors(this);
      }
    }

    IEnumerable<ScriptDescriptor> IScriptControl.GetScriptDescriptors()
    {
      return this.GetScriptDescriptors();
    }

    IEnumerable<ScriptReference> IScriptControl.GetScriptReferences()
    {
      return this.GetScriptReferences();
    }
  }
}
```

As Listing 17-4 shows, the ScriptControl base class derives from the WebControl base class and overrides its OnPreRender and Render methods. Next, I'll walk you through the ScriptControl base class's implementation of the OnPreRender method. As you can see, this method begins by invoking the OnPreRender method of its base class to raise the PreRender event and consequently to invoke the event handlers registered for this event:

```
base.OnPreRender(e);
```

If you need to run some custom code when a script server control such as
`TextBoxWatermarkScriptControl` *enters its PreRender life-cycle phase, you must*
encapsulate this code in a method and register the method as event handler for the `PreRender`
event of the script server control.

Next, it calls the `GetCurrent` static method on our replica `ScriptManager` class to return a reference to
the current replica `ScriptManager` server control:

```
ScriptManager scriptManager = ScriptManager.GetCurrent(Page);
```

Finally, it calls the `RegisterScriptControl` method on the current replica `ScriptManager` server
control to register the script server control.

```
scriptManager.RegisterScriptControl<ScriptControl>(this);
```

Next, I'll walk you through the implementation of the `Render` method. As you can see from Listing 17-4,
this method first invokes the `Render` method of its base class, which in turn invokes the `RenderControl`
method of the child controls of the script server control.

```
base.Render(writer);
```

Next, it calls the `GetCurrent` static method on our replica `ScriptManager` class to return a reference to
the current replica `ScriptManager` server control:

```
ScriptManager scriptManager = ScriptManager.GetCurrent(Page);
```

Finally, it calls the `RegisterScriptDescriptors` method on the current replica `ScriptManager` server
control to allow the script server control to register its scripts:

```
scriptManager.RegisterScriptDescriptors(this);
```

As you can see from Listing 17-4, the `ScriptControl` base class derives from the `WebControl` base class
instead of the `Control` base class. Therefore, if you decide to derive your custom script server control
from the `ScriptControl` base class instead of explicitly implementing the `IScriptControl` interface,
you must make sure that you override the `WebControl` base class's overridable methods as opposed to
the `Control` base class. You'll see an example of this later in this chapter.

ScriptDescriptor

Recall from Listings 17-1 and 17-3 that the `GetScriptDescriptors` method of the `IExtenderControl`
and `IScriptControl` interfaces return an `IEnumerable` collection of the `ScriptDescriptor` objects.
Listing 17-5 presents the implementation of the replica `ScriptDescriptor` abstract base class. As you
can see, this class exposes two methods:

❑ `GetScript`: The subclasses of the `ScriptDescriptor` abstract base class must implement
the `GetScript` abstract method to return a string that contains the client script that supports the
client functionality of a script server control or extender server control. This client script normally
performs these tasks:

  ❑ Instantiates the ASP.NET AJAX component associated with the script server control or
  extender server control

❑   Initializes the properties of this ASP.NET AJAX component and registers event handlers for the events of this ASP.NET AJAX component

❑   Adds this ASP.NET AJAX component to the current ASP.NET AJAX application

❑   `RegisterDisposeForDescriptor`: The subclasses of the `ScriptDescriptor` base class can override the `RegisterDisposeForDescriptor` method to generate the client script that registers the dispose script for the ASP.NET AJAX component associated with the script server control or extender server control. Such a dispose script normally performs final cleanup before the ASP.NET AJAX component is disposed of. As you can see, the `ScriptDescriptor` base class does not mark the `RegisterDisposeForDescriptor` method as abstract. Therefore the implementation of this method is optional.

Listing 17-5: The ScriptDescriptor Base Class

```
namespace CustomComponents3
{
  using System.Web.UI;

  public abstract class ScriptDescriptor
  {
    protected internal abstract string GetScript();
    internal virtual void RegisterDisposeForDescriptor(ScriptManager scriptManager,
                                                       Control owner)

    {
    }
  }
}
```

The ASP.NET AJAX Framework comes with a class named `ScriptComponentDescriptor` that derives from the `ScriptDescriptor` abstract base class, implements its `GetScript` method, and extends its functionality to add support for new methods and properties. We'll discuss all this in the next section.

ScriptComponentDescriptor

Listing 17-6 presents the implementation of the replica `ScriptComponentDescriptor` class. I'll discuss the implementation of the methods and properties of this class in the following sections.

Listing 17-6: The ScriptComponentDescriptor

```
namespace CustomComponents3
{
  using System.Collections.Generic;
  using System.Web.Script.Serialization;
  using System.Web.UI;
  using System.Text;
  using System;

  public class ScriptComponentDescriptor : ScriptDescriptor
  {
    // Fields
    private string _elementIDInternal;
```

(continued)

Listing 17-6 *(continued)*

```
        private SortedList<string, string> _events;
        private string _id;
        private SortedList<string, string> _properties;
        private SortedList<string, string> _references;
        private bool _registerDispose;
        private JavaScriptSerializer _serializer;
        private string _type;

        // Methods
        public ScriptComponentDescriptor(string type)
        {
          this._registerDispose = true;
          this._type = type;
        }

        internal ScriptComponentDescriptor(string type, string elementID) : this(type)
        {
          this._elementIDInternal = elementID;
        }

        public void AddComponentProperty(string name, string componentID)
        {
          string value = "\"";
          value += HelperMethods.QuoteString(componentID);
          value += "\"";
          References[name] = value;
        }

        public void AddElementProperty(string name, string elementID)
        {
          string value = "$get(\"";
          value += HelperMethods.QuoteString(elementID);
          value += "\")";
          Properties[name] = value;
        }

        public void AddEvent(string name, string handler)
        {
          this.Events[name] = handler;
        }

        public void AddProperty(string name, object val)
        {
          string value = this.Serializer.Serialize(val);
          Properties[name] = value;
        }

        public void AddScriptProperty(string name, string script)
        {
          Properties[name] = script;
        }
```

```
    private void AppendScript(SortedList<string, string> list,
                              StringBuilder builder)
{
  bool flag = true;
  if ((list != null) && (list.Count > 0))
  {
    foreach (KeyValuePair<string, string> pair in list)
    {
      if (flag)
      {
        builder.Append("{");
        flag = false;
      }

      else
        builder.Append(",");

      builder.Append('"');
      builder.Append(HelperMethods.QuoteString(pair.Key));
      builder.Append('"');
      builder.Append(':');
      builder.Append(pair.Value);
    }
  }

  if (flag)
    builder.Append("null");
  else
    builder.Append("}");
}

protected internal override string GetScript()
{
  if (!string.IsNullOrEmpty(this.ID))
    this.AddProperty("id", this.ID);

  StringBuilder builder = new StringBuilder();
  builder.Append("$create(");
  builder.Append(this.Type);
  builder.Append(", ");
  this.AppendScript(this._properties, builder);
  builder.Append(", ");
  this.AppendScript(this._events, builder);
  builder.Append(", ");
  this.AppendScript(this._references, builder);
  if (this.ElementIDInternal != null)
  {
    builder.Append(", ");
    builder.Append("$get(\"");
    builder.Append(HelperMethods.QuoteString(this.ElementIDInternal));
    builder.Append("\")");
  }
```

(continued)

Listing 17-6 (continued)

```
    builder.Append(");");
    return builder.ToString();
}

public virtual string ClientID
{
  get { return this.ID; }
}

internal string ElementIDInternal
{
  get { return this._elementIDInternal; }
}

private SortedList<string, string> Events
{
  get
  {
    if (this._events == null)
      this._events = new SortedList<string, string>(StringComparer.Ordinal);
    return this._events;
  }
}

public virtual string ID
{
  get { return (this._id ?? string.Empty); }
  set { this._id = value; }
}

private SortedList<string, string> Properties
{
  get
  {
    if (this._properties == null)
      this._properties =
                    new SortedList<string, string>(StringComparer.Ordinal);
    return this._properties;
  }
}

private SortedList<string, string> References
{
  get
  {
    if (this._references == null)
      this._references =
                    new SortedList<string, string>(StringComparer.Ordinal);
    return this._references;
  }
}
```

```
internal bool RegisterDispose
{
  get { return this._registerDispose; }
  set { this._registerDispose = value; }
}

private JavaScriptSerializer Serializer
{
  get
  {
    if (this._serializer == null)
      this._serializer = new JavaScriptSerializer();
    return this._serializer;
  }
}

public string Type
{
  get { return this._type; }
  set { this._type = value; }
}
  }
}
```

GetScript

The ScriptComponentDescriptor overrides the GetScript abstract method that it inherits from the ScriptDescriptor abstract base class, as shown in Listing 17-6.

The main responsibility of the GetScript method of the ScriptComponentDescriptor class is to generate the client script that performs the following tasks:

- ❑ Instantiates the ASP.NET AJAX component associated with the script or extender server control
- ❑ Initializes the properties of this ASP.NET AJAX component
- ❑ Registers event handlers for the events of this ASP.NET AJAX component
- ❑ Attaches this ASP.NET AJAX component to its associated script or extender server control
- ❑ Adds this ASP.NET AJAX component to the current ASP.NET AJAX application

As the following excerpt from Listing 16-64 shows, all of this is achieved through a call into the $create global JavaScript function:

```
var properties = {name : "MyTextBoxWatermarkBehaviorName",
                  id : "MyTextBoxWatermarkBehaviorID",
                  WatermarkText : "Enter text here",
                  WatermarkCssClass : "WatermarkCssClass"};

var textBox1 = $get("TextBox1");
textBoxWatermarkBehavior =
              $create(AjaxControlToolkit.TextBoxWatermarkBehavior, properties,
                      null, null, textBox1);
```

This example does not register any event handlers. However, in general, the $create function takes five parameters:

❑ The first parameter references the constructor of the ASP.NET AJAX component being created. The current example passes the reference to the constructor of the `TextBoxWatermarkBehavior` because this behavior is the ASP.NET AJAX component being created in this case:

```
$create(AjaxControlToolkit.TextBoxWatermarkBehavior, properties,
        null, null, textBox1);
```

❑ The second parameter references the dictionary that contains the names and initial values of the properties of the ASP.NET AJAX component being created:

```
$create(AjaxControlToolkit.TextBoxWatermarkBehavior, properties,
        null, null, textBox1);
```

❑ The third parameter references the dictionary that contains the names of the events of the ASP.NET AJAX component being created, and the event handlers being registered for these events. This example passes `null` for this parameter because the page shown in Listing 16-64 does not register any event handlers:

```
$create(AjaxControlToolkit.TextBoxWatermarkBehavior, properties,
        null, null, textBox1);
```

❑ The fourth parameter is a dictionary that contains the names and values of those properties of the ASP.NET AJAX component that reference other ASP.NET AJAX components in the current ASP.NET AJAX application:

```
$create(AjaxControlToolkit.TextBoxWatermarkBehavior, properties,
        null, null, textBox1);
```

❑ The fifth parameter references the associated DOM element of the ASP.NET AJAX component being instantiated (if any):

```
$create(AjaxControlToolkit.TextBoxWatermarkBehavior, properties,
        null, null, textBox1);
```

As you can see from Listing 17-6, the `GetScript` method takes these steps to generate the client script that calls into the $create global JavaScript function, passing in the preceding five parameters. As you'll see later, the `ScriptComponentDescriptor` exposes a method named `AddProperty` that takes two parameters, the first parameter containing the name of the property being added and the second containing the value of this property. The `AddProperty` method under the hood adds the specified property name and value to an internal dictionary. As Listing 17-6 shows, the `GetScript` method calls the `AddProperty` method to add the `id` property and its value to this internal dictionary:

```
if (!string.IsNullOrEmpty(this.ID))
    this.AddProperty("id", this.ID);
```

As the following code fragment shows, the `ScriptComponentDescriptor` exposes a read-only property named `ClientID`, which returns the value of another property named `ID`. The `ID` property is a read/write property that specifies the `id` of the ASP.NET AJAX component being created. Recall that the `id` of an ASP.NET AJAX component uniquely identifies that component among other components in the current ASP.NET AJAX application:

```
public virtual string ClientID
{
  get { return this.ID; }
}

public virtual string ID
{
  get { return (this._id ?? string.Empty); }
  set { this._id = value; }
}
```

Now back to the implementation of the `GetScript` method. Next, `GetScript` instantiates a `StringBuilder` and populates it with the script that invokes the `$create` function:

```
StringBuilder builder = new StringBuilder();
```

Then, `GetScript` appends the string `"$create("` to the `StringBuilder`:

```
builder.Append("$create(");
```

Next, it passes the value of the `Type` property of the `ScriptComponentDescriptor` as the first parameter of the `$create` function. Recall that the first parameter references the constructor of the ASP.NET AJAX component being created:

```
builder.Append(this.Type);
```

As you can see from the following code fragment, the constructor of the `ScriptComponentDescriptor` takes a string parameter that contains the fully qualified name of the type of the ASP.NET AJAX component being initialized. Note that this constructor assigns this string parameter to a private field named `_type`, which can be then accessed via the read/write `Type` property of the `ScriptComponentDescriptor`:

```
public ScriptComponentDescriptor(string type)
{
  this._registerDispose = true;
  this._type = type;
}

public string Type
{
  get { return this._type; }
  set { this._type = value; }
}
```

Now back to the implementation of the `GetScript` method. Next, this method invokes another method, `AppendScript`, and passes two parameters into it. The first parameter references an internal collection named _properties, and the second parameter references the `StringBuilder`. As you'll see later, the _properties collection is a `SortedList` of `KeyValuePair<string, string>` objects for which each object represents a property of the ASP.NET AJAX component being created. The `Key` and `Value` properties of each object contain the name and value of the associated property, respectively.

As you'll see later, the `AppendScript` method serializes the _properties collection into an object literal whose name/value pairs are the object literal representations of the `KeyValuePair<string, string>` objects in the collection. The `AppendScript` method then passes this object literal into the `$create` method as its second argument. Recall that the second argument of the `$create` method is a dictionary that contains one name/value pair for each property being initialized, the name part of the pair containing the name of the property and the value part containing the value:

```
this.AppendScript(this._properties, builder);
```

Next, the `GetScript` method invokes the `AppendScript` method once again and passes two parameters into it. The first parameter references an internal collection named _events and the second parameter references the `StringBuilder`. As you'll see later, the _events collection is another `SortedList` of `KeyValuePair<string, string>` objects. The `Key` and `Value` properties contain an event name of the ASP.NET AJAX component being initialized and the event handler being registered for this event, respectively.

As you'll see later, the `AppendScript` method serializes the _events collection into an object literal whose name/value pairs are the object literal representations of `KeyValuePair<string, string>` objects in the collection. The `AppendScript` method then passes this object literal into the `$create` method as its third argument. Recall that the third argument of the `$create` method is an object literal whose name/value pairs represent event names and the event handlers being registered for these events.

```
this.AppendScript(this._events, builder);
```

Next, the `GetScript` method invokes the `AppendScript` method once more and passes two parameters into it. The first parameter references an internal collection named _references and the second parameter references the `StringBuilder`. As you'll see later, the _references collection is another `SortedList` of `KeyValuePair<string, string>` objects for which the `Key` and `Value` properties contain the name of a property of the ASP.NET AJAX component being initialized and the id of another ASP.NET AJAX component that the property references, respectively.

As you'll see later, the `AppendScript` method serializes the _references collection into an object literal whose name/value pairs are the object literal representation of `KeyValuePair<string, string>` objects in the collection. The `AppendScript` method then passes this object literal into the `$create` method as its fourth argument.

```
this.AppendScript(this._references, builder);
```

Next, `GetScript` generates the script that invokes the `$get` global JavaScript function to return a reference to the associated DOM element of the ASP.NET AJAX component being created. Note that `GetScript` passes the value of the `ElementIDInternal` property of the `ScriptComponentDescriptor` into the

$get function. The value returned from the $get function is then passed into the $create global JavaScript function as its last parameter. Recall that the last parameter of this function references the associated DOM element of the ASP.NET AJAX component being created.

```
builder.Append("$get(\"");
builder.Append(HelperMethods.QuoteString(this.ElementIDInternal));
```

The `ScriptComponentDescriptor` comes with an internal constructor that takes two parameters. The first parameter is a string that contains the fully qualified name of the type of the ASP.NET AJAX component being instantiated, including its complete namespace containment hierarchy (for example, this parameter is the string `AjaxControlToolkit.TextBoxWatermarkBehavior` in the case of the `TextBoxWatermarkBehavior`). The second parameter is a string that contains the id HTML attribute value of the associated DOM element of the component. As you can see, this constructor stores its second parameter in a private field named `_elementIDInternal`, whose value is returned by an internal property named `ElementIDInternal`:

```
internal ScriptComponentDescriptor(string type, string elementID) : this(type)
{
  this._elementIDInternal = elementID;
}

internal string ElementIDInternal
{
  get { return this._elementIDInternal; }
}
```

HelperMethods

As Listing 17-6 shows, the `GetScript` method calls the `QuoteString` static method on a class named `HelperMethods` and passes the value of the `ElementIDInternal` property of the `ScriptComponentDescriptor` into it:

```
builder.Append(HelperMethods.QuoteString(this.ElementIDInternal));
```

To understand what the `QuoteString` static method does, you need to understand the definition of a string in the JSON jargon. According to the JSON specification, a string is a collection of zero or more Unicode characters wrapped in double quotes and using backlash escapes. As you can see from Listing 17-7, the `QuoteString` method ensures that the string passed into it as its argument meets these JSON requirements. Note that the `QuoteString` static method makes use of another static method of the `HelperMethods` class, `AppendCharAsUnicode`, to ensure that all the characters in the specified string are Unicode characters.

Listing 17-7: The HelperMethods Class

```
using System;
using System.Data;
using System.Configuration;
using System.Web;
using System.Web.Security;
using System.Web.UI;
using System.Web.UI.WebControls;
using System.Web.UI.WebControls.WebParts;
```

(continued)

Listing 17-7 *(continued)*

```csharp
using System.Web.UI.HtmlControls;
using System.Text;

namespace CustomComponents3
{
  public class HelperMethods
  {
    public static string QuoteString(string value)
    {
      if (string.IsNullOrEmpty(value))
        return string.Empty;

      StringBuilder builder = null;
      int startIndex = 0;
      int count = 0;
      for (int i = 0; i < value.Length; i++)
      {
        char c = value[i];
        if ((((c == '\r') || (c == '\t')) || ((c == '"') ||
            (c == '\''))) || ((((c == '<') || (c == '>')) ||
            ((c == '\\') || (c == '\n'))) || (((c == '\b') ||
            (c == '\f')) || (c < ' '))))
        {
          if (builder == null)
            builder = new StringBuilder(value.Length + 5);

          if (count > 0)
            builder.Append(value, startIndex, count);

          startIndex = i + 1;
          count = 0;
        }

        switch (c)
        {
          case '<':
          case '>':
          case '\'':
            HelperMethods.AppendCharAsUnicode(builder, c);
            continue;
          case '\\':
            builder.Append(@"\\");
            continue;
          case '\b':
            builder.Append(@"\b");
            continue;
          case '\t':
            builder.Append(@"\t");
            continue;
          case '\n':
            builder.Append(@"\n");
            continue;
```

```
          case '\f':
             builder.Append(@"\f");
             continue;
          case '\r':
             builder.Append(@"\r");
             continue;
          case '"':
             builder.Append("\\\"");
             continue;
       }

       if (c < ' ')
          HelperMethods.AppendCharAsUnicode(builder, c);

       else
          count++;
    }

    if (builder == null)
      return value;

    if (count > 0)
      builder.Append(value, startIndex, count);

    return builder.ToString();
  }

  public static void AppendCharAsUnicode(StringBuilder builder, char c)
  {
    builder.Append(@"\u");
    builder.AppendFormat("{0:x4}", new object[] { (int)c });
  }
 }
}
```

Public Methods

The `ScriptComponentDescriptor` class exposes five important public methods that you can call from your managed code. I'll present and discuss the implementation of these public methods in the following sections.

AddComponentProperty

Use the `AddComponentProperty` method to initialize those properties of an ASP.NET AJAX component that reference other ASP.NET AJAX components in the current ASP.NET AJAX application. These properties are known as *component properties*.

The `AddComponentProperty` method takes two parameters, the first being a string that contains the name of the property being initialized and the second being a string that contains the `id` property value of the ASP.NET AJAX component that this property references. Recall that the `id` property value of an ASP.NET AJAX component uniquely identifies the component among other components in the current ASP.NET AJAX application.

Keep in mind that an ASP.NET AJAX component is any ASP.NET AJAX class that directly or indirectly inherits from the ASP.NET AJAX Component *base class. Since all ASP.NET AJAX controls and behaviors inherit from this base class, they are all ASP.NET AJAX components.*

Listing 17-6 presents the implementation of the AddComponentProperty method. As you can see, this method takes the following two steps to ensure that the id property value passed into the method as its second argument is a valid JSON string. (Keep in mind that this id property is the id property value of the component referenced by the property being initialized.) Recall that a valid JSON string is a collection of zero or more Unicode characters wrapped in double quotes and using backslash escapes:

❏   First, the AddComponentProperty method calls the QuoteString static method, passing in the component id. Recall from Listing 17-7 that the QuoteString method ensures that the specified string, which is the component id in this case, is a collection of Unicode characters using backslash escapes.

❏   Second, it wraps the component id in double quotes.

The AddComponentProperty method then stores the property name and its associated value, which is the id property value of the component that the property references, in an internal collection named References.

As you can see from Listing 17-6, the References collection is a SortedList of KeyValuePair<string, string> objects for which each object represents a component property. The Key and Value properties of each object in the References collection respectively contain the name of the associated property and its value, which is nothing but the id property value of the component that the property references.

AddElementProperty

Use the AddElementProperty method to initialize those properties of an ASP.NET AJAX component that reference DOM elements on the current page. These properties are known as *element properties*. As you can see from Listing 17-6, the AddElementProperty method takes two arguments: a string that contains the name of the property whose value is being initialized, and a string that contains the id HTML attribute value of a DOM element on the current page.

As Listing 17-6 shows, the AddElementProperty method begins by evaluating the value of the property, which is a reference to the DOM element with the specified id HTML attribute value. As such, this method generates the script that contains a call into the $get global JavaScript function. The method takes the following steps to ensure that this script is a valid JSON string:

❏   Calls the QuoteString static method, passing in the element id. Recall from Listing 17-7 that the QuoteString method ensures that the specified string, which is the element id in this case, is a collection of Unicode characters using backslash escapes.

❏   Wraps the element id in double quotes.

Finally, the AddElementProperty method adds the name of the property and its value, which is the above script, to an internal collection named Properties. Notice that the Properties collection is again a SortedList of KeyValuePair<string, string> objects where each object represents an element property. The Key and Value properties of each in the Properties collection respectively contain the name of the associated property and its value, which is nothing but the script that returns a reference to the DOM element with the specified element id.

AddEvent

The `AddEvent` method takes two parameters: a string that contains an event name, and a string that contains an event handler. In other words, this method enables you to register an event handler for the specified event of an ASP.NET AJAX component. As Listing 17-6 shows, this method adds the specified event name and its associated event handler to an internal dictionary named `Events`. Notice that the `Events` collection is a `SortedList` of `KeyValuePair<string, string>` objects. The `Key` and `Value` properties of each object in the `Events` collection contain an event name and its associated event handler, respectively.

AddProperty

The `AddProperty` public method takes the name of the property being initialized as its first argument and the value of the property as its second argument. The value could be any .NET object that the `JavaScriptSerializer` can serialize into a valid JSON string. As you can see from Listing 17-6, this method first invokes the `Serialize` method on the `JavaScriptSerializer`, passing in the property value, which is a .NET object. The `Serialize` method serializes the specified .NET object into its JSON representation and returns a string that contains this JSON representation. The `AddProperty` method then adds the name of this property and its value, which is the string that contains the JSON representation of the original .NET object, to the `Properties` collection.

As you can see from Listing 17-6, our replica `ScriptComponentDescriptor` exposes a property of type `JavaScriptSerializer` named `Serializer` that instantiates and returns a `JavaScriptSerializer` object.

AddScriptProperty

The `AddScriptProperty` method enables you to initialize those properties of an ASP.NET AJAX component whose values are client scripts. As you can see from Listing 17-6, this method takes the name of the property being initialized as its first argument and the script that constitutes the value of the property as its second argument. This method stores the name of the property and its associated value in the `Properties` collection.

AppendScript

Recall from Listing 17-6 that the `GetScript` method of the `ScriptComponentDescriptor` instantiates a `StringBuilder` and populates it with the script that invokes the `$create` global JavaScript function to create a new ASP.NET AJAX component. As you saw, this method invokes the `AppendScript` method three times, as follows:

❏   The first time, it passes the `Properties` collection into the method to have the method to serialize this collection into its object literal representation and to append a string to the specified `StringBuilder` that contains this representation. Recall that this representation contains one name/value pair for each item in the `Properties` collection.

❏   The second time, it passes the `Events` collection into the method to have the method to serialize this collection into its object literal representation and to append a string to the specified `StringBuilder` that contains this representation. Recall that this representation contains one name/value pair for each item in the `Events` collection.

❑ The third time, it passes the References collection into the method to have the method to serialize this collection into its object literal representation and to append a string to the specified StringBuilder that contains this representation. Recall that this representation contains one name/value pair for each item in the References collection.

Next, I'll walk you through the implementation of the AppendScript method, as shown in Listing 17-6. This method takes two arguments: a SortedList of KeyValuePair<string, string> objects, and a StringBuilder. The main responsibility of this method is to serialize the specified SortedList into its JSON representation, which is a JSON object. This JSON object, like any other JSON object, starts with an open curly brace ({):

```
builder.Append("{");
```

This JSON object also contains a comma-separated list of name/value pairs, for which each name/value pair is the JSON serialization of a KeyValuePair<string, string> object in the SortedList. Here is how the AppendScript method serializes each KeyValuePair<string, string> object in the SortedList: since the AddComponentProperty, AddElementProperty, AddEvent, AddProperty, and AddScriptProperty methods have already ensured that the value contained in the Value property of each KeyValuePair<string, string> object in the References, Properties, and Events collections is a valid JSON representation, the AppendScript method must only serialize the value contained in the Key property of each KeyValuePair<string, string> object. To do so, the method performs these tasks:

❑ Invokes the QuoteString static method on the HelperMethods class once for each KeyValuePair<string, string> object in the SortedList, passing in the value of the Key property of the KeyValuePair object to ensure that this value is a collection of Unicode characters using backslash escapes:

```
builder.Append(HelperMethods.QuoteString(pair.Key));
```

❑ Wraps the return value of the QuoteString static method in double quotes:

```
builder.Append('"');
builder.Append(HelperMethods.QuoteString(pair.Key));
builder.Append('"');
```

Finally, the AppendScript method appends a colon character followed by the value of the Value property of the KeyValuePair object as is:

```
builder.Append(':');
builder.Append(pair.Value);
```

ScriptControlDescriptor

Listing 17-8 presents the implementation of the replica ScriptControlDescriptor. As you can see, this class derives from the ScriptComponentDescriptor base class discussed in the previous sections. Note that the constructor of the ScriptControlDescriptor class makes use of the internal constructor of the ScriptComponentDescriptor base class. As discussed earlier, this internal constructor takes two parameters, the first containing the fully qualified name of the type of the ASP.NET AJAX control being instantiated and initialized, and the second containing the id HTML attribute of the associated DOM element of this ASP.NET AJAX control.

Listing 17-8: The ScriptControlDescriptor

```
namespace CustomComponents3
{
  using System;

  public class ScriptControlDescriptor : ScriptComponentDescriptor
  {
    public ScriptControlDescriptor(string type, string elementID) : base(type,
                                                                         elementID)

    {
      base.RegisterDispose = false;
    }

    public override string ClientID
    {
      get { return this.ElementID; }
    }

    public string ElementID
    {
      get { return base.ElementIDInternal; }
    }

    public override string ID
    {
      get { return base.ID; }
      set { throw new InvalidOperationException("ID Not Settable"); }
    }
  }
}
```

ScriptBehaviorDescriptor

Listing 17-9 presents the implementation of the replica ScriptBehaviorDescriptor. As you can see, this class, just like the ScriptControlBehavior class, derives from the ScriptComponentDescriptor base class. Note that the constructor of the ScriptBehaviorDescriptor class, just like the constructor of the ScriptControlBehavior class, makes use of the internal constructor of the ScriptComponentDescriptor base class. In this case, the first parameter passed into this internal constructor contains the fully qualified name of the type of the ASP.NET AJAX behavior being instantiated and initialized, and the second parameter contains the id HTML attribute of the associated DOM element of this ASP.NET AJAX behavior.

As discussed in Chapter 16, every ASP.NET AJAX behavior exposes a property named name that contains the name of the behavior. As a result, the ScriptBehaviorDescriptor overrides the GetScript method of its base class — that is, the ScriptComponentDescriptor — to make a call to the AddProperty method to add the value of its _name field as the value of the name property of the behavior being instantiated and initialized:

```
if (!string.IsNullOrEmpty(this._name))
  base.AddProperty("name", this._name);

return base.GetScript();
```

As you can see from Listing 17-9, the ScriptBehaviorDescriptor class exposes a read/write property named Name that enables you to get and to set the value of the _name field of the class. Note that the getter of this property first checks whether the value of the _name field is set — that is, whether the setter method has been called to set this value. If so, it simply returns the value of the _name field. If not, it invokes another method named GetTypeName, passing in the fully qualified name of the type of the behavior being instantiated and initialized to generate and return an appropriate value for the Name property.

As Listing 17-9 shows, the GetTypeName method simply extracts the name of the type of the behavior being instantiated and initialized from its fully qualified name. Recall that the fully qualified name of the type of an ASP.NET AJAX component such as a behavior contains both the name and the complete namespace containment hierarchy of the component.

Listing 17-9: The ScriptBehaviorDescriptor

```
namespace CustomComponents3
{
  public class ScriptBehaviorDescriptor : ScriptComponentDescriptor
  {
    private string _name;

    public ScriptBehaviorDescriptor(string type, string elementID)
      : base(type, elementID)
    {
      base.RegisterDispose = false;
    }

    protected internal override string GetScript()
    {
      if (!string.IsNullOrEmpty(this._name))
        base.AddProperty("name", this._name);

      return base.GetScript();
    }

    private static string GetTypeName(string type)
    {
      int num = type.LastIndexOf('.');
      if (num == -1)
        return type;
```

```
          return type.Substring(num + 1);
      }

      public override string ClientID
      {
        get
        {
          if (string.IsNullOrEmpty(this.ID))
            return (this.ElementID + "$" + this.Name);
          return this.ID;
        }
      }

      public string ElementID
      {
        get { return base.ElementIDInternal; }
      }

      public string Name
      {
        get
        {
          if (string.IsNullOrEmpty(this._name))
            return GetTypeName(base.Type);
          return this._name;
        }
        set { this._name = value; }
      }
    }
  }
```

ScriptReference

Listing 17-10 presents the implementation of the replica ScriptReference class. The main responsibility of a ScriptReference object is to specify and represent a reference to a JavaScript file. The ASP.NET AJAX ScriptReference class provides you with two approaches to specify the location of the JavaScript file. The first approach requires you to set the value of the Path property of the ScriptReference object to the URL of the JavaScript file. The second approach, which only applies to JavaScript files embedded in an assembly, requires you to assign a string that contains the assembly information to the Assembly property of the ScriptReference object and to assign a string that specifies the name of the JavaScript file to the Name property of the ScriptReference object. To keep our discussions focused, the replica ScriptReference class only supports the first approach. However, you can easily extend the replica to add support for the second approach as well.

Listing 17-10: The ScriptReference Class

```
using System;
using System.Web.UI;
using System.ComponentModel;

namespace CustomComponents3
{
  public class ScriptReference
  {
    private Control _containingControl;
    private bool _isStaticReference;
    private string _path;

    public ScriptReference() {}

    public ScriptReference(string path) : this()
    {
      this.Path = path;
    }

    [DefaultValue(""), Category("Behavior")]
    public string Path
    {
      get
      {
        if (this._path != null)
          return this._path;

        return string.Empty;
      }
      set { this._path = value; }
    }

    internal bool IsStaticReference
    {
      get { return this._isStaticReference; }
      set { this._isStaticReference = value; }
    }

    internal Control ContainingControl
    {
      get { return this._containingControl; }
      set { this._containingControl = value; }
    }
  }
}
```

ScriptReferenceCollection

Listing 17-11 presents the implementation of the replica `ScriptReferenceCollection` class. As the name suggests, this collection contains objects of type `ScriptReference`. As you'll see in the next section, the `ScriptManager` exposes a property of type `ScriptReferenceCollection` named `Scripts`. Thanks to the .NET 2.0 generics, implementing a new collection class such as `ScriptReferenceCollection` is as easy as declaring a class that derives from one of the standard .NET generic collections.

Listing 17-11: The ScriptReferenceCollection Class

```
using System.Collections.ObjectModel;

namespace CustomComponents3
{
  public class ScriptReferenceCollection : Collection<ScriptReference> { }
}
```

ScriptManager

Listing 17-12 contains the implementation of the replica `ScriptManager` class. As you can see, this class drives from the `Control` base class. This derivation turns the `ScriptManager` into a server control and consequently allows it to participate in the typical ASP.NET page/control life-cycle phases. I'll discuss the implementation of the methods and properties of the replica `ScriptManager` server control in the following sections.

Listing 17-12: The ScriptManager Class

```
using System;
using System.Web;
using System.Text;
using System.Web.UI;
using System.ComponentModel;
using System.Collections.Generic;

namespace CustomComponents3
{
  [ParseChildren(true), DefaultProperty("Scripts"),
  NonVisualControl, PersistChildren(false)]
  public class ScriptManager : Control
  {
    public event EventHandler<ScriptReferenceEventArgs> ResolveScriptReference
    {
      add
      {
        base.Events.AddHandler(ResolveScriptReferenceEvent, value);
      }
      remove
```

(continued)

Listing 17-12 *(continued)*

```
    {
      base.Events.RemoveHandler(ResolveScriptReferenceEvent, value);
    }
  }

  private ScriptReferenceCollection _scripts;

  [PersistenceMode(PersistenceMode.InnerProperty),
  Editor("System.Web.UI.Design.CollectionEditorBase,
  System.Web.Extensions.Design, Version=1.0.61025.0, Culture=neutral,
  PublicKeyToken=31bf3856ad364e35", typeof(System.Drawing.Design.UITypeEditor)),
        DefaultValue((string)null), MergableProperty(false),
        Category("Behavior")]
  public ScriptReferenceCollection Scripts
  {
    get
    {
      if (this._scripts == null)
        this._scripts = new ScriptReferenceCollection();

      return this._scripts;
    }
  }

  protected override void OnInit(EventArgs e)
  {
    base.OnInit(e);
    Page.Items[typeof(ScriptManager)] = this;
    this.Page.PreRenderComplete += new EventHandler(Page_PreRenderComplete);
  }

  public static ScriptManager GetCurrent(Page page)
  {
    return (page.Items[typeof(ScriptManager)] as ScriptManager);
  }

  private static readonly object ResolveScriptReferenceEvent = new object();

  protected virtual void OnResolveScriptReference(ScriptReferenceEventArgs e)
  {
    EventHandler<ScriptReferenceEventArgs> handler =
                (EventHandler<ScriptReferenceEventArgs>)
                                    base.Events[ResolveScriptReferenceEvent];
    if (handler != null)
      handler(this, e);
  }

  void Page_PreRenderComplete(object sender, EventArgs e)
  {
    List<ScriptReference> list1 = new List<ScriptReference>();
    this.CollectScripts(list1);

    ScriptReferenceEventArgs args;
```

```
      foreach (ScriptReference reference3 in list1)
      {
        args = new ScriptReferenceEventArgs(reference3);
        this.OnResolveScriptReference(args);
      }

      foreach (ScriptReference reference4 in list1)
      {
        string url = reference4.Path;
        if (this.LoadScriptsBeforeUI)
          this.Page.ClientScript.RegisterClientScriptInclude(typeof(ScriptManager),
                                                  url, url);
        else
        {
          string script = "\r\n<script src=\"" +
                          HttpUtility.HtmlAttributeEncode(url) +
                          "\" type=\"text/javascript\"></script>";
          this.Page.ClientScript.RegisterStartupScript(typeof(ScriptManager),
                                                  url, script, false);
        }
      }
    }

    private void CollectScripts(List<ScriptReference> scripts)
    {
      if (this._scripts != null)
      {
        foreach (ScriptReference reference1 in this._scripts)
        {
          reference1.ContainingControl = this;
          reference1.IsStaticReference = true;
          scripts.Add(reference1);
        }
      }
      this.AddScriptReferencesForScriptControls(scripts);
      this.AddScriptReferencesForExtenderControls(scripts);
    }

    private void AddScriptReferencesForScriptControls(
                                      List<ScriptReference> scriptReferences)
    {
      if (this._scriptControls != null)
      {
        foreach (IScriptControl scriptControl in this._scriptControls.Keys)
        {
          IEnumerable<ScriptReference> enumerable1 =
                                      scriptControl.GetScriptReferences();
          if (enumerable1 != null)
          {
            using (IEnumerator<ScriptReference> enumerator1 =
                                            enumerable1.GetEnumerator())
            {
              while (enumerator1.MoveNext())
              {
```

(continued)

Listing 17-12 *(continued)*

```
                ScriptReference reference1 = enumerator1.Current;
                if (reference1 != null)
                {
                  reference1.ContainingControl = (Control)scriptControl;
                  reference1.IsStaticReference = false;
                  scriptReferences.Add(reference1);
                }
              }
            }
          }
        }
      }
    }
  }
}
private void AddScriptReferencesForExtenderControls(List<ScriptReference>
                                              scriptReferences)
{
  if (this._extenderControls != null)
  {
    foreach (IExtenderControl extenderControl in this._extenderControls.Keys)
    {
      IEnumerable<ScriptReference> enumerable1 =
                              extenderControl.GetScriptReferences();
      if (enumerable1 != null)
      {
        using (IEnumerator<ScriptReference> enumerator1 =
                                      enumerable1.GetEnumerator())
        {
          while (enumerator1.MoveNext())
          {
            ScriptReference reference1 = enumerator1.Current;
            if (reference1 != null)
            {
              reference1.IsStaticReference = false;
              reference1.ContainingControl = (Control)extenderControl;
              scriptReferences.Add(reference1);
            }
          }
        }
      }
    }
  }
}


public void RegisterScriptControl<TScriptControl>(TScriptControl scriptControl)
          where TScriptControl : Control, IScriptControl
{
  int num;
  this.ScriptControls.TryGetValue(scriptControl, out num);
  num++;
  this.ScriptControls[scriptControl] = num;
}
```

```
private Dictionary<IScriptControl, int> _scriptControls;
private Dictionary<IScriptControl, int> ScriptControls
{
  get
  {
    if (this._scriptControls == null)
      this._scriptControls = new Dictionary<IScriptControl, int>();

    return this._scriptControls;
  }
}

public void RegisterExtenderControl<TExtenderControl>(TExtenderControl
    extenderControl, Control targetControl) where TExtenderControl :
    Control, IExtenderControl
{
  List<Control> list;
  if (!this.ExtenderControls.TryGetValue(extenderControl, out list))
  {
    list = new List<Control>();
    this.ExtenderControls[extenderControl] = list;
  }
  list.Add(targetControl);
}

private Dictionary<IExtenderControl, List<Control>> _extenderControls;
private Dictionary<IExtenderControl, List<Control>> ExtenderControls
{
  get
  {
    if (this._extenderControls == null)
      this._extenderControls = new Dictionary<IExtenderControl,
                                      List<Control>>();

    return this._extenderControls;
  }
}

private bool _loadScriptsBeforeUI;

[Category("Behavior"), DefaultValue(true)]
public bool LoadScriptsBeforeUI
{
  get { return this._loadScriptsBeforeUI; }
  set { this._loadScriptsBeforeUI = value; }
}

public void RegisterScriptDescriptors(IExtenderControl extenderControl)
{
  List<Control> list;
  Control control = extenderControl as Control;
  if (!this.ExtenderControls.TryGetValue(extenderControl, out list))
    throw new ArgumentException("Extender Control Not Registered");
```

(continued)

Listing 17-12 (continued)

```
    foreach (Control control2 in list)
    {
      if (control2.Visible)
      {
        IEnumerable<ScriptDescriptor> scriptDescriptors =
                            extenderControl.GetScriptDescriptors(control2);
        if (scriptDescriptors != null)
        {
          StringBuilder builder = null;
          foreach (ScriptDescriptor descriptor in scriptDescriptors)
          {
            if (builder == null)
            {
              builder = new StringBuilder();
              builder.AppendLine("Sys.Application.add_init(function() {");
            }

            builder.Append(" ");
            builder.AppendLine(descriptor.GetScript());
            descriptor.RegisterDisposeForDescriptor(this, control);
          }

          if (builder != null)
          {
            builder.AppendLine("});");
            string key = builder.ToString();
            Page.ClientScript.RegisterStartupScript(typeof(ScriptManager),
                                              key, key, true);
          }
        }
      }
    }
  }

  public void RegisterScriptDescriptors(IScriptControl scriptControl)
  {
    int num;
    Control control = scriptControl as Control;
    if (!this.ScriptControls.TryGetValue(scriptControl, out num))
      throw new ArgumentException("Script Control Not Registered");

    for (int i = 0; i < num; i++)
    {
      IEnumerable<ScriptDescriptor> scriptDescriptors =
                                  scriptControl.GetScriptDescriptors();
      if (scriptDescriptors != null)
      {
        StringBuilder builder = null;
        foreach (ScriptDescriptor descriptor in scriptDescriptors)
        {
          if (builder == null)
          {
```

```
                  builder = new StringBuilder();
                  builder.AppendLine("Sys.Application.add_init(function() {");
              }

              builder.Append(" ");
              builder.AppendLine(descriptor.GetScript());
              descriptor.RegisterDisposeForDescriptor(this, control);
          }

          if (builder != null)
          {
              builder.AppendLine("});");
              string key = builder.ToString();
              Page.ClientScript.RegisterStartupScript(typeof(ScriptManager),
                                                      key, key, true);
          }
      }
   }
 }
}
```

Scripts

As you can see from Listing 17-12, the ScriptManager server control exposes a collection property of the type ScriptReferenceCollection named Scripts that contains the ScriptReference objects that reference JavaScript files. Note that this property is marked with the PersistenceMode(PersistenceMode.InnerProperty) metadata attribute to enable you to add ScriptReference objects to this collection in a purely declarative fashion, without writing a single line of imperative code.

LoadScriptsBeforeUI

As Listing 17-12 shows, the ScriptManager server control exposes a Boolean property named LoadScriptsBeforeUI that specifies whether the script files referenced by the ScriptReference objects in the Scripts collection must be loaded before the HTML markup text. The default is true. The decision as to whether to load the scripts before or after UI depends on whether the scripts contain any references to the UI elements. If they do, they must be loaded after UI to ensure that the UI elements that the scripts reference are already loaded. You'll see an example of this property later in this chapter.

ScriptControls

The replica ScriptManager server control maintains the list of all script server controls on the current page in an internal collection named ScriptControls (see Listing 17-12).

RegisterScriptControl

The RegisterScriptControl method of the ScriptManager server control adds the specified script server control to the ScriptControls collection discussed in the previous section (see Listing 17-12).

ExtenderControls

The replica ScriptManager server control also maintains the list of all extender server controls on the current page in an internal collection named ExtenderControls (see Listing 17-12).

RegisterExtenderControl

As you saw in the previous section, the ExtenderControls collection is a dictionary of items, each of which contains a list of server controls associated with a particular extender server control. The RegisterExtenderControl method takes two parameters, the first referencing the extender server control being registered and the second the server control whose client-side functionality the specified extender server control extends. Recall that this server control is known as the *target server control* of the extender server control. The RegisterExtenderControl simply accesses the item associated with the specified extender server control and adds the specified target server control to the associated server control list of this item. Recall also that each item in the ExtenderControls dictionary contains a list of server controls associated with a particular extender server control.

GetCurrent

As Listing 17-12 shows, the GetCurrent static method of the ScriptManager server control returns a reference to the current ScriptManager server control. Recall that the ScriptManager server control maintains this reference in the Items collection of the current Page object. This ensures that the same ScriptManager server control is used throughout the current request.

OnInit

As Listing 17-12 shows, the ScriptManager server control overrides the OnInit method that inherits from the Control base class. This method performs three tasks. First, it invokes the OnInit method of its base class to raise the Init event and consequently to invoke all the event handlers registered for the Init event of the current ScriptManager server control:

```
base.OnInit(e);
```

Next, it stores the reference to the current ScriptManager server control in the Items collection of the current Page object. As discussed earlier, the GetCurrent static method returns this reference to its caller to ensure that the same instance of the ScriptManager server control is used during processing of the current request.

```
Page.Items[typeof(ScriptManager)] = this;
```

Finally, the OnInit method registers a method named Page_PreRenderComplete as an event handler for the PreRenderComplete event of the current Page object:

```
this.Page.PreRenderComplete += new EventHandler(Page_PreRenderComplete);
```

Page_PreRenderComplete

When the current `Page` enters its `PreRenderComplete` phase, it automatically invokes the `Page_PreRenderComplete` method of the current `ScriptManager` server control shown in Listing 17-12. As you can see, this method first instantiates a `List<ScriptReference>` collection:

```
List<ScriptReference> list1 = new List<ScriptReference>();
```

Next, it invokes another method named `CollectScripts`, passing in the `List<ScriptReference>` collection to have this method to populate this collection with the list of `ScriptReference` objects that reference JavaScript files:

```
this.CollectScripts(list1);
```

Then it iterates through the `ScriptReference` objects in the `List<ScriptReference>` collection and performs these two tasks for each enumerated `ScriptReference` object. First, it instantiates a `ScriptReferenceEventArgs` instance, passing in a reference to the enumerated `ScriptReference` object. As you'll see later, the `ScriptReferenceEventArgs` is the event data class associated with an event named `ResolveScriptReference`. Next, it invokes a method named `OnResolveScriptReference`, passing in the `ScriptReferenceEventArgs` object to raise the `ResolveScriptReference` event. As you'll see later, this enables the page developer to register an event handler for this event whereby he or she can use custom code to resolve the reference to the JavaScript file specified by the enumerated `ScriptReference` object.

```
foreach (ScriptReference reference3 in list1)
{
    args = new ScriptReferenceEventArgs(reference3);
    this.OnResolveScriptReference(args);
}
```

Next, the `Page_PreRenderComplete` method iterates through the `ScriptReference` objects in the `List<ScriptReference>` collection once more and takes these steps for each enumerated `ScriptReference` object. It checks whether the `LoadScriptsBeforeUI` property is set to `true`. If so, this indicates that the page developer has requested the referenced JavaScript files to be loaded before the UI is loaded. As a result, the `Page_PreRenderComplete` method invokes the `RegisterClientScriptInclude` method on the `ClientScript` property of the current `Page` object to have the current page render the script block associated with the enumerated `ScriptReference` at the beginning of the current page. Note that the `src` attribute of this script block is set to the value of the `Path` property of the enumerated `ScriptReference` object because this property contains the URL of the JavaScript file that the object references.

```
foreach (ScriptReference reference4 in list1)
{
    string url = reference4.Path;
    if (this.LoadScriptsBeforeUI)
        this.Page.ClientScript.RegisterClientScriptInclude(typeof(ScriptManager),
                                                           url, url);
```

If the `LoadScriptBeforeUI` property is set to `false`, this indicates that the page developer wants the JavaScript file referenced by the enumerated `ScriptReference` object to be loaded after the UI. As a result, the `Page_PreRenderComplete` method first generates a string that contains a script include block whose `src` attribute is set to the value of the `Path` property of the enumerated `ScriptReference` object. Then it invokes the `RegisterStartupScript` method to have the current page render this string right before the closing tag of the form HTML element:

```
else
{
  string script = "\r\n<script src=\"" +
                HttpUtility.HtmlAttributeEncode(url) +
                "\" type=\"text/javascript\"></script>";
  this.Page.ClientScript.RegisterStartupScript(typeof(ScriptManager),
                                            url, script, false);

}
}
```

CollectScripts

As you saw in the previous section, the `Page_PreRenderComplete` method invokes the `CollectScripts` method of the current `ScriptManager` server control, passing in a `List<ScriptReference>` collection to that method to populate this collection with the list of all `ScriptReference` objects. In general, there are three groups of `ScriptReference` objects that the `CollectScripts` method needs to collect. The first group contains the `ScriptReference` objects that the page developers declaratively or imperatively add to the `Scripts` collection of the current `ScriptManager` server control. As a result, the `CollectScripts` method iterates through the `ScriptReference` objects in the `Scripts` collection and performs these tasks for each `ScriptReference` object. First it assigns the reference to the current `ScriptManager` server control as the `ContainingControl` property of the `ScriptReference` object:

```
reference1.ContainingControl = this;
```

Next, it sets the `IsStaticReference` property of the `ScriptReference` object to `true` to signal that this `ScriptReference` object was defined statically by the page developer:

```
reference1.IsStaticReference = true;
```

Finally, it adds the `ScriptReference` object to the `List<ScriptReference>` collection passed into the `CollectScripts` method:

```
scripts.Add(reference1);
```

The second group of `ScriptReference` objects includes the `ScriptReference` objects of the script server controls on the current page. Next, the `CollectScripts` method invokes another method named `AddScriptReferencesForScriptControls`, passing in the `List<ScriptReference>` collection to have this method add the `ScriptReference` objects in the second group to this collection:

```
this.AddScriptReferencesForScriptControls(scripts);
```

The third group of `ScriptReference` objects includes the `ScriptReference` objects of the extender server controls on the current page. Next, the `CollectScripts` method invokes another method named `AddScriptReferencesForExtenderControls`, passing in the `List<ScriptReference>` collection to have this method add the `ScriptReference` objects in the third group to this collection:

```
this.AddScriptReferencesForExtenderControls(scripts);
```

As you can see, when the `CollectScripts` method finally returns, the `List<ScriptReference>` collection passed into it is populated with `ScriptReference` objects defined for the current page.

AddScriptReferencesForScriptControls

As you saw earlier, the `CollectScripts` method invokes the `AddScriptReferencesForScriptControls` method, passing in a `List<ScriptReference>` collection to have this method to add the `ScriptReference` objects of all the script server controls on the current page to this collection. Recall that the current `ScriptManager` server control maintains references of all script server controls on the current page in an internal collection of type `Dictionary<IScriptControl, int>` named `ScriptControls`. This dictionary exposes a collection property named `Keys` that contains the actual references to all the script server controls on the current page. Keep in mind that all script server controls implement the `IScriptControl` interface.

As you can see from Listing 17-12, this method iterates through the script server controls in the `Keys` collection of this collection and takes these steps for each script server control to collect its `ScriptReference` objects. First, it invokes the `GetScriptReferences` method on the script server control to return an `IEnumerable<ScriptReference>` collection that contains all the `ScriptReference` objects associated with the script server control.

```
IEnumerable<ScriptReference> enumerable1 = scriptControl.GetScriptReferences();
```

Next, it calls the `GetEnumerator` method on this `IEnumerable<ScriptReference>` collection to return a reference to the `IEnumerator<ScriptReference>` object that knows how to iterate through the items of this collection in a generic fashion:

```
IEnumerator<ScriptReference> enumerator1 = enumerable1.GetEnumerator()
```

Next, it uses this `IEnumerator<ScriptReference>` object to iterate through the `ScriptReference` objects in this collection and performs these steps for each enumerated `ScriptReference` object. First, it assigns a reference to the script server control to the `ContainingControl` property of the enumerated `ScriptReference` object:

```
reference1.ContainingControl = (Control)scriptControl;
```

Next, it sets the `IsStaticReference` property of the `ScriptReference` object to `false` to indicate that the enumerated `ScriptReference` object is not one of those `ScriptReference` objects that the page developer has statically added to the `Scripts` collection of the `ScriptManager` server control:

```
reference1.IsStaticReference = false;
```

Finally, it adds the enumerated `ScriptReference` object to the `List<ScriptReference>` collection passed into the method:

```
scriptReferences.Add(reference1);
```

As you can see, by the time the `AddScriptReferencesForScriptControls` method returns, all the `ScriptReference` objects of all the script server controls on the current page have been added to the `List<ScriptReference>` collection passed into the method.

RegisterScriptDescriptors For Extender Controls

The `ScriptManager` exposes a public method named `RegisterScriptDescriptors` that you can use from your server-side code to add `ScriptDescriptor` objects for your extender server control. As Listing 17-12 shows, this method begins by checking whether the `ExtenderControls` collection of the current `ScriptManager` server control contains the specified extender server control. Recall from previous sections that you must invoke the `RegisterExtenderControl` method on the current `ScriptManager` server control to add your extender server control to the `ExtenderControls` collection. Note that if the `ExtenderControls` collection does not contain the specified extender server control, the `RegisterScriptDescriptors` method raises an exception and does not allow you to add `ScriptDescriptors` for your extender server control:

```
if (!this.ExtenderControls.TryGetValue(extenderControl, out list))
    throw new ArgumentException("Extender Control Not Registered");
```

You must invoke the `RegisterExtenderControl` method on the current `ScriptManager` server control to register your extender server control with the current `ScriptManager` server control before you can register any `ScriptDescriptor` objects for your extender server control. You do not have to worry about this issue if you're deriving your extender server control from the `ExtenderControl` base class. As Listing 17-2 shows, the `ExtenderControl` base class invokes the `RegisterExtenderControl` method when it enters its `PreRender` life-cycle phase and the `RegisterScriptDescriptors` method when it enters its `Render` life-cycle phase.

Since the `PreRender` life-cycle phase always occurs before the `Render` life-cycle phase, the `RegisterExtenderControl` method is always invoked before the `RegisterScriptDescriptors` method.

The `RegisterScriptDescriptors` method then calls the `GetScriptDescriptors` method on the specified extender server control, passing in the reference to the target server control to return an `IEnumerable<ScriptDescriptor>` collection that contains all the `ScriptDescriptor` objects associated with this extender server control:

```
IEnumerable<ScriptDescriptor> scriptDescriptors =
                    extenderControl.GetScriptDescriptors(control2);
```

Next, it instantiates a `StringBuilder` and adds the following string to it. As you can see, this string contains a client script that invokes the `add_init` method on the `Application` object that represents the current ASP.NET AJAX application, in order to register the JavaScript function being defined as an event handler for the `init` event of the `Application` object. As you'll see shortly, the rest of the `RegisterScriptDescriptors` method will define the rest of this JavaScript function. In other words, this method is generating the script code that both defines this JavaScript function and registers it as an event handler for the `init` event.

```
"Sys.Application.add_init(function() {"
```

Next, the `RegisterScriptDescriptors` method iterates through the `ScriptDescriptor` objects in the previously mentioned `IEnumerable<ScriptDescriptor>` collection and takes these two steps for each enumerated `ScriptDescriptor` object. First, it calls the `GetScript` method on the enumerated `ScriptDescriptor` object to return a string that contains the client script being registered and adds this string to the `StringBuilder`:

```
builder.AppendLine(descriptor.GetScript());
```

When the `RegisterScriptDescriptors` method gets out of the loop, it invokes the `RegisterStartupScript` method to have the current page to render the content of the `StringBuilder` right before the closing tag of the form element. Recall that the content of the `StringBuilder` is a string that defines and registers a JavaScript function as event handler for the `init` event of the client-side `Application` object.

```
if (builder != null)
{
  builder.AppendLine("});");
  string key = builder.ToString();
  Page.ClientScript.RegisterStartupScript(typeof(ScriptManager),
                                          key, key, true);
}
```

As you can see, by the time the `RegisterScriptDescriptors` method returns, all the `ScriptDescriptor` objects associated with the specified extender server control are registered.

ResolveScriptReference Event

Recall from Listing 17-12 that the current `ScriptManager` server control registers its `Page_PreRenderComplete` method as an event handler for the `PreRenderComplete` event of the current page. When the current page enters its `PreRenderComplete` phase, it automatically invokes the `Page_PreRenderComplete` method. As you saw earlier (and will also see in the following code fragment), this method first invokes the `CollectScripts` method to collect all `ScriptReference` objects in a `List<ScriptReference>` collection. Next, it iterates through the `ScriptReference` objects in this collection and takes the following two steps for each enumerated `ScriptReference` object. First, it instantiates a `ScriptReferenceEventArgs` object, passing in the enumerated `ScriptReference` object. Then it invokes the `OnResolveScriptReference` method, passing in this `ScriptReferenceEventArgs` object to raise the `ResolveScriptReference` event for the enumerated `ScriptReference` object. As you can see, the current `ScriptManager` server control raises its `ResolveScriptReference` event once for each `ScriptReference` object. The page developer can register an event handler for this event in order to be notified when this event is raised. As you can see from the highlighted portions of the following code listing, the current `ScriptManager` server control raises its `ResolveScriptReference` event before it invokes the `RegisterClientScriptInclude` or `RegisterStartupScript` method to have the current page render the associated script block. This allows the event handlers registered for this event to make any required updates to each `ScriptReference` object before their associated script blocks are rendered to the current page.

```
void Page_PreRenderComplete(object sender, EventArgs e)
{
  List<ScriptReference> list1 = new List<ScriptReference>();
  this.CollectScripts(list1);

  ScriptReferenceEventArgs args;
  foreach (ScriptReference reference3 in list1)
  {
    args = new ScriptReferenceEventArgs(reference3);
    this.OnResolveScriptReference(args);
  }

  foreach (ScriptReference reference4 in list1)
  {
    string url = reference4.Path;
    if (this.LoadScriptsBeforeUI)

      this.Page.ClientScript.RegisterClientScriptInclude(typeof(ScriptManager),
                                                         url, url);

    else
    {
      string script = "\r\n<script src=\"" +
                      HttpUtility.HtmlAttributeEncode(url) +
                      "\" type=\"text/javascript\"></script>";

      this.Page.ClientScript.RegisterStartupScript(typeof(ScriptManager),
                                                   url, script, false);

    }
  }
}
```

The `ScriptManager` server control follows the typical .NET event implementation pattern to implement its `ResolveScriptReference` event:

❑ It defines an event data class named `ScriptReferenceEventArgs` to hold the event data for this event. Listing 17-13 presents the implementation of this event data class. As you can see from this code listing, the constructor of this event data class takes a single argument of type `ScriptReference` and stores it in a private field named `_script`. Note that the class exposes a single read-only property named `Script` that returns the value of this private field.

❑ It defines an event property as follows:

```
public event EventHandler<ScriptReferenceEventArgs> ResolveScriptReference
{
  add
  {
    base.Events.AddHandler(ResolveScriptReferenceEvent, value);
  }
  remove
  {
    base.Events.RemoveHandler(ResolveScriptReferenceEvent, value);
  }
}
```

❑   It defines a private static read-only object that will be used as a key to the `Events` collection that the `ScriptManager` server control inherits from the `Control` base class in order to add an event handler to and remove an event handler from this collection:

```
private static readonly object ResolveScriptReferenceEvent = new object();
```

❑   It defines a protected virtual method named `OnResolveReference` that raises the following event:

```
protected virtual void OnResolveScriptReference(ScriptReferenceEventArgs e)
{
  EventHandler<ScriptReferenceEventArgs> handler =
          (EventHandler<ScriptReferenceEventArgs>)
                                    base.Events[ResolveScriptReferenceEvent];
  if (handler != null)
    handler(this, e);
}
```

❑   Note that the `OnResolveScriptReference` method passes the `ScriptReferenceEventArgs` object into the event handlers registered for this event. Recall that this object exposes a read-only property named `Script` that returns a reference to the `ScriptReference` object for which the event was raised in the first place. This means that the event handler registered for this event can use this property to access the `ScriptReference` object to change the properties of this object. For example, this enables you to dynamically specify the value of the `Path` or `Assembly` property of the `ScriptReference` object instead of statically setting them in the `.aspx` page.

Listing 17-13: The ScriptReferenceEventArgs Event Data Class

```
using System;

namespace CustomComponents3
{
  public class ScriptReferenceEventArgs : EventArgs
  {
    private readonly ScriptReference _script;

    public ScriptReferenceEventArgs(ScriptReference script)
    {
      if (script == null)
        throw new ArgumentNullException("script");

      this._script = script;
    }

    public ScriptReference Script
    {
      get { return this._script; }
    }
  }
}
```

Putting it All Together

The next chapter will show you how to implement custom extender and script server controls and will implement pages that use these custom controls. Since we would like to put the replica components that we developed in the previous sections to the test and run our custom server controls in the context of these replicas, you need to set up a Web application that uses these replicas. Follow these steps to accomplish this task:

1. Create an AJAX-enabled Web site in Visual Studio.

2. Add an App_Code directory to this Web site.

3. Add a new source file named IExtenderControl.cs to the App_Code directory and add the code shown in Listing 17-1 to this source file.

4. Add a new source file named ExtenderControl.cs to the App_Code directory and add the code shown in Listing 17-2 to this source file.

5. Add a new source file named IScriptControl.cs to the App_Code directory and add the code shown in Listing 17-3 to this source file.

6. Add a new source file named ScriptControl.cs to the App_Code directory and add the code shown in Listing 17-4 to this source file.

7. Add a new source file named ScriptDescriptor.cs to the App_Code directory and add the code shown in Listing 17-5 to this source file.

8. Add a new source file named ScriptComponentDescriptor.cs to the App_Code directory and add the code shown in Listing 17-6 to this source file.

9. Add a new source file named HelperMethods.cs to the App_Code directory and add the code shown in Listing 17-7 to this source file.

10. Add a new source file named ScriptControlDescriptor.cs to the App_Code directory and add the code shown in Listing 17-8 to this source file.

11. Add a new source file named ScriptBehaviorDescriptor.cs to the App_Code directory and add the code shown in Listing 17-9 to this source file.

12. Add a new source file named ScriptReference.cs to the App_Code directory and add the code shown in Listing 17-10 to this source file.

13. Add a new source file named ScriptReferenceCollection.cs to the App_Code directory and add the code shown in Listing 17-11 to this source file.

14. Add a new source file named ScriptManager.cs to the App_Code directory and add the code shown in Listing 17-12 to this source file.

15. Add a new source file named ScriptReferenceEventArgs.cs to the App_Code directory and add the code shown in Listing 17-13 to this source file.

Developing a Custom Extender Server Control

In this section, I'll implement a custom extender server control named `TextBoxWatermarkExtenderControl` to help you gain the skills that you need to develop your own custom extender server controls. Listing 17-15 presents the implementation of the `TextBoxWatermarkExtenderControl` server control.

Recall that Chapter 16 developed an ASP.NET AJAX behavior named `TextBoxWatermarkBehavior`. When this behavior is attached to a textbox DOM element, it extends the functionality of the DOM element to add support for watermark capability. As discussed earlier in this chaper, the page that uses the `TextBoxWatermarkBehavior` must take the steps shown in boldfaced portions of the following code listing:

Listing 17-14: A Page that Uses the TextBoxWatermarkBehavior

```
<%@ Page Language="C#" %>
. . .
<html xmlns="http://www.w3.org/1999/xhtml">
<head runat="server">
  <title>Untitled Page</title>
  . . .
  <script type="text/javascript" language="javascript">
    var textBoxWatermarkBehavior;

    function submitCallback()
    {
      textBoxWatermarkBehavior._onSubmit();
    }

    function pageLoad()
    {
      var properties = [];
      properties["name"] = "MyTextBoxWatermarkBehaviorName";
      properties["id"] = "MyTextBoxWatermarkBehaviorID";
      properties["WatermarkText"] = "Enter text here";
      properties["WatermarkCssClass"] = "WatermarkCssClass";

      var textBox1 = $get("TextBox1");
      textBoxWatermarkBehavior =
              $create(AjaxControlToolkit.TextBoxWatermarkBehavior, properties,
                      null, null, textBox1);
    }
  </script>
</head>
<body>
  <form id="form1" runat="server" onsubmit="submitCallback()">
    <asp:ScriptManager runat="server" ID="ScriptManager1">
      <Scripts>
        <asp:ScriptReference Path="BehaviorBase.js" />
        <asp:ScriptReference Path="TextBoxWatermarkBehavior.js" />
      </Scripts>
```

(continued)

Listing 17-14 *(continued)*

```
            </asp:ScriptManager>
            . . .
        </form>
    </body>
</html>
```

The `TextBoxWatermarkExtenderControl` server control encapsulates the logic that the boldfaced portions of Listing 17-14 implement and presents page developers with an object-oriented ASP.NET based API that allows them to use the same imperative and declarative ASP.NET techniques to program against the underlying `TextBoxwatermark` behavior. I'll discuss the implementation of the methods and properties of the `TextBoxWatermarkExtenderControl` server control, shown in Listing 17-15, in the following sections.

Listing 17-15: The TextBoxWatermarkExtenderControl

```csharp
using System;
using System.ComponentModel;
using System.Collections.Generic;
using System.Globalization;
using System.Text;
using System.Web;
using System.Web.UI;
using System.Web.UI.WebControls;

namespace CustomComponents3
{
    [TargetControlType(typeof(IEditableTextControl))]
    public class TextBoxWatermarkExtenderControl : ExtenderControl
    {
        protected override IEnumerable<ScriptReference> GetScriptReferences()
        {
            ScriptReference reference1 = new ScriptReference();
            reference1.Path = ResolveClientUrl("BehaviorBase.js");

            ScriptReference reference2 = new ScriptReference();
            reference2.Path = ResolveClientUrl("TextBoxWatermarkBehavior.js");

            return new ScriptReference[] { reference1, reference2 };
        }

        protected override IEnumerable<ScriptDescriptor> GetScriptDescriptors(
                                                    Control targetControl)
        {
            ScriptBehaviorDescriptor descriptor =
                new ScriptBehaviorDescriptor("AjaxControlToolkit.TextBoxWatermarkBehavior",
                                    targetControl.ClientID);
            descriptor.AddProperty("WatermarkText", this.WatermarkText);
            descriptor.AddProperty("WatermarkCssClass", this.WatermarkCssClass);
            descriptor.AddProperty("id", this.BehaviorID);
```

```
      return new ScriptDescriptor[] { descriptor };
    }

    private string _clientState;
    [Browsable(false)]

    [DesignerSerializationVisibility(DesignerSerializationVisibility.Hidden)]
    public string ClientState
    {
      get { return _clientState; }
      set { _clientState = value; }
    }

    public string BehaviorID
    {
      get
      {
        return ViewState["BehaviorID"] != null ?
                              (string)ViewState["BehaviorID"] : ClientID;
      }
      set
      {
        ViewState["BehaviorID"] = value;
      }
    }

    protected override void OnPreRender(EventArgs e)
    {
      base.OnPreRender(e);
      Control targetControl = base.FindControl(TargetControlID);
      Control nc = NamingContainer;
      while ((targetControl == null) && (nc != null))
      {
        targetControl = nc.FindControl(TargetControlID);
        nc = nc.NamingContainer;
      }

      if (targetControl.Visible)
      {
        HiddenField hiddenField = null;

        if (string.IsNullOrEmpty(ClientStateFieldID))
          hiddenField = CreateClientStateField();

        else
          hiddenField =
                    (HiddenField)NamingContainer.FindControl(ClientStateFieldID);

        if (hiddenField != null)
          hiddenField.Value = ClientState;
      }
    }
```

(continued)

Listing 17-15 *(continued)*

```csharp
private HiddenField CreateClientStateField()
{
  HiddenField field = new HiddenField();
  field.ID = string.Format(CultureInfo.InvariantCulture,
                           "{0}_ClientState", ID);
  Controls.Add(field);
  ClientStateFieldID = field.ID;
  return field;
}

protected override void Render(HtmlTextWriter writer)
{
  if (Page != null)
    Page.VerifyRenderingInServerForm(this);
  base.Render(writer);
}

protected override void OnInit(EventArgs e)
{
  CreateClientStateField();
  Page.PreLoad += new EventHandler(Page_PreLoad);
  base.OnInit(e);
}

void Page_PreLoad(object sender, EventArgs e)
{
  if (!string.IsNullOrEmpty(ClientStateFieldID))
  {
    HiddenField hiddenField =
                (HiddenField)NamingContainer.FindControl(ClientStateFieldID);

    if ((hiddenField != null) && !string.IsNullOrEmpty(hiddenField.Value))
      ClientState = hiddenField.Value;
  }
}

[Browsable(false)]
[EditorBrowsable(EditorBrowsableState.Never)]
[IDReferenceProperty(typeof(HiddenField))]
[DefaultValue("")]
[DesignerSerializationVisibility(DesignerSerializationVisibility.Hidden)]
public string ClientStateFieldID
{
  get { return ViewState["ClientStateFieldID"] != null ?
                      (string)ViewState["ClientStateFieldID"] : string.Empty; }
  set { ViewState["ClientStateFieldID"] = value; }
}

protected override void OnLoad(EventArgs e)
{
  base.OnLoad(e);
```

```
      string key;
      string script;

      key = string.Format(CultureInfo.InvariantCulture, "{0}_onSubmit", ID);
      script = string.Format(CultureInfo.InvariantCulture, "var o = $find('{0}');
                                    if(o) {{ o._onSubmit(); }}", BehaviorID);
      System.Web.UI.ScriptManager.RegisterOnSubmitStatement(this,
                            typeof(TextBoxWatermarkExtenderControl), key, script);

      ClientState = (string.Compare(Page.Form.DefaultFocus, TargetControlID,
            StringComparison.InvariantCultureIgnoreCase) == 0) ? "Focused" : null;
    }

    private string watermarkText;
    [DefaultValue("")]
    public string WatermarkText
    {
      get { return this.watermarkText; }
      set { this.watermarkText = value; }
    }

    private string watermarkCssClass;
    [DefaultValue("")]
    public string WatermarkCssClass
    {
      get { return this.watermarkCssClass; }
      set { this.watermarkCssClass = value; }
    }
  }
}
```

WatermarkText

The `TextBoxWatermarkExtenderControl` server control exposes a string property named
`WatermarkText` that you can use to get and set the watermark text. This is the text that will be
shown to the end user when the associated text box is empty and does not have the mouse focus.

WatermarkCssClass

As the name suggests, you can use the `WatermarkCssClass` to get and to set the watermark style. This
is the style that will be automatically applied to the associated text box when the text box is empty and
does not have the focus.

ClientState

The `ClientState` property of the `TextBoxWatermarkExtenderControl` server control gets and sets
the client state of the underlying `TextBoxWatermarkBehavior`. Recall that the the client state of this
behavior is a string that specifies whether the associated textbox DOM element has the focus.

ClientStateFieldID

The `ClientStateFieldID` property gets and sets the `ID` attribute HTML value of the hidden field that stores the client state of the underlying `TextBoxWatermarkBehavior`. As you'll see shortly, the server and client side code use this hidden field to communicate the client state.

CreateClientStateField

The `CreateClientStateField` method of the `TextBoxWatermarkExtenderControl` creates the hidden field where the client state of the underlying `TextBoxWatermarkBehavior` is stored.

BehaviorID

The `BehaviorID` property gets and sets the `id` of the underlying `TextBoxWatermarkBehavior`. Recall that the `id` of an ASP.NET AJAX component such as a behavior uniquely identifies the component among other components in the current ASP.NET AJAX application.

GetScriptReferences

The `TextBoxWatermarkExtenderServer` control overrides the `GetScriptReferences` method that it inherits from its base class, that is, the `ExtenderControl` base class. First, it creates a `ScriptReference` object. Then, it sets the `Path` property of this object to the URL of the JavaScript file that contains the definition of the `BehaviorBase` class. Next, it creates another `ScriptReference` object and sets its `Path` property to the URL of the `JavaScript` file that contains the definition of the `TextBoxWatermarkBehavior` class. You need to copy over the `BehaviorBase.js` and `TextBoxWatermarkBehavior.js` files from Chapter 16 to include them in this `Website`. Finally, the `GetScriptReferences` method instantiates and returns an array that contains these two `ScriptReference` objects.

GetScriptDescriptors

The `TextBoxWatermarkExtenderControl` overrides the `GetScriptDescriptors` method that it inherits from the `ExtenderControl` base class to instantiate and return the `ScriptDescriptor` object that instantiates and initializes the `TextBoxWatermarkBehavior`. As you can see from Listing 17-15, this method begins by creating a `ScriptBehaviorDescriptor` object, passing in two parameters. The first parameter is a string that contains the fully qualified name of the `TextBoxWatermarkBehavior`, including its namespace. The second parameter is the `ClientID` property value of the target server control. Recall that the target server control of an extender server control is the server control whose client side functionality the extender server control is extending, which is an ASP.NET `TextBox` server control in this case.

```
ScriptBehaviorDescriptor descriptor =
        new ScriptBehaviorDescriptor("AjaxControlToolkit.TextBoxWatermarkBehavior",
                                targetControl.ClientID);
```

Next, I digress from our discussion of the implementation of the `GetScriptDescriptors` method to use the discussions of the previous sections to show you what happens to the `AjaxControlToolkit` `.TextBoxWatermarkBehavior` and `targetControl.ClientID` parameters passed into the `ScriptBehaviorDescriptor` constructor.

Every server control renders its `ClientID` property value as the value of the `id` HTML attribute of its containing DOM element. In this case, the ASP.NET `TextBox` server control renders its `ClientID` property value as the value of the `id` HTML attribute of its containing `<input type="text"/>` DOM element. Recall from Listing 17-8 that the constructor of the `ScriptBehaviorDescriptor` passes its parameters to the internal constructor of its base class, that is, that `ScriptComponentDescriptor`, which means that the `AjaxControlToolkit.TextBoxWatermarkBehavior` and `targetControl.ClientID` parameters are passed into the constructor of the `ScriptComponentDescriptor`:

```
public ScriptBehaviorDescriptor(string type, string elementID)
  : base(type, elementID)
{
  base.RegisterDispose = false;
}
```

Now, recall from Listing 17-6 that the constructor of the `ScriptComponentDescriptor` stores the `AjaxControlToolkit.TextBoxWatermarkBehavior` and `targetControl.ClientID` parameters in `_type` and `_elementIDInternal` private fields:

```
public ScriptComponentDescriptor(string type)
{
  this._registerDispose = true;
  this._type = type;
}

internal ScriptComponentDescriptor(string type, string elementID) : this(type)
{
  this._elementIDInternal = elementID;
}
```

Now, recall from Listing 17-6 (shown again in the following code listing) that the `GetScript` method of the `ScriptComponentDescriptor` generates the script that makes the call into the `$create` global JavaScript function to create an instance of the `TextBoxWatermarkBehavior` behavior. As you can see from the bold faced portions of the following code listing, the `GetScript` method passes the value of the `Type` property of the `ScriptComponentDescriptor` as the first parameter of the `$create` global function. This property simply returns the value of the `_type` private field, that is, the string `AjaxControlToolkit.TextBoxWatermarkBehavior`. As the boldfaced portion of the following code fragment shows, the `GetScript` method passes the value of the `ElementIDInternal` property into the `$get` JavaScript function, which is then passed into the `$create` function as its last argument. This property simply returns the value of the `_elementIDInternal` private field, that is, the value of the `targetControl.ClientID` property.

```
protected internal override string GetScript()
{
    . . .
    builder.Append("$create(");
    builder.Append(this.Type);
    . . .
    if (this.ElementIDInternal != null)
    {
        builder.Append(", ");
        builder.Append("$get(\"");
        builder.Append(HelperMethods.QuoteString(
                                    this.ElementIDInternal));
        builder.Append("\")");
    }
    . . .
}
```

Now back to the implementation of the GetScriptDescriptors method. Next, this method invokes the AddProperty method on the newly-instantiated ScriptBehaviorDescriptor object to specify the value of the WatermarkText property of the TextBoxWatermarkExtenderControl as the value of the WatermarkText property of the underlying TextBoxWatermarkBehavior:

```
descriptor.AddProperty("WatermarkText", this.WatermarkText);
```

Next, the GetScriptDescriptors method invokes the AddProperty method once again to specify the value of the WatermarkCssClass property of the TextBoxWatermarkExtenderControl as the value of the WatermarkCssClass property of the underlying TextBoxWatermarkBehavior:

```
descriptor.AddProperty("WatermarkCssClass", this.WatermarkCssClass);
```

Then, it invokes the AddProperty method once more to specify the value of the BehaviorID property of the TextBoxWatermarkExtenderControl as the value of the id property of the underlying TextBoxWatermarkBehavior:

```
descriptor.AddProperty("id", this.BehaviorID);
```

Finally, it instantiates and returns an array that contains the above ScriptBehaviorDescriptor object:

```
return new ScriptDescriptor[] { descriptor };
```

OnInit

The TextBoxWatermarkExtenderControl server control overrides the OnInit method that it inherits from the Control base class where it performs these tasks (see Listing 17-15). First, it invokes the CreateClientStateField method to create the hidden field where the client state will be stored as discussed earlier:

```
CreateClientStateField();
```

Next, it registers a method named Page_PreLoad as an event handler for the PreLoad event of the current page:

```
Page.PreLoad += new EventHandler(Page_PreLoad);
```

Finally it invokes the OnInit method of its base class:

```
base.OnInit(e);
```

> *Your extender server control's implementation of the methods of any of its base classes such as* ExtenderControl *and* Control *must always invoke the associated method of its base classes unless you have a very good reason to skip the calls into these base methods.*

Page_PreLoad

As you saw in Listing 17-15, the OnInit method registers the Page_PreLoad method as an event handler for the PreLoad event of the containing page. When the current page enters its PreLoad lifecycle phase, it automatically invokes the Page_PreLoad method. The main responsibility of this method is to set the value of the ClientState property. As you can see from Listing 17-15, this method first invokes the FindControl method on the naming container of the TextBoxWatermarkExtenderControl server control passing in the value of the ClientStateFieldID property to return a reference to the hidden field that contains the client state. Finally, the Page_PreLoad method extracts the client state from this hidden field and assigns it to the ClientState property.

> *Every server control including the* TextBoxWatermarkExtenderControl, *inherits the* NamingContainer *property from the* Control *base class. The* NamingContainer *property of a server control such as* TextBoxWatermarkExtenderControl *references the first ancestor of the server control that implements the* INamingContainer *interface. This interface is a marker interface and does not contain any methods, properties, and events. Implementing this interface allows a server control to act as a naming scope or container for its descendant server controls.*

OnLoad

As you can see from Listing 17-15, the TextBoxWatermarkExtenderControl server control overrides the OnLoad method of its base class to perform the following tasks. First, it invokes the OnLoad method of its base class to raise the Load event and consequently to invoke all the event handlers registered for the Load event of the TextBoxWatermarkExtenderControl:

```
base.OnLoad(e);
```

To understand what the rest of the code in the OnLoad method does, you need to revisit Listing 17-14 as repeated in Listing 17-16. Recall that this code listing contains a page that directly uses the TextBoxWatermarkBehavior. As the boldfaced portion of this code listing shows, this page registers a JavaScript function named submitCallback as event handler for the submit event of the form DOM element. When the end user clicks the Submit button to submit this form, the form automatically invokes the submitCallback function before the actual form submission takes place. As you can see from the boldfaced portion of Listing 17-16, the submitCallback method in turn invokes the _onSubmit method on the TextBoxWatermarkBehavior.

Recall from Listing 16-40 (repeated in the following code listing) that the _onSubmit method of the TextBoxWatermarkBehavior calls the clearText method to remove the watermark text from the text box before the form is submitted. This ensures that the form submission does not contain the watermark text.

```
function AjaxControlToolkit$TextBoxWatermarkBehavior$_onSubmit()
{
  if(this._watermarked)
  {
    this.clearText(false);
    this._clearedForSubmit = true;
  }
}
```

Now back to the implementation of the OnLoad method of the TextBoxWatermarkExtenderControl. The main objective of this method is to render the script that registers the _onSubmit method of the underlying TextBoxWatermarkBehavior as event handler for the submit event of the form DOM element. The OnLoad method takes these steps to achieve this objective. First, it generates the script that makes a call into the $find global JavaScript function to return a reference to the underlying TextBoxWatermarkBehavior. Note that this script passes the value of the BehaviorID property of the TextBoxWatermarkExtenderControl server control as the argument of the $find function. Next, the OnLoad method generates the script that invokes the _onSubmit method on the TextBoxWatermarkBehavior. For example, if the BehaviorID property of the TextBoxWatermarkExtenderControl is set to the string value of MyTextBoxWatermarkBehavior, the OnLoad method will generate the following script:

```
var o = $find ('MyTextBoxWatermarkBehavior');
if (o)
  o._onSubmit();
```

Next, the OnLoad method invokes the RegisterOnSubmitStatement static method on the ScriptManager class to have the current page to render the script into the page being sent to the client:

```
System.Web.UI.ScriptManager.RegisterOnSubmitStatement(this,
                    typeof(TextBoxWatermarkExtenderControl), key, script);
```

Finally, the OnLoad method determines whether the target server control of the TextBoxWatermarkExtenderControl server control has the focus. If so, it assigns the string value Focused to the ClientState property:

```
ClientState = (string.Compare(Page.Form.DefaultFocus, TargetControlID,
            StringComparison.InvariantCultureIgnoreCase) == 0) ? "Focused" : null;
```

As you'll see later, the TextBoxWatermarkExtenderControl server control will store this value of the ClientState property into the client state hidden field before the response is sent back to the client. This will allow the TextBoxWatermarkBehavior to retrieve the client state from this hidden field to determine whether the target server control has the focus. If the target server control does not have the focus, the TextBoxWatermarkBehavior displays the watermark text to the end user and applies the watermark CSS class to the text box.

Listing 17-16: A Page that Directly Uses the TextBoxWatermarkBehavior

```
<%@ Page Language="C#" %>
. . .
<html xmlns="http://www.w3.org/1999/xhtml">
<head runat="server">
  . . .
  <script type="text/javascript" language="javascript">
    . . .
    function submitCallback()
    {
      textBoxWatermarkBehavior._onSubmit();
    }
    . . .
  </script>
</head>
<body>
  <form id="form1" runat="server" onsubmit="submitCallback()">
    . . .
  </form>
</body>
</html>
```

OnPreRender

The `TextBoxWatermarkExtenderControl` server control overrides the `OnPreRender` method as shown in Listing 17-15. This method begins by invoking the `OnPreRender` method of its base class to raise the `PreRender` event and consequently to invoke all the event handlers registered for the `PreRender` event of the `TextBoxWatermarkExtenderControl` server control:

```
base.OnPreRender(e);
```

Next, it invokes the `FindControl` method, passing in the value of the `TargetControlID` property to return a reference to the target server control of the `TextBoxWatermarkExtenderControl`. Recall that the target server control of an extender server control is a server control whose client-side function-ality the extender server control extends, which is the ASP.NET `TextBox` server control in this case:

```
Control targetControl = base.FindControl(TargetControlID);
```

If the `FindControl` method returns null, the `OnPreRender` method invokes the `FindControl` method on the naming container of the `TextBoxWatermarkExtenderControl`, passing in the value of the `TargetControlID` property to return a reference to the target server control. The `OnPreRender` method keeps repeating this process until it reaches the first naming container in the naming container hierarchy of the `TextBoxWatermarkExtenderControl` whose `FindControl` method returns a non-null value, that is, until it finally accesses the reference to the target server control. Repeating this process is necessary because the `FindControl` method only searches the server controls in the current naming container.

```
Control targetControl = base.FindControl(TargetControlID);
Control nc = NamingContainer;
while ((targetControl == null) && (nc != null))
{
  targetControl = nc.FindControl(TargetControlID);
  nc = nc.NamingContainer;
}
```

You may be wondering how the target server control of the `TextBoxWatermarkExtenderControl` server control (the `TextBox` server control) is not in the same naming container as the `TextBoxWatermarkExtenderControl` server control. The answer lies in the fact that the `TextBox` server control could be a child control of a composite server control that implements the `INamingContainer` interface. Since the logic discussed in the code listing repeats the call into the `FindControl` method until it locates the naming container that contains the target server control, you can rest assured that the target server control will eventually be located.

Next, the `OnPreRender` method invokes the `FindControl` method on the naming container of the `TextBoxWatermarkExtenderControl` server control, passing in the value of the `ClientStateFieldID` property to return a reference to the hidden field where the client state must be stored:

```
hiddenField = (HiddenField)NamingContainer.FindControl(ClientStateFieldID);
```

You may be wondering why this time around we're not searching through all the ancestor naming containers of the `TextBoxWatermarkExtenderControl` server control. This is because the `CreateClientStateField` method creates and adds the hidden field in the naming container of the `TextBoxWatermarkExtenderControl` server control. In other words, we're one hundred percent sure that this hidden field is in the naming container of the `TextBoxWatermarkExtenderControl` server control. If it is not in this naming container, it simply has not been created yet. That is why the `OnPreRender` method invokes the `CreateClientStateField` method when the current naming container does not include the specified hidden field to create the hidden field.

This is one of the features of the `FindControl` method that you must take into account when you're using this method in your own code to locate a server control. The `FindControl` method is designed to search only through the server controls in the current naming container. It does not search through the server controls in other naming containers. The `FindControl` method is designed this way on purpose to allow you to limit the search to the current naming container and consequently improve the performance of your application. If you know for a fact that the control that you're looking for belongs to a specific naming container, you must invoke the `FindControl` method on that naming container to limit the search to that naming container.

Finally, the `OnPreRender` method stores the value of the `ClientState` property in this hidden field before the response is sent back to the client:

```
if (hiddenField != null)
   hiddenField.Value = ClientState;
```

Render

As Listing 17-15 shows, the `TextBoxWatermarkExtenderControl` server control overrides the `Render` method to make a call to the `VerfyRenderingInServerForm` method of the current page to ensure that the `TextBoxWatermarkExtenderControl` server control has been declared within a form DOM element whose `runat` attribute is set to the string value `server`. A form DOM element with the `runat="server"` attribute is known as server form.

> *One of the fundamental artichitectural aspects of the ASP.NET Framework is that every page can contain only one server form, that is, only one form DOM element on the page can have the `runat="server"` attribute.*

Using the Extender Server Control

Add a new source file named `TextBoxWatermarkExtenderControl.cs` to the `App_Code` directory of the same Web application that contains the replica components developed earlier in this chapter and add the code shown in Listing 17-15 to this source file. Next, add a new Web page named `TextBoxWatermarkExtenderControl.aspx` to this application and add the code shown in Listing 17-17 to this page. As you can see, this page uses the `TextBoxWatermarkExtenderControl` server control developed in the previous sections.

Note that this page contains both the standard ASP.NET AJAX `ScriptManager` server control and the replica `ScriptManager` server control. This is because the replica does not implement every single feature of the standard ASP.NET `ScriptManager` server control. It just implements those features that relate to extender and script server controls. As such, this page uses the standard ASP.NET AJAX `ScriptManager` server control for other features such as downloading the main JavaScript files, such as `MicrosoftAjax.js` and so on.

Listing 17-17: A Page that Uses the TextBoxWatermarkExtenderControl Server Control

```
<%@ Page Language="C#" %>

<%@ Register Namespace="CustomComponents3" TagPrefix="custom" %>
<!DOCTYPE html PUBLIC "-//W3C//DTD XHTML 1.0 Transitional//EN"
"http://www.w3.org/TR/xhtml11/DTD/xhtml11-transitional.dtd">

<script runat="server">
  void ClickCallback(object sender, EventArgs e)
  {
    Info.Text = TextBox1.Text;
  }
</script>

<html xmlns="http://www.w3.org/1999/xhtml">
<head id="Head1" runat="server">
  <title>Untitled Page</title>
  <style type="text/css">
    .WatermarkCssClass
    {
      background-color: #dddddd
    }
```

(continued)

Listing 17-17 (continued)

```
      </style>
  </head>
  <body>
    <form id="form1" runat="server">
      <asp:ScriptManager runat="server" ID="ScriptManager1" />

      <custom:ScriptManager runat="server" ID="CustomScriptManager1" />

      <custom:TextBoxWatermarkExtenderControl BehaviorID="Behavior1"
        ID="TextBoxWatermarkExtender1"
         runat="server" TargetControlID="TextBox1"
        WatermarkCssClass="WatermarkCssClass"
        WatermarkText="Enter value" />

      <asp:TextBox ID="TextBox1" runat="server" />
      <asp:Button ID="Button1" runat="server" OnClick="ClickCallback"
        Text="Submit" /><br />
      <br />
      <asp:Label ID="Info" runat="server" />
    </form>
  </body>
  </html>
```

Developing a Script Control

As you saw in the previous section, the `TextBoxWatermarkExtenderControl` server control encapsulates the logic that the boldfaced portions of Listing 17-14 implement and presents developers with an object-oriented ASP.NET based API that allows them to use the same imperative and declarative ASP.NET techniques to program against the underlying `TextBoxWatermark` behavior.

Another approach to encapsulating the logic that the boldfaced portions of Listing 17-14 implement is to develop a script server control. In this section, I'll implement a script server control named `TextBoxWatermarkScriptControl` that does what the `TextBoxWatermarkExtenderControl` does, that is, it encapsulates the logic that the boldfaced portions of Listing 17-14 implement and presents developers with an object-oriented ASP.NET based API that allows them to use the same imperative and declarative ASP.NET techniques to program against the underlying `TextBoxwatermark` behavior.

Listing 17-18 presents the implementation of the `TextBoxWatermarkScriptControl` server control. As you can see, this control derives from the ASP.NET `TextBox` server control and implements the `IScriptControl` interface.

You may be wondering why we don't derive the `TextBoxWatermarkScriptControl` server control from the `ScriptControl` base class to save ourselves from having to implement the base functionality that the `ScriptControl` base class already supports. The answer lies in the fact that object-oriented languages such as C# and VB.NET do not support multiple class inheritances. In other words, the `TextBoxWatermarkScriptControl` server control cannot derive from both the `TextBox` and `ScriptControl` classes. We have two options here. One option is to derive the

`TextBoxWatermarkScriptControl` server control from the `ScriptControl` base class and implement the functionality that the `TextBox` server control already supports. Another option is to derive the `TextBoxWatermarkScriptControl` server control from the `TextBox` server control and implement the functionality that the `ScriptControl` server control already supports. As you can see, both options require you to implement functionality that an existing ASP.NET server control already supports. Which option you choose is completely up to you and very much depends on which option requires less coding. In this case it is somewhat easier to implement the functionality that the `ScriptControl` server control supports than the functionality that the `TextBox` server control supports.

There are two ways to implement the functionality that an existing server control provides. One approach is to have the `TextBoxWatermarkScriptControl` server control compose the `ScriptControl` server control and delegate to this control. This is known as *object composition* in object-oriented jargon and *composite controls* in ASP.NET jargon. Another approach is to implement the functionality from scratch. The object composition approach is not possible in this case because the `ScriptControl` server control is an abstract class and cannot be instantiated.

Comparision of Listings 17-18 and 17-15 shows that the `TextBoxWatermarkScriptControl` exposes some of the same properties and methods that the `TextBoxWatermarkExtenderControl` exposes. In the following sections, I'll discuss the implementation of only those methods and properties of the `TextBoxWatermarkScriptControl` server control that are different from the `TextBoxWatermarkExtenderControl`.

Listing 17-18: The TextBoxWatermarkScriptControl

```
using System;
using System.ComponentModel;
using System.Collections.Generic;
using System.Globalization;
using System.Text;
using System.Web;
using System.Web.UI;
using System.Web.UI.WebControls;

namespace CustomComponents3
{
  [TargetControlType(typeof(IEditableTextControl))]
  public class TextBoxWatermarkScriptControl : TextBox, IScriptControl
  {
    protected virtual IEnumerable<ScriptReference> GetScriptReferences()
    {
      ScriptReference reference1 = new ScriptReference();
      reference1.Path = ResolveClientUrl("BehaviorBase.js");

      ScriptReference reference2 = new ScriptReference();
      reference2.Path = ResolveClientUrl("TextBoxWatermarkBehavior.js");

      return new ScriptReference[] { reference1, reference2 };
    }

    protected virtual IEnumerable<ScriptDescriptor> GetScriptDescriptors()
    {
      ScriptBehaviorDescriptor descriptor =
```

(continued)

Listing 17-18 *(continued)*

```
      new ScriptBehaviorDescriptor("AjaxControlToolkit.TextBoxWatermarkBehavior",
                                this.ClientID);
    descriptor.AddProperty("WatermarkText", this.WatermarkText);
    descriptor.AddProperty("WatermarkCssClass", this.WatermarkCssClass);
    descriptor.AddProperty("id", this.BehaviorID);

    return new ScriptDescriptor[] { descriptor };
}

private string _clientState;
[Browsable(false)]
[DesignerSerializationVisibility(DesignerSerializationVisibility.Hidden)]
public string ClientState
{
  get { return _clientState; }
  set { _clientState = value; }
}

public string BehaviorID
{
  get
  {
    return ViewState["BehaviorID"] != null ?
                                (string)ViewState["BehaviorID"] : ClientID;
  }
  set { ViewState["BehaviorID"] = value; }
}

protected override void OnPreRender(EventArgs e)
{
  if (!this.DesignMode)
  {
    ScriptManager sm = ScriptManager.GetCurrent(Page);
    sm.RegisterScriptControl(this);
  }

  base.OnPreRender(e);
  HiddenField hiddenField = null;

  if (string.IsNullOrEmpty(ClientStateFieldID))
    hiddenField = CreateClientStateField();

  else
    hiddenField = (HiddenField)NamingContainer.FindControl(ClientStateFieldID);

  if (hiddenField != null)
    hiddenField.Value = ClientState;
}

private HiddenField CreateClientStateField()
{
```

```
      HiddenField field = new HiddenField();
      field.ID = string.Format(CultureInfo.InvariantCulture,
                        "{0}_ClientState", ID);
      Controls.Add(field);
      ClientStateFieldID = field.ID;
      return field;
   }

   protected override void Render(HtmlTextWriter writer)
   {
     if (!this.DesignMode)
     {
       ScriptManager sm = ScriptManager.GetCurrent(Page);
       sm.RegisterScriptDescriptors(this);
     }

     if (Page != null)
       Page.VerifyRenderingInServerForm(this);
     base.Render(writer);
   }

   protected override void OnInit(EventArgs e)
   {
     CreateClientStateField();
     Page.PreLoad += new EventHandler(Page_PreLoad);
     base.OnInit(e);
   }

   void Page_PreLoad(object sender, EventArgs e)
   {
     if (!string.IsNullOrEmpty(ClientStateFieldID))
     {
       HiddenField hiddenField =
                  (HiddenField)NamingContainer.FindControl(ClientStateFieldID);

       if ((hiddenField != null) && !string.IsNullOrEmpty(hiddenField.Value))
         ClientState = hiddenField.Value;
     }
   }

[Browsable(false)]
[EditorBrowsable(EditorBrowsableState.Never)]
[IDReferenceProperty(typeof(HiddenField))]
[DefaultValue("")]
[DesignerSerializationVisibility(DesignerSerializationVisibility.Hidden)]
public string ClientStateFieldID
{
   get { return ViewState["ClientStateFieldID"] != null ?
                    (string)ViewState["ClientStateFieldID"] : string.Empty; }
   set { ViewState["ClientStateFieldID"] = value; }
}
```

(continued)

Listing 17-18 *(continued)*

```csharp
protected override void OnLoad(EventArgs e)
  {
    base.OnLoad(e);

    string key;
    string script;

    key = string.Format(CultureInfo.InvariantCulture, "{0}_onSubmit", ID);
    script = string.Format(CultureInfo.InvariantCulture,
                       "var o = $find('{0}'); if(o) {{ o._onSubmit(); }}",
                       BehaviorID);
    System.Web.UI.ScriptManager.RegisterOnSubmitStatement(this,
                       typeof(TextBoxWatermarkScriptControl), key, script);

    ClientState = (string.Compare(Page.Form.DefaultFocus, this.ID,
                          StringComparison.InvariantCultureIgnoreCase) == 0)
                       ? "Focused" : null;
  }

  private string watermarkText;
  [DefaultValue("")]
  public string WatermarkText
  {
    get { return this.watermarkText; }
    set { this.watermarkText = value; }
  }

  private string watermarkCssClass;
  [DefaultValue("")]
  public string WatermarkCssClass
  {
    get { return this.watermarkCssClass; }
    set { this.watermarkCssClass = value; }
  }

  IEnumerable<ScriptDescriptor> IScriptControl.GetScriptDescriptors()
  {
    return this.GetScriptDescriptors();
  }

  IEnumerable<ScriptReference> IScriptControl.GetScriptReferences()
  {
    return this.GetScriptReferences();
  }
 }
}
```

PreRender

As you can see from Listing 17-18, the `TextBoxWatermarkScriptControl` server control overrides the `OnPreRender` method of its base class to perform these tasks. First, it invokes the `GetCurrent` static method on the ScriptManager class to return a reference to the current ScriptManager server control on the current page:

```
ScriptManager sm = ScriptManager.GetCurrent(Page);
```

Next, it invokes the RegisterScriptControl method on the current ScriptManager server control to register the TextBoxWatermarkScriptControl server control with the current ScriptManager server control. As discussed earlier, this method simply adds the specified TextBoxWatermarkScriptControl server control to an internal collection named ScriptControls:

```
sm.RegisterScriptControl(this);
```

Next, the OnPreRender method invokes the OnPreRender method of its base class to raise the PreRender event and consequently invokes all the event handlers registered for this event:

```
base.OnPreRender(e);
```

Next, it invokes the FindControl method on the naming container of the TextBoxWatermarkScriptControl server control, passing in the value of the ClientStateFieldID property to return a reference to the hidden field that contains the client state:

```
hiddenField = (HiddenField)NamingContainer.FindControl(ClientStateFieldID);
```

Finally, it stores the value of the ClientState property in this hidden field:

```
if (hiddenField != null)
    hiddenField.Value = ClientState;
```

Render

As Listing 17-18 shows, the TextBoxWatermarkScriptControl overrides the Render method of its base class, where it accesses the current ScriptManager server control:

```
ScriptManager sm = ScriptManager.GetCurrent(Page);
```

Next, it invokes the RegisterScriptDescriptors method on the current ScriptManager server control to register the ScriptDescriptor object associated with the TextBoxWatermarkScriptControl server control:

```
sm.RegisterScriptDescriptors(this);
```

Using the Script Server Control

Add a new source file named TextBoxWatermarkScriptControl.cs to the App_Code directory of the same Web application that contains the replica components developed earlier in this chapter and add the code shown in Listing 17-18 to this source file. Next, add a new Web page named TextBoxWatermarkScriptControl.aspx to this application and add the code shown in Listing 17-19 to this page. As you can see, this page uses the TextBoxWatermarkScriptControl server control developed in the previous sections.

Listing 17-19: A Page that Uses the TextBoxWatermarkScriptControl

```
<%@ Page Language="C#" %>

<%@ Register Namespace="CustomComponents3" TagPrefix="custom" %>
<!DOCTYPE html PUBLIC "-//W3C//DTD XHTML 1.0 Transitional//EN"
"http://www.w3.org/TR/xhtml1/DTD/xhtml1-transitional.dtd">

<script runat="server">
  void ClickCallback(object sender, EventArgs e)
  {
    Info.Text = TextBoxWatermarkScriptControl1.Text;
  }
</script>

<html xmlns="http://www.w3.org/1999/xhtml">
<head id="Head1" runat="server">
  <title>Untitled Page</title>
  <style type="text/css">
    .WatermarkCssClass
    {
      background-color: #dddddd
    }
  </style>
</head>
<body>
  <form id="form1" runat="server">
    <asp:ScriptManager runat="server" ID="ScriptManager1" />
    <custom:ScriptManager runat="server" ID="CustomScriptManager1" />
    <custom:TextBoxWatermarkScriptControl BehaviorID="Behavior1"
               ID="TextBoxWatermarkScriptControl1"
     runat="server" WatermarkCssClass="WatermarkCssClass"WatermarkText="Hi there"/>
    <asp:Button ID="Button1" runat="server" OnClick="ClickCallback" Text="Submit"
               /><br />
    <br />
    <asp:Label ID="Info" runat="server" />
  </form>
</body>
</html>
```

Script Server Controls versus Extender Server Controls

You may be wondering what the differences are between script and extender server controls considering the fact that both types of controls serve the same purpose, that is, they both encapsulate the logic such as the one that the boldfaced portions of Listing 17-14 implement and present the page developers with an object-oriented ASP.NET based API that allows them to use the same imperative and declarative ASP.NET techniques to program against the underlying ASP.NET AJAX component.

The main difference between a script server control and an extender server control is that while the extender server control extends the client-side functionality of an existing ASP.NET server control, the script server control defines a new server control that directly includes this client-side functionality. This means that you can attach the same extender server control to different server controls to enhance their client-side functionality. However, the functionality contained in a script server control only applies to the script server control itself and cannot be attached to other server controls.

Therefore, if you're implementing a functionality that can be used by lot of other server controls, you may want to encapsulate this functionality in an extender server control that can be attached to other server controls. However, if you're implementing a functionality that does not make sense to apply to other server controls, you may want to encapsulate this functionality in a script server control.

Summary

This chapter first implemented fully functional replicas of those components of the ASP.NET AJAX server side Framework that play important roles in the internal working of script and extender server controls. Then, it used practical examples to teach you how to implement your own custom script and extender server controls. The next chapter will implement a custom script server control that uses a Web services bridge to communicate with Amazon Web services.

Web Services Bridges and Transformers

This chapter will first provide an overview of the Amazon E-Commerce Web service. It will then implement a script server control that uses a Web services bridge to invoke a specified Web method of this Web service and display the results to end users. Finally, I will provide an in-depth coverage of ASP.NET AJAX transformers.

Amazon Web Services

At the end of Chapter 14, I promised that I'd present a more complete example of Web services bridges. In this chapter you'll learn how to develop a custom script server control that uses a bridge to enable the client code to interact with the Amazon Web services. Before diving into the implementation of this custom script server control you need to do the following things:

❑ Visit the Amazon Web service site at www.amazon.com/gp/aws/landing.html and follow the instructions on this site to create an Amazon Web service account and get an access key. As you'll see later, you have to include this access key with every single call that you make to the Amazon Web services. This site comes with the complete documentation and sample code for using the Amazon Web services.

❑ Acquire a good understanding of the Amazon Web services. In particular, we're interested in the Amazon E-Commerce Web service (AWSECommerceService), a particular Web method of this Web service named ItemSearch, and a particular set of parameters of this Web method. Therefore, in this chapter we'll focus on these items. Complete coverage of the Amazon Web services is beyond the scope of this book.

The following code listing presents the declaration of the Amazon E-Commerce Web service:

```
public class AWSECommerceService
{
  public ItemSearchResponse ItemSearch(ItemSearch ItemSearch1);
}
```

As you can see, the `ItemSearch` method takes an argument of type `ItemSearch` and returns an object of type `ItemSearchResponse`. I'll discuss the `ItemSearch` and `ItemSearchResponse` types in the following sections.

ItemSearch

The `ItemSearch` type or class is defined in Listing 18-1. As you can see, this class exposes two important properties, `SubscriptionId` and `Request`. As the name suggests, the `SubscriptionId` property is a string that contains your Amazon access key or subscription ID. The `Request` property references the `ItemSearchRequest` object that represents a request to the Amazon service.

Listing 18-1: The ItemSearch Class

```
public class ItemSearch
{
  public string SubscriptionId {get; set;}
  public ItemSearchRequest Request {get; set;}
}
```

Listing 18-2 defines the `ItemSearchRequest` type or class. As you can see, this class contains four properties:

❑ `ItemPage`, a positive integer number. This is basically the index of the page that we want to download from the Web service. Since there could be thousands of records for our query keyword, we need to specify which page of records we're interested in. If you don't specify the page index, the first page of records is returned by default.

❑ `Keywords`, a string that contains our query.

❑ `ResponseGroup`, a string that contains certain of our search criteria, as you'll see in the following example.

❑ `SearchIndex`, a string that contains the type of the query. For example, if you pass `Books` as the `SearchIndex` parameter into the `ItemSearch` Web method, you're telling this method that you're searching for books.

Listing 18-2: The ItemSearchRequest Class

```
public class ItemSearchRequest
{
  public int ItemPage {get; set;}
  public string Keywords {get; set;}
  public string ResponseGroup {get; set;}
  public string SearchIndex {get; set;}
}
```

Listing 18-3 defines the `ItemSearchResponse` class, which exposes an array property of type `Items` named `Items`.

Listing 18-3: The ItemSearchResponse Class

```
public class ItemSearchResponse
{
  public Items[] Items { get; set;}
}
```

Listing 18-4 defines the Items type, which exposes an array property of type Item named Item.

Listing 18-4: The Items Class

```
public class Items
{
  public Item[] Item { get; set; }
}
```

As you can see from Listing 18-5, the Item type or class exposes four properties:

❑   DetailPageURL, a string that contains the URL of the page with more detailed information about the item. For example, if the item represents a book, this URL takes the end user to the page that provides more detailed information about the book.

❑   MediumImage, which is of type Image.

❑   ItemsAttributes and Offers, which you'll learn about later in the chapter.

Listing 18-5: The Item Class

```
public partial class Item
{
  public string DetailPageURL {get; set; }
  public Image MediumImage {get; set;}
  public ItemAttributes ItemAttributes {get; set;}
  public Offers Offers {get; set;}
}
```

As Listing 18-6 shows, the Image type or class exposes a string property named URL, which contains the URL of the image associated with the item. For example, if the item is a book, this is the URL of the image of the book.

Listing 18-6: The Image Class

```
public partial class Image
{
  public string URL {get; set;}
}
```

As Listing 18-7 shows, the Offers type exposes an array property named Offer that contains objects of type Offer.

Listing 18-7: The Offers Class

```
public partial class Offers
{
   public Offer[] Offer {get; set;}
}
```

As you can see from Listing 18-8, the Offer type exposes an array property named OfferListing that contains an object of type OfferListing.

Listing 18-8: The Offer Class

```
public partial class Offer
{
   public OfferListing[] OfferListing {get; set;}
}
```

As Listing 18-9 shows, the OfferListing type or class exposes a property of type Price named Price.

Listing 18-9: The OfferListing Class

```
public partial class OfferListing
{
   public Price Price {get; set;}
}
```

As you can see from Listing 18-10, the Price type exposes a property of type string named FormattedPrice.

Listing 18-10: The Price Class

```
public class Price
{
   public string FormattedPrice { get; set; }
}
```

As Listing 18-11 shows, the ItemAttributes type exposes a string property named Author, a property of type Price named ListPrice, and a string property named Title.

Listing 18-11: The ItemAttributes Class

```
public class ItemAttributes
{
   public string[] Author { get;set;}
   public Price ListPrice { get; set;}
   public string ProductGroup { get; set;}
   public string Title { get; set;}
}
```

Now that you have a good understanding of the `AWSECommerceService` Web service, its `ItemSearch` Web method, the names and types of parameters you need to pass into this Web method, and the type of return value you should expect to receive from it, we're ready to use this Web service.

As you learned from the WSDL document, you need to make a HTTP SOAP request to the `http://soap.amazon.com/onca/soap?Service=AWSECommerceService` URL to invoke the `ItemSearch` Web method. You could go ahead and write the SOAP message yourself, but then you would have to get involved in the dirty little details of SOAP messaging. A better approach is to generate the code for a class known as `proxy` that hides the underlying SOAP messaging and enables you to program against the remote Web service object as if you were programming against a local object.

There are different ways to create the `proxy` class. If you're working in the Visual Studio environment, you have the following options:

❑ Launch the `Add Web References` dialog, navigate to `http://webservices.amazon.com/AWSECommerceService/AWSECommerceService.wsdl` and click the Add Reference button to add a reference to the `AWSECommerceService` Web service. This will automatically download the `AWSECommerceService.wsdl` WSDL document from the amazon.com site, create the code for the proxy class, compile the proxy class into an assembly, and add a reference to the assembly.

❑ Download the `AWSECommerceService.wsdl` WSDL document from `http://webservices.amazon.com/AWSECommerceService/AWSECommerceService.wsdl` and store the WSDL file in your favorite directory on your machine. If you're using the built-in Web server, launch the Add Web Reference dialog and follow the same steps as in the previous item, but this time navigate to the directory where the WSDL file is located. The URL should look something like the following:

```
file:///d:/download/AWSECommerceService.wsdl
```

❑ If you're using IIS, you have to copy the `AWSECommerceService.wsdl` document to the root directory of your application. The path to this directory should look something like `C:\Inetpub\wwwroot\ApplicationRoot`. Then launch the Add Web References dialog and follow the steps discussed in the previous item to navigate to the application root where the WSDL document is located. The URL for the WSDL document should look something like this:

```
http://localhost/(ApplicationRoot)/AWSECommerceService.wsdl
```

❑ If you're using `App_Code` directory, copy the `AWSECommerceService.wsdl` document to this directory. That's it. The Visual Studio automatically generates the code for the proxy, compiles the proxy code into an assembly, and adds a reference to the assembly.

If you're not working in the Visual Studio environment, and you like to do things from the command line, first download the `AWSECommerceService.wsdl` document from `http://webservices.amazon.com/AWSECommerceService/AWSECommerceService.wsdl` and store the document in a file in your favorite directory. Go to this directory and use the following command to generate the code for the proxy class and to save the code to the `AWSECommerceService.cs` file (give it any name you wish):

```
wsdl /out:AWSECommerceService.cs AWSECommerceService.wsdl
```

The `wsdl.exe` tool comes with different options. For example, you can use `/namespace:`
`AWSECommerceService` to specify your desired namespace for the proxy class. Then use the following
command to compile the `AWSECommerceService.cs` into the `AWSECommerceService.dll` assembly
and use the assembly as you would use any other:

```
csc /t:library /out: AWSECommerceService.dll AWSECommerceService.cs
```

Since we want to use the ASP.NET AJAX Web services bridges to enable our client-side code to invoke the
`ItemSearch` Web method of the `AWSECommerceService` Web service, first we need to create and add an
`.asbx` file to our application. (These files were thoroughly discussed earlier in this book.) Listing 18-12
presents the content of an `.asbx` file named `AmazonSearch.asbx` that we will use in our example. This
file instructs the ASP.NET AJAX framework to generate a client-side proxy class named `AmazonService`
that belongs to a namespace named `MyServices` and contains a method named `Search` that takes two
parameters, `pageIndex` and `searchQuery`. The `pageIndex` parameter specifies the page of records
being retrieved and the `searchQuery` parameter specifies the search keywords.

Listing 18-12: The AmazonSearch.asbx File

```xml
<?xml version="1.0" encoding="utf-8" ?>
<bridge namespace="MyServices" className="AmazonService">
  <proxy type="CustomComponents3.AmazonService, App_Code"/>
  <method name="Search">
    <input>
      <parameter name="pageIndex" />
      <parameter name="searchQuery" />
    </input>
  </method>
</bridge>
```

As Listing 18-12 shows, this bridge is a wrapper around a .NET class named `AmazonService` that
belongs to a namespace called `CustomComponents3` and is located in the `App_Code` directory of the
current application. Listing 18-13 presents the implementation of this class. Store this code listing in a
file named `AmazonService.cs` and add the file to the `App_Code` directory.

Listing 18-13: The AmazonService Class

```csharp
using System;
using System.Data;
using System.Configuration;
using System.Web;
using System.Web.Security;
using System.Web.UI;
using System.Web.UI.WebControls;
using System.Web.UI.WebControls.WebParts;
using System.Web.UI.HtmlControls;
using System.IO;
using System.Xml;
using System.Collections;
using com.amazon.webservices;

namespace CustomComponents3
{
    public class AmazonService
```

```
{
  public Items Search(int pageIndex, string searchQuery)
  {
    ItemSearchRequest itemSearchRequest = new ItemSearchRequest();
    itemSearchRequest.Keywords = searchQuery;
    itemSearchRequest.SearchIndex = "Books";
    itemSearchRequest.ResponseGroup =
            new string[] { "Small", "Images", "ItemAttributes", "OfferFull" };
    itemSearchRequest.ItemPage = pageIndex.ToString();

    ItemSearch itemSearch = new ItemSearch();
    itemSearch.SubscriptionId =
                        ConfigurationManager.AppSettings["SubscriptionID"];
    itemSearch.AssociateTag = "";
    itemSearch.Request = new ItemSearchRequest[1] { itemSearchRequest };

    ItemSearchResponse itemSearchResponse;
    try
    {
      AWSECommerceService amazonService = new AWSECommerceService();
      itemSearchResponse = amazonService.ItemSearch(itemSearch);
    }

    catch (Exception e)
    {
      throw e;
    }

    Items[] itemsResponse = itemSearchResponse.Items;

    // Check for errors in the reponse
    if (itemsResponse == null)
      throw new Exception("Response from amazon.com contains not items!");

    if (itemsResponse[0].Request.Errors != null)
      throw new Exception(
                  "Response from amazon.com contains this error message: " +
                  itemsResponse[0].Request.Errors[0].Message);

    Items items = itemsResponse[0];
    return items;
  }
  }
}
```

As you can see from Listing 18-13, the `AmazonService` class exposes a single method named `Search` that performs these tasks. First, it instantiates an `ItemSearchRequest` object:

```
ItemSearchRequest itemSearchRequest = new ItemSearchRequest();
```

Next, it assigns the search query to the `Keywords` property of this object. For example, the search query could be the string `asp.net`.

```
itemSearchRequest.Keywords = searchQuery;
```

Then, it assigns the string `Books` to the `SearchIndex` property of the `ItemSearchRequest` object to instruct the Amazon Web service that the end user is searching for books. For example, if the search query is the string `asp.net` and the search index is the string `Books`, the Amazon Web service will return the list of books on ASP.NET:

```
itemSearchRequest.SearchIndex = "Books";
```

Next, it assigns the specified array of strings to the `ResponseGroup` property of the `ItemSearchRequest` object:

```
itemSearchRequest.ResponseGroup =
        new string[] { "Small", "Images", "ItemAttributes", "OfferFull" };
```

Then it specifies the page of records that the Amazon Web service should return. For example, if the search query is the string `asp.net`, the search index is the string `Books`, and the page index is 4, the Amazon Web service will return the fourth page of records, where each record describes an ASP.NET book:

```
itemSearchRequest.ItemPage = pageIndex.ToString();
```

Next, the `Search` method instantiates an `ItemSearch` object:

```
ItemSearch itemSearch = new ItemSearch();
```

Then it assigns the access key to the `SubscriptionId` property of this `ItemSearchObject`. As discussed earlier, you need to create an Amazon Web services account and get an access key. For security reasons, you may want to store your access key in the `appSettings` section of the `web.config` file. The great thing about doing this is that the ASP.NET framework enables you to encrypt selected sections of the `web.config` file to protect your data. You can then use your access key through the `AppSettings` static collection property of the `ConfigurationManager` class:

```
itemSearch.SubscriptionId =
                        ConfigurationManager.AppSettings["SubscriptionID"];
```

Next, the `Search` method assigns an array that contains the previously instantiated and initialized `ItemSearchRequest` object to the `Request` property of the `ItemSearch` object:

```
itemSearch.Request = new ItemSearchRequest[1] { itemSearchRequest };
```

Then it instantiates an instance of the `AWSECommerceService` proxy class:

```
AWSECommerceService amazonService = new AWSECommerceService();
```

Next, it invokes the `ItemSearch` method of the proxy class, passing in the `ItemSearch` object:

```
ItemSearchResponse itemSearchResponse = amazonService.ItemSearch(itemSearch);
```

The `ItemSearch` method returns an `ItemSearchResponse` object that contains the server response data. As discussed earlier, this object exposes an array property named `Items` that contains an object of type `Items`:

```
Items[] itemsResponse = itemSearchResponse.Items;
```

Finally, the Search method returns the first Items object in the Items collection property:

```
Items items = itemsResponse[0];
return items;
```

Developing Web Services Bridge-Enabled Script Server Controls

Next, I'll present and discuss the implementation of a custom ASP.NET AJAX script server control that uses the AWSECommerceService Web service to search the amazon.com site for books that meet particular search criteria. This involves implementing the following four components:

❑ AspNetAjaxAmazonSearch: An ASP.NET AJAX client control that uses the ASP.NET AJAX Web services bridges to invoke the ItemSearch Web method of the AWSECommerceService Web service

❑ AmazonSearchScriptControl: An ASP.NET script server control that encapsulates the logic, enabling page developers to use the same imperative and declarative ASP.NET techniques to program against the underlying AspNetAjaxAmazonSearch ASP.NET AJAX client-side control

❑ HtmlGenerator: An ASP.NET AJAX client-side component that displays the results returned from the call into the ItemSearch Web method of the AWSECommerceService Web service

❑ HtmlGeneratorScriptControl: An ASP.NET script server control that encapsulates the logic, enabling page developers to use the same imperative and declarative ASP.NET techniques to program against the underlying HtmlGenerator ASP.NET AJAX client-side component

AspNetAjaxAmazonSearch

Listing 18-14 presents the implementation of the AspNetAjaxAmazonSearch client control. I'll discuss the methods and properties of this control in the following sections.

Listing 18-14: The AspNetAjaxAmazonSearch Client-side Control

```
Type.registerNamespace("CustomComponents3");

CustomComponents3.AspNetAjaxAmazonSearch =
function CustomComponents3$AspNetAjaxAmazonSearch(associatedElement)
{
  CustomComponents3.AspNetAjaxAmazonSearch.initializeBase(this,
                                                 [associatedElement]);
}

function CustomComponents3$AspNetAjaxAmazonSearch$get_searchTextBox()
{
  return this._searchTextBox;
}

function CustomComponents3$AspNetAjaxAmazonSearch$set_searchTextBox(value)
{
```

(continued)

Listing 18-14 *(continued)*

```
    this._searchTextBox = value;
}

function CustomComponents3$AspNetAjaxAmazonSearch$get_searchButton()
{
  return this._searchButton;
}

function CustomComponents3$AspNetAjaxAmazonSearch$set_searchButton(value)
{
  this._searchButton = value;
}

function CustomComponents3$AspNetAjaxAmazonSearch$get_htmlGenerator()
{
  return this._htmlGenerator;
}

function CustomComponents3$AspNetAjaxAmazonSearch$set_htmlGenerator(value)
{
  this._htmlGenerator = value;
}

function CustomComponents3$AspNetAjaxAmazonSearch$get_searchResultAreaDiv()
{
  return this._searchResultAreaDiv;
}

function CustomComponents3$AspNetAjaxAmazonSearch$set_searchResultAreaDiv(value)
{
  this._searchResultAreaDiv = value;
}

function CustomComponents3$AspNetAjaxAmazonSearch$get_commandBarAreaDiv()
{
  return this._commandBarAreaDiv;
}

function CustomComponents3$AspNetAjaxAmazonSearch$set_commandBarAreaDiv(value)
{
  this._commandBarAreaDiv = value;
}

function CustomComponents3$AspNetAjaxAmazonSearch$get_nextButton()
{
  return this._nextButton;
}

function CustomComponents3$AspNetAjaxAmazonSearch$set_nextButton(value)
{
  this._nextButton = value;
}
```

```
function CustomComponents3$AspNetAjaxAmazonSearch$get_previousButton()
{
  return this._previousButton;
}

function CustomComponents3$AspNetAjaxAmazonSearch$set_previousButton(value)
{
  this._previousButton = value;
}

function CustomComponents3$AspNetAjaxAmazonSearch$get_pageIndex()
{
  return this._pageIndex;
}

function CustomComponents3$AspNetAjaxAmazonSearch$set_pageIndex(value)
{
  this._pageIndex = value;
}

function CustomComponents3$AspNetAjaxAmazonSearch$get_searchMethod()
{
  return this._searchMethod;
}

function CustomComponents3$AspNetAjaxAmazonSearch$set_searchMethod(value)
{
  this._searchMethod = value;
}

function CustomComponents3$AspNetAjaxAmazonSearch$initialize()
{
  CustomComponents3.AspNetAjaxAmazonSearch.callBaseMethod(this, "initialize");

  this._searchButtonClickHandler =
                    Function.createDelegate(this, this._onSearchButtonClick);

  this._nextButtonClickHandler =
                    Function.createDelegate(this, this._onNextButtonClick);

  this._previousButtonClickHandler =
                    Function.createDelegate(this, this._onPreviousButtonClick);

  $addHandler(this._searchButton, "click", this._searchButtonClickHandler);
  $addHandler(this._nextButton, "click", this._nextButtonClickHandler);
  $addHandler(this._previousButton, "click", this._previousButtonClickHandler);

  this._onSuccessHandler = Function.createDelegate(this, this._onSuccess);
  this._onFailureHandler = Function.createDelegate(this, this._onFailure);
}

function CustomComponents3$AspNetAjaxAmazonSearch$_onSearchButtonClick(evt)
{
```

(continued)

Listing 18-14 *(continued)*

```
  this._pageIndex = 1;
  this._searchQuery = this._searchTextBox.value;
  this._searchMethod(
               {"pageIndex": this._pageIndex, "searchQuery": this._searchQuery},
               this._onSuccessHandler, this._onFailureHandler, null);
}

function CustomComponents3$AspNetAjaxAmazonSearch$_onPreviousButtonClick(evt)
{
  this._pageIndex--;
  if (this._pageIndex < 0)
    this._pageIndex = 1;

  this._searchQuery = this._searchTextBox.value;
  this._searchMethod(
    {"pageIndex": this._pageIndex, "searchQuery": this._searchQuery},
    this._onSuccessHandler, this._onFailureHandler, null);
}

function CustomComponents3$AspNetAjaxAmazonSearch$_onNextButtonClick(evt)
{
  this._pageIndex++;
  this._searchQuery = this._searchTextBox.value;

  this._searchMethod(
               {"pageIndex": this._pageIndex, "searchQuery": this._searchQuery},
               this._onSuccessHandler, this._onFailureHandler, null);
}

function CustomComponents3$AspNetAjaxAmazonSearch$_onSuccess(items,
                                          userContext, methodName)
{
  var html = this._htmlGenerator.generateHtml(items);

  this._searchResultAreaDiv.innerHTML = html;
  this._commandBarAreaDiv.style.display = "block";
  this._searchResultAreaDiv.style.display = "block";
}

function CustomComponents3$AspNetAjaxAmazonSearch$_onFailure(result,
                                          userContext, methodName)
{
  var builder = new Sys.StringBuilder();
   builder.append("timedOut: ");
  builder.append(result.get_timedOut());
  builder.appendLine();
  builder.appendLine();
  builder.append("message: ");
  builder.append(result.get_message());
  builder.appendLine();
```

```
    builder.appendLine();
    builder.append("stackTrace: ");
    builder.appendLine();
    builder.append(result.get_stackTrace());
    builder.appendLine();
    builder.appendLine();
    builder.append("exceptionType: ");
    builder.append(result.get_exceptionType());
    builder.appendLine();
    builder.appendLine();
    builder.append("statusCode: ");
    builder.append(result.get_statusCode());
    builder.appendLine();
    builder.appendLine();
    builder.append("methodName: ");
    builder.append(methodName);

    alert(builder.toString());
}

CustomComponents3.AspNetAjaxAmazonSearch.prototype =
{
  get_searchTextBox: CustomComponents3$AspNetAjaxAmazonSearch$get_searchTextBox,
  set_searchTextBox: CustomComponents3$AspNetAjaxAmazonSearch$set_searchTextBox,
  get_searchButton: CustomComponents3$AspNetAjaxAmazonSearch$get_searchButton,

  set_searchButton:
            CustomComponents3$AspNetAjaxAmazonSearch$set_searchButton,

  get_searchResultAreaDiv:
            CustomComponents3$AspNetAjaxAmazonSearch$get_searchResultAreaDiv,

  set_searchResultAreaDiv:
            CustomComponents3$AspNetAjaxAmazonSearch$set_searchResultAreaDiv,

  get_commandBarAreaDiv:
            CustomComponents3$AspNetAjaxAmazonSearch$get_commandBarAreaDiv,

  set_commandBarAreaDiv:
            CustomComponents3$AspNetAjaxAmazonSearch$set_commandBarAreaDiv,

  get_nextButton: CustomComponents3$AspNetAjaxAmazonSearch$get_nextButton,
  set_nextButton: CustomComponents3$AspNetAjaxAmazonSearch$set_nextButton,
  get_previousButton: CustomComponents3$AspNetAjaxAmazonSearch$get_previousButton,
  set_previousButton: CustomComponents3$AspNetAjaxAmazonSearch$set_previousButton,
  get_pageIndex: CustomComponents3$AspNetAjaxAmazonSearch$get_pageIndex,
  set_pageIndex: CustomComponents3$AspNetAjaxAmazonSearch$set_pageIndex,
  get_htmlGenerator: CustomComponents3$AspNetAjaxAmazonSearch$get_htmlGenerator,
  set_htmlGenerator: CustomComponents3$AspNetAjaxAmazonSearch$set_htmlGenerator,
  get_searchMethod: CustomComponents3$AspNetAjaxAmazonSearch$get_searchMethod,
  set_searchMethod: CustomComponents3$AspNetAjaxAmazonSearch$set_searchMethod,
  initialize: CustomComponents3$AspNetAjaxAmazonSearch$initialize,
```

(continued)

Listing 18-14 *(continued)*

```
    _onSearchButtonClick:
                CustomComponents3$AspNetAjaxAmazonSearch$_onSearchButtonClick,
    _onPreviousButtonClick:
                CustomComponents3$AspNetAjaxAmazonSearch$_onPreviousButtonClick,
    _onNextButtonClick: CustomComponents3$AspNetAjaxAmazonSearch$_onNextButtonClick,
    _onSuccess: CustomComponents3$AspNetAjaxAmazonSearch$_onSuccess,
    _onFailure: CustomComponents3$AspNetAjaxAmazonSearch$_onFailure
}

CustomComponents3.AspNetAjaxAmazonSearch.registerClass(
                    "CustomComponents3.AspNetAjaxAmazonSearch", Sys.UI.Control);

if (typeof(Sys) !== 'undefined')
    Sys.Application.notifyScriptLoaded();
```

Properties

The following table describes the getters and setters associated with the properties of the AspNetAjaxAmazonSearch client control:

Getter or Setter Method	Description
get_searchTextBox	Gets a reference to the search text box DOM element
set_searchTextBox	Sets a reference to the search text box DOM element
get_searchButton	Gets a reference to the search button DOM element
set_searchButton	Sets a reference to the search button DOM element
get_htmlGenerator	Gets a reference to the HtmlGenerator client control that displays the results returned from the call into the ItemSearch Web method of the AWSECommerceService Web service
set_htmlGenerator	Sets a reference to the HtmlGenerator client control that displays the results returned from the call into the ItemSearch Web method of the AWSECommerceService Web service
get_searchResultAreaDiv	Gets a reference to the div DOM element that displays the search result
set_searchResultAreaDiv	Sets a reference to the div DOM element that displays the search result
get_commandBarAreaDiv	Gets a reference to the div DOM element that displays the command bar
set_commandBarAreaDiv	Sets a reference to the div DOM element that displays the command bar

Getter or Setter Method	Description
get_nextButton	Gets a reference to the next button DOM element
set_nextButton	Sets a reference to the next button DOM element
get_previousButton	Gets a reference to the previous button DOM element
set_previousButton	Sets a reference to the previous button DOM element
get_pageIndex	Gets the current page index
set_pageIndex	Sets the current page index
get_searchMethod	Gets a reference to the search method
set_searchMethod	Sets the reference to the search method

initialize

As you can see from Listing 18-14, the AspNetAjaxAmazonSearch client control overrides the initialize method that it inherits from its base class, where it performs the following tasks. First, it uses the callBaseMethod method to invoke the initialize method of the base class to allow the base class to initialize itself:

```
CustomComponents3.AspNetAjaxAmazonSearch.callBaseMethod(this, "initialize");
```

Next, it creates three delegates to represents the _onSearchButtonClick, _onNextButtonClick, and _onPreviousButtonClick methods and stores these delegates in private fields named _searchButtonClickHandler, _nextButtonClickHandler, and _previousButtonClickHandler, respectively:

```
this._searchButtonClickHandler =
                Function.createDelegate(this, this._onSearchButtonClick);
this._nextButtonClickHandler =
                Function.createDelegate(this, this._onNextButtonClick);
this._previousButtonClickHandler =
                Function.createDelegate(this, this._onPreviousButtonClick);
```

Then it registers the above delegates as event handlers for the click events of the search, next, and previous button DOM elements, respectively. Therefore, when the end user clicks one of these buttons, the associated delegate and consequently the method that the delegate represents is automatically invoked:

```
$addHandler(this._searchButton, "click", this._searchButtonClickHandler);
$addHandler(this._nextButton, "click", this._nextButtonClickHandler);
$addHandler(this._previousButton, "click", this._previousButtonClickHandler);
```

Finally, the AspNetAjaxAmazonSearch client control creates two more delegates to represent the _onSuccess and _onFailure methods and stores them in _onSuccessHandler and _onFailureHandler private fields, respectively:

```
this._onSuccessHandler = Function.createDelegate(this, this._onSuccess);
this._onFailureHandler = Function.createDelegate(this, this._onFailure);
```

_onSearchButtonClick

As Listing 18-14 shows, this method first reset the current page index to 1 because we're about to make a new search query for which we need to download the first page of the search results:

```
this._pageIndex = 1;
```

Next, it retrieves the search query from the search text box DOM element and stores it in a private field named _searchQuery:

```
this._searchQuery = this._searchTextBox.value;
```

Finally, it invokes the search method, passing in four parameters. The first parameter is an object literal that describes the names and values of the parameters of the Web method being invoked. In our case, the Web method expects two parameters, pageIndex and searchQuery. The second and third parameters reference the _onSuccessHandler and _onFailureHandler delegates. Recall that these delegates respectively represent the _onSuccess and _onFailure methods.

```
this._searchMethod(
                   {"pageIndex": this._pageIndex, "searchQuery": this._searchQuery},
                   this._onSuccessHandler, this._onFailureHandler, null);
```

_onPreviousButtonClick

As you can see from Listing 18-14, this method begins by decrementing the current page index because we're moving back to the previous page:

```
this._pageIndex--;
```

Next, it checks whether the new current page index is negative. If so, it resets the current page index to 1:

```
if (this._pageIndex < 0)
   this._pageIndex = 1;
```

Then, it retrieves the search query from the search text box DOM element and stores it in the _searchQuery field:

```
this._searchQuery = this._searchTextBox.value;
```

Finally, it invokes the search method, passing in the same parameters we discussed earlier:

```
this._searchMethod(
   {"pageIndex": this._pageIndex, "searchQuery": this._searchQuery},
   this._onSuccessHandler, this._onFailureHandler, null);
```

_onNextButtonClick

This method (see Listing 18-14) first increments the current page index because we need to download the next page of search results from the Web service:

```
this._pageIndex++;
```

The next two steps are the same as in the previous example:

```
this._searchQuery = this._searchTextBox.value;

this._searchMethod(
          {"pageIndex": this._pageIndex, "searchQuery": this._searchQuery},
          this._onSuccessHandler, this._onFailureHandler, null);
```

_onSuccess

As discussed earlier, the _onSearchButtonClick, _onPreviousButtonClick, and _onNextButtonClick methods internally pass the _onSuccessHandler delegate into the _searchMethod as its second argument. This delegate represents the _onSucccess method, which means that when the search results finally arrive, the _onSuccessHandler delegate and consequently the _onSuccess method are automatically invoked. This method takes three parameters. The first parameter contains the search results, the second references the context object, and the third contains the name of the invoked method.

As you can see from Listing 18-14, the _onSuccess method invokes the generateHtml instance method on the HtmlGenenrator component, passing in the search results. As you'll see later, this method is responsible for generating and returning the HTML markup that displays the search results:

```
var html = this._htmlGenerator.generateHtml(items);
```

Next, _onSuccess assigns this HTML markup to the innerHTML property of the search result area div DOM element to display the search results in this div element:

```
this._searchResultAreaDiv.innerHTML = html;
```

Finally, it sets the values of the display properties of the style properties of the div elements that display the search results and command bar to "block":

```
this._commandBarAreaDiv.style.display = "block";
this._searchResultAreaDiv.style.display = "block";
```

AmazonSearchScriptControl

Listing 18-15 presents the implementation of the AmazonSearchScriptControl script server control. As I mentioned earlier, this script server control enables page developers to use familiar imperative and declarative ASP.NET techniques to program against the underlying AspNetAjaxAmazonSearch ASP.NET AJAX client-side control. I'll discuss the methods and properties of this server control in the following sections.

Listing 18-15: The AmazonSearchScriptControl Script Server Control

```
using System;
using System.Data;
using System.Configuration;
using System.Web;
using System.Web.Security;
using System.Web.UI;
using System.Web.UI.WebControls;
using System.Web.UI.WebControls.WebParts;
using System.Web.UI.HtmlControls;
using System.Collections.Specialized;
using System.Xml;
using System.IO;
using System.Collections.Generic;
using com.amazon.webservices;

namespace CustomComponents3
{
  public class AmazonSearchScriptControl : ScriptControl
  {
    public string HtmlGeneratorID
    {
      get
      {
        return ViewState["HtmlGeneratorID"] != null ?
                            (string)ViewState["HtmlGeneratorID"] : string.Empty;
      }
      set
      {
        ViewState["HtmlGeneratorID"] = value;
      }
    }

    public string SearchMethod
    {
      get
      {
        return ViewState["SearchMethod"] != null ?
                              (string)ViewState["SearchMethod"] : string.Empty;
      }
      set
      {
        ViewState["SearchMethod"] = value;
      }
    }

    public string Path
    {
      get
      {
        return ViewState["Path"] != null ?
                                (string)ViewState["Path"] : string.Empty;
      }
```

```
    set
    {
      ViewState["Path"] = value;
    }
}

public string ClientControlType
{
  get
  {
    return ViewState["ClientControlType"] != null ?
                    (string)ViewState["ClientControlType"] : string.Empty;
  }
  set
  {
    ViewState["ClientControlType"] = value;
  }
}

protected override IEnumerable<ScriptDescriptor> GetScriptDescriptors()
{
  ScriptControlDescriptor descriptor =
          new ScriptControlDescriptor(this.ClientControlType, this.ClientID);

  descriptor.AddProperty("pageIndex", 1);
  descriptor.AddScriptProperty("searchMethod", this.SearchMethod);

  descriptor.AddElementProperty("searchTextBox",
                          this.ClientID + "_SearchTextBox");

  descriptor.AddElementProperty("searchButton",
                          this.ClientID + "_SearchButton");

  descriptor.AddElementProperty("searchResultAreaDiv",
                          this.ClientID + "_SearchResultArea");

  descriptor.AddElementProperty("commandBarAreaDiv",
                          this.ClientID + "_CommandBarArea");

  descriptor.AddElementProperty("previousButton",
                          this.ClientID + "_PreviousButton");

  descriptor.AddElementProperty("nextButton", this.ClientID + "_NextButton");
  descriptor.AddComponentProperty("htmlGenerator", this.HtmlGeneratorID);
  return new ScriptDescriptor[] { descriptor };
}

protected override IEnumerable<ScriptReference> GetScriptReferences()
{
  ScriptReference reference = new ScriptReference();
  reference.Path = Path;
  return new ScriptReference[] { reference };
}
```

(continued)

Listing 18-15 *(continued)*

```
protected override void RenderContents(HtmlTextWriter writer)
{
    writer.RenderBeginTag(HtmlTextWriterTag.Tr);

    writer.RenderBeginTag(HtmlTextWriterTag.Td);
    writer.AddStyleAttribute(HtmlTextWriterStyle.BorderWidth, "0");
    writer.AddStyleAttribute("cellpadding", "0");
    writer.AddStyleAttribute("cellspacing", "0");

    writer.RenderBeginTag(HtmlTextWriterTag.Table);
    writer.RenderBeginTag(HtmlTextWriterTag.Tr);

    writer.RenderBeginTag(HtmlTextWriterTag.Td);
    writer.AddAttribute(HtmlTextWriterAttribute.Type, "text");
    writer.AddAttribute(HtmlTextWriterAttribute.Id, ClientID + "_SearchTextBox");
    writer.AddAttribute(HtmlTextWriterAttribute.Size, "41");
    writer.RenderBeginTag(HtmlTextWriterTag.Input);
    writer.RenderEndTag();
    writer.Write("  ");
    writer.AddAttribute(HtmlTextWriterAttribute.Type, "button");
    writer.AddAttribute(HtmlTextWriterAttribute.Id,
                        this.ClientID + "_SearchButton");

    writer.RenderBeginTag(HtmlTextWriterTag.Button);
    writer.Write("Search");
    writer.RenderEndTag();
    writer.RenderEndTag();
    writer.RenderEndTag();
    writer.RenderEndTag();
    writer.RenderEndTag();

    writer.RenderEndTag();

    writer.RenderBeginTag(HtmlTextWriterTag.Tr);
    writer.AddAttribute(HtmlTextWriterAttribute.Colspan, "3");
    writer.RenderBeginTag(HtmlTextWriterTag.Td);
    writer.AddStyleAttribute(HtmlTextWriterStyle.Display, "none");

    writer.AddAttribute(HtmlTextWriterAttribute.Id,
                        this.ClientID + "_SearchResultArea");

    writer.RenderBeginTag(HtmlTextWriterTag.Div);
    writer.RenderEndTag();

    writer.RenderEndTag();
    writer.RenderEndTag();

    writer.RenderBeginTag(HtmlTextWriterTag.Tr);
    writer.AddAttribute(HtmlTextWriterAttribute.Align, "center");
    writer.AddAttribute(HtmlTextWriterAttribute.Colspan, "3");
    writer.RenderBeginTag(HtmlTextWriterTag.Td);
    writer.AddStyleAttribute(HtmlTextWriterStyle.Display, "none");
```

```
      writer.AddAttribute(HtmlTextWriterAttribute.Id,
                          this.ClientID + "_CommandBarArea");

    writer.RenderBeginTag(HtmlTextWriterTag.Div);
    writer.AddAttribute(HtmlTextWriterAttribute.Type, "button");
    writer.AddAttribute(HtmlTextWriterAttribute.Id,
                          this.ClientID + "_PreviousButton");

    writer.RenderBeginTag(HtmlTextWriterTag.Button);
    writer.Write("<< Prev");
    writer.RenderEndTag();
    writer.Write("         ");
    writer.AddAttribute(HtmlTextWriterAttribute.Type, "button");
    writer.AddAttribute(HtmlTextWriterAttribute.Id, ClientID + "_NextButton");
    writer.RenderBeginTag(HtmlTextWriterTag.Button);
    writer.Write("Next >>");
    writer.RenderEndTag();

    writer.RenderEndTag();
    writer.RenderEndTag();
    writer.RenderEndTag();
}

protected override HtmlTextWriterTag TagKey
{
  get { return HtmlTextWriterTag.Table; }
}

protected override Style CreateControlStyle()
{
  return new TableStyle(ViewState);
}

public virtual int CellPadding
{
  get { return ((TableStyle)ControlStyle).CellPadding; }
  set { ((TableStyle)ControlStyle).CellPadding = value; }
}

public virtual int CellSpacing
{
  get { return ((TableStyle)ControlStyle).CellSpacing; }
  set { ((TableStyle)ControlStyle).CellSpacing = value; }
}

public virtual HorizontalAlign HorizontalAlign
{
  get { return ((TableStyle)ControlStyle).HorizontalAlign; }
  set { ((TableStyle)ControlStyle).HorizontalAlign = value; }
}

public virtual string BackImageUrl
{
```

(continued)

Listing 18-15 *(continued)*

```
      get { return ((TableStyle)ControlStyle).BackImageUrl; }
      set { ((TableStyle)ControlStyle).BackImageUrl = value; }
    }

    public virtual GridLines GridLines
    {
      get { return ((TableStyle)ControlStyle).GridLines; }
      set { ((TableStyle)ControlStyle).GridLines = value; }
    }
  }
}
```

Properties

The following table describes four of the non-style properties of the `AmazonSearchScriptControl` script server control.

Property	Description
HtmlGeneratorID	Gets or sets the id property value of the HTML generator component, which is responsible for generating the HTML markup that displays the search results.
SearchMethod	Gets or sets the fully qualified name of the proxy method to invoke, including the name of the proxy class to which the method belongs and the complete namespace containment hierarchy to which the proxy class belongs.
Path	Gets or sets the virtual path of the JavaScript file that contains the implementation of the client control that the `AmazonSearchScriptControl` script server control represents.
ClientControlType	Gets or sets the fully qualified name of the client control that the `AmazonSearchScriptControl` script server control represents. This name must contain the complete namespace containment hierarchy of the client control.

`AmazonSearchScriptControl` overrides the `TagKey` property that it inherits from the `WebControl` base class to specify a table HTML element as its containing or outermost HTML element. As the name suggests, the containing HTML element of a server control is an element that contains the rest of the HTML markup that makes up the user interface of the control:

```
    protected override HtmlTextWriterTag TagKey
    {
      get { return HtmlTextWriterTag.Table; }
    }
```

Since `AmazonSearchScriptControl` uses a table HTML element as its containing HTML element, it also overrides the `CreateControlStyle` method of its base class to specify a `TableStyle` as a `Style` object for styling its containing HTML element. This `TableStyle` object enables page developers to style the containing HTML element in a strongly-typed fashion:

```
protected override Style CreateControlStyle()
{
  return new TableStyle(ViewState);
}
```

Every server control that overrides the `CreateControlStyle` method must also expose the properties of the associated `Style` object as its own top-level properties. As a result, the `AmazonSearchScriptControl` exposes five style properties, `CellPadding`, `CellSpacing`, `HorizonalAlign`, `BackImageUrl`, and `GridLines`, that respectively get or set the values of the `CellPadding`, `CellSpacing`, `HorizonalAlign`, `BackImageUrl`, and `GridLines` properties of the underlying `TableStyle` object that styles the containing `table` HTML element of the `AmazonSearchScriptControl` script server control.

GetScriptDescriptors

`AmazonSearchScriptControl`, like any other script server control, overrides the `GetScriptDescriptors` method of its base class, where it takes the following steps (see Listing 18-14). First, it instantiates a `ScriptControlDescriptor` object, passing the values of its `ClientControlType` and `ClientID` properties. Recall that the `ClientControlType` property contains the fully qualified name of the client control that `AmazonSearchScriptControl` represents:

```
ScriptControlDescriptor descriptor =
          new ScriptControlDescriptor(this.ClientControlType, this.ClientID);
```

Next, it invokes the `AddProperty` method on this `ScriptControlDescriptor` object to specify the value of the `pageIndex` property of the client control that `AmazonSearchScriptControl` represents:

```
descriptor.AddProperty("pageIndex", 1);
```

Then it calls the `AddScriptProperty` method on the `ScriptControlDescriptor` object to specify the value of the `searchMethod` property of the client control that `AmazonSearchScriptControl` represents. Recall that the `searchMethod` property references the proxy method to be invoked:

```
descriptor.AddScriptProperty("searchMethod", this.SearchMethod);
```

Next, it calls the `AddElementProperty` method six times to specify the values of the `searchTextBox`, `searchButton`, `searchResultAreaDiv`, `commandBarAreaDiv`, `previousButton`, and `nextButton` properties of the client control that `AmazonSearchScriptControl` represents:

```
descriptor.AddElementProperty("searchTextBox",
                      this.ClientID + "_SearchTextBox");
descriptor.AddElementProperty("searchButton",
                      this.ClientID + "_SearchButton");
descriptor.AddElementProperty("searchResultAreaDiv",
                      this.ClientID + "_SearchResultArea");
descriptor.AddElementProperty("commandBarAreaDiv",
                      this.ClientID + "_CommandBarArea");
descriptor.AddElementProperty("previousButton",
                      this.ClientID + "_PreviousButton");
descriptor.AddElementProperty("nextButton", this.ClientID + "_NextButton");
```

Next, it calls the `AddComponentProperty` method on the `ScriptControlDescriptor` object to specify the value of the `htmlGenerator` property that the `AmazonSearchScriptControl` represents. Recall that the `htmlGenerator` property references the client component responsible for generating and returning the HTML markup that renders the search results:

```
descriptor.AddComponentProperty("htmlGenerator", this.HtmlGeneratorID);
```

Finally, it instantiates and populates an array with the `ScriptControlDescriptor` object and returns the array to its caller:

```
return new ScriptDescriptor[] { descriptor };
```

GetScriptReferences

`AmazonSearchScriptControl`, like any other script server control, overrides the `GetScriptReferences` method of its base class, where it instantiates a `ScriptReference` object:

```
ScriptReference reference = new ScriptReference();
```

Next, it assigns to the `Path` property of this `ScriptReference` object the virtual path of the JavaScript file that contains the implementation of the client control that `AmazonSearchScriptControl` represents:

```
reference.Path = Path;
```

Finally, it instantiates and populates an array with this `ScriptReference` object and returns the array to its caller:

```
return new ScriptReference[] { reference };
```

RenderContents

`AmazonSearchScriptControl`, like any other `WebControl` subclass, overrides the `RenderContents` method of the `WebControl` base class to render its content HTML markup. The content HTML markup of a server control is the portion of its HTML markup that goes within the opening and closing tags of its containing HTML element, which is the `table` HTML element in the case of `AmazonSearchScriptControl`.

As you can see from Listing 18-14, `RenderContents` renders three `tr` HTML elements. The first `tr` HTML element contains the search text box and the search button:

```
writer.RenderBeginTag(HtmlTextWriterTag.Tr);
writer.RenderBeginTag(HtmlTextWriterTag.Td);
writer.RenderBeginTag(HtmlTextWriterTag.Table);
writer.RenderBeginTag(HtmlTextWriterTag.Tr);
writer.RenderBeginTag(HtmlTextWriterTag.Td);
writer.AddAttribute(HtmlTextWriterAttribute.Type, "text");
writer.AddAttribute(HtmlTextWriterAttribute.Id, ClientID + "_SearchTextBox");
```

```
        writer.AddAttribute(HtmlTextWriterAttribute.Size, "41");
        writer.RenderBeginTag(HtmlTextWriterTag.Input);
        writer.RenderEndTag();
        writer.Write("  ");
        writer.AddAttribute(HtmlTextWriterAttribute.Type, "button");
        writer.AddAttribute(HtmlTextWriterAttribute.Id,
                            this.ClientID + "_SearchButton");
        writer.RenderBeginTag(HtmlTextWriterTag.Button);
        writer.Write("Search");
        writer.RenderEndTag();
        writer.RenderEndTag();
        writer.RenderEndTag();
        writer.RenderEndTag();
        writer.RenderEndTag();
        writer.RenderEndTag();
```

Notice that RenderContents uses the following as the value of the id HTML attributes of the text box and search button elements:

```
ClientID + "_SearchTextBox"
ClientID + "_SearchButton"
```

Notice also that these are the same two values that GetScriptDescriptors passes into the AddElementProperty methods that specify the values of the searchTextBox and searchButton properties of the client script that AmazonSearchScriptControl represents.

Next, RenderContents renders the tr HTML element that contains the div HTML element that displays the search results:

```
        writer.RenderBeginTag(HtmlTextWriterTag.Tr);
        writer.AddAttribute(HtmlTextWriterAttribute.Colspan, "3");
        writer.RenderBeginTag(HtmlTextWriterTag.Td);
        writer.AddStyleAttribute(HtmlTextWriterStyle.Display, "none");
        writer.AddAttribute(HtmlTextWriterAttribute.Id,
                            this.ClientID + "_SearchResultArea");
        writer.RenderBeginTag(HtmlTextWriterTag.Div);
        writer.RenderEndTag();
        writer.RenderEndTag();
        writer.RenderEndTag();
```

Notice that RenderContents uses ClientID plus "_SearchResultArea" as the value of the id HTML attribute of the div HTML element that displays the search result. This value is the same one that the GetScriptDescriptors method passes into the AddElementProperty method that specifies the value of the searchResultArea property of the client control that AmazonSearchScriptControl represents.

Finally, RenderContents renders the tr HTML element that contains the div HTML element that displays the command bar, which consists of the Previous and Next buttons. Again notice that the id HTML attributes of these two buttons are set to the same values that GetScriptDescriptors passes into the AddElementProperty methods that specify the values of the previousButton and nextButton properties of the client control that AmazonSearchScriptControl represents.

```
            writer.RenderBeginTag(HtmlTextWriterTag.Tr);
            writer.AddAttribute(HtmlTextWriterAttribute.Align, "center");
            writer.AddAttribute(HtmlTextWriterAttribute.Colspan, "3");
            writer.RenderBeginTag(HtmlTextWriterTag.Td);
            writer.AddStyleAttribute(HtmlTextWriterStyle.Display, "none");
            writer.AddAttribute(HtmlTextWriterAttribute.Id,
                            this.ClientID + "_CommandBarArea");
            writer.RenderBeginTag(HtmlTextWriterTag.Div);
            writer.AddAttribute(HtmlTextWriterAttribute.Type, "button");
            writer.AddAttribute(HtmlTextWriterAttribute.Id,
                            this.ClientID + "_PreviousButton");
            writer.RenderBeginTag(HtmlTextWriterTag.Button);
            writer.Write("<< Prev");
            writer.RenderEndTag();
            writer.Write("         ");
            writer.AddAttribute(HtmlTextWriterAttribute.Type, "button");
            writer.AddAttribute(HtmlTextWriterAttribute.Id, ClientID + "_NextButton");
            writer.RenderBeginTag(HtmlTextWriterTag.Button);
            writer.Write("Next >>");
            writer.RenderEndTag();
            writer.RenderEndTag();
            writer.RenderEndTag();
            writer.RenderEndTag();
```

HtmlGenerator

Listing 18-16 presents the implementation of the HtmlGenerator client component. I'll discuss the methods and properties of this component in the following sections.

Listing 18-16: The HtmlGenerator Client Component

```
Type.registerNamespace("CustomComponents3");

CustomComponents3.HtmlGenerator =
function CustomComponents3$HtmlGenerator()
{
  CustomComponents3.HtmlGenerator.initializeBase(this);
}

function CustomComponents3$HtmlGenerator$get_tableStyle()
{
  return this._tableStyle;
}

function CustomComponents3$HtmlGenerator$set_tableStyle(value)
{
  this._tableStyle = value;
}

function CustomComponents3$HtmlGenerator$get_rowStyle()
{
  return this._rowStyle;
}
```

```
function CustomComponents3$HtmlGenerator$set_rowStyle(value)
{
  this._rowStyle = value;
}

function CustomComponents3$HtmlGenerator$get_alternatingRowStyle()
{
  return this._alternatingRowStyle;
}

function CustomComponents3$HtmlGenerator$set_alternatingRowStyle(value)
{
  this._alternatingRowStyle = value;
}

function CustomComponents3$HtmlGenerator$generateHtml(items)
{
  var title;
  var author;
  var amazonUrl;
  var imageUrl;
  var listPrice;
  var price;
  var item;

   var results = items.Item;
  if (!results)
    return;

  var builder = new Sys.StringBuilder();
  builder.append("<table cellspacing='10' style='");
  builder.append(this._tableStyle);
  builder.append("'>");

  for (var i=0; i<results.length-1; i++)
  {
    item = results[i];
    if (!item)
      continue;

    if (item.ItemAttributes.Title)
      title = item.ItemAttributes.Title;

    if (item.ItemAttributes.Author)
      author = item.ItemAttributes.Author[0];

    if (item.DetailPageURL)
      amazonUrl = item.DetailPageURL;

    if (item.MediumImage)
      imageUrl = item.MediumImage.URL;

    if (item.ItemAttributes.ListPrice)
      listPrice = item.ItemAttributes.ListPrice.FormattedPrice;
```

(continued)

Listing 18-16 *(continued)*

```
if (item.Offers)
{
  var offerArray = item.Offers.Offer;
  if (offerArray)
  {
    if (offerArray[0].OfferListing)
    {
      if (offerArray[0].OfferListing[0].Price)
        price = item.Offers.Offer[0].OfferListing[0].Price.FormattedPrice;
    }
  }
}

builder.append("<tr>");
builder.append("<td valign='top' width='100%'>");
builder.append("<table cellspacing='10' style='");
if (i % 2 == 0)
  builder.append(this._rowStyle);
else
  builder.append(this._alternatingRowStyle);
builder.append("'>");
builder.append("<tr>");
builder.append("<td align='center' valign='top' width='20%'>");
builder.append("<img alt='' src='");
builder.append(imageUrl);
builder.append("'/>");
builder.append("</td>");
builder.append("<td align='left' valign='top'>");
builder.append("<p>");
builder.append("<a href='");
builder.append(amazonUrl);
builder.append("'>");
builder.append(title);
builder.append("</a>");
builder.append("<br/>");
builder.append("by ");
builder.append(author);
builder.append(" (Author)");
builder.append("</p>");
builder.append("<p>");
builder.append("<b>List Price:</b> <s>");
builder.append(listPrice);
builder.append("</s></br>");
builder.append("<b>       Price:</b>");
builder.append(price);
builder.append("</br>");
builder.append("</td>");
builder.append("</tr>");
builder.append("<tr>");
builder.append("<td colspan='2'>");
builder.append("</td>");
```

```
      builder.append("</tr>");
      builder.append("</table>");
      builder.append("</td>");
      builder.append("</tr>");
  }

  builder.append("</table>");
  return builder.toString();
}

function CustomComponents3$HtmlGenerator$initialize()
{
  CustomComponents3.HtmlGenerator.callBaseMethod(this, "initialize");
}

CustomComponents3.HtmlGenerator.prototype =
{
  get_tableStyle: CustomComponents3$HtmlGenerator$get_tableStyle,
  set_tableStyle: CustomComponents3$HtmlGenerator$set_tableStyle,
  get_rowStyle: CustomComponents3$HtmlGenerator$get_rowStyle,
  set_rowStyle: CustomComponents3$HtmlGenerator$set_rowStyle,
  get_alternatingRowStyle: CustomComponents3$HtmlGenerator$get_alternatingRowStyle,
  set_alternatingRowStyle: CustomComponents3$HtmlGenerator$set_alternatingRowStyle,
  generateHtml: CustomComponents3$HtmlGenerator$generateHtml,
  initialize: CustomComponents3$HtmlGenerator$initialize
}

CustomComponents3.HtmlGenerator.registerClass("CustomComponents3.HtmlGenerator",
                                   Sys.Component);
if (typeof(Sys) !== 'undefined')
  Sys.Application.notifyScriptLoaded();
```

Properties

The following table describes the properties of the HtmlGenerator client component.

Getter or Setter	Description
get_tableStyle	Gets a string that contains the value that can be directly assigned to the style property of the table HTML element that the generateHtml method renders as the containing HTML element
set_tableStyle	Specifies a string that contains the value that can be directly assigned to the style property of the table HTML element that the generateHtml method renders as the containing HTML element
get_rowStyle	Gets a string that contains the value that can be directly assigned to the style property of the even tr HTML elements that the generateHtml method renders

(continued)

Getter or Setter	Description
set_rowStyle	Specifies a string that contains the value that can be directly assigned to the style property of the even tr HTML elements that the generateHtml method renders
get_alternatingRowStyle	Gets a string that contains the value that can be directly assigned to the style property of the odd tr HTML elements that the generateHtml method renders
set_alternatingRowStyle	Specifies a string that contains the value that can be directly assigned to the style property of the odd tr HTML elements that the generateHtml method renders

generateHtml

This method takes the search results as its argument and generates and returns the HTML markup that displays them. This method first invokes the Item property on the object passed into it to return the actual search results:

```
var results = items.Item;
if (!results)
    return;
```

Next, it instantiates a StringBuilder, which will accumulate the HTML markup that displays the search results:

```
var builder = new Sys.StringBuilder();
```

Then it adds the string that contains the containing table HTML element. Notice that it directly assigns the value of the _tableStyle field to the style property of the table element:

```
builder.append("<table cellspacing='10' style='");
builder.append(this._tableStyle);
builder.append("'>");
```

Next, it iterates through the search results and takes the following steps for each enumerated search result. (Keep in mind that each enumerated search result contains data about a particular book.) First it retrieves the book data that the enumerated search result contains and stores the data in the associated private fields:

```
title = item.ItemAttributes.Title;
author = item.ItemAttributes.Author[0];
amazonUrl = item.DetailPageURL;
imageUrl = item.MediumImage.URL;
listPrice = item.ItemAttributes.ListPrice.FormattedPrice;
var offerArray = item.Offers.Offer;
price = item.Offers.Offer[0].OfferListing[0].Price.FormattedPrice;
```

Next, it generates a string that contains a `tr` HTML element with a single `td` HTML element, which in turn contains a `table` HTML element:

```
builder.append("<tr>");
builder.append("<td valign='top' width='100%'>");
builder.append("<table cellspacing='10' style='");
```

Then it generates a string that contains a `tr` HTML element that displays a particular piece of information about the book, such as its title. Note that `generateHTML` assigns the value of the `_rowStyle` field to the `style` property of the `tr` HTML element if the element represents an even row. Otherwise it assigns the value of the `_alternatingRowStyle` field to this style property.

```
if (i % 2 == 0)
   builder.append(this._rowStyle);
else
   builder.append(this._alternatingRowStyle);
```

HtmlGeneratorScriptControl

Listing 18-17 contains the implementation of the `HtmlGeneratorScriptControl` script server control. I'll discuss the methods and properties of this server control in the following sections.

Listing 18-17: The HtmlGeneratorScriptControl Script Server Control

```
using System;
using System.Data;
using System.Configuration;
using System.Web;
using System.Web.Security;
using System.Web.UI;
using System.Web.UI.WebControls;
using System.Web.UI.WebControls.WebParts;
using System.Web.UI.HtmlControls;
using System.Collections.Specialized;
using System.Xml;
using System.IO;
using System.Collections.Generic;
using com.amazon.webservices;
using System.ComponentModel;

namespace CustomComponents3
{
   public class HtmlGeneratorScriptControl : ScriptControl
   {
      protected override Style CreateControlStyle()
      {
         return new TableStyle(ViewState);
      }
```

(continued)

Listing 18-17 *(continued)*

```
private TableItemStyle rowStyle;
[PersistenceMode(PersistenceMode.InnerProperty)]
[NotifyParentProperty(true)]
[DesignerSerializationVisibility(DesignerSerializationVisibility.Content)]
public virtual TableItemStyle RowStyle
{
  get
  {
    if (rowStyle == null)
    {
      rowStyle = new TableItemStyle();
      if (IsTrackingViewState)
        ((IStateManager)rowStyle).TrackViewState();
    }
    return rowStyle;
  }
}

private TableItemStyle alternatingRowStyle;
[PersistenceMode(PersistenceMode.InnerProperty)]
[NotifyParentProperty(true)]
[DesignerSerializationVisibility(DesignerSerializationVisibility.Content)]
public virtual TableItemStyle AlternatingRowStyle
{
  get
  {
    if (alternatingRowStyle == null)
    {
      alternatingRowStyle = new TableItemStyle();
      if (IsTrackingViewState)
        ((IStateManager)alternatingRowStyle).TrackViewState();
    }
    return alternatingRowStyle;
  }
}

protected override object SaveViewState()
{
  object[] state = new object[3];
  state[0] = base.SaveViewState();
  if (this.rowStyle != null)
    state[1] = ((IStateManager)rowStyle).SaveViewState();
  if (this.alternatingRowStyle != null)
    state[2] = ((IStateManager)alternatingRowStyle).SaveViewState();

  foreach (object obj in state)
  {
    if (obj != null)
      return state;
  }
```

```
      return null;
    }

    protected override void LoadViewState(object savedState)
    {
      if (savedState == null)
      {
        base.LoadViewState(savedState);
        return;
      }

      object[] state = savedState as object[];
      if (state == null || state.Length != 3)
        return;

      base.LoadViewState(state[0]);
      if (state[1] != null)
        ((IStateManager)RowStyle).LoadViewState(state[1]);
      if (state[2] != null)
        ((IStateManager)AlternatingRowStyle).LoadViewState(state[2]);
    }

    protected override void TrackViewState()
    {
      base.TrackViewState();
      if (rowStyle != null)
        ((IStateManager)RowStyle).TrackViewState();
      if (alternatingRowStyle != null)
        ((IStateManager)AlternatingRowStyle).TrackViewState();
    }

    protected override IEnumerable<ScriptDescriptor> GetScriptDescriptors()
    {
      ScriptComponentDescriptor descriptor =
                        new ScriptComponentDescriptor(this.ClientControlType);
      descriptor.AddProperty("id", this.ClientID);
      CssStyleCollection col;
      if (ControlStyleCreated)
      {
        col = ControlStyle.GetStyleAttributes(this);
        descriptor.AddProperty("tableStyle", col.Value);
      }

      if (this.rowStyle != null)
      {
        col = rowStyle.GetStyleAttributes(this);
        descriptor.AddProperty("rowStyle", col.Value);
      }
```

(continued)

Listing 18-17 *(continued)*

```
if (this.alternatingRowStyle != null)
    {
        col = alternatingRowStyle.GetStyleAttributes(this);
        descriptor.AddProperty("alternatingRowStyle", col.Value);
    }

    return new ScriptDescriptor[] { descriptor };
}

protected override IEnumerable<ScriptReference> GetScriptReferences()
{
    ScriptReference reference = new ScriptReference();
    reference.Path = this.Path;
    return new ScriptReference[] { reference };
}

public string Path
{
    get
    {
        return ViewState["Path"] != null ?
                                    (string)ViewState["Path"] : string.Empty;
    }
    set
    {
        ViewState["Path"] = value;
    }
}

public string ClientControlType
{
    get
    {
        return ViewState["ClientControlType"] != null ?
                        (string)ViewState["ClientControlType"] : string.Empty;
    }
    set
    {
        ViewState["ClientControlType"] = value;
    }
}

public virtual int CellPadding
{
    get { return ((TableStyle)ControlStyle).CellPadding; }
    set { ((TableStyle)ControlStyle).CellPadding = value; }
}
```

```
    public virtual int CellSpacing
    {
      get { return ((TableStyle)ControlStyle).CellSpacing; }
      set { ((TableStyle)ControlStyle).CellSpacing = value; }
    }

    public virtual HorizontalAlign HorizontalAlign
    {
      get { return ((TableStyle)ControlStyle).HorizontalAlign; }
      set { ((TableStyle)ControlStyle).HorizontalAlign = value; }
    }

    public virtual string BackImageUrl
    {
      get { return ((TableStyle)ControlStyle).BackImageUrl; }
      set { ((TableStyle)ControlStyle).BackImageUrl = value; }
    }

    public virtual GridLines GridLines
    {
      get { return ((TableStyle)ControlStyle).GridLines; }
      set { ((TableStyle)ControlStyle).GridLines = value; }
    }
  }
}
```

Properties

The following table describes the properties of the HtmlGeneratorScriptControl script server control:

Property	Description
RowStyle	Gets the TableItemStyle object that styles the even rows of the table that the underlying HTML generator client component generates
AlternatingRowStyle	Gets the TableItemStyle object that styles the odd rows of the table that the underlying HTML generator client component generates
ClientControlType	Gets or sets the string that contains the fully qualified name of the type of the underlying HTML generator client component, including its complete namespace containment hierarchy
Path	Gets or sets the string that contains the virtual path of the JavaScript file that contains the implementation of the underlying HTML generator client component

CreateControlStyle

As Listing 18-17 shows, HtmlGeneratorScriptControl overrides the CreateControlStyle method that it inherits from the WebControl base class to instantiate and to return a TableStyle object. This object will enable page developers to style the containing table HTML element of the HTML markup text that the underlying HTML generator client component generates:

```
protected override Style CreateControlStyle()
{
  return new TableStyle(ViewState);
}
```

As I mentioned earlier, every server control that overrides the CreateControlStyle method must also expose the properties of the associated Style object as its own top-level properties. As a result, the HtmlGeneratorScriptControl exposes five style properties — CellPadding, CellSpacing, HorizontalAlign, BackImageUrl, and GridLines — that get or set the values of the CellPadding, CellSpacing, HorizontalAlign, BackImageUrl, and GridLines properties, respectively, of the underlying TableStyle object that styles the containing table HTML element of the HtmlGeneratorScriptControl script server control. As you'll see later, HtmlGeneratorScriptControl will apply the TableStyle settings to the containing table HTML element of the HTML markup text that the underlying HTML generator client component generates.

GetScriptDescriptors

As Listing 18-17 shows, HtmlGeneratorScriptControl, like any other script server control, overrides the GetScriptDescriptors method, where it takes the following steps. First, it instantiates a ScriptComponentDescriptor object, passing in the value of the ClientControlType property. Recall that this property contains the fully qualified name of the type of the underlying HTML generator client component:

```
ScriptComponentDescriptor descriptor =
                    new ScriptComponentDescriptor(this.ClientControlType);
```

Next, it invokes the AddProperty method on this ScriptComponentDescriptor object to specify the value of the ClientID property of the HtmlGeneratorScriptControl server control as the id property value of the underlying HTML generator client component:

```
descriptor.AddProperty("id", this.ClientID);
```

Then it calls the ControlStyleCreated property to check whether the ControlStyle property of the HtmlGeneratorScriptControl server control has been specified. If so, it invokes the GetStyleAttributes method on the ControlStyle property to return a CssStyleCollection that contains the CSS styles of the containing table HTML element of the server control:

```
col = ControlStyle.GetStyleAttributes(this);
```

Next, it invokes the AddProperty method on the ScriptComponentDescriptor object to specify the value of the Value property of the CssStyleCollection as the value of the tableStyle property of the underlying HTML generator client components. Keep in mind that the value of the Value property is a string that contains a semicolon-separated list of items in which each item consists of two parts separated by a colon. In other words, the value of this property is a string that can be directly assigned to the `style` property of the containing `table` HTML element:

```
descriptor.AddProperty("tableStyle", col.Value);
```

Then `HtmlGeneratorScriptControl` repeats the preceding process to specify the value of the `rowStyle` and `alternatingRowStyle` properties of the underlying HTML generator client component:

```
if (this.rowStyle != null)
{
  col = rowStyle.GetStyleAttributes(this);
  descriptor.AddProperty("rowStyle", col.Value);
}

if (this.alternatingRowStyle != null)
{
  col = alternatingRowStyle.GetStyleAttributes(this);
  descriptor.AddProperty("alternatingRowStyle", col.Value);
}
```

Finally, it instantiates and populates an array with the preceding `ScriptComponentDescriptor` object, and returns the array to its caller:

```
return new ScriptDescriptor[] { descriptor };
```

GetScriptReferences

`HtmlGeneratorScriptControl`, like any other script server control, overrides the `GetScriptReferences` method. As you can see from Listing 18-17, this method first instantiates a `ScriptReference` object:

```
ScriptReference reference = new ScriptReference();
```

Next, it assigns the value of the `Path` property of the `HtmlGeneratorScriptControl` to the `Path` property of the `ScriptReference` object. Recall that the `Path` property specifies the virtual path of the JavaScript file that contains the implementation of the underlying HTML generator client component:

```
reference.Path = this.Path;
```

Finally, it instantiates and populates an array with the `ScriptReference` object, and returns the array to its caller:

```
return new ScriptReference[] { reference };
```

State Management

As Listing 18-17 shows, `HtmlGeneratorScriptControl` overrides the `SaveViewState`, `LoadViewState`, and `TrackViewState` methods to manage the state of its `RowStyle` and `AlternatingRowStyle` properties across page postbacks, as discussed in the following sections.

SaveViewState

HtmlGeneratorScriptControl, like any other server control, overrides the SaveViewState method to save the state of its complex properties into view state before the current server response is sent to the client. As you can see from Listing 18-17, this method begins by instantiating an array of length 3:

```
object[] state = new object[3];
```

Next, it invokes the base SaveViewState method to return an object that contains the base state of HtmlGeneratorScriptControl:

```
state[0] = base.SaveViewState();
```

If the rowStyle field has been set, it invokes the SaveViewState on this field to return an object that contains the state of the field:

```
if (this.rowStyle != null)
    state[1] = ((IStateManager)rowStyle).SaveViewState();
```

If the alternatingRowStyle field has been set, it invokes the SaveViewState on this field to return an object that contains the state of this field as well:

```
if (this.alternatingRowStyle != null)
    state[2] = ((IStateManager)alternatingRowStyle).SaveViewState();
```

Finally, it returns the array that contains these three objects.

LoadViewState

This method takes an array of three objects. This array is the same one that the SaveViewState returns. As you can see, LoadViewState does the opposite of SaveViewState. First, it invokes the base LoadViewState, passing in the first object in the array to load the base state:

```
base.LoadViewState(state[0]);
```

Next, it calls the LoadViewState method on the RowStyle property, passing in the second object in the array to have this property load its state:

```
if (state[1] != null)
    ((IStateManager)RowStyle).LoadViewState(state[1]);
```

Finally, it calls the LoadViewState method on the AlternatingRowStyle property, passing in the third object in the array to have this property load its state as well:

```
if (state[2] != null)
    ((IStateManager)AlternatingRowStyle).LoadViewState(state[2]);
```

TrackViewState

As you can see from Listing 18-17, this method first invokes the base TrackViewState method to start tracking the base state:

```
base.TrackViewState();
```

If the `rowStyle` field is set, it invokes the `TrackViewState` on this field to have this field start tracking its state:

```
if (rowStyle != null)
    ((IStateManager)RowStyle).TrackViewState();
```

If the `alternatingRowStyle` field is set, it invokes the `TrackViewState` on this field to have this field start tracking its state as well:

```
if (alternatingRowStyle != null)
    ((IStateManager)AlternatingRowStyle).TrackViewState();
```

Using the Components

Follow these steps to use the components we've developed in the last few sections:

1. Follow the steps discussed in the previous chapter to create a new AJAX-enabled Web application in Visual Studio that contains all the replicas developed in the previous chapter.

2. Make sure that the `web.config` file contains the following section:

```
<configuration>
  <system.web>
    <compilation debug="true">
      <assemblies>
        <add assembly="System.Web.Extensions, Version=1.0.61025.0, Culture=neutral,
                       PublicKeyToken=31bf3856ad364e35" />
      </assemblies>
      <buildProviders>
        <add extension=".asbx"
        type="Microsoft.Web.Preview.Services.BridgeBuildProvider" />
      </buildProviders>
    </compilation>
  </system.web>
</configuration>
```

3. Make sure that IIS is configured to hand the incoming requests for resources with the `.asbx` file extension over to the appropriate handler, as discussed in Chapter 14. For example, if you're using IIS 5.1 (running on the XP operating system), IIS 6.0 (running on Windows 2000 Server), or IIS 7.0 in ISAPI mode (running on the Vista operating system), you need to register the `aspnet_isapi.dll` ISAPI extension module with IIS to have IIS hand requests for resources with the `.asbx` file extension to this ISAPI extension module.

As you can see from Listing 18-14, the `AspNetAjaxAmazonSearch` ASP.NET AJAX control catches request failures in a method named `_onFailure`. This method displays a pop-up box that contains the complete information about the failure, including stack trace and the HTTP status code. If you run the page shown in Listing 18-18 and get this pop-up with the HTTP status code of 404, you know that the code could not find the specified file with the `.asbx` file extension. This normally happens when IIS has not been configured to hand the request for resources with the `.asbx` file extension to the appropriate handler. When IIS does not find a handler that can process the request, it returns a response with the status code of 404.

4. Add a new file named `AmazonSearch.asbx` to the root directory of the application and add the code shown in Listing 18-12 to this file.

5. Add a new Web page, `AmazonSearch.aspx`, to the root directory of the application, and add the code shown in Listing 18-18 to this file. As you can see, this page uses our components.

6. Add a new source file named `AspNetAjaxAmazonSearch.js` to the root directory of the application and add the code shown in Listing 18-14 to this file.

7. Add a new source file named `HtmlGenerator.js` to the root directory of the application and add the code shown in Listing 18-16 to this file.

8. Add a new source file named `AmazonSearchScriptControl.cs` to the `App_Code` directory and add the code shown in Listing 18-15 to this source file.

9. Add a new source file named `HtmlGeneratorScriptControl.cs` to the `App_Code` directory and add the code shown in Listing 18-17 to this source file.

10. Add a new source file named `AmazonService.cs` to the `App_Code` directory and add the code shown in Listing 18-13 to this source file.

Listing 18-18: A Page that Uses Our Components

```
<%@ Page Language="C#" %>

<%@ Register Namespace="CustomComponents3" TagPrefix="custom" %>
<!DOCTYPE html PUBLIC "-//W3C//DTD XHTML 1.0 Transitional//EN"
"http://www.w3.org/TR/xhtml1/DTD/xhtml1-transitional.dtd">
<html xmlns="http://www.w3.org/1999/xhtml">
<head id="Head1" runat="server">
  <title>Untitled Page</title>
</head>
<body>
  <form id="form1" runat="server">
    <asp:ScriptManager runat="server" ID="ScriptManager1">
      <Services>
        <asp:ServiceReference InlineScript="true"
        Path="AmazonSearch.asbx" />
      </Services>
    </asp:ScriptManager>

    <custom:ScriptManager runat="server" ID="CustomScriptManager1" />

    <custom:AmazonSearchScriptControl runat="server" ID="MyControl"
    SearchMethod="MyServices.AmazonService.Search"
    HtmlGeneratorID="MyHtmlGenerator"
    Path="AspNetAjaxAmazonSearch.js"
    ClientControlType="CustomComponents3.AspNetAjaxAmazonSearch"/>

    <custom:HtmlGeneratorScriptControl runat="server" ID="MyHtmlGenerator"
    Path="HtmlGenerator.js"
    ClientControlType="CustomComponents3.HtmlGenerator">
      <RowStyle BackColor="#eeeeee" Width="100%" />
      <AlternatingRowStyle BackColor="#cccccc" Width="100%" />
    </custom:HtmlGeneratorScriptControl>
  </form>
</body>
</html>
```

Transformers

Run the page shown in Listing 18-18 in debug mode. Go to the following directory on your machine:

```
%WinDir%\Microsoft.NET\Framework\v2.0.50727\Temporary ASP.NET Files
```

If you have installed the .NET framework in a directory different from the standard %WinDir%, you need to locate the Temporary ASP.NET Files directory in that directory.

Look for a directory with the same name as your application. For example, if your application name is AJAXTCPEnabledWebSite2, look for the directory named ajaxtcpenabledwebsite2 (all in lowercase). Then go to a couple of directories below this directory (note that ASP.NET uses a random hash algorithm to generate the names of these two directories). Then look for a source file with the name similar to the following:

```
App_Web_amazonsearch.asbx.cdcab7d2.rxua8pbv.0.cs
```

Note that the name of the file consists of the keyword App_Web_, the name of the file that that this source file represents (which is amazonsearch.aspx in this case), some random hash (cdcab7d2), another random hash (rxua8pbv), the number 0, and finally the file extension .cs. Open this file in your favorite directory. You should see the code shown in Listing 18-19.

Listing 18-19: The Content of App_Web_amazonsearch.asbx.cdcab7d2.rxua8pbv.0.cs

```
namespace MyServices
{
  using System;
  using System.Net;
  using System.Web.Services;
  using System.Collections;
  using System.Xml.Serialization;
  using Microsoft.Web.Preview.Services;
  using System.Web.Script.Services;
  using System.Collections.Generic;

  [ScriptService()]
  [WebService(Name = "http://tempuri.org/")]
  [WebServiceBinding(ConformsTo = WsiProfiles.BasicProfile1_1)]
  public partial class AmazonService : BridgeHandler
  {
    public AmazonService()
    {
      this.VirtualPath = "/AJAXFuturesEnabledWebSite3/AmazonSearch.asbx";

      this.BridgeXml = @"<?xml version=""1.0"" encoding=""utf-8"" ?>
                        <bridge namespace=""MyServices""
                        className=""AmazonService"">
                          <proxy
                          type=""CustomComponents3.AmazonService, App_Code""/>
                            <method name=""Search"">
                              <input>
                                <parameter name=""pageIndex"" />
```

(continued)

Listing 18-19 *(continued)*

```
                                <parameter name=""searchQuery"" />
                            </input>
                        </method>
                    </bridge>";
    }

    [WebMethodAttribute()]
    [ScriptMethodAttribute(UseHttpGet = false,
                            ResponseFormat = ResponseFormat.Json)]
    public virtual object Search(IDictionary args)
    {
        return this.Invoke(new BridgeRequest("Search", args));
    }

    public override object CallServiceClassMethod(string method,
                                        Dictionary<string, object> args,
                                        ICredentials credentials,
                                        string url)
    {
        if ("Search".Equals(method))
        {
            CustomComponents3.AmazonService proxy =
                                    new CustomComponents3.AmazonService();
            object obj;
            args.TryGetValue("pageIndex", out obj);
            int arg0 = ((int)(BridgeHandler.ConvertToType(obj, typeof(int))));
            args.TryGetValue("searchQuery", out obj))
            string arg1 = ((string)(BridgeHandler.ConvertToType(obj, typeof(string))));
            return proxy.Search(arg0, arg1);
        }
    }
}
```

If you're wondering who generated this code, open the `web.config` file and look for the compilation section. You should see the XML fragment shown in the following listing:

```
<configuration>
  <system.web>
    <compilation debug="true">
      <buildProviders>
        <add extension=".asbx"
        type="Microsoft.Web.Preview.Services.BridgeBuildProvider" />
      </buildProviders>
    </compilation>
  </system.web>
</configuration>
```

As you can see, the `buildProviders` subsection of the `compilation` section registers a build provider named `BridgeBuildProvider` for the `.asbx` file extension. A build provider is an ASP.NET class that knows how to parse a file with a specific extension into a .NET class. For example, the `BridgeBuildProvider` knows how to parse a file with the extension `.asbx` into a .NET class such as the one shown in Listing 18-19.

The ASP.NET framework enables you to implement and register your own custom build provider.

In other words, the `BridgeBuildProvider` parses the `AmazonSearch.asbx` file shown in Listing 18-12 (repeated in the following listing) into the `AmazonService` class shown in Listing 18-19. Note that the value of the `className` attribute of the `bridge` element in the following code listing determines the name of this dynamically generated class, and the value of the `namespace` attribute of this element determines the name of the namespace of this dynamically generated class, which is `MyServices` in this case. Also, note that the `AmazonService` class shown in Listing 18-19 contains a method named `Search`. The value of the `name` attribute of the `method` subelement of the proxy element determines the name of this method. Also note that the names and number of the parameters of this method are determined by the `parameter` subelements of the input subelement of this method element. Basically, each `parameter` subelement specifies the name of a particular parameter of the method.

```xml
<?xml version="1.0" encoding="utf-8" ?>
<bridge namespace="MyServices" className="AmazonService">
  <proxy type="CustomComponents3.AmazonService, App_Code"/>
  <method name="Search">
    <input>
      <parameter name="pageIndex" />
      <parameter name="searchQuery" />
    </input>
  </method>
</bridge>
```

Note that the `AmazonService` class shown in Listing 18-19 is annotated with the `WebService` metadata attribute. This means that this class is a Web service. In other words, the `BridgeBuildProvider` creates a Web service out of the content of the `.asbx` that it parses. The base class of a normal Web service is a class named `WebService`. However, as you can see from Listing 18-19, the base class of the `AmazonService` Web service is not the `WebService` class. Instead it is an ASP.NET class named `BridgeHandler`. I'll discuss this class shortly.

Keep in mind that ASP.NET Web services are not required to inherit from the `WebService` base class. Inheriting from this optional class provides the ASP.NET Web service with typical ASP.NET objects such as `Request`, `Response`, `Server`, and so on.

As you can see from Listing 18-19, the constructor of the `AmazonSearch` class sets two of its properties. The first is a string property named `VirtualPath`, whose value is set to the virtual path of the `.asbx` file, which is /AJAXFuturesEnabledWebSite3/AmazonSearch.asbx in our case. The second is a string property named BridgeXml, whose value is set to a string that contains the content of the .aspx file:

```
public AmazonService()
{
  this.VirtualPath = "/AJAXFuturesEnabledWebSite3/AmazonSearch.asbx";

  this.BridgeXml = @"<?xml version=""1.0"" encoding=""utf-8"" ?>
                    <bridge namespace=""MyServices""
                    className=""AmazonService"">
                      <proxy
                      type=""CustomComponents3.AmazonService, App_Code""/>
                        <method name=""Search"">
                          <input>
                            <parameter name=""pageIndex"" />
                            <parameter name=""searchQuery"" />
                          </input>
                        </method>
                      </bridge>";
}
```

As I mentioned earlier, the AmazonSearch Web service contains a Web method named Search. Note that this method takes an IDictionary collection that contains the arguments that will be passed into the Search Web method of the AWSECommerceService Web service. As you can see, this method calls a method named Invoke and passes an instance of an ASP.NET class named BridgeRequest into it. As the name suggests, this class represents the current request:

```
public class BridgeRequest
{
  private IDictionary _args;
  private string _method;
  private string _serviceUrl;

  public BridgeRequest(string method, IDictionary args)
  {
    _method = method;
    if (args == null)
      args = new Hashtable();
    _args = args;
  }

  public IDictionary Args { get {return _args;} set {_args = value;} }
  public string Method { get {return _method;} set {_method = value;} }
  public string ServiceUrl { get{return _serviceUrl;} set{_serviceUrl = value;}}
}
```

What matters to us here is that the Search method of the AmazonSearch class calls the Invoke method. This class inherits the Invoke method from its base class — that is, the BridgeHandler. This is an important method, which will be discussed shortly.

```
[WebMethodAttribute()]
[ScriptMethodAttribute(UseHttpGet = false,
                       ResponseFormat = ResponseFormat.Json)]
public virtual object Search(IDictionary args)
{
  return this.Invoke(new BridgeRequest("Search", args));
}
```

Before diving into the implementation of the `Invoke` method, let's wrap up our discussions of the `AmazonSearch` class shown in Listing 18-19 by briefly discussing its `CallServiceClassMethod`. The `AmazonSearch` class inherits this method from its base class (that is, `BridgeHandler`) and overrides this method. First, it instantiates an instance of a class named `CustomComponents3.AmazonService`. If you check with the `AmazonSearch.asbx` file, you'll notice that this class is nothing but the class that we registered through the `type` attribute of the `proxy` subelement of the `bridge` element. This class is shown in Listing 18-13. Next the `CallServiceClassMethod` simply invokes the `Search` method on the newly created instance of the `CustomComponents3.AmazonService`:

```
public override object CallServiceClassMethod(string method,
                                              Dictionary<string, object> args,
                                              ICredentials credentials,
                                              string url)
{
  if ("Search".Equals(method))
  {
    CustomComponents3.AmazonService proxy =
                                       new CustomComponents3.AmazonService();
    object obj;
    args.TryGetValue("pageIndex", out obj);
    int arg0 = ((int)(BridgeHandler.ConvertToType(obj, typeof(int))));
    args.TryGetValue("searchQuery", out obj))
    string arg1 = ((string)(BridgeHandler.ConvertToType(obj, typeof(string))));
    return proxy.Search(arg0, arg1);
  }
}
```

As I discussed earlier, the `AmazonService` class shown in Listing 18-19 exposes a method named `Search` that calls the `Invoke` method that this class inherits from its base class, the `BridgeHandler`. When you run the page shown in Listing 18-18, enter a search query into the search text box, and hit the Search button to perform an Amazon search, the `Search` method of the `AmazonService` class shown in Listing 18-19 is invoked, which in turn calls the `Invoke` method of its base class, the `BridgeHandler`. The `Invoke` method performs two important tasks. First, it calls the `CallServiceClassMethod` method shown in Listing 18-19 to process the request. As I mentioned earlier, the `CallServiceClassMethod` method ends up calling the `Search` method of the `CustomComponents3.AmazonService` class shown in Listing 18-13. Recall that this method is the one that makes the actual request to the `AWSECommerce` Web service and receives the response or the search results from the Amazon Web service.

The `Invoke` method does not directly return to the client the result returned from the `Search` method of the `Customcomponents3.AmazonService` class. Instead it checks whether the associated `.asbx` file contains any transformers for the specified method. As the name suggests, a transformer is a component that transforms the return value of the method call before the value is sent back to the client. As you'll see later, different types of transformers perform different types of transformations on the return value of the method call. For example, the ASP.NET AJAX framework comes with a transformer named

XmlBridgeTransformer that transforms this return value into its XML representation. You can even write your own custom transformer to perform custom transformation on this return value. This will all be clear by the end of this chapter.

The AmazonSearch.asbx file that we've been using so far does not contain any transformers. Listing 18-20 presents the contents of a new file named AmazonSearch2.asbx that contains a transformer for the Search method. Take these steps to add a transformer for a specified method:

1. If you haven't already done so, add a child element named transforms to the method element that represents the specified method in the .asbx file:

```
<method name="Search">
  <input>
    <parameter name="pageIndex" />
    <parameter name="searchQuery" />
  </input>

  <transforms>

    <transform type="CustomComponents3.XmlBridgeTransformer"/>

  </transforms>

</method>
```

2. Add a child element named transform to the transforms element:

```
<method name="Search">
  <input>
    <parameter name="pageIndex" />
    <parameter name="searchQuery" />
  </input>
  <transforms>

    <transform

    type="CustomComponents3.XmlBridgeTransformer"/>
  </transforms>
</method>
```

3. Set the value of the type attribute of this transform element to the fully qualified name of the desired transformer:

```
<method name="Search">
    <input>
      <parameter name="pageIndex" />
      <parameter name="searchQuery" />
    </input>
    <transforms>
      <transform

      type="CustomComponents3.XmlBridgeTransformer"/>

    </transforms>
  </method>
```

You must repeat steps 2 and 3 if you need to add more transformers for the same method. You'll see an example of adding more transformers later in this chapter.

Listing 18-20: The AmazonSearch2.asbx

```xml
<?xml version="1.0" encoding="utf-8" ?>
<bridge namespace="MyServices2" className="AmazonService2">
  <proxy type="CustomComponents3.AmazonService2, App_Code"/>
  <method name="Search">
    <input>
      <parameter name="pageIndex" />
      <parameter name="searchQuery" />
    </input>
    <transforms>
      <transform type="CustomComponents3.XmlBridgeTransformer"/>
    </transforms>
  </method>
</bridge>
```

As I discussed earlier, after invoking the `CallServiceClassMethod` method (which in turn invokes the `Search` method on the `CustomComponents3.AmazonService` class), the `Invoke` method of the `BridgeHandler` checks whether the associated `.asbx` file contains transformers for the specified method. In the case of Listing 18-20, the `.asbx` file contains a transformer of type `XmlBridgeTransformer` for the `Search` method. As you'll see later, the `.asbx` file may contain more than one transformer for the same method.

The `Invoke` method then instantiates these transformers by means of the .NET reflection and the values of the `type` attributes of the transform subelements of the `transforms` subelement of the `method` element that represents the specified method. The transformers are then linked together to form a pipeline: the output of a transformer in the pipeline becomes an input into the next. Since the `.asbx` file shown in Listing 18-11 contains a single transformer named `XmlBridgeTransformer`, this pipeline contains a single transformer.

The `Invoke` method passes the return value of the `CallServiceClassMethod` method into the first transformer in the pipeline, which is the `XmlBridgeTransform` in the case of Listing 18-11. The first transformer performs its specific transformation on its input. In other words, the output of this transformer is the transformed version of the return value of the `CallServiceClassMethod` method.

The `Invoke` method then passes this output as an input to the second transformer in the pipeline. In other words, the second transformer receives a transformed version of the return value of the `CallServiceClassMethod` method. The second transformer, in turn, performs its own transformation on its input and outputs the transformed version. The `Invoke` method then repeats the same process with any subsequent transformers in the pipeline. The `Invoke` method finally returns the output of the last transformer to the client.

Every ASP.NET AJAX transformer implements an interface named `IBridgeResponseTransformer`. As you can see from Listing 18-21, this interface exposes two methods:

❑　Initialize: This method allows a transformer to initialize itself. It takes a single argument of type BridgeTransformData, which will be discussed shortly.

❑　Transform: The Invoke method calls the Transform method of a transformer, passing in an object to allow the transform to perform its specific transformation on this object. As I discussed earlier, this object is the output of the previous transformer in the pipeline. The Invoke method then passes the return value of the Transform method of the transformer as input into the Transform method of the next transformer. What a Transform method of a transformer does to the object passed into it is completely up to the transformer. The Transform methods of different transformers perform different types of transformations on their input. As you'll see later, you can implement your own transformer whose Transform method performs some custom transformation on its input.

Listing 18-21: The IBridgeResponseTransformer Interface

```
public interface IBridgeResponseTransformer
{
  void Initialize(BridgeTransformData data);
  object Transform(object results);
}
```

Listing 18-22 presents the declaration of the BridgeTransformData class. As you can see, the constructor of BridgeTransformData creates two dictionaries. The first dictionary is a dictionary of dictionaries in which each dictionary is uniquely identified by a key, which is a string. The BridgeTransformData class exposes a property named Dictionaries that returns a reference to the first dictionary. The second dictionary is a dictionary of string values in which each string value is uniquely identified by a key, which is a string. The BridgeTransformData class exposes a property named Attributes that returns a reference to the second dictionary.

Listing 18-22: The BridgeTransformData Class

```
public class BridgeTransformData
{
  private Dictionary<string, string> _attributes;
  private Dictionary<string, Dictionary<string, string>> _dictionaries;

  public BridgeTransformData()
  {
    this._dictionaries = new Dictionary<string, Dictionary<string, string>>();
    this._attributes = new Dictionary<string, string>();
  }

  public Dictionary<string, string> Attributes
  {
    get { return this._attributes; }
  }

  public Dictionary<string, Dictionary<string, string>> Dictionaries
  {
    get { return this._dictionaries; }
  }
}
```

To understand the role of the `Dictionaries` and `Attributes` properties of `BridgeTransformData` we need to revisit a typical `.asbx` file, shown in Listing 18-23. As you can see, each `transform` element contains a subelement named `data`, which in turn contains zero or more `attribute` elements and zero or more `dictionary` elements. The value of the `name` attribute of each `attribute` element uniquely identifies that `attribute` element among other `attribute` elements of the specified transformer. The value of the `value` attribute of each `attribute` element contains the string representation of a particular parameter of the associated transformer. What this parameter means depends completely on the transformer.

The value of the `name` attribute of each `dictionary` element uniquely identifies that `dictionary` element among other `dictionary` elements. Note that each `dictionary` element contains one or more `item` subelements. The value of the `name` attribute of each `item` element uniquely identifies that `item` element among others of the specified dictionary. The value of the `value` attribute of each `item` element contains the string representation of a particular parameter of the associated transformer. What the values of the `value` attributes of the `item` elements of a given dictionary of a transformer mean depends completely on the transformer. You'll see an example of using different `value` attributes later in this chapter.

Listing 18-23: A typical .asbx File

```xml
<?xml version="1.0" encoding="utf-8" ?>
<bridge namespace="..." className="...">
  <proxy type="..."/>
  <method name="...">
    <input>
      <parameter name="..." />
      <parameter name="..." />
          .
          .
          .
      <parameter name="..." />
    </input>
    <transforms>
      <transform type="...">
        <data>
          <attribute name="..." value="..." />
          <attribute name="..." value="..." />
              .
              .
              .
          <attribute name="..." value="..." />

          <dictionary name="...">
            <item name="..." value="..." />
            <item name="..." value="..." />
                .
                .
                .
            <item name="..." value="..." />
          </dictionary>
              .
              .
              .
```

(continued)

Listing 18-23 (continued)

```
            <dictionary name="...">
                <item name="..." value="..." />
                <item name="..." value="..." />
                                .
                                .
                                .
                <item name="..." value="..." />
            </dictionary>
          </data>
        </transform>
      </transforms>
    </method>
</bridge>
```

As I discussed earlier, the `Initialize` method of a transformer takes a single parameter of type
`BridgeTransformData`. The ASP.NET AJAX framework performs these tasks for each transform
element in the `.asbx` file (recall that each `transform` element represents a transformer):

❏ Parses the content of the `data` subelement of the `transform` element. Recall that the content of
the `data` subelement consists of a bunch of `attribute` elements and a bunch of `dictionary`
elements.

❏ Instantiates a `BridgeTransformData` object.

❏ Populates the `Attributes` dictionary of the `BridgeTransformData` object with the values of
the `name` and `value` attributes of the `attribute` elements. This means that the `Initialize`
method of a transformer can use the value of the `name` attribute of an `attribute` element as an
index into the `Attributes` property of the `BridgeTransformData` object passed into it to
access the value of the `value` attribute of the `attribute` element as shown in the following
code snippet. As I discussed earlier, the value that the `Attributes` collection returns is the
string representation of some .NET object. The `Initialize` method can then use the appropriate converter to convert this string to the actual .NET object.

```
public class SomeTransformer : IBridgeResponseTransformer
{
  void IBridgeResponseTransformer.Initialize(BridgeTransformData data)
  {
    string valueOfTheValueAttributeOfTheAttributeElement =
          data.Attributes["ValueOfTheNameAttributeOfTheAttributeElement"];

    . . .
  }
  object Transform(object results);
}
```

❏ Populates the `Dictionaries` collection of the `BridgeTransformData` object with the content
of the `dictionary` elements. Since each `dictionary` element is uniquely identified by
the value of its `name` attribute, the `Initialize` method of a transformer can use the value of the
`name` attribute of a `dictionary` element as an index into the `Dictionaries` property of
the `BridgeTransformData` object passed into it to access the `Dictionary` object that
contains the content of the `dictionary` element. Since the value of the `name` attribute of an

item subelement of a dictionary element uniquely identifies the item element, the Initialize method can use the value of the name attribute of an item element as an index into this Dictionary object to return the value of the value attribute of the item element. As I discussed earlier, the value of the value attribute of an item element is the string representation of some .NET object. The Initialize method can then use the appropriate type converter to convert this string representation to the actual .NET object:

```
public class SomeTransformer : IBridgeResponseTransformer
{
  void IBridgeResponseTransformer.Initialize(BridgeTransformData data)
  {
    Dictionary<string, string> dictionary =
                data.Dictionaries["ValueOfTheNameAttributeOfTheDictionaryElement"];
    string valueOfTheValueAttributeOfTheItemElement =
                          dictionary["ValueOfTheNameAttributeOfTheItemElement"];
    . . .
  }
  object Transform(object results);
}
```

Using Transformers

In this section, first I'll implement fully functional replicas of the XmlBridgeTransformer and XsltBridgeTransformer transformers and present several examples in which these transformers are used. I'll then show you how to implement your own custom transformer and plug it into the ASP.NET AJAX transformation infrastructure.

XmlBridgeTransformer

Listing 18-24 presents the implementation of the replica XmlBridgeTransformer. The XmlBridgeTransformer, like any other ASP.NET AJAX transformer, derives from the IBridgeResponseTransformer interface and implements the Initialize and Transform methods of this interface.

Listing 18-24: The XmlBridgeTransformer

```
using System;
using System.Data;
using System.Configuration;
using System.Web;
using System.Web.Security;
using System.Web.UI;
using System.Web.UI.WebControls;
using System.Web.UI.WebControls.WebParts;
using System.Web.UI.HtmlControls;
using Microsoft.Web.Preview.Services;
using System.Xml.Serialization;
using System.Xml;
```

(continued)

Listing 18-24 *(continued)*

```
using System.IO;
using System.Text;

namespace CustomComponents3
{
  public class XmlBridgeTransformer : IBridgeResponseTransformer
  {
    public void Initialize(BridgeTransformData data) { }

    public object Transform(object results)
    {
      object obj2;
      XmlSerializer serializer = new XmlSerializer(results.GetType());
      MemoryStream w = new MemoryStream();
      using (XmlTextWriter writer = new XmlTextWriter(w, Encoding.UTF8))
      {
        serializer.Serialize((XmlWriter)writer, results);
        w.Position = 0;
        using (StreamReader reader = new StreamReader(w))
        {
          obj2 = reader.ReadToEnd();
        }
      }
      return obj2;
    }
  }
}
```

As you can see from the .asbx file shown in Listing 18-20, the transform element that represents the XmlBridgeTransformer does not have the data subelement because the XmlBridgeTransformer does not have any parameters. That is why the Initialize method of the XmlBridgeTransformer doesn't do anything:

```
public void Initialize(BridgeTransformData data) { }
```

Next I'll walk you through the implementation of the Transform method of the replica XmlBridgeTransformer. As I discussed earlier, the Invoke method of the BridgeHandler passes the return value of the Transform method of the transformer that comes before a given transformer in the pipeline as an input into the Transform method of the transformer. The main responsibility of the Transform method is to perform its own transformation on the input and return the transformed object as output to the Invoke method. The type of transformation a transformer performs on the object passed into its Transform method depends on the type of transformer.

As you can see from Listing 18-24, the Transform method of the XmlBridgeTransformer simply serializes the object passed into it into an XML document and returns this document to its caller — that is, the Invoke method of the BridgeHandler. The Transform method of the XmlBridgeTransformer takes the following steps to perform its transformation. First, it instantiates an XmlSerializer. Note that it passes into the constructor of the XmlSerializer class the Type object that represents the type of the object being serialized:

```
XmlSerializer serializer = new XmlSerializer(results.GetType());
```

Next, it instantiates a MemoryStream into which the XML document will be written:

```
MemoryStream w = new MemoryStream();
```

Then it instantiates an XmlTextWriter to write the XML document into the MemoryStream:

```
XmlTextWriter writer = new XmlTextWriter(w, Encoding.UTF8)
```

Next, it invokes the Serialize method on the XmlSerializer to serialize the object passed into it into its XML representation, and uses the XmlTextWriter to write this XML representation into the MemoryStream:

```
serializer.Serialize((XmlWriter) writer, results);
```

Next, it instantiates a StreamReader to read the XML document from the MemoryStream:

```
StreamReader reader = new StreamReader(w)
```

Finally, it invokes the ReadToEnd method on the StreamReader to read the entire XML representation or document from the MemoryStream, which is then returned to the caller of the Transform method, the BridgeHandler.

Next, I'll present an example that shows the replica XmlBridgeTransformer in action. This example uses the .asbx file shown in Listing 18-11, which contains only one transformer, XmlBridgeTransformer. This means that the Invoke method of the BridgeHandler directly passes the return value of the Search method of the CustomComponents3.AmazonService class into the Transform method of the XmlBridgeTransformer and returns the return value of this Transform method to the client. In other words, the XmlBridgeTransformer simply serializes the return value of the Search method of the CustomComponents3.AmazonService class into its XML representation, which is subsequently sent to the client. To put it differently, the generateHtml method of the HtmlGenerator client component receives the XML representation of the data that the Search method returns.

Since the generateHtml method must extract the title, author, amazonUrl, imageUrl, listPrice, and price values of each book from this XML representation to display them to the end user, it expects the XML representation to have a specific schema. Listing 18-25 presents a new ASP.NET AJAX client control named HtmlGenerator2, which derives from HtmlGenerator and overrides its generateHtml method.

Listing 18-25: The HtmlGenerator2 Client Control

```
CustomComponents3.HtmlGenerator2 =
function CustomComponents3$HtmlGenerator2()
{
  CustomComponents3.HtmlGenerator2.initializeBase(this);
}

function CustomComponents3$HtmlGenerator2$generateHtml(xml)
{
  var title;
  var author;
  var amazonUrl;
  var imageUrl;
  var listPrice;
  var price;

  var builder = new Sys.StringBuilder();
  builder.append("<table cellspacing='10' style='");
  builder.append(this._tableStyle);
  builder.append("'>");
  var xmlDocument = new XMLDOM(xml);
  var items = xmlDocument.documentElement;
  var item = items.firstChild;
  var i = 0;
  while (item != null)
  {
    title = item.getAttribute("title");
    author = item.getAttribute("author");
    amazonUrl = item.getAttribute("amazonUrl");
    imageUrl = item.getAttribute("imageUrl");
    listPrice = item.getAttribute("listPrice");
    price = item.getAttribute("price");

    builder.append("<tr>");
    builder.append("<td valign='top' width='100%'>");
    builder.append("<table cellspacing='10' style='");
    if (i % 2 == 0)
      builder.append(this._rowStyle);
    else
      builder.append(this._alternatingRowStyle);
    builder.append("'>");
    builder.append("<tr>");
    builder.append("<td align='center' valign='top' width='20%'>");
    builder.append("<img alt='' src='");
    builder.append(imageUrl);
    builder.append("'/>");
    builder.append("</td>");
    builder.append("<td align='left' valign='top'>");
    builder.append("<p>");
    builder.append("<a href='");
    builder.append(amazonUrl);
    builder.append("'>");
    builder.append(title);
```

```
        builder.append("</a>");
        builder.append("<br/>");
        builder.append("by ");
        builder.append(author);
        builder.append(" (Author)");
        builder.append("</p>");
        builder.append("<p>");
        builder.append("<b>List Price:</b> <s>");
        builder.append(listPrice);
        builder.append("</s></br>");
        builder.append("<b>       Price:</b> ");
        builder.append(price);
        builder.append("</br>");
        builder.append("</td>");
        builder.append("</tr>");
        builder.append("<tr>");
        builder.append("<td colspan='2'>");
        builder.append("</td>");
        builder.append("</tr>");
        builder.append("</table>");
        builder.append("</td>");
        builder.append("</tr>");
        item = item.nextSibling;
        i++;
    }

    builder.append("</table>");
    return builder.toString();
}


function CustomComponents3$HtmlGenerator2$initialize()
{
    CustomComponents3.HtmlGenerator2.callBaseMethod(this, "initialize");
}


CustomComponents3.HtmlGenerator2.prototype =
{
    generateHtml: CustomComponents3$HtmlGenerator2$generateHtml,
    initialize: CustomComponents3$HtmlGenerator2$initialize
}

CustomComponents3.HtmlGenerator2.registerClass("CustomComponents3.HtmlGenerator2",
                                    CustomComponents3.HtmlGenerator);
```

As you can see from Listing 18-38, the generateHtml method of the HtmlGenerator2 client component assumes that the XML representation it receives from the server has the schema shown in Listing 18-26. As you can see, this schema defines an XML document with a document element named results, which contains zero or more child elements named result, each having six attributes: title, author, amazonUrl, imageUrl, listPrice, and price.

Listing 18-26: The Expected XML Schema of the XML Representation Received from the Server

```xml
<?xml version="1.0" encoding="utf-8" ?>
<xs:schema id="Results" xmlns:xs="http://www.w3.org/2001/XMLSchema">
  <xs:element name="results" type="results"/>
  <xs:complexType name="results">
    <xs:sequence>
      <xs:element name="result" type="result" minOccurs="0" maxOccurs="unbounded"/>
    </xs:sequence>
  </xs:complexType>

  <xs:complexType name="result">
    <xs:attribute name="title" type="xs:string"/>
    <xs:attribute name="author" type="xs:string"/>
    <xs:attribute name="amazonUrl" type="xs:string"/>
    <xs:attribute name="imageUrl" type="xs:string"/>
    <xs:attribute name="listPrice" type="xs:string"/>
    <xs:attribute name="price" type="xs:string"/>
  </xs:complexType>
</xs:schema>
```

This raises the following question: how can we make sure that the XmlBridgeTransformer serializes the return value of the Search method of the CustomComponents3.AmazonService class into an XML representation or document with the XML schema presented in Listing 18-26 — that is, the XML schema that the generateHtml method of the HtmlGenerator2 client component expects to receive from the server? Since the XmlBridgeTransformer internally uses an XmlSerializer to serialize the return value of the Search method into an XML document, the question then becomes: how can we communicate to this XmlSerializer that we want it to serialize the return value of the Search method into an XML document with the schema presented in Listing 18-26?

The ASP.NET framework provides you with two means to communicate with XmlSerializer:

❑   You can annotate your types and their public properties and fields with the appropriate metadata attributes such as XmlAttribute, XmlElement, and so on to tell the XmlSerializier how you want it to serialize the public properties and fields and the return values of these types.

❑   You can have your types implement the IXmlSerializer interface to let them take complete control over their serialization. This is the most flexible way to achieve the desired serialization.

Before diving into the details of these two approaches, we need to implement a new version of the CustomComponents3.AmazonService named CustomComponents3.AmazonService2, as shown in Listing 18-27. The boldface portions of Listing 18-27 are the only differences between AmazonService and AmazonService2.

To understand the significance of these boldface portions, you'll need to revisit Listing 18-16. Recall that this code listing defines the HtmlGenerator ASP.NET AJAX client control. Listing 18-28 presents a portion of Listing 18-16. If you compare the bottom boldface portion of Listing 18-27 with the highlighted portion of Listing 18-28, you'll notice that they're the same. In other words, we've moved this logic from the HtmlGenerator ASP.NET AJAX client control to the AmazonService2 class. Moving this logic from the client side to the server side enables us to filter the search results on the server side to avoid sending useless data over the wire to the client.

Listing 18-27: The AmazonService2 Class

```csharp
using System;
using System.Data;
using System.Configuration;
using System.Web;
using System.Web.Security;
using System.Web.UI;
using System.Web.UI.WebControls;
using System.Web.UI.WebControls.WebParts;
using System.Web.UI.HtmlControls;
using System.IO;
using System.Xml;
using System.Collections;
using com.amazon.webservices;
using System.Xml.Serialization;
using System.Xml.Schema;

namespace CustomComponents3
{
  [XmlRootAttribute(ElementName = "results")]
  public partial class Results
  {
    private Result[] resultField;

    [XmlElementAttribute("result")]
    public Result[] Result
    {
      get { return this.resultField; }
      set { this.resultField = value; }
    }
  }

  public class Result
  {
    private string title;

    [XmlAttribute(AttributeName = "title")]
    public string Title
    {
      get { return this.title; }
      set { this.title = value; }
    }

    private string author;

    [XmlAttribute(AttributeName = "author")]
    public string Author
    {
      get { return this.author; }
      set { this.author = value; }
    }
```

(continued)

Listing 18-27 *(continued)*

```csharp
    private string amazonUrl;

    [XmlAttribute(AttributeName = "amazonUrl")]
    public string AmazonUrl
    {
      get { return this.amazonUrl; }
      set { this.amazonUrl = value; }
    }

    private string imageUrl;

    [XmlAttribute(AttributeName = "imageUrl")]
    public string ImageUrl
    {
      get { return this.imageUrl; }
      set { this.imageUrl = value; }
    }

    private string listPrice;

    [XmlAttribute(AttributeName = "listPrice")]
    public string ListPrice
    {
      get { return this.listPrice; }
      set { this.listPrice = value; }
    }

    private string price;

    [XmlAttribute(AttributeName = "price")]
    public string Price
    {
      get { return this.price; }
      set { this.price = value; }
    }
  }

public class AmazonService2
{
  public Results Search(int pageIndex, string searchQuery)
  {
    ItemSearchRequest itemSearchRequest = new ItemSearchRequest();
    itemSearchRequest.Keywords = searchQuery;
    itemSearchRequest.SearchIndex = "Books";
    itemSearchRequest.ResponseGroup =
            new string[] { "Small", "Images", "ItemAttributes", "OfferFull" };
    itemSearchRequest.ItemPage = pageIndex.ToString();

    ItemSearch itemSearch = new ItemSearch();
    itemSearch.SubscriptionId =
                        ConfigurationManager.AppSettings["SubscriptionID"];
```

```
itemSearch.AssociateTag = "";
itemSearch.Request = new ItemSearchRequest[1] { itemSearchRequest };

ItemSearchResponse itemSearchResponse;
try
{
  AWSECommerceService amazonService = new AWSECommerceService();
  itemSearchResponse = amazonService.ItemSearch(itemSearch);
}

catch (Exception e)
{
  throw e;
}

Items[] itemsResponse = itemSearchResponse.Items;

// Check for errors in the reponse
if (itemsResponse == null)
  throw new Exception("Response from amazon.com contains not items!");
if (itemsResponse[0].Request.Errors != null)
  throw new Exception(
                  "Response from amazon.com contains this error message: " +
                  itemsResponse[0].Request.Errors[0].Message);

Items items = itemsResponse[0];

Item[] results = items.Item;
if (results == null || results.Length == 0)
  return null;

Item item;
Result result;
ArrayList list = new ArrayList();

for (int i = 0; i < results.Length; i++)
{
  item = results[i];
  if (item == null)
    continue;

  result = new Result();

  if (!string.IsNullOrEmpty(item.ItemAttributes.Title))
    result.Title = item.ItemAttributes.Title;

  if (item.ItemAttributes.Author != null &&
      item.ItemAttributes.Author.Length != 0)
    result.Author = item.ItemAttributes.Author[0];

  if (!string.IsNullOrEmpty(item.DetailPageURL))
    result.AmazonUrl = item.DetailPageURL;
```

(continued)

Listing 18-27 *(continued)*

```
            if (item.MediumImage != null)
              result.ImageUrl = item.MediumImage.URL;

            if (item.ItemAttributes.ListPrice != null)
              result.ListPrice = item.ItemAttributes.ListPrice.FormattedPrice;

            if (item.Offers != null)
            {
              Offer[] offerArray = item.Offers.Offer;
              if (offerArray != null && offerArray.Length != 0)
              {
                if (offerArray[0].OfferListing != null &&
                    offerArray[0].OfferListing.Length != 0)
                {
                  if (offerArray[0].OfferListing[0].Price != null)
                  result.Price =
                            item.Offers.Offer[0].OfferListing[0].Price.FormattedPrice;
                }
              }
            }
            list.Add(result);
          }

          Results results2 = new Results();
          results2.Result = new Result[list.Count];
          list.CopyTo(results2.Result);
          return results2;
        }
      }
    }
```

Listing 18-27 contains the definition of a custom class named `Result`, the instances of which are used to contain the filtered data sent to the clients. As you can see, the `Result` class exposes six properties — `Title`, `Author`, `AmazonUrl`, `ImageUrl`, `ListPrice`, and `Price` — that precisely represent the data that the client side displays.

As I discussed earlier, there are two ways to tell the `XmlSerializer` that the `XmlBridgeTranformer` uses internally how to serialize the return value of the `Search` method of the `AmazonService2` class. Listing 18-27 shows the first approach, where two classes, `Results` and `Result`, are defined and annotated as follows:

❑   The `Results` class itself is annotated with an `XmlRootAttribute` metadata attribute with the `ElementName` value of `results`, to instruct the `XmlSerializer` to serialize a given instance of the `Results` class as an XML document with the document element named `results`:

```
<?xml version="1.0" encoding="utf-8" ?>
<results>
  . . .
</results>
```

❑ The Results class exposes an array property of type Result named Result, which is annotated with an XmlElementAttribute metadata attribute with the ElementName value of result, to instruct the XmlSerializer to serialize a given instance of the Result class as an XML element named result, as shown in the highlighted portion of the following XML fragment:

```
<?xml version="1.0" encoding="utf-8" ?>
<results>
    <result . . . />
    <result . . . />
            .
            .
            .
    <result . . . />
</results>
```

❑ The Title property of the Result class is annotated with an XmlAttribute metadata attribute with the AttributeName value of title, to instruct the XmlSerializer to serialize the Title property of a given instance of the Result class as an attribute named title on the XML element that represents the instance, which is the result element in this case, as shown in the boldface portions of the following XML fragment:

```
<?xml version="1.0" encoding="utf-8" ?>
<results>
    <result title="..." . . . />
    <result title="..." . . . />
            .
            .
            .
    <result title="..." . . . />
</results>
```

❑ The Author property of the Result class is annotated with an XmlAttribute metadata attribute with the AttributeName value of author, to instruct the XmlSerializer to serialize the Author property of a given instance of the Result class as an attribute named author on the XML element that represents the instance, which is the result element in this case, as shown in the boldface portions of the following XML fragment:

```
<?xml version="1.0" encoding="utf-8" ?>
<results>
    <result title="..." author="..." . . . />
    <result title="..." author="..." . . . />
            .
            .
            .
    <result title="..." author="..." . . . />
</results>
```

❑ The `AmazonUrl` property of the `Result` class is annotated with an `XmlAttribute` metadata attribute with the `AttributeName` value of `amazonUrl`, to instruct the `XmlSerializer` to serialize the `AmazonUrl` property of a given instance of the `Result` class as an attribute named `amazonUrl` on the XML element that represents the instance, which is the `result` element in this case, as shown in the boldface portions of the following XML fragment:

```
<?xml version="1.0" encoding="utf-8" ?>
<results>
  <result title="..." author="..." amazonUrl="..." . . . />
  <result title="..." author="..." amazonUrl="..." . . . />
                .
                .
                .
  <result title="..." author="..." amazonUrl="..." . . . />
</results>
```

❑ The `ImageUrl` property of the `Result` class is annotated with an `XmlAttribute` metadata attribute with the `AttributeName` value of `imageUrl`, to instruct the `XmlSerializer` to serialize the `ImageUrl` property of a given instance of the `Result` class as an attribute named `imageUrl` on the XML element that represents the instance, which is the `result` element in this case, as shown in the boldface portions of the following XML fragment:

```
<?xml version="1.0" encoding="utf-8" ?>
<results>
  <result title="..." author="..." amazonUrl="..." imageUrl="..." ... />
  <result title="..." author="..." amazonUrl="..." imageUrl="..." ... />
                .
                .
                .
  <result title="..." author="..." amazonUrl="..." imageUrl="..." ... />
</results>
```

❑ The `ListPrice` property of the `Result` class is annotated with an `XmlAttribute` metadata attribute with the `AttributeName` value of `listPrice`, to instruct the `XmlSerializer` to serialize the `ListPrice` property of a given instance of the `Result` class as an attribute named `listPrice` on the XML element that represents the instance, which is the `result` element in this case, as shown in the boldface portions of the following XML fragment:

```
<?xml version="1.0" encoding="utf-8" ?>
<results>
  <result title="..." author="..." amazonUrl="..." imageUrl="..."
               listPrice="..." . . . />
  <result title="..." author="..." amazonUrl="..." imageUrl="..."
               listPrice="..." . . . />
                .
                .
                .
  <result title="..." author="..." amazonUrl="..." imageUrl="..."
               listPrice="..." . . . />
</results>
```

The Price property of the Result class is annotated with an XmlAttribute metadata attribute with the AttributeName value of price, to instruct the XmlSerializer to serialize the Price property of a given instance of the Result class as an attribute named price on the XML element that represents the instance, which is the result element in this case, as shown in the boldface portions of the following XML fragment:

```
<?xml version="1.0" encoding="utf-8" ?>
<results>
 <result title="..." author="..." amazonUrl="..." imageUrl="..."
                listPrice="..." price="..."/>
 <result title="..." author="..." amazonUrl="..." imageUrl="..."
                listPrice="..." price="..."/>
            .
            .
            .
 <result title="..." author="..." amazonUrl="..." imageUrl="..."
                listPrice="..." price="..."/>
</results>
```

Listing 18-28: Portion of Listing 18-16

```
function CustomComponents3$HtmlGenerator$generateHtml(items)
{
  var title;
  var author;
  var amazonUrl;
  var imageUrl;
  var listPrice;
  var price;
  var item;

   var results = items.Item;
  if (!results)
    return;

  var builder = new Sys.StringBuilder();
  builder.append("<table cellspacing='10' style='");
  builder.append(this._tableStyle);
  builder.append("'>");

  for (var i=0; i<results.length-1; i++)
  {
    item = results[i];
    if (!item)
      continue;

    if (item.ItemAttributes.Title)
      title = item.ItemAttributes.Title;

    if (item.ItemAttributes.Author)
      author = item.ItemAttributes.Author[0];
```

(continued)

Listing 18-28 *(continued)*

```
if (item.DetailPageURL)
  amazonUrl = item.DetailPageURL;

if (item.MediumImage)
  imageUrl = item.MediumImage.URL;

if (item.ItemAttributes.ListPrice)
  listPrice = item.ItemAttributes.ListPrice.FormattedPrice;

if (item.Offers)
{
  var offerArray = item.Offers.Offer;
  if (offerArray)
  {
    if (offerArray[0].OfferListing)
    {
      if (offerArray[0].OfferListing[0].Price)
        price = item.Offers.Offer[0].OfferListing[0].Price.FormattedPrice;
    }
  }
}
```

```
builder.append("<tr>");
builder.append("<td valign='top' width='100%'>");
builder.append("<table cellspacing='10' style='");
if (i % 2 == 0)
  builder.append(this._rowStyle);
else
  builder.append(this._alternatingRowStyle);
builder.append("'>");
builder.append("<tr>");
builder.append("<td align='center' valign='top' width='20%'>");
builder.append("<img alt='' src='");
builder.append(imageUrl);
builder.append("'/>");
builder.append("</td>");
builder.append("<td align='left' valign='top'>");
builder.append("<p>");
builder.append("<a href='");
builder.append(amazonUrl);
builder.append("'>");
builder.append(title);
builder.append("</a>");
builder.append("<br/>");
builder.append("by ");
builder.append(author);
builder.append(" (Author)");
builder.append("</p>");
builder.append("<p>");
```

```
            builder.append("<b>List Price:</b> <s>");
            builder.append(listPrice);
            builder.append("</s></br>");
            builder.append("<b>       Price:</b> ");
            builder.append(price);
            builder.append("</br>");
            builder.append("</td>");
            builder.append("</tr>");
            builder.append("<tr>");
            builder.append("<td colspan='2'>");
            builder.append("</td>");
            builder.append("</tr>");
            builder.append("</table>");
            builder.append("</td>");
            builder.append("</tr>");
        }

    builder.append("</table>");
    return builder.toString();
    }
```

As you can see, you can manually annotate classes such as `Results` and `Result` and their public properties and fields with the appropriate metadata attributes to tell the `XmlSerializer` used internally by the `XmlBridgeTransformer` how to serialize the return value of the `Search` method of the `CustomComponents3.AmazonService2`. The manual annotation of a class and its public properties and fields can get really cumbersome for large classes, especially when the desired schema is not as simple as Listing 18-26.

The ASP.NET framework comes with a command-line tool named `xsd.exe` that takes a schema file such as the one shown in Listing 18-26 and automatically generates the classes, such as `Results` and `Result`, with the appropriate annotations. Follow these steps to use this tool:

1. Store Listing 18-26 in a file named `Result.xsd`.

2. Launch the Visual Studio Command Prompt.

3. Go to the directory where the `Result.xsd` file is located.

4. Run the following command:

```
xsd.exe Result.xsd /c
```

This will automatically generate a file named `Result.cs` that contains the definitions of the `Results` and `Result` classes shown in Listing 18-27. Both classes and their public properties are automatically annotated with the metadata attributes shown in this code listing. This saves you from having to implement the `Results` and `Result` classes and annotate these classes and their public properties with the appropriate metadata attributes.

Before we go any further with our discussions, let's implement a Web page that uses the components we've implemented so far to give you chance to play with the code and get a better understanding of how these components operate. Recall from the previous sections that we developed a Web application that contains all the replica components we developed in the previous chapter and the components we developed in the previous sections of this chapter. Add the following files to this Web application:

1. Add the content of Listing 18-25 to the existing `HtmlGenerator.js` file. Recall that this code listing contains the definition of the `HtmlGenerator2`. Since `HtmlGenerator2` derives from `HtmlGenerator`, we need to include the definitions of both `HtmlGenerator` and `HtmlGenerator2` client components. The best way to do this is to put them in the same `HtmlGenerator.js` file.

2. Add a new source file named `AmazonService2.cs` to the `App_Code` directory of the application and add Listing 18-27 to this source file.

3. Add a new file named `AmazonSearch2.asbx` to the root directory of the application and add Listing 18-20 to this file.

4. Add a new source file named `XmlBridgeTransformer.cs` to the `App_Code` directory of the application and add Listing 18-24 to this file.

5. Add a new Web form named `AmazonSearch2.aspx` to the root directory of the application and add Listing 18-29 to this file.

Listing 18-29: The AmazonSearch2.aspx Page

```
<%@ Page Language="C#" %>

<%@ Register Namespace="CustomComponents3" TagPrefix="custom" %>
<!DOCTYPE html PUBLIC "-//W3C//DTD XHTML 1.0 Transitional//EN"
"http://www.w3.org/TR/xhtml1/DTD/xhtml1-transitional.dtd">
<html xmlns="http://www.w3.org/1999/xhtml">
<head id="Head1" runat="server">
  <title>Untitled Page</title>
</head>
<body>
  <form id="form1" runat="server">
    <asp:ScriptManager runat="server" ID="ScriptManager1">
      <Services>
        <asp:ServiceReference InlineScript="true" Path="AmazonSearch2.asbx" />
      </Services>
    </asp:ScriptManager>

    <custom:ScriptManager runat="server" ID="CustomScriptManager1" />

    <custom:AmazonSearchScriptControl runat="server" ID="MyControl1"
    SearchMethod="MyServices2.AmazonService2.Search"
    HtmlGeneratorID="MyHtmlGenerator"
    Path="/AJAXFuturesEnabledWebSite3/AmazonSearchScriptControl.js"
    ClientControlType="CustomComponents3.AspNetAjaxAmazonSearch" />

    <custom:HtmlGeneratorScriptControl runat="server" ID="MyHtmlGenerator"
    Path="/AJAXFuturesEnabledWebSite3/HtmlGenerator.js"
    ClientControlType="CustomComponents3.HtmlGenerator2">
      <RowStyle BackColor="#eeeeee" Width="100%" />
```

```
            <AlternatingRowStyle BackColor="#cccccc" Width="100%" />
        </custom:HtmlGeneratorScriptControl>
    </form>
</body>
</html>
```

IXmlSerializable

As I discussed earlier, there are two ways to tell the XmlSerializer used internally by the XmlBridgeTransformer how to serialize the return value of the Search method. So far I've discussed the first approach, which involves annotating the Results and Result classes and their properties with the appropriate metadata attributes.

The second approach requires you to have the Results class implement the IXmlSerializable interface. Listing 18-30 presents the definition of this interface.

Listing 18-30: The IXmlSerializable Interface

```
public interface IXmlSerializable
{
    XmlSchema GetSchema();
    void ReadXml(XmlReader reader);
    void WriteXml(XmlWriter writer);
}
```

Implementing the IXmlSerializable interface allows a class such as Results to take full control of its serialization and deserialization mechanisms. As you can see, this interface exposes three methods: GetSchema, ReadXml, and WriteXml. The GetSchema method takes no arguments and returns an instance of the XmlSchema class. This method is reserved and shouldn't be used.

A class implements the ReadXml method to take full control of its deserialization mechanism. This method allows a class to deserialize itself from a given XML representation or document. The ReadXml method takes an XmlReader instance as its argument, which the class uses to access the contents of the XML document and to populate its own properties with the appropriate values from the XML document. Since our example does not involve deserialization of the Results class, this class's implementation of this method does not do anything.

A class implements the WriteXml method to take full control of its serialization mechanism. The WriteXml method takes an XmlWriter instance, which the class uses to generate the appropriate XML representations.

You must annotate your class with the XmlSchemaProvider metadata attribute. This attribute is used to specify the name of the method that generates the XML schema document that fully describes the structure of the XML document that the WriteXml method generates and the ReadXml method consumes.

Listing 18-31 presents the implementation of the Results and Result classes. Note that neither the classes nor their properties are annotated with any of the previously mentioned metadata attributes. I'll discuss the implementation of the methods of the Results class in the following sections.

Listing 18-31: The Results and Result Classes

```csharp
using System;
using System.Web;
using System.Xml;
using System.Xml.Schema;
using System.Xml.Serialization;

namespace CustomComponents
{
  [XmlSchemaProvider("ResultsSchema")]
  public class Results: IXmlSerializable
  {
    private Result[] resultField;
    public Result[] Result
    {
      get { return this.resultField; }
      set { this.resultField = value; }
    }

    XmlSchema IXmlSerializable.GetSchema()
    {
      return null;
    }

    void IXmlSerializable.ReadXml(XmlReader reader)
    {
    }

    public static XmlQualifiedName ResultsSchema(XmlSchemaSet xs)
    {
      XmlSerializer serializer = new XmlSerializer(typeof(XmlSchema));
      XmlReader reader =
              XmlReader.Create(HttpContext.Current.Server.MapPath("Results.xsd"));
      XmlSchema schema = (XmlSchema)serializer.Deserialize(reader);
      xs.Add(schema);
      return new XmlQualifiedName("results");
    }

    void IXmlSerializable.WriteXml(XmlWriter writer)
    {
      foreach (Result result in this.Result)
      {
        writer.WriteStartElement("result");
        writer.WriteAttributeString("title", result.Title);
        writer.WriteAttributeString("author", result.Author);
        writer.WriteAttributeString("amazonUrl", result.AmazonUrl);
        writer.WriteAttributeString("imageUrl", result.ImageUrl);
        writer.WriteAttributeString("listPrice", result.ListPrice);
        writer.WriteAttributeString("price", result.Price);
        writer.WriteEndElement();
      }
    }
  }
}
```

```
public class Result
{
  private string title;
  public string Title
  {
    get { return this.title; }
    set { this.title = value; }
  }

  private string author;
  public string Author
  {
    get { return this.author; }
    set { this.author = value; }
  }

  private string amazonUrl;
  public string AmazonUrl
  {
    get { return this.amazonUrl; }
    set { this.amazonUrl = value; }
  }

  private string imageUrl;
  public string ImageUrl
  {
    get { return this.imageUrl; }
    set { this.imageUrl = value; }
  }

  private string listPrice;
  public string ListPrice
  {
    get { return this.listPrice; }
    set { this.listPrice = value; }
  }

  private string price;
  public string Price
  {
    get { return this.price; }
    set { this.price = value; }
  }
}
}
```

WriteXml

As you can see from Listing 18-32, the `Results` class implements the `WriteXml` method of the `IXmlSerializable` interface to generate its XML representation. The `WriteXml` method of the `Results` class, like the `WriteXml` method of any other class that implements the `IXmlSerializable` interface, writes its XML representation or document into the `XmlWrite` passed into it as its only argument. This method iterates through the `Result` objects in the `Result` collection property of the `Results` class and takes the following steps to generate the XML representation of each enumerated `Result` object. First, it invokes the `WriteStartElement` method on the `XmlWrite` object to write out a new element named `result`:

```
writer.WriteStartElement("result");
```

Next, it invokes the `WriteAttributeString` method on the `XmlWriter` object six times to write out six attributes — `title`, `author`, `amazonUrl`, `imageUrl`, `listPrice`, and `price` — on the `Result` element and set the values of these attributes to the value of the `Title`, `Author`, `AmazonUrl`, `ImageUrl`, `ListPrice`, and `Price` properties of the enumerated `Result` object, respectively.

Listing 18-32: The WriteXml Method of the Results Class

```
void IXmlSerializable.WriteXml(XmlWriter writer)
{
  foreach (Result result in this.Result)
  {
    writer.WriteStartElement("result");
    writer.WriteAttributeString("title", result.Title);
    writer.WriteAttributeString("author", result.Author);
    writer.WriteAttributeString("amazonUrl", result.AmazonUrl);
    writer.WriteAttributeString("imageUrl", result.ImageUrl);
    writer.WriteAttributeString("listPrice", result.ListPrice);
    writer.WriteAttributeString("price", result.Price);
    writer.WriteEndElement();
  }
}
```

ResultsSchema

Every class that implements the `IXmlSerializable` interface must implement a method with the following signature:

```
public static XmlQualifiedName MethodName (XmlSchemaSet xs);
```

You can give this method any name you wish as long as the following conditions are met:

- ❏ It takes a single argument of type `XmlSchemaSet`.
- ❏ It returns a value of type `XmlQualifiedName`.
- ❏ It is static.
- ❏ It is public.

You must also annotate the class that implements the IXmlSerializable interface with the XmlSchemaProvider metadata attribute, to specify which method of the class is responsible for generating the XML schema of the XML document that WriteXml generates and ReadXml consumes:

```
namespace CustomComponents
{

   [XmlSchemaProvider("ResultsSchema")]
   public class Results: IXmlSerializable

   {
      . . .

      public static XmlQualifiedName ResultsSchema(XmlSchemaSet xs)

      {
         XmlSerializer serializer = new XmlSerializer(typeof(XmlSchema));
         XmlReader reader =
                 XmlReader.Create(HttpContext.Current.Server.MapPath("Results.xsd"));
         XmlSchema schema = (XmlSchema)serializer.Deserialize(reader);
         xs.Add(schema);
         return new XmlQualifiedName("results");
      }
      . . .

   }
}
```

Listing 18-33 presents the implementation of the ResultsSchema method of the Results class. This method is the one that is responsible for generating the XML schema of the XML document that WriteXml generates and ReadXml consumes. In general, there are two ways to implement this method. We will only discuss the first approach in this chapter. The second approach requires you to make use of the classes in the System.Xml.Schema namespace.

Listing 18-33 uses the first approach, which requires you to create a separate XSD file that contains the XML schema document. Our example uses the XSD document shown in Listing 18-26. As you can see, the ResultsSchema method first instantiates an XmlSerializer, passing in the Type object that represents the XmlSchema type:

```
XmlSerializer serializer = new XmlSerializer(typeof(XmlSchema));
```

Passing a Type *object into the constructor of the* XmlSerializer *allows the* XmlSerializer *to use .NET reflection to extract the complete information about the specified class, which is the* XmlSchema *class. The* XmlSerializer *uses this information when it is serializing an instance of this class.*

Next, the ResultsSchema method instantiates an XmlReader and loads the content of the Results.xsd schema file into this XmlReader:

```
XmlReader reader =
        XmlReader.Create(HttpContext.Current.Server.MapPath("Results.xsd"));
```

Then `ResultsSchema` invokes the `Deserialize` method on the `XmlSerializer` to deserialize an `XmlSchema` object from the XML schema document loaded into the `XmlReader`:

```
XmlSchema schema = (XmlSchema)serializer.Deserialize(reader);
```

Next, `ResultsSchema` adds this `XmlSchema` object into the `XmlSchemaSet` collection passed into the method as its argument:

```
xs.Add(schema);
```

Finally, `ResultsSchema` returns an `XmlQualifiedName` that contains the qualified name of the XSD type of the document element of the XML document that `WriteXml` generates and `ReadXml` consumes:

```
return new XmlQualifiedName("results");
```

Listing 18-33: The ResultsSchema Method

```
public static XmlQualifiedName ResultsSchema(XmlSchemaSet xs)
{
  XmlSerializer serializer = new XmlSerializer(typeof(XmlSchema));
  XmlReader reader =
          XmlReader.Create(HttpContext.Current.Server.MapPath("Results.xsd"));
  XmlSchema schema = (XmlSchema)serializer.Deserialize(reader);
  xs.Add(schema);
  return new XmlQualifiedName("results");
}
```

Now let's implement a page that uses the components developed in this section. In previous sections we developed a Web application that contains all the replica components we developed in the previous chapter and the components we developed in the previous sections of this chapter. Now do the following:

1. Add a new source file named `Results.cs` to the `App_Code` directory of the application and add Listing 18-31 to this source file.

2. Add a new source file named `AmazonService3.cs` to the `App_Code` directory of the application and add Listing 18-34 to this source file. This code listing contains a new version of the `AmazonService2` class, named `AmazonService3`, that makes use of the `Results` and `Result` classes defined in Listing 18-31.

3. Add a new file named `AmazonSearch3.asbx` to the root directory of the application and add Listing 18-35 to this file. Every time we introduce a new version of our `AmazonService` class we must also introduce a new version of our `.asbx` file to reference this class.

4. Add a new XSD file named `Results.xsd` to the root directory of the application and add Listing 18-26 to this file.

5. Add a new Web form named `AmazonSearch3.aspx` to the root directory of the application and add Listing 18-36 to this file.

Listing 18-34: The AmazonService3.cs

```csharp
using System;
using System.Data;
using System.Configuration;
using System.Web;
using System.IO;
using System.Xml;
using System.Collections;
using com.amazon.webservices;
using System.Xml.Serialization;
using System.Xml.Schema;

namespace CustomComponents3
{
  public class AmazonService3
  {
    public CustomComponents.Results Search(int pageIndex, string searchQuery)
    {
      ItemSearchRequest itemSearchRequest = new ItemSearchRequest();
      itemSearchRequest.Keywords = searchQuery;
      itemSearchRequest.SearchIndex = "Books";
      itemSearchRequest.ResponseGroup =
              new string[] { "Small", "Images", "ItemAttributes", "OfferFull" };
      itemSearchRequest.ItemPage = pageIndex.ToString();

      ItemSearch itemSearch = new ItemSearch();
      itemSearch.SubscriptionId =
                              ConfigurationManager.AppSettings["SubscriptionID"];
      itemSearch.AssociateTag = "";
      itemSearch.Request = new ItemSearchRequest[1] { itemSearchRequest };

      ItemSearchResponse itemSearchResponse;
      try
      {
        AWSECommerceService amazonService = new AWSECommerceService();
        itemSearchResponse = amazonService.ItemSearch(itemSearch);
      }

      catch (Exception e)
      {
        throw e;
      }

      Items[] itemsResponse = itemSearchResponse.Items;

      // Check for errors in the reponse
      if (itemsResponse == null)
        throw new Exception("Response from amazon.com contains not items!");
```

(continued)

Listing 18-34 *(continued)*

```
    if (itemsResponse[0].Request.Errors != null)
      throw new Exception(
                    "Response from amazon.com contains this error message: " +
                    itemsResponse[0].Request.Errors[0].Message);

    Items items = itemsResponse[0];
    Item[] results = items.Item;
    if (results == null || results.Length == 0)
      return null;

    Item item;
    CustomComponents.Result result;
    ArrayList list = new ArrayList();

    for (int i = 0; i < results.Length; i++)
    {
      item = results[i];
      if (item == null)
        continue;

      result = new CustomComponents.Result();

      if (!string.IsNullOrEmpty(item.ItemAttributes.Title))
        result.Title = item.ItemAttributes.Title;

      if (item.ItemAttributes.Author != null &&
          item.ItemAttributes.Author.Length != 0)
        result.Author = item.ItemAttributes.Author[0];

      if (!string.IsNullOrEmpty(item.DetailPageURL))
        result.AmazonUrl = item.DetailPageURL;

      if (item.MediumImage != null)
        result.ImageUrl = item.MediumImage.URL;

      if (item.ItemAttributes.ListPrice != null)
        result.ListPrice = item.ItemAttributes.ListPrice.FormattedPrice;

      if (item.Offers != null)
      {
        Offer[] offerArray = item.Offers.Offer;
        if (offerArray != null && offerArray.Length != 0)
        {
          if (offerArray[0].OfferListing != null &&
              offerArray[0].OfferListing.Length != 0)
          {
            if (offerArray[0].OfferListing[0].Price != null)
              result.Price =
                    item.Offers.Offer[0].OfferListing[0].Price.FormattedPrice;
          }
        }
      }
```

```
            list.Add(result);
        }

        CustomComponents.Results results2 = new CustomComponents.Results();
        results2.Result = new CustomComponents.Result[list.Count];
        list.CopyTo(results2.Result);
        return results2;
    }
  }
}
```

Listing 18-35: The AmazonSearch3.asbx

```xml
<?xml version="1.0" encoding="utf-8" ?>
<bridge namespace="MyServices3" className="AmazonService3">
  <proxy type="CustomComponents3.AmazonService3, App_Code"/>
  <method name="Search">
    <input>
      <parameter name="pageIndex" />
      <parameter name="searchQuery" />
    </input>
    <transforms>
      <transform type="CustomComponents3.XmlBridgeTransformer"/>
    </transforms>
    </method>
</bridge>
```

Listing 18-36: The AmazonSearch3.aspx

```aspx
<%@ Page Language="C#" %>

<%@ Register Namespace="CustomComponents3" TagPrefix="custom" %>
<!DOCTYPE html PUBLIC "-//W3C//DTD XHTML 1.0 Transitional//EN"
"http://www.w3.org/TR/xhtml1/DTD/xhtml1-transitional.dtd">
<html xmlns="http://www.w3.org/1999/xhtml">
<head id="Head1" runat="server">
  <title>Untitled Page</title>
</head>
<body>
  <form id="form1" runat="server">
    <asp:ScriptManager runat="server" ID="ScriptManager1">
      <Services>
        <asp:ServiceReference InlineScript="true" Path="AmazonSearch3.asbx" />
      </Services>
    </asp:ScriptManager>
    <custom:ScriptManager runat="server" ID="CustomScriptManager1" />

    <custom:AmazonSearchScriptControl runat="server" ID="MS"
    SearchMethod="MyServices3.AmazonService3.Search"
    HtmlGeneratorID="MyHtmlGenerator"
    Path="/AJAXFuturesEnabledWebSite3/AmazonSearchScriptControl.js"
    ClientControlType="CustomComponents3.AspNetAjaxAmazonSearch" />
```

(continued)

Listing 18-36 *(continued)*

```
      <custom:HtmlGeneratorScriptControl runat="server" ID="MyHtmlGenerator"
      Path="/AJAXFuturesEnabledWebSite3/HtmlGenerator.js"
      ClientControlType="CustomComponents3.HtmlGenerator2">
        <RowStyle BackColor="#eeeeee" Width="100%" />
        <AlternatingRowStyle BackColor="#cccccc" Width="100%" />
      </custom:HtmlGeneratorScriptControl>
    </form>
  </body>
</html>
```

XsltBridgeTransformer

The ASP.NET AJAX framework comes with another transformer, named XsltBridgeTransformer. As the name suggests, this transformer performs XSLT transformation on a specified XML document. The XsltBridgeTransformer, like any other ASP.NET AJAX transformer, derives from the IBridgeResponseTransformer interface and implements its Initialize and Transform methods.

Listing 18-37 presents the implementation of the replica XsltBridgeTransformer. Next I'll walk you through the implementation of the Initialize method of the replica. Recall that when this method is invoked, a BridgeTransformData object is passed into it. As thoroughly discussed earlier, this object exposes a collection property named Attributes that contains the values of the name and value attributes of the attribute subelements of the data subelement of the transform element that represents the transformer in the .asbx file. The data subelement of the transform element that represents the XsltBridgeTransformer contains a single attribute subelement whose name attribute is set to the keyword stylesheetFile and whose value attribute is set to the virtual path of the XSLT file. For example, Listing 18-38 shows an .asbx file that uses our replica XsltBridgeTransformer, where the value of the value attribute element is set to the virtual path of an XSLT file named MyFile.xsl:

```
<attribute name="stylesheetFile" value="/AJAXFuturesEnabledWebSite3/MyFile.xsl"/>
```

The Initialize method of the XsltBridgeTransformer uses the keyword stylesheetFile as an index into the Attributes collection to return the value of the value attribute of the attribute subelement. Note that the Initialize method stores this value in a private field named _xsltVirtualPath.

Next, I'll walk you through the implementation of the Transform method of our replica XsltBridgeTransformer. This method first checks whether the object passed into it is a string. If not, it raises an exception. As you'll see shortly, the Transform method expects the value passed into it to be an XML document.

```
        string xml = results as string;
        if (xml == null)
          throw new ArgumentException("String Only", "results");
```

The fact that the Transform method expects an XML document has a significant consequence. Since the return value of a method such as the Search method of the AmazonService is a .NET object, not an XML document, it cannot be directly passed into the Transform method of the XsltBridgeTransformer. In other words, the Transform method of the

XsltBridgeTransformer *expects to receive the XML representation of a .NET object, not the object itself. Therefore, you must use the* XmlBridgeTransformer *before the* XsltBridgeTransformer *in the transformer pipeline to have the* Invoke *method of the* BridgeHandler *pass the return value of a method, such as the* Search *method of the* AmazonService, *into the* Transform *method of the* XmlBridgeTransformer *to serialize this value into its XML representation before it is passed into the* Transform *method of the* XsltBridgeTransformer. *For example, the* .asbx *file shown in Listing 18-38 uses an* XmlBridgeTransformer *before the* XsltBridgeTransformer.

Next, the Transform method instantiates an XmlDocument:

```
XmlDocument document = new XmlDocument();
```

Then it populates this XmlDocument with the XML document contained in the string passed into the method:

```
document.LoadXml(xml);
```

Next, it instantiates an XslCompiledTransform, which will be used to perform XSLT transformation on the above XML document:

```
XslCompiledTransform transform = new XslCompiledTransform();
```

Then it instantiates a StringWriter into which the transformed XML document will be written:

```
using (StringWriter writer = new StringWriter(CultureInfo.CurrentCulture))
```

Next, it evaluates the absolute path of the XSLT file. Recall that the .asbx file such as the one shown in Listing 18-38 provides the virtual path to the XSLT file:

```
this._xsltVirtualPath =
                VirtualPathUtility.ToAbsolute(this._xsltVirtualPath);
```

Then it invokes the OpenFile static method to load the content of the XSLT file into a Stream:

```
using (Stream input = VirtualPathProvider.OpenFile(this._xsltVirtualPath))
```

Next, it loads this Stream into an XmlReader:

```
using (XmlReader stylesheet = XmlReader.Create(input))
```

Then it loads this XmlReader into the XsltCompiledTransform. Keep in mind that this XmlReader contains the content of the XSLT file:

```
transform.Load(stylesheet);
```

Next, it invokes the Transform method on the XsltCompiledTransform to transform the XML document based on the XSLT rules specified in the XSLT files. Note that the transformed XML document is written into the StringWriter:

```
transform.Transform((IXPathNavigable)document, null,
                (TextWriter)writer);
```

Finally, it returns the content of this `StringWriter`:

```
          return writer.GetStringBuilder().ToString();
```

Listing 18-37: The XsltBridgeTransformer

```csharp
using System;
using System.Data;
using System.Configuration;
using System.Web;
using Microsoft.Web.Preview.Services;
using System.Xml.Serialization;
using System.Xml;
using System.IO;
using System.Text;
using System.Xml.XPath;
using System.Xml.Xsl;
using System.Web.Hosting;
using System.Globalization;

namespace CustomComponents3
{
  public class XsltBridgeTransformer : IBridgeResponseTransformer
  {
    private string _xsltVirtualPath;

    public XsltBridgeTransformer()
    {
      this._xsltVirtualPath = string.Empty;
    }

    public void Initialize(BridgeTransformData data)
    {
      this._xsltVirtualPath = data.Attributes["stylesheetFile"];
    }

    public object Transform(object results)
    {
      string xml = results as string;
      if (xml == null)
        throw new ArgumentException("String Only", "results");

      XmlDocument document = new XmlDocument();
      document.LoadXml(xml);
      XslCompiledTransform transform = new XslCompiledTransform();
      using (StringWriter writer = new StringWriter(CultureInfo.CurrentCulture))
      {
        this._xsltVirtualPath =
                      VirtualPathUtility.ToAbsolute(this._xsltVirtualPath);
```

```
      using (Stream input = VirtualPathProvider.OpenFile(this._xsltVirtualPath))
      {
        using (XmlReader stylesheet = XmlReader.Create(input))
        {
          transform.Load(stylesheet);
          transform.Transform((IXPathNavigable)document, null,
                              (TextWriter)writer);
        }
      }
      return writer.GetStringBuilder().ToString();
    }
  }
}
```

Listing 18-38: The AmazonSearch4.asbx

```xml
<?xml version="1.0" encoding="utf-8" ?>
<bridge namespace="MyServices4" className="AmazonService4">
  <proxy type="CustomComponents3.AmazonService4, App_Code"/>
  <method name="Search">
    <input>
      <parameter name="pageIndex" />
      <parameter name="searchQuery" />
    </input>

    <transforms>
      <transform type="CustomComponents3.XmlBridgeTransformer"/>

      <transform type="CustomComponents3.XsltBridgeTransformer">
        <data>
          <attribute name="stylesheetFile"
          value="/AJAXFuturesEnabledWebSite3/MyFile.xsl"/>
        </data>
      </transform>
    </transforms>
  </method>
</bridge>
```

Next, I'll implement an example that uses the replica XsltBridgeTransformer. This example uses the .asbx file shown in Listing 18-38. Note that this file uses an XSLT file named MyFile.xsl. Listing 18-39 presents the content of this XSLT file. As you can see, this XSLT file basically transforms the original XML document, which is the XML representation of the return value of the Search method of the CustomComponents3.AmazonService4 class shown in Listing 18-40, into an XML document that the HtmlGenerator2 expects. Recall that the generateHtml method of the HtmlGenerator2 client component expects the XML document with the schema shown in Listing 18-33.

Listing 18-39: The MyFile.xsl File

```
<?xml version="1.0" encoding="utf-8"?>

<xsl:stylesheet version="1.0"
    xmlns:xsl="http://www.w3.org/1999/XSL/Transform">

  <xsl:template match="/">
    <results>
      <xsl:apply-templates select="//Result" />
    </results>
  </xsl:template>

  <xsl:template match="//Result">
    <result title="{Title}" author="{Author}" amazonUrl="{AmazonUrl}"
            imageUrl="{ImageUrl}" listPrice="{ListPrice}" price="{Price}" />
  </xsl:template>
</xsl:stylesheet>
```

Listing 18-40 presents a new version of our `AmazonService` class named `AmazonService4`. Note that this file makes use of the `Result` class (not the `Results` class) defined in Listing 18-31.

Listing 18-40: The AmazonService4 Class

```
using System;
using System.Data;
using System.Configuration;
using System.Web;
using System.Web.Security;
using System.Web.UI;
using System.Web.UI.WebControls;
using System.Web.UI.WebControls.WebParts;
using System.Web.UI.HtmlControls;
using System.IO;
using System.Xml;
using System.Collections;
using com.amazon.webservices;
using System.Xml.Serialization;

namespace CustomComponents3
{
  public class AmazonService4
  {
    public CustomComponents.Result[] Search(int pageIndex, string searchQuery)
    {
      ItemSearchRequest itemSearchRequest = new ItemSearchRequest();
      itemSearchRequest.Keywords = searchQuery;
      itemSearchRequest.SearchIndex = "Books";
      itemSearchRequest.ResponseGroup =
              new string[] { "Small", "Images", "ItemAttributes", "OfferFull" };
      itemSearchRequest.ItemPage = pageIndex.ToString();

      ItemSearch itemSearch = new ItemSearch();
```

```
itemSearch.SubscriptionId =
                      ConfigurationManager.AppSettings["SubscriptionID"];
itemSearch.AssociateTag = "";
itemSearch.Request = new ItemSearchRequest[1] { itemSearchRequest };

ItemSearchResponse itemSearchResponse;
try
{
  AWSECommerceService amazonService = new AWSECommerceService();
  itemSearchResponse = amazonService.ItemSearch(itemSearch);
}

catch (Exception e)
{
  throw e;
}

Items[] itemsResponse = itemSearchResponse.Items;

// Check for errors in the reponse
if (itemsResponse == null)
  throw new Exception("Response from amazon.com contains not items!");

if (itemsResponse[0].Request.Errors != null)
  throw new Exception("Response from amazon.com contains this error message:"
+ itemsResponse[0].Request.Errors[0].Message);

Items items = itemsResponse[0];
Item[] results = items.Item;
if (results == null || results.Length == 0)
  return null;

Item item;
CustomComponents.Result result;
ArrayList list = new ArrayList();

for (int i = 0; i < results.Length; i++)
{
  item = results[i];
  if (item == null)
    continue;

  result = new CustomComponents.Result();

  if (!string.IsNullOrEmpty(item.ItemAttributes.Title))
    result.Title = item.ItemAttributes.Title;

  if (item.ItemAttributes.Author != null &&
      item.ItemAttributes.Author.Length != 0)
    result.Author = item.ItemAttributes.Author[0];

  if (!string.IsNullOrEmpty(item.DetailPageURL))
    result.AmazonUrl = item.DetailPageURL;
```

(continued)

Listing 18-40 *(continued)*

```
      if (item.MediumImage != null)
        result.ImageUrl = item.MediumImage.URL;

      if (item.ItemAttributes.ListPrice != null)
        result.ListPrice = item.ItemAttributes.ListPrice.FormattedPrice;

      if (item.Offers != null)
      {
        Offer[] offerArray = item.Offers.Offer;
        if (offerArray != null && offerArray.Length != 0)
        {
          if (offerArray[0].OfferListing != null &&
              offerArray[0].OfferListing.Length != 0)
          {
            if (offerArray[0].OfferListing[0].Price != null)
              result.Price =
                      item.Offers.Offer[0].OfferListing[0].Price.FormattedPrice;
          }
        }
      }
      list.Add(result);
    }

    CustomComponents.Result[] list2 = new CustomComponents.Result[list.Count];
    list.CopyTo(list2);
    return list2;
  }
}
}
```

Recall from the previous sections that we developed a Web application that contains all the replica components we developed in the previous chapter and the components we developed in the previous sections of this chapter. Then take the following steps:

1. Add a new source file named `XsltBridgeTransformer.cs` to the `App_Code` directory of the application and add Listing 18-37 to this source file.

2. Add a new source file named `AmazonService4.cs` to the `App_Code` directory of the application and add Listing 18-40 to this source file.

3. Add a new file named `AmazonSearch4.asbx` to the root directory of the application and add Listing 18-38 to this file.

4. Add a new XSLT file named `MyFile.xsl` to the root directory of the application and add Listing 18-39 to this file.

5. Add a new Web form named `AmazonSearch4.aspx` to the root directory of the application and add Listing 18-41 to this file.

Listing 18-41: The AmazonSearch4.aspx

```
<%@ Page Language="C#" %>

<%@ Register Namespace="CustomComponents3" TagPrefix="custom" %>
<!DOCTYPE html PUBLIC "-//W3C//DTD XHTML 1.0 Transitional//EN"
"http://www.w3.org/TR/xhtml1/DTD/xhtml1-transitional.dtd">
<html xmlns="http://www.w3.org/1999/xhtml">
<head id="Head1" runat="server">
  <title>Untitled Page</title>
</head>
<body>
  <form id="form1" runat="server">
    <asp:ScriptManager runat="server" ID="ScriptManager1">
      <Services>
        <asp:ServiceReference InlineScript="true" Path="AmazonSearch4.asbx" />
      </Services>
    </asp:ScriptManager>
    <custom:ScriptManager runat="server" ID="CustomScriptManager1" />

    <custom:AmazonSearchScriptControl runat="server" ID="MS"
SearchMethod="MyServices4.AmazonService4.Search" HtmlGeneratorID="MyHtmlGenerator"
Path="/AJAXFuturesEnabledWebSite3/AmazonSearchScriptControl.js"
    ClientControlType="CustomComponents3.AspNetAjaxAmazonSearch"/>

    <custom:HtmlGeneratorScriptControl runat="server" ID="MyHtmlGenerator"
Path="/AJAXFuturesEnabledWebSite3/HtmlGenerator.js"
    ClientControlType="CustomComponents3.HtmlGenerator2">
      <RowStyle BackColor="#eeeeee" Width="100%" />
      <AlternatingRowStyle BackColor="#cccccc" Width="100%" />
    </custom:HtmlGeneratorScriptControl>
  </form>
</body>
</html>
```

Summary

This chapter implemented custom script server controls that use ASP.NET AJAX Web services bridges to retrieve data from external Web services such as Amazon Web services. The chapter also discussed ASP.NET AJAX transformers in detail.

In the next chapter, we'll move on to the important topic of asynchronous partial page rendering and the associated `UpdatePanel` and `ScriptManager` server controls.

19

UpdatePanel and ScriptManager

The ASP.NET AJAX Framework extends the ASP.NET Framework to add support for a new type of page postback that enables what is known as *asynchronous partial page rendering* or *updates*. The asynchronous partial page rendering is characterized by the following characteristics:

❑ The values of the form elements are posted through an asynchronous HTTP request, allowing the end user to interact with the page while the request makes its way to the server and processed by the server-side code and the server response makes its way back to the client. The asynchronous nature of the client-server communications goes a long way to improve the interactivity, responsiveness, and performance of ASP.NET AJAX applications.

❑ When the server response arrives, only designated portions of the page are updated and re-rendered. The rest of the page remains intact, hence the name "partial page rendering." ASP.NET AJAX developers must use UpdatePanel server controls to tell the ASP.NET AJAX Framework which regions of a page must be updated on an asynchronous page postback.

Enabling Asynchronous Partial Page Rendering

One of the great advantages of the ASP.NET AJAX partial page rendering feature is that you can enable it declaratively without writing a single line of client script. Enabling partial page rendering for an ASP.NET page takes two simple steps:

❑ Add a single instance of the ScriptManager server control to the .aspx page

Every ASP.NET page can contain only one instance of the ScriptManager server control.

❑ Add one or more UpdatePanel server controls to designate portions of the page that you want to have updated when an asynchronous page postback occurs

Listing 19-1 presents a page that consists of two sections. The page uses an UpdatePanel server control to designate the top section as a partially updatable portion of the page. The bottom portion is an area of the page that can be updated only on a regular synchronous page postback.

If you run this page, you should see the result shown in Figure 19-1. As you can see from this figure, each section of the page contains an ASP.NET Label and Button server control, where the Label displays the last time at which the associated section was refreshed.

Now click the Update button in the top section. Notice that:

❑ The browser does not display the little animation that it normally displays when a page is posted back to the server. This is because the page postback is done asynchronously in the background.

❑ Only the timestamp of the top portion of the page changes. In other words, this asynchronous page postback does not affect the bottom portion of the page — hence the name "partial page rendering."

Listing 19-1: Enabling a Page for Partial Page Rendering

```
<%@ Page Language="C#" %>

<%@ Import Namespace="System.Drawing" %>
<!DOCTYPE html PUBLIC "-//W3C//DTD XHTML 1.1//EN"
"http://www.w3.org/TR/xhtml11/DTD/xhtml11.dtd">

<script runat="server">
  void Page_Load(object sender, EventArgs e)
  {
    string text = "Refreshed at " + DateTime.Now.ToString();
    UpdatePanel1Label.Text = text;
    NonPartiallyUpdatableLabel.Text = text;
  }
</script>

<html xmlns="http://www.w3.org/1999/xhtml">
<head id="Head1" runat="server">
  <title>Untitled Page</title>
</head>
<body>
  <form id="form1" runat="server">
    <asp:ScriptManager ID="ScriptManager1" runat="server"/>
    <asp:UpdatePanel ID="UpdatePanel1" runat="server">
      <ContentTemplate>
        <table cellspacing="10" style="background-color: #dddddd">
          <tr>
            <th colspan="2" align="center">
              Partially Updatable Portion (UpdatePanel1) </th>
          </tr>
          <tr>
            <td>
              <asp:Label ID="UpdatePanel1Label" runat="server" />
            </td>
```

```
                  <td>
                    <asp:Button ID="UpdatePanelButton" runat="server"
                    Text="Update" />
                  </td>
                </tr>
              </table>
            </ContentTemplate>
          </asp:UpdatePanel>
          <br />
          <br />
          <table cellspacing="10" style="background-color: #dddddd">
            <tr>
              <th colspan="2"> Non Partially Updatable Portion </th>
            </tr>
            <tr>
              <td>
                <asp:Label ID="NonPartiallyUpdatableLabel" runat="server" />
              </td>
              <td>
                <asp:Button runat="server" Text="Update" />
              </td>
            </tr>
          </table>
        </form>
      </body>
    </html>
```

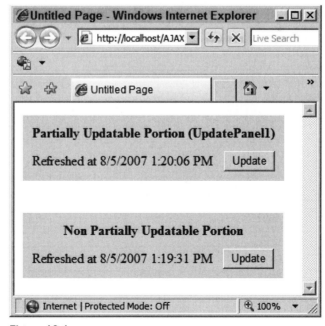

Figure 19-1

Conditional Updates

By default, every `UpdatePanel` server control on a page is updated on every single asynchronous page postback. You can see this from the following example.

Listing 19-2 presents a page that uses two `UpdatePanel` server controls. If you run this page, you should get the result shown in Figure 19-2. Now click the Update button in the top `UpdatePanel` server control (`UpdatePanel1`). Note that both `UpdatePanel` server controls are updated. Here is the reason. The `UpdatePanel` server control exposes `UpdateMode`, a property of type `UpdatePanelUpdateMode` enumerator with possible values of `Always` and `Conditional`. The default value of this property is `Always`, which means that the `UpdatePanel` server control is updated on every single asynchronous page postback.

Listing 19-2: A Page that Uses Two UpdatePanel Server Controls

```
<%@ Page Language="C#" %>

<script runat="server">
  void Page_Load(object sender, EventArgs e)
  {
    string text = "Refreshed at " + DateTime.Now.ToString();
    UpdatePanel1Label.Text = text;
    UpdatePanel2Label.Text = text;
    NonPartiallyUpdatableLabel.Text = text;
  }
</script>

<html xmlns="http://www.w3.org/1999/xhtml">
<body>
  <form id="form1" runat="server">
    <asp:ScriptManager ID="ScriptManager1" runat="server"/>
    <asp:UpdatePanel ID="UpdatePanel1" runat="server">
      <ContentTemplate>
        <table cellspacing="10" style="background-color: #dddddd">
          <tr>
            <th colspan="2" align="center">
              Partially Updatable Portion (UpdatePanel1) </th>
          </tr>
          <tr>
            <td>
              <asp:Label ID="UpdatePanel1Label" runat="server" />
            </td>
            <td>
              <asp:Button ID="UpdatePanelButton" runat="server" Text="Update" />
            </td>
          </tr>
        </table>
      </ContentTemplate>
    </asp:UpdatePanel>
```

```
        <br />
        <br />
        <asp:UpdatePanel ID="UpdatePanel2" runat="server">
          <ContentTemplate>
            <table cellspacing="10"
          style="background-color: #dddddd">
              <tr>
                <th colspan="2">
                  Partially Updatable Portion (UpdatePanel2) </th>
              </tr>
              <tr>
                <td>
                  <asp:Label ID="UpdatePanel2Label" runat="server" />
                </td>
                <td>
                  <asp:Button  runat="server" Text="Update" />
                </td>
              </tr>
            </table>
          </ContentTemplate>
        </asp:UpdatePanel>
        <br />
        <br />
        <table cellspacing="10" style="background-color: #dddddd">
          <tr>
            <th colspan="2"> Non Partially Updatable Portion </th>
          </tr>
          <tr>
            <td>
              <asp:Label ID="NonPartiallyUpdatableLabel" runat="server" />
            </td>
            <td>
              <asp:Button runat="server" Text="Update" />
            </td>
          </tr>
        </table>
    </form>
  </body>
</html>
```

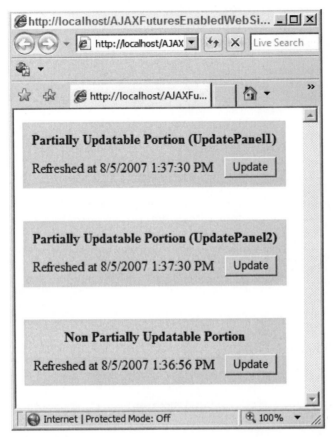

Figure 19-2

Listing 19-3 shows a new version of Listing 19-2 for which the UpdateMode properties of both UpdatePanel server controls are set to Conditional. Note that the boldface portions of Listing 19-3 are the only differences between Listings 19-2 and 19-3. Now if you run this code listing and click the Update button in the top UpdatePanel server control, only the top UpdatePanel server control will update; the bottom UpdatePanel server control will be left as is.

Listing 19-3: A Page that Uses Conditional Updates

```
<%@ Page Language="C#" %>

<script runat="server">
  void Page_Load(object sender, EventArgs e)
  {
    // Same as Listing 19-2
  }
</script>
```

```
<html xmlns="http://www.w3.org/1999/xhtml">
<body>
  <form id="form1" runat="server">
    <asp:ScriptManager ID="ScriptManager1" runat="server"/>
    <asp:UpdatePanel ID="UpdatePanel1" runat="server"
    UpdateMode="Conditional">
      <ContentTemplate>

        <!-- Same as Listing 19-2 -->

      </ContentTemplate>
    </asp:UpdatePanel>
    <br />
    <br />
    <asp:UpdatePanel ID="UpdatePanel2" runat="server"
    UpdateMode="Conditional">
      <ContentTemplate>

        <!-- Same as Listing 19-2 -->

      </ContentTemplate>
    </asp:UpdatePanel>

    <!-- Same as Listing 19-2 -->

  </form>
</body>
</html>
```

As the name of the setting suggests, when the UpdateMode property of an UpdatePanel server control is set to Conditional, the UpdatePanel server control updates only when one of the conditions discussed in the following sections is met.

Children as Triggers

The UpdatePanel server control exposes a Boolean property named ChildrenAsTriggers, which is true by default. When this property is set to true, every asynchronous page postback originating from a server control inside the UpdatePanel server control causes the UpdatePanel server control to update. Listing 19-3 showed an example of this scenario.

Listing 19-4 shows you what happens if you explicitly set the ChildrenAsTriggers property of an UpdatePanel server control to false. This code listing is a new version of Listing 19-3 in which the ChildrenAsTriggers property of the top UpdatePanel server control is set to false, as shown in the boldface portion of this code listing.

If you run this code listing and click the Update button in the top UpdatePanel server control, you'll see that this UpdatePanel server control does not update.

Listing 19-4: A Page that Uses ChildrenAsTriggers Property

```
<%@ Page Language="C#" %>

<script runat="server">
  void Page_Load(object sender, EventArgs e)
  {
    // Same as Listing 19-2
  }
</script>

<html xmlns="http://www.w3.org/1999/xhtml">
<body>
  <form id="form1" runat="server">
    <asp:ScriptManager ID="ScriptManager1" runat="server"/>
    <asp:UpdatePanel ID="UpdatePanel1" runat="server"
     UpdateMode="Conditional" ChildrenAsTriggers="false">
      <ContentTemplate>

        <!-- Same as Listing 19-2 -->

      </ContentTemplate>
    </asp:UpdatePanel>
    <br />
    <br />
    <asp:UpdatePanel ID="UpdatePanel2" runat="server"
     UpdateMode="Conditional">
      <ContentTemplate>

        <!-- Same as Listing 19-2 -->

      </ContentTemplate>
    </asp:UpdatePanel>

    <!-- Same as Listing 19-2 -->

  </form>
</body>
</html>
```

Inclusion of One UpdatePanel in another UpdatePanel

As mentioned earlier, when the UpdateMode property of an UpdatePanel server control is set to Conditional, the UpdatePanel server control updates only when one of the predefined conditions is met. I discussed one of these conditions in the preceding section. Here is the second condition. When an UpdatePanel server control updates, all its descendant UpdatePanel server controls update as well. This happens in several different scenarios, which I will discuss in the following sections.

Direct Inclusion of One UpdatePanel in another UpdatePanel

In this scenario the descendant UpdatePanel server controls are directly declared inside the UpdatePanel control.

Listing 19-5 presents an example of the first scenario. Here `UpdatePanel2` is declared directly inside `UpdatePanel1`. If you run this page, you should see the result shown in Figure 19-3. Now click the Update button in the parent `UpdatePanel` server control. Note that both parent and child `UpdatePanel` server controls are updated. Now click the Update button in the child `UpdatePanel` server control. Note that only the child `UpdatePanel` server control is updated.

Listing 19-5: An Example of the Scenario where One UpdatePanel Contains Another UpdatePanel

```
<%@ Page Language="C#" %>

<%@ Import Namespace="System.Drawing" %>
<!DOCTYPE html PUBLIC "-//W3C//DTD XHTML 1.1//EN"
"http://www.w3.org/TR/xhtml11/DTD/xhtml11.dtd">

<script runat="server">
  void Page_Load(object sender, EventArgs e)
  {
    string text = "Refreshed at " + DateTime.Now.ToString();
    UpdatePanel1Label.Text = text;
    UpdatePanel2Label.Text = text;
    NonPartiallyUpdatableLabel.Text = text;
  }
</script>

<html xmlns="http://www.w3.org/1999/xhtml">
<head id="Head1" runat="server">
  <title>Untitled Page</title>
</head>
<body>
  <form id="form1" runat="server">
    <asp:ScriptManager ID="ScriptManager1" runat="server" />
    <table>
      <tr>
        <td>
          <asp:UpdatePanel ID="UpdatePanel1" runat="server"
          UpdateMode="Conditional">
            <ContentTemplate>
              <table cellspacing="10" style="background-color: #dddddd">
                <tr>
                  <th colspan="2" align="center">
                    Parent UpdatePanel Server Control (UpdatePanel1)
                  </th>
                </tr>
                <tr>
                  <td>
                    <asp:Label ID="UpdatePanel1Label" runat="server" />
                  </td>
```

(continued)

Listing 19-5 *(continued)*

```
                    <td>
                      <asp:Button ID="UpdatePanelButton" runat="server"
                      Text="Update" />
                    </td>
                </tr>
                <tr>
                  <td colspan="2">
                    <br />
                    <br />
                    <asp:UpdatePanel ID="UpdatePanel2" runat="server"
                    UpdateMode="Conditional">
                      <ContentTemplate>
                        <table cellspacing="10"
                        style="background-color: #aaaaaa">
                          <tr>
                            <th colspan="2">
                              Child UpdatePanel Server Control(UpdatePanel2)
                            </th>
                          </tr>
                          <tr>
                            <td>
                              <asp:Label ID="UpdatePanel2Label"
                              runat="server" />
                            </td>
                            <td>
                              <asp:Button ID="Button1" runat="server"
                              Text="Update" />
                            </td>
                          </tr>
                        </table>
                      </ContentTemplate>
                    </asp:UpdatePanel>
                  </td>
                </tr>
              </table>
            </ContentTemplate>
          </asp:UpdatePanel>
        </td>
      </tr>
      <tr>
        <td>
          <br />
          <br />
          <table cellspacing="10"
          style="background-color: #eeeeee" width="100%">
```

```
            <tr>
              <th colspan="2">
                Non Partially Updatable Portion </th>
            </tr>
            <tr>
              <td>
                <asp:Label ID="NonPartiallyUpdatableLabel" runat="server" />
              </td>
              <td>
                <asp:Button ID="Button2" runat="server" Text="Update" />
              </td>
            </tr>
          </table>
        </td>
      </tr>
    </table>
  </form>
</body>
</html>
```

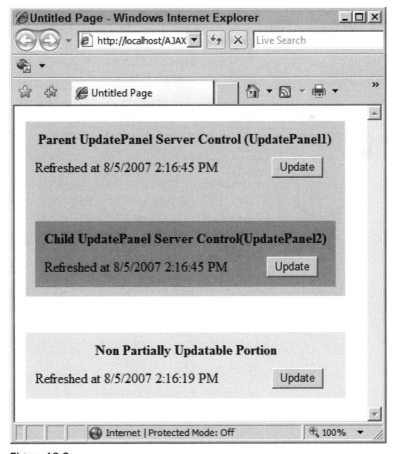

Figure 19-3

Indirect Inclusion of One UpdatePanel in Another UpdatePanel via a User Control

This scenario occurs when an UpdatePanel server control is part of a user control that is added to another UpdatePanel server control.

Listing 19-6 contains a user control that encapsulates an UpdatePanel server control.

Listing 19-6: A User Control that Encapsulates an UpdatePanel Server Control

```
<%@ Control Language="C#" ClassName="WebUserControl" %>

<script runat="server">
  void Page_Load(object sender, EventArgs e)
  {
    UpdatePanel2Label.Text = "Refreshed at " + DateTime.Now.ToString();
  }
</script>
<table style="background-color: #aaaaaa" cellspacing="20">
 <tr>
  <th>
    User Control
  </th>
 </tr>
  <tr>
    <td>
      <asp:UpdatePanel ID="UpdatePanel2" runat="server"
      UpdateMode="Conditional">
        <ContentTemplate>
          <table cellspacing="10" style="background-color: #cccccc">
            <tr>
              <th colspan="2" align="center">
                UpdatePanel Server Control
              </th>
            </tr>
            <tr>
              <td>
                <asp:Label ID="UpdatePanel2Label" runat="server" />
              </td>
              <td>
                <asp:Button runat="server" Text="Update" />
              </td>
            </tr>
          </table>
        </ContentTemplate>
      </asp:UpdatePanel>
    </td>
  </tr>
</table>
```

Listing 19-7 presents a page where this user control is added within an UpdatePanel server control that acts as the parent of this user control.

Listing 19-7: A Page that Uses the User Control from Listing 19-6

```
<%@ Page Language="C#" %>
<%@ Register Src="~/WebUserControl.ascx" TagName="MyUserControl" TagPrefix="custom" %>
<%@ Import Namespace="System.Drawing" %>
<!DOCTYPE html PUBLIC "-//W3C//DTD XHTML 1.1//EN"
"http://www.w3.org/TR/xhtml11/DTD/xhtml11.dtd">

<script runat="server">
  void Page_Load(object sender, EventArgs e)
  {
    string text = "Refreshed at " + DateTime.Now.ToString();
    UpdatePanel1Label.Text = text;
    NonPartiallyUpdatableLabel.Text = text;
  }
</script>

<html xmlns="http://www.w3.org/1999/xhtml">
<head id="Head1" runat="server">
  <title>Untitled Page</title>
</head>
<body>
  <form id="form1" runat="server">
    <asp:ScriptManager ID="ScriptManager1" runat="server" />
    <table>
      <tr>
        <td>
          <asp:UpdatePanel ID="UpdatePanel1" runat="server"
          UpdateMode="Conditional">
            <ContentTemplate>
              <table cellspacing="10" style="background-color: #dddddd">
                <tr>
                  <th colspan="2" align="center">
                    Parent UpdatePanel Server Control
                  </th>
                </tr>
                <tr>
                  <td>
                    <asp:Label ID="UpdatePanel1Label" runat="server" />
                  </td>
```

(continued)

869

Listing 19-7 *(continued)*

```
              <td>
                <asp:Button ID="UpdatePanelButton" runat="server"
                Text="Update" />
              </td>
            </tr>
            <tr>
              <td colspan="2">
              <br />
              <br />
                <custom:MyUserControl runat="server" />
              </td>
            </tr>
          </table>
        </ContentTemplate>
      </asp:UpdatePanel>
    </td>
  </tr>
  <tr>
    <td>
    <br />
    <br />
      <table cellspacing="10" style="background-color: #eeeeee" width="100%">
        <tr>
          <th colspan="2">
            Non Partially Updatable Portion
          </th>
        </tr>
        <tr>
          <td>
            <asp:Label ID="NonPartiallyUpdatableLabel" runat="server" />
          </td>
          <td>
            <asp:Button ID="Button2" runat="server" Text="Update" />
          </td>
        </tr>
      </table>
    </td>
  </tr>
</table>
</form>
</body>
</html>
```

If you run the page in Listing 19-7, you should get the result shown in Figure 19-4. Now click the Update button in the parent UpdatePanel server control. Note that both the parent UpdatePanel server control and the UpdatePanel server control defined as part of the user control are updated.

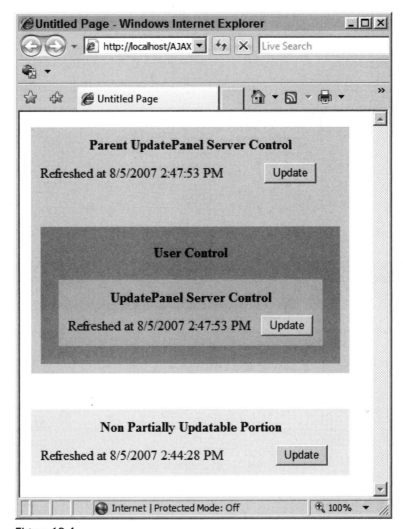

Figure 19-4

Indirect Inclusion of an UpdatePanel in Another UpdatePanel via a Content Page

The third scenario occurs when the following conditions are met:

❑ A master page includes an UpdatePanel server control that contains a ContentPlaceHolder server control.

❑ A content page includes a Content server control, associated with the above ContentPlaceHolder server control, which contain one or more UpdatePanel server controls.

Listing 19-8 shows a master page that includes an UpdatePanel server control that contains a ContentPlaceHolder server control.

Listing 19-8: A Master Page that Includes an UpdatePanel Server Control

```
<%@ Master Language="C#" %>
<!DOCTYPE html PUBLIC
"-//W3C//DTD XHTML 1.0 Transitional//EN"
"http://www.w3.org/TR/xhtml1/DTD/xhtml1-transitional.dtd">

<script runat="server">
  void Page_Load(object sender, EventArgs e)
  {
    string text = "Refreshed at " + DateTime.Now.ToString();
    UpdatePanel1Label.Text = text;
    NonPartiallyUpdatableLabel.Text = text;
  }
</script>


<html xmlns="http://www.w3.org/1999/xhtml">
<head runat="server">
  <title>Untitled Page</title>
</head>
<body>
  <form id="form1" runat="server">
    <asp:ScriptManager ID="ScriptManager1" runat="server" />
    <table>
      <tr>
        <td>
          <asp:UpdatePanel ID="UpdatePanel1" runat="server"
          UpdateMode="Conditional">
            <ContentTemplate>
              <table cellspacing="10" style="background-color: #dddddd">
                <tr>
                  <th colspan="2" align="center">
                    Parent UpdatePanel Server Control </th>
                </tr>
                <tr>
                  <td>
                    <asp:Label ID="UpdatePanel1Label" runat="server" />
                  </td>
                  <td>
                    <asp:Button ID="UpdatePanelButton" runat="server"
                    Text="Update" />
                  </td>
                </tr>
                <tr>
                  <td colspan="2">
                  <br />
                  <br />
                    <asp:ContentPlaceHolder ID="ContentPlaceHolder1"
                    runat="server" /> </td>
                </tr>
              </table>
            </ContentTemplate>
          </asp:UpdatePanel>
```

```
                </td>
              </tr>
              <tr>
               <td>
              <br />
              <br />
                <table cellspacing="10" style="background-color: #eeeeee" width="100%">
                  <tr>
                    <th colspan="2">
                      Non Partially Updatable Portion </th>
                  </tr>
                  <tr>
                    <td>
                      <asp:Label ID="NonPartiallyUpdatableLabel" runat="server" />
                    </td>
                    <td>
                      <asp:Button ID="Button2" runat="server" Text="Update" />
                    </td>
                  </tr>
                </table>
              </td>
            </tr>
          </table>
        </form>
    </body>
</html>
```

Listing 19-9 shows a content page that contains a Content server control associated with the ContentPlaceHolder server control specified within the UpdatePanel server control shown in Listing 19-8. Note that this Content server control contains an UpdatePanel server control. If you run this page, you'll get the result shown in Figure 19-5. Note that if you click the Update button in the master UpdatePanel server control, it automatically updates the UpdatePanel server control declared in the content page.

Listing 19-9: A Content Page that Uses the Master Page from Listing 19-8

```
<%@ Page Language="C#" MasterPageFile="MasterPage.master" %>

<script runat="server">
  void Page_Load(object sender, EventArgs e)
  {
    UpdatePanel2Label.Text = "Refreshed at " + DateTime.Now.ToString();
  }
</script>

<asp:Content ContentPlaceHolderID="ContentPlaceHolder1" runat="server">
  <table style="background-color: #aaaaaa" cellspacing="20">
    <tr>
      <th>
        Content Page
      </th>
    </tr>
```

Listing 19-9 *(continued)*

```
        <tr>
          <td>
            <asp:UpdatePanel ID="UpdatePanel2" runat="server"
            UpdateMode="Conditional">
              <ContentTemplate>
                <table cellspacing="10" style="background-color: #cccccc">
                  <tr>
                    <th colspan="2" align="center">
                      UpdatePanel Server Control
                    </th>
                  </tr>
                  <tr>
                    <td>
                      <asp:Label ID="UpdatePanel2Label" runat="server" />
                    </td>
                    <td>
                      <asp:Button runat="server" Text="Update" />
                    </td>
                  </tr>
                </table>
              </ContentTemplate>
            </asp:UpdatePanel>
          </td>
        </tr>
      </table>
    </asp:Content>
```

Note also that this example declares the ScriptManager server control on the master page, which means that all content pages that use this master page will automatically inherit this ScriptManager server control. The side effect of this approach is that the partial page rendering is automatically enabled for all content pages that use this master page. If this is not what you want, do one of the following:

❑   Programmatically disable the partial page rendering for the desired content pages (see Listing 19-10).

❑   Declare a separate ScriptManager server control on each content page instead of declaring the ScriptManager server control on the master page. Keep in mind that if you choose to declare ScriptManager server controls on content pages, you mustn't declare a ScriptManager server control on the master page. This is because when you access a content page from your browser, the ASP.NET merges the content and master pages together, which means that they form a single page. As I mentioned earlier, every page can contain only a single instance of the ScriptManager server control.

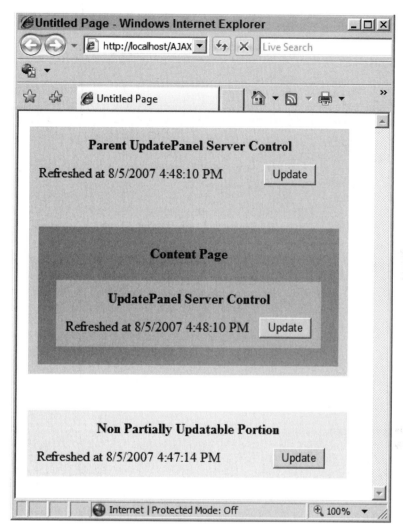

Figure 19-5

The boldface portion of Listing 19-10 shows how to programmatically disable partial page rendering for a specific content page. As this portion demonstrates, you must disable partial page rendering in the Init life-cycle phase of the current page.

Listing 19-10: Disabling Partial Page Rendering for a Content Page

```
<%@ Page Language="C#" MasterPageFile="~/MasterPage.master" %>

<asp:Content ContentPlaceHolderID="ContentPlaceHolder1" runat="server">

  <script runat="server">
    void Page_Init(object sender, EventArgs e)
    {
        ScriptManager sm = ScriptManager.GetCurrent(this.Page);
        sm.EnablePartialRendering = false;
    }

    void Page_Load(object sender, EventArgs e)
    {
      UpdatePanel2Label.Text = "Refreshed at " + DateTime.Now.ToString();
    }
  </script>

  <table style="background-color: #aaaaaa" cellspacing="20">
    <tr>
      <th>
        Content Page
      </th>
    </tr>
    <tr>
      <td>
        <asp:UpdatePanel ID="UpdatePanel2" runat="server" UpdateMode="Conditional">
          <ContentTemplate>
            <table cellspacing="10" style="background-color: #cccccc">
              <tr>
                <th colspan="2" align="center">
                  UpdatePanel Server Control </th>
              </tr>
              <tr>
                <td>
                  <asp:Label ID="UpdatePanel2Label" runat="server" />
                </td>
                <td>
                  <asp:Button ID="Button1" runat="server" Text="Update" />
                </td>
              </tr>
            </table>
          </ContentTemplate>
        </asp:UpdatePanel>
      </td>
    </tr>
  </table>
</asp:Content>
```

Using Triggers

As I mentioned earlier, when the UpdateMode property of an UpdatePanel server control is set to Conditional, the UpdatePanel server control updates only when one of the predefined conditions is met. Here is the third condition. The UpdatePanel server control exposes Triggers, a collection property of type UpdatePanelTriggerCollection that contains objects known as triggers. As the name implies, a trigger is an object that triggers the update of the UpdatePanel server control whose Triggers collection property contains the trigger.

Listing 19-11 presents a page that contains an UpdatePanel server control that uses a trigger that causes an asynchronous page postback. As you can see, an asynchronous page postback trigger is an instance of a class named AsyncPostBackTrigger, which is declaratively added to the <Triggers> child element of the associated <asp:UpdatePanel> tag. If you run this page, you should see the result shown in Figure 19-6. Note that the trigger in this case is an ASP.NET Button server control located in the non-partially updatable section of the page. In other words, a trigger enables you to trigger the update of a specified UpdatePanel server control from outside the control. This approach is different from the approach discussed earlier in which you set the ChildrenAsTriggers property of the UpdatePanel server control to true to have the server controls residing inside the control trigger the update of the control.

Listing 19-11: A Page that Contains an UpdatePanel Server Control that Uses a Trigger

```
<%@ Page Language="C#" %>

<%@ Import Namespace="System.Drawing" %>
<!DOCTYPE html PUBLIC "-//W3C//DTD XHTML 1.1//EN"
"http://www.w3.org/TR/xhtml11/DTD/xhtml11.dtd">

<script runat="server">
  void Page_Load(object sender, EventArgs e)
  {
    string text = "Refreshed at " + DateTime.Now.ToString();
    UpdatePanel1Label.Text = text;
    NonPartiallyUpdatableLabel.Text = text;
  }
</script>

<html xmlns="http://www.w3.org/1999/xhtml">
<head id="Head1" runat="server">
  <title>Untitled Page</title>
</head>
<body>
  <form id="form1" runat="server">
    <asp:ScriptManager ID="ScriptManager1" runat="server" />
    <asp:UpdatePanel ID="UpdatePanel1" runat="server">
      <ContentTemplate>
        <table cellspacing="10" style="background-color: #dddddd">
          <tr>
            <th colspan="2" align="center">
              Partially Updatable Portion (UpdatePanel1) </th>
          </tr>
```

(continued)

Listing 19-11 *(continued)*

```
                  <tr>
                    <td>
                      <asp:Label ID="UpdatePanel1Label" runat="server" />
                    </td>
                    <td>
                      <asp:Button ID="UpdatePanelButton" runat="server" Text="Update" />
                    </td>
                  </tr>
                </table>
              </ContentTemplate>
              <Triggers>
                <asp:AsyncPostBackTrigger ControlID="AsyncPostBackButton"
                EventName="Click" />
              </Triggers>
            </asp:UpdatePanel>
            <br />
            <br />
            <table cellspacing="10" style="background-color: #dddddd">
              <tr>
                <th colspan="2"> Non Partially Updatable Portion </th>
              </tr>
              <tr>
                <td>
                  <asp:Label ID="NonPartiallyUpdatableLabel" runat="server" />
                </td>
                <td>
                  <asp:Button ID="Button1" runat="server" Text="Update" />
                </td>
              </tr>
              <tr>
                <td colspan="2" align="center">
                <br />
                  <asp:Button ID="AsyncPostBackButton" runat="server"
                  Text="Async Postback Trigger" />
                </td>
              </tr>
            </table>
          </form>
      </body>
      </html>
```

Imperative Update

The `UpdatePanel` server control exposes a public method named `Update` that you can call from within your managed code to imperatively update the control. You must set the `UpdateMode` property of the `UpdatePanel` server control to `Conditional` if you want to update the control imperatively. Otherwise an exception will be raised.

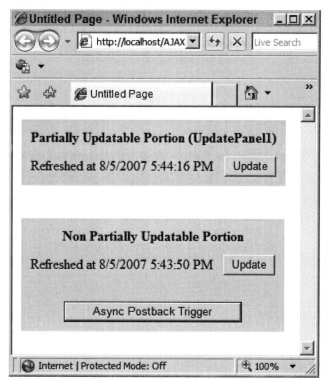

Figure 19-6

Listing 19-12 presents a page that updates an UpdatePanel server control imperatively. This page first adds an ASP.NET Button server control to the non-partially updatable part of the page and registers a method named AsyncPostBackButtonCallback as an event handler for the Click event of this button:

```
<asp:Button ID="AsyncPostBackButton" runat="server"
Text="Async Postback Trigger"
OnClick="AsyncPostbackButtonCallback" />
```

Next, it implements the AsyncPostbackButtonCallback method, where it invokes the Update method on the UpdatePanel server control to update the control. This means that every time the end user clicks the ASP.NET Button server control, the callback for the Click event of this button automatically updates the UpdatePanel server control:

```
void AsyncPostbackButtonCallback(object sender, EventArgs e)
{
  UpdatePanel1.Update();
}
```

We're not done yet! If you don't take the next step, the ASP.NET `Button` server control will trigger a regular synchronous page postback to the server, where not only the `UpdatePanel` server control but also the non-partially updatable section of the page will be updated. The next step adds the following line of code to the `Page_Load` method. As you can see, this line of code calls the `RegisterAsyncPostBackControl` method on the current `ScriptManager` server control to register the ASP.NET `Button` server control as the trigger for asynchronous page postbacks:

```
ScriptManager1.RegisterAsyncPostBackControl(AsyncPostBackButton);
```

Listing 19-12: A Page that Imperatively Updates an UpdatePanel Server Control

```
<%@ Page Language="C#" %>

<%@ Import Namespace="System.Drawing" %>
<!DOCTYPE html PUBLIC "-//W3C//DTD XHTML 1.1//EN"
"http://www.w3.org/TR/xhtml11/DTD/xhtml11.dtd">

<script runat="server">
  void AsyncPostbackButtonCallback(object sender, EventArgs e)
  {
    UpdatePanel1.Update();
  }

  void Page_Load(object sender, EventArgs e)
  {
    string text = "Refreshed at " + DateTime.Now.ToString();
    UpdatePanel1Label.Text = text;
    NonPartiallyUpdatableLabel.Text = text;

    ScriptManager1.RegisterAsyncPostBackControl(AsyncPostBackButton);
  }
</script>

<html xmlns="http://www.w3.org/1999/xhtml">
<head id="Head1" runat="server">
  <title>Untitled Page</title>
</head>
<body>
  <form id="form1" runat="server">
    <asp:ScriptManager ID="ScriptManager1" runat="server" />
    <asp:UpdatePanel ID="UpdatePanel1" runat="server" UpdateMode="Conditional">
      <ContentTemplate>
        <table cellspacing="10" style="background-color: #dddddd">
          <tr>
            <th colspan="2" align="center">
              Partially Updatable Portion (UpdatePanel1) </th>
          </tr>
```

```
          <tr>
            <td>
              <asp:Label ID="UpdatePanel1Label" runat="server" />
            </td>
            <td>
              <asp:Button ID="UpdatePanelButton" runat="server" Text="Update" />
            </td>
          </tr>
        </table>
      </ContentTemplate>
    </asp:UpdatePanel>
    <br />
    <br />
    <table cellspacing="10" style="background-color: #dddddd">
      <tr>
        <th colspan="2"> Non Partially Updatable Portion </th>
      </tr>
      <tr>
        <td>
          <asp:Label ID="NonPartiallyUpdatableLabel" runat="server" />
        </td>
        <td>
          <asp:Button ID="Button1" runat="server" Text="Update" />
        </td>
      </tr>
      <tr>
        <td colspan="2" align="center">
        <br />
          <asp:Button ID="AsyncPostBackButton" runat="server"
          Text="Async Postback Trigger"
          OnClick="AsyncPostbackButtonCallback" />
        </td>
      </tr>
    </table>
  </form>
</body>
</html>
```

Developing Partial-Rendering Enabled Custom Composite Server Controls

Master/detail forms play an important role in ASP.NET applications. As the name suggests, a master/detail form consists of two main components, the master and the detail. The master displays a set of selectable records to the end users. When an end user selects a record from the master, the detail displays detailed information about the selected record.

Several different ASP.NET server controls can be used as master and detail components, and a master/detail form can be made up of any combination of these server controls. For example, you could have a master/detail form in which ASP.NET `GridView` and `DetailsView` controls are used as master and detail components, respectively. Or you could have a master/detail form in which ASP.NET `DropDownList` and `DetailsView` controls are used as master and detail components.

As you can see, different types of master/detail forms can use different types of ASP.NET server controls as master and detail components. All these different types of master/detail forms have certain characteristics in common. I'll first develop an abstract base class named `BaseMasterDetailControl` that captures these common characteristics.

Some of the important characteristics that all master/detail forms share are their usability, responsiveness, and performance. Let's take a look at a scenario where these common characteristics play significant roles. When the end user selects a record from the master, two things must happen:

❑ A round trip must be made to the server to retrieve the detailed information about the selected record. As you can imagine, such round trips can easily degrade the usability, responsiveness, and performance of the master/detail form if they block the user from further interaction with the page until the server response arrives. As a result, it is of paramount importance that such round trips are made asynchronously in the background, allowing the user to interact with the page while the data is being downloaded from the server.

❑ The detail component of the master/detail form must be updated with the new information. As you can imagine, such updates can easily degrade the usability, responsiveness, and performance of the master/detail form if they cause the entire page — including those parts of the page that have absolutely nothing to do with the master/detail form — to update. This is especially a problem for graphics-heavy pages. As a result, it is of paramount importance that such updates are limited to the master/detail form itself and do not propagate to the entire page.

Therefore, a master/detail form must be designed to meet these two requirements. First, all round trips to the server must be performed asynchronously in the background without interrupting the user's interaction with the page. Second, all updates must be limited to the master/detail form without causing the entire page to reload.

The ASP.NET AJAX Framework provides you with two main approaches to designing a master/detail form that meets these two requirements. One approach is to use the ASP.NET AJAX Web service consumption infrastructure to make asynchronous round trips to a Web service to retrieve the required data, and to use the ASP.NET AJAX client-side Framework to dynamically update the master/detail form with the retrieved data. Another approach is to use the ASP.NET AJAX partial page rendering infrastructure to make asynchronous page postbacks to the server and to dynamically update the master/detail form. As I discussed earlier, this infrastructure requires you to use a `ScriptManager` and one or more `UpdatePanel` server controls. In this chapter I will use the second approach.

BaseMasterDetailControl

In this section I'll implement an abstract base class named `BaseMasterDetailControl` that will capture the logic that all types of master/detail forms have in common, as shown in Listing 19-13. Since the `BaseMasterDetailControl` consists of two components — master and detail — it is an example of what is known as a *composite server control*.

The controls from which a composite server control such as `BaseMasterDetailControl` is assembled are known as *child controls*. Composite controls delegate most of their responsibilities — such as rendering content HTML and handling postback events — to their child controls. Implementing a custom composite server control such as the `BaseMasterDetailControl` control involves the following actions:

1. Deriving from `CompositeControl`
2. Choosing child controls
3. Choosing layout
4. Implementing a custom container control
5. Creating a container control
6. Creating the child controls of a container control
7. Applying style to a container control
8. Adding a container control to the custom composite server control
9. Rendering a container control
10. Overriding the `CreateChildControls` method
11. Overriding the `TagKey` property
12. Overriding the `CreateControlStyle` method
13. Exposing the `ControlStyle`'s properties as if they were the properties of the composite control
14. Overriding the `RenderContents` method
15. Exposing the properties of the child controls as if they were the properties of the composite control

Listing 19-13 uses the above recipe to implement the BaseMasterDetailControl composite server control as discussed in the following sections.

Listing 19-13: The BaseMasterDetailControl Server Control

```
using System;
using System.Data;
using System.Configuration;
using System.Web;
using System.Web.UI;
using System.Web.UI.WebControls;
using System.Web.UI.HtmlControls;
using System.Collections;
using System.Drawing;
using System.ComponentModel;
```

(continued)

Listing 19-13 *(continued)*

```csharp
namespace CustomComponents
{
  public abstract class BaseMasterDetailControl : CompositeControl
  {
    Control master;
    Control detail;
    UpdatePanel masterUpdatePanel;
    UpdatePanel detailUpdatePanel;
    MasterDetailContainer masterContainer;
    MasterDetailContainer detailContainer;

    protected abstract Control CreateMaster();
    protected abstract Control CreateDetail();
    protected abstract void RegisterMasterEventHandlers();
    protected abstract void RegisterDetailEventHandlers();

    public Control Master
    {
      get { EnsureChildControls(); return this.master; }
    }

    public Control Detail
    {
      get { EnsureChildControls(); return this.detail; }
    }

    public string MasterSkinID
    {
      get
      {
        EnsureChildControls();
        return master.SkinID;
      }
      set
      {
        EnsureChildControls();
        master.SkinID = value;
      }
    }

    public string DetailSkinID
    {
      get
      {
        EnsureChildControls();
        return detail.SkinID;
      }
      set
      {
        EnsureChildControls();
        detail.SkinID = value;
      }
    }
```

```
public virtual object SelectedValue
{
  get { return ViewState["SelectedValue"]; }
  set { ViewState["SelectedValue"] = value; }
}

protected override Style CreateControlStyle()
{
  return new TableStyle(ViewState);
}

public virtual GridLines GridLines
{
  get { return ((TableStyle)ControlStyle).GridLines; }
  set { ((TableStyle)ControlStyle).GridLines = value; }
}

public virtual int CellSpacing
{
  get { return ((TableStyle)ControlStyle).CellSpacing; }
  set { ((TableStyle)ControlStyle).CellSpacing = value; }
}

public virtual int CellPadding
{
  get { return ((TableStyle)ControlStyle).CellPadding; }
  set { ((TableStyle)ControlStyle).CellPadding = value; }
}

public virtual HorizontalAlign HorizontalAlign
{
  get { return ((TableStyle)ControlStyle).HorizontalAlign; }
  set { ((TableStyle)ControlStyle).HorizontalAlign = value; }
}

public virtual string BackImageUrl
{
  get { return ((TableStyle)ControlStyle).BackImageUrl; }
  set { ((TableStyle)ControlStyle).BackImageUrl = value; }
}

protected virtual void CreateContainerChildControls(
                                        MasterDetailContainer container)
{
  switch (container.ContainerType)
  {
    case ContainerType.Master:
      masterUpdatePanel = new UpdatePanel();
      masterUpdatePanel.UpdateMode = UpdatePanelUpdateMode.Conditional;
      master = this.CreateMaster();
      if (string.IsNullOrEmpty(master.ID))
        master.ID = "MasterServerControl";
```

(continued)

Listing 19-13 *(continued)*

```
            this.RegisterMasterEventHandlers();
            masterUpdatePanel.ContentTemplateContainer.Controls.Add(master);
            container.Controls.Add(masterUpdatePanel);
            break;
          case ContainerType.Detail:
            detailUpdatePanel = new UpdatePanel();
            detailUpdatePanel.UpdateMode = UpdatePanelUpdateMode.Conditional;
            detail = this.CreateDetail();
            if (string.IsNullOrEmpty(detail.ID))
              detail.ID = "DetailServerControl";
            this.RegisterDetailEventHandlers();
            detailUpdatePanel.ContentTemplateContainer.Controls.Add(detail);
            container.Controls.Add(detailUpdatePanel);
            break;
      }
    }

    protected void UpdateMaster(object sender, EventArgs e)
    {
      master.DataBind();
      masterUpdatePanel.Update();
    }

    protected void UpdateDetail(object sender, EventArgs e)
    {
      detail.DataBind();
      detailUpdatePanel.Update();
    }

    protected virtual void AddContainer(MasterDetailContainer container)
    {
      Controls.Add(container);
    }

    protected virtual void RenderContainer(MasterDetailContainer container,
                                           HtmlTextWriter writer)
    {
      container.RenderControl(writer);
    }

    protected virtual MasterDetailContainer CreateContainer
                           (ContainerType containerType)
    {
      return new MasterDetailContainer(containerType);
    }
```

```
  private TableItemStyle masterContainerStyle;
  [DefaultValue((string)null)]
  [PersistenceMode(PersistenceMode.InnerProperty)]
  [NotifyParentProperty(true)]
  [DesignerSerializationVisibility(DesignerSerializationVisibility.Content)]
  public TableItemStyle MasterContainerStyle
  {
    get
    {
      if (masterContainerStyle == null)
      {
        masterContainerStyle = new TableItemStyle();
        if (IsTrackingViewState)
          ((IStateManager)masterContainerStyle).TrackViewState();
      }

      return masterContainerStyle;
    }
  }

  private TableItemStyle detailContainerStyle;
  [DefaultValue((string)null)]
  [PersistenceMode(PersistenceMode.InnerProperty)]
  [NotifyParentProperty(true)]
  [DesignerSerializationVisibility(DesignerSerializationVisibility.Content)]
  public TableItemStyle DetailContainerStyle
  {
    get
    {
      if (detailContainerStyle == null)
      {
        detailContainerStyle = new TableItemStyle();
        if (IsTrackingViewState)
          ((IStateManager)detailContainerStyle).TrackViewState();
      }

      return detailContainerStyle;
    }
  }

  protected override void TrackViewState()
  {
    base.TrackViewState();

    if (masterContainerStyle != null)
      ((IStateManager)masterContainerStyle).TrackViewState();
```

(continued)

Listing 19-13 *(continued)*

```
      if (detailContainerStyle != null)
        ((IStateManager)detailContainerStyle).TrackViewState();
    }

    protected override object SaveViewState()
    {
      object[] state = new object[3];

      state[0] = base.SaveViewState();

      if (masterContainerStyle != null)
        state[1] = ((IStateManager)masterContainerStyle).SaveViewState();

      if (detailContainerStyle != null)
        state[2] = ((IStateManager)detailContainerStyle).SaveViewState();

      foreach (object obj in state)
      {
        if (obj != null)
          return state;
      }

      return null;
    }

    protected override void LoadViewState(object savedState)
    {
      if (savedState != null)
      {
        object[] state = savedState as object[];
        if (state != null && state.Length == 3)
        {
          base.LoadViewState(state[0]);

          if (state[1] != null)
            ((IStateManager)MasterContainerStyle).LoadViewState(state[1]);

          if (state[2] != null)
            ((IStateManager)DetailContainerStyle).LoadViewState(state[2]);
        }
      }

      else
        base.LoadViewState(savedState);
    }
```

```csharp
      protected virtual void ApplyContainerStyles()
      {
        foreach (MasterDetailContainer container in Controls)
        {
          switch (container.ContainerType)
          {
            case ContainerType.Master:
              if (masterContainerStyle != null)
                container.ApplyStyle(masterContainerStyle);
              break;
            case ContainerType.Detail:
              if (detailContainerStyle != null)
                container.ApplyStyle(detailContainerStyle);
              break;
          }
        }
      }

      protected override void CreateChildControls()
      {
        Controls.Clear();

        masterContainer = CreateContainer(ContainerType.Master);
        CreateContainerChildControls(masterContainer);
        AddContainer(masterContainer);

        detailContainer = CreateContainer(ContainerType.Detail);
        CreateContainerChildControls(detailContainer);
        AddContainer(detailContainer);

        ChildControlsCreated = true;
      }

      protected override HtmlTextWriterTag TagKey
      {
        get { return HtmlTextWriterTag.Table; }
      }

      protected override void RenderContents(HtmlTextWriter writer)
      {
        ApplyContainerStyles();
        writer.RenderBeginTag(HtmlTextWriterTag.Tr);
        RenderContainer(masterContainer, writer);
        writer.RenderEndTag();

        writer.RenderBeginTag(HtmlTextWriterTag.Tr);
        RenderContainer(detailContainer, writer);
        writer.RenderEndTag();
      }
    }
  }
}
```

Deriving from CompositeControl

The ASP.NET Framework comes with a base class named `CompositeControl` that provides the basic features that every composite control must support. These features will be discussed later in this chapter. You must derive your custom composite control from the `CompositeControl` base class to save yourself from having to re-implement the features that your control can easily inherit from this base class.

```
public class BaseMasterDetailControl: CompositeControl
```

Choosing the Child Controls

The next order of business in developing a custom composite control is to choose the child controls that you'll need in order to assemble your custom control. You'll need the following server controls to assemble the `BaseMasterDetailControl` control (each child control is named for ease of reference):

❑   A server control to display the master data records (`master`)

❑   A server control to display the detailed information about the selected record of the master control (`detail`)

The `BaseMasterDetailControl` control exposes two abstract methods that its subclasses must override to create the appropriate master and detail server controls:

```
protected abstract Control CreateMaster();
protected abstract Control CreateDetail();
```

Choosing the Layout

Next you need to choose the desired layout for your child controls. As Figure 19-7 shows, the `BaseMasterDetailControl` control uses a tabular layout for its child controls, in which each table cell contains a child control. Note that the table cells in Figure 19-7 are numbered for ease of reference. Keep in mind that cell numbers 1 and 2 contain the master and detail server controls, respectively.

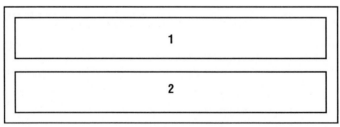

Figure 19-7

Implementing a Custom Container Control

Since the `BaseMasterDetailControl` control uses a tabular layout for its child controls, in which each table cell contains a child control, the appropriate container for the child controls is `TableCell` control. However, the `TableCell` control doesn't meet the following requirements:

❑   It doesn't implement the `INamingContainer` interface. I'll discuss later why it's important for a container control to implement this interface. You'll also see that this is a marker interface and doesn't have any methods or properties.

❑   It doesn't expose a property that uniquely locates or identifies a cell among other cells. It's important to know which cell you're dealing with because different cells contain different types of child controls. For example, cell number 1 contains the `master` control while cell number 2 contains the `detail` control.

Therefore, I'll implement a custom container control named `MasterDetailContainer` that derives from `TableCell`, implements the `INamingContainer` interface, and exposes a property named `ContainerType` whose value uniquely locates or identifies each cell among other cells.

As Figure 19-7 shows, the number of a cell is used to identify or locate the cell among other cells. The `BaseMasterDetailControl` control defines an enumeration named `ContainerType` whose values correspond to the cell numbers shown in Figure 19-7. Listing 19-14 presents the definition of this enumerator.

Listing 19-14: The ContainerType Enumerator

```
namespace CustomComponents
{
  public enum ContainerType
  {
    Master = 1,
    Detail = 2
  }
}
```

Listing 19-15 shows the implementation of the `MasterDetailContainer` container control.

Listing 19-15: The MasterDetailContainer Container Control

```
using System;
using System.Data;
using System.Configuration;
using System.Web;
using System.Web.UI;
using System.Web.UI.WebControls;
using System.Web.UI.HtmlControls;
```

(continued)

Listing 19-15 *(continued)*

```
namespace CustomComponents
{
  public class MasterDetailContainer : TableCell, INamingContainer
  {
    private ContainerType containerType;

    public MasterDetailContainer(ContainerType containerType)
    {
      this.containerType = containerType;
    }

    public ContainerType ContainerType
    {
      get { return containerType; }
    }
  }
}
```

Creating a Container Control

The extensibility of a custom control is of paramount importance. As a matter of fact, the extensibility of your custom control is much more important than its feature set. You'd be better off developing an extensible custom control with fewer features than a non-extensible one with more features. An extensible control enables others to extend it to add support for missing features, but the non-extensible one is pretty much it — if it doesn't support the features the clients of your control need, they have no choice but to dump it.

That said, you can't design a custom control that can be extended to support all possible features. This is simply not practical, for two reasons. First, you can't see the future, which means you can't plan for all possible extensions. Second, extensibility comes with a price in terms of both time and budget. The more extensible you want your custom control to be, the more time and effort you have to put into it.

This chapter will show you a few examples of how you can make your custom controls more extensible. Listing 19-13 shows the first example, in which the protected virtual CreateContainer method encapsulates and isolates the instantiation of the container control. This will enable others to write new container controls that derive from the MasterDetailContainer control and override this method to return their own container controls.

Creating the Child Controls of a Container Control

As discussed earlier, a MasterDetailContainer control is used to represent each numbered cell shown in Figure 19-7. The next order of business is to create the child controls that go into each container control. This is a tricky one because you have to do it in such a way that it doesn't tie your custom control to a specific set of child controls. The trick is to implement a new protected virtual method (CreateContainerChildControls, shown in Listing 19-13) that encapsulates the code that does the dirty job of creating the child controls. This method must take the container control as its argument, create the child controls, and add them to the container. Therefore the only dependency between your custom control and its child controls is the container control. This dependency is weak, considering the fact that others can override the CreateContainer method to use their own custom container controls.

You can think of the container control as a bucket. Your custom control first calls the `CreateContainer` method to create the bucket. The `CreateContainer` method isolates your custom control from the code that does the dirty job of creating the bucket. Your custom control then passes the bucket to the `CreateContainerChildControls` method shown in Listing 19-13. `CreateContainerChildControls` creates the child controls and puts them in the bucket. Your custom control doesn't know or care what this method puts into the bucket because your custom control deals only with the bucket, not its contents.

The `CreateContainerChildControls` method first uses the `ContainerType` property of the container control to identify the table cell into which the respective child control will go. Recall that the values of the `ContainerType` property correspond to the cell numbers shown in Figure 19-7. The containing cell matters because it determines what types of child controls the `CreateContainerChildControls` method must create. For example, the child control responsible for displaying the master data records goes into the cell number 1 in Figure 19-7. The child control responsible for displaying the details of the record that the end user selects from the master, on the other hand, goes into the cell number 2. The method then creates the child control that goes into the specified cell or container control, as follows.

If the container type is `Master`, the method first instantiates an `UpdatePanel` server control:

```
masterUpdatePanel = new UpdatePanel();
```

This `UpdatePanel` server control will contain the master server control — that is, the server control that will display the master records. Placing the master server control in an `UpdatePanel` server control provides the following important benefit: any postback originating from the inside the master server control, such as selecting a record, will be treated as an asynchronous page postback, which means that the page will be posted back asynchronously in the background without interrupting the end user interaction with the page.

As Listing 19-13 shows, the `CreateContainerChildControls` method sets the `UpdateMode` property of the master `UpdatePanel` server control to `Conditional`:

```
masterUpdatePanel.UpdateMode = UpdatePanelUpdateMode.Conditional;
```

As you'll see later, this ensures that the master server control is updated only when one of these conditions is met:

- ❑   The user selects a record from the master server control
- ❑   The user updates the record shown in the detail server control
- ❑   The user deletes the record shown in the detail server control
- ❑   The user inserts a new record in the detail server control

Next, the `CreateContainerChildControls` method invokes the `CreateMaster` method to create the master server control. As mentioned earlier, the `CreateMaster` method is an abstract method. It is the responsibility of the subclasses of the `BaseMasterDetailControl` to override this method to create the appropriate master server control. For example, one subclass may override this method to create and return a `GridView` server control. Another subclass, on the other hand, may override this method to create and return a `DropDownList` server control. In other words, it is completely up to the subclass to decide what type of server control should be used to display the master records:

```
master = this.CreateMaster();
```

Next, the `CreateContainerChildControls` method invokes the `RegisterMasterEventHandlers` method:

```
this.RegisterMasterEventHandlers();
```

The `RegisterMasterEventHandlers` method is an abstract method:

```
protected abstract void RegisterMasterEventHandlers();
```

As such, it is the responsibility of the subclass of the `BaseMasterDetailControl` to override this method to register the appropriate event handlers for those events of the master server control that require the detail server control to update. For example, if the master server control is a `DropDownList` control, the subclass must register an event handler for the `SelectedIndexChanged` event of the `DropDownList` control because when this event fires, the detail server control must be updated with the detailed information about the newly selected record.

Next, the `CreateContainerChildControls` method adds the master server control to the `Controls` collection of the content template container server control of the master `UpdatePanel` server control:

```
masterUpdatePanel.ContentTemplateContainer.Controls.Add(master);
```

In general, there are two ways to add content to a `UpdatePanel` server control: declarative and programmatic. The declarative approach requires you to add HTML or ASP.NET server controls within the opening and closing tags of the `ContentTemplate` child element of the tag that represents the `UpdatePanel` server control on an `.aspx` or `.ascx` file. Here is an example:

```
<asp:UpdatePanel runat="server" ID="UpdatePanel1">
  <ContentTemplate>
      <!-- HTML and/or ASP.NET server control goes here -->
  </ContentTemplate>
</asp:UpdatePanel>
```

The imperative approach, on the other hand, requires you to add ASP.NET server controls to the `Controls` collection of the content template container control of the `UpdatePanel` server control from your C# or VB.NET code.

Next, the `CreateContainerChildControls` method adds the master `UpdatePanel` server control to the `Controls` collection of the container server control:

```
container.Controls.Add(masterUpdatePanel);
```

If the container type is `Detail`, the `CreateContainerChildControls` method first instantiates an `UpdatePanel` server control:

```
detailUpdatePanel = new UpdatePanel();
```

This UpdatePanel server control will contain the detail server control — that is, the server control that will display the details of the record that the user selects from the master server control. Placing the detail server control in an UpdatePanel server control provides the following two important benefits. First, any postback originating from the inside the detail server control such as clicking an Update button to update a record will be treated as an asynchronous page postback, which means that the page will be posted back asynchronously in the background without interrupting the end-user interaction with the page. Second, when the end user selects a new record from the master records, the detail server control is the only part of the page that gets updated. That is, this update does not trigger the entire page to reload. This gives an important performance, usability, and responsiveness boost in graphics-heavy pages.

As Listing 19-13 shows, the CreateContainerChildControls method sets the UpdateMode property of the detail UpdatePanel server control to Conditional:

```
detailUpdatePanel.UpdateMode = UpdatePanelUpdateMode.Conditional;
```

As you'll see later and as I mentioned earlier, this ensures that the detail server control is updated only when one of these conditions is met:

- ❑ The user selects a new record from the master server control
- ❑ The user updates the record shown in the detail server control
- ❑ The user deletes the record shown in the detail server control
- ❑ The user inserts a new record in the detail server control

Next, the CreateContainerChildControls method invokes the CreateDetail method to create the detail server control. As mentioned earlier, the CreateDetail method is an abstract method. It is the responsibility of the subclasses of the BaseMasterDetailControl to override this method to create the appropriate detail server control. For example, one subclass may override this method to create and to return a DetailsView server control. Another subclass, on the other hand, may override this method to create and to return a different type of server control. In other words, it is completely up to the subclass to decide what type of server control should be used to display the detail record:

```
detail = this.CreateDetail();
```

Next, the CreateContainerChildControls method invokes the RegisterDetailEventHandlers method:

```
this.RegisterDetailEventHandlers();
```

The RegisterDetailEventHandlers method is an abstract method:

```
protected abstract void RegisterDetailEventHandlers();
```

Because of this, it is the responsibility of the subclass of the BaseMasterDetailControl to override this method to register the appropriate event handlers for those events of the detail server control that require the master server control to update. For example, if the detail server control is a DetailsView control, the subclass must register an event handler for the ItemDeleted event of the DetailsView control, because when this event fires, the master server control must be updated to "undisplay" the deleted record.

Next, the `CreateContainerChildControls` method adds the detail server control to the `Controls` collection of the content template container server control of the detail `UpdatePanel` server control:

```
detailUpdatePanel.ContentTemplateContainer.Controls.Add(detail);
```

Finally, the `CreateContainerChildControls` method adds the detail `UpdatePanel` server control to the `Controls` collection of the container server control:

```
container.Controls.Add(detailUpdatePanel);
```

Note that the `CreateContainerChildControls` method assigns unique values to the ID properties of the child controls. Also note that the `CreateContainerChildControls` method initializes the child controls before they are added to the `Controls` collection.

> *You must initialize your child controls before you add them to the `Controls` collection of your custom control, because if you initialize them afterward these initialized property values will be saved to the view state. This will unnecessarily increase the size of your custom control's view state. Recall that the containing page stores the string representation of your control's view state in a hidden field on the page, which means that any increase in the size of your control's view state will increase the size of the page that the requesting browser has to download from the server.*

Applying Style to a Container Control

Recall that container controls are of type `MasterDetailContainer`. As Listing 19-15 shows, the `MasterDetailContainer` class derives from the `TableCell` control, which in turn derives from `WebControl`. Every control that derives from `WebControl` exposes a property named `ControlStyle`. The real type of this property may vary from one control to another; the `ControlStyle` property of the `TableCell` control is of type `TableItemStyle`.

The `TableItemStyle` class exposes the following 12 style properties: `ForeColor`, `BorderColor`, `BackColor`, `BorderWidth`, `BorderStyle`, `Width`, `Height`, `Font`, `CssClass`, `HorizontalAlign`, `VerticalAlign`, and `Wrap`. This means that the `ControlStyle` of each container control exposes these style properties.

The `BaseMasterDetailControl` server control exposes two properties of type `TableItemStyle`, each of which internally maps to the `ControlStyle` property of its associated container control, as shown in the following table.

Style Property	Associated Container Control
masterContainerStyle	ContainerType.Master
detailContainerStyle	ContainerType.Detail

These two properties enable page developers to set the `ControlStyle` property of a container control as if they were setting the style properties of the `BaseMasterDetailControl` server control itself. In other words, the `BaseMasterDetailControl` server control hides the `ControlStyle` properties of its container controls and exposes them as its own properties.

As Listing 19-13 shows, the `ApplyContainerStyles` method iterates through the container controls in the `Controls` collection of the `BaseMasterDetailControl` server control and calls the `ApplyStyle` method of each enumerated container control if its associated style property isn't `null`. Notice that the `ApplyContainerStyles` method uses the `ContainerType` property of each enumerated container control to determine which container control it's dealing with.

State Management

Object-oriented applications use objects to service their users. Each object normally keeps the information that it needs to function properly in memory. This information includes, but is not limited to, the property and field values of the object. This in-memory information is known as the *state* of the object. Invoking the methods and properties of an object normally changes its state. The state of an object is lost forever when the object is disposed of. This isn't an issue in a desktop application, because the objects are disposed of only when they're no longer needed. However, it causes a big problem in a Web application where each user session normally consists of more than one request.

Due to the stateless nature of the HTTP protocol, the objects are disposed of at the end of each request, even though the session that the request belongs to still needs the objects. That is, the states of these objects are lost at the end of each request and new objects of the same types are recreated at the beginning of the next request. These newly created objects have no memory of the previous objects and start off with their default states.

The ASP.NET view state mechanism enables you to save the states of your objects at the end of each request and load them at the beginning of the next request. The next request does the following:

❑ Creates new objects of the same types as those that were disposed of at the end of the previous request

❑ Loads the states of the old objects into the new objects

Since the newly created objects at the beginning of each request have the same types and states as the objects disposed of at the end of the previous request, it gives the illusion that objects are not disposed of at the end of each request and that the same objects are being used all along.

Now you'll see how the ASP.NET view state mechanism works. Every server control inherits three methods from the `Control` class: `TrackViewState`, `SaveViewState`, and `LoadViewState`. At the end of each request, the following sequence of events occurs:

1. The page automatically calls the `SaveViewState` method of the controls in its `Controls` collection. Remember, the `Controls` collection contains all the controls that were declared in the `.aspx` file. Page developers can also programmatically create server controls and manually add them to the `Controls` collection of the page.

2. The `SaveViewState` method of each control must save the state of the control and its child controls into an appropriate object and return the object.

3. The page collects the objects returned from the `SaveViewState` methods of the controls in its `Controls` collection and forms a tree of objects known as an *object graph*.

4. The page framework then uses the type converter associated with each object to convert the object into a string representation, and combines these string representations into a single string that represents the entire object graph.

5. The page framework then stores the string representation of the entire object graph in a hidden field named __VIEWSTATE, which looks something like the following:

```
<input type="hidden" name="__VIEWSTATE" id="__VIEWSTATE"
value="/wEPDwULLTE3MDU5MjY4MTkPZBYCAgMPZBYCAgEPFCsAAmRkFgZm
D2QWAmYPDxYCHgRUZXh0BQ5Q
YX1tZW50IE11dGhvZGRkAgEPZBYCZg8PDxY
CHgtfIURhdGFCb3VuZGdkZGQCBw9kFgRmDw8PFgIfAWdkZGQ
CAg8PDxYCHw
FnZGRkZJDAqbyjCj4rjagRWSiVYTp7nQfM" />
```

Therefore the __VIEWSTATE hidden field is sent to the client browser as part of the containing page. When the page is posted back to the server, the following sequence of events occurs:

1. The page framework retrieves the string representation of the object graph from the __VIEWSTATE hidden field.

2. The page framework extracts the string representation of each object.

3. The page framework uses the type converter associated with each object to recreate the object from its string representation.

4. The page calls the LoadViewState method of each control in its Controls collection and passes the respective object into it. (Remember that this object contains the state of the control and its child controls at the end of the previous request.)

5. The LoadViewState method of each control must load the contents (the state of the control at the end of the previous request) of this object into itself. Therefore the control will have the same state as in the previous request.

6. The page calls the TrackViewState method of each control in its Controls collection.

7. The TrackViewState of each control must set an internal Boolean field to true to specify that it's tracking the control's state. What this means is that from this point on, any changes in the state of the object will be marked as dirty and saved at the end of the request (as discussed before).

As I mentioned, the state of a control includes, but is not limited to, its property values. In general, there are two types of properties:

❑ **Simple properties:** A simple property is one whose type doesn't expose any properties. For example, the MasterSkinID property of the BaseMasterDetailControl server control is of type string, which doesn't expose any properties.

❑ **Complex properties:** A complex property is one whose type exposes properties. For example, the MasterContainerStyle and DetailContainerStyle properties of the BaseMasterDetailControl server control are of type TableItemStyle, which exposes properties such as Font, Width, Height, and so on.

Simple properties use the ViewState collection as their backing store to manage their states across page postbacks. How about the MasterContainerStyle and DetailContainerStyle complex properties of the BaseMasterDetailControl server control? How do they manage their states across page postbacks?

This is where the `IStateManager` interface comes into play. The type of `MasterContainerStyle` and `DetailContainerStyle` complex properties — that is, the `TableItemStyle` — implements this interface.

`IStateManager` exposes one Boolean property, `IsTrackingViewState`, and three methods, `TrackViewState`, `SaveViewState`, and `LoadViewState`.

When the `TrackViewState` method of a control is called, the method calls the `TrackViewState` methods of its complex properties. The `TrackViewState` method of a complex property does exactly what the `TrackViewState` method of a control does — sets an internal Boolean field to `true` to specify that any state changes will be marked as dirty and saved at the end of the current request.

When the `SaveViewState` method of a control is called, the method calls the `SaveViewState` methods of its complex properties. The `SaveViewState` method of a complex property does exactly what the `SaveViewState` method of a control does — it saves its state into an appropriate object and returns the object.

It then collects the objects returned from the `SaveViewState` methods of its complex properties and saves them into the same object to which it saves its own state. Finally, it returns the object that contains the states of both the control and its complex properties.

When the `LoadViewState` method of a control is called, it retrieves the objects that contain the states of its complex properties. It then calls the `LoadViewState` method of each complex property and passes the object that contains the saved state into it. The `LoadViewState` method of a complex property does exactly what the `LoadViewState` of a control does.

As you can see from the implementation of the `MasterContainerStyle` and `DetailContainerStyle` properties shown in Listing 19-13, when these two style properties are created and `BaseMasterDetailControl` server control is tracking its view state, the control calls the `TrackViewState` method of these two properties to inform them that they must start tracking their view states.

TrackViewState

`BaseMasterDetailControl` overrides `TrackViewState` to call the `TrackViewState` methods of its style properties, as shown in Listing 19-13. Note that `TrackViewState` calls the `TrackViewState` method of a style property if and only if the style isn't null — that is, if the page developer has specified the style.

SaveViewState

`BaseMasterDetailControl` overrides `SaveViewState` to call the `SaveViewState` methods of its style properties, as shown in Listing 19-13. The `SaveViewState` method of each style property stores its view state in an appropriate object and returns the object to the `SaveViewState` method of `BaseMasterDetailControl`, which in turn puts all these objects, and the object that contains the view state of its base class, in an array and returns the array to its caller.

Notice that `SaveViewState` checks whether all the objects that the array contains are `null`. If they are, it returns `null`. If at least one of the objects isn't `null`, it returns the whole array.

LoadViewState

BaseMasterDetailControl overrides LoadViewState to call the LoadViewState methods of its style properties, as shown in Listing 19-13. As you can see, the LoadViewState method of BaseMasterDetailControl retrieves the array of objects that contains the saved view state of its base class and style properties. The method then calls the LoadViewState methods of its base class and properties in the order in which the SaveViewState method of BaseMasterDetailControl called their SaveViewState methods. The LoadViewState method of each style property loads its view state with the saved view state.

Adding a Container Control to a Composite Control

The BaseMasterDetailControl server control implements a method named AddContainer, shown in Listing 19-13, that encapsulates the code that adds a container control to the Controls collection of the BaseMasterDetailControl control. Note that this method is marked as *protected virtual* to enable others to override it — in order, for example, to raise an event before or after the container is added to the Controls collection.

Rendering a Container Control

The BaseMasterDetailControl server control exposes a method named RenderContainer, shown in Listing 19-13, which encapsulates the code that renders a container. This method is marked as protected virtual to enable others to override it.

Overriding CreateChildControls: One-Stop Shopping for All Your Child Controls

The Control class exposes a method named CreateChildControls that you must override to create the child controls that you need in order to assemble your custom control. One important thing to keep in mind about child controls is that they're created on demand. Don't assume that they're created at a particular stage of your custom control's life cycle. They can be created at any time. In other words, the CreateChildControls method can be called at any stage of your custom control's life cycle to create the child controls.

This has important consequences. One of these is that you must create the child controls of your custom control in one and only one place — the CreateChildControls method. Your custom control mustn't create any of its child controls in any other place. If you create your child controls in any other place, they cannot be created on demand because the on-demand child-control creation feature of the ASP.NET Framework is accomplished via calling the CreateChildControls method. Think of CreateChildControls as your one-stop shopping place for all your child controls. You mustn't shop anywhere else!

Next, I'll walk you through the implementation of the CreateChildControls method shown in Listing 19-13. This method first calls the Clear method of the Controls collection to clear the collection. This ensures that multiple copies of child controls aren't added to the Controls collection when the CreateChildControls method is called multiple times:

```
Controls.Clear();
```

If you examine the implementation of the `BaseMasterDetailControl` *server control, you'll notice that this method is never called multiple times. You may be wondering, then, why you should bother with clearing the collection. You're right as far as the implementation of the* `BaseMasterDetailControl` *server control goes, because you're the author of this control and you can make sure your implementation of it doesn't call the* `CreateChildControls` *method multiple times. However, you have no control over others when they're deriving from your control to author their own custom controls. There's nothing that would stop them from calling the* `CreateChildControls` *method multiple times. This example shows that when you're writing a custom control you must take the subclasses of your custom control into account.*

Then it takes the following actions for each cell shown in Figure 19-7 to create the child control that goes into the cell:

❑ It calls the `CreateContainer` method to create the container control that represents the cell. For example, the following call to the `CreateContainer` method creates the container control that represents the cell number 2 in Figure 19-7:

```
detailContainer = CreateContainer(ContainerType.Detail);
```

❑ It calls the `CreateContainerChildControls` method and passes the container control into it. As I mentioned earlier, the `CreateContainerChildControls` method creates the child controls, initializes them, and adds them to the container control. For example, the following call to the `CreateContainerChildControls` method creates the detail server control and adds it to the `detailContainer` server control:

```
CreateContainerChildControls(detailContainer);
```

❑ It calls the `AddContainer` method to add the container control to the `BaseMasterDetailControl` server control. For example, the following code adds the container control that represents the cell number 2 in Figure 19-7 to the `BaseMasterDetailControl` control:

```
AddContainer(detailContainer);
```

After all the child controls are created, the method then sets the `ChildControlsCreated` property to `true`:

```
ChildControlsCreated = true;
```

As I mentioned, the child controls aren't created at any particular stage of your custom control's life cycle. They're created on demand. This means that the `CreateChildControls` method can be called multiple times, though this will waste server resources because this method recreates the child controls every single time it's called, regardless of whether or not the child controls have already been created.

To address this problem, the `Control` class exposes a method named `EnsureChildControls` and a Boolean property named `ChildControlsCreated`. The `EnsureChildControls` method checks whether the `ChildControlsCreated` property is set to `false`. If it is, the method first calls the `CreateChildControls` method and then sets the `ChildControlsCreated` property to `true`. The `EnsureChildControls` method uses this property to avoid multiple invocations of the `CreateChildControls` method.

That is why your custom control's implementation of the `CreateChildControls` method must set the `ChildControlsCreated` property to `true` to signal the `EnsureChildControls` method that child controls have been created and the `CreateChildControls` mustn't be called again.

Overriding the TagKey Property

Your custom control must use the `TagKey` property to specify the HTML element that will contain the entire contents of your custom control — that is, the containing element of your custom control. Since `BaseMasterDetailControl` displays its contents in a table, the control overrides the `TagKey` property to specify the `table` HTML element as its containing element (see Listing 19-13).

Overriding the CreateControlStyle Method

Your custom control must override the `CreateControlStyle` method to specify the appropriate `Style` subclass. The properties of this `Style` subclass are rendered as CSS style attributes on the containing HTML element. Since `BaseMasterDetailControl` uses a table HTML element as its containing element, it overrides the `CreateControlStyle` method to use a `TableStyle` instance (see Listing 19-13). The `TableStyle` class exposes properties such as `GridLines`, `CellSpacing`, `CellPadding`, `HorizontalAlign`, and `BackImageUrl` that are rendered as CSS table style attributes.

Exposing Style Properties

When you override the `CreateControlStyle` method, you must also define new style properties for your custom control that expose the corresponding properties of the `Style` subclass. This provides page developers with a convenient mechanism to set the CSS style properties of the containing HTML element.

`BaseMasterDetailControl` exposes five properties named `GridLines`, `CellSpacing`, `CellPadding`, `HorizonalAlign`, and `BackImageUrl` that correspond to the properties of the `TableStyle` class with the same names as shown in Listing 19-13.

Overriding the RenderContents Method

The `CreateChildControls` method is where you create and initialize the child controls that you need in order to assemble your custom control. The `RenderContents` method is where you do the assembly — that is, where you assemble your custom control from the child controls. First you need to understand how the default implementation (the `WebControl` class's implementation) of the `RenderContents` method assembles your custom control from the child controls.

The `WebControl` class's implementation of `RenderContents` calls the `Render` method of its base class, the `Control` class:

```
protected internal virtual void RenderContents(HtmlTextWriter writer)
{
  base.Render(writer);
}
```

Render calls the RenderChildren method of the Control class:

```
protected internal virtual void Render(HtmlTextWriter writer)
{
  RenderChildren(writer);
}
```

RenderChildren calls the RenderControl methods of the child controls in the order in which they are added to the Controls collection:

```
protected internal virtual void RenderChildren(HtmlTextWriter writer)
{
  foreach (Control childControl in Controls)
    childControl.RenderControl(writer);
}
```

In conclusion, the default implementation of the RenderContents method assembles the child controls in the order in which the CreateChildControls method adds them to the Controls collection. This default assembly of the BaseMasterDetailControl custom control will simply lay down the child controls on the page one after another in a linear fashion, which is not the layout you want. As Listing 19-13 shows, the BaseMasterDetailControl server control overrides the RenderContents method to compose or assemble the child controls in a tabular fashion.

As Figure 19-7 shows, the BaseMasterDetailControl server control renders its contents in a table that consists of two rows. The RenderContents method in Listing 19-13 first calls the ApplyContainerStyles method to apply container styles. Then, for each table row, it calls the RenderBeginTag method of the HtmlTextWriter object passed in as its argument to render the opening tag of the tr HTML element that represents the row:

```
writer.RenderBeginTag(HtmlTextWriterTag.Tr);
```

It then calls the RenderContainer method to render the masterContainer and detailContainer container controls that represent the cells numbered 1 and 2, respectively, in Figure 19-7:

```
RenderContainer(masterContainer,writer);
RenderContainer(detailContainer,writer);
```

Finally, it calls the RenderEndTag method of the HtmlTextWriter object to render the closing tag of the tr HTML element that represents the row:

```
writer.RenderEndTag();
```

Exposing the Properties of Child Controls

Your composite control must expose the properties of its child controls as if they were its own properties in order to enable page developers to treat these properties as attributes on the tag that represents your custom control on an ASP.NET page. BaseMasterDetailControl exposes the following properties of its child master and detail controls as its own properties, as shown in Listing 19-13.

Since the child controls of your custom composite control are created on demand, there are no guarantees that the child controls are created when the getters and setters of these properties access them. That's why the getters and setters of these properties call EnsureChildControls before they access the respective child controls. In general, your custom control must call EnsureChildControls before it accesses any of its child controls.

Exposing the properties of child controls as the top-level properties of your composite control provides page developers with the following benefits:

- ❏ They can set the property values of child controls as attributes on the tag that represents your composite control on an ASP.NET page.

- ❏ If your custom composite control doesn't expose the properties of its child controls as its top-level properties, page developers will have no choice but to use the error-prone approach of indexing the Controls collection of the composite control to access the desired child control and set its properties.

- ❏ They can treat your custom control as a single entity. In other words, your composite control enables page developers to set the properties of its child controls as if they were setting its own properties.

What Your Custom Control Inherits from CompositeControl

The ASP.NET CompositeControl provides the basic features that every composite control must support:

- ❏ Overriding the Controls collection

- ❏ Implementing INamingInterface

- ❏ Overriding the DataBind method

- ❏ Implementing the ICompositeControlDesignerAccessor interface. This interface exposes a single method named RecreateChildControls that enables designer developers to recreate the child controls of a composite control on the designer surface. This is useful if you want to develop a custom designer for your composite control. A designer is a component that enables page developers to work with your custom composite control in a designer such as Visual Studio. (This chapter doesn't cover designers.)

- ❏ Overriding the Render method to call EnsureChildControls when the control is in design mode before the actual rendering begins. This ensures that child controls are created before they are rendered.

Overriding the Controls Collection

As I discussed earlier, the child controls that you need in order to assemble your custom control aren't created at any particular phase of your control's life cycle. They're created on demand. Therefore, there are no guarantees that the child controls are created when the Controls collection is accessed. That's why `CompositeControl` overrides the `Collection` property to call the `EnsureChildControls` method to ensure that the child controls are created before the collection is accessed:

```
public override ControlCollection Controls
{
  get
  {
    EnsureChildControls();
    return base.Controls;
  }
}
```

INamingContainer Interface

As Listing 19-13 shows, the `BaseMasterDetailControl` server control assigns unique values to the ID properties of all of its child controls. For example, it assigns the string value `MasterServerControl` to the ID property of the master child control. This string value is unique in that no other child control of the `BaseMasterDetailControl` control has the same ID property.

Now let's examine what happens when page developers use two instances of the `BaseMasterDetailControl` control on the same ASP.NET Web page. Call the first instance `MasterDetailControl_1` and the second instance `MasterDetailControl_2`. Even though the ID properties of the child controls of each instance are unique within the scope of the instance, they aren't unique within the page scope, because the ID property of a given child control of one instance is the same as the ID property of the corresponding child control of the other instance. For example, the ID property of the `master` child control of the `MasterDetailControl_1` instance is the same as the ID property of the `master` child control of the `MasterDetailControl_2` instance.

So can the ID property value of a child control of a composite control be used to locate the control? It depends. Any code within the scope of the composite control can use the ID property value of a child control to locate it, because the ID property values are unique within the scope of the composite control.

However, if the code isn't within the scope of the composite control, it can't use the ID property to locate the child control on the page if the page contains more than one instance of the composite control. Two very good examples of this circumstance are as follows:

❑ The client-side code uses the `id` attribute of a given HTML element to locate it on the page. This scenario is very common, because DHTML is so popular.

❑ The page needs to uniquely identify and locate a server control on the page to delegate postback and postback data events to it.

So what property of the child control should the code from outside the scope of the composite control use to locate the child control on the page? The `Control` class exposes two important properties named `ClientID` and `UniqueID`. The page is responsible for assigning values to these two properties that are unique on the page. The `ClientID` and `UniqueID` properties of a control are rendered as the `id` and name HTML attributes on the HTML element that contains the control. As you know, client code uses the id attribute to locate the containing HTML element on the page while the page uses the name attribute to locate the control on the page.

The page doesn't automatically assign unique values to the ClientID and UniqueID properties of the child controls of a composite control. The composite control must implement the INamingContainer interface to request the page to assign unique values to these two properties. The INamingContainer interface is a marker interface and doesn't expose any methods, properties, or events.

You may wonder how the page assigns unique values to the ClientID and UniqueID properties of the child controls of a composite control. A child control, like any other control, inherits the NamingContainer property from the Control class. This property refers to the first ascendant control of the child control that implements the INamingContainer interface. If your custom composite control implements this interface, it becomes the NamingContainer of its child controls. The page concatenates the ClientID of the NamingContainer of a child control to its ID with an underscore character as the separator to create a unique string value for the ClientID of the child control. The page does the same thing to create a unique string value for the UniqueID of the child control with one difference — the separator character is a dollar sign character rather than an underscore character.

BaseMasterDetailControl2

One of the best choices for a detail server control is the ASP.NET DetailsView server control, and one of the best choices for a master server control is the subclasses of BaseDataBoundControl, which include GridView, BulletedList, ListBox, CheckBoxList, RadioButtonList, and so on. I'll implement another abstract base class named BaseMasterDetailControl2 that derives from BaseMasterDetailControl and extends its functionality to use a DetailsView server control as detail server control and a BaseDataBoundControl server control as master server control, as shown in Listing 19-16.

Listing 19-16: The BaseMasterDetailControl2 Server Control

```
using System;
using System.Data;
using System.Configuration;
using System.Web;
using System.Web.Security;
using System.Web.UI;
using System.Web.UI.WebControls;
using System.Web.UI.WebControls.WebParts;
using System.Web.UI.HtmlControls;
using System.Collections;
using System.Drawing;
using System.ComponentModel;
```

```csharp
namespace CustomComponents
{
  public abstract class BaseMasterDetailControl2 : BaseMasterDetailControl
  {
    protected override Control CreateMaster()
    {
      BaseDataBoundControl master = this.CreateBaseDataBoundControlMaster();
      master.DataBound += new EventHandler(Master_DataBound);
      return master;
    }

    protected abstract void Master_DataBound(object sender, EventArgs e);
    protected abstract BaseDataBoundControl CreateBaseDataBoundControlMaster();

    protected override Control CreateDetail()
    {
      DetailsView detail = new DetailsView();
      detail.AllowPaging = false;
      detail.AutoGenerateDeleteButton = true;
      detail.AutoGenerateEditButton = true;
      detail.AutoGenerateInsertButton = true;
      detail.AutoGenerateRows = true;
      detail.ID="DetailDetailsView";

      return detail;
    }

    protected override void RegisterDetailEventHandlers()
    {
      ((DetailsView)Detail).ItemDeleted +=
                          new DetailsViewDeletedEventHandler(UpdateMaster);
      ((DetailsView)Detail).ItemInserted +=
                          new DetailsViewInsertedEventHandler(UpdateMaster);
      ((DetailsView)Detail).ItemUpdated +=
                          new DetailsViewUpdatedEventHandler(UpdateMaster);
    }

    public string MasterDataSourceID
    {
      get
      {
        return ((BaseDataBoundControl)Master).DataSourceID;
      }
      set
      {
        ((BaseDataBoundControl)Master).DataSourceID = value;
      }
    }
```

(continued)

Listing 19-16 (continued)

```
      public string DetailDataSourceID
      {
        get
        {
          return ((DetailsView)Detail).DataSourceID;
        }
        set
        {
          ((DetailsView)Detail).DataSourceID = value;
        }
      }
    }
  }
```

CreateMaster

As you can see from Listing 19-16, the `CreateMaster` method first invokes another method named `CreateBaseDataBoundControlMaster` to create and return a `BaseDataBoundControl` server control as the master server control:

```
BaseDataBoundControl master = this.CreateBaseDataBoundControlMaster();
```

Next, it registers a method named `Master_DataBound` as event handler for the `DataBound` event of the master server control:

```
master.DataBound += new EventHandler(Master_DataBound);
```

As you'll see later, the master server control is normally bound to an ASP.NET data source control such as `SqlDataSource`. A `BaseDataBoundControl` server control raises the `DataBound` event every time it is bound or rebound to the underlying data source control. This normally happens when the `DataBind` method of the control is invoked. Since rebinding the master server control causes the control to download fresh data from the underlying data store and to reload, you need to ensure that the selected record is set back to the original record if the fresh data contains the original record. That is why the `BaseMasterDetailControl2` registers the `Master_DataBound` method as an event handler for the `DataBound` event of the master server control.

As Listing 19-16 shows, the `CreateBaseDataBoundControlMaster` method is an abstract method and must be implemented by the subclasses of `BaseMasterDetailControl2`. This allows each subclass to use a different subclass of `BaseDataBoundControl` as a master server control:

```
protected abstract BaseDataBoundControl CreateBaseDataBoundControlMaster();
```

As you can see from Listing 19-16, the `Master_DataBound` is an abstract method and must be implemented by the subclasses of `BaseMasterDetailControl2`. This allows each subclass to perform tasks specific to the specific type of the `BaseDataBoundControl` server control being used:

```
protected abstract void Master_DataBound(object sender, EventArgs e);
```

CreateDetail

As you can see from Listing 19-16, the BaseMasterDetailControl2 control implements the CreateDetail method of its base class to instantiate and initialize a DetailsView server control as the detail server control.

RegisterDetailEventHandlers

The main responsibility of the RegisterDetailEventHandlers method is to register event handlers for those events of the detail server control that require the master server control to update. As you can see from Listing 19-16, in the case of the DetailsView server control, the following events are of interest:

- ItemDeleted: The DetailsView server control raises this event when the end user deletes the selected data record. The BaseMasterDetailControl2 registers a method named UpdateMaster as an event handler for this event to update the master server control accordingly:

```
((DetailsView)Detail).ItemDeleted +=
                    new DetailsViewDeletedEventHandler(UpdateMaster);
```

- ItemInserted: The DetailsView server control raises this event when the end user inserts a new data record into the underlying data store. The BaseMasterDetailControl2 registers the UpdateMaster as an event handler for this event to update the list of records that the master server control is displaying:

```
((DetailsView)Detail).ItemInserted +=
                    new DetailsViewInsertedEventHandler(UpdateMaster);
```

- ItemUpdated: The DetailsView server control raises this event when the end user updates the selected data record. The BaseMasterDetailControl2 registers the UpdateMaster as an event handler for this event to update the master server control accordingly:

```
((DetailsView)Detail).ItemUpdated +=
                    new DetailsViewUpdatedEventHandler(UpdateMaster);
```

The BaseMasterDetailControl2 inherits the UpdateMaster method from the BaseMasterDetailControl. The main responsibility of this method is to retrieve fresh data from the underlying data store and to update the master server control with this data. As Listing 19-16 shows, the UpdateMaster method first invokes the DataBind method on the master server control to rebind the control and consequently to retrieve fresh data from the underlying data store. Next, the method calls the Update method on the master UpdatePanel server control to cause this control to update.

If you don't call the Update method on the UpdatePanel server control after rebinding the master server control, the master server control will retrieve the data from the underlying data store but will not refresh itself with the retrieved data. You'll see the logic behind this process in the following chapters.

Properties

As you can see from Listing 19-16, the `BaseMasterDetailControl2` control, like any other composite server control, exposes the properties of its child controls as its own top-level properties, as follows:

❑ `MasterDataSourceID`: This string property exposes the `DataSourceID` property of the master server control, which is a `BaseDataBoundControl` control, as a top-level property.

❑ `DetailDataSourceID`: This string property exposes the `DataSourceID` property of the detail server control, which is a `DetailsView` control, as a top-level property.

Summary

This chapter used numerous examples to provide you with an introduction to the ASP.NET AJAX partial page rendering. I then developed two base custom partial-page-enabled server controls named `BaseMasterDetailControl` and `BaseMasterDetailControl2`, which we will use in the next chapter to build partial-page-enabled server controls.

Using UpdatePanel in User Controls and Custom Controls

The previous chapter developed two partial-rendering-enabled custom controls named
`BaseMasterDetailControl` and `BaseMasterDetailControl2`, which I will use in this chapter
to develop partial-rendering-enabled custom server controls. I'll then use examples to show you
how to use ASP.NET AJAX partial page rendering in your own Web applications.

MasterDetailControl

`MasterDetailControl` is a server control that inherits from `BaseMasterDetailControl2` and
extends its functionality to use the ASP.NET `GridView` as a master server control, as shown in
Listing 20-1.

Listing 20-1: The MasterDetailControl Server Control

```
using System;
using System.Data;
using System.Configuration;
using System.Web;
using System.Web.Security;
using System.Web.UI;
using System.Web.UI.WebControls;
using System.Web.UI.WebControls.WebParts;
using System.Web.UI.HtmlControls;
using System.Collections;
using System.Drawing;
using System.ComponentModel;
```

(continued)

Listing 20-1 *(continued)*

```
namespace CustomComponents
{
  public class MasterDetailControl : BaseMasterDetailControl2
  {
    protected override BaseDataBoundControl CreateBaseDataBoundControlMaster()
    {
      GridView master = new GridView();
      master.AllowPaging = true;
      master.AllowSorting = true;
      master.AutoGenerateColumns = true;
      master.AutoGenerateSelectButton = true;
      master.ID = "MasterGridView";
      return master;
    }

    protected override void RegisterMasterEventHandlers()
    {
      ((GridView)Master).SelectedIndexChanged +=
                            new EventHandler(Master_SelectedIndexChanged);
      ((GridView)Master).PageIndexChanged +=
                            new EventHandler(Master_ResetSelectedValue);
      ((GridView)Master).Sorted += new EventHandler(Master_ResetSelectedValue);
    }

    public int PageSize
    {
      get
      {
        EnsureChildControls();
        return ((GridView)Master).PageSize;
      }
      set
      {
        EnsureChildControls();
        ((GridView)Master).PageSize = value;
      }
    }

    [TypeConverter(typeof(StringArrayConverter))]
    public string[] DataKeyNames
    {
      get
      {
        EnsureChildControls();
        return ((GridView)Master).DataKeyNames;
      }
      set
```

```
        {
          EnsureChildControls();
          ((GridView)Master).DataKeyNames = value;
          ((DetailsView)Detail).DataKeyNames = value;
        }
      }

      protected override void Master_DataBound(object sender, EventArgs e)
      {
        for (int i = 0; i < ((GridView)Master).Rows.Count; i++)
        {
          if (((GridView)Master).DataKeys[i].Value == this.SelectedValue)
          {
            ((GridView)Master).SelectedIndex = i;
            break;
          }
        }

        Master_SelectedIndexChanged(null, null);
      }

      void Master_ResetSelectedValue(object sender, EventArgs e)
      {
        if (((GridView)Master).SelectedIndex != -1)
        {
          ((GridView)Master).SelectedIndex = -1;
          Master_SelectedIndexChanged(null, null);
        }
      }

      protected virtual void Master_SelectedIndexChanged(object sender, EventArgs e)
      {
        if (((GridView)Master).SelectedIndex == -1)
          this.Detail.Visible = false;
        else
          this.Detail.Visible = true;

        this.SelectedValue = ((GridView)Master).SelectedValue;
        UpdateDetail(sender, e);
      }
    }
  }
}
```

I'll discuss the methods and properties of the `MasterDetailControl` server control in the following sections.

CreateBaseDataBoundControlMaster

As Listing 20-1 shows, the `MasterDetailControl` server control overrides the `CreateBaseDataBoundControlMaster` method of its base class to create and return a `GridView` server control as the master server control. As you can see, this method instantiates a `GridView` server control and sets its `AllowPaging`, `AllowSorting`, `AutoGenerateColumns`, and `AutoGenerateSelectButton` properties.

RegisterMasterEventHandlers

The main responsibility of the `RegisterMasterEventHandlers` method is to register event handlers for those events of the master server control that require the detail server control to update. The `GridView` server control exposes the following three important events that meet that description, as shown in Listing 20-1:

❑ `SelectedIndexChanged`: The `GridView` server control raises this event when the end user selects a new record from the records that the control is displaying. Since the detail server control displays the details of the selected record, every time a new record is selected — that is, every time the `SelectedIndexChanged` event is raised — the detail server control must be updated with the details of the newly selected record. Because of this, the `MasterDetailControl` registers a method named `Master_SelectedIndexChanged` as an event handler for the `SelectedIndexChanged` event of the `GridView` server control:

```
((GridView)Master).SelectedIndexChanged +=
                          new EventHandler(Master_SelectedIndexChanged);
```

❑ `PageIndexChanged`: The `GridView` server control raises this event when the end user clicks an element in the pager user interface to display a new page of records. Since the new page of records may not include the selected record, you need to hide the detail server control until the end user makes a new selection. That is why the `MasterDetailControl` registers a method named `Master_ResetSelectedValue` as an event handler for the `PageIndexChanged` event of the `GridView` server control:

```
((GridView)Master).PageIndexChanged +=
                          new EventHandler(Master_ResetSelectedValue);
```

❑ `Sorted`: The `GridView` server control raises this event when the end user clicks the header text of a column to sort the displayed records. Again, the newly sorted records may not include the selected record, so you need to hide the detail server control. That is why the `MasterDetailControl` registers the `Master_ResetSelectedValue` method as an event handler for the `Sorted` event of the `GridView` server control:

```
((GridView)Master).Sorted += new EventHandler(Master_ResetSelectedValue);
```

Master_SelectedIndexChanged

As you can see from Listing 20-1, this method hides the detail server control if the `SelectedIndex` property of the master server control is set to -1 — that is, if no record is selected. There is no point in rendering the detail server control if there is no selected record to display:

```
if (((GridView)Master).SelectedIndex == -1)
    this.Detail.Visible = false;
else
    this.Detail.Visible = true
```

Next, the method stores the value of the `SelectedValue` of the `GridView` server control in the `SelectedValue` property of the `MasterDetailControl`:

```
this.SelectedValue = ((GridView)Master).SelectedValue;
```

The `MasterDetailControl` inherits the `SelectedValue` property from the `BaseMasterDetailControl`. As Listing 20-1 shows, this property stores its value in the view state for future reference. It is necessary to store the selected record in the view state because the following requests may end up rebinding the `GridView` server control and consequently resetting the `SelectedValue` property of the control. In such situations, you can retrieve the selected value from the view state and assign it to the `SelectedValue` property of the `GridView` server control after rebinding the control if the control still contains the selected record.

As Listing 20-1 shows, the `Master_SelectedIndexChanged` method finally calls the `UpdateDetail` method to update the detail server control. This is necessary because a new record has been selected.

`MasterDetailControl` inherits the `UpdateDetail` method from its base class — that is, from the `BaseMasterDetailControl`. As you can see from Listing 20-1, this method first calls the `DataBind` method on the detail server control to rebind the control and consequently to retrieve fresh data from the underlying data store:

```
detail.DataBind();
```

Next, the method calls the `Update` method on the detail `UpdatePanel` server control to force this control to update.

Master_ResetSelectedValue

As you can see from Listing 20-1, this method simply sets the `SelectedIndex` property of the `GridView` server control to -1 to signal that no record is selected, and then invokes the `Master_SelectedIndexChanged` method discussed in the previous section.

Master_DataBound

As you can see from Listing 20-1, this method first searches through the `GridViewRow` server controls in the `Rows` collection of the `GridView` server control for a `GridViewRow` server control with the same primary key field value as the one stored in the `SelectedValue` property. If the search succeeds, the method assigns the index of the `GridViewRow` server control to the `SelectedIndex` property of the `GridView` server control to specify this `GridViewRow` server control as the selected row:

```
for (int i = 0; i < ((GridView)Master).Rows.Count; i++)
{
  if (((GridView)Master).DataKeys[i].Value == this.SelectedValue)
  {
    ((GridView)Master).SelectedIndex = i;
    break;
  }
}
```

The `GridView` server control uses an instance of a server control named `GridViewRow` to display each of its data records. The `Rows` collection property of the `GridView` server control contains all the `GridViewRow` server controls that display the data records of the server control.

The `GridView` server control exposes a collection property named `DataKeys`, which contains one `DataKey` object for each displayed data record in which the names and values of the primary key datafields of the record are stored. In other words, each `DataKey` object in the `DataKeys` collection corresponds to a `GridViewRow` server control in the `Rows` collection.

Next, the method invokes the `Master_SelectedIndexChanged` method discussed earlier:

```
Master_SelectedIndexChanged(null, null);
```

Properties

As you can see from Listing 20-1, the `MasterDetailControl`, like any other composite server control, exposes the properties of its child controls as its own top-level properties, as follows:

❑ `PageSize`: This string property exposes the `PageSize` property of the `GridView` server control as top-level property. Recall that the `PageSize` property of a `GridView` server control specifies the total number of records to display.

❑ `DataKeyNames`: This array property exposes the `DataKeyNames` property of the `GridView` server control as top-level property. Recall that the `DataKeyNames` property of a `GridView` server control contains the list of primary key datafield names.

Note that the `DataKeyNames` property is annotated with the `TypeConverter(typeof(StringArray Converter))` metadata attribute to instruct the page parser that it must use the `StringArrayConverter` to convert the declarative value of the `DataKeyNames` to the array. This declarative value is the value that the page developer declaratively assigns to the `DataKeyNames` attribute on the tag that represents the `MasterDetailControl` server control on an .aspx or .ascx file. This declarative value is a string of comma-separated list of substrings in which each substring contains the name of a primary key datafield name. As the name suggests, the `StringArrayConverter` converts this string into an array, which the page parser then automatically assigns to the `DataKeyNames` property of the `MasterDetailControl` server control.

Note that the getters and setters of these properties of the `MasterDetailControl` invoke the `EnsureChildControls` method before they attempt to access the associated child server controls, as I mentioned earlier.

Using MasterDetailControl in a Web Page

Add the following files to the `App_Code` directory of the application that contains the page that uses the `MasterDetailControl` control:

❑ `BaseMasterDetailControl.cs`: Listing 19-12 presents the content of this file.

❑ `ContainerType.cs`: Listing 19-13 presents the content of this file.

❑ `MasterDetailContainer.cs`: Listing 19-14 presents the content of this file.

❑ `BaseMasterDetailControl2.cs`: Listing 19-15 presents the content of this file.

❑ `MasterDetailControl.cs`: Listing 20-1 presents the content of this file.

Listing 20-2 presents a page that uses the `MasterDeatilControl`. Note that this page uses a theme, a database with two tables named Products and Categories, and a connections string named MyConnectionString. I'll discuss this theme, database, and connection string shortly. If you run this page, you'll get the result shown in Figure 20-1.

Listing 20-2: A Page that Uses the MasterDetailControl

```
<%@ Page Language="C#" Theme="Theme1" %>

<%@ Register Namespace="CustomComponents" TagPrefix="custom" %>
<!DOCTYPE html PUBLIC "-//W3C//DTD XHTML 1.0 Transitional//EN"
"http://www.w3.org/TR/xhtml1/DTD/xhtml1-transitional.dtd">
<html xmlns="http://www.w3.org/1999/xhtml">
<head runat="server">
  <title>Untitled Page</title>
</head>
<body>
  <form id="form1" runat="server">
    <asp:ScriptManager ID="ScriptManager1" runat="server" />

    <custom:MasterDetailControl ID="MasterDetailControl1" runat="server"
     DataKeyNames="ProductID" DetailDataSourceID="DetailDataSource"
     MasterDataSourceID="MasterDataSource" PageSize="3"
     MasterSkinID="GridView1" DetailSkinID="DetailsView1" CellSpacing="20"
     HorizontalAlign="Center" GridLines="both" BorderStyle="Ridge"
     BorderWidth="20" BorderColor="Yellow" BackImageUrl="images.jpg">
      <MasterContainerStyle HorizontalAlign="center" BorderStyle="Ridge"
        BorderWidth="20" BorderColor="Yellow" />
      <DetailContainerStyle BorderStyle="Ridge" BorderWidth="20"
        BorderColor="Yellow" />
    </custom:MasterDetailControl>

    <asp:SqlDataSource runat="server" ID="MasterDataSource"
     ConnectionString="<%$ ConnectionStrings:MyConnectionString %>"
     SelectCommand="Select ProductID, ProductName, UnitPrice From Products" />

    <asp:SqlDataSource ID="DetailDataSource" runat="server"
     ConnectionString="<%$ ConnectionStrings:MyConnectionString %>"
     SelectCommand="Select * From Products where ProductID=@ProductID"
     UpdateCommand="Update Products Set ProductName=@ProductName,
                                 CategoryID=@CategoryID,
                                 UnitPrice=@UnitPrice,
                                 DistributorName=@DistributorName
                where ProductID=@ProductID"
     DeleteCommand="Delete From Products where ProductID=@ProductID"
     InsertCommand="Insert Into Products (ProductName, CategoryID, UnitPrice,
                                    DistributorName)
                            Values (@ProductName, @CategoryID, @UnitPrice,
                                    @DistributorName)">
      <SelectParameters>
        <asp:ControlParameter ControlID="MasterDetailControl1" Name="ProductID"
          PropertyName="SelectedValue" DefaultValue="1" />
      </SelectParameters>
    </asp:SqlDataSource>
  </form>
</body>
</html>
```

Figure 20-1

As you can see, the MasterDetailControl displays only the master portion of the control. Now if you select a record from the GridView control, you'll get the result shown in Figure 20-2: the DetailsView server control displays the detail of the selected record.

Note that the DetailsView server control displays the standard Edit and Delete buttons to enable end users to edit and delete the current record from the underlying data store. The DetailsView server control also contains the New button to enable the end user to add a new record to the data store.

Thanks to the ASP.NET AJAX partial page rendering infrastructure, all the user interactions with the GridView and DetailsView server controls are handled asynchronously in the background without interrupting the user or reloading the entire page.

Note that the page shown in Listing 20-2 takes advantage of ASP.NET 2.0 themes. A theme is implemented as a subfolder under the App_Themes folder. The subfolder must have the same name as the theme. A theme subfolder consists of one or more skin files and their respective image and Cascading Style Sheet files. Since ASP.NET 2.0 merges all the skin files of a theme into a single skin file, page developers can use as many skin files as necessary to organize the theme folder. Themes are assigned to the containing page, not to the the individual controls.

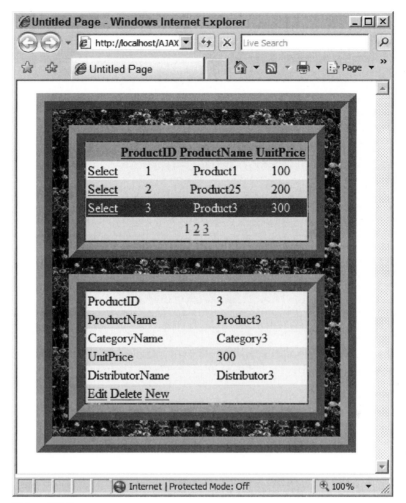

Figure 20-2

The @Page directive in ASP.NET 2.0 exposes a new attribute named Theme, which is set to the name of the desired theme. Since all themes are subfolders of the App_Themes folder, the ASP.NET framework knows where to find the assigned theme. A skin file includes one or more control skins. A control skin defines the appearance properties of a class of server controls. The definition of a control skin is very similar to the declaration of an instance of the control on an ASP.NET page. This doesn't mean that all properties of a server control can be set in its skin. In general, only the appearance properties can be included and set in a control skin. If the SkinID property of a control skin isn't set, the control skin is treated as the default skin. A default skin is automatically applied to the control instances whose SkinID properties aren't set. If the SkinID property of a control skin is set, it will be applied only to the control instances whose SkinID property is set to the same value.

The page shown in Listing 20-2 uses a theme named `Theme1` that contains a skin file with the following content:

```
<asp:GridView SkinID="GridView1" runat="server" BackColor="LightGoldenrodYellow"
  BorderColor="Tan" BorderWidth="1px" CellPadding="2" ForeColor="Black"
  GridLines="None">
    <FooterStyle BackColor="Tan" />
    <SelectedRowStyle BackColor="DarkSlateBlue" ForeColor="GhostWhite" />
    <PagerStyle BackColor="PaleGoldenrod" ForeColor="DarkSlateBlue"
     HorizontalAlign="Center" />
    <HeaderStyle BackColor="Tan" Font-Bold="True" />
    <AlternatingRowStyle BackColor="PaleGoldenrod" />
</asp:GridView>

<asp:DetailsView SkinID="DetailsView1" runat="server" Width="100%"
 BackColor="LightGoldenrodYellow" BorderColor="Tan" BorderWidth="1px"
 CellPadding="2" ForeColor="Black" GridLines="None" HorizontalAlign="Center">
    <FooterStyle BackColor="Tan" />
    <EditRowStyle BackColor="DarkSlateBlue" ForeColor="GhostWhite" />
    <PagerStyle BackColor="PaleGoldenrod" ForeColor="DarkSlateBlue"
     HorizontalAlign="Center" />
    <HeaderStyle BackColor="Tan" Font-Bold="True" />
    <AlternatingRowStyle BackColor="PaleGoldenrod" />
</asp:DetailsView>
```

Also note that the page shown in Listing 20-2 connects to a database named `ProductsDB` that consists of two database tables named `Products` and `Categories`. The following table describes the `Products` database table:

Column Name	Data Type
ProductID	int
ProductName	varchar (50)
CategoryID	int
UnitPrice	decimal (18, 0)
DistributorName	varchar (50)

The following table describes the `Categories` database table:

Column Name	Data Type
CategoryID	int
CategoryName	varchar (50)
CategoryDescription	varchar (255)
DateCreated	datetime

Note that the data source controls in Listing 20-2 make use of a connection string named
`MyConnectionString`. You need to add the following fragment to the `web.config` file of your
application:

```
<configuration>
  <connectionStrings>
    <add
    connectionString="server=YOUR_SERVER_NAME;initial catalog=ProductsDB;integrated
                                security=SSPI" name="MyConnectionString"/>
  </connectionStrings>
</configuration>
```

MasterDetailControl2

In this section, you'll implement a new server control named `MasterDetailControl2` that derives from
`BaseMasterDetailControl2` and extends its functionality to use a `DropDownList` server control as the
master server control, as shown in Listing 20-3.

Listing 20-3: The MasterDetailControl2 Server Control

```csharp
using System;
using System.Data;
using System.Configuration;
using System.Web;
using System.Web.Security;
using System.Web.UI;
using System.Web.UI.WebControls;
using System.Web.UI.WebControls.WebParts;
using System.Web.UI.HtmlControls;
using System.Collections;
using System.Drawing;
using System.ComponentModel;

namespace CustomComponents
{
  public class MasterDetailControl2 : BaseMasterDetailControl2
  {
    protected override BaseDataBoundControl CreateBaseDataBoundControlMaster()
    {
      DropDownList master = new DropDownList();
      master.AutoPostBack = true;
      master.ID = "DropDownList";
      return master;
    }

    protected override void RegisterMasterEventHandlers()
    {
      ((ListControl)Master).SelectedIndexChanged +=
                              new EventHandler(Master_SelectedIndexChanged);
    }
```

(continued)

Listing 20-3 *(continued)*

```csharp
protected override void Master_DataBound(object sender, EventArgs e)
{
  ListItem selectedItem =
                ((ListControl)Master).Items.FindByValue((string)SelectedValue);
  int selectedIndex = ((ListControl)Master).Items.IndexOf(selectedItem);
  ((ListControl)Master).SelectedIndex = selectedIndex;
  Master_SelectedIndexChanged(null, null);
}

protected virtual void Master_SelectedIndexChanged(object sender, EventArgs e)
{
  if (((ListControl)Master).SelectedIndex == -1)
    this.Detail.Visible = false;
  else
    this.Detail.Visible = true;

  this.SelectedValue = ((ListControl)Master).SelectedValue;
  this.UpdateDetail(sender, e);
}

public string DataTextField
{
  get
  {
    return ((ListControl)Master).DataTextField;
  }
  set
  {
    ((ListControl)Master).DataTextField = value;
  }
}

public string DataValueField
{
  get
  {
    return ((ListControl)Master).DataValueField;
  }
  set
  {
    ((ListControl)Master).DataValueField = value;
  }
}

[TypeConverter(typeof(StringArrayConverter))]
public string[] DataKeyNames
{
  get
  {
    return ((DetailsView)Detail).DataKeyNames;
  }
```

```
      set
      {
         ((DetailsView)Detail).DataKeyNames = value;
      }
   }
  }
}
```

CreateBaseDataBoundControlMaster

As you can see from Listing 20-3, the `MasterDetailControl2`'s implementation of this method instantiates and initializes a `DropDownList` server control as the master server control.

RegisterMasterEventHandlers

As Listing 20-3 shows, this method registers a method named `Master_SelectedIndexChanged` as an event handler for the `SelectedIndexChanged` event of the master server control. Note that this method treats the master server control as a `ListControl` object rather than a `DropDownList`. This is possible because the ASP.NET `DropDownList` server control derives from the `ListControl` base class. As you'll see in the next section, treating the master server control as a `ListControl` enables you to use the same implementation of the `RegisterMasterEventHandlers` method for all types of `ListControl` controls, such as `DropDownList` and `ListBox`.

Master_SelectedIndexChanged

When the `ListControl` control raises the `SelectedIndexChanged` event, the `Master_SelectedIndexChanged` method shown in Listing 20-3 is automatically invoked. This method first checks whether any item has been selected from the `ListControl` control. If not, it hides the detail server control, as I mentioned earlier:

```
if (((ListControl)Master).SelectedIndex == -1)
   this.Detail.Visible = false;
else
   this.Detail.Visible = true;
```

Next, it assigns the value of the `SelectedValue` property of the `ListControl` control to the `SelectedValue` property of the `MasterDetailControl2` control:

```
this.SelectedValue = ((ListControl)Master).SelectedValue;
```

Finally, it invokes the `UpdateDetail` method to update the detail server control. As discussed earlier, the detail server control picks up the new value of the `SelectedValue` property of the `MasterDetailControl2` and displays the detail information about the selected item:

```
this.UpdateDetail(sender, e);
```

Master_DataBound

Recall that the `Master_DataBound` method is automatically invoked when the `DataBound` event of the master server control is fired. As you can see from Listing 20-3, this method first accesses the `ListItem` object whose value is given by the `SelectedValue` property of the `MasterDetailControl2`. Recall that this property contains the value associated with the selected item:

```
ListItem selectedItem =
                ((ListControl)Master).Items.FindByValue((string)SelectedValue);
```

Next, it accesses the index of the selected item:

```
int selectedIndex = ((ListControl)Master).Items.IndexOf(selectedItem);
```

Then it assigns this index to the `SelectedIndex` property of the `ListControl` master:

```
((ListControl)Master).SelectedIndex = selectedIndex;
```

Finally, it invokes the `SelectedIndexChanged` method discussed earlier:

```
Master_SelectedIndexChanged(null, null);
```

Properties

`MasterDetailControl2`, like any other composite control, exposes the properties of its child controls as its own top-level properties, as shown in Listing 20-3. Note that the `DataKeyNames` property is annotated with the `[TypeConverter(typeof(StringArrayConverter))]` metadata attribute to instruct the page parser that it must use the `StringArrayConverter` to convert the declarative value of this property to its imperative value. The declarative value is the string containing a list of comma-separated substrings that the page developer assigns to the `DataKeyNames` attribute on the tag that represents the `MasterDetailControl2` control on the `.aspx` page. The imperative value is the value that the `DataKeyNames` property expects — that is, an array of strings. The `StringArrayConverter` knows how to convert the string containing a list of comma-separated substrings to a .NET array that contains these substrings.

Using MasterDetailControl2

Listing 20-4 presents a page that uses the `MasterDetailControl2`. Figure 20-3 shows what you'll see on your browser when you access this page. Note that this page uses a theme named `Theme1` that contains a skin file with the following content:

```
<asp:DetailsView SkinID="DetailsView1" runat="server" Width="100%"
 BackColor="LightGoldenrodYellow" BorderColor="Tan" BorderWidth="1px"
 CellPadding="2" ForeColor="Black" GridLines="None" HorizontalAlign="Center">
    <FooterStyle BackColor="Tan" />
    <EditRowStyle BackColor="DarkSlateBlue" ForeColor="GhostWhite" />
    <HeaderStyle BackColor="Tan" Font-Bold="True" />
    <AlternatingRowStyle BackColor="PaleGoldenrod" />
</asp:DetailsView>
```

```
<asp:DropDownList SkinID="DropDownList1" runat="server"
  BackColor="LightGoldenrodYellow" BorderColor="Tan" BorderWidth="1px"
  CellPadding="2" ForeColor="Black" GridLines="None" Width="100%"/>
```

This page assumes that the following files are added to the App_Code directory of the application that contains the page:

- ❑ BaseMasterDetailControl.cs: Listing 19-12 presents the content of this file.
- ❑ ContainerType.cs: Listing 19-13 presents the content of this file.
- ❑ MasterDetailContainer.cs: Listing 19-14 presents the content of this file.
- ❑ BaseMasterDetailControl2.cs: Listing 19-15 presents the content of this file.
- ❑ MasterDetailControl.cs: Listing 20-1 presents the content of this file.
- ❑ MasterDetailControl2.cs: Listing 20-3 presents the content of this file.

Also note that this page uses the same database (ProductsDB) and connection string discussed in the previous section.

Again, thanks to the ASP.NET AJAX partial page infrastructure, every time the end user selects a new item from the DropDownList master control, or deletes, inserts, or updates a record in the DetailsView detail control, the following things happen:

- ❑ The current page is posted back to the server asynchronously in the background, without interrupting the user interaction with the current page.
- ❑ When the server response finally arrives, only the MasterDetailControl2 is updated, without causing the entire page to reload.

Listing 20-4: A Page that Uses MasterDetailControl2

```
<%@ Page Language="C#" Theme="Theme1" %>

<%@ Register Namespace="CustomComponents" TagPrefix="custom" %>
<!DOCTYPE html PUBLIC "-//W3C//DTD XHTML 1.0 Transitional//EN"
"http://www.w3.org/TR/xhtml1/DTD/xhtml1-transitional.dtd">
<html xmlns="http://www.w3.org/1999/xhtml">
<head runat="server">
  <title>Untitled Page</title>
</head>
<body>
  <form id="form1" runat="server">
    <asp:ScriptManager ID="ScriptManager1" runat="server" />
```

(continued)

Listing 20-4 *(continued)*

```
   <custom:MasterDetailControl2 ID="MasterDetailControl21" runat="server"
    DataKeyNames="ProductID" DetailDataSourceID="DetailDataSource"
    MasterDataSourceID="MasterDataSource" MasterSkinID="DropDownList1"
    DetailSkinID="DetailsView1" CellSpacing="20" HorizontalAlign="Center"
    GridLines="both" BorderStyle="Ridge" BorderWidth="20" BorderColor="Yellow"
    BackImageUrl="images.jpg" DataTextField="ProductName"
    DataValueField="ProductID">
        <MasterContainerStyle HorizontalAlign="center" BorderStyle="Ridge"
         BorderWidth="20" BorderColor="Yellow" />
        <DetailContainerStyle BorderStyle="Ridge" BorderWidth="20"
         BorderColor="Yellow" />
   </custom:MasterDetailControl2>

   <asp:SqlDataSource runat="server" ID="MasterDataSource"
    ConnectionString="<%$ ConnectionStrings:MyConnectionString %>"
    SelectCommand="Select ProductID, ProductName From Products" />

   <asp:SqlDataSource ID="DetailDataSource" runat="server"
    ConnectionString="<%$ ConnectionStrings:MyConnectionString %>"
    SelectCommand="Select * From Products where ProductID=@ProductID"
    UpdateCommand="Update Products Set ProductName=@ProductName,
                             CategoryID=@CategoryID,
                             UnitPrice=@UnitPrice,
                             DistributorName=@DistributorName
                          where ProductID=@ProductID"
    DeleteCommand="Delete From Products where ProductID=@ProductID"
    InsertCommand="Insert Into Products (ProductName, CategoryID, UnitPrice,
                             DistributorName)
                          Values (@ProductName, @CategoryID, @UnitPrice,
                             @DistributorName)">
     <SelectParameters>
       <asp:ControlParameter ControlID="MasterDetailControl21" Name="ProductID"
        PropertyName="SelectedValue" DefaultValue="1" />
     </SelectParameters>
   </asp:SqlDataSource>
    
 </form>
</body>
</html>
```

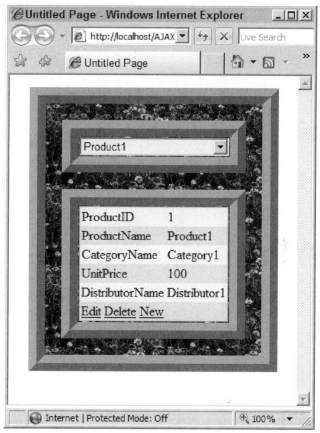

Figure 20-3

MasterDetailControl3

In this section, you'll implement a new server control named MasterDetailControl3 that derives from MasterDetailControl2 and extends its functionality to use a ListBox server control rather than the DropDownList server control as master server control, as shown in Listing 20-5. As you can see, MasterDetailControl3 simply overrides the CreateBaseDataBoundControlMaster method that it inherits from MasterDetailControl2 and replaces the DropDownList server control with a ListBox server control.

Listing 20-5: The MasterDetailControl3 Control

```
using System;
using System.Data;
using System.Configuration;
```

(continued)

Listing 20-5 *(continued)*

```
using System.Web;
using System.Web.UI;
using System.Web.UI.WebControls;
using System.Web.UI.HtmlControls;
using System.Collections;
using System.Drawing;
using System.ComponentModel;

namespace CustomComponents
{
  public class MasterDetailControl3 : MasterDetailControl2
  {
    protected override BaseDataBoundControl CreateBaseDataBoundControlMaster()
    {
      ListBox master = new ListBox();
      master.AutoPostBack = true;
      master.ID = "ListBox";
      return master;
    }
  }
}
```

Using MasterDetailControl3

Listing 20-6 contains a page that uses `MasterDetailControl3`. Note that this page uses a theme named `Theme1`, which contains a skin file with the following content:

```
<asp:DetailsView SkinID="DetailsView1" runat="server" Width="100%"
  BackColor="LightGoldenrodYellow" BorderColor="Tan" BorderWidth="1px"
  CellPadding="2" ForeColor="Black" GridLines="None" HorizontalAlign="Center">
    <FooterStyle BackColor="Tan" />
    <EditRowStyle BackColor="DarkSlateBlue" ForeColor="GhostWhite" />
    <HeaderStyle BackColor="Tan" Font-Bold="True" />
    <AlternatingRowStyle BackColor="PaleGoldenrod" />
</asp:DetailsView>

<asp:ListBox SkinID="ListBox1" runat="server" BackColor="LightGoldenrodYellow"
  BorderColor="Tan" BorderWidth="1px" ForeColor="Black" Width="200"/>
```

Note also that this page assumes that the following files are added to the `App_Code` directory of the application that contains this page:

❏   `BaseMasterDetailControl.cs`: Listing 19-12 presents the content of this file.

❏   `ContainerType.cs`: Listing 19-13 presents the content of this file.

❏   `MasterDetailContainer.cs`: Listing 19-14 presents the content of this file.

❏   `BaseMasterDetailControl2.cs`: Listing 19-15 presents the content of this file.

❑ `MasterDetailControl.cs`: Listing 20-1 presents the content of this file.

❑ `MasterDetailControl2.cs`: Listing 20-3 presents the content of this file.

❑ `MasterDetailControl3.cs`: Listing 20-5 presents the content of this file.

Also note that this page uses the same database (`ProductsDB`) and connection string as the pages in the previous sections.

Figure 20-4 shows what you'll get when you access this page. As you can see, the master server control is now a `ListBox` server control. Again, thanks to the ASP.NET AJAX partial page infrastructure, every time the end user selects a new item from the `ListBox` master control or deletes, inserts, or updates a record in the `DetailsView` detail control, the following things happen:

❑ The current page is posted back to the server asynchronously in the background, without interrupting the user interaction with the current page.

❑ When the server response finally arrives, only the `MasterDetailControl3` is updated, without causing the entire page to reload.

Listing 20-6: A Page that Uses the MasterDetailControl3 Control

```
<%@ Page Language="C#" Theme="Theme1" %>

<%@ Register Namespace="CustomComponents" TagPrefix="custom" %>
<!DOCTYPE html PUBLIC "-//W3C//DTD XHTML 1.0 Transitional//EN"
"http://www.w3.org/TR/xhtml1/DTD/xhtml1-transitional.dtd">
<html xmlns="http://www.w3.org/1999/xhtml">
<head runat="server">
  <title>Untitled Page</title>
</head>
<body>
  <form id="form1" runat="server">
    <asp:ScriptManager ID="ScriptManager1" runat="server" />

    <custom:MasterDetailControl3 ID="MasterDetailControl21" runat="server"
      DataKeyNames="ProductID" DetailDataSourceID="DetailDataSource"
      MasterDataSourceID="MasterDataSource" MasterSkinID="ListBox1"
      DetailSkinID="DetailsView1" CellSpacing="20" HorizontalAlign="Center"
      GridLines="both" BorderStyle="Ridge" BorderWidth="20" BorderColor="Yellow"
      BackImageUrl="images.jpg" DataTextField="ProductName"
      DataValueField="ProductID">
        <MasterContainerStyle HorizontalAlign="center" BorderStyle="Ridge"
          BorderWidth="20" BorderColor="Yellow" />
        <DetailContainerStyle BorderStyle="Ridge" BorderWidth="20"
          BorderColor="Yellow" />
    </custom:MasterDetailControl3>
```

(continued)

929

Listing 20-6 *(continued)*

```
        <asp:SqlDataSource runat="server" ID="MasterDataSource"
         ConnectionString="<%$ ConnectionStrings:MyConnectionString %>"
         SelectCommand="Select ProductID, ProductName From Products" />

        <asp:SqlDataSource ID="DetailDataSource" runat="server"
         ConnectionString="<%$ ConnectionStrings:MyConnectionString %>"
         SelectCommand="Select * From Products where ProductID=@ProductID"
         UpdateCommand="Update Products Set ProductName=@ProductName,
                                       CategoryID=@CategoryID,
                                       UnitPrice=@UnitPrice,
                                       DistributorName=@DistributorName
                                       where ProductID=@ProductID"
         DeleteCommand="Delete From Products where ProductID=@ProductID"
         InsertCommand="Insert Into Products (ProductName, CategoryID, UnitPrice,
                                       DistributorName)
                             Values (@ProductName, @CategoryID, @UnitPrice,
                                       @DistributorName)">
          <SelectParameters>
            <asp:ControlParameter ControlID="MasterDetailControl21" Name="ProductID"
             PropertyName="SelectedValue" DefaultValue="1" />
          </SelectParameters>
        </asp:SqlDataSource>
         
      </form>
  </body>
  </html>
```

MasterDetailControl4

In this section I'll implement a server control named `MasterDetailControl4` that derives from the `MasterDetailControl2` and overrides its `SelectedValue` property. Recall that the `MasterDetailControl2` inherits this property from the `BaseMasterDetailControl`. `MasterDetailControl4` overrides this property to use the ASP.NET `Session` object as the backing store. Recall that the `BaseMasterDetailControl`'s implementation of this property uses the `ViewState` as the backing store. In the next section we'll implement a custom data control field that will demonstrate the significance of using the ASP.NET `Session` object as the backing store. Listing 20-7 presents the implementation of `MasterDetailControl4`.

Listing 20-7: The MasterDetailControls4 Server Control

```
namespace CustomComponents
{
  public class MasterDetailControl4 : MasterDetailControl2
  {
    public override object SelectedValue
    {
      get { return this.Page.Session["SelectedValue"]; }
      set { this.Page.Session["SelectedValue"] = value; }
    }
  }
}
```

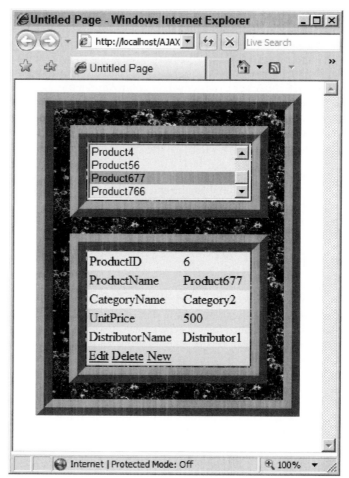

Figure 20-4

Developing Partial-Rendering-Enabled Data Control Fields

The foreign and primary key pairs establish relationships among database tables. The value of a foreign key field in a given record is one of the existing values of its corresponding primary key field. Most database tables automatically generate the primary key value of a record when the record is added to the table. Therefore the actual foreign key value is an auto-generated integer that doesn't mean anything to end users. However, the table that contains the primary key field normally contains other field values that are more meaningful to them.

For instance, consider a database that contains tables named Products and Categories. The Products table has a foreign key field named CategoryID. The Categories table contains the corresponding primary key field, CategoryID. The Categories table also exposes fields such as CategoryName and

CategoryDescription, which provide more meaningful information to end users. Wouldn't it be great if you could provide end users the appropriate user interface with which to view more meaningful information about the available categories, so they can make more intelligent decisions as to which category to choose for a given record? This is exactly what you're going to do in this section. You'll implement a custom data control field named MasterDetailField that will present the end users with a user interface that consists of a DropDownList master server control and a DetailsView detail server control, so users can view more detailed information about a given foreign key field. The MasterDetailField will take advantage of the ASP.NET AJAX partial rendering infrastructure to retrieve the required data from the server asynchronously and to update only the necessary part of the page — that is, the detail server control — without forcing a complete page reload.

As you'll see, the MasterDetailField data control field not only displays detailed information about a selected foreign key field value but also enables the end user to update this information. In other words, the end user gets to update the records of both the table that contains the primay key field values and the table that contains the associated foreign key field values, simultaneously.

Extending BoundField

Most standard data control fields internally use server controls to display the values of their respective database fields. For example, the ImageField and CheckBoxField data control fields internally use Image and CheckBox server controls, respectively, to display their field values. The data type of the field and the state of its containing row determine the type of server control used to display the value of the field. For instance, an ImageField data control field uses an Image server control to display its field value when its containing row is in the normal state, and a TextBox server control when its containing row is in the Edit or Insert state.

The MasterDetailField custom data control field will use a MasterDetailControl4 server control to display all the legal values of its field when its containing row is in the Edit or Insert state. The MasterDetailField data control field will display the current value of its field as simple text when its containing row isn't in the Edit or Insert state. The MasterDetailField data control field derives from the BoundField data control field because BoundField provides all the necessary base functionality when the containing row isn't in the Edit or Insert state, such as:

❑ Extracting the current value of the field whose name is the value of the DataField property. The MasterDetailField overrides this property and defines a new property named DataTextField to replace it because DataTextField is a more appropriate name than DataField.

❑ Displaying the current value as simple text if the current value isn't null.

❑ Displaying the value of the NullDisplayText property if the current value is null.

❑ Displaying the value of the HeaderText property as simple text if sorting is disabled and as a hyperlink if sorting is enabled.

❑ Raising the sort event when sorting is enabled and the header hyperlink is clicked.

The main shortcoming of the BoundField data control field is that it displays the current value of the field in a TextBox control when the containing row is in the Edit or Insert state. The TextBox control is not the appropriate server control for editing foreign key fields because it enables users to enter any value instead of restricting values to the legal ones. The MasterDetailField data control field overrides the InitializeDataCell, OnDataBindField, and ExtractValuesFromCell methods of the

BoundField data control field to add the support needed when the containing row is in the Edit or Insert state. Listing 20-8 shows all the properties and methods of the MasterDetailField data control field. In the following sections I'll walk you through the implementation of these properties and methods.

Listing 20-8: The MasterDetailField Data Control Field

```
namespace CustomComponents
{
    using System;
    using System.Web;
    using System.Web.UI;
    using System.Web.UI.WebControls;
    using System.ComponentModel;
    using System.Collections.Specialized;
    using System.Collections;
    using System.Data;

    public class MasterDetailField : BoundField
    {
        public override string DataField
        {
            get
            {
                return base.DataField;
            }

            set
            {
                throw new global::System.NotImplementedException();
            }
        }

        public virtual string DataTextField
        {
            get
            {
                return base.DataField;
            }
            set
            {
                base.DataField = value;
            }
        }

        public virtual string MasterSkinID
        {
            get
            {
                return (ViewState["MasterSkinID"] != null) ?
                                    (string)ViewState["MasterSkinID"] : String.Empty;
            }
```

(continued)

Listing 20-8 *(continued)*

```
      set
      {
        ViewState["MasterSkinID"] = value;
      }
    }

    public virtual string DetailSkinID
    {
      get
      {
        return (ViewState["DetailSkinID"] != null) ?
                            (string)ViewState["DetailSkinID"] : String.Empty;
      }
      set
      {
        ViewState["DetailSkinID"] = value;
      }
    }

    [TypeConverter(typeof(StringArrayConverter))]
    public virtual string[] DataKeyNames
    {
      get
      {
        return (ViewState["DataKeyNames"] != null) ?
                              (string[])ViewState["DataKeyNames"] : null;
      }
      set
      {
        ViewState["DataKeyNames"] = value;
      }
    }

    public virtual bool EnableTheming
    {
      get
      {
        return (ViewState["EnableTheming"] != null) ?
                              (bool)ViewState["EnableTheming"] : true;
      }
      set
      {
        ViewState["EnableTheming"] = value;
      }
    }

    public virtual string DataValueField
    {
      get
      {
        return (ViewState["DataValueField"] != null) ?
                          (string)ViewState["DataValueField"] : String.Empty;
      }
```

```csharp
    set
    {
      ViewState["DataValueField"] = value;
    }
  }

  public virtual string MasterDataSourceID
  {
    get
    {
      return (ViewState["MasterDataSourceID"] != null) ?
                      (string)ViewState["MasterDataSourceID"] : String.Empty;
    }
    set
    {
      ViewState["MasterDataSourceID"] = value;
    }
  }

  public virtual string DetailDataSourceID
  {
    get
    {
      return (ViewState["DetailDataSourceID"] != null) ?
                      (string)ViewState["DetailDataSourceID"] : String.Empty;
    }
    set
    {
      ViewState["DetailDataSourceID"] = value;
    }
  }

  protected override void OnDataBindField(Object sender, EventArgs e)
  {
    DropDownList ddl = sender as DropDownList;
    if (ddl == null)
    {
      base.OnDataBindField(sender, e);
      return;
    }

    Control parent = ddl.Parent;
    DataControlFieldCell cell = null;
    while (parent != null)
    {
      cell = parent as DataControlFieldCell;
      if (cell != null)
        break;
      parent = parent.Parent;
    }
```

(continued)

Listing 20-8 (continued)

```
    IDataItemContainer container = (IDataItemContainer)cell.Parent;
    object dataItem = container.DataItem;
    if (dataItem == null || String.IsNullOrEmpty(DataValueField))
      return;
    object dataValueField = DataBinder.Eval(dataItem, DataValueField);

    if (dataValueField.Equals(DBNull.Value))
      ddl.SelectedIndex = 0;
    else
      ddl.SelectedIndex =
            ddl.Items.IndexOf(ddl.Items.FindByValue(dataValueField.ToString()));
}

protected override void InitializeDataCell(DataControlFieldCell cell,
                                    DataControlRowState rowState)
{
  if ((rowState & DataControlRowState.Edit) != 0 ||
      (rowState & DataControlRowState.Insert) != 0)
  {
    MasterDetailControl4 mdc = new MasterDetailControl4();
    mdc.MasterSkinID = MasterSkinID;
    mdc.DetailSkinID = DetailSkinID;
    mdc.EnableTheming = EnableTheming;
    mdc.MasterDataSourceID = this.MasterDataSourceID;
    mdc.DetailDataSourceID = this.DetailDataSourceID;
    mdc.DataKeyNames = DataKeyNames;
    ((DropDownList)mdc.Master).DataTextField = DataTextField;
    ((DropDownList)mdc.Master).DataValueField = DataValueField;
    if (DataTextField.Length != 0 && DataValueField.Length != 0)
      ((DropDownList)mdc.Master).DataBound +=
                                    new EventHandler(OnDataBindField);
    cell.Controls.Add(mdc);
  }
  else
    base.InitializeDataCell(cell, rowState);
}

public override void ExtractValuesFromCell(IOrderedDictionary dictionary,
                                    DataControlFieldCell cell,
                                    DataControlRowState rowState,
                                    bool includeReadOnly)
{
  if (cell.Controls.Count > 0)
  {
    MasterDetailControl4 mdc = cell.Controls[0] as MasterDetailControl4;
    if (mdc == null)
      throw new InvalidOperationException(
                        "MasterDetailField could not extract control.");

    string dataValueField = ((DropDownList)mdc.Master).SelectedValue;
```

```
        if (dictionary.Contains(DataValueField))
          dictionary[DataValueField] = int.Parse(dataValueField);

        else
          dictionary.Add(DataValueField, int.Parse(dataValueField));
      }
    }
  }
}
```

Overriding InitializeDataCell

The BoundField data control field exposes a method named InitializeDataCell that contains the code that generates the appropriate HTML markup text for the data cell. The InitializeDataCell method takes two arguments. The first argument is the DataControlFieldCell cell being initialized. The second argument is the state of the containing row.

What HTML markup text the BoundField class's implementation of the InitializeDataCell method emits depends on the state of its containing row. If the containing row is not in the Edit or Insert state, the method simply registers the OnDataBindField method as the callback for the DataBinding event of the respective DataControlFieldCell instance. When the DataBinding event of the cell is raised, the OnDataBindField method extracts the current value of the respective field (the name of the field is the value of the DataField property). If the current value is null, the value of the NullDisplayText property is displayed. Otherwise the current value is displayed as simple text.

The BoundField class's implementation of the InitializeDataCell method in normal state is exactly what you need. However, the BoundField class's implementation of the method when the containing row is in the Edit or Insert state is not acceptable, because the method instantiates an instance of the TextBox control. You need an implementation that instantiates an instance of the MasterDetailControl4 control. That is why the MasterDetailField data control field overrides the InitializeDataCell method. The MasterDetailField data control field calls the base version of the InitializeDataCell method when the containing row is in the normal state, because the behavior of the base version is exactly what you need. However, the MasterDetailField data control field provides its own implementation when the containing row is in the Edit or Insert state.

As Listing 20-8 shows, the MasterDetailField data control field's implementation of the InitializeDataCell method instantiates an instance of the MasterDetailControl4 control and sets its MasterDataSourceID and DetailDataSourceID properties to the values of the MasterDataSourceID and DetailDataSourceID properties of the MasterDetailField data control field, respectively. It is the responsibility of page developers to set the MasterDataSourceID and DetailDataSourceID properties of the MasterDetailField data control field to the values of the ID properties of the appropriate data source controls in the containing page. Page developers must also set the DataTextField and DataValueField properties of the MasterDetailField data control field to the names of the appropriate database fields. This allows the MasterDetailField data control field to automatically populate its MasterDetailControl4 control with the valid values of the foreign key field. Note that InitializeDataCell method also sets the DataKeyNames property of the MasterDetailControl4 control to the value of the DataKeyNames property of the

`MasterDetailField`. Again, it's the responsibility of page developers to assign the comma-separated list of primary key field names to the `DataKeyNames` property of the `MasterDetailField`:

```
MasterDetailControl4 mdc = new MasterDetailControl4();
mdc.MasterSkinID = MasterSkinID;
mdc.DetailSkinID = DetailSkinID;
mdc.EnableTheming = EnableTheming;
mdc.MasterDataSourceID = this.MasterDataSourceID;
mdc.DetailDataSourceID = this.DetailDataSourceID;
mdc.DataKeyNames = DataKeyNames;
((DropDownList)mdc.Master).DataTextField = DataTextField;
((DropDownList)mdc.Master).DataValueField = DataValueField;
```

One of the requirements for the `MasterDetailField` data control field is that it has to set the selected value of the `MasterDetailControl4` control to the current value of the respective foreign key field. This is done in a callback registered for the `DataBound` event of the `DropDownList` master server control of the `MasterDetailControl4` control. The `DropDownList` control inherits the `DataBound` event from the `BaseDataBoundControl` class. There is a difference between the `DataBound` event that the `BaseDataBoundControl` class exposes and the `DataBinding` event that the `Control` class exposes: the `DataBinding` event is raised before the data is actually bound, while the `DataBound` event is raised after the data binding process finishes.

Since the selected value of the `MasterDetailControl4` control must be set after the control is bound to its data source, it is set within the callback for the `DataBound` event. The `InitializeDataCell` method registers the `OnDataBindField` method as the callback for the `DataBound` event of the `DropDownList` master server control:

```
if (DataTextField.Length != 0 && DataValueField.Length != 0)
    ((DropDownList)mdc.Master).DataBound += new EventHandler(OnDataBindField);
```

Handling the DataBound Event

When the `DataBinding` event of the cell is raised, the `OnDataBindField` method is called to display the current value in display mode — that is, as a simple text. When the `DataBound` event of the `DropDownList` master server control of the `MasterDetailControl4` control is raised, the `OnDataBindField` method is called to display the current value in edit mode — that is, as the selected item of the `MasterDetailControl4` control.

Before the `OnDataBindField` method can display the current value in the edit or insert mode, it has to extract the value. The `OnDataBindField` method uses the parent control of the cell to access the value:

```
Control parent = ddl.Parent;
DataControlFieldCell cell = null;
while (parent != null)
{
    cell = parent as DataControlFieldCell;
    if (cell != null)
        break;
    parent = parent.Parent;
}
```

```
IDataItemContainer container = (IDataItemContainer)cell.Parent;
object dataItem = container.DataItem;
```

The parent of the cell is a row of type `GridViewRow` in `GridView` controls and of type `DetailsViewRow` in `DetailsView` controls. Both these types implement the `IDataItemContainer` interface. `IDataItemContainer` exposes a property named `DataItem` of type `Object`. The `DataItem` object represents the record of the database that the row is bound to. After you access the `dataItem` object, you can use the `DataBinder` class to extract the current value of the field whose name is the value of the `DataValueField` property:

```
object dataValueField = DataBinder.Eval(dataItem, DataValueField);
```

The value of the `DataValueField` property is the name of the foreign key field.

The `OnDataBindField` method then sets the `SelectedIndex` of the `DropDownList` master server control of the `MasterDetailControl4` control to the index of `dataValueField` if `dataValueField` is not equal to `DBNull`. Otherwise it configures this `DropDownList` server control to display the newly added item as its selected item:

```
if (dataValueField.Equals(DBNull.Value))
    ddl.SelectedIndex = 0;
else
    ddl.SelectedIndex =
        ddl.Items.IndexOf(ddl.Items.FindByValue(dataValueField.ToString()));
```

Extracting Values from Cells

Data-bound controls such as `GridView` and `DetailsView` enable users to edit database fields. Users click on the Update button after they make the desired changes. `GridView` and `DetailsView` controls are equipped with internal handlers to handle the `Update` event. These handlers call the `ExtractRowValues` method of the `GridView` or `DetailsView` control, which in turn calls the `ExtractValuesFromCell` methods of its cells. The `ExtractRowValues` method provides each `ExtractValuesFromCell` method with a container of type `IOrderedDictionary`. Each `ExtractValuesFromCell` method extracts the value of its cell and inserts the value into the container. The internal handler for the `Update` event then uses these values in its internal data access code to update the underlying database fields.

The `ExtractValuesFromCell` method of the `MasterDetailField` data control field extracts the selected value of the `MasterDetailControl4` control and inserts it into the `IOrderedDictionary` container passed in as its first input argument.

Appearance Properties

The `DataControlField` class exposes a property of type `Style` named `ControlStyle`. The `DataControlField` class internally uses the value of the `ControlStyle` property to set the style properties of the server control that the `DataControlField` instance renders. In the case of the `MasterDetailField` data control field, the `ControlStyle` property is applied to the `MasterDetailControl4` control that the class contains.

The `ControlStyle` property is not the only styling option available. Another styling option is the ASP.NET 2.0 themes.

The `MasterDetailField` class exposes two new properties named `MasterSkinID` and `DetailSkinID`. It's the responsibility of page developers to set these two properties to the values of the `SkinID` properties of the desired `DropDownList` and `DetailsView` control skins, respectively. The `InitializeDataCell` method sets the `MasterSkinID` and `DetailSkinID` properties of the `MasterDetailControl4` control to the values of the `MasterSkinID` and `DetailSkinID` properties of the `MasterDetailField` object. Themes give page developers full control over the appearance properties of the `MasterDetailControl4` control that the `MasterDetailField` object renders.

Using MasterDetailField

Page developers can use the `MasterDetailField` data control field declaratively. Listing 20-9 shows a page that uses an instance of the `MasterDetailField` declaratively. Note that this page uses a theme that contains the following skin file:

```
<asp:DetailsView SkinID="RainyDay" runat="server" Width="100%" BackColor="White"
BorderColor="#999999" BorderStyle="None" BorderWidth="1px" CellPadding="3"
GridLines="Vertical">
   <FooterStyle BackColor="#CCCCCC" ForeColor="Black" />
   <EditRowStyle BackColor="#008A8C" Font-Bold="True" ForeColor="White" />
   <RowStyle BackColor="#EEEEEE" ForeColor="Black" />
   <PagerStyle BackColor="#999999" ForeColor="Black" HorizontalAlign="Center" />
   <HeaderStyle BackColor="#000084" Font-Bold="True" ForeColor="White" />
   <AlternatingRowStyle BackColor="#DCDCDC" />
</asp:DetailsView>

<asp:DropDownList SkinID="RainyDay2" runat="server" BackColor="White"
BorderColor="#999999" BorderStyle="None" BorderWidth="1px" CellPadding="3"
GridLines="Vertical" Width="100%"/>
```

As Listing 20-9 shows, the `SkinID` property values of the preceding two control skins are assigned to the `MasterSkinID` and `DetailSkinID` properties, respectively, of the `MasterDetailField` data control field.

Note that this page assumes that the following files are added to the `App_Code` directory of the application that contains this page:

❑ `BaseMasterDetailControl.cs`: Listing 19-12 presents the content of this file.

❑ `ContainterType.cs`: Listing 19-13 presents the content of this file.

❑ `MasterDetailContainer.cs`: Listing 19-14 presents the content of this file.

❑ `BaseMasterDetailControl2.cs`: Listing 19-15 presents the content of this file.

❑ `MasterDetailControl.cs`: Listing 20-1 presents the content of this file.

❑ `MasterDetailControl2.cs`: Listing 20-3 presents the content of this file.

❑ `MasterDetailControl4.cs`: Listing 20-7 presents the content of this file.

❑   `MasterDetailField.cs`: Listing 20-8 presents the content of this file.

❑   `Product.cs`: The following code listing presents the content of this file. (Notice that the `ObjectDataSource` control shown in Listing 20-9 uses the `Product` class defined in this file.)

```
using System;
using System.Data;
using System.Configuration;
using System.Collections;
using System.Data.SqlClient;

public class Product
{
  public static IEnumerable Select(string sortExpression)
  {
    string connectionString =
    ConfigurationManager.ConnectionStrings["MyConnectionString"].ConnectionString;

    string commandText = "Select CategoryName, ProductName, ProductID," +
                "Products.CategoryID As CategoryID From Products, Categories " +
                "Where Products.CategoryID = Categories.CategoryID";

    if (!string.IsNullOrEmpty(sortExpression))
      commandText += " Order By " + sortExpression;

    SqlConnection con = new SqlConnection(connectionString);
    SqlCommand com = new SqlCommand(commandText, con);
    con.Open();
    return com.ExecuteReader(CommandBehavior.CloseConnection);
  }

  public static void Update(int ProductID, string ProductName, int CategoryID)
  {
    string connectionString =
    ConfigurationManager.ConnectionStrings["MyConnectionString"].ConnectionString;

    string commandText = "Update Products Set ProductName=@ProductName," +
                "CategoryID=@CategoryID Where ProductID=@ProductID";

    SqlConnection con = new SqlConnection(connectionString);
    SqlCommand com = new SqlCommand(commandText, con);
    com.Parameters.AddWithValue("@ProductName", ProductName);
    com.Parameters.AddWithValue("@CategoryID", CategoryID);
    com.Parameters.AddWithValue("@ProductID", ProductID);

    con.Open();
    com.ExecuteNonQuery();
    con.Close();
  }
}
```

Also note that the page shown in Listing 20-9 uses the same database (`ProductsDB`) and connection string as the pages in the previous sections.

Listing 20-9: Using the MasterDetailField Data Control Field Declaratively

```
<%@ Page Language="C#" Theme="Theme1" %>

<%@ Register TagPrefix="custom" Namespace="CustomComponents" %>
<!DOCTYPE html PUBLIC "-//W3C//DTD XHTML 1.1//EN"
"http://www.w3.org/TR/xhtml11/DTD/xhtml11.dtd">

<script runat="server">
</script>

<html xmlns="http://www.w3.org/1999/xhtml">
<head id="Head1" runat="server">
  <title>Untitled Page</title>
</head>
<body>
  <form id="form1" runat="server">
    <asp:ScriptManager runat="server" ID="ScriptManager1" />

    <asp:GridView ID="gv2" runat="Server" AutoGenerateColumns="false"
      AllowSorting="true" DataSourceID="GridViewSource"
      AutoGenerateEditButton="true" DataKeyNames="ProductID"
      BackColor="LightGoldenrodYellow" BorderColor="Tan" BorderWidth="1px"
      CellPadding="2" ForeColor="Black" GridLines="None">
        <FooterStyle BackColor="Tan" />
        <SelectedRowStyle BackColor="DarkSlateBlue" ForeColor="GhostWhite" />
        <PagerStyle BackColor="PaleGoldenrod" ForeColor="DarkSlateBlue"
         HorizontalAlign="Center" />
        <HeaderStyle BackColor="Tan" Font-Bold="True" />
        <AlternatingRowStyle BackColor="PaleGoldenrod" />
        <Columns>
          <asp:BoundField DataField="ProductName" HeaderText="Product Name"
            SortExpression="ProductName"/>

          <custom:MasterDetailField MasterSkinID="RainyDay2"
            DetailSkinID="RainyDay" EnableTheming="true"
            DataValueField="CategoryID" DataKeyNames="CategoryID, DateCreated"
            DataTextField="CategoryName" MasterDataSourceID="MasterSource"
            SortExpression="CategoryName" HeaderText="Category Name"
            NullDisplayText="Unknown" DetailDataSourceID="DetailSource" />

        </Columns>
      </asp:GridView>
      <asp:ObjectDataSource ID="GridViewSource" runat="Server"
       SortParameterName="sortExpression" TypeName="Product" SelectMethod="Select"
       UpdateMethod="Update" />

      <asp:SqlDataSource ID="MasterSource" runat="Server"
       ConnectionString="<%$ ConnectionStrings:MyConnectionString %>"
       SelectCommand="Select * From Categories" />
```

```
        <asp:SqlDataSource ID="DetailSource" runat="Server"
        ConnectionString="<%$ ConnectionStrings:MyConnectionString %>"
        SelectCommand="Select * From Categories Where CategoryID=@CategoryID"
        UpdateCommand="Update Categories Set CategoryName=@CategoryName,
                                    CategoryDescription=@CategoryDescription,
                                    DateCreated=@DateCreated
                                Where CategoryID=@CategoryID"
        InsertCommand="Insert Into Categories (CategoryName, CategoryDescription)
                            Values (@CategoryName, @CategoryDescription)"
        DeleteCommand="Delete From Categories Where CategoryID=@CategoryID2">
            <SelectParameters>
                <asp:SessionParameter Name="CategoryID" SessionField="SelectedValue" />
            </SelectParameters>
            <UpdateParameters>
                <asp:SessionParameter Name="CategoryID" SessionField="SelectedValue" />
            </UpdateParameters>
            <DeleteParameters>
                <asp:SessionParameter Name="CategoryID2" SessionField="SelectedValue" />
            </DeleteParameters>
        </asp:SqlDataSource>
    </form>
</body>
</html>
```

If you run this page, you'll get the result shown in Figure 20-5. Now, if you click the Edit link on the fifth row, you'll get the result shown in Figure 20-6. As you can see, the `Category` cell now contains the `MasterDetailControl4` server control, which consists of a `DropDownList` master server control and a `DetailsView` detail server control.

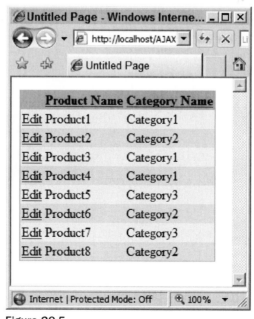

Figure 20-5

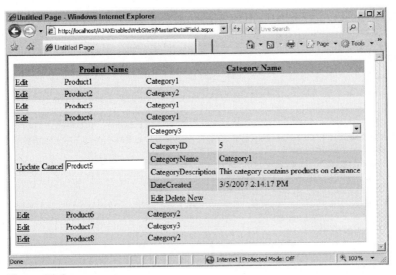

Figure 20-6

Note that the `DetailsView` detail server control contains the standard Edit, Delete, and New buttons to enable the end user to edit an existing category, delete a category, and add a new category. If you click the Edit button, you'll get the result shown in Figure 20-7.

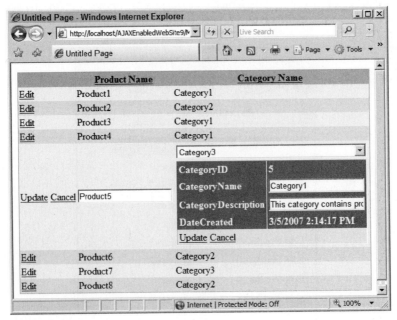

Figure 20-7

The great thing about the `MasterDetailField` is that it takes full advantage of the ASP.NET AJAX partial page rendering infrastructure where all these operations are performed asynchronously in the background without interrupting the user interaction with the current page and without causing the entire page to reload.

Developing Partial-Rendering-Enabled User Controls

The previous section showed you how to develop custom server controls that take full advantage of the ASP.NET AJAX partial page rendering infrastructure to:

❑ Perform page postbacks to the server asynchronously, without interrupting the user interaction

❑ Update themselves without causing the entire page to reload

This section will show you how to develop user controls that achieve similar goals. To make our discussions more concrete, I'll develop a partial-rendering-enabled threaded discussion forum user control that you can use in your own Web applications. Before diving into the details of the implementation of this user control, let's see what it looks like in action. Figure 20-8 shows this user control.

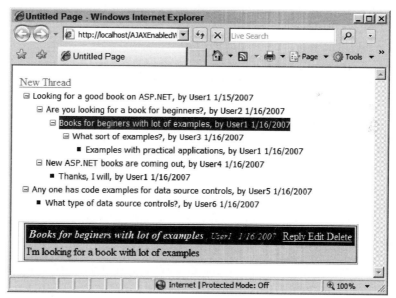

Figure 20-8

As you can see, this user control consists of two main parts: the top part is a `TreeView` server control that displays the subjects of all the messages of the threaded discussion forum. When the end user clicks a given subject, the `DetailsView` control at the bottom of the user control displays detailed information about the message, including its body. Note that this `DetailsView` control contains the standard Reply, Edit, and Delete buttons to enable the end user to reply to, edit, or delete a message. For example, when the end user clicks the Reply button, the page shown in Figure 20-9 is displayed, which includes the user interface that enables the user to enter the reply to the specified message.

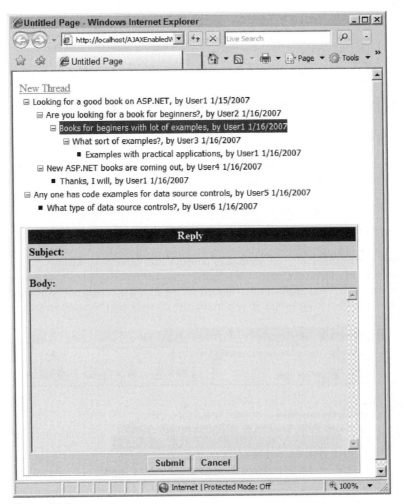

Figure 20-9

Listing 20-10 presents the implementation of the partial-rendering-enabled threaded discussion forum user control. As you can see from this code listing, this user control consists of two UpdatePanel server controls with ID property values of MasterUpdatePanel and DetailUpdatePanel. Note that the UpdateMode properties of both UpdatePanel server controls are set to Conditional to ensure that they get updated only when the required conditions are met.

Notice that the top and bottom UpdatePanel server controls respectively contain the TreeView and DetailsView server controls discussed earlier. Since the TreeView and DetailsView server controls are the children of these UpdatePanel server controls and since these UpdatePanel server controls update conditionally, the partial-rendering-enabled threaded discussion forum user control takes full advantage of the ASP.NET AJAX partial rendering infrastructure to ensure that all the communications with the backend server are done asynchronously in the background without interrupting the end user's interactions with the page that contains the user control, and to ensure that all the page updates are limited to the associated UpdatePanel server controls without reloading the entire page all over again.

Listing 20-10: The Partial-Rendering-Enabled Threaded Discussion Forum User Control

```
<%@ Control Language="C#" ClassName="ThreadedDiscussionForum" %>
<%@ Import Namespace="System.Xml" %>
<%@ Import Namespace="System.IO" %>
<%@ Import Namespace="System.Xml.XPath" %>

<script runat="server">
  public string DataFile
  {
    get { return MySource.DataFile; }
    set
    {
      MySource.DataFile = value;
      MySource2.DataFile = value;
    }
  }

  void DataBound(Object sender, TreeNodeEventArgs e)
  {
    if (((XmlNode)e.Node.DataItem).LocalName == "Message")
      e.Node.Text = XPathBinder.Eval(e.Node.DataItem, "Subject").ToString() +
                    ", by " +
                    XPathBinder.Eval(e.Node.DataItem, "@UserName").ToString() +
                    "   " +
                    XPathBinder.Eval(e.Node.DataItem, "@AddedDate").ToString();
  }

  void SelectedNodeChanged(object sender, EventArgs e)
  {
    MySource2.XPath = TreeView1.SelectedNode.DataPath;

    if (DetailsView1.CurrentMode != DetailsViewMode.ReadOnly)
      DetailsView1.ChangeMode(DetailsViewMode.ReadOnly);

    DetailUpdatePanel.Update();
  }
  void DetailsView_ItemCommand(object sender, DetailsViewCommandEventArgs e)
  {
    switch (e.CommandName)
    {
      case "SubmitUpdate":
        Update();
        break;
      case "SubmitInsert":
        Insert();
        break;
      case "SubmitDelete":
        Delete();
        break;
    }
```

(continued)

Listing 20-10 *(continued)*

```
      MasterUpdatePanel.Update();
}

void Insert()
{
   TextBox subject1 = (TextBox)DetailsView1.FindControl("InsertSubject");
   TextBox body1 = (TextBox)DetailsView1.FindControl("InsertBody");

   XmlDocument doc = MySource2.GetXmlDocument();
   XmlElement message = doc.CreateElement("Message");
   XmlNode parent;

   if (ViewState["NewThread"] == null)
      parent = doc.SelectSingleNode(TreeView1.SelectedNode.DataPath);

   else
   {
      ViewState.Remove("NewThread");
      parent = doc.DocumentElement;
   }

   parent.AppendChild(message);
   message.SetAttribute("AddedDate", DateTime.Now.ToShortDateString());
   message.SetAttribute("UserName", this.Context.User.Identity.Name);
   XmlElement subject = doc.CreateElement("Subject");
   message.AppendChild(subject);
   subject.InnerText = subject1.Text;
   XmlElement body = doc.CreateElement("Body");
   message.AppendChild(body);
   body.InnerText = body1.Text;
   Save();
}

void Update()
{
   TextBox subject1 = (TextBox)DetailsView1.FindControl("EditSubject");
   TextBox body1 = (TextBox)DetailsView1.FindControl("EditBody");

   XmlDocument doc = MySource2.GetXmlDocument();

   string subjectPath = TreeView1.SelectedNode.DataPath + "/Subject";
   XmlNode subject = doc.SelectSingleNode(subjectPath);
   subject.InnerText = subject1.Text;

   string bodyPath = TreeView1.SelectedNode.DataPath + "/Body";
   XmlNode body = doc.SelectSingleNode(bodyPath);
   body.InnerText = body1.Text;

   Save();
}
```

```
  void Delete()
  {
    XmlDocument doc = MySource2.GetXmlDocument();
    XmlNode message = doc.SelectSingleNode(TreeView1.SelectedNode.DataPath);
    message.ParentNode.RemoveChild(message);
    MySource2.XPath = "";
    Save();
  }

  void Save()
  {
    MySource2.Save();
    if (DetailsView1.CurrentMode != DetailsViewMode.ReadOnly)
      DetailsView1.ChangeMode(DetailsViewMode.ReadOnly);

    Cache.Remove("MyKey");
    TreeView1.DataBind();
  }

  void NewThreadClick(object sender, EventArgs e)
  {
    DetailsView1.ChangeMode(DetailsViewMode.Insert);
    ViewState["NewThread"] = "NewThread";
  }

</script>

<asp:LinkButton ID="NewThread" runat="server"
 OnClick="NewThreadClick">New Thread</asp:LinkButton>

<asp:UpdatePanel runat="server" ID="MasterUpdatePanel" UpdateMode="Conditional">
  <ContentTemplate>
    <asp:TreeView ID="TreeView1" runat="Server" AutoGenerateDataBindings="False"
      OnSelectedNodeChanged="SelectedNodeChanged" DataSourceID="MySource"
      OnTreeNodeDataBound="DataBound" ImageSet="Simple">
        <SelectedNodeStyle BackColor="DarkSlateBlue" ForeColor="GhostWhite" />
        <DataBindings>
          <asp:TreeNodeBinding DataMember="Message" TextField="UserName" />
        </DataBindings>
        <NodeStyle Font-Names="Tahoma" Font-Size="10pt" ForeColor="Black" />
      <HoverNodeStyle BackColor="DarkSlateBlue" ForeColor="GhostWhite" />
    </asp:TreeView>
  </ContentTemplate>
</asp:UpdatePanel>
<br />
```

(continued)

Listing 20-10 *(continued)*

```
<asp:UpdatePanel runat="server" ID="DetailUpdatePanel" UpdateMode="Conditional">
  <ContentTemplate>
    <asp:DetailsView ID="DetailsView1" runat="Server" DataSourceID="MySource2"
    AutoGenerateRows="false" OnItemCommand="DetailsView_ItemCommand">
      <Fields>
        <asp:TemplateField>
          <ItemTemplate>
            <table bgcolor="#DCDCDC" border="1" width="500px">
              <tr bgcolor="#000080" style="color: white">
                <td style="border: 0px">
                  <table border="0" width="100%" bgcolor="#00008"
                  style="color: white">
                    <tr>
                      <td align="left" style="font-style: italic">
                        <b>
                          <%# XPath("Subject/text()") %>
                        <b><small>, <%# XPath("@UserName") %>  
                          <%# XPath("@AddedDate") %>
                        </small>
                      </td>
                      <td align="right">
                        <asp:LinkButton ID="LinkButton1" ForeColor="White"
                         runat="server" CommandName="New"
                         Visible='<%# Context.User.Identity.IsAuthenticated %>'>
                           Reply
                        </asp:LinkButton>

                        <asp:LinkButton ID="LinkButton2" ForeColor="White"
                         runat="server" CommandName="Edit"
                         Visible='<%# Context.User.Identity.IsAuthenticated %>'>
                           Edit
                        </asp:LinkButton>

                        <asp:LinkButton ID="LinkButton3" ForeColor="White"
                         runat="server" CommandName="SubmitDelete"
                         Visible='<%# Context.User.Identity.IsAuthenticated %>'>
                           Delete
                        </asp:LinkButton>
                      </td>
                    </tr>
                  </table>
                </td>
              </tr>
              <tr>
              <td style="border: 0px">
                <%# XPath("Body/text()") %>
              </td>
            </tr>
```

```
          </table>
        </ItemTemplate>
        <InsertItemTemplate>
          <table width="500px" style="color: black; background-color: #dcdcdc">
            <thead align="center"
             style="font-weight: bold; color: white; background-color: #000084">
              <tr>
                <td>
                  <strong>Reply</strong></td>
              </tr>
            </thead>
            <tr>
              <td>
                <strong>Subject: </strong>
                <br>
                <asp:TextBox BackColor="#EEEEEE" ID="InsertSubject"
                 runat="server" Width="100%" />
              </td>
            </tr>
            <tr>
              <td>
                <strong>Body: </strong>
                <br>
                <asp:TextBox ID="InsertBody" runat="server" BackColor="#EEEEEE"
                 Width="100%" TextMode="MultiLine" Rows="15" />
              </td>
            </tr>
            <tr>
              <td align="center">
                <asp:Button ID="Submit" runat="server" Text="Submit"
                 Font-Bold="True" CommandName="SubmitInsert" />
                <asp:Button ID="Button2" runat="server" Text="Cancel"
                 Font-Bold="True" CommandName="Cancel" />
              </td>
            </tr>
          </table>
        </InsertItemTemplate>
        <EditItemTemplate>
          <table width="500px" style="color: black; background-color: #dcdcdc">
            <thead align="center"
             style="font-weight: bold; color: white; background-color: #000084">
              <tr>
                <td>
                  <strong>Edit</strong></td>
              </tr>
            </thead>
```

(continued)

Listing 20-10 *(continued)*

```
                  <tr>
                    <td>
                      <strong>Subject: </strong>
                      <br>
                      <asp:TextBox BackColor="#EEEEEE" ID="EditSubject" runat="server"
                       Width="100%" Text='<%# XPath("Subject/text()") %>' />
                    </td>
                  </tr>
                  <tr>
                    <td>
                      <strong>Body: </strong>
                      <br>
                      <asp:TextBox ID="EditBody" runat="server" BackColor="#EEEEEE"
                       Width="100%" TextMode="MultiLine" Rows="15" />
                    </td>
                  </tr>
                  <tr>
                    <td align="center">
                      <asp:Button ID="EditSubmit" runat="server" Text="Update"
                       Font-Bold="True" CommandName="SubmitUpdate" />
                      <asp:Button ID="Button1" runat="server" Text="Cancel"
                       Font-Bold="True" CommandName="Cancel" />
                    </td>
                  </tr>
                </table>
              </EditItemTemplate>
            </asp:TemplateField>
          </Fields>
        </asp:DetailsView>
      </ContentTemplate>
      <Triggers>
        <asp:AsyncPostBackTrigger ControlID="NewThread" EventName="Click" />
      </Triggers>
    </asp:UpdatePanel>

    <asp:XmlDataSource ID="MySource" runat="Server" EnableCaching="true"
     CacheDuration="300" CacheExpirationPolicy="Sliding" CacheKeyDependency="MyKey"
     XPath="/Messages/Message" />

    <asp:XmlDataSource ID="MySource2" runat="Server" />
```

The partial-rendering-enabled threaded discussion forum uses an XML document as its underlying data store. Listing 20-11 shows part of the XML document.

Listing 20-11: Part of the XML Document that Stores the Messages

```xml
<?xml version="1.0" encoding="utf-8"?>
<Messages>
  <Message AddedDate="1/15/2007" UserName="User1">
    <Subject>Looking for a good book on ASP.NET</Subject>
    <Body>I'm looking for a book with lot of examples.</Body>
    <Message AddedDate="1/16/2007" UserName="User2">
      <Subject>Are you looking for a book for beginners?</Subject>
      <Body>What kind of book are you looking for?</Body>
      <Message AddedDate="1/16/2007" UserName="User1">
        <Subject>Books for beginers with lot of examples</Subject>
        <Body>I'm looking for a book with lot of examples</Body>
        <Message AddedDate="1/16/2007" UserName="User3">
          <Subject>What sort of examples?</Subject>
          <Body>Could you be more specific?</Body>
          <Message AddedDate="1/16/2007" UserName="User1">
            <Subject>Examples with practical applications</Subject>
            <Body>Code examples that I could use in my work</Body>
          </Message>
        </Message>
      </Message>
    </Message>
    <Message AddedDate="1/16/2007" UserName="User4">
      <Subject>New ASP.NET books are coming out</Subject>
      <Body>You may want to checkout amazon.com for new books on ASP.NET</Body>
      <Message AddedDate="1/16/2007" UserName="User1">
        <Subject>Thanks, I will</Subject>
        <Body>I will check out amazon.com. I may get lucky there.</Body>
      </Message>
    </Message>
  </Message>
  <Message AddedDate="1/16/2007" UserName="User5">
    <Subject>Any one has code examples for data source controls</Subject>
    <Body>I need code examples that show how to use data source controls in big
    applications</Body>
    <Message AddedDate="1/16/2007" UserName="User6">
      <Subject>What type of data source controls?</Subject>
      <Body>There are all kinds of data source controls. Which ones are you
      planning on using?</Body>
    </Message>
  </Message>
</Messages>
```

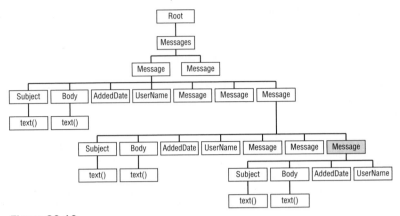

Figure 20-10

A <Message> element represents a posted message in which the <Subject> and <Body> child elements contain the subject and body, respectively. The AddedDate and UserName attributes of a given <Message> element represent the date on which the message was added and the user name of the author, respectively. As Listing 20-10 shows, the partial-rendering-enabled threaded discussion forum user control uses an XmlDataSource server control to interact with the underlying XML document.

The XmlDataSource control must first load the document into memory. The XmlDataSource control uses the W3C DOM model to load the entire contents of the messages.xml file into an instance of the XmlDocument class and generates the in-memory tree representation of the document, as shown in Figure 20-10.

Let us compare the XmlDataSource and SqlDataSource loading models. The SqlDataSource control loads the underlying database tables into an instance of the DataSet class, and generates the in-memory tabular representation of the underlying tables. The in-memory tabular representation consists of inter-connected rows, each of which is an instance of the DataRow class.

Now compare that with the in-memory tree representation such as the one shown in Figure 20-10, which consists of interconnected nodes, each of which is an instance of the XmlNode class. The XmlNode class is an abstract class that represents any type of node. Each of its subclasses represents a particular type of node. For instance, the XmlElement subclass represents element nodes, such as <Message>, <Subject>, and <Body>, while the XmlAttribute subclass represents attribute nodes, such as AddedDate and UserName.

When you select, delete, insert, or update a row in a DataSet object, you do not directly select, delete, insert, or update the corresponding row in the underlying database table because the DataSet object is not connected to the database. In other words, you select, delete, insert, or update the row in the in-memory tabular representation of the database table, not the database table itself. That is why the changes made to the in-memory tabular representation must be explicitly committed to the underlying database tables.

The same logic applies to the XmlDocument object that has been loaded with the data from the underlying messages.xml file. When you select, delete, insert, or update a node in the XmlDocument object, you do not directly select, delete, insert, or update the corresponding node in the underlying XML document, because the XmlDocument object is not connected to the underlying XML file itself. You are really manipulating the node in the in-memory tree representation of the XML document, not the file itself.

Again, that is why the changes to made the in-memory tree representation must be explicitly committed to the underlying XML file.

In order to select, delete, insert, or update a row or node, you have to first select, delete, insert, or update the row or node in the corresponding tabular or tree representation and then commit the changes to the underlying data store. Since a tabular or tree representation is a collection of rows or nodes, you cannot select, delete, insert, or update a row or node in the collection unless you have a way to locate and identify that row or node.

Page developers use the primary key of a row to uniquely locate and identify the row in the underlying tabular representation. The primary key of a row plays a crucial role in data operations because without it there is no way to know which row is being selected, deleted, updated, or inserted. The XPath data model uses a concept known as *hierarchical* or *location path* to uniquely locate or identify a node in the tree hierarchy. The hierarchical or location paths play the same role in a tree hierarchy that primary keys play in a tabular representation. Without it there is no way to know which node is being selected, deleted, updated, or inserted.

As Figure 20-10 shows, every node in the tree is the root node of yet another tree, unless the node is a leaf node. This means the tree is a hierarchy of trees of which each tree is built out of smaller trees. Since you have to locate the root node of a subtree in order to locate the subtree itself, the location of the root node of a subtree uniquely identifies the subtree in the hierarchy of trees. This means that the hierarchical path of a node in a tree hierarchy uniquely identifies and locates not only the node itself but also the subtree associated with the node.

The primary key of a row is normally an autogenerated integer number with a unique value. The hierarchical or location path of a node, on the other hand, is built out of the location steps of its ancestor nodes all the way up to the root node of the entire tree hierarchy. The hierarchical path of a node is based on an imaginary journey from the root node of the tree all the way down to the node itself. The journey consists of several location steps. Each location step takes you from your current node to the next. Let us consider an example. Suppose you want to locate the gray node in Figure 20-10.

The journey begins at the root node of the entire tree hierarchy. The XPath data model uses the notation / to represent the root node. The first location step, `Messages[position()=1]`, takes you from the root node to the `Messages` node. So far the location path is `/Messages[position()=1]`.

The second location step, `Message[position()=1]`, takes you from the `Messages` node to the first `Message` node. The location path so far is `/Messages[position()=1]/Message[position()=1]`. The third location step, `Message[position()=3]`, takes you from the current `Message` node to the next `Message` node. The location path is now `/Messages[position()=1]/Message[position()=1]/Message[position()=3]`. The final location step, `Message[position()=3]`, takes you to the destination, the gray node. Therefore the location path of the gray node is as follows:

```
/Messages[position()=1]/Message[position()=1]/Message[position()=3]/
Message[position()=3]
```

As the example shows, the loation path of a node, such as the gray node, uniquely identifies and locates the node and its associated subtree in the tree hierarchy.

The `XmlDataSource` control provides hierarchical data-bound controls such as `TreeView` and `Menu` with the hierarchical views of the underlying XML document. A hierarchical view represents a particular subtree in the in-memory tree representation of the document. Therefore the hierarchical path of the root node of a subtree uniquely identifies the hierarchical view that represents the subtree. That is why the hierarchical path of the root node of a subtree is also referred to as a view path. Every hierarchical view has a unique view path.

As we discussed earlier, the user interface of the partial-rendering-enabled threaded discussion forum user control consists of a `TreeView` and a `DetailsView` control. The `TreeView` control displays the subject, added date, and user name of all the message nodes of the tree hierarchy. The `TreeView` and `DetailsView` controls create a master/detail form in which the user selects a message from the `TreeView` control to see its details in the `DetailsView` control. The `DetailsView` control also enables users to edit, delete, or reply to the selected message, or to start a new thread of discussion.

The `DetailsView` control therefore does not display, edit, delete, or reply to all the message nodes of the tree. It only displays, edits, deletes, or replies to the message node that the user has selected from the `TreeView` control. This means that the `DetailsView` control must first locate the selected message node in the underlying tree representation. The only way to locate a node in a tree is to find out its hierarchical or location path. Let us see how the `DetailsView` control accesses the hierarchical path of the selected message.

The `TreeView` control creates an instance of the `TreeNode` class for each message node it displays and sets its `DataPath` property to the hierarchical or location path of the message node. When the user selects a message from the `TreeView` control, the `SelectedNode` property of the control is set to the `TreeNode` object that represents the selected message node. Therefore the `DetailsView` control can easily use the `DataPath` property of the `SelectedNode` object of the `TreeView` control to access the hierarchical path of the selected message node, `TreeView1.SelectedNode.DataPath`.

One of the responsibilities of the `DetailsView` control is to use the hierarchical path of the selected message node to locate the node in the underlying tree representation, extract its details, and display them to users. Thanks to the new ASP.NET 2.0 data source and data-bound model this is all done automatically. All you need to do is to set the `XPath` property of the `XmlDataSource` associated with the `DetailsView` control to the hierarchical path of the selected message node. You an do this easily in the callback for the `SelectedNodeChanged` event of the `TreeView` control:

```
void SelectedNodeChanged(object sender, EventArgs e)
{
    MySource2.XPath = TreeView1.SelectedNode.DataPath;
    if (dv.CurrentMode != DetailsViewMode.ReadOnly)
        dv.ChangeMode(DetailsViewMode.ReadOnly);
}
```

Setting the XPath property of the `XmlDataSource` control associated with the `DetailsView` control (`MySource2`) to the hierarchical path of the selected message node is all it takes to have the `DetailsView` control extract the details of the selected message node from the tree and display them. Let us see what makes this possible.

The `DetailsView` control internally registers a callback for the `DataSourceChanged` event of its associated `XmlDataSource` control, i.e. `MySource2`. The `XmlDataSource` control raises the event when one of the following conditions is met:

❑ One or more of its properties change value.

❑ The underlying data store changes because of a delete, update, or insert operation.

Therefore, setting the XPath property of the XmlDataSource control raises the DataSourceChanged event and calls the internal callback function by which the DetailsView control uses the XmlDataSource control to automatically extract the details of the selected message node from the underlying tree and displays them to users.

The great thing about the DetailsView control is that it allows all operations (display, edit, delete, reply, and add a new thread) to be handled within the same server control, the DetailsView control. You switch from one operation to another by switching the mode of the DetailsView control. The DetailsView control can be in one of the three possible modes: DetailsViewMode.ReadOnly, DetailsViewMode.Edit, and DetailsViewMode.Insert.

When the user selects a message from the TreeView control, the DetailsView control is switched to the DetailsViewMode.ReadOnly mode, in which the details of the selected message are displayed. When the user clicks the Edit button of the DetailsView control, the DetailsView control is switched to the DetailsViewMode.Edit mode, in which the user can edit the selected message. When the user clicks the Reply button of the DetailsView control, the DetailsView control is switched to the DetailsViewMode.Insert mode, in which the user can reply to the selected message. When the user clicks the New Thread button, the DetailsView control is switched to the DetailsViewMode.Insert mode, in which the user can start a new thread.

Displaying all Messages

The TreeView control uses the following XmlDataSource control to extract all the message nodes from the tree:

```
<asp:XmlDataSource ID="MySource" Runat="Server"
EnableCaching="true" CacheDuration="300"
CacheExpirationPolicy="Sliding" CacheKeyDependency="MyKey"
DataFile="messages.xml" XPath="/Messages/Message" />
```

The XPath property operates like the SelectCommand attribute of the SqlDataSource control — that is, it specifies which message nodes will be selected. In this case it is set to the value "/Messages/ Message" to extract all the message nodes.

Accessing the underlying data store is one of the most time-consuming operations in data-driven Web applications. Page developers normally cache data query results in the Cache object to improve performance. The XmlDataSource control enables you to cache data without writing a single line of code. All you have to do is to set the EnableCaching, CacheDuration, and CacheExpirationPolicy properties of the XmlDataSource control. The possible values of CacheExpirationPolicy are Sliding and Absolute.

Automatic caching is possible because the XmlDataSource control uses W3C DOM APIs to load the entire XML document into memory. The streaming load model, on the other hand, does not allow caching because only the current node is kept in memory.

The downside of every caching is the problem of stale data. The problem occurs when the underlying data store changes but the application still displays out-of-date information. The XmlDataSource control, like any other ASP.NET component, internally uses the Insert method of the Cache object to cache the XML document if its caching feature is enabled. The Insert method takes an argument that specifies a cache key. This cache key is an arbitrary key under which some arbitrary information is cached in the Cache object. The Insert method internally establishes a dependency between the cache key under which the XML document is cached and the cache key passed into the method. This means that if you invalidate the cache key passed into the Insert method as its argument, you'll automatically invalidate the cache key under which the XML document is cached, because of the dependency between these two cache keys. The XmlDataSource control exposes a public property named CacheKeyDependency, which you must set to the cache key that you want the control to pass into the Insert method of the Cache object when it is caching the XML document.

You will see later that the callbacks for the Delete, Update, and Edit operations in the DetailsView control call the Remove method of the Cache object to invalidate the data cached under the key specified in the CacheKeyDependency property, and consequently to invalidate the cached XML document. The next time the page is accessed, the XmlDataSource control will extract fresh data from the underlying XML document. This automatically resolves the problem of stale data.

The application also registers the DataBound method as the callback for the TreeNodeDataBound event of the TreeView control, in which it specifies what information to display for each message:

```
void DataBound(Object sender, TreeNodeEventArgs e)
{
    if (((XmlNode)e.Node.DataItem).LocalName == "Message")
        e.Node.Text = XPathBinder.Eval(e.Node.DataItem, "Subject").ToString() +
                ", by " +
                    XPathBinder.Eval(e.Node.DataItem, "@UserName").ToString() +
                    "   " +
                    XPathBinder.Eval(e.Node.DataItem, "@AddedDate").ToString();
}
```

The Eval method of the XPathBinder takes two arguments. The first argument is the object against which a given XPath expression is evaluated. The second argument is the XPath expression being evaluated. The first argument accepts only objects whose classes implement the IXPathNavigable interface. This is because the Eval method simply calls the CreateNavigator method of the object to access its XPathNavigator object. The Eval method then calls the Select method of the XPathNavigator object and passes the XPath expression as its argument.

Let us take a look at the XPath expressions used as the second arguments of the Eval method calls Subject, @UserName, and @AddedDate. These expressions refer to the <Subject> child element and the UserName and AddedDate attributes of the selected message node. As Figure 20-10 shows, the <Subject> child element and UserName and AddedDate attributes are themselves nodes of the tree hierarchy. Therefore the XPath expressions are nothing but the location steps that take you from the selected message node to the Subject, UserName, and AddedDate nodes. The Select method of the XPathNavigator object uses these location steps to locate these nodes and return references to them.

Displaying the Details of a Message

Since the DetailsView control is bound to an XmlDataSource control in which every data item implements the IXPathNavigable interface, it uses XPathBinder in its data-binding expressions. XPath is the short version of `XPathBinder.Eval(Container.DataItem, xpathexpression, format)`. The `DetailsView` control uses four XPath data-binding expressions:

1. `XPath("Subject/text()")` returns the subject of the selected message node. The `text()` function returns the text within the opening and closing tags of the `<Subject>` element in the XML document. As Figure 20-10 shows, the text itself is a node in the tree hierarchy. The XPath expression `Subject/text()` is therefore a location path that takes us from the selected `message` node to the text node.

2. `XPath("Body/text()")` returns the body of the selected message node.

3. `XPath("@AddedDate")` returns the value of the `AddedDate` attribute of the selected `<Message>` element. As Figure 20-10 shows, the attribute itself is a node.

4. `XPath("@UserName")` returns the value of the `UserName` attribute of the selected `<Message>` element.

The `DetailsView` control and its associated `XmlDataSource` control work together to automatically display the details of the `message` node that the user selects from the `TreeView` control. In other words, the select operation is done automatically. However, `XmlDataSource` does not provide automatic support for delete, update, and insert operations. The application must explicitly handle these operations.

Deleting a Message

The `ItemTemplate` section of the `DetailsView` control contains the Delete button. The `DetailsView` control provides built-in support for deleting items. Page developers need only add a new Delete button to the `ItemTemplate` section and set its `CommandName` property to `Delete`. When the user clicks the Delete button, the `DetailsView` control checks the value of the `CanDelete` property of its associated view object. If it is `true`, the control calls the `Delete` method of the view object; otherwise it throws an exception. The `CanDelete` property value is `true` only when the view object implements the `Delete` method.

However, the `XmlDataSourceView` class does not implement the `Delete` method. Therefore the application must not set the `CommandName` property of the Delete button to the value `"Delete,"` or an exception will be thrown when the button is clicked. The application sets the `CommandName` property of the Delete button to the value `"SubmitDelete"` instead, and registers the `DetailsView_ItemCommand` method as the callback for the `ItemCommand` event of the `DetailsView` control to handle the delete event. Later you will see that the `DetailsView_ItemCommand` method will also be used to handle the update and insert events.

The method calls the `Delete` method to handle the delete event. As discussed before, the `XmlDataSource` control uses the W3C DOM APIs to load the entire `messages.xml` file into memory and creates an in-memory tree representation of the XML document. The great thing about the W3C DOM model is that it enables page developers to add, update, and delete nodes from the in-memory tree. The `XmlDataSource` control exposes a method named `GetXmlDocument` that returns a reference to the underlying `XmlDocument` object.

As you can see from the implementation of the `Delete` method shown in Listing 20-10, deleting a node from the tree hierarchy involves the following four steps:

1. Find out the hierarchical path of the node to be deleted. Since the message node being deleted is the node that the user selected from the `TreeView` control, the value of the `DataPath` property of the `SelectedNode` of the `TreeView` control is the hierarchical path of the node being deleted.

2. Call the `SelectSingleNode` method of the `XmlDocument` object and pass the hierarchical path of the node as its argument. The method uses the hierarchical path to locate the message node in the tree:

```
XmlNode message = doc.SelectSingleNode(TreeView1.Selected.DataPath);
```

3. Access the parent node of the node being deleted:

```
XmlNode parent = message.ParentNode;
```

4. Call the `RemoveChild` method of the parent node to delete the node from the tree:

```
parent.RemoveChild(message);
```

The `Delete` method then calls the `Save` method. As you can see from Listing 20-10, the `Save` method takes care of the following issues:

❑ Removing the selected message node from the in-memory tree hierarchy does not automatically remove the message from the underlying data store — that is, the XML document. The `Save` method calls the `Save` method of the associated `XmlDataSource` control to propagate the changes to the XML document.

❑ Recall that the `XmlDataSource` control associated with the `TreeView` control caches the XML document in the `Cache` object. Since the `Delete` method changes the underlying data store, it must call the `Remove` method of the `Cache` object to invalidate the cached data, otherwise the `TreeView` control will show out-of-date data.

❑ The `DataBind` method of the `TreeView` control must be called to update the `TreeView` control display. Since the cached data has already been invalidated, the `DataBind` method will extract fresh data from the underlying XML document.

❑ The `DetailsView` control must be switched back to its `ReadOnly` mode.

Updating a Message

The `ItemTemplate` section of the `DetailsView` control contains the Edit button. Since the `CommandName` property of the button is set to "`Edit`", when the user clicks the button the `DetailsView` control automatically switches to `DetailsViewMode.Edit` mode, in which it renders the contents of its `EditItemTemplate` section, including the Update and Cancel buttons.

When the Cancel button is clicked, the `DetailsView` control automatically switches back to the `DetailsViewMode.ReadOnly` mode, in which it renders the contents of its `ItemTemplate` section. Notice that the `CommandName` property of the Update button is not set to "`Update`" for the same reason that the CommandName property of the Delete button was not set to "Delete". The application sets the property to "SubmitUpdate" and uses the DetailsView_ItemCommand method to handle the event. The method calls the Update method to handle the Update event. As you can see from Listing 20-10, the Update method first extracts the new values for the subject and body of the selected message. Updating a node in the tree hierarchy involves the following steps:

1. Find out the hierarchical path of the node to be updated.

Since the message node being updated is the message that the user selected from the TreeView control, the value of the DataPath property of the SelectedNode of the TreeView control is the hierarchical path of the message node. However, you want to update the child nodes (the subject and body nodes) of the message node, not the message node itself.

Recall that the hierarchical path of a node takes you from the root node of the tree, node by node, all the way down to the node itself. The hierarchical path consists of location steps, each of which takes you from your current node to the next. This means that you need to add another location step to the hierarchical path of the message node to go from the message node to its child nodes, the subject and body nodes. Therefore the hierarchical paths of the subject and body nodes are as follows:

```
string subjectPath = TreeView1.SelectedNode.DataPath + "/Subject";
sring bodyPath = TreeView1.SelectedNode.DataPath + "/Body";
```

2. Call the SelectSingleNode method of the XmlDocument object and pass the hierarchical path of the node to access the node in the tree:

```
XmlNode subject = doc.SelectSingleNode(subjectPath);
XmlNode body = doc.SelectSingleNode(bodyPath);
```

3. Update the node:

```
subject.InnerText = subject1.Text;
body.InnerText = body1.Text;
```

Notice that the SelectSingleNode method returns the reference to the actual node in the tree. This enables you to directly update the properties of the subject and body nodes. At the end, the Update method calls the Save method, exactly as the Delete method did.

Replying to a Message

The ItemTemplate property of the DetailsView control contains the Reply button. Since the CommandName property of the button is set to "New", when the user clicks the button the DetailsView control automatically switches to the DetailsViewMode.Insert mode, in which the control renders the contents of its InsertItemTemplate section that also includes the Insert button.

Notice that the CommandName property of the Insert button is not set to "Insert" for the same reason that the CommandName properties of the Delete and Update buttons were not set to "Delete" and "Update". The application sets the property to "SubmitInsert" and uses the DetailsView_ItemCommand method to handle the event. The method calls the Insert method to handle the `Insert` event. Listing 20-10 shows the code for the `Insert` method. Adding a new element node to the tree hierarchy involves the following six steps:

1. Call the `CreateElement` method of the `XmlDocument` object to create the new element node.

2. Set the properties of the new element node.

3. Call the `SetAttribute` method of the new element node to set its attributes.

4. Find out the hierarchical path of the element node that will act as the parent node of the new element node.

5. Call the `SelectSingleNode` method of the `XmlDocument` object and pass the hierarchical path of the parent node as its argument to access the parent node in the tree.

6. Call the `AppendChild` method of the parent node to add the new element node to the tree as its child node.

The `Insert` method creates three element nodes and adds them to the tree hierarchy. The first element node represents the reply message itself. The second and third element nodes represent the subject and body of the reply message, respectively. The `Insert` method follows the preceding six steps for each element node that it creates and adds to the tree hierarchy. For instance, consider the six steps for the creation and addition of the element node that represents the reply message itself:

1. Create the element node:

```
XmlElement message = doc.CreateElement("Message");
```

2. Not applicable.

3. Since the message element exposes two attributes, you have to call the `SetAttribute` method twice:

```
message.SetAttribute("AddedDate", DateTime.Now.ToShortDateString());
message.SetAttribute("UserName", User.Identity.Name);
```

4. Since the message node being added is the reply to the message node that the user selected from the `TreeView` control, the selected message node will be the parent of the new message node. Therefore the value of the `DataPath` property of the `SelectedNode` of the `TreeView` control is the hierarchical path of the parent node of the new element node.

5. Access the parent element node in the tree hierarchy:

```
XmlNode parent = doc.SelectSingleNode(TreeView1.SelectedNode.DataPath);
```

6. Add the new element node to the tree hierarchy as the child node of the parent node:

```
parent.AppendChild(message);
```

At the end, the `Insert` method calls the `Save` method to commit all the changes to the disk and update the `TreeView` and `DetailsView` controls.

Starting a New Thread

The NewThreadClick method is registered as the callback for the Click event of the NewThread button, as shown in Listing 20-10. As you can see from this code listing, the method calls the ChangeMode method of the DetailsView control to change its mode to DetailsViewMode.Insert, in which the control renders the contents of its InsertItemTemplate property. The method also stores "NewThread" in ViewState under the key "NewThread".

Since replying to a message and creating a new thread both switch the DetailsView control to its Insert mode, the same discussions presented in the previous section apply here. The only difference is that the Insert method appends the newly created message node as the child node of the document element because it starts a new thread. The Insert method uses ViewState["NewThread"] as the signal to find out whether the user is starting a new thread or replying to an existing message.

Note that the partial-rendering-enabled threaded discussion forum user control registers the NewThread button as the trigger for the automatic update of the UpdatePanel server control that contains the DetailsView server control. This ensures that when the end user clicks the NewThread button to add a new thread of discussions, this UpdatePanel server control and consequently its child DetailsView server control are automatically updated.

```
<Triggers>
  <asp:AsyncPostBackTrigger ControlID="NewThread" EventName="Click" />
</Triggers>
```

The following code listing presents a page that uses the partial-rendering-enabled threaded discussion forum user control:

```
<%@ Page Language="C#" %>

<%@ Register TagName="DiscussionForum" TagPrefix="custom"
Src="~/DiscussionForum.ascx" %>
<!DOCTYPE html PUBLIC "-//W3C//DTD XHTML 1.0 Transitional//EN"
"http://www.w3.org/TR/xhtml1/DTD/xhtml1-transitional.dtd">
<html xmlns="http://www.w3.org/1999/xhtml">
<head runat="server">
  <title>Untitled Page</title>
</head>
<body>
  <form id="form1" runat="server">
    <asp:ScriptManager runat="server" ID="ScriptManager1" />
    <custom:DiscussionForum runat="server" ID="DiscussionForum1"
    DataFile="messages.xml" />
  </form>
</body>
</html>
```

This page assumes that you've stored Listing 20-10 in a file named `DiscussionForum.ascx` and Listing 20-11 in a file named `messages.xml`. Note that Listing 20-10 uses the value of the `IsAuthenticated` property of the `Identity` property of the `User` object to determine whether to display the following `LinkButton` server controls:

```
<asp:LinkButton ID="LinkButton1" ForeColor="White" runat="server" CommandName="New"
Visible='<%# Context.User.Identity.IsAuthenticated %>'>Reply</asp:LinkButton>

<asp:LinkButton ID="LinkButton2" ForeColor="White" runat="server"
 CommandName="Edit" Visible='<%# Context.User.Identity.IsAuthenticated %>'>Edit
</asp:LinkButton>

<asp:LinkButton ID="LinkButton3" ForeColor="White" runat="server"
 CommandName="SubmitDelete" Visible='<%# Context.User.Identity.IsAuthenticated %>'>
Delete</asp:LinkButton>
```

This means that you need to use the ASP.NET Web Site Administration Tool to configure your application to use the ASP.NET 2.0 security features. You can launch this tool from the Website menu of Visual Studio 2005.

Summary

This chapter used numerous examples to show you how to use ASP.NET AJAX partial page rendering in your own Web applications. You also learned how to develop custom partial-page-rendering-enabled server controls and user controls. The next chapter will delve deeper into the ASP.NET AJAX partial-page-rendering infrastructure, and you'll learn a great deal about the constituent components of this infrastructure.

21

Page Life Cycle and Asynchronous Partial Page Rendering

The main goal of this and the next few chapters is to help you gain a solid understanding of the ASP.NET AJAX asynchronous page postback or partial-page-rendering-request-processing infrastructure. This infrastructure consists of two groups of components:

❑ **Server-side components:** This group includes the `ScriptManager`, `UpdatePanel`, `PageRequestManager`, and `ScriptRegistrationManager` classes.

❑ **Client-side components:** This group includes the `PageRequestManager`, `WebRequest`, `WebRequestExecutor`, `WebRequestManager`, `XMLHttpExecutor`, and `Application` classes, among others.

Note that both the server and client sides contain a component named `PageRequestManager`. Even though they have the same name, they are two different components defined in two different frameworks. One is defined in the ASP.NET AJAX server-side framework while the other is defined in the ASP.NET AJAX client-side framework. For ease of reference, I'll refer to the one defined in the server-side framework as the server-side `PageRequestManager` and the other as the client-side `PageRequestManager`. These components are at the heart of ASP.NET AJAX partial page rendering, which, as you'll see later, is the result of the communications between the client-side and server-side `PageRequestManager` components. As their names suggest, they're the ones that are responsible for managing and processing asynchronous partial-page-rendering requests.

Here is how these two components work together. The current client-side `PageRequestManager` instance makes an asynchronous page postback request to the server. The current server-side `PageRequestManager` instance picks up and processes the request and sends the reponse text back to the client. The current client-side `PageRequestManager` instance then picks up and processes the response text and updates the regions of the page enclosed within the specified `UpdatePanel` server controls.

Your server-side code cannot directly access the current server-side `PageRequestManager` instance. Your code gets to interact with the current server-side `PageRequestManager` instance via the current `ScriptManager` server control, as you'll see later in this chapter. Your client-side code, on the other hand, can directly access the current client-side `PageRequestManager` instance. This will all be cleared up later in this and the following chapters.

Processing a Request

When an HTTP request — be it synchronous, asynchronous, partial-page-update, or normal postback — for an ASP.NET Web page arrives, the ASP.NET framework parses the requested page into a dynamically generated class that inherits the ASP.NET `Page` class. By default, the name of this class consists of two parts separated by an underscore character (_). The first part is the name of the file that contains the page and the second part is the string `aspx`. For example, if the requested page is in a file named `default .aspx`, ASP.NET parses the content of this file into a dynamically generated class named `default_aspx` that inherits the `Page` class.

All ASP.NET dynamically generated classes, such as `default_aspx`, belong to a standard namespace named `ASP`. As a matter of fact, Visual Studio provides IntelliSense support for this namespace and its constituent dynamically generated classes. To see this, open the file that contains the code-behind file for an ASP.NET Web page (for example, the `default.aspx.cs`) in Visual Studio and type the first letter of the `ASP` namespace, that is, the letter A. You should see the popup that displays all the namespaces whose names begin with that letter, including the `ASP` namespace. Now, if you select ASP from this popup and type the dot character (.) you should see the name of the dynamically generated class (for example, `default_aspx`) associated with the current Web page.

After parsing the requested page into a dynamically generated class that inherits from the ASP.NET `Page` class, the ASP.NET framework temporarily stores the code for this class in a source file a couple of directories below the directory named after the current Web application, in a standard directory named `Temporary ASP.NET Files`, under the directory on your machine where the .NET framework is installed:

```
%windir%\Microsoft.NET\Framework\v2.0.50727\Temporary ASP.NET Files\
ajaxenabledwebsite11\de910baf\54181126
```

The name of this source file follows this format: `App_Web_FileName.aspx.RandomHash.0.cs`, where the `FileName` is the name of the `.aspx` file and the `RandomHash` is a randomly generated hash value that ensures the uniqueness of the source-file name.

Figure 21-1 shows an example that represents this file structure for an ASP.NET application named `AjaxEnabledWebSite11`. This Web application is a very simple one that consists of a single page named `default.aspx`, as shown in the following code listing. The file named `App_Web_default.aspx.cdcab7d2.a5hjdn-i.0` shown in Figure 21-1 contains the source code for the `ASP.default_aspx` class that represents the `default.aspx` file.

```
<%@ Page Language="C#" %>
<script runat="server">
  void SubmitCallback(object sender, EventArgs e)
  {
    Info.Text = TextBox1.Text;
  }
</script>
<html xmlns="http://www.w3.org/1999/xhtml">
<body>
  <form id="form1" runat="server">
    <asp:ScriptManager ID="ScriptManager1" runat="server" />
    <asp:UpdatePanel runat="server" ID="UpdatePanel1">
      <ContentTemplate>
        Enter text:
        <asp:TextBox runat="server" ID="TextBox1" />
        <asp:Button runat="server" ID="Button1" Text="Submit"
         OnClick="SubmitCallback" /><br />
        <asp:Label runat="server" ID="Info" />
      </ContentTemplate>
    </asp:UpdatePanel>
  </form>
</body>
</html>
```

If you're curious to see what this dynamically generated class looks like, go to the previously mentioned directory and open the file that contains the source code for this class in your favorite editor. For example, the file associated with the preceding page contains the following source code (note that I've cleaned it up for presentation purposes):

> As I said earlier, the ASP.NET compilation system temporarily stores the source code in the previously mentioned source file. Therefore, if you want the file to remain in the directory so you can open it in your favorite editor, you must run the page in debug mode to instruct ASP.NET not to delete the file.

```
using System;
using System.Web;
using System.Web.UI;
using System.Web.UI.WebControls;
using System.Web.UI.HtmlControls;
namespace ASP
{
  public class default_aspx : Page
  {
    protected ScriptManager ScriptManager1;
    protected TextBox TextBox1;
    protected Button Button1;
    protected Label Info;
    protected UpdatePanel UpdatePanel1;
    protected HtmlForm form1;

    . . .
```

(continued)

(continued)

```csharp
    private UpdatePanel @__BuildControlUpdatePanel1()
    {
        . . .
    }
    private HtmlForm @__BuildControlform1()
    {
        . . .
    }
    private void @__BuildControlTree(default_aspx @__ctrl)
    {
        IParserAccessor @__parser = ((IParserAccessor)(@__ctrl));
        @__parser.AddParsedSubObject(
                new LiteralControl("<html xmlns=\"http://www.w3.org/1999/xhtml\">"));
        @__parser.AddParsedSubObject(new LiteralControl("\r\n<body>\r\n "));
        HtmlForm @__ctrl2 = this.@__BuildControlform1();
        @__parser.AddParsedSubObject(@__ctrl2);
        @__parser.AddParsedSubObject(
                            new LiteralControl("\r\n</body>\r\n</html>\r\n"));
    }
    protected override void FrameworkInitialize()
    {
        base.FrameworkInitialize();
        this.@__BuildControlTree(this);
    }
}
}
```

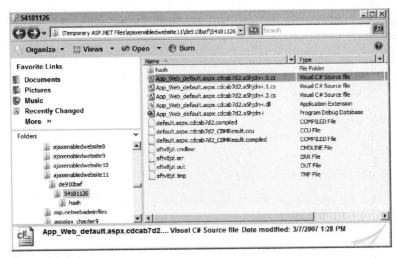

Figure 21-1

The ASP.NET framework then dynamically compiles the content of the source file that contains the dynamically generated class into an assembly, stores the assembly in the same directory as the source file, and deletes the source file afterward. If you run the application in debug mode, the ASP.NET framework will not delete the source file after the compilation. As I mentioned earlier, this will enable you to open the file in your favorite editor and study its content. The name of this assembly follows the naming convention `App_Web_FileName.aspx.RandomHash.0.dll`, where `FileName` is the name of the `.aspx` file and `RandomHash` is a randomly generated hash value that ensures the uniqueness of the DLL file name. For example, in the case of Figure 21-1, the DLL's name is `App_Web_default.aspx.cdcab7d2.a5hjdn-i.dll`.

The ASP.NET Framework then loads this assembly — keep in mind that it contains the dynamically generated class — into the application domain where the current application is running, dynamically instantiates an instance of this compiled class, and calls the `ProcessRequest` method on this instance. For ease of reference, I'll refer to this instance as the `Page` object or the `Page`, because this is an instance of a class that inherits the ASP.NET `Page` class.

You can think of this instance (the `Page` object) as the ASP.NET representation of the requested Web page. It inherits the `ProcessRequest` method from the ASP.NET `Page` class. As the name suggests, this method processes the current request. The call into this method causes the `Page` object to start its life cycle, which consists of different phases. The best way to understand the ASP.NET AJAX asynchronous page postback or partial-rendering-request-processing infrastructure and its constituent components is to follow the `Page` object as it goes through its life cycle phases.

The Page Life Cycle

Listing 21-1 presents the internal implementation of the `ProcessRequest` method of the ASP.NET `Page` class. As you can see, this method consists of a bunch of method calls, each of which defines a particular phase of the `Page` object's life cycle, as discussed in the following sections. Figure 21-2 presents the flowchart associated with the `ProcessRequest` method. Keep this flowchart in mind as you're reading through this chapter.

Listing 21-1: The ProcessRequest Method of the Page Class

```
public void ProcessRequest(HttpContext context)
{
  this._context = context;
  this.RetrievePostedData();
  if (this.MaintainScrollPositionOnPostBack)
    this.LoadScrollPosition();

  this.PerformPreInit();
  this.InitRecursive(null);
  this.OnInitComplete(EventArgs.Empty);
  if (this.IsPostBack)
  {
    this.LoadAllState();
    this.ProcessPostData(this._requestValueCollection, true);
  }
  this.OnPreLoad(EventArgs.Empty);
  this.LoadRecursive();
```

(continued)

Listing 21-1 *(continued)*

```
    if (this.IsPostBack)
    {
      this.ProcessPostData(this._leftoverPostData, false);
      this.RaiseChangedEvents();
      this.RaisePostBackEvent(this._requestValueCollection);
    }
    this.OnLoadComplete(EventArgs.Empty);
    this.PreRenderRecursive();

    this.PerformPreRenderComplete();
    this.SaveAllState();
    this.OnSaveStateComplete(EventArgs.Empty);
    this.RenderControl(this.CreateHtmlTextWriter(this.Response.Output));
}
```

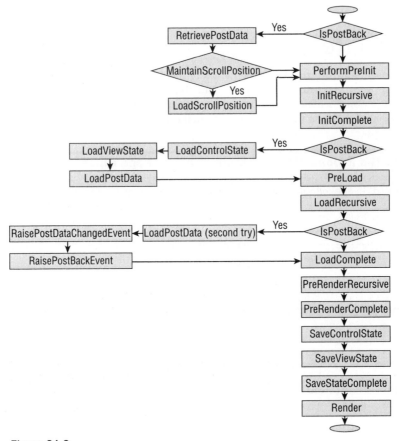

Figure 21-2

Keep in mind that our goal in this chapter is to follow the Page object through its life cycle phases in order to understand the ASP.NET AJAX asynchronous page postback or partial-page-rendering-request-processing infrastructure and its constituent server-side and client-side components. As discussed in the previous chapter, an ASP.NET Web page enabled for partial page rendering contains a single instance of the ScriptManager server control and one or more instances of the UpdatePanel server controls.

I'll begin with the first request that the requesting browser makes to the server to visit an ASP.NET Web page enabled for partial page rendering. This first request is an HTTP GET request that downloads the Web page for the first time. Obviously this first request is not a postback or asynchronous postback request. I'll first follow the Page object through its life cycle phases to process this very first request, even though it is not an asynchronous postback request because the first request instantiates and initializes many of the components that come into play in the subsequent asynchronous page postback requests to the same Web page.

The First Visit to a Partial-Page-Rendering-Enabled Web Page

As just discussed, to visit for the first time an ASP.NET Web page enabled for partial page rendering, the browser must send an HTTP GET request to the server. In this section I'll follow the Page object through its life cycle phases to process this HTTP GET request. As Figure 21-2 shows, the current Page skips some of its life cycle phases when it is processing a non-postback request such as the first HTTP GET request.

InitRecursive

I'll begin when the page enters its InitRecursive (or Init) life cycle phase, where the ProcessRequest method invokes the InitRecursive method on the current Page (see Listing 21-1 and Figure 21-2). All server controls, including the Page, ScriptManager, and UpdatePanel, inherit the InitRecursive method from the Control base class. The InitRecursive method of a server control such as Page and UpdatePanel recursively invokes the InitRecursive methods of its child server controls. The InitRecursive method of a server control takes these actions:

- Sets the NamingContainer, ID (if it hasn't already been set), and Page properties of its child server controls. This step does not apply to the ScriptManager because it does not contain any child server controls. However, it does apply to the UpdatePanel server controls on the current page because they do contain other server controls.

- Calls the ApplySkin to apply its associated skins if theming is enabled. This step does not apply to the ScriptManager because it does not render visual HTML, but it does apply to the UpdatePanel server controls because they may contain child server controls that use skins.

- Calls the OnInit method to raise its Init event and consequently invoke all the event handlers registered for this event.

❑ Calls the `TrackViewState` method to start tracking its view state. After the call into the `TrackViewState` method goes through, any changes made to the state of a server control, such as to its property values, will be marked as dirty and stored in the view state at the end of the current request and consequently sent to the client as part of the current page. As you can see, the bigger the view state the bigger the current page.

The `Init` life cycle phase of the `Page` object is very complex in that it involves a lot of method calls on the `Page`, `ScriptManager`, `PageRequestManager`, and `UpdatePanel` classes. Because of this, it's really easy to lose track of these method calls and their surrounding discussions. To make things a little easier on you, I'll present these method calls in a diagram. At the end of each section I'll update this diagram with the method calls discussed in the section. Therefore, by the time I'm done with our discussions of the `Init` life cycle phase of the `Page` object, you'll have a single diagram that contains all the method calls in the order in which they're made. I'll do the same for other complex life cycle phases of the `Page` object. This way, for each complex life cycle phase you'll have one diagram that contains all the method calls made in that phase in the order in which they're made. Keep in mind that the vertical line in each diagram represents the timeline. The method calls positioned higher on these vertical lines occur earlier.

Figure 21-3 presents the diagram that contains the method calls I've discussed so far. As you can see, when the `Page` enters its `Init` phase, it first invokes its own `InitRecursive` method. Since the `Page` calls this method on itself, the diagram uses an arrow that starts and ends with the vertical timeline associated with the page. The `InitRecursive` method then calls the `InitRecusive` methods of the `ScriptManager` and `UpdatePanel` before calling its own `ApplySkin`, `OnInit`, and `TrackViewState` methods. The `InitRecursive` methods of the `ScriptManager` and `UpdatePanel`, like the `InitRecusive` method of any other server control, call their own `ApplySkin`, `OnInit`, and `TrackViewState` methods.

Now the question is: what happens when the `OnInit` methods of the `ScriptManager` and `UpdatePanel` server controls are invoked? In other words, what sequence of method calls do the calls into the `OnInit` methods of the `ScriptManager` and `UpdatePanel` server controls trigger? The dashed lines in Figure 21-3 are the placeholders for these missing method calls, which will be discussed in the following sections.

The OnInit Method of ScriptManager

Listing 21-2 presents the `ScriptManager` class's internal implementation of the `OnInit` method, which it inherits from the `Control` base class. This implementation takes these steps. First, it calls the `GetCurrent` static method on the `ScriptManager` class to determine whether the current page already contains an instance of the `ScriptManager` server control. If so, it raises an exception because every page can contain only one instance of the `ScriptManager` server control.

Next, the `OnInit` method adds the current instance of the `ScriptManager` server control to the `Items` collection of the current `Page` object. The next calls into the `GetCurrent` static method will return the instance stored in the `Items` collection of the current page. This ensures that the same instance will always be used for the entire lifespan of the current request.

```
this.Page.Items[typeof(ScriptManager)] = this;
```

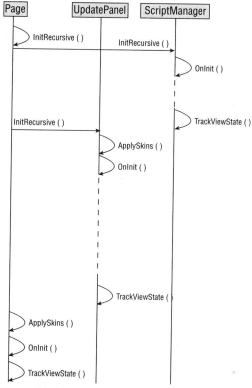

Figure 21-3

This behavior of the Items collection has significant consequences when you're enabling partial page rendering for a user control or a content page. Since a user control or a content page merges into its parent page and consequently forms a single page with its parent, you have to make sure that you do not declare separate instances of the ScriptManager server control in the parent page and the child page — be they user controls or content pages.

You have two choices in these situations. You can declare the ScriptManager server control either in the parent or the child page (that is, user control or content page). Each option has its own pluses and minuses. If you declare the ScriptManager server control in the parent page, this automatically enables partial page rendering for all child pages — that is, for all user controls and content pages — which may not be the effect you're looking for. Doing this also means that if you need to access the current ScriptManager server control from within your user control or content page, you must call the GetCurrent static method on the ScriptManager class to return a reference to the ScriptManager server control declared in the parent page.

If you declare the ScriptManager in the child page you can directly access the current ScriptManager server control from the child page without using the GetCurrent static method. However, this also means that partial page rendering is only enabled for those user controls or content pages that directly contain the ScriptManager server control, which may not be the effect you're looking for. Another side effect of this approach is that you cannot directly access the current

ScriptManager server control from your parent page because the parent page does not directly contain this server control. Instead you must use the GetCurrent *static method to return a reference to this server control. Using this approach also means that if your parent page contains a partial-page-rendering-related functionality you must add code to check whether the child control does indeed contain an instance of the* ScriptManager *server control. If not, you must disable this functionality for this child control.*

OnInit then registers the OnPagePreRenderComplete method as an event handler for the PreRenderComplete event of the current Page object:

```
this.Page.PreRenderComplete += new EventHandler(this.OnPagePreRenderComplete);
```

Next, OnInit checks whether the page has been posted back to the server. If so, it calls the IsAsyncPostBackRequest static method on the current server-side PageRequestManager instance, passing in the request header collection to determine whether the page has been posted back asynchronously. (You'll learn more about the server-side PageRequestManager class later.) As you'll see, the ScriptManager server control delegates some of its responsibilities to this class, especially those responsibilities that handle asynchronous page postback or partial-rendering requests.

The IsAsyncPostBackRequest static method will be thoroughly discussed later. For now, suffice it to say that this method uses the request headers to determine whether the page is posted back asynchronously — that is, whether the current request is an asynchronous partial-page-rendering request. Note that OnInit assigns the return value of this method to the _isInAsyncPostback Boolean field:

```
if (this.Page.IsPostBack)
    this._isInAsyncPostBack =
            PageRequestManager.IsAsyncPostBackRequest(this.Page.Request.Headers);
```

The ScriptManager *exposes a read-only Boolean property named* IsInAsyncPostBack *that returns the value of the* _isInAsyncPostBack *field. Call this property on the current* ScriptManager *server control if you need to know whether the current request is an asynchronous page postback or partial-page-rendering request.*

Since the current Page object is processing the first HTTP GET request made to the server to visit the Web page for the first time, the IsAsyncPostBackRequest method of the current server-side PageRequestMananager instance is not invoked for this request.

Next, OnInit calls the OnInit method on the current server-side PageRequestManager instance to initialize this instance. Unlike the ScriptManager, the PageRequestManager class is not a server control, which means that its OnInit method will not be automatically invoked by the containing page. That is why the OnInit method of the ScriptManager server control explicitly calls the OnInit method of the current server-side PageRequestManager instance:

```
this.PageRequestManager.OnInit();
```

This is an example of a situation in which a server control such as ScriptManager *has to work hand in hand with a non–server control object such as* PageRequestManager *throughout its life cycle. Thanks to the* Page *object, the server control's life cycle methods, such as* OnInit, *are automatically called as the control goes through its life cycle phases. The same does not apply to the non–server control objects, such as* PageRequestManager. *In these cases, the server control's life cycle methods, such as* OnInit, *must call the corresponding methods of the non–server control object to ensure that the non–server control object gets to run its appropriate life cycle methods as the server control is moving through its own life cycle phases. This pattern allows a server control, such as* ScriptManager, *to delegate some of its responsibilities to a non–server control object, such as* PageRequestManager.

Listing 21-2: The OnInit Method of the ScriptManager Class

```
protected override void OnInit(EventArgs e)
{
  base.OnInit(e);
  if (ScriptManager.GetCurrent(this.Page) != null)
    throw new InvalidOperationException("OnlyOneScriptManager");
  this.Page.Items[typeof(ScriptManager)] = this;
  this.Page.PreRenderComplete += new EventHandler(this.OnPagePreRenderComplete);
  if (this.Page.IsPostBack)
    this._isInAsyncPostBack =
            PageRequestManager.IsAsyncPostBackRequest(this.Page.Request.Headers);
  this.PageRequestManager.OnInit();
}
```

The OnInit Method of PageRequestManager

Listing 21-3 presents the internal implementation of the OnInit method of the server-side PageRequestManager.

Listing 21-3: The OnInit Method of the PageRequestManager Class

```
internal void OnInit()
{
  if (this._owner.EnablePartialRendering &&
      !this._owner._supportsPartialRenderingSetByUser)
  {
    IHttpBrowserCapabilities capabilities1 = this._owner.Page.Request.Browser;
    this._owner.SupportsPartialRendering =
                      (capabilities1.W3CDomVersion >= new Version(1, 0)) &&
                      (capabilities1.EcmaScriptVersion >= new Version(1, 0)) &&
                      capabilities1.SupportsCallback;
  }
  if (this._owner.IsInAsyncPostBack)
    this._owner.Page.Error += new EventHandler(this.OnPageError);
}
```

Note that the current server-side PageRequestManager instance exposes a field named _owner that references the current ScriptManager server control. Also note that the ScriptManager server control exposes the following two Boolean properties:

❑   EnablePartialRendering: Gets or sets a Boolean value that specifies whether the partial-rendering feature is enabled.

Set this property to false if you need to turn off the partial page rendering for a page. Keep in mind that if the current ScriptManager server control is declared on a parent page such as a master page, setting this property to false will disable partial page rendering for all its child pages — that is, for all its child user controls and content pages, which may not be the effect you're looking for. In this situation, you must take the following steps to explicitly turn on partial page rendering for a particular child page. First, call the GetCurrent static method on the `ScriptManager` class to return a reference to the `ScriptManager` server control declared on the parent page. Then set the `EnablePartialRendering` property of this `ScriptManager` server control to `true`. Keep in mind that this will enable partial rendering only for this specific child page, which means that you have to take these same two steps for every child page for which you need to enable partial page rendering.

This may seem to suggest that you should always declare the `ScriptManager` server control on the child pages, which is not the case; it all depends on the specifics of your application. The downside of declaring the `ScriptManager` server control on child pages is that you must now disable partial page rendering for every single child page if you need to disable partial page rendering for all child pages of a given parent page.

❑ `SupportsPartialRendering`: Gets or sets a Boolean value that specifies whether the browser supports partial rendering. If you explicitly set the value of this property, the `ScriptManager` sets an internal flag named `_supportPartialRenderingSetByUser` to signal to the `OnInit` method of the current server-side `PageRequestManager` instance that it does not need to determine whether the browser indeed supports partial rendering because the user (you) has explicitly set the value of this property.

The same argument presented before regarding the effects of setting the value of the `EnablePartialRendering` property in parent/child page scenarios also applies to the `SupportsPartialRendering` property.

Now let's walk through Listing 21-3. As you can see, if partial rendering is enabled but the value of the `SupportsPartialRendering` property of the `ScriptManager` object has not been explicitly set, the `OnInit` method of the `PageRequestManager` object takes the following steps to set the value of the `SupportsPartialRendering` property. First, it accesses the `HttpBrowserCapabilities` object that contains the complete information about the requesting browser's capabilities:

```
HttpBrowserCapabilities capabilities1 = this._owner.Page.Request.Browser;
```

The ASP.NET framework uses the browser files to determine the capabilities of the requesting browser and caches this information in an instance of the `HttpBrowserCapabilities` class, which is then assigned to the `Browser` property of the ASP.NET `Request` object. The browser files are files with extension `.browser`, which are located in the standard directory on your machine. Each browser file normally describes the capabilities of a particular type of browser. For example, `ie.browser` describes capabilities of the IE browser. As you can see, the information stored in the `Browser` property of the ASP.NET `Request` object comes from an offline database on your machine. The ASP.NET framework enables you to extend the existing browser files by introducing one of your own:

```
%WinDir%\Microsoft.NET\Framework\v2.0.50727\CONFIG\Browsers
```

Next, `OnInit` checks whether the requesting browser supports version 1.0 of W3C DOM and `EcmaScript` and the client callbacks:

```
this._owner.SupportsPartialRendering =
                    (capabilities1.W3CDomVersion >= new Version(1, 0)) &&
                    (capabilities1.EcmaScriptVersion >= new Version(1, 0)) &&
                    capabilities1.SupportsCallback;
```

As I mentioned earlier, you can explicitly set the value of the `SupportsPartialRendering` property to instruct the current server-side `PageRequestManager` instance to bypass this check. This is a *great option when you know for a fact that the browsers that your clients use to access your application support (or do not support) partial page rendering.*

If the current request is an asynchronous page postback or partial rendering request, the `OnInit` method of the current server-side `PageRequestManager` instance registers its `OnPageError` method as an event handler for the `Error` event of the current `Page` object. This does not apply to the first request to the page because the first request is not an asynchronous page postback.

```
if (this._owner.IsInAsyncPostBack)
   this._owner.Page.Error += new EventHandler(this.OnPageError);
```

Recall that the second dashed line from the left in Figure 21-3 represents the method calls triggered by the call into the `OnInit` method of the current `ScriptManager` server control. As you saw in this section, this call triggers a call into the `OnInit` method of the current server-side `PageRequestManager` instance. Figure 21-4 extends Figure 21-3 to add this method call. Note that Figure 21-4 still contains the first dashed line, which represents the method calls triggered by the call into the `OnInit` method of the `UpdatePanel` server control. I'll discuss these methods in the following section.

At this point, we'll digress from our main discussions to cover two related topics in the following two subsections.

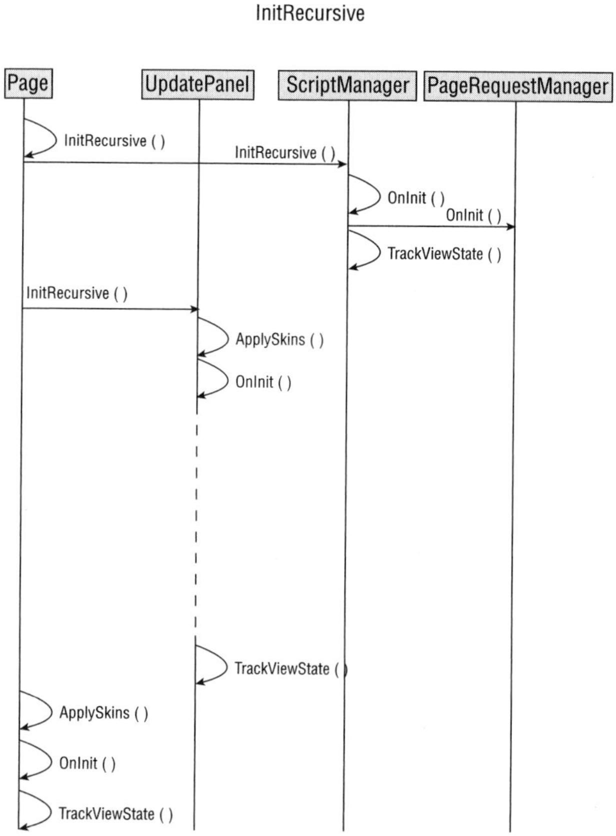

Figure 21-4

Handling the Error Event

As I mentioned earlier, errors that occur during the first request to a Web page enabled for partial page rendering are handled through normal ASP.NET error-handling practices. (Complete coverage of these practices is beyond the scope of this book.) For example, one typical practice is to define a page-level event handler such as the following:

```
protected void Page_Error (object sender, EventArgs e)
{
  Exception error = Server.GetLastError();
  if (error is ArgumentException)
    Server.Transfer("ArgumentException.aspx");
  else if (error is ArgumentOutOfRangeException)
    Server.Transfer("ArgumentOutOfRangeException.aspx");
  //. . .
  Server.ClearError();
}
```

Such an event handler begins by invoking the GetLastError static method on the ASP.NET Server object to return a reference to the last unhandled Exception object:

```
Exception error = Server.GetLastError();
```

Next, it determines the type of the Exception object and redirects the request to the Web page that displays more information about the specified type of error. Note that such redirects are normally done on the server side and does not involve a round trip to the client. Finally, the event handler invokes the ClearError static method on the Server object to remove the Exception object.

Instead of writing an event handler named Page_Error, you could register an event handler for the Error event of the current Page object. However, as you can see from Listing 21-3, such registration must be done in the Init life cycle phase of the current Page to ensure that your event handler does not miss any errors. Here is an example:

```
<%@ Page Language="C#" %>
<script runat="server">
  void MyErrorHandler(object sender, EventArgs e)
  {
    Exception error = Server.GetLastError();
    if (error is ArgumentException)
      Server.Transfer("ArgumentException.aspx");
    else if (error is ArgumentOutOfRangeException)
      Server.Transfer("ArgumentOutOfRangeException.aspx");
    //. . .
    Server.ClearError();
  }

  protected override void OnInit(EventArgs e)
  {
    base.OnInit(e);
    this.Error += new EventHandler(MyErrorHandler);
  }
</script>
```

```
<html xmlns="http://www.w3.org/1999/xhtml">
<head runat="server">
  <title>Untitled Page</title>
</head>
<body>
  <form id="form1" runat="server">
    . . .
  </form>
</body>
</html>
```

As you can see from Listing 21-3, the OnInit method of the current server-side PageRequestManager instance registers a method named OnPageError as an event handler for the Error event of the current Page when an asynchronous page postback request is made to a Web page enabled for partial page rendering. I'll discuss the OnPageError method later because the first request to a partial-page-rendering-enabled Web page is not an asynchronous page postback.

Handling the Init Event

As you saw in Listing 21-2, the current ScriptManager server control invokes the OnInit method of its base class to raise the Init event and consequently invoke the event handlers registered for this event. If you need to run some custom code when the current ScriptManger server control raises its Init event, you have two options. If your custom code is something that you think a lot of your clients might be interested in, and is not specific to a particular application, you can write a custom server control that derives from the ScriptManager server control and overrides its OnInit method to include this custom code. Here is an example:

```
public class MyScriptManager : ScriptManager
{
  protected override void OnInit(EventArgs e)
  {
    base.OnInit(e);
    // Your custom code should go here
  }
}
```

It's very important that your custom server control's implementation of the OnInit method invoke the OnInit method of its base class — that is, the ScriptManager server control. Otherwise none of the following code will run and consequently the ASP.NET AJAX partial rendering will not work:

```
this.Page.Items[typeof(ScriptManager)] = this;
this.Page.PreRenderComplete += new EventHandler(this.OnPagePreRenderComplete);
if (this.Page.IsPostBack)
  this._isInAsyncPostBack =
        PageRequestManager.IsAsyncPostBackRequest(this.Page.Request.Headers);
this.PageRequestManager.OnInit();
```

If your custom code is specific to a particular application, you need to wrap the code in a method and register the method as the event handler for the `Init` method of the current `ScriptManager` server control instead of writing a custom server control. Here is an example:

```
<%@ Page Language="C#" %>
<script runat="server">
  void MethodContainingYourCustomCode(object sender, EventArgs e)
  {
    // Your custom code should go here
  }
</script>
<html xmlns="http://www.w3.org/1999/xhtml">
<head runat="server">
  <title>Untitled Page</title>
</head>
<body>
  <form id="form1" runat="server">
  <asp:ScriptManager runat="server" ID="ScriptManager1"
   OnInit="MethodContainingYourCustomCode" />
    . . .
  </form>
</body>
</html>
```

The OnInit Method of UpdatePanel

Keep in mind that we're following the `Page` object as it goes through its life cycle phases to process the first request made to a Web page enabled for partial page rendering. As you follow the `Page` object, keep in mind where you are at every moment of the journey. Currently we're at the `Init` life cycle phase where the `OnInit` methods of the `ScriptManager` and `UpdatePanel` server controls are invoked. (I covered the `OnInit` method of the `ScriptManager` server control in the previous section.) In this section I'll discuss the `OnInit` method of the `UpdatePanel` server control. Listing 21-4 presents the internal implementation of this method.

Listing 21-4: The OnInit Method of the UpdatePanel Control

```
protected override void OnInit(EventArgs e)
{
  base.OnInit(e);
  this.RegisterPanel();
  this.CreateContents(base.DesignMode);
}
```

As you can see, the `OnInit` method calls the `RegisterPanel` and `CreateContents` methods of the `UpdatePanel` server control. I'll discuss these methods in the following sections.

Recall that the dashed line in Figure 21-4 represents the method calls triggered by the call into the `OnInit` method of the `UpdatePanel` server control. As you saw in this section, these triggered method calls are the calls into the `RegisterPanel` and `CreateContents` methods of the `UpdatePanel` server control. Figure 21-5 extends Figure 21-4 to add these two method calls. Note that Figure 21-5 now contains two dashed lines, which represent the method calls triggered by the calls into the RegisterPanel and CreateContents methods. I'll discuss these two methods in the following sections.

I'll wrap up the this section with the following note on handling the Init event of UpdatePanel server controls.

InitRecursive

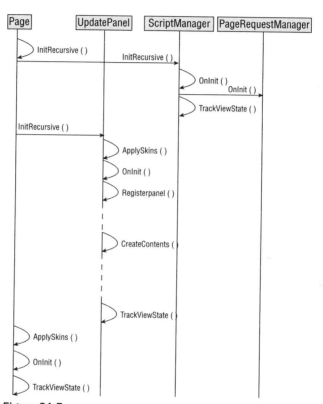

Figure 21-5

As you saw in Listing 21-4, the UpdatePanel server control invokes the OnInit method of its base class to raise the Init event and consequently invoke the event handlers registered for this event. If you need to run some custom code when a specific UpdatePanel server control on the current page raises its Init event, you have two options. If your custom code is something that you think a lot of your clients might be interested in and is not specific to a particular application, you can write a custom server control that derives from the UpdatePanel server control and overrides its OnInit method to include this custom code. Here is an example:

```
public class MyUpdatePanel : UpdatePanel
{
  protected override void OnInit(EventArgs e)
  {
    base.OnInit(e);
    // Your custom code should go here
  }
}
```

It's very important that your custom server control's implementation of the OnInit method invoke the OnInit method of its base class — that is, the UpdatePanel server control. Otherwise none of the following code will run and consequently the ASP.NET AJAX partial rendering will not work:

```
base.OnInit(e);
this.RegisterPanel();
this.CreateContents(base.DesignMode);
```

If your custom code is specific to a particular application, you need to wrap the code in a method and register the method as the event handler for the Init method of the desired UpdatePanel server control instead of writing a custom server control. Here is an example:

```
<%@ Page Language="C#" %>
<script runat="server">
  void MethodContainingYourCustomCode(object sender, EventArgs e)
  {
    // Your custom code should go here
  }
</script>
<html xmlns="http://www.w3.org/1999/xhtml">
<head runat="server">
  <title>Untitled Page</title>
</head>
<body>
  <form id="form1" runat="server">
    . . .
    <asp:UpdatePanel runat="server" ID="UpdatePanel1"
    OnInit="MethodContainingYourCustomCode">
    . . .
    </asp:UpdatePanel>
    . . .
  </form>
</body>
</html>
```

The RegisterPanel Method of the UpdatePanel

Listing 21-5 contains the code for the RegisterPanel method, which calls the RegisterUpdatePanel method on the current ScriptManager server control to register the UpdatePanel control with the current ScriptManager control. Note that the RegisterPanel method first determines whether the UpdatePanel control is contained in another UpdatePanel control. If so, it calls the RegisterPanel method of the container UpdatePanel control before calling the RegisterUpdatePanel method to register the current UpdatePanel. This has two consequences:

❑ The container UpdatePanel control of an UpdatePanel control is registered before the UpdatePanel control itself. You'll see shortly what this registration entails.

❑ When the RegisterPanel method of an UpdatePanel control returns, you can rest assured that its container UpdatePanel control, the container UpdatePanel control of its container UpdatePanel control, the container UpdatePanel control of the container UpdatePanel control of its container UpdatePanel control, and so on are all registered with the current ScriptManager server control.

Note that the RegisterPanel method finally sets the _panelRegistered Boolean field to true to mark the completion of the registration process:

```
this._panelRegistered = true;
```

Listing 21-5: The RegisterPanel Method

```
private void RegisterPanel()
{
  if (!this._panelRegistered)
  {
    for (Control control1 = this.Parent; control1 != null;
        control1 = control1.Parent)
    {
      UpdatePanel panel1 = control1 as UpdatePanel;
      if (panel1 != null)
      {
        panel1.RegisterPanel();
        break;
      }
    }
    this.ScriptManager.RegisterUpdatePanel(this);
    this._panelRegistered = true;
  }
}
```

The RegisterUpdatePanel Method of the ScriptManager

Next, I'll show you the implementation of the RegisterUpdatePanel method of the ScriptManager class. As you can see from Listing 21-6, this method delegates the responsibility of registering the specified UpdatePanel control to the RegisterUpdatePanel method of the current server-side PageRequestManager instance.

Listing 21-6: The RegisterUpdatePanel Method of ScriptManager

```
void IScriptManagerInternal.RegisterUpdatePanel(UpdatePanel updatePanel)
{
  this.PageRequestManager.RegisterUpdatePanel(updatePanel);
}
```

The RegisterUpdatePanel Method of the PageRequestManager

The current server-side `PageRequestManager` instance maintains all `UpdatePanel` server controls on the current page in an internal collection named `_allUpdatePanels`. As Listing 21-7 shows, the `RegisterUpdatePanel` method of the `PageRequestManager` simply adds the specified `UpdatePanel` control to this collection.

Listing 21-7: The RegisterUpdatePanel Method of the PageRequestManager

```
internal void RegisterUpdatePanel(UpdatePanel updatePanel)
{
  if (this._allUpdatePanels == null)
    this._allUpdatePanels = new List<UpdatePanel>();

  this._allUpdatePanels.Add(updatePanel);
}
```

Now let's update Figure 21-5 with the latest method calls. Recall that the top dashed line in Figure 21-5 represents the method calls triggered by the call into the `RegisterPanel` method of the `UpdatePanel` server control. As we discussed earlier, the `RegisterPanel` method triggers the call into the `RegisterUpdatePanel` method of the current `ScriptManager` server control, which in turn triggers the call into the `RegisterUpdatePanel` method of the current server-side `PageRequestManager` instance, which in turn triggers the call into the `Add` method of the `_allUpdatePanels` collection to add the `UpdatePanel` server control to this collection. Figure 21-6 extends Figure 21-5 to add the latest triggered method calls.

Note that Figure 21-6 inherits the bottom dashed line from Figure 21-5, and remember that this dashed line represents the method calls triggered by the call into the `CreateContents` method of the `UpdatePanel` server control. These method calls will also be discussed in the following section.

The CreateContents Method of the UpdatePanel

Recall from Listing 21-4 that the `OnInit` method of the `UpdatePanel` calls the `CreateContents` method, and Listing 21-8 presents its internal implementation. This method takes a Boolean parameter that specifies whether the contents of the `UpdatePanel` must be recreated from scratch. If so, the method first clears the `Controls` collection of the content template container server control:

```
this.ContentTemplateContainer.Controls.Clear();
```

As Listing 21-8 shows, the `CreateControl` method first checks whether it is asked to recreate the content of the `UpdatePanel` from scratch. If so, it takes the following steps. First, it clears the `Controls` collection of the template container server control. This collection contains the server controls that represent the markup text enclosed within the opening and closing tags of the `<ContentTemplate>` child element that represents the `ContentTemplate` property on the `.aspx` page.

```
this.ContentTemplateContainer.Controls.Clear();
```

As I mentioned in the previous chapter, you can access the `ContentTemplateContainer` property of an `UpdatePanel` server control from within your C# or VB.NET code and imperatively add server controls to the `Controls` collection of the content template container server control from right within your code.

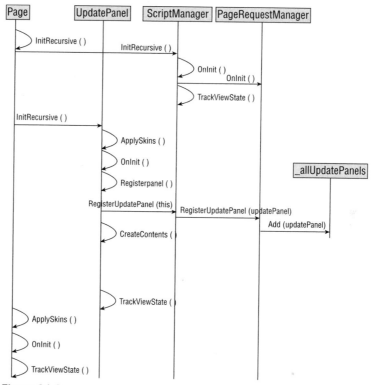

Figure 21-6

Next, the `CreateContents` method calls the `CreateContentTemplateContainer` method to create the template container server control that will act as the container for the server controls that represent the markup text enclosed within the opening and closing tags of the `<ContentTemplate>` child element:

```
this._contentTemplateContainer = this.CreateContentTemplateContainer();
```

Then the `CreateContents` method calls the `InstantiateIn` method on the `ContentTemplate` property, passing in the template container server control. Keep in mind that ASP.NET has already parsed the markup text enclosed within the opening and closing tags of the `<ContentTemplate>` child element into a class, compiled this class, and assigned an instance of it to the `ContentTemplate` property. This means that when the `CreateContents` method calls the `InstantiateIn` method on the `ContentTemplate` property, it actually calls the `InstantiateIn` method of this class instance. As discussed earlier, this method adds the server controls that represent the markup text enclosed within the opening and closing tags of the `<ContentTemplate>` child element to the `Controls` collection of the template container server control:

```
this._contentTemplate.InstantiateIn(this._contentTemplateContainer);
```

Next, the `CreateContents` method calls the `AddContentTemplateContainer` method to add the template container server control to the `Controls` collection of the `UpdatePanel` control:

```
        this.AddContentTemplateContainer();
```

Listing 21-8: The CreateContents Method of the UpdatePanel

```
    private void CreateContents(bool recreate)
    {
      if (recreate)
      {
        this.ContentTemplateContainer.Controls.Clear();
        this._contentTemplateContainer = null;
        this.ChildControls.ClearInternal();
      }
      if (this._contentTemplateContainer == null)
      {
        this._contentTemplateContainer = this.CreateContentTemplateContainer();
        this._contentTemplate.InstantiateIn(this._contentTemplateContainer);
        this.AddContentTemplateContainer();
      }
    }
```

The following code listing contains the implementation of the `CreateContentTemplateContainer` method of the `UpdatePanel` control. As you can see, the `UpdatePanel` uses an instance of the `Control` base class as the template container server control.

```
    protected virtual Control CreateContentTemplateContainer()
    {
      return new Control();
    }
```

Now let's update Figure 21-6 with the latest method calls. Recall that the dashed line in Figure 21-6 represents the method calls triggered by the call into the `CreateContents` method of the `UpdatePanel`, and that this method triggers the call into the `CreateContentTemplateContainer` and `AddContentTemplateContainer` methods of the `UpdatePanel`, as well as the `InstantiateIn` method of the `ITemplate` interface. Figure 21-7 extends Figure 21-6 to add these three latest triggered method calls. This wraps up our discussions of the `Init` life cycle phase of the current `Page`.

At this point, we digress from our main discussions to cover the related topic of templated controls in the following subsection.

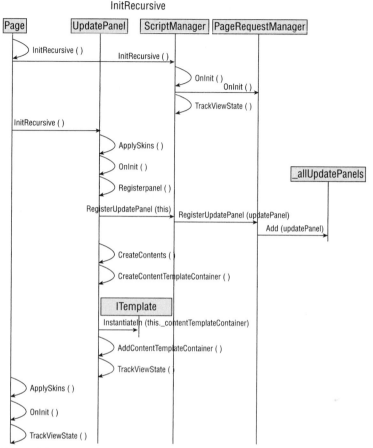

Figure 21-7

Templated Controls

The UpdatePanel is a templated control that exposes a template property named ContentTemplate. The ContentTemplate property, just like any other template property, is of type ITemplate, and as such it exposes a method named InstantiateIn. This method takes a server control known as a *template container* as its argument.

The great thing about a template property is that you can specify its value declaratively on an .ascx or .aspx page without writing a single line of imperative code such as C# or VB.NET. This declarative value is the markup, including HTML and server controls, that you place within the opening and closing tags of the element that represents the template property on an .ascx or .aspx page. In the case of the UpdatePanel, this declarative value is the markup that you place between the opening and closing tags of the <ContentTemplate> child element of the UpdatePanel, because this child element represents the ContentTemplate property on the .ascx or .aspx page.

ASP.NET automatically parses the markup enclosed within the opening and closing tags of the <ContentTemplate> child element and dynamically generates an instance of a class named CompiledTemplateBuilder that implements the ITemplate interface, which means that this class implements the InstantiateIn method of the interface. This class's implementation of this method adds the server controls that represent the markup enclosed within the opening and closing tags of the <ContentTemplate> child element to the Controls collection of the server control passed into the InstantiateIn method. As mentioned earlier, this server control is known as the template container. As you can see, the template container server control acts as a container for the server controls that represent the markup enclosed within the opening and closing tags of the <ContentTemplate> child element. ASP.NET then assigns this CompiledTemplateBuilder instance to the ContentTemplate property of the UpdatePanel.

As discussed earlier, ASP.NET dynamically generates a class that inherits from the Page class to represent the current page, and stores the source file for this class a couple of directories underneath the directory associated with your Web application under the following standard directory on your machine:

```
%windir%\Microsoft.NET\Framework\v2.0.50727\Temporary ASP.NET Files
```

If you're curious to see the these principles in action, create a Web application that contains a page named default.aspx, as shown in the following code listing. In my case this application is named AjaxEnabledWebSite11.:

```
<%@ Page Language="C#" %>
<script runat="server">
  void SubmitCallback(object sender, EventArgs e)
  {
    Info.Text = TextBox1.Text;
  }
</script>
<html xmlns="http://www.w3.org/1999/xhtml">
<body>
  <form id="form1" runat="server">
    <asp:ScriptManager ID="ScriptManager1" runat="server" />
    <asp:UpdatePanel runat="server" ID="UpdatePanel1">
      <ContentTemplate>
        Enter text:
        <asp:TextBox runat="server" ID="TextBox1" />
        <asp:Button runat="server" ID="Button1" Text="Submit"
        OnClick="SubmitCallback" /><br />
        <asp:Label runat="server" ID="Info" />
      </ContentTemplate>
    </asp:UpdatePanel>
  </form>
</body>
</html>
```

If you go to a couple of directories (these two directories have weird-looking names because the ASP.NET framework uses auto-generated hash values to create these names) underneath the directory named ajaxenabledwebsite11 (which is nothing but the name of the application) underneath the standard directory Temporary ASP.NET Files, and open the file that contains the source code for the dynamically generated class that represents the preceding page, as discussed earlier in this chapter, you'll see the following code. The boldface portion of this code listing shows how ASP.NET manages to initialize the value of the ContentTemplate property of the UpdatePanel server control.

```
namespace ASP
{
  public class default_aspx : Page
  {
    protected ScriptManager ScriptManager1;
    protected TextBox TextBox1;
    protected Button Button1;
    protected Label Info;
    protected UpdatePanel UpdatePanel1;
    protected HtmlForm form1;
    . . .
    private UpdatePanel @__BuildControlUpdatePanel1()
    {
      UpdatePanel @__ctrl = new UpdatePanel();
      this.UpdatePanel1 = @__ctrl;
      BuildTemplateMethod templateMethod =
                          new BuildTemplateMethod(this.@__BuildControl__control4);
      @__ctrl.ContentTemplate = new CompiledTemplateBuilder(templateMethod);
      @__ctrl.ID = "UpdatePanel1";
      return @__ctrl;
    }
    . . .
  }
}
```

Interestingly enough, the CompiledTemplateBuilder class is a public class, which means that you can use it within your own C# or VB.NET code. As we discussed in the previous chapter, if you need to imperatively add server controls to an UpdatePanel server control, you must add these server controls to the Controls collection of the ContentTemplateContainer property of the UpdatePanel server control.

You can use the CompiledTemplateBuilder class to enhance the functionality of the ASP.NET UpdatePanel server control to add support for default templates. The following code listing shows the implementation of such a custom UpdatePanel server control. To understand the implementation of this custom server control, you first need to understand how the CompiledTemplateBuilder class works. The constructor of this class takes an instance of a .NET delegate named BuildTemplateMethod, which represents a method that takes a single argument of type Control and returns no value. It is the responsibility of this method to populate the Controls collection of the Control passed into it with the appropriate server controls. As you'll see shortly, these server controls will constitute the content of the custom UpdatePanel server control.

Now back to the implementation of the CustomUpdatePanel server control. As you can see from the following code listing, the CustomUpdatePanel server control exposes two public properties named BuildTemplateMethodProviderType and BuildTemplateMethodProviderMethod. The BuildTemplateMethodProviderType property specifies the assembly-qualified name of a .NET type. The assembly-qualified name of a .NET type consists of five parts, which includes the fully qualified name of the type (including its complete namespace containment hierarchy) and the name, version, culture, and public key token of the assembly where the type resides. The

`BuildTemplateMethodProviderMethod` property specifies the name of the method of this .NET type that takes no arguments and returns an instance of the `BuildTemplateMethod` delegate.

Next, I'll walk you through the implementation of the `OnInit` method of the `CustomUpdatePanel` server control, where all the action is. This method begins by checking whether the values of the `BuildTemplateMethodProviderType` and `BuildTemplateMethodProviderMethod` properties are set. If not, the method simply invokes the `OnInit` method on its base class — that is, the `UpdatePanel` server control. If so, it performs the following tasks. First, it extracts the fully qualified name of the specified .NET type, excluding the assembly information, from the `BuildTemplateMethodProviderType` property:

```
string typeName = BuildTemplateMethodProviderType.Trim().Split(
                                     new char[] { ',' })[0];
```

Next, it extracts the assembly information for the `BuildTemplateMethodProviderType` property:

```
string assemblyName = BuildTemplateMethodProviderType.Trim().Remove(
                BuildTemplateMethodProviderType.IndexOf(typeName),
                typeName.Length);
```

Then, if the `BuildTemplateMethodProviderType` property does not contain the assembly information, the `CustomUpdatePanel` server control assumes that the specified .NET type resides in the executing assembly, and consequently invokes the `GetExecutingAssembly` static method on the `Assembly` class to return a reference to the `Assembly` object that represents the executing assembly:

```
Assembly assembly;
if (string.IsNullOrEmpty(assemblyName))
  assembly = Assembly.GetExecutingAssembly();
```

If the `BuildTemplateMethodProviderType` property does contain the assembly information, it invokes the `Load` static method on the `Assembly` class to load the specified assembly into the current application domain and to return a reference to the `Assembly` object that represents this assembly:

```
else
{
  assemblyName = assemblyName.Trim().Remove(0, 1);
  assembly = Assembly.Load(assemblyName);
}
```

Next, the `OnInit` method invokes the `CreateInstance` method on the `Assembly` object, passing in the fully qualified name of the specified .NET type to instantiate an instance of this .NET type:

```
object provider = assembly.CreateInstance(typeName);
```

Then it invokes the `GetType` method on the newly-created instance to return a reference to the `Type` object that represents the type of this instance:

```
Type type = provider.GetType();
```

Next, it invokes the GetMethod on this Type object, passing in the value of the BuildTemplateMethodProviderMethod property to return a reference to the MethodInfo object that represents the specified method of the specified .NET type. Recall that this is the method that returns the BuildTemplateMethod delegate that you must pass into the CompiledTemplateBuilder constructor:

```
MethodInfo methodInfo =
                type.GetMethod(BuildTemplateMethodProviderMethod);
```

Then it calls the Invoke method on the MethodInfo object to dynamically invoke the specified method on the newly created instance and consequently to return the BuildTemplateMethod delegate that you need:

```
BuildTemplateMethod method =
                (BuildTemplateMethod)methodInfo.Invoke(provider, null);
```

Next, the OnInit method passes the BuildTemplateMethod instance into the CompiledTemplateBuilder constructor to instantiate a CompiledTemplateBuilder object, which is subsequently assigned to the ContentTemplate property that the CustomUpdatePanel server control inherits from the UpdatePanel server control:

```
ContentTemplate = new CompiledTemplateBuilder(method);
```

Finally, it invokes the OnInit method of its base class — that is, the UpdatePanel server control. This step is very important because, as thoroughly discussed earlier, the OnInit method of the UpdatePanel server control is the method that actually calls the InstantiateIn method on the ContentTemplate property to create the content of the UpdatePanel control. Nothing will take effect if this last step is not taken.

Listing 21-9: The CustomUpdatePanel Server Control

```csharp
using System;
using System.Web;
using System.Web.UI;
using System.Web.UI.WebControls;
using System.Reflection;
namespace CustomComponents5
{
  public class CustomUpdatePanel : UpdatePanel
  {
    public string BuildTemplateMethodProviderType
    {
      get
      {
        return ViewState["BuildTemplateMethodProviderType"] != null ?
          (string)ViewState["BuildTemplateMethodProviderType"] : string.Empty;
      }
      set
      {
        ViewState["BuildTemplateMethodProviderType"] = value;
      }
    }
```

(continued)

Listing 21-9 *(continued)*

```
    public string BuildTemplateMethodProviderMethod
    {
      get
      {
        return ViewState["BuildTemplateMethodProviderMethod"] != null ?
        (string)ViewState["BuildTemplateMethodProviderMethod"] : string.Empty;
      }
      set
      {
        ViewState["BuildTemplateMethodProviderMethod"] = value;
      }
    }
    protected override void OnInit(EventArgs e)
    {
      if (!string.IsNullOrEmpty(BuildTemplateMethodProviderType) &&
          !string.IsNullOrEmpty(BuildTemplateMethodProviderMethod))
      {
        string typeName = BuildTemplateMethodProviderType.Trim().Split(
                                             new char[] { ',' })[0];
        string assemblyName = BuildTemplateMethodProviderType.Trim().Remove(
                        BuildTemplateMethodProviderType.IndexOf(typeName),
                        typeName.Length);
        Assembly assembly;
        if (string.IsNullOrEmpty(assemblyName))
          assembly = Assembly.GetExecutingAssembly();
        else
        {
          assemblyName = assemblyName.Trim().Remove(0, 1);
          assembly = Assembly.Load(assemblyName);
        }
        object provider = assembly.CreateInstance(typeName);
        Type type = provider.GetType();
        MethodInfo methodInfo =
                          type.GetMethod(BuildTemplateMethodProviderMethod);
        BuildTemplateMethod method =
                    (BuildTemplateMethod)methodInfo.Invoke(provider, null);
        ContentTemplate = new CompiledTemplateBuilder(method);
      }
      base.OnInit(e);
    }
  }
}
```

Listing 21-10 contains an example of a .NET type that supports a method that returns a
`BuildTemplateMethod` delegate. This code listing shows a class named
`BuildTemplateMethodProvider` that exposes a method named `GetBuildTemplateMethod` that
instantiates and returns an instance of the `BuildTemplateMethod` delegate. Note that this method
passes another method named `BuildTemplate` as an argument into the constructor of
the `BuildTemplateMethod` delegate. When the `CompiledTemplateBuilder` invokes the
`BuildTemplateMethod` delegate, this delegate in turn invokes the method passed into its constructor,
which is the `BuildTemplate` method in this case. Note that the method passed into this constructor must
take a single argument of type `Control` and return no value.

The `BuildTemplate` method is where the `BuildTemplateMethodProvider` class builds the server controls that go into the `UpdatePanel` server control. The method can be as complex as you want it to be and can build any type of server controls that you want to put in. In this simple example, the `BuildTemplate` method first creates a `Label` control, sets its `Text` property value to the current date and time, and adds the `Label` control to the `Controls` collection of the `Control` passed into it. Since the `CompiledTemplateBuilder` passes the `ContentTemplateContainer` of the `UpdatePanel` server control as the argument of the `BuildTemplate` method, any server control you add to the `Controls` collection of this control goes right into the `UpdatePanel` server control.

```
label1 = new Label();
label1.Text = DateTime.Now.ToString();
c.Controls.Add(label1);
```

The `BuildTemplate` method then creates a `Button` control, registers a method named `Button1_Click` as an event handler for its `Click` event, and adds the `Button` to the `Controls` collection of the `Control` passed into it:

```
Button button1 = new Button();
button1.Text = "Update";
button1.Click += new EventHandler(Button1_Click);
c.Controls.Add(button1);
```

The `Button1_Click` method doesn't do much in this case. It simply displays the current date and time in the `Label` control.

21-10: An Example of a .NET Type that Supports a Method that Returns a BuildTemplateMethod Delegate

```
using System;
using System.Web;
using System.Web.UI;
using System.Web.UI.WebControls;
using System.Reflection;
namespace CustomComponents5
{
  public class BuildTemplateMethodProvider
  {
    Label label1;
    public void BuildTemplate(Control c)
    {
      label1 = new Label();
      label1.Text = DateTime.Now.ToString();
      c.Controls.Add(label1);
      Button button1 = new Button();
      button1.Text = "Update";
      button1.Click += new EventHandler(Button1_Click);
      c.Controls.Add(button1);
    }
```

(continued)

21-10 *(continued)*

```
      void Button1_Click(object sender, EventArgs e)
      {
        label1.Text = DateTime.Now.ToString();
      }
      public BuildTemplateMethod GetBuildTemplateMethod()
      {
        return new BuildTemplateMethod(BuildTemplate);
      }
    }
  }
```

The following code listing contains a page that uses the `CustomUpdatePanel` server control:

```
<%@ Page Language="C#" %>
<%@ Register Namespace="CustomComponents5" TagPrefix="custom" %>
<script runat="server">
  void Page_Load(object sender, EventArgs e)
  {
    Info.Text = DateTime.Now.ToString();
  }
</script>
<html xmlns="http://www.w3.org/1999/xhtml">
<head runat="server">
  <title>Untitled Page</title>
</head>
<body>
  <form id="form1" runat="server">
  <asp:ScriptManager runat="server" ID="ScriptManager1" />

  <custom:CustomUpdatePanel runat="server" ID="CustomUpatePanel1"
    BuildTemplateMethodProviderType="CustomComponents5.BuildTemplateMethodProvider"
    BuildTemplateMethodProviderMethod="GetBuildTemplateMethod"/>
  <br />
  <asp:Label runat="server" ID="Info" />
  </form>
</body>
</html>
```

The official ASP.NET 2.0 documentation from Microsoft makes the following statement about the `CompiledTemplateBuilder` class:

This class supports the .NET Framework infrastructure and is not intended to be used directly from your code.

That said, there is nothing technically wrong with directly using this class from your code. Another important point is that as you've seen in the preceding examples, this class makes a great educational tool for learning about the `UpdatePanel` server control, which is one of our main goals in this chapter.

LoadRecursive

Keep in mind, again, that you're following the current Page object as it goes through its life cycle phases to process the first HTTP GET request made to a Web page enabled for partial page rendering. Since the first request is not a postback, the current Page skips all the postback-related life cycle phases and enters directly into its LoadRecusive (or Load) life cycle phase, in which the ProcessRequest method of the current Page (see Listing 21-1) invokes the LoadRecursive method on the current Page. The following code listing presents the internal implementation of the LoadRecursive method. All server controls, including the Page, ScriptManager, and UpdatePanel, inherit the LoadRecursive method from the Control base class. As the following code listing shows, the LoadRecursive method of a server control such as Page or UpdatePanel first calls its own OnLoad method and then calls the LoadRecursive methods of its child server controls.

```
internal virtual void LoadRecursive()
{
  this.OnLoad(EventArgs.Empty);
  foreach (Control control in this.Controls)
  {
    control.LoadRecursive();
  }
}
```

Therefore, the following sequence of method calls occurs when the current Page enters its LoadRecusive phase:

1. The call into the LoadRecusive method of the current Page
2. The call into the OnLoad method of the current Page
3. The call into the LoadRecusive method of the ScriptManager
4. The call into the OnLoad method of the ScriptManager
5. The call into the LoadRecusive method of the UpdatePanel
6. The call into the OnLoad method of the UpdatePanel

The OnLoad methods of the current Page and the current ScriptManager server control simply raise the Load event.

If you need to execute some application-specific logic when the current ScriptManager server control or a particular UpdatePanel server control enters its Load life cycle phase, you must encapsulate this logic in a method and register this method as an event handler for the Load event of the current ScriptManager server control or the specified UpdatePanel server control.

If you want the ScriptManager server control to do more work than just raising the Load event, you can write your own custom ScriptManager server control that inherits from the ScriptManager server control and overrides its OnLoad method to do whatever else you need the control to do when it enters its Load life cycle phase. Make sure your custom ScriptManager server control's implementation of the OnLoad method calls the OnLoad method of its base class. Otherwise your custom ScriptManager server control will not raise the Load event when it enters its Load life cycle phase.

Listing 21-11 presents the internal implementation of the OnLoad method of the UpdatePanel server control. As you can see, this method checks whether the current request is an asynchronous page postback. If not, it calls the Initialize method of the UpdatePanel to initialize it. Keep in mind that the current Page is processing the first request to a Web page enabled for partial page rendering. Since the first request is not a postback, the OnLoad method of the UpdatePanel server control calls its Initialize method, which will be discussed in the following section.

Implement a custom UpdatePanel server control that overrides the OnLoad method if you want the UpdatePanel server control to do more work than just raising the Load event and invoking the Initialize method.

Listing 21-11: The OnLoad Method of the UpdatePanel

```
protected override void OnLoad(EventArgs e)
{
    base.OnLoad(e);
    if (!this.ScriptManager.IsInAsyncPostBack)
        this.Initialize();
}
```

Figure 21-8 presents a diagram that contains the method calls that occur when the current Page enters the LoadRecusive life cycle phase:

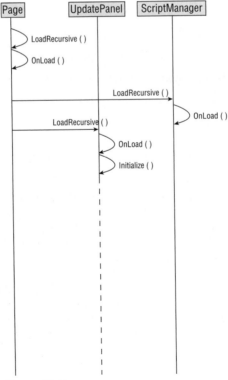

Figure 21-8

As mentioned earlier, the current `ScriptManager` server control's `OnLoad` method simply raises the `Load` event and consequently invokes the event handlers registered for this event. If you need to run some custom code when the current `ScriptManger` server control raises its `Load` event, you have two options. If your custom code is something that you think a lot of your clients might be interested in and is not specific to a particular application, you can write a custom server control that derives from the `ScriptManager` server control and overrides its `OnLoad` method to include this custom code. Here is an example:

```csharp
public class MyScriptManager : ScriptManager
{
  protected override void OnLoad(EventArgs e)
  {
    base.OnInit(e);
    // Your custom code should go here
  }
}
```

It's very important that your custom server control's implementation of the `OnLoad` method invoke the `OnLoad` method of its base class — that is, the `ScriptManager` server control. Otherwise the `Load` event of your custom server control will not be raised and consequently the event handlers registered for this event will not be invoked.

If your custom code is specific to a particular application, you need to wrap the code in a method and register the method as the event handler for the `Load` method of the current `ScriptManager` server control instead of writing a custom server control. Here is an example:

```aspx
<%@ Page Language="C#" %>
<script runat="server">
  void MethodContainingYourCustomCode(object sender, EventArgs e)
  {
    // Your custom code should go here
  }
</script>
<html xmlns="http://www.w3.org/1999/xhtml">
<head runat="server">
  <title>Untitled Page</title>
</head>
<body>
  <form id="form1" runat="server">
  <asp:ScriptManager runat="server" ID="ScriptManager1"
   OnLoad="MethodContainingYourCustomCode" />
    . . .
  </form>
</body>
</html>
```

As you saw in Listing 21-11, the `UpdatePanel` server control invokes the `OnLoad` method of its base class to raise the `Load` event and consequently invoke the event handlers registered for this event. If you need to run some custom code when a specific `UpdatePanel` server control on the current page raises its `Load` event, you have the same two options that you have with the `ScriptManager`, as just discussed.

The Initialize Method of the UpdatePanel

The UpdatePanel server control maintains an internal collection of type UpdatePanelTriggerCollection named _triggers that contains objects of type UpdatePanelTrigger. As the name suggests, an UpdatePanelTrigger object triggers automatic updates of its associated UpdatePanel server control. Note that an UpdatePanelTrigger object is an instance of a class, which itself is not a server control. This raises the following question: what causes an UpdatePanelTrigger object to trigger the automatic updates of its associated UpdatePanel server control? The answer is "it depends." Different types of triggers use different types of mechanisms. The UpdatePanelTrigger class is an abstract base class whose methods and properties define an API that all triggers must implement in order to act as triggers for automatic updates of their associated UpdatePanel server controls.

The UpdatePanel exposes a property of type UpdatePanelTriggerCollection named Triggers that returns a reference to the _triggers collection, as shown in Listing 21-12.

Listing 21-12: The Triggers Collection Property of the UpdatePanel

```
[DefaultValue((string)null),
PersistenceMode(PersistenceMode.InnerProperty)]
public UpdatePanelTriggerCollection Triggers
{
  get
  {
    if (this._triggers == null)
      this._triggers = new UpdatePanelTriggerCollection(this);
    return this._triggers;
  }
}
```

As Listing 21-13 shows, the Initialize method of the UpdatePanel first checks whether the _triggers collection contains any UpdatePanelTrigger objects and whether the partial rendering is supported. If both of these conditions are met, it calls the Initialize method on the _triggers collection to initialize the collection.

Listing 21-13: The Initialize Method of the UpdatePanel

```
protected internal virtual void Initialize()
{
  if ((this._triggers != null) && this.ScriptManager.SupportsPartialRendering)
    this._triggers.Initialize();
}
```

The Initialize Method of the UpdatePanelTriggerCollection

As Listing 21-14 shows, the Initialize method of the UpdatePanelTriggerCollection iterates through its constituent UpdatePanelTrigger objects and calls their Initialize methods to initialize them. Note that the Initialize method sets an internal flag named _initialized to true to mark the end of the initialization phase.

Listing 21-14: The Initialize Method of the UpdatePanelTriggerCollection

```
internal void Initialize()
{
  using (IEnumerator<UpdatePanelTrigger> enumerator1 = base.GetEnumerator())
  {
    while (enumerator1.MoveNext())
    {
      enumerator1.Current.Initialize();
    }
  }
  this._initialized = true;
}
```

Before diving into the implementation of the `Initialize` method of the `UpdatePanelTrigger` class, let's update Figure 21-8 with the latest method calls. Recall that the dashed line in Figure 21-8 represents the method calls triggered by the call into the `Initialize` method of the `UpdatePanel` server control. As mentioned earlier, the `Initialize` method triggers the call into the `Initialize` method of the `UpdatePanelTriggersCollection`, which in turn triggers the call into the `Initialize` method of the `UpdatePanelTrigger`. Figure 21-9 extends Figure 21-8 to add these two latest triggered method calls.

Note that Figure 21-9 contains a dashed line, which represents the method calls triggered by the call into the `Initialize` method of the `UpdatePanelTrigger`, which will be discussed in the following sections. I'll wrap up the discussions of this subsection with the following note on the `Initialize` method of the `UpdatePanel` server control.

As you can see from Listing 21-11, when the `UpdatePanel` server control enters its `Load` life cycle phase it automatically invokes its `Initialize` method if the current request is not an asynchronous partial-page-rendering request:

```
protected override void OnLoad(EventArgs e)
{
  base.OnLoad(e);
  if (!this.ScriptManager.IsInAsyncPostBack)
    this.Initialize();
}
```

As Listing 21-13 shows, the `Initialize` method of the `UpdatePanel` server control is marked as `protected virtual`. This means that you can write a custom server control that derives from the `UpdatePanel` server control and overrides its `Initialize` method to extend its functionality. Keep in mind that any custom code you include in the `Initialize` method will *not* be executed when the current request is an asynchronous partial page rendering. Also make sure that your custom control's implementation of the `Initialize` method invokes the `Initialize` method of its base class — that is, the `UpdatePanel` server control. Otherwise, none of the triggers registered with your custom controls will be initialized.

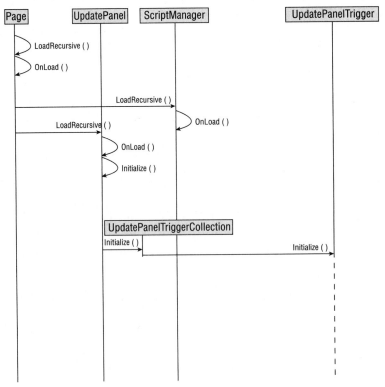

LoadRecursive

Figure 21-9

The Initialize Method of the UpdatePanelTrigger

As you can see from Listing 21-15, the `UpdatePanelTrigger` is an abstract class whose `Initialize` method does not do anything. However, the subclasses of this abstract class override this method to perform subclass-specific initialization. At this point, we digress from our main discussion to study the `UpdatePanelTrigger` and its subclasses.

Listing 21-15: The Initialize Method of the UpdatePanelTrigger

```
public abstract class UpdatePanelTrigger
{
  protected internal abstract bool HasTriggered();
  protected internal virtual void Initialize() { }
  internal void SetOwner(UpdatePanel owner)
  {
    this._owner = owner;
  }
  private UpdatePanel _owner;
}
```

UpdatePanelTrigger and its Subclasses

The methods of the `UpdatePanelTrigger` base class define the API that every `UpdatePanelTrigger` subclass must implement in order to trigger updates of its owner `UpdatePanel` server control. Keep in mind that the owner of an `UpdatePanelTrigger` object is the `UpdatePanel` server control whose `Triggers` collection contains the object.

As Listing 21-15 shows, this API consists of two methods:

❑ `Initialize`: A subclass of the `UpdatePanelTrigger` base class can override this optional method to perform any subclass-specific initialization task. You'll see an example of this later in this section.

❑ `HasTriggered`: A subclass of the `UpdatePanelTrigger` base class must override this mandatory method, where the subclass's implementation of this method must use subclass-specific logic to determine when the trigger has been triggered. You'll see an example of this later in this section.

Note that the `UpdatePanelTrigger` exposes a method named `SetOwner` that specifies an `UpdatePanel` control as the owner of the trigger. This method is marked as `internal`, which means that you can never set the owner `UpdatePanel` server control of a given `UpdatePanelTrigger` from your code. You may be wondering who calls this method. The answer is the `Add` method of the `UpdatePanelTriggerCollection`. Recall from Listing 21-12 that when the `Triggers` property of the `UpdatePanel` instantiates the `UpdatePanelTriggerCollection`, it passes a reference to the `UpdatePanel` control into the constructor of the `UpdatePanelTriggerCollection`, as shown in the highlighted portion of the following code listing:

```
[DefaultValue((string)null),
PersistenceMode(PersistenceMode.InnerProperty)]
public UpdatePanelTriggerCollection Triggers
{
  get
  {
    if (this._triggers == null)
      this._triggers = new UpdatePanelTriggerCollection(this);

    return this._triggers;
  }
}
```

Listing 21-16 presents the internal implementation of the constructor of the `UpdatePanelTriggerCollection`. As you can see, this constructor stores the reference to the owner `UpdatePanel` server control in a field named `_owner` for future reference.

Listing 21-16: The Constructor of the UpdatePanelTriggerCollection

```
public UpdatePanelTriggerCollection(UpdatePanel owner)
{
  if (owner == null)
    throw new ArgumentNullException("owner");

  this._owner = owner;
}
```

As a matter of fact, the `UpdatePanelTriggerCollection` exposes a public read-only property named `Owner` that returns the value of the `_owner` field, as shown in Listing 21-17.

Listing 21-17: The Owner Property of the UpdatePanelTriggerCollection

```
public UpdatePanel Owner
{
  get {return this._owner;}
}
```

The `UpdatePanelTriggerCollection` exposes a method named `InsertItem`, as shown in Listing 21-18. When you call the `Add` method on the `Triggers` collection of an `UpdatePanel` server control to add a new `UpdatePanelTrigger` object to the collection, the `Add` method internally calls the `InsertItem` method. As you can see from Listing 21-18, the `InsertItem` method takes these steps. First, it calls the `SetOwner` method on the `UpdatePanelTrigger` object being inserted, to set its owner `UpdatePanel` server control:

```
item.SetOwner(this.Owner);
```

Therefore, when the `Add` method is invoked on the `Triggers` collection of an `UpdatePanel` server control to add a new `UpdatePanelTrigger` object to the collection, under the hood the `Add` method automatically sets the owner of the newly added `UpdatePanelTrigger` object.

In general, there are two ways to add a new `UpdatePanelTrigger` object to the `Triggers` collection of an `UpdatePanel` server. The first approach, which is the most common, is to do it declaratively. Here is an example:

```
<asp:UpdatePanel runat="server" ID="UpdatePanel1">
  . . .
  <Triggers>
    <asp:AsyncPostBackTrigger ControlID="Button1" EventName="Click" />
  </Triggers>
</asp:UpdatePanel>
```

When you do this declaratively, the page parser automatically calls the `Add` method under the hood to add the specified trigger to the `Triggers` collection.

The second approach is to do it imperatively from your code:

```
UpdatePanel up;
AsyncPostBackTrigger trigger = new AsyncPostBackTrigger();
trigger.ControlID = "Button1";
trigger.EventName = "Click";
up.Triggers.Add(trigger);
```

As you can see, the imperative approach requires you to explicitly invoke the `Add` method on the `Triggers` collection.

Back to the implementation of the `InsertItem` method. Next, this method checks whether its `_intialized` field has been set. If so, it initializes the object by calling the `Initialize` method on the `UpdatePanelTrigger` object being inserted:

```
if (this._initialized)
   item.Initialize();
```

Recall from Listing 21-14 that the `Initialize` method of the `UpdatePanelTriggerCollection` is the one that sets the value of the `_initialized` field.

Therefore, you can add new `UpdatePanelTrigger` objects to the `Triggers` collection of a given `UpdatePanel` server control, even after the `Init` life cycle phase and rest assured that the `Initialize` method of your newly added `UpdatePanelTrigger` object will be automatically invoked. A good place for imperative addition of new `UpdatePanelTrigger` objects to the `Triggers` collection of an `UpdatePanel` server control is within the `Page_Load` method of the current page — that is, where the current `Page` enters its `Load` life cycle phase.

Listing 21-18: The Add Method of the UpdatePanelTriggerCollection

```
protected override void InsertItem(int index, UpdatePanelTrigger item)
{
  item.SetOwner(this.Owner);
  if (this._initialized)
    item.Initialize();

  base.InsertItem(index, item);
}
```

Note that the `UpdatePanelTrigger` API does not contain any reference to any server control (see Listing 21-15). This means that this API does not put a restriction on how a particular subclass of `UpdatePanelTrigger` is triggered. In other words, you could implement a subclass of the `UpdatePanelTrigger` base class that is triggered by a mechanism other than a server control.

The immediate subclass of the `UpdatePanelTrigger` abstract class is another abstract class named `UpdatePanelControlTrigger` (see Listing 21-19), which exposes a property named `ControlID` and a method named `FindTargetControl`. Every `UpdatePanelControlTrigger` trigger is associated with a server control. The user interaction with the associated server control of an `UpdatePanelControlTrigger` trigger triggers the `UpdatePanelControlTrigger`, which in turn triggers the update of its owner `UpdatePanel` server control.

The `ControlID` property of the `UpdatePanelControlTrigger` contains the `UniqueID` property value of the trigger's associated server control. As the name suggests, the `FindTargetControl` method finds and returns a reference to the associated server control of the `UpdatePanelControlTrigger` trigger.

As Listing 21-19 shows, the `FindTargetControl` method first checks whether it is asked to limit the search for the associated server control to the child controls of the `UpdatePanel` control that owns the `UpdatePanelControlTrigger` trigger. If so, the method simply calls the `FindControl` method on the owner `UpdatePanel` control to search for the associated server control. Otherwise, the method searches through all the naming containers of the `UpdatePanel` control and its ancestor controls for the associated server control.

Note that the `FindTargetControl` method is marked as `protected`. This means that only subclasses of this base class can access this method. Therefore, when you're writing your own custom subclass of the `UpdatePanelControlTrigger` class, you can call this method from within your subclass scope to return a reference to the associated server control of your subclass. Also note that the `FindTargetControl` method cannot be overridden because it is not marked as virtual. Your custom subclass must use this method as is.

Listing 21-19: The UpdatePanelControlTrigger Class

```
public abstract class UpdatePanelControlTrigger : UpdatePanelTrigger
{
  protected Control FindTargetControl(bool searchNamingContainers)
  {
    if (searchNamingContainers)
    {
      Control control2 = base.Owner;
      Control control1 = null;
      while ((control1 == null) && (control2 != base.Owner.Page))
      {
        control2 = control2.NamingContainer;
        if (control2 == null)
          return control1;

        control1 = control2.FindControl(this.ControlID);
      }
      return control1;
    }
    return base.Owner.FindControl(this.ControlID);
  }
  [DefaultValue("")]
  public string ControlID
  {
    get { return (this._controlID ?? string.Empty); }
    set { this._controlID = value; }
  }
  private string _controlID;
}
```

The ASP.NET AJAX framework comes with two subclasses of the `UpdatePanelControlTrigger` abstract base class: `PostBackTrigger` and `AsyncPostBackTrigger`. As the names suggest, these two triggers are associated with server controls that trigger synchronous and asynchronous page postbacks, respectively.

Back to the Initialize Method of UpdatePanelTrigger

Recall that we digressed from our discussions of the `Initialize` method of the `UpdatePanelTrigger` class to study this class and its subclasses in more detail. As you may recall from Listing 21-14, the `Initialize` method of the `UpdatePanelTriggerCollection` invokes the `Initialize` method of its constituent `UpdatePanelTrigger` objects. As Listing 21-15 shows, the `Initialize` method of the `UpdatePanelTrigger` abstract base class doesn't do anything. However, the `AsyncPostBackTrigger` subclass of this base class overrides this method, providing the implementations shown in Listing 21-20.

Before diving into the AsyncPostBackTrigger's implementation of the Initialize method, we need to get some facts straight about an AsyncPostBackTrigger and how it works. An AsyncPostBackTrigger, like any other subclass of the UpdatePanelControlTrigger base class, is triggered when its associated server control raises a specified type of event. That is why, as you can see from Listing 21-20, the AsyncPostBackTrigger exposes two read/write properties named ControlID and EventName. You must set the ControlID property to the value of the ID property of its associated server control. Even though it's mandatory that you set the value of the ControlID property, it is not mandatory to set the EventName property. However, if you decide to set this property, you must set it to the name of a specified event of the associated server control.

```
public string ControlID
{
  get { return base.ControlID; }
  set { base.ControlID = value; }
}
[DefaultValue("")]
public string EventName
{
  get
  {
    if (this._eventName == null)
      return string.Empty;
    return this._eventName;
  }
  set { this._eventName = value; }
}
```

Here is an example:

```
<asp:UpdatePanel runat="server" ID="UpdatePanel1">
  <Triggers>
    <asp:AsyncPostBackTrigger ControlID="Button1" EventName="Click" />
  </Triggers>
  <ContentTemplate>
    . . .
  </ContentTemplate>
</asp:UpdatePanel>
<asp:Button runat="server" ID="Button1" Text="Submit" />
```

As you can see, this code listing sets the ControlID property of the AsyncPostBackTrigger to the value of the ID property of the specified ASP.NET Button server control, and the EventName property to the string "Click" to specify that the AsyncPostBackTrigger must be triggered when the Click event of the specified Button server control is raised.

Now let's walk through the Initialize method of the AsyncPostBackTrigger. The whole idea behind the Initialize method is to register a method named OnEvent as an event handler for the specified event — that is, the event whose name is given by the EventName property — of the associated server control so that when the server control raises this event, the OnEvent method of the AsyncPostBackTrigger is automatically invoked, allowing the AsyncPostBackTrigger to mark itself as triggered. As Listing 21-21 shows, the OnEvent method simply sets an internal flag to mark the current AsyncPostBackTrigger as triggered:

```
public void OnEvent(object sender, EventArgs e)
{
  this._eventHandled = true;
}
```

As Listing 21-20 shows, the AsyncPostBackTrigger class' implementation of the Initialize method is complex. This makes you wonder what is so difficult about registering the OnEvent method as the event handler for the specified event of the associated server control.

The difficulty arises from the fact that the only information you're providing to the AsyncPostBackTrigger is the value of the ID property of its associated server control and the name of the event of the associated server control that you want the AsyncPostBackTrigger to respond to:

```
<asp:UpdatePanel runat="server" ID="UpdatePanel1">
  <Triggers>
    <asp:AsyncPostBackTrigger ControlID="Button1" EventName="Click" />
  </Triggers>
  <ContentTemplate>
    . . .
  </ContentTemplate>
</asp:UpdatePanel>
<asp:Button runat="server" ID="Button1" Text="Submit" />
```

To register a method as an event handler for an event of a server control:

❑   You need a reference to the server control.

❑   You need to know the actual delegate type of the event so you can instantiate an instance of this delegate to represent your method.

For example, to register the OnEvent method as an event handler for the Click event of the ASP.NET Button server control shown in the previous example:

❑   You need a reference to the ASP.NET Button server control with the ID property value of Button1. Let's assume that some variable named myButton references this server control.

❑   You need to know that the Click event of the ASP.NET Button server control is a delegate of type EventHandler so you can instantiate an instance of the EventHandler delegate to represent the OnEvent method, and add this delegate to the Click event delegate:

```
myButton.Click += new EventHandler(OnEvent);
```

The `AsyncPostBackTrigger` only knows the following things:

- ❑ The value of the `ID` property of the server control instead of the actual reference to the control itself

- ❑ The name of the event instead of the actual type of the event delegate

That is why the `Initialize` method must take extra steps to use the value of the `ID` property of the server control to somehow access a reference to the control itself, and to use the name of the event to somehow access the actual type of the event delegate. Now let's walk through the implementation of the `Initialize` method of the `AsyncPostBackTrigger` shown in Listing 21-20 to see how this method manages to register the `OnEvent` method as an event handler for the specified event of the server control with the specified `ID` property value.

Listing 21-20: The AsyncPostBackTrigger Class

```
public class AsyncPostBackTrigger : UpdatePanelControlTrigger
{
  public AsyncPostBackTrigger() { }
  internal AsyncPostBackTrigger(IScriptManagerInternal scriptManager)
  {
    this._scriptManager = scriptManager;
  }
  protected internal override bool HasTriggered()
  {
    if (!string.IsNullOrEmpty(this.EventName))
      return this._eventHandled;
    string text1 = this.ScriptManager.AsyncPostBackSourceElementID;
    if (text1 != this._associatedControl.UniqueID)
      return text1.StartsWith(this._associatedControl.UniqueID + "$",
                        StringComparison.Ordinal);
    return true;
  }
  protected internal override void Initialize()
  {
    base.Initialize();
    this._associatedControl = base.FindTargetControl(true);
    this.ScriptManager.RegisterAsyncPostBackControl(this._associatedControl);
    Type associatedControlType = this._associatedControl.GetType();

    EventInfo eventInfo = associatedControlType.GetEvent(this.EventName,
          BindingFlags.Public | BindingFlags.Instance | BindingFlags.IgnoreCase);
    Type eventDelegateType = eventInfo.EventHandlerType;
    MethodInfo methodInfo = eventDelegateType.GetMethod("Invoke");
    Delegate delegate = Delegate.CreateDelegate(eventDelegateType, this,
                              AsyncPostBackTrigger.EventHandler);
    eventInfo.AddEventHandler(this._associatedControl, delegate);
  }
  public void OnEvent(object sender, EventArgs e)
  {
    this._eventHandled = true;
  }
```

(continued)

Listing 21-20 *(continued)*

```
public override string ToString()
{
  if (string.IsNullOrEmpty(this.ControlID))
    return "AsyncPostBack";
  return ("AsyncPostBack: " + this.ControlID +
          (string.IsNullOrEmpty(this.EventName) ? string.Empty :
                                  ("." + this.EventName)));
}
public string ControlID
{
  get { return base.ControlID; }
  set { base.ControlID = value; }
}
private static MethodInfo EventHandler
{
  get
  {
    if (AsyncPostBackTrigger._eventHandler == null)
      AsyncPostBackTrigger._eventHandler =
                      typeof(AsyncPostBackTrigger).GetMethod("OnEvent");
    return AsyncPostBackTrigger._eventHandler;
  }
}
[DefaultValue("")]
public string EventName
{
  get
  {
    if (this._eventName == null)
      return string.Empty;
    return this._eventName;
  }
  set { this._eventName = value; }
}
internal IScriptManagerInternal ScriptManager
{
  get
  {
    if (this._scriptManager == null)
    {
      this._scriptManager = ScriptManager.GetCurrent(base.Owner.Page);
      if (this._scriptManager == null)
        throw new InvalidOperationException("ScriptManagerRequired");
    }
    return this._scriptManager;
  }
}
private Control _associatedControl;
private bool _eventHandled;
private static MethodInfo _eventHandler;
private string _eventName;
private IScriptManagerInternal _scriptManager;
}
```

This method first calls the FindTargetControl method that it inherits from its base class to return a reference to its associated server control. Recall from Listing 21-19 that the FindTargetControl method searches through the child controls of all the naming containers of the owner UpdatePanel server control and the owner ancestor server controls for the server control with the specified ID property value. In the case of the previous example, this method will return a reference to the Button server control with the ID property value of Button1. Therefore, the call into the FindTargetControl method provides the AsyncPostBackTrigger with a reference to the server control for whose event the OnEvent method is being registered as an event handler:

```
this._associatedControl = base.FindTargetControl(true);
```

The method then calls the RegisterAsyncPostBackControl method on the current ScriptManager instance, passing in the reference to its associated server control to register this control as the trigger for asynchronous page postbacks. As you'll see later, the server-side PageRequestManager instance passes the list of the UniqueID property values of the controls registered as triggers for asynchronous page post backs to the client-side PageRequestManager instance, where they're stored in an internal client-side collection for future reference. When the end user clicks a control to post the form back to the server, the client-side PageRequestManager intercepts the postback before the actual postback request is made to the server, and determines whether the end user has clicked a control whose UniqueID property value belongs to the internal collection. If so, it treats the postback as asynchronous and makes an asynchronous page postback request to the server, bypassing the normal browser's form submission. This will all be made clear in the next few chapters.

```
this.ScriptManager.RegisterAsyncPostBackControl(this._associatedControl);
```

The RegisterAsyncPostBackControl *method of the* ScriptManager *class is a public method that you can use in your own C# or VB.NET code. In other words, the application of this method is not limited to the* AsyncPostBackTrigger *class.*

The rest of the code in the Initialize method is there to access the actual type of the event delegate in a generic fashion. As you can see, the method first calls the GetType method on its associated server control to return a reference to the Type object that represents the type of the control:

```
Type associatedControlType = this._associatedControl.GetType();
```

Next, it calls the GetEvent method on this Type object, passing in the event name to return a reference to the EventInfo object that represents the specified event of its associated control:

```
EventInfo eventInfo = associatedControlType.GetEvent(this.EventName,
        BindingFlags.Public | BindingFlags.Instance | BindingFlags.IgnoreCase);
```

Then it accesses the Type object that represents the type of the event delegate:

```
Type eventDelegateType = eventInfo.EventHandlerType;
```

Next, it calls GetMethod on this Type object to return a reference to the MethodInfo object that represents the Invoke method of the event delegate:

```
MethodInfo methodInfo = eventDelegateType.GetMethod("Invoke");
```

Then it calls the `CreateDelegate` static method on the `Delegate` class, passing in three parameters to create a `Delegate` object. The first parameter references the `Type` object that represents the type of the delegate object being created. The second parameter references the current `AsyncPostBackTrigger` object. (This parameter is automatically passed into the delegate object being created as its first argument when the delegate is finally invoked.) The third parameter references the `MethodInfo` object that represents the method that the delegate object being created encapsulates. As you'll see shortly, the `AsyncPostBackTrigger` exposes a static property of type `MethodInfo` named `EventHandler` that represents the `OnEvent` method.

```
Delegate delegate = Delegate.CreateDelegate(eventDelegateType, this,
                                            AsyncPostBackTrigger.EventHandler);
```

Finally, the method calls the `AddEventHandler` method on the `EventInfo` object that represents the event whose name is given by the `EventName` property, to register the newly created delegate object as event handler for this event:

```
eventInfo.AddEventHandler(this._associatedControl, delegate);
```

As mentioned earlier, the `AsyncPostBackTrigger` class exposes a static property of type `MethodInfo` named `EventHandler`. As you can see from the following code listing, this property represents the `OnEvent` method of the `AsyncPostBackTrigger` class. Therefore, the delegate object that the `CreateDelegate` method creates represents the `OnEvent` method of the `AsyncPostBackTrigger`. This means that when the associated server control finally raises the event whose name is given by the `EventName` property of the `AsyncPostBackTrigger`, the `OnEvent` method of the `AsyncPostBackTrigger` is automatically invoked:

```
private static MethodInfo EventHandler
{
  get
  {
    if (AsyncPostBackTrigger._eventHandler == null)
      AsyncPostBackTrigger._eventHandler =
                        typeof(AsyncPostBackTrigger).GetMethod("OnEvent");
    return AsyncPostBackTrigger._eventHandler;
  }
}
```

As discussed earlier, the `OnEvent` method of the `AsyncPostBackTrigger` simply sets an internal flag named `_eventHandler` to `true` to mark the `AsyncPostBackTrigger` as triggered:

```
public void OnEvent(object sender, EventArgs e)
{
  this._eventHandled = true;
}
```

As you'll see later, at some point in the `UpdatePanel` server control's life cycle the `HasTriggered` property is invoked on each `UpdatePanelTrigger`, including the `AsyncPostBackTrigger` in the `Triggers` collection of the `UpdatePanel` server control, to determine whether it has been triggered. As the following code listing shows, the `HasTriggered` method of the `AsyncPostBackTrigger` takes the following steps. If the `EventName` property of the `AsyncPostBackTrigger` has been set, it simply returns the value of the `_eventHandled` flag. Otherwise it compares the value of the `AsyncPostBackSourceElementID` property of the `ScriptManager` with the value of the `UniqueID` property of its associated server control.

If they are the same, or if the value of the `AsyncPostBackSourceElementID` property begins with the value of the `UniqueID` property of its associated server control plus the dollar sign, the `HasTriggered` method returns `true` to signal to its caller that the current `AsyncPostBackTrigger` has indeed been triggered:

```
protected internal override bool HasTriggered()
{
  if (!string.IsNullOrEmpty(this.EventName))
    return this._eventHandled;
  string text1 = this.ScriptManager.AsyncPostBackSourceElementID;
  if (text1 != this._associatedControl.UniqueID)
    return text1.StartsWith(this._associatedControl.UniqueID + "$",
                            StringComparison.Ordinal);
  return true;
}
```

As mentioned earlier, the `HasTriggered` method returns `true` if the value of the `AsyncPostBackSourceElementID` property begins with the value of the `UniqueID` property of its associated server control plus the dollar sign. This happens when the associated server control of the `AsyncPostBackTrigger` is a composite control that contains a child control that triggers the asynchronous postbacks. This means that the associated server control of an `AsyncPostBackTrigger` does not have to be a simple server control.

Before diving into the implementation of the `RegisterAsyncPostBackControl` method of the `ScriptManager` class, let's update Figure 21-9 with the latest method calls. Recall that the dashed line in Figure 21-9 represents the method calls triggered by the call into the `Initialize` method of the `UpdatePanelTrigger`. In this case the trigger is the `AsyncPostBackTrigger` subclass of the `UpdatePanelTrigger`. Because of this, we need to replace the `UpdatePanelTrigger` class shown in Figure 21-9 with `AsyncPostBackTrigger`. Again, the `Initialize` method of the `AsyncPostBackTrigger` triggers the call into the `FindTargetControl` method of the `AsyncPostBackTrigger` and the `RegisterAsyncPostBackControl` method of the `ScriptManager`. Figure 21-10 extends Figure 21-9 to add these two latest triggered method calls.

Note that Figure 21-10 contains a dashed line that represents the method calls triggered by the call into `RegisterAsyncPostBackControl` method of the `ScriptManager`, which will be discussed in the following sections.

The RegisterAsyncPostBackControl Method of the ScriptManager

As you saw earlier, the `Initialize` method of the `AsyncPostBackTrigger` calls the `RegisterAsyncPostBackControl` method on the `ScriptManager` to register its associated server control as a trigger for asynchronous page postbacks. Listing 21-21 presents the internal implementation of the `RegisterAsyncPostBackControl` method of the `ScriptManager`. As you can see, this method delegates the responsibility of registering the specified server control to the `RegisterAsyncPostBackControl` method of the current server-side `PageRequestManager` instance.

Listing 21-21: The RegisterAsyncPostBackControl Method of the ScriptManager

```
public void RegisterAsyncPostBackControl(Control control)
{
  this.PageRequestManager.RegisterAsyncPostBackControl(control);
}
```

LoadRecursive

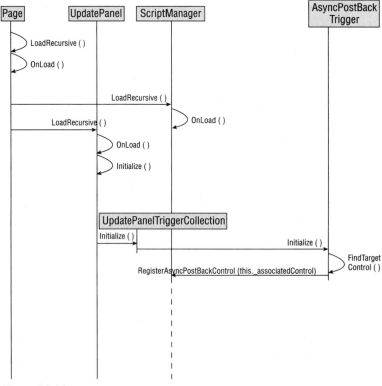

Figure 21-10

The RegisterAsyncPostBackControl Method of PageRequestManager

Listing 21-22 contains the code for the `RegisterAsyncPostBackControl` method of the `PageRequestManager`. As you can see, this method takes the following steps. First, it raises an exception if the control being registered is the `Page` object:

```
if (control is Page)
    throw new ArgumentException("CannotRegisterPage");
```

The `Page` cannot be registered as a trigger for asynchronous page postbacks.

Next, it raises an exception if the control being registered implements none of the `INamingContainer`, `IPostBackDataHandler`, and `IPostBackEventHandler` interfaces:

```
if ((!(control is INamingContainer) &&
        !(control is IPostBackDataHandler)) &&
        !(control is IPostBackEventHandler))
    throw new ArgumentException("InvalidControlRegistration");
```

Only server controls that implement at least one of the INamingContainer, IPostBackDataHandler, and IPostBackEventHandler interfaces can be registered as triggers for asynchronous page postbacks. For example, the ASP.NET Button server control can be registered as a trigger for asynchronous page postbacks because it implements the IPostBackEventHandler interface.

Note that the current server-side PageRequestManager instance maintains two internal collections named _postBackControls and _asyncPostBackControls, where it stores the server controls registered as triggers for synchronous and asynchronous page postbacks, respectively. As you can see from Listing 21-22, the RegisterAsyncPostBackControl method raises an exception if the server control being registered has already been added to the _postBackControls collections:

```
if ((this._postBackControls != null) && this._postBackControls.Contains(control))
    throw new ArgumentException("CannotRegisterBothPostBacks");
```

The same server control cannot be registered as a trigger for both synchronous and asynchronous page postbacks.

Finally, the RegisterAsyncPostBack method adds the server control being registered to the _asyncPostBackControls collection if the collection does not already contain the server control:

```
if (!this._asyncPostBackControls.Contains(control))
    this._asyncPostBackControls.Add(control);
```

The same server control can be registered multiple times as a trigger for asynchronous page postbacks, because the RegisterAsyncPostBack method ensures that the same server control is not added multiple times to the _asyncPostBackControls collection.

Listing 21-22: The RegisterAsyncPostBackControl Method of the PageRequestManager

```
public void RegisterAsyncPostBackControl(Control control)
{
  if (control == null)
    throw new ArgumentNullException("control");

  if (control is Page)
    throw new ArgumentException("CannotRegisterPage");

  if (!(control is INamingContainer) &&
      !(control is IPostBackDataHandler) &&
      !(control is IPostBackEventHandler))
    throw new ArgumentException("InvalidControlRegistration");
  if ((this._postBackControls != null) && this._postBackControls.Contains(control))
    throw new ArgumentException("CannotRegisterBothPostBacks");

  if (this._asyncPostBackControls == null)
    this._asyncPostBackControls = new List<Control>();

  if (!this._asyncPostBackControls.Contains(control))
    this._asyncPostBackControls.Add(control);
}
```

Now let's update Figure 21-10 with the latest method calls. Recall that the dashed line in Figure 21-10 represents the method calls triggered by the call into the `RegisterAsyncPostBackControl` method of the `ScriptManager`. As I mentioned earlier, this method triggers the call into the `RegisterAsyncPostBackControl` method of the `PageRequestManager`, which in turn triggers the call into the `Add` method of the `_asyncPostBackControls` field, which is a collection of type `List<Control>`. Figure 21-11 extends Figure 21-10 to add these two latest triggered method calls. This wraps up the `LoadRecursive` life cycle phase.

LoadRecursive

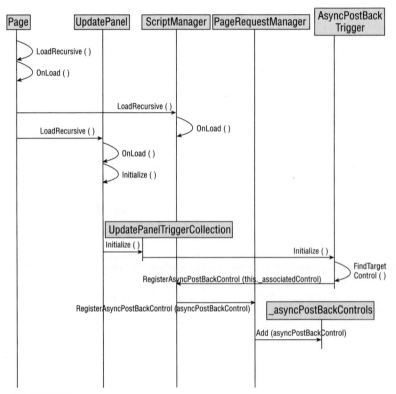

Figure 21-11

Before diving into the next life cycle phase, that of `PreRenderRecursive`, let's take a look at an example that shows you how to develop your own custom `UpdatePanelTrigger` triggers.

Developing a Custom UpdatePanelTrigger

In this section, I'll develop a custom `UpdatePanelTrigger` named `AsyncMultiPostBackTrigger` that is associated with a list of server controls. Listing 21-23 presents the implementation of this trigger. As you can see, it inherits from the `UpdatePanelTrigger` base class and overrides its `HasTriggered` and `Initialize` methods.

As you can also see, `AsyncMultiPostBackTrigger` exposes two collection properties named `ControlIDs` and `EventNames`. It is the responsibility of the page developer to assign a comma-separated list of `UniqueID` property values and event names, respectively, to these two properties. Each value in the former list must be the `UniqueID` property value of a server control on the current page. There must be a one-to-one correspondence between the `UniqueID` property value and event names.

Note that the `AsyncMultiPostBackTrigger` exposes a method named `FindTargetControls`, which repeats the logic used in the `FindTargetControl` method shown in Listing 21-19 once for each `UniqueID` property value in the `ControlIDs` collection. In other words, the `FindTargetControls` method returns an array that contains references to the associated server controls of the `AsyncMultiPostBackTrigger`.

Also note that the `AsyncMultiPostBackTrigger`'s implementation of the `HasTriggered` and `Initialize` methods repeats the logic used in the `HasTriggered` and `Initialize` methods shown in Listing 21-20 once for each server control in the list of associated server controls. As the boldface portion of Listing 21-23 shows, the `AsyncMultiPostBackTrigger` is considered triggered when the first server control in the list of its associated server control triggers.

Listing 21-23: The AsyncMultiPostBackTrigger Class

```
using System;
using System.Configuration;
using System.Web;
using System.Web.UI;
using System.Web.UI.WebControls;
using System.Web.UI.HtmlControls;
using System.Reflection;
using System.ComponentModel;
using System.Collections;
namespace CustomComponents
{
  public class AsyncMultiPostBackTrigger : UpdatePanelTrigger
  {
    protected Control[] FindTargetControls(bool searchNamingContainers)
    {
      ArrayList list = new ArrayList();
      if (searchNamingContainers)
      {
        Control control2 = null;
        Control control1 = null;
        foreach (string controlID in this._controlIDs)
        {
          control2 = base.Owner;
          control1 = null;
          while ((control1 == null) && (control2 != base.Owner.Page))
          {
            control2 = control2.NamingContainer;
            if (control2 == null)
              break;
            control1 = control2.FindControl(controlID);
          }
          list.Add(control1);
        }
      }
```

(continued)

Listing 21-23 *(continued)*

```
    else
    {
      foreach (string controlID in this._controlIDs)
      {
        list.Add(base.Owner.FindControl(controlID));
      }
    }
    Control[] controls = new Control[list.Count];
    list.CopyTo(controls);
    return controls;
  }
  protected override bool HasTriggered()
  {
    if (this.EventNames != null && this.EventNames.Length > 0 &&
        !String.IsNullOrEmpty(this.EventNames[0]))
      return this._eventHandled;
    ScriptManager sm = ScriptManager.GetCurrent(this.Owner.Page);
    foreach (Control associatedControl in this._associatedControls)
    {
      if (sm.AsyncPostBackSourceElementID != associatedControl.UniqueID)
      return sm.AsyncPostBackSourceElementID.StartsWith(
                  associatedControl.UniqueID + "$", StringComparison.Ordinal);
    }
    return true;
  }
  protected override void Initialize()
  {
    base.Initialize();
    this._associatedControls = this.FindTargetControls(true);
    ScriptManager sm = ScriptManager.GetCurrent(this.Owner.Page);
    Control associatedControl = null;
    string eventName = "";
    Type associatedControlType;
    EventInfo eventInfo;
    Type eventDelegateType;
    MethodInfo methodInfo;
    Delegate delegate1;
    for (int i = 0; i < this._associatedControls.Length; i++)
    {
      associatedControl = this._associatedControls[i];
      eventName = this.EventNames[i];
      sm.RegisterAsyncPostBackControl(associatedControl);
      associatedControlType = associatedControl.GetType();
      eventInfo = associatedControlType.GetEvent(eventName,
                    BindingFlags.Public | BindingFlags.Instance |
                    BindingFlags.IgnoreCase);
      eventDelegateType = eventInfo.EventHandlerType;
      methodInfo = eventDelegateType.GetMethod("Invoke");
      delegate1 = Delegate.CreateDelegate(eventDelegateType, this,
                          AsyncMultiPostBackTrigger.EventHandler);
      eventInfo.AddEventHandler(associatedControl, delegate1);
    }
  }
```

```
    public void OnEvent(object sender, EventArgs e)
    {
      this._eventHandled = true;
    }
    [TypeConverter(typeof(StringArrayConverter))]
    public string[] ControlIDs
    {
      get { return this._controlIDs; }
      set { this._controlIDs = value; }
    }
    private static MethodInfo EventHandler
    {
      get
      {
        if (AsyncMultiPostBackTrigger._eventHandler == null)
          AsyncMultiPostBackTrigger._eventHandler =
                  typeof(AsyncMultiPostBackTrigger).GetMethod("OnEvent");
        return AsyncMultiPostBackTrigger._eventHandler;
      }
    }
    [TypeConverter(typeof(StringArrayConverter))]
    public string[] EventNames
    {
      get { return this._eventNames; }
      set { this._eventNames = value; }
    }
    private bool _eventHandled;
    private Control[] _associatedControls;
    private static MethodInfo _eventHandler;
    private string[] _eventNames;
    private string[] _controlIDs;
  }
}
```

The following code listing presents a page that uses the AsyncMultiPostBackTrigger. As the boldface portion of this code listing shows, the AsyncMultiPostBackTrigger has two associated server controls, which have the UniqueID property values AsyncPostBackButton1 and AsyncPostBackButton2.

```
<%@ Page Language="C#" %>
<%@ Register TagPrefix="custom" Namespace="CustomComponents" %>
<%@ Import Namespace="System.Drawing" %>
<!DOCTYPE html PUBLIC "-//W3C//DTD XHTML 1.1//EN"
"http://www.w3.org/TR/xhtml11/DTD/xhtml11.dtd">
<script runat="server">
  void Page_Load(object sender, EventArgs e)
  {
    string text = "Refreshed at " + DateTime.Now.ToString();
    UpdatePanel1Label.Text = text;
    NonPartiallyUpdatableLabel.Text = text;
  }
</script>
```

(continued)

(continued)

```
<html xmlns="http://www.w3.org/1999/xhtml">
<head id="Head1" runat="server">
  <title>Untitled Page</title>
</head>
<body>
  <form id="form1" runat="server">
    <asp:ScriptManager ID="ScriptManager1" runat="server" />
    <asp:UpdatePanel ID="UpdatePanel1" runat="server">
      <ContentTemplate>
        <table cellspacing="10"
          style="background-color: #dddddd" width="100%">
          <tr>
            <th colspan="2" align="center">
              Partially Updatable Portion (UpdatePanel1)</th>
          </tr>
          <tr>
            <td>
              <asp:Label ID="UpdatePanel1Label" runat="server" />
            </td>
            <td>
              <asp:Button ID="UpdatePanelButton" runat="server"
               Text="Update" />
            </td>
          </tr>
        </table>
      </ContentTemplate>
      <Triggers>
        <custom:AsyncMultiPostBackTrigger
          ControlIDs="AsyncPostBackButton1,AsyncPostBackButton2"
          EventNames="Click,Click" />
      </Triggers>
    </asp:UpdatePanel>
    <br />
    <br />
    <table cellspacing="10" style="background-color: #dddddd" width="100%">
      <tr>
        <th colspan="2">
          Non Partially Updatable Portion</th>
      </tr>
      <tr>
        <td>
          <asp:Label ID="NonPartiallyUpdatableLabel" runat="server" />
        </td>
        <td>
          <asp:Button ID="Button1" runat="server" Text="Update" />
        </td>
      </tr>
```

```
    <tr>
      <td align="left">
        <asp:Button ID="AsyncPostBackButton1" runat="server"
        Text="Async Postback Trigger1" />
      </td>
      <td align="left">
        <asp:Button ID="AsyncPostBackButton2" runat="server"
        Text="Async Postback Trigger2" />
      </td>
    </tr>
  </table>
</form>
</body>
</html>
```

Rendering

Once again, keep in mind that we're following the current `Page` object as it goes through its life cycle phases to process the first HTTP GET request made to a Web page enabled for partial page rendering. In the previous sections, you saw what happens when the `Page` enters its `PreInit`, `InitRecursive`, `LoadRecursive`, and `PreRenderRecursive` life cycle phases. In this section, you'll see what happens when the `Page` enters its rendering life cycle phase, where the `ProcessRequest` method (see Listing 21-1) calls the `RenderControl` method on the current `Page`.

The current `Page` inherits the `RenderControl` from the ASP.NET `Control` base class. The `RenderControl` method internally calls the `Render` method, which in turn calls the `RenderChildren` method. Listing 21-24 presents the internal implementation of the `RenderChildren` method of the `Control` base class. As you can see, the `RenderChildren` method first calls the `GetRenderMethod` to return a reference to the `RenderMethod` delegate registered with the server control, if any. Since this part of the implementation of the `RenderChildren` method does not apply to the first request, I'll postpone the discussion of this part of the code to later when we're discussing asynchronous page postback requests.

In other words, only the boldface portion of the `RenderChildren` method is executed for the first request. As you can see, this portion iterates through the child controls in the `Controls` collection of the current `Page` and invokes the `RenderControl` method on each enumerated child control.

Synchronous page postbacks and the first requests always end up rendering all visible server controls on the current page. As you'll see, asynchronous page postbacks, on the other hand, end up rendering only specified `UpdatePanel` *server controls on the current page.*

Listing 21-24: The RenderChildren Method of the Control Base Class

```
protected internal virtual void RenderChildren(HtmlTextWriter writer)
{
  RenderMethod renderMethod = this.GetRenderMethod();
  if (renderMethod != null)
  {
    writer.BeginRender();
    renderMethod(writer, this);
    writer.EndRender();
  }

  else if (this.Controls != null)
  {
    foreach (Control control in this.Controls)
    {
      control.RenderControl(writer);
    }
  }
}
```

Therefore, the `RenderControl` method of the `ScriptManager` and `UpdatePanel` server controls is automatically invoked when the current `Page` enters its rendering life cycle phase. As just discussed, the `RenderControl` method calls the `Render` method. Figure 21-12 depicts the method calls that we've covered so far. Note that this figure contains two dashed lines. These dashed lines represent the method calls that the `Render` methods of the `ScriptManager` and `UpdatePanel` server controls trigger, as discussed in the following sections.

The Render Method of ScriptManager

The `Render` method of the current `ScriptManager` server control internally calls the `RenderPageRequestManagerScript` method on the current server-side `PageRequestManager` instance. Listing 21-25 presents the implementation of the `RenderPageRequestManagerScript` method. This method renders the script that instantiates and initializes the client-side `PageRequestManager` class.

The instantiation and initialization of the current client-side `PageRequestManager` instance involves two steps. First, the `_initialize` static method must be called on the client-side `PageRequestManager` class. Second, the `_updateControls` instance method must be called on the current client-side `PageRequestManager` instance. As Listing 21-25 shows, the `RenderPageRequestManagerScript` method takes these steps to render the script that instantiates and initializes the current client-side `PageRequestManager` instance.

Rendering Lifecycle Phase

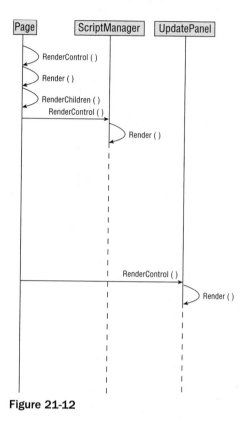

Figure 21-12

Listing 21-25: The RenderPageRequestManagerScript Method of PageRequestManager

```
internal void RenderPageRequestManagerScript(HtmlTextWriter writer)
{
  writer.Write("<script type=\"text/javascript\">\r\n");
  writer.Write("//<![CDATA[\r\nSys.WebForms.PageRequestManager._initialize('");
  writer.Write(this._owner.UniqueID);
  writer.Write("', document.getElementById('");
  writer.Write(this._owner.IPage.Form.ClientID);
  writer.Write("'));\r\n");
  writer.Write("Sys.WebForms.PageRequestManager.getInstance()._updateControls([");
  PageRequestManager.RenderUpdatePanelIDsFromList(writer, this._allUpdatePanels);
  writer.Write("], [");
  writer.Write(this.GetAsyncPostBackControlIDs(true));
  writer.Write("], [");
  writer.Write(this.GetPostBackControlIDs(true));
  writer.Write("], ");
  writer.Write(this.GetAsyncPostBackTimeout());
  writer.WriteLine(");");
  writer.Write("//]]>\r\n</script>\r\n");
}
```

The method begins by rendering the opening tag of the script HTML element that will contain the entire instantiation/initialization script:

```
writer.Write("<script type=\"text/javascript\">\r\n");
```

Next, the method renders the part of the script that invokes the _initialize static method on the client-side PageRequestManager class:

```
writer.Write("//<![CDATA[\r\nSys.WebForms.PageRequestManager._initialize('");
```

Next, the method renders the parameters that are passed into the _initialize method. The _initialize method takes two parameters. The first is a string that contains the value of the UniqueID property of the current ScriptManager server control:

```
writer.Write(this._owner.UniqueID);
```

The second references the form HTML element that contains the current ScriptManager server control (recall that the ScriptManager server control is always declared inside a <form runat="server"> element):

```
writer.Write("', document.getElementById('");
writer.Write(this._owner.IPage.Form.ClientID);
writer.Write("'));\r\n");
```

Next, the RenderPageRequestManagerScript method renders the portion of the script that invokes the _updateControls method on the current client-side PageRequestManager instance. It begins by rendering the method invocation:

```
writer.Write("Sys.WebForms.PageRequestManager.getInstance()._updateControls([");
```

Next, it renders the parameters passed into the _updateControls method. This method takes three parameters. The first is an array that contains the values of the UniqueID properties of all the UpdatePanel server controls on the current page. The RenderPageRequestManagerScript method calls the RenderUpdatePanelIDsFromList static method to return an array that contains these UniqueID property values:

```
PageRequestManager.RenderUpdatePanelIDsFromList(writer, this._allUpdatePanels);
writer.Write("], [");
```

The second parameter of the _updateControls method is an array that contains the values of the UniqueID properties of all the server controls that cause asynchronous page postbacks. The RenderPageRequestManagerScript method calls the GetAsyncPostBackControlIDs method to return an array that contains these UniqueID property values:

```
writer.Write(this.GetAsyncPostBackControlIDs(true));
writer.Write("], [");
```

The third parameter of the _updateControls method is an array that contains the values of the UniqueID properties of all the server controls that cause synchronous page postbacks. The RenderPageRequestManagerScript method calls the GetPostBackControlIDs method to return an array that contains these UniqueID property values:

```
writer.Write(this.GetPostBackControlIDs(true));
writer.Write("], ");
```

The fourth parameter of the _updateControls method is a string that contains the asynchronous postback timeout. Recall that the server-side PageRequestManager class exposes a field named _owner that references the current ScriptManager server control. Also recall that the ScriptManager server control exposes an integer property named AsyncPostBackTimeout that returns the asynchronous postback request timeout:

```
writer.Write(this._owner.AsyncPostBackTimeout.ToString());
writer.WriteLine(");");
writer.Write("//]]>\r\n</script>\r\n");
```

Here is an example. Suppose the current page contains a ScriptManager server control with UniqueID value of "ScriptManager1" enclosed in a form element with the id HTML attribute value of "Form1", three UpdatePanel server controls with UniqueID values of "UpdatePanel1", "UpdatePanel2", and "UpdatePanel3", two Button server controls that cause synchronous page postbacks, with UniqueID values of "SyncButton1" and "SyncButton2", and finally three Button server controls that cause asynchronous page postbacks, with UniqueID values of "AsyncButton1", "AsyncButton2", and "AsyncButton3". The following code fragment shows the script that the RenderPageRequestManagerScript method will render:

```
<script type="text/javascript">
//<![CDATA[
Sys.WebForms.PageRequestManager._initialize('ScriptManager1',
                                      document.getElementById('Form1'));
Sys.WebForms.PageRequestManager.getInstance()._updateControls(
                        ['tUpdatePanel1', 'fUpdatePanel2', 'tUpdatePanel3'],
                        ['SyncButton1', 'SyncButton2'],
                        ['AsyncButton1', 'AsyncButton2']);
//]]
</script>
```

Before diving into the implementations of the RenderUpdatePanelIDsFromList, GetAsyncPostBackConrolIDs, and GetPostBackControlIDs of the server-side PageRequestManager, let's update Figure 21-12 with the latest method calls.

Figure 21-13 extends Figure 21-12 to add the new method calls. Note that this figure contains three dashed lines. The figure inherits the left dashed line from Figure 21-12. Recall that this dashed line represents the method calls triggered by the call into the Render method of the UpdatePanel. The remaining two dashed lines represent the method calls triggered by the calls into the GetAsynchPostBackControlIDs and GetPostBackControlIDs, which will be discussed in the next sections.

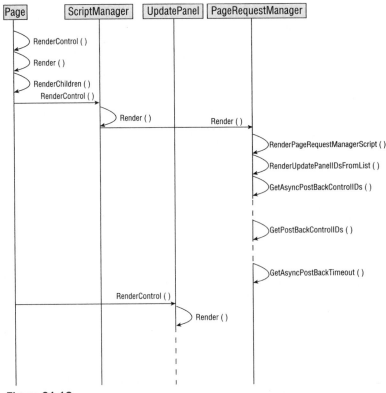

Figure 21-13

The RenderUpdatePanelIDsFromList Method of the Server-Side PageRequestManager

Listing 21-26 presents the implementation of the RenderUpdatePanelIDsFromList method of PageRequestManager. This method takes two parameters. The first references an HtmlTextWriter object. The second is a List<UpdatePanel> collection that contains the list of all UpdatePanel server controls on the current page. The main responsibility of this method is to retrieve the values of the UniqueID and ChildrenAsTriggers properties of all UpdatePanel server controls in this collection and render them into the HtmlTextWriter object as a comma-separated list of strings, one for each UpdatePanel server control, each of which contains the following two parts:

❑ The character t if the ChildrenAsTrigger property of the associated UpdatePanel server control is true; the character f otherwise

❑ The UniqueID property value of the associated UpdatePanel server control

Listing 21-26: The RenderUpdatePanelIDsFromList Method of PageRequestManager

```
private static void RenderUpdatePanelIDsFromList(HtmlTextWriter writer,
                                                 List<UpdatePanel> list)
{
  if ((list != null) && (list.Count > 0))
  {
    bool flag1 = true;
    for (int num1 = 0; num1 < list.Count; num1++)
    {
      if (list[num1].Visible)
      {
        if (!flag1)
          writer.Write(",");

        flag1 = false;
        writer.Write("'");
        writer.Write(list[num1].ChildrenAsTriggers ? "t" : "f");
        writer.Write(list[num1].UniqueID);
        writer.Write("'");
      }
    }
  }
}
```

The GetAsyncPostBackControlIDs Method of the Server-Side PageRequestManager

Listing 21-27 presents the implementation of the `GetAsyncPostBackControlIDs` method of the `PageRequestManager`. As you can see, this method simply delegates to the `GetControlIDsFromList` method, passing in the `_asyncPostBackControls` collection. Recall that the `PageRequestManager` server class features a private collection named `_asyncPostBackControls` that contains all the server controls that cause asynchronous page postbacks.

Listing 21-27: The GetAsyncPostBackControlIDs Method of the PageRequestManager

```
private string GetAsyncPostBackControlIDs(bool includeQuotes)
{
  return PageRequestManager.GetControlIDsFromList(this._asyncPostBackControls,
                                                  includeQuotes);
}
```

The GetControlIDsFromList Method of the Server-Side PageRequestManager

Listing 21-28 contains the code for the `GetControlIDsFromList` method of the `PageRequestManager`. This method takes a `List<Control>` collection that contains a list of server controls. The main responsibility of this method is to return a comma-separated list of strings, each of which contains the `UniqueID` property value of a server control in the `List<Control>` collection. Note that this method takes a second Boolean argument that specifies whether these `UniqueID` property values must be rendered in quotes.

Listing 21-28: The GetControlIDsFromList Method of the PageRequestManager

```
private static string GetControlIDsFromList(List<Control> list, bool includeQuotes)
{
  if ((list == null) || (list.Count <= 0))
    return string.Empty;

  StringBuilder builder1 = new StringBuilder();
  bool flag1 = true;
  for (int num1 = 0; num1 < list.Count; num1++)
  {
    if (list[num1].Visible)
    {
      if (!flag1)
        builder1.Append(",");

      flag1 = false;
      if (includeQuotes)
        builder1.Append("'");

      builder1.Append(list[num1].UniqueID);
      if (includeQuotes)
        builder1.Append("'");
    }
  }
  return builder1.ToString();
}
```

The GetPostBackControlIDs Method of the Server-Side PageRequestManager

Listing 21-29 presents the implementation of the GetPostBackControlIDs method of the PageRequestManager. As you can see, this method simply delegates to the GetControlIDsFromList method, passing in the _postBackControls collection. The current server-side PageRequestManager instance features a private collection field named _postBackControls that contains all the server controls on the current page that cause synchronous page postbacks.

Listing 21-29: The GetPostBackControlIDs Method of the PageRequestManager

```
private string GetPostBackControlIDs(bool includeQuotes)
{
  return PageRequestManager.GetControlIDsFromList(this._postBackControls,
                                                  includeQuotes);
}
```

The GetAsyncPostBackTimeout Method of the Server-Side PageRequestManager

As Listing 21-30 shows, this method simply returns the value of the AsyncPostBacktimeout property of the current ScriptManager server control. Recall that the _owner field of the current server-side PageRequestManager instance references the current ScriptManager server control.

Listing 21-30: The GetAsyncPostBackTimeout Method of the PageRequestManager

```
private string GetAsyncPostBackTimeout()
{
  return this._owner.AsyncPostBackTimeout.ToString();
}
```

Figure 21-14 updates Figure 21-13 with the latest method calls. Note that Figure 21-14 contains a dashed line that it inherits from Listing 21-13. Recall that this dashed line represents the method calls triggered by the call into the RenderControl method of the UpdatePanel server control.

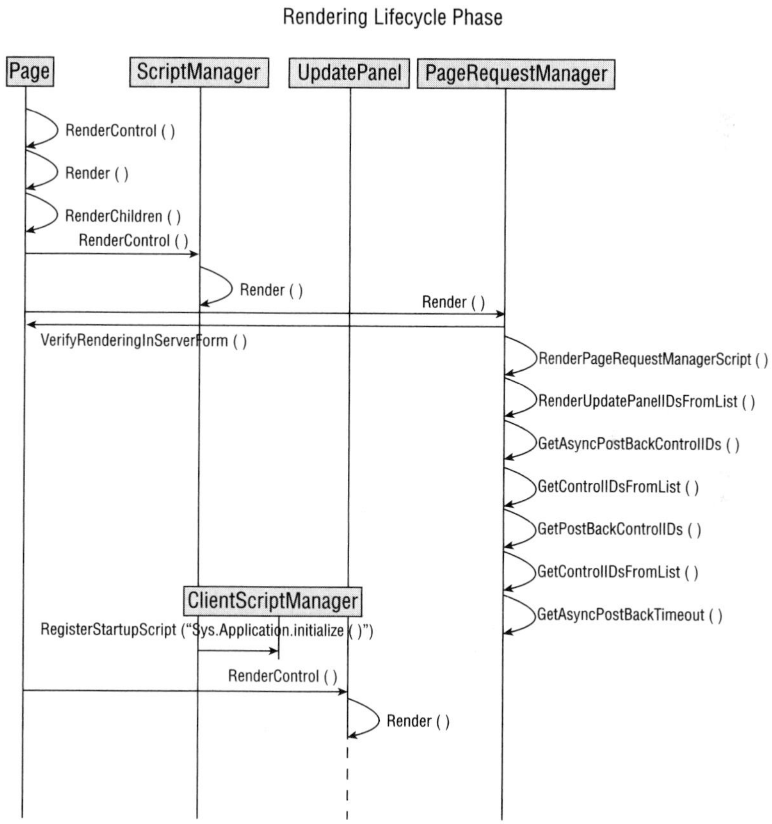

Figure 21-14

The Render Method of the UpdatePanel

The `UpdatePanel` server control inherits the `RenderControl` method from the `Control` base class. The base class's implementation of the `RenderControl` method calls the `Render` method, shown in Listing 21-31. As you can see, this method takes two actions. First, it calls the `VerifyRenderingInServerForm` method on the current `Page` to raise an exception if the `UpdatePanel` server control is not inside a `<form runat="server">` element:

```
this.Page.VerifyRenderingInServerForm(this);
```

Next, it calls the `Render` method of its base class, which in turn calls the `RenderChildren` method, as shown in Listing 21-32.

Listing 21-31: The Render Method of the UpdatePanel

```
protected override void Render(HtmlTextWriter writer)
{
  this.Page.VerifyRenderingInServerForm(this);
  base.Render(writer);
}
```

Listing 21-32 presents the implementation of the `RenderChildren` method of the `UpatePanel` server control. The method first checks whether the `UpdatePanel` control is in asynchronous postback mode — that is, if the current request is an asynchronous page postback. Since the current request is the first request to a Web page enabled for partial page rendering, and since the first request is not an asynchronous postback, only the boldface portion of the `RenderChildren` method of the `UpdatePanel` server control is executed for the first request. I'll discuss the non-boldface portion of this method later when we're studying the next request, which will be an asynchronous page postback.

As the boldface portion of the Listing 21-32 shows, the `UpdatePanel` server control renders its child controls within either a `div` or `span` HTML element, depending on the value of its `UpdatePanelRenderMode` property. This property is of type `UpdatePanelRenderMode` enumerator, which can have one of the following possible enumeration values:

```
public enum UpdatePanelRenderMode
{
  Block,
  Inline
}
```

As the boldface portion of Listing 21-32 shows, the `RenderChildren` method of the `UpdatePanel` server control encapsulates its child controls in a `div` HTML element if its `UpdatePanelRenderMode` is set to the enumeration value `Block`, and in a `span` HTML element otherwise:

```
if (this.RenderMode == UpdatePanelRenderMode.Block)
  writer.RenderBeginTag(HtmlTextWriterTag.Div);
else
  writer.RenderBeginTag(HtmlTextWriterTag.Span);
```

Note that the UpdatePanel server control renders the value of its ClientID property as the value of the id HTML attribute of the outermost div or span HTML element:

```
writer.AddAttribute(HtmlTextWriterAttribute.Id, this.ClientID);
```

Listing 21-32: The RenderChildren Method of the UpdatePanel

```
protected override void RenderChildren(HtmlTextWriter writer)
{
  if (this._asyncPostBackMode)
  {
    if (this._rendered)
      return;
    HtmlTextWriter writer1 = new HtmlTextWriter(new StringWriter());
    base.RenderChildren(writer1);
    PageRequestManager.EncodeString(writer, "updatePanel", this.ClientID,
                                    writer1.InnerWriter.ToString());
  }
  else
  {
    writer.AddAttribute(HtmlTextWriterAttribute.Id, this.ClientID);
    if (this.RenderMode == UpdatePanelRenderMode.Block)
      writer.RenderBeginTag(HtmlTextWriterTag.Div);
    else
      writer.RenderBeginTag(HtmlTextWriterTag.Span);
    base.RenderChildren(writer);
    writer.RenderEndTag();
  }
  this._rendered = true;
}
```

Figure 21-15 updates Figure 21-14 with the latest method calls, which wraps up our discussions of the Rendering phase of the current Page object.

Summary

This chapter followed the Page object through its life cycle phases to process the first request to a Web page enabled for partial page rendering. As you saw, the server response to this request contains a script block generated by the current server-side PageRequestManager instance. Recall that this script block takes the following two important actions:

❑ Calls the _initialize static method on the client-side PageRequestManager class to instantiate and to initialize the current client-side PageRequestManager instance

❑ Calls the _updateControls instance method on the current client-side PageRequestManager instance, passing in three parameters:

    ❑ The first parameter is an array containing one string for each UpdatePanel server control on the current page, each string consisting of two substrings. The first substring contains

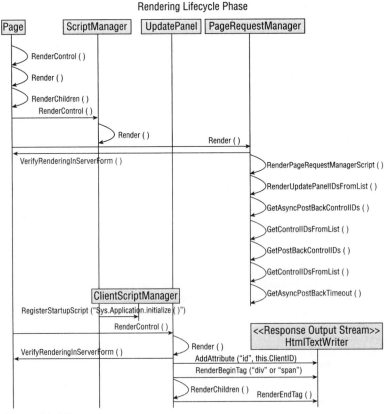

Figure 21-15

the letter t if the `ChildrenAsTriggers` property of the associated `UpdatePanel` server control has been set to `true`, and the letter f otherwise. The second substring contains the value of the `UniqueID` property of the associated `UpdatePanel` server control.

❏   The second parameter is an array that contains the `UniqueID` property values of all server controls on the current page that cause synchronous page postbacks.

❏   The third parameter is an array that contains the `UniqueID` property values of all server controls on the current page that cause asynchronous page postbacks.

The following code listing presents an example of the script block rendered by the current server-side `PageRequestManager` instance:

```
<script type="text/javascript">
  //<![CDATA[
    Sys.WebForms.PageRequestManager._initialize('ScriptManager1',
                                  document.getElementById('Form1'));
    Sys.WebForms.PageRequestManager.getInstance()._updateControls(
                       ['tUpdatePanel1', 'fUpdatePanel2', 'tUpdatePanel3'],
                       ['SyncButton1', 'SyncButton2'],
                       ['AsyncButton1', 'AsyncButton2']);
  //]]
</script>
```

In the next chapter we'll move on to the client side where the server response, including this script block, arrives. We'll study what happens when the this script block invokes the _initialize and _updateControls methods of the client-side PageRequestManager.

ASP.NET AJAX Client-Side PageRequestManager

The last chapter followed the Page object through its life cycle phases to process the first request to a Web page enabled for partial page rendering. As you saw, the server response to this request contains a script block generated by the current server-side PageRequestManager instance. Recall that this script block takes the following two important actions:

❑ Calls the _initialize static method on the client-side PageRequestManager class to instantiate and initialize the current client-side PageRequestManager instance

❑ Calls the _updateControls instance method on the current client-side PageRequestManager instance, passing in four parameters:

❑ The first parameter is an array containing one string for each UpdatePanel server control on the current page. This string consists of two substrings. The first substring contains the letter t if the ChildrenAsTriggers property of the associated UpdatePanel server control has been set to true and the letter f otherwise. The second substring contains the value of the UniqueID property of the associated UpdatePanel server control.

❑ The second parameter is an array that contains the UniqueID property values of all server controls on the current page that cause synchronous page postbacks.

❑ The third parameter is an array that contains the UniqueID property values of all server controls on the current page that cause asynchronous page postbacks.

❑ The fourth parameter is a string that contains the asynchronous postback request timeout.

Listing 22-1 presents an example of the script block rendered by the current server-side PageRequestManager instance.

Listing 22-1: The Sample Script Block that Arrives on the Client Side as Part of the Server Response

```
<script type="text/javascript">
//<![CDATA[
    Sys.WebForms.PageRequestManager._initialize('ScriptManager1',
                                    document.getElementById('Form1'));
    Sys.WebForms.PageRequestManager.getInstance()._updateControls(
                            ['tUpdatePanel1', 'fUpdatePanel2', 'tUpdatePanel3'],
                            ['SyncButton1', 'SyncButton2'],
                            ['AsyncButton1', 'AsyncButton2'], '90');
//]]
</script>
```

In this chapter we'll move on to the client side, where the server response — including this script block — arrives. As you can see, this script block automatically invokes the _intialize and _updateControls methods of the client-side PageRequestManager. Figure 22-1 depicts the instantiation and initialization of the current PageRequestManager instance. As you can see, this figure diplays the two method calls I've discussed. Note that this figure contains two dashed lines. The top one represents the method calls triggered by the call into the _initialize method of the PageRequestManager. The bottom one represents the method calls triggered by the call into the _updateControls method. I'll discuss these two sets of triggered method calls in the following sections, and update this figure with new method calls as we move through the chapter.

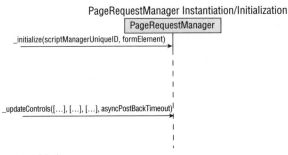

Figure 22-1

Instantiating and Initializing the Client-Side PageRequestManager

Listing 22-2 presents the internal implementation of the _initialize static method of the client-side PageRequestManager.

Listing 22-2: The _initialize Static Method of the PageRequestManager Client Class

```
Sys.WebForms.PageRequestManager._initialize =
function Sys$WebForms$PageRequestManager$_initialize(scriptManagerID, formElement)
{
    Sys.WebForms.PageRequestManager._ensureSinglePageRequestManagerInstance();
    Sys.WebForms.PageRequestManager._createPageRequestManagerInstance();
    Sys.WebForms.PageRequestManager._initializePageRequestManagerInstance(
                                          scriptManagerID, formElement);
}
```

Note that this method takes two parameters. The first is a string that contains the value of the `UniqueID` property of the current `ScriptManager` instance; the second references the `form` HTML element that contains the current `ScriptManager` instance.

This method first calls the `_ensureSinglePageRequestManagerInstance` static method on the `PageRequestManager` to ensure that the current page contains a single `PageRequestManager` instance. As the following code listing shows, `_ensureSinglePageRequestManagerInstance` calls the `getInstance` static method on the client-side `PageRequestManager` to check whether the current page already contains an instance of the client-side `PageRequestManager` class. If so, it raises an exception, because every page can contain only one instance of this class:

```
Sys.WebForms.PageRequestManager._ensureSinglePageRequestManagerInstance =
function Sys$WebForms$PageRequestManager$_ ensureSinglePageRequestManagerInstance()
{
    if (Sys.WebForms.PageRequestManager.getInstance())
        throw Error.invalidOperation(Sys.WebForms.Res.PRM_CannotRegisterTwice);
}
```

Next, `_initialize` calls the `_createPageRequestManagerInstance` static method on the `PageRequestManager` to create a new instance of the `PageRequestManager`. As the following code listing shows, this method instantiates an instance of the client-side `PageRequestManager` class and assigns it to the `_instance` static field of this class:

```
Sys.WebForms.PageRequestManager._createPageRequestManagerInstance =
function Sys$WebForms$PageRequestManager$_createPageRequestManagerInstance()
{
    Sys.WebForms.PageRequestManager._instance =
                                  new Sys.WebForms.PageRequestManager();
}
```

Finally, the `_initialize` method calls the `_initializePageRequestManagerInstance` static method to initialize the newly created `PageRequestManager` instance. As the following code listing shows, this method calls the `_initializeInternal` private instance method on the newly instantiated client-side `PageRequestManager`, passing in the value of the `UniqueID` property of the `ScriptManager` server control and the reference to the `form` HTML element of the current page:

```
Sys.WebForms.PageRequestManager._initializePageRequestManagerInstance =
function Sys$WebForms$PageRequestManager$_createPageRequestManagerInstance(
                                                scriptManagerID, formElement)
{
  Sys.WebForms.PageRequestManager.getInstance()._initializeInternal(
                                                scriptManagerID, formElement);
}
```

Figure 22-2 updates Figure 22-1 to add the method calls triggered by the _initialize static method of
the PageRequestManager.

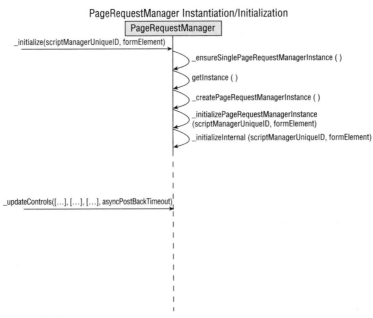

Figure 22-2

The getInstance Method of the Client-Side PageRequestManager

Listing 22-3 presents the internal implementation of the getInstance static method of the client-side
PageRequestManager class. As you can see, this method returns the value of the _instance static field
of the PageRequestManager client class.

If you need to access this instance from your client-side code, call the getInstance static method
on the client-side PageRequestManager class to return a reference to the current client-side
PageRequestManager instance.

Listing 22-3: The getInstance Static Method of the PageRequestManager Client Class

```
Sys.WebForms.PageRequestManager.getInstance =
function Sys$WebForms$PageRequestManager$getInstance()
{
  /// <returns type="Sys.WebForms.PageRequestManager"></returns>
  return Sys.WebForms.PageRequestManager._instance || null;
}
```

The Constructor of the Client-Side PageRequestManager Class

Listing 22-4 presents the implementation of the constructor of the client-side PageRequestManager class. As this code listing shows, this class contains the following private fields:

❑ _form: This field references the form DOM element associated with the HtmlForm server control. Keep in mind that an ASP.NET page may have more than one instance of the <form> HTML element. However, only one of these <form> HTML elements can have the runat="server" attribute. The ASP.NET framework represents this <form> HTML element with an instance of the HtmlForm server control. The _form field of the client-side PageRequestManager references the <form> HTML element that contains the runat="server" attribute.

❑ _updatePanelIDs: This field is an array that contains the values of the UniqueID properties of all UpdatePanel server controls on the current page after update.

❑ _updatePanelClientIDs: This field is an array that contains the values of the ClientID properties of all UpdatePanel server controls on the current page after update.

❑ _oldUpdatePanelIDs: This field is an array that contains the values of the UniqueID properties of all UpdatePanel server controls on the current page before update.

❑ _childUpdatePanelIDs: This field is an array that contains the values of the UniqueID properties of all child UpdatePanel server controls after update.

❑ _panelsToRefreshIDs: This field is an array that contains the values of the UniqueID properties of all parent UpdatePanel server controls that need refreshing.

❑ _updatePanelHasChildrenAsTriggers: This field is an array that contains the values of the UniqueID properties of all UpdatePanel server controls on the current page whose ChildrenAsTriggers Boolean property have been set to true.

❑ _asyncPostBackControlIDs: This field is an array that contains the values of the UniqueID properties of all server controls on the current page that cause asynchronous page postbacks.

❑ _asyncPostBackControlClientIDs: This field is an array that contains the values of the ClientID properties of all server controls on the current page that cause asynchronous page postbacks.

❑ _postBackControlIDs: This field is an array that contains the values of the UniqueID properties of all server controls on the current page that cause synchronous page postbacks.

❑ _postBackControlClientIDs: This field is an array that contains the values of the ClientID properties of all server controls on the current page that cause synchronous page postbacks.

❑ _scriptManagerID: This field contains the value of the UniqueID property of the current ScriptManager server control.

❑ _pageLoadedHandler: This field references the delegate registered as an event handler for the load event of the window object.

❑ _additionalInput: This field contains additional optional information.

❑ _onsubmit: This field references the original onsubmit method of the form DOM element that the _form field references. As you'll see later, the client-side PageRequestManager instance replaces this method with another method when it needs to make an asynchronous page post-back to the server. Before replacing this method, the current client-side PageRequestMananger instance stores the function in the _onsubmit field so it can be used later when the page needs to make a synchronous page postback.

❑ _onSubmitStatements: This field is an array that contains dynamically added form submit statements.

❑ * _originalDoPostBack: This field references the _doPostBack JavaScript function that performs a regular synchronous page postback to the server. As you'll see later, the client-side PageRequestManager instance replaces this JavaScript function with the one that performs an asynchronous page postback to the server when PageRequestManager needs to make an asynchronous postback request. Before replacing the _doPostBack JavaScript function, the current client-side PageRequestManager instance stores the function in the _originalDoPostBack field so it can be used later when the page needs to make a synchronous page postback.

❑ _postBackSettings: This field references an object literal with three name/value pairs that describe the postback settings for the postback request that the current client-side PageRequestManager instance is about to make to the server. The name part of the first name/value pair is the keyword async, and the value part is a Boolean value that specifies whether the current postback request is asynchronous. The name part of the second name/value pair is the keyword panelID, and the value part is a string that contains the value of the UniqueID property of the UpdatePanel server control whose trigger triggered the current asynchronous page postback. The name part of the third name/value pair is the keyword sourceElement, and the value part references the DOM element that triggered the asynchronous page postback.

❑ _request: This field references the WebRequest object that represents the current asynchronous page postback request.

❑ _onFormSubmitHandler: This field references the delegate that represents the _onFormSubmit method of the current PageRequestManager instance. As you'll see later, this instance registers this delegate as an event handler for the submit event of the form DOM element referenced by the _form field.

❑ _onFormElementClickHandler: This field references the delegate that represents the _onFormElementClick method of the current PageRequestManager instance. As you'll see later, this instance registers this delegate as an event handler for the click event of the form DOM element referenced by the _form field.

❑ _onWindowUnloadHandler: This field references the delegate that represents the _onWindowUnload method of the current PageRequestManager instance. As you'll see later, this instance registers this delegate as an event handler for the unload event of the form DOM element referenced by the _form field.

❑ _asyncPostBackTimeout: This field is a string that contains the asynchronous page postback request timeout.

❑ _controlIDToFocus: This field is a string that contains the value of the UniqueID property of the server control that has the mouse focus.

❑ _scrollPosition: This field references an object literal with two name/value pairs that describe the current position of the scroll. The name part of the first name/value pair is the keyword x, and the value part is an integer that specifies the x coordinate of the scroll bar. The name part of the second name/value pair is the keyword y, and the value part is an integer that specifies the y coordinate of the scroll bar.

❑ _dataItems: This field references a dictionary of data items.

❑ _response: This field references the WebRequestExecutor object responsible for executing the current asynchronous page postback request.

❑ _processingRequest: This field is a Boolean value that specifies whether the current PageRequestManager is processing the server response.

❑ _scriptDisposes: This field references a dictionary of script disposes.

Listing 22-4: The Constructor of the PageRequestManager Client Class

```
Sys.WebForms.PageRequestManager = function Sys$WebForms$PageRequestManager()
{
    this._form = null;
    this._updatePanelIDs = null;
    this._updatePanelClientIDs = null;
    this._oldUpdatePanelIDs = null;
    this._childUpdatePanelIDs = null;
    this._panelsToRefreshIDs = null;
    this._updatePanelHasChildrenAsTriggers = null;
    this._asyncPostBackControlIDs = null;
    this._asyncPostBackControlClientIDs = null;
    this._postBackControlIDs = null;
    this._postBackControlClientIDs = null;
    this._scriptManagerID = null;
    this._pageLoadedHandler = null;
    this._additionalInput = null;
    this._onsubmit = null;
    this._onSubmitStatements = [];
    this._originalDoPostBack = null;
    this._postBackSettings = null;
    this._request = null;
    this._onFormSubmitHandler = null;
    this._onFormElementClickHandler = null;
    this._onWindowUnloadHandler = null;
    this._asyncPostBackTimeout = null;
    this._controlIDToFocus = null;
    this._scrollPosition = null;
    this._dataItems = null;
    this._response = null;
    this._processingRequest = false;
    this._scriptDisposes = {};
}
Sys.WebForms.PageRequestManager.registerClass('Sys.WebForms.PageRequestManager');
```

The _initializeInternal Method of the Client-Side PageRequestManager

Understanding the internal implementation of the _initializeInternal method of the current PageRequestManager instance requires a good understanding of the two common types of page postback. Therefore, before diving into the implementation of this method, we need to study these two different types.

The first relies on the Submit button. As you know, when the user clicks the Submit button, the form DOM element raises the submit event and consequently invokes the onsubmit event handler. If the onsubmit event handler does not return false, the browser takes these steps:

1. Collects the names and values of the form elements.

2. Generates a list of items separated by the & character, where each item contains the name and value of a form element. Each item consists of two parts separated by the equals sign (=), the first containing the name of the form element and the second containing the value.

3. Creates an HTTP POST request.

4. Adds the list of items to the body of the request.

5. Sets the request headers, such as Content-Type, Content-Length, Host, etc.

6. Submits the request to the server synchronously.

The onsubmit event handler normally validates the values of the form elements and returns false to cancel the form submission if the validation fails.

The main problem with the first type of page postback is its strict reliance on the Submit button for form submission. There are times when the form must be submitted via DOM elements other than the Submit button. For example, you may want the form submission to occur when the user selects an item from a certain HTML element. This is where the second type of page postback comes into play.

This type relies on the __doPostBack JavaScript function. The ASP.NET server controls, such as the DropDownList, register this JavaScript function as an event handler for one of their events. For example, the DropDownList server control registers the _doPostBack JavaScript function as event handler for the onchange event of the <select> HTML element associated with the server control if the AutoPostBack property of the server control is set to true.

Listing 22-5 contains the definition of the _doPostBack JavaScript function. Since this JavaScript function is a global one, it is automatically considered as a method on the window object. As you can see, _doPostBack takes two arguments. The first is the value of the UniqueID property of the server control that caused the postback. For example, in the case of the DropDownList server control, this will be the value of the UniqueID property of the DropDownList control itself. The second argument is optional. In the case of the DropDownList server control, this will be the value of the value property of the selected <option> element of the <select> element associated with the server control.

As you can see from Listing 22-5, the _doPostBack JavaScript function takes the following steps. First, it invokes the onsubmit event handler. Recall that this event handler normally validates the values of the form elements and returns false if the validation fails. As Listing 22-5 shows, if the onsubmit event handler does not return false, the _doPostBack JavaScript function assigns its first parameter to the value property of a hidden field named __EVENTTARGET and its second parameter to the value property of a hidden field named __EVENTARGUMENT. For example, in the case of the DropDownList server control, the _doPostBack JavaScript function assigns the UniqueID property value of the server control to the value property of the __EVENTTARGET hidden field and the value of the value property of the selected option subelement of the select element associated with the server control to the value property of the __EVENTARGUMENT hidden field.

```
theForm.__EVENTTARGET.value = eventTarget;
theForm.__EVENTARGUMENT.value = eventArgument;
```

Finally, the _doPostBack JavaScript function invokes the submit method on the form DOM element to submit the values of the form elements to the server. When the submit method is invoked, under the hood, the browser takes these steps:

1. Collects the names and values of the form elements.

2. Generates a list of items separated by the & character, where each item contains the name and value of a form element. Each item consists of two parts separated by the equals sign (=), the first containing the name of the form element and the second containing the value.

3. Creates an HTTP POST request.

4. Adds to the body of the request the list of items shown in Step 2.

5. Sets the request headers, such as Content-Type, Content-Length, Host, etc.

6. Submits the request to the server synchronously.

Note that the preceding six steps are the same ones the browser takes for the first type of page postback — that is, the page postback via the Submit button. In other words, both the page postback via the Submit button and the page postback via the _doPostBack JavaScript function rely on the browser to take these steps.

Listing 22-5: The Standard __doPostBack JavaScript Function

```
<script type='text/javascript'>
<!--
  var theForm = document.forms['Form1'];
  if (!theForm)
    theForm = document.Form1;
  function __doPostBack(eventTarget, eventArgument)
  {
    if (!theForm.onsubmit || (theForm.onsubmit() != false))
    {
      theForm.__EVENTTARGET.value = eventTarget;
      theForm.__EVENTARGUMENT.value = eventArgument;
      theForm.submit();
    }
  }
// -->
</script>
```

Both the page postback via the Submit button and page postback via the _doPostBack JavaScript function suffer from the following fundamental shortcomings:

❑ The browser submits the request to the server synchronously. A synchronous request is *blocking*, meaning that the end user cannot interact with the page until the server response arrives. This dramatically degrades the responsiveness, performance, and usability of a Web application that relies heavily on normal synchronous page postbacks.

❑ In both types of page postbacks, when the server response finally arrives, the entire page reloads even though only a small portion of the page requires refreshing. This also dramatically degrades the responsiveness, performance, and usability of a graphic-heavy Web page, which takes a lot of time to re-render.

As you'll see in this chapter, the current `PageRequestManager` instance resolves both of these problems, as follows:

❑ Unlike page postback via the Submit button or the `_doPostBack` JavaScript function, it does not rely on the browser's default synchronous form submission. Instead, the current `PageRequestManager` instance uses the ASP.NET AJAX client-server communication layer discussed in previous chapters to make asynchronous page postback requests to the server.

❑ Unlike page postback via the Submit button or the `_doPostBack` JavaScript function, it does not rely on the browser's default rendering mechanism, which re-renders the entire page when the server response arrives. Instead, the current `PageRequestManager` instance uses the ASP.NET AJAX client-side framework to refresh only those parts of the page that need refreshing.

Now that you have a good understanding of the two main types of page postbacks and their shortcomings, you're ready to dive into the internal implementation of the `_initializeInternal` method of the `PageRequestManager`, as shown in Listing 22-6.

Listing 22-6: The _initializeInternal Intance Method of the PageRequestManager Client Class

```
function Sys$WebForms$PageRequestManager$_initializeInternal(scriptManagerID,
                                                             formElement)
{
    this._scriptManagerID = scriptManagerID;
    this._form = formElement;
    this._detachAndStoreOriginalFormOnSubmit();
    this._registerHandlerForFormSubmitEvent ();
    this._detachAndStoreOriginalDoPostBack();
    this._attachNewDoPostBack();
    this._registerHandlerForWindowLoadEvent();
    this._registerHandlerForFormClickEvent();
    this._registerHandlerForWindowUnloadEvent();
    this._storeOriginalFormAction();
}
```

As you can see, this method takes two arguments. The first is a string that contains the value of the `UniqueID` property of the `ScriptManager` server control. The second references the `form` DOM element of the current page. The method assigns the following two parameters to the `_scriptManagerID` and `_form` private fields of the current `PageRequestManager` instance:

```
this._scriptManagerID = scriptManagerID;
this._form = formElement;
```

Next, the `_initializeInternal` method calls the `_detachAndStoreOriginalFormOnSubmit` method shown in the following code listing. As you can see, this method detaches the `onsubmit` method from the `form` DOM element and stores it in a local field named `_onsubmit` for future reference:

```
function Sys$WebForms$PageRequestManager$_detachAndStoreOriginalFormOnSubmit()
{
  this._onsubmit = this._form.onsubmit;
  this._form.onsubmit = null;
}
```

Then the `_initializeInternal` method calls the `_registerHandlerForFormSubmitEvent` method shown in the following code listing. As you can see, this method first creates a delegate that represents the `_onFormSubmit` method of the current `PageRequestManager` instance, and then registers this delegate as an event handler for the `submit` event of the `form` element:

```
function Sys$WebForms$PageRequestManager$_registerHandlerForFormSubmitEvent ()
{
  this._onFormSubmitHandler = Function.createDelegate(this, this._onFormSubmit);
  Sys.UI.DomEvent.addHandler(this._form, 'submit', this._onFormSubmitHandler);
}
```

Recall that page postback via the Submit button causes the `form` DOM element to fire its `submit` event. Since the current `PageRequestManager` instance has registered the `_onFormSubmitHandler` delegate for this event, this delegate and consequently the `_onFormSubmit` method of the current `PageRequestManager` instance are automatically invoked. This allows the current `PageRequestManager` instance to take complete control over the first type of page postback mechanism before the page is actually posted back to the server. As you'll see later, the `_onFormSubmit` method of the current `PageRequestManager` instance will first determine whether the form submission must be done asynchronously. If so, it will bypass the browser's default synchronous form submission and use the ASP.NET AJAX client-server communication layer discussed in previous chapters to make an asynchronous page postback to the server. If the `_onFormSubmit` method of the current `PageRequestManager` instance comes to the conclusion that the form must be submitted synchronously, the method gets out of the way and allows the browser to take over the form submission and submit the form synchronously.

Now back to the discussion of the implementation of the `_initializeInternal` method of the `PageRequestManager`. Next, this method calls the `_detachAndStoreOriginalDoPostBack` method shown in the following code listing. As you can see, this method detaches the `_doPostBack` JavaScript function shown in Listing 22-5 from the `window` object and stores it in the `_originalDoPostBack` field of the current `PageRequestManager` instance for future reference:

```
function Sys$WebForms$PageRequestManager$_detachAndStoreOriginalDoPostBack()
{
  this._originalDoPostBack = window.__doPostBack;
  window.__doPostBack = null;
}
```

The `_initializeInternal` method then calls the `_attachNewDoPostBack` method shown in the following code listing. As you can see, this method first creates a delegate that represents the `_doPostBack` method of the current `PageRequestManager` instance and then attaches this method to the `window` object as its `_doPostBack` method:

```
function Sys$WebForms$PageRequestManager$_attachNewDoPostBack()
{
    window.__doPostBack = Function.createDelegate(this, this._doPostBack);
}
```

Recall that the second type of page postback invokes the _doPostBack method of the window object to submit the form to the server. Since the current PageRequestManager instance has replaced the original _doPostBack method (that is, the one shown in Listing 22-5) with the delegate that represents the _doPostBack method of the current PageRequestManager instance, when a server control such as DropDownList calls the _doPostBack method of the window object, this delegate and consequently the _doPostBack method of the current PageRequestManager instance will be called instead of the original _doPostBack method shown in Listing 22-5. This allows the current PageRequestManager instance to take complete control of the second type of page postback mechanism before the page is actually posted back to the server. As you'll see later in this chapter, the _doPostBack method of the current PageRequestManager instance will first determine whether the form submission must be done asynchronously. If so, it will bypass the browser's default synchronous form submission and use the ASP.NET AJAX client-server communication layer discussed in previous chapters to make an asynchronous page postback to the server. If the _doPostBack method of the current PageRequestManager instance comes to the conclusion that the form must be submitted synchronously, the method gets out of the way and allows the browser to take over the form submission and submit the form synchronously.

Now back to the discussion of the implementation of the _initializeInternal method. Next, this method calls the _registerHandlerForWindowLoadEvent method shown in the following code listing. As you can see, this method first creates a delegate that represents the _pageLoadedInitialLoad method of the current PageRequestManager instance, and then registers this delegate as an event handler for the load event of the window object. Therefore, when the window raises its load event, this delegate and consequently the _pageLoadedInitialLoad method of the current PageRequestManager instance are invoked:

```
function Sys$WebForms$PageRequestManager$_registerHandlerForWindowLoadEvent()
{
    this._pageLoadedHandler =
                            Function.createDelegate(this, this._pageLoadedInitialLoad);
    Sys.UI.DomEvent.addHandler(window, 'load', this._pageLoadedHandler);
}
```

Next, the _initializeInternal method calls the _registerHandlerFormClickEvent method shown in the following code listing. As you can see, this method first creates a delegate that represents the _onFormElementClick method of the current PageRequestManager instance, and then registers this delegate as an event handler for the click event of the form element:

```
function Sys$WebForms$PageRequestManager$_registerHandlerForFormClickEvent()
{
    this._onFormElementClickHandler =
                            Function.createDelegate(this, this._onFormElementClick);
    Sys.UI.DomEvent.addHandler(this._form, 'click', this._onFormElementClickHandler);
}
```

Then the _initializeInternal method calls the _registerHandlerForWindowUnloadEvent method shown in the following code listing. As you can see, this method first creates a delegate that represents the _onWindowUnload method of the current PageRequestManager instance, and then registers this delegate as an event handler for the unload event of the window object:

```
function Sys$WebForms$PageRequestManager$_registerHandlerForWindowUnloadEvent()
{
   this._onWindowUnloadHandler =
                              Function.createDelegate(this, this._onWindowUnload);
   Sys.UI.DomEvent.addHandler(window, 'unload', this._onWindowUnloadHandler);
}
```

Finally, the method calls the _storeOriginalFormAction method shown in the following code listing. As you can see, this method stores the value of the action property of the form DOM element in a custom property on the form named _initialAction for future reference. As you'll see later, the current PageRequestManager instance uses the initial action value to determine whether a given request is a cross-page postback.

```
function Sys$WebForms$PageRequestManager$_storeOriginalFormAction()
{
   this._form._initialAction = this._form.action;
}
```

Figure 22-3 updates Figure 22-2 with the method calls that the _initializeInternal method triggers. Note that Figure 22-3 inherits the bottom dashed line from Figure 22-2. Recall that this dashed line represents the method calls triggered by the call into the _updateControls method.

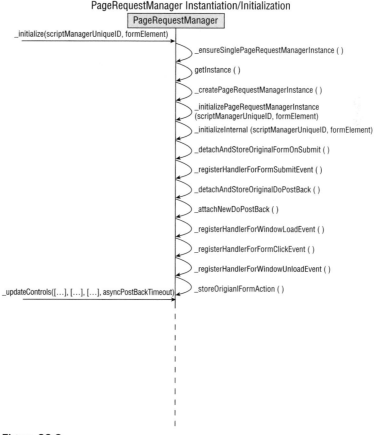

Figure 22-3

_updateControls

Listing 22-7 presents the internal implementation of the _updateControls method of the PageRequestManager. This method takes the following four parameters:

- ❑ updatePanelIDs: This parameter is an array that contains the values of the UniqueID properties of all the UpdatePanel server controls on the current page.

- ❑ asyncPostBackControlIDs: This parameter is an array that contains the values of the UniqueID properties of all the server controls on the current page that cause asynchronous page postbacks.

- ❑ postBackControlIDs: This parameter is an array that contains the values of the UniqueID properties of all the server controls on the current page that cause synchronous page postbacks.

- ❑ asyncPostBackTimeout: This parameter is a string that contains the asynchronous page postback request timeout.

Listing 22-7: The _updateControls Method of the PageRequestManager

```
function Sys$WebForms$PageRequestManager$_updateControls(updatePanelIDs,
                                                  asyncPostBackControlIDs,
                                                  postBackControlIDs,
                                                  asyncPostBackTimeout)
{
  if (updatePanelIDs)
  {
    this._updatePanelIDs = new Array(updatePanelIDs.length);
    this._updatePanelClientIDs = new Array(updatePanelIDs.length);
    this._updatePanelHasChildrenAsTriggers = new Array(updatePanelIDs.length);
    for (var i = 0; i < updatePanelIDs.length; i++)
    {
      this._updatePanelHasChildrenAsTriggers[i] =
                                        (updatePanelIDs[i].charAt(0) === 't');
      this._updatePanelIDs[i] = updatePanelIDs[i].substr(1);
      this._updatePanelClientIDs[i] =
                          this._uniqueIDToClientID(updatePanelIDs[i].substr(1));
    }
    this._asyncPostBackTimeout = asyncPostBackTimeout * 1000;
  }

  else
  {
    this._updatePanelIDs = [];
    this._updatePanelClientIDs = [];
    this._updatePanelHasChildrenAsTriggers = [];
    this._asyncPostBackTimeout = 0;
  }
  this._asyncPostBackControlIDs = [];
  this._asyncPostBackControlClientIDs = [];
```

```
for (var i = 0; i < asyncPostBackControlIDs.length; i++)
{
  Array.add(this._asyncPostBackControlIDs, asyncPostBackControlIDs[i]);
  Array.add(this._asyncPostBackControlClientIDs,
            this._uniqueIDToClientID(asyncPostBackControlIDs[i]));
}
this._postBackControlIDs = [];
this._postBackControlClientIDs = [];
for (var i = 0; i < postBackControlIDs.length; i++)
{
  Array.add(this._postBackControlIDs, postBackControlIDs [i]);
  Array.add(this._postBackControlClientIDs,
            this._uniqueIDToClientID(postBackControlIDs [i]));
}
}
```

The _updateControls method takes the following steps. First, it instantiates the _updatePanelIDs, _updatePanelClientIDs, and _updatePanelHasChildrenAsTriggers array fields of the current PageRequestManager instance:

```
this._updatePanelIDs = new Array(updatePanelIDs.length);
this._updatePanelClientIDs = new Array(updatePanelIDs.length);
this._updatePanelHasChildrenAsTriggers = new Array(updatePanelIDs.length);
```

Next, it iterates through the UniqueID property values in the updatePanelIDs parameter and takes the following actions for each enumerated UniqueID property value. (Keep in mind that this value consists of two substrings, the first containing the character t or f, and the second containing the actual UniqueID property value):

❑ As mentioned, the current PageRequestManager instance contains a private array field named _updatePanelIDs that contains the UniqueID property values of all the UpdatePanel server controls on the current page. The _updateControls method retrieves the second substring of the enumerated value and adds it to the _updatePanelIDs array:

```
this._updatePanelIDs[i] = updatePanelIDs[i].substr(1);
```

❑ The current PageRequestManager instance also contains a private array field named _updatePanelClientIDs that contains the ClientID property values of all the UpdatePanel server controls on the current page. The _updateControls method calls the _uniqueIDToClientID method to return the ClientID property value associated with the UniqueID property value and adds this ClientID property value to the _updatePanelClientIDs array:

```
this._updatePanelClientIDs[i] = this._uniqueIDToClientID(this._updatePanelIDs[i]);
```

❑ The current PageRequestManager instance contains a private Boolean array field named _updatePanelHasChildrenAsTriggers that contains one Boolean value for each UpdatePanel server control on the page, which specifies whether its child server controls trigger partial page updates. The _updateControls method retrieves the first substring of the enumerated value. If this substring contains the character t, asynchronous updates of the server control are triggered by the child controls of the UpdatePanel server control whose UniqueID property is given by the second substring, and the _updateControls method adds the Boolean value of true to the _updatePanelHasChildrenAsTriggers collection. Otherwise it adds false.

```
this._updatePanelHasChildrenAsTriggers[i] =
                              (updatePanelIDs[i].charAt(0) === 't');
```

❏ The current `PageRequestManager` instance also contains an integer field named `_asyncPostBackTimeout` that specifies the timeout (in seconds) for all asynchronous page postback requests. The `_updateControls` method converts to seconds the value passed into it as its last parameter, and assigns the value to this field:

```
this._asyncPostBackTimeout = asyncPostBackTimeout * 1000;
```

Next, the `_updateControls` method iterates through the `UniqueID` property values in the `asyncPostBackControlIDs` array and takes these actions for each value:

❏ The current `PageRequestManager` instance contains a private array field named `_asyncPostBackControlIDs` that contains the `UniqueID` property values of all the server controls on the current page that trigger asynchronous page postbacks. The `_updateControls` method adds the enumerated `UniqueID` property value to this array field:

```
Array.add(this._asyncPostBackControlIDs, asyncPostBackControlIDs[i]);
```

❏ The current `PageRequestManager` instance contains a private array field named `_asyncPostBackControlClientIDs` that contains the `ClientID` property values of all the server controls on the current page that trigger asynchronous page postbacks. The `_updateControls` method first calls the `_uniqueIDToClientID` method to return the `ClientID` property value associated with the enumerated `UniqueID` property value, and then adds this return value to this array field:

```
Array.add(this._asyncPostBackControlClientIDs,
        this._uniqueIDToClientID(asyncPostBackControlIDs[i]));
```

Next, the `_updateControls` method iterates through the `UniqueID` property values in the `postBackControlIDs` array and takes these actions for each value:

❏ The current `PageRequestManager` instance contains a private array field named `_postBackControlIDs` that contains the `UniqueID` property values of all the server controls on the current page that trigger synchronous page postbacks. The `_updateControls` method adds the enumerated `UniqueID` property value to this array field:

```
Array.add(this._postBackControlIDs, postBackControlIDs[i]);
```

❏ The current `PageRequestManager` instance contains a private array field named `_postBackControlClientIDs` that contains the `ClientID` property values of all the server controls on the current page that trigger asynchronous page postbacks. The `_updateControls` method first calls the `_uniqueIDToClientID` method to return the `ClientID` property value associated with the enumerated `UniqueID` property value, and then adds this return value to this array field:

```
Array.add(this._postBackControlClientIDs,
        this._uniqueIDToClientID(postBackControlIDs[i]));
```

As Listing 22-8 shows, the `_uniqueIDToClientID` method takes an `UniqueID` value as its argument and replaces all the dollar signs ($) with the underscore character (_).

The `UniqueID` and `ClientID` property values of an ASP.NET server control are read-only, which means that only the ASP.NET can set their values. The `UniqueID` property value of a server control is a string that consists of two substrings separated by the dollar sign ($), the first containing the value of the `ID` property of the server control and the second containing the value of the `UniqueID` property of the parent of the server control. The `ClientID` property value of a server control is a string that consists of two substrings separated by the underscore character (_), the first containing the value of the `ID` property of the server control and the second containing the value of the `ClientID` property of the parent of the server control. As you can see, the only difference between the `UniqueID` and the `ClientID` property values of a server control is the separator. That is why the `_uniqueIDToClientID` method replaces the dollar signs with the underscore characters to arrive at the `ClientID` property value.

Listing 22-8: The _uniqueIDToClientID Method of the PageRequestManager

```
function Sys$WebForms$PageRequestManager$_uniqueIDToClientID(uniqueID)
{
    // Convert unique IDs to client IDs by replacing all '$' with '_'
    return uniqueID.replace(/\$/g, '_');
}
```

Figure 22-4 updates Figure 22-3 with the new method calls.

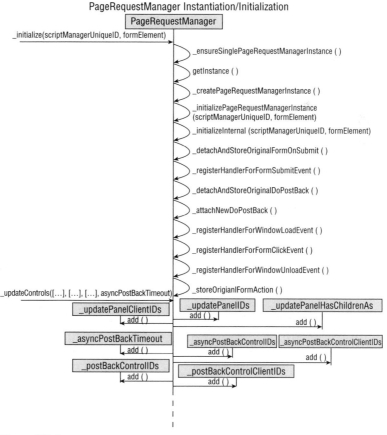

Figure 22-4

The _pageLoadedInitialLoad Method of the Client-Side PageRequestManager

When the current page is finally loaded, the `window` object raises the `load` event and calls the `_pageLoadedHandler` delegate, which in turn calls the `_pageLoadedInitialLoad` instance method of the current client-side `PageRequestManager` instance, as shown in Listing 22-9.

Listing 22-9: The _pageLoadedInitialLoad Method of the PageRequestManager Client Class

```
function Sys$WebForms$PageRequestManager$_pageLoadedInitialLoad(evt)
{
    this._pageLoaded(true);
}
```

As you can see, the `_pageLoadedInitialLoad` method calls the `_pageLoaded` method of the current client-side `PageRequestManager` instance, passing in `true` as its argument.

The _pageLoaded Method of the Client-Side PageRequestManager

Listing 22-10 presents the internal implementation of the `_pageLoaded` method of the client-side `PageRequestManager` instance.

Listing 22-10: The _pageLoaded Method of the PageRequestManager Client Class

```
function Sys$WebForms$PageRequestManager$_pageLoaded(initialLoad)
{
    var handler = this._get_eventHandlerList().getHandler("pageLoaded");
    if (handler)
        handler(this, this._getPageLoadedEventArgs(initialLoad));

    if (!initialLoad)
    {
        // If this isn't the first page load (i.e. we are doing an async postback), we
        // need to re-raise the Application's load event.
        Sys.Application.raiseLoad();
    }
}
```

This method first calls the `_get_eventHandlerList` method to return a reference to the `EventHandlerList` object that contains all the event handlers registered for the events of the current client-side `PageRequestManager` instance, and then calls the `getHandler` method on the `EventHandlerList` to return a reference to the JavaScript function whose invocation automatically invokes all the event handlers registered for the `pageLoaded` event of the current client-side `PageRequestManager` instance. I'll discuss this event later in the chapter.

```
var handler = this._get_eventHandlerList().getHandler("pageLoaded");
```

Next, the `_pageLoaded` method calls the `_getPageLoadedEventArgs` method to create and return a `PageLoadedEventArgs` object. As you'll see later, the `PageLoadedEventArgs` class is the event data class for the `pageLoaded` event of the client-side `PageRequestManager` instance.

```
var pageLoadedEventArgs = this._getPageLoadedEventArgs(initialLoad);
```

Then it calls the JavaScript function, passing in a reference to the current client-side `PageRequestManager` instance and a reference to the `PageLoadedEventArgs` instance. This JavaScript function in turn calls all the event handlers registered for the `pageLoaded` event of the current client-side `PageRequestManager` instance, passing in the same two references.

```
if (handler)
   handler(this, this._getPageLoadedEventArgs(initialLoad));
```

This enables you to perform application-specific tasks by registering an event handler for the `pageLoaded` event of the current `PageRequestManager` instance.

Figure 22-5 updates Figure 22-4 with the latest method calls. This wraps up our discussion of the instantiation/initialization process of the current client-side `PageRequestManager` instance. Keep in mind that this process occurs only for the first request and subsequent normal synchronous page post-back requests. In other words, it does not occur for subsequent asynchronous page postback requests.

In summary, the previous chapter followed the first request from the time it arrived in ASP.NET to the time the server response text, including the `PageRequestManager` instantiation/initialization script block — such as the one shown in Listing 22-1 — was sent back to the client. The previous sections of this chapter then followed this server response text from the time it arrived on the client side to the time the instantiation and initialization of the current `PageRequestManager` instance were completed.

Now the current `PageRequestManager` instance is sitting there waiting for the first or second type of page postback to occur. Recall that there are two types of page postbacks, via the Submit button and via the `_doPostBack` method of the `window` object. As we discussed earlier, as soon as the first type of page postback occurs, the `_onFormSubmit` method of the current `PageRequestManager` instance will intercept it before the page is actually posted back to the server; and as soon as the second type of page postback occurs, the `_doPostBack` method of the current `PageRequestManager` instance will intercept it before the page is actually posted back to the server. Both the `_onFormSubmit` and `_doPostBack` methods of the current `PageRequestManager` instance will first determine whether the page postback must be done asynchronously. If so, both methods bypass the browser's default synchronous form submission and use the ASP.NET AJAX client-server communication layer (discussed in previous chapters) to submit the form asynchronously. If these methods determine that the page postback must be done synchronously, they simply get out of the way and let the browser's default synchronous form submission take over and submit the form synchronously.

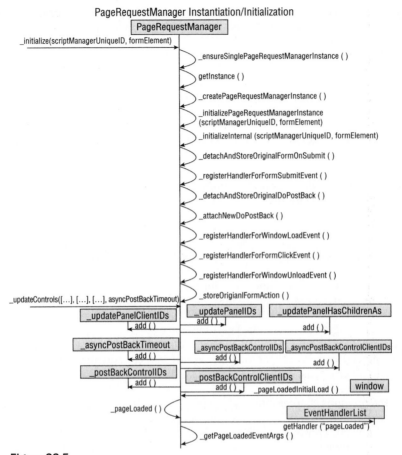

Figure 22-5

The pageLoaded Event

The previous sections followed the current client-side PageRequestManager instance through its instantiation/initialization life cycle phases. As you can see from Figure 22-5, the current client-side PageRequestManager instance fires its pageLoaded event at the end of its instantiation/initialization phase to enable you to perform application-specific tasks that must be performed right after the current client-side PageRequestManager instance is instantiated and initialized.

The client-side PageRequestManager class uses the standard ASP.NET AJAX event-implementation pattern to implement its pageLoaded event as follows:

1. The PageRequestManager class defines a collection property of type EventHandlerList to store all the event handlers registered for the events of the current client-side PageRequestManager instance.

2. It defines a getter method that returns a reference to this EventHandlerList object:

```
function Sys$WebForms$PageRequestManager$_get_eventHandlerList()
{
  if (!this._events)
    this._events = new Sys.EventHandlerList();

  return this._events;
}
```

3. It defines a method named `add_pageLoaded` that enables you to register event handlers for the `pageLoaded` event of the current client-side `PageRequestManager` instance. As the following code fragment shows, this method first calls the `get_eventHandlerList` method on the current `PageRequestManager` instance to return a reference to the `EventHandlerList` object. Then it calls the `addHandler` method on this `EventHandlerList` object to register the specified handler as an event handler for the `pageLoaded` event of the current `PageRequestManager` instance:

```
function Sys$WebForms$PageRequestManager$add_pageLoaded(handler)
{
  this._get_eventHandlerList().addHandler("pageLoaded", handler);
}
```

4. It defines a method named `remove_pageLoaded` that allows you to unregister an event handler registered for the `pageLoaded` event of the instance:

```
function Sys$WebForms$PageRequestManager$remove_pageLoaded(handler)
{
  this._get_eventHandlerList().removeHandler("pageLoaded", handler);
}
```

5. It defines a method named `_pageLoaded` that raises the `pageLoaded` event and consequently invokes all the event handlers registered for this event, as shown in Listing 22-10.

The `pageLoaded` event, like any other, is associated with an event data class whose instance acts as a container for the associated event data. The event data class associated with the `pageLoaded` event is an ASP.NET AJAX client class named `PageLoadedEventArgs`. Listing 22-11 presents the internal implementation of the `PageLoadedEventArgs` class.

Listing 22-11: The Internal Implementation of the PageLoadedEventArgs Class

```
Sys.WebForms.PageLoadedEventArgs =
function Sys$WebForms$PageLoadedEventArgs(panelsUpdated, panelsCreated, dataItems)
{
  /// <param name="panelsUpdated" type="Array"></param>
  /// <param name="panelsCreated" type="Array"></param>
  /// <param name="dataItems" type="Object" mayBeNull="true"></param>

  Sys.WebForms.PageLoadedEventArgs.initializeBase(this);
  this._panelsUpdated = panelsUpdated;
  this._panelsCreated = panelsCreated;
  // Need to use "new Object()" instead of "{}", since the latter breaks code
  // coverage.
  this._dataItems = dataItems || new Object();
}
```

(continued)

Listing 22-11 *(continued)*

```
function Sys$WebForms$PageLoadedEventArgs$get_dataItems()
{
  /// <value type="Object"></value>
  return this._dataItems;
}
function Sys$WebForms$PageLoadedEventArgs$get_panelsCreated()
{
  /// <value type="Array"></value>
  return this._panelsCreated;
}
function Sys$WebForms$PageLoadedEventArgs$get_panelsUpdated()
{
  /// <value type="Array"></value>
  return this._panelsUpdated;
}

Sys.WebForms.PageLoadedEventArgs.prototype =
{
  get_dataItems: Sys$WebForms$PageLoadedEventArgs$get_dataItems,
  get_panelsCreated: Sys$WebForms$PageLoadedEventArgs$get_panelsCreated,
  get_panelsUpdated: Sys$WebForms$PageLoadedEventArgs$get_panelsUpdated
}
Sys.WebForms.PageLoadedEventArgs.registerClass('Sys.WebForms.PageLoadedEventArgs',
                                    Sys.EventArgs);
```

As you can see, the constructor of the `PageLoadedEventArgs` class takes three parameters. The first is an array that contains the list of updated `UpdatePanel` server controls on the current page, the second is an array that contains the list of newly created `UpdatePanel` server controls, and the last is optional. The last parameter is `null` when the `pageLoaded` event is raised at the end of the instantiation/initialization of the current `PageRequestManager` instance. However, as you'll see in the following chapters, the current client-side `PageRequestManager` instance also raises the `pageLoaded` event when it is processing the server response to an asynchronous page postback request where the last parameter of the constructor of the `PageLoadedEventArgs` class comes into play.

As you can see from Listing 22-11, the constructor of the `PageLoadedEventArgs` class stores its parameters in private fields named _panelsUpdated, _panelsCreated, and _dataItems. Note that the `PageLoadedEventArgs` class exposes three getters named get_panelsUpdated, get_panelsCreated, and get_dataItems, that return these private fields.

Now let's revisit Listing 22-10, as shown again in the following code listing:

```
function Sys$WebForms$PageRequestManager$_pageLoaded(initialLoad)
{
  var handler = this._get_eventHandlerList().getHandler("pageLoaded");
  if (handler)
  {
    var args = this._getPageLoadedEventArgs(initialLoad));
    handler(this, args);
  }
}
```

```
if (!initialLoad)
{
  // If this isn't the first page load (i.e. we are doing an async postback), we
  // need to re-raise the Application's load event.
  Sys.Application.raiseLoad();
}
}
```

As you can see, for the highlighted portion of the preceding code listing, this method invokes the
_getPageLoadedEventArgs(initialLoad) internal method on the current PageRequestManager
instance to instantiate and return an instance of the PageLoadedEventArgs class, which is then passed into
the event handlers registered for the pageLoaded event of the current PageRequestManager instance.
(I'll present and discuss the internal implementation of the _getPageLoadedEventArgs method in
Chapter 28.)

Using the pageLoaded Event

As I mentioned earlier, the current client-side PageRequestManager instance fires its pageLoaded event
at the end of its instantiation/initialization process to enable you to perform application-specific tasks
that must be performed right after the current PageRequestManager instance is instantiated and initialized. Follow these steps to ensure that your required application-specific logic is executed right after the
current PageRequestManager instance is instantiated and initialized:

1. If your required application-specific logic is encapsulated in a method of an ASP.NET AJAX client class, invoke the createDelegate static method on the Function to instantiate a delegate
that represents this method. If your required application-specific logic is not already encapsulated in a method of an ASP.NET AJAX client class, write a new JavaScript function that encapsulates this logic.

2. Implement a JavaScript function that performs the following tasks:

❑ Invokes the getInstance static method on the client-side PageRequestManager class to
return a reference to the current client-side PageRequestManager instance

❑ Invokes the add_pageLoaded method on the current client-side PageRequestManager
instance to register the delegate or the JavaScript function from Step 1 as the event handler
for the pageLoaded event of the current client-side PageRequestManager instance

3. Register the JavaScript function from Step 3 as an event handler for the load event of the
window object.

Listing 22-12 contains a page that uses this recipe. If you run this page, you should see the results shown
in Figures 22-6 and 22-7. As Figure 22-6 shows, this page consists of a parent UpdatePanel server control
that contains two child UpdatePanel server controls: one is added statically and the other is added
dynamically — that is, via code. When you run this page, the page also displays the popup shown in
Figure 22-7. As you can see, this popup contains a message that displays, right after the current client-side
PageRequestManager instance is instantiated and initialized, some of the information that is available to
an event handler registered for the pageLoaded event. What you do with this information is completely
up to you. Your event handler can use it information to perform application-specific tasks that must be
performed right after the current client-side PageRequestManager instance is instantiated and initialized.

Listing 22-12: A Page that Uses the pageLoaded Event to Execute Application-Specific Logic

```
<%@ Page Language="C#" %>
<%@ Import Namespace="System.Drawing" %>
<!DOCTYPE html PUBLIC "-//W3C//DTD XHTML 1.1//EN"
"http://www.w3.org/TR/xhtml11/DTD/xhtml11.dtd">
<script runat="server">
  void Page_Load(object sender, EventArgs e)
  {
    Label parentUpdatePanelLabel =
                         (Label)Page.FindControl("ParentUpdatePanelLabel");
    parentUpdatePanelLabel.Text = "UpdatePanel refreshed at " +
                          DateTime.Now.ToString();
    Label staticChildUpdatePanelLabel =
                      (Label)Page.FindControl("StaticChildUpdatePanelLabel");
    staticChildUpdatePanelLabel.Text = "UpdatePanel refreshed at " +
                              DateTime.Now.ToString();
    UpdatePanel dynamicChildUpdatePanel = new UpdatePanel();
    dynamicChildUpdatePanel.ID = "DynamicChildUpdatePanel";
    Table table = new Table();
    table.BackColor = Color.FromArgb(90, 90, 90);
    table.ForeColor = Color.FromName("White");
    TableRow headerRow = new TableRow();
    table.Rows.Add(headerRow);
    TableHeaderCell headerCell = new TableHeaderCell();
    headerCell.Text = "Dynamic Child UpdatePanel Control";
    headerRow.Cells.Add(headerCell);
    TableRow bodyRow = new TableRow();
    table.Rows.Add(bodyRow);
    TableCell bodyCell = new TableCell();
    bodyRow.Cells.Add(bodyCell);
    Label label = new Label();
    label.ID = "DynamicChildUpdatePanelLabel";
    label.Text = "UpdatePanel refreshed at " + DateTime.Now.ToString() +
                "   ";
    bodyCell.Controls.Add(label);
    Button button = new Button();
    button.Text = "Update";
    button.ID = "DynamicChildUpdatePanelButton";
    button.Click += new EventHandler(ClickCallback);
    bodyCell.Controls.Add(button);
    dynamicChildUpdatePanel.ContentTemplateContainer.Controls.Add(table);
    PlaceHolder1.Controls.Add(dynamicChildUpdatePanel);
  }
  void ClickCallback (object sender, EventArgs e)
  {
    Label label = (Label)Page.FindControl("DynamicChildUpdatePanelLabel");
    label.Text = "UpdatePanel refreshed at " + DateTime.Now.ToString() +
                "   ";
  }
</script>
<html xmlns="http://www.w3.org/1999/xhtml">
<head runat="server">
```

```
<title>Untitled Page</title>
<script type="text/javascript" language="javascript">
  window.onload = function ()
  {
    var prm = Sys.WebForms.PageRequestManager.getInstance();
    prm.remove_pageLoaded(pageLoadedHandler);
    prm.add_pageLoaded(pageLoadedHandler);
  }

  function pageLoadedHandler(sender, e)
  {
    var panelsUpdated = e.get_panelsUpdated();
    var panelsCreated = e.get_panelsCreated();
    var dataItems = e.get_dataItems();

    var builder = new Sys.StringBuilder();
    builder.append("panelsUpdated: ");
    builder.appendLine();
    for (var i in panelsUpdated)
    {
      builder.append(panelsUpdated[i].id);
      builder.appendLine();
    }

    builder.appendLine();
    builder.append("panelsCreated: ");
    builder.appendLine();
    for (var j in panelsCreated)
    {
      builder.append(panelsCreated[j].id);
      builder.appendLine();
    }
    builder.appendLine();
    builder.append("_updatePanelIDs: ");
    builder.append(sender._updatePanelIDs);
    builder.appendLine();
    builder.appendLine();
    builder.append("_updatePanelClientIDs: ");
    builder.append(sender._updatePanelClientIDs);
    builder.appendLine();
    builder.appendLine();
    builder.append("_updatePanelHasChildrenAsTriggers: ");
    builder.append(sender._updatePanelHasChildrenAsTriggers);
    builder.appendLine();
    builder.appendLine();
    builder.append("_asyncPostBackTimeout: ");
    builder.append(sender._asyncPostBackTimeout);
    builder.appendLine();
    builder.appendLine();
    builder.append("_asyncPostBackControlIDs: ");
    builder.append(sender._asyncPostBackControlIDs);
    builder.appendLine();
    builder.appendLine();
    builder.append("_asyncPostBackControlClientIDs: ");
    builder.append(sender._asyncPostBackControlClientIDs);
```

(continued)

Listing 22-12 *(continued)*

```
        builder.appendLine();
        builder.appendLine();
        builder.append("_postBackControlIDs: ");
        builder.append(sender._postBackControlIDs);
        builder.appendLine();
        builder.appendLine();
        builder.append("_postBackControlClientIDs: ");
        builder.append(sender._postBackControlClientIDs);
        alert(builder.toString());
      }
    </script>
  </head>
  <body>
    <form id="form1" runat="server">
      <asp:ScriptManager ID="ScriptManager1" runat="server" />
      <table cellspacing="10">
        <tr>
          <td align="center" colspan="2">
            <asp:UpdatePanel ID="ParentUpdatePanel" UpdateMode="Conditional"
              runat="server">
              <ContentTemplate>
                <table cellspacing="20" style="background-color: #dddddd">
                  <tr>
                    <th>
                      Parent UpdatePanel Control</th>
                  </tr>
                  <tr>
                    <td>
                      <asp:Label ID="ParentUpdatePanelLabel" runat="server" />
                         
                      <asp:Button ID="ParentUpdatePanelButton" runat="server"
                      Text="Update" />
                    </td>
                  </tr>
                  <tr>
                    <td style="width: 100%">
                      <asp:UpdatePanel ID="StaticChildUpdatePanel" runat="server">
                        <ContentTemplate>
                          <table style="background-color: #aaaaaa">
                            <tr>
                              <th>
                                Static Child UpdatePanel Control
                              </th>
                            </tr>
                            <tr>
                              <td>
                                <asp:Label ID="StaticChildUpdatePanelLabel"
                                  runat="server" />   
                                <asp:Button ID="StaticChildUpdatePanelButton"
                                  runat="server" Text="Update" />
                              </td>
                            </tr>
```

```
                                         <tr>
                                           <td>
                                           </td>
                                         </tr>
                                       </table>
                                     </ContentTemplate>
                                     <Triggers>
                                       <asp:AsyncPostBackTrigger EventName="Click"
                                       ControlID="StaticChildUpdatePanelTrigger" />
                                     </Triggers>
                                   </asp:UpdatePanel>
                               </td>
                             </tr>
                             <tr>
                               <td style="width: 100%">
                                 <asp:PlaceHolder runat="server" ID="PlaceHolder1" />
                               </td>
                             </tr>
                           </table>
                         </ContentTemplate>
                         <Triggers>
                           <asp:AsyncPostBackTrigger ControlID="ParentUpdatePanelTrigger"
                           EventName="Click" />
                         </Triggers>
                       </asp:UpdatePanel>
                   </td>
                 </tr>
                 <tr>
                   <td style="width:50%">
                     <asp:Button ID="StaticChildUpdatePanelTrigger" runat="server"
                     Text="Static Child UpdatePanel Trigger" Width="100%" />
                   </td>
                   <td>
                     <asp:Button ID="ParentUpdatePanelTrigger" runat="server" Text="Parent
                     UpdatePanel Trigger" Width="100%" />
                   </td>
                 </tr>
               </table>
             </form>
           </body>
         </html>
```

Now let's walk through the code shown in Listing 22-12. As you can see, this page contains a server-side and a client-side script block. The server-side script block contains the implementation of the Page_Load method. This method first calls the FindControl method twice on the current Page to return references to the ParentUpdatePanelLabel and StaticChildUpdatePanelLabel server controls, and then sets the values of their Text properties to the current time:

```
Label parentUpdatePanelLabel = (Label)Page.FindControl("ParentUpdatePanelLabel");
parentUpdatePanelLabel.Text = "UpdatePanel refreshed at " +
                          DateTime.Now.ToString();
Label staticChildUpdatePanelLabel =
                          (Label)Page.FindControl("StaticChildUpdatePanelLabel");
staticChildUpdatePanelLabel.Text = "UpdatePanel refreshed at " +
                          DateTime.Now.ToString();
```

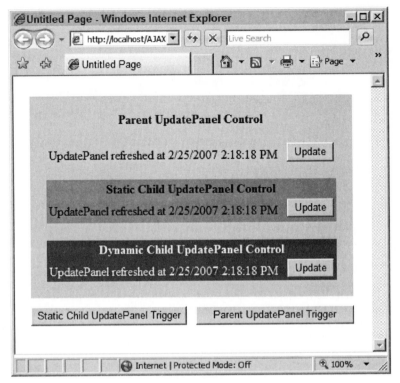

Figure 22-6

Next, the Page_Load method instantiates an UpdatePanel server control and sets its ID property value:

```
UpdatePanel dynamicChildUpdatePanel = new UpdatePanel();
dynamicChildUpdatePanel.ID = "DynamicChildUpdatePanel";
```

Then the method instantiates a Table server control with the specified background and foreground colors:

```
Table table = new Table();
table.BackColor = Color.FromArgb(90, 90, 90);
table.ForeColor = Color.FromName("White");
```

Next, it instantiates a TableRow server control to represent the header of the table:

```
TableRow headerRow = new TableRow();
table.Rows.Add(headerRow);
TableHeaderCell headerCell = new TableHeaderCell();
headerCell.Text = "Dynamic Child UpdatePanel Control";
headerRow.Cells.Add(headerCell);
```

Figure 22-7

Then it creates another `TableRow` server control with two cells that contain a `Label` and a `Button` server control, respectively:

```
TableRow bodyRow = new TableRow();
    table.Rows.Add(bodyRow);
    TableCell bodyCell = new TableCell();
    bodyRow.Cells.Add(bodyCell);
    Label label = new Label();
    label.ID = "DynamicChildUpdatePanelLabel";
    label.Text = "UpdatePanel refreshed at " + DateTime.Now.ToString() +
                 "   ";
    bodyCell.Controls.Add(label);
    Button button = new Button();
    button.Text = "Update";
    button.ID = "DynamicChildUpdatePanelButton";
    button.Click += new EventHandler(ClickCallback);
    bodyCell.Controls.Add(button);
```

Note that the `ClickCallback` method is registered as an event handler for the `Click` event of the `Button` server control. Next, the `Page_Load` method adds the `Table` server control to the `Controls` collection of the `ContentTemplateContainer` property of the `UpdatePanel` server control:

```
dynamicChildUpdatePanel.ContentTemplateContainer.Controls.Add(table);
```

As Listing 22-12 shows, the client-side script block consists of two parts. The first part registers the following JavaScript function as an event handler for the `load` event of the window object:

```
window.onload = function ()
{
    var prm = Sys.WebForms.PageRequestManager.getInstance();
    prm.add_pageLoaded(pageLoadedHandler);
}
```

As you can see from the code fragment, this JavaScript function first calls the `getInstance` static method on the client-side `PageRequestManager` class to return a reference to the current client-side `PageRequestManager` instance:

```
var prm = Sys.WebForms.PageRequestManager.getInstance();
```

Next, the function invokes the `add_pageLoaded` method on the current `PageRequestManager` instance to register the `pageLoadedHandler` JavaScript function as an event handler for the `pageLoaded` event of the current `PageRequestManager` instance:

```
prm.add_pageLoaded(pageLoadedHandler);
```

Now let's walk through the implementation of the `pageLoadedHandler` JavaScript function. When the current client-side `PageRequestManager` instance invokes this function, it passes two parameters into it. The first parameter references the current client-side `PageRequestManager` instance and the second references the `PageLoadedEventArgs` object that contains the event data for the `pageLoaded` event.

As Listing 22-12 shows, the `pageLoadedHandler` method first calls the `get_panelsUpdated` method on the `PageLoadedEventArgs` object to return a reference to the array that contains all the `UpdatePanel` server controls on the current page that were updated during the instantiation/ initialization phase of the current client-side `PageRequestManager` instance. Since this phase occurs when the current page is accessed for the first time, there are no prior `UpdatePanel` server controls to update and therefore the call to the `get_panelsUpdated` method is bound to return an empty array:

```
var panelsUpdated = e.get_panelsUpdated();
```

Next, the `pageLoadedHandler` method calls the `get_panelsCreated` method on the `PageLoadedEventArgs` object to return a reference to the array that contains all the `UpdatePanel` server controls that were created and added to the current page during the instantiation/initialization phase of the current client-side `PageRequestManager` instance. As I mentioned earlier, because this phase occurs when the current page is accessed for the first time, all the `UpdatePanel` server controls on the current page are created and added to the current page, which means that the call into the `get_panelsCreated` method returns an array that contains all the `UpdatePanel` server controls on the current page:

```
var panelsCreated = e.get_panelsCreated();
```

Next, the `pageLoadedHandler` method instantiates a `StringBuilder`:

```
var builder = new Sys.StringBuilder();
```

Then it populates the `StringBuilder` with the `UniqueID` property values of all the `UpdatePanel` server controls in the `panelsUpdated` array. As I just mentioned, this array is empty:

```
builder.append("panelsUpdated: ");
builder.appendLine();
for (var i in panelsUpdated)
{
  builder.append(panelsUpdated[i].id);
  builder.appendLine();
}
```

Next, it populates the `StringBuilder` with the `UniqueID` property values of the all the `UpdatePanel` server controls in the `panelsCreated` array. As I just mentioned, this array contains all the `UpdatePanel` server controls on the current page:

```
for (var j in panelsCreated)
{
  builder.append(panelsCreated[j].id);
  builder.appendLine();
}
```

Then the `pageLoadedHandler` method adds the content of the `_updatePanelIDs` field of the current client-side `PageRequestManager` instance to the `StringBuilder`. Recall that the first parameter (that is, the sender parameter) of the `pageLoadedHandler` method references the current client-side `PageRequestManager` instance. Also recall that the `_updatePanelIDs` field of the current `PageRequestManager` instance contains the comma-separated list of the `UniqueID` property values of all the `UpdatePanel` server controls on the current page, both updated and created:

```
builder.appendLine();
builder.append("_updatePanelIDs: ");
builder.append(sender._updatePanelIDs);
```

Next, it adds the content of the `_updatePanelClientIDs` field of the current client-side `PageRequestManager` instance to the `StringBuilder`. Recall that the `_updatePanelClientIDs` field contains the comma-separated list of the `ClientID` property values of all the `UpdatePanel` server controls on the current page, both updated and created:

```
builder.appendLine();
builder.appendLine();
builder.append("_updatePanelClientIDs: ");
builder.append(sender._updatePanelClientIDs);
```

Then it adds the content of the `_updatePanelHasChildrenAsTriggers` field of the current client-side `PageRequestManager` instance to the `StringBuilder`. Recall that the `_updatePanelHasChildrenAsTriggers` field contains the comma-separated list of Boolean values, one for each `UpdatePanel` server control in the `_updatePanelIDs`:

```
builder.appendLine();
builder.appendLine();
builder.append("_updatePanelHasChildrenAsTriggers: ");
builder.append(sender._updatePanelHasChildrenAsTriggers);
```

Next, the pageLoadedHandler method adds the value of the _asyncPostBackTimeout field of the current client-side PageRequestManager instance to the StringBuilder. Recall that this field contains the asynchronous page postback request timeout:

```
builder.appendLine();
builder.appendLine();
builder.append("_asyncPostBackTimeout: ");
builder.append(sender._asyncPostBackTimeout);
```

Next, it adds the content of the _asyncPostBackControlIDs field of the current client-side PageRequestManager instance to the StringBuilder. Recall that the _asyncPostBackControlIDs field contains the comma-separated list of the UniqueID property values of all the server controls on the current page that cause asynchronous page postbacks:

```
builder.appendLine();
builder.appendLine();
builder.append("_asyncPostBackControlIDs: ");
builder.append(sender._asyncPostBackControlIDs);
```

Then it adds the content of the _asyncPostBackControlClientIDs field of the current client-side PageRequestManager instance to the StringBuilder. Recall that the _asyncPostBackControlClientIDs field contains the comma-separated list of the ClientID property values of all the server controls on the current page that cause asynchronous page postbacks:

```
builder.appendLine();
builder.appendLine();
builder.append("_asyncPostBackControlClientIDs: ");
builder.append(sender._asyncPostBackControlClientIDs);
```

Next, it adds the content of the _postBackControlIDs field of the current client-side PageRequestManager instance to the StringBuilder. Recall that the _postBackControlIDs field contains the comma-separated list of the UniqueID property values of all the server controls on the current page that cause synchronous page postbacks:

```
builder.appendLine();
builder.appendLine();
builder.append("_postBackControlIDs: ");
builder.append(sender._postBackControlIDs);
```

Then it adds the content of the _postBackControlClientIDs field of the current client-side PageRequestManager instance to the StringBuilder. Recall that the _postBackControlClientIDs field contains the comma-separated list of the ClientID property values of all the server controls on the current page that cause synchronous page postbacks:

```
builder.appendLine();
builder.appendLine();
builder.append("_postBackControlClientIDs: ");
builder.append(sender._postBackControlClientIDs);
```

Finally, the `pageLoadedHandler` method displays the content of the `StringBuilder` in a popup, shown in Figure 22-7.

```
alert(builder.toString());
```

As Figure 22-7 shows:

❑ The `panelsUpdated` array is empty as expected.

❑ The `panelsCreated` array contains all the `UpdatePanel` server controls on the current page: `ParentUpdatePanel`, `StaticChildUpdatePanel`, and `DynamicChildUpdatePanel`, as expected. As we discussed, when the current page is loaded for the first time, all the `UpdatePanel` server controls are created and added to the current page.

❑ The `_updatePanelIDs` field of the current `PageRequestManager` instance returns the comma-separated list of the `UniqueID` properties of all the `UpdatePanel` server controls on the current page: `ParentUpdatePanel`, `StaticChildUpdatePanel`, and `DynamicChildUpdatePanel`. Note that the `UniqueID` property values in this example are the same as the `ID` property values because none of the `UpdatePanel` server controls in this example belongs to a parent server control that implements the `INamingContainer` interface.

❑ The `_updatePanelClientIDs` field of the current `PageRequestManager` instance returns the comma-separated list of the `ClientID` properties of all the `UpdatePanel` server controls on the current page: `ParentUpdatePanel`, `StaticChildUpdatePanel`, and `DynamicChildUpdatePanel`. Note that the `ClientID` property values in this example are the same as the `ID` property values because none of the `UpdatePanel` server controls in this example belongs to a parent server control that implements the `INamingContainer` interface.

❑ The `_updatePanelHasChildrenAsTriggers` field of the current `PageRequestManger` instance returns the comma-separated list of the Boolean values, one for each `UpdatePanel` server control. Because this example contains three `UpdatePanel` server controls and because the `ChildrenAsTriggers` properties of all three `UpdatePanel` server controls are set to `true` by default, the `_updatePanelHasChildrenAsTrigger` field contains a comma-separated list of three `true` values.

❑ The `_asyncPostBackTimeout` field of the current `PageRequestManager` instance returns the default value, which is `90000`.

❑ The `_asyncPostBackControlIDs` field of the current `PageRequestManager` instance returns the comma-separated list of the `UniqueID` property values of all asynchronous postback server controls. This example contains two asynchronous postback `Button` server controls: `ParentUpdatePanelTrigger` and `StaticChildUpdatePanelTrigger`.

❑ The `_asyncPostBackControlClientIDs` field of the current `PageRequestManager` instance returns the comma-separated list of the `ClientID` property values of all asynchronous postback server controls. This example contains two asynchronous postback `Button` server controls: `ParentUpdatePanelTrigger` and `StaticChildUpdatePanelTrigger`. Again, because these two `Button` server controls do not belong to a server control that implements the `INamingContainer` interface, their `UniqueID`, `ClientID`, and `ID` properties have the same values.

Keep in mind that the arrays returned from the calls into the `get_panelsUpdated` and `get_panelsCreated` methods contain references to the actual updated and created `UpdatePanel` server controls. This gives your event handler (registered for the `pageLoaded` event of the current

PageRequestManager instance) a powerful tool with which to modify the contents of these UpdatePanel server controls or to enhance their functionality. The next example should give you an idea of the types of things you could do within your event handler.

Listing 22-13 contains a page that registers an event handler for the pageLoaded event of the current PageRequestManager instance, where it attaches a Mover object to each UpdatePanel server control. Recall from Chapter 7 that we developed an ASP.NET AJAX component named Mover. When an instance of this component is attached to a control, the end user can freely move the control.

As you can see, the page shown in Listing 22-12 contains two UpdatePanel server controls. I've intentionally kept the contents of these UpdatePanel server controls simple so we can focus on what matters to our discussions. However, you can make these contents as complex as you want.

Listing 22-13: A Page that Attaches Movers to UpdatePanel Server Controls

```
<%@ Page Language="C#" %>
<%@ Import Namespace="System.Drawing" %>
<!DOCTYPE html PUBLIC "-//W3C//DTD XHTML 1.1//EN"
"http://www.w3.org/TR/xhtml11/DTD/xhtml11.dtd">
<html xmlns="http://www.w3.org/1999/xhtml">
<head runat="server">
  <title>Untitled Page</title>
  <script type="text/javascript" language="javascript">
    window.onload = function ()
    {
      var prm = Sys.WebForms.PageRequestManager.getInstance();
      prm.remove_pageLoaded(pageLoadedHandler);
      prm.add_pageLoaded(pageLoadedHandler);
    }

    function pageLoadedHandler(sender, e)
    {

      var updatePanelMover;
      var updatePanelProvider;
      var addUpdatePanelDelegate;

      var panelsCreated = e.get_panelsCreated();

      for (var j in panelsCreated)
      {
        updatePanelMover = new Delegates.Mover("container"+j);
        updatePanelProvider = new Delegates.UpdatePanelProvider(panelsCreated[j]);
        addUpdatePanelDelegate = Function.createDelegate(updatePanelProvider,
                                        updatePanelProvider.addUpdatePanel);
        updatePanelMover.addContent(addUpdatePanelDelegate);
      }
    }
  </script>
</head>
```

```
<body>
  <form id="form1" runat="server">
    <asp:ScriptManager ID="ScriptManager1" runat="server">
      <Scripts>
        <asp:ScriptReference Path="Delegate.js" />
      </Scripts>
    </asp:ScriptManager>
    <asp:UpdatePanel ID="UpdatePanel1" runat="server">
      <ContentTemplate>
        <asp:Image ImageUrl="~/images.jpg" runat="server" />
      </ContentTemplate>
    </asp:UpdatePanel>
    <asp:UpdatePanel ID="UpdatePanel2" runat="server">
      <ContentTemplate>
        <a href="Javascript:">Wrox Web Site</a>
      </ContentTemplate>
    </asp:UpdatePanel>
  </form>
</body>
</html>
```

Now let's walk through the implementation of the pageLoadedHandler JavaScript function.

This function invokes the get_panelsCreated method on the PageLoadedEventArgs object to return a reference to the array that contains all the newly created UpdatePanel server control on the current page:

```
var panelsCreated = e.get_panelsCreated();
```

Next, the function iterates through the UpdatePanel server controls in the panelsCreated array and takes the following steps for each enumerated UpdatePanel control. First it instantiates a Mover object:

```
updatePanelMover = new Delegates.Mover("container"+j);
```

Next, it instantiates an UpdatePanelProvder object, passing in the enumerated UpdatePanel server control as its argument:

```
updatePanelProvider = new Delegates.UpdatePanelProvider(panelsCreated[j]);
```

Then it calls the createDelegate static method on the Function to create a delegate that represents the addUpdatePanel method of the UpdatePanelProvider object:

```
addUpdatePanelDelegate = Function.createDelegate(updatePanelProvider,
                                    updatePanelProvider.addUpdatePanel);
```

Finally, it invokes the addContent method on the Mover object, passing in the delegate. Recall from Chapter 7 that the addContent method automatically invokes this delegate and consequently the addUpdatePanel method on the UpdataPanelProvider object.

```
updatePanelMover.addContent(addUpdatePanelDelegate);
```

Listing 22-14 presents the content of the Delegates.js JavaScript file. The boldfaced portion of this code listing contains the code for a new ASP.NET AJAX client class named UpdatePanelProvider.

Listing 22-14: The Content of the Delegates.js JavaScript File

```
Type.registerNamespace("Delegates");
Delegates.Mover = function (containerId)
{
  var container = $get(containerId);
  Delegates.Mover.incrementMoversCount();
  if (!container)
  {
    container = document.createElement("div");
    this.containerId = container.id = containerId;
    container.style.position = "absolute";
    document.body.insertBefore(container, document.forms[0]);
    $addHandlers(container, { mousedown: this.mousedowncb }, this);
  }
}

Delegates.Mover.prototype =
{
  addContent : Delegates$Mover$invokeAddContentDelegate,
  mousedowncb : Delegates$Mover$mousedowncb,
  mouseupcb : Delegates$Mover$mouseupcb,
  mousemovecb : Delegates$Mover$mousemovecb
}

Delegates.Mover.incrementMoversCount = function()
{
  if (typeof(this.moversCount) == "undefined")
    this.moversCount = 0;
  this.moversCount++;
}

Delegates.Mover.get_moversCount = function()
{
  return this.moversCount;
}

function Delegates$Mover$invokeAddContentDelegate(addContentDelegate)
{
  addContentDelegate(this.containerId);
}

function Delegates$Mover$mousedowncb(domEvent)
{
  var container = $get(this.containerId);
  this.oldClientX = domEvent.clientX;
  this.oldClientY = domEvent.clientY;
  var events = {mousemove: this.mousemovecb, mouseup: this.mouseupcb}
```

```
    $addHandlers(document, events, this);
    container.style.zIndex += Delegates.Mover.get_moversCount();
    domEvent.preventDefault();
}

function Delegates$Mover$mouseupcb(domEvent)
{
  var container = $get(this.containerId);
  $clearHandlers(document);
  container.style.zIndex -= Delegates.Mover.get_moversCount();
  domEvent.preventDefault();
}

function Delegates$Mover$mousemovecb(domEvent)
{
  var container = $get(this.containerId);
  var deltaClientX = domEvent.clientX - this.oldClientX;
  var deltaClientY = domEvent.clientY - this.oldClientY;
  var containerLocation = Sys.UI.DomElement.getLocation(container);
  Sys.UI.DomElement.setLocation(container, containerLocation.x+deltaClientX,
  containerLocation.y+deltaClientY);
  this.oldClientX = domEvent.clientX;
  this.oldClientY = domEvent.clientY;
  domEvent.preventDefault();
}

Delegates.UpdatePanelProvider = function (updatePanel)
{
  this.updatePanel = updatePanel;
}

Delegates.UpdatePanelProvider.prototype =
{
  addUpdatePanel : Delegates$UpdatePanelProvider$addUpdatePanel
}

function Delegates$UpdatePanelProvider$addUpdatePanel(containerId)
{
  var container = $get(containerId);
  container.appendChild(this.updatePanel);
}

Delegates.Mover.registerClass("Delegates.Mover");
Delegates.UpdatePanelProvider.registerClass("Delegates.UpdatePanelProvider");

if (typeof(Sys) !== 'undefined')
    Sys.Application.notifyScriptLoaded();
```

As you can see, because the `PageLoadedEventArgs` event data class provides you with references to the actual updated and created `UpdatePanel` server controls, you can do really cool things within your event handler for the `pageLoaded` event.

I'll wrap up this section by drawing your attention to something important in Listings 22-12 and 22-13. Note that both code listings perform the registration of the `pageLoadedHandler` function for the `pageLoaded` event inside an event handler for the `load` event of the `window` object, as opposed to the `pageLoad` method. To find out why this is, we need to visit the internal implementation of the `Render` method of the `ScriptManager` server control, as shown in Listing 22-15.

Listing 22-15: The Render Method of the Current ScriptManager Server Control

```
protected override void Render(HtmlTextWriter writer)
{
  this.PageRequestManager.Render(writer);
  if (!this.IsInAsyncPostBack)
    this.IPage.ClientScript.RegisterStartupScript(typeof(ScriptManager),
                                                  "AppInitialize",
  "Sys.Application.initialize();\r\n", true);
  base.Render(writer);
}
```

As you can see from the highlighted portions of Listing 22-15, the `Render` method of the current `ScriptManager` server control calls the following two methods:

1. First, it calls the `Render` method on the current server-side `PageRequestManager` instance. As discussed thoroughly in the previous chapter, the `Render` method of the current server-side `PageRequestManager` instance renders the following script block, which is then sent to the requesting browser:

```
<script type="text/javascript">
  //<![CDATA[
    Sys.WebForms.PageRequestManager._initialize('ScriptManager1',
                                    document.getElementById('Form1'));
    Sys.WebForms.PageRequestManager.getInstance()._updateControls(
                    ['tUpdatePanel1', 'fUpdatePanel2', 'tUpdatePanel3'],
                    ['SyncButton1', 'SyncButton2'],
                    ['AsyncButton1', 'AsyncButton2']);
  //]]
</script>
```

As you can see, the script block shown calls the `_initialize` static method on the client-side `PageRequestManager` class to instantiate and to initialize the current client-side `PageRequestManager` instance. As discussed thoroughly earlier in this chapter, the `_initialize` static method is the one that finally raises the `pageLoaded` event of the current client-side `PageRequestManager` instance.

2. Next, the `Render` method of the current `ScriptManager` server control calls the `RegisterStartupScript` method on the `ClientScript` property of the current page to render the following script block at the bottom of the current page:

```
<script type="text/javascript">
  //<![CDATA[
    Sys.Application.initialize();
  //]]
</script>
```

As you can see, the script block calls the initialize method on the Application object that represents the current ASP.NET AJAX application. As discussed thoroughly in Chapter 8, the call into the initialize method finally calls the pageLoad method.

As you can see, the script block that raises the pageLoaded event of the current client-side PageRequestManager instance is rendered before the script block that calls the pageLoad method. That is why, if you register a JavaScript function as an event handler for the pageLoaded event of the current client-side PageRequestManager instance inside the pageLoad method, your JavaScript function will not be invoked when the pageLoaded event is raised at the end of the instantiation/initialization phase.

Making an Asynchronous Page Postback

The previous section followed the current client-side PageRequestManager instance through its instantiation and initialization life cycle phases. As discussed earlier, the current client-side pageRequestManager instance goes through these life cycle phases only once during its entire lifetime.

In this section we'll follow the current client-side PageRequestManager instance through its life cycle phases to make an asynchronous page postback request to the server. As discussed earlier, ASP.NET provides two different mechanisms for triggering a page postback: the Submit button and the _doPostBack method.

Assume that a page postback via the _doPostBack method of the window object has just occurred and that consequently the _doPostBack method of the current PageRequestManager instance has just been invoked.

Helper Methods

The implementation of the _doPostBack method of the PageRequestManager makes use of four other helper methods of the current PageRequestManager instance. I'll present and discuss the implementations of these four helper methods first.

_createPostBackSettings

The PageRequestManager exposes an private method named _createPostBackSettings, as shown in Listing 22-16, that takes three parameters: the first is a Boolean value that specifies whether the current page postback request is asynchronous, the second is a string that contains the value of the UniqueID property of the UpdatePanel server control whose child server control causes the current postback, and the third references the DOM element that caused the current postback. This private method creates and returns an object literal with three name/value pairs. The name part of the first name/value pair is the keyword async, and the value part contains the value of the first parameter of the method. The name part of the second name/value pair is the keyword panelID, and the value part contains the value of the second parameter of the method. The name part of the third name/value pair is the keyword sourceElement, and the value part contains the value of the third parameter of the method.

Listing 22-16: The _createPostBackSettings Private Method of PageRequestManager

```
function Sys$WebForms$PageRequestManager$_createPostBackSettings(async, panelID,
                                                                  sourceElement)
{
  return { async: async, panelID: panelID, sourceElement: sourceElement };
}
```

_findNearestElement

The PageRequestManager exposes a private method named _findNearestElement that takes a UniqueID property value and returns a reference to the nearest element. As Listing 22-17 shows, this method uses the fact that the UniqueID property value of an ASP.NET server control is a string that contains one or more substrings separated by the dollar sign ($), each of which contains the UniqueID property value of an ancestor of the server control. As you can see, the _findNearestElement method first calls the _uniqueIDToClientID method on the current PageRequestManager instance to return the ClientID property value associated with the specified UniqueID property value (see Listing 22-10):

```
var clientID = this._uniqueIDToClientID(uniqueID);
```

Next, the method invokes the getElementById method on the document object to return a reference to the DOM element with the preceding ClientID property value:

```
var element = document.getElementById(clientID);
```

If the current document does indeed contain a DOM element with the desired ClientID property value, the _findNearestElement method simply returns this reference. However, if the current document does not contain a DOM element with the specified ClientID property value, the _findNearestElement method accesses the last substring in the UniqueID property value string and repeats the previous steps:

```
var indexOfLastDollar = uniqueID.lastIndexOf('$');
uniqueID = uniqueID.substring(0, indexOfLastDollar);
```

The _findNearestElement method keeps repeating the same steps for each substring of the UniqueID property value string until it locates the substring or UniqueID property value whose associated DOM element exists in the current document, or it returns null. (Keep in mind that each substring is itself a UniqueID property value.)

Listing 22-17: The _findNearestElement Private Method of PageRequestManager

```
function Sys$WebForms$PageRequestManager$_findNearestElement(uniqueID)
{
  while (uniqueID.length > 0)
  {
    var clientID = this._uniqueIDToClientID(uniqueID);
    var element = document.getElementById(clientID);
    if (element)
      return element;
```

```
      var indexOfLastDollar = uniqueID.lastIndexOf('$');
      if (indexOfLastDollar === -1)
        return null;

      uniqueID = uniqueID.substring(0, indexOfLastDollar);
    }
  return null;
}
```

_matchesParentIDInList

The current `PageRequestManager` instance features an internal method named `_matchesParentIDInList` that takes two parameters. The first is a string that contains a `ClientID` property value and the second is an array of `ClientID` property values. As you can see from Listing 22-18, this method searches the array for the `ClientID` property value of the parent server control of the server control whose `ClientID` property value is given by the first parameter. The method return `true` if the search succeeds and `false` otherwise.

Listing 22-18: The _matchesParentIDInList Method of PageRequestManager

```
function Sys$WebForms$PageRequestManager$_matchesParentIDInList(clientID,
                                                   parentClientIDList)
{
  for (var i = 0; i < parentClientIDList.length; i++)
  {
    if (clientID.startsWith(parentClientIDList[i] + "_")) return true;
  }
  return false;
}
```

_getPostBackSettings

The `_getPostBackSettings` method of the `PageRequestManager` takes two parameters, as shown in Listing 22-19. The second parameter is a `UniqueID` property value of the server control that caused the current postback. The first parameter references the server control whose `UniqueID` property value best matches this `UniqueID` property value. This method has two main responsibilities:

❑ Determine whether the current postback is asynchronous

❑ Determine whether the server control that the second parameter references resides inside an `UpdatePanel` server control whose `ChildrenAsTriggers` property is set to `true`

The `_getPostBackSettings` method walks up the DOM hierarchy of the server control that the first parameter references and takes the following steps for each server control in this DOM hierarchy:

❑ If the server control resides in an `UpdatePanel` server control whose `ChildrenAsTriggers` property is set to `true`, the `_getPostBackSettings` method creates an object literal whose:

  ❑ `async` property is set to `true` to specify that the current postback is asynchronous

When a server control that resides in an UpdatePanel *server control whose* ChildrenAsTriggers *property is set to* true *causes a page postback, the current* PageRequestManager *instance treats the page postback as asynchronous page postback regardless of whether or not the server control has been explicitly registered as a trigger for asynchronous page postback.*

❑ panelID property is set to a string that contains two substrings separated by the | character, where the first substring contains the UniqueID property value of the UpdatePanel server control and the second contains the UniqueID property value of the server control. As you'll see later, the presence of the UniqueID property value of this UpdatePanel server control signals the server that this UpdatePanel server control must be updated.

When a server control that resides in an UpdatePanel *server control whose* ChildrenAsTriggers *property is set to* true *causes a page postback, it automatically triggers the update of its parent* UpdatePanel *server control.*

❑ sourceElement property contains a reference to the server control.

❑ If the _asyncPostBackControlIDs collection contains the UniqueID property value of the server control or one of its ancestor server controls, but the server control does not reside in an UpdatePanel server control whose ChildrenAsTrigger property is set to true, the _getPostBackSettings method creates an object literal whose:

❑ async property is set to true to specify that the current postback is asynchronous.

When a server control whose UniqueID *property value belongs to the* _asyncPostBackControlIDs *collection of the current* PageRequestManager *instance causes a page postback, the current* PageRequestManager *instance treats the page postback as asynchronous.*

❑ panelID property is set to a string that contains two substrings separated by the | character where the first substring contains the UniqueID property value of the ScriptManager server control and the second contains the UniqueID property value of the server control.

❑ sourceElement property contains a reference to the server control.

❑ If the _postBackControlIDs collection contains the UniqueID property value of the server control or one of its ancestor server controls, the _getPostBackSettings method creates an object literal whose:

❑ async property is set to false to specify that the current postback is a regular synchronous postback. This instructs the current PageRequestManager instance that the responsibility of posting the current page back to the server must be delegated to the browser to allow the browser to perform a regular page postback to the server.

❑ panelID property is set to null.

❑ sourceElement is set to null.

When a server control whose UniqueID *property value belongs to the* _postBackControlIDs *collection of the current* PageRequestManager *instance causes a page postback, the current* PageRequestManager *instance doesn't get involved in the form submission.*

Listing 22-19: The _getPostBackSettings Method of the PageRequestManager

```
function Sys$WebForms$PageRequestManager$_getPostBackSettings(element,
                                                              elementUniqueID)
{
  var originalElement = element;
  // Keep track of whether we have an AsyncPostBackControl but still
  // want to see if we're inside an UpdatePanel anyway.
  var proposedSettings = null;
  // Walk up DOM hierarchy to find out the nearest container of
  // the element that caused the postback.
  while (element)
  {
    if (element.id)
    {
      // First try an exact match for async postback, regular postback,
      // or UpdatePanel
      if (!proposedSettings &&
          Array.contains(this._asyncPostBackControlClientIDs, element.id))
      {
        // The element explicitly causes an async postback
        proposedSettings = this._createPostBackSettings(true,
                         this._scriptManagerID + '|' + elementUniqueID,
                                                      originalElement);
      }

      else
      {
        if (!proposedSettings &&
            Array.contains(this._postBackControlClientIDs, element.id))
        {
          // The element explicitly doesn't cause an async postback
          return this._createPostBackSettings(false, null, null);
        }

        else
        {
          var indexOfPanel = Array.indexOf(this._updatePanelClientIDs, element.id);
          if (indexOfPanel !== -1)
          {
            // The element causes an async postback because it is inside
            // an UpdatePanel
            if (this._updatePanelHasChildrenAsTriggers[indexOfPanel])
            {
              // If it was in an UpdatePanel and the panel has
              // ChildrenAsTriggers=true, then
              // we do an async postback and refresh the given panel
              // Although we do the search by looking at ClientIDs, we end
              // up sending a UniqueID back to the server so that we can
              // call FindControl() with it.
              return this._createPostBackSettings(true,
                        this._updatePanelIDs[indexOfPanel] + '|' + elementUniqueID,
                                              originalElement);
            }
```

(continued)

Listing 22-19 (continued)

```
                    else
                    {
                        // The element was inside an UpdatePanel so we do an async postback,
                        // but because it has ChildrenAsTriggers=false we don't update
                        // this panel.
                        return this._createPostBackSettings(true,
                                        this._scriptManagerID + '|' + elementUniqueID,
                                                    originalElement);
                    }
                }
            }
        }
    }
    // Then try near matches
    if (!proposedSettings &&
        this._matchesParentIDInList(element.id,
                                    this._asyncPostBackControlClientIDs))
    {
        // The element explicitly causes an async postback
        proposedSettings = this._createPostBackSettings(true,
                            this._scriptManagerID + '|' + elementUniqueID,
                                            originalElement);
    }

    else
    {
        if (!proposedSettings &&
            this._matchesParentIDInList(element.id,
                                    this._postBackControlClientIDs))
        {
            // The element explicitly doesn't cause an async postback
            return this._createPostBackSettings(false, null, null);
        }
    }
}
element = element.parentNode;
}
// If we have proposed settings that means we found a match for an
// AsyncPostBackControl but were still searching for an UpdatePanel.
// If we got here that means we didn't find the UpdatePanel so we
// just fall back to the original AsyncPostBackControl settings that
// we created.
if (!proposedSettings)
{
    // The element doesn't cause an async postback
    return this._createPostBackSettings(false, null, null);
}

else
    return proposedSettings;
}
```

_doPostBack

Now back to the main topic of discussion: the implementation of the _doPostBack method of the current PageRequestManager instance. As discussed earlier, this method is invoked when a page postback occurs via the _doPostBack method of the window object. An example of such a page postback is the one that occurs when an end user selects a new item from a DropDownList server control whose AutoPostBack property has been set to true.

Listing 22-20 presents the internal implementation of the _doPostBack method of the current PageRequestManager instance. This method takes the same two parameters that the original _doPostBack method takes. The first is the value of the UniqueID property of the server control that caused the page postback. For example, in the case of the DropDownList server control whose AutoPostBack property is set to true, the first parameter is the value of the UniqueID property of the DropDownList control. The second parameter is optional. For example, in the case of the DropDownList server control whose AutoPostBack property is set to true, the second parameter is the selected value of the server control.

Listing 22-20: The _doPostBack Method of the PageRequestManager

```
function Sys$WebForms$PageRequestManager$_doPostBack(eventTarget, eventArgument)
{
   this._additionalInput = null;
   var form = this._form;

   if (form.action !== form._initialAction)
   {
      // Allow the default form submit to take place. Since the current
      // form action is different from the initial one, it's a cross-page postback.
      this._postBackSettings = this._createPostBackSettings(false, null, null);
   }

   else
   {
      // If it's not a cross-page post, see if we can find the DOM element
      // that caused the postback
      var clientID = this._uniqueIDToClientID(eventTarget);
      var postBackElement = document.getElementById(clientID);
      if (!postBackElement)
      {
         // If the control has no matching DOM element we look for an exact
         // match from RegisterAsyncPostBackControl or RegisterPostBackControl.
         // If we can't find anything about it then we do a search based on
         // naming containers to still try and find a match.
         if (Array.contains(this._asyncPostBackControlIDs, eventTarget))
         {
            // Exact match for async postback
            this._postBackSettings = this._createPostBackSettings(true,
                                    this._scriptManagerID + '|' + eventTarget, null);
         }

      else
         {
            if (Array.contains(this._postBackControlIDs, eventTarget))
```

(continued)

Listing 22-20 *(continued)*

```
            {
                // Exact match for regular postback
                this._postBackSettings = this._createPostBackSettings(false, null, null);
            }

            else
            {
                // Find nearest element based on UniqueID in case the element calling
                // __doPostBack doesn't have an ID. GridView does this for its Update
                // button and without this we can't do async postbacks.
                var nearestUniqueIDMatch = this._findNearestElement(eventTarget);
                if (nearestUniqueIDMatch)
                {
                    // We found a related parent element, so walk up the DOM to find out
                    // what kind of postback we should do.
                    this._postBackSettings =
                            this._getPostBackSettings(nearestUniqueIDMatch, eventTarget);
                }

                else
                {
                    // Can't find any DOM element at all related to the eventTarget,
                    // so we just give up and do a regular postback.
                    this._postBackSettings = this._createPostBackSettings(false, null,
                                                                          null);
                }
            }
        }
    }
    else
    {
        // The element was found, so walk up the DOM to find out what kind
        // of postback we should do.
        this._postBackSettings = this._getPostBackSettings(postBackElement,
                                                           eventTarget);
    }
}
if (!this._postBackSettings.async)
{
    // Temporarily restore the form's onsubmit handler expando while calling
    // the original ASP.NET 2.0 __doPostBack() function.
    form.onsubmit = this._onsubmit;
    this._originalDoPostBack(eventTarget, eventArgument);
    form.onsubmit = null;
    return;
}
form.__EVENTTARGET.value = eventTarget;
form.__EVENTARGUMENT.value = eventArgument;
this._onFormSubmit();
}
```

As Listing 22-20 shows, the _doPostBack method first checks whether the current value of
the action property of the form is different from its original value. Recall from Listing 22-5 that the
_initializeInternal method of the current PageRequestManager instance stores the original

`action` value in a custom property on the form named `_initialAction`. If the current `action` value is different from the original `action` value, this indicates that the current postback is a cross-page postback. Therefore, the `_doPostBack` method calls the `_createPostBackSettings` method on the current `PageRequestManager` instance to create a postback settings — an object literal with `async` property value of `false` — to indicate that the current postback is not asynchronous. (Recall from Listing 22-16 that the `_createPostBackSettings` method creates an object literal, known as postback settings, with three properties named `async`, `panelID`, and `sourceElement`.)

```
if (form.action !== form._initialAction)
    this._postBackSettings = this._createPostBackSettings(false, null, null);
```

If the current form `action` value is the same as the original form `action` value, the `_doPostBack` method calls the `_uniqueIDToClientID` method on the current `PageRequestManager` instance, passing in its first parameter. Recall that the first parameter is a string that contains the `UniqueID` property value of the server control that caused the current page postback. Also recall from Listing 22-8 that the `_uniqueIDToClientID` method simply returns the `ClientID` property value of the server control with the specified `UniqueID` property value.:

```
var clientID = this._uniqueIDToClientID(eventTarget);
```

The `_doPostBack` method then calls the `getElementById` method on the document object, passing in the `ClientID` property value to return a reference to the DOM element that caused the current page postback.

```
var postBackElement = document.getElementById(clientID);
```

If the `getElementById` method does not return `null`, the `_doPostBack` method calls the `_getPostBackSettings` method discussed earlier to create the appropriate postback settings object:

```
this._postBackSettings = this._getPostBackSettings(postBackElement, eventTarget);
```

If the `getElementById` method does return `null`, the `_doPostBack` method takes the following steps to get a reference to the DOM element that caused the current page postback:

❑ If the `_asyncPostBackControlIDs` collection of the current `PageRequestManager` instance contains the `UniqueID` property value of the server control that caused the current postback, the `_doPostBack` method creates an object literal whose:

   ❑ `async` property is set to `true` to specify that the current postback is asynchronous

   ❑ `panelID` property is set to a string that contains two substrings separated by the | character, where the first substring contains the `UniqueID` property value of the `ScriptManager` server control and the second contains the `UniqueID` property value of the server control that caused the current page postback

   ❑ `sourceElement` property is set to null:

```
if (Array.contains(this._asyncPostBackControlIDs, eventTarget))
{
  // Exact match for async postback
  this._postBackSettings = this._createPostBackSettings(true,
                           this._scriptManagerID + '|' + eventTarget, null);
}
```

❑ If the `_postBackControlIDs` collection of the current `PageRequestManager` instance contains the `UniqueID` property value of the server control that caused the current postback, the `_doPostBack` method creates an object literal whose

   ❑ `async` property is set to `false` to specify that the current postback is a regular synchronous postback. This instructs the current `PageRequestManager` instance that the responsibility of posting the current page back to the server must be delegated to the browser to allow the browser to perform a regular page postback to the server.

   ❑ `panelID` property is set to `null`.

   ❑ `sourceElement` is set to `null`:

```
if (Array.contains(this._postBackControlIDs, eventTarget))
{
  // Exact match for regular postback
  this._postBackSettings = this._createPostBackSettings(false, null, null);
}
```

❑ If neither the `_asyncPostBackControlIDs` nor the `_postBackControlIDs` collections of the current `PageRequestManager` instance contains the `UniqueID` property value of the server control that caused the current postback, the `_doPostBack` method calls the `_findNearestElement` method on the current `PageRequestManager` instance to return a reference to the DOM element that best matches the specified `UniqueID` property:

```
var nearestUniqueIDMatch = this._findNearestElement(eventTarget);
```

❑ If it finds such an element on the current page, it calls the `_getPostBackSettings` method on the current `PageRequestManager` instance to return the appropriate postback settings object, as discussed earlier:

```
if (nearestUniqueIDMatch)
{
  // We found a related parent element, so walk up the DOM to find out
  // what kind of postback we should do.
  this._postBackSettings =
        this._getPostBackSettings(nearestUniqueIDMatch, eventTarget);
}
```

❑ If it doesn't find such an element on the current page, it gives up the search for the element with the specified `UniqueID` and creates a postback settings object whose:

   ❑ `async` property is set to `false` to specify that the current postback is a regular synchronous postback. This instructs the current `PageRequestManager` instance that the responsibility of posting the current page back to the server must be delegated to the browser to allow the browser to perform a regular page postback to the server.

   ❑ `panelID` property is set to `null`.

   ❑ `sourceElement` is set to `null`:

```
            else
            {
                // Can't find any DOM element at all related to the eventTarget,
                // so we just give up and do a regular postback.
                this._postBackSettings = this._createPostBackSettings(false, null,
                                                                       null);
            }
```

Next, the _doPostBack method checks whether the async property of the postback settings object is set. If not, this is an indication that the current page postback is not asynchronous, and consequently the _doPostBack method first assigns the _onsubmit method of the current PageRequestManager instance as the onsubmit method on the form element. Recall that the _onsubmit method references the original value of the onsubmit property of the form. Next, the _doPostBack method of the current PageRequestManager instance invokes the _originalDoPostBack method of the current PageRequestManager instance. Recall that the _originalDoPostBack method references the ASP.NET 2.0 standard __doPostBack global JavaScript function, which performs normal synchronous page postbacks to the server:

```
    if (!this._postBackSettings.async)
    {
        // Temporarily restore the form's onsubmit handler expando while calling
        // the original ASP.NET 2.0 __doPostBack() function.
        form.onsubmit = this._onsubmit;
        this._originalDoPostBack(eventTarget, eventArgument);
        form.onsubmit = null;
        return;
    }
```

If the async property of the postback settings object has been set, this is an indication that the current page postback is asynchronous page and consequently that the _doPostBack method of the current PageRequestManager instance first stores the UniqueID property value of the server control that caused the current postback in a hidden field named __EVENTTARGET:

```
    form.__EVENTTARGET.value = eventTarget;
```

Next, it stores the optional event argument parameter in a hidden field named __EVENTARGUMENT:

```
    form.__EVENTARGUMENT.value = eventArgument;
```

Finally, it invokes the _onFormSubmit method on the current PageRequestManager instance to submit the form to the server. As you'll see in the next section, the _onFormSubmit method uses the ASP.NET AJAX client-server communication layer to post the page back to the server asynchronously:

```
    this._onFormSubmit();
```

_onFormSubmit

As we discussed earlier, the ASP.NET framework provides an ASP.NET page with two types of post-backs: through the Submit button and through the ASP.NET 2.0 standard __doPostBack global JavaScript function. As you can see, both approaches end up calling the _onFormSubmit method of the current PageRequestManager instance. Listing 22-21 presents the internal implementation of the _onFormSubmit method of the PageRequestManager.

Listing 22-21: The _onFormSubmit Method of the Client-Side PageRequestManager Instance

```
function Sys$WebForms$PageRequestManager$_onFormSubmit(evt)
{
  var continueSubmit = true;
  if (this._onsubmit)
    continueSubmit = this._onsubmit();
  if (continueSubmit)
  {
    for (var i = 0; i < this._onSubmitStatements.length; i++)
    {
      if (!this._onSubmitStatements[i]())
      {
        continueSubmit = false;
        break;
      }
    }
  }
  if (!continueSubmit)
  {
    if (evt)
      evt.preventDefault();

    return;
  }
  var form = this._form;
  if (form.action !== form._initialAction)
    return;
  if (!this._postBackSettings.async)
    return;
  var formBody = new Sys.StringBuilder();
  formBody.append(this._scriptManagerID + '=' +
                  this._postBackSettings.panelID + '&');
  var count = form.elements.length;
  for (var i = 0; i < count; i++)
  {
    var element = form.elements[i];
    var name = element.name;
    if (typeof(name) === "undefined" || (name === null) || (name.length === 0))
      continue;
    var tagName = element.tagName;
    if (tagName === 'INPUT')
    {
      var type = element.type;
      if ((type === 'text') ||
          (type === 'password') ||
          (type === 'hidden') ||
          (((type === 'checkbox') || (type === 'radio')) && element.checked))
      {
        formBody.append(name);
        formBody.append('=');
```

```
          formBody.append(encodeURIComponent(element.value));
          formBody.append('&');
        }
      }

      else if (tagName === 'SELECT')
      {
        var optionCount = element.options.length;
        for (var j = 0; j < optionCount; j++)
        {
          var option = element.options[j];
          if (option.selected)
          {
            formBody.append(name);
            formBody.append('=');
            formBody.append(encodeURIComponent(option.value));
            formBody.append('&');
          }
        }
      }

      else if (tagName === 'TEXTAREA')
      {
        formBody.append(name);
        formBody.append('=');
        formBody.append(encodeURIComponent(element.value));
        formBody.append('&');
      }
    }
    if (this._additionalInput)
    {
      formBody.append(this._additionalInput);
      this._additionalInput = null;
    }
    var request = new Sys.Net.WebRequest();
    request.set_url(form.action);
    request.get_headers()['X-MicrosoftAjax'] = 'Delta=true';
    request.get_headers()['Cache-Control'] = 'no-cache';
    request.set_timeout(this._asyncPostBackTimeout);
    request.add_completed(Function.createDelegate(this,
                                            this._onFormSubmitCompleted));
    request.set_body(formBody.toString());
    var handler = this._get_eventHandlerList().getHandler("initializeRequest");
    if (handler)
    {
      var eventArgs = new Sys.WebForms.InitializeRequestEventArgs(request,
                                        this._postBackSettings.sourceElement);
      handler(this, eventArgs);
      continueSubmit = !eventArgs.get_cancel();
    }
```

(continued)

Listing 22-21 *(continued)*

```
    if (!continueSubmit)
    {
      if (evt)
        evt.preventDefault();
      return;
    }
    this._scrollPosition = this._getScrollPosition();
    this.abortPostBack();
    handler = this._get_eventHandlerList().getHandler("beginRequest");
    if (handler)
    {
      var eventArgs = new Sys.WebForms.BeginRequestEventArgs(request,
                                    this._postBackSettings.sourceElement);
      handler(this, eventArgs);
    }
    this._request = request;
    request.invoke();
    if (evt)
      evt.preventDefault();
}
```

As you can see, this method takes the following steps. First, it calls the _onsubmit method on the current PageRequestManager instance. Recall from Listing 22-5 that the _initializeInternal method assigned the original value of the onsubmit property of the window object to the _onsubmit property of the current PageRequestManager instance. The original onsubmit method is normally where the values of the form elements are validated. This method returns false if the data validation fails:

```
    if (this._onsubmit)
      continueSubmit = this._onsubmit();
```

If the call into the original onsubmit method returns true — that is, if the data validation succeeds — the _onFormSubmit method iterates through the JavaScript statements in the _onSubmitStatements array and executes each statement. As you'll see later, the _onSubmitStatements array contains the dynamically added form onsubmit statements:

```
    for (var i = 0; i < this._onSubmitStatements.length; i++)
    {
      if (!this._onSubmitStatements[i]())
      {
        continueSubmit = false;
        break;
      }
    }
```

If either the original onsubmit method or one of the dynamically added form onsubmit statements returns false, the _onFormSubmit method cancels the form submission by invoking the preventDefault method on the DomEvent object that represents the current event:

```
    evt.preventDefault();
```

Next, the _onFormSubmit method compares the current value of the action property of the form with its original value. If these two values are different, this is an indication that the current form is being posted back to a different page and consequently that the current request is a cross-page postback. As such, the _onFormSubmit method simply returns. Recall that the _onFormSubmit method is the event handler registered for the submit event of the form. The form submission proceeds as normal if all the event handlers registered for the submit event either return true or don't return a value.

As you can see, the asynchronous page postback mechanism of the ASP.NET AJAX client-side framework does not apply to cross-page postback requests. This means that these requests proceed as usual with no intervention from the ASP.NET AJAX framework:

```
var form = this._form;
if (form.action !== form._initialAction)
    return;
```

Next, the _onFormSubmit method checks whether the current request is an asynchronous page postback. If not, it simply returns, which means that the form submission proceeds as usual: the page is synchronously posted back to the server and the entire page is re-rendered when the server response arrives:

```
if (!this._postBackSettings.async)
    return;
```

As you can see, the ASP.NET AJAX client-side framework falls back to the normal page postback for synchronous requests.

If the current request is neither a cross-page nor a normal synchronous page postback, the _onSubmitForm method takes complete control over the submission of the values of the form elements, bypassing the normal form submission mechanism and taking the following steps.

First it creates a StringBuilder to accumulate the strings that will constitute the body of the asynchronous Web request being made to the server, where each string will contain the value of a form element. Therefore, each string consists of two parts separated by an equals sign (=), the first part being a string that normally contains the value of the name HTML attribute of the form element and the second part being a string that contains the value of the form element. Keep in mind that every server control renders its UniqueID property value as the value of the name HTML attribute of its associated HTML element. For example, the DropDownList server control renders its UniqueID property value as the value of the name HTML attribute of its associated <select> HTML element:

```
var formBody = new Sys.StringBuilder();
```

The first part of the first string contains the value of the UniqueID property of the current ScriptManager server control and the second part of the first string contains the value of the panelID property of the postback settings object:

```
formBody.append(this._scriptManagerID + '=' +
                this._postBackSettings.panelID + '&');
```

Next, the _onFormSubmit method iterates through the form elements and takes the following steps for each enumerated element. If the element is a text, password, hidden, checkbox, or radio input form element, the _onFormSubmit method appends a string that consists of two parts: the first contains the name of the element and the second contains its value:

```
if (tagName === 'INPUT')
{
  var type = element.type;
  if ((type === 'text') ||
      (type === 'password') ||
      (type === 'hidden') ||
      (((type === 'checkbox') || (type === 'radio')) && element.checked))
  {
    formBody.append(name);
    formBody.append('=');
    formBody.append(encodeURIComponent(element.value));
    formBody.append('&');
  }
}
```

If the enumerated form element is a select input element, the _onFormSubmit method iterates through the options collection of the element and creates one string for each selected option, the first part of the string containing the name of the select element and the second part containing the option value:

```
else if (tagName === 'SELECT')
{
  var optionCount = element.options.length;
  for (var j = 0; j < optionCount; j++)
  {
    var option = element.options[j];
    if (option.selected)
    {
      formBody.append(name);
      formBody.append('=');
      formBody.append(encodeURIComponent(option.value));
      formBody.append('&');
    }
  }
}
```

If the form input element is a textarea, the _onFormSubmit method appends a string that consists of two parts, the first containing the name of the element and the second part containing its value:

```
else if (tagName === 'TEXTAREA')
{
  formBody.append(name);
  formBody.append('=');
  formBody.append(encodeURIComponent(element.value));
  formBody.append('&');
}
}
```

If there's additional information that needs to be sent to the server, the _onSubmitForm method appends this information as well:

```
if (this._additionalInput)
{
  formBody.append(this._additionalInput);
  this._additionalInput = null;
}
```

So far, you've populated the `StringBuilder` object with a bunch of strings, each of which contains the value of a specific input form element. Next, the `_onSubmitForm` method creates a `WebRequest` object to represent the current asynchronous Web request:

```
var request = new Sys.Net.WebRequest();
```

Next, it specifies the target URL for the current request:

```
request.set_url(form.action);
```

Then it adds a header named `'X-MicrosoftAjax'` and sets its value to `'Delta=true'` to signal the server-side `PageRequestManager` instance that the current request is an asynchronous page postback:

```
request.get_headers()['X-MicrosoftAjax'] = 'Delta=true';
```

Next, the `_onFormSubmit` method adds a header named `'Cache-Control'` and sets its value to `'no-cache'` to signal the server that it mustn't cache the response, because the current request is an asynchronous page postback:

```
request.get_headers()['Cache-Control'] = 'no-cache';
```

Next, it specifies the request timeout. If the server response does not arrive within the specified time, the `WebRequest` will abort the current request:

```
request.set_timeout(this._asyncPostBackTimeout);
```

Then it calls the `createDelegate` static method on the `Function` to create a delegate that represents the `_onFormSubmitCompleted` method of the current `PageRequestManager` instance and registers this delegate as an event handler for the completed event of the `WebRequest` object. This object will automatically call this delegate and consequently the `_onFormSumitCompleted` method when the server response finally arrives:

```
request.add_completed(Function.createDelegate(this, this._onFormSubmitCompleted));
```

Next, the `_onFormSubmit` method populates the body of the current request with the content of the `StringBuilder` object. Recall that this object accumulated the strings that contain the values of the form elements. In other words, the values of the form elements will be sent to the server in the body of the request:

```
request.set_body(formBody.toString());
```

Next, the `_onFormSubmit` method calls the `getHandler` method on the `EventHandlerList` object that contains all the event handlers registered for the events of the current `PageRequestManager` instance, in order to return a reference to a JavaScript function whose invocation automatically invokes all the event handlers registered for the `initializeRequest` event of the current `PageRequestManager` instance:

```
var handler = this._get_eventHandlerList().getHandler("initializeRequest");
```

Then the _onFormSubmit method creates an instance of an ASP.NET AJAX class named InitializeRequestEventArgs, passing in a reference to the WebRequest object that represents the current request and the DOM element that caused the postback. As you'll see later in this chapter, InitializeRequestEventArgs is the event data class for the initializeRequest event of the current PageRequestManager instance:

```
var eventArgs = new Sys.WebForms.InitializeRequestEventArgs(request,
                                   this._postBackSettings.sourceElement);
```

Then, it invokes the previously mentioned JavaScript function, passing in a reference to the current PageRequestManager and InitializeRequestEventArgs instances. Invoking this JavaScript function automatically invokes the event handlers registered for the initializeRequest event of the current PageRequestManager instance, passing in the same two references — that is, a reference to the current PageRequestManager instance and a reference to the InitializeRequestEventArgs instance:

```
handler(this, eventArgs);
```

If you register an event handler for the initializeRequest event of the current PageRequestManager instance, your event handler will receive the two references previously mentioned. Your handler can then use these two references to get the complete information about the current request and use this information to determine whether the execution of the current request will violate application-specific business rules. If so, your event handler must call the set_cancel method on the InitializeRequestEventArgs object to ask the current PageRequestManager instance to cancel the current request.

Next, the _onSubmitForm method checks whether any of the event handlers has requested the cancellation of the current request:

```
continueSubmit = !eventArgs.get_cancel();
```

If so, the method invokes the preventDefault method on the DomEvent object that represents the current submit event to abort the form submission:

```
if (!continueSubmit)
{
  if (evt)
    evt.preventDefault();
  return;
}
```

Next, the _onFormSubmit method stores the current scroll position in a field named _scrollPosition for future use. As you'll see later, when the server response finally arrives, the current PageRequestManager instance will compare the new scroll position with the old one to determine whether the scroll position has changed:

```
this._scrollPosition = this._getScrollPosition();
```

Then the _onFormSubmit method calls the abortPostBack method on the current PageRequestManager instance to abort any ongoing requests. This ensures two things. First, only the latest request takes effect. Second, you don't exhaust the browser's two-connections-per-server limit:

```
this.abortPostBack();
```

Then the _onFormSubmit method calls the getHandler method on the EventHandlerList that contains all the event handlers registered for the events of the current PageRequestManager instance, in order to return a reference to the JavaScript function whose invocation automatically invokes all the event handlers registered for the beginRequest event of the current PageRequestManager instance:

```
handler = this._get_eventHandlerList().getHandler("beginRequest");
```

Next, it creates an instance of the BeginRequestEventArgs class, passing in a reference to the WebRequest object that represents the current request and a reference to the DOM element that causes the current form submission. As you'll see later in this chapter, BeginRequestEventArgs is the event data class for the beginRequest event of the PageRequestManager:

```
var eventArgs = new Sys.WebForms.BeginRequestEventArgs(request,
                                      this._postBackSettings.sourceElement);
```

Then it invokes the previously mentioned JavaScript function, and consequently invokes the event handlers registered for the beginRequest event passing in a reference to the current PageRequestManager instance and a reference to the BeginRequestEventArgs class:

```
handler(this, eventArgs);
```

> *If you register an event handler for the beginRequest event of the current PageRequestManager instance, your event handler will receive the two references previously mentioned. Your handler can then use these two references to get the complete information about the current request and use this information to perform application-specific request-beginning tasks.*

Next, for future use, the _onSubmitForm method stores the reference to the WebRequest object that represents the current request in a private field of the current PageRequestManager instance named _request:

```
this._request = request;
```

Then, to submit the request to the server, the method calls the invoke method on the WebRequest object that represents the current request:

```
request.invoke();
```

Finally, the method calls the preventDefault method on the DomEvent object that represents the current submit event of the form, in order to prevent the form from performing a regular synchronous page postback to the server:

```
evt.preventDefault();
```

Figure 22-8 contains a diagram that shows all the method calls involved in making an asynchronous page postback request.

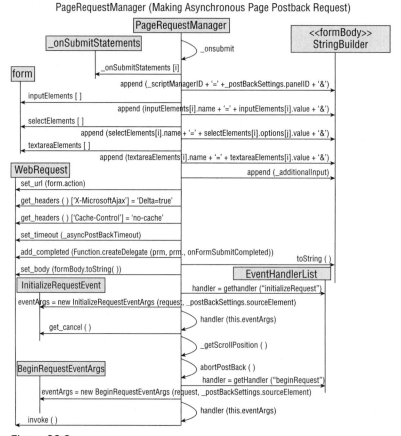

Figure 22-8

The initializeRequest Event

As you can see from Figure 22-8, the current client-side PageRequestManager instance fires its initializeRequest event right after completing the instantiation and initialization of the WebRequest object that represents the current asynchronous page postback request. This enables you to do the following:

❑ Perform application-specific tasks that must be performed right after the WebRequest object is instantiated and initialized.

❑ Run application-specific validation logic to determine whether the current form submission violates any application-specific rules. If so, you can have the current PageRequestManager instance abort the request.

The client-side `PageRequestManager` class uses the standard ASP.NET AJAX event implementation pattern to implement its `initializeRequest` event as follows:

1. The class defines a method named `add_initializeRequest` that enables you to register event handlers for the `initializeRequest` event of the current client-side `PageRequestManager` instance. As the following code fragment shows, this method first calls the `get_eventHandlerList` method on the current `PageRequestManager` instance to return a reference to the `EventHandlerList` object that contains all the event handlers registered for the events of the current `PageRequestManager` instance. Then the `add_initializeRequest` method calls the `addHandler` method on this `EventHandlerList` object to register the specified handler as an event handler for the `initializeRequest` event of the current `PageRequestManager` instance:

```
function Sys$WebForms$PageRequestManager$add_initializeRequest(handler)
{
    this._get_eventHandlerList().addHandler("initializeRequest", handler);
}
```

2. The class defines a method named `remove_initializeRequest` that enables you to unregister an event handler registered for the `initializeRequest` event of the instance:

```
function Sys$WebForms$PageRequestManager$remove_initializeRequest(handler)
{
    this._get_eventHandlerList().removeHandler("initializeRequest", handler);
}
```

The `initializeRequest` event, like any other, is associated with an event data class whose instance acts as a container for the associated event data. The event data class associated with the `initializeRequest` event is an ASP.NET AJAX client class named `InitializeRequestEventArgs`. Listing 22-22 presents the internal implementation of the `InitializeRequestEventArgs` class.

Listing 22-22: The InitializeRequestEventArgs Class

```
Sys.WebForms.InitializeRequestEventArgs =
function Sys$WebForms$InitializeRequestEventArgs(request, postBackElement)
{
    /// <param name="request" type="Sys.Net.WebRequest"></param>
    /// <param name="postBackElement" domElement="true"></param>

    Sys.WebForms.InitializeRequestEventArgs.initializeBase(this);
    this._request = request;
    this._postBackElement = postBackElement;
}
function Sys$WebForms$InitializeRequestEventArgs$get_postBackElement()
{
    /// <value domElement="true"></value>
    return this._postBackElement;
}
```

(continued)

Listing 22-22 *(continued)*

```
function Sys$WebForms$InitializeRequestEventArgs$get_request()
{
  /// <value type="Sys.Net.WebRequest"></value>
  return this._request;
}
Sys.WebForms.InitializeRequestEventArgs.prototype =
{
  get_postBackElement: Sys$WebForms$InitializeRequestEventArgs$get_postBackElement,
  get_request: Sys$WebForms$InitializeRequestEventArgs$get_request
}
Sys.WebForms.InitializeRequestEventArgs.registerClass(
                  'Sys.WebForms.InitializeRequestEventArgs',
                  Sys.CancelEventArgs);
```

As you can see, the constructor of the `InitializeRequestEventArgs` event data class takes two parameters, the first referencing the `WebRequest` object that represents the current asynchronous page postback request being made, and the second referencing the DOM element that caused the current asynchronous page postback. This constructor assigns these parameters to two internal fields named `_request` and `_postBackElement`:

```
this._request = request;
this._postBackElement = postBackElement;
```

Note that the `InitializeRequestEventArgs` class exposes two getters named `get_request` and `get_postBackElement` that return references to these two fields.

As Listing 22-22 shows, the `InitializeRequestEventArgs` class derives from the `CancelEventArgs` base class:

```
Sys.WebForms.InitializeRequestEventArgs.registerClass(
                  'Sys.WebForms.InitializeRequestEventArgs',
                  Sys.CancelEventArgs);
```

Because of this, the `InitializeRequestEventArgs` class inherits the `get_cancel` and `set_cancel` methods from the `CancelEventArgs` base class. As you'll see later, an event handler registered for the `initializeRequest` event of the current `PageRequestManager` instance can call the `set_cancel` method, passing in `true` as its argument to request the current `PageRequestManager` instance to cancel the request.

Using the initializeRequest Event

Listing 22-23 contains a page that handles the `initializeRequest` event of the current `PageRequestManager` instance. If you run this page you should see the result shown in Figure 22-6. Now, if you click on the Parent UpdatePanel Trigger button shown in Figure 22-6, you should get the popup shown in Figure 22-9.

Listing 22-23: A Page that Uses the initializeRequest Event

```
<%@ Page Language="C#" %>
<%@ Import Namespace="System.Drawing" %>
<!DOCTYPE html PUBLIC "-//W3C//DTD XHTML 1.1//EN"
"http://www.w3.org/TR/xhtml11/DTD/xhtml11.dtd">
<script runat="server">
  void Page_Load(object sender, EventArgs e)
  {
    Label parentUpdatePanelLabel =
          (Label)Page.FindControl("ParentUpdatePanelLabel");
    parentUpdatePanelLabel.Text = "UpdatePanel refreshed at " +
                                  DateTime.Now.ToString();
    Label staticChildUpdatePanelLabel =
                  (Label)Page.FindControl("StaticChildUpdatePanelLabel");
    staticChildUpdatePanelLabel.Text = "UpdatePanel refreshed at " +
                                       DateTime.Now.ToString();
    UpdatePanel dynamicChildUpdatePanel = new UpdatePanel();
    dynamicChildUpdatePanel.ID = "DynamicChildUpdatePanel";
    Table table = new Table();
    table.BackColor = Color.FromArgb(90, 90, 90);
    table.ForeColor = Color.FromName("White");
    TableRow headerRow = new TableRow();
    table.Rows.Add(headerRow);
    TableHeaderCell headerCell = new TableHeaderCell();
    headerCell.Text = "Dynamic Child UpdatePanel Control";
    headerRow.Cells.Add(headerCell);
    TableRow bodyRow = new TableRow();
    table.Rows.Add(bodyRow);
    TableCell bodyCell = new TableCell();
    bodyRow.Cells.Add(bodyCell);
    Label label = new Label();
    label.ID = "DynamicChildUpdatePanelLabel";
    label.Text = "UpdatePanel refreshed at " + DateTime.Now.ToString() +
                 "   ";
    bodyCell.Controls.Add(label);
    Button button = new Button();
    button.Text = "Update";
    button.ID = "DynamicChildUpdatePanelButton";
    button.Click += new EventHandler(button_Click);
    bodyCell.Controls.Add(button);
    dynamicChildUpdatePanel.ContentTemplateContainer.Controls.Add(table);
    PlaceHolder1.Controls.Add(dynamicChildUpdatePanel);
  }
  void button_Click(object sender, EventArgs e)
  {
    Label label = (Label)Page.FindControl("DynamicChildUpdatePanelLabel");
    label.Text = "UpdatePanel refreshed at " + DateTime.Now.ToString() +
 "   ";
  }
</script>
```

(continued)

Listing 22-23 *(continued)*

```html
<html xmlns="http://www.w3.org/1999/xhtml">
<head runat="server">
  <title>Untitled Page</title>
  <script type="text/javascript" language="javascript">
    function pageLoad()
    {
      var prm = Sys.WebForms.PageRequestManager.getInstance();
      prm.remove_initializeRequest(initializeRequestHandler);
      prm.add_initializeRequest(initializeRequestHandler);
    }

    function initializeRequestHandler(sender, e)
    {
      var request = e.get_request();
      var postBackElement = e.get_postBackElement();

      var builder = new Sys.StringBuilder();

      builder.append("Postback Element: ");
      builder.append(postBackElement.id);
      builder.appendLine();
      builder.appendLine();

      builder.append("Request Target URL: ");
      builder.appendLine();
      builder.append(request.get_url());
      builder.appendLine();
      builder.appendLine();

      builder.append("Request Headers: ");
      builder.appendLine();
      var headers = request.get_headers();
      var headerValue;
      for (var headerName in headers)
      {
        builder.append(headerName);
        builder.append(" = '");
        headerValue = headers[headerName];
        builder.append(headerValue);
        builder.append("'");
        builder.appendLine();
      }

      builder.appendLine();
      builder.append("Request Timeout: ");
      builder.append(request.get_timeout());
      builder.appendLine();
      builder.appendLine();

      builder.append("Request Body: ");
      builder.appendLine();
      builder.append(request.get_body());
```

```
            builder.appendLine();
            alert(builder.toString());
        }
    </script>
</head>
<body>
  <form id="form1" runat="server">
    <asp:ScriptManager ID="ScriptManager1" runat="server" />
    <table cellspacing="10">
      <tr>
        <td align="center" colspan="2">
          <asp:UpdatePanel ID="ParentUpdatePanel" UpdateMode="Conditional"
          runat="server">
            <ContentTemplate>
              <table cellspacing="20" style="background-color: #dddddd">
                <tr>
                  <th>
                    Parent UpdatePanel Control</th>
                </tr>
                <tr>
                  <td>
                    <asp:Label ID="ParentUpdatePanelLabel" runat="server" />
                       
                    <asp:Button ID="ParentUpdatePanelButton" runat="server"
                    Text="Update" />
                  </td>
                </tr>
                <tr>
                  <td style="width: 100%">
                    <asp:UpdatePanel ID="StaticChildUpdatePanel" runat="server">
                      <ContentTemplate>
                        <table style="background-color: #aaaaaa">
                          <tr>
                            <th>
                              Static Child UpdatePanel Control</th>
                          </tr>
                          <tr>
                            <td>
                              <asp:Label ID="StaticChildUpdatePanelLabel"
                              runat="server" />   
                              <asp:Button ID="StaticChildUpdatePanelButton"
                              runat="server" Text="Update" />
                            </td>
                          </tr>
                          <tr>
                            <td>
                            </td>
                          </tr>
                        </table>
                      </ContentTemplate>
                      <Triggers>
                        <asp:AsyncPostBackTrigger
                          ControlID="StaticChildUpdatePanelTrigger"
                          EventName="Click" />
                      </Triggers>
```

(continued)

Listing 22-23 *(continued)*

```
                    </asp:UpdatePanel>
                  </td>
                </tr>
                <tr>
                  <td style="width: 100%">
                    <asp:PlaceHolder runat="server" ID="PlaceHolder1" />
                  </td>
                </tr>
              </table>
            </ContentTemplate>
            <Triggers>
              <asp:AsyncPostBackTrigger ControlID="ParentUpdatePanelTrigger"
                EventName="Click" />
            </Triggers>
          </asp:UpdatePanel>
        </td>
      </tr>
      <tr>
        <td style="width:50%">
          <asp:Button ID="StaticChildUpdatePanelTrigger" runat="server"
          Text="Static Child UpdatePanel Trigger" Width="100%" />
        </td>
        <td>
          <asp:Button ID="ParentUpdatePanelTrigger" runat="server"
          Text="Parent UpdatePanel Trigger" Width="100%" />
        </td>
      </tr>
    </table>
  </form>
</body>
</html>
```

Now let's walk through the `pageLoad` method shown in Listing 22-23.

```
function pageLoad()
{
  var prm = Sys.WebForms.PageRequestManager.getInstance();
  prm.remove_initializeRequest(initializeRequestHandler);
  prm.add_initializeRequest(initializeRequestHandler);
}
```

As you can see, this method first calls the `getInstance` static method on the `PageRequestManager` class to return a reference to the current `PageRequestManager` instance:

```
var prm = Sys.WebForms.PageRequestManager.getInstance();
```

Next, it calls the `add_initializeRequest` method on the current `PageRequestManager` instance to register the `initializeRequestHandler` JavaScript function as an event handler for the `initializeRequest` event of the current `PageRequestManager` instance:

```
prm.add_initializeRequest(initializeRequestHandler);
```

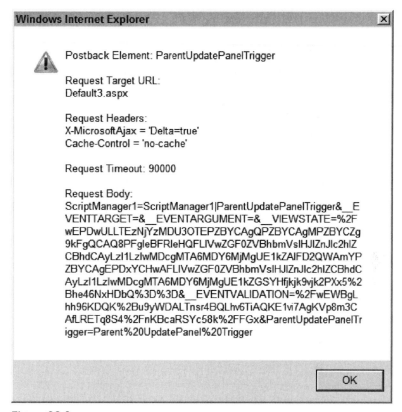

Figure 22-9

Next I'll walk you through the implementation of the `initializeRequestHandler` JavaScript function. Note that this method takes two parameters, the first referencing the current `PageRequestManager` instance, and the second referencing the `InitializeRequestEventArgs` object that contains the event data for the `initializeRequest` event.

As you can see from Listing 22-23, this `initializeRequestHandler` function first invokes the `get_request` method on the `InitializeRequestEventArgs` object to return a reference to the `WebRequest` object that represents the current asynchronous page postback request being made to the server:

```
var request = e.get_request();
```

Next, it invokes the `get_postBackElement` method on the `InitializeRequestEventArgs` object to return a reference to the DOM element that caused the current page postback:

```
var postBackElement = e.get_postBackElement();
```

Then it instantiates a `StringBuilder`:

```
var builder = new Sys.StringBuilder();
```

Next, the `initializeRequestHandler` function appends a string that contains the value of the id HTML attribute of the DOM element that caused the current page postback to the `StringBuilder`:

```
builder.append("Postback Element: ");
builder.append(postBackElement.id);
builder.appendLine();
builder.appendLine();
```

Then it invokes the `get_url` method on the `WebRequest` object that represents the current request to return a string that contains the target URL and appends a string that contains this target URL to the `StringBuilder`:

```
builder.append("Request Target URL: ");
builder.appendLine();
builder.append(request.get_url());
builder.appendLine();
builder.appendLine();
```

Next, it invokes the `get_headers` method on the `WebRequest` object to return a dictionary that contains the names and values of the headers of the current request:

```
builder.append("Request Headers: ");
builder.appendLine();
var headers = request.get_headers();
```

Then the `initializeRequestHandler` function iterates through the items in the dictionary and adds to the `StringBuilder` a string for each item that contains the name and value of the associated header:

```
var headerValue;
for (var headerName in headers)
{
   builder.append(headerName);
   builder.append(" = '");
   headerValue = headers[headerName];
   builder.append(headerValue);
   builder.append("'");
   builder.appendLine();
}
```

Next, it invokes the `get_timeout` method on the `WebRequest` object to return the request timeout value, and appends a string that contains this value to the `StringBuilder`:

```
builder.appendLine();
builder.append("Request Timeout: ");
builder.append(request.get_timeout());
builder.appendLine();
builder.appendLine();
```

Then it calls the `get_body` method on the `WebRequest` object to return a string that contains the body of the current request and appends that string to the `StringBuilder`:

```
builder.append("Request Body: ");
builder.appendLine();
builder.append(request.get_body());
builder.appendLine();
```

Finally, it calls the `alert` function to display a popup that contains the content of the `StringBuilder`:

```
alert(builder.toString());
```

One of the great things about the `initializeRequest` event is that it is cancelable. This enables you to register a callback for this event whereby you can run application-specific validation code to determine whether the current request should be aborted. If so, your callback can invoke the `set_cancel` method on the `InitializeRequestEventArgs` object, passing in `true` as its argument, to have the current `PageRequestManager` instance abort the current request.

The beginRequest Event

As you can see from Figure 22-8, the current client-side `PageRequestManager` instance fires its `beginRequest` event right before it calls the `invoke` method on the `WebRequest` object that represents the current asynchronous page postback request to begin the request, to enable you to perform application-specific tasks that must be performed right before the request is made to the server.

The client-side `PageRequestManager` class uses the standard ASP.NET AJAX event-implementation pattern to implement its `beginRequest` event, as follows:

1. `PageRequestManager` defines a method named `add_beginRequest` that enables you to register event handlers for the `beginRequest` event of the current client-side `PageRequestManager` instance. As the following code fragment shows, this method first calls the `get_eventHandlerList` method on the current `PageRequestManager` instance to return a reference to the `EventHandlerList` object that contains all the event handlers registered for the events of the current `PageRequestManager` instance. Then it calls the `addHandler` method on this `EventHandlerList` object to register the specified handler as event handler for the `beginRequest` event of the current `PageRequestManager` instance:

```
function Sys$WebForms$PageRequestManager$add_beginRequest(handler)
{
   this._get_eventHandlerList().addHandler("beginRequest", handler);
}
```

2. `PageRequestManager` defines a method named `remove_beginRequest` that enables you to unregister an event handler registered for the `beginRequest` event of the instance:

```
function Sys$WebForms$PageRequestManager$remove_beginRequest(handler)
{
   this._get_eventHandlerList().removeHandler("beginRequest", handler);
}
```

The `beginRequest` event, like any other, is associated with an event data class whose instance acts as a container for the associated event data. The event data class associated with the `beginRequest` event is an ASP.NET AJAX client class named `beginRequestEventArgs`. Listing 22-24 presents the internal implementation of the `beginRequestEventArgs` class.

As you can see, the constructor of the `beginRequestEventArgs` event data class takes two parameters, the first referencing the `WebRequest` object that represents the current asynchronous page postback request being made, and the second referencing the DOM element that caused the current asynchronous page postback. This constructor assigns these parameters to two internal fields named `_request` and `_postBackElement`:

```
this._request = request;
this._postBackElement = postBackElement;
```

Note that the `beginRequestEventArgs` class exposes two getters named `get_request` and `get_postBackElement` that return references to these two fields.

Listing 22-24: The beginRequestEventArgs Class

```
Sys.WebForms.BeginRequestEventArgs =
function Sys$WebForms$BeginRequestEventArgs(request, postBackElement)
{
   /// <param name="request" type="Sys.Net.WebRequest"></param>
   /// <param name="postBackElement" domElement="true"></param>
   Sys.WebForms.BeginRequestEventArgs.initializeBase(this);
   this._request = request;
   this._postBackElement = postBackElement;
}
function Sys$WebForms$BeginRequestEventArgs$get_postBackElement()
{
   /// <value domElement="true"></value>
   return this._postBackElement;
}
function Sys$WebForms$BeginRequestEventArgs$get_request()
{
   /// <value type="Sys.Net.WebRequest"></value>
   return this._request;
}
Sys.WebForms.BeginRequestEventArgs.prototype =
{
   get_postBackElement: Sys$WebForms$BeginRequestEventArgs$get_postBackElement,
   get_request: Sys$WebForms$BeginRequestEventArgs$get_request
}
Sys.WebForms.BeginRequestEventArgs.registerClass(
                       'Sys.WebForms.BeginRequestEventArgs', Sys.EventArgs);
```

Using the beginRequest Event

Listing 22-25 contains a page that uses the `beginRequest` event. If you run this page, you'll see the result shown in Figure 22-10. If you click the Update button, you'll see the result shown in Figure 22-11. As you can see, Figure 22-11 displays the latest two refresh times. This very simple example will teach you an important technique that you can use in your own applications to perform complex tasks.

Listing 22-25: A Page that Uses the beginRequest Event

```
<%@ Page Language="C#" %>
<%@ Import Namespace="System.Drawing" %>
<!DOCTYPE html PUBLIC "-//W3C//DTD XHTML 1.1//EN"
"http://www.w3.org/TR/xhtml11/DTD/xhtml11.dtd">
<script runat="server">
  void Page_Load(object sender, EventArgs e)
  {
    if (Request.Form["OldTime"] != null)
      info.Text = "UpdatePanel refreshed at " + Request.Form["OldTime"];
    Label updatePanelLabel = (Label)Page.FindControl("UpdatePanelLabel");
    updatePanelLabel.Text = "UpdatePanel refreshed at " + DateTime.Now.ToString();
  }
</script>
<html xmlns="http://www.w3.org/1999/xhtml">
<head runat="server">
  <title>Untitled Page</title>
  <script type="text/javascript" language="javascript">
    function pageLoad()
    {
      var prm = Sys.WebForms.PageRequestManager.getInstance();
      prm.remove_beginRequest(beginRequestHandler);
      prm.add_beginRequest(beginRequestHandler);
    }

    function beginRequestHandler(sender, e)
    {
      var request = e.get_request();
      var postBackElement = e.get_postBackElement();
      var body = request.get_body();
      var updatePanelLabel = $get("UpdatePanelLabel");
      var oldTime = updatePanelLabel.innerText.slice(25);

      var body2 = body.concat("&OldTime="+oldTime);
      request.set_body(body2);
    }
  </script>
</head>
```

(continued)

Listing 22-25 *(continued)*

```
<body>
  <form id="form1" runat="server">
    <asp:ScriptManager ID="ScriptManager1" runat="server" />
    <asp:UpdatePanel ID="UpdatePanel" runat="server">
      <ContentTemplate>
        <table cellspacing="20" style="background-color: #dddddd">
          <tr>
            <td>
              <asp:Label ID="UpdatePanelLabel" runat="server"/>
                 
              <asp:Button ID="UpdatePanelButton" runat="server" Text="Update" />
            </td>
          </tr>
          <tr>
            <td>
              <asp:Label runat="server" ID="info" />
            </td>
          </tr>
        </table>
      </ContentTemplate>
    </asp:UpdatePanel>
  </form>
</body>
</html>
```

Next, we'll walk through the implementation of this page, beginning with the `pageLoad` function:

```
function pageLoad()
{
  var prm = Sys.WebForms.PageRequestManager.getInstance();
  prm.remove_beginRequest(beginRequestHandler);
  prm.add_beginRequest(beginRequestHandler);
}
```

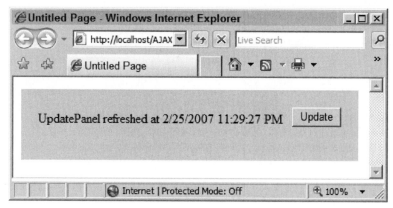

Figure 22-10

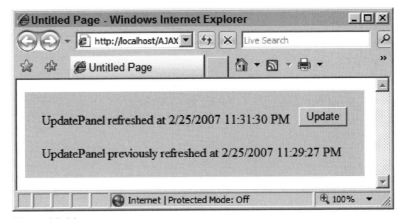

Figure 22-11

As you can see, this function first invokes the `getInstance` static method on the `PageRequestManager` class to return a reference to the current `PageRequestManager` instance:

```
var prm = Sys.WebForms.PageRequestManager.getInstance();
```

Next, it calls the `add_beginRequest` method on the current `PageRequestManager` instance to register the `beginRequestHandler` JavaScript function as an event handler for the `beginRequest` event of the current `PageRequestManager` instance:

```
prm.add_beginRequest(beginRequestHandler);
```

Now let's walk through the implementation of the `beginRequestHandler` function:

```
function beginRequestHandler(sender, e)
{
    var request = e.get_request();
    var body = request.get_body();
    var updatePanelLabel = $get("UpdatePanelLabel");
    var oldTime = updatePanelLabel.innerText.slice(25);

    var body2 = body.concat("&OldTime="+oldTime);
    request.set_body(body2);
}
```

This function begins by calling the `get_request` method on the `BeginRequestEventArgs` object to return a reference to the `WebRequest` object that represents the current request. Recall that when the current `PageRequestManager` instance invokes the `beginRequestHandler` function, it passes the `BeingRequestEventArgs` object containing the event data as the second parameter of this function.

```
var request = e.get_request();
```

Next, the `beginRequestHandler` function calls the `get_body` method on the `WebRequest` object to return a string that contains the body of the current request:

```
var body = request.get_body();
```

Then it calls the $get global JavaScript function to return a reference to the UpdatePanelLabel DOM element:

```
var updatePanelLabel = $get("UpdatePanelLabel");
```

Next, it extracts the old time from the innerText property of the UpdatePanelLabel DOM element. Twenty-five is the number of characters in the string UpdatePanel refreshed at, which precedes the time:

```
var oldTime = updatePanelLabel.innerText.slice(25);
```

Then it concatenates a string with the format &name=value, where the name part will be used on the server side to access the value part. As you can see, the name part contains the string OldTime (you can use any string value you wish as long as it is different from the values of the name parts of other name/value pairs in the body of request) and the value part contains the old time:

```
var body2 = body.concat("&OldTime="+oldTime);
```

Finally, it calls the set_body method on the WebRequest object to set the body of the request to the new value:

```
request.set_body(body2);
```

As you can see from Listing 22-25, when the current asynchronous page postback request arrives on the server side, the Page_Load method is invoked:

```
void Page_Load(object sender, EventArgs e)
{
  if (Request.Form["OldTime"] != null)
    info.Text = "UpdatePanel refreshed at " + Request.Form["OldTime"];
  Label updatePanelLabel = (Label)Page.FindControl("UpdatePanelLabel");
  updatePanelLabel.Text = "UpdatePanel refreshed at " + DateTime.Now.ToString();
}
```

As you can see, this method uses the string OldTime as an index into the Form collection of the Request object to return the old time, which is then displayed in an ASP.NET Label server control.

Summary

This chapter followed the current client-side PageRequestManager instance as it made an asynchronous page postback to the server. The next chapter will move on to the server side, where we will follow this asynchronous page postback request from the time it arrives in ASP.NET to the time the server response text is finally sent back to the client.

Asynchronous Partial Page Rendering: Server Side Processing

The previous chapter followed the current client-side `PageRequestManager` instance as it made an asynchronous page postback or partial-page-rendering request to the server. This chapter will move on to the server side to follow the asynchronous page postback request from the time it arrives in ASP.NET to the time the final response text is sent back to the server.

Chapter 21 followed the `Page` object as it went through its life cycle phases to process the first request made to a Web page enabled for partial page rendering. Since the first request wasn't a postback, the `Page` object skipped the postback-related life cycle phases when it was processing the first request. This chapter, on the other hand, follows the current `Page` object as it goes through its life cycle phases to process an asynchronous page postback request to the same page that the first request downloaded. Since an asynchronous page postback is a postback request, the current `Page` will go through both postback and non-postback life cycle phases, shown in Listing 21-1 and Figure 21-2.

Since the non-postback life cycle phases were discussed thoroughly in Chapter 21, I'll discuss only the postback-related life cycle phases in this chapter.

RetrievePostData

This is the life cycle phase in which the `Page` object populates an internal collection of type `NameValueCollection` named `_requestValueCollection` with the posted data, as shown in Listing 23-1. As such, this phase makes sense for postback requests — whether synchronous or asynchronous.

Listing 23-1: The RetrievePostData Method of the Page Object

```
private void RetrievePostData()
{
  if (this._request.HttpVerb == HttpVerb.POST && this._request.HasForm)
    this._requestValueCollection = this._request.Form;
  else if (this._request.HasQueryString)
    this._requestValueCollection = this._request.QueryString;
}
```

Depending on the HTTP verb used to make a request, the clients of a page will use one of the following two approaches to submit data to the server.

If the HTTP POST verb is used to make a request, the clients of the page include the data in the body of the request. The data consists of a list of data items separated by the & character, each of which consists of two parts separated by the equals sign (=). The first part of each data item helps the server determine what type of information the item contains. The second part of each data item contains the actual data or information being submitted. As an example, consider the ASP.NET page shown in Listing 23-2. As you can see, this page contains a TextBox and a DropDownList server control.

Every ASP.NET server control inherits a property named UniqueID from the Control base class. The value of this property is automatically set by ASP.NET when the page containing the server control is accessed. This value is a string that contains one or more substrings separated by the dollar sign, of which the first substring contains the value of the ID property of the control and the subsequent substrings contain the values of the UniqueID properties of those parent controls of the control that implement the INamingContainer interface. In the case of Listing 23-2, none of the parent controls of the TextBox and DropDownList server controls (other than the Page itself whose UniqueID property returns an empty string) implements this interface, which means that ASP.NET sets the values of the UniqueID properties of these two server controls to the respective values of their ID properties.

You may be wondering what the significance of the UniqueID property of a server control is. As the name suggests, this property uniquely identifies the server control among other server controls on the current page.

Listing 23-2: A Page that Contains a TextBox and a DropDownList Server Control

```
<%@ Page Language="C#" %>
<!DOCTYPE html PUBLIC "-//W3C//DTD XHTML 1.0 Transitional//EN"
  "http://www.w3.org/TR/xhtml1/DTD/xhtml1-transitional.dtd">
<html xmlns="http://www.w3.org/1999/xhtml">
<head runat="server">
  <title>Untitled Page</title>
</head>
<body>
  <form id="form1" runat="server">
    <asp:TextBox runat="server" ID="TextBox1" />
    <asp:DropDownList runat="server" ID="DropDownList1">
      <asp:ListItem Text="Text1" Value="Value1" />
      <asp:ListItem Text="Text2" Value="Value2" />
      <asp:ListItem Text="Text3" Value="Value3" />
    </asp:DropDownList>
```

```
        <asp:Button runat="server" Text="Submit" />
    </form>
</body>
</html>
```

When the browser accesses this page, it receives the HTML markup text shown in Listing 23-3. Each server control renders the value of its `UnqiueID` property as the value of the name attribute of the HTML element that represents the control. Therefore, the `TextBox` and `DropDownList` server controls render the values of their `UniqueID` properties as the values of the name attributes of the input and select HTML elements, respectively, as shown in the boldface portions of the following code listing:

```
<input name="TextBox1" type="text" id="TextBox1" />
<select name="DropDownList1" id="DropDownList1">
  <option value="Value1">Text1</option>
  <option value="Value2">Text2</option>
  <option value="Value3">Text3</option>
</select>
```

Listing 23-3: The HTML Markup Text Sent to the Client

```
<!DOCTYPE html PUBLIC "-//W3C//DTD XHTML 1.0 Transitional//EN"
 "http://www.w3.org/TR/xhtml11/DTD/xhtml11-transitional.dtd">
<html xmlns="http://www.w3.org/1999/xhtml">
<head>
  <title>Untitled Page </title>
</head>
<body>
  <form name="form1" method="post" action="Default7.aspx" id="form2">
    <div>
      <input type="hidden" name="__VIEWSTATE" id="__VIEWSTATE"
      value="/wEPDwUKMTAxNzk2MjY2OWRkxj+0HeO0c5N0xVutp03x6OdaSpw=" />
    </div>
    <input name="TextBox1" type="text" id="TextBox1" />
    <select name="DropDownList1" id="DropDownList1">
      <option value="Value1">Text1</option>
      <option value="Value2">Text2</option>
      <option value="Value3">Text3</option>
    </select>
    <input type="submit" name="ctl02" value="Submit" />
  </form>
</body>
</html>
```

Now imagine that the end user enters the string `MyText` into the text field, selects the `Text2` option from the select element, and clicks the Submit button. The browser retrieves the following information:

❑   The value of the name HTML attribute of the text field — that is, the string `"TextBox1"`. Recall that this value is the value of the `UniqueID` property of the `TextBox` server control.

❑   The value of the name HTML attribute of the select HTML element — that is, the string `"DropDownList1"`. Recall that this value is that of the `UniqueID` property of the `DropDownList` server control.

❑ The string that the end user has entered into the text field — that is, the string `MyText`.

❑ The value of the `value` HTML attribute of the selected `option` of the `select` HTML element — that is, the string `"Value2"`.

Therefore, the data that the browser needs to send to the server consists of two data items. The first contains the string that the end user has entered into the text field, and the second contains the value of the `value` HTML attribute of the selected `option` of the `select` HTML element:

```
TextBox1=MyText&DropDownList1=Value2
```

As you can see, each data item consists of two parts. The first part is the value of the `UniqueID` property of the server control and the second part is the value associated with the server control. The `UniqueID` property values allow ASP.NET to determine which data item is associated with which server control.

So far, I've covered the case in which the client uses the HTTP POST verb to make its request to the server. The second scenario is when the client uses the HTTP GET verb. This scenario often involves e-commerce Web applications. For example, consider a page that displays the list of product names to the end users. When a user selects a product to see more details about it, the primary key values of the product and its distributor are passed as a query string to the server:

```
http://www.mysite.com/Product.aspx?ProductID=2&DistributorID=3
```

As you can see, the query string consists of a list of data items separated by the ampersand character, each of which consists of two parts separated by the equals sign.

ASP.NET represents each request with an instance of a class named `HttpRequest`, which exposes two collection properties of type `NameValueCollection` named `Form` and `QueryString`. ASP.NET automatically populates the `Form` collection with the posted data if the request was made using the HTTP POST verb; otherwise it populates the `QueryString` collection with the posted data.

Keep in mind that we're following the current `Page` through its life cycle phases to process the asynchronous page postback method that the current client-side `PageRequestManager` instance has made to the server. As we just discussed, the clients of a page have two options when it comes to submitting data to the server. Which option did the current client-side `PageRequestManager` instance use to submit its data to the server? The answer lies in Listing 22-22. Recall that this code listing presents the internal implementation of the _onFormSubmit method of the current client-side `PageRequestManager` instance. As we discussed in the previous chapter, this method is automatically invoked when a page postback occurs, allowing the current client-side `PageRequestManager` instance to intercept the page postback before the page is actually posted back to the server. The current client-side `PageRequestManager` instance then determines whether the page must be posted back asynchronously. If so, it takes over the form submission, bypassing the browser's default synchronous form submission.

As Listing 22-22 shows, the current client-side `PageRequestManager` instance iterates through all the input form elements on the current page, generates for each input form element one string that consists of two substrings separated by the equals sign (the first substring containing the value of the `name` HTML attribute of the `form` element and the second containing the value of the `form` element), and finally packs all these strings into a single string using the & character as the separator. Recall from Listing 22-22 that the current client-side `PageRequestManager` instance adds this string to the body of the request being made to the server. As you can see, the current client-side `PageRequestManager` instance submits its data to the server via the body of an HTTP POST request.

Now back to the implementation of the `RetrievePostData` method of the `Page` object, as shown in Listing 23-1. Recall that the `Page` object calls this method when it enters the Retrieve Post Data life cycle phase. As this code listing shows, this method simply stores the content of the `Form` or `QueryString` collection of the `HttpRequest` object that represents the current request in an internal collection named `_requestValueCollection`. This collection contains one name/value pair for each posted data item. Recall that each posted data item consists of two parts separated by the equals sign. The name part of each name/value pair in this collection contains the first part of the data item and the value part contains the second part of the data item. This means that the first part of the data item can be used as an index into the collection to access the second part of the data item. For example, in the case of the examples discussed earlier, the following items are true:

❑   The `UniqueID` property value of the `TextBox` server control can be used as an index into the `_requestValueCollection` to access the text that the end user has entered into the text field:

```
string text1 = this._requestValueCollection["TextBox1"];
```

❑   The `UniqueID` property value of the `DropDownList` server control can be used as an index into the `_requestValueCollection` to access the value of the `value` HTML attribute of the selected option of the select HTML element associated with the server control:

```
string text1 = this._requestValueCollection["DropDownList1"];
```

❑   The string `"ProductID"` can be used as an index into the `_requestValueCollection` to access the primary key value of the product:

```
string text1 = this._requestValueCollection["ProductID"];
```

❑   The string `"DistributorID"` can be used as an index into the `_requestValueCollection` to access the primary key value of the distributor:

```
string text1 = this._requestValueCollection["DistributorID"];
```

Since the current `Page` is processing the asynchronous request shown in Listing 22-22, the `_requestValueCollection` of the current `Page` contains all the name/value pairs that Listing 22-22 stuffed into the body of the request.

LoadScrollPosition

This is the life cycle phase in which the `Page` object retrieves the scroll x and y positions from the `_requestValueCollection` and assigns them to the `_scrollPositionX` and `_scrollPositionY` fields, respectively, as shown in Listing 23-4. As you'll see later, the `Page` object uses these two fields to set the scroll position in the response text before submitting the response back to the client. This life cycle phase takes effect only if the `MaintainScrollPositionOnPostBack` property of the `Page` object has been set to `true`. As the name suggests, this property instructs the `Page` to maintain the scroll position on page postbacks — be they synchronous or asynchronous.

Listing 23-4: The LoadScrollPosition Method of the Page Object

```
Private void LoadScrollPosition()
{
  if (this._requestValueCollection != null)
  {
    string text1 = this._requestValueCollection["__SCROLLPOSITIONX"];
    if ((text1 != null) && !int.TryParse(text1, out this._scrollPositionX))
      this._scrollPositionX = 0;
    string text2 = this._requestValueCollection["__SCROLLPOSITIONY"];
    if ((text2 != null) && !int.TryParse(text2, out this._scrollPositionY))
      this._scrollPositionY = 0;
  }
}
```

Since the current Page is processing the asynchronous request made by the current client-side PageRequestManager instance, and since the _requestValueCollection contains only the name/value pairs that the current client-side PageRequestManager instance stuffed into the body of the request, you may be wondering where the scroll x and y values come from. The answer lies in Listing 22-22 itself, which is partially repeated in the following code listing.

Recall that this code listing contains the code for the _onFormSubmit method of the current client-side PageRequestManager instance. As discussed earlier, this method is automatically invoked when a post-back occurs. As the highlighted portions of the following code listing show, the current client-side PageRequestManager instance iterates through all the input form elements on the page, including the hidden fields named __SCROLLPOSITIONX and __SCROLLPOSITIONY, and forms for each input form element one string that consists of two substrings, the first containing the value of the name HTML attribute of the input form element (in this case, these values are __SCROLLPOSITIONX and __SCROLLPOSITIONY) and the second containing the value of the value HTML attribute of the input form element (in this case, these values are the scroll x and y positions).

As the boldface portion of the following code listing shows, the current client-side PageRequestManager instance stores the current scroll x and y positions in an internal field named _scrollPostion before it submits the request to the server. As you'll see later, when the server response arrives, the current client-side PageRequestManager instance retrieves the new scroll x and y positions from the response and compares them with the old values stored in the _scrollPosition field to determine whether the scroll x and y positions have indeed changed.

```
function Sys$WebForms$PageRequestManager$_onFormSubmit(evt)
{
    . . .
    if (tagName === 'INPUT')
    {
      var type = element.type;
      if ((type === 'text') ||
          (type === 'password') ||
          (type === 'hidden') ||
          (((type === 'checkbox') || (type === 'radio')) && element.checked))
      {
          formBody.append(name);
          formBody.append('=');
```

```
            formBody.append(encodeURIComponent(element.value));
            formBody.append('&');
        }
      }
      . . .
  }
  . . .
  this._scrollPosition = this._getScrollPosition();
  . . .
}
```

InitRecursive

I covered the non-postback-related parts of the `InitRecursive` life cycle phase of the `Page` object in Chapter 21; therefore I'll just cover the postback-related parts of this phase in this section. Recall from Chapter 21 that the `OnInit` method of the current `ScriptManager` instance is automatically invoked when the current `Page` enters its `Init` phase. Listing 23-5 presents the `ScriptManager` class's internal implementation of the `OnInit` method, which it inherits from the `Control` base class. I discussed all the parts of Listing 23-6 in Chapter 21 except for the highlighted portion, which is applicable only to post-back requests. As you can see, this portion calls the `IsAsyncPostBackRequest` static method on the server-side `PageRequestManager`, passing in the `NameValueCollection` that contains the names and values of the request headers. The main responsibility of this method is to determine whether the current request is an asynchronous page postback.

Listing 23-5: The OnInit Method of the ScriptManager Class

```
protected override void OnInit(EventArgs e)
{
  base.OnInit(e);
  if (ScriptManager.GetCurrent(this.Page) != null)
    throw new InvalidOperationException("OnlyOneScriptManager");
  this.IPage.Items[typeof(ScriptManager)] = this;
  this.IPage.PreRenderComplete += new EventHandler(this.OnPagePreRenderComplete);

  if (this.IPage.IsPostBack)
    this._isInAsyncPostBack =
            PageRequestManager.IsAsyncPostBackRequest(this.IPage.Request.Headers);

  this.PageRequestManager.OnInit();
}
```

The IsAsyncPostBackRequest Method of the PageRequestManager

Listing 23-6 presents the internal implementation of this method. As you can see, the `IsAsyncPostBackRequest` method first calls the `GetValues` method on the `NameValueCollection` that contains the names and values of the request headers, in order to access all the values of the request header named `"X-MicrosoftAjax"`:

```
string[] textArray1 = headers.GetValues("X-MicrosoftAjax");
```

Then it iterates through these values searching for a value that contains the string `"Delta=true"`. If it finds a value that contains this string, it returns `true` to signal its caller that the current request is an asynchronous page postback.

Listing 22-22 contains the client-side code that made the current asynchronous page postback. The following code listing repeats a portion of Listing 22-22. As the highlighted portion of the following code shows, the current client-side `PageRequestManager` instance added the `"Delta=true"` header value to a custom request header named `"X-MicrosoftAjax"` to signal the server-side `PageRequestManager` instance that the current request is an asynchronous page postback.

```
function Sys$WebForms$PageRequestManager$_onFormSubmit(evt)
{
  . . .
  var request = new Sys.Net.WebRequest();
  request.set_url(form.action);

  request.get_headers()['X-MicrosoftAjax'] = 'Delta=true';

  request.get_headers()['Cache-Control'] = 'no-cache';
  . . .
}
```

Listing 23-6: The IsAsyncPostBackRequest Static Method of the PageRequestManager Class

```
internal static bool IsAsyncPostBackRequest(NameValueCollection headers)
{
  string[] textArray1 = headers.GetValues("X-MicrosoftAjax");
  if (textArray1 != null)
  {
    for (int num1 = 0; num1 < textArray1.Length; num1++)
    {
      string[] textArray2 = textArray1[num1].Split(new char[] { ',' });
      for (int num2 = 0; num2 < textArray2.Length; num2++)
      {
        if (textArray2[num2].Trim() == "Delta=true")
          return true;
      }
    }
  }
  return false;
}
```

The OnInit Method of PageRequestManager

Recall from Chapter 21 that the `OnInit` method of the current server-side `PageRequestManager` instance is automatically invoked when the `Page` object enters its `Init` life cycle phase. Listing 23-7 presents the internal implementation of the `OnInit` method of the server-side `PageRequestManager`. I covered all the parts of this method in Chapter 21, except for the highlighted portion, because this portion is run only when the current request is an asynchronous page postback. As you can see, this portion simply registers the `OnPageError` method of the current server-side `PageRequestManager` instance as an event handler for the `Error` event of the current `Page` object.

Listing 23-7: The OnInit Method of the PageRequestManager Class

```
internal void OnInit()
{
    . . .

    if (this._owner.IsInAsyncPostBack)
        this._owner.IPage.Error += new EventHandler(this.OnPageError);

}
```

Load Post Data

Currently we're at the Load Post Data life cycle phase, in which the `ProcessRequest` method (see Listing 21-1) invokes the `ProcessPostData` method of the current `Page`, passing in two parameters. The first parameter is the `_requestValueCollection` field of the current `Page`. Recall that this field is a collection of type `NameValueCollection` that contains one name/value pair for each posted data item, the name part containing the `UniqueID` property value of a server control and the value part containing the value associated with that server control. For example, the name part of the name/value pair associated with a `TextBox` server control contains the value of the `UniqueID` property of the `TextBox` control, and the value part contains the text that the end user has entered into the text field.

As Listing 21-1 shows, the `ProcessRequest` method of the current `Page` passes `true` as the second argument of the `ProcessPostData` method to instruct this method that the `Page` is currently in a pre-Load life cycle phase. As you'll see later, the same `ProcessPostData` method will also be called after the Load life cycle phase. The second Boolean argument allows this method to distinguish between these two calls.

Listing 23-8 presents the internal implementation of the `ProcessPostData` method of the `Page`.

Listing 23-8: The ProcessPostData Method of the Page Object

```
private void ProcessPostData(NameValueCollection postData, bool fBeforeLoad)
{
    if (this._changedPostDataConsumers == null)
        this._changedPostDataConsumers = new ArrayList();
    foreach (string text1 in postData)
    {
        if (!Page.IsSystemPostField(text1))
        {
            Control control1 = this.FindControl(text1);
            if (control1 == null)
            {
                if (fBeforeLoad)
                {
                    if (this._leftoverPostData == null)
                        this._leftoverPostData = new NameValueCollection();
                    this._leftoverPostData.Add(text1, null);
                }
            }
            else
            {
                IPostBackDataHandler handler1 = control1 as IPostBackDataHandler;
```

(continued)

Listing 23-8 *(continued)*

```
            if (handler1 == null)
            {
              if (control1 as IPostBackEventHandler != null)
                this.RegisterRequiresRaiseEvent(control1.PostBackEventHandler);
            }
            else
            {
              if (handler1.LoadPostData(text1, this._requestValueCollection))
                this._changedPostDataConsumers.Add(control1);

              if (this._controlsRequiringPostBack != null)
                this._controlsRequiringPostBack.Remove(text1);
            }
          }
        }
      }
    }
    ArrayList list1 = null;
    if (this._controlsRequiringPostBack != null)
    {
      foreach (string text2 in this._controlsRequiringPostBack)
      {
        Control control2 = this.FindControl(text2);
        if (control2 != null)
        {
          IPostBackDataHandler handler2 = control2 as IPostBackDataHandler;
          if (handler2.LoadPostData(text2, this._requestValueCollection))
            this._changedPostDataConsumers.Add(control2);
        }
        else if (fBeforeLoad)
        {
          if (list1 == null)
            list1 = new ArrayList();
          list1.Add(text2);
        }
      }
      this._controlsRequiringPostBack = list1;
    }
  }
}
```

This method first instantiates an `ArrayList` field named _changePostDataConsumers, if it hasn't
already been instantiated. You'll see the significance of this field later.

```
    if (this._changedPostDataConsumers == null)
      this._changedPostDataConsumers = new ArrayList();
```

Next, it iterates through the name/value pairs in the `NameValueCollection` passed into it as its first
argument, and takes the following actions for each enumerated name/value pair if the name part of the
pair does not contain the name attribute value of one of the standard hidden fields such as __VIEWSTATE
(the name/value pairs associated with standard hidden fields will be processed later):

❑   The `ProcessPostData` method calls the `FindControl` method on the current `Page` object to
     return a reference to the server control whose `UniqueID` property value is given by the name
     part of the enumerated name/value pair:

```
Control control1 = this.FindControl(text1);
```

❑ If the current Page does not contain a server control with this UniqueID property value, this indicates that the server control has been dynamically added to the Page during the Page's Load life cycle phase. For example, the page developers could add server controls to the current Page within the Page_Load method, which is invoked when the Page enters its Load life cycle phase. Since we're currently at the Load Post Data life cycle phase, which occurs before the Load life cycle phase (see Figure 21-2), the ProcessPostData method does not process the enumerated name/value pair and instead stores the value of the name part of the pair in a collection named _leftOverPostData so that this name/value pair can be processed after the Load life cycle phase — that is, after the associated server control is added to the current Page:

```
if (this._leftoverPostData == null)
    this._leftoverPostData = new NameValueCollection();
this._leftoverPostData.Add(text1, null);
```

❑ If the current Page contains a server control whose UniqueID property value is given by the name part of the enumerated name/value pair, the ProcessPostData method takes the following steps to process the enumerated name/value pair. First, it checks whether the server control implements the IPostBackDataEventHandler interface:

❑ If not, it checks whether the server control implements the IPostBackEventHandler interface. If so, it calls the RegisterRequiresRaiseEvent method of the current Page, passing in the server control. This method stores this server control in an internal field for future reference. As you'll see later, when the current Page enters its RaisePostBackEvent life cycle phase, it will automatically call the RaisePostBackEvent method of this server control. In general, controls that implement the IPostBackEventHandler interface raise postback events.

```
IPostBackDataHandler handler1 = control1 as IPostBackDataHandler;
if (handler1 == null)
{
   if (control1 as IPostBackEventHandler != null)
      this.RegisterRequiresRaiseEvent((IPostBackEventHandler)control1);
}
```

❑ If so, it calls the LoadPostData method on the associated server control, passing in two parameters. The first parameter is the name part of the enumerated name/value pair, and the second parameter is the _requestValueCollection field. Recall that this field contains all the name/value pairs (or data items) that the client has posted back to the server.

❑ It is the responsibility of the LoadPostData method of the server control to use its first parameter as an index into the second parameter to retrieve the value of the value part of the associated name/value pair (or data item). For example, the LoadPostData method of an ASP.NET TextBox server control uses its UniqueID property value as an index into the _requestValueCollection to retrieve the text that the end user has entered into the text field. This method then compares this text with the value of the Text property of the TextBox control. If these two values are different, the end user has changed the original value of the text field. As a result, the LoadPostData method returns true to signal the ProcessPostData method that its value has changed and that therefore its RaisePostDataChangedEvent method must be invoked when the current Page enters its RaisePostDataChangedEvent life cycle phase (see Figure 21-2).

❑ Note that if the `LoadPostData` method returns `true`, the `ProcessPostData` method adds the server control to an internal collection named _changedPostDataConsumers. As you'll see later, when the current `Page` object enters its `RaisePostDataChangedEvent` life cycle phase, it will iterate through the server controls in the _changedPostDataConsumers collection and invoke their `RaisePostDataChangedEvent` methods.

```
if (handler1.LoadPostData(text1, this._requestValueCollection))
    this._changedPostDataConsumers.Add(control1);
```

❑ Finally, the `ProcessPostData` method removes the current `UniqueID` property value from the _controlsRequiringPostBack collection. This collection maintains the `UniqueID` property values of those server controls whose `RaisePostBackEvent` methods must be called when the current `Page` enters the `RaisePostBackEvent` life cycle phase.

```
this._controlsRequiringPostBack.Remove(text1);
```

Next, the `ProcessPostData` method iterates through the items in the _controlsRequiringPostBack collection. Recall that this collection contains the `UniqueID` property values of those server controls whose `RaisePostBackEvent` method must be invoked when the current `Page` enters the `RaisePostBackEvent` life cycle phase. The `ProcessPostData` method takes the following actions for each enumerated `UniqueID` property value in this collection:

❑ First, it calls the `FindControl` method on the current `Page` to return a reference to the server control with the enumerated `UniqueID` property value:

```
Control control2 = this.FindControl(text2);
```

❑ If the current `Page` object contains a server control with the enumerated `UniqueID` property value, the `ProcessPostData` method calls the `LoadPostData` method on the server control, and if this method returns `true`, it adds the server control to the _changedPostDataConsumers collection:

```
if (control2 != null)
{
    IPostBackDataHandler handler2 = control2 as IPostBackDataHandler;
    if (handler2.LoadPostData(text2, this._requestValueCollection))
        this._changedPostDataConsumers.Add(control2);
}
```

❑ If the current page does not contain a server control with the enumerated `UniqueID` property value, the `ProcessPostData` method adds the server control to a local array, which is finally added to the _controlsRequiringPostBack collection:

```
else if (fBeforeLoad)
{
    if (list1 == null)
        list1 = new ArrayList();
    list1.Add(text2);
}
}
this._controlsRequiringPostBack = list1;
```

UpdatePanel

As these discussions show, the Load Post Data life cycle phase of the current Page object is applicable only to those server controls that implement the IPostBackDataHandler interface. Since the current implementation of the UpdatePanel server control does not implement this interface, none of the UpdatePanel server controls on the current Page will participate in the current Page's Load Post Data life cycle phase. However, you can write a custom UpdatePanel server control that inherits the UpdatePanel server control and implements the IPostBackDataHandler interface. If you do so, the current Page object will automatically call the LoadPostData method of your custom UpdatePanel server control, and if your implementation of this method returns true, the current Page object will also automatically call the RaisePostDataChangedEvent method of your custom control.

ScriptManager

As the boldface portion of Listing 23-9 shows, the ScriptManager implements the IPostBackDataHandler interface. As I already mentioned, this interface exposes two methods named LoadPostData and RaisePostDataChangedEvent.

Listing 23-9: The Declaration of the ScriptManager Class

```
[ParseChildren(true), DefaultProperty("Scripts"), NonVisualControl,
PersistChildren(false)]
public class ScriptManager : Control, IPostBackDataHandler, IControl,
                             IClientUrlResolver, IScriptManagerInternal
{
  protected virtual bool LoadPostData(string postDataKey,
                                      NameValueCollection postCollection)
  {
    this.PageRequestManager.LoadPostData(postDataKey, postCollection);
                                      return false;
  }
  protected virtual void RaisePostDataChangedEvent()
  {
  }
}
```

Since the ScriptManager server control implements the IPostBackDataHandler interface, when the current Page enters its Load Post Data life cycle phase, it automatically calls the LoadPostData method on the current ScriptManager server control, passing in two parameters. The first parameter is a string that contains the UniqueID property value of the current ScriptManager server control, and the second is the NameValueCollection that contains all the name/value pairs that the current ASP.NET AJAX client-side PageRequestManager instance has posted back to the server.

As Listing 23-9 shows, the LoadPostData method of the ScriptManager delegates to the LoadPostData method of the current server-side PageRequestManager instance. Note that the LoadPostData method of the current ScriptManager instance passes the same two parameters that were passed into it into the LoadPostData method of the current server-side PageRequestManager instance.

The LoadPostData Method of PageRequestManager

Listing 23-10 presents the internal implementation of the `LoadPostData` method of the server-side `PageRequestManager`. Recall that when the `LoadPostData` method of the current `ScriptManager` server control calls the `LoadPostData` method of the current server-side `PageRequestManager` instance, it passes two parameters into it. The first parameter is a string that contains the value of the `UniqueID` property of the current `ScriptManager` server control. The second parameter is the `NameValueCollection` that contains all the name/value pairs (each pair represents a posted data item) that the current client-side `PageRequestManager` instance has posted back to the server.

Recall that Listing 22-22 presents the internal implementation of the `_onFormSubmit` method of the current client-side `PageRequestManager` instance. This method is where the current client-side `PageRequestManager` instance posts all its name/value pairs back to the server asynchronously. The following code listing repeats a portion of Listing 22-22:

```
function Sys$WebForms$PageRequestManager$_onFormSubmit(evt)
{
    . . .
    var formBody = new Sys.StringBuilder();

    formBody.append(this._scriptManagerID + '=' +
                    this._postBackSettings.panelID + '&');

    . .
}
```

As the highlighted portion of this code listing shows, the current client-side `PageRequestManager` instance posts a name/value pair whose name part contains the `UniqueID` property value of the current `ScriptManager` server control, and whose value part contains the value of the `panelID` property of the postback settings JavaScript object.

Recall that Listing 22-22 shows where the value of the `panelID` property of the postback settings JavaScript object is set. This code listing contains the implementation of the `_getPostBackSettings` method of the current client-side `PageRequestManager` instance. As discussed in Chapter 22, this method uses the following logic to set the value of the `panelID` property of the postback settings JavaScript object:

❑   If the server control that caused the current page postback resides in an `UpdatePanel` server control whose `ChildrenAsTriggers` property is set to `true`, the `_getPostBackSettings` method sets the value of the `panelID` property to a string that contains two substrings separated by the pipe character (|), of which the first substring contains the `UniqueID` property value of the `UpdatePanel` server control, and the second the `UniqueID` property value of the server control that caused the current page postback. As you'll see shortly, the presence of the `UniqueID` property value of this `UpdatePanel` server control signals the current server-side `PageRequestManager` instance that this `UpdatePanel` server control must be updated.

> When a page postback is caused by a server control that resides in an `UpdatePanel` server control whose `ChildrenAsTriggers` property is set to `true`, it automatically triggers the update of its parent `UpdatePanel` server control.

❑   If the `_asyncPostBackControlIDs` collection of the current client-side `PageRequestManager` instance contains the `UniqueID` property value of the server control that caused the current page postback, or one of its ancestor server controls, but the server control itself does not reside in an `UpdatePanel` server control whose `ChildrenAsTrigger` property is set to `true`, `_getPostBackSettings` sets the value of the `panelID` property to a string that contains two substrings separated by the | character: the first substring contains the `UniqueID` property value of the `ScriptManager` server control, and the second substring contains the `UniqueID` property value of the server control that caused the current page postback.

Keep this logic in mind as we're walking through the implementation of the `LoadPostData` method of the server-side `PageReqeustManager`. As you can see from Listing 23-10, this method first uses its first parameter, which is nothing but the `UniqueID` property value of the current `ScriptManager` server control, as an index into the `NameValueCollection` to return the associated posted string value data.

```
string text1 = postCollection[postDataKey];
```

This string value consists of up to two substrings separated by the | character. As we discussed earlier, the second substring is the `UniqueID` property value of the server control that caused the current page postback. The `LoadPostData` method assigns this substring to the `_asyncPostBackSourceElementID` field for future reference.

As we also discussed earlier, the first substring contains the value of the `UniqueID` property of either the `ScriptManager` server control or the `UpdatePanel` control whose content must be updated. If the substring does not contain the value of the `UniqueID` property of the `ScriptManager` server control — that is, if it contains the value of the `UniqueID` property of a specific `UpdatePanel` server control — the `LoadPostData` method assigns this substring to the `_updatePanelRequestUpdate` field:

```
this._updatePanelRequiresUpdate = text2;
```

Next, the `LoadPostData` method iterates through all the `UpdatePanel` server controls on the current page and calls their `Initialize` methods. The server-side `PageRequestManager` maintains references to all the `UpdatePanel` server controls on the page in an internal collection named `_allUpdatePanels`. (The `Initialize` method of the `UpdatePanel` server control was thoroughly discussed in Chapter 21.)

```
if ((this._allUpdatePanels != null) && (this._allUpdatePanels.Count != 0))
{
    List<UpdatePanel>.Enumerator enumerator1 =
                                    this._allUpdatePanels.GetEnumerator();
    while (enumerator1.MoveNext())
    {
        enumerator1.Current.Initialize();
    }
}
```

Finally, the `LoadPostData` method sets an internal flag named `_panelsInitialized` to signal that all `UpdatePanel` controls on the page have been initialized:

```
this._panelsInitialized = true;
```

Listing 23-10: The LoadPostData Method of the PageRequestManager

```
internal void LoadPostData(string postDataKey, NameValueCollection postCollection)
{
  string postData = postCollection[postDataKey];
  if (postData != null)
  {
    int separatorIndex = postData.IndexOf('|');
    this._asyncPostBackSourceElementID = postData.Substring(separatorIndex + 1);
    string text = postData.Substring(0, separatorIndex);

    if (text != this._owner.UniqueID)
      this._updatePanelRequiresUpdate = text;
  }
  if ((this._allUpdatePanels != null) && (this._allUpdatePanels.Count != 0))
  {
    List<UpdatePanel>.Enumerator enumerator1 =
                                 this._allUpdatePanels.GetEnumerator();
    while (enumerator1.MoveNext())
    {
      enumerator1.Current.Initialize();
    }
  }
  this._panelsInitialized = true;
}
```

Figure 23-1 contains all the method calls that occur when the current `Page` object enters its Load Post Data life cycle phase.

LoadPostData

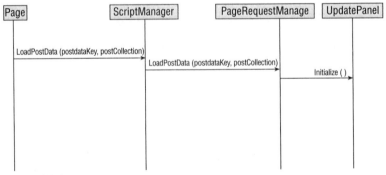

Figure 23-1

The Raise Post Data Changed Event

When the `Page` object enters its Raise Post Data Changed Event phase (see Figure 21-2), it calls the `RaisePostDataChangedEvent` methods of those server controls that meet the following two requirements:

❑ They implement the `IPostBackDataHandler` interface.

❑ Their implementation of the `LoadPostData` method returns `true`.

The `ScriptManager` server control meets the first requirement. However, it does not meet the second requirement because its `LoadPostData` method returns `false`, as shown in Listing 23-9. Therefore, the `RaisePostDataChangedEvent` method of the `ScriptManager` server control is never invoked. As the following code listing shows, this method does not do anything anyway:

```
protected virtual void RaisePostDataChangedEvent()
{
}
```

That said, you can implement a custom `ScriptManager` that extends the functionality of the `ScriptManager` server control, where its implementation of the `LoadPostData` method returns `true`, to have the `Page` object invoke its `RaisePostDataChangedEvent`. Your custom `ScriptManager` control's implementation of this method can then take the appropriate actions in response.

PreRender

The `PreRender` life cycle phase of the `Page` was thoroughly discussed in Chapter 21. In this section, I'll focus only on the postback-related topics that weren't covered in Chapter 21. As we discussed in Chapter 21, the `OnPreRender` method of the current `ScriptManager` server control is automatically invoked when the current page enters its `PreRender` life cycle phase.

Listing 23-11 presents the internal implementation of the `OnPreRender` method of the `ScriptManager` server control. This method checks whether the current request is an asynchronous page postback. If so, it delegates to the `OnPreRender` method of the server-side `PageRequestManager`. This applies to the current request because the current request is indeed an asynchronous page postback.

Listing 23-11: The OnPreRender Method of the ScriptManager

```
protected override void OnPreRender(EventArgs e)
{
  base.OnPreRender(e);
  if (this.IsInAsyncPostBack)
    this.PageRequestManager.OnPreRender();
}
```

The OnPreRender Method of PageRequestManager

Listing 23-12 presents the implementation of the `OnPreRender` method of the server-side `PageRequestManager`. The `Page` object, like any other server control, inherits a method named `SetRenderMethodDelegate` from the `Control` base class. This method registers a delegate of type `RenderMethod` that represents another method. In the case of Listing 23-12, the `SetRenderMethodDelegate` method registers a delegate that represents the `RenderPageCallback` method of the server-side `PageRequestManager`.

As you'll see later in this chapter, when the server control on which the `SetRenderMethodDelegate` method was invoked enters its rendering phase, in which its `RenderChildren` method is invoked, the `RenderChildren` method invokes the `RenderMethod` delegate, and consequently the method that the delegate represents, bypassing the normal rendering logic that renders the child controls of the server control.

In the case of Listing 23-12, when the Page server control enters its rendering phase in which its RenderChildren method is called, the RenderChildren method will invoke the delegate that represents the RenderPageCallback method of the PageRequestManager, bypassing the normal rendering logic that renders the server controls in the Controls collection of the Page. This allows the server-side PageRequestManager to take complete control of the rendering of the server controls in the Controls collection of the Page object when the current request is an asynchronous page postback.

Listing 23-12: The OnPreRender Method of the PageRequestManager

```
internal void OnPreRender()
{
    RenderMethod renderMethod = new RenderMethod(this.RenderPageCallback);
    this._owner.IPage.SetRenderMethodDelegate(renderMethod);
}
```

Rendering

In this section, we'll see what happens when the Page enters its rendering life cycle phase, in which the Render method of the Page is invoked. The Page inherits the Render method from the Control base class. Listing 23-13 presents the implementation of the Render method of the Control base class.

Listing 23-13: The Render Method of the Control Base Class

```
protected internal override void Render(HtmlTextWriter writer)
{
    this.RenderChildren(writer);
}
```

As you can see, the Render method of the Control base class simply calls the RenderChildren method shown in Listing 23-14. Recall from Listing 23-12 that the OnPreRender method of the server-side PageRequestManager created a RenderMethod delegate that represents the RenderPageCallback method of the server-side PageRequestManager and invoked the SetRenderMethodDelegate method on the Page object, passing in this RenderMethod delegate.

Every server control, including the Page object, inherits the RenderChildren method shown in Listing 23-14 from the Control base class. As you can see, the RenderChildren method of a server control first calls the GetRenderMethod to return a reference to the RenderMethod delegate registered with the server control, if any. In the case of the Page server control, since the current request is an asynchronous page postback, the GetRenderMethod returns a reference to the RenderMethod delegate that represents the PageRenderCallback method of the PageRequestManager.

As Listing 23-14 shows, the RenderChildren method of a server control bypasses the normal rendering logic of the server control's child controls if a RenderMethod delegate has been registered with the server control. As the boldface portion of Listing 23-14 shows, the normal rendering logic of the server control's child controls simply iterates through the child controls in the server control's Controls collection and invokes the RenderControl method on each enumerated child control.

In the case of the Page server control, if the current request is an asynchronous page postback, the RenderChildren method invokes the registered RenderMethod delegate, which in turn invokes the

PageRenderCallback method of the server-side PageRequestManager. The end result of all this is that the server-side PageRequestManager takes complete control over what gets rendered when the current request is an asynchronous page postback.

Listing 23-14: The RenderChildren Method of the Control Base Class

```
protected internal virtual void RenderChildren(HtmlTextWriter writer)
{
  RenderMethod renderMethod = this.GetRenderMethod();
  if (renderMethod != null)
  {
    writer.BeginRender();
    renderMethod(writer, this);
    writer.EndRender();
  }
  else if (this.Controls != null)
  {
    foreach (Control control in this.Controls)
    {
      control.RenderControl(writer);
    }
  }
}
```

The Encode Method of PageRequestManager

Since the implementation of the RenderPageCallback method makes use of another method of PageRequestManager named EncodeString, I'll discuss the implementation of this method first.

Listing 23-15 presents the internal implementation of the EncodeString method of the server-side PageRequestManager. This method takes four parameters as follows, encodes the values of its second through fourth parameters into a string, and writes this encoded string into the TextWriter object referenced by its first parameter.

- ❑ writer: This parameter references the TextWriter instance in which the encoded string is stored. This is normally an HtmlTextWriter instance that wraps the response output stream.

- ❑ type: This parameter is a string that specifies the type of information that the encoded string contains. As you'll see later, the current client-side PageRequestManager instance will use this string to determine what type of information it is dealing with. For example, if the encoded string contains the value of a hidden field, the server-side PageRequestManager instance uses the string "hiddenField" as the type to tell the current client-side PageRequestManager instance that the encoded string contains the name and value of a hidden field.

- ❑ id: As you'll see later, if the encoded string contains the value associated with a server control, this optional parameter contains the value of the ClientID property of the server control.

- ❑ content: This parameter contains the actual value being encoded.

As Listing 23-15 shows, the EncodeString method generates a string that contains four substrings separated by the | character, where the second, third, and fourth substrings contain the second and third parameters, and the encoded form of the fourth parameter, of the EncodeString method.

Listing 23-15: The EncodeString Method of PageRequestManager

```
internal static void EncodeString(TextWriter writer, string type, string id,
                                  string content)
{
  int num1 = 0;
  for (int num2 = 0; num2 < content.Length; num2++)
  {
    if (content[num2] == '\x00ff')
      num1++;

    else if (content[num2] == '\0')
      num1 += 2;
  }
  writer.Write((content.Length + num1).ToString());
  writer.Write('|');
  writer.Write(type);
  writer.Write('|');
  writer.Write(id);
  writer.Write('|');
  int num3 = 0;
  char[] chArray1 = content.ToCharArray();
  for (int num4 = 0; num4 < chArray1.Length; num4++)
  {
    if (chArray1[num4] == '\x00ff')
    {
      writer.Write(chArray1, num3, num4 - num3);
      writer.Write("\x00ff\x00ff");
      num3 = num4 + 1;
    }
    else if (chArray1[num4] == '\0')
    {
      writer.Write(chArray1, num3, num4 - num3);
      writer.Write("\\\x00ff\\");
      num3 = num4 + 1;
    }
  }
  writer.Write(chArray1, num3, chArray1.Length - num3);
  writer.Write('|');
}
```

The RenderPageCallback Method of PageRequestManager

Now back to the implementation of the RenderPageCallback method of the server-side PageRequestManager, as shown in Listing 23-16. As you can see, this method takes two arguments. The first references the HtmlTextWriter instance that wraps the response output stream, which means that anything that this method writes into this HtmlTextWriter instance will be automatically written into the response output stream. The second argument references the Page object. The main responsibility of this method is to render the Page object and its contents to the specified HtmlTextWriter instance and consequently to the response output stream.

As you can see, the RenderPageCallback method first calls the ProcessUpdatePanels method on the current server-side PageRequestManager instance. As you'll see later in this chapter, the main responsibility of this method is to determine which UpdatePanel server controls on the current page must be updated.

```
this.ProcessUpdatePanels();
```

The RenderPageCallback method then sets the ContentType property of the ASP.NET Response object to text/plain to inform the current client-side PageRequestManager instance that the body of the response contains plain text:

```
IHttpResponse response1 = this._owner.IPage.Response;
response1.ContentType = "text/plain";
```

Next, it calls the SetNoServerCaching on the ASP.NET Cache object to turn off server-side output caching for the current response, because the current request is an asynchronous page postback, which only updates specific portions of the page — that is, the portions encapsulated in the UpdatePanel server controls. If the output caching were allowed, the next synchronous request for the page would be served from the cache and consequently the client would get HTML that contains only portions of the original page:

```
response1.Cache.SetNoServerCaching();
```

Next, the RenderPageCallback method creates a delegate of type RenderMethod that represents the RenderFormCallback method of the server-side PageRequestManager:

```
RenderMethod renderMethod = new RenderMethod(this.RenderFormCallback);
```

Then it calls the SetRenderMethodDelegate method on the HtmlForm server control that represents the <form runat="server"> HTML element of the current page to register the RenderMethod delegate with the HtmlForm server control. As we discussed earlier, the HtmlForm server control, like any other, inherits the SetRenderMethodDelegate method from the Control base class. When the HtmlForm server control enters its rendering phase, in which its RenderChildren method is invoked, the RenderChildren method will call the delegate and consequently the RenderFormCallback method that the delegate represents, bypassing the normal rendering logic of the HtmlForm server control's child controls. Recall that this normal logic simply iterates through all the visible child controls of the HtmlForm server control and calls the RenderControl method on each child control to render the control, which means that the normal rendering logic renders all the visible child controls of the form. Obviously, the normal rendering logic makes sense only in a normal page postback. In an asynchronous partial page rendering, on the other hand, only the portions of the page contained within specified UpdatePanel server controls must be rendered; the rest of the page must be left alone.

```
IHtmlForm form1 = this._owner.IPage.Form;
form1.SetRenderMethodDelegate(renderMethod);
```

Next, for future use, the RenderPageCallback method stores a reference to the HtmlTextWriter object passed into it as its first argument, in an internal field named _updatePanelWriter. Recall that this HtmlTextWriter object wraps the response output stream. Because of this, anything written into this object will automatically be written into the response output stream and sent to the client as part of the server response.

```
this._updatePanelWriter = writer;
```

Then the method instantiates an instance of an internal `StringWriter` subclass named `ParserStringWriter`. A string writer is a stream that contains an internal string in which it accumulates the information written into the stream.

```
PageRequestManager.ParserStringWriter writer1 =
                            new PageRequestManager.ParserStringWriter();
```

Next, the `RenderPageCallback` method instantiates an instance of an internal `HtmlTextWriter` subclass named `ParserHtmlTextWriter` that wraps the `ParserStringWriter` instance. Note the difference between the `ParserHtmlTextWriter` instance and the `HtmlTextWriter` instance stored in the `_updatePanelWriter` field. While the former wraps the `ParserStringWriter`, the latter wraps the response output stream. This means that anything written into the former will be automatically written into the `ParserStringWriter`, which is nothing but a string writer, and anything written into the latter will be automatically written into the response output stream, which is sent back to the client. In other words, what's written into the `ParserHtmlTextWriter` instance remains in the server memory for the duration of the current request, while what's written into the `HtmlTextWriter` instance stored in the `_updatePanelWriter` field is sent to the client.

```
PageRequestManager.ParserHtmlTextWriter writer2 =
                        new PageRequestManager.ParserHtmlTextWriter(writer1);
    writer1.ParseWrites = true;
```

Then the `RenderPageCallback` method calls the `RenderControl` method on the `HtmlForm` server control to render the control and its child controls into the `ParserHtmlTextWriter` instance. Since the `RenderControl` method renders the `HtmlForm` server control and its child controls into an in-memory stream, as opposed to the response output stream, what gets rendered remains in memory, allowing the `RenderPageCallback` method to decide which part of this rendered HTML markup must be sent to the client.

```
    form1.RenderControl(writer2);
    writer1.ParseWrites = false;
```

The `HtmlForm` server control may contain hidden fields. When the `RenderControl` method of the `HtmlForm` server control renders these hidden fields into the `ParserHtmlTextWriter` instance, this instance stores these hidden fields in a collection named `HiddenFields`. This collection contains one `KeyValuePair` object for each hidden field: the name part of the pair contains the name of the hidden field and the value part contains the value.

The `RenderPageCallback` method iterates through the `KeyValuePair` objects in this collection and takes the following steps for each enumerated pair. First, it checks whether the enumerated pair represents a standard hidden field. If so, it calls the `EncodeString` static method on the `PageRequestManager` class.

As we discussed earlier, the `EncodeString` method first creates an encoded string that consists of three main substrings separated by the | character — "hiddentField"|pair1.Key.ToString()|pair1 .Value.ToString() — in which the `Key` and `Value` properties of the `KeyValuePair` object contain the name and value of the hidden field, respectively. Next, the `EncodeString` method writes this encoded string into the `HtmlTextWriter` object that wraps the response output stream.

```
foreach (KeyValuePair<string, string> pair1 in writer1.HiddenFields)
{
    if (PageRequestManager.IsBuiltInHiddenField(pair1.Key))
        PageRequestManager.EncodeString(writer, "hiddenField", pair1.Key,
                                        pair1.Value);
}
```

Next, the `RenderPageCallback` method calls the `EncodeString` method eight more times to write the following encoded strings to the response output stream:

❑ `"asyncPostBackControlIDs"|""|this.GetAsycnPostBackControlIDs(false)`: The first part of this encoded string tells the current client-side `PageRequestMananger` instance that this string contains the list of the `UniqueID` property values of all server controls on the current page that cause asynchronous page postbacks:

```
PageRequestManager.EncodeString(writer, "asyncPostBackControlIDs", string.Empty,
                                this.GetAsyncPostBackControlIDs(false));
```

❑ `"postBackControlIDs"|""|this.GetPostBackControlIDs(false)`: The first part of this encoded string tells the current client-side `PageRequestMananger` instance that this string contains the list of the `UniqueID` property values of all server controls on the current page that cause synchronous page postbacks:

```
PageRequestManager.EncodeString(writer, "postBackControlIDs", string.Empty,
                                this.GetPostBackControlIDs(false));
```

❑ `"updatePanelIDs"|""|this.GetAllUpdatePanelIDs()`: The first part of this encoded string tells the current client-side `PageRequestMananger` instance that this string contains the list of the `UniqueID` property values of all `UpdatePanel` server controls on the current page:

```
PageRequestManager.EncodeString(writer, "updatePanelIDs", string.Empty,
                                this.GetAllUpdatePanelIDs());
```

❑ `"childUpdatePanelIDs"|""|this.GetChildUpdatePanelIDs()`: The first part of this encoded string tells the current client-side `PageRequestMananger` instance that this string contains the list of the `UniqueID` property values of all `UpdatePanel` server controls on the current page that reside inside another `UpdatePanel` server control:

```
PageRequestManager.EncodeString(writer, "childUpdatePanelIDs", string.Empty,
                                this.GetChildUpdatePanelIDs());
```

❑ `"panelsToRefreshIDs"|""|this.GetRefreshingUpdatePanelIDs()`: The first part of this encoded string tells the current client-side `PageRequestMananger` instance that this string contains the list of the `UniqueID` property values of all `UpdatePanel` server controls on the current page that need refreshing:

```
PageRequestManager.EncodeString(writer, "panelsToRefreshIDs", string.Empty,
                                this.GetRefreshingUpdatePanelIDs());
```

❑ `"asyncPostBackTimeout"|""|this._owner.AsyncPostBackTimeout.ToString()`: The first part of this encoded string tells the current client-side `PageRequestMananger` instance that this string contains the value of the asynchronous page postback timeout:

```
PageRequestManager.EncodeString(writer, "asyncPostBackTimeout", string.Empty,
                            this._owner.AsyncPostBackTimeout.ToString());
```

❑ `"formAction"|""|writer2.FormAction`: The first part of this encoded string tells the current client-side `PageRequestMananger` instance that this string contains the value of the form action:

```
if (writer2.FormAction != null)
   PageRequestManager.EncodeString(writer, "formAction", string.Empty,
                            writer2.FormAction);
```

❑ `"pageTitle"|""|this._owner.IPage.Title`: The first part of this encoded string tells the current client-side `PageRequestMananger` instance that this string contains the value of the page title:

```
if (this._owner.IPage.Header != null)
{
  string text1 = this._owner.IPage.Title;
  if (!string.IsNullOrEmpty(text1))
    PageRequestManager.EncodeString(writer, "pageTitle", string.Empty, text1);
}
```

Next, the `RenderPageCallback` method calls the `RenderDataItems` method on the current server-side `PageRequestManager` instance to render the data items into the server output stream:

```
this.RenderDataItems(writer);
```

Then the method calls the `ProcessScriptRegistration` method on the current server-side `PageRequestManager` instance to render all the required client scripts:

```
this.ProcessScriptRegistration(writer);
```

Finally, the `RenderPageCallback` method calls the `ProcessFocus` method on the current server-side `PageRequestManager` instance to give the mouse focus to the appropriate server control.

```
this.ProcessFocus(writer);
```

Listing 23-16: The RenderPageCallback Method of the PageRequestManager

```
private void RenderPageCallback(HtmlTextWriter writer, Control pageControl)
{
  this.ProcessUpdatePanels();
  IHttpResponse response1 = this._owner.IPage.Response;
  response1.ContentType = "text/plain";
  response1.Cache.SetNoServerCaching();
  IHtmlForm form1 = this._owner.IPage.Form;
  form1.SetRenderMethodDelegate(new RenderMethod(this.RenderFormCallback));
```

```
        this._updatePanelWriter = writer;
        PageRequestManager.ParserStringWriter writer1 =
                                    new PageRequestManager.ParserStringWriter();
        PageRequestManager.ParserHtmlTextWriter writer2 =
                                    new PageRequestManager.ParserHtmlTextWriter(writer1);
        writer1.ParseWrites = true;
        form1.RenderControl(writer2);
        writer1.ParseWrites = false;
        foreach (KeyValuePair<string, string> pair1 in writer1.HiddenFields)
        {
            if (PageRequestManager.IsBuiltInHiddenField(pair1.Key))
                PageRequestManager.EncodeString(writer, "hiddenField", pair1.Key,
                                        pair1.Value);
        }
        PageRequestManager.EncodeString(writer, "asyncPostBackControlIDs", string.Empty,
                                this.GetAsyncPostBackControlIDs(false));
        PageRequestManager.EncodeString(writer, "postBackControlIDs", string.Empty,
                                this.GetPostBackControlIDs(false));
        PageRequestManager.EncodeString(writer, "updatePanelIDs", string.Empty,
                                this.GetAllUpdatePanelIDs());
        PageRequestManager.EncodeString(writer, "childUpdatePanelIDs", string.Empty,
                                this.GetChildUpdatePanelIDs());
        PageRequestManager.EncodeString(writer, "panelsToRefreshIDs", string.Empty,
                                this.GetRefreshingUpdatePanelIDs());
        PageRequestManager.EncodeString(writer, "asyncPostBackTimeout", string.Empty,
                                this._owner.AsyncPostBackTimeout.ToString());
        if (writer2.FormAction != null)
            PageRequestManager.EncodeString(writer, "formAction", string.Empty,
                                    writer2.FormAction);
        if (this._owner.IPage.Header != null)
        {
            string text1 = this._owner.IPage.Title;
            if (!string.IsNullOrEmpty(text1))
                PageRequestManager.EncodeString(writer, "pageTitle", string.Empty, text1);
        }
        this.RenderDataItems(writer);
        this.ProcessScriptRegistration(writer);
        this.ProcessFocus(writer);
}
```

The ProcessUpdatePanels Method of PageRequestManager

As we discussed, the current page consists of a bunch of UpdatePanel server controls, each of which designates a particular region of the page as a partially updatable region. When an asynchronous page postback request arrives — that is, when a request for a partial page rendering arrives, how does the page know which UpdatePanel server controls need updating or refreshing? An UpdatePanel server control needs updating if it meets one or more of the following requirements:

❑   The first substring of the string that the LoadPostData method retrieves from the post collection contains the value of the UniqueID property of the UpdatePanel server control. (Recall from Listing 23-10 that the LoadPostData method assigns this substring to the _updatePanelRequestUpdate field.) As we discussed earlier in this chapter, this scenario occurs when the server control that caused the current asynchronous page postback resides inside an UpdatePanel server control whose ChildrenAsTriggers property is set to true.

❑ The UpdateMode property of the UpdatePanel server control is set to Always.

❑ The Update method of the UpdataPanel server control is explicitly invoked. As you can see from Listing 23-17, this method simply sets the internal Boolean _explicitUpdate field of the UpdatePanel server control on which the method is invoked to true, to specify that this UpdatePanel server control must be updated.

Use the Update *method to imperatively force an* UpdatePanel *server control to refresh regardless of what triggered the current asynchronous page postback.*

If you call the Update *method on an* UpdatePanel *server control whose* UpdateMode *property is set to* Always, *the method will raise an invalid operation exception.*

❑ The second substring of the string that the LoadPostData method retrieves from the post collection contains the value of the UniqueID property of the associated server control of one of the triggers in the Triggers collection of the UpdatePanel server control. Recall from Listing 23-10 that the LoadPostData method assigns this substring to the _asyncPostBackSourceElementID field.

❑ The UpdatePanel server control is a child of an UpdatePanel server control that needs updating.

As you can see, the update of an UpdatePanel server control automatically triggers the updates of all its descendant UpdatePanel server controls. However, the update of an UpdatePanel server control does not automatically trigger the updates of its ancestor UpdatePanel server controls. If you want to force the ancestor UpdatePanel server controls to update as well, you must take one of these extra steps.

❑ Set the UpdateMode properties of the ancestor UpdatePanel server controls to Always.

❑ Add the triggers that trigger the update of a child UpdatePanel server control to the Triggers collections of the ancestor UpdatePanel server controls.

❑ Imperatively call the Update methods of the ancestor UpdatePanel server controls.

Listing 23-17: The Update Method of the UpdatePanel Server Control

```
public void Update()
{
  if (this.UpdateMode == UpdatePanelUpdateMode.Always)
    throw new InvalidOperationException("UpdateConditional");

  if (this._asyncPostBackModeInitialized)
    throw new InvalidOperationException("UpdateTooLate");
  this._explicitUpdate = true;
}
```

As you saw back in Listing 23-16, the RenderPageCallback method of the current server-side PageRequestManager instance calls the ProcessUpdatePanels method on the current server-side PageRequestManager instance to determine which UpdatePanel server controls on the current page must be updated. Recall that the current server-side PageRequestManager instance maintains the list of all UpdatePanel server controls on the current page in an internal collection named _allUpdatePanels.

As you can see from Listing 23-18, the `ProcessUpdatePanels` method iterates through the `UpdatePanel` server controls in this collection and takes the following steps for each enumerated `UpdatePanel` server control to determine whether the control needs refreshing. (Note that this method sets a local Boolean variable named `updatePanelNeedsToUpdate` to specify whether the enumerated `UpdatePanel` server control needs updating.)

Listing 23-18: The ProcessUpdatePanels Method of the PageRequestManager

```
private void ProcessUpdatePanels()
{
  if (this._allUpdatePanels != null)
  {
    this._updatePanelsToRefresh =
                        new List<UpdatePanel>(this._allUpdatePanels.Count);
    this._childUpdatePanelsToRefresh =
                        new List<UpdatePanel>(this._allUpdatePanels.Count);
    HtmlForm form1 = this._owner.Page.Form;
    for (int num1 = 0; num1 < this._allUpdatePanels.Count; num1++)
    {
      UpdatePanel panel1 = this._allUpdatePanels[num1];
      bool updatePanelNeedsToUpdate = false;
      if ((this._updatePanelRequiresUpdate != null) &&
          string.Equals(panel1.UniqueID, this._updatePanelRequiresUpdate))
        updatePanelNeedsToUpdate = true;
      else
        updatePanelNeedsToUpdate = panel1.RequiresUpdate;
      Control control1 = panel1.Parent;
      while (control1 != form1)
      {
        UpdatePanel panel2 = control1 as UpdatePanel;
        if ((panel2 != null) &&
            (this._updatePanelsToRefresh.Contains(panel2) ||
            this._childUpdatePanelsToRefresh.Contains(panel2)))
        {
          updatePanelNeedsToUpdate = false;
          this._childUpdatePanelsToRefresh.Add(panel1);
          break;
        }
        control1 = control1.Parent;
        if (control1 == null)
        {
          updatePanelNeedsToUpdate = false;
          break;
        }
      }
      if (updatePanelNeedsToUpdate)
      {
        panel1.SetAsyncPostBackMode(true);
        this._updatePanelsToRefresh.Add(panel1);
      }
      else
        panel1.SetAsyncPostBackMode(false);
    }
  }
}
```

The `ProcessUpdatePanels` method first checks whether the `_updatePanelRequiresUpdate` field of the current server-side `PageRequestManager` instance contains the `UniqueID` property value of the enumerated `UpdatePanel` server control. Recall from Listing 23-10 that the `LoadPostData` method of the current server-side `PageRequestManager` instance retrieves from the posted data the `UniqueID` property value of the `UpdatePanel` server control that requires refreshing (if any) and stores the value in the `_updatePanelRequestUpdate` field of the current server-side `PageRequestManager` instance.

```
if ((this._updatePanelRequiresUpdate != null) &&
        string.Equals(panel1.UniqueID, this._updatePanelRequiresUpdate))
    updatePanelNeedsToUpdate = true;
```

If this check fails — that is, if the `_updatePanelRequiresUpdate` field does not contain the `UniqueID` property value of the enumerated `UpdatePanel` server control — the `ProcessUpdatePanels` method sets the value of the `updatePanelNeedsToUpdate` Boolean variable to the value of the `RequiresUpdate` property of the enumerated `UpdatePanel` server control.

```
else
    updatePanelNeedsToUpdate = panel1.RequiresUpdate;
```

Next, I'll digress from our discussion of the implementation of the `ProcessUpdatePanels` method to discuss the implementation of the `RequiresUpdate` property of the `UpdatePanel` server control.

As Listing 23-19 shows, the `RequiresUpdate` property returns true if:

❏ The `_explicitUpdate` field of the `UpdatePanel` server control is set to `true`. Recall from Listing 23-17 that the value of this field is set to `true` only when you explicitly invoke the `Update` method of the `UpdatePanel` server control from within your code.

❏ The `UpdateMode` property of the `UpdatePanel` server control is set to `Always`.

❏ The `HasTriggered` method of the `Triggers` collection of the `UpdatePanel` server control returns true. As Listing 23-20 shows, the `HasTriggered` method of this collection returns `true` if the `HasTriggered` method of at least one of its `UpdatePanelTrigger` objects returns `true`. (I discussed the `HasTriggered` method of the `AsyncPostBackTrigger` class in Chapter 21.)

Listing 23-19: The RequiresUpdate Method of the UpdatePanel Server Control

```
protected internal virtual bool RequiresUpdate
{
  get
  {
    if (this._explicitUpdate || (this.UpdateMode == UpdatePanelUpdateMode.Always))
      return true;

    if ((this._triggers != null) && (this._triggers.Count != 0))
      return this._triggers.HasTriggered();

    return false;
  }
}
```

Listing 23-20: The HasTriggered Method of the UpdatePanelTriggerCollection Class

```
internal bool HasTriggered()
{
  using (IEnumerator<UpdatePanelTrigger> enumerator1 = base.GetEnumerator())
  {
    while (enumerator1.MoveNext())
    {
      if (enumerator1.Current.HasTriggered())
        return true;
    }
  }
  return false;
}
```

Now back to the implementation of the ProcessUpdatePanels method shown in Listing 23-21. So far, you've learned that this method sets the value of the updatePanelNeedsToUpdate variable to true if the _updatePanelRequiresUpdate field contains the UniqueID property of the enumerated UpdatePanel server control, or if the RequiresUpdate property of the enumerated UpdatePanel server control returns true. As the name suggests, the updatePanelNeedsToUpdate variable specifies whether the enumerated UpdatePanel server control needs to update.

Next, the ProcessUpdatePanels method walks up the control hierarchy of the enumerated UpdatePanel server control to determine whether it resides inside another UpdatePanel server control. If so, it checks whether the _updatePanelsToRefresh or _childUpdatePanelsToRefresh collection of the current server-side PageRequestManager instance already contains the container UpdatePanel server control. If so, this indicates that the container UpdatePanel server control of the enumerated UpdatePanel server control needs to update. Since updating the container UpdatePanel server control automatically updates all its content, including the enumerated UpdatePanel server control, the ProcessUpdatePanels method first sets the updatePanelNeedsToUpdate local Boolean variable to false to signal that the enumerated UpdatePanel server control mustn't be added to the _updatePanelsToRefresh collection. This avoids duplicate updates. The ProcessUpdatePanels method then adds the enumerated UpdatePanel server control to the _childUpdatePanelsToRefresh collection.

```
while (control1 != form1)
{
  UpdatePanel panel2 = control1 as UpdatePanel;
  if ((panel2 != null) &&
      (this._updatePanelsToRefresh.Contains(panel2) ||
       this._childUpdatePanelsToRefresh.Contains(panel2)))
  {
    updatePanelNeedsToUpdate = false;
    this._childUpdatePanelsToRefresh.Add(panel1);
    break;
  }
  control1 = control1.Parent;
  if (control1 == null)
  {
    updatePanelNeedsToUpdate = false;
    break;
  }
}
```

Recall from Listing 21-31 that the markup text that makes up an UpdatePanel server control consists of two main parts. The first part is a div or span HTML element. The second is the rest of the markup text that makes up the UpdatePanel server control. The first part is known as the *containing* or *outermost* HTML element because it contains or encapsulates the second part. The second part is known as *content* because it is contained or enclosed within the opening and closing tags of the containing or outermost HTML element.

As you'll see later in this chapter, the current server-side PageRequestManager instance renders the content of an UpdatePanel server control that needs updating into a string, which is then sent back to the current client-side PageRequestManager instance for processing.

As you'll see in the next chapter, the current client-side PageRequestManager instance simply assigns the string that contains the content of the UpdatePanel server control to the innerHTML property of the containing or outermost HTML element of the UpdatePanel server control. This means that the original content of the UpdatePanel server control is completely wiped out and replaced with the new content. This has an important consequence when the UpdatePanel server control contains child UpdatePanel server controls, because updating the UpdatePanel server control deletes the current child UpdatePanel server controls and replaces them with brand-new child UpdatePanel server controls, even though the new child UpdatePanel server controls have the same UniqueID and ClientID property values as the deleted ones.

Therefore, as far as the current client-side PageRequestManager instance is concerned, when an UpdatePanel server control updates, its child UpdatePanel server controls do *not*. Instead they are completely deleted from the current page and replaced with brand-new child UpdatePanel server controls with the same UniqueID and ClientID property values as the deleted ones.

So far, we've assumed that the new content simply deleted the old child UpdatePanel server controls and replaced them with the brand-new child UpdatePanel server controls with the same UniqueID and ClientID property values as the deleted ones. However, it is quite possible that the new content may also include new child UpdatePanel server controls that are not replacing the old ones. It is also quite possible that some of the old child UpdatePanel server controls are indeed deleted from the new content, which means that the new content may have fewer child server controls than the old.

Finally, the ProcessUpdatePanels method checks whether the updatePanelNeedsToUpdate variable is set to true. If so, it first calls the SetAsyncPostBackMode method on the enumerated UpdatePanel server control and then adds the control to the _updatePanelsToRefresh collection of the current server-side PageRequestManager instance. As Listing 23-21 shows, the SetAsyncPostBackMode method sets an internal flag of the specified UpdatePanel server control, named _asyncPostBackMode, to true.

```
if (updatePanelNeedsToUpdate)
{
  panel1.SetAsyncPostBackMode(true);
  this._updatePanelsToRefresh.Add(panel1);
}
```

If the updatePanelNeedsToUpdate variable is set to false, the ProcessUpdatePanels method calls the SetAsyncPostBackMode method on the enumerated UpdatePanel server control to set its _asyncPostBackMode field to false.

```
      else
         panel1.SetAsyncPostBackMode(false);
```

As you'll see later, when the UpdatePanel server control enters its rendering phase, it checks the value of its _asyncPostBackMode field to determine how to render its content.

Listing 23-21: The SetAsyncPostBackMode Method of the UpdatePanel

```
internal void SetAsyncPostBackMode(bool asyncPostBackMode)
{
  if (this._asyncPostBackModeInitialized)
    throw new InvalidOperationException("SetPartialRenderingModeCalledOnce");
  this._asyncPostBackMode = asyncPostBackMode;
  this._asyncPostBackModeInitialized = true;
}
```

RenderControl Method of HtmlForm

Recall from Listing 23-16 that the RenderPageCallback method creates a delegate of type RenderMethod that represents the RenderFormCallback method of the current server-side PageRequestManager instance and calls the SetRenderMethodDelegate method on the HtmlForm server control that represents the <form runat="server"> HTML element of the current page to register this RenderMethod delegate with the HtmlForm server control.

Also recall from Listing 23-16 that the RenderPageCallback method calls the RenderControl method on the HtmlForm server control to have this server control render itself to the ParserHtmlTextWriter instance passed into the RenderControl method as its argument. Listing 23-22 presents the internal implementation of the RenderControl method of the HtmlForm server control. As you can see, this method calls the RenderControl method of the Control base class, which in turn calls the Render method of the Control base class. As Listing 23-13 shows, the Render method of the Control base class calls the RenderChildren method.

Listing 23-22: The RenderControl Method of the HtmlForm Server Control

```
public override void RenderControl(HtmlTextWriter writer)
{
  if (base.DesignMode)
    base.RenderChildren(writer);

  else
    base.RenderControl(writer);
}
```

Listing 23-23 presents the internal implementation of the RenderChildren method of the HtmlForm server control. This method first invokes the OnFormRender method on the Page:

```
this.Page.OnFormRender();
```

Next, it calls the `BeginFormRender` method on the `Page`:

```
this.Page.BeginFormRender(writer, this.UniqueID);
```

Then it calls the `RenderChildren` method of the `Control` base class:

```
base.RenderChildren(writer);
```

Next, the `RenderChildren` method calls the `EndFormRender` method on the `Page`:

```
this.Page.EndFormRender(writer, this.UniqueID);
```

Finally, it calls the `OnFormPostRender` method on the `Page`:

```
this.Page.OnFormPostRender();
```

Listing 23-23: The RenderChildren Method of the HtmlForm Server Control

```
protected internal override void RenderChildren(HtmlTextWriter writer)
{
  if (this.Page != null)
  {
    this.Page.OnFormRender();
    this.Page.BeginFormRender(writer, this.UniqueID);
  }
  base.RenderChildren(writer);
  if (this.Page!= null)
  {
    this.Page.EndFormRender(writer, this.UniqueID);
    this.Page.OnFormPostRender();
  }
}
```

The `RenderChildren` method of the `Control` base class (see Listing 23-14) calls the `GetRenderMethod` to return a reference to the `RenderMethod` delegate that represents the `RenderFormCallback` method and calls this delegate, and consequently the `RenderFormCallback` method, bypassing the normal rendering logic of the child controls of the `HtmlForm` server control. Recall that this normal logic simply iterates through the child controls in the `Controls` collection of the `HtmlForm` server control and calls the `RenderControl` method on each child control, as shown in the boldface portion of Listing 23-14.

The RenderFormCallback Method of PageRequestManager

Listing 23-24 presents the internal implementation of the `RenderFormCallback` method of the server-side `PageRequestManager`. Recall that the `ProcessUpdatePanels` method populates an internal collection named _updatePanelsToRefresh with all the `UpdatePanel` server controls that need refreshing. The `RenderFormCallback` method iterates through the `UpdatePanel` server controls in this collection and calls the `RenderControl` method on each enumerated `UpdatePanel` server control to have the control render itself into the `HtmlTextWriter` object that the _updatePanelWriter field references. Recall from Listing 23-16 that the `RenderPageCallback` method of the `PageRequestManager` stores a reference to the `HtmlTextWriter` object that wraps the response output stream in the _updatePanelWriter field. Therefore, the `RenderControl` method of the enumerated `UpdatePanel` server control ends up rendering itself into the response output stream. The response output stream is the stream that contains the response text that is sent back to the requesting browser.

As you can see, the RenderFormCallback method renders the UpdatePanels in the _updatePanelsToRefresh collection only. In other words, none of the other server controls on the current page is rendered when the current request is an asynchronous page postback. The other server controls go through all their life cycle phases as usual, except for the rendering phase. This phase is what makes an asynchronous page postback request different from a synchronous page postback request. While the HTML markup contained in the response output stream in the case of a synchronous page postback contains HTML markup text from all visible server controls on the current page, the HTML markup text contained in the response output stream in the case of an asynchronous page postback contains HTML markup text only from the visible UpdatePanel server controls in the _updatePanelsToRefresh collection.

Listing 23-24: The RenderFormCallback Method of the PageRequestManager

```
private void RenderFormCallback(HtmlTextWriter writer, Control containerControl)
{
    PageRequestManager.ParserStringWriter writer1 =
                    writer.InnerWriter as PageRequestManager.ParserStringWriter;
    writer1.ParseWrites = false;
    if (this._updatePanelsToRefresh != null)
    {
        foreach (UpdatePanel panel1 in this._updatePanelsToRefresh)
        {
            if (panel1.Visible)
                panel1.RenderControl(this._updatePanelWriter);
        }
    }
    writer1.ParseWrites = true;
}
```

The RenderControl Method of the UpdatePanel

The UpdatePanel server control inherits the RenderControl method from the Control base class. The base class's implementation of the RenderControl method calls the Render method shown in Listing 23-25. As you can see, this method calls the VerifyRenderingInServerForm method on the Page object to raise an exception if the UpdatePanel server control is not inside a <form runat="server"> element:

```
this.IPage.VerifyRenderingInServerForm(this);
```

Next, it calls the Render method of its base class, which in turn calls the RenderChildren method.

Listing 23-25: The Render Method of the UpdatePanel

```
protected override void Render(HtmlTextWriter writer)
{
    this.IPage.VerifyRenderingInServerForm(this);
    base.Render(writer);
}
```

Listing 23-26 presents the implementation of the RenderChildren method of the UpatePanel server control. This method checks whether the UpdatePanel control is in asynchronous postback mode. Recall from Listing 23-21 that the ProcessUpdatePanels method calls the SetAsyncPostBackMode method on each UpdatePanel server control in the _allUpdatePanels collection of the current server-side PageRequestManager instance to set the value of the _asyncPostBackMode field of the UpdatePanel server control to specify whether the UpdatePanel server control must be rendered in asynchronous postback mode.

As Listing 23-26 shows, the RenderChildren method of an UpdatePanel server control instantiates an HtmlTextWriter instance when the control is in asynchronous postback mode :

```
HtmlTextWriter writer1 = new HtmlTextWriter(new StringWriter());
```

Next, it calls the RenderChildren method of its base class — that is, the Control base class — passing in the HtmlTextWriter instance. Recall from Listing 23-14 that the RenderChildren method of the Control base class iterates through the child controls in the Controls collection and invokes the RenderControl method on each child control to have the child control render itself into the preceding HtmlTextWriter instance. In other words, this HtmlTextWriter instance accumulates the HTML markup text generated by the server controls and HTML enclosed within the opening and closing tags of the <ContentTemplate> child element of the <UpdatePanel> tag.

```
base.RenderChildren(writer1);
```

Finally, the RenderChildren method of the UpdatePanel control calls the EncodeString static method on the server-side PageRequestManager class, passing in four parameters: the first references the HtmlTextWriter instance that wraps the response output stream, the second is the string "updatePanel", the third contains the value of the ClientID property of the UpdatePanel server control, and the last is a string that contains all the HTML markup of the child controls of the UpdatePanel server control. The main responsibility of the EncodeString method is to encode the last three parameters into a string and render the string into the HtmlTextWriter object that the first parameter references — that is, the HtmlTextWriter instance that wraps the response output stream.

Listing 23-26: The RenderChildren Method of the UpdatePanel

```
protected override void RenderChildren(HtmlTextWriter writer)
{
  if (this._asyncPostBackMode)
  {
    if (this._rendered)
      return;
    HtmlTextWriter writer1 = new HtmlTextWriter(new StringWriter());
    base.RenderChildren(writer1);
    PageRequestManager.EncodeString(writer, "updatePanel", this.ClientID,
                          writer1.InnerWriter.ToString());
  }
  else
  {
    writer.AddAttribute(HtmlTextWriterAttribute.Id, this.ClientID);
```

```
      if (this.RenderMode == UpdatePanelRenderMode.Block)
        writer.RenderBeginTag(HtmlTextWriterTag.Div);
      else
        writer.RenderBeginTag(HtmlTextWriterTag.Span);
      base.RenderChildren(writer);
      writer.RenderEndTag();
    }
    this._rendered = true;
}
```

The GetAsyncPostBackControlIDs Method of the Server-Side PageRequestManager

Listing 23-27 presents the implementation of the GetAsyncPostBackControlIDs method of the PageRequestManager. As you can see, this method simply delegates to the GetControlIDsFromList method, passing in the _asyncPostBackControls collection. Recall that the PageRequestManager server class features a private collection named _asyncPostBackControl that contains all the server controls that cause asynchronous page postbacks.

Listing 23-27: The GetAsyncPostBackControlIDs Method of the PageRequestManager

```
private string GetAsyncPostBackControlIDs(bool includeQuotes)
{
   return PageRequestManager.GetControlIDsFromList(this._asyncPostBackControls,
                                                   includeQuotes);
}
```

The GetControlIDsFromList Method of the Server-Side PageRequestManager

Listing 23-28 contains the code for the GetControlIDsFromList method of the server-side PageRequestManager. This method takes a List<Control> collection that contains a list of server controls. The main responsibility of this method is to return a comma-separated list of strings, each of which contains the UniqueID property value of a server control in the List<Control> collection. Note that this method takes a second Boolean argument that specifies whether these UniqueID property values must be rendered in quotes.

Listing 23-28: The GetControlIDsFromList Method of the PageRequestManager

```
private static string GetControlIDsFromList(List<Control> list, bool includeQuotes)
{
   if ((list == null) || (list.Count <= 0))
     return string.Empty;

   StringBuilder builder1 = new StringBuilder();
   bool flag1 = true;
   for (int num1 = 0; num1 < list.Count; num1++)
   {
     if (list[num1].Visible)
     {
       if (!flag1)
         builder1.Append(",");
```

(continued)

1139

Listing 23-28 *(continued)*

```
        flag1 = false;
        if (includeQuotes)
          builder1.Append("'");

        builder1.Append(list[num1].UniqueID);
        if (includeQuotes)
          builder1.Append("'");
      }
    }
    return builder1.ToString();
  }
```

The GetPostBackControlIDs Method of the Server-Side PageRequestManager

Listing 23-29 presents the implementation of the GetPostBackControlIDs method of the server-side PageRequestManager. As you can see, this method simply delegates to the GetControlIDsFromList method, passing in the _postBackControls collection. Recall that the PageRequestManager features a private collection field named _postBackControls that contains all the server controls on the current page that cause synchronous page postbacks.

Listing 23-29: The GetPostBackControlIDs Method of the PageRequestManager

```
private string GetPostBackControlIDs(bool includeQuotes)
{
    return PageRequestManager.GetControlIDsFromList(this._postBackControls,
                                                    includeQuotes);
}
```

GetAllUpdatePanelIDs

Recall from Listing 23-16 that the RenderPageCallback method of the server-side PageRequestManager calls the GetAllUpdatePanelIDs method to return a comma-separated list of strings that contain the values of the UniqueID properties of all the UpdatePanel server controls on the current page:

```
PageRequestManager.EncodeString(writer, "updatePanelIDs", string.Empty,
                                this.GetAllUpdatePanelIDs());
```

Listing 23-30 presents the internal implementation of the GetAllUpdatePanelIDs method. As you can see, this method simply delegates to the GetUpdatePanelIDsFromList static method of the server-side PageRequestManager.

Listing 23-30: The GetAllUpdatePanelIDs Method of the PageRequestManager

```
private string GetAllUpdatePanelIDs()
{
    return PageRequestManager.GetUpdatePanelIDsFromList(this._allUpdatePanels, true);
}
```

GetUpdatePanelIDsFromList

This method takes two arguments. The first argument is a `List<UpdatePanel>` collection of `UpdatePanel` server controls. The main responsibility of this method is to create and return a string that contains a comma-separated list of substrings, each of which consists of up to two parts. The first part of the each substring is optional and consists of the letter `f` or `t`. The second part contains the `UniqueID` property value of an `UpdatePanel` server control in the `List<UpdatePanel>` collection. Note that the `GetUpdatePanelIDsFromList` method takes a second Boolean argument that specifies whether each substring must contain the first part — that is, the letter `f` or `t`.

As you can see from Listing 23-31, the `GetUpdatePanelIDsFromList` method instantiates a `StringBuilder`, iterates through the `UpdatePanel` server controls in the `List<UpdatePanel>` collection, and appends a substring to the `StringBuilder` for each `UpdatePanel` server control. Note that the content of the first part of this substring depends on the value of the `ChildrenAsTriggers` property of the associated `UpdatePanel` server control. If this property is set to `true`, the first part of the substring contains the letter `t`. Otherwise the first part of the substring contains the letter `f`.

Listing 23-31: The GetUpdatePanelIDsFromList Static Method of the PageRequestManager

```
private static string GetUpdatePanelIDsFromList(List<UpdatePanel> list,
                                                bool includeChildrenAsTriggersPrefix)
{
  if ((list == null) || (list.Count <= 0))
    return string.Empty;

  StringBuilder builder1 = new StringBuilder();
  bool flag1 = true;
  for (int num1 = 0; num1 < list.Count; num1++)
  {
    if (list[num1].Visible)
    {
      if (!flag1)
        builder1.Append(',');

      flag1 = false;
      if (includeChildrenAsTriggersPrefix)
        builder1.Append(list[num1].ChildrenAsTriggers ? 't' : 'f');

      builder1.Append(list[num1].UniqueID);
    }
  }
  return builder1.ToString();
}
```

GetChildUpdatePanelIDs

Recall from Listing 23-16 that the `RenderPageCallback` method of the server-side `PageRequestManager` calls the `GetChildUpdatePanelIDs` method to return a comma-separated list of strings that contain the values of the `UniqueID` properties of all the child `UpdatePanel` server controls on the current page:

```
PageRequestManager.EncodeString(writer, "childUpdatePanelIDs", string.Empty,
                      this.GetChildUpdatePanelIDs());
```

As Listing 23-32 shows, the `GetChildUpdatePanelIDs` method simply delegates to the `GetUpdatePanelIDsFromList` static method of the server-side `PageRequestManager`, passing in the `_childUpdatePanelsToRefresh` collection of the current server-side `PageRequestManager` instance. Recall that this collection contains all the child `UpdatePanel` server controls on the current page that need refreshing.

Listing 23-32: The GetChildUpdatePanelIDs Method of the PageRequestManager

```
private string GetChildUpdatePanelIDs()
{
  return PageRequestManager.GetUpdatePanelIDsFromList(
                                   this._childUpdatePanelsToRefresh, false);
}
```

GetRefreshingUpdatePanelIDs

Recall from Listing 23-16 that the `RenderPageCallback` method of the server-side `PageRequestManager` calls the `GetRefreshingUpdatePanelIDs` method to return a comma-separated list of strings that contain the values of the `UniqueID` properties of all the `UpdatePanel` server controls on the current page that need refreshing and updating:

```
PageRequestManager.EncodeString(writer, "panelsToRefreshIDs", string.Empty,
                         this.GetRefreshingUpdatePanelIDs());
```

As you can see from Listing 23-33, the `GetRefreshingUpdatePanelIDs` method simply delegates to the `GetUpdatePanelIDsFromList` static method of the server-side `PageRequestManager`, passing in the `_updatePanelsToRefresh` collection of the current server-side `PageRequestManager` instance. Recall that this collection contains all the `UpdatePanel` server controls on the current page that need refreshing.

Listing 23-33: The GetRefreshingUpdatePanelIDs Method of the PageRequestManager

```
private string GetRefreshingUpdatePanelIDs()
{
  return PageRequestManager.GetUpdatePanelIDsFromList(
                                    this._updatePanelsToRefresh, false);
}
```

The RenderDataItems Method of PageRequestManager

Recall from Listing 23-16 that the `RenderPageCallback` method of the current server-side `PageRequestManager` instance calls the `RenderDataItems` method on the current server-side `PageRequestManager` instance to render data items. The current server-side `PageRequestManager` instance maintains all data items in an internal collection named `_scriptDataItems`. Each data item in this collection is represented by an instance of an internal class named `ScriptDataItem`, which exposes three important properties. The first property is a Boolean property named `IsJsonSerialized`, which specifies whether the data item is in JSON format. The second property is of type `Control`, which references the server control associated with the data item. The third property is of type `string`, and contains the actual data item.

As you can see from Listing 23-34, the `RenderDataItems` method of the current server-side `PageRequestManager` instance invokes the `EncodeString` static method on the server-side `PageRequestManager` for each `ScriptDataItem` object in the `_scriptDataItems` collection. As we discussed earlier, the `EncodeString` method takes four parameters. The first references the `HtmlTextWriter` object that wraps the response output stream. The second is a string that specifies the type of data item being encoded, which is `"dataItemJson"` if the data item is in JSON format, and `"dataItem"` otherwise. The third parameter is the `ClientID` property value of the server control associated with the data item. The last parameter is the string that contains the data item itself.

> *Currently the ASP.NET AJAX Timer is the only client-side component that makes use of data items. However, you can use data items in your own ASP.NET AJAX custom components. The only restriction that the ASP.NET AJAX framework puts on the data item is that it must be a string. However, it does not put any restriction on the content and the format of the content of this string. You can pack anything you want to in any format you wish in this string. For example, the string could contain an XML document.*

Listing 23-34: The RenderDataItems Method of PageRequestManager

```
private void RenderDataItems(HtmlTextWriter writer)
{
  if (this._scriptDataItems != null)
  {
    foreach (PageRequestManager.ScriptDataItem item1 in this._scriptDataItems)
    {
      PageRequestManager.EncodeString(writer,
                      item1.IsJsonSerialized ? "dataItemJson" : "dataItem",
                      item1.Control.ClientID, item1.DataItem);
    }
  }
}
```

As I mentioned earlier, the current server-side `PageRequestManager` instance maintains all data items in an internal collection named `_scriptDataItems`. Since the current server-side `PageRequestManager` instance is not public and consequently cannot be accessed from your code, you may be wondering how you can add new data items to the `_scriptDataItems` collection.

The current `ScriptManager` server control exposes a method named `RegisterDataItem` that takes two parameters. The first references the server control associated with the data item and the second is a string that contains the actual data item.

> *Take the following steps to register a new data item. First, call the `GetCurrent` static method on the `ScriptManager` to return a reference to the current `ScriptManager` server control. Next, call the `RegisterDataItem` instance method on the current `ScriptManager` server control, passing in two parameters. The first parameter must reference the server control associated with the data item being registered. The second must be a string that contains the actual data item being registered.*

Listing 23-35 presents the internal implementation of the `RegisterDataItem` static method of the `ScriptManager` server control. As you can see, this method delegates the responsibility of registering the specified data item associated with the specified server control to the `RegisterDataItem` method of the current server-side `PageRequestManager` instance.

Note that the current `ScriptManager` server control comes with two overloads of the `RegisterDataItem` method. Under the hood, one overload delegates to the other. If your data item is not in JSON format, use the overload that takes two parameters. Otherwise, use the second overload.

Listing 23-35: The RegisterDataItem Method of ScriptManager

```
public void RegisterDataItem(Control control, string dataItem)
{
  this.RegisterDataItem(control, dataItem, false);
}
public void RegisterDataItem(Control control, string dataItem,
                            bool isJsonSerialized)
{
  this.PageRequestManager.RegisterDataItem(control, dataItem, isJsonSerialized);
}
```

Listing 23-36 presents the internal implementation of the `RegisterDataItem` method of the current server-side `PageRequestManager` instance. Note that this method raises an argument-null exception if the data item is not associated with a server control:

```
if (control == null)
   throw new ArgumentNullException("control");
```

Also note that this method raises an invalid operation exception if the current request is not an asynchronous page post-back:

```
if (!this._owner.IsInAsyncPostBack)
   throw new InvalidOperationException("RegisterDataItemInNonAsyncRequest");
```

The `RegisterDataItem` method instantiates the `_scriptDataItems` collection if it hasn't already been instantiated:

```
if (this._scriptDataItems == null)
   this._scriptDataItems = new ScriptDataItemCollection();
```

Note that the method raises an argument exception if the `_scriptDataItems` collection already contains the same server control. In other words, you can register one data item for each server control. This is not a real restriction because the string that contains the data item can contain anything you want to, in any format you wish, as long as you do the data item registration in one shot. In other words, you cannot divide your data into multiple data items and register each data item separately.

```
else if (this._scriptDataItems.ContainsControl(control))
   throw new ArgumentException("RegisterDataItemTwice");
```

Next, the `RegisterDataItem` method instantiates a `ScriptDataItem` instance that contains the reference to the server control associated with the data item, the string that contains the data item, and the Boolean value that specifies whether the data item is in JSON format:

```
ScriptDataItem scriptDataItem =
                         new ScriptDataItem(control, dataItem, isJsonSerialized);
```

Finally, the method adds this `ScriptDataItem` object to the `_scriptDataItems` collection of the current server-side `PageRequestManager` instance:

```
    this._scriptDataItems.Add(scriptDataItem);
```

Listing 23-36: The RegisterDataItem Method of PageRequestManager

```
public void RegisterDataItem(Control control, string dataItem,
                             bool isJsonSerialized)
{
  if (control == null)
    throw new ArgumentNullException("control");

  if (!this._owner.IsInAsyncPostBack)
    throw new InvalidOperationException("RegisterDataItemInNonAsyncRequest");

  if (this._scriptDataItems == null)
    this._scriptDataItems = new ScriptDataItemCollection();
  else if (this._scriptDataItems.ContainsControl(control))
    throw new ArgumentException("RegisterDataItemTwice");
  ScriptDataItem scriptDataItem =
                      new ScriptDataItem(control, dataItem, isJsonSerialized);
  this._scriptDataItems.Add(scriptDataItem);
}
```

Listing 23-37 presents the internal implementation of the ScriptDataItem class, just in case you're wondering what this class looks like. As you can see, it is nothing but a bag of properties.

Listing 23-37: The ScriptDataItem Class

```
private sealed class ScriptDataItem
{
  // Methods
  public ScriptDataItem(Control control, string dataItem, bool isJsonSerialized)
  {
    this._control = control;
    this._dataItem = (dataItem == null) ? string.Empty : dataItem;
    this._isJsonSerialized = isJsonSerialized;
  }
  // Properties
  public Control Control
  {
    get { return this._control; }
  }
  public string DataItem
  {
    get { return this._dataItem; }
  }
  public bool IsJsonSerialized
  {
    get { return this._isJsonSerialized; }
  }
  // Fields
  private Control _control;
  private string _dataItem;
  private bool _isJsonSerialized;
}
```

As Listing 23-36 shows, before adding the specified data item associated with the specified server control to the _scriptDataItems collection, the RegisterDataItem method of the current server-side PageRequestManager instance invokes the ContainsControl method on the _scriptDataItems collection to check whether the collection already contains the same server control. If so, it raises an exception, because you cannot register more that one data item per server control.

Listing 23-38 presents the internal implementation of the ScriptDataItemCollection class. Keep in mind that the _scriptDataItems collection is of type ScriptDataItemCollection. As you can see, the ScriptDataItemCollection simply extends the List<ScriptDataItem> to add support for the ContainsControl method. Note that the ContainsControl method simply searches through the ScriptDataItem objects in the collection for a ScriptDataItem object associated with the specified server control. If the search fails, it returns false to inform its caller that the collection does not contain a data item associated with the specified server control. Otherwise, it returns true.

Listing 23-38: The ScriptDataItemCollection Class

```
private sealed class ScriptDataItemCollection : List<ScriptDataItem>
{
  public bool ContainsControl(Control control)
  {
    using(List<ScriptDataItem>.Enumerator enumerator1 = base.GetEnumerator())
    {
      while (enumerator1.MoveNext())
      {
        if (enumerator1.Current.Control == control)
          return true;
      }
    }

    return false;
  }
}
```

The ProcessScriptRegistration Method of the PageRequestManager

Recall from Listing 23-16 that the RenderPageCallback method of the current server-side PageRequestManager instance calls the ProcessScriptRegistration method on the current server-side PageRequestManager instance to register the required client scripts. Listing 23-39 presents the internal implementation of the ProcessScriptRegistration method.

As you can see, this method delegates the responsibility of registering the specified client scripts to the appropriate methods of the ScriptRegistration property of the current ScriptManager server control. Keep in mind that the _owner field of the current server-side PageRequestManager instance references the current ScriptManager server control. The ScriptRegistration property of the ScriptManager server control is of type ScriptRegistrationManager, which is an internal class that manages the registration and rendering of the client scripts when the current request is an asynchronous page postback.

As you can see from Listing 23-39, the `ProcessScriptRegistration` method passes the same two parameters to all the methods of the `ScriptRegistrationManager` class that it invokes. The first parameter references the _updatePanelsToRefresh collection of the current server-side PageRequestManager and the second references the `HtmlTextWriter` object that wraps the response output stream. Recall that the _updatePanelsToRefresh collection contains all the UpdatePanels server controls on the current page that need refreshing.

Listing 23-39: The ProcessScriptRegistration Method of the PageRequestManager

```
private void ProcessScriptRegistration(HtmlTextWriter writer)
{
  this._owner.ScriptRegistration.RenderActiveArrayDeclarations(
                                    this._updatePanelsToRefresh, writer);
  this._owner.ScriptRegistration.RenderActiveScripts(
                                    this._updatePanelsToRefresh, writer);
  this._owner.ScriptRegistration.RenderActiveSubmitStatements(
                                    this._updatePanelsToRefresh, writer);
  this._owner.ScriptRegistration.RenderActiveExpandos(
                                    this._updatePanelsToRefresh, writer);
  this._owner.ScriptRegistration.RenderActiveHiddenFields(
                                    this._updatePanelsToRefresh, writer);
  this._owner.ScriptRegistration.RenderActiveScriptDisposes(
                                    this._updatePanelsToRefresh, writer);
}
```

The ScriptRegistrationManager Class

As we discussed in the previous sections, the `ScriptRegistrationManager` is an internal ASP.NET responsible for registering and rendering the required client scripts when the current request is an asynchronous page postback.

The current `ScriptRegistrationManager` instance contains the collections shown in Listing 23-40.

Listing 23-40: The Internal Collections of the Current ScriptRegistrationManager Instance

```
Dictionary<Control, List<ScriptArrayEntry>> ScriptArrays { get; }
Dictionary<Control, List<ScriptBlockEntry>> ScriptBlocks { get; }
List<ScriptDisposeEntry> ScriptDisposes { get; }
Dictionary<Control, List<ScriptExpandoEntry>> ScriptExpandos { get; }
Dictionary<Control, List<ScriptHiddenFieldEntry>> ScriptHiddenFields {get;}
Dictionary<Control, List<ScriptBlockEntry>> ScriptStartupBlocks { get; }
Dictionary<Control, List<ScriptSubmitStatementEntry>> ScriptSubmitStatements {get;}
```

Here is what each collection contains:

❑ ScriptArrays: This dictionary contains one List<ScriptArrayEntry> for each server control, where the List<ScriptArrayEntry> collection contains all the ScriptArrayEntry objects associated with the server control. As the following code listing shows, each `ScriptArrayEntry` represents a JavaScript array with a specified name and value:

```
private sealed class ScriptArrayEntry
{
  public ScriptArrayEntry(string arrayName, string arrayValue)
  {
    this._arrayName = arrayName;
    this._arrayValue = arrayValue;
  }
  public string ArrayName { get { return this._arrayName; } }
  public string ArrayValue { get { return this.ArrayValue; } }
  private string _arrayName;
  private string _arrayValue;
}
```

❏   **ScriptBlocks**: This dictionary contains one `List<ScriptBlockEntry>` for each server control, where the `List<ScriptBlockEntry>` collection contains all the `ScriptBlockEntry` objects associated with the server control. As the following code listing shows, each `ScriptBlockEntry` represents a JavaScript script block with the specified `Type` and `key`, where the `Type` and `key` together form a unique identifier under which the script block is registered. Note that the `ScriptBlockEntry` exposes two constructors. The first is used to instantiate a `ScriptBlockEntry` object that represents a JavaScript `include` block. Because of this, the third argument of this constructor is a string that contains the `include` path. The second constructor is used to instantiate a `ScriptBlockEntry` object that represents a JavaScript script block. Because of this, the third and fourth arguments of this constructor are a string that contain the script block and a Boolean value that specifies whether the script block contains the script tags, respectively.

```
private sealed class ScriptBlockEntry
{
  public ScriptBlockEntry(Type type, string key, string includePath)
  {
    this._type = type;
    this._key = key;
    this._includePath = includePath;
  }
  public ScriptBlockEntry(Type type, string key, string script, bool addScriptTags)
  {
    this._type = type;
    this._key = key;
    this._script = script;
    this._addScriptTags = addScriptTags;
  }
  public bool AddScriptTags { get {return this._addScriptTags; } }
  public string IncludePath { get { return this._includePath; } }
  public string Key { get { return this._key; } }
  public string Script { get {return this._script; } }
  public Type Type { get {return this._type; } }
```

```
    private bool _addScriptTags;
    private string _includePath;
    private string _key;
    private string _script;
    private Type _type;
}
```

❑   ScriptDisposes: This List<ScriptDisposeEntry> collection contains a bunch of
    ScriptDisposeEntry objects, each of which represents a JavaScript script that will be
    executed when a specified UpdatePanel server control is disposed of.

```
private sealed class ScriptDisposeEntry
{
  public ScriptDisposeEntry(string disposeScript, UpdatePanel parentUpdatePanel)
  {
    this._disposeScript = disposeScript;
    this._parentUpdatePanel = parentUpdatePanel;
  }
  public string DisposeScript { get { return this._disposeScript; } }
  public UpdatePanel ParentUpdatePanel { get {return this._parentUpdatePanel; } }
  private string _disposeScript;
  private UpdatePanel _parentUpdatePanel;
}
```

❑   ScriptExpandos: This dictionary contains one List<ScriptExpandoEntry> for each
    server control, where the List<ScriptExpandoEntry> collection contains all the
    ScriptExpandoEntry objects associated with the server control. As the following code list-
    ing shows, each ScriptExpandoEntry represents, with a specified name and value, an
    expando attribute of a control with a specified ID:

```
private sealed class ScriptExpandoEntry
{
  public ScriptExpandoEntry(string controlId, string attributeName,
                            string attributeValue)
  {
    this._controlId = controlId;
    this._attributeName = attributeName;
    this._attributeValue = attributeValue;
  }
  public string AttributeName { get {return this._attributeName; } }
  public string AttributeValue { get {return this._attributeValue; } }
  public string ControlId { get {return this._controlId; } }
  private string _attributeName;
  private string _attributeValue;
  private string _controlId;
}
```

❑ `ScriptHiddenFields`: This dictionary contains one `List<ScriptHiddenFieldEntry>` for each server control, where the `List<ScriptHiddenFieldEntry>` collection contains all the `ScriptHiddenFieldEntry` objects associated with the server control. As the following code listing shows, each `ScriptHiddenFieldEntry` represents a hidden field with a specified name and initial value:

```
private sealed class ScriptHiddenFieldEntry
{
  public ScriptHiddenFieldEntry(string hiddenFieldName,
                                string hiddenFieldInitialValue)
  {
    this._hiddenFieldName = hiddenFieldName;
    this._hiddenFieldInitialValue = hiddenFieldInitialValue;
  }
  public string HiddenFieldInitialValue{get{return this._hiddenFieldInitialValue;}}
  public string HiddenFieldName { get {return this._hiddenFieldName; } }
  private string _hiddenFieldInitialValue;
  private string _hiddenFieldName;
}
```

❑ `ScriptStartupBlocks`: This dictionary contains one `List<ScriptBlockEntry>` for each server control, where the `List<ScriptBlockEntry>` collection contains all the `ScriptBlockEntry` objects associated with the server control.

❑ `ScriptSubmitStatements`: This dictionary contains one `List<ScriptSubmitStatementEntry>` for each server control, where the `List<ScriptSubmitStatementEntry>` collection contains all the `ScriptSubmitStatementEntry` objects associated with the server control. As the following code listing shows, each `ScriptSubmitStatementEntry` represents a submit script, which will be executed when the `submit` event of the current form is fired:

```
private sealed class ScriptSubmitStatementEntry
{
  public ScriptSubmitStatementEntry(Type type, string key, string script)
  {
    this._type = type;
    this._key = key;
    this._script = script;
  }
  public string Key { get {return this._key; } }
  public string Script { get {return this._script; } }
  public Type Type { get {return this._type; } }
  private string _key;
  private string _script;
  private Type _type;
}
```

The current `ScriptRegistrationManager` instance exposes the static methods shown in Listing 23-41 that can be used to add script entries into its `ScriptArrays`, `ScriptBlocks`, `ScriptDisposes`, `ScriptExpandos`, `ScriptHiddenFields`, `ScriptStartupBlocks`, and `ScriptSubmitStatements` collections.

Listing 23-41: The Script Registration Methods of the ScriptRegistrationManager

```
public static void RegisterArrayDeclaration(Control control, string arrayName,
                                            string arrayValue)
{
  . . .
  ScriptManager manager1 = ScriptManager.GetCurrent(control.Page);
  if (manager1.IsInAsyncPostBack)
  {
    ScriptArrayEntry entry1 = new ScriptArrayEntry(arrayName, arrayValue);
    List<ScriptArrayEntry> list1 = this.ScriptArrays.TryGetValue(control,
                                      out (List<ScriptArrayEntry>)list1);
    if (!list1)
    {
      list1 = new List<ScriptArrayEntry>();
      this.ScriptArrays[control] = (List<ScriptArrayEntry>)list1;
    }
    list1.Add(entry1);
  }
}
public static void RegisterClientScriptBlock(Control control, Type type,
                                             string key, string script,
                                             bool addScriptTags)
{
  . . .
  ScriptManager manager1 = ScriptManager.GetCurrent(control.Page);
  if (manager1.IsInAsyncPostBack)
  {
    ScriptBlockEntry entry1 =
                    new ScriptBlockEntry(type, key, script, addScriptTags);
    List<ScriptBlockEntry> list1 = this.ScriptBlocks.TryGetValue(control,
                                      out (List<ScriptBlockEntry>)list1);
    if (!list1)
    {
      list1 = new List<ScriptBlockEntry>();
      this.ScriptBlocks[control] = (List<ScriptBlockEntry>)list1;
    }
    list1.Add(entry1);
  }
}
public static void RegisterClientScriptInclude(Control control, Type type,
                                               string key, string url)
{
  . . .
  ScriptManager manager1 = ScriptManager.GetCurrent(control.Page);
  if (manager1.IsInAsyncPostBack)
  {
    ScriptBlockEntry entry1 = new ScriptBlockEntry(type, key, includePath);
    List<ScriptBlockEntry> list1 = this.ScriptBlocks.TryGetValue(control,
                                      out (List<ScriptBlockEntry>)list1);
    if (!list1)
    {
      list1 = new List<ScriptBlockEntry>();
      this.ScriptBlocks[control] = (List<ScriptBlockEntry>)list1;
    }
```

(continued)

1151

Listing 23-41 *(continued)*

```
      list1.Add(entry1);
  }
}
public static void RegisterClientScriptResource(Control control, Type type,
                                                string resourceName)
{
    . . .
  ScriptManager manager1 = ScriptManager.GetCurrent(control.Page);
  string includePath = manager1.GetScriptResourceUrl(resourceName, type.Assembly);
  ScriptBlockEntry entry1 = new ScriptBlockEntry(type, key, includePath);
  List<ScriptBlockEntry> list1 = this.ScriptBlocks.TryGetValue(control,
                                            out (List<ScriptBlockEntry>)list1);
  if (!list1)
  {
    list1 = new List<ScriptBlockEntry>();
    this.ScriptBlocks[control] = (List<ScriptBlockEntry>)list1;
  }
  list1.Add(entry1);
}
public static void RegisterExpandoAttribute(Control control, string controlId,
                                            string attributeName,
                                            string attributeValue, bool encode)
{
    . . .
  ScriptManager manager1 = ScriptManager.GetCurrent(control.Page);
  if (manager1.IsInAsyncPostBack)
  {
    if (encode)
      attributeValue = JavaScriptString.QuoteString(attributeValue);

    ScriptExpandoEntry entry1 =
                new ScriptExpandoEntry(controlId, attributeName, attributeValue);
    List<ScriptExpandoEntry> list1 = this.ScriptExpandos.TryGetValue(control,
                                          out (List<ScriptExpandoEntry>)list1);
    if (!list1)
    {
      list1 = new List<ScriptExpandoEntry>();
      this.ScriptExpandos[control] = (List<ScriptExpandoEntry>)list1;
    }
    list1.Add(entry1);
  }
}
public static void RegisterHiddenField(Control control, string hiddenFieldName,
                                       string hiddenFieldInitialValue)
{
    . . .
  ScriptManager manager1 = ScriptManager.GetCurrent(control.Page);
  if (manager1.IsInAsyncPostBack)
  {
    manager1.ScriptRegistration.RegisterHiddenFieldInternal(control,
                                hiddenFieldName, hiddenFieldInitialValue);
```

```
          ScriptHiddenFieldEntry entry1 =
                  new ScriptHiddenFieldEntry(hiddenFieldName, hiddenFieldInitialValue);
        List<ScriptHiddenFieldEntry> list1 =
              this.ScriptHiddenFields.TryGetValue(control,
                                          out (List<ScriptHiddenFieldEntry>)list1);
        if (!list1)
        {
          list1 = new List<ScriptHiddenFieldEntry>();
          this.ScriptHiddenFields[control] = (List<ScriptHiddenFieldEntry>)list1;
        }
        list1.Add(entry1);
    }
}
public static void RegisterOnSubmitStatement(Control control, Type type,
                                        string key, string script)
{
    . . .
    ScriptManager manager1 = ScriptManager.GetCurrent(control.Page);
    if (manager1.IsInAsyncPostBack)
    {
      manager1.ScriptRegistration.RegisterOnSubmitStatementInternal(control, type,
                                            key, script);
      ScriptSubmitStatementEntry entry1 =
                          new ScriptSubmitStatementEntry(type, key, script);
      List<ScriptSubmitStatementEntry> list1 =
          this.ScriptSubmitStatements.TryGetValue(control,
                              out (List<ScriptSubmitStatementEntry>)list1);
      if (!list1)
      {
        list1 = new List<ScriptSubmitStatementEntry>();
        this.ScriptSubmitStatements[control] =
                              (List<ScriptSubmitStatementEntry>)list1;
      }
      list1.Add(entry1);
    }
}
public static void RegisterStartupScript(Control control, Type type, string key,
                                  string script, bool addScriptTags)
{
    . . .
    ScriptManager manager1 = ScriptManager.GetCurrent(control.Page);
    if (manager1.IsInAsyncPostBack)
    {
      manager1.ScriptRegistration.RegisterStartupScriptInternal(control, type, key,
                                        script, addScriptTags);
      ScriptBlockEntry entry1 =
                      new ScriptBlockEntry(type, key, script, addScriptTags);
      List<ScriptBlockEntry> list1 =
            this.ScriptStartupBlocks.TryGetValue(control,
                                    out (List<ScriptBlockEntry>)list1);
```

(continued)

Listing 23-41 *(continued)*

```
        if (!list1)
        {
          list1 = new List<ScriptBlockEntry>();
          this.ScriptStartupBlocks[control] = (List<ScriptBlockEntry>)list1;
        }
        list1.Add(entry1);
      }
    }
    internal void RegisterDispose(Control control, string disposeScript)
    {
      Control control1 = control.Parent;
      UpdatePanel panel1 = null;
      while (control1 != null)
      {
        panel1 = control1 as UpdatePanel;
        if (panel1 != null)
          break;
        control1 = control1.Parent;
      }
      if (panel1 != null)
      {
        if (this._scriptManager.IsInAsyncPostBack)
        {
          ScriptDisposeEntry entry = new ScriptDisposeEntry(disposeScript, panel1);
          this.ScriptDisposes.Add(entry);
        }
        else
        {
          JavaScriptSerializer serializer1 = new JavaScriptSerializer();
          StringBuilder builder1 = new StringBuilder(0x100);
          Builder1.Append("var prm = Sys.WebForms.PageRequestManager.getInstance();");
          builder1.Append("prm._registerDisposeScript(");
          serializer1.Serialize(panel1.ClientID, builder1);
          builder1.Append(", ");
          serializer1.Serialize(disposeScript, builder1);
          builder1.AppendLine(");");
          ScriptRegistrationManager.RegisterStartupScript(
                                     control,
                                     typeof(ScriptRegistrationManager),
                                     this._scriptManager.CreateUniqueScriptKey(),
                                     builder1.ToString(),
                                     true);
        }
      }
    }
}
```

Since the current `ScriptRegistrationManager` instance is internal to the ASP.NET framework, you may be wondering how you can add script entries to these collections. The current `ScriptManager` server control exposes the public static methods shown in Listing 23-42, which under the hood delegate to the methods of the current `ScriptRegistrationMananger` instance shown in Listing 23-41.

Listing 23-42: The Public Static Registration Methods of the ScriptManager Server Control

```
public static void RegisterArrayDeclaration(Control control, string arrayName,
                                            string arrayValue)
{
  ScriptRegistrationManager.RegisterArrayDeclaration(control, arrayName,
                                            arrayValue);
}
public static void RegisterArrayDeclaration(Page page, string arrayName,
                                            string arrayValue)
{
  ScriptRegistrationManager.RegisterArrayDeclaration(page, arrayName, arrayValue);
}
public static void RegisterClientScriptBlock(Control control, Type type,
                                            string key, string script,
                                            bool addScriptTags)
{
  ScriptRegistrationManager.RegisterClientScriptBlock(control, type, key, script,
                                            addScriptTags);
}
public static void RegisterClientScriptBlock(Page page, Type type, string key,
                                            string script, bool addScriptTags)
{
  ScriptRegistrationManager.RegisterClientScriptBlock(page, type, key, script,
                                            addScriptTags);
}
public static void RegisterClientScriptInclude(Control control, Type type,
                                            string key, string url)
{
  ScriptRegistrationManager.RegisterClientScriptInclude(control, type, key, url);
}
public static void RegisterClientScriptInclude(Page page, Type type, string key,
                                            string url)
{
  ScriptRegistrationManager.RegisterClientScriptInclude(page, type, key, url);
}
public static void RegisterClientScriptResource(Control control, Type type,
                                            string resourceName)
{
  ScriptRegistrationManager.RegisterClientScriptResource(control, type,
                                            resourceName);
}
```

(continued)

1155

Listing 23-42 *(continued)*

```
public static void RegisterClientScriptResource(Page page, Type type,
                                                string resourceName)
{
  ScriptRegistrationManager.RegisterClientScriptResource(page, type, resourceName);
}
public static void RegisterExpandoAttribute(Control control, string controlId,
                                            string attributeName,
                                            string attributeValue, bool encode)
{
  ScriptRegistrationManager.RegisterExpandoAttribute(control, controlId,
                                                     attributeName, attributeValue,
                                                     encode);
}
public void RegisterExtenderControl<TExtenderControl>(
  TExtenderControl extenderControl, Control targetControl) where TExtenderControl :
                                    Control, IExtenderControl
{
  this.ScriptControlManager.RegisterExtenderControl<TExtenderControl>(
                                    extenderControl, targetControl);
}
public static void RegisterHiddenField(Control control, string hiddenFieldName,
                                       string hiddenFieldInitialValue)
{
  ScriptRegistrationManager.RegisterHiddenField(control, hiddenFieldName,
                                                hiddenFieldInitialValue);
}
public static void RegisterHiddenField(Page page, string hiddenFieldName,
                                       string hiddenFieldInitialValue)
{
  ScriptRegistrationManager.RegisterHiddenField(page, hiddenFieldName,
                                                hiddenFieldInitialValue);
}
public static void RegisterOnSubmitStatement(Control control, Type type,
                                             string key, string script)
{
  ScriptRegistrationManager.RegisterOnSubmitStatement(control, type, key, script);
}
public static void RegisterOnSubmitStatement(Page page, Type type, string key,
                                             string script)
{
  ScriptRegistrationManager.RegisterOnSubmitStatement(page, type, key, script);
}
public static void RegisterStartupScript(Control control, Type type, string key,
                                         string script, bool addScriptTags)
{
  ScriptRegistrationManager.RegisterStartupScript(control, type, key, script,
                                                  addScriptTags);
}
```

```
public static void RegisterStartupScript(Page page, Type type, string key,
                                         string script, bool addScriptTags)
{
    ScriptRegistrationManager.RegisterStartupScript(page, type, key, script,
                                                    addScriptTags);
}
public void RegisterDispose(Control control, string disposeScript)
{
    this.ScriptRegistration.RegisterDispose(control, disposeScript);
}
```

As Listing 23-39 shows, when the current Page enters its rendering phase, the
ProcessScriptRegistration method of the current server-side PageRequestManager instance is
invoked, by means of which the methods of the current ScriptRegistrationManager instance
shown in Listing 23-43 are called to render the script entries in the ScriptArrays, ScriptBlocks,
ScriptDisposes, ScriptExpandos, ScriptHiddenFields, ScriptStartupBlocks, and
ScriptSubmitStatements collections.

Listing 23-43: The Script-Rendering Methods of the ScriptRegistrationMananger

```
public void RenderActiveArrayDeclarations(List<UpdatePanel> updatePanels,
                                          HtmlTextWriter writer)
{
    List<ScriptArrayEntry> list1 = new List<ScriptArrayEntry>();
    foreach (KeyValuePair<Control, List<ScriptArrayEntry>> pair1 in
                                                      this.ScriptArrays)
    {
        foreach (UpdatePanel panel1 in updatePanels)
        {
            if (this.IsControlRegistrationActive(panel1, pair1.Key, true))
            {
                foreach (ScriptArrayEntry entry1 in pair1.Value)
                {
                    if (!list1.Contains(entry1))
                        list1.Add(entry1);
                }
            }
        }
    }
    foreach (ScriptArrayEntry entry3 in list1)
    {
        PageRequestManager.EncodeString(writer, "arrayDeclaration",
                                        entry3.ArrayName, entry3.ArrayValue);
    }
}
```

(continued)

Listing 23-43 (continued)

```
public void RenderActiveExpandos(List<UpdatePanel> updatePanels,
                                 HtmlTextWriter writer)
{
  List<ScriptExpandoEntry> list1 = new List<ScriptExpandoEntry>();
  using (Dictionary<Control, List<ScriptExpandoEntry>>.Enumerator enumerator1 =
                                        this.ScriptExpandos.GetEnumerator())
  {
    while (enumerator1.MoveNext())
    {
      KeyValuePair<Control, List<ScriptExpandoEntry>> pair1 = enumerator1.Current;
      foreach (UpdatePanel panel1 in updatePanels)
      {
        if (this.IsControlRegistrationActive(panel1, pair1.Key, false))
        {
          foreach (ScriptExpandoEntry entry1 in pair1.Value)
          {
            if (!list1.Contains(entry1))
              list1.Add(entry1);
          }
        }
      }
    }
  }
  foreach (ScriptExpandoEntry entry2 in list1)
  {
    string id = "document.getElementById('" +
                  entry2.ControlId + "')['" + entry2.AttributeName + "']";
    string content = "null";
    if (entry2.AttributeValue != null)
      content = "'" + entry2.AttributeValue + "'";
    PageRequestManager.EncodeString(writer, "expando", id, content);
  }
}
public void RenderActiveHiddenFields(List<UpdatePanel> updatePanels,
                                     HtmlTextWriter writer)
{
  List<ScriptHiddenFieldEntry> list1 = new List<ScriptHiddenFieldEntry>();
  foreach (KeyValuePair<Control, List<ScriptHiddenFieldEntry>> pair1 in
                                                this.ScriptHiddenFields)
  {
    foreach (UpdatePanel panel1 in updatePanels)
    {
      if (this.IsControlRegistrationActive(panel1, pair1.Key, true))
      {
        foreach (ScriptHiddenFieldEntry entry1 in pair1.Value)
        {
```

```
              if (!list1.Contains(entry1))
                list1.Add(entry1);
            }
          }
        }
      }
      foreach (ScriptHiddenFieldEntry entry3 in list1)
      {
        PageRequestManager.EncodeString(writer, "hiddenField", entry3.HiddenFieldName,
                                    entry3.HiddenFieldInitialValue);
      }
    }
    public void RenderActiveScriptDisposes(List<UpdatePanel> updatePanels,
                                    HtmlTextWriter writer)
    {
      List<ScriptDisposeEntry> list1 = new List<ScriptDisposeEntry>();
      using(List<ScriptDisposeEntry>.Enumerator enumerator1 =
                                    this.ScriptDisposes.GetEnumerator())
      {
        while (enumerator1.MoveNext())
        {
          ScriptDisposeEntry entry1 = enumerator1.Current;
          foreach (UpdatePanel panel1 in updatePanels)
          {
            if (this.IsControlRegistrationActive(panel1,
                                    entry1.ParentUpdatePanel, false))
              list1.Add(entry1);
          }
        }
      }
      foreach (ScriptDisposeEntry entry2 in list1)
      {
        PageRequestManager.EncodeString(writer, "scriptDispose",
                                    entry2.ParentUpdatePanel.ClientID,
                                    entry2.DisposeScript);
      }
    }
    public void RenderActiveScripts(List<UpdatePanel> updatePanels,
                              HtmlTextWriter writer)
    {
      this.RenderActiveScriptBlocks(updatePanels, writer, this.ScriptBlocks);
      this.RenderActiveScriptBlocks(updatePanels, writer, this.ScriptStartupBlocks);
    }
```

(continued)

Listing 23-43 *(continued)*

```
public void RenderActiveSubmitStatements(List<UpdatePanel> updatePanels,
                                         HtmlTextWriter writer)
{
  List<ScriptSubmitStatementEntry> list1 = new List<ScriptSubmitStatementEntry>();
  foreach (KeyValuePair<Control, List<ScriptSubmitStatementEntry>> pair1 in
                                                   this.ScriptSubmitStatements)
  {
    foreach (UpdatePanel panel1 in updatePanels)
    {
      if (this.IsControlRegistrationActive(panel1, pair1.Key, true))
      {
        foreach (ScriptSubmitStatementEntry entry1 in pair1.Value)
        {
          if (!list1.Contains(entry1))
            list1.Add(entry1);
        }
      }
    }
  }
  foreach (ScriptSubmitStatementEntry entry3 in list1)
  {
    PageRequestManager.EncodeString(writer, "onSubmit", null, entry3.Script);
  }
}
```

ProcessFocus

The current `ScriptManager` server control exposes two overloads of a method named `SetFocus` that you can call from within your code to set the focus to a particular server control. Listing 23-44 presents the internal implementation of these two overloads. The first takes the `ClientID` property value of the server control to which the focus is being set. The second takes the reference to the actual server control to which the focus is being set.

As you can see from Listing 23-44, both overloads delegate to the associated overload of the `SetFocus` method of the current server-side `PageRequestManager` instance.

Listing 23-44: The Internal Implementations of the SetFocus Overloads of the Current ScriptManager Server Control

```
public void SetFocus(string clientID)
{
  this.PageRequestManager.SetFocus(clientID);
}
public void SetFocus(Control control)
{
  this.PageRequestManager.SetFocus(control);
}
```

Listing 23-45 presents the internal implementations of the two overloads of the `SetFocus` method of the current server-side `PageRequestManager` instance. As you can see, each overload checks whether the current request is an asynchronous page postback request and whether the `ClientSupportsFocus` property of the current server side PageRequestMananger instance is set to true. If these things are true, the overloads assign their input parameters to the _focusedControl and focusedControlID properties, respectively, of the current server-side PageRequestManager instance. Note that both overloads set the _requiresFocusScript field of the current server-side PageRequestManager instance to true.

Listing 23-45: The Focus-Related Methods of the PageRequestManager

```
public void SetFocus(Control control)
{
  this._owner.IPage.SetFocus(control);
  if (this._owner.IsInAsyncPostBack && this.ClientSupportsFocus)
  {
    this._focusedControl = control;
    this._focusedControlID = null;
    this._requireFocusScript = true;
  }
}
public void SetFocus(string clientID)
{
  this._owner.IPage.SetFocus(clientID);
  if (this._owner.IsInAsyncPostBack && this.ClientSupportsFocus)
  {
    this._focusedControlID = clientID.Trim();
    this._focusedControl = null;
    this._requireFocusScript = true;
  }
}
```

As Listing 23-39 shows, when the current Page finally enters its rendering phase, the ProcessFocus method of the current server-side PageRequestManager instance is invoked. As Listing 23-46 shows, this method checks whether the _requiresFocusScript field is set to true. If so, it takes the following steps. First, it evaluates the ClientID property value of the server control that must gain the focus:

```
string focusedControlID = string.Empty;
  if (!string.IsNullOrEmpty(this._focusedControlID))
    focusedControlID = this._focusedControlID;
  else if ((this._focusedControl != null) && this._focusedControl.Visible)
    focusedControlID = this._focusedControl.ClientID;
```

Next, it calls the GetScriptResouseUrl method on the current ScriptManager server control to return the URL to the Focus.js JavaScript file. This file contains all the focus-related client scripts:

```
string scriptPath = this._owner.GetScriptResourceUrl("Focus.js",
                                            typeof(HtmlForm).Assembly);
```

Next, it invokes the EncodeString static method on the server-side PageRequestManager to write a string that consists of four substrings into the response output stream. The first substring specifies the length of the last substring. The second substring is the string "scriptBlock", to signal the current client-side PageRequestManager instance that the encoded string contains a script block. The third substring is the string "ScriptPath", to signal the current client-side PageRequestManager instance that the encoded string contains the URL of a JavaScript file. The fourth substring is a string that contains the actual URL for the JavaScript file.

1161

```
PageRequestManager.EncodeString(writer, "scriptBlock", "ScriptPath",
                                scriptPath);
```

Next, the `ProcessFocus` method invokes the `EncodeString` static method once more on the server-side `PageRequestManager` to write a string that consists of four substrings into the response output stream. The first substring specifies the length of the last substring. The second substring is the string `"focus"`, to signal the current client-side `PageRequestManager` instance that the encoded string contains the `ClientID` property value of the server control that must have the focus. The third substring is an empty string. The fourth substring is a string that contains the actual `ClientID` property value.

```
PageRequestManager.EncodeString(writer, "focus", string.Empty,
                                focusedControlID);
```

Listing 23-46: The ProcessFocus Method of PageRequestMananger

```
private void ProcessFocus(HtmlTextWriter writer)
{
  if (this._requireFocusScript)
  {
    string focusedControlID = string.Empty;
    if (!string.IsNullOrEmpty(this._focusedControlID))
      focusedControlID = this._focusedControlID;
    else if ((this._focusedControl != null) && this._focusedControl.Visible)
      focusedControlID = this._focusedControl.ClientID;
    if (focusedControlID.Length > 0)
    {
      string scriptPath = this._owner.GetScriptResourceUrl("Focus.js",
                                           typeof(HtmlForm).Assembly);
      PageRequestManager.EncodeString(writer, "scriptBlock", "ScriptPath",
                                      scriptPath);
      PageRequestManager.EncodeString(writer, "focus", string.Empty,
                                      focusedControlID);
    }
  }
}
```

Server Response

Keep in mind that we have been following the current `Page` as it goes through its life cycle phases to process the asynchronous page postback request that the current client-side `PageRequestMananger` instance made to the server. The end result of this request-processing activity is the server response text, which is sent back to the current client-side `PageRequestMananger` instance.

As you saw in the previous sections, the current `Page` delegates the responsibility of generating the server response text to the `RenderPageCallback` method of the current server-side `PageRequestManager` instance (see Listing 23-16). Listing 23-47 repeats Listing 23-16.

Listing 23-47: The RenderPageCallback Method of the Current Server-Side PageRequestManager Instance

```
private void RenderPageCallback(HtmlTextWriter writer, Control pageControl)
{
  this.ProcessUpdatePanels();
  IHttpResponse response1 = this._owner.IPage.Response;
  response1.ContentType = "text/plain";
  response1.Cache.SetNoServerCaching();
  IHtmlForm form1 = this._owner.IPage.Form;
  form1.SetRenderMethodDelegate(new RenderMethod(this.RenderFormCallback));
  this._updatePanelWriter = writer;
  PageRequestManager.ParserStringWriter writer1 =
                                  new PageRequestManager.ParserStringWriter();
  PageRequestManager.ParserHtmlTextWriter writer2 =
                            new PageRequestManager.ParserHtmlTextWriter(writer1);
  writer1.ParseWrites = true;
  form1.RenderControl(writer2);
  writer1.ParseWrites = false;
  foreach (KeyValuePair<string, string> pair1 in writer1.HiddenFields)
  {
    if (PageRequestManager.IsBuiltInHiddenField(pair1.Key))

      PageRequestManager.EncodeString(writer, "hiddenField", pair1.Key,
                                      pair1.Value);

  }

  PageRequestManager.EncodeString(writer, "asyncPostBackControlIDs", string.Empty,
                            this.GetAsyncPostBackControlIDs(false));
  PageRequestManager.EncodeString(writer, "postBackControlIDs", string.Empty,
                            this.GetPostBackControlIDs(false));
  PageRequestManager.EncodeString(writer, "updatePanelIDs", string.Empty,
                            this.GetAllUpdatePanelIDs());
  PageRequestManager.EncodeString(writer, "childUpdatePanelIDs", string.Empty,
                            this.GetChildUpdatePanelIDs());
  PageRequestManager.EncodeString(writer, "panelsToRefreshIDs", string.Empty,
                            this.GetRefreshingUpdatePanelIDs());
  PageRequestManager.EncodeString(writer, "asyncPostBackTimeout", string.Empty,
                            this._owner.AsyncPostBackTimeout.ToString());

  if (writer2.FormAction != null)

    PageRequestManager.EncodeString(writer, "formAction", string.Empty,
                              writer2.FormAction);

  if (this._owner.IPage.Header != null)
  {
    string text1 = this._owner.IPage.Title;
    if (!string.IsNullOrEmpty(text1))

      PageRequestManager.EncodeString(writer, "pageTitle", string.Empty, text1);

  }
  this.RenderDataItems(writer);
  this.ProcessScriptRegistration(writer);
  this.ProcessFocus(writer);
}
```

The highlighted portions of Listing 23-47 present the calls into the `EncodeString` static method of the server-side `PageRequestManager`. Each call into this method generates an encoded string and writes the string into the response output stream. Each encoded string is in the format `length|type|id|content|`. As you can see, each string consists of four parts separated by the pipe character. The first part specifies the length of the content. The second part is a string that tells the current client-side `PageRequestMananger` what type of information the encoded string contains. The third part is an optional string that contains the `ClientID` property value of the server control associated with the encoded string. The last part is the actual encoded information.

As you can see, the final response text is a string that consists of a bunch of substrings of the format `length|type|id|content|`. The highlighted portions of Listing 23-47 are the only calls into the `EncodeString` method. The boldface method calls in Listing 23-47 — that is, `RenderFormCallback`, `RenderDataItems`, `ProcessScriptRegistration`, and `ProcessFocus` calls — trigger more calls into the `EncodeString` static method as follows.

The highlighted portion of Listing 23-48 presents the `EncodeString` method call triggered by the call into the `RenderFormCallback` method. Recall that the call into the `RenderFormCallback` method triggers the call into the `RenderChildren` method of the `UpdatePanel` server control, which in turn triggers the call into the `EncodeString` method. As we discussed earlier, this call into the `EncodeString` method renders the content of the `UpdatePanel` server control into the response output stream. There will be one call into the `EncodeString` method for each `UpdatePanel` server control that needs updating.

Listing 23-48: The EncodeString Method Call Triggered by the RenderChildren Method of the UpdatePanel Server Control

```
protected override void RenderChildren(HtmlTextWriter writer)
{
  if (this._asyncPostBackMode)
  {
    . . .
    HtmlTextWriter writer1 = new HtmlTextWriter(new StringWriter());
    base.RenderChildren(writer1);

    PageRequestManager.EncodeString(writer, "updatePanel", this.ClientID,
                        writer1.InnerWriter.ToString());

  }
  . . .
}
```

The highlighted portion of Listing 23-49 presents the `EncodeString` method call triggered by the call into the `RenderDataItems` method. As you can see, there will be one `EncodeString` method call for each data item in the `ScriptDataItem` collection of the current `PageRequestManager` instance.

Listing 23-49: The RenderDataItems Method of the Server-Side PageRequestManager

```
private void RenderDataItems(HtmlTextWriter writer)
{
  if (this._scriptDataItems != null)
  {
    foreach (PageRequestManager.ScriptDataItem item1 in this._scriptDataItems)
    {
      PageRequestManager.EncodeString(writer,
                          item1.IsJsonSerialized ? "dataItemJson" : "dataItem",
                          item1.Control.ClientID, item1.DataItem);
    }
  }
}
```

The highlighted portions of Listing 23-50 present the EncodeString method calls triggered by the call into the ProcessScriptRegistration method of the server-side PageRequestMananger.

Listing 23-50: The Method Calls into the EncodeString Method Triggered by the ProcessScriptRegistration Method

```
public void RenderActiveArrayDeclarations(List<UpdatePanel> updatePanels,
                                        HtmlTextWriter writer)
{
  List<ScriptArrayEntry> list1 = new List<ScriptArrayEntry>();
  . . .
  foreach (ScriptArrayEntry entry3 in list1)
  {
    PageRequestManager.EncodeString(writer, "arrayDeclaration",
                          entry3.ArrayName, entry3.ArrayValue);
  }
}
public void RenderActiveExpandos(List<UpdatePanel> updatePanels,
                                HtmlTextWriter writer)
{
  List<ScriptExpandoEntry> list1 = new List<ScriptExpandoEntry>();
  . . .
  foreach (ScriptExpandoEntry entry2 in list1)
  {
    string id = "document.getElementById('" +
                  entry2.ControlId + "')['" + entry2.AttributeName + "']";
    string content = "null";
    if (entry2.AttributeValue != null)
      content = "'" + entry2.AttributeValue + "'";

    PageRequestManager.EncodeString(writer, "expando", id, content);
  }
}
```

(continued)

Listing 23-50 *(continued)*

```
public void RenderActiveHiddenFields(List<UpdatePanel> updatePanels,
                                     HtmlTextWriter writer)
{
  List<ScriptHiddenFieldEntry> list1 = new List<ScriptHiddenFieldEntry>();
  . . .
  foreach (ScriptHiddenFieldEntry entry3 in list1)
  {
      PageRequestManager.EncodeString(writer, "hiddenField", entry3.HiddenFieldName,
                                      entry3.HiddenFieldInitialValue);
  }
}
public void RenderActiveScriptDisposes(List<UpdatePanel> updatePanels,
                                       HtmlTextWriter writer)
{
  List<ScriptDisposeEntry> list1 = new List<ScriptDisposeEntry>();
  . . .
  foreach (ScriptDisposeEntry entry2 in list1)
  {
      PageRequestManager.EncodeString(writer, "scriptDispose",
                                      entry2.ParentUpdatePanel.ClientID,
                                      entry2.DisposeScript);
  }
}
public void RenderActiveSubmitStatements(List<UpdatePanel> updatePanels,
                                         HtmlTextWriter writer)
{
  List<ScriptSubmitStatementEntry> list1 = new List<ScriptSubmitStatementEntry>();
  . . .
  foreach (ScriptSubmitStatementEntry entry3 in list1)
  {
      PageRequestManager.EncodeString(writer, "onSubmit", null, entry3.Script);
  }
}
```

The highlighted portions of Listing 23-51 present the EncodeString method calls triggered by the call into the ProcessFocus method.

Listing 23-51: The EncodeString Method Calls Triggered by the ProcessFocus Method of the PageRequestManager

```
private void ProcessFocus(HtmlTextWriter writer)
{
  if (this._requireFocusScript)
  {
    . . .
    if (focusedControlID.Length > 0)
    {
      string scriptPath = this._owner.GetScriptResourceUrl("Focus.js",
                                             typeof(HtmlForm).Assembly);

      PageRequestManager.EncodeString(writer, "scriptBlock", "ScriptPath",
                              scriptPath);
      PageRequestManager.EncodeString(writer, "focus", string.Empty,
                              focusedControlID);

    }
  }
}
```

Listing 23-52 puts together all the EncodeString method calls triggered by the call into the RenderPageCallback method of the current server-side PageRequestMananger instance.

Listing 23-52: All EncodeString Method Calls Triggered by the RenderPageCallback Method

```
private void RenderPageCallback(HtmlTextWriter writer, Control pageControl)
{
  IHttpResponse response1 = this._owner.IPage.Response;
  response1.ContentType = "text/plain";
  response1.Cache.SetNoServerCaching();
  foreach (UpdatePanel updatePanel in this._updatePanelsToRefresh)
  {
    . . .
    HtmlTextWriter writer2 = new HtmlTextWriter(new StringWriter());
    base.RenderChildren(writer2);

    PageRequestManager.EncodeString(writer, "updatePanel", updatePanel.ClientID,
                           Writer2.InnerWriter.ToString());

  }
  foreach (KeyValuePair<string, string> pair1 in writer1.HiddenFields)
  {
    if (PageRequestManager.IsBuiltInHiddenField(pair1.Key))

      PageRequestManager.EncodeString(writer, "hiddenField", pair1.Key,
                             pair1.Value);

  }
```

(continued)

Listing 23-52 *(continued)*

```
      PageRequestManager.EncodeString(writer, "asyncPostBackControlIDs", string.Empty,
                                 this.GetAsyncPostBackControlIDs(false));
      PageRequestManager.EncodeString(writer, "postBackControlIDs", string.Empty,
                                 this.GetPostBackControlIDs(false));
      PageRequestManager.EncodeString(writer, "updatePanelIDs", string.Empty,
                                 this.GetAllUpdatePanelIDs());
      PageRequestManager.EncodeString(writer, "childUpdatePanelIDs", string.Empty,
                                 this.GetChildUpdatePanelIDs());
      PageRequestManager.EncodeString(writer, "panelsToRefreshIDs", string.Empty,
                                 this.GetRefreshingUpdatePanelIDs());
      PageRequestManager.EncodeString(writer, "asyncPostBackTimeout", string.Empty,
                                 this._owner.AsyncPostBackTimeout.ToString());

    if (writer2.FormAction != null)

      PageRequestManager.EncodeString(writer, "formAction", string.Empty,
                                 writer2.FormAction);

    if (this._owner.IPage.Header != null)
    {
      string text1 = this._owner.IPage.Title;
      if (!string.IsNullOrEmpty(text1))

        PageRequestManager.EncodeString(writer, "pageTitle", string.Empty, text1);

    }
    foreach (PageRequestManager.ScriptDataItem item1 in this._scriptDataItems)
    {

      PageRequestManager.EncodeString(writer,
                            item1.IsJsonSerialized ? "dataItemJson" : "dataItem",
                            item1.Control.ClientID, item1.DataItem);

    }
    foreach (ScriptArrayEntry entry3 in list1)
    {

      PageRequestManager.EncodeString(writer, "arrayDeclaration",
                              entry3.ArrayName, entry3.ArrayValue);

    }
    foreach (ScriptExpandoEntry entry2 in list2)
    {
      string id = "document.getElementById('" +
                  entry2.ControlId + "')['" + entry2.AttributeName + "']";
      string content = "null";
      if (entry2.AttributeValue != null)
        content = "'" + entry2.AttributeValue + "'";

      PageRequestManager.EncodeString(writer, "expando", id, content);

    }
    foreach (ScriptHiddenFieldEntry entry3 in list3)
    {

      PageRequestManager.EncodeString(writer, "hiddenField", entry3.HiddenFieldName,
                              entry3.HiddenFieldInitialValue);

    }
```

```csharp
foreach (ScriptDisposeEntry entry2 in list4)
{

  PageRequestManager.EncodeString(writer, "scriptDispose",
                              entry2.ParentUpdatePanel.ClientID,
                              entry2.DisposeScript);

}
foreach (ScriptSubmitStatementEntry entry3 in list5)
{

  PageRequestManager.EncodeString(writer, "onSubmit", null, entry3.Script);

}
    string scriptPath = this._owner.GetScriptResourceUrl("Focus.js",
                                                typeof(HtmlForm).Assembly);

  PageRequestManager.EncodeString(writer, "scriptBlock", "ScriptPath",
                          scriptPath);
  PageRequestManager.EncodeString(writer, "focus", string.Empty,
                          focusedControlID);

}
```

Just by looking at the `EncodeString` calls shown in the highlighted portions of Listing 23-52, and considering the fact that each `EncodeString` call generates a string of the format `length|type|id|content`, can you guess what the final server response text sent to the current client-side `PageRequestManagner` instance looks like?

Listing 23-53 presents a page that shows you the actual server response text sent to the current client-side `PageRequestManager` instance. If you access this page, you should get the result shown in Figure 23-2. As you can see, this page consists of two text fields and a button. Now enter some text into the text fields and click the button. You should see the actual server response text on a popup like the one shown in Figure 23-3.

Listing 23-53: A Page that Shows What the Server Response Text Looks Like

```
<%@ Page Language="C#" %>
<!DOCTYPE html PUBLIC "-//W3C//DTD XHTML 1.1//EN"
"http://www.w3.org/TR/xhtml11/DTD/xhtml11.dtd">
<html xmlns="http://www.w3.org/1999/xhtml">
<head runat="server">
  <title>Untitled Page</title>
  <script type="text/javascript" language="javascript">
    function requestCompleted(sender, args)
    {
      var reply = sender.get_responseData();
      alert(reply);
    }
```

(continued)

Listing 23-53 *(continued)*

```
      function beginRequestHandler(sender, args)
      {
        var request = args.get_request();
        request.add_completed(requestCompleted);
      }

      function pageLoad()
      {
        var prm = Sys.WebForms.PageRequestManager.getInstance();
        prm.add_beginRequest(beginRequestHandler);
      }
    </script>
  </head>
<body>
    <form id="form1" runat="server">
      <asp:ScriptManager ID="ScriptManager1" runat="server" />
      <asp:UpdatePanel ID="UpdatePanel1" runat="server">
        <ContentTemplate>
          <table>
            <tr>
              <td>
                First Name:</td>
              <td>
                <asp:TextBox ID="TextBox1" runat="server"></asp:TextBox></td>
            </tr>
            <tr>
              <td>
                Last Name:</td>
              <td>
                <asp:TextBox ID="TextBox2" runat="server"></asp:TextBox></td>
            </tr>
            <tr>
              <td colspan="2">
                <asp:Button ID="Button1" runat="server" Text="Submit" /></td>
            </tr>
          </table>
        </ContentTemplate>
      </asp:UpdatePanel>
      <div id="info">
      </div>
      <div>
      </div>
    </form>
  </body>
</html>
```

Figure 23-2

Figure 23-3

As shown in these images, the server response text is a string that consists of a bunch of substrings with the format length|type|id|content, where the length part specifies the number of characters in the content part of the substring, the type part specifies the type of information stored in the content part of the substring, the id part specifies the ClientID property value of the server control associated with the information stored in the content part of the substring, and finally the content part contains the actual information or data being sent to the current client-side PageRequestManager instance.

The server response text shown in Figure 23-3 consists of 11 substrings as follows:

Here is the first substring:

```
586|updatePanel|UpdatePanel1|
        <table>
          <tr>
            <td>
              First Name:</td>
            <td>
              <input name="TextBox1" type="text" value="Shahram" id="TextBox1"
                /></td>
          </tr>
          <tr>
            <td>
              Last Name:</td>
            <td>
              <input name="TextBox2" type="text" value="Khosravi" id="TextBox2"
                /></td>
          </tr>
          <tr>
            <td colspan="2" align="center">
              <input type="submit" name="Button1" value="Submit" id="Button1"
                /></td>
          </tr>
        </table>
  |
```

The first substring is the one the EncodeString method call shown in Listing 23-52 generates and renders into the response output stream:

```
PageRequestManager.EncodeString(writer, "updatePanel", this.ClientID,
                        writer1.InnerWriter.ToString());
```

As you can see, the first substring consists of the following four parts:

❑   586: This first part of the substring tells the current client-side PageRequestManager that the fourth part of the substring contains 586 characters (with spaces).

❑   updatePanel: This second part of the substring tells the current client-side PageRequestManager that the fourth part of the substring contains the HTML markup text enclosed within the UpdatePanel server control whose UniqueID property value is given by the third part of the substring.

❑ UpdatePanel1: The third part of the substring tells the current client-side PageRequestManager that the HTML markup text contained in the fourth part of the string belongs to the UpdatePanel server control with the UniqueID property value of UpdatePanel1.

❑ The fourth part of the substring provides the current client-side PageRequestManager instance with the HTML markup text of the UpdatePanel server control with the UniqueID property value of UpdatePanel1. Recall from Listing 23-48 that the RenderChildren method of the UpdatePanel server control generates this HTML markup text.

Here is the second substring:

```
52|hiddenField|__VIEWSTATE|/wEPDwULLTIxMjYzMDU2NzJkZJ0ptWJFvcbB81530BKz9PRMaPrd|
```

This is the substring that the first EncodeString method call shown in Listing 23-52 generates and renders into the response output stream:

```
PageRequestManager.EncodeString(writer, "hiddenField", pair1.Key,
                        pair1.Value);
```

As you can see, the second substring consists of the following four parts:

❑ 52: This first part of the substring tells the client-side PageRequestManager instance that the fourth part of this substring contains 52 characters (with spaces).

❑ hiddenField: This second part of the substring tells the client-side PageRequestManager instance that this substring contains the name and value of a hidden field.

❑ __VIEWSTATE: This third part of the substring tells the client-side PageRequestManager instance that the name of this hidden field is __VIEWSTATE.

❑ The fourth part of the substring tells the client-side PageRequestManager instance that the value of this hidden field is as follows:

```
/wEPDwULLTIxMjYzMDU2NzJkZJ0ptWJFvcbB81530BKz9PRMaPrd
```

Here is the third substring:

```
64|hiddenField|__EVENTVALIDATION|/wEWBAKj4cTUAgLs0bLrBgLs0fbZDAKM54rGBv6aI9H0
                        BYIx273PdOWCCpAOOHzF|
```

This is the substring that the first EncodeString method call shown in Listing 23-52 generates and renders into the response output stream:

```
PageRequestManager.EncodeString(writer, "hiddenField", pair1.Key,
                        pair1.Value);
```

As you can see, the third substring consists of the following four parts:

❑ 64: This first part of the substring tells the client-side PageRequestManager instance that the fourth part of this substring contains 64 characters (with spaces).

❑ hiddenField: This second part of the substring tells the client-side PageRequestManager instance that this substring contains the name and value of a hidden field.

❑ __EVENTVALIDATION: This third part of the substring tells the client-side `PageRequestManager` instance that the name of this hidden field is __EVENTVALIDATION.

❑ The fourth part of the substring tells the client-side `PageRequestManager` instance that the value of this hidden field is as follows:

```
/wEWBAKj4cTUAgLs0bLrBgLs0fbZDAKM54rGBv6aI9H0BYIx273PdOWCCpAOOHzF
```

Here is the fourth substring:

```
0|asyncPostBackControlIDs|||
```

This is the substring that the following `EncodeString` method call in Listing 23-52 generates and renders into the response output stream:

```
PageRequestManager.EncodeString(writer, "asyncPostBackControlIDs", string.Empty,
                    this.GetAsyncPostBackControlIDs(false));
```

As you can see, the fourth substring consists of the following four parts:

❑ 0: This first part of the substring tells the client-side `PageRequestManager` instance that the fourth part of this substring contains zero characters.

❑ `asyncPostBackControlIDs`: This second part of the substring tells the client-side `PageRequestManager` instance that the fourth part of this substring contains the comma-separated list of the `UniqueID` property values of all the server controls on the current page that cause asynchronous page postbacks. Since our example does not contain any server control causing asynchronous page postbacks, this list is empty.

❑ Since the third part of this substring does not play any role in this case, it is an empty string.

❑ Since the current example does not contain any server controls causing asynchronous page postbacks, the fourth part of this substring is an empty string.

Here is the fifth substring:

```
0|postBackControlIDs|||
```

This is the substring that the following `EncodeString` method call in Listing 23-52 generates and renders into the response output stream:

```
PageRequestManager.EncodeString(writer, "postBackControlIDs", string.Empty,
                    this.GetPostBackControlIDs(false));
```

As you can see, the fifth substring consists of the following four parts:

❑ a: This first part of the substring tells the client-side `PageRequestManager` instance that the fourth part of this substring contains zero characters.

❑ `postBackControlIDs`: This second part of the substring tells the client-side `PageRequestManager` instance that the fourth part of this substring contains the comma-separated list of the `UniqueID` property values of all the server controls on the current page that cause synchronous page postbacks. Since our example does not contain any server control causing synchronous page postbacks, this list is empty.

❑ Since the third part of this substring does not play any role in this case, it is an empty string,

❑ Since the current example does not contain any server controls causing synchronous page postbacks, the fourth part of the substring is an empty string.

Here is the sixth substring:

```
13|updatePanelIDs||tUpdatePanel1|
```

This is the substring that the following EncodeString method call in Listing 23-52 generates and renders into the response output stream:

```
PageRequestManager.EncodeString(writer, "updatePanelIDs", string.Empty,
                        this.GetAllUpdatePanelIDs());
```

As you can see, the sixth substring consists of the following four parts:

❑ 13: This first part of the substring tells the client-side PageRequestManager instance that the fourth part of this substring contains 13 characters.

❑ updatePanelIDs: This second part of the substring tells the client-side PageRequestManager instance that the fourth part of this substring contains the comma-separated list of the UniqueID property values of all the UpdatePanel server controls on the current page.

❑ Since the third part of this substring does not play any role in this case, it is an empty string.

❑ tUpdatePanel1: This fourth part of the substring provides the current client-side PageRequestManager instance with the comma-separated list of all the UpdatePanel server controls on the current page. Since our example includes a single UpdatePanel server control, this list has a single member. Note that the member consists of two parts, where the first part contains the letter t, which tells the current client-side PageRequestMananger instance that the ChildrenAsTriggers property of this UpdatePanel server control has been set to true, and the second part contains the UniqueID property value of the UpdatePanel server control.

Here is the seventh substring:

```
0|childUpdatePanelIDs|||
```

This is the substring that the following EncodeString method call in Listing 23-52 generates and renders into the response output stream:

```
PageRequestManager.EncodeString(writer, "childUpdatePanelIDs", string.Empty,
                        this.GetChildUpdatePanelIDs());
```

As you can see, the seventh substring consists of the following four parts:

- ❏ `0`: This first part of the substring tells the client-side `PageRequestManager` instance that the fourth part of this substring contains zero characters.

- ❏ `childUpdatePanelIDs`: This second part of the substring tells the client-side `PageRequestManager` instance that the fourth part of this substring contains the comma-separated list of the `UniqueID` property values of all the child `UpdatePanel` server controls on the current page.

- ❏ Since the third part of this substring does not play any role in this case, it is an empty string.

- ❏ Since the current example does not contain any child `UpdatePanel` server controls, the fourth part of the substring is an empty string.

Here is the eighth substring:

```
12|panelsToRefreshIDs||UpdatePanel1|
```

This is the substring that the following `EncodeString` method call in Listing 23-52 generates and renders into the response output stream:

```
PageRequestManager.EncodeString(writer, "panelsToRefreshIDs", string.Empty,
                       this.GetRefreshingUpdatePanelIDs());
```

As you can see, the eighth substring consists of the following four parts:

- ❏ `12`: This first part of the substring tells the client-side `PageRequestManager` instance that the fourth part of this substring contains 12 characters.

- ❏ `panelsToRefreshIDs`: This second part of the substring tells the client-side `PageRequestManager` instance that the fourth part of this substring contains the comma-separated list of the `UniqueID` property values of all the `UpdatePanel` server control on the current page that need refreshing.

- ❏ Since the third part of the substring does not play any role in this case, it is an empty string.

- ❏ `UpdatePanel1`: This fourth part of the substring provides the current client-side `PageRequestManager` instance with the comma-separated list of all the `UpdatePanel` server controls on the current page that need refreshing. Since our example includes a single `UpdatePanel` server control, this list has a single member.

Here is the ninth substring:

```
2|asyncPostBackTimeout||90|
```

This is the substring that the following `EncodeString` method call in Listing 23-52 generates and renders into the response output stream:

```
PageRequestManager.EncodeString(writer, "asyncPostBackTimeout", string.Empty,
                       this._owner.AsyncPostBackTimeout.ToString());
```

As you can see, the ninth substring consists of the following four parts:

- ❑ 2: This first part of the substring tells the client-side `PageRequestManager` instance that the fourth part of this substring contains two characters.

- ❑ `asyncPostBackTimeout`: This second part of the substring tells the client-side `PageRequestManager` instance that the fourth part of this substring contains the asynchronous page postback timeout value.

- ❑ Since the third part of this substring does not play any role in this case, it is an empty string.

- ❑ 90: This fourth part of the substring tells the current client-side `PageRequestManager` instance that the asynchronous page postback timeout value is 90.

Here is the tenth substring:

```
12|formAction||Default.aspx|
```

The tenth substring is the substring that the following `EncodeString` method call in Listing 23-52 generates and renders into the response output stream:

```
PageRequestManager.EncodeString(writer, "formAction", string.Empty,
                                writer2.FormAction);
```

As you can see, the tenth substring consists of the following four parts:

- ❑ 12: This first part of the substring tells the client-side `PageRequestManager` instance that the fourth part of this substring contains 12 characters.

- ❑ `formAction`: This second part of the substring tells the client-side `PageRequestManager` instance that the fourth part of this substring contains the form action.

- ❑ Since the third part of this substring does not play any role in this case, it is an empty string.

- ❑ `Default.aspx`: This fourth part of the substring tells the current client-side `PageRequestManager` instance that the form action for the current page is `Default.aspx`.

Here is the eleventh substring:

```
13|pageTitle||Untitled Page
```

This is the substring that the following `EncodeString` method call in Listing 23-52 generates and renders into the response output stream:

```
PageRequestManager.EncodeString(writer, "pageTitle", string.Empty, text1);
```

As you can see, the eleventh substring consists of the following four parts:

- ❑ 13: This first part of the substring tells the client-side `PageRequestManager` instance that the fourth part of this substring contains 13 characters.

- ❑ `pageTitle`: This second part of the substring tells the client-side `PageRequestManager` instance that the fourth part of this substring contains the page title.

❏ Since the third part of this substring does not play any role in this case, it is an empty string.

❏ Untitled Page: This fourth part of the substring tells the current client-side PageRequestManager instance that the page title is "Untitled Page."

Summary

This chapter followed the Page through its life cycle phases to process the asynchronous page postback request made by the current client-side PageRequestMananger instance. We followed the request from the time it arrived in the ASP.NET to the time the server response text was finally sent back to the client.

The next chapter will move on to the client side, where this server response text arrives, and follow the client-side PageRequestManager instance through its life cycle phases to process the server response.

Asynchronous Partial Page Rendering: Client-Side Processing

The previous chapter followed the Page through its life cycle phases to process the asynchronous page postback request made by the current client-side `PageRequestMananger` instance. We followed the request from the time it arrived in ASP.NET to the time the server response text was finally sent back to the client.

This chapter will move on to the client side, where this server response text arrives, and follow the client-side `PageRequestManager` instance through its life cycle phases to process the server response.

Arrival of the Server Response Text

Recall from Listing 22-22 that the `_onFormSubmit` method of the current client-side `PageRequestManager` instance is where the current client-side `PageRequestManager` instance made its asynchronous page postback to the server. Listing 24-1 presents a portion of the `_onFormSubmit` method. As the highlighted portion of this code listing shows, the current client-side `PageRequestManager` instance registers its `_onFormSubmitCompleted` method as an event handler for the `completed` event of the `WebRequest` object that represents the current request.

```
request.add_completed(Function.createDelegate(this,
                                   this._onFormSubmitCompleted));
```

As the name suggests, the `WebRequest` object fires its `completed` event when the current request is finally completed.

Listing 24-1: The _onFormSubmit Method of the Client-Side PageRequestManager Instance

```
function Sys$WebForms$PageRequestManager$_onFormSubmit(evt)
{
    . . .
    var formBody = new Sys.StringBuilder();
    formBody.append(this._scriptManagerID + '=' +
                    this._postBackSettings.panelID + '&');
    var count = form.elements.length;
    for (var i = 0; i < count; i++)
    {
        . . .
    }
    . . .
    var request = new Sys.Net.WebRequest();
    request.set_url(form.action);
    request.get_headers()['X-MicrosoftAjax'] = 'Delta=true';
    request.get_headers()['Cache-Control'] = 'no-cache';
    request.set_timeout(this._asyncPostBackTimeout);

    request.add_completed(Function.createDelegate(this,
                                        this._onFormSubmitCompleted));

    request.set_body(formBody.toString());
    . . .
    this._request = request;
    request.invoke();
    . . .
}
```

Recall from Listing 12-41 of Chapter 12 that when the request is finally completed, the _onReadyStateChange method of the current XMLHttpExecutor is invoked, as shown again in Listing 24-2. As you can see from the highlighted portion of this code listing, the _onReadyStateChange method invokes the completed method on the WebRequest object that represents the current request.

Listing 24-2: The _onReadyStateChange Method

```
this._onReadyStateChange = function ()
{
    if (_this._xmlHttpRequest.readyState === 4 /*complete*/)
    {
        _this._clearTimer();
        _this._responseAvailable = true;

        _this._webRequest.completed(Sys.EventArgs.Empty);

        if (_this._xmlHttpRequest != null)
        {
            _this._xmlHttpRequest.onreadystatechange = Function.emptyMethod;
            _this._xmlHttpRequest = null;
        }
    }
}
```

Recall from Listing 12-11 of Chapter 12 that the `completed` method of the `WebRequest` object in turn calls the event handlers registered for the `completed` event of the `WebRequest` object, as shown again in the highlighted portion of Listing 24-3.

Listing 24-3: The Completed Method

```
function Sys$Net$WebRequest$completed(eventArgs)
{
  var handler = Sys.Net.WebRequestManager._get_eventHandlerList().getHandler(
  "completedRequest");
  if (handler)
    handler(this._executor, eventArgs);

  handler = this._get_eventHandlerList().getHandler("completed");
  if (handler)
    handler(this._executor, eventArgs);

}
```

As the boldface portion of Listing 24-3 shows, when the `completed` method of the `WebRequest` object invokes the event handlers registered for its `completed` event, it passes a reference to the `WebRequestExecutor` object responsible for executing the current request. This means that the first parameter of the `_onFormSubmitCompleted` method of the current client-side `PageRequestManager` instance references this `WebResquestExecutor` object. You'll see the internal implementation of the `_onFormSubmitCompleted` method later in the chapter.

As I mentioned earlier, our goal in this chapter is to follow the current `PageRequestMananger` instance through its life cycle phases to process the server response. Since the current `PageRequestManager` instance's life cycle is rather complex and involves a lot of method calls, I've captured almost all of them in a two-part diagram shown in Figures 24-1 and 24-2 to make it easier for you to follow our discussions. The vertical axis in this two-part diagram measures increasing time (early on the top, late on the bottom).

Keep this two-part diagram in mind as you're reading through this chapter. Also keep in mind where we are on this diagram at every stage of the current `PageRequestManager` instance's life cycle.

As you can see from Listing 24-3, the `_onFormSubmitCompleted` method of the current `PageRequestManager` instance sets the `_processingRequest` field on the current client-side `PageRequestManager` instance to `true` to signal that the request is now being processed:

```
this._processingRequest = true;
```

Just because the `WebRequest` object has fired the `completed` event and consequently called the `_onFormSubmitCompleted` method does not mean that everything went fine and the server response has arrived. The `WebRequest` object fires the `completed` event for a number of reasons. Therefore, the `_onFormSubmitCompleted` method takes the following steps to determine why the `completed` event was raised. First, it calls the `get_timedOut` method on the `WebRequestExecutor` object to return a

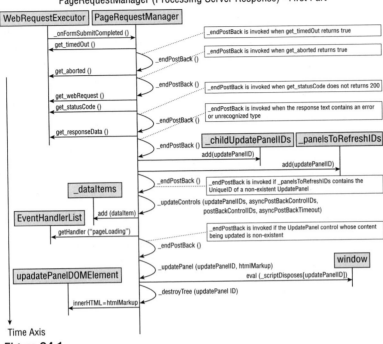

Figure 24-1

Boolean value that specifies whether the `completed` event was raised because of a timeout. If so, it calls the `_endPostBack` method on the current `PageRequestManager` instance to end the ongoing asynchronous postback request and returns the following:

```
if (sender.get_timedOut())
{
  this._endPostBack(this._createPageRequestManagerTimeoutError(), sender);
  return;
}
```

Next, it calls the `get_aborted` method on the `WebRequestExecutor` to return a Boolean value that specifies whether the `completed` event was raised because the request aborted. If so, it calls the `_endPostBack` method on the current `PageRequestManager` instance to end the ongoing request and returns this:

```
if (sender.get_aborted())
{
  this._endPostBack(null, sender);
  return;
}
```

Next, the `_onFormSubmitCompleted` method calls the `get_webRequest` method on the `WebRequestExecutor` to return a reference to the `WebRequest` object that represents the request that the `WebRequestExecutor` executed. It then compares this with the `WebRequest` object that the `_request` property of the current `PageRequestManager` instance references. (As the boldface portion

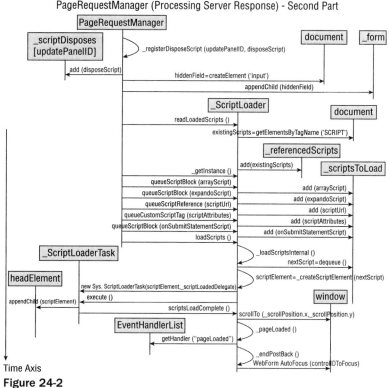

PageRequestManager (Processing Server Response) - Second Part

Figure 24-2

of Listing 24-1 shows, the current `PageRequestManager` instance assigns the `WebRequest` object to an internal field named `_request` before it executes the request.) If these two `WebRequest` objects are different, the `completed` event was raised for a different request and consequently the `_onFormSubmitCompleted` method simply returns this:

```
if (!this._request || sender.get_webRequest() !== this._request)
  return;
```

As you can see, if an application makes several overlapping asynchronous page postback requests to the server, the last request wins.

Next, the `_onFormSubmitCompleted` method calls the `get_statusCode` method on the `WebRequestExecutor` object to return an integer that contains the response status code. If this code is not `200`, it is an indication that a server error occurred, and consequently the method calls the `_endPostBack` method on the current `PageRequestManager` instance to end the current request and returns this:

```
if (sender.get_statusCode() !== 200)
{
  this._endPostBack(
    this._createPageRequestManagerServerError(sender.get_statusCode()), sender);
  return;
}
```

Next, the _onFormSubmitCompleted method calls the get_responseData method on the
WebRequestExecutor object to return the string that contains the server response:

```
var reply = sender.get_responseData();
```

Recall from Listing 23-52 that the server response text is a string that contains a bunch of substrings in
the format length|type|id|content, where:

- ❑ The length part tells the current client-side PageRequestManager instance how many
  characters there are in the content part of the substring.

- ❑ The type part tells the current client-side PageRequestManager instance what type of
  information the content part contains.

- ❑ The optional id part specifies the ClientID property value of the server control associated with
  the information contained in the content part.

- ❑ The content part contains the actual information that the current server-side
  PageRequestManager instance has sent to the current client-side PageRequestManager
  instance.

Listing 24-4 contains an example of a server response text that the current server-side PageRequestManager
instance sends to the current client-side PageRequestManager instance. Keep this code listing in mind as
we're walking through the implementation of the _onFormSubmitCompleted method. The main
responsibility of this method is to parse a response text similar to Listing 24-4.

**Listing 24-4: An Example of a Server Response Text that the Current Client-Side
PageRequestManager Might Receive**

```
586|updatePanel|UpdatePanel1|
        <table>
          <tr>
            <td>
              First Name:</td>
            <td>
              <input name="TextBox1" type="text" value="Shahram" id="TextBox1"
                  /></td>
          </tr>
          <tr>
            <td>
              Last Name:</td>
            <td>
              <input name="TextBox2" type="text" value="Khosravi" id="TextBox2"
                  /></td>
          </tr>
          <tr>
            <td colspan="2" align="center">
              <input type="submit" name="Button1" value="Submit" id="Button1"
                  /></td>
          </tr>
        </table>
```

```
|52|hiddenField|__VIEWSTATE|/wEPDwULLTIxMjYzMDU2NzJkZJ0ptWJFvcbB81530BKz9PRMaPrd|64
|hiddenField|__EVENTVALIDATION|/wEWBAKj4cTUAgLs0bLrBgLs0fbZDAKM54rGBv6aI9H0BYIx273P
dOWCCpAOOHzF|0|asyncPostBackControlIDs|||0|postBackControlIDs|||13|updatePanelIDs||
tUpdatePanel1|0|childUpdatePanelIDs|||12|panelsToRefreshIDs||UpdatePanel1|2|asyncPo
stBackTimeout||90|12|formAction||Default.aspx|13|pageTitle||Untitled Page
```

The _onFormSubmitCompleted method recursively takes the following steps to parse each substring in the server response string:

❑   It accesses the index of the first delimiter | character of the substring:

```
delimiterIndex = reply.indexOf('|', replyIndex);
```

❑   If the substring does not contain this delimiter, the _onFormSubmitCompleted method calls another method named _findText, stores the return value of this method in a local field named parserErrorDetails, and exits the while loop that loops through the substrings in the server response string. In other words, it does not attempt to parse the rest of the server response string. There is no point in processing an erroneous server response. As you'll see shortly, the first statement after this while loop checks whether the value of the parserErrorDetails field is set. If so, it takes the appropriate action to end the current request.

```
if (delimiterIndex === -1)
{
  parserErrorDetails = this._findText(reply, replyIndex);
  break;
}
```

❑   The following code listing presents the implementation of the _findText method:

```
function Sys$WebForms$PageRequestManager$_findText(text, location)
{
  var startIndex = Math.max(0, location - 20);
  var endIndex = Math.min(text.length, location + 20);
  return text.substring(startIndex, endIndex);
}
```

❑   The _onFormSubmitCompleted method parses the first part (that is, the length part) of the substring:

```
len = parseInt(reply.substring(replyIndex, delimiterIndex), 10);
replyIndex = delimiterIndex + 1;
```

❑   It accesses the index of the second delimiter:

```
delimiterIndex = reply.indexOf(delimitByLengthDelimiter, replyIndex);
```

❑   If the substring does not contain this delimiter, the _onFormSubmitCompleted method calls the _findText method, stores the return value of this method in the parserErrorDetails local field, and exits the while loop, as discussed earlier.

```
if (delimiterIndex === -1)
{
  parserErrorDetails = this._findText(reply, replyIndex);
  break;
}
```

❑ The _onFormSubmitCompleted method parses the second part (that is, the type part) of the substring:

```
type = reply.substring(replyIndex, delimiterIndex);
replyIndex = delimiterIndex + 1;
```

❑ It accesses the index of the third delimiter |:

```
delimiterIndex = reply.indexOf(delimitByLengthDelimiter, replyIndex);
```

❑ If the substring does not contain this delimiter, the _onFormSubmitCompleted method calls the _findText method, stores the return value of this method in the parserErrorDetails local field, and exits the while loop, as discussed earlier.

```
if (delimiterIndex === -1)
{
  parserErrorDetails = this._findText(reply, replyIndex);
  break;
}
```

❑ The _onFormSubmitCompleted method parses the third part (that is, the id part) of the substring:

```
id = reply.substring(replyIndex, delimiterIndex);
replyIndex = delimiterIndex + 1;
```

❑ Recall that the len local field contains the length of the content part of the substring. _onFormSubmitCompleted first checks whether the index of the expected last character of the content part of the substring is a value that exceeds the length of the substring. If so, this is an indication that the server response has problems and consequently _onFormSubmitCompleted takes the same steps discussed earlier and exits the while loop.

```
if ((replyIndex + len) >= reply.length)
{
  parserErrorDetails = this._findText(reply, reply.length);
  break;
}
```

❑ The _onFormSubmitCompleted method accesses the fourth part (that is, the content part) of the substring. (Note that the length of the fourth part is given by the first part of the length|type|id|content format.)

```
content = this._decodeString(reply.substr(replyIndex, len));
replyIndex += len;
```

❑ Next, _onFormSubmitCompleted checks whether the last character of the substring is the delimiter character (|). If not, this is an indication that the server response has problems and consequently _onFormSubmitCompleted method takes the same steps discussed earlier and exits the while loop.

```
if (reply.charAt(replyIndex) !== delimitByLengthDelimiter)
{
  parserErrorDetails = this._findText(reply, replyIndex);
  break;
}
```

❑ The _onFormSubmitCompleted method creates an object literal with three name/value pairs. The name part of the first pair is the word type and its value part is the second part of the substring (that is, the type part). The name part of the second name/value pair is the word id and its value part is the third part of the substring (that is, the id part). The name part of the third name/value pair is the word content and its value part is the fourth part of the substring (that is, the content part).

```
var obj = {type: type, id: id, content: content};
```

❑ The _onFormSubmitCompleted method stores the above object literal in a local array named delta.

```
Array.add(delta, obj);
```

As you can see, the _onSubmitFormCompleted method parses each substring (in the length|type|id|content format) into an object literal and stores the object in a local array named delta.

After existing the while loop, the _onSubmitFormCompleted method first checks whether the value of the parseErrorDetails local field is set. If so, this is an indication that the server response had some problems and consequently _onSubmitFormCompleted invokes the _endPostBack method to end the current asynchronous page postback request.

```
if (parserErrorDetails)
{
  this._endPostBack(this._createPageRequestManagerParserError(
                    String.format(Sys.WebForms.Res.PRM_ParserErrorDetails,
                                  parserErrorDetails)), sender);
  return;
}
```

Next, the method iterates through the object literals in the delta array and checks the value of the type property of each enumerated object (recall that the value associated with the type property of the object contains the second part of the length|type|id|content format):

❑ If the type is the string "updatePanel", the _onFormSubmitCompleted method adds the enumerated object to a local array named updatePanelNodes. The value of the id property of this object is a string that contains the value of the UniqueID property of an UpdatePanel server control. The value of the content property of this object is a string that contains the markup text for this UpdatePanel server control.

```
case "updatePanel":
    Array.add(updatePanelNodes, deltaNode);
    break;
```

❏ If the type is the string "hiddenField", the _onFormSubmitCompleted method adds the enumerated object to a local array named hiddenFieldNodes. The value of the id property of this object is a string that contains the name of the hidden field and the value of the content property is a string that contains the value of the hidden field.

```
case "hiddenField":
    Array.add(hiddenFieldNodes, deltaNode);
    break;
```

❏ If the type is the string "arrayDeclaration", the _onFormSubmitCompleted method adds the enumerated object to a local array named arrayDeclarationNodes. This object describes an array declaration in which the value of the id property of the object is a string that contains the name of the JavaScript array. The value of the content property of this object is a string that contains the value being added to the array.

```
case "arrayDeclaration":
    Array.add(arrayDeclarationNodes, deltaNode);
    break;
```

❏ If the type is the string "scriptBlock", the _onFormSubmitCompleted method adds the enumerated object to a local array named scriptBlockNodes. This object describes a script block in which the value of the id property of the object is one of the following string values: "ScriptContentNoTags", "ScriptContentWithTags", or "ScriptPath", and in which the value of the content property is a string that contains the associated script block:

```
case "scriptBlock":
    Array.add(scriptBlockNodes, deltaNode);
    break;
```

❏ If the type is the string "expando", the _onFormSubmitCompleted method adds the enumerated object to a local array named expandoNodes. This object describes an expando attribute in which the value of the id property of the object is a string that contains the name of the expando attribute, and the value of the content property is a string that contains the value of the expando attribute.

```
case "expando":
    Array.add(expandoNodes, deltaNode);
    break;
```

❏ If the type is the string "onSubmit", the _onFormSubmitCompleted method adds the enumerated object to a local array named onSubmitNodes. This object describes a dynamically added form onsubmit statement in which the value of the id property of the object is an empty string and the value of the content property of the object is a string that contains the dynamically added form onsubmit statement.

```
case "onSubmit":
  Array.add(onSubmitNodes, deltaNode);
  break;
```

❏ If the type is the string `"asyncPostBackControlIDs"`, the `_onFormSubmitCompleted`
method assigns the enumerated object to a local field named `asyncPostBackControlIDsNode`.
This object describes all the server controls on the page that cause asynchronous page postbacks.
The value of the `id` property of this object is an empty string, and the value of the `content`
property is a string that contains a comma-separated list of substrings, each substring containing
the value of the `UniqueID` property of a server control that causes an asynchronous page
postback.

```
case "asyncPostBackControlIDs":
  asyncPostBackControlIDsNode = deltaNode;
  break;
```

❏ If the `type` is the string `"postBackControlIDs"`, the `_onFormSubmitCompleted` method
assigns the enumerated object to a local field named `postBackControlIDsNode`. This object
describes all the server controls on the page that cause normal synchronous page postbacks. The
value of the `id` property of this object is an empty string, and the value of the `content` property
is a string that contains a comma-separated list of substrings, each substring containing the
value of the `UniqueID` property of a server control that causes a synchronous page postback.

```
case "postBackControlIDs":
  postBackControlIDsNode = deltaNode;
  break;
```

❏ If the `type` is the string `"updatePanelIDs"`, the `_onFormSubmitCompleted` method assigns
the enumerated object to a local field named `updatePanelIDsNode`. This object describes all the
`UpdatePanel` server controls on the current page. The value of the `id` property of this object is
an empty string, and the value of the `content` property is a string that contains a comma-
separated list of substrings, each substring containing the value of the `UniqueID` property of an
`UpdatePanel` server control.

```
case "updatePanelIDs":
  updatePanelIDsNode = deltaNode;
  break;
```

❏ If the `type` is the string `"asyncPostBackTimeout"`, the `_onFormSubmitCompleted` method
assigns the enumerated object to a local field named `asyncPostBackTimeoutNode`. This object
describes timeout value for asynchronous page postbacks. The value of the `id` property of this
object is an empty string, and the value of the `content` property is a string that contains the
value of the asynchronous page postback timeout:

```
case "asyncPostBackTimeout":
  asyncPostBackTimeoutNode = deltaNode;
  break;
```

❑   If the `type` is the string `"childUpdatePanelIDs"`, the `_onFormSubmitCompleted` method assigns the enumerated object to a local field named `childUpdatePanelIDsNode`. This object describes all the child `UpdatePanel` server controls on the current page that need updating because their parent `UpdatePanel` server controls need updating. The value of the `id` property of this object is an empty string, and the value of the `content` property is a string that contains a comma-separated list of substrings, each substring containing the value of the `UniqueID` property of a child `UpdatePanel` server control.

```
case "childUpdatePanelIDs":
    childUpdatePanelIDsNode = deltaNode;
    break;
```

❑   If the `type` is the string `"panelsToRefreshIDs"`, the `_onFormSubmitCompleted` method assigns the enumerated object to a local field named `panelsToRefreshNode`. This object describes all the `UpdatePanel` server controls on the current page that need updating. The value of the `id` property of this object is an empty string, and the value of the `content` property is a string that contains a comma-separated list of substrings, each substring containing the value of the `UniqueID` property of an `UpdatePanel` server control.

```
case "panelsToRefreshIDs":
    panelsToRefreshNode = deltaNode;
    break;
```

❑   If the `type` is the string `"formAction"`, the `_onFormSubmitCompleted` method assigns the enumerated object to a local field named `formActionNode`. This object describes the current form action. The value of the `id` property of this object is an empty string, and the value of the `content` property is a string that contains the value of the action property of the form.

```
case "formAction":
    formActionNode = deltaNode;
    break;
```

❑   If the `type` is the string `"dataItem"`, the `_onFormSubmitCompleted` method adds the enumerated object to a local array named `dataItemNodes`. This object describes a data item associated with a server control. The value of the `id` property of the object is the value of the `ClientID` property of the server control, and the value of the `content` property is a string that contains the string representation of the data item. For example, this string representation could be an XML representation of the data item.

```
case "dataItem":
    Array.add(dataItemNodes, deltaNode);
    break;
```

❑   If the `type` is the string `"dataItemJson"`, the `_onFormSubmitCompleted` method adds the enumerated object to a local array named `dataItemJsonNodes`. This object describes a data item associated with a server control. The value of the `id` property of the object is the value of the `ClientID` property of the server control, and the value of the `content` property is a string that contains the JSON representation of the data item.

```
case "dataItemJson":
    Array.add(dataItemJsonNodes, deltaNode);
    break;
```

❏ If the `type` is the string `"scriptDispose"`, the `_onFormSubmitCompleted` method adds the enumerated object to a local array named `scriptDisposeNodes`. This object describes a script that contains a call into a `dispose` method associated with an `UpdatePanel` server control. The value of the `id` property of the object is the value of the `ClientID` property of the `UpdatePanel` server control, and the value of the `content` property is a string that contains the calls into the `dispose` method.

```
case "scriptDispose":
  Array.add(scriptDisposeNodes, deltaNode);
  break;
```

❏ The following code fragment shows an example of the value of the `content` property. This example registers the `$find('UpdatePanel1').dispose();` script for the `UpdatePanel` server control whose `ClientID` property has the value of `"UpdatePanel1"`:

```
Sys.WebForms.PageRequestManager.getInstance()._registerDisposeScript("UpdatePanel1"
                           ,"$find('UpdatePanel1').dispose();");
```

❏ If the `type` is the string `"pageRedirect"`, the `_onFormSubmitCompleted` method assigns the value of the `content` property of the enumerated object to the `href` property of the `location` property of the `window` object. As you can see, the value of the `content` property of this object is a string that contains the URL to which the current window will be redirected:

```
case "pageRedirect":
  window.location.href = deltaNode.content;
  return;
```

❏ If the `type` is the string `"error"`, the enumerated object describes a server error: the value of the `id` property of the object is a string that contains the number associated with the error, and the value of the `content` property of the object is a string that contains the error message. As you can see, the `_onFormSubmitCompleted` method calls the `_endPostBack` method on the current `PageRequestManager` instance to end the current request:

```
case "error":
  this._endPostBack(this._createPageRequestManagerServerError(
        Number.parseInvariant(deltaNode.id), deltaNode.content), sender);
  return;
```

❏ If the `type` is the string `"pageTitle"`, the enumerated object describes the title of the current page: the value of the `content` property of the object is a string that contains the new title of the page. Because of this, the `_onFormSubmitCompleted` method assigns the value of the `content` property to the `title` property of the `document` object.

```
case "pageTitle":
  document.title = deltaNode.content;
  break;
```

❑ If the type is the string `"focus"`, the enumerated object describes the HTML element that must have the focus. The value of the `id` property of this object is an empty string, and the value of the `content` property is a string that contains the value of the `ClientID` property of the server control that must have the focus. As you can see, the `_onFormSubmitCompleted` method assigns the value of the `content` property of the object to the `_controlIDToFocus` field of the current `PageRequestManager` instance:

```
case "focus":
    this._controlIDToFocus = deltaNode.content;
    break;
```

❑ If the type is none of the preceding strings, the `_onFormSubmitCompleted` method calls the `_endPostBack` method on the current `PageRequestManager` instance to end the current post-back request:

```
default:
    this._endPostBack(this._createPageRequestManagerParserError(
    String.format(Sys.WebForms.Res.PRM_UnknownToken, deltaNode.type)), sender);
    return;
```

Next, the `_onFormSubmitCompleted` method stores the contents of the `_updatePanelIDs` array in the `_oldUpdatePanelIDs` array field of the current `PageRequestManager` instance:

```
this._oldUpdatePanelIDs = this._updatePanelIDs;
```

Then the method uses the `childUpdatePanelIDsNode` to populate the `_childUpdatePanelIDs` array of the current `PageRequestManager` instance. Keep in mind that this array contains the value of the `UniqueID` properties of the `UpdatePanel` server controls that need updating because their parent `UpdatePanel` server control needs updating:

```
var childUpdatePanelIDsString = childUpdatePanelIDsNode.content;
this._childUpdatePanelIDs =
    childUpdatePanelIDsString.length ? childUpdatePanelIDsString.split(',') : [];
```

Next, the method uses the `panelsToRefreshNode` to populate the `_panelsToRefreshIDs` array of the current `PageRequestManager` instance. Keep in mind that this array contains the value of the `UniqueID` properties of the `UpdatePanel` server controls that need updating:

```
this._panelsToRefreshIDs = this._splitNodeIntoArray(panelsToRefreshNode);
```

Next the method iterates through the `UniqueID` property values in the `_panelsToRefreshIDs` array, passes each enumerated value into the `_uniqueIDToClientID` method to return the value of its associated `ClientID` property, and finally calls the `getElementById` method, passing in this `ClientID` property value to check whether the current page contains an `UpdatePanel` server control with the specified `UniqueID` and `ClientID` property values. If not, it calls the `_endPostBack` method to end the current request:

```
for (i = 0; i < this._panelsToRefreshIDs.length; i++)
{
  var panelClientID = this._uniqueIDToClientID(this._panelsToRefreshIDs[i]);
  if (!document.getElementById(panelClientID))
  {
    this._endPostBack(Error.invalidOperation(
      String.format(Sys.WebForms.Res.PRM_MissingPanel, panelClientID)), sender);
    return;
  }
}
```

Next, the _onFormSubmitCompleted method calls the _splitNodeIntoArray method of the PageRequestManager three times to convert asyncPostBackControlIDsNode, postBackControlIDsNode, and updatePanelIDsNode into arrays:

```
var asyncPostBackControlIDsArray =
                  this._splitNodeIntoArray(asyncPostBackControlIDsNode);
var postBackControlIDsArray = this._splitNodeIntoArray(postBackControlIDsNode);
var updatePanelIDsArray = this._splitNodeIntoArray(updatePanelIDsNode);
var asyncPostBackTimeout = asyncPostBackTimeoutNode.content;
```

Next, it calls the _updateControls method on the current PageRequestManager instance, passing in the following parameters:

❑ updatePanelIDsArray: This parameter is an array that contains the values of the UniqueID properties of all UpdatePanel server controls on the current page after the update. I say "after the update" because this array has just arrived from the server. Because of this, the content of the _updatePanelIDs array of the current PageRequestManager instance could be out of date: the server code may have added a new UpdatePanel server control or deleted an existing UpdatePanel server control.

❑ asyncPostBackControlIDsArray: This parameter is an array that contains the values of the UniqueID properties of all the server controls on the current page that cause asynchronous page postbacks.

❑ postBackControlIDsArray: This parameter is an array that contains the values of the UniqueID properties of all the server controls on the current page that cause normal synchronous page postbacks.

❑ asyncPostBackTimeout: This parameter is a string that contains the timeout value for asynchronous page postbacks:

```
this._updateControls(updatePanelIDsArray, asyncPostBackControlIDsArray,
                  postBackControlIDsArray, asyncPostBackTimeout);
```

I thoroughly discussed the _updateControls method of the PageRequestManager in Chapter 22.

Next, the _onFormSubmitCompleted method iterates through the objects in the dataItemNodes array (recall that this array contains all the objects that represent data items) and uses the value of the id property of each enumerated object as an index into the _dataItems collection of the current

PageRequestManager instance to store the value of the content property of the enumerated object into the collection. Recall that the value of the content property of the enumerated object is a string that contains the string representation of the data item associated with the server control whose UniqueID property value is given by the value of the id property of the enumerated object. In other words, each item in the _dataItems collection of the current PageRequestManager instance contains the string representation of a data item associated with a server control that has a specified UniqueID property value:

```
this._dataItems = {};
for (i = 0; i < dataItemNodes.length; i++)
{
  var dataItemNode = dataItemNodes[i];
  this._dataItems[dataItemNode.id] = dataItemNode.content;
}
```

Next, the _onFormSubmitCompleted method iterates through the objects in the dataItemJsonNodes array (recall that this array contains all the objects that represent JSON data items) and uses the value of the id property of each enumerated object as an index into the _dataItems collection of the current PageRequestManager instance to store the value of the content property of the enumerated object into the collection. Recall that the value of the content property of the enumerated object is a string that contains the JSON representation of the data item associated with the server control whose UniqueID property value is given by the value of the id property of the enumerated object:

```
for (i = 0; i < dataItemJsonNodes.length; i++)
{
  var dataItemJsonNode = dataItemJsonNodes[i];
  this._dataItems[dataItemJsonNode.id] = eval(dataItemJsonNode.content);
}
```

Next, the _onFormSubmitCompleted method calls the get_eventHandlerList method on the current PageRequestManager instance to return a reference to the EventHandlerList that contains all the event handlers registered for the events of the PageRequestManager instance. Then it calls the getHandler method on this EventHandlerList to return a reference to a JavaScript function whose invocation automatically invokes all the event handlers registered for the pageLoading event of the current PageRequestManager instance:

```
var handler = this._get_eventHandlerList().getHandler("pageLoading");
```

Next, it calls the _getPageLoadingEventArgs method on the current PageRequestManager instance to instantiate and return a PageLoadingEventArgs object. As you'll see later, the PageLoadingEventArgs is the event data class for the pageLoading event of the PageRequestManager class:

```
var Sys.WebForms.PageLoadingEventArgs args = this._getPageLoadingEventArgs();
```

Then it calls the previously mentioned JavaScript function and consequently all the event handlers registered for the pageLoading event of the current PageRequestManager instance, passing in a reference to the current PageRequestManager instance and the PageLoadingEventArgs object:

```
handler(this, args);
```

If you register an event handler for the `pageLoading` *event of the current* `PageRequestManager` *instance, your event handler will receive the previously mentioned two references. Your handler can then use these two references to get the complete information about the current request and use this information to perform application-specific page-loading tasks.*

Next, the `_onFormSubmitCompleted` method checks whether the `formActionNode` local variable is `null`. Recall that this variable references the object that describes the `action` property of the current form. If the variable is not `null`, the method assigns the value of the `content` property of this object to the action property of the form. You may be wondering why an asynchronous page postback may end up changing the `action` property of the current form. This normally happens when cookieless sessions are used, in which the session ID is embedded in the target URL, which changes the `action` value:

```
if (formActionNode)
  this._form.action = formActionNode.content;
```

Next, the method iterates through the objects in the `updatePanelNodes` array (recall that each object in this array describes an `UpdatePanel` server control that needs updating) and takes the following steps for each enumerated object. First, it calls the `getElementById` method on the document object, passing in the value of the `id` property of the enumerated object. Recall that the value of this property is a string that contains the value of the `ClientID` property of the `UpdatePanel` server control that the object describes. Therefore, the `getElementById` method returns a reference to the DOM element associated with the `UpdatePanel` server control:

```
var deltaUpdatePanel = updatePanelNodes[i];
var updatePanelElement = document.getElementById(deltaUpdatePanel.id);
```

If the current page does not contain a DOM element associated with the `UpdatePanel` server control, the `_onFormSubmitCompleted` method calls the `_endPostBack` method on the current `PageRequestManager` instance to end the current request:

```
if (!updatePanelElement)
{
  this._endPostBack(Error.invalidOperation(
    String.format(Sys.WebForms.Res.PRM_MissingPanel, deltaPanelID)), sender);
  return;
}
```

Next, the method calls the `_updatePanel` method on the current `PageRequestManager` instance, passing in a reference to the DOM element that represents the `UpdatePanel` server control and the value of the `content` property of the enumerated object. Recall that the value of this property is a string that contains the markup text for the `UpdatePanel` server control. As you'll see later, the `_updatePanel` server control updates the content of the specified `UpatePanel` server control with the specified HTML markup text.

```
this._updatePanel(updatePanelElement, deltaUpdatePanel.content);
```

Next, the method iterates through the objects in the `scriptDisposeNodes` array. Recall that the value of the `content` property of each object in this array contains a script that disposes the server control whose `ClientID` property value is given by the value of the `id` property of the object. The `_onFormSubmitCompleted` method calls the `_registerDisposeScript` method on the current `PageRequestManager` instance, passing in the values of the `id` and `content` properties of the enumerated object. As you'll see later, the _registerDisposeScript method of the current PageRequestManager instances registers the specified dispose script for the specified UpdatePanel server control:

```
for (i = 0; i < scriptDisposeNodes.length; i++)
{
  var disposePanelId = scriptDisposeNodes[i].id;
  var disposeScript = scriptDisposeNodes[i].content;
  this._registerDisposeScript(disposePanelId, disposeScript);
}
```

Next, the method iterates through the objects in the hiddenFieldNodes array. Recall that each object in this array describes a hidden field for which the value of the id property of the object contains the value of the id HTML attribute of the hidden field, and the value of the content property of the object contains the value that must be stored in the hidden field. The _onFormSubmitCompleted method takes the following steps for each enumerated object. First, it calls the getElementById method on the document object to check whether the current page already contains a hidden field with the specified id HTML attribute value.

```
var hiddenFieldElement = document.getElementById(hiddenFieldNodes[i].id);
```

If so, it simply stores the value of the content property of the enumerated object in the existing hidden field:

```
hiddenFieldElement.value = value;
```

If not, it takes the following steps to create a new hidden field. First, it calls the createElement method on the document object to create a new input HTML element:

```
hiddenFieldElement = document.createElement('input');
```

Then it assigns the value of the id property of the enumerated object to the id property of the newly instantiated input HTML element:

```
hiddenFieldElement.id = hiddenFieldNodes[i].id;
```

Next, the _onFormSubmitCompleted method assigns the value of the id property of the enumerated object to the name property of the newly instantiated input HTML element:

```
hiddenFieldElement.name = hiddenFieldNodes[i].id;
```

Next, it sets the type property of the newly instantiated input HTML element to hidden:

```
hiddenFieldElement.type = 'hidden';
```

Finally, it calls the appendChild method on the form element to append the newly instantiated hidden field as the child of the form element:

```
this._form.appendChild(hiddenFieldElement);
```

Next, the _onFormSubmitCompleted method iterates through the objects in the arrayDeclarationNodes array. Recall that each object in this array represents an array declaration for which the value of the id property of the object contains the name of the array being declared, and the value of the content property of the object contains the value being stored in the array. As you can see, the method takes the following steps for each object in the arrayDeclarationNodes array. First, it creates a string that contains a call into the _addArrayElement static method of the PageRequestManager class, passing in the values of the id and content properties of the object as the arguments of the method. Next, it adds this string to a local string named arrayScript that accumulates all the strings associated with the objects in the arrayDeclarationNodes array:

```
var arrayScript = '';
for (i = 0; i < arrayDeclarationNodes.length; i++)
{
    arrayScript += "Sys.WebForms.PageRequestManager._addArrayElement('" +
            arrayDeclarationNodes[i].id + "', " +
            arrayDeclarationNodes[i].content + ");\r\n";
}
```

Next, the _onFormSubmitCompleted method iterates through the objects in the expandoNodes array. Recall that each object in this array describes an expando attribute for which the values of the id and content properties of the object contain the name and value, respectively of the expando attribute. As you can see, the _onFormSubmitCompleted method forms a string for each object that consists of two substrings separated by the equals sign, these substrings containing the name and value, respectively, of the associated expando attribute. Note that the expandoScript string accumulates all these strings.

```
var expandoScript = '';
for (i = 0; i < expandoNodes.length; i++)
{
    var propertyReference = expandoNodes[i].id;
    var propertyValue = expandoNodes[i].content;
    expandoScript += propertyReference + " = " + propertyValue + "\r\n";
}
```

As you can see, the server response to an asynchronous page postback may contain scripts. The current page may also contain scripts. Therefore, you need a way to avoid duplicate scripts. The ASP.NET AJAX client-side framework comes with an internal class named _ScriptLoader that provides the current PageRequestManager instance with script-loading services. The _onFormSubmitCompleted method of the current PageRequestManager instance, shown in Listing 24-5, uses these services to avoid loading duplicate scripts as follows:

❑ The method begins by calling the readLoadedScripts static method on the _ScriptLoader class. As you'll see later, this static method populates an internal static collection named _referencedScripts with the values of the src HTML attributes of all the script HTML elements that *currently* exist on the current page. I say *currently* because the server response to the current asynchronous page postback request may contain references to script files that the existing script HTML elements on the current page may or may not reference.

```
Sys._ScriptLoader.readLoadedScripts();
```

❑ The method then calls the getInstance static method of the _ScriptLoader class to access the current _ScriptLoader instance. Each page can have only one instance of the _ScriptLoader class. As you'll see later, the getInstance method checks whether an internal static field named _instance references an instance of the _ScriptLoader class. If so, it simply returns this reference. If not, it creates and returns a new instance of the _ScriptLoader class and stores this instance in this internal field for future use. This ensures that the current page always uses the same instance of the _ScriptLoader class.

```
var scriptLoader = Sys._ScriptLoader.getInstance();
```

❑ Next, the method calls the queueScriptBlock method on the current _ScriptLoader instance to queue the script contained in the arrayScript string. Recall that the arrayScript string contains the script that declares one or more JavaScript arrays. The current page may or may not contain the same ones.

❑ As you'll see later, the queueScriptBlock method simply adds the specified script to an internal collection named _scriptsToLoad:

```
if (arrayScript.length)
  scriptLoader.queueScriptBlock(arrayScript);
```

❑ Next, the method calls the queueScriptBlock method on the current _ScriptLoader instance to queue the script contained in the expandoScript string. Recall that the expandoScript string contains the script that defines one or more expando attributes:

```
if (expandoScript.length)
  scriptLoader.queueScriptBlock(expandoScript);
```

❑ Then the method iterates through the objects in the scriptBlockNodes array and takes the following steps for each enumerated object:

  ❑ If the value of the id property of the object is the string "ScriptContentNoTags", this is an indication that the value of the content property of the object contains a script block. Therefore, the method calls the queueScriptBlock method on the current _ScriptLoader instance to queue this script block:

```
case "ScriptContentNoTags":
  scriptLoader.queueScriptBlock(scriptBlockNodes[i].content);
  break;
```

  ❑ If the value of the id property of the object is the string "ScriptContentWithTags", this is an indication that the value of the content property of the object does not contain a script block. Instead it contains the JSON representation of the attributes of a script HTML element. You can think of this JSON representation as the serialized form of these attributes. It contains one name/value pair for each attribute, where the name part of the pair is a string that contains the name of the attribute, and the value part is a string that contains the value of the attribute. Keep in mind that some of these attributes may be custom attributes.

❑ The _onFormSubmitCompleted method first checks whether this JSON representation contains a name/value pair for the src HTML attribute. If so, it uses the name part of this pair — that is, the keyword src — to access the value part of the pair — that is, the URL of the referenced script file — and calls the isScriptLoaded static method on the _ScriptLoader class to check whether the internal _referencedScripts collection contains an entry for this URL. (Recall that this collection contains the URLs of all the *currently* referenced script files.) If so, the _onFormSubmitCompleted method skips the enumerated object. If not, it calls the queueCustomScriptTag method on the current _ScriptLoader instance, passing in the JSON representation of the script attributes. As you'll see later, this method simply adds this JSON representation to an internal collection named _scriptsToLoad. This collection contains one object for each script file that needs to be loaded, and describes the HTML standard and custom script attributes.

```
case "ScriptContentWithTags":
  var scriptTagAttributes;
  eval("scriptTagAttributes = " + scriptBlockNodes[i].content);
  if (scriptTagAttributes.src &&
      Sys._ScriptLoader.isScriptLoaded(scriptTagAttributes.src))
    continue;
  scriptLoader.queueCustomScriptTag(scriptTagAttributes);
  break;
```

❑ If the value of the id property of the object is the string "ScriptPath", this is an indication that the value of the content property of the object does not contain a script block. Instead it contains the URL of a script file. The _onFormSubmitCompleted method first calls the isScriptLoaded static method on the _ScriptLoader class to check whether the internal _referencedScripts collection contains an entry for this URL. If so, it simply skips the enumerated object because the associated script has already been loaded.

If not, it calls the queueScriptReference method on the current _ScriptLoader instance, passing in the value of the content property of the enumerated object — that is, the URL. As you'll see later, this method creates an object with a single name/value pair and adds the object to the internal _scriptsToLoad collection. The name part of this name/value pair is the keyword src and the value part is the URL.

❑ Keep in mind that _scriptsToLoad is a collection of objects in which each object describes the HTML standard and custom script attributes associated with a particular script file. To put it differently, this collection contains information about the script files that need to be downloaded from the server.

```
case "ScriptPath":
  if (Sys._ScriptLoader.isScriptLoaded(scriptBlockNodes[i].content))
    continue;
  scriptLoader.queueScriptReference(scriptBlockNodes[i].content);
  break;
```

❑ Next, the _onFormSubmitCompleted method iterates through the objects in the onSubmitNodes array. Recall that each object in this array describes a dynamically added form onsubmit statement for which the value of the id property of the object is an empty string and the value of the content property is a string that contains the dynamically added form onsubmit statement.

❑ The _onFormSubmitCompleted method creates a local string named onSubmitStatementScript that contains a script that adds a dynamically generated JavaScript function to the _onSubmitStatements collection of the current PageRequestManager instance. Note that the method iterates through the objects in the onSubmitNodes collection and adds the value of the content property of each enumerated object to the body of this dynamically generated JavaScript function.

```
var onSubmitStatementScript = '';
for (var i = 0; i < onSubmitNodes.length; i++)
{
    if (i === 0)
       onSubmitStatementScript = 'Array.add(Sys.WebForms.PageRequestManager
                      .getInstance()._onSubmitStatements, function() {\r\n';
    onSubmitStatementScript += onSubmitNodes[i].content + "\r\n";
}
```

❑ Next, the method calls the queueScriptBlock method on the current _ScriptLoader instance that is passing in the local onSubmitStatementScript string. As you'll see later, the queueScriptBlock method creates a object with a single name/value pair and adds the object to the internal _scriptsToLoad collection of the current _ScriptLoader instance. The name part of this name/value pair is the keyword text and the value part contains the content of the onSubmitStatementScript string.

```
if (onSubmitStatementScript.length)
{
    onSubmitStatementScript += "\r\nreturn true;\r\n});\r\n";
    scriptLoader.queueScriptBlock(onSubmitStatementScript);
}
```

❑ Next, the _onFormSubmitCompleted method stores the reference to the WebRequestExecutor object responsible for executing the current request in the _response field of the current PageRequestManager instance:

```
this._response = sender;
```

❑ Next, the _onFormSubmitCompleted method calls the createDelegate static method on the function to create a delegate that represents the _scriptsLoadComplete method of the current PageRequestManager instance:

```
var scriptLoadCompleteDelegate = Function.createDelegate(this,
                                          this._scriptsLoadComplete);
```

❑ Finally, the _onFormSubmitCompleted method calls the loadScripts method on the current _ScriptLoader instance, passing in the delegate. As you'll see later, this method will load the scripts in the _scriptsToLoad collection:

```
scriptLoader.loadScripts(0, scriptLoadCompleteDelegate, null, null);
```

Listing 24-5 : The _onFormSubmitCompleted Method of the PageRequestManager

```
function Sys$WebForms$PageRequestManager$_onFormSubmitCompleted(sender, eventArgs)
{
  this._processingRequest = true;
  var delimitByLengthDelimiter = '|';

  if (sender.get_timedOut())
  {
    this._endPostBack(this._createPageRequestManagerTimeoutError(), sender);
    return;
  }
  if (sender.get_aborted())
  {
    this._endPostBack(null, sender);
    return;
  }
  if (!this._request || sender.get_webRequest() !== this._request)
    return;
  var errorMessage;
  var delta = [];
  if (sender.get_statusCode() !== 200)
  {
    this._endPostBack(
        this._createPageRequestManagerServerError(sender.get_statusCode()), sender);
    return;
  }
  var reply = sender.get_responseData();
  var delimiterIndex, len, type, id, content;
  var replyIndex = 0;
  var parserErrorDetails = null;
  while (replyIndex < reply.length)
  {
    delimiterIndex = reply.indexOf(delimitByLengthDelimiter, replyIndex);
    if (delimiterIndex === -1)
    {
      parserErrorDetails = this._findText(reply, replyIndex);
      break;
    }

    len = parseInt(reply.substring(replyIndex, delimiterIndex), 10);
    if ((len % 1) !== 0)
    {
      parserErrorDetails = this._findText(reply, replyIndex);
      break;
    }
    replyIndex = delimiterIndex + 1;
    delimiterIndex = reply.indexOf(delimitByLengthDelimiter, replyIndex);
```

(continued)

Listing 24-5 (continued)

```
      if (delimiterIndex === -1)
      {
        parserErrorDetails = this._findText(reply, replyIndex);
        break;
      }
      type = reply.substring(replyIndex, delimiterIndex);
      replyIndex = delimiterIndex + 1;
      delimiterIndex = reply.indexOf(delimitByLengthDelimiter, replyIndex);
      if (delimiterIndex === -1)
      {
        parserErrorDetails = this._findText(reply, replyIndex);
        break;
      }
      id = reply.substring(replyIndex, delimiterIndex);
      replyIndex = delimiterIndex + 1;
      if ((replyIndex + len) >= reply.length)
      {
        parserErrorDetails = this._findText(reply, reply.length);
        break;
      }
      content = this._decodeString(reply.substr(replyIndex, len));
      replyIndex += len;
      if (reply.charAt(replyIndex) !== delimitByLengthDelimiter)
      {
        parserErrorDetails = this._findText(reply, replyIndex);
        break;
      }
      replyIndex++;
      var obj = {type: type, id: id, content: content};
      Array.add(delta, obj);
    }
    if (parserErrorDetails)
    {
      this._endPostBack(this._createPageRequestManagerParserError(
                        String.format(Sys.WebForms.Res.PRM_ParserErrorDetails,
                                      parserErrorDetails)), sender);
      return;
    }
    var updatePanelNodes = [];
    var hiddenFieldNodes = [];
    var arrayDeclarationNodes = [];
    var scriptBlockNodes = [];
    var expandoNodes = [];
    var onSubmitNodes = [];
    var dataItemNodes = [];
    var dataItemJsonNodes = [];
    var scriptDisposeNodes = [];
    var asyncPostBackControlIDsNode, postBackControlIDsNode,
        updatePanelIDsNode, asyncPostBackTimeoutNode,
        childUpdatePanelIDsNode, panelsToRefreshNode, formActionNode;
```

```
for (var i = 0; i < delta.length; i++)
{
  var deltaNode = delta[i];
  switch (deltaNode.type)
  {
    case "updatePanel":
      Array.add(updatePanelNodes, deltaNode);
      break;
    case "hiddenField":
      Array.add(hiddenFieldNodes, deltaNode);
      break;
    case "arrayDeclaration":
      Array.add(arrayDeclarationNodes, deltaNode);
      break;
    case "scriptBlock":
      Array.add(scriptBlockNodes, deltaNode);
      break;
    case "expando":
      Array.add(expandoNodes, deltaNode);
      break;
    case "onSubmit":
      Array.add(onSubmitNodes, deltaNode);
      break;
    case "asyncPostBackControlIDs":
      asyncPostBackControlIDsNode = deltaNode;
      break;
    case "postBackControlIDs":
      postBackControlIDsNode = deltaNode;
      break;
    case "updatePanelIDs":
      updatePanelIDsNode = deltaNode;
      break;
    case "asyncPostBackTimeout":
      asyncPostBackTimeoutNode = deltaNode;
      break;
    case "childUpdatePanelIDs":
      childUpdatePanelIDsNode = deltaNode;
      break;
    case "panelsToRefreshIDs":
      panelsToRefreshNode = deltaNode;
      break;
    case "formAction":
      formActionNode = deltaNode;
      break;
    case "dataItem":
      Array.add(dataItemNodes, deltaNode);
      break;
    case "dataItemJson":
      Array.add(dataItemJsonNodes, deltaNode);
      break;
    case "scriptDispose":
      Array.add(scriptDisposeNodes, deltaNode);
      break;
```

(continued)

Listing 24-5 *(continued)*

```
          case "pageRedirect":
            window.location.href = deltaNode.content;
            return;
          case "error":
            this._endPostBack(this._createPageRequestManagerServerError(
                    Number.parseInvariant(deltaNode.id), deltaNode.content), sender);
            return;
          case "pageTitle":
            document.title = deltaNode.content;
            break;
          case "focus":
            this._controlIDToFocus = deltaNode.content;
            break;
          default:
            this._endPostBack(this._createPageRequestManagerParserError(
            String.format(Sys.WebForms.Res.PRM_UnknownToken, deltaNode.type)), sender);
            return;
        }
    }
    var i;
    if (asyncPostBackControlIDsNode && postBackControlIDsNode &&
        updatePanelIDsNode && panelsToRefreshNode &&
        asyncPostBackTimeoutNode && childUpdatePanelIDsNode)
    {
      this._oldUpdatePanelIDs = this._updatePanelIDs;
      var childUpdatePanelIDsString = childUpdatePanelIDsNode.content;
      this._childUpdatePanelIDs =
        childUpdatePanelIDsString.length ? childUpdatePanelIDsString.split(',') : [];
      var asyncPostBackControlIDsArray =
                             this._splitNodeIntoArray(asyncPostBackControlIDsNode);
      var postBackControlIDsArray = this._splitNodeIntoArray(postBackControlIDsNode);
      var updatePanelIDsArray = this._splitNodeIntoArray(updatePanelIDsNode);
      this._panelsToRefreshIDs = this._splitNodeIntoArray(panelsToRefreshNode);
      for (i = 0; i < this._panelsToRefreshIDs.length; i++)
      {
        var panelClientID = this._uniqueIDToClientID(this._panelsToRefreshIDs[i]);
        if (!document.getElementById(panelClientID))
        {
          this._endPostBack(Error.invalidOperation(
            String.format(Sys.WebForms.Res.PRM_MissingPanel, panelClientID)), sender);
          return;
        }
      }
      var asyncPostBackTimeout = asyncPostBackTimeoutNode.content;
      this._updateControls(updatePanelIDsArray, asyncPostBackControlIDsArray,
                      postBackControlIDsArray, asyncPostBackTimeout);
    }
```

```
this._dataItems = {};
for (i = 0; i < dataItemNodes.length; i++)
{
  var dataItemNode = dataItemNodes[i];
  this._dataItems[dataItemNode.id] = dataItemNode.content;
}

for (i = 0; i < dataItemJsonNodes.length; i++)
{
  var dataItemJsonNode = dataItemJsonNodes[i];
  this._dataItems[dataItemJsonNode.id] = eval(dataItemJsonNode.content);
}
var handler = this._get_eventHandlerList().getHandler("pageLoading");
if (handler)
  handler(this, this._getPageLoadingEventArgs());
if (formActionNode)
{
  this._form.action = formActionNode.content;
  this._form._initialAction = this._form.action;
}
for (i = 0; i < updatePanelNodes.length; i++)
{
  var deltaUpdatePanel = updatePanelNodes[i];
  var deltaPanelID = deltaUpdatePanel.id;
  var deltaPanelRendering = deltaUpdatePanel.content;
  var updatePanelElement = document.getElementById(deltaPanelID);
  if (!updatePanelElement)
  {
    this._endPostBack(Error.invalidOperation(
        String.format(Sys.WebForms.Res.PRM_MissingPanel, deltaPanelID)), sender);
    return;
  }
  this._updatePanel(updatePanelElement, deltaPanelRendering);
}
for (i = 0; i < scriptDisposeNodes.length; i++)
{
  var disposePanelId = scriptDisposeNodes[i].id;
  var disposeScript = scriptDisposeNodes[i].content;
  this._registerDisposeScript(disposePanelId, disposeScript);
}
for (i = 0; i < hiddenFieldNodes.length; i++)
{
  var id = hiddenFieldNodes[i].id;
  var value = hiddenFieldNodes[i].content;
  var hiddenFieldElement = document.getElementById(id);
  if (!hiddenFieldElement)
  {
    hiddenFieldElement = document.createElement('input');
    hiddenFieldElement.id = id;
    hiddenFieldElement.name = id;
    hiddenFieldElement.type = 'hidden';
    this._form.appendChild(hiddenFieldElement);
  }
  hiddenFieldElement.value = value;
}
```

(continued)

Listing 24-5 *(continued)*

```
var arrayScript = '';
for (i = 0; i < arrayDeclarationNodes.length; i++)
{
  arrayScript += "Sys.WebForms.PageRequestManager._addArrayElement('" +
              arrayDeclarationNodes[i].id + "', " +
              arrayDeclarationNodes[i].content + ");\r\n";
}
var expandoScript = '';
for (i = 0; i < expandoNodes.length; i++)
{
  var propertyReference = expandoNodes[i].id;
  var propertyValue = expandoNodes[i].content;
  expandoScript += propertyReference + " = " + propertyValue + "\r\n";
}
Sys._ScriptLoader.readLoadedScripts();
Sys.Application.beginCreateComponents();
var scriptLoader = Sys._ScriptLoader.getInstance();
if (arrayScript.length)
  scriptLoader.queueScriptBlock(arrayScript);

if (expandoScript.length)
  scriptLoader.queueScriptBlock(expandoScript);
for (i = 0; i < scriptBlockNodes.length; i++)
{
  var scriptBlockType = scriptBlockNodes[i].id;
  switch (scriptBlockType)
  {
    case "ScriptContentNoTags":
      scriptLoader.queueScriptBlock(scriptBlockNodes[i].content);
      break;
    case "ScriptContentWithTags":
      var scriptTagAttributes;
      eval("scriptTagAttributes = " + scriptBlockNodes[i].content);
      if (scriptTagAttributes.src &&
          Sys._ScriptLoader.isScriptLoaded(scriptTagAttributes.src))
        continue;
      scriptLoader.queueCustomScriptTag(scriptTagAttributes);
      break;
    case "ScriptPath":
      if (Sys._ScriptLoader.isScriptLoaded(scriptBlockNodes[i].content))
        continue;
      scriptLoader.queueScriptReference(scriptBlockNodes[i].content);
      break;
  }
}
```

```
    var onSubmitStatementScript = '';
    for (var i = 0; i < onSubmitNodes.length; i++)
    {
        if (i === 0)
            onSubmitStatementScript =
    'Array.add(Sys.WebForms.PageRequestManager.getInstance()._onSubmitStatements,
    function() {\r\n';
        onSubmitStatementScript += onSubmitNodes[i].content + "\r\n";
    }

    if (onSubmitStatementScript.length)
    {
        onSubmitStatementScript += "\r\nreturn true;\r\n});\r\n";
        scriptLoader.queueScriptBlock(onSubmitStatementScript);
    }
    this._response = sender;
    scriptLoader.loadScripts(0,
            Function.createDelegate(this, this._scriptsLoadComplete), null, null);
}
```

The _updatePanel Method
of PageRequestManager

Recall from Listing 24-5 that the _onFormSubmitCompleted method of the current PageRequestManager instance invokes the _updatePanel method on itself, passing in two parameters, the first of which references an UpdatePanel server control that needs refreshing and the second of which is a string that contains the new HTML markup text for this UpdatePanel server control. The main responsibility of the _updatePanel method is to the update the content of the specified UpdatePanel server control with the specified HTML markup text.

As Listing 24-6 shows, this method searches through the _scriptDisposes dictionary of the current PageRequestManager instance for the collection or array that contains all the script disposes associated with the specified UpdatePanel server control. If it finds such a collection, it iterates through the script disposes in this collection and calls the eval JavaScript function on each script dispose to execute the script. This will allow these script disposes to release the resources that the UpdatePanel server control and its constituent client components are holding before the server control and its content are disposed of. It is necessary to release these resources because the UpdatePanel server control and its content is about to reload or refresh.

```
    var disposeScripts = this._scriptDisposes[updatePanelID];
    for (var i = 0; i < disposeScripts.length; i++)
    {
        eval(disposeScripts[i]);
    }
```

Recall from Listing 23-41 that you can use the `RegisterDispose` *public method of the current* `ScriptManager` *server control to register dispose scripts for a specified child server control of a specified* `UpdatePanel` *server control on the current page. Recall that the* `RegisterDispose` *method takes two parameters. The first references the child server control for which the dispose script is being registered; the second is a string that contains the actual dispose script being registered.*

Next, the `_onFormSubmitCompleted` method deletes the collection from the `_scriptDisposes` dictionary.

```
delete this._scriptDisposes[updatePanelID];
```

Next, it invokes the `_destroyTree` method on the current `PageRequestManager` instance, passing in the reference to the specified `UpdatePanel` server control to delete the DOM hierarchy associated with the server control and its content:

```
this._destroyTree(updatePanelElement);
```

Finally, it assigns the string that contains the updated HTML markup text to the `innerHTML` property of the specified `UpdatePanel` server control:

```
updatePanelElement.innerHTML = rendering;
```

Listing 24-6 : The _updatePanel Method of the PageRequestManager

```
function Sys$WebForms$PageRequestManager$_updatePanel(updatePanelElement,
                                                      rendering)
{
  for (var updatePanelID in this._scriptDisposes)
  {
    var runDisposeScripts = false;
    var element = document.getElementById(updatePanelID);
    while (element)
    {
      if (element === updatePanelElement)
      {
        runDisposeScripts = true;
        break;
      }
      element = element.parentNode;
    }

    if (runDisposeScripts)
    {
      var disposeScripts = this._scriptDisposes[updatePanelID];
      for (var i = 0; i < disposeScripts.length; i++)
      {
        eval(disposeScripts[i]);
      }
      delete this._scriptDisposes[updatePanelID];
    }
  }
  this._destroyTree(updatePanelElement);
  updatePanelElement.innerHTML = rendering;
}
```

The registerDisposeScript Method of PageRequestManager

Recall from Listing 24-5 that the _onFormSubmitCompleted method of the current PageRequestManager instance iterates through a local collection named scriptDisposeNodes, as shown again in the following code listing:

```
for (i = 0; i < scriptDisposeNodes.length; i++)
{
  var disposePanelId = scriptDisposeNodes[i].id;
  var disposeScript = scriptDisposeNodes[i].content;
  this._registerDisposeScript(disposePanelId, disposeScript);
}
```

As discussed earlier, the scriptDisposeNodes is a collection of objects, each of which describes a dispose script. Recall that the value of the id property of each object is a string that contains the ClientID property value of the UpdatePanel server control for which the dispose script is being registered, and that the value of the content property of this object is a string that contains the actual dispose script being registered. As the preceding code listing shows, the _onFormSubmitCompleted method calls the _registerDisposeScript method on the current PageRequestManager instance to register the specified dispose script for the UpdatePanel server control with the specified ClientID property value.

Listing 24-7 presents the internal implementation of the _registerDisposeScript method. As you can see, this method first uses the ClientID property value as an index into the _scriptDisposes collection to return the array that holds all the dispose scripts registered for the UpdatePanel server control that has the specified ClientID property value. (Recall that the _scriptDisposes collection of the current PageRequestManager instance maintains one array for each server control.) Next, the _registerDisposeScript method adds the specified dispose script to the associated array.

Listing 24-7 : The _registerDisposeScript Method of the PageRequestManager

```
function Sys$WebForms$PageRequestManager$_registerDisposeScript(panelID,
                                                     disposeScript)
{
  if (!this._scriptDisposes[panelID])
    this._scriptDisposes[panelID] = [disposeScript];

  else
    Array.add(this._scriptDisposes[panelID], disposeScript);
}
```

_destroyTree

Recall from Listing 24-6 that the _updatePanel method of the current PageRequestManager instance invokes the _destroyTree method on the current PageRequestMananger instance to destroy the entire DOM hierarchy that has the specified root DOM element. The _destroyTree method takes a reference to a DOM element and deletes it and all its descendant DOM elements. As Listing 24-8 shows, this method first makes sure that its argument is indeed an element. Then it iterates through the child DOM elements of the element and takes these steps for each. If the enumerated child DOM element supports the dispose method, _destroyTree invokes this method on the child element. If the enumerated child DOM element does not support the method but does expose a property named control that supports the method, _destroyTree calls the method on this property. (Recall that the control property of a DOM element references the client control associated with the element.) Next, it calls the getBehaviors method to return an array that contains all the behaviors associated with the enumerated DOM element and calls the dispose methods of these behaviors. Finally, it calls _destroyTree to destroy all the descendant DOM elements of the enumerated child element. As you can see, _destroyTree is a recursive method.

Listing 24-8: The _destroyTree Method of PageRequestManager

```
function Sys$WebForms$PageRequestManager$_destroyTree(element)
{
  if (element.nodeType === 1)
  {
    var childNodes = element.childNodes;
    for (var i = childNodes.length - 1; i >= 0; i--)
    {
      var node = childNodes[i];
      if (node.nodeType === 1)
      {
        if (node.dispose && typeof(node.dispose) === "function")
          node.dispose();

        else if (node.control && typeof(node.control.dispose) === "function")
          node.control.dispose();

        var behaviors = Sys.UI.Behavior.getBehaviors(node);
        for (var j = behaviors.length - 1; j >= 0; j--)
        {
          behaviors[j].dispose();
        }
        this._destroyTree(node);
      }
    }
  }
}
```

_ScriptLoader

The main responsibility of the _ScriptLoader class is to load the required scripts. As you saw, Listing 24-5 makes extensive use of this class. In this section, I'll walk you though the implementation of the methods of the class.

readLoadedScripts

Recall from Listing 24-5 that the _onSubmitFormCompleted method invokes the readLoadedScripts static method on the _ScriptLoader class. As Listing 24-9 shows, the readLoadedScripts method first instantiates the _referencedScripts static field of the class:

```
Sys._ScriptLoader._referencedScripts = [];
```

Next, it calls the `getElementByTagName` method on the document object to return an array that contains references to all the script HTML elements on the current page:

```
var existingScripts = document.getElementsByTagName('SCRIPT');
```

Finally, `readLoadedScripts` iterates through these `script` HTML elements and adds the value of the `src` HTML attribute of each element to the `_referencedScripts` static collection of the `_ScriptLoader` class:

```
Array.add(Sys._ScriptLoader._referencedScripts, existingScripts[i].src);
```

Listing 24-9: The readLoadedScripts Static Method of the _ScriptLoader Class

```
Sys._ScriptLoader.readLoadedScripts =
function Sys$_ScriptLoader$readLoadedScripts()
{
  if(!Sys._ScriptLoader._referencedScripts)
  {
    var existingScripts = document.getElementsByTagName('SCRIPT');
    for (i = existingScripts.length - 1; i >= 0; i--)
    {
      if (existingScripts[i].src.length)
      {
        if (!Array.contains(Sys._ScriptLoader._referencedScripts,
                            existingScripts[i].src))
          Array.add(Sys._ScriptLoader._referencedScripts, existingScripts[i].src);
      }
    }
  }
}
```

getInstance

As Listing 24-10 shows, the `getInstance` static method of the `_ScriptLoader` class ensures that each page can have only one instance of the `_ScriptLoader` class.

Listing 24-10: The getInstance Static Method of the _ScriptLoader Class

```
Sys._ScriptLoader.getInstance = function Sys$_ScriptLoader$getInstance()
{
  if(!Sys._ScriptLoader._activeInstance)
    Sys._ScriptLoader._activeInstance = new Sys._ScriptLoader();

  return Sys._ScriptLoader._activeInstance;
}
```

queueScriptBlock

As you can see from Listing 24-11, the queueScriptBlock method of the _ScriptLoader class creates an object with a single name/value pair and adds it to the _scriptToLoad array of the current _ScriptLoader instance. Note that the name part of this name/value pair is the keyword text and the value part contains the script being queued.

Listing 24-11: The queueScriptBlock Method of the _ScriptLoader Class

```
function Sys$_ScriptLoader$queueScriptBlock(scriptContent)
{
  if(!this._scriptsToLoad)
    this._scriptsToLoad = [];

  Array.add(this._scriptsToLoad, {text: scriptContent});
}
```

queueCustomScriptTag

Recall from Listing 24-5 that the _onFormSubmitCompleted method of the current PageRequestManager instance calls the queueCustomScriptTag method on the current _ScriptLoader instance, passing in the object that represents the serialized form of the attributes of a script HTML element. As Listing 24-12 shows, the queueCustomScriptTag method adds this object to the _scriptsToLoad collection of the current _scriptLoader instance.

Listing 24-12: The queueCustomScriptTag Method of the _ScriptLoader Class

```
function Sys$_ScriptLoader$queueCustomScriptTag(scriptAttributes)
{
  if(!this._scriptsToLoad)
    this._scriptsToLoad = [];

  Array.add(this._scriptsToLoad, scriptAttributes);
}
```

isScriptLoaded

Recall from Listing 24-5 that the _onFormSubmitCompleted method of the current PageRequestManager instance invokes the isScriptLoaded static method on the _ScriptLoader class to determine whether the script file with the specified URL has already been loaded. Listing 24-13 presents the implementation of this method.

Listing 24-13: The isScriptLoaded Static Method of the _ScriptLoader Class

```
Sys._ScriptLoader.isScriptLoaded =
function Sys$_ScriptLoader$isScriptLoaded(scriptSrc)
{
  var dummyScript = document.createElement('script');
  dummyScript.src = scriptSrc;
  return Array.contains(Sys._ScriptLoader._getLoadedScripts(), dummyScript.src);
}
```

_getLoadedScript

As Listing 24-14 shows, the _getLoadedScripts static method of the _ScriptLoader class simply returns a reference to the _referencedScripts collection, which contains the values of the src HTML attributes of all the script HTML elements that *currently* exist on the current page.

Listing 24-14: The _getLoadedScripts Static Method of the _ScriptLoader Class

```
Sys._ScriptLoader._getLoadedScripts =
function Sys$_ScriptLoader$_getLoadedScripts()
{
  if(!Sys._ScriptLoader._referencedScripts)
  {
    Sys._ScriptLoader._referencedScripts = [];
    Sys._ScriptLoader.readLoadedScripts();
  }

  return Sys._ScriptLoader._referencedScripts;
}
```

queueScriptReference

Recall from Listing 24-5 that the _onFormSubmitCompleted method of the current client script PageRequestManager instance calls the queueScriptReference method on the current _ScriptLoader instance to queue the specified script reference. As Listing 24-15 shows, this method creates an object with a single name/value pair, the name part of the pair being the keyword src and the value part the URL of the JavaScript file passed into the method as its only argument. The method then adds this object to the _scriptsToLoad collection of the current _ScriptLoader instance.

Listing 24-15: The queueScriptReference Method of the _ScriptLoader Class

```
function Sys$_ScriptLoader$queueScriptReference(scriptUrl)
{
  if(!this._scriptsToLoad)
    this._scriptsToLoad = [];

  Array.add(this._scriptsToLoad, {src: scriptUrl});
}
```

loadScripts

Recall from Listing 24-5 that the _onFormSubmitCompleted method of the current client-side PageRequestManager instance calls the loadScripts method on the current _ScriptLoader instance to load the scripts in the _scriptsToLoad collection. As Listing 24-16 shows, this method takes four parameters. The first contains the script loading timeout, the second references the JavaScript function that will be automatically invoked if all the scripts in the _scriptsToLoad collection are loaded, the third references the JavaScript function that will be automatically invoked if the script loading fails, and the fourth parameter references the JavaScript function that will be automatically invoked if the scripts in the _scriptsToLoad collection do not load within the time specified by the first parameter of the method.

As you can see from Listing 24-16, the loadScripts method first checks whether the _loading field of the current _ScriptLoader instance is set to true. If so, this is an indication that the scripts in the _scriptsToLoad collection are already being loaded. Therefore, an invalid operation exception is raised:

```
if(this._loading)
    throw Error.invalidOperation(Sys.Res.scriptLoaderAlreadyLoading);
```

Next, the loadScripts method sets the _loading flag to true to signal that the scripts in the _scriptsToLoad collection are being loaded:

```
this._loading = true;
```

Then it stores its second parameter in the _allScriptsLoadedCallback field of the current _ScriptLoader instance:

```
this._allScriptsLoadedCallback = allScriptsLoadedCallback;
```

Recall from Listing 24-5 that the _onFormSubmitCompleted method of the current PageRequestManager instance passes the following delegate as the second parameter of the loadScripts method:

```
Function.createDelegate(this, this._scriptsLoadComplete)
```

As you can see, this delegate represents the _scriptLoadComplete method of the current PageRequestManager instance. This means that when all the scripts in the _scriptsToLoad collection of the current PageRequestManager instance are finally loaded, the current _ScriptLoader instance will automatically invoke this delegate and consequently the _scriptsLoadComplete method that it represents.

As Listing 24-16 shows, the loadScripts method finally invokes the _loadScriptsInternal method on the current _ScriptLoader instance to load the scripts in the _scriptsToLoad collection of the current _ScriptLoader instance:

```
this._loadScriptsInternal();
```

Listing 24-16: The loadScripts Method of the _ScriptLoader Class

```
function Sys$_ScriptLoader$loadScripts(scriptTimeout, allScriptsLoadedCallback,
                                        scriptLoadFailedCallback,
                                        scriptLoadTimeoutCallback)
{
  if(this._loading)
     throw Error.invalidOperation(Sys.Res.scriptLoaderAlreadyLoading);

  this._loading = true;
  this._allScriptsLoadedCallback = allScriptsLoadedCallback;
  this._scriptLoadFailedCallback = scriptLoadFailedCallback;
  this._scriptLoadTimeoutCallback = scriptLoadTimeoutCallback;

  this._loadScriptsInternal();
}
```

_loadScriptsInternal

Listing 24-17 presents the internal implementation of the _loadScriptsInternal method of the current _ScriptLoader instance. Recall that the _scriptsToLoad array of the current _ScriptLoader instance contains one object for each script that needs to be loaded. This object contains the complete information about its associated script.

Note that the _loadScriptsInternal method is a recursive function, meaning that the method calls itself to load the script described by the next object in the _scriptsToLoad array. This method checks whether the _scriptsToLoad collection contains any more objects. If not, it first calls the _stopLoading method on the current _ScriptLoader instance to end the script-loading process and then calls the _allScriptsLoadedCallback method to notify its caller that all the scripts have been loaded. As discussed earlier, the _allScriptsLoadedCallback field of the current _ScriptLoader instance references the delegate that represents the _scriptsLoadComplete method of the current PageRequestManager instance.

```
var callback = this._allScriptsLoadedCallback;
this._stopLoading();
if(callback)
  callback(this);
```

If the _scriptsToLoad collection contains more objects, the _loadScriptsInternal method calls the dequeue static method on the Array to dequeue the next object from the _scriptsToLoad collection:

```
var nextScript = Array.dequeue(this._scriptsToLoad);
```

Next, it calls the _createScriptElement method on the current _ScriptLoader instance that is passing in the dequeued object. As you'll see later, this method creates an HTML script element and uses the values of the properties of the object to initialize the attributes of this script element.

```
var scriptElement = this._createScriptElement(nextScript);
```

Next, the _loadScriptsInternal method checks whether the object contains a name/value pair associated with the src script attribute. If so, this is an indication that the object describes a script file that must be downloaded from the server. Because of this, we have to worry about issues such as timeout. Therefore, the _loadScriptsInternal method instantiates an instance of an ASP.NET AJAX class named _ScriptLoaderTask, passing a reference to the newly instantiated script element and a reference to the delegate referenced by the _scriptLoadedDelegate field of the current _ScriptLoader instance. As you'll see later, the constructor of the _ScriptLoader class creates a delegate that represents the _scriptLoadedHandler method of the current _ScriptLoader instance and assigns this delegate to the _scriptLoadedDelegate field.

```
this._currentTask = new Sys._ScriptLoaderTask(scriptElement,
                                              this._scriptLoadedDelegate);
```

Next, the _loadScriptsInternal method invokes the execute method on the current ScriptLoaderTask instance to execute the task. The execute method basically downloads the script file referenced by the specified script element:

```
this._currentTask.execute();
```

If the object does not contain a name/value pair associated with the `src` script attribute, this indicates that the object does not describe a script file to be downloaded from the server. Instead it describes a literal script. Therefore the `_loadScriptsInternal` method first accesses the head HTML element:

```
var headElement = document.getElementsByTagName('HEAD')[0];
```

Next, it calls the `appendChild` method on the head HTML element to append the script element as its child element. Appending this script element immediately runs the script enclosed within the opening and closing tags of the script element:

```
headElement.appendChild(scriptElement);
```

Next, the `_loadScriptsInternal` method removes the script element because you do not need the element after running its contained script:

```
scriptElement.parentNode.removeChild(scriptElement);
```

Finally, it calls the `_loadScriptsInternal` method to load the script associated with the next object in the `_scriptsToLoad` collection:

```
this._loadScriptsInternal();
```

Listing 24-17: The _loadScriptsInternal Method of the _ScriptLoader Class

```
function Sys$_ScriptLoader$_loadScriptsInternal()
{
  if (this._scriptsToLoad && this._scriptsToLoad.length > 0)
  {
    var nextScript = Array.dequeue(this._scriptsToLoad);
    var scriptElement = this._createScriptElement(nextScript);

    if (scriptElement.text && Sys.Browser.agent === Sys.Browser.Safari)
    {
      scriptElement.innerHTML = scriptElement.text;
      delete scriptElement.text;
    }
    if (typeof(nextScript.src) === "string")
    {
      this._currentTask = new Sys._ScriptLoaderTask(scriptElement,
                                          this._scriptLoadedDelegate);
      this._currentTask.execute();
    }

    else
    {
      document.getElementsByTagName('HEAD')[0].appendChild(scriptElement);
      Sys._ScriptLoader._clearScript(scriptElement);
      this._loadScriptsInternal();
    }
  }
}
```

```
    else
    {
      var callback = this._allScriptsLoadedCallback;
      this._stopLoading();
      if(callback)
        callback(this);
    }
  }
```

_createScriptElement

Listing 24-18 presents the internal implementation of the _createScriptElement method of the _ScriptLoader class. This method takes a single object that describes the standard and custom HTML attributes of the HTML script element being created. As you can see, this method first calls the createElement method on the document object to create the script HTML element:

```
var scriptElement = document.createElement('SCRIPT');
```

Next, it sets the type attribute of the script HTML element to a default value. Note that the object may contain a name/value pair for the type HTML attribute, which means that this default value may be overridden:

```
scriptElement.type = 'text/javascript';
```

Finally, it iterates through the name/value pairs of the object, uses the name part of each as an index into the object to return the value part of the pair, and finally uses the name part of each as an index into the newly instantiated script element to store the value part of the pair.

```
for (var attr in queuedScript)
{
  scriptElement[attr] = queuedScript[attr];
}
```

Listing 24-18: The _createScriptElement Method of the _ScriptLoader Class

```
function Sys$_ScriptLoader$_createScriptElement(queuedScript)
{
  var scriptElement = document.createElement('SCRIPT');
  scriptElement.type = 'text/javascript';
  for (var attr in queuedScript)
  {
    scriptElement[attr] = queuedScript[attr];
  }

  return scriptElement;
}
```

The Constructor of the _ScriptLoader Class

As Listing 24-19 shows, the constructor of the _ScriptLoader class sets the _scriptsToLoad collection to null, creates a delegate the represents the _scriptLoadedHandler method of the current _ScriptLoader instance, and stores this delegate in a field named _scriptLoadedDelegate.

Listing 24-19: The Constructor of the _ScriptLoader Class

```
Sys._ScriptLoader = function Sys$_ScriptLoader()
{
    this._scriptsToLoad = null;
    this._scriptLoadedDelegate =
                    Function.createDelegate(this, this._scriptLoadedHandler);
}
```

_scriptLoaderHandler

Listing 24-20 presents the internal implementation of the _scriptLoadedHandler method of the _ScriptLoader class. As discussed earlier, the current ScriptLoaderTask instance calls this method when it is finished loading the specified script in the _scriptsToLoad collection. As you can see, this method calls the _getLoadedScripts static method on the _ScriptLoader class to return a reference to the _referencedScripts static collection of the class. (Recall that this collection stores the URLs of all the loaded script files.) The _scriptLoadedHandler method adds the URL of the newly loaded script file into this collection:

```
Array.add(Sys._ScriptLoader._getLoadedScripts(), scriptElement.src);
```

Next, it calls the dispose method on the current ScriptLoaderTask instance to allow the instance to release the resources it is holding before the instance is disposed of:

```
this._currentTask.dispose();
```

Next, the _scriptLoadedHandler method calls the _loadScriptsInternal method to load the script described by the next object in the _scriptsToLoad collection. As you can see, the scripts described by the objects in the _scriptsToLoad collection are loaded one at a time; in other words, the loading of the next script does not start until the previous script is completely loaded.

Listing 24-20: The _scriptLoadedHandler Method of the _ScriptLoader Class

```
function Sys$_ScriptLoader$_scriptLoadedHandler(scriptElement, loaded)
{
    if(loaded && this._currentTask._notified)
    {
        if(this._currentTask._notified > 1)
            this._raiseError(true);
```

```
    else
    {
        Array.add(Sys._ScriptLoader._getLoadedScripts(), scriptElement.src);
        this._currentTask.dispose();
        this._currentTask = null;
        this._loadScriptsInternal();
    }
  }
  else
    this._raiseError(false);
}
```

_ScriptLoaderTask

In this section I'll discuss the methods of the ASP.NET AJAX _ScriptLoaderTask class.

The Constructor of the_ScriptLoaderTask Class

As Listing 24-21 shows, this constructor takes two parameters. The first references a script HTML element, and the second references the JavaScript function that will be automatically called when the specified script is downloaded for the server. Recall from Listing 24-17 that the _loadScriptsInternal method of the current _ScriptLoader instance passes the _scriptLoadedDelegate field of the current _ScriptLoader instance as the second parameter into the constructor of the _ScriptLoaderTask:

```
this._currentTask = new Sys._ScriptLoaderTask(scriptElement,
                                    this._scriptLoadedDelegate);
```

Recall from Listing 24-19 that the _scriptLoadedDelegate field references the delegate that represents the _scriptLoadedHandler method of the current _ScriptLoader instance:

```
this._scriptLoadedDelegate =
                    Function.createDelegate(this, this._scriptLoadedHandler);
```

Listing 24-21: The Constructor Method of the _ScriptLoaderTask Class

```
Sys._ScriptLoaderTask =
function Sys$_ScriptLoaderTask(scriptElement, completedCallback)
{
    this._scriptElement = scriptElement;
    this._completedCallback = completedCallback;
    this._notified = 0;
}
```

execute

Listing 24-22 presents the internal implementation of the execute method of the current _ScriptLoaderTask instance. As you can see, this method first creates a delegate the represents the _scriptLoadHandler method of the current _ScriptLoaderTask instance, and stores this delegate in a local variable named scriptLoadDelegate:

```
var scriptLoadDelegate = Function.createDelegate(this, this._scriptLoadHandler);
```

Next, if the current browser is Internet Explorer, it invokes the $addHandler global JavaScript function to register the delegate as an event handler for the script HTML element that the _scriptElement references:

```
$addHandler(this._scriptElement, 'load', scriptLoadDelegate);
```

Internet Explorer will automatically call this delegate, and consequently the _scriptLoadHandler method that the delegate represents, when the script associated with the specified script HTML element is downloaded from the server.

If the current browser is not Internet Explorer, the execute method invokes the $addHandler global JavaScript function to register the delegate as an event handler for the readystatechange event of the script HTML element referenced by the _scriptElement field:

```
$addHandler(this._scriptElement, 'readystatechange', scriptLoadDelegate);
```

The browser will automatically call this delegate, and consequently the _scriptLoadHandler method that the delegate represents, when the script associated with the specified script HTML element is downloaded from the server.

Next, the execute method calls the getElementByTagName method on the current document object to return a reference to the head HTML element:

```
var headElement = document.getElementsByTagName('HEAD')[0];
```

Finally, it calls the appendChild method on the head HTML element to append the script HTML element referenced by the _scriptElement field as the child element of the head HTML element. As soon as this script HTML element is added to the DOM hierarchy of the current document, the browser automatically downloads the JavaScript file whose URL is specified by the src attribute of the newly added script HTML element, and calls the previously mentioned delegates after the download is completed.

Listing 24-22: The Execute Method of the _ScriptLoaderTask Class

```
function Sys$_ScriptLoaderTask$execute()
{
  var scriptLoadDelegate = Function.createDelegate(this, this._scriptLoadHandler);

  if (Sys.Browser.agent !== Sys.Browser.InternetExplorer)
  {
    this._scriptElement.readyState = 'loaded';
    $addHandler(this._scriptElement, 'load', scriptLoadDelegate);
  }
```

```
    else
      $addHandler(this._scriptElement, 'readystatechange', scriptLoadDelegate);
    var headElement = document.getElementsByTagName('HEAD')[0];
    headElement.appendChild(this._scriptElement);
}
```

_scriptLoadHandler

As you saw from Listing 24-22, the execute method of the current _ScriptLoader instance registers a delegate that represents the _scriptLoadHandler method of the current _ScriptLoaderTask instance as an event handler for the load or readystatechange event of the script HTML element referenced by the _scriptElement field of the current _ScriptLoaderTask instance.

Listing 24-23 presents the internal implementation of the _scriptLoadhandler method. As you can see, this method simply calls the JavaScript function referenced by the _completedCallback field of the current _ScriptLoaderTask instance.

Listing 24-23: The _scriptLoadHandler Method of the _ScriptLoaderTask Class

```
function Sys$_ScriptLoaderTask$_scriptLoadHandler()
{
  if(this._disposed)
    return;
  var scriptElement = this.get_scriptElement();
  if ((scriptElement.readyState !== 'loaded') &&
      (scriptElement.readyState !== 'complete'))
    return;

  window.setTimeout(
          function() {this._completedCallback(this._scriptElement, true);}, 0);
}
```

_scriptsLoadComplete

Recall from Listing 24-23 that the current _ScriptLoaderTask instance invokes the _completedCallback delegate after loading all the scripts. Also recall that this delegate represents the _scriptsLoadComplete method of the current PageRequestMananger instance. Listing 24-24 presents the internal implementation of the _scriptsLoadComplete method. This method first calls the scrollTo method on the window object to set the scroll position:

```
window.scrollTo(this._scrollPosition.x, this._scrollPosition.y);
```

Next, this method invokes the _pageLoaded method on the current PageRequestManager instance to raise the pageLoaded event:

```
    this._pageLoaded(false);
```

Then it calls the _endPostBack method to end the current postback:

```
this._endPostBack(null, this._response);
```

Finally, the _scriptsLoadComplete method calls the WebForm_AutoFocus global JavaScript function to set the focus to the specified element:

```
WebForm_AutoFocus(this._controlIDToFocus);
```

Listing 24-24: The _scriptsLoadComplete Method of the Current PageRequestMananger

```
function Sys$WebForms$PageRequestManager$_scriptsLoadComplete()
{
  if (window.__theFormPostData)
    window.__theFormPostData = "";

  if (window.__theFormPostCollection)
    window.__theFormPostCollection = [];

  if (window.WebForm_InitCallback)
    window.WebForm_InitCallback();
  if (this._scrollPosition)
  {
    if (window.scrollTo)
      window.scrollTo(this._scrollPosition.x, this._scrollPosition.y);

    this._scrollPosition = null;
  }
  Sys.Application.endCreateComponents();
  this._pageLoaded(false);
  this._endPostBack(null, this._response);
  this._response = null;
  if (this._controlIDToFocus)
  {
    var focusTarget;
    var oldContentEditableSetting;
    if (Sys.Browser.agent === Sys.Browser.InternetExplorer)
    {
      var targetControl = $get(this._controlIDToFocus);
      var focusTarget = targetControl;
      if (targetControl && (!WebForm_CanFocus(targetControl)))
        focusTarget = WebForm_FindFirstFocusableChild(targetControl);

      if (focusTarget && (typeof(focusTarget.contentEditable) !== "undefined"))
      {
        oldContentEditableSetting = focusTarget.contentEditable;
        focusTarget.contentEditable = false;
      }
    }
```

```
      else
        focusTarget = null;
    }
    WebForm_AutoFocus(this._controlIDToFocus);
    if (focusTarget)
    {
        focusTarget.contentEditable = oldContentEditableSetting;
    }
    this._controlIDToFocus = null;
  }
}
```

_pageLoaded

As Listing 24-24 shows, the _scriptsLoadComplete method of the current PageRequestManager instance invokes the _pageLoaded method on the current PageRequestManager instance. Listing 24-25 presents the internal implementation of the _pageLoaded method. As you can see, this method first calls the _get_eventHandlerList method on the current PageRequestManager instance to return a reference to the EventHandlerList object that contains all the event handlers registered for the events of the current PageRequestManager instance. Then it calls the getHandler method on the EventHandlerList to return a reference to a JavaScript function whose invocation automatically invokes all the event handlers registered for the pageLoaded event of the current PageRequestManager instance:

```
var handler = this._get_eventHandlerList().getHandler("pageLoaded");
```

Next, the _scriptsLoadComplete method calls the _getPageLoadedEventArgs method to create and to return the PageLoadedEventArgs object that contains the event data for the current pageLoaded event:

```
var args = this._getPageLoadedEventArgs(initialLoad);
```

Next, it calls the previously mentioned JavaScript function, passing the reference to the current PageRequestManager instance and the preceding PageLoadedEventArgs object. This JavaScript function in turn calls all the event handlers registered for the pageLoaded event of the current PageRequestManager instance, passing the reference to the current PageRequestManager instance and the preceding PageLoadedEventArgs object:

```
handler(this, args);
```

Note that the _pageLoaded method takes a Boolean parameter named initialLoad. As the name suggests, this parameter specifies whether the _pageLoaded method is being called during the initialization phase of the current PageRequestManager instance. In other words, the _pageLoaded method is invoked in two different life cycle phases of the current PageRequestManager instance:

❑ During the instantiation/initialization phase (see Figure 22-5). Recall from Listing 22-6 that the current PageRequestManager instance invokes the _pageLoaded method, passing in true as its argument during its initialization phase when the current PageRequestManager instance is being loaded for the first time.

❏ When the server response for an asynchronous page postback is processed and consequently the page is reloaded. Recall from Listing 24-24 that the _scriptsLoadComplete method invokes the _pageLoaded method, passing in false as its argument.

As Listing 24-25 shows, if the _pageLoaded method is invoked with false as its argument, the method invokes the raiseLoad method on the Application object that represents the current ASP.NET AJAX application. The raiseLoad method was thoroughly discussed in Chapter 7 (see Listing 7-28).

Listing 24-25: The _pageLoaded Method of the Current PageRequestManager Instance

```
function Sys$WebForms$PageRequestManager$_pageLoaded(initialLoad)
{
  var handler = this._get_eventHandlerList().getHandler("pageLoaded");
  if (handler)
  {
    var args = this._getPageLoadedEventArgs(initialLoad);
    handler(this, args);
  }

  if (!initialLoad)
    Sys.Application.raiseLoad();
}
```

_endPostBack

Listing 24-26 presents a portion of Listing 24-5. Recall that Listing 24-5 presents the internal implementation of the _onFormSubmitCompleted method of the current PageRequestManager instance. As the highlighted portions of Listing 24-26 show, the current PageRequestManager instance may invoke its _endPostBack method for a number of reasons:

❏ The current request has timed out:

```
if (sender.get_timedOut())
{
  this._endPostBack(this._createPageRequestManagerTimeoutError(), sender);
  return;
}
```

❏ The current request has aborted:

```
if (sender.get_aborted())
{
  this._endPostBack(null, sender);
  return;
}
```

❏ The status code of the server response is a number other than 200:

```
if (sender.get_statusCode() !== 200)
{
  this._endPostBack(
     this._createPageRequestManagerServerError(sender.get_statusCode()), sender);
  return;
}
```

❑ The server response text is not in the expected format and has some problems:

```
if (parserErrorDetails)
{
  this._endPostBack(this._createPageRequestManagerParserError(
                 String.format(Sys.WebForms.Res.PRM_ParserErrorDetails,
                              parserErrorDetails)), sender);
  return;
}
```

❑ The type part of a substring in the server response text is the string `"error"`. Recall that the server response text consists of a bunch of substrings in the format `length|type|id|content`, where the `type` part of the substring specifies the type of information that the `content` part contains. The server-side `PageRequestManager` instance sets the `type` part of a substring to the string `"error"` to signal the current client-side `PageRequestManager` instance that the `id` part of the substring contains the error code and the `content` part contains an error message:

```
case "error":
   this._endPostBack(this._createPageRequestManagerServerError(
          Number.parseInvariant(deltaNode.id), deltaNode.content), sender);
   return;
```

❑ The `type` part of a substring in the server response text is a string that the current client-side `PageRequestManager` instance does not recognize:

```
default:
   this._endPostBack(this._createPageRequestManagerParserError(
   String.format(Sys.WebForms.Res.PRM_UnknownToken, deltaNode.type)), sender);
   return;
```

❑ The `_panelsToRefreshIDs` collection that the current client-side `PageRequestManager` instance has received from the server-side `PageRequestManager` instance contains the `UniqueID` property value of an `UpdatePanel` server control that does not exist on the current page. Recall that the `_panelsToRefreshIDs` collection contains the list of the `UniqueID` property values of all `UpdatePanel` server controls that need refreshing.

```
for (i = 0; i < this._panelsToRefreshIDs.length; i++)
{
  var panelClientID = this._uniqueIDToClientID(this._panelsToRefreshIDs[i]);
  if (!document.getElementById(panelClientID))
  {
    this._endPostBack(Error.invalidOperation(
    String.format(Sys.WebForms.Res.PRM_MissingPanel, panelClientID)), sender);
    return;
  }
}
```

Recall that the server response text contains one or more substrings with the type value of updatePanel, to signal the current client-side PageRequestManager instance that the id part of the specified substring contains the ClientID property value of an UpdatePanel server control, and that the content part of the substring contains the HTML markup text that makes up the content of the UpdatePanel server control.

Also recall that the _onFormSubmitCallback method parses these substrings into a local array named updatePanelNodes, which contains one object for each substring: the value of the id property of the object is a string that contains the id part of the associated substring, and the value of the content part of the object is a string that contains the content part of the associated substring.

The id part of a substring (or the value of the id property of the associated object in the updatePanelNodes collection) contains the ClientID property value of an UpdatePanel server control that does not exist on the current page:

```
for (i = 0; i < updatePanelNodes.length; i++)
{
  var deltaUpdatePanel = updatePanelNodes[i];
  var deltaPanelID = deltaUpdatePanel.id;
  var deltaPanelRendering = deltaUpdatePanel.content;
  var updatePanelElement = document.getElementById(deltaPanelID);
  if (!updatePanelElement)
  {
    this._endPostBack(Error.invalidOperation(
        String.format(Sys.WebForms.Res.PRM_MissingPanel, deltaPanelID)), sender);
    return;
  }
  this._updatePanel(updatePanelElement, deltaPanelRendering);
}
```

As the last highlighted portion of Listing 24-26 shows, the _onFormSubmitCompleted method registers the _scriptsLoadComplete method with the current _ScriptLoader instance. As discussed earlier, this instance invokes this method when it is done with downloading all scripts:

```
scriptLoader.loadScripts(0,
        Function.createDelegate(this, this._scriptsLoadComplete), null, null);
```

❏ Recall from Listing 24-24 that the _scriptsLoadComplete method calls the _endPostBack method after calling the _pageLoaded method, as shown again in the following code fragment:

```
this._pageLoaded(false);
this._endPostBack(null, this._response);
this._response = null;
```

Listing 24-26: The _onFormSubmitCompleted Method of the PageRequestManager Instance

```
function Sys$WebForms$PageRequestManager$_onFormSubmitCompleted(sender, eventArgs)
{
  this._processingRequest = true;
  var delimitByLengthDelimiter = '|';

  if (sender.get_timedOut())
  {
    this._endPostBack(this._createPageRequestManagerTimeoutError(), sender);
    return;
  }
  if (sender.get_aborted())
  {
    this._endPostBack(null, sender);
    return;
  }

  if (!this._request || sender.get_webRequest() !== this._request)
    return;
  var errorMessage;
  var delta = [];

  if (sender.get_statusCode() !== 200)
  {
    this._endPostBack(
        this._createPageRequestManagerServerError(sender.get_statusCode()), sender);
    return;
  }

  var reply = sender.get_responseData();
  . . .

  if (parserErrorDetails)
  {
    this._endPostBack(this._createPageRequestManagerParserError(
                   String.format(Sys.WebForms.Res.PRM_ParserErrorDetails,
                                 parserErrorDetails)), sender);
    return;
  }

  . . .
  for (var i = 0; i < delta.length; i++)
  {
    var deltaNode = delta[i];
    switch (deltaNode.type)
    {
      case "updatePanel":
        Array.add(updatePanelNodes, deltaNode);
        break;
      case "hiddenField":
        Array.add(hiddenFieldNodes, deltaNode);
        break;
      . . .
```

(continued)

Listing 24-26 *(continued)*

```
      case "error":
        this._endPostBack(this._createPageRequestManagerServerError(
              Number.parseInvariant(deltaNode.id), deltaNode.content), sender);
        return;

      case "pageTitle":
        document.title = deltaNode.content;
        break;
      case "focus":
        this._controlIDToFocus = deltaNode.content;
        break;

      default:
        this._endPostBack(this._createPageRequestManagerParserError(
        String.format(Sys.WebForms.Res.PRM_UnknownToken, deltaNode.type)), sender);
        return;
    }
  }
  var i;
  if (asyncPostBackControlIDsNode && postBackControlIDsNode &&
      updatePanelIDsNode && panelsToRefreshNode &&
      asyncPostBackTimeoutNode && childUpdatePanelIDsNode)
  {
    . . .

    for (i = 0; i < this._panelsToRefreshIDs.length; i++)
    {
      var panelClientID = this._uniqueIDToClientID(this._panelsToRefreshIDs[i]);
      if (!document.getElementById(panelClientID))
      {
        this._endPostBack(Error.invalidOperation(
        String.format(Sys.WebForms.Res.PRM_MissingPanel, panelClientID)), sender);
        return;
      }
    }

    var asyncPostBackTimeout = asyncPostBackTimeoutNode.content;
    this._updateControls(updatePanelIDsArray, asyncPostBackControlIDsArray,
                      postBackControlIDsArray, asyncPostBackTimeout);
  }
  . . .

  for (i = 0; i < updatePanelNodes.length; i++)
  {
    var deltaUpdatePanel = updatePanelNodes[i];
    var deltaPanelID = deltaUpdatePanel.id;
    var deltaPanelRendering = deltaUpdatePanel.content;
    var updatePanelElement = document.getElementById(deltaPanelID);
```

```
    if (!updatePanelElement)
    {
      this._endPostBack(Error.invalidOperation(
          String.format(Sys.WebForms.Res.PRM_MissingPanel, deltaPanelID)), sender);
      return;
    }
    this._updatePanel(updatePanelElement, deltaPanelRendering);
}

    . . .

    scriptLoader.loadScripts(0,
            Function.createDelegate(this, this._scriptsLoadComplete), null, null);
}
```

As you can see from these discussions, the _endPostBack method of the current PageRequestManager instance can be invoked for a number of reasons. Listing 24-27 presents the internal implementation of this method. It first sets an internal flag named _processingRequest to false to signal that it is done with processing the request:

```
this._processingRequest = false;
```

Then it sets the _request field of the current PageRequestManager instance to null so the same WebRequest object is not used to make the next asynchronous page postback requests to the server:

```
this._request = null;
```

Next, it calls the get_eventHandlerList method on the current PageRequestManager instance to return a reference to the EventHandlerList object that contains the list of event handlers registered for the events of the current PageRequestManager instance. Then it invokes the getHandler method on this EventHandlerList object to return a reference to the JavaScript function whose invocation automatically invokes all the event handlers registered for the endRequest event of the current PageRequestManager instance:

```
var handler = this._get_eventHandlerList().getHandler("endRequest");
```

Then the _endPostBack method instantiates an EndRequestEventArgs object, passing in three parameters: the first references the error object, the second the _dataItems collection of the current PageRequestManager instance (recall that the current PageRequestManager instance maintains all data items in this collection), and the last the WebRequestExecutor object responsible for executing the current request. As you'll see later, the EndRequestEventArgs is the event data class associated with the endRequest event.

```
var eventArgs =
        new Sys.WebForms.EndRequestEventArgs(error, this._dataItems, response);
```

Finally, the _endPostBack method invokes the previously mentioned JavaScript function and consequently all the event handlers registered for the endRequest event of the current PageRequestManager instance. Note that the _endPostBack method passes two parameters into each event handler: the first references the current `PageRequestManager` instance and the second references the preceding `EndRequestEventArgs` object:

```
handler(this, eventArgs);
```

If you register an event handler for the `endRequest` *event of the current* `PageRequestManager` *instance, your event handler will receive these two parameters. Your handler can then use them to retrieve all the required information about the current response and* `PageRequestManager` *instance and use that information to perform any necessary application-specific tasks that must be done when a request ends.*

Finally, the `_endPostBack` method calls the `get_errorHandled` method on the `EndRequestEventArgs` instance to return a Boolean value that specifies whether any of the event handlers has indeed handled the error (if any):

```
errorHandled = eventArgs.get_errorHandled();
```

As you'll see later, the `EndRequestEventArgs` *event data class exposes a Boolean property named* `errorHandled`. *Your event handler can call the* `set_errorHandled` *method on the* `EndRequestEventArgs` *object to set the value of this property to* `true` *to signal the current* `PageRequestManager` *instance that the specified error has already been handled. This enables you to use a custom error-handling technique to handle the error, bypassing the standard ASP.NET AJAX error-handling logic. As you'll see shortly, this standard logic simply displays a popup that contains the error message.*

If none of the event handlers has processed the error, the `_endPostBack` method simply calls the `alert` method to display the error message to the end user:

```
if (error && !errorHandled)
  alert(error.message);
```

Listing 24-27: The _endPostBack Method of the Current PageRequestManager Instance

```
function Sys$WebForms$PageRequestManager$_endPostBack(error, response)
{
  this._processingRequest = false;
  this._request = null;
  this._additionalInput = null;
  var handler = this._get_eventHandlerList().getHandler("endRequest");
  var errorHandled = false;
  if (handler)
  {
    var eventArgs =
            new Sys.WebForms.EndRequestEventArgs(error, this._dataItems, response);
    handler(this, eventArgs);
    errorHandled = eventArgs.get_errorHandled();
  }

  this._dataItems = null;
  if (error && !errorHandled)
    alert(error.message);
}
```

pageLoading

Recall from Figure 24-1 that the current client-side `PageRequestManager` instance fires its `pageLoading` event right before it calls the `_updatePanel` method once for each `UpdatePanel` control that needs updating. This enables you to run application-specific code that must be run before the `UpdatePanel` controls on the current page are updated.

The client-side `PageRequestManager` class uses the standard ASP.NET AJAX event-implementation pattern to implement its `pageLoading` event, as follows:

1. It defines a method named `add_pageLoading` that enables you to register event handlers for the `pageLoading` event of the current client-side `PageRequestManager` instance. As the following code fragment shows, this method first calls the `get_eventHandlerList` method on the current `PageRequestManager` instance, to return a reference to the `EventHandlerList` object that contains all the event handlers registered for the events of the current `PageRequestManager` instance. Then it calls the `addHandler` method on this `EventHandlerList` object to register the specified handler as an event handler for the `pageLoading` event of the current `PageRequestManager` instance:

```
function Sys$WebForms$PageRequestManager$add_pageLoading(handler)
{
    this._get_eventHandlerList().addHandler("pageLoading", handler);
}
```

2. It defines a method named `remove_ pageLoading` that enables you to unregister an event handler registered for the `pageLoading` event of the instance:

```
function Sys$WebForms$PageRequestManager$remove_pageLoading(handler)
{
    this._get_eventHandlerList().removeHandler("pageLoading", handler);
}
```

The `pageLoading` event, like any other, is associated with an event data class whose instance acts as a container for the associated event data. The event data class associated with the `pageLoading` event is an ASP.NET AJAX client class named `PageLoadingEventArgs`. Listing 24-28 presents the internal implementation of the `PageLoadingEventArgs` class.

Listing 24-28: The Internal Implementation of the PageLoadingEventArgs Class

```
Sys.WebForms.PageLoadingEventArgs =
function Sys$WebForms$PageLoadingEventArgs(panelsUpdating, panelsDeleting,
                                           dataItems)
{
    Sys.WebForms.PageLoadingEventArgs.initializeBase(this);
    this._panelsUpdating = panelsUpdating;
    this._panelsDeleting = panelsDeleting;
    this._dataItems = dataItems || new Object();
}
```

(continued)

Listing 24-28 *(continued)*

```
function Sys$WebForms$PageLoadingEventArgs$get_dataItems()
{
  return this._dataItems;
}
function Sys$WebForms$PageLoadingEventArgs$get_panelsDeleting()
{
  return this._panelsDeleting;
}
function Sys$WebForms$PageLoadingEventArgs$get_panelsUpdating()
{
  return this._panelsUpdating;
}

Sys.WebForms.PageLoadingEventArgs.prototype =
{
  get_dataItems: Sys$WebForms$PageLoadingEventArgs$get_dataItems,
  get_panelsDeleting: Sys$WebForms$PageLoadingEventArgs$get_panelsDeleting,
  get_panelsUpdating: Sys$WebForms$PageLoadingEventArgs$get_panelsUpdating
}
Sys.WebForms.PageLoadingEventArgs.registerClass(
                    'Sys.WebForms.PageLoadingEventArgs', Sys.EventArgs);
```

As you can see, the constructor of the `PageLoadingEventArgs` class takes three parameters. The first is an array that contains the list of `UpdatePanel` server controls on the current page *to be* updated. Note the emphasis on *to be*. As I mentioned earlier, the current `PageRequestManager` instance first raises the `pageLoading` event before it invokes the `_updatePanel` method, once for each updating `UpdatePanel` control, to update the `UpdatePanel` controls on the current page. In other words, when the `pageLoading` event is raised, the `UpdatePanel` controls that need updating haven't been updated yet.

The second parameter is an array that contains the list of the `UpdatePanel` server controls on the current page *to be* deleted. Again, notice the emphasis on *to be*. In other words, when the `pageLoading` event is raised, the `UpdatePanel` controls that must be deleted haven't been deleted yet.

The last parameter, which is optional, returns an object that contains one name/value pair for each data item. Recall that the current client-side `PageRequestManager` instance stores all data items in an internal collection named `_dataItems`. This optional parameter basically returns a reference to this collection.

As you can see from Listing 24-28, the constructor of the `PageLoadingEventArgs` class stores its parameters in private fields named `_panelsUpdating`, `_panelsDeleting`, and `_dataItems`. Note that the `PageLoadingEventArgs` class exposes three getters named `get_panelsUpdating`, `get_panelsDeleting`, and `get_dataItems`, which return these private fields.

Next, I'll examine what is and is not in effect or available when the current `PageRequestManager` instance raises its `pageLoading` event:

❏ As you can see from the following portion of Listing 24-5, the title of the current document has already taken effect. Note that even though the _controlIDToFocus field of the current PageRequestManager instance has already been set to the ClientID property value of the server control to receive the focus, the focus has not yet been given to this server control. Therefore the older server control, whatever it is, is still holding the focus at this point.

```
for (var i = 0; i < delta.length; i++)
{
  var deltaNode = delta[i];
  switch (deltaNode.type)
  {
    . . .
    case "pageTitle":
      document.title = deltaNode.content;
      break;
    case "focus":
      this._controlIDToFocus = deltaNode.content;
      break;
    . . .
  }
}
```

❏ As you can see from the following portion of Listing 24-5, the current PageRequestManager instance has already made sure that the current page contains all the UpdatePanel server controls to be refreshed. In other words, your code can safely program against these UpdatePanel server controls:

```
for (i = 0; i < this._panelsToRefreshIDs.length; i++)
{
  var panelClientID = this._uniqueIDToClientID(this._panelsToRefreshIDs[i]);
  if (!document.getElementById(panelClientID))
  {
    this._endPostBack(Error.invalidOperation(
      String.format(Sys.WebForms.Res.PRM_MissingPanel, panelClientID)), sender);
    return;
  }
}
```

❏ As you can see from the following portion of Listing 24-5, the current PageRequestManager instance has already invoked the _updateControls method:

```
this._updateControls(updatePanelIDsArray, asyncPostBackControlIDsArray,
                     postBackControlIDsArray, asyncPostBackTimeout);
```

❏ Listing 24-29 presents the internal implementation of _updateControls. As discussed in Chapter 22, this method populates the following collections of the current PageRequestManager instance:

   ❏ _updatePanelIDs: This collection contains the UniqueID property values of all UpdatePanel server controls on the current page *after* processing of the current asynchronous page postback request on the server side and *before* processing of the server response to this request. This means that when the current PageRequestManager instance

1233

fires its pageLoading event, the current document has not yet been updated with the contents of the _updatePanelsIDs collection. Therefore, if your event handler for the pageLoading event attempts to access the UpdatePanel controls in the current document, it will receive references to the old UpdatePanel controls, which may or may not be there after the current PageRequestManager instance updates the current document with the contents of the _updatePanelIDs.

In other words, the current document may contain UpdatePanel controls whose UniqueID property values are not included in the _updatePanelIDs collection, which means that these UpdatePanel controls have been deleted during processing of the current asynchronous page postback on the server side. Or the _updatePanelIDs collection may contain UniqueID property values associated with UpdatePanel server controls that do not exist in the current document, which means that these UpdatePanel server controls have been added during processing of the current asynchronous page postback on the server side.

❑ _updatePanelClientIDs: This collection is the same as the _updatePanelIDs collection, with one difference: it contains the ClientID property values of all the UpdatePanel server controls on the current page instead of their UniqueID property values. Therefore, all the same discussions apply equally to the _updatePanelClientIDs collection.

❑ _updatePanelHasChildrenAsTriggers: This collection contains one Boolean value for each UpdatePanel server control in the _updatePanelIDs collection, which specifies whether the ChildrenAsTriggers property of the UpdatePanel server control is set to true. Again, keep in mind that when the current PageRequestManager instance fires its pageLoading event, the UpdatePanel controls on the current document have not yet been updated with the contents of the _updatePanelHasChildrenAsTriggers collection.

❑ _asyncPostBackControlIDs: This collection is the same as the _syncPostBackControlIDs collection, with one main difference: this one contains the UniqueID property values of all the asynchronous page postback controls on the current page *after* processing of the current asynchronous page postback request on the server side but *before* processing of the server response to this request on the client side. Therefore, all the same discussions presented earlier about the _syncPostBackControlIDs equally apply to the _asyncPostBackControlIDs collection.

❑ _asyncPostBackControlClientIDs: This collection is much like the _asyncPostBackControlIDs collection. The only difference is that this one contains the ClientID property values of all the asynchronous postback server controls on the current page instead of their UniqueID property values.

❑ _postBackControlIDs: This collection is much like syncPostBackControlIDs. The main difference is that this one contains the UniqueID property values of all the synchronous page postback controls on the current page *after* processing of the current asynchronous page postback request on the server side but *before* processing of the server response to this request on the client side.

❑ _postBackControlClientIDs: This collection is the same as _postBackControlIDs collection, with one difference: it contains the ClientID property values of all the synchronous postback server controls on the current page instead of their UniqueID property values.

❑ As you can see from the following portion of Listing 24-5, the current `PageRequestManager` instance has populated the `_dataItems` collection. Recall that this collection contains all data items after processing of the current asynchronous page postback request on the server side and before processing of the server response to this request on the client side.

This means that when the current `PageRequestManager` instance fires its `pageLoading` event, the current document has not yet been updated with the contents of the `_dataItems` collection. Therefore, if your event handler for the `pageLoading` event attempts to access the data items associated with the existing controls in the current document, it will receive references to the old data items.

```
this._dataItems = {};
for (i = 0; i < dataItemNodes.length; i++)
{
  var dataItemNode = dataItemNodes[i];
  this._dataItems[dataItemNode.id] = dataItemNode.content;
}

for (i = 0; i < dataItemJsonNodes.length; i++)
{
  var dataItemJsonNode = dataItemJsonNodes[i];
  this._dataItems[dataItemJsonNode.id] = eval(dataItemJsonNode.content);
}
```

❑ As you can see from Listing 24-5, when the current `PageRequestManager` instance raises the `pageLoading` event:

   ❑ The `action` property of the form element of the current document has not yet been updated. This means two things: first, if the value of this property has been changed during processing of the current asynchronous page postback, your event handler for the `pageLoading` event will receive the old value of this property if it attempts to access the value of this property from the current document. Second, if some part of the logic of your application depends on the value of this property, and if you need to run some application-specific code before the value of this property changes, your event handler for the `pageLoading` event must contain this application-specific code.

   ❑ The `_updatePanel` method has not yet been invoked. This means that the content of none of the `UpdatePanel` server controls on the current page whose `UniqueID` property values are contained in the `_updatePanelsToRefresh` collection has yet been updated.

   ❑ The content of an `UpdatePanel` server control is what goes between the opening and closing tags of the `<ContentTemplate>` child element of the `<UpdatePanel>` tag on an `.aspx` page. Therefore, this content contains a bunch of HTML elements and scripts. If your event handler attempts to access any of these content HTML elements and scripts, it will get the current HTML elements and scripts, which may or may not be there after the current `PageRequestManager` instance is done with processing the server response.

   ❑ None of the scripts contained in the server response to the current asynchronous page postback request has yet been processed, and consequently they cannot be accessed from your event handler for the `pageLoading` event. For example, if the server response contains script blocks that reference new JavaScript files, these files have not been downloaded from the server yet. Or if the server response contains new JavaScript array declarations or form submit statements, they have not yet been added to the current document. Therefore, your event handler for the pageLoading event mustn't attempt to use these scripts.

❑   If the current server response contains new hidden fields, these fields have not been yet added to the current document. Therefore, your event handler for the pageLoading event will not be able to use the DOM API to access these hidden fields from the current document.

❑   If the current server response contains new expando attributes, they have not yet been added to the current document. Therefore, your event handler for the pageLoading event will not be able to use the DOM API to access these attributes from the current document.

Listing 24-29: The _updateControls Method

```
function Sys$WebForms$PageRequestManager$_updateControls(updatePanelIDs,
                                         asyncPostBackControlIDs,
                                         postBackControlIDs,
                                         asyncPostBackTimeout)
{
  if (updatePanelIDs)
  {
    this._updatePanelIDs = new Array(updatePanelIDs.length);
    this._updatePanelClientIDs = new Array(updatePanelIDs.length);
    this._updatePanelHasChildrenAsTriggers = new Array(updatePanelIDs.length);
    for (var i = 0; i < updatePanelIDs.length; i++)
    {
      this._updatePanelHasChildrenAsTriggers[i] =
                              (updatePanelIDs[i].charAt(0) === 't');
      this._updatePanelIDs[i] = updatePanelIDs[i].substr(1);
      this._updatePanelClientIDs[i] =
                        this._uniqueIDToClientID(updatePanelIDs[i].substr(1));
    }
    this._asyncPostBackTimeout = asyncPostBackTimeout * 1000;
  }

  else
  {
    this._updatePanelIDs = [];
    this._updatePanelClientIDs = [];
    this._updatePanelHasChildrenAsTriggers = [];
    this._asyncPostBackTimeout = 0;
  }
  this._asyncPostBackControlIDs = [];
  this._asyncPostBackControlClientIDs = [];
  for (var i = 0; i < asyncPostBackControlIDs.length; i++)
  {
    Array.add(this._asyncPostBackControlIDs, asyncPostBackControlIDs[i]);
    Array.add(this._asyncPostBackControlClientIDs,
            this._uniqueIDToClientID(asyncPostBackControlIDs[i]));
  }
```

```
    this._postBackControlIDs = [];
    this._postBackControlClientIDs = [];
    for (var i = 0; i < postBackControlIDs.length; i++)
    {
      Array.add(this._postBackControlIDs, postBackControlIDs [i]);
      Array.add(this._postBackControlClientIDs,
              this._uniqueIDToClientID(postBackControlIDs [i]));
    }
  }
}
```

As I discussed earlier, when the current `PageRequestManager` instance fires its `pageLoading` event and invokes your event handler, it passes two parameters to your event handler. The first parameter references the current `PageRequestManager` instance. The second references a `PageLoadingEventArgs` object that contains the event data for the current `pageLoading` event. This event data contains three arrays: data items, panels deleting, and panels updating.

What is the significance of these three arrays and what can your event handler do with them? First, let's see the significance of the panels updating array. As you can see from Listing 24-5, and as discussed earlier, after your event handler finally returns, the current `PageRequestManager` instance calls the `_updatePanel` method shown in Listing 24-6 once for each `UpdatePanel` server control in the `_updatePanelsToRefreshIDs` to update the contents of these `UpdatePanel` server controls. As you can see from the highlighted portions of Listing 24-30, which repeats Listing 24-6, updating an `UpdatePanel` server control does the following:

❑ Runs all the dispose scripts associated with the `UpdatePanel` server control. If your application logic depends on resources released by these dispose scripts, your event handler for the `pageLoading` event must take the necessary steps before these resources are released:

```
    var disposeScripts = this._scriptDisposes[updatePanelID];
    for (var i = 0; i < disposeScripts.length; i++)
    {
      eval(disposeScripts[i]);
    }
```

❑ Deletes all the dispose scripts associated with the `UpdatePanel` server control:

```
    delete this._scriptDisposes[updatePanelID];
```

❑ Invokes the `_destroyTree` method:

```
  this._destroyTree(updatePanelElement);
```

❑ The `_destroyTree` method recursively takes these steps for each element in the DOM descendant hierarchy of the `UpdatePanel` server control, as shown in the highlighted portions of Listing 24-31, which repeats Listing 24-8:

❑ Invokes the `dispose` method on client controls associated with the DOM element. If your application logic depends on these client controls, your event handler for the `pageLoading` event must take the necessary steps before these controls are disposed of:

```
    node.control.dispose();
```

❑ Invokes the dispose method on all behaviors associated with the DOM element. If your application logic depends on these behaviors, your event handler for the pageLoading event must take the necessary steps before these behaviors are disposed of:

```
var behaviors = Sys.UI.Behavior.getBehaviors(node);
for (var j = behaviors.length - 1; j >= 0; j--)
{
  behaviors[j].dispose();
}
```

❑ Invokes the _destroyTree method, passing in the DOM element. This method in turn repeats the same steps — that is, it recursively invokes the dispose method on client controls and behaviors associated with each element in the DOM descendant hierarchy of the element. If your application logic depends on these client controls and behaviors, your event handler for the pageLoading event must take the necessary steps before these controls and behaviors are disposed of:

```
this._destroyTree(node);
```

❑ Assigns the string that contains the new content to the innerHTML property of the UpdatePanel control. This wipes out all the old content, including the child server controls, and replaces them with the new content. If your application logic depends on any of the DOM elements enclosed within the UpdatePanel server control, your event handler for the pageLoading event must take the necessary steps before these DOM elements are wiped out and replaced.

Listing 24-30: The _updatePanel Method

```
function Sys$WebForms$PageRequestManager$_updatePanel(updatePanelElement,
                                                      htmlMarkup)
{
  for (var updatePanelID in this._scriptDisposes)
  {
    var runDisposeScripts = false;
    var element = document.getElementById(updatePanelID);
    while (element)
    {
      if (element === updatePanelElement)
      {
        runDisposeScripts = true;
        break;
      }
      element = element.parentNode;
    }
```

```
    if (runDisposeScripts)
    {
        var disposeScripts = this._scriptDisposes[updatePanelID];
        for (var i = 0; i < disposeScripts.length; i++)
        {
            eval(disposeScripts[i]);
        }
        delete this._scriptDisposes[updatePanelID];
    }
    }

    this._destroyTree(updatePanelElement);
    updatePanelElement.innerHTML = rendering;

}
```

Listing 24-31: The _destroyTree Method

```
function Sys$WebForms$PageRequestManager$_destroyTree(element)
{
    if (element.nodeType === 1)
    {
        var childNodes = element.childNodes;
        for (var i = childNodes.length - 1; i >= 0; i--)
        {
            var node = childNodes[i];
            if (node.nodeType === 1)
            {
                if (node.dispose && typeof(node.dispose) === "function")
                    node.dispose();

                else if (node.control && typeof(node.control.dispose) === "function")

                    node.control.dispose();

                var behaviors = Sys.UI.Behavior.getBehaviors(node);
                for (var j = behaviors.length - 1; j >= 0; j--)
                {
                    behaviors[j].dispose();
                }

                this._destroyTree(node);
            }
        }
    }
}
```

Keep in mind that we're discussing the significance of the three event data arrays — data items, panels updating, and panels deleting — associated with the pageLoading event. So far, I've discussed the panels updating array. Now, let's study the significance of the panels deleting array. This array contains the list of all UpdatePanel server controls that are deleted after processing of the current asynchronous page postback request on the server side and before processing of the server response to this request on the client side. If your application logic depends on any of these UpdatePanel controls, the DOM elements and scripts that they contain or the client controls and behaviors associated with these DOM elements, your event handler for the pageLoading event must take the necessary steps before these UpdatePanel server controls are deleted from the current document.

Next, let's study the significance of the data items dictionary. This dictionary contains all the new data items after processing of the current asynchronous page postback request on the server side and before processing of the server response to this request on the client side. Each data item in this dictionary is associated with a particular control on the current page. You can access this dictionary from within your event handler to enable the pageLoading event to do whatever application-specific tasks you deem necessary. However, keep in mind that some of these data items could be associated with the server controls that have not yet been added to the current document.

Now that we've covered the significance of the panels deleting, panels updating, and data items collections of the PageLoadingEventArgs event data class, let revisit the following portion of Listing 24-5. Recall that this portion of the _onFormSubmitCompleted method of the current PageRequestManager instance invokes the _getPageLoadingEventArgs method on the current PageRequestManager instance to instantiate and to return an instance of the PageLoadingEventArgs class, which is then passed into the event handlers registered for the pageLoading event of the current PageRequestManager instance:

```
var handler = this._get_eventHandlerList().getHandler("pageLoading");
if (handler)
    handler(this, this._getPageLoadingEventArgs());
```

Listing 24-32 presents the internal implementation of the _getPageLoadingEventArgs method.

Since the main responsibility of the _getPageLoadingEventArgs method is to instantiate an instance of the PageLoadingEventArgs class, and since the constructor of this class requires the list of updating and deleting UpdatePanel server controls, the _getPageLoadedEventArgs method first populates two local collections named updating and deleting with the list of the UpdatePanel server controls *to be updated* and the list of UpdatePanel server controls *to be deleted*, respectively.

As you can see, the method iterates through the UniqueID property values in the _panelsToRefreshIDs collection of the current PageRequestManager instance and takes the following steps for each enumerated UniqueID property value. First, it invokes the _uniqueIDToClientID method on the current PageRequestManager instance, passing in the enumerated UniqueID property value to return its associated ClientID property value:

```
updatePanelClientID = this._uniqueIDToClientID(refreshIDs[i]);
```

Next, it invokes the getElementById method on the document object passing the ClientID property value to return a reference to the associated UpdatePanel server control:

```
updatePanel = document.getElementById(updatePanelClientID);
```

Finally, the _getPageLoadingEventArgs method adds the UpdatePanel server control to the updating local collection:

```
Array.add(updating, updatePanel);
```

The next order of business for the _getPageLoadingEventArgs method is to populate the deleting collection with the list of UpdatePanel server controls *to be deleted*.

As discussed in the previous chapter, as far as the current client-side PageRequestManager *instance is concerned, when an* UpdatePanel *server control updates, its child* UpdatePanel *server controls do* not*. Instead they are deleted from the current page and replaced with brand-new child* UpdatePanel *server controls that have the same* UniqueID *and* ClientID *property values as the deleted ones.*

In other words, the current client-side PageRequestManager *instance treats* all *child* UpdatePanel *server controls of the* UpdatePanel *server control being updated as brand-new* UpdatePanel *server controls created during processing of the current asynchronous page postback request. This includes both those child* UpdatePanel *server controls replacing the deleted ones (that is, those with the same* UniqueID *and* ClientID *property values as the deleted ones) and those child* UpdatePanel *server controls that are not replacing the deleted ones (those with completely different* UniqueID *and* ClientID *property values from the deleted ones). Keep in mind that the server-side code may add new child* UpdatePanel *server controls to an* UpdatePanel *server control.*

As Listing 24-32 shows, the _getPageLoadingEventArgs method searches through the oldIDs collection for those UpdatePanel server controls that are being deleted from the current document, and adds them to the deleting collection:

```
for (var i = 0; i < oldIDs.length; i++)
{
  if (Array.indexOf(refreshedIDs, oldIDs[i]) === -1 &&
     (Array.indexOf(newIDs, oldIDs[i]) === -1 ||
      Array.indexOf(childIDs, oldIDs[i]) > -1))
   Array.add(deleting,
            document.getElementById(this._uniqueIDToClientID(oldIDs[i])));
}
```

Finally, the _getPageLoadingEventArgs method instantiates and returns an instance of the PageLoadingEventArgs event data class passing in three collections: updating, deleting, and _dataItems.

```
return new Sys.WebForms.PageLoadedEventArgs(updated, created, this._dataItems);
```

Listing 24-32: The _getPageLoadingEventArgs Method of the PageRequestManager

```
function Sys$WebForms$PageRequestManager$_getPageLoadingEventArgs()
{
  var updating = [];
  var deleting = [];
  var oldIDs = this._oldUpdatePanelIDs;
  var newIDs = this._updatePanelIDs;
  var childIDs = this._childUpdatePanelIDs;
  var refreshedIDs = this._panelsToRefreshIDs;
  var updatePanelClientID;
  var updatePanel;
```

(continued)

1241

Listing 24-32 (continued)

```
      for (var i = 0; i < refreshedIDs.length; i++)
      {
        updatePanelClientID = this._uniqueIDToClientID(refreshIDs[i]);
        updatePanel = document.getElementById(updatePanelClientID);
        Array.add(updating, updatePanel);
        Array.add(updating,
                  document.getElementById(this._uniqueIDToClientID(refreshedIDs[i])));
      }
      for (var i = 0; i < oldIDs.length; i++)
      {
        if (Array.indexOf(refreshedIDs, oldIDs[i]) === -1 &&
           (Array.indexOf(newIDs, oldIDs[i]) === -1 ||
            Array.indexOf(childIDs, oldIDs[i]) > -1))
          Array.add(deleting,
                    document.getElementById(this._uniqueIDToClientID(oldIDs[i])));
      }
      return new Sys.WebForms.PageLoadingEventArgs(updating, deleting,
                                                   this._dataItems);
}
```

Using the pageLoading Event

As discussed earlier, the current client-side `PageRequestManager` instance fires its `pageLoading` event right before loading new content into the current page, to enable you to perform application-specific tasks that must be performed right before the new content is loaded. Follow these steps to ensure that your required application-specific logic is executed right before the loading takes place:

1. If your required application-specific logic is encapsulated in a method of an ASP.NET AJAX client class, invoke the `createDelegate` static method on the `Function` to instantiate a delegate that represents this method. For example, if this logic is contained in a method named `myMethod` that belongs to an ASP.NET AJAX class named `MyClass`, you'll need to create a delegate such as the following:

```
var myObj = new CustomComponents.MyClass();
. . .
var myDelegate = Function.createDelegate(myObj, myObj.myMethod);
```

2. If your required application-specific logic in not already encapsulated in a method of an ASP. NET AJAX client class, write a new JavaScript function that encapsulates this logic.

3. Take the following steps inside the `pageLoad` method:

    ❑   Invoke the `getInstance` static method on the client-side `PageRequestManager` class to return a reference to the current client-side `PageRequestManager` instance:

```
function pageLoad()
{
  var prm = Sys.WebForms.PageRequestManager.getInstance();
  . . .
}
```

❑ Invoke the `add_pageLoading` method on the current client-side `PageRequestManager` instance to register the delegate from Step 1 or the JavaScript function from Step 2 as the event handler for the `pageLoading` event of the current client-side `PageRequestManager` instance:

```
function pageLoad()
{
  var myObj = new CustomComponents.MyClass();
  . . .
  var myDelegate = Function.createDelegate(myObj, myObj.myMethod);
  var prm = Sys.WebForms.PageRequestManager.getInstance();
  prm.add_pageLoading(myDelegate);
  . . .
}
```

Listing 24-33 contains a page that uses this recipe. If you run this page you should see the results shown in Figure 24-3. As this figure shows, this page consists of a parent `UpdatePanel` server control that contains a child `UpdatePanel` server control. If you click the button labeled Parent UpdatePanel Trigger, the page will display the popup shown in Figure 24-4. If you click the button labeled Child UpdatePanel Trigger, the page will display the popup shown in Figure 24-5. As you can see, each popup contains a message that displays some of the information available to an event handler registered for the `pageLoading` event right before the actual loading takes place. What you do with this information is completely up to you. Your event handler can use it to perform application-specific tasks that must be performed right before the actual loading occurs.

Listing 24-33: A Page that Uses the Preceding Recipe

```
<%@ Page Language="C#" %>
<%@ Import Namespace="System.Drawing" %>
<!DOCTYPE html PUBLIC "-//W3C//DTD XHTML 1.1//EN"
"http://www.w3.org/TR/xhtml11/DTD/xhtml11.dtd">
<script runat="server">
  void Page_Load(object sender, EventArgs e)
  {
    Label parentUpdatePanelLabel =
                            (Label)Page.FindControl("ParentUpdatePanelLabel");
    parentUpdatePanelLabel.Text = "UpdatePanel refreshed at " +
                              DateTime.Now.ToString();
    Label childUpdatePanelLabel =
                            (Label)Page.FindControl("childUpdatePanelLabel");
    childUpdatePanelLabel.Text = "UpdatePanel refreshed at " +
                                DateTime.Now.ToString();
  }
  void ClickCallback (object sender, EventArgs e)
  {
    Label label = (Label)Page.FindControl("DynamicChildUpdatePanelLabel");
    label.Text = "UpdatePanel refreshed at " + DateTime.Now.ToString() +
                "   ";
  }
</script>
```

(continued)

Listing 24-33 *(continued)*

```html
<html xmlns="http://www.w3.org/1999/xhtml">
<head id="Head1" runat="server">
  <title>Untitled Page</title>
  <script type="text/javascript" language="javascript">
    function pageLoad()
    {
      var prm = Sys.WebForms.PageRequestManager.getInstance();
      prm.remove_pageLoading(pageLoadingHandler);
      prm.add_pageLoading(pageLoadingHandler);
    }

    function pageLoadingHandler(sender, e)
    {
      var panelsUpdating = e.get_panelsUpdating();
      var panelsDeleting = e.get_panelsDeleting();
      var dataItems = e.get_dataItems();

      var builder = new Sys.StringBuilder();
      builder.append("panelsUpdating: ");
      builder.appendLine();
      for (var i in panelsUpdating)
      {
        builder.append(panelsUpdating[i].id);
        builder.appendLine();
      }

      builder.appendLine();
      builder.append("panelsDeleting: ");
      builder.appendLine();
      for (var j in panelsDeleting)
      {
        builder.append(panelsDeleting[j].id);
        builder.appendLine();
      }
      builder.appendLine();
      builder.append("_updatePanelIDs: ");
      builder.append(sender._updatePanelIDs);
      builder.appendLine();
      builder.appendLine();
      builder.append("_updatePanelClientIDs: ");
      builder.append(sender._updatePanelClientIDs);
      builder.appendLine();
      builder.appendLine();
      builder.append("_updatePanelHasChildrenAsTriggers: ");
      builder.append(sender._updatePanelHasChildrenAsTriggers);
      builder.appendLine();
      builder.appendLine();
      builder.append("_asyncPostBackTimeout: ");
      builder.append(sender._asyncPostBackTimeout);
      builder.appendLine();
```

```
            builder.appendLine();
            builder.append("_asyncPostBackControlIDs: ");
            builder.append(sender._asyncPostBackControlIDs);
            builder.appendLine();
            builder.appendLine();
            builder.append("_asyncPostBackControlClientIDs: ");
            builder.append(sender._asyncPostBackControlClientIDs);
            builder.appendLine();
            builder.appendLine();
            builder.append("_postBackControlIDs: ");
            builder.append(sender._postBackControlIDs);
            builder.appendLine();
            builder.appendLine();
            builder.append("_postBackControlClientIDs: ");
            builder.append(sender._postBackControlClientIDs);
            alert(builder.toString());
        }
    </script>
</head>
<body>
    <form id="form1" runat="server">
        <asp:ScriptManager ID="ScriptManager1" runat="server" />
        <table cellspacing="10">
            <tr>
                <td align="center" colspan="2">
                    <asp:UpdatePanel ID="ParentUpdatePanel" UpdateMode="Conditional"
                        runat="server">
                        <ContentTemplate>
                            <table cellspacing="20" style="background-color: #dddddd">
                                <tr>
                                    <th>
                                        Parent UpdatePanel Control</th>
                                </tr>
                                <tr>
                                    <td>
                                        <asp:Label ID="ParentUpdatePanelLabel" runat="server" />
                                           
                                        <asp:Button ID="ParentUpdatePanelButton" runat="server"
                                        Text="Update" />
                                    </td>
                                </tr>
                                <tr>
                                    <td style="width: 100%">
                                        <asp:UpdatePanel ID="ChildUpdatePanel" runat="server">
                                            <ContentTemplate>
                                                <table style="background-color: #aaaaaa">
                                                    <tr>
                                                        <th>
                                                            Child UpdatePanel Control</th>
                                                    </tr>
```

(continued)

Listing 24-33 *(continued)*

```
                            <tr>
                              <td>
                                <asp:Label ID="childUpdatePanelLabel"
                                 runat="server" />   
                                <asp:Button ID="ChildUpdatePanelButton"
                                 runat="server" Text="Update" />
                              </td>
                            </tr>
                            <tr>
                              <td>
                              </td>
                            </tr>
                          </table>
                        </ContentTemplate>
                        <Triggers>
                          <asp:AsyncPostBackTrigger EventName="Click"
                          ControlID="ChildUpdatePanelTrigger" />
                        </Triggers>
                      </asp:UpdatePanel>
                    </td>
                  </tr>
                </table>
              </ContentTemplate>
              <Triggers>
                <asp:AsyncPostBackTrigger ControlID="ParentUpdatePanelTrigger"
                EventName="Click" />
              </Triggers>
            </asp:UpdatePanel>
          </td>
        </tr>
        <tr>
          <td width="50%">
            <asp:Button ID="ChildUpdatePanelTrigger" runat="server"
             Text="Child UpdatePanel Trigger" Width="100%" />
          </td>
          <td>
            <asp:Button ID="ParentUpdatePanelTrigger" runat="server"
             Text="Parent UpdatePanel Trigger" Width="100%" />
          </td>
        </tr>
      </table>
    </form>
  </body>
</html>
```

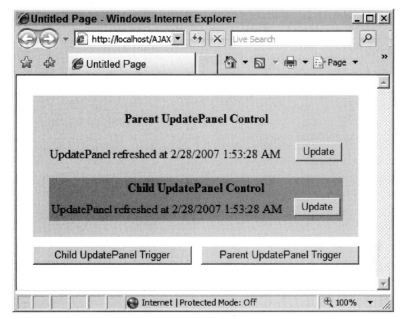

Figure 24-3

Now let's walk through the code shown in Listing 24-33. As you can see, this page contains a server-side and a client-side script block. The server-side script block contains the implementation of the `Page_Load` method. As you can see, this method first calls the `FindControl` method twice on the current `Page` to return references to the `ParentUpdatePanelLabel` and `ChildUpdatePanelLabel` server controls, and then sets the values of their `Text` properties to the current time:

```
Label parentUpdatePanelLabel = (Label)Page.FindControl("ParentUpdatePanelLabel");
parentUpdatePanelLabel.Text = "UpdatePanel refreshed at " +
                              DateTime.Now.ToString();
Label childUpdatePanelLabel = (Label)Page.FindControl("ChildUpdatePanelLabel");
childUpdatePanelLabel.Text = "UpdatePanel refreshed at " + DateTime.Now.ToString();
```

As Listing 24-33 shows, the client-side script block consists of two parts. The first part contains the implementation of the `pageLoad` method:

```
function pageLoad()
{
  var prm = Sys.WebForms.PageRequestManager.getInstance();
  prm.add_pageLoading(pageLoadingHandler);
}
```

As you can see, `pageLoad` first calls the `getInstance` static method on the client-side `PageRequestManager` class to return a reference to the current client-side `PageRequestManager` instance:

```
var prm = Sys.WebForms.PageRequestManager.getInstance();
```

Figure 24-4

Next, the method invokes the `add_pageLoading` method on the current `PageRequestManager` instance to register the `pageLoadingHandler` JavaScript function as an event handler for the `pageLoading` event of the current `PageRequestManager` instance:

```
prm.add_pageLoading(pageLoadingHandler);
```

Now, let's walk through the implementation of the `pageLoadingHandler` JavaScript function. When the current client-side `PageRequestManager` instance invokes this function, it passes two parameters into it. The first parameter references the current client-side `PageRequestManager` instance. The second parameter references the `PageLoadingEventArgs` object that contains the event data for the `pageLoading` event.

As Listing 24-33 shows, the `pageLoadingHandler` method first calls the `get_panelsUpdating` method on the `PageLoadingEventArgs` object to return a reference to the array that contains all the `UpdatePanel` server controls that need to be updated:

```
var panelsUpdating = e.get_panelsUpdating();
```

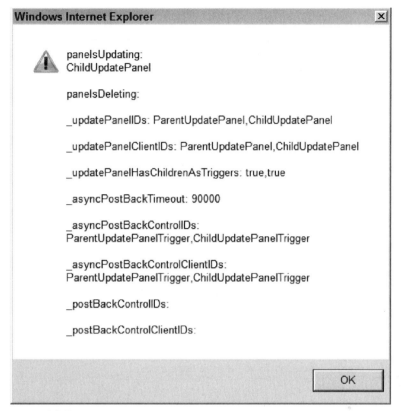

Figure 24-5

Next, it calls the `get_panelsDeleting` method on the `PageLoadingEventArgs` object to return a reference to the array that contains all the `UpdatePanel` server controls that need to be deleted:

```
var panelsDeleting = e.get_panelsDeleting();
```

Next, the `pageLoadingHandler` method instantiates a `StringBuilder`:

```
var builder = new Sys.StringBuilder();
```

Then it populates the `StringBuilder` with the `UniqueID` property values of all the `UpdatePanel` server controls in the `panelsUpdating` array:

```
builder.append("panelsUpdating: ");
builder.appendLine();
for (var i in panelsUpdating)
{
  builder.append(panelsUpdating[i].id);
  builder.appendLine();
}
```

Next, it populates the `StringBuilder` with the `UniqueID` property values of the all the `UpdatePanel` server controls in the `panelsDeleting` array:

```
for (var j in panelsDeleting)
{
    builder.append(panelsDeleting[j].id);
    builder.appendLine();
}
```

Then the `pageLoadingHandler` method adds the content of the `_updatePanelIDs` field of the current client-side `PageRequestManager` instance to the `StringBuilder`. Recall that the first parameter (that is, the sender parameter) of the `pageLoadingHandler` method references the current client-side `PageRequestManager` instance. Also recall that the `_updatePanelIDs` field of the current `PageRequestManager` instance contains the comma-separated list of the `UniqueID` property values of all the `UpdatePanel` server controls on the current page after processing of the current request on the server side and before processing of the server response to this request on the client side:

```
builder.appendLine();
builder.append("_updatePanelIDs: ");
builder.append(sender._updatePanelIDs);
```

Next, it adds the content of the `_updatePanelClientIDs` field of the current client-side `PageRequestManager` instance to the `StringBuilder`. Recall that the `_updatePanelClientIDs` field contains the comma-separated list of the `ClientID` property values of all the `UpdatePanel` server controls on the current page after processing of the current request on the server side and before processing of the server response to this request on the client side:

```
builder.appendLine();
builder.appendLine();
builder.append("_updatePanelClientIDs: ");
builder.append(sender._updatePanelClientIDs);
```

Then it adds the content of the `_updatePanelHasChildrenAsTriggers` field of the current client-side `PageRequestManager` instance to the `StringBuilder`. Recall that the `_updatePanelHasChildrenAsTriggers` field contains the comma-separated list of Boolean values, one for each `UpdatePanel` server control in the `_updatePanelIDs`.

```
builder.appendLine();
builder.appendLine();
builder.append("_updatePanelHasChildrenAsTriggers: ");
builder.append(sender._updatePanelHasChildrenAsTriggers);
```

Next, the `pageLoadingHandler` method adds the value of the `_asyncPostBackTimeout` field of the current client-side `PageRequestManager` instance to the `StringBuilder`. Recall that this field contains the asynchronous page postback request timeout.

```
builder.appendLine();
builder.appendLine();
builder.append("_asyncPostBackTimeout: ");
builder.append(sender._asyncPostBackTimeout);
```

Next, it adds the content of the _asyncPostBackControlIDs field of the current client-side PageRequestManager instance to the StringBuilder. Recall that the _asyncPostBackControlIDs field contains the comma-separated list of the UniqueID property values of all the asynchronous postback controls on the current page after processing of the current request on the server side and before processing of the server response to this request on the client side:

```
builder.appendLine();
builder.appendLine();
builder.append("_asyncPostBackControlIDs: ");
builder.append(sender._asyncPostBackControlIDs);
```

Then it adds the content of the _asyncPostBackControlClientIDs field of the current client-side PageRequestManager instance to the StringBuilder. Recall that the _asyncPostBackControlClientIDs field contains the comma-separated list of the ClientID property values of all the server controls on the current page that cause asynchronous page postback:

```
builder.appendLine();
builder.appendLine();
builder.append("_asyncPostBackControlClientIDs: ");
builder.append(sender._asyncPostBackControlClientIDs);
```

Next, the pageLoadingHandler method adds the content of the _postBackControlIDs field of the current client-side PageRequestManager instance to the StringBuilder. Recall that the _postBackControlIDs field contains the comma-separated list of the UniqueID property values of all the server controls on the current page that cause synchronous page postback:

```
builder.appendLine();
builder.appendLine();
builder.append("_postBackControlIDs: ");
builder.append(sender._postBackControlIDs);
```

Then it adds the content of the _postBackControlClientIDs field of the current client-side PageRequestManager instance to the StringBuilder. Recall that the _postBackControlClientIDs field contains the comma-separated list of the ClientID property values of all the server controls on the current page that cause synchronous page postback:

```
builder.appendLine();
builder.appendLine();
builder.append("_postBackControlClientIDs: ");
builder.append(sender._postBackControlClientIDs);
```

Finally, it displays the content of the StringBuilder in a popup, shown in Figure 24-4 or 24-5.

```
alert(builder.toString());
```

Next, let's study the messages shown in Figurers 24-4 and 24-5. As Figure 24-4 shows,

❑ The panelsUpdating array contains ParentUpdatePanel because the user clicked the button labeled Parent UpdatePanel Trigger, which triggers the update of ParentUpdatePanel.

❑ The `panelsDeleting` array contains the `ChildUpdatePanel`. This is because updating the `ParentUpdatePanel` wipes out the `ChildUpdatePanel` and replaces it with a new `ChildUpdatePanel` that has the same `UniqueID` and `ClientID` property values as the deleted one.

❑ The `_updatePanelIDs` field of the current `PageRequestManager` instance returns the comma-separated list of the `UniqueID` properties of all the `UpdatePanel` server controls on the current page — that is, `ParentUpdatePanel` and `ChildUpdatePanel`. Note that the `UniqueID` property values in this example are the same as the `ID` property values because none of the `UpdatePanel` server controls in this example belongs to a parent server control that implements the `INamingContainer` interface.

❑ The `_updatePanelClientIDs` field of the current `PageRequestManager` instance returns the comma-separated list of the `ClientID` properties of all the `UpdatePanel` server controls on the current page — that is, `ParentUpdatePanel` and `ChildUpdatePanel`. Note that the `ClientID` property values in this example are the same as the `ID` property values because none of the `UpdatePanel` server controls in this example belongs to a parent server control that implements the `INamingContainer` interface.

❑ The `_updatePanelHasChildrenAsTriggers` field of the current `PageRequestManger` instance returns the comma-separated list of Boolean values, one for each `UpdatePanel` server control. Because this example contains two `UpdatePanel` server controls and because the `ChildrenAsTriggers` properties of both `UpdatePanel` server controls are set to `true` by default, the `_updatePanelHasChildrenAsTriggers` field contains a comma-separated list of two `true` values.

❑ The `_asyncPostBackTimeout` field of the current `PageRequestManager` instance returns the default value, which is `90000`.

❑ The `_asyncPostBackControlIDs` field of the current `PageRequestManager` instance returns the comma-separated list of the `UniqueID` property values of all asynchronous postback server controls. Our example contains two asynchronous postback `Button` server controls: `ParentUpdatePanelTrigger` and `ChildUpdatePanelTrigger`.

❑ The `_asyncPostBackControlClientIDs` field of the current `PageRequestManger` instance returns the comma-separated list of the `ClientID` property values of all asynchronous postback server controls. Our example contains two asynchronous postback `Button` server controls: `ParentUpdatePanelTrigger` and `ChildUpdatePanelTrigger`. Again, because these two `Button` server controls do not belong to a server control that implements the `INamingContainer` interface, their `UniqueID`, `ClientID`, and `ID` properties have the same values.

Keep in mind that the arrays returned from the calls into the `get_panelsUpdating` and `get_panelsDeleting` methods contain references to the actual `updating` and `deleting` `UpdatePanel` server controls, respectively. This gives your event handler (registered for the `pageLoading` event of the current `PageRequestManager` instance) a powerful tool with which to modify the contents of these `UpdatePanel` server controls or to enhance their functionality.

pageLoaded

The current client-side `PageRequestManager` instance raises the `pageLoaded` event in two separate occasions:

❑ At the end of its instantiation/initialization phase, as shown in Figure 22-5. Recall that this phase occurs only once during the entire lifetime of the current `PageRequestManager` instance — when it is loaded for the first time. This scenario was thoroughly discussed in Chapter 22.

❑ At the end of the processing of the server response for an asynchronous page postback request, as shown in Figure 24-2. This could happen as many times as the current `PageRequestManager` instance makes asynchronous page postback requests to the server, because the current `PageRequestManager` instance raises the `pageLoaded` event at the end of the processing of the server response for every single asynchronous page postback request it makes to the server.

The client-side `PageRequestManager` class uses the standard ASP.NET AJAX event implementation pattern to implement its `pageLoaded` event, as thoroughly discussed in Chapter 22. Recall that the `PageRequestManager` exposes a method named `_pageLoaded` that raises its `pageLoaded` event, as shown again in the highlighted portion of Listing 24-34.

Listing 24-34: The _pageLoaded Method of the PageRequestManager

```
function Sys$WebForms$PageRequestManager$_pageLoaded(initialLoad)
{

    var handler = this._get_eventHandlerList().getHandler("pageLoaded");
    if (handler)
      handler(this, this._getPageLoadedEventArgs(initialLoad));

    if (!initialLoad)
      Sys.Application.raiseLoad();
}
```

As you can see in the highlighted portion of this code listing, this method invokes the `_getPageLoadedEventArgs(initialLoad)` internal method on the current `PageRequestManager` instance to instantiate and to return an instance of the `PageLoadedEventArgs` event data class, which is then passed into the event handlers registered for the `pageLoaded` event of the current `PageRequestManager` instance. Listing 24-35 presents the internal implementation of the `_getPageLoadedEventArgs` method.

Since the main responsibility of the `_getPageLoadedEventArgs` method is to instantiate an instance of the `PageLoadedEventArgs` class, and since the constructor of this class requires the list of updated and created `UpdatePanel` server controls, the `_getPageLoadedEventArgs` method first populates two local collections named `updated` and `created` with the list of the updated `UpdatePanel` server controls and the list of newly-created `UpdatePanel` server controls, respectively.

As you can see, the method iterates through the `UniqueID` property values in the `_panelsToRefreshIDs` collection of the current `PageRequestManager` instance and takes the following steps for each enumerated `UniqueID` property value. First, it invokes the `_uniqueIDToClientID` method on the current

`PageRequestManager` instance, passing in the enumerated `UniqueID` property value to return its associated `ClientID` property value:

```
updatePanelClientID = this._uniqueIDToClientID(refreshIDs[i]);
```

Next, the `_getPageLoadedEventArgs` method invokes the `getElementById` method on the document object, passing the `ClientID` property value to return a reference to the `UpdatePanel` server control with the specified `ClientID` property value:

```
updatePanel = document.getElementById(updatePanelClientID);
```

Finally, it adds the `UpdatePanel` server control to the `updated` local collection:

```
Array.add(updated, updatePanel);
```

The next order of business for the `_getPageLoadedEventArgs` method is to populate the `created` collection with the list of all `UpdatePanel` server controls that the server-side `PageRequestManager` instance has created during processing of the current asynchronous page postback request.

As Listing 24-35 shows, the `_getPageLoadedEventArgs` method searches through the `newIDs` collection for those `UpdatePanel` server controls that are child `UpdatePanel` server controls of other `UpdatePanel` server controls. Since the current client-side `PageRequestManager` instance treats every child `UpdatePanel` server control as a newly-created `UpdatePanel` server control during processing of the current asynchronous page postback request, all child `UpdatePanel` server controls are added to the `created` collection. This includes both those child `UpdatePanel` server controls that have the same `UniqueID` property values as the ones they're replacing, and those child `UpdatePanel` server controls that do not correspond to any of the old child `UpdatePanel` server controls.

```
for (var i = 0; i < newIDs.length; i++)
{
  if (initialLoad || Array.indexOf(childIDs, newIDs[i]) !== -1)
  {
    updatePanelClientID = this._uniqueIDToClientID(newIDs[i]);
    updatePanel = document.getElementById(updatePanelClientID);
    Array.add(created, updatePanel);
  }
}
```

Finally, the `_getPageLoadedEventArgs` method instantiates and returns an instance of the `PageLoadedEventArgs` event data class passing in three collections: updated, created, and `_dataItems`.

```
return new Sys.WebForms.PageLoadedEventArgs(updated, created, this._dataItems);
```

Listing 24-35: The _getPageLoadedEventArgs Method of PageRequestManager

```
function Sys$WebForms$PageRequestManager$_getPageLoadedEventArgs(initialLoad)
{
  var updated = [];
  var created = [];
  var oldIDs = this._oldUpdatePanelIDs || [];
  var newIDs = this._updatePanelIDs;
```

```
      var childIDs = this._childUpdatePanelIDs || [];
      var refreshedIDs = this._panelsToRefreshIDs || [];
      var updatePanelClientID;
      var updatePanel;
      for (var i = 0; i < refreshedIDs.length; i++)
      {
        updatePanelClientID = this._uniqueIDToClientID(refreshIDs[i]);
        updatePanel = document.getElementById(updatePanelClientID);
        Array.add(updated, updatePanel);
      }
      for (var i = 0; i < newIDs.length; i++)
      {
        if (initialLoad || Array.indexOf(childIDs, newIDs[i]) !== -1)
        {
          updatePanelClientID = this._uniqueIDToClientID(newIDs[i]);
          updatePanel = document.getElementById(updatePanelClientID);
          Array.add(created, updatePanel);
        }
      }
      return new Sys.WebForms.PageLoadedEventArgs(updated, created, this._dataItems);
}
```

endRequest

As thoroughly discussed earlier in this chapter, the current `PageRequestManager` instance invokes its `_endPostBack` on numerious occasions. As the highlighted portion of Listing 24-36, which repeats Listing 24-27, shows, the `_endPostBack` method raises the `endRequest` event.

Listing 24-36: The _endPostBack Method

```
function Sys$WebForms$PageRequestManager$_endPostBack(error, response)
{
  this._processingRequest = false;
  this._request = null;
  this._additionalInput = null;

  var handler = this._get_eventHandlerList().getHandler("endRequest");
  var errorHandled = false;
  if (handler)
  {
    var eventArgs =
            new Sys.WebForms.EndRequestEventArgs(error, this._dataItems, response);
    handler(this, eventArgs);
    errorHandled = eventArgs.get_errorHandled();
  }

  this._dataItems = null;
  if (error && !errorHandled)
    alert(error.message);
}
```

As you can see from this code listing, the _endPostBack method instantiates an instance of an ASP.NET AJAX class named EndRequestEventArgs and passes this instance to the event handlers registered for the endRequest event of the current PageRequestManager instance. This class is the event data class associated with the endRequest event. Listing 24-37 presents the internal implementation of this class.

Listing 24-37: The EndRequestEventArgs Class

```
Sys.WebForms.EndRequestEventArgs =
function Sys$WebForms$EndRequestEventArgs(error, dataItems, response)
{
  Sys.WebForms.EndRequestEventArgs.initializeBase(this);
  this._errorHandled = false;
  this._error = error;
  this._dataItems = dataItems || new Object();
  this._response = response;
}
function Sys$WebForms$EndRequestEventArgs$get_dataItems()
{
  return this._dataItems;
}
function Sys$WebForms$EndRequestEventArgs$get_error()
{
  return this._error;
}
function Sys$WebForms$EndRequestEventArgs$get_errorHandled()
{
  return this._errorHandled;
}
function Sys$WebForms$EndRequestEventArgs$set_errorHandled(value)
{
  this._errorHandled = value;
}
function Sys$WebForms$EndRequestEventArgs$get_response()
{
  return this._response;
}
Sys.WebForms.EndRequestEventArgs.prototype =
{
  get_dataItems: Sys$WebForms$EndRequestEventArgs$get_dataItems,
  get_error: Sys$WebForms$EndRequestEventArgs$get_error,
  get_errorHandled: Sys$WebForms$EndRequestEventArgs$get_errorHandled,
  set_errorHandled: Sys$WebForms$EndRequestEventArgs$set_errorHandled,
  get_response: Sys$WebForms$EndRequestEventArgs$get_response
}
Sys.WebForms.EndRequestEventArgs.registerClass('Sys.WebForms.EndRequestEventArgs',
                                               Sys.EventArgs);
```

As you can see from this code listing, the constructor of the EndRequestEventArgs class takes three parameters. The first parameter references the error object, if any. The second parameter references the object that contains one name/value pair for each data item. As the highlighted portion of Listing 24-36 shows, this parameter basically returns a reference to the _dataItems collection of the current PageRequestManager instance. The third parameter references the WebRequestExecutor object responsible for executing the current asynchronous page postback request. As Listing 24-37 shows, this constructor stores these three parameters in three internal fields named _error, _dataItems, and _response, respectively. Your event handler for the endRequest event can then invoke the get_error, get_dataItems, and get_response methods on the EndRequestEventArgs object passed into it to access these internal fields.

As you can see from Listing 24-37, the EndRequestEventArgs event data class also exposes a Boolean property named _errorHandled and two methods named get_errorHandled and set_errorHandled that get and set the values of this property. If your event handler for the endRequest event chooses to use a custom error handler to handle the error (if any), it must call the set_errorHandled method on the EndRequestEventArgs object passed into it to set the value of the _errorHandled property to true to signal the current PageRequestManager instance that it mustn't use the default error handler to handle the error because the error has already been handled by your custom error handler. As the boldface portions of Listing 24-36 show, when your event handler for the endRequest event finally returns, the _endPostBack method calls the get_errorHandled method on the EndRequestEventArgs object passed into your event handler to access the value of the _errorHandled property to determine whether your event handler has set this property to true. If so, the _endPostBack method bypasses the default error-handling mechanism. As the boldface portion of Listing 24-36 shows, the default error-handling mechanism simply calls the alert function to display the error message in a popup.

As you should expect by now, the PageRequestManager instance exposes two methods, add_endRequest and remove_endRequest, that enable you to register and unregister an event handler for the endRequest method of the current PageRequestManager instance, as shown in the following code listing:

```
function Sys$WebForms$PageRequestManager$add_endRequest(handler)
{
  this._get_eventHandlerList().addHandler("endRequest", handler);
}
function Sys$WebForms$PageRequestManager$remove_endRequest(handler)
{
  this._get_eventHandlerList().removeHandler("endRequest", handler);
}
```

Using the endRequest Event

As the name suggests, the current PageRequestManager instance raises the endRequest event to mark the end of the current asynchronous page postback request. Since the _endPostBack method can be invoked for a number of reasons, the endRequest event can be raised for a number of reasons as well. In other words, your event handler for the endRequest event must *not* assume that everything went fine and the server response successfully arrived. It must include the necessary logic to determine why the endRequest event was fired.

Follow these steps to ensure that your required application-specific logic is executed when the current PageRequestManager instance fires its endRequest event:

1. If your required application-specific logic is encapsulated in a method of an ASP.NET AJAX client class, invoke the createDelegate static method on the Function to instantiate a delegate that represents this method. For example, if this logic is contained in a method named `myMethod` that belongs to an ASP.NET AJAX class named `MyClass`, you'll need to create a delegate such as the following:

```
var myObj = new CustomComponents.MyClass();
. . .
Var myDelegate = Function.createDelegate(myObj, myObj.myMethod);
```

2. If your required application-specific logic in not already encapsulated in a method of an ASP.NET AJAX client class, write a new JavaScript function that encapsulates this logic.

3. Take the following steps inside the `pageLoad` method:

   ❑ Invoke the `getInstance` static method on the client-side `PageRequestManager` class to return a reference to the current client-side `PageRequestManager` instance:

```
function pageLoad()
{
  var prm = Sys.WebForms.PageRequestManager.getInstance();
  . . .
}
```

   ❑ Invoke the `add_endRequest` method on the current client-side `PageRequestManager` instance to register the delegate from Step 1 or the JavaScript function from Step 2 as the event handler for the `endRequest` event of the current client-side `PageRequestManager` instance:

```
function pageLoad()
{
  var myObj = new CustomComponents.MyClass();
  . . .
  var myDelegate = Function.createDelegate(myObj, myObj.myMethod);
  var prm = Sys.WebForms.PageRequestManager.getInstance();
  prm.add_endRequest(myDelegate);
  . . .
}
```

As Listing 24-36 shows, the `_endPostBack` method uses a default error-handling mechanism to handle an error if your event handler for the `endRequest` event does not handle it and does not set the `_errorHandled` property of the `EndRequestEventArgs` object passed into it to `true`. As you can see from the bottom boldface portion of Listing 24-36, this default error-handling mechanism simply calls the `alert` JavaScript function to display the value of the `message` property of the error object in a popup.

If you're not happy with this default error mechanism, you can write your own custom error-handling routine. Such a routine normally needs to know the type of error being handled. As thoroughly discussed in Chapter 4, every error object exposes a property named `name`, which specifies the name or type of the exception. Your custom error-handling routine must contain a `switch` statement with one `case` statement for each type of error, something like the following:

```
function myCustomErrorHandler(error)
{
  switch (error.name)
  {
    case "...":
      // Handle error here
      break;
    case "...":
      // Handle error here
      break;
    case "...":
      // Handle error here
      break;
  }
}
```

As you can see from this code fragment, your custom error handler needs to know exactly what type of errors it is supposed to handle. This raises the following question: what types of exceptions could the current PageRequestManager instance throw when it is firing its endRequest event? To find the answer to this question we need to revisit those places where the current PageRequestManager instance invokes its _endPostBack method, because those are the places where the current PageRequestManager instance creates the error object and passes it as the first argument into the _endPostBack method. As we discussed earlier, the _endPostBack method, in turn, passes the error object to your event handler when it invokes your handler.

As we also discussed earlier, the current PageRequestManager instance invokes the _endPostBack method on eight different occasions, as follows (the variable sender in all the following code fragments references the current WebRequestExecutor object responsible for executing the current asynchronous page postback request):

1. When the current request times out, the current PageRequestManager instance invokes its _endPostBack method, passing in a parameter that calls the _createPageRequestManagerTimeoutError method on the current PageRequestManager instance to instantiate and return an exception of type PageRequestManagerTimeoutException. (I'll discuss this method shortly.)

```
if (sender.get_timedOut())
{
  this._endPostBack(this._createPageRequestManagerTimeoutError(), sender);
  return;
}
```

2. When the current request aborts, the current PageRequestManager instance invokes its _endPostBack method, passing in null as an error. As you can see, the absence of an error does not mean that everything went fine and the server response successfully arrived.

```
if (sender.get_aborted())
{
  this._endPostBack(null, sender);
  return;
}
```

3. When the status code of the server response is a number other than 200, the current `PageRequestManager` instance invokes its `_endPostBack` method, passing in a parameter that calls the `_createPageRequestManagerServerError` method on the current `PageRequestManager` instance to instantiate and return an exception of type `PageRequestManagerServerErrorException`. (I'll discuss this method shortly.)

```
if (sender.get_statusCode() !== 200)
{
  this._endPostBack(
      this._createPageRequestManagerServerError(sender.get_statusCode()), sender);
  return;
}
```

4. Recall that the server response text consists of a bunch of substrings with the format `length|type|id|content`. When the `type` part of a substring in the server response text is the string `"error"`, the current `PageRequestManager` instance invokes its `_endPostBack` method, passing in a parameter that calls the `_createPageRequestManagerServerError` method on the current `PageRequestManager` instance to instantiate and return an exception of type `PageRequestManagerServerErrorException`. Note that the current `PageRequestManager` instance passes the `id` and `content` parts of the substring into the `_createPageRequestManagerServerError` method. Recall that these two parts respectively contain the error code and the error message.

```
this._endPostBack(this._createPageRequestManagerServerError(
                Number.parseInvariant(deltaNode.id), deltaNode.content), sender);
```

5. When the `type` part of a substring in the server response text is a string that the current client-side `PageRequestManager` instance does not recognize, the current `PageRequestManager` instance invokes its `_endPostBack` method, passing in a parameter that calls the `_createPageRequestManagerParserError` method to instantiate and to return an exception of type `PageRequestManagerParserErrorException`. Note that the current `PageRequestManager` instance passes the `type` part of the substring into the `_createPageRequestManagerParserError` method.

```
this._endPostBack(this._createPageRequestManagerParserError(
        String.format(Sys.WebForms.Res.PRM_UnknownToken, deltaNode.type)), sender);
```

6. When the `_panelsToRefreshIDs` collection that the current client-side `PageRequestManager` instance has received from the server-side `PageRequestManager` instance contains the `UniqueID` property value of an `UpdatePanel` server control that does not exist on the current page, the current `PageRequestManager` instance invokes its `_endPostBack` method, passing in a parameter that calls the `invalidOperation` static method on the `Error` to instantiate and return an exception of type `InvalidOperationException`. Note that the current `PageRequestManager` instance passes the `ClientID` property value of the nonexistent `UpdatePanel` server control as a parameter into the `invalidOperation` method.

```
for (i = 0; i < this._panelsToRefreshIDs.length; i++)
{
  var panelClientID = this._uniqueIDToClientID(this._panelsToRefreshIDs[i]);
  if (!document.getElementById(panelClientID))
  {
    this._endPostBack(Error.invalidOperation(
      String.format(Sys.WebForms.Res.PRM_MissingPanel, panelClientID)), sender);
    return;
  }
}
```

7. When the `type` part of a substring in the server response text is the string `"updatePanel"` and the `id` part contains the `UniqueID` property value of an `UpdatePanel` server control that does not exist on the current page, the current `PageRequestManager` instance invokes its `_endPostBack` method, passing in a parameter that calls the `invalidOperation` static method on the `Error` to instantiate and return an exception of type `InvalidOperationException`. Note that the current `PageRequestManager` instance passes the `ClientID` property value of the nonexistent `UpdatePanel` server control as a parameter into the `invalidOperation` method.

```
for (i = 0; i < updatePanelNodes.length; i++)
{
  var deltaUpdatePanel = updatePanelNodes[i];
  var deltaPanelID = deltaUpdatePanel.id;
  var deltaPanelRendering = deltaUpdatePanel.content;
  var updatePanelElement = document.getElementById(deltaPanelID);
  if (!updatePanelElement)
  {
    this._endPostBack(Error.invalidOperation(
        String.format(Sys.WebForms.Res.PRM_MissingPanel, deltaPanelID)), sender);
    return;
  }
  this._updatePanel(updatePanelElement, deltaPanelRendering);
}
```

8. When all the scripts are loaded, the current `PageRequestManager` instance invokes its `_endPostBack` method, passing in `null` as its argument. This scenario happens when everything goes fine and the server response is successfully processed.

```
this._pageLoaded(false);
this._endPostBack(null, this._response);
this._response = null;
```

As you can see, the current `PageRequestManager` instance passes one of the following exceptions into the `_endPostBack` method when it invokes the method and thereafter fires its `endRequest` event:

❑ `PageRequestManagerTimeoutException`

❑ `PageRequestManagerServerErrorException`

❑ `PageRequestManagerParserErrorException`

❑ `InvalidOperationException`

To understand what these exceptions are we need to study the methods that generate them, which we'll do in the following sections.

PageRequestManagerTimeoutException

Listing 24-38 presents the internal implementation of the `_createPageRequestManagerTimeoutError` method of the `PageRequestManager` class. As you can see, this method creates an error object with the following two properties:

❑   `message`: This property specifies the following error message:

```
var displayMessage = "Sys.WebForms.PageRequestManagerTimeoutException: " +
                     Sys.WebForms.Res.PRM_TimeoutError;
```

❑   `name`: This property specifies the name of the exception, `Sys.WebForms`
    `.PageRequestManagerTimeoutException`.

Listing 24-38: The _createPageRequestManagerTimeoutError Method of PageRequestManager

```
function Sys$WebForms$PageRequestManager$_createPageRequestManagerTimeoutError()
{
  var displayMessage = "Sys.WebForms.PageRequestManagerTimeoutException: " +
                       Sys.WebForms.Res.PRM_TimeoutError;
  var e = Error.create(displayMessage,
                       {name: 'Sys.WebForms.PageRequestManagerTimeoutException'});
  e.popStackFrame();
  return e;
}
```

PageRequestManagerServerErrorException

Listing 24-39 presents the internal implementation of the `_createPageRequestManagerServerError` method of the `PageRequestManager` class. As you can see, this method creates an error object with the following three properties:

❑   `message`: This property specifies the following error message:

```
var displayMessage "Sys.WebForms.PageRequestManagerServerErrorException: " +
                   String.format(Sys.WebForms.Res.PRM_ServerError, httpStatusCode));
```

❑   `name`: This property specifies the name of the exception, `Sys.WebForms`
    `.PageRequestManagerServerErrorException`.

❑   `httpStatusCode`: This property specifies the HTTP status code of the server response.

Listing 24-39: The _createPageRequestManagerServerError Method of PageRequestManager

```
function Sys$WebForms$PageRequestManager$_createPageRequestManagerServerError(
                                                    httpStatusCode, message)
{
  var displayMessage = message ||
              ("Sys.WebForms.PageRequestManagerServerErrorException: " +
                  String.format(Sys.WebForms.Res.PRM_ServerError, httpStatusCode));
  var e = Error.create(displayMessage,
        {name: 'Sys.WebForms.PageRequestManagerServerErrorException',
          httpStatusCode: httpStatusCode});
  e.popStackFrame();
  return e;
}
```

PageRequestManagerParserErrorException

Listing 24-40 presents the internal implementation of the _createPageRequestManagerParserError method of the PageRequestManager class. As you can see, this method creates an error object with the following two properties:

❑ message: This property specifies the following error message:

```
var displayMessage = "Sys.WebForms.PageRequestManagerParserErrorException: " +
              String.format(Sys.WebForms.Res.PRM_ParserError, parserErrorMessage);
```

❑ name: This property specifies the name of the exception, Sys.WebForms
.PageRequestManagerParserErrorException.

Listing 24-40: The _createPageRequestManagerParserError Method of PageRequestManager

```
function Sys$WebForms$PageRequestManager$_createPageRequestManagerParserError(
                                                    parserErrorMessage)
{
  var displayMessage = "Sys.WebForms.PageRequestManagerParserErrorException: " +
            String.format(Sys.WebForms.Res.PRM_ParserError, parserErrorMessage);
  var e = Error.create(displayMessage,
                  {name: 'Sys.WebForms.PageRequestManagerParserErrorException'});
  e.popStackFrame();
  return e;
}
```

InvalidOperationException

Listing 24-41 presents the internal implementation of the invalidOperation static method of the Error class. As you can see, this method creates an error object with the following two properties:

❑ message: This property specifies the following error message:

```
var displayMessage = "Sys.InvalidOperationException: " +
                    (message ? message : Sys.Res.invalidOperation);
```

❑   name: This property specifies the name of the exception, Sys.InvalidOperationException.

Listing 24-41: The invalidOperation Static Method of Error

```
Error.invalidOperation = function Error$invalidOperation(message)
{
  var displayMessage = "Sys.InvalidOperationException: " +
                       (message ? message : Sys.Res.invalidOperation);
  var e = Error.create(displayMessage, {name: 'Sys.InvalidOperationException'});
  e.popStackFrame();
  return e;
}
```

Listing 24-42 presents the skeleton of a sample custom error handler that you can use to handle errors that the current PageRequestManager raises when it fires its endRequest event. Use this error handler if you want to handle the error on the client side by simply displaying the appropriate error to the end user.

Listing 24-42: A Custom Error Handler Skeleton

```
function myCustomErrorHandler(error)
{
  switch (error.name)
  {
    case 'Sys.WebForms.PageRequestManagerTimeoutException':
      // Handle error here
      break;
    case 'Sys.WebForms.PageRequestManagerServerErrorException':
      switch (error.httpStatusCode)
      {
        case 300:
          // Handle error here
          break;
        case 301:
          // Handle error here
          break;
        case 302:
          // Handle error here
          break;
        case 303:
          // Handle error here
          break;
        case 305:
          // Handle error here
          break;
        case 307:
          // Handle error here
          break;
        case 400:
          // Handle error here
          break;
        case 401:
          // Handle error here
          break;
```

```
        case 403:
          // Handle error here
          break;
        case 404:
          // Handle error here
          break;
        // . . .
      }
      break;
    case 'Sys.WebForms.PageRequestManagerParserErrorException':
      // Handle error here
      break;
    case 'Sys.InvalidOperationException':
      // Handle error here
      break;
    default:
      // Handle error here
      break;
  }
}
```

Another thing that a custom error handler can do is quietly send an e-mail to the site administration when an error occurs. Listing 24-43 presents an example of a page that uses this approach.

Listing 24-43: A Page that Uses a Custom Error Handler

```
<%@ Page Language="C#" %>
<%@ Import Namespace="System.Drawing" %>
<%@ Import Namespace="System.Net.Mail" %>
<!DOCTYPE html PUBLIC "-//W3C//DTD XHTML 1.1//EN"
"http://www.w3.org/TR/xhtml11/DTD/xhtml11.dtd">
<script runat="server">
  void Page_Load(object sender, EventArgs e)
  {
    if (Request.Form["ErrorName"] != null)
    {
      MailMessage mail = new MailMessage();
      MailAddress fromAddress = new MailAddress("admin@somesite.com");
      mail.From = fromAddress;
      MailAddress toAddress = new MailAddress("admin@somesite.com");
      mail.To.Add(toAddress);
      mail.Subject = "Asynchronous Page Postback Request Error at " + DateTime.Now;
      mail.Body = "Error Name: " + Request.Form["ErrorName"];
      if (Request.Form["HttpStatusCode"] != null)
        mail.Body += ("<br/>" + "HTTP Status Code: " +
                    Request.Form["HttpStatusCode"]);
      mail.IsBodyHtml = true;
      SmtpClient smtp = new SmtpClient();
      smtp.Host = "HostName";
      smtp.Send(mail);
      Response.End();
    }
```

(continued)

Listing 24-43 *(continued)*

```
      Label parentUpdatePanelLabel =
                              (Label)Page.FindControl("ParentUpdatePanelLabel");
      parentUpdatePanelLabel.Text = "UpdatePanel refreshed at " +
                              DateTime.Now.ToString();
      Label childUpdatePanelLabel = (Label)Page.FindControl("ChildUpdatePanelLabel");
      childUpdatePanelLabel.Text = "UpdatePanel refreshed at " +
                              DateTime.Now.ToString();
    }
</script>
<html xmlns="http://www.w3.org/1999/xhtml">
<head runat="server">
  <title>Untitled Page</title>
  <script type="text/javascript" language="javascript">
    function customErrorHandler(error)
    {
      var formBody = new Sys.StringBuilder();
      formBody.append('ErrorName=');

      if (!error)
        formBody.append(
              encodeURIComponent(
  'Sys.WebForms.PageRequestManagerRequestAbortedException'));
      else
        formBody.append(encodeURIComponent(error.name));

      formBody.append('&');

      if (error && error.name ==
  'Sys.WebForms.PageRequestManagerServerErrorException')
      {
        formBody.append('HttpStatusCode=');
        formBody.append(encodeURIComponent(error.httpStatusCode));
        formBody.append('&');
      }

      var request = new Sys.Net.WebRequest();
      request.set_url(document.form1.action);
      request.set_body(formBody.toString());
      request.invoke();
    }
    function pageLoad ()
    {
      var prm = Sys.WebForms.PageRequestManager.getInstance();
      prm.remove_endRequest(endRequestHandler);
      prm.add_endRequest(endRequestHandler);
    }
```

```
         function endRequestHandler(sender, e)
         {
           var error = e.get_error();
           if (error)
           {
             customErrorHandler(error);
             return;
           }

           var response = e.get_response();
           if (response.get_aborted())
           {
             customErrorHandler(null);
             return;
           }

           var dataItems = e.get_dataItems();
           var builder = new Sys.StringBuilder();
           builder.append("dataItems: ");
           builder.appendLine();
           for (var controlID in dataItems)
           {
             builder.append("Control ID: ");
             builder.append(controlID);
             builder.appendLine();
             builder.append("Data Item: ");
             builder.append(dataItem[controlID]);
             builder.appendLine();
           }

           alert(builder.toString());
         }
       </script>
     </head>
     <body>
       <form id="form1" runat="server">
         <asp:ScriptManager ID="ScriptManager1" runat="server" />
         <table cellspacing="10">
           <tr>
             <td align="center" colspan="2">
               <asp:UpdatePanel ID="ParentUpdatePanel" UpdateMode="Conditional"
               runat="server">
                 <ContentTemplate>
                   <table cellspacing="20" style="background-color: #dddddd">
                     <tr>
                       <th>
                         Parent UpdatePanel Control</th>
                     </tr>
```

(continued)

Listing 24-43 *(continued)*

```
                  <tr>
                   <td>
                     <asp:Label ID="ParentUpdatePanelLabel" runat="server" />
                        
                     <asp:Button ID="ParentUpdatePanelButton" runat="server"
                     Text="Update" />
                   </td>
                  </tr>
                  <tr>
                   <td style="width: 100%">
                     <asp:UpdatePanel ID="ChildUpdatePanel" runat="server">
                       <ContentTemplate>
                         <table style="background-color: #aaaaaa">
                           <tr>
                             <th>
                               Child UpdatePanel Control</th>
                           </tr>
                           <tr>
                             <td>
                               <asp:Label ID="ChildUpdatePanelLabel"
                               runat="server" />
                                  
                               <asp:Button ID="ChildUpdatePanelButton"
                               runat="server" Text="Update" />
                             </td>
                           </tr>
                           <tr>
                             <td>
                             </td>
                           </tr>
                         </table>
                       </ContentTemplate>
                       <Triggers>
                         <asp:AsyncPostBackTrigger
                         ControlID="ChildUpdatePanelTrigger" EventName="Click" />
                       </Triggers>
                     </asp:UpdatePanel>
                   </td>
                  </tr>
                </table>
            </ContentTemplate>
            <Triggers>
              <asp:AsyncPostBackTrigger ControlID="ParentUpdatePanelTrigger"
              EventName="Click" />
            </Triggers>
          </asp:UpdatePanel>
       </td>
     </tr>
```

```
    <tr>
      <td style="width:50%">
        <asp:Button ID="ChildUpdatePanelTrigger" runat="server"
        Text="Child UpdatePanel Trigger" Width="100%" />
      </td>
      <td>
        <asp:Button ID="ParentUpdatePanelTrigger" runat="server"
        Text="Parent UpdatePanel Trigger" Width="100%" />
      </td>
    </tr>
  </table>
</form>
</body>
</html>
```

As you can see, the `pageLoad` JavaScript function is where we register a JavaScript function named `endRequestHandler` as an event handler for the `endRequest` event of the current `PageRequestManager` instance:

```
function pageLoad ()
{
  var prm = Sys.WebForms.PageRequestManager.getInstance();
  prm.remove_endRequest(endRequestHandler);
  prm.add_endRequest(endRequestHandler);
}
```

When the current `PageRequestManager` instance finally fires the `endRequest` event and invokes the `endRequestHandler` function, it passes two parameters into this function. The first references the current `PageRequestManager` instance. The second references the `EndRequestEventArgs` object that contains the event data for the current `endRequest` event.

Now let's walk through the code for the `endRequestHandler` function. As you can see from Listing 24-43, this function first invokes the `get_error` method on the `EndRequestEventArgs` object to return a reference to the error object, if any.

```
var error = e.get_error();
```

If the current `PageRequestManager` instance has indeed raised an error, the `endRequestHandler` method invokes the custom error handler function, passing in the error object. Note that the `endRequestHandler` method simply returns after invoking the error handler function. I'll discuss the `customErrorHandler` function shortly.

```
if (error)
{
  customErrorHandler(error);
  return;
}
```

Next, the `endRequestHandler` function invokes the `get_response` method on the `EndRequestEventArgs` object to return a reference to the `WebRequestExecutor` object responsible for executing the current request:

```
var response = e.get_response();
```

Then the function calls the `get_aborted` method on the `WebRequestExecutor` object to return a Boolean value that specifies whether the current request has been aborted. If so, it invokes our custom error handler function, passing in `null`:

```
if (response.get_aborted())
{
  customErrorHandler(null);
  return;
}
```

Next, it invokes the `get_dataItems` method on the `EndRequestEventArgs` object to return the dictionary that contains all data items:

```
var dataItems = e.get_dataItems();
```

Then it instantiates a `StringBuilder` and populates it with the data items in this dictionary. Note that the `endRequestHandler` function uses the control ID as an index into the dictionary to access its associated data item. As we discussed earlier, each data item is associated with a particular server control on the current page.

```
var builder = new Sys.StringBuilder();
builder.append("dataItems: ");
builder.appendLine();
for (var controlID in dataItems)
{
  builder.append("Control ID: ");
  builder.append(controlID);
  builder.appendLine();
  builder.append("Data Item: ");
  builder.append(dataItem[controlID]);
  builder.appendLine();
}

alert(builder.toString());
```

Next, I'll walk you through the implementation of the `customErrorHandler` function. The main responsibility of this method is to make an asynchronous request containing the error information to the server. What the server does with this error information is completely up to your application. As you'll see later in this example, the server will simply send an e-mail containing the error information to the system administrator.

As you can see from Listing 24-43, the `customErrorHandler` function first instantiates a `StringBuilder`, which will accumulate a list of ampersand-separated strings that will make up the body of the request that will subsequently be sent to the server. Each string will consist of two parts separated by the equals sign (=), where the first part will be used as a key on the server side to access the second part. The second part contains a piece of error information.

```
var formBody = new Sys.StringBuilder();
```

The `customErrorHandler` function adds two strings to the `StringBuilder`. The first part (the key) of the first string is the string `ErrorName`:

```
formBody.append('ErrorName=');
```

The second part of the first string contains the name of the error. Recall that the `endRequestHandler` function passes `null` into the `customErrorHandler` function if the request has been aborted. As such, the `customErrorHandler` appends the string `Sys.WebForms.PageRequestManagerRequestAbortedException` as the error name. Keep in mind that the ASP.NET AJAX client-side framework does not contain an error with this name. I've added this for consistency.

```
if (!error)
    formBody.append(
            encodeURIComponent(
'Sys.WebForms.PageRequestManagerRequestAbortedException'));
```

If the error object passed into the `customErrorHandler` function is not `null`, the function simply appends the value of the `name` property of the error object as the error name:

```
else
    formBody.append(encodeURIComponent(error.name));
```

The `customErrorHandler` function appends an & character before it starts rendering the second string. Keep in mind that the strings that make up the body of the request must be separated by & character:

```
formBody.append('&');
```

Next, the `customErrorHandler` function checks whether the error is of type `Sys.WebForms.PageRequestManagerServerErrorException`. If so, it appends a second string as follows. First, it appends the string `HttpStatusCode` as the first part (that is, the key) of the string:

```
formBody.append('HttpStatusCode=');
```

Then it appends the value of the `httpStatusCode` property of the error object as the second part of the string:

```
formBody.append(encodeURIComponent(error.httpStatusCode));
formBody.append('&');
```

Next, it instantiates a `WebRequest` object to represent a new asynchronous request:

```
var request = new Sys.Net.WebRequest();
```

1271

Then it calls the set_url method on the WebRequest object to set the target URL of the request to the value of the action property of the form DOM element:

```
request.set_url(document.form1.action);
```

Next, it calls the toString method on the StringBuilder to return a string that makes up the body of the request, and passes this string into the set_body method of the WebRequest object:

```
request.set_body(formBody.toString());
```

Finally the customErrorHandler function calls the invoke method on the WebRequest object to send the request to the server:

```
request.invoke();
```

Next, we need to go to the server side, where this request is processed. As you can see from Listing 24-43, the Page_Load method checks whether the Form collection of the current ASP.NET Request object contains an item with the key ErrorName. If so, it takes the following steps to send an e-mail to the administrator. First, it instantiates a MailMessage object to represent the e-mail being sent:

```
MailMessage mail = new MailMessage();
```

Next, it instantiates a MailAddress object to represent the e-mail address of the sender and assigns this object to the From property of the MailMessage object that represents the e-mail being sent:

```
MailAddress fromAddress = new MailAddress("error@somesite.com");
mail.From = fromAddress;
```

Next, it instantiates another MailAddress object to represent the e-mail address of the receiver, that is, the administrator, and adds this object to the To collection property of the MailMessage that represents the e-mail being sent:

```
MailAddress toAddress = new MailAddress("admin@somesite.com");
mail.To.Add(toAddress);
```

Then it specifies the subject of the e-mail:

```
mail.Subject = "Asynchronous Page Postback Request Error at " + DateTime.Now;
```

Next, it specifies the body of the e-mail. Note that the body contains the error name and HTTP status code (if any):

```
mail.Body = "Error Name: " + Request.Form["ErrorName"];
if (Request.Form["HttpStatusCode"] != null)
   mail.Body += ("<br/>" + "HTTP Status Code: " +
                Request.Form["HttpStatusCode"]);
mail.IsBodyHtml = true;
```

Then it instantiates a `SmtpClient` object to send the e-mail:

```
SmtpClient smtp = new SmtpClient();
smtp.Host = "HostName";
smtp.Send(mail);
```

Finally the `Page_Load` method calls the `End` method on the ASP.NET `Response` object to end processing of the current request:

```
Response.End();
```

Summary

This chapter followed the current `PageRequestManager` instance thorough its life cycle phases to process the asynchronous server response text and update the associated `UpdatePanel` server controls and scripts.

The chapters of this book used numerous examples, code walkthroughs, and under-the-hood looks to help you gain the skills, knowledge, and experience you need to take full advantage of the rich features of the ASP.NET AJAX framework in your own Web application. The earlier chapters of the book showed you how the ASP.NET AJAX client-side framework manages to simulate the rich features of the ASP.NET/.NET framework on the client side to enable you to use an ASP.NET/.NET-like programming style and techniques in your own client code. These earlier chapters covered a wide range of topics such as JavaScript base type extensions, object-oriented programming, exception programming, type inspection/description, event programming, and component/control development.

We then dived into the client-server communication layer of the ASP.NET AJAX framework, where you learned how to use a .NET-like network programming style in your client-side code to communicate with the backend server. From there we moved on to Web services, where you learned how to enable your client code to exchange SOAP and JSON messages with Web services. You also learned four different ways to make a remote method call from your client code. Those discussions took us to the next related topic, proxy classes, where you learned how to use these classes to save yourself from having to write a lot of code to make remote method calls.

We then moved on to the ASP.NET AJAX behaviors, where we also discussed the ASP.NET AJAX control toolkit. Next we covered script and extender server controls, where you learned how to develop your own custom versions. Finally, we covered `UpdatePanel` and `ScriptManager` server controls and ASP.NET AJAX partial page rendering.

The appendices of the book will begin by providing an in-depth coverage of ASP.NET AJAX XML-script and showing you how it enables you to implement most features of your ASP.NET AJAX application in a purely declarative fashion, without writing imperative JavaScript code. This is great news to those of you who prefer declarative programming over imperative programming. These appendices will then cover ASP.NET AJAX actions, where you'll learn how to encapsulate your favorite client-side functionality in a component known as an action and how to execute this component in response to a specified event of a specified ASP.NET AJAX object.

We'll then move on to ASP.NET AJAX binding, which will teach you how to bind specified properties of a given ASP.NET AJAX object to specified properties of another ASP.NET AJAX object. The appendices will then take us to data controls, and you'll learn how to implement your own custom data controls that can bind to your favorite data collections to display the records of these collections. We'll then dive into templated controls, where you'll learn how to develop your own custom templated data controls. Finally, you'll get a complete coverage of the ASP.NET AJAX `ListView` templated data control.

XML Script

The xml-script is an XML document enclosed within the opening and closing tags of an HTML `script` element whose `type` attribute is set to `text/xml-script`. The xml-script, like any other XML document, has a single element known as the *document element* that encapsulates the rest of the xml-script. In other words, the document element is the outermost or containing element of an XML document. The document element in the case of the xml-script XML document is an element named `page` that belongs to an XML namespace named `http://schemas.microsoft.com/xml-script/2005`. The `page` document element contains a child element named `components`, which belongs to the same XML namespace as the `page` element. The descendants of the `components` element are the declarative representations of ASP.NET AJAX client-side objects.

The ASP.NET AJAX client-side framework comes with an extensible JavaScript library that parses the descendants of the `components` element, instantiates and initializes the ASP.NET AJAX client-side objects that these descendant elements represent, and adds these ASP.NET AJAX client-side objects to the current ASP.NET AJAX application. As you'll see later, an ASP.NET AJAX client class named `MarkupContext` plays an important role in the logic that parses the xml-script document. Therefore, I'll begin by discussing this class.

MarkupContext

Every instance of the `MarkupContext` ASP.NET AJAX class contains two important pieces of information:

❑ An XML document that contains a subtree of DOM elements. As you'll see later, the `MarkupContext` class comes with methods that you can use to search this document for a particular DOM element.

❑ An object collection that contains a list of ASP.NET AJAX components. As you'll see later, the `MarkupContext` class comes with methods that you can use to search this collection for a particular ASP.NET AJAX component, or to add a new component to this collection.

In general, there're two types of markup contexts:

❏ Global markup context: The XML document of the global markup context contains all the DOM elements in the current document, including those in the xml-script. In other words, the document object is the XML document of the global markup context. The object collection of the global markup context contains all the ASP.NET AJAX components in the current page.

❏ Local markup context: The XML document of a local markup context contains a subtree of DOM elements that do not belong to the document object. In other words, you cannot call the getElementById method on the document object to access the DOM elements in this subtree. That is why MarkupContext comes with methods that enable you to access the DOM elements in the XML document of a local markup context. Local markup contexts are normally used in ASP.NET templates. As you'll see later, the createInstance method of the ASP.NET AJAX Template class instantiates and initializes a local MarkupContext.

The following code listing presents the constructor of the MarkupContext class:

```
Sys.Preview.MarkupContext =
function Sys$Preview$MarkupContext(document, global, parentContext, dataContext)
{
  this._document = document;
  this._global = global;
  this._parentContext = parentContext;
  this._objects = { };
  this._pendingReferences = [];
  this._pendingEndUpdates = [];
}
```

This constructor takes the four parameters shown in the following table:

Parameter	Description
document	This parameter references the XML document associated with the MarkupContext.
global	This Boolean parameter specifies whether the MarkupContext is global.
parentContext	This parameter references the parent markup context of the current markup context. The parent markup context of the global markup context is null.
dataContext	This parameter references the current data context. (I'll cover data contexts later.)

Note that the constructor of the MarkupContext instantiates an internal collection named _objects, in which it will maintain the list of its associated ASP.NET AJAX client-side components. The MarkupContext class exposes a method named addComponent that adds a new ASP.NET AJAX component to the _objects collection.

As you'll see later, every time the xml-script parser parses a node in xml-script and instantiates the ASP .NET AJAX component that the node represents, it calls the `addComponent` method on the current `MarkupContext` class to add this component to its `_objects` collection. As you can see from the following code listing, each component is stored in this collection under its `id`. (Recall that every ASP.NET AJAX component is uniquely identified by its `id`.) Note that `addComponent` takes a second argument of type Boolean that specifies whether the specified component must also be added to the `Application` object that represents the current application. Also note that the `addComponent` method does not add the specified component to the current `Application` if the current markup context is a local markup context.

```
function Sys$Preview$MarkupContext$addComponent(component, noRegisterWithApp)
{
  var id = component.get_id();
  if(id)
    this._addComponentByID(id, component, noRegisterWithApp);
}
function Sys$Preview$MarkupContext$_addComponentByID(id, object, noRegisterWithApp)
{
  this._objects[id] = object;
  if(!noRegisterWithApp && this._global && Sys.Component.isInstanceOfType(object))
    Sys.Application.addComponent(object);
}
```

This makes finding an ASP.NET AJAX component interesting. The `MarkupContext` exposes a method named `findComponent` that takes two parameters, the first being a string that contains the `id` of the component that you're looking for. If the second parameter is not specified, `findComponent` first searches through the `_objects` collection of the current markup context for the component with the specified `id`. If it can't find it there, `findComponent` then calls the `findComponent` method on the parent `MarkupContext` object. In most cases, the parent `MarkupContext` object is the global markup context.

If the second parameter is specified, the `findComponent` method simply calls the `findComponent` method on the `Application` object that represents the current application, to look for the component among the child components of the specified parent.

```
function Sys$Preview$MarkupContext$findComponent(id, parent)
{
  if(parent)
    return Sys.Application.findComponent(id, parent);

  else
  {
    var object = this._objects[id];
    if (!object)
    {
        parent = this._parentContext || Sys.Application;
        object = parent.findComponent(id);
    }
    return object;
  }
}
```

The `MarkupContext` class also exposes a method named `getComponents` that returns all the components in its `_objects` collection of the current markup context.

```
function Sys$Preview$MarkupContext$getComponents()
{
  var res = [];
  var objects = this._objects;
  for (var id in objects)
    res[res.length] = objects[id];

  return res;
}
```

Another interesting method of the `MarkupContext` class is one named `findElement`. As the name implies, this method returns a reference to the DOM element with the specified `id` HTML attribute value. It's interesting to see how the search for this DOM element is performed. The `findElement` method first calls the `getElementById` method to search for the DOM element in the `_document` XML document fragment. Recall that the `_document` field of `MarkupContext` contains the XML document fragment associated with `MarkupContext`. In other words, `MarkupContext` assumes that the DOM element you're looking for is in this XML document fragment. If it can't find the element there, it searches the XML document fragment of its parent `MarkupContext` for the DOM element.

```
function Sys$Preview$MarkupContext$findElement(id)
{
  if (this._opened)
  {
    var element = Sys.UI.DomElement.getElementById(id, this._document);
    if (!element && this._parentContext)
      element = Sys.UI.DomElement.getElementById(id, this._parentContext);

    return element;
  }
  return null;
}
```

Note that the constructor of the `MarkupContext` class instantiates another internal collection named `_pendingReferences`. As we discussed earlier, when the xml-script parser parses a node in the xml-script into its associated ASP.NET AJAX component, it calls the `addComponent` method on the current `MarkupContext` to add the component to its `_objects` collection. If this component contains a property that references another ASP.NET AJAX component, the parser also invokes the `addReference` method on the current `MarkupContext` to add a reference to the `_pendingReferences` collection for this property. This reference is a JavaScript object literal that has three properties: o, which refers to the ASP.NET AJAX component that owns the property that references another ASP.NET AJAX component, p, which refers to the `propertyInfo` object that represents this property, and r, which refers to the `id` of the referenced ASP.NET AJAX component. In other words, instead of trying to initialize the property that references another ASP.NET AJAX component, the parser makes a note of it by adding this JavaScript object literal to the `_pendingReferences` collection of the current `MarkupContext` so it can initialize the property when it's done with parsing all the xml-script nodes associated with the current `MarkupContext`. This is necessary because the property could be referencing an ASP.NET AJAX component associated with an xml-script node that hasn't yet been parsed. To put it differently, the parser performs all the cross-references when it's done with parsing all the xml-script nodes associated with the current markup context.

```
function Sys$Preview$MarkupContext$addReference(instance, propertyInfo, reference)
{
  Array.add(this._pendingReferences,
          { o: instance, p: propertyInfo, r: reference });
}
```

When the xml-script parser is finally done with parsing all the xml-script nodes associated with the current markup context, it invokes the `close` method of the current `MarkupContext` to resolve the previously mentioned cross-references, as shown in the following code listing. The `close` method iterates through the JavaScript object literals in the `_pendingReferences` collection and takes the following steps for each enumerated object. First, it calls the `findComponent` method on the `MarkupContext`, passing in the value of the `r` property of the enumerated JavaScript object literal. Recall that this property contains the `id` of the component referenced by the property being initialized. Also recall that the `findComponent` method first looks for the referenced component in its own `_objects` collection. If it can't find the component there, it calls the `findComponent` method on its parent `MarkupContext` to look for the referenced component in the `_objects` collection of the parent `MarkupContext`. This search finally ends when the referenced component is located in the `_objects` collection of the first ancestor `MarkupContext` of the current `MarkupContext`.

Next, the `close` method creates the string that contains the name of the setter method of the property being initialized, and uses this string as an index into the ASP.NET AJAX component whose property is being initialized to return a reference to this setter method:

```
var setter = instance['set_' + propertyInfo.name];
```

Next, the `close` method invokes the setter method to set the value of the specified property of the referenced component.

```
function Sys$Preview$MarkupContext$close()
{
  this._opened = false;
  var i;
  for (i = 0; i < this._pendingReferences.length; i++)
  {
    var pendingReference = this._pendingReferences[i];
    var instance = pendingReference.o;
    var propertyInfo = pendingReference.p;
    var propertyValue = pendingReference.r;
    var object = this.findComponent(propertyValue);
    var setter = instance['set_' + propertyInfo.name];
    setter.call(instance, object);
  }
  this._pendingReferences = null;
}
```

The open method of MarkupContext instantiates the _pendingReferences collection and marks the MarkupContext as open:

```
function Sys$Preview$MarkupContext$open()
{
  this._pendingReferences = [];
  this._pendingEndUpdates = [];
  this._opened = true;
}
```

MarkupContext exposes a static method named createGlobalContext that creates the global MarkupContext. Note that the document object is passed into the constructor of the MarkupContext class to create the global markup context.

```
Sys.Preview.MarkupContext.createGlobalContext =
function Sys$Preview$MarkupContext$createGlobalContext()
{
  return new Sys.Preview.MarkupContext(document, true);
}
```

The MarkupContext class also exposes a static method named createLocalContext that creates a local MarkupContext. Note that the XML document fragment associated with this local markup context is passed into the constructor of the MarkupContext class. Also note that the parent MarkupContext is passed as the third argument to this constructor.

```
Sys.Preview.MarkupContext.createLocalContext =
function Sys$Preview$MarkupContext$createLocalContext(documentFragment,
                                        parentContext, dataContext)
{
  return new Sys.Preview.MarkupContext(documentFragment, false,
                              parentContext, dataContext);
}
```

Processing the xml-script XML Document

Listing A-1 presents the script that starts the processing of the xml-script XML document. This script is part of the PreviewScript.js JavaScript file and is loaded and executed automatically. As you can see, this script first invokes the createGlobalContext static method on the MarkupContext class to create the global MarkupContext. Recall that the XML document associated with the global markup context is the document object. Note that the script shown in Listing A-1 stores this global MarkupContext in the _markupContext private field of the Application object that represents the current ASP.NET AJAX application.

```
Sys.Application._markupContext = Sys.Preview.MarkupContext.createGlobalContext();
```

Next, the script shown in Listing A-1 registers a method of the Application object named __initHandler as an event handler for the init event of the Application object:

```
Sys.Application.add_init(Sys.Application.__initHandler);
```

Listing A-1: The Script that Starts the Processing of the xml-script XML Document

```
if(!Sys.Application._markupContext)
{
   Sys.Application._markupContext = Sys.Preview.MarkupContext.createGlobalContext();
   Sys.Application.add_init(Sys.Application.__initHandler);
   Sys.Application.add_unload(Sys.Application.__unloadHandler);
}
```

When the `Application` object that represents the current ASP.NET AJAX application finally raises its `init` event, the Application object automatically invokes the `__initHandler` method. As you can see from Listing A-2, this method in turn invokes the `processDocument` static method on an ASP.NET AJAX client class named `MarkupParser`, passing in the global `MarkupContext`:

```
Sys.Preview.MarkupParser.processDocument(Sys.Application._markupContext);
```

Listing A-2: The __initHandler Method

```
Sys.Application.__initHandler = function
Sys$Application$__initHandler()
{
    Sys.Application.remove_init(Sys.Application.__initHandler);

Sys.Preview.MarkupParser.processDocument(Sys.Application._markupContext);
}
```

processDocument

Listing A-3 presents a simplified version of the implementation of the `processDocument` method.

Listing A-3: The processDocument Method

```
Sys.Preview.MarkupParser.processDocument =
function Sys$Preview$MarkupParser$processDocument(markupContext)
{
   var pageNodes = [];
   var scriptElements = document.getElementsByTagName('script');
   var xmlScriptElement = null;

   for (var e = 0; e < scriptElements.length; e++)
   {
     if (scriptElements[e].type == 'text/xml-script')
     {
       xmlScriptElement = scriptElements[e];
       break;
     }
   }
}
```

(continued)

Listing A-3 *(continued)*

```
    if (xmlScriptElement)
    {
      var xmlDocument;
      if (Sys.Net.XMLDOM)
        xmlDocument = new Sys.Net.XMLDOM(scriptMarkup);
      else
        xmlDocument = new XMLDOM(xmlScriptElement.innerHTML);

      var documentElement = xmlDocument.documentElement;
      if (!documentElement ||
          Sys.Preview.MarkupParser.getNodeName(documentElement) != ="page")
        throw Error.create('Missing page element in xml script block.',
                            scriptMarkup);

      Sys.Preview.MarkupParser.processDocumentScripts(markupContext,
                                                      documentElement);

    }
  }
```

This method first calls the `getElementsByTagName` method on the `document` object to return an array that contains references to all `script` HTML elements on the current page:

```
    var scriptElements = document.getElementsByTagName('script');
```

Next, it searches through the `script` HTML elements in this array for a `script` HTML element with the `type` attribute value of `text/xml-script`:

```
    for (var e = 0; e < scriptElements.length; e++)
    {
      if (scriptElements[e].type == 'text/xml-script')
      {
        xmlScriptElement = scriptElements[e];
        break;
      }
    }
```

As I mentioned earlier, Listing A-3 presents a simplified version of the `ProcessDocument` method. The full version of this method supports multiple `script` HTML elements with a `type` attribute value of `text/xml-script`.

Next the `processDocument` method loads the content of this `script` HTML element into an XMLDOM document:

```
    var xmlDocument = new XMLDOM(xmlScriptElement.innerHTML);
```

Then it references the document element of the xml-script XML document. As we discussed earlier, the document element of the xml-script XML document is an element named `page`. If the document element does not exist or if it is anything other than the page element, the processDocument method raises an exception:

```
var documentElement = xmlDocument.documentElement;
if (!documentElement ||
    Sys.Preview.MarkupParser.getNodeName(documentElement) != ="page")
    throw Error.create('Missing page element in xml script block.',
                       scriptMarkup);
```

Finally, processDocument invokes the processDocumentScripts static method on the MarkupParser class, passing in the global MarkupContext and the document element of the xml-script XML document — that is, the page element or node:

```
Sys.Preview.MarkupParser.processDocumentScripts(markupContext,
                                                documentElement);
```

processDocumentScripts

Listing A-4 presents the implementation of the processDocumentScripts method.

Listing A-4: The processDocumentScripts Method

```
Sys.Preview.MarkupParser.processDocumentScripts =
function Sys$Preview$MarkupParser$processDocumentScripts(markupContext, pageNode)
{
  markupContext.open();
  var componentNodes = [];
  var pageChildNodes = pageNode.childNodes;
  for (var i = pageChildNodes.length - 1; i > =0; i--)
  {
    var pageChildNode = pageChildNodes[i];
    if (pageChildNode.nodeType != =1)
      continue;
    var pageChildNodeName = Sys.Preview.MarkupParser.getNodeName(pageChildNode);
    pageChildNodeName = pageChildNodeName.toLowerCase();

    if (pageChildNodeName === 'components')
    {
      for (var c = 0; c < pageChildNode.childNodes.length; c++)
      {
        var componentNode = pageChildNode.childNodes[c];
        if (componentNode.nodeType != =1)
          continue;
        Array.add(componentNodes, componentNode);
      }
    }
  }

  Sys.Preview.MarkupParser.parseNodes(componentNodes, markupContext);

  markupContext.close();
}
```

This method first invokes the open method on the global MarkupContext. Recall that the open method instantiates the _pendingReferences collection:

```
markupContext.open();
```

Next, the processDocumentScripts method searches through the child elements of the page node for a child element named components. It then iterates through the child elements of the components element and adds each enumerated child element to a local collection named componentNodes. (Keep in mind that each child element of the components element is a declarative representation of an ASP.NET AJAX client component. In other words, each child element of the components element is a component node.)

```
if (pageChildNodeName === 'components')
{
  for (var c = 0; c < pageChildNode.childNodes.length; c++)
  {
    var componentNode = pageChildNode.childNodes[c];
    if (componentNode.nodeType !== 1)
      continue;
    Array.add(componentNodes, componentNode);
  }
}
```

Next, the processDocumentScripts method invokes the parseNodes static method on the MarkupParser class, passing in two parameters. The first parameter is the array that contains the references to all the component child nodes of the components element. The second parameter references the global MarkupContext.

As you'll see later, the parseNodes method parses the nodes in its first parameter, determines the ASP.NET AJAX type associated with each node, instantiates this type, and adds it to the _objects collection of the MarkupContext object that is passed into the method as its second argument.

```
Sys.Preview.MarkupParser.parseNodes(componentNodes, markupContext);
```

Finally, the processDocumentScripts method invokes the close method on the global MarkupContext. Recall that the close method resolves the component cross-references.

```
markupContext.close();
```

parseNodes

The parseNodes static method of the MarkupParser class takes two parameters, as shown in the following table:

Parameter	Description
Nodes	An array that contains references to xml-script nodes being parsed.
markupContext	References the current MarkupContext. For example, as you'll see later, each `<template>` element in xml-script is associated with a local markup context, which means that all descendant nodes of this element are parsed within this local markup context.

The main responsibility of the parseNodes method is to parse the specified xml-script nodes into their associated ASP.NET AJAX objects.

As Listing A-5 shows, the parseNodes method iterates through these xml-script nodes and takes the following steps for each enumerated xml-script node. First, it invokes the parseNode static method on the MarkupParser class, passing in two parameters: the first is the reference to the enumerated xml-script node, and the second is the reference to the current MarkupContext.

```
var processedObject = Sys.Preview.MarkupParser.parseNode(node, markupContext);
```

As you'll see later, the parseNode method parses the specified xml-script node into its associated ASP.NET AJAX object, and returns this object. The parseNodes method then adds the object to an internal collection:

```
if (processedObject)
   Array.add(objects, processedObject);
```

As you can see, this internal collection basically collects all the ASP.NET AJAX objects associated with the xml-script nodes passed into the parseNodes method as its first argument. The parseNodes method then returns this collection to its caller:

```
if (processedObject)
   Array.add(objects, processedObject);
```

Listing A-5: The parseNodes Method

```
Sys.Preview.MarkupParser.parseNodes =
function Sys$Preview$MarkupParser$parseNodes(nodes, markupContext)
{
  var objects = [];
  for (var i = 0; i < nodes.length; i++)
  {
    var node = nodes[i];
    if (node.nodeType != =1)
      continue;
    var processedObject = Sys.Preview.MarkupParser.parseNode(node, markupContext);
    if (processedObject)
      Array.add(objects, processedObject);
  }
  return objects;
}
```

parseNode

The `parseNode` method, shown in Listing A-6, takes two parameters, as shown in the following table:

Parameter	Description
node	References the xml-script node being parsed
markupContext	References the current `MarkupContext`

The main responsibility of the `parseNode` method is to parse the specified xml-script node to its associated ASP.NET AJAX object. It begins by invoking the `_getTagType` static method on the `MarkupParser` class, passing in the reference to the xml-script node being parsed. As you'll see later, the `_getTagType` name determines and returns the `Type` object that represents the type of the ASP.NET AJAX class associated with the xml-script node being parsed:

```
var tagType = Sys.Preview.MarkupParser._getTagType(node);
```

Next, the `parseNode` method checks whether the ASP.NET AJAX class associated with the xml-script node being parsed contains a static method named `parseFromMarkup`. If so, it uses this method as the parsing method. If not, it walks up the ancestors of this ASP.NET AJAX class until it reaches an ancestor that supports the `parseFromMarkup` static method, and assigns this method as the static method of the ASP.NET AJAX class.

```
var parseMethod = tagType.parseFromMarkup;
if (!parseMethod)
{
  var baseType = tagType.getBaseType();
  while (baseType)
  {
    parseMethod = baseType.parseFromMarkup;
    if (parseMethod)
      break;

    baseType = baseType.getBaseType();
  }
  tagType.parseFromMarkup = parseMethod;
}
```

Next, it invokes the `parseFromMarkup` static method, passing in four parameters: the first is `null`, the second references the `Type` object that represents the ASP.NET AJAX class associated with the xml-script node being parsed, the third references the xml-script node being parsed, and the fourth references the current `MarkupContext`.

```
parsedObject = parseMethod.call(null, tagType, node, markupContext);
```

As you'll see later, the `parseFromMarkup` static method of the ASP.NET AJAX class that's associated with the xml-script node being parsed instantiates, initializes, and returns an instance of this class.

Listing A-6: The parseNode Method

```
Sys.Preview.MarkupParser.parseNode =
function Sys$Preview$MarkupParser$parseNode(node, markupContext)
{
  var parsedObject = null;
  var tagType = Sys.Preview.MarkupParser._getTagType(node);
  if (tagType)
  {
    var parseMethod = tagType.parseFromMarkup;
    if (!parseMethod)
    {
      var baseType = tagType.getBaseType();
      while (baseType)
      {
        parseMethod = baseType.parseFromMarkup;
        if (parseMethod)
          break;

        baseType = baseType.getBaseType();
      }
      tagType.parseFromMarkup = parseMethod;
    }
    if (parseMethod)
      parsedObject = parseMethod.call(null, tagType, node, markupContext);

  }
  return parsedObject;
}
```

_getTagType

The _getTagType static method of the MarkupParser class, shown in Listing A-7, takes a single parameter that references the node being parsed.

The main responsibility of the _getTagType method is to determine the ASP.NET AJAX type associated with the specified xml-script node. This method begins by invoking the getNodeName static method on the MarkupParser class to return the name of the xml-script node being parsed:

```
var tagName = Sys.Preview.MarkupParser.getNodeName(node);
```

It then determines the XML namespace to which the node being parsed belongs:

```
var namespaceURI = node.namespaceURI ||
                   Sys.Preview.MarkupParser._defaultNamespaceURI;
```

Note that the MarkupParser class exposes a static field named _defaultNamespaceURI with the following value:

```
Sys.Preview.MarkupParser._defaultNamespaceURI =
                          'http://schemas.microsoft.com/xml-script/2005';
```

The `MarkupParser` class also exposes another static collection field named `_cachedNamespaceURILists`, which caches the ASP.NET AJAX namespaces associated with each XML namespace.

```
Sys.Preview.MarkupParser._cachedNamespaceURILists = {};
```

The `_getTagType` method uses the XML namespace of the node being parsed as an index into this cache to return the list of ASP.NET AJAX namespaces associated with the node:

```
var nspaceList = Sys.Preview.MarkupParser._cachedNamespaceURILists[namespaceURI];
```

If the cache does not contain any ASP.NET AJAX namespaces associated with the XML namespace of the node being parsed, the `_getTagType` method invokes the `_processNamespaceURI` static method on the `MarkupParser` class to evaluate and return the list of ASP.NET AJAX namespaces associated with this XML namespace:

```
nspaceList = Sys.Preview.MarkupParser._processNamespaceURI(namespaceURI);
```

The `_getTagType` method then uses the XML namespace as an index into the cache to add this list of ASP.NET AJAX namespaces to the cache. As a result, the next request for this list will be serviced directly from the cache to improve performance:

```
Sys.Preview.MarkupParser._cachedNamespaceURILists[namespaceURI] = nspaceList;
```

Next, `_getTagType` uses the `toUpperCase` method to convert all lowercase characters in the name of the xml-script node to uppercase:

```
var upperTagName = tagName.toUpperCase();
```

Next, `_getTagType` iterates through the list of ASP.NET AJAX namespaces associated with the XML namespace of the xml-script node being parsed, and invokes the `parse` static method on the `Type` class, passing in the name of the xml-script node and the enumerated ASP.NET AJAX namespace. The `parse` static method determines whether the enumerated ASP.NET AJAX namespace contains an ASP.NET AJAX type with the same name as the xml-script node. If so, the method returns a reference to the constructor of the ASP.NET AJAX type.

```
for(var i=0; i < nspaceList.length; i++)
{
  var nspace = nspaceList[i];
  var type = Type.parse(tagName, nspace);
  if(typeof(type) === 'function')
    return type;
}
```

If none of the ASP.NET AJAX namespaces associated with the specified XML namespace contains an ASP.NET AJAX type with the same name as the xml-script node, the `_getTagType` checks whether the xml-script node's name is `APPLICATION`. If so, it simply returns a reference to the `Sys._Application` constructor.

```
if(upperTagName === "APPLICATION")
  return Sys._Application;
```

If the xml-script node's name is not APPLICATION either, the _getTagType checks whether the xml-script node's name is WEBREQUESTMANAGER. If so, it simply returns a reference to the Sys.Net._WebRequestManager constructor:

```
if(upperTagName === "WEBREQUESTMANAGER")
    return Sys.Net._WebRequestManager;
```

If the xml-script node's name is not WEBREQUESTMANAGER either, the _getTagType gives up and returns null to tell its caller that there's no ASP.NET AJAX type with the same name as the xml-script node whose type is being determined:

```
return null;
```

Listing A-7: The _getTagType Method

```
Sys.Preview.MarkupParser._getTagType =
function Sys$Preview$MarkupParser$_getTagType(node)
{
  var tagName = Sys.Preview.MarkupParser.getNodeName(node);
  var namespaceURI = node.namespaceURI ||
                     Sys.Preview.MarkupParser._defaultNamespaceURI;
  var nspaceList = Sys.Preview.MarkupParser._cachedNamespaceURILists[namespaceURI];
  if (typeof(nspaceList) === 'undefined')
  {
    nspaceList = Sys.Preview.MarkupParser._processNamespaceURI(namespaceURI);
    Sys.Preview.MarkupParser._cachedNamespaceURILists[namespaceURI] = nspaceList;
  }

  var upperTagName = tagName.toUpperCase();
  for(var i=0; i < nspaceList.length; i++)
  {
    var nspace = nspaceList[i];
    var type = Type.parse(tagName, nspace);
    if(typeof(type) === 'function')
      return type;
  }

  if(upperTagName === "APPLICATION")
    return Sys._Application;

  if(upperTagName === "WEBREQUESTMANAGER")
    return Sys.Net._WebRequestManager;

  return null;
}
```

_processNamespaceURI

The main responsibilities of the _processNamespaceURI static method of the MarkupParser class are to create and return an array that contains all the ASP.NET AJAX namespaces associated with the specified XML namespace URI. Listing A-8 contains the implementation of this method.

Listing A-8: The _processNamespaceURI Method

```
Sys.Preview.MarkupParser._processNamespaceURI =
function Sys$Preview$MarkupParser$_processNamespaceURI(namespaceURI)
{
  if(!namespaceURI ||
     namespaceURI === Sys.Preview.MarkupParser._defaultNamespaceURI)
    return Sys.Preview.MarkupParser._getDefaultNamespaces();

  var start = namespaceURI.slice(0, 12).toLowerCase();
  if(start === "javascript:")
  {
    namespaceURI = namespaceURI.slice(11);
    if(!namespaceURI.length)
      return [];
  }
  var nspaceList = namespaceURI.split(',');
  list = [];
  for(var i=0; i < nspaceList.length; i++)
  {
    var nspaceName = nspaceList[i];
    if(nspaceName.startsWith(' '))
      nspaceName = nspaceName.trimStart();
    if(nspaceName.endsWith(' '))
      nspaceName = nspaceName.trimEnd();
    if(!nspaceName.length)
      continue;
    var nspace = null;
    try
    {
      nspace = eval(nspaceName);
    }
    catch(e) { }

    if (!nspace || !Type.isNamespace(nspace))
      throw Error.invalidOperation(String.format("'{0}' is not a valid namespace.",
                                                  nspaceName));

    if(nspace)
      Array.add(list, nspace);
  }
  return list;
}
```

If the specified XML namespace URI is the default namespace (that is, the standard `http://schemas` `.microsoft.com/xml-script/2005` XML namespace) the `_processNamespaceURI` delegates to the `_getDefaultNamespaces` static method of the `MarkupParser` class the responsibility of creating and returning the array that contains all the ASP.NET AJAX namespaces associated with this standard XML namespace. I'll discuss this static method in the following section.

```
if(!namespaceURI ||
   namespaceURI === Sys.Preview.MarkupParser._defaultNamespaceURI)
  return Sys.Preview.MarkupParser._getDefaultNamespaces();
```

Next, the `_processNamespaceURI` splits the specified XML namespace URI into an array of XML namespace names:

```
var nspaceList = namespaceURI.split(',');
list = [];
```

Then it iterates through these XML namespace names and invokes the `eval` JavaScript function once for each XML namespace name, to return one reference for each namespace to the actual XML namespace.

```
nspace = eval(nspaceName);
```

As you can see, the xml-script is very strict about the names of the custom XML namespaces. They cannot include strings such as `http://`; they must be the name of the actual ASP.NET AJAX namespaces. The `eval` JavaScript function basically takes the string that contains the name of an ASP.NET AJAX namespace and returns a reference to the actual namespace.

Note that if the value that the `eval` method returns is not a valid ASP.NET AJAX namespace, the `_processNamespaceURI` raises an exception:

```
if (!nspace || !Type.isNamespace(nspace))
   throw Error.invalidOperation(String.format("'{0}' is not a valid namespace.",
                                              nspaceName));
```

Also note that the `_processNamespaceURI` collects in a local array the return values of the calls into the `eval` method (that is, the actual ASP.NET AJAX namespaces). This array is then returned to the caller of the method:

```
Array.add(list, nspace);
```

_getDefaultNamespaces

As you can see from Listing A-9, the `_getDefaultNamespaces` method populates the `_defaultNamespace` static array field of the `MarkupParser` class with the list of standard ASP.NET AJAX namespaces such as `Sys`, `Sys.UI`, `Sys.Net`, and so on.

Listing A-9: The _getDefaultNamespaces Method

```
Sys.Preview.MarkupParser._getDefaultNamespaces =
function Sys$Preview$MarkupParser$_getDefaultNamespaces()
{
  if(!Sys.Preview.MarkupParser._defaultNamespaces)
  {
    var list = [ Sys, Sys.UI, Sys.Net, Sys.Preview, Sys.Preview.UI,
                 Sys.Preview.Net, Sys.Preview.Data, Sys.Preview.UI.Data,
                 Sys.Preview.Services.Components ];

    if(Sys.Preview.UI.Effects)
      Array.add(list, Sys.Preview.UI.Effects);
    Sys.Preview.MarkupParser._defaultNamespaces = list;
  }
  return Sys.Preview.MarkupParser._defaultNamespaces;
}
```

parseFromMarkup

Each ASP.NET AJAX type either defines a static method named `parseFromMarkup` or inherits this method from its first ancestor, which defines this method through the process discussed earlier. This method takes the three parameters shown in the following table:

Parameter	Description
type	This parameter references the constructor of the ASP.NET AJAX type associated with the xml-script node being parsed. Recall that this ASP.NET AJAX type has the same name as the xml-node being parsed.
node	This parameter references the xml-node being parsed.
markupContext	This parameter references the current `MarkupContext`. Recall that the current `MarkupContext` internally maintains three important entities. The first one is a document fragment that contains a subtree of nodes (`_document`). The second is a collection of ASP.NET AJAX components (`_objects`). The third is a collection of JavaScript object literals, each of which represents a property of an ASP.NET AJAX component that references another ASP.NET AJAX component (`_pendingReferences`).

As mentioned earlier, the `parseFromMarkup` method is a static method: it is defined on an ASP.NET AJAX type itself, not its `prototype` property. The `parseFromMarkup` static method of a given ASP.NET AJAX type has the following main responsibilities:

❑ It must instantiate an instance of the ASP.NET AJAX type. Since the first parameter of the `parseFromMarkup` method references the constructor of this type, instantiating an instance is normally as simple as invoking the `new` JavaScript operator on this constructor:

```
var instance = new type();
```

❑ It must initialize this instance. Initializing an ASP.NET AJAX object involves two main tasks:

    ❑ Initializing the properties of the instance: The second parameter of the `parseFromMarkup` method references the xml-script node that represents this instance in xml-script. This xml-script node contains attributes or child nodes with the same names as the properties of this ASP.NET AJAX instance. The `parseFromMarkup` method must parse the values of these attributes or child nodes and assign them to the properties of the ASP.NET AJAX instance with the same names. For some properties of this ASP.NET AJAX instance, such as those simple properties that directly map to the attributes on the xml-script node, the `parseFromMarkup` method may simply use the DOM API to access the values of these attributes and directly assign them to the properties of the instance. For some more complex properties, the `parseFromMarkup` method delegates the responsibility of initialization to the `initializeObject` static method of the `MarkupParser` class.

    ❑ Registering event handlers for the events of the instance: As just mentioned, the second parameter of the `parseFromMarkup` method references the xml-script node that represents this instance in xml-script. This xml-script node contains attributes or child nodes with the same names as the events of this ASP.NET AJAX instance. The `parseFromMarkup` method must parse the values of these attributes or child nodes. These values are nothing but the names of the event handlers that must be registered for the specified events. Since the `initializeObject` static method of the `MarkupParser` class already contains the logic that knows how to get a reference to the event handler with the specified name, the `parseFromMarkup` method normally delegates the responsibility of registering event handlers for the events of the instance to the `initializeObject` method.

❑ It must add this ASP.NET AJAX instance to the `_objects` collection of the current `MarkupContext`. Recall that this collection maintains the list of all the ASP.NET AJAX instances parsed within the current `MarkupContext`. As we discussed earlier, the current `MarkupContext` exposes a method named `addComponent` that the `parseFromMarkup` method can use to add the newly parsed ASP.NET AJAX instance to this collection.

The `parseFromMarkup` method is the most important extensibility point of the ASP.NET AJAX xml-script-parsing infrastructure. Your custom classes can define a custom `parseFromMarkup` method to take complete control over how the xml-script node that represents an instance of your custom class in xml-script must be parsed. The custom `parseFromMarkup` method of your custom class must meet the following requirements:

❑ It must be named `parseFromMarkup`.

❑ It must take three parameters. The first references the constructor of your custom class, the second references the xml-script node that represents the current instance of your custom class in xml-script, and the third references the current `MarkupContext`.

❑ It must instantiate, initialize, and return the instance of your custom class that represents the xml-script node referenced by the second parameter.

❑ It must be static — that is, it must be defined on your custom class, not its `prototype` property.

You'll see an example of a custom `parseFromMarkup` method in Appendix E. If your custom component does not define its own `parseFromMarkup` method, the ASP.NET AJAX xml-script-parsing infrastructure walks up the ancestors of your custom class searching for the first ancestor that support this method and assigns it to your custom class. In other words, your custom class will end up using the `parseFromMarkup` method of its first ancestor that supports this method.

For example, if you implement a custom control that derives from the `Control` base class, and if your custom control does not directly support its own `parseFromMarkup` method, it will end up using the `parseFromMarkup` method of the `Control` base class, as shown in Listing A-10.

Listing A-10: The parseFromMarkup Method

```
Sys.UI.Control.parseFromMarkup =
function Sys$UI$Control$parseFromMarkup(type, node, markupContext)
{
  var idAttribute = node.attributes.getNamedItem('id');
  var id = idAttribute.nodeValue;
  var associatedElement = markupContext.findElement(id);
  var dataContextHidden = false;
  var dataContext = markupContext.get_dataContext();
  if (dataContext)
    dataContextHidden = markupContext.hideDataContext();
```

(continued)

Listing A-10 *(continued)*

```
var newControl = new type(associatedElement);
var control = Sys.Preview.MarkupParser.initializeObject(newControl, node,
                                                         markupContext);

if (control)
{
  var id = control.get_id();
  markupContext.addComponent(control);
  if (dataContext)
    control.set_dataContext(dataContext);
}

else
  newControl.dispose();
if (dataContextHidden)
  markupContext.restoreDataContext();
return control;
}
```

This listing shows an example of the implementation of the `parseFromMarkup` method. You can follow this example to implement your own custom `parseFromMarkup` method for your own custom classes. Next, I'll walk you through this sample `parseFromMarkup` method.

As you can see, it begins by calling the `getNamedItem` method on the `attributes` collection of the xml-script node that represents the current control in xml-script to return a reference to the attribute node that represents the `id` attribute of the xml-script node:

```
var idAttribute = node.attributes.getNamedItem('id');
```

Next, it invokes the `nodeValue` property on this attribute node to access the value of the `id` attribute:

```
var id = idAttribute.nodeValue;
```

Then it invokes the `findElement` method on the current `MarkupContext`, passing in the `id` attribute value to return a reference to the associated DOM element of the control. Recall that each ASP.NET AJAX client control is associated with a DOM element whose `id` HTML attribute is given by the `id` attribute of the xml-script node that represents the client control in xml-script:

```
var associatedElement = markupContext.findElement(id);
```

Next, it invokes the `new` JavaScript operator on the constructor of the client control, passing in the reference to the associated DOM element of the control to instantiate the client control associated with the specified xml-script node. Recall that the first parameter of the `parseFromMarkup` method references the constructor of the ASP.NET AJAX type associated with the specified xml-script node:

```
var newControl = new type(associatedElement);
```

Then the `parseFromMarkup` method delegates the responsibility of initializing the properties of the newly instantiated client control, and the responsibility of registering event handlers for its events, to the `initializeObject` static method of the `MarkupParser` class:

```
var control = Sys.Preview.MarkupParser.initializeObject(newControl, node,
                                                        markupContext);
```

Next, the `parseFromMarkup` method calls the `addComponent` method on the current `MarkupContext` to add the client control to its `_objects` collection. Recall that the current `MarkupContext` maintains the list of all the ASP.NET AJAX components parsed in the current markup context in this collection:

```
markupContext.addComponent(control);
```

initializeObject

The `initializeObject` method takes the three parameters described in the following table:

Parameter	Description
instance	References the ASP.NET AJAX object being initialized
node	References the xml-script node that represents the ASP.NET AJAX object being initialized
markupContext	References the current `MarkupContext`

As the name suggests, the `initializeObject` method initializes the ASP.NET AJAX object that its first parameter references. This initialization involves two main tasks:

❏ Initializing the properties of the ASP.NET AJAX object: The xml-script node referenced by the second parameter of the `initializeObject` method exposes attributes or child nodes with the same names as the properties of the ASP.NET AJAX object being initialized. The `initializeObject` method extracts the required values from these attributes or child nodes and assigns them to the properties of the ASP.NET AJAX object with the same names.

❏ Registering event handlers for the events of the ASP.NET AJAX object: The xml-script node referenced by the second parameter of the `initializeObject` method exposes attributes or child nodes with the same names as the events of the ASP.NET AJAX object being initialized. The `initializeObject` method extracts the required event handlers from these attributes or child nodes and registers them as event handlers for the events of the ASP.NET AJAX object with the same names.

Before diving into the implementation of the `initializeObject` method we need to revisit the ASP.NET AJAX `TypeDescriptor` class, because the `initializeObject` method makes extensive use of this class and its methods. Recall from Chapter 10 that every ASP.NET AJAX type, such as a class, is associated with an object known as a type descriptor, which generically describes the properties, events, methods, and metadata attributes of the type. This object allows the client of an ASP.NET AJAX type to inspect the type generically without knowing the actual type of the type.

The ASP.NET AJAX `TypeDescriptor` class comes with a static method named `getTypeDescriptor` that takes an ASP.NET AJAX object as its argument and returns a reference to the type descriptor object that describes the type of this ASP.NET AJAX object.

As you'll see shortly, to initialize the ASP.NET AJAX object passed into it in a generic way, the `initializeObject` method uses the type descriptor object returned by the `getTypeDescriptor` static method of the `TypeDescriptor` class. Therefore, the type descriptor object associated with a given ASP.NET AJAX type determines how an instance of the type is initialized from the attributes and child nodes of the xml-script node that represents the instance in xml-script.

Therefore, if you want to enable the clients of your custom ASP.NET AJAX type to instantiate and initialize instances of your custom type in xml-script in a purely declarative fashion, without their writing any JavaScript code, you must take extra steps to make sure that the `getTypeDescriptor` static method of the `TypeDescriptor` class returns the appropriate type descriptor object to the `initializeObject` method. You have two options:

❑ Have your custom type implement the `ICustomTypeProvider` interface, so the `getTypeDescriptor` static method returns your own custom type descriptor object.

❑ Define a `descriptor` static property on your custom type to describe the properties, events, methods, and metadata attributes of your type, as we discussed earlier.

Which approach is better? It depends on the specifics of your application requirements. In general, the first approach is more flexible than the second but requires more coding. Keep in mind that your custom type must either implement the `ICustomTypeProvider` interface or expose a static property named `descriptor`. Otherwise no one will be able to use your custom type declaratively in xml-script.

The implementation of the `initializeObject` method is quite complex. To help you get a better understanding of this method, I'll present an example of its implementation. This example consists of four ASP.NET AJAX client classes named `MyCustomType`, `MyEnumeration`, `MyType`, and `MyType2`. A JavaScript file named `MyClientTypes.js` contains the implementation of these three client classes. Listing A-11 presents the content of this JavaScript file.

Listing A-11: The Content of the MyClientTypes.js JavaScript File

```
Type.registerNamespace("CustomComponents");
CustomComponents.MyType2 =
function CustomComponents$MyType2(param1, param2, param3)
{
   this._param1 = param1;
   this._param2 = param2;
   this._param3 = param3;
}
CustomComponents.MyType2.registerClass("CustomComponents.MyType2");
CustomComponents.MyType2.parse = function (value)
{
   var params = value.split(',');
   alert("Instantiating a MyType2 object and initializing it with " + params);
   return new CustomComponents.MyType2(params[0], params[1], params[2]);
}
/////////////////////////////////
CustomComponents.MyEnumeration = function CustomComponents$MyEnumeration()
{
   throw Error.invalidOperation();
}
```

```
CustomComponents.MyEnumeration.prototype =
{
  EnumValue1: 0,
  EnumValue2: 1,
  EnumValue3: 2
}
CustomComponents.MyEnumeration.registerEnum("CustomComponents.MyEnumeration");
/////////////////////////////////
CustomComponents.MyType = function CustomComponents$MyType()
{
}
function CustomComponents$MyType$set_myTypeProperty(value)
{
  this._myTypeProperty = value;
  alert("myTypeProperty was set to " + value);
}
function CustomComponents$MyType$get_myTypeProperty()
{
  return this._myTypeProperty;
}
CustomComponents.MyType.prototype =
{
  get_myTypeProperty : CustomComponents$MyType$get_myTypeProperty,
  set_myTypeProperty : CustomComponents$MyType$set_myTypeProperty
}
CustomComponents.MyType.registerClass("CustomComponents.MyType");
CustomComponents.MyType.descriptor =
{
  properties : [{name : "myTypeProperty", type : String}]
}
/////////////////////////////////
CustomComponents.MyCustomType = function CustomComponents$MyCustomType()
{
  CustomComponents.MyCustomType.initializeBase(this);
}
function CustomComponents$MyCustomType$add_myEvent(eventHandler)
{
  this.get_events().addHandler("myEvent", eventHandler);
  alert(eventHandler + " \n\nwas registered as event handler for myEvent event!");
}
function CustomComponents$MyCustomType$remove_myEvent(eventHandler)
{
  this.get_events().removeHandler("myEvent", eventHandler);
}
function CustomComponents$MyCustomType$set_myProperty(value)
{
  this._myProperty = value;
  alert("myProperty was set to the DOM element with id HTML attribute value of " +
        value.id);
}
```

(continued)

Listing A-11 *(continued)*

```
function CustomComponents$MyCustomType$get_myProperty()
{
  return this._myProperty;
}
function CustomComponents$MyCustomType$set_myNonReadOnlyStringProperty(value)
{
  this._myNonReadOnlyStringProperty = value;
  alert("myNonReadOnlyStringProperty was set to " + value);
}
function CustomComponents$MyCustomType$get_myNonReadOnlyStringProperty()
{
  return this._myNonReadOnlyStringProperty;
}
function CustomComponents$MyCustomType$set_myProperty2(value)
{
  this._myProperty2 = value;
  alert("myProperty2 was set to " + value);
}
function CustomComponents$MyCustomType$get_myProperty2()
{
  return this._myProperty2;
}
function CustomComponents$MyCustomType$set_myReferenceProperty(value)
{
  this._myReferenceProperty = value;
  alert("myReferenceProperty was set to the component with the id value of " +
        value.get_id());
}
function CustomComponents$MyCustomType$get_myReferenceProperty()
{
  return this._myReferenceProperty;
}
function CustomComponents$MyCustomType$set_myArrayProperty(value)
{
  this._myArrayProperty = value;
  alert("myArrayProperty was set to " + value);
}
function CustomComponents$MyCustomType$get_myArrayProperty()
{
  return this._myArrayProperty;
}
function CustomComponents$MyCustomType$get_myReadOnlyArrayProperty()
{
  alert("The value of myReadOnlyArrayProperty is being retrieved!");
  return this._myReadOnlyArrayProperty;
}
```

```
function CustomComponents$MyCustomType$get_myObjectProperty()
{
  alert("The value of myObjectProperty is being retrieved!");
  return this._myObjectProperty;
}
function CustomComponents$MyCustomType$get_myNonObjectNonArrayProperty()
{
  alert("The value of myNonObjectNonArrayProperty is being retrieved!");
  if (!this._myNonObjectNonArrayProperty)
    this._myNonObjectNonArrayProperty = new CustomComponents.MyType();
  return this._myNonObjectNonArrayProperty;
}
function CustomComponents$MyCustomType$set_myEnumProperty(value)
{
  this._myEnumProperty = value;
  alert("myEnumProperty was set to " + value);
}
function CustomComponents$MyCustomType$get_myEnumProperty()
{
  return this._myEnumProperty;
}
CustomComponents.MyCustomType.prototype =
{
  _myReadOnlyArrayProperty : [],
  _myObjectProperty : {},
  set_myProperty : CustomComponents$MyCustomType$set_myProperty,
  get_myProperty : CustomComponents$MyCustomType$get_myProperty,
  set_myNonReadOnlyStringProperty :
                CustomComponents$MyCustomType$set_myNonReadOnlyStringProperty,
  get_myNonReadOnlyStringProperty :
                CustomComponents$MyCustomType$get_myNonReadOnlyStringProperty,
  set_myProperty2 : CustomComponents$MyCustomType$set_myProperty2,
  get_myProperty2 : CustomComponents$MyCustomType$get_myProperty2,
  set_myReferenceProperty : CustomComponents$MyCustomType$set_myReferenceProperty,
  get_myReferenceProperty : CustomComponents$MyCustomType$get_myReferenceProperty,
  set_myArrayProperty : CustomComponents$MyCustomType$set_myArrayProperty,
  get_myArrayProperty : CustomComponents$MyCustomType$get_myArrayProperty,
  set_myEnumProperty : CustomComponents$MyCustomType$set_myEnumProperty,
  get_myEnumProperty : CustomComponents$MyCustomType$get_myEnumProperty,
  get_myReadOnlyArrayProperty :
                CustomComponents$MyCustomType$get_myReadOnlyArrayProperty,
  get_myObjectProperty : CustomComponents$MyCustomType$get_myObjectProperty,
  get_myNonObjectNonArrayProperty :
                CustomComponents$MyCustomType$get_myNonObjectNonArrayProperty,
  add_myEvent : CustomComponents$MyCustomType$add_myEvent,
  remove_myEvent : CustomComponents$MyCustomType$remove_myEvent
}
```

(continued)

Listing A-11 *(continued)*

```
CustomComponents.MyCustomType.registerClass("CustomComponents.MyCustomType",
                                            Sys.Component);
CustomComponents.MyCustomType.descriptor =
{
  properties : [{name : 'myProperty', type : null, isDomElement : true},
               {name : 'myNonReadOnlyStringProperty', type : String},
               {name : 'myReferenceProperty',
                type : CustomComponents.MyCustomType},
               {name : 'myProperty2', type : CustomComponents.MyType2},
               {name : 'myArrayProperty', type : Array},
               {name : 'myEnumProperty', type : CustomComponents.MyEnumeration},
               {name : 'myReadOnlyArrayProperty', type : Array, readOnly : true},
               {name : 'myObjectProperty', type : Object, readOnly : true},
               {name : 'myNonObjectNonArrayProperty',
                type : CustomComponents.MyType, readOnly : true}],
  events : [{name : "myEvent"}]
}
if(typeof(Sys)!=='undefined')
  Sys.Application.notifyScriptLoaded();
```

Listing A-12 presents a page that uses these client classes in xml-script in a purely declarative fashion.

Listing A-12: A Page that Uses the Client Classes Defined in Listing A-11 in xml-script

```
<%@ Page Language="C#" %>
<!DOCTYPE html PUBLIC "-//W3C//DTD XHTML 1.0 Transitional//EN"
"http://www.w3.org/TR/xhtml1/DTD/xhtml1-transitional.dtd">
<html xmlns="http://www.w3.org/1999/xhtml">
<head id="Head1" runat="server">
  <title>Untitled Page</title>
  <script language="text/javascript" type="text/javascript">
    function myEventHandler (sender, eventArgs) { }
  </script>
</head>
<body>
  <form id="form1" runat="server">
    <asp:ScriptManager runat="server" ID="ScriptManager1">
      <Scripts>
        <asp:ScriptReference Assembly="Microsoft.Web.Preview"
        Name="PreviewScript.js" />
        <asp:ScriptReference Path="MyClientTypes.js" />
      </Scripts>
    </asp:ScriptManager>
    <div id="mydiv" />
    <div id="mydiv2" />
  </form>
```

```
<script type="text/xml-script">
  <page xmlns="http://schemas.microsoft.com/xml-script/2005"
  xmlns:custom="CustomComponents">
    <components>
      <custom:MyCustomType id="myCustomType1" myReferenceProperty="myCustomType2"
      myProperty="mydiv" myProperty2="'valuevvv1','valuevvv2','valuevvv3'"
      myArrayProperty="'value1','value2'"
      myEnumProperty="EnumValue2" myEvent="myEventHandler">
        <myReadOnlyArrayProperty>
          <custom:MyType myTypeProperty="'value1'" />
          <custom:MyType myTypeProperty="'value2'" />
        </myReadOnlyArrayProperty>
        <myObjectProperty myObjectPropertyProperty1="'value1'"
        myObjectPropertyProperty2="'value2'" />
        <myNonReadOnlyStringProperty>value1</myNonReadOnlyStringProperty>
        <myNonObjectNonArrayProperty myTypeProperty="'value1'" />
      </custom:MyCustomType>

      <custom:MyCustomType id="myCustomType2" myProperty="mydiv2" />
    </components>
  </page>
</script>
</body>
</html>
```

I'll walk you through the implementation of these client classes (that is, Listing A-11) as we're walking through the implementation of the `initializeObject` method, shown in Listing A-13.

Listing A-13: The initializeObject Method

```
Sys.Preview.MarkupParser.initializeObject =
function Sys$Preview$MarkupParser$initializeObject(instance, node, markupContext)
{
  var td = Sys.Preview.TypeDescriptor.getTypeDescriptor(instance);
  if (!td)
    return null;

  var supportsBatchedUpdates = false;
  if ((instance.beginUpdate && instance.endUpdate && instance !==Sys.Application))
  {
    supportsBatchedUpdates = true;
    instance.beginUpdate();
  }
  var i, a;
  var attr, attrName;
  var propertyInfo, propertyName, propertyType, propertyValue;
  var eventInfo, eventValue;
  var setter, getter;
  var properties = td._getProperties();
  var events = td._getEvents();
  var attributes = node.attributes;
```

(continued)

Listing A-13 *(continued)*

```
if (attributes)
{
  for (a = attributes.length - 1; a > =0; a--)
  {
    attr = attributes[a];
    attrName = attr.nodeName;

    if(attrName === "id" && Sys.UI.Control.isInstanceOfType(instance))
      continue;
    propertyInfo = properties[attrName];
    if (propertyInfo)
    {
      propertyType = propertyInfo.type;
      propertyValue = attr.nodeValue;
      if (propertyType &&
          (propertyType === Object ||
           propertyType === Sys.Component ||
           propertyType.inheritsFrom(Sys.Component)))
        markupContext.addReference(instance, propertyInfo, propertyValue);

      else
      {
        if (propertyInfo.isDomElement || propertyType === Sys.UI.DomElement)
          propertyValue = markupContext.findElement(propertyValue);

        else
        {
          if (propertyType === Array)
            propertyValue = Array.parse('[' + propertyValue + ']');

          else if (propertyType && propertyType != =String)
          {
            if(Type.isEnum(propertyType))
              propertyValue = propertyType.parse(propertyValue, true);

            else
            {
              if(propertyValue === "" && propertyType === Number)
                propertyValue = 0;

              else
                propertyValue =
                    (propertyType.parseInvariant || propertyType.parse)
                    (propertyValue);
            }
          }
        }
        propertyName = propertyInfo.name;
        setter = instance['set_' + propertyName];
        setter.call(instance, propertyValue);
      }
    }
  }
```

```
      else
      {
        eventInfo = events[attrName];
        if (eventInfo)
        {
          var handler = Function.parse(attr.nodeValue);
          if (handler)
          {
            eventValue = instance['add_' + eventInfo.name];
            if (eventValue)
              eventValue.apply(instance, [handler]);
            else
              throw Error.invalidOperation(String.format(
"The event '{0}' is specified in the type descriptor, but add_{0} was not found.",
                                          eventInfo.name));
          }
        }
        else
          throw Error.invalidOperation(
              String.format('Unrecognized attribute "{0}" on object of type "{1}"',
                          attrName, Object.getTypeName(instance)));
      }
    }
  }
}
var childNodes = node.childNodes;
if (childNodes && (childNodes.length ! =0))
{
  for (i = childNodes.length - 1; i >= 0; i--)
  {
    var childNode = childNodes[i];
    if (childNode.nodeType != 1)
      continue;
    var nodeName = Sys.Preview.MarkupParser.getNodeName(childNode);
    propertyInfo = properties[nodeName];
    if (propertyInfo)
    {
      propertyName = propertyInfo.name;
      propertyType = propertyInfo.type;
      if (propertyInfo.readOnly)
      {
        getter = instance['get_' + propertyName];
        var nestedObject = getter.call(instance);
        if (propertyType === Array)
        {
          if (childNode.childNodes.length)
          {
            var items = Sys.Preview.MarkupParser.parseNodes(childNode.childNodes,
                                                markupContext);
            for (var itemIndex = 0; itemIndex < items.length; itemIndex++)
            {
              var item = items[itemIndex];
              if(typeof(nestedObject.add) === "function")
                nestedObject.add(item);
```

(continued)

Listing A-13 *(continued)*

```
          else
          {
            Array.add(nestedObject, item);
            if(typeof(item.setOwner) === "function")
              item.setOwner(instance);
          }
        }
      }
    }

    else if (propertyType === Object)
    {
      attributes = childNode.attributes;
      for (a = attributes.length - 1; a >= 0; a--)
      {
        attr = attributes[a];
        nestedObject[attr.nodeName] = attr.nodeValue;
      }
    }
    else
      Sys.Preview.MarkupParser.initializeObject(nestedObject, childNode,
                                                markupContext);
  }

  else
  {
    propertyValue = null;
    if (propertyType == String)
      propertyValue = childNode.text;

    else if (childNode.childNodes.length != 0)
    {
      var valueNode;
      for (var childNodeIndex = 0;
           childNodeIndex < childNode.childNodes.length; childNodeIndex++)
      {
        if (childNode.childNodes[childNodeIndex].nodeType != 1)
          continue;

        valueNode = childNode.childNodes[childNodeIndex];
        break;
      }
      if (valueNode)
        propertyValue = Sys.Preview.MarkupParser.parseNode(valueNode,
                                                           markupContext);
    }
    if (propertyValue)
    {
      setter = instance['set_' + propertyName];
      setter.call(instance, propertyValue);
    }
  }
}
```

```
      else
      {
        eventInfo = events[nodeName];
        if (eventInfo)
        {
          var actions = Sys.Preview.MarkupParser.parseNodes(childNode.childNodes,
                                                markupContext);
          if (actions.length)
          {
            eventValue = instance["add_" + eventInfo.name];
            if(eventValue)
            {
              for (var e = 0; e < actions.length; e++)
              {
                var action = actions[e];
                action.set_eventName(eventInfo.name);
                action.set_eventSource(instance);
              }
            }
            else
              throw Error.invalidOperation(String.format(
"The event '{0}' is specified in the type descriptor, but add_{0} was not found.",
                                              eventInfo.name));
          }
        }

        else
        {
          var type = null;
          var upperName = nodeName.toUpperCase();
          if(upperName === 'BINDINGS')
            type = Sys.Preview.BindingBase;

          else if(upperName === 'BEHAVIORS')
            type = Sys.UI.Behavior;

          if(type)
          {
            if (childNode.childNodes.length)
            {
              var items = Sys.Preview.MarkupParser.parseNodes(childNode.childNodes,
                                                markupContext);
              for (var itemIndex = 0; itemIndex < items.length; itemIndex++)
              {
                var item = items[itemIndex];
                debug.assert(type.isInstanceOfType(item),
                  String.format("The '{0}' element may only contain child elements
                            of type '{1}'.", nodeName, type.getName()));
                if(typeof(item.setOwner) === "function")
                  item.setOwner(instance);
              }
            }
          }
        }
```

(continued)

Listing A-13 *(continued)*

```
        else
            throw Error.invalidOperation(String.format(
            'Unrecognized child node "{0}" on object of type "{1}"', nodeName,
                Object.getTypeName(instance))));
        }
      }
    }
  }
  if (supportsBatchedUpdates)
    markupContext.addEndUpdate(instance);
  return instance;
}
```

As you can see from Listing A-13, the `initializeObject` method begins by invoking the `getTypeDescriptor` static method on the `TypeDescriptor` class, passing in the reference to the ASP.NET AJAX object being initialized. This method returns a reference to the type descriptor object that describes the type of the ASP.NET AJAX object being initialized.

```
    var td = Sys.Preview.TypeDescriptor.getTypeDescriptor(instance);
```

Next, the `initializeObject` method invokes the `getProperties` method on the type descriptor object to return a dictionary that contains the complete information about the properties of the ASP.NET AJAX object being initialized:

```
    var properties = td._getProperties();
```

Next, the `initializeObject` method invokes the `getEvents` method on the type descriptor object to return a dictionary that contains the complete information about the events of the ASP.NET AJAX object being initialized:

```
    var events = td._getEvents();
```

Then the method accesses the `attributes` collection of the xml-script node referenced by the second parameter of the method. (Recall that this xml-script node represents the ASP.NET AJAX object being initialized.) The `attributes` collection contains one attribute node for each attribute on this xml-script node:

```
    var attributes = node.attributes;
```

Next, the `initializeObject` method iterates through the attribute nodes in the `attributes` collection and performs several tasks for each enumerated attribute node. First, the `initializeObject` method accesses the name of the attribute that the attribute node represents:

```
        attr = attributes[a];
        attrName = attr.nodeName;
```

The `initializeObject` method ignores the `id` attribute if the ASP.NET AJAX object being initialized is a client control. Recall from Listing A-10 that the `parseFromMarkup` method of the `Control` class has already taken care of the `id` attribute:

```
if(attrName === "id" && Sys.UI.Control.isInstanceOfType(instance))
    continue;
```

The method then uses the attribute name as an index into the `properties` collection, to return a reference to the property info object that contains the complete information about the property with the same name as the attribute. Recall that the `properties` collection is the return value of the call into the `_getProperties` method:

```
propertyInfo = properties[attrName];
```

If the `properties` collection does contain a property with the same name as the attribute, the `initializeObject` method accesses a reference to the constructor of the type of the property:

```
propertyType = propertyInfo.type;
```

It then accesses the attribute value:

```
propertyValue = attr.nodeValue;
```

If the property references a JavaScript object, or an instance of the ASP.NET AJAX `Component` class, or an instance of the ASP.NET AJAX class that derives from the ASP.NET AJAX `Component` class, the `initializeObject` method invokes the `addReference` method on the current `MarkupContext` to add a reference for this property to the `_pendingReferences` collection of the current `MarkupContext`. Recall that this collection contains one JavaScript object literal for each property that references another component. This JavaScript object literal exposes three properties: the first references the object that owns the property (which is the object being initialized), the second references the property info object that represents the property, and the last is the attribute value, which will be used to evaluate the property value. Recall that the actual evaluation takes place when the `close` method is invoked on the current `MarkupContext`. This is to ensure that the object being referenced is instantiated and initialized before it is referenced:

```
if (propertyType &&
    (propertyType === Object ||
     propertyType === Sys.Component ||
     propertyType.inheritsFrom(Sys.Component)))
    markupContext.addReference(instance, propertyInfo, propertyValue);
```

Next, I'll present an example of this case. As Listing A-11 shows, the `MyCustomType` class exposes a property named `myReferenceProperty` that references another `MyCustomType` component in the current application:

```
function CustomComponents$MyCustomType$set_myReferenceProperty(value)
{
    this._myReferenceProperty = value;
    alert("myReferenceProperty was set to the component with the id value of " +
        value.get_id());
}
```

Note that the setter method associated with this property pops up an alert that displays the new value of the property. As Listing A-11 shows, the value of the `properties` property of the `descriptor` static property of the `MyCustomType` contains the object literal shown in the boldface portion of the following code fragment, where the value of the `type` property of this object literal references the constructor of the `MyCustomType` type:

```
CustomComponents.MyCustomType.descriptor =
{
    properties : [. . .
        {name : 'myReferenceProperty', type : CustomComponents.MyCustomType}, . . . ],
    . . .
}
```

This object literal tells the `initializeObject` method that the `myReferenceProperty` property of the `MyCustomType` object references another `MyCustomType` object in the current application. As Listing A-12 shows, this enables you to use the boldface declarative syntax shown in the following code fragment to specify the value of this property in xml-script if the value of the `myReferenceProperty` attribute on the `<custom:MyCustomType>` element with an `id` property value of `myCustomType1` is set to the value of the `id` property of the `<custom:MyCustomType>` element with an `id` property value of `myCustomType2`:

```
<custom:MyCustomType id="myCustomType1" myReferenceProperty="myCustomType2" . . . >
    . . .
</custom:MyCustomType>

<custom:MyCustomType id="myCustomType2" . . .  />
```

Now back to the implementation of the `initializeObject` method. If the property references a DOM element, the `initializeObject` invokes the `findElement` method on the current `MarkupContext`, passing in the attribute value to return a reference to the DOM element that will be used as the value of the property:

```
if (propertyInfo.isDomElement || propertyType === Sys.UI.DomElement)
    propertyValue = markupContext.findElement(propertyValue);
```

Listing A-11 shows an example of this case, in which the `MyCustomType` component exposes a property named `myProperty` that references a DOM element. As you can see from this code listing, the value of the `properties` property of the `descriptor` property of the `MyCustomType` component contains an object literal, shown in the boldface portion of the following excerpt from this code listing:

```
CustomComponents.MyCustomType.descriptor =
{
    properties : [ {name : 'myProperty', type : null, isDomElement : true}, . . . ],
    . . .
}
```

This enables you to declaratively specify the value of the `myProperty` property by declaring an attribute named `myProperty` on an xml-script `<custom:MyCustomType>` node in xml-script, and setting the value of this attribute to the id HTML attribute value of the DOM element that the myProperty property is supposed to reference, as shown in the boldface portion of the following excerpt from Listing A-12:

```
<form id="form1" runat="server">
  . . .
  <div id="mydiv" />
</form>

<script type="text/xml-script">
  <page xmlns="http://schemas.microsoft.com/xml-script/2005"
  xmlns:custom="CustomComponents">
    <components>
      <custom:MyCustomType myProperty="mydiv" . . . >
        . . .
      </custom:MyCustomType>
    </components>
  </page>
</script>
```

Since the descriptor static property of the MyCustomType ASP.NET AJAX type specifies true as the value of the isDomElement property, the initializeObject method automatically passes the value of the myProperty attribute into the findElement method to return a reference to the referenced <div> DOM element, which is the actual value of the myProperty property.

Now back to the implementation of the initializeObject method. If the property is a JavaScript array, the initializeObject generates a string that encloses the attribute value within square brackets and parses this string into a JavaScript array, which will be used as the value of the property:

```
if (propertyType === Array)
  propertyValue = Array.parse('[' + propertyValue + ']');
```

Listing A-11 also shows an example of this case, in which MyCustomType exposes a property of type Array named myArrayProperty. Note that the properties property of the descriptor static property of MyCustomType contains the object literal shown in the boldface portion of the following excerpt from Listing A-11:

```
CustomComponents.MyCustomType.descriptor =
{
  properties : [. . . , {name : 'myArrayProperty', type : Array}, . . . ],
  . . .
}
```

This enables you to declaratively specify the value of the myArrayProperty property by declaring in xml-script an attribute named myArrayProperty on the xml-script <custom:MyCustomType> node and setting the value of this attribute to a comma-separated list of values, as shown in the boldface portion of the following excerpt from Listing A-12:

```
<custom:MyCustomType . . .  myArrayProperty="'value1','value2'" . . . >
  . . .
</custom:MyCustomType>
```

This excerpt sets the value of the myArrayProperty attribute on the <custom:MyCustomType> xml-script node to a comma-separated list of two values. Since the descriptor static property of MyCustomType specifies Array as the type of the myArrayProperty property, the initializeObject method automatically encloses the preceding comma-separated list of values in square brackets and passes the result into the parse method of the Array class to parse the list into a valid JavaScript array, to arrive at the actual value of the myArrayProperty property.

Now back to the implementation of the initializeObject method. If the property is not a string, the initializeObject method checks whether the property is an enumeration. If so, it parses the attribute value into the appropriate enumeration value, which will be used as the value of the property.

```
if (Type.isEnum(propertyType))
    propertyValue = propertyType.parse(propertyValue, true);
```

Next, we'll look at the portions of Listings A-11 and A-12 that cover this case. As Listing A-11 shows, MyCustomType exposes a property of type MyEnumeration named myEnumProperty, which has three possible values named EnumValue1, EnumValue2, and EnumValue3. Notice that the properties property of the descriptor static property of MyCustomType contains an object literal with the type value of CustomComponents.MyEnumeration, as shown in the boldface portion of the following excerpt from Listing A-11:

```
CustomComponents.MyCustomType.descriptor =
{
  properties : [. . .,
        {name : 'myEnumProperty', type : CustomComponents.MyEnumeration}, . . . ],
  . . .
}
```

This enables you to declaratively specify the value of the myEnumProperty property by declaring in xml-script an attribute named myEnumProperty on the xml-script <custom:MyCustomType> node and setting the value of this attribute to one of the possible values of the MyEnumeration — that is, EnumValue1, EnumValue2, or EnumValue3 — without having to specify the complete name of the value, as shown in the boldface portion of the following excerpt from Listing A-12. The complete name is prefixed by CustomComponents.MyEnumeration.

```
<custom:MyCustomType . . .   myEnumProperty="EnumValue2" . . . >
    . . .
</custom:MyCustomType>
```

This example sets the value of the myEnumProperty attribute on the <custom:MyCustomType> xml-script node to the enumeration value of EnumValue2 without your having to specify the complete name of the enumeration value, MyNamespace.MyEnumeration.MyEnumValue2. Since the descriptor static property of MyCustomType specifies CustomComponents.MyEnumeration as the type of the myEnumProperty property, the initializeObject method automatically calls the parse method to parse this attribute value to the actual MyNamespace.MyEnumeration.MyEnumValue2 enumeration value.

Now back to the implementation of the initializeObject method. If the property is not an enumeration, the initializeObject method simply invokes the parse static method on the type of the property to parse the attribute value, which will be used as the value of the property. In other words, `initializeObject` assumes that the `parse` static method of this type knows how to parse this attribute value to the type that the property expects.

```
            else
                propertyValue = propertyType.parse(propertyValue);
```

Next, I'll take a look at an example of this case. As you can see from Listing A-11, `MyCustomType` features a property named `myProperty2`:

```
function CustomComponents$MyCustomType$set_myProperty2(value)
{
    this._myProperty2 = value;
    alert("myProperty2 was set to " + value);
}
```

As you can see from the boldface portion of the following excerpt from Listing A-11, the `myProperty2` is of type `CustomComponents.MyType2`:

```
CustomComponents.MyCustomType.descriptor =
{
    properties : [. . . , {name : 'myProperty2', type : CustomComponents.MyType2},
                    . . . ],
    . . .
}
```

As Listing A-11 shows, `CustomComponents.MyType2` exposes the following `parse` static method, which parses the specified value into a `CustomComponents.MyType2` object and returns this object to its caller (the caller in our case being the `initializeObject` method):

```
CustomComponents.MyType2.parse = function (value)
{
    var params = value.split(',');
    alert("Instantiating a MyType2 object and initializing it with " + params);
    return new CustomComponents.MyType2(params[0], params[1], params[2]);
}
```

This is a powerful technique that you can use in your own client code to enable page developers to instantiate instances of your custom client classes from xml-script in a purely declarative fashion, as you can from the boldface portion of the following excerpt from Listing A-12. Here the page developer uses a declarative approach to instantiate an instance of `CustomComponents.MyType2` and to assign this instance to the `myProperty2` property of the specified `MyCustomType` component:

```
<custom:MyCustomType . . .  myProperty2="'value1','value2','value3'" . . . >
    . . .
</custom:MyCustomType>
```

Now back to the implementation of the `initializeObject` method. Now that the property's value has been determined, it's time to assign this value to the property. The `initializeObject` method takes several steps to accomplish this.

❑ First, it accesses the property name:

```
propertyName = propertyInfo.name;
```

❑ Then it generates a string that contains the name of the setter method for the property and uses this string as an index into the object being initialized to return a reference to this setter method:

```
setter = instance['set_' + propertyName];
```

❑ Finally, it invokes the `call` method on this reference to set the value of the property to the specified value:

```
setter.call(instance, propertyValue);
```

As you can see, the `initializeObject` method expects the getter and setter methods associated with a given property to follow these naming conventions:

```
get_PropertyName
set_PropertyName
```

PropertyName stands for the name of the property. Following these naming conventions will enable page developers to declare an attribute with the same name as the property on the xml-script node that represents an instance of your custom type in xml-script, and to assign the appropriate value to this attribute and rest assured that the `initializeObject` method will automatically invoke the underlying setter method to assign the specified value to the property.

Your custom ASP.NET AJAX type must explicitly describe its properties in the value of the `properties` property of its `descriptor` static property, as you saw in the previous examples.

It's very important to realize that the `initializeObject` method does not pick up the property information, such as name and type, from the `prototype` property of your custom type. Such information is picked up from the `descriptor` property. If you do not add object literals describing your properties to the value of the `properties` property of the `descriptor` property of your custom type, the `initializeObject` will have no way of knowing that your type exposes those properties. As we discussed earlier, another approach is to have your type implement the `ICustomTypeProvider` interface to return a type descriptor that describes these properties.

If the `properties` collection does not contain a property with the same name as the attribute, the `initializeObject` method uses the attribute name as an index into the `events` collection to return a reference to the event info object that contains the complete information about the event with the same name as the attribute. Recall that the `events` collection is the return value of the call into the `_getEvents` method:

```
eventInfo = events[attrName];
```

If the `events` collection does indeed contain an event with the same name as the attribute, the `initializeObject` method performs the following tasks:

❑ First, it invokes the `parse` static method on the `Function` class, passing in the attribute value to return a reference to the event handler being registered. As you can see, the `initializeObject` method assumes that the value assigned to the attribute is the name of the event handler being registered for the event with the same name as the attribute name:

```
var handler = Function.parse(attr.nodeValue);
```

❑ Next, it generates a string that contains the name of the method that registers event handlers for the event with the specified name, and uses this string as an index into the object being initialized in order to return a reference to this method:

```
eventValue = instance['add_' + eventInfo.name];
```

❑ Then the `initializeObject` method calls the `apply` method on this reference to invoke the method and consequently to register the specified event handler for the specified event of the object being initialized:

```
eventValue.apply(instance, [handler]);
```

As you can see, the `initializeObject` method expects the methods of your custom ASP.NET AJAX type that register event handlers for events with specified names to follow this naming convention:

add_*EventName*

EventName stands for the name of the event. Following this naming convention will enable page developers to declare an attribute with the same name as the event on the xml-script node that represents an instance of your custom type in xml-script, and to assign the name of the desired event handler to this attribute and rest assured that the `initializeObject` method will automatically invoke the underlying `add` method to register the specified event handler for the event with the specified name.

For example, as you can see from Listing A-11, `MyCustomType` exposes a method named `add_myEvent`:

```
function CustomComponents$MyCustomType$add_myEvent(eventHandler)
{
  this.get_events().addHandler("myEvent", eventHandler);
  alert(eventHandler + " \n\nwas registered as event handler for myEvent event!");
}
```

Notice that the value of the `events` property of the `descriptor` property of `MyCustomType` includes the object literal shown in the boldface portion of the following excerpt from Listing A-11:

```
CustomComponents.MyCustomType.descriptor =
{
  . . .
  events : [ {name : "myEvent"} ]
}
```

This object literal tells the `initializeObject` method that the attribute named `myEvent` contains the name of an event handler that must be registered for the `myEvent` event of the specified `MyCustomType` object. This enables the page developer to register an event handler such as `myEventHandler` in a purely declarative fashion in xml-script, as shown in the boldface portion of the following excerpt from Listing A-12:

```
<custom:MyCustomType . . .  myEvent="myEventHandler" . . . >
    . . .
</custom:MyCustomType>
```

When the `initializeObject` method encounters this boldface portion, it automatically calls the `parse` method to return a reference to the `myEventHandler` JavaScript function:

```
var refTomyEventHandler = Function.parse("myEventHandler");
```

It then creates the `"add_myEvent"` string and uses it as an index to return a reference to the `add_myEvent` method of your custom type:

```
var refToadd_myEvent = instance["add_" + "myEvent"];
```

It then calls the `apply` method on the `refToadd_myEvent` reference to invoke the `add_myEvent` method of `MyCustomType` to register the `myEventHandler` JavaScript function for `myEvent` event:

```
refToadd_MyEvent.apply(instance, [refTomyEventHandler]);
```

Again, it's very important to realize that the `initializeObject` method does not pick up the event information from the `prototype` property of your custom type. That information is picked up from the `descriptor` property. If you do not describe the events of your custom type in the `events` property of the `descriptor` property of your custom type, the `initializeObject` will have no way of knowing that your type exposes those events.

If neither the `properties` nor the `events` collection contains an entry with the same name as the attribute, the `initializeObject` method raises an exception because the specified attribute on the xml-script node referenced by the second parameter of the `initializeObject` method is unrecognized.

```
else
   throw Error.invalidOperation(
            String.format('Unrecognized attribute "{0}" on object of type "{1}"',
                         attrName, Object.getTypeName(instance)));
```

As you can see, the xml-script does not support expando *or* custom *attributes. Every attribute on an xml-script node that represents an ASP.NET AJAX object must map into either a property or an event of the ASP.NET AJAX object with the same name as the attribute.*

Next, the `initializeObject` method accesses the collection that contains the child nodes of the xml-script node referenced by the second parameter of the `initializeObject` method. Recall that this xml-script node represents the ASP.NET AJAX object being initialized:

```
var childNodes = node.childNodes;
```

Next, the `initialize` method iterates through these child xml-script nodes and performs several tasks for each enumerated child xml-script node.

First, the `initialize` method ignores the child xml-script node if the node is not an element node:

```
var childNode = childNodes[i];
if (childNode.nodeType ! =1)
  continue;
```

Next, it invokes the `getNodeName` static method on the `MarkupParser` class, passing in the child xml-script node to access the name of the node:

```
var nodeName = Sys.Preview.MarkupParser.getNodeName(childNode);
```

The `initialize` method then uses the node name as an index into the `properties` collection to return a reference to the property info object that contains the complete information about the property with the same name as the child xml-script node. Recall that the `properties` collection is the return value of the call into the `_getProperties` method:

```
propertyInfo = properties[nodeName];
```

If the `properties` collection contains a property with the same name as the child xml-script node, this is an indication that this child xml-script node represents this property. This means that the attributes and child nodes of this child xml-script node are there to specify the value of this property. Therefore, the value of this property must be an object. In other words, this property references a nested object. This is very similar to what is known in object-oriented programming as *object composition,* wherein one object composes or encapsulates another object. In this case, the object that owns the property encapsulates or composes the object referenced by the property. The `initializeObject` method performs the following tasks to initialize this property:

❑   Accesses the name of the property:

```
propertyName = propertyInfo.name;
```

❑   Accesses the `Type` object that represents the type of the property — that is, the type of the object represented by the property, or the type of the nested or composed object:

```
propertyType = propertyInfo.type;
```

If the property is read-only, the `initializeObject` takes the following steps. First, it generates a string that contains the name of the getter method that gets the value of the property, and uses this string as an index into the object being initialized (which is the object that owns the property), to return a reference to this getter method:

```
getter = instance['get_' + propertyName];
```

Next, it invokes the `call` method on this reference to invoke this getter method and to return the value of the property, which is the object encapsulated by the object that owns the property:

```
var nestedObject = getter.call(instance);
```

What happens next depends on the type of the property. If the property is a JavaScript array, the `initializeObject` method invokes the `parseNodes` static method on the `MarkupParser` class to parse the child xml-script nodes of the current child xml-script node:

```
var items = Sys.Preview.MarkupParser.parseNodes(childNode.childNodes,
                                                markupContext);
```

As we discussed earlier, the `parseNodes` method parses the specified xml-script nodes into their associated ASP.NET AJAX objects and returns a collection that contains these parsed objects. The `initializeObject` method then adds each parsed object to the property. Recall that the property is a JavaScript array:

```
for (var itemIndex = 0; itemIndex < items.length; itemIndex++)
{
  var item = items[itemIndex];
  if(typeof(nestedObject.add) === "function")
    nestedObject.add(item);

  else
  {
    Array.add(nestedObject, item);
    if(typeof(item.setOwner) === "function")
      item.setOwner(instance);
  }
}
```

For example, `MyCustomType`, shown in Listing A-11, exposes a property of type `Array` named `myReadOnlyArrayProperty`:

```
function CustomComponents$MyCustomType$get_myReadOnlyArrayProperty()
{
  alert("The value of myReadOnlyArrayProperty is being retrieved!");
  return this._myReadOnlyArrayProperty;
}
```

As the boldface portion of the following excerpt from Listing A-11 shows, the value of the `properties` property of the `descriptor` static property of `MyCustomType` contains an object literal that contains metadata information about the `myReadOnlyArrayProperty` property:

```
CustomComponents.MyCustomType.descriptor =
{
  properties : [. . .
                {name : 'myReadOnlyArrayProperty', type : Array, readOnly : true},
                . . . ],
  . . .
}
```

This enables you to declaratively specify the value of the `myReadOnlyArrayProperty` property in xml-script by declaring an xml-script node named `myReadOnlyArrayProperty` as the child node of the xml-script `<custom:MyCustomType>` node, which contains a bunch of `<custom:MyType>` child nodes. each of these nodes represents an item in the `myReadOnlyArrayProperty` array property, as shown in the boldface portion of the following excerpt from Listing A-12:

```
<custom:MyCustomType . . . >
  <myReadOnlyArrayProperty>
    <custom:MyType myTypeProperty="'value1'" />
    <custom:MyType myTypeProperty="'value2'" />
  </myReadOnlyArrayProperty>
  . . .
</custom:MyCustomType>
```

As you can see, each child node of a read-only array property such as `myReadOnlyArrayProperty` has its own attributes and child nodes. For example, each `<custom:MyType>` child node has its own `myTypeProperty` attribute. That is why the `initializeObject` method invokes the `parseNodes` method and passes all these child nodes into it to parse them into the appropriate ASP.NET AJAX objects. In our case, the `parseNodes` method will parse the `<custom:MyType>` child nodes into instances of the `CustomComponents.MyType` client class.

Now back to the implementation of the `initializeObject` method. If the property is not a JavaScript array, the `initializeObject` checks whether the property is a JavaScript object. If so, it first accesses the `attributes` collection of the child xml-script node. This collection contains one attribute node for each attribute on the child xml-script node. Then it uses the attribute name as an index into the JavaScript object to access the property of the object with the same name as the attribute, and assigns the attribute value as the value of this property:

```
else if (propertyType === Object)
{
  attributes = childNode.attributes;
  for (a = attributes.length - 1; a > =0; a--)
  {
    attr = attributes[a];
    nestedObject[attr.nodeName] = attr.nodeValue;
  }
}
```

Now let's take a look at an example before we continue with the implementation of the `initializeObject` method. As Listing A-11 shows, `MyCustomType` exposes a property named `myObjectProperty` with the following associated getter method:

```
function CustomComponents$MyCustomType$get_myObjectProperty()
{
  alert("The value of myObjectProperty is being retrieved!");
  return this._myObjectProperty;
}
```

As you can see from the boldface portion of the following excerpt from Listing A-12, the `descriptor` static property of `MyCustomType` describes this property as a read-only property of type `Object`:

```
CustomComponents.MyCustomType.descriptor =
{
  properties : [. . . ,
               {name : 'myObjectProperty', type : Object, readOnly : true},. . . ],
  . . .
}
```

This enables you to specify the value of the `myObjectProperty` property by declaring a `<myObjectProperty>` xml-script node as the child node of the `<custom:MyCustomType>` xml-script node and setting its `myObjectPropertyProperty1` and `myObjectPropertyProperty2` properties as the attributes with the same names on the `<myObjectProperty>` xml-script node, as shown in the boldface portion of the following excerpt from Listing A-12:

```
<custom:MyCustomType . . . >
   . . .
   <myObjectProperty myObjectPropertyProperty1="'value1'"
myObjectPropertyProperty2="'value2'" />
   . . .
</custom:MyCustomType>
```

In this case, the `initializeObject` method takes the following steps.

❑ First, it generates the string that contains the name of the getter method — that is, the string `"get_myObjectProperty"`. Next, it will use this string as an index into the ASP.NET AJAX object that represents the `<custom:MyCustomType>` xml-script node, in order to return a reference to the `get_myObjectProperty` getter method:

```
var refToget_myObjectPropertyMethod = instance['get_myObjectProperty'];
```

❑ Next, it will invoke the `call` method on `refToget_myObjectPropertyMethod` to invoke this method and consequently to return a reference to the object that the `myObjectProperty` property references — that is, the nested or composed object:

```
var nestedObject = refToget_myObjectPropertyMethod.call(instance);
```

❑ Then it uses `'myObjectPropertyProperty1'` and `'myObjectPropertyProperty2'` as indexes into the `nestedObject`, and assigns `'value1'` and `'value2'`:

```
nestedObject['myObjectPropertyProperty1'] = 'Value1';
nestedObject['myObjectPropertyProperty2'] = 'Value1';
```

Now back to the implementation of the `initializeObject` method. If the property is neither a JavaScript array nor a JavaScript `Object`, the `initializeObject` method invokes the `initializeObject` method once again to initialize this property. As you can see, `initializeObject` is a recursive method.

```
              else
                  Sys.Preview.MarkupParser.initializeObject(nestedObject, childNode,
                                                            markupContext);
```

Here is an example of this case. As you can see from Listing A-11, `MyCustomType` features a property named `myNonObjectNonArrayProperty` with the following associated getter method:

```
function CustomComponents$MyCustomType$get_myNonObjectNonArrayProperty()
{
  alert("The value of myNonObjectNonArrayProperty is being retrieved!");
  if (!this._myNonObjectNonArrayProperty)
    this._myNonObjectNonArrayProperty = new CustomComponents.MyType();
  return this._myNonObjectNonArrayProperty;
}
```

Notice that the value of the `properties` property of the `descriptor` static property of `MyCustomType` contains the object literal, which is shown in the boldface portion of the following excerpt from Listing A-11:

```
CustomComponents.MyCustomType.descriptor =
{
  properties : [ . . . , {name : 'myNonObjectNonArrayProperty',
                          type : CustomComponents.MyType, readOnly : true} . . . ],
  . . .
}
```

This object literal describes `myNonObjectNonArrayProperty` as a read-only property of type `CustomComponents.MyType`, which is neither an `Array` nor an `Object`. As the boldface portion of the following excerpt from Listing A-12 shows, you can specify the value of the `myNonObjectNonArrayProperty` property by declaring a `myNonObjectNonArrayProperty` xml-script node as the child node of the `<custom:MyCustomType>` xml-script node:

```
            <custom:MyCustomType . . . >
              . . .
              <myNonObjectNonArrayProperty myTypeProperty="'value1'" />
            </custom:MyCustomType>
```

Note that the xml-script node that represents a non-object, non-array property in xml-script may have its own attributes and child xml-script nodes. For example, the `<myNonObjectNonArrayProperty>` xml-script node in the preceding xml-script fragment contains an attribute named `myTypeProperty`, which maps to the `myTypeProperty` property of the `CustomComponents.MyType` object represented by this xml-script node. That is why the `initializeObject` method invokes the `initializeObject` method once again to have this method use these attributes and child nodes to initialize the `CustomComponents.MyType` object represented by the `<myNonObjectNonArrayProperty>` xml-script node.

Now back to the implementation of the `initializeObject` method. If the property is not read-only, the `initializeObject` method assigns the value of the `text` property of the child xml-script node as the value of the property if the property is a string:

```
            propertyValue = null;
            if (propertyType == String)
              propertyValue = childNode.text;
```

For example, `MyCustomType` shown in Listing A-11 features a property named `myNonReadOnlyStringProperty` with the following associated setter method:

```
function CustomComponents$MyCustomType$set_myNonReadOnlyStringProperty(value)
{
    this._myNonReadOnlyStringProperty = value;
    alert("myNonReadOnlyStringProperty was set to " + value);
}
```

As the boldface portion of the following excerpt from Listing A-11 shows, the value of the `properties` property of the `descriptor` property of `MyCustomType` contains an object literal that describes `myNonReadOnlyStringProperty` as a non-read-only property of type `String`:

```
CustomComponents.MyCustomType.descriptor =
{
    properties : [. . . ,
                  {name : 'myNonReadOnlyStringProperty', type : String}, . . . ],
    . . .
}
```

This enables you to specify the value of the `myNonReadOnlyStringProperty` property by declaring a `<myNonReadOnlyStringProperty>` xml-script node as the child node of the `<custom:MyCustomType>` xml-script node and setting the content of this child node as shown in the boldface portion of the following excerpt from Listing A-12:

```
<custom:MyCustomType . . . >
    . . .
    <myNonReadOnlyStringProperty>value1</myNonReadOnlyStringProperty>
    . . .
</custom:MyCustomType>
```

Now back to the implementation of the `initializeObject` method. If the property is not a string, the method first searches the child xml-script nodes of the current xml-script node for the first child xml-script node, which is an element node:

```
var valueNode;
for (var childNodeIndex = 0;
     childNodeIndex < childNode.childNodes.length; childNodeIndex++)
{
    if (childNode.childNodes[childNodeIndex].nodeType ! =1)
        continue;

    valueNode = childNode.childNodes[childNodeIndex];
    break;
}
```

Then it invokes the `parseNode` method to parse this element node.

```
if (valueNode)
    propertyValue = Sys.Preview.MarkupParser.parseNode(valueNode,
                                                       markupContext);
```

As we discussed earlier, the `parseNode` method parses the specified xml-script node into its associated ASP.NET AJAX object and returns this object. Now that we know the value of the property, we need to assign this value to the property. The `intializeObject` method first generates a string that contains the name of the setter method for this property and uses this string as an index into the object being initialized to return a reference to this setter method:

```
setter = instance['set_' + propertyName];
```

Next, it invokes the `call` method on this reference to invoke the setter method and consequently to assign the specified value as the value of the property:

```
setter.call(instance, propertyValue);
```

If the `properties` collection does not contain a property with the same name as the child xml-script node, the `initializeObject` method uses the child xml-script node's name as an index into the `events` collection, in order to return a reference to the event info object that provides complete information about the event with the same name as the child xml-script node:

```
eventInfo = events[nodeName];
```

If the `events` collection does contain an event with the same name as the child xml-script node, the `initializeObject` method performs the following tasks:

❏ Invokes the `parseNodes` static method on the `MarkupParser` class to parse the child xml-script nodes of this child xml-script node:

```
var actions = Sys.Preview.MarkupParser.parseNodes(childNode.childNodes,
                                                   markupContext);
```

The `parseNodes` method parses the specified xml-script nodes to their associated ASP.NET AJAX objects and returns a collection that contains these parsed objects. These objects in this case are instances of an ASP.NET AJAX class named `Action` or one of its subclasses. (I'll discuss the `Action` class and its subclasses in Appendix C.)

❏ Generates a string that contains the name of the method that registers an event handler for the specified event, and uses this string as an index into the object being initialized to return a reference to this method:

```
eventValue = instance["add_" + eventInfo.name];
```

❏ If the object being initialized does contain such a method, the `initializeObject` performs the following tasks for each parsed object in the collection of parsed objects returned from the `parseNodes` method. (Recall that each parsed object is an instance of the `Action` ASP.NET AJAX class or one of its subclasses.)

    ❏ First, the `initializeObject` method calls the `set_eventName` method on the enumerated parsed object or action to set the value of the `eventName` property of the parsed object to the specified event name. Recall that the `Action` ASP.NET AJAX class exposes a property named `eventName`.

❏ Next, the `initializeObject` method calls the `set_eventSource` method on the enumerated parsed object or action to set the value of the `eventSource` property of the parsed object or action to the object being initialized. In other words, this tells this action that the object being initialized is the source of the event with the specified name.

```
if(eventValue)
{
  for (var e = 0; e < actions.length; e++)
  {
    var action = actions[e];
    action.set_eventName(eventInfo.name);
    action.set_eventSource(instance);
  }
}
```

❏ If neither the `properties` nor the `events` collection contains an entry with the same name as the child xml-script node, the `initializeObject` method takes the following steps:

   ❏ Calls the `toUpperCase` method to convert lowercase characters of the child xml-script node's name to uppercase:

```
var type = null;
var upperName = nodeName.toUpperCase();
```

   ❏ If the child xml-script node's name is BINDINGS, sets a local variable named `type` to reference the constructor of the `Sys.Preview.BindingBase` class. (I'll discuss ASP.NET AJAX binding in Appendix B.)

```
if(upperName === 'BINDINGS')
  type = Sys.Preview.BindingBase;
```

   ❏ If the child xml-script node's name is BEHAVIORS, sets the `type` local variable to reference the constructor of the `Sys.UI.Behavior` class:

```
else if(upperName === 'BEHAVIORS')
  type = Sys.UI.Behavior;
```

   ❏ If the `type` local variable is not `null` — that is, if it references the constructor of either the `BindingBase` or the `Behavior` class, the `initializeObject` method first invokes the `parseNodes` static method on the `MarkupParser` class to parse the child xml-script nodes of the child xml-script node to their associated ASP.NET AJAX objects. Then it returns a collection that contains these parsed objects.

```
var items = Sys.Preview.MarkupParser.parseNodes(childNode.childNodes,
                                                markupContext);
```

   ❏ If the child xml-script node's name is BEHAVIORS, these parsed objects are instances of the `Behavior` ASP.NET AJAX class or its sub-classes. If the child xml-script node's name is BINDINGS, these parsed objects are instances of the `BindingBase` ASP.NET AJAX class or its subclasses.

❑ Next, the `initializeObject` method iterates through the parsed objects in the collection returned from the call into the `parseNodes` method and takes the following steps for each enumerated parsed object. As just mentioned, each enumerated parsed object is either a behavior or a binding object. First, the method checks whether the enumerated parsed object supports a method named `setOwner`. If so, it invokes this method on the enumerated parsed object, passing in the reference to the object being initialized. This specifies the object being initialized as the owner of the behavior or binding object.

```
for (var itemIndex = 0; itemIndex < items.length; itemIndex++)
{
    var item = items[itemIndex];
    debug.assert(type.isInstanceOfType(item),
        String.format("The '{0}' element may only contain child elements
                      of type '{1}'.", nodeName, type.getName()));
    if(typeof(item.setOwner) === "function")
        item.setOwner(instance);
}
```

❑ If the `type` local variable is `null` — that is, if the child xml-script node does not represent `BindingBase` or `Behaviors`, the `initializeObject` raises an exception because the child xml-script node is not recognized:

```
else
  throw Error.invalidOperation(
          String.format('Unrecognized child node "{0}" on object of type "{1}"',
                        nodeName, Object.getTypeName(instance)));
```

B

Binding

The best way to understand what a binding is and what it does is to use it in an example. Listing B-1 contains a page that binds the text property of the `Label` ASP.NET AJAX client control with an `id` property value of `span1` to the `text` property of the `TextBox` ASP.NET AJAX client control with an `id` property value of `text1`. Thanks to this binding, every time you enter a different value in the text box, the `span` element associated with the `Label` control will be automatically updated with the new value.

Listing B-1: A Page that Uses Binding

```
<%@ Page Language="C#" %>
<!DOCTYPE html PUBLIC "-//W3C//DTD XHTML 1.0 Transitional//EN"
"http://www.w3.org/TR/xhtml1/DTD/xhtml1-transitional.dtd">
<html xmlns="http://www.w3.org/1999/xhtml">
<head id="Head1" runat="server">
  <title>Untitled Page</title>
</head>
<body>
  <form id="form1" runat="server">
    <asp:ScriptManager runat="server" ID="ScriptManager1">
      <Scripts>
        <asp:ScriptReference Assembly="Microsoft.Web.Preview"
        Name="PreviewScript.js" />
      </Scripts>
    </asp:ScriptManager>
    <input type="text" id="text1" />
    <span id="span1" />
  </form>
```

(continued)

Listing B-1 *(continued)*

```
<script type="text/xml-script">
  <page xmlns="http://schemas.microsoft.com/xml-script/2005">
    <components>
      <textBox id="text1" />
      <label id="span1">
        <bindings>
          <binding dataContext="text1" dataPath="text" property="text" />
        </bindings>
      </label>
    </components>
  </page>
</script>
</body>
</html>
```

As this example shows, the ASP.NET AJAX binding enables you to bind a specified property of a specified ASP.NET AJAX object to a specified property of another ASP.NET AJAX object. Every time the value of the specified property of the latter ASP.NET AJAX object changes, the value of the specified property of the former ASP.NET AJAX object automatically changes as well. The latter ASP.NET AJAX object is known as the *data context* and its associated property is known as the *data path*. As Listing B-1 shows, the <label> xml-script node that represents the Label ASP.NET AJAX client control contains a child node named <bindings>. This makes it seem that the Label ASP.NET AJAX client control exposes a property named bindings, which is not true. Neither the Label ASP.NET AJAX client control nor its base classes exposes such a property. As a matter of fact, none of the ASP.NET AJAX client classes currently exposes the bindings property. The only exception to this rule is the Action class.

Yet the only way to use the ASP.NET AJAX binding feature in xml-script is to declare a <bindings> xml-script node. The answer to this apparent contradiction lies in the initializeObject method shown in Listing A-11. Listing B-2 presents the portion of Listing A-11 (I've cleaned up Listing B-2 for presentation purposes) that parses the Bindings subelement of the xml-script node that represents an ASP.NET AJAX object in xml-script. Let's study Listing B-2 in the context of the example shown in Listing B-1.

When the initializeObject method is invoked to initialize the Label ASP.NET AJAX client control shown in Listing B-1, three parameters are passed into this method. The first parameter references the Label ASP.NET AJAX client control, and the second references the <label> xml-script node that represents this Label ASP.NET AJAX client control in xml-script. As you can see from Listing B-2, if the name of the child node of the <label> xml-script node is Bindings, the initializeObject method invokes the parseNodes method, passing in the child nodes of the <bindings> node. Recall that the child nodes of the <bindings> node are the <binding> nodes. The parseNodes method parses these <binding> nodes into instances of Binding ASP.NET AJAX class and uses the attributes on each <binding> element to set the associated properties of the associated Binding ASP.NET AJAX object.

Note that the initializeObject method then iterates through these Binding ASP.NET AJAX objects and invokes the setOwner method on each object to specify the Label ASP.NET AJAX object as its owner.

Listing B-2: The Portion of Listing A-11 that Initializes a Binding Object

```
Sys.Preview.MarkupParser.initializeObject =
function Sys$Preview$MarkupParser$initializeObject(instance, node, markupContext)
{
  var childNodes = node.childNodes;
  for (i = childNodes.length - 1; i >= 0; i--)
  {
    var childNode = childNodes[i];
    var nodeName = Sys.Preview.MarkupParser.getNodeName(childNode);
    var upperName = nodeName.toUpperCase();
    if(upperName === 'BINDINGS')
    {
      var bindings = Sys.Preview.MarkupParser.parseNodes(childNode.childNodes,
                                                         markupContext);
      for (var bindingIndex = 0; bindingIndex < bindings.length; bindingIndex++)
      {
        var binding = bindings[bindingIndex];
        binding.setOwner(instance);
      }
    }
  }
}
```

BindingBase

As you saw in the previous section, each `<binding>` subelement of the `<bindings>` subelement binds a specified property of an ASP.NET AJAX object (also known as the owner) to the specified property of another ASP.NET AJAX object in xml-script. Recall from Listing B-2 that the `parseNodes` method parses each `<binding>` subelement of the `<bindings>` subelement into an instance of an ASP.NET AJAX class named `Binding`. The `Binding` class derives from a base class named `BindingBase`. This means that if you're not happy with the `Binding` class you can implement your own custom `Binding` class that derives from the `BindingBase` class.

The `BindingBase` class derives from the `Component` base class:

```
Sys.Preview.BindingBase.registerClass('Sys.Preview.BindingBase', Sys.Component,
                                      Sys.IDisposable);
```

The following table presents the methods of the `BindingBase` class:

Method	Description
get_automatic	Gets a Boolean value that specifies whether the binding object should evaluate the binding automatically.
set_automatic	Sets a Boolean value that specifies whether the binding object should evaluate the binding automatically.

(continued)

(continued)

Method	Description
get_dataContext	Gets the current data context. The data context references the ASP.NET AJAX object whose property the specified property of the ASP.NET AJAX object that owns the binding object binds to.
set_dataContext	Sets the current data context.
get_dataPath	Gets the data path. The data path contains the name of the property of the data context that the specified property of the ASP.NET AJAX object that owns the binding object binds to.
set_dataPath	Sets the data path.
get_target	Gets the binding target. The binding target references the ASP.NET AJAX object that owns the binding object.
set_target	Sets the binding target.
get_property	Gets the name of the property of the binding target that binds to the specified property of the data context.
set_property	Sets the name of the property of the binding target that binds to the specified property of the data context.
get_propertyKey	Gets the property key. The property key enables you to bind the subproperty of a property of a binding target to the specified property of the data context.
set_propertyKey	Sets the property key.
get_transformerArgument	Gets the transformer argument.
set_transformerArgument	Sets the transformer argument.
add_transform	Adds a new event handler to the list of event handlers registered for the transform event of the binding object. This event handler is known as the *transformer*. In other words, transformers are treated as event handlers registered for the transform event.
remove_transform	Removes an event handler from the list of event handlers registered for the transform event of the binding object. In other words, this method removes a transformer from the list of registered transformers.
dispose	Performs the final cleanup before the binding object is disposed of.
evaluate	Takes an enumeration parameter of type BindingDirection. The method delegates to the evaluateIn method if the value of this parameter is BindingDirection.In; otherwise it delegates to the evaluateOut method.

evaluateIn	This method retrieves the value of the data path from the data context and assigns it to the target property.
evaluateOut	The BindingBase class does not implement this method; it delegates the implementation to its subclasses.
initialize	Initializes the binding object. The BindingBase class inherits this method from the Component base class.
setOwner	Specifies the ASP.NET AJAX object that owns the binding object. The setOwner internally invokes the set_target method.

evaluate

Listing B-3 presents the implementation of the evaluate method of the BindingBase class. As you can see, this method delegates to the evaluateIn method if the BindingDirection.In value is passed into it, and delegates to the evaluateOut method otherwise. The BindingDirection is an enumeration type with three possible values: In, Out, and InOut. As you can see, the evaluateOut method handles both the BindingDirection.Out and BindingDirection.InOut cases.

Listing B-3: The evaluate Method

```
function Sys$Preview$BindingBase$evaluate(direction)
{
  /// <param name="direction" type="Number"></param>
  if (this._bindingExecuting)
    return;

  this._bindingExecuting = true;
  if (direction === Sys.Preview.BindingDirection.In)
    this.evaluateIn();

  else
    this.evaluateOut();

  this._bindingExecuting = false;
}
```

evaluateIn

As Listing B-4 shows, the evaluateIn method first invokes the getPropertyType static method on the TypeDescriptor class to return the type object that provides complete information about the type of the property whose value is being set. Recall that this is the property of the target ASP.NET AJAX object.

```
var targetPropertyType =
    Sys.Preview.TypeDescriptor.getPropertyType(this._target, this._property,
                                               this._propertyKey);
```

Under the hood, the `getPropertyType` method extracts the required information about the target property from the `descriptor` static property of the target ASP.NET AJAX object (assuming that the target ASP.NET AJAX type does not implement the `ICustomTypeProvider` interface). As you can see, the `evaluteIn` method and consequently the whole ASP.NET AJAX binding infrastructure only supports target ASP.NET AJAX objects whose types expose a `descriptor` static property with an entry for the target property.

For example, if we have a target ASP.NET AJAX type named `MyNamespace.MyType` with a property of type `MyNamespace.MyPropertyType` named `myProperty`, the `MyNamespace.MyType` type must expose a `descriptor` static property that has an entry for the `myProperty` property, as follows:

```
MyNamespace.MyType.descriptor =
{
    properties: [{name: "myProperty", type: MyNamespace.MyPropertyType}]
}
```

Next, the `evaluateIn` method invokes an internal method named `_getSourceValue` to retrieve the value of the source property to which the target property is bound:

```
var value = this._getSourceValue(targetPropertyType);
```

Then, the `evaluateIn` method fires the `transform` event of the `BindingBase` class and consequently invokes the event handlers registered for this event. These event handlers are known as *transformers* because they're used to transforme the source property value before it is assigned to the target property. As you can see, ASP.NET AJAX transformers are treated as event handlers.

Note that the `evaluateIn` method instantiates an instance of `BindingEventArgs`, passing in four parameters. The first parameter is the value of the source property, the second is the enumeration value `BindingDirection.In`, the third is the reference to the constructor of the type of the property, and the fourth is the transformer argument. Note that the `evaluateIn` method passes this `BindingEventArgs` object into these event handlers.

These event handlers or transformers can then invoke the following getters on this `BindingEventArgs` object to access the same parameters that the `evaluateIn` method passed into the `BindingEventArgs` object:

❑ `get_value`: Returns the source property value that the `evaluateIn` method passed into the `BindingEventArgs` object

❑ `get_direction`: Returns the `BindingDirection.In` value that the `evaluateIn` method passed into the `BindingEventArgs` object

❑ `get_targetPropertyType`: Returns the type object that the `evaluateIn` method passed into the `BindingEventArgs` object

❑ `get_transformerArgument`: Returns the transformer argument value that the `evaluateIn` method passed into the `BindingEventArgs` object

Note that `BindingEventArgs` also exposes a setter named `set_value` that the event handlers can optionally invoke to request the `evaluateIn` method to assign a value other than the original source property value to the target property.

Since the `BindingEventArgs` class derives from the `CancelEventArgs` base class, it inherits the `set_cancel` method from this class. The event handlers or transformers can optionally invoke the `set_cancel` method, passing in `true` as its argument, to request the `evaluateIn` method not to assign the source property value to the target property. This in effect cancels the binding.

As Listing B-4 shows, when these event handlers finally return, the `evaluateIn` method first invokes the `get_cancel` method on the `BindingEventArgs` object to check whether any of the handlers or transformers has placed a request for the cancellation of the assignment of the source property value to the target property. If so, the `evaluateIn` method does not assign the source property value to the target property. If not, the `evaluateIn` method invokes the `get_value` method on the `BindingEventArgs` object to return the value that must be assigned to the target property. Recall that this value is different from the original source property value if any of the event handlers or transformers has invoked the `set_value` method on the `BindingEventArgs` object to specify a different value.

Finally, the `evaluateIn` method invokes the `setProperty` static method on the `TypeDescriptor` class to set the value of the target property:

```
Sys.Preview.TypeDescriptor.setProperty(this._target, this._property,
                                       value, this._propertyKey);
```

Listing B-4: The evaluateIn Method

```
function Sys$Preview$BindingBase$evaluateIn()
{
  var targetPropertyType =
      Sys.Preview.TypeDescriptor.getPropertyType(this._target, this._property,
                                                 this._propertyKey);
  var value = this._getSourceValue(targetPropertyType);

  var canceled = false;
  var handler = this.get_events().getHandler("transform");
  if (handler)
  {
    var be = new Sys.Preview.BindingEventArgs(value,
                                              Sys.Preview.BindingDirection.In,
                                              targetPropertyType,
                                              this._transformerArgument);
    handler(this, be);
    canceled = be.get_cancel();
    value = be.get_value();
  }
  if (!canceled)
    Sys.Preview.TypeDescriptor.setProperty(this._target, this._property,
                                           value, this._propertyKey);
}
```

evalulateOut

As you can see from the following code listing, the `BindingBase` class does not implement the `evaluateOut` method and delegates the responsibility of implementing this method to its subclasses. Recall that the `evaluateOut` method handles the `BindingDirection.Out` and `BindingDirection.InOut` cases.

```
function Sys$Preview$BindingBase$evaluateOut()
{
  throw Error.createError('evaluateOut is not supported for this binding');
}
```

initialize

The `BindingBase` class overrides the `initialize` method that inherits from the `Component` base class, as shown in Listing B-5.

Listing B-5: The initialize Method

```
function Sys$Preview$BindingBase$initialize()
{
  Sys.Preview.BindingBase.callBaseMethod(this, 'initialize');
  this._source = this._dataContext;
  if (!this._source)
    this._source = this._target.get_dataContext();
  if (this._dataPath && this._dataPath.indexOf('.') > 0)
    this._dataPathParts = this._dataPath.split('.');
}
```

Recall that `BindingBase` exposes a property named `dataContext` that you can set to reference the source ASP.NET AJAX object. If this property has not been explicitly set, the `initialize` method invokes the `get_dataContext` method on the target ASP.NET AJAX object to use as the source ASP.NET AJAX object the current data context associated with the target.

```
    this._source = this._dataContext;
    if (!this._source)
      this._source = this._target.get_dataContext();
```

You'll see an example of this case in Appendix F, where we'll use a `Binding` object to bind the `text` property of a `Label` ASP.NET AJAX client control to the specified data field of data records in a data collection bound to the `ListView` client control that contains this `Label` ASP.NET AJAX client control. As you'll see, this example will not explicitly specify the `dataContext` property of this `Binding` object. Thanks to the `initialize` method of the `BindingBase` class, the `Binding` object will pick up the current data context, which references the current data record of the data collection bound to the `ListView` control. This will enable us to display the specified data field of the current data record in this `Label` ASP.NET AJAX client control.

Next, the `initialize` method splits the `dataPath` into its constituent parts:

```
    if (this._dataPath && this._dataPath.indexOf('.') > 0)
      this._dataPathParts = this._dataPath.split('.');
```

As you can see, if you assign a string that consists of a dot-separated list of names to the `dataPath` property of a `Binding` object, the `initialize` method treats each name in the list as a subproperty of the previous name in the list. Here is an example. Let's say you have an ASP.NET AJAX type named `CustomComponents.MyType` that exposes a property of type `CustomComponents.MyPropertyType` named `myProperty`, where the `CustomComponents.MyPropertyType` type itself exposes two properties, `mySubProperty1` and `mySubProperty2`. You can then use the following `Binding` object to bind the `text` property of a `Label` ASP.NET AJAX client control to the `mySubProperty2` property of the `myProperty` property of an instance of the `CustomComponents.MyPropertyType` type:

```
<html>
    <body>
        <form runat="server">
            . . .
            <span id="span1" />
        </form>
        <script type="text/xml-script">
            <page xmlns="http://schemas.microsoft.com/xml-script/2005"
            xmlns:custom="CustomComponents">
                <components>
                    <custom:MyType id="mytype1" />
                    <label id="span1">
                        <bindings>
                            <binding dataContext=="mytype1" property=="text"
                                dataPath=="myProperty.mySubProperty1" />
                        </bindings>
                    </label>
                </components>
            </page>
        </script>
    </body>
</html>
```

descriptor

The `descriptor` static property of the `BindingBase` class specifies those properties, methods, and events of the class that the clients of the class such as the xml-script parser can access using the ASP.NET AJAX type inspection facilities. This means that you can use these properties, methods, and events only in xml-script.

```
Sys.Preview.BindingBase.descriptor =
{
  properties: [    {name: 'target', type: Object},
                   {name: 'automatic', type: Boolean},
                   {name: 'dataContext', type: Object},
                   {name: 'dataPath', type: String},
                   {name: 'property', type: String},
                   {name: 'propertyKey' },
                   {name: 'transformerArgument', type: String} ],
  methods: [ {name: 'evaluateIn'} ],
  events: [ {name: 'transform'} ]
}
```

Transformers

As you saw from Listing B-4, a transformer is an event handler registered for the `transform` event of a given binding object: it transforms the source property value before the value is assigned to the target property. The `BindingBase` class exposes a method named `add_transform` that you can use from your client code to imperatively add a transformer. As you can see, writing a custom transformer is as easy as implementing a new event handler for the `transform` event. This event handler takes two parameters, the first referencing the binding object that raises the transform event and the second referencing an instance of the `BindingEventArgs` event data class that contains the event data for the `transform` event. As discussed earlier, you can use the methods of the `BindingEventArgs` event data class to access the event data.

Listing B-6 contains a page that defines a new transformer. This transformer simply adds the transformer argument to the beginning of the source property value and displays a pop-up that contains the return values of the getter methods of the `BindingEventArgs` object.

Listing B-6: A Page that Defines a Custom Transformer

```
<%@ Page Language="C#" %>
<!DOCTYPE html PUBLIC "-//W3C//DTD XHTML 1.0 Transitional//EN"
"http://www.w3.org/TR/xhtml1/DTD/xhtml1-transitional.dtd">
<html xmlns="http://www.w3.org/1999/xhtml">
<head id="Head1" runat="server">
  <title>Untitled Page</title>
  <script type="text/javascript" language="javascript">
    function transformCallback(sender, e)
    {
      var builder = new Sys.StringBuilder();
      builder.append("old value: ");
      builder.append(e.get_value());
      builder.appendLine();
      builder.append("direction: ");
      builder.append(e.get_direction());
      builder.appendLine();
      builder.append("target property type: ");
      builder.append(e.get_targetPropertyType());
      builder.appendLine();
      builder.append("transformer argument: ");
      builder.append(e.get_transformerArgument());
      builder.appendLine();

      e.set_value(e.get_transformerArgument()+e.get_value());
      builder.append("new value: ");
      builder.append(e.get_value());
      alert(builder.toString());
    }
  </script>
</head>
```

```
<body>
  <form id="form1" runat="server">
    <asp:ScriptManager runat="server" ID="ScriptManager1">
      <Scripts>
        <asp:ScriptReference Assembly="Microsoft.Web.Preview"
        Name="PreviewScript.js" />
      </Scripts>
    </asp:ScriptManager>
    <input type="text" id="text1" />
    <span id="span1" />
  </form>
  <script type="text/xml-script">
    <page xmlns="http://schemas.microsoft.com/xml-script/2005">
      <components>
        <textBox id="text1" />
        <label id="span1">
          <bindings>
            <binding dataContext="text1" dataPath="text" property="text"
            transform="transformCallback" transformerArgument="MyArg" />
          </bindings>
        </label>
      </components>
    </page>
  </script>
</body>
</html>
```

In the following sections I'll discuss some of the standard built-in ASP.NET AJAX transformers.

ToString

As you can see, the `ToString` transformer transforms the source property value into its string representation. You can optionally pass a format string as the value of the `transformerArgument` property. As the following code listing shows, the `ToString` transformer simply passes this format string into the `format` static method of the `String` class as its first argument and the `source` property value as its second argument.

```
Sys.Preview.BindingBase.Transformers.ToString =
function Sys$Preview$BindingBase$Transformers$ToString(sender, eventArgs)
{
  var value = eventArgs.get_value();
  var newValue = '';
  var formatString = eventArgs.get_transformerArgument();
  var placeHolder = (formatString && (formatString.length !== 0)) ?
                    formatString.indexOf('{0}') : -1;
```

(continued)

(continued)

```
  if (placeHolder != -1)
    newValue = String.format(formatString, value);

  else if (value)
    newValue = value.toString();

  else
    newValue = formatString;
  eventArgs.set_value(newValue);
}
```

Here is an example:

```
<%@ Page Language="C#" %>
<!DOCTYPE html PUBLIC "-//W3C//DTD XHTML 1.0 Transitional//EN"
"http://www.w3.org/TR/xhtml1/DTD/xhtml1-transitional.dtd">
<html xmlns="http://www.w3.org/1999/xhtml">
<head id="Head1" runat="server">
  <title>Untitled Page</title>
</head>
<body>
  <form id="form1" runat="server">
    <asp:ScriptManager runat="server" ID="ScriptManager1">
      <Scripts>
        <asp:ScriptReference Assembly="Microsoft.Web.Preview"
                             Name="PreviewScript.js" />
      </Scripts>
    </asp:ScriptManager>
    <input type="text" id="text1" />
    <span id="span1" />
  </form>
  <script type="text/xml-script">
    <page xmlns="http://schemas.microsoft.com/xml-script/2005">
      <components>
        <textBox id="text1" />
        <label id="span1">
          <bindings>
            <binding dataContext="text1" dataPath="text" property="text"
            transform="ToString" transformerArgument="${0}" />
          </bindings>
        </label>
      </components>
    </page>
  </script>
</body>
</html>
```

Invert

As you can see from the following code listing, the Invert transformer simply inverts the source property value. This means that if the source property value is null, this transformer sets the value to true. Otherwise it sets the value to false.

```
Sys.Preview.BindingBase.Transformers.Invert =
function Sys$Preview$BindingBase$Transformers$Invert(sender, eventArgs)
{
  eventArgs.set_value(!eventArgs.get_value());
}
```

Compare

As the following code listing shows, the `Compare` transformer compares the source property value with the value assigned to the `transformerArgument` property. If they're equal, the transformer sets the value to `true`. Otherwise it sets the value to `false`.

```
Sys.Preview.BindingBase.Transformers.Compare =
function Sys$Preview$BindingBase$Transformers$Compare(sender, eventArgs)
{
  var value = eventArgs.get_value();
  var compareValue = eventArgs.get_transformerArgument();
  if (compareValue === null)
    value = value ? true : false;

  else
    value = (value === compareValue);

  eventArgs.set_value(value);
}
```

CompareInverted

As the following code listing shows, the `CompareInverted` transformer is the opposite of the `Compare` transformer. In other words, if the source property value is equal to the value assigned to the `transformerArgument` property, this transformer sets the value to `false`. Otherwise it sets the value to `true`.

```
Sys.Preview.BindingBase.Transformers.CompareInverted =
function Sys$Preview$BindingBase$Transformers$CompareInverted(sender, eventArgs)
{
  Sys.Debug.assert(eventArgs.get_direction() === Sys.Preview.BindingDirection.In);
  var value = eventArgs.get_value();
  var compareValue = eventArgs.get_transformerArgument();
  if (compareValue === null)
    value = value ? false : true;

  else
    value = (value !== compareValue);
  eventArgs.set_value(value);
}
```

Binding

The `Binding` class derives from the `BindingBase` class and extends its functionality to add support for a new property of type `Sys.Preview.BindingDirection` named `direction`. You can use the `get_direction` and `set_direction` methods of the `Binding` object to imperatively get and set the value of the `direction` property from your code.

```
Sys.Preview.Binding.registerClass('Sys.Preview.Binding', Sys.Preview.BindingBase);
```

The `direction` property specifies the direction of binding. By default, the target property is bound to the source property, so that changes in the source property value are reflected in the target property. The `direction` property value of `Sys.Preview.BindingDirection.In` represents this default behavior. However, you can set the direction property to the `Sys.Preview.BindingDirection.Out` value to instruct the `Binding` object that you want the binding in the opposite direction, so that the changes made in the target property are reflected in the source property. You can also set the direction property to `Sys.Preview.BindingDirection.InOut` to instruct the `Binding` object that you want a two-way binding, so that changes made in the target property are reflected in the source property and vice versa.

The `Binding` class also overrides the `evaluateOut` method that it inherits from the `BindingBase` class. Recall that this base class did not implement this method. Listing B-3 showed that the `evaluate` method of the `BindingBase` class invokes the `evaluateOut` method when the binding direction is not `Sys.Preview.BindingDirection.In`. In other words, the `evaluateOut` method handles the reverse and two-way binding scenarios.

Note that the binding direction affects the results of some built-in transformers such as `Add` and `Multiply`. The following code listing presents the implementation of the `Add` transformer. As you can see, this transformer adds the value specified in the `transformerArgument` property to the source property value if the binding direction is `Sys.Preview.BindingDirection.In` and subtracts this value from the source property value if the binding direction is `Sys.Preview.BindingDirection.Out`.

```
Sys.Preview.BindingBase.Transformers.Add =
function Sys$Preview$BindingBase$Transformers$Add(sender, eventArgs)
{
  var value = eventArgs.get_value();
  if (typeof(value) !== 'number')
  {
    if(value === "")
      value = 0;

    else
      value = Number.parseInvariant(value);
  }
  var delta = eventArgs.get_transformerArgument();
  if (!delta)
    delta = 1;

  if (typeof(delta) !== 'number')
  {
    if(value === "")
      delta = 0;
```

```
      else
        delta = Number.parseInvariant(delta);
    }
    if (eventArgs.get_direction() === Sys.Preview.BindingDirection.Out)
      delta = -delta;
    var newValue = value + delta;
    if (eventArgs.get_targetPropertyType() !== 'number')
      newValue = newValue.toString();
    eventArgs.set_value(newValue);
}
```

The Binding class exposes a descriptor static property that specifies the members of this class that you can invoke declaratively in xml-script. As the following code listing shows, you can set the direction property of a Binding object in xml-script. You can also invoke the evaluateOut method in xml-script.

```
Sys.Preview.Binding.descriptor =
{
  properties: [ {name: 'direction', type: Sys.Preview.BindingDirection} ],
  methods: [ {name: 'evaluateOut'} ]
}
```

Actions

Most ASP.NET AJAX client classes expose events. An *action* is an ASP.NET AJAX object that encapsulates a piece of client-side functionality that gets executed in response to a specified event of a specified ASP.NET AJAX object. All ASP.NET AJAX actions implement an interface named IAction, defined in Listing C-1. As you can see, this interface exposes the two methods described in the following table:

Method	Description
execute	This method executes the action's encapsulated client-side functionality in response to a specified event of a specified ASP.NET AJAX object.
setOwner	This method specifies the owner of the action. The owner of the action is the ASP.NET AJAX object that fires the event that triggers the execution of the action's encapsulated client-side functionality.

Listing C-1: The IAction Interface

```
Sys.Preview.IAction = function Sys$Preview$IAction()
{
  throw Error.notImplemented();
}
function Sys$Preview$IAction$execute()
{
  throw Error.notImplemented();
}
function Sys$Preview$IAction$setOwner()
{
  throw Error.notImplemented();
}
Sys.Preview.IAction.prototype =
{
  execute: Sys$Preview$IAction$execute,
  setOwner: Sys$Preview$IAction$setOwner
}
Sys.Preview.IAction.registerInterface('Sys.Preview.IAction');
```

Action

The ASP.NET AJAX client-side framework comes with an implementation of the `IAction` interface named `Action`, which encapsulates the base functionality that every action must support. Because of this, you should derive your custom actions from the `Action` base class instead of directly implementing the `IAction` interface, to save yourself from having to re-implement the base functionality that the `Action` base class already supports. The following table presents the methods of the `Action` class:

Method	Description
get_eventSource	Gets the reference to the ASP.NET AJAX object whose event triggers the execution of the client-side functionality that the action encapsulates.
set_eventSource	Sets the reference to the ASP.NET AJAX object whose event triggers the execution of the client-side functionality that the action encapsulates.
get_eventName	Gets the name of the event that triggers the execution of the client-side functionality that the action encapsulates.
set_eventName	Sets the name of the event that triggers the execution of the client-side functionality that the action encapsulates.
get_target	Gets the target of the action. The target of an action is an ASP.NET AJAX object to which the client-side functionality that the action encapsulates is applied. Note the difference between the target and event source of an action. The event source of an action is the ASP.NET AJAX object whose event triggers the execution of the encapsulated client-side functionality of the action.
set_target	Sets the target of the action.
get_dataContext	Returns a reference to the action. The `Action` inherits this method from the `Component` base class. This method allows the action to act as a data context for other ASP.NET AJAX objects. (A data context is an ASP.NET AJAX object that acts as a source of data for other ASP.NET AJAX objects.)
get_eventArgs	The `initialize` method of the `Action` class registers the `execute` method as an event handler for the event (whose name is given by the `eventName` property) of the event source (referenced by the `eventSource` property). When event source raises the event and consequently invokes the `execute` method, it passes two parameters into this method. The first parameter references the event source. The second parameter references an instance of the event data class associated with the event. The `execute` method stores this instance in an internal field named `_eventArgs` before it invokes the `performAction` method. The `get_eventArgs` method simply returns the value of this field. This allows the subclasses of the `Action` to invoke the `get_eventArgs` method from within their implementation of the `performAction` method in order to access the event data class instance that holds the event data. The `execute` method sets the

	_eventArgs field to null before it returns. Therefore, you must call the get_eventArgs method only inside the performAction method of your custom action class. If you call this method after the execute method returns or before the execute method is invoked, you'll get a null value.
get_result	Returns the return value of the performAction method of the action. The execute method invokes the performAction method and stores the return value of this method in an internal field named _result. The get_result method basically returns the value of this internal field. The execute method sets the _results field to null before it returns. Therefore, you must call the get_result method only inside the performAction method of your custom action class. If you call this method after the execute method returns or before the execute method is invoked, you'll get a null value.
get_sender	Returns a reference to the event source — in other words, the same object that get_eventSource returns.
get_bindings	Gets an array of Binding objects, each of which binds a particular property of the action to a particular property of the current data context.
dispose	Performs the final cleanup before the action is disposed of. The Action class inherits this method from the Component base class.
performAction	The subclasses of the Action base class must implement this method to encapsulate the client-side functionality that they want executed in response to a specified event of the specified ASP.NET AJAX object.
execute	Executes the client-side functionality encapsulated by the action. The Action class inherits this method from the IAction interface. Your custom action mustn't override this method; it must instead override the performAction method.
initialize	Initializes the action. The Action class inherits this method from the Component base class. Your custom action can override this optional method to initialize itself. If you do decide to override this method, make sure you invoke the initialize method of the base class to allow the base class to perform its own initialization.
setOwner	Sets the owner of the action. The Action class inherits this method from the IAction interface. The owner of an Action object is the same as its event source.

The Action class derives from the Component base class and implements the IAction interface:

```
Sys.Preview.Action.registerClass('Sys.Preview.Action',
                        Sys.Component, Sys.Preview.IAction);
```

The Action class exposes a property named eventSource, as well as a getter named get_eventSource and a setter named set_eventSource that you can use to get and set this property. The eventSource property references the ASP.NET AJAX object whose event triggers the execution of the client-side functionality encapsulated by the action.

Listing C-2 presents an excerpt from Listing A-13. I've cleaned up this excerpt for presentation purposes. As you can see, it contains the logic that initializes the ASP.NET AJAX object whose event triggers the execution of the client-side functionality encapsulated by the action. In other words, the first parameter of the `initializeObject` method references the ASP.NET AJAX object whose event triggers the execution of the action, and the second parameter of this method references the xml-script node that represents this ASP.NET AJAX object in xml-script.

Listing C-2: An Excerpt from Listing A-13

```
Sys.Preview.MarkupParser.initializeObject =
function Sys$Preview$MarkupParser$initializeObject(instance, node, markupContext)
{
  var td = Sys.Preview.TypeDescriptor.getTypeDescriptor(instance);
  var events = td._getEvents();
  var childNodes = node.childNodes;
  for (i = childNodes.length - 1; i >= 0; i--)
  {
    var childNode = childNodes[i];
    var nodeName = Sys.Preview.MarkupParser.getNodeName(childNode);
    eventInfo = events[nodeName];
    if (eventInfo)
    {
      var actions = Sys.Preview.MarkupParser.parseNodes(childNode.childNodes,
                                                        markupContext);
      if (actions.length)
      {
        eventValue = instance["add_" + eventInfo.name];
        if(eventValue)
        {
          for (var e = 0; e < actions.length; e++)
          {
            var action = actions[e];
            action.set_eventName(eventInfo.name);
            action.set_eventSource(instance);
          }
        }
      }
    }
  }
}
```

Let's study this excerpt in the context of the example shown in Listing C-3. This example shows a page that uses an instance of an action named `SetPropertyAction`, which is a subclass of the `Action` base class. `SetPropertyAction` encapsulates the client-side functionality that sets the specified property of a specified ASP.NET AJAX object. In the example shown in Listing C-3, `SetPropertyAction` sets the value of the `text` property of a `Label` ASP.NET AJAX control with `id` property value of `myspan`, which represents a span HTML element with an `id` HTML attribute value of `myspan`. Note that the `target` property of this `SetPropertyAction` contains the `id` property value of this `Label` ASP.NET AJAX control. Recall that the `target` property references the ASP.NET AJAX object to which the action applies.

The except shown in Listing C-2 basically parses the boldface portion of Listing C-3, that is,

```
<button id="button1">
  <click>
    <SetPropertyAction target="myspan" property="text"
    value="This is a message!" />
  </click>
</button>
```

In other words, the first parameter of the `initializeObject` method references the `Button` ASP.NET AJAX client control with the `id` property value of `button1`, and the second parameter of this method references the xml-script node that represents this `Button` ASP.NET AJAX client control in xml-script — that is, the `<button id="button1">` node.

Note that this excerpt invokes the `set_eventName` setter of the `SetPropertyAction` action to set its `eventName` property to `click`, because this is the event that triggers this action, and invokes the `set_eventSource` setter of the `SetPropertyAction` action to set its `eventSource` property to a reference to the `Button` ASP.NET AJAX control with the `id` property value of `button1`, because this is the ASP.NET AJAX object whose event triggers the action. As you can see, the `initializeObject` method sets only the `eventName` and `eventSource` properties of an action. You may be wondering who is responsible for setting the rest of the properties. The answer is the `parseFromMarkup` static method of the `Action` class, as shown in Listing C-4.

Listing C-3: An Example of an Action

```
<%@ Page Language="C#" %>
<!DOCTYPE html PUBLIC "-//W3C//DTD XHTML 1.0 Transitional//EN"
"http://www.w3.org/TR/xhtml1/DTD/xhtml1-transitional.dtd">
<html xmlns="http://www.w3.org/1999/xhtml">
<head runat="server">
  <title>Untitled Page</title>
</head>
<body>
  <form id="form1" runat="server">
    <asp:ScriptManager runat="server" ID="ScriptManager1">
      <Scripts>
        <asp:ScriptReference Assembly="Microsoft.Web.Preview"
                             Name="PreviewScript.js" />
      </Scripts>
    </asp:ScriptManager>
    <button id="button1">
      Print Message</button>
    <span id="myspan" />
  </form>
```

(continued)

Listing C-3 *(continued)*

```
<script type="text/xml-script">
  <page xmlns="http://schemas.microsoft.com/xml-script/2005">
    <components>
      <label id="myspan"/>
      <button id="button1">
        <click>
          <SetPropertyAction target="myspan" property="text"
          value="This is a message!" />
        </click>
      </button>
    </components>
  </page>
</script>
</body>
</html>
```

Listing C-4: The parseFormMarkup Method

```
Sys.Preview.Action.parseFromMarkup =
function Sys$Preview$Action$parseFromMarkup(type, node,
                                           markupContext)
{
  var newAction = new type();
  var action = Sys.Preview.MarkupParser.initializeObject(newAction, node,
                                                         markupContext);
  if (action)
  {
    markupContext.addComponent(action);
    return action;
  }

  else
    newAction.dispose();
  return null;
}
```

As you can see, the parseFromMarkup method first invokes the new operator on the first parameter of the method. In the case of Listing C-3, the first parameter references the constructor of the SetPropertyAction class, which means that the following statement basically instantiates an instance of the SetPropertyAction class:

```
var newAction = new type();
```

Next, the parseFromMarkup method invokes the initializeObject static method on the MarkupParser class, passing in four parameters. The first parameter references the newly instantiated action, which is the newly instantiated SetPropertyAction in the case of listing C-3. The second parameter references the xml-script node that represents the action in xml-script, which is the following node in the case of Listing C-3:

```
<SetPropertyAction target="myspan" property="text" value="This is a message!" />
```

The third parameter references the current `MarkupContext`. The `initializeObject` method first parses the xml-script node referenced by its second parameter, which is the following node:

```
<SetPropertyAction target="myspan" property="text" value="This is a message!" />
```

The method then extracts the values of the `target`, `property`, and `value` attributes on the xml-script node and assigns them to the `target`, `property`, and `value` properties of the newly instantiated `SetPropertyAction` action.

Note that the `get_target` and `set_target` methods of the `Action` base class get and set the actual reference to the target ASP.NET AJAX object. If you plan to invoke the `set_target` method imperatively from your client code to set the `target` property, you must ensure that you pass the actual reference to the target ASP.NET AJAX object into this method.

You may be wondering why the xml-script shown in Listing C-3 enables page developers to assign the `id` property value of the `Label` ASP.NET AJAX control to the `target` property of the `SetPropertyAction`, as opposed to assigning the actual reference to the `Label` ASP.NET AJAX control, as shown in the bold-face portions of the following excerpt from Listing C-3:

```
<label id="myspan"/>
<button id="button1">
  <click>
    <SetPropertyAction target="myspan" property="text"
    value="This is a message!" />
  </click>
</button>
```

The answer lies in what the `parseFromMarkup` static method of the `Action` base class does when the xml-script is being parsed. As discussed earlier, this method invokes the `initializeObject` method. As thoroughly discussed in Appendix A, this method automatically uses the value of the target attribute to access the actual reference to the `Label` ASP.NET AJAX control.

execute

The `Action` class implements the `execute` method of the `IAction` interface, as shown in Listing C-5. As mentioned earlier, this method is registered as an event handler for a specified event of a specified ASP.NET AJAX object. Therefore, like any other ASP.NET AJAX event handler, it takes two arguments: the first references the object that raised the event and consequently called the method, and the second references the event data class instance that contains the event data associated with the event.

As Listing C-5 shows, the `execute` method stores this event data class instance in a private field named `_eventArgs`. As I mentioned earlier, the `Action` class exposes a getter named `get_eventArgs`, which returns the value of this private field.

```
this._eventArgs = eventArgs;
```

The `execute` method then calls the `get_bindings` method to return an array that contains all the binding objects associated with the action:

```
var bindings = this.get_bindings();
```

Then the `execute` method iterates through the binding objects in this array and takes the following steps for each enumerated binding object. If the binding object is of type `Binding` or one of its subclasses, and if the binding direction of the binding object is not reverse — that is, if the `get_direction` method of the binding object does not return the enumeration value of `Out` — the `execute` method invokes the `evaluateIn` method on the binding object to have the object assign the value of the specified property of the current data context to the specified property of the action. Which property of the current data context is bound to which property of the action is determined when the associated binding object is defined and added to the `bindings` collection property of the action. Keep in mind that the `get_bindings` method of the `Action` class returns a reference to this `bindings` collection property.

This logic ensures that the values of those properties of the action that are bound to the properties of some other ASP.NET AJAX objects are updated before the `performAction` method is invoked to execute the action.

Next, the `execute` method invokes the `performAction` method to execute the action and stores the return value of this method in a private field named `_result`. As a matter of fact, the `Action` base class exposes a getter named `get_result` that returns the value of this private field.

```
this._result = this.performAction();
```

Then the `execute` method iterates through the binding objects in the `bindings` collection property of the action once more, and takes the following steps for each enumerated binding object. If the enumerated binding object is of type `Binding` or one of its subclasses, and if the binding direction of the binding object is reverse or two-way — that is, if the call into the `get_direction` method of the binding object does not return an `In` enumeration value — the `execute` method invokes the `evalutateOut` method on the binding object to have this object evaluate the value of the specified property of the action and to assign this value to the specified property of the specified ASP.NET AJAX object. This ensures that if the `performAction` method causes one or more properties of the action to change, these changes are reflected in the properties of those ASP.NET AJAX objects that are bound to the changed properties of the action.

Finally, the `execute` method resets the values of the `_eventArgs` and `_result` private fields. This means that the values of these two fields, and consequently the return values of the `get_eventArgs` and `get_result` getter methods, are only valid during the execution of the `execute` method — that is, after the `execute` method is invoked and before this method returns.

```
this._eventArgs = null;
this._result = null;
```

Note that the `Action` base class does not implement the `performAction` method; it delegates the responsibility of implementing this method to its subclasses.

Listing C-5: The Execute Method of the Action Base Class

```
function Sys$Preview$Action$execute(sender, eventArgs)
{
  this._eventArgs = eventArgs;

  var bindings = this.get_bindings();
  var binding;
  var bindingType;
  if(bindings)
  {
    var i;
    for (i = 0; i < bindings.length; i++)
    {
      binding = bindings[i];
      bindingType = binding ? Object.getType(binding) : null;
      if(bindingType && (bindingType === Sys.Preview.Binding ||
                    Sys.Preview.Binding.inheritsFrom(bindingType)))
      {
        if(binding.get_direction() !== Sys.Preview.BindingDirection.Out)  :
          binding.evaluateIn(); :         } :      else  :
          binding.evaluateIn();
      }
    }
  }

  this._result = this.performAction();
  if(bindings)
  {
    for (i = 0; i < bindings.length; i++)
    {
      binding = bindings[i];
      bindingType = binding ? Object.getType(binding) : null;
      if(bindingType && (bindingType === Sys.Preview.Binding ||
                    Sys.Preview.Binding.inheritsFrom(bindingType)))
      {
        if(binding.get_direction() !== Sys.Preview.BindingDirection.In)
          binding.evaluateOut();
      }
      else
        binding.evaluateOut();
    }
  }

  this._eventArgs = null;
  this._result = null;
}
```

descriptor

The following code listing presents the descriptor property of the Action class. This property specifies those properties that can be set declaratively from xml-script.

```
Sys.Preview.Action.descriptor =
{
   properties: [    {name: 'eventSource', type: Object},
                    {name: 'eventName', type: String},
                    {name: 'bindings', type: Array, readOnly: true},
                    {name: 'eventArgs', type: Sys.EventArgs, readOnly: true},
                    {name: 'result', type: Object, readOnly: true},
                    {name: 'sender', type: Object, readOnly: true},
                    {name: 'target', type: Object} ]
}
```

InvokeMethodAction

The InvokeMethodAction ASP.NET AJAX action, like any other, derives from the Action base class:

```
Sys.Preview.InvokeMethodAction.registerClass('Sys.Preview.InvokeMethodAction',
                                  Sys.Preview.Action);
```

As the name suggests, the InvokeMethodAction encapsulates the client-side functionality that invokes a specified method on a specified ASP.NET AJAX object. The following table presents the members of the InvokeMethodAction:

Member	Description
get_method	Gets the name of the method invoked by the InvokeMethodAction
set_method	Sets the name of the method invoked by the InvokeMethodAction
get_parameters	Returns the JavaScript object literal that contains the names and values of the parameters of the method invoked by the InvokeMethodAction

The InvokeMethodAction implements the performAction method that it inherits from the Action base class, as shown in the following code fragment. As you can see, this method calls the invokeMethod static method on the TypeDescriptor class, passing in three parameters: the first references the ASP.NET AJAX object whose method is being invoked, the second contains the name of the method being invoked, and the third is the JavaScript object literal that contains the names and values of the parameters of the method being invoked.

```
function Sys$Preview$InvokeMethodAction$performAction()
{
   return Sys.Preview.TypeDescriptor.invokeMethod(this.get_target(),
                                  this._method, this._parameters);
}
```

The invokeMethod static method of the TypeDescriptor class searches for the method with the specified name in the descriptor property of the ASP.NET AJAX object that owns the method. Therefore, the ASP.NET AJAX object whose method the InvokeMethodAction invokes must expose a static descriptor property with an entry for the method. Suppose you have an ASP.NET AJAX type named MyNamespace.MyType that exposes a method named MyMethod that takes a parameter of type MyNamespace.MyParameterType named MyParameter. The MyNamespace.MyType type must expose a descriptor static property with the following entry to allow the InvokeMethodAction to invoke its MyMethod method:

```
MyNamespace.MyType.descriptor =
{
  methods: [{name: "MyMethod",
             parameters: [{name: "Parameter1",
                           type: MyNamespace.MyParameterType}]}]
}
```

The InvokeMethodAction class exposes the following descriptor static property:

```
Sys.Preview.InvokeMethodAction.descriptor =
{
  properties: [ {name: 'method', type: String},
                {name: 'parameters', type: Object, readOnly: true} ]
}
```

This means that you can set the method and parameters properties of the InvokeMethodAction declaratively in xml-script.

> *Keep in mind that only those properties and events of an ASP.NET AJAX class specified in the* descriptor *static property of the class can be set in xml-script. If a class exposes a property but does not include an entry for it in its* descriptor *static property, you cannot set the value of this property in xml-script. You must set it imperatively from your client code. As I mentioned earlier, another option is for the class to implement the* ICustomTypeProvider *interface.*

The following code listing contains a page that uses the InvokeMethodAction to invoke the toggleCssClass method on the Label ASP.NET AJAX client control with an id property value of myspan.

```
<%@ Page Language="C#" %>
<!DOCTYPE html PUBLIC "-//W3C//DTD XHTML 1.0 Transitional//EN"
"http://www.w3.org/TR/xhtml1/DTD/xhtml1-transitional.dtd">
<html xmlns="http://www.w3.org/1999/xhtml">
<head id="Head1" runat="server">
  <title>Untitled Page</title>
  <style type="text/css">
    .myCssClass {
      background-color: #dddddd;
    }
  </style>
</head>
```

(continued)

(continued)

```
<body>
  <form id="form1" runat="server">
    <asp:ScriptManager runat="server" ID="ScriptManager1">
      <Scripts>
        <asp:ScriptReference Assembly="Microsoft.Web.Preview"
                             Name="PreviewScript.js" />
      </Scripts>
    </asp:ScriptManager>
    <button id="button1">Toggle CSS Class</button>
    <span id="myspan">Wrox Web Site</span>
  </form>
  <script type="text/xml-script">
    <page xmlns="http://schemas.microsoft.com/xml-script/2005">
      <components>
        <label id="myspan"/>
        <button id="button1">
          <click>
            <InvokeMethodAction target="myspan" method="toggleCssClass">
              <parameters className="myCssClass" />
            </InvokeMethodAction>
          </click>
        </button>
      </components>
    </page>
  </script>
</body>
</html>
```

It is very important that you use the same exact names for the method and its parameters that the
`descriptor` property of the class that owns the method uses. For example, in this case, the Label
ASP.NET AJAX client control derives from the `Control` base class, which exposes the following
`descriptor` property. As the boldface portion of this code fragment shows, the `descriptor` property
contains an entry for a method named `toggleCssClass`, which takes a parameter of type string named
`className`, which are the same exact names we've used (as shown in the boldfaced portion of the
previous code listing).

```
Sys.UI.Control.descriptor =
{
    properties: [ {name: 'element', type: Object, readOnly: true},
                  {name: 'role', type: String, readOnly: true},
                  {name: 'parent', type: Object},
                  {name: 'visible', type: Boolean},
                  {name: 'visibilityMode', type: Sys.UI.VisibilityMode} ],
    methods:    [ {name: 'addCssClass',
                   parameters: [ {name: 'className', type: String} ] },
                  {name: 'removeCssClass',
                   parameters: [ {name: 'className', type: String} ] },
                  {name: 'toggleCssClass',
                   parameters: [ {name: 'className', type: String} ] } ]
}
```

SetPropertyAction

The SetPropertyAction ASP.NET AJAX action, like any other, derives from the Action base class:

```
Sys.Preview.SetPropertyAction.registerClass('Sys.Preview.SetPropertyAction',
                                             Sys.Preview.Action);
```

As the name suggests, the SetPropertyAction encapsulates the client-side functionality that sets the value of a specified property of a specified ASP.NET AJAX object. The following table presents the members of the SetPropertyAction:

Member	Description
get_property	Gets the name of the property set by SetPropertyAction.
set_property	Sets the name of the property set by SetPropertyAction.
get_propertyKey	Gets the name of the subproperty set by SetPropertyAction. If both the property and propertyKey properties are specified, SetPropertyAction assumes that the specified propertyKey is a subproperty of the specified property and sets the value of the subproperty.
set_propertyKey	Sets the name of the subproperty set by SetPropertyAction.
get_value	Gets the value that SetPropertyAction assigns to the specified property or subproperty.
set_value	Sets the value that SetPropertyAction assigns to the specified property or subproperty.

SetPropertyAction, like any other action, implements the performAction method that it inherits from the Action base class, as shown in the following code fragment. As you can see, this method calls the setProperty static method on the TypeDescriptor class, passing in four parameters: the first references the ASP.NET AJAX object whose property is being set, the second contains the name of the property being set, the third contains the value to be assigned to the specified property or subproperty, and the last specifies the name of the subproperty being set:

```
function Sys$Preview$SetPropertyAction$performAction()
{
  Sys.Preview.TypeDescriptor.setProperty(this.get_target(), this._property,
                                  this._value, this._propertyKey);
  return null;
}
```

The setProperty static method of the TypeDescriptor class searches for the property with the specified name in the descriptor property of the ASP.NET AJAX object that owns the property. Therefore, the ASP.NET AJAX object whose property the InvokeMethodAction sets must expose a static descriptor property with an entry for the property.

The `SetPropertyAction` class exposes the following `descriptor` static property:

```
Sys.Preview.SetPropertyAction.descriptor =
{
  properties: [    {name: 'property', type: String},
                   {name: 'propertyKey' },
                   {name: 'value', type: String} ]
}
```

This means that you can set in xml-script only those properties of the `SetPropertyAction` specified in this `descriptor` property.

The following code listing contains a page that uses `SetPropertyAction` to set the `className` subproperty of the `element` property of the `Label` ASP.NET AJAX client control with an `id` property value of `myspan` to the value `myCssClass`:

```
<%@ Page Language="C#" %>
<!DOCTYPE html PUBLIC "-//W3C//DTD XHTML 1.0 Transitional//EN"
"http://www.w3.org/TR/xhtml1/DTD/xhtml1-transitional.dtd">
<html xmlns="http://www.w3.org/1999/xhtml">
<head id="Head1" runat="server">
  <title>Untitled Page</title>
  <style type="text/css">
    .myCssClass
    {
      background-color: #dddddd;
    }
  </style>
</head>
<body>
  <form id="form1" runat="server">
    <asp:ScriptManager runat="server" ID="ScriptManager1">
      <Scripts>
        <asp:ScriptReference Assembly="Microsoft.Web.Preview"
                             Name="PreviewScript.js" />
      </Scripts>
    </asp:ScriptManager>
    <button id="button1">Toggle CSS Class</button>
    <span id="myspan">Wrox Web Site</span>
  </form>
  <script type="text/xml-script">
    <page xmlns="http://schemas.microsoft.com/xml-script/2005">
      <components>
        <label id="myspan"/>
        <button id="button1">
          <click>
            <SetPropertyAction target="myspan" property="element"
                               propertyKey="className" value="myCssClass" />
          </click>
        </button>
      </components>
    </page>
  </script>
</body>
</html>
```

PostBackAction

The `PostBackAction` ASP.NET AJAX action also derives from the `Action` base class:

```
Sys.Preview.PostBackAction.registerClass('Sys.Preview.PostBackAction',
                                          Sys.Preview.Action);
```

As the name implies, `PostBackAction` encapsulates the client-side functionality that enables an ASP.NET AJAX object to post the current page back to the server. The best way to understand the significance of the `PostBackAction` action is to study its implementation of the `performAction` method, as shown in the following code listing:

```
function Sys$Preview$PostBackAction$performAction()
{
    __doPostBack(this.get_target(), this.get_eventArgument());
    return null;
}
```

As you can see, the `performAction` method calls the `__doPostBack` global JavaScript function, passing in two parameters, the return values of the `get_target` and `get_eventArgument` getter methods, respectively. Recall that the `__doPostBack` global JavaScript function posts the page back to the server. Also recall that this JavaScript function takes two parameters. The first is a string that contains the value of the `name` HTML attribute of the HTML element responsible for the postback. This HTML element is known as the *event target*. The second parameter is an optional string that contains extra information that helps the server-side code process the page postback. This optional parameter is known as the *event argument*.

The following table presents the members of `PostBackAction`:

Member	Description
`get_target`	Gets the value of the name HTML attribute of the event target
`set_target`	Sets the value of the name HTML attribute of the event target
`get_eventArgument`	Gets the event argument
`set_eventArgument`	Sets the event argument

The `PostBackAction` class exposes the following descriptor static property:

```
Sys.Preview.PostBackAction.descriptor =
{
    properties: [   {name: 'eventArgument', type: String},
                    {name: 'target', type: String} ]
}
```

This means that you can set in xml-script only those properties of `PostBackAction` specified in the preceding descriptor property.

The great thing about the `PostBackAction` action is that it lets you enable your ASP.NET AJAX classes to perform a page postback. For example, the `Button` ASP.NET AJAX client control associated with the `<button>` HTML element normally does not post the page back to the server. The page shown in the following code listing demonstrates how to use `PostBackAction` to enable the `Button` ASP.NET AJAX client control associated with the `<button>` HTML element to perform a page postback:

```
<%@ Page Language="C#" %>
<!DOCTYPE html PUBLIC "-//W3C//DTD XHTML 1.0 Transitional//EN"
"http://www.w3.org/TR/xhtml1/DTD/xhtml1-transitional.dtd">
<html xmlns="http://www.w3.org/1999/xhtml">
<head id="Head1" runat="server">
  <title>Untitled Page</title>
</head>
<body>
  <form id="form1" runat="server">
    <asp:ScriptManager runat="server" ID="ScriptManager1">
      <Scripts>
        <asp:ScriptReference Assembly="Microsoft.Web.Preview"
                             Name="PreviewScript.js" />
      </Scripts>
    </asp:ScriptManager>
    <button id="button1" type="button">Submit</button>
  </form>
  <script type="text/xml-script">
    <page xmlns="http://schemas.microsoft.com/xml-script/2005">
      <components>
        <button id="button1">
          <click>
            <PostBackAction target="button1" eventArgument="myArg" />
          </click>
        </button>
      </components>
    </page>
  </script>
</body>
</html>
```

Data Control

The ASP.NET framework comes with a server control named DataBoundControl that acts as the base class for important server controls such as GridView and DetailsView. The DataBoundControl base server control encapsulates the basic functionality that all data-bound controls must support. The ASP.NET AJAX client-side framework comes with a client control named DataControl that acts as the base control for important client controls such as ListView. The DataControl client control, just like its DataBoundControl server-side counterpart, encapsulates the base functionality that all data-bound client controls must support. In this appendix I'll present and discuss the members of the DataControl base class to:

❑ Help you gain the skills you need to derive from this base class in order to implement your own custom data controls.

❑ Set the stage for the Appendix F, where you'll see how the ASP.NET AJAX ListView client control extends the functionality of the DataControl base class.

The DataControl base class belongs to a namespace named Sys.Preview.UI.Data, as defined in the following:

```
Type.registerNamespace('Sys.Preview.UI.Data');
```

Constructor

Listing D-1 presents the internal implementation of the constructor of the DataControl base class. This constructor takes a single argument that references the DOM element that the DataControl base class represents. In other words, you can think of the DataControl base class as the ASP.NET AJAX representation of this DOM element. This constructor, like that of any other subclass, first calls the initializeBase method to invoke the constructor of its base class:

```
Sys.Preview.UI.Data.DataControl.initializeBase(this, [associatedElement]);
```

The base class in this case is the `Control` client class:

```
Sys.Preview.UI.Data.DataControl.registerClass('Sys.Preview.UI.Data.DataControl',
                                              Sys.UI.Control);
```

The constructor then sets the value of a property named `dataIndex` to 0. The value of this property will be used as an index into the collection that contains the data records to access the associated record:

```
this._dataIndex = 0;
```

Listing D-1: The Internal Implementation of the Constructor of the DataControl Base Class

```
Sys.Preview.UI.Data.DataControl = function
Sys$Preview$UI$Data$DataControl(associatedElement)
{
    Sys.Preview.UI.Data.DataControl.initializeBase(this, [associatedElement]);
    this._dataIndex = 0;
}
Sys.Preview.UI.Data.DataControl.registerClass('Sys.Preview.UI.Data.DataControl',
                                              Sys.UI.Control);
```

prepareChange

As you can see from Listing D-2, the `DataControl` base class comes with a method named `prepareChange` that returns a JavaScript object literal that contains three name/value pairs, which describe the `dataIndex`, `canMoveNext`, and `canMovePrevious` properties of the class, respectively. I'll discuss these three properties shortly. As you'll see later, other methods of the `DataControl` base class call the `prepareChange` method every time the values of these properties are about to change. These methods store the JavaScript object containing the current values of these properties so they can compare those values with the new ones and raise the necessary events if the values have indeed changed (hence the name `prepareChange`).

Listing D-2: The prepareChange Method of the DataControl Base Class

```
function Sys$Preview$UI$Data$DataControl$prepareChange()
{
    return {dataIndex: this.get_dataIndex(),
            canMoveNext: this.get_canMoveNext(),
            canMovePrevious: this.get_canMovePrevious()};
}
```

triggerChangeEvents

As you can see from Listing D-3, the `triggerChangeEvents` method of the `DataControl` base class takes a JavaScript object literal as its sole argument. This object is the same one that the `prepareChange` method returns. As we discussed earlier, other methods of the `DataControl` base class invoke the prepareChange method to return the object that contains the current values of the dataIndex, canMoveNext, and canMovePrevious properties every time the values of these properties are about to change. After the changes occur, these methods call the triggerChangeEvents method, passing in the object containing the old values of these properties. This method takes the following steps for each of these properties. First, it calls the associated getter method of the DataControl base class to access the current value of the property:

```
var dataIndex = this.get_dataIndex();
```

Next, it compares the current value with the old value and calls the raisePropertyChanged method to raise the propertyChanged event if the two values are different:

```
this.raisePropertyChanged('dataIndex');
this.raisePropertyChanged('dataItem');
```

The DataControl class inherits the raisePropertyChanged method from its base class — that is, the Control class. Recall from the previous chapters that this method raises an event named propertyChanged.

Finally, the triggerChangeEvents method assigns the new value to the respective property of the object. In other words, the new value is now the old value:

```
oldState.dataIndex = dataIndex;
```

Listing D-3: The triggerChangeEvent Method of the DataControl Base Class

```
function Sys$Preview$UI$Data$DataControl$triggerChangeEvents(oldState)
{
  var dataIndex = this.get_dataIndex();
  if (oldState.dataIndex !== dataIndex)
  {
    this.raisePropertyChanged('dataIndex');
    this.raisePropertyChanged('dataItem');
    oldState.dataIndex = dataIndex;
  }

  var canMoveNext = this.get_canMoveNext();
  if (oldState.canMoveNext !== canMoveNext)
  {
    this.raisePropertyChanged('canMoveNext');
    oldState.canMoveNext = canMoveNext;
  }

  var canMovePrevious = this.get_canMovePrevious();
  if (oldState.canMovePrevious !== canMovePrevious)
  {
    this.raisePropertyChanged('canMovePrevious');
    oldState.canMovePrevious = canMovePrevious;
  }
}
```

get_canMoveNext

The `DataControl` class exposes a read-only Boolean property named `canMoveNext` that specifies whether the data control can move to the next data record in the internal data record collection. As Listing D-4 shows, the `DataControl` class features a getter method named `get_canMoveNext` that you can use to access the value of this property. This method first checks whether the internal data collection exists to begin with. If not, it returns `false`:

```
if (!this._data)
    return false;
```

`DataControl` exposes a collection property named `data` that contains the data records. If the data collection does exist, it checks whether the current data index is less than the total number of data records in the data record collection:

```
return (this._dataIndex < this.get_length() - 1);
```

As you'll see later, the `DataControl` class exposes a getter method named `get_length` that returns the total number of data records in the data collection.

Listing D-4: The get_canMoveNext Method of the DataControl Base Class

```
function Sys$Preview$UI$Data$DataControl$get_canMoveNext()
{
  if (!this._data)
    return false;

  return (this._dataIndex < this.get_length() - 1);
}
```

get_canMovePrevious

The `DataControl` base class exposes a read-only Boolean property named `canMovePrevious` that specifies whether the data control can move to the previous record in the data record collection. As you can see from Listing D-5, the `DataControl` base class comes with a getter method named `get_canMovePrevious` that you can use to access the value of the `canMovePrevious` property. This method first checks whether the data record collection exists. If not, it returns `false` to inform its caller that the data control cannot move to the previous record:

```
if (!this._data)
    return false;
```

If so, it checks whether the current data index is greater than 0. If so, it returns `true` to inform its caller that the data control can indeed move to the previous record.

Listing D-5: The get_canMovePrevious Method of the DataControl Base Class

```
function Sys$Preview$UI$Data$DataControl$get_canMovePrevious()
{
  if (!this._data)
    return false;

  return (this._dataIndex > 0);
}
```

get_data

As I mentioned earlier, the DataControl base class exposes a collection property named data that contains the data records. The get_data getter method of the DataControl class returns a reference to this collection, as shown in Listing D-6.

Listing D-6: The get_data Method of the DataControl Base Class

```
function Sys$Preview$UI$Data$DataControl$get_data()
{
  return this._data;
}
```

set_data

The set_data setter method of the DataControl base class enables you to set the value of the data property of the class. As you can see from Listing D-7, this method takes a collection of data records as its single argument and assigns that collection to the data property. Here are the steps that the set_data method takes to accomplish this task. First, it calls the prepareChange method to return the JavaScript object that contains the current values of the dataIndex, canMoveNext, and canMovePrevious properties of the data control:

```
var oldState = this.prepareChange();
```

As you'll see shortly, every time the value of the data property is set — that is, every time a new data record collection is assigned to the data property — the set_data method registers a delegate named _dataChangedDelegate as an event handler for the collectionChanged event of the new data record collection, if the collection implements the INotifyCollectionChanged interface. That is why, before assigning the new data collection to the data property, the set_data setter first invokes the remove_collectionChanged method on the old data collection to remove the _dataChangedDelegate delegate from the list of event handlers registered for the collectionChanged event of the old data collection. This ensures that the old data collection no longer invokes this delegate, because it is being replaced with the new data collection:

```
if (this._data &&
        Sys.Preview.INotifyCollectionChanged.isImplementedBy(this._data))
{
    this._data.remove_collectionChanged(this._dataChangedDelegate);
    this._dataChangedDelegate = null;
}
```

Next, the set_data method assigns the new data collection to the data property:

```
this._data = value;
```

Next, the set_data method checks whether the new data collection implements the INotifyCollectionChanged interface. If so, it calls the createDelegate static method on the Function to create a delegate that represents a method named onDataChanged, and stores this delegate in the _dataChangedDelegate field. Next, it invokes the add_collectionChanged method on the new data collection to register this delegate as event handler for the collectionChanged event of the new data collection:

```
if (this._data &&
        Sys.Preview.INotifyCollectionChanged.isImplementedBy(this._data))
{
    this._dataChangedDelegate = Function.createDelegate(this, this.onDataChanged);
    this._data.add_collectionChanged(this._dataChangedDelegate);
}
```

Next, the set_data setter calls the get_length method to determine the total number of records in the new data collection. If the current data index of the data control is greater or equal to this number, the set_data setter method invokes the set_dataIndex setter to reset the current data index to 0:

```
if (this._dataIndex >= this.get_length())
    this.set_dataIndex(0);
```

If the data control is not already updating, the set_data setter invokes the render method to update the data control:

```
if (!this.get_isUpdating())
    this.render();
```

Next, the set_data setter invokes the raisePropertyChanged method to raise the propertyChanged event and consequently to invoke all the event handlers registered for this event:

```
this.raisePropertyChanged('data');
```

If you need to run some custom code when the data control is bound to a new data collection, encapsulate this custom code in a method and register this method as an event handler for the propertyChanged event of the data control.

Finally, the `set_data` setter invokes `triggerChangedEvents`, passing in the JavaScript object that contains the old values of the `dataIndex`, `canMoveNext`, and `canMovePrevious` properties to raise the associated events as discussed earlier:

```
this.triggerChangeEvents(oldState);
```

Listing D-7: The set_data Method of the DataControl Base Class

```
function Sys$Preview$UI$Data$DataControl$set_data(value)
{
    var oldState = this.prepareChange();
    if (this._data &&
        Sys.Preview.INotifyCollectionChanged.isImplementedBy(this._data))
    {
        this._data.remove_collectionChanged(this._dataChangedDelegate);
        this._dataChangedDelegate = null;
    }

    this._data = value;
    if (this._data &&
        Sys.Preview.INotifyCollectionChanged.isImplementedBy(this._data))
    {
        this._dataChangedDelegate = Function.createDelegate(this, this.onDataChanged);
        this._data.add_collectionChanged(this._dataChangedDelegate);
    }

    if (this._dataIndex >= this.get_length())
        this.set_dataIndex(0);
    if (!this.get_isUpdating())
        this.render();
    this.raisePropertyChanged('data');
    this.triggerChangeEvents(oldState);
}
```

get_length

The `DataControl` base class exposes a getter named `get_length` that returns the total number of records in the data collection to which the data control is bound. As Listing D-8 shows, this getter returns 0 if the data property is `null` — that is, if the data control is not bound any data collection:

```
if(!this._data)
    return 0;
```

Next, the `get_length` getter checks whether the bound data collection implements the `IData` interface. If so, it invokes the `get_length` method on the data collection to return the total number of records in the collection:

```
if (Sys.Preview.Data.IData.isImplementedBy(this._data))
    return this._data.get_length();
```

Then, it checks whether the bound data collection is a JavaScript array. If so, it returns the value of the `length` property of the data collection:

```
if (this._data instanceof Array)
    return this._data.length;
```

If the bound data collection does not implement the `IData` interface and is not a JavaScript array, the `get_length` method returns 0 because the bound data collection is not supported:

```
return 0;
```

Listing D-8: The get_length Getter

```
function Sys$Preview$UI$Data$DataControl$get_length()
{
  if(!this._data)
    return 0;

  if (Sys.Preview.Data.IData.isImplementedBy(this._data))
    return this._data.get_length();

  if (this._data instanceof Array)
    return this._data.length;

  return 0;
}
```

get_dataIndex

The `get_dataIndex` getter method of the `DataControl` base class returns the index of the current record in the data collection to which the data control is bound. This getter simply returns the value of the `_dataIndex` field, as shown in Listing D-9.

Listing D-9: The get_dataIndex Getter

```
function Sys$Preview$UI$Data$DataControl$get_dataIndex()
{
  return this._dataIndex;
}
```

set_dataIndex

The `set_dataIndex` setter of the `DataControl` base class takes the following steps (see Listing D-10). First, it checks whether the new value is different from the old value. If not, it doesn't do anything. If so, it begins by calling the `prepareChange` method to return the JavaScript object that contains the current values of the `dataIndex`, `canMoveNext`, and `canMovePrevious` properties:

```
var oldState = this.prepareChange();
```

Next, it assigns the new value to the `dataIndex` property:

```
this._dataIndex = value;
```

Finally, it invokes the `triggerChangeEvents` method, passing in the preceding JavaScript object to raise the required events, as discussed earlier:

```
this.triggerChangeEvents(oldState);
```

Listing D-10: The set_dataIndex Setter

```
function Sys$Preview$UI$Data$DataControl$set_dataIndex(value)
{
  if (this._dataIndex !== value)
  {
    var oldState = this.prepareChange();
    this._dataIndex = value;
    if (!this._suspendChangeNotifications)
      this.triggerChangeEvents(oldState);
  }
}
```

onDataChanged

Recall that the `set_data` setter method registers a delegate that represents the `onDataChanged` method as event handler for the `collectionChanged` event of the bound data collection if this collection implements the `INotifyCollectionChanged` interface. As we discussed earlier, a collection raises this event when it changes. As you can see from Listing D-11, the `onDataChanged` method simply invokes the `render` method of the data control to update the data control.

Listing D-11: The onDataChanged Method

```
function Sys$Preview$UI$Data$DataControl$onDataChanged(sender, args)
{
  this.render();
}
```

get_dataItem

The `get_dataItem` getter method of the `DataControl` base class returns a reference to the current data record in the data collection bound to the data control. As Listing D-12 shows, this method first checks whether the current data index is a positive number. If not, it returns `null` because the data collection does not contain a data record with a negative index! If so, it checks whether the data collection implements the `IData` interface. If so, it invokes the `getItem` method on the data collection, passing in the current data index to return a reference to the data record with the specified index:

```
if (Sys.Preview.Data.IData.isImplementedBy(this._data))
  return this._data.getItem(this._dataIndex);
```

If the data collection is a JavaScript array, the getter method simply uses the value of the data index as an index into the data collection to return a reference to the data item with the specified index:

```
if (this._data instanceof Array)
    return this._data[this._dataIndex];
```

Listing D-12: The get_dataItem Getter Method

```
function Sys$Preview$UI$Data$DataControl$get_dataItem()
{
  if (this._data && (this._dataIndex >= 0))
  {
    if (Sys.Preview.Data.IData.isImplementedBy(this._data))
      return this._data.getItem(this._dataIndex);

    if (this._data instanceof Array)
      return this._data[this._dataIndex];
  }
  return null;
}
```

get_dataContext

The `DataControl` base class overrides the `get_dataContext` method that it inherits from the `Control` base class, in which `DataControl` invokes the `get_dataItem` method to return a reference to the current data record in the bound data collection, as shown in Listing D-13:

```
return this.get_dataItem();
```

Listing D-13: The get_dataContext Getter

```
function Sys$Preview$UI$Data$DataControl$get_dataContext()
{
  return this.get_dataItem();
}
```

addItem

The `addItem` method of the `DataControl` base class enables you to add an empty record to the bound data collection. As Listing D-14 shows, this method first checks whether the data control is bound to any data collection. If not, it doesn't do anything and returns. If so, it begins by calling the `prepareChange` method to return the JavaScript object that contains the current values of the `dataIndex`, `canMoveNext`, and `canMovePrevious` properties:

```
var oldState = this.prepareChange();
```

Next, it checks whether the bound data collection implements the IData interface. If so, it invokes the add method on the data collection to add an empty record to the collection:

```
if (Sys.Preview.Data.IData.isImplementedBy(this._data))
    this._data.add({});
```

If the bound data collection is a JavaScript array, and if it exposes a method named add, the addItem method simply calls this method to add an empty record to the data collection:

```
else if (this._data instanceof Array)
{
    if(typeof(this._data.add) === "function")
        this._data.add({});
```

If the bound data collection is a JavaScript array but it does not expose the add method, the addItem method simply calls the add static method on the Array class to add an empty record to the data collection:

```
else if (this._data instanceof Array)
{
    if(typeof(this._data.add) === "function")
        this._data.add({});

    else
        Array.add(this._data, {});
}
```

Next, the addItem method sets the current data index to the index of the newly added data record:

```
this.set_dataIndex(this.get_length() - 1);
```

Finally, the addItem method calls the triggerChangeEvents method, passing the JavaScript object that contains the old values of the dataIndex, canMoveNext, and canMovePrevious properties to raise the appropriate events, as discussed earlier:

```
this.triggerChangeEvents(oldState);
```

Listing D-14: The addItem Method

```
function Sys$Preview$UI$Data$DataControl$addItem()
{
    if (this._data)
    {
        var oldState = this.prepareChange();
        if (Sys.Preview.Data.IData.isImplementedBy(this._data))
            this._data.add({});
```

(continued)

```
      else if (this._data instanceof Array)
      {
        if(typeof(this._data.add) === "function")
          this._data.add({});

        else
          Array.add(this._data, {});
      }
      this.set_dataIndex(this.get_length() - 1);
      this.triggerChangeEvents(oldState);
    }
  }
```

deleteCurrentItem

As the name suggests, the deleteCurrentItem method deletes the current data record from the bound
data collection — if the data control is indeed bound to a data collection. As Listing D-15 shows, this
method begins by invoking the prepareChange method to return the JavaScript object that contains the
current values of the dataIndex, canMoveNext, and canMovePrevious properties:

```
      var oldState = this.prepareChange();
```

Next, it sets an internal flag to true to signal that all change notifications must be suspended because
we're about to introduce new changes:

```
      this._suspendChangeNotifications = true;
```

Then it calls the get_dataItem getter to return a reference to the current data record:

```
      var item = this.get_dataItem();
```

Next, it resets the current data index if the current data record is the last data record in the data
collection:

```
      if (this.get_dataIndex() === this.get_length() - 1)
        this.set_dataIndex(Math.max(0, this.get_length() - 2));
```

Then it checks whether the bound data collection implements the IData interface. If so, it invokes the
remove method on the bound data collection to remove the current data record:

```
      if (Sys.Preview.Data.IData.isImplementedBy(this._data))
        this._data.remove(item);
```

Next, the deleteCurrentItem method checks whether the bound data collection is a JavaScript array
and whether it supports the remove method. If so, it invokes the remove method on the data collection
to remove the current data record:

```
      else if (this._data instanceof Array)
      {
        if(typeof(this._data.remove) === "function")
          this._data.remove(item);
```

If the bound data collection is a JavaScript array but does not support the `remove` method, it calls the `remove` static method on the `Array` class to remove the current data record for the data collection:

```
      else if (this._data instanceof Array)
      {
        if(typeof(this._data.remove) === "function")
          this._data.remove(item);

        else
          Array.remove(this._data, item);
      }
```

Next, it resets the `_suspendChangeNotifications` flag to allow change notifications:

```
      this._suspendChangeNotifications = false;
```

Finally, it invokes the `triggerChangeEvents` method, passing in the JavaScript object that contains the old values of the `dataIndex`, `canMoveNext`, and `canMovePrevious` properties, to trigger the required events, as discussed earlier:

```
      this.triggerChangeEvents(oldState);
```

Listing D-15: The deleteCurrentItem Method

```
function Sys$Preview$UI$Data$DataControl$deleteCurrentItem()
{
  if (this._data)
  {
    var oldState = this.prepareChange();
    this._suspendChangeNotifications = true;
    var item = this.get_dataItem();
    if (this.get_dataIndex() === this.get_length() - 1)
      this.set_dataIndex(Math.max(0, this.get_length() - 2));

    if (Sys.Preview.Data.IData.isImplementedBy(this._data))
      this._data.remove(item);

    else if (this._data instanceof Array)
    {
      if(typeof(this._data.remove) === "function")
        this._data.remove(item);

      else
        Array.remove(this._data, item);
    }
    this._suspendChangeNotifications = false;
    this.triggerChangeEvents(oldState);
  }
}
```

getItem

The getItem method of the DataControl base class enables you to return a reference to the data record with the specified data index. As you can see from Listing D-16, this method first checks whether the data control is indeed bound to a data collection. If not, it returns null. If so, it checks whether the bound data collection implements the IData interface. If so, it simply calls the getItem method on the data collection to return a reference to the data record with the specified index:

```
if (Sys.Preview.Data.IData.isImplementedBy(this._data))
    return this._data.getItem(index);
```

If not, it checks whether the bound data collection is a JavaScript array. If so, it uses the specified data index as an index into the data collection to return a reference to the data record with the specified index:

```
if (this._data instanceof Array)
    return this._data[index];
```

Listing D-16: The getItem Method

```
function Sys$Preview$UI$Data$DataControl$getItem(index)
{
  if (this._data)
  {
    if (Sys.Preview.Data.IData.isImplementedBy(this._data))
      return this._data.getItem(index);

    if (this._data instanceof Array)
      return this._data[index];
  }
  return null;
}
```

moveNext

The moveNext method of the DataControl base class enables you to move to the next data record in the bound data collection. As Listing D-17 shows, if the data control is not bound to any data collection, the moveNext method does not do anything. This method begins by invoking the prepareChange method, as usual:

```
var oldState = this.prepareChange();
```

Next, it calls the get_dataIndex getter to return the current data index, and increments this value by one to arrive at the new value for the current data index:

```
var newIndex = this.get_dataIndex() + 1;
```

If the new value is not greater than or equal to the total number of data records in the bound collection, it calls the `set_dataIndex` setter to set the current data index to the new value:

```
if (newIndex < this.get_length())
    this.set_dataIndex(newIndex);
```

Finally, it invokes the `triggerChangeEvents` method as usual to trigger the necessary events:

```
this.triggerChangeEvents(oldState);
```

Listing D-17: The moveNext Method

```
function Sys$Preview$UI$Data$DataControl$moveNext()
{
  if (this._data)
  {
    var oldState = this.prepareChange();
    var newIndex = this.get_dataIndex() + 1;
    if (newIndex < this.get_length())
      this.set_dataIndex(newIndex);

    this.triggerChangeEvents(oldState);
  }
}
```

movePrevious

As the name suggests, the `movePrevious` method of the `DataControl` base class enables you to move to the previous data record of the bound data collection. As Listing D-18 shows, this method begins by calling the `prepareChange` method as usual:

```
var oldState = this.prepareChange();
```

Next, it calls the `get_dataIndex` getter to return the current data index and decrements this value by one to arrive at the new value:

```
var newIndex = this.get_dataIndex() - 1;
```

If the new value is a positive number, it invokes the `set_dataIndex` setter to set the current data index to the new value:

```
if (newIndex >=0)
    this.set_dataIndex(newIndex);
```

Finally, it invokes the `triggerChangeEvents` method as usual:

```
this.triggerChangeEvents(oldState);
```

Listing D-18: The movePrevious Method

```
function Sys$Preview$UI$Data$DataControl$movePrevious()
{
  if (this._data)
  {
      var oldState = this.prepareChange();
      var newIndex = this.get_dataIndex() - 1;
      if (newIndex >=0)
        this.set_dataIndex(newIndex);

      this.triggerChangeEvents(oldState);
  }
}
```

onBubbleEvent

The DataControl base class overrides the onBubbleEvent method that it inherits from the Control base class, as shown in Listing D-19. Recall that the onBubbleEvent method is where a client control captures the command events raised by its child controls. The DataControl base class' implementation of this method only handles the select event; that is why the method begins by calling the get_commandName method on its second parameter to determine whether the current event is a select event. If so, it takes these steps to handle the event. First, it calls the get_argument method on its second parameter to return the index of the selected data record:

```
var arg = args.get_argument();
```

If no data index has been specified, the onBubbleEvent takes these steps to access the current data index, and uses this index as the selected index. First, it invokes the get_dataContext to return a reference to the current data record:

```
var dataContext = source.get_dataContext();
```

Next, it invokes the get_index method on the current data record to return its index, and uses this index as the selected index:

```
arg = dataContext.get_index();
```

Next, it calls the set_dataIndex method to specify the selected index as the current data index:

```
this.set_dataIndex(arg);
```

Listing D-19: The onBubbleEvent Method

```
function Sys$Preview$UI$Data$DataControl$onBubbleEvent(source, args)
{
  if (args.get_commandName() === "select")
  {
    var arg = args.get_argument();
    if (!arg && arg !== 0)
    {
      var dataContext = source.get_dataContext();
      if (dataContext)
        arg = dataContext.get_index();
    }

    if (arg && String.isInstanceOfType(arg))
      arg = Number.parseInvariant(arg);

    if (arg || arg === 0)
    {
      this.set_dataIndex(arg);
      return true;
    }
  }
  return false;
}
```

descriptor

The DataControl base class, like any other ASP.NET AJAX client class, exposes a static property named descriptor that describes its methods and properties to enable its clients to use the ASP.NET AJAX client-side type inspection facilities to inspect its methods and properties generically, without knowing the actual type of the class, as shown in Listing D-20.

Listing D-20: The descriptor Property

```
Sys.Preview.UI.Data.DataControl.descriptor =
{
  properties: [ { name: 'canMoveNext', type: Boolean, readOnly: true },
                { name: 'canMovePrevious', type: Boolean, readOnly: true },
                { name: 'data', type: Sys.Preview.Data.DataTable },
                { name: 'dataIndex', type: Number },
                { name: 'dataItem', type: Object, readOnly: true },
                { name: 'length', type: Number, readOnly: true } ],
  methods: [ { name: 'addItem' },
             { name: 'deleteCurrentItem' },
             { name: 'moveNext' },
             { name: 'movePrevious' } ]
}
```

Developing a Custom Data Control

Listing D-21 presents the content of a JavaScript file named `CustomTable.js` that contains the implementation of a new version of the `CustomTable` control that derives from the `DataControl` base class. As you can see, the `render` method is where all the action is. This is the method that renders the user interface of the `CustomTable` custom data control. As you can see, this method begins by invoking the `get_data` method to return a reference to the data collection bound to the `CustomTable` data control. This control, like any other data control, inherits the `get_data` method from the `DataControl` base class:

```
var dataSource = this.get_data();
```

Next, the `render` method raises an exception if the data collection bound to the data control is neither a JavaScript array nor an `IData` object:

```
if (Sys.Preview.Data.IData.isImplementedBy(dataSource))
  isArray = false;

else if (!Array.isInstanceOfType(dataSource))
  throw Error.createError('Unknown data source type!');
```

Next, the `render` method simply iterates through the data records in the data collection bound to the data control to render each record in a `<tr>` DOM element.

Listing D-21: The Content of the CustomTable.js JavaScript File that Contains the Implementation of the CustomTable Custom Data Control

```
Type.registerNamespace("CustomComponents");
CustomComponents.CustomTable = function
CustomComponents$CustomTable(associatedElement)
{
  CustomComponents.CustomTable.initializeBase(this, [associatedElement]);
}
function CustomComponents$CustomTable$set_dataFieldNames(value)
{
  this._dataFieldNames = value;
}
function CustomComponents$CustomTable$get_dataFieldNames()
{
  return this._dataFieldNames;
}
function CustomComponents$CustomTable$render()
{
  var isArray = true;
  var dataSource = this.get_data();

  if (Sys.Preview.Data.IData.isImplementedBy(dataSource))
    isArray = false;

  else if (!Array.isInstanceOfType(dataSource))
    throw Error.createError('Unknown data source type!');
```

```
var sb = new Sys.StringBuilder('<table align="center" id="products" ');
sb.append('style="background-color:LightGoldenrodYellow; border-color:Tan;');
sb.append('border-width:1px; color:Black"');
sb.append(' cellpadding="5">');

var propertyNames = [];

var length = isArray ? dataSource.length : dataSource.get_length();

for (var i=0; i<length; i++)
{
  var dataItem = isArray? dataSource[i] : dataSource.getItem(i);

  if (i == 0)
  {
    sb.append('<tr style="background-color:Tan; font-weight:bold">');
    for (var c in this._dataFieldNames)
    {
      sb.append('<td>');
      sb.append(this._dataFieldNames[c]);
      sb.append('</td>');
    }
    sb.append('</tr>');
  }

  if (i % 2 == 1)
    sb.append('<tr style="background-color:PaleGoldenrod">');
  else
    sb.append('<tr>');

  for (var j in this._dataFieldNames)
  {
    var dataFieldName = this._dataFieldNames[j];

    var dataFieldValue = Sys.Preview.TypeDescriptor.getProperty(dataItem,
                                               dataFieldName, null);
    var typeName = Object.getTypeName(dataFieldValue);

    if (typeName !== 'String' && typeName !== 'Number' && typeName !== 'Boolean')
    {
      var convertToStringMethodName =
          Sys.Preview.TypeDescriptor.getAttribute(dataFieldValue,
                                          "convertToStringMethodName");

      if (convertToStringMethodName)
        dataFieldValue = Sys.Preview.TypeDescriptor.invokeMethod(dataFieldValue,
                                          convertToStringMethodName);
    }

    sb.append('<td>')
    sb.append(dataFieldValue);
    sb.append('</td>');
  }
```

(continued)

Listing D-21 *(continued)*

```
      sb.append('</tr>');
    }

    sb.append('</table>');
    this.get_element().innerHTML = sb.toString();
}
function CustomComponents$CustomTable$initialize()
{
    CustomComponents.CustomTable.callBaseMethod(this, "initialize");
}
CustomComponents.CustomTable.prototype =
{
    get_dataFieldNames : CustomComponents$CustomTable$get_dataFieldNames,
    set_dataFieldNames : CustomComponents$CustomTable$set_dataFieldNames,
    render : CustomComponents$CustomTable$render,
    initialize : CustomComponents$CustomTable$initialize
}
CustomComponents.CustomTable.registerClass("CustomComponents.CustomTable",
                                    Sys.Preview.UI.Data.DataControl);
CustomComponents.CustomTable.descriptor =
{
    properties: [{name : "dataFieldNames", type: Array}]
}
if(typeof(Sys)!=='undefined')
    Sys.Application.notifyScriptLoaded();
```

Listing D-22 shows a page that uses the `CustomTable` data control. If you run this page, you'll get the result shown in Figure D-1.

Listing D-22: A Page that Uses the CustomTable Data Control

```
<%@ Page Language="C#" %>
<!DOCTYPE html PUBLIC "-//W3C//DTD XHTML 1.0 Transitional//EN"
"http://www.w3.org/TR/xhtml11/DTD/xhtml1-transitional.dtd">
<html xmlns="http://www.w3.org/1999/xhtml">
<head id="Head1" runat="server">
  <title>Untitled Page</title>
  <script type="text/javascript" language="javascript">
    function onSuccess(result, userContext, methodName)
    {
      userContext.set_data(result);
    }

    function onFailure(result, userContext, methodName)
    {
      var builder = new Sys.StringBuilder();
      builder.append("timedOut: ");
      builder.append(result.get_timedOut());
      builder.appendLine();
      builder.appendLine();
```

```
                builder.append("message: ");
                builder.append(result.get_message());
                builder.appendLine();
                builder.appendLine();
                builder.append("stackTrace: ");
                builder.appendLine();
                builder.append(result.get_stackTrace());
                builder.appendLine();
                builder.appendLine();
                builder.append("exceptionType: ");
                builder.append(result.get_exceptionType());
                builder.appendLine();
                builder.appendLine();
                builder.append("statusCode: ");
                builder.append(result.get_statusCode());
                builder.appendLine();
                builder.appendLine();
                builder.append("methodName: ");
                builder.append(methodName);

                alert(builder.toString());
            }

        function pageLoad()
        {
            var properties = [];
            properties["dataFieldNames"] = ['Title', 'AuthorName', 'Publisher'];
            var customTable = $create(CustomComponents.CustomTable, properties,
                                    null, null, $get("mydiv"));
            MyWebService.GetBooks(onSuccess, onFailure, customTable);
        }
    </script>
</head>
<body>
    <form id="form1" runat="server">
        <asp:ScriptManager runat="server" ID="ScriptManager1">
            <Services>
                <asp:ServiceReference InlineScript="true" Path="WebService.asmx" />
            </Services>
            <Scripts>
                <asp:ScriptReference Assembly="Microsoft.Web.Preview"
                Name="PreviewScript.js" />
                <asp:ScriptReference Path="CustomTable.js" />
            </Scripts>
        </asp:ScriptManager>
        <div id="myDiv">
        </div>
    </form>
</body>
</html>
```

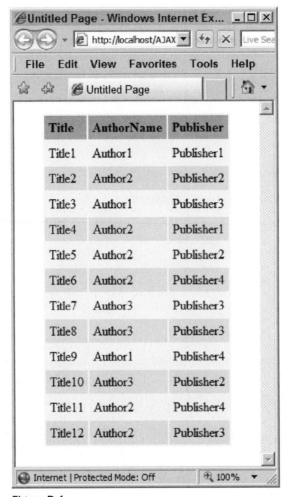

Figure D-1

Listing D-22 retrieves the data from the Web service shown in Listing D-23. This code listing presents the content of the WebService.asmx file that contains the implementation of our Web service. As you can see, this Web service exposes a method named GetBooks that retrieves the data from the underlying database and populates an array of Book objects with them.

Note that the underlying database is a database named BooksDB that contains two tables named Books and Authors. The following table describes the Books database table:

Column Name	Data Type
BookID	int
Title	nvarchar(50)
Publisher	nvarchar(50)
Price	decimal(18, 0)
AuthorID	int

The following table describes the Authors database table:

Column Name	Data Type
AuthorID	int
AuthorName	nvarchar(50)

Make sure you add the following fragment to the Web.config file of the application that contains the Web service:

```
<configuration>
  <connectionStrings>
    <add connectionString="Data Source=ServerName;Initial Catalog=BooksDB;
                          Integrated Security=SSPI" name="MyConnectionString" />
  </connectionStrings>
</configuration>
```

Listing D-23: The Content of the WebService.asmx File that Contains the Implementation of the Web Service Used by the Page Shown in Listing D-22

```
<%@ WebService Language="C#" Class="MyWebService" %>
using System;
using System.Web;
using System.Web.Services;
using System.Web.Services.Protocols;
using System.Data;
using System.Data.SqlClient;
using System.Configuration;
using System.Web.Script.Services;
using System.Web.Script.Serialization;
using System.Collections;
public class Book
{
  private string title;
  public string Title
  {
    get { return this.title; }
    set { this.title = value; }
  }
```

(continued)

```csharp
  private string authorName;
  public string AuthorName
  {
    get { return this.authorName; }
    set { this.authorName = value; }
  }
  private string publisher;
  public string Publisher
  {
    get { return this.publisher; }
    set { this.publisher = value; }
  }
  private decimal price;
  public decimal Price
  {
    get { return this.price; }
    set { this.price = value; }
  }
}
[WebService(Namespace = "http://tempuri.org/")]
[WebServiceBinding(ConformsTo = WsiProfiles.BasicProfile1_1)]
[ScriptService]
public class MyWebService : System.Web.Services.WebService
{
  [WebMethod]
  public Book[] GetBooks()
  {
    ConnectionStringSettings settings =
      ConfigurationManager.ConnectionStrings["MyConnectionString"];
    string connectionString = settings.ConnectionString;
    string commandText = "Select Title, AuthorName, Publisher, Price " +
  "From Books Inner Join Authors " +
  "On Books.AuthorID = Authors.AuthorID ";
    DataTable dt = new DataTable();
    SqlDataAdapter ad = new SqlDataAdapter(commandText, connectionString);
    ad.Fill(dt);
    Book[] books = new Book[dt.Rows.Count];
    for (int i=0; i<dt.Rows.Count; i++)
    {
      books[i] = new Book();
      books[i].Title = (string)dt.Rows[i]["Title"];
      books[i].AuthorName = (string)dt.Rows[i]["AuthorName"];
      books[i].Publisher = (string)dt.Rows[i]["Publisher"];
      books[i].Price = (decimal)dt.Rows[i]["Price"];
    }
    return books;
  }
}
```

Templated Controls

Appendix D implemented a client control named `CustomTable` that uses predetermined HTML content to render its user interface to display the specified data records. This client control is an example of one that hard-codes its HTML content. A templated client control is a control that enables page developers to customize the HTML content that makes up its user interface. In other words, a templated client control does not hard-code its HTML. Every ASP.NET AJAX templated client control exposes a property of type `ITemplate`. As Listing E-1 shows, the `ITemplate` interface exposes the methods discussed in the following table:

Method	Description
createInstance	Every subclass of the `ITemplate` interface must implement this method. The subclass must contain the appropriate logic to create the DOM subtree that the template represents and to attach this subtree to the document object.
initialize	Every subclass of the `ITemplate` interface must implement this method to initialize itself.
disposeInstance	A static method that must be used as is. This method simply disposes the current `MarkupContext`. Recall that the current `MarkupContext` maintains two important pieces of information: the DOM subtree that the template represents and its associated ASP.NET AJAX components.

Listing E-1: The ITemplate Interface

```
}
Sys.Preview.UI.ITemplate = function Sys$Preview$UI$ITemplate()
{
   throw Error.notImplemented();
}
function Sys$Preview$UI$ITemplate$createInstance()
{
   throw Error.notImplemented();
}
```

(continued)

Listing E-1 *(continued)*

```
function Sys$Preview$UI$ITemplate$initialize()
{
  throw Error.notImplemented();
}
Sys.Preview.UI.ITemplate.prototype =
{
  createInstance: Sys$Preview$UI$ITemplate$createInstance,
  initialize: Sys$Preview$UI$ITemplate$initialize
}
Sys.Preview.UI.ITemplate.registerInterface('Sys.Preview.UI.ITemplate');
Sys.Preview.UI.ITemplate.disposeInstance =
function Sys$Preview$UI$ITemplate$disposeInstance(container)
{
  if (container.markupContext)
  {
    container.markupContext.dispose();
    container.markupContext = null;
  }
}
```

TemplateInstance

Property	Description
instanceElement	References the root DOM element of the subtree of DOM elements represented by the template and its associated MarkupContext
callbackResult	Normally references a DOM element with a specified id HTML attribute value

A subclass of the ITemplate interface normally instantiates and initializes an instance of the TemplateInstance class inside the createInstance method, and returns this instance as the return value of the createInstance method.

Listing E-2: The TemplateInstance Type

```
Sys.Preview.UI.TemplateInstance = function Sys$Preview$UI$TemplateInstance()
{
  this.instanceElement = null;
  this.callbackResult = null;
}
```

Template

The ASP.NET AJAX client-side framework comes with an implementation of the `ITemplate` interface named `Template`, as shown in Listing E-3, which is used in ASP.NET AJAX `templated` controls such as `ListView`. I'll discuss the members of this class in the following sections.

Listing E-3: The Template Type

```
Sys.Preview.UI.Template =
function Sys$Preview$UI$Template(layoutElement, scriptNode, parentMarkupContext)
{
  Sys.Preview.UI.Template.initializeBase(this);
  this._layoutElement = layoutElement;
  this._scriptNode = scriptNode;
  this._parentMarkupContext = parentMarkupContext;
}
Sys.Preview.UI.Template.prototype =
{
  createInstance: Sys$Preview$UI$Template$createInstance,
  dispose: Sys$Preview$UI$Template$dispose,
  initialize: Sys$Preview$UI$Template$initialize
}
Sys.Preview.UI.Template.registerClass('Sys.Preview.UI.Template', null,
                          Sys.Preview.UI.ITemplate, Sys.IDisposable);
```

Constructor

The constructor of the `Template` class takes three parameters, as shown in the following table:

Parameter	Description
layoutElement	References the DOM element, such as a `<div>` HTML element, that represents the template on the current page. Every ASP.NET AJAX template must be associated with an HTML element. This HTML element is known as a layout element.
scriptNode	References the xml-script `<template>` element that represents the template in the xml-script.
parentMarkupContext	References the parent `MarkupContext` of the local `MarkupContext` that the template uses to represent the subtree of nodes associated with the template. The parent `MarkupContext` is normally the global `MarkupContext`. Recall that the global `MarkupContext` represents the current `document` object.

parseFromMarkup

Every ASP.NET AJAX component either exposes a `parseFromMarkup` static method or inherits this static method from its parent component through the process discussed in Appendix A. When the xml-script parser is parsing an xml-script node that represents an ASP.NET AJAX client class of type `Component`, it first accesses a reference to the type and then invokes the `parseFromMarkup` method of the type, passing in three parameters to have the type parse the child xml-script nodes of the xml-script node that represents the type. The following table presents these three parameters:

Parameter	Description
Type	References the ASP.NET AJAX type associated with the xml-script node being parsed, which is the `<template>` xml-script node in this case.
Node	References the xml-script node being parsed.
markupContext	References the current `MarkupContext`. (Recall that the current `MarkupContext` maintains two important pieces of information: a DOM subtree and its associated ASP.NET AJAX components.)

As you can see from Listing E-4, the `parseFromMarkup` static method of the `Template` class first calls the `getNamedItem` method on the attributes collection property of the node that references the `<template>` xml-script element to return a reference to the attribute node named `layoutElement`:

```
var layoutElementAttribute = node.attributes.getNamedItem('layoutElement');
```

Next, it calls the `nodeValue` property on the attribute node to return the value of the attribute node. This value is a string that contains the value of the `id` HTML attribute of the HTML element, such as a `<div>` element, that represents the template:

```
var layoutElementID = layoutElementAttribute.nodeValue;
```

Next, it calls the `findElement` instance method on the current `MarkupContext` to return a reference to the HTML DOM element in the subtree of nodes represented by the current `MarkupContext`. Keep in mind that this subtree of nodes is not part of the document object. As a result, you cannot call the `getElementById` method on the `document` object to return a reference to this DOM element. The `document` object is part of the global `MarkupContext`, not the local `MarkupContext`, which is local to the current template:

```
var layoutElement = markupContext.findElement(layoutElementID);
```

Finally, it instantiates a `Template` object, passing in three parameters. The first parameter references the HTML DOM element returned by the call into the `findElement` method. This DOM element is the root node of the subtree that the current `MarkupContext` represents. The second parameter references the xml-script `<template>` node that represents the template in the xml-script XML document. The third parameter references the current `MarkupContext`.

Listing E-4: The parseFromMarkup Static Method of the Template Class

```
Sys.Preview.UI.Template.parseFromMarkup =
function Sys$Preview$UI$Template$parseFromMarkup(type, node, markupContext)
{
  var layoutElementAttribute = node.attributes.getNamedItem('layoutElement');
  var layoutElementID = layoutElementAttribute.nodeValue;
  var layoutElement = markupContext.findElement(layoutElementID);
  return  new Sys.Preview.UI.Template(layoutElement, node, markupContext);
}
```

createInstance

The `Template` client class, like any other template class, implements the `createInstance` method of the `ITemplate` interface. This method takes the parameters shown in the following table:

Parameter	Description
containerElement	References the DOM element on the current page that will contain the subtree of DOM elements generated by the call into the `createInstance` method. The `createInstance` method basically parses the specified `<template>` node in xmlscript to extract the information that it needs to generate this subtree of DOM nodes.
dataContext	References the current data context, which is normally the current data record in the underlying data record collection.
instanceElementCreatedCallback	References a JavaScript function or delegate that will be invoked right after the parsing of the child nodes of the `<template>` node that represents the template in the xml-script document.
callbackContext	References contextual information that will be passed into the JavaScript function or delegate as is.

As Listing E-5 shows, the `Template` class's implementation of the `createInstance` method performs the following tasks. First, it instantiates an instance of the `TemplateInstance` class:

```
var result = new Sys.Preview.UI.TemplateInstance();
```

Next, it invokes the `cloneNode` method on the DOM element that represents the template on the current page. Note that the `createInstance` method passes `true` to the `cloneNode` method to instruct it to clone the descendants of this DOM element as well. In other words, the return value of the `cloneNode` is a subtree of DOM nodes, in which the root is the clone of the DOM element that represents the template on the current page. The `createInstance` method then stores this subtree in the `instanceElement` property of the newly instantiated `TemplateInstance` object:

```
result.instanceElement = this._layoutElement.cloneNode(true);
```

Then, it invokes the `createDocumentFragment` method on the document object to create a new document fragment:

```
var documentFragment = document.createDocumentFragment();
```

Next, it appends the cloned sub tree of DOM nodes to this document fragment:

```
documentFragment.appendChild(result.instanceElement);
```

Then the `createInstance` method invokes the `createLocalContext` static method on the `MarkupContext` class to create a new local `MarkupContext` to represent the preceding document fragment. Note that the `createInstance` method passes three parameters into the `createLocalContext` method. The first parameter references the new document fragment, which contains the preceding cloned subtree. The second parameter references the current `MarkupContext`, which is normally the global `MarkupContext`. While the global `MarkupContext` represents the document object, the local markup context represents this document fragment. (Keep in mind that this document fragment, which contains the cloned subtree, is not part of the document object. In other words, you cannot invoke the `getElementById` method on the document object to access the DOM elements in this closed subtree.) The third parameter is the reference to the current data context. The data context is normally the current data record in the underlying data record collection:

```
var markupContext =
        Sys.Preview.MarkupContext.createLocalContext(documentFragment,
                                        this._parentMarkupContext, dataContext);
```

Next, the `createInstance` method invokes the `open` method on the newly created `MarkupContext` object. Recall that the `open` method simply instantiates the `_pendingReferences` collection of the `MarkupContext` object.

```
markupContext.open();
```

Then it invokes the `parseNodes` static method on the `MarkupParser` class to parse the child nodes of the `<template>` node that represents the template in xml-script. Note that the `createInstance` method passes two parameters into the `parseNodes` method. The first is an array that contains the references to all the child nodes of the `<template>` node that represents the template in xml-script. (These child nodes are normally the ASP.NET AJAX components that the page developer declares between the opening and closing of the template element.) The second parameter references the newly instantiated local `MarkupContext`. This is the `MarkupContext` that represents a cloned subtree of nodes:

```
Sys.Preview.MarkupParser.parseNodes(this._scriptNode.childNodes, markupContext);
```

The caller of the `createInstance` method can pass a reference to a JavaScript function or delegate that represents a JavaScript function, and use this as the third parameter of the `createInstance` method. The `createInstance` method invokes this JavaScript function or delegate at this point and passes three parameters into it. The first parameter references the cloned subtree of nodes. The second parameter references the newly created `MarkupContext`. The third parameter references the JavaScript object that the caller of the `createInstance` method has passed into the method as its last parameter (if any). As you can see, the `createInstance` method doesn't do anything with its last parameter. It simply passes it back into its caller through the JavaScript function, or the delegate that the caller passed into the `createInstance` method as its third argument. It is the responsibility of this JavaScript function or delegate to use the parameters passed into it to run the necessary custom code and return the result to the `createInstance` method. The `createInstance` method simply stores the returned value of this JavaScript function or delegate in the `callbackResult` property of the `TemplateInstance` object. The caller of the `createInstance` method can then access this return value via the `callbackResult` property of this object.

```
if (instanceElementCreatedCallback)
  result.callbackResult = instanceElementCreatedCallback(result.instanceElement,
                                            markupContext, callbackContext);
```

Next, the `createInstance` method stores the newly created `markupContext` in the `markupContext` property of the `instanceElement` property of the `TemplateInstance` object.

```
result.instanceElement.markupContext = markupContext;
```

Then the `createInstance` method appends the cloned subtree of nodes as the child element of the DOM element passed into the method as its first parameter:

```
containerElement.appendChild(result.instanceElement);
```

Next, the `createInstance` method invokes the `close` method on the newly created `MarkupContext`. Recall that this method resolves the cross-references among the ASP.NET AJAX objects that represent the parsed nodes:

```
markupContext.close();
```

Finally, the `createInstance` method returns the `TemplateInstance` object to its caller:

```
return result;
```

Listing E-5: The createInstance Method

```
function Sys$Preview$UI$Template$createInstance(containerElement, dataContext,
                                          instanceElementCreatedCallback,
                                          callbackContext)
{
  var result = new Sys.Preview.UI.TemplateInstance();
  result.instanceElement = this._layoutElement.cloneNode(true);
  var documentFragment = document.createDocumentFragment();
  documentFragment.appendChild(result.instanceElement);
  var markupContext =
      Sys.Preview.MarkupContext.createLocalContext(documentFragment,
                                      this._parentMarkupContext, dataContext);
  markupContext.open();
  Sys.Preview.MarkupParser.parseNodes(this._scriptNode.childNodes, markupContext);
```

(continued)

```
    if (instanceElementCreatedCallback)
      result.callbackResult = instanceElementCreatedCallback(result.instanceElement,
                                          markupContext, callbackContext);
    result.instanceElement.markupContext = markupContext;
    containerElement.appendChild(result.instanceElement);
    markupContext.close();
    return result;
  }
```

Developing a Custom Template

Listing E-6 presents the content of a JavaScript file named `TemplateField.js` that contains the implementation of a custom template named `TemplateField`. (You'll see an application of this custom template later in this appendix.) As you can see, the `TemplateField` inherits from the `Template` class and extends its functionality to add support for a new property named `headerText`:

```
CustomComponents.TemplateField.registerClass("CustomComponents.TemplateField",
                                      Sys.Preview.UI.Template);
```

I'll walk you through the implementation of the members of this template in the following sections.

Listing E-6: The Content of the TemplateField.js JavaScript File that Contains the Implementation of the TemplateField Custom Template

```
Type.registerNamespace("CustomComponents");
CustomComponents.TemplateField =
function CustomComponents$TemplateField(layoutElement, scriptNode,
                                    parentMarkupContext, headerText)
{
  CustomComponents.TemplateField.initializeBase(this,
                          [layoutElement, scriptNode, parentMarkupContext]);
  this._headerText = headerText;
}
function CustomComponents$TemplateField$get_headerText()
{
  return this._headerText;
}
CustomComponents.TemplateField.prototype =
{
  get_headerText : CustomComponents$TemplateField$get_headerText
}
CustomComponents.TemplateField.registerClass("CustomComponents.TemplateField",
                                    Sys.Preview.UI.Template);
CustomComponents.TemplateField.parseFromMarkup =
function Sys$Preview$UI$Template$parseFromMarkup(type, node, markupContext)
{
  var layoutElementAttribute = node.attributes.getNamedItem('layoutElement');
  Sys.Debug.assert(!!(layoutElementAttribute &&
                  layoutElementAttribute.nodeValue.length),
                  'Missing layoutElement attribute on template definition');
```

```
        var layoutElementID = layoutElementAttribute.nodeValue;
        var layoutElement = markupContext.findElement(layoutElementID);
        Sys.Debug.assert(!!layoutElement,
                    String.format('Could not find the HTML element with ID "{0}"
                                   associated with the template',
                                   layoutElementID));
        var headerTextAttribute = node.attributes.getNamedItem('headerText');
        var headerText = headerTextAttribute.nodeValue;
        return new CustomComponents.TemplateField(layoutElement, node,
                                         markupContext, headerText);
    }
    if(typeof(Sys)!=='undefined')
        Sys.Application.notifyScriptLoaded();
```

Constructor

As Listing E-7 shows, the constructor of the `TemplateField` custom template takes a fourth parameter, in addition to the parameters that the `Template` constructor takes. This fourth parameter is used to set the `headerText` property of this custom template:

```
        this._headerText = headerText;
```

Note that the constructor of the `TemplateField` custom template passes its first three parameters to the constructor of the `Template` class:

```
        CustomComponents.TemplateField.initializeBase(this,
                                [layoutElement, scriptNode, parentMarkupContext]);
```

Listing E-7: The Constructor of the TemplateField Custom Template

```
CustomComponents.TemplateField =
function CustomComponents$TemplateField(layoutElement, scriptNode,
parentMarkupContext, headerText)
{
    CustomComponents.TemplateField.initializeBase(this,
                               [layoutElement, scriptNode, parentMarkupContext]);
    this._headerText = headerText;
}
```

headerText

The `TemplateField` custom template extends the functionality of the `Template` base class to add support for a read-only string property named `headerText`. You can set this property only through the constructor of the `TemplateField` custom template. Therefore, this custom template does not expose a setter method for setting this property. Listing E-8 presents the implementation of the getter method for this property.

Listing E-8: The Getter Method for the HeaderText Property

```
function CustomComponents$TemplateField$get_headerText()
{
    return this._headerText;
}
```

parseFromMarkup

Every time you implement a custom template that derives from the `Template` class, you must also implement a method for your custom template that meets the following criteria:

- ❑ It must be named `parseFromMarkup`.

- ❑ It must be static — that is, it must be defined on your custom template, not its `prototype` property.

- ❑ This method must take the following three parameters:

  - ❑ `type`: This parameter references the `Type` object that describes the ASP.NET AJAX type that represents the DOM node referenced by the second parameter.

  - ❑ `node`: This parameter references the DOM node that represents your custom template in xml-script.

  - ❑ `markupContext`: This parameter references the current `MarkupContext`, which is normally the global `MarkupContext`.

- ❑ This method must instantiate an instance of your custom template and return the instance to its caller.

Listing E-9 presents the `TemplateField` custom template's implementation of the `parseFromMarkup` method. This method begins by invoking the `getNamedItem` method on the `attributes` collection property of the DOM node that represents your custom template in xml-script, in order to return a reference to the DOM node that represents the `layoutElement` attribute on your custom template:

```
var layoutElementAttribute = node.attributes.getNamedItem('layoutElement');
```

Next, it invokes the `nodeValue` property on the DOM node that represents the `layoutElement` attribute, to access the value of this attribute:

```
var layoutElementID = layoutElementAttribute.nodeValue;
```

Then it invokes the `findElement` method on the current `MarkupContext` to return a reference to the associated DOM element of the `TemplateField` custom template:

```
var layoutElement = markupContext.findElement(layoutElementID);
```

Note that `parseFromMarkup` raises an exception if the current page does not contain the specified DOM element.

Next, the `parseFromMarkup` method invokes the `getNamedItem` method on the `attributes` collection property of the DOM node that represents the `TemplateField` in xml-script, in order to return a reference to the DOM node that represents the `headerText` attribute:

```
var headerTextAttribute = node.attributes.getNamedItem('headerText');
```

Then it invokes the `nodeValue` property on the attribute node to access the value of this attribute:

```
var headerText = headerTextAttribute.nodeValue;
```

Next, it instantiates and returns an instance of the `TemplateField`, passing in the reference to the associated DOM element of the template, the reference to the DOM element that represents the template in xml-script, the reference to the current `MarkupContext`, and the header text.

```
return new CustomComponents.TemplateField(layoutElement, node,
                                          markupContext, headerText);
```

Listing E-9: The parseFromMarkup Method

```
CustomComponents.TemplateField.parseFromMarkup =
function Sys$Preview$UI$Template$parseFromMarkup(type, node, markupContext)
{
  var layoutElementAttribute = node.attributes.getNamedItem('layoutElement');
  Sys.Debug.assert(!!(layoutElementAttribute &&
                    layoutElementAttribute.nodeValue.length),
                    'Missing layoutElement attribute on template definition');
  var layoutElementID = layoutElementAttribute.nodeValue;

  var layoutElement = markupContext.findElement(layoutElementID);
  Sys.Debug.assert(!!layoutElement,
                  String.format('Could not find the HTML element with ID "{0}"
                                associated with the template',
                                layoutElementID));
  var headerTextAttribute = node.attributes.getNamedItem('headerText');
  var headerText = headerTextAttribute.nodeValue;
  return new CustomComponents.TemplateField(layoutElement, node,
                                            markupContext, headerText);
}
```

Developing a Custom Templated Data Control

Recall that we developed a custom data control named `CustomTable` in Appendix D. The main problem with this data control is that its user interface is not customizable. The great thing about templates is that they enable page developers to customize the HTML content of their associated client controls. In this section, I'll present and discuss the implementation of a new version of the `CustomTable` data control that enables page developers to declare instances of the `TemplateField` custom template in xml-script to customize the HTML content of the `CustomTable` client control and the appearance of the control. Listing E-10 presents the content of a JavaScript file named `CustomTable.js` that contains the implementation of the CustomTable templated data control. This is a data control because it derives from the DataControl base class:

```
CustomComponents.CustomTable.registerClass("CustomComponents.CustomTable",
                                    Sys.Preview.UI.Data.DataControl);
```

I'll discuss the members of this custom templated data control in the following sections.

Listing E-10: The Content of the CustomTable.js JavaScript File that Contains the Implementation of the CustomTable Templated Data Control

```javascript
Type.registerNamespace("CustomComponents");
CustomComponents.CustomTable =
function CustomComponents$CustomTable(associatedElement)
{
  CustomComponents.CustomTable.initializeBase(this, [associatedElement]);
  this._fields = [];
}
function CustomComponents$CustomTable$get_fields()
{
  return this._fields;
}
function CustomComponents$CustomTable$get_cssClass()
{
  return this._cssClass;
}
function CustomComponents$CustomTable$set_cssClass(value)
{
  this._cssClass = value;
}
function CustomComponents$CustomTable$get_hoverCssClass()
{
  return this._hoverCssClass;
}
function CustomComponents$CustomTable$set_hoverCssClass(value)
{
  this._hoverCssClass = value;
}
function CustomComponents$CustomTable$get_headerCssClass()
{
  return this._headerCssClass;
}
function CustomComponents$CustomTable$set_headerCssClass(value)
{
  this._headerCssClass = value;
}
function CustomComponents$CustomTable$get_itemCssClass()
{
  return this._itemCssClass;
}
function CustomComponents$CustomTable$set_itemCssClass(value)
{
  this._itemCssClass = value;
}
```

```
function CustomComponents$CustomTable$get_alternatingItemCssClass()
{
  return this._alternatingItemCssClass;
}
function CustomComponents$CustomTable$set_alternatingItemCssClass(value)
{
  this._alternatingItemCssClass = value;
}
function CustomComponents$CustomTable$render()
{
  var isArray = true;
  var dataSource = this.get_data();

  if (Sys.Preview.Data.IData.isImplementedBy(dataSource))
    isArray = false;

  else if (!Array.isInstanceOfType(dataSource))
    throw Error.createError('Unknown data source type!');

  var table = document.createElement("table");
  if (this._cssClass)
    table.className = this._cssClass;

  var length = isArray ? dataSource.length : dataSource.get_length();
  var dataRow;
  var dataItem;
  var dataCell;
  var index = 0;
  var headerRow;
  var headerCell;

  if (this._fields)
  {
    headerRow = table.insertRow(index);
    if (this._headerCssClass)
      headerRow.className = this._headerCssClass;

    index++;
    for (var c in this._fields)
    {
      headerCell = headerRow.insertCell(c);
      headerCell.innerText = this._fields[c].get_headerText();
    }
  }

  this._toggleCssClassHandler =
                      Function.createDelegate(this, this._toggleCssClass);

  for (var i=0; i<length; i++)
  {
    dataItem = isArray? dataSource[i] : dataSource.getItem(i);
```

(continued)

Listing E-10 *(continued)*

```
      if (this._fields)
      {
        dataRow = table.insertRow(index + i);
        $addHandler(dataRow, "mouseover", this._toggleCssClassHandler);
        $addHandler(dataRow, "mouseout", this._toggleCssClassHandler);

        if ((i % 2 === 1) && (this._alternatingItemCssClass))
          dataRow.className = this._alternatingItemCssClass;

        else if (this._itemCssClass)
          dataRow.className = this._itemCssClass;
        for (var c in this._fields)
        {
          dataCell = dataRow.insertCell(c);
          this._fields[c].createInstance(dataCell, dataItem);
        }
      }
    }
  }

  this.get_element().appendChild(table);
}
function CustomComponents$CustomTable$_toggleCssClass(evt)
{
  var s = evt.target;
  while (s && (typeof(s.insertCell) === 'undefined'))
  {
    s = s.parentNode;
  }

  Sys.UI.DomElement.toggleCssClass(s, this._hoverCssClass);
}
CustomComponents.CustomTable.prototype =
{
  render : CustomComponents$CustomTable$render,
  get_cssClass : CustomComponents$CustomTable$get_cssClass,
  set_cssClass : CustomComponents$CustomTable$set_cssClass,
  get_hoverCssClass : CustomComponents$CustomTable$get_hoverCssClass,
  set_hoverCssClass : CustomComponents$CustomTable$set_hoverCssClass,
  get_headerCssClass : CustomComponents$CustomTable$get_headerCssClass,
  set_headerCssClass : CustomComponents$CustomTable$set_headerCssClass,
  get_itemCssClass : CustomComponents$CustomTable$get_itemCssClass,
  set_itemCssClass : CustomComponents$CustomTable$set_itemCssClass,
  get_alternatingItemCssClass :
                      CustomComponents$CustomTable$get_alternatingItemCssClass,
  set_alternatingItemCssClass :
                      CustomComponents$CustomTable$set_alternatingItemCssClass,
  _toggleCssClass : CustomComponents$CustomTable$_toggleCssClass,
  get_fields : CustomComponents$CustomTable$get_fields
}
CustomComponents.CustomTable.registerClass("CustomComponents.CustomTable",
                                     Sys.Preview.UI.Data.DataControl);
```

```
CustomComponents.CustomTable.descriptor =
{
  properties: [{name: "fields", type: Array, readOnly: true},
              {name: 'cssClass', type: String },
              {name: 'hoverCssClass', type: String },
              {name: 'headerCssClass', type: String },
              {name: 'itemCssClass', type: String },
              {name: 'alternatingItemCssClass', type: String }
              ]
}
if(typeof(Sys)!=='undefined')
  Sys.Application.notifyScriptLoaded();
```

fields

The CustomTable template data control exposes an array property named fields, as shown in Listing E-11. As you'll see later, page developers declaratively add instances of the TemplateField template to this array in xml-script. They do this in order to specify which data fields of each data record of the data collection bound to the CustomTable must be displayed, and what header text must be used for each data column.

Listing E-11: The Getter Method for the Fields Property

```
function CustomComponents$CustomTable$get_fields()
{
  return this._fields;
}
```

Style Properties

The following table describes the style properties of the CustomTable templated data control:

Property	Description
cssClass	Specifies the name of the CSS class for the containing <table> element of the CustomTable control
headerCssClass	Specifies the name of the CSS class for the header row
hoverCssClass	Specifies the name of the CSS class for the data row when the mouse hovers over the data row
itemCssClass	Specifies the name of the CSS class for the even-numbered data rows
alternatingItemCssClass	Specifies the name of the CSS class for the odd-numbered data rows

render

Every data control that inherits from the DataControl base class must implement a method named render. Listing E-12 presents the CustomTable class's implementation of this method. As you can see, it begins by calling the `get_data` method to return a reference to the data collection bound to the `CustomTable` control. The `CustomTable` control, like any other data control, inherits the `get_data` method from the `DataControl` base class:

```
var dataSource = this.get_data();
```

Next, it raises an exception if the bound data collection is not a JavaScript array and does not implement the `IData` interface:

```
if (Sys.Preview.Data.IData.isImplementedBy(dataSource))
   isArray = false;

else if (!Array.isInstanceOfType(dataSource))
   throw Error.createError('Unknown data source type!');
```

Then it creates a table DOM element:

```
var table = document.createElement("table");
```

Next, it assigns the value of the `cssClass` style property to the `className` property of the table DOM element:

```
if (this._cssClass)
   table.className = this._cssClass;
```

Next, the `CustomTable` control determines the total number of data records in the data collection bound to the `CustomTable` data control:

```
var length = isArray ? dataSource.length : dataSource.get_length();
```

Then it inserts a new row into the table DOM element and sets its `className` property to the value of the `headerCssClass` property:

```
headerRow = table.insertRow(index);
if (this._headerCssClass)
   headerRow.className = this._headerCssClass;

index++;
```

Next, it iterates through the template objects in the `fields` collection, inserts a cell into the newly added row, and sets the inner text of this cell to the value of the `headerText` property of the enumerated template object:

```
for (var c in this._fields)
{
   headerCell = headerRow.insertCell(c);
   headerCell.innerText = this._fields[c].get_headerText();
}
```

Then it creates a delegate that represents the `_toggleCssClass` method:

```
this._toggleCssClassHandler =
                        Function.createDelegate(this, this._toggleCssClass);
```

1396

Next, the `CustomTable` control iterates through the data records in the data collection bound to the `CustomTable` control and performs the following tasks for each enumerated data record.

```
dataItem = isArray? dataSource[i] : dataSource.getItem(i);
```

First, it inserts a new row into the table DOM element and registers the `_toggleCssClassHandler` delegate as the event handler for the `mouseover` and `mouseout` events of the newly added row.

```
dataRow = table.insertRow(index + i);
$addHandler(dataRow, "mouseover", this._toggleCssClassHandler);
$addHandler(dataRow, "mouseout", this._toggleCssClassHandler);
```

If the row is an even-numbered row, the `CustomTable` control assigns the value of the `itemCssClass` property to the `className` property of the row. Otherwise, it assigns the value of the `alternatingItemCssClass` property to the `className` property:

```
if ((i % 2 === 1) && (this._alternatingItemCssClass))
   dataRow.className = this._alternatingItemCssClass;

else if (this._itemCssClass)
   dataRow.className = this._itemCssClass;
```

Next, it iterates through the template objects in the `fields` collection, inserts a new cell for each template object, and calls the `createInstance` method of the template object to render the HTML enclosed within the template object into the newly added cell to display the current data record:

```
for (var c in this._fields)
{
   dataCell = dataRow.insertCell(c);
   this._fields[c].createInstance(dataCell, dataItem);
}
```

Finally, it appends the table DOM element to the associated DOM element of the `CustomTable` control as a child element:

```
this.get_element().appendChild(table);
```

Listing E-12: The Render Method

```
function CustomComponents$CustomTable$render()
{
   var isArray = true;
   var dataSource = this.get_data();

   if (Sys.Preview.Data.IData.isImplementedBy(dataSource))
      isArray = false;

   else if (!Array.isInstanceOfType(dataSource))
      throw Error.createError('Unknown data source type!');
```

(continued)

Listing E-12 *(continued)*

```javascript
    var table = document.createElement("table");
    if (this._cssClass)
      table.className = this._cssClass;

    var length = isArray ? dataSource.length : dataSource.get_length();
    var dataRow;
    var dataItem;
    var dataCell;
    var index = 0;
    var headerRow;
    var headerCell;

    if (this._fields)
    {
      headerRow = table.insertRow(index);
      if (this._headerCssClass)
        headerRow.className = this._headerCssClass;

      index++;
      for (var c in this._fields)
      {
        headerCell = headerRow.insertCell(c);
        headerCell.innerText = this._fields[c].get_headerText();
      }
    }

    this._toggleCssClassHandler =
                        Function.createDelegate(this, this._toggleCssClass);

    for (var i=0; i<length; i++)
    {
      dataItem = isArray? dataSource[i] : dataSource.getItem(i);

      if (this._fields)
      {
        dataRow = table.insertRow(index + i);
        $addHandler(dataRow, "mouseover", this._toggleCssClassHandler);
        $addHandler(dataRow, "mouseout", this._toggleCssClassHandler);

        if ((i % 2 === 1) && (this._alternatingItemCssClass))
          dataRow.className = this._alternatingItemCssClass;

        else if (this._itemCssClass)
          dataRow.className = this._itemCssClass;
        for (var c in this._fields)
        {
          dataCell = dataRow.insertCell(c);
          this._fields[c].createInstance(dataCell, dataItem);
        }
      }
    }

    this.get_element().appendChild(table);
}
```

_toggleCssClass

Recall from Listing E-12 that the `render` method registers the delegate that represents the `_toggleCssClass` method as an event handler for the `mouseout` and `mouseover` events of the `CustomTable` control. As Listing E-13 shows, the `_toggleCssClass` method invokes the `toggleCssClass` static method on the `DomElement` to toggle the CSS class name.

Listing E-13: The _toggleCssClass Method

```
function CustomComponents$CustomTable$_toggleCssClass(evt)
{
  var s = evt.target;
  while (s && (typeof(s.insertCell) === 'undefined'))
  {
    s = s.parentNode;
  }

  Sys.UI.DomElement.toggleCssClass(s, this._hoverCssClass);
}
```

Descriptor

The `CustomTable` control exposes a `descriptor` static property to expose its properties to the ASP.NET AJAX type inspection infrastructure, as shown in Listing E-14. This will enable page developers to set these properties in xml-script.

Listing E-14: The Descriptor Static Property

```
CustomComponents.CustomTable.descriptor =
{
  properties: [{name: "fields", type: Array, readOnly: true},
              {name: 'cssClass', type: String },
              {name: 'hoverCssClass', type: String },
              {name: 'headerCssClass', type: String },
              {name: 'itemCssClass', type: String },
              {name: 'alternatingItemCssClass', type: String }
              ]
}
```

Using the TemplateField and CustomTable Templated Data Controls

Follow these steps to use the `TemplateField` and `CustomTable` templated data controls:

1. Create a new Ajax-enabled Web site in Visual Studio 2005.

2. Add a new JavaScript file named `TemplateField.js` to the root directory of this application and add Listing E-6 to this file.

3. Add a new JavaScript file named `CustomTable.js` to the root directory of this application and add Listing E-10 to this file.

4. Add a new Web page named `CustomTable.aspx` to the root directory of this application and add Listing E-15 to this file.

5. Add a new Web service named `WebService.asmx` to the root directory of this application and add Listing E-16 to this file.

Keep in mind that this example uses the same `BooksDB` database discussed in Appendix D.

Listing E-15: A Page that Uses the TemplateField and CustomTable Templated Data Controls

```
<%@ Page Language="C#" %>
<!DOCTYPE html PUBLIC "-//W3C//DTD XHTML 1.0 Transitional//EN"
"http://www.w3.org/TR/xhtml1/DTD/xhtml1-transitional.dtd">
<html xmlns="http://www.w3.org/1999/xhtml">
<head id="Head1" runat="server">
  <title>Untitled Page</title>
  <style type="text/css">
    .cssClass
    {
      background-color: LightGoldenrodYellow;
      border-color: Tan;
      border-width: 1px;
    }

    .headerCssClass
    {
      background-color: Tan;
      font-weight: bold;
    }

    .alternatingItemCssClass
    {
      background-color: PaleGoldenrod
    }

    .hoverCssClass
    {
      background-color: DarkSlateBlue;
      color: GhostWhite;
    }

  </style>
  <script type="text/javascript" language="javascript">
    function onSuccess(result, userContext, methodName)
    {
      userContext.set_data(result);
    }
```

```
        function onFailure(result, userContext, methodName)
        {
          var builder = new Sys.StringBuilder();
          builder.append("timedOut: ");
          builder.append(result.get_timedOut());
          builder.appendLine();
          builder.appendLine();
          builder.append("message: ");
          builder.append(result.get_message());
          builder.appendLine();
          builder.appendLine();
          builder.append("stackTrace: ");
          builder.appendLine();
          builder.append(result.get_stackTrace());
          builder.appendLine();
          builder.appendLine();
          builder.append("exceptionType: ");
          builder.append(result.get_exceptionType());
          builder.appendLine();
          builder.appendLine();
          builder.append("statusCode: ");
          builder.append(result.get_statusCode());
          builder.appendLine();
          builder.appendLine();
          builder.append("methodName: ");
          builder.append(methodName);

          alert(builder.toString());
        }

        function pageLoad()
        {
          var customTable = Sys.Application.findComponent("customTable");
          MyWebService.GetBooks(onSuccess, onFailure, customTable);
        }
    </script>
</head>
<body>
  <form id="form1" runat="server">
    <asp:ScriptManager runat="server" ID="ScriptManager1">
      <Services>
        <asp:ServiceReference InlineScript="true" Path="WebService.asmx" />
      </Services>
      <Scripts>
        <asp:ScriptReference Assembly="Microsoft.Web.Preview"
        Name="PreviewScript.js" />
        <asp:ScriptReference Path="CustomTable.js" />
        <asp:ScriptReference Path="TemplateField.js" />
      </Scripts>
    </asp:ScriptManager>
```

(continued)

1401

Listing E-15 *(continued)*

```
      <div id="customTable" />
      <div style="display: none;" >
        <div id="field1">
          <span id="title"></span>
        </div>
        <div id="field2">
          <span id="publisher"></span>
        </div>
        <div id="field3">
          <span id="price"></span>
        </div>
      </div>
  </form>
  <script type="text/xml-script">
    <page xmlns="http://schemas.microsoft.com/xml-script/2005"
    xmlns:custom="CustomComponents">
      <components>
        <custom:CustomTable id="customTable" cssClass="cssClass"
        headerCssClass="headerCssClass" hoverCssClass="hoverCssClass"
        alternatingItemCssClass="alternatingItemCssClass" >
          <fields>
            <custom:TemplateField layoutElement="field1" headerText="Title">
              <label id="title">
                <bindings>
                  <binding dataPath="Title" property="text" />
                </bindings>
              </label>
            </custom:TemplateField>
            <custom:TemplateField layoutElement="field2" headerText="Publisher">
              <label id="publisher">
                <bindings>
                  <binding dataPath="Publisher" property="text" />
                </bindings>
              </label>
            </custom:TemplateField>
            <custom:TemplateField layoutElement="field3" headerText="Price">
              <label id="price">
                <bindings>
                  <binding dataPath="Price" property="text" transform="ToString"
                                   transformerArgument="${0}" />
                </bindings>
              </label>
            </custom:TemplateField>
          </fields>
        </custom:CustomTable>
      </components>
    </page>
  </script>
</body>
</html>
```

Listing E-16: The MyWebService Web Service

```csharp
<%@ WebService Language="C#" Class="MyWebService" %>
using System;
using System.Web;
using System.Web.Services;
using System.Web.Services.Protocols;
using System.Data;
using System.Data.SqlClient;
using System.Configuration;
using System.Web.Script.Services;
using System.Web.Script.Serialization;
using System.Collections;
public class Book
{
  private string title;
  public string Title
  {
    get { return this.title; }
    set { this.title = value; }
  }
  private string authorName;
  public string AuthorName
  {
    get { return this.authorName; }
    set { this.authorName = value; }
  }
  private string publisher;
  public string Publisher
  {
    get { return this.publisher; }
    set { this.publisher = value; }
  }
  private decimal price;
  public decimal Price
  {
    get { return this.price; }
    set { this.price = value; }
  }
}
[WebService(Namespace = "http://tempuri.org/")]
[WebServiceBinding(ConformsTo = WsiProfiles.BasicProfile1_1)]
[ScriptService]
public class MyWebService : System.Web.Services.WebService
{
  [WebMethod]
  public Book[] GetBooks()
  {
    ConnectionStringSettings settings =
      ConfigurationManager.ConnectionStrings["MyConnectionString"];
    string connectionString = settings.ConnectionString;
    string commandText = "Select Title, AuthorName, Publisher, Price " +
                         "From Books Inner Join Authors " +
                         "On Books.AuthorID = Authors.AuthorID ";
```

(continued)

Listing E-16 *(continued)*

```
       DataTable dt = new DataTable();
       SqlDataAdapter ad = new SqlDataAdapter(commandText, connectionString);
       ad.Fill(dt);
       Book[] books = new Book[dt.Rows.Count];
       for (int i=0; i<dt.Rows.Count; i++)
       {
         books[i] = new Book();
         books[i].Title = (string)dt.Rows[i]["Title"];
         books[i].AuthorName = (string)dt.Rows[i]["AuthorName"];
         books[i].Publisher = (string)dt.Rows[i]["Publisher"];
         books[i].Price = (decimal)dt.Rows[i]["Price"];
       }
       return books;
     }
   }
```

Using a custom ASP.NET AJAX class in xml-script requires you to define on the `<page>` element an XML namespace prefix that maps to the ASP.NET AJAX namespace containing the custom ASP.NET AJAX class. In this case, Listing E-15 defines an XML namespace prefix named `custom` that maps to the ASP.NET AJAX `CustomComponents` namespace, because this is the namespace that contains the `TemplateField` and `CustomTable` ASP.NET AJAX client classes:

```
<script type="text/xml-script">
  <page xmlns="http://schemas.microsoft.com/xml-script/2005"
    xmlns:custom="CustomComponents">
    <components>
      <custom:CustomTable id="customTable" cssClass="cssClass"
      headerCssClass="headerCssClass" hoverCssClass="hoverCssClass"
      alternatingItemCssClass="alternatingItemCssClass" >
      </custom:CustomTable>
      . . .
    </components>
  </page>
</script>
```

You must qualify with this XML namespace prefix the names of the XML elements that represent instances of your custom client class in xml-script. In this case, Listing E-15 qualifies the names of the `TemplateField` and `CustomTable` XML elements with the prefix `custom`, as shown in the highlighted portions of the following excerpt from Listing E-15:

```
<script type="text/xml-script">
  <page xmlns="http://schemas.microsoft.com/xml-script/2005"
  xmlns:custom="CustomComponents">
    <components>
      <custom:CustomTable
      id="customTable" cssClass="cssClass"
      headerCssClass="headerCssClass" hoverCssClass="hoverCssClass"
```

```
                    alternatingItemCssClass="alternatingItemCssClass" >
                <fields>

                    <custom:TemplateField

                    layoutElement="field1" headerText="Title">
                      <label id="title">
                        <bindings>
                          <binding dataPath="Title" property="text" />
                        </bindings>
                      </label>
                    </custom:TemplateField>

                    <custom:TemplateField

                    layoutElement="field2" headerText="Publisher">
                      <label id="publisher">
                        <bindings>
                          <binding dataPath="Publisher" property="text" />
                        </bindings>
                      </label>
                    </custom:TemplateField>

                    <custom:TemplateField

                    layoutElement="field3" headerText="Price">
                      <label id="Price">
                        <bindings>
                          <binding dataPath="Price" property="text" transform="ToString"
                          transformerArgument="${0}" />
                        </bindings>
                      </label>
                    </custom:TemplateField>
                </fields>
              </custom:CustomTable>
            </components>
        <page>
    <script>
```

As you can see, each TemplateField in Listing E-15 is associated with an HTML element on the page. For example, consider the following excerpt from Listing E-15 that contains one of these TemplateFields:

```
            <custom:TemplateField layoutElement="field1" headerText="Title">
              <label id="title">
                <bindings>
                  <binding dataPath="Title" property="text" />
                </bindings>
              </label>
            </custom:TemplateField>
```

The following excerpt from Listing E-15 shows the HTML element associated with the TemplateField:

```
        <div id="field1">
          <span id="title"> </span>
        </div>
```

Also note that each `TemplateField` contains a `<label>` element that represents a `<span>` element, which is the subelement of the associated HTML element of the `TemplateField`. For example, in the preceding two excerpts, the `<label>` subelement of the `<custom:TemplateField>` represents the `<span>` subelement of the `<div>` element associated with this `TemplateField`.

Note that each `<label>` element contains a `<bindings>` subelement, which in turn contains a `<binding>` subelement. This `<binding>` subelement binds the text property of its associated `<label>` element to the specified data field of the current data record of the data collection bound to the `CustomTable` data control. For example, in the case of the following excerpt from Listing E-15, the `<binding>` subelement binds the `text` property of the `<label>` element that has the `id` attribute value of `title` to the `Title` data field of the current data record:

```
<custom:TemplateField layoutElement="field1" headerText="Title">
  <label id="title">
    <bindings>

      <binding dataPath="Title" property="text" />

    </bindings>
  </label>
</custom:TemplateField>
```

Also note that all `<custom:TemplateField>` elements are declared as child elements of the `<fields>` element:

```
<custom:CustomTable id="customTable" cssClass="cssClass"
headerCssClass="headerCssClass" hoverCssClass="hoverCssClass"
alternatingItemCssClass="alternatingItemCssClass" >
  <fields>
    <custom:TemplateField layoutElement="field1" headerText="Title">
    . . .

    </custom:TemplateField>
    <custom:TemplateField layoutElement="field2" headerText="Publisher">
    . . .

    </custom:TemplateField>
    <custom:TemplateField layoutElement="field3" headerText="Price">

    . . .

    </custom:TemplateField>
  </fields>

</custom:CustomTable>
```

Also note that Listing E-15 sets the `cssClass, headerCssClass, hoverCssClass,` and `alternatingItemCssClass` properties of the `CustomTable` to the names of the CSS classes defined on the page:

```
<script type="text/xml-script">
  <page xmlns="http://schemas.microsoft.com/xml-script/2005"
  xmlns:custom="CustomComponents">
    <components>

      <custom:CustomTable id="customTable" cssClass="cssClass"
      headerCssClass="headerCssClass" hoverCssClass="hoverCssClass"
      alternatingItemCssClass="alternatingItemCssClass" >

        <fields>
          . . .
        </fields>
      </custom:CustomTable>
    </components>
  </page>
</script>
```

ListView

The ASP.NET AJAX `ListView` client control is a templated data control for displaying data records. A good understanding of the implementation of the `ListView` templated data control and its surrounding ASP.NET AJAX classes and interfaces will provide you with the skills, knowledge, and experience that you need to implement templated data controls as complex as the `ListView`.

However, before diving into the implementation of the `ListView` control and its surrounding ASP.NET AJAX classes and interfaces, I'll uses a few examples to show you how to take advantage of the rich features of this control in your own Web applications.

Overview of ListView

The `ListView` templated data control offers two sets of properties to customize the control:

❑ Style properties: These enable you to style the DOM elements that make up the `ListView` templated data control. In other words, you cannot use the style properties to customize the DOM elements themselves — that is, to replace them with a new set of DOM elements; you can only customize the appearances of these DOM elements.

❑ Template properties: These enable you to customize the DOM elements that make up the `ListView` control. In other words, you get to decide what types of DOM elements are used to build the `ListView` control's UI.

The following table presents the getter and setter methods of the style properties of the `ListView` templated data control:

Style Property	Description
`get_itemCssClass`	Gets the name of the CSS class that styles the even-numbered data rows or items of the `ListView` control. (A data row is a row that displays a data record.)

(continued)

(continued)

Style Property	Description
set_itemCssClass	Sets the name of the CSS class that styles the even-numbered data rows or items of the ListView control.
get_alternatingItemCssClass	Gets the name of the CSS class that styles the odd-numbered data rows or items of the ListView control.
set_alternatingItemCssClass	Sets the name of the CSS class that styles the odd-numbered data rows or items of the ListView control
get_separatorCssClass	Gets the name of the CSS class that styles the separator rows or items of the ListView control. (A separator row is a row that separates two consecutive data rows.)
set_separatorCssClass	Sets the name of the CSS class that styles the separator rows or items of the ListView control.
get_selectedItemCssClass	Gets the name of the CSS class that styles the selected data row or item of the ListView control.
set_selectedItemCssClass	Sets the name of the CSS class that styles the selected data row or item of the ListView control.

The following table presents the template properties of the ListView templated data control:

Template Property	Description
get_emptyTemplate	Gets a reference to the empty template. (The empty template is the one that specifies the markup that will be shown to the end user when the data collection bound to the ListView control does not contain any data records.)
set_emptyTemplate	Sets the empty template. (Take the following steps to specify the empty template. First, add an <emptyTemplate> subelement to the <listView> element in the xml-script. Next, add a <template> subelement to the <emptyTemplate> element. Finally, add the desired markup text between the opening and closing tags of the template subelement. The ListView control will automatically display this markup text if the bound data collection does not contain any data records.)
get_itemTemplate	Gets a reference to the item template. (The item template is the one that specifies the markup that displays a data record.)
set_itemTemplate	Sets the item template. (Take these steps to specify the item template. First, add an <itemTemplate> subelement to the <listView> element in the xml-script. Next, add a <template> subelement to the <itemTemplate> element. Finally, add the desired markup text between the opening and closing tags of the template subelement. The ListView control will automatically use this markup to display a data record.)

Template Property	Description
get_layoutTemplate	Gets a reference to the layout template. (The layout template is the one that specifies the layout markup for the whole ListView control.)
set_layoutTemplate	Sets the layout template. (Take these steps to specify the layout template. First, add a <layoutTemplate> subelement to the <listView> element in the xml-script. Next, add a <template> subelement to the <layoutTemplate> element. Finally, add the desired markup text between the opening and closing tags of the template subelement. The ListView control will automatically use this markup to layout the ListView control.)
get_separatorTemplate	Gets a reference to the separator template. (The separator template is the one that specifies the markup that separates two consecutive data rows of the ListView control.)
set_separatorTemplate	Sets the separator template. (Take the following steps to specify the separator template. First, add a <separatorTemplate> subelement to the <listView> element in the xml-script. Next, add a <template> subelement to the <separatorTemplate> element. Finally, add the desired markup text between the opening and closing tags of the template subelement. The ListView control will automatically use this markup to separate data rows.)

Besides the getters and setters that get and set the style and template properties, the ListView control also exposes the getters and setters shown in the following table that get and set other properties:

Property	Descriptor
set_dataIndex	Sets the current data index. (The current data index is the index of the current data record in the data collection bound to the ListView control.)
get_itemTemplateParentElementId	Gets the id HTML attribute value of the parent DOM element of the DOM element that represents the item template. (Keep in mind that every ASP.NET AJAX template, including the item template, is associated with a DOM element on the current page.)
set_itemTemplateParentElementId	Sets the id HTML attribute value of the parent DOM element of the DOM element that represents the item template. You can specify this id HTML attribute value declaratively in the xml-script by setting the itemTemplateParentElementId attribute on the <listView> element.
getItemElement	Returns a reference to the item DOM element with the specified data index. (An item DOM element is a DOM element that displays a data record.)

The ListView control also exposes an event named renderComplete. This event is fired when the rendering of the ListView control completes:

Method	Description
add_renderComplete	Adds a new event handler to the list of event handlers registered for the renderComplete event of the ListView control.
remove_renderComplete	Removes an event handler from the list of event handlers registered for the renderComplete event of the ListView control.

The following table presents some of the important methods of the ListView control:

Method	Description
Initialize	This method initializes the ListView control. Since the ListView control is normally added declaratively to the current page, that is, since it is declared in the xml-script, you do not have to worry about this method because the ASP.NET AJAX client side Framework automatically invokes this method behind the scenes. However, it you decide to use the ListView control imperatively and if you do not use the $create global JavaScript function to instantiate the control, you do have to invoke the initialize method to initialize the control.
Dispose	Performs the final cleanup before the ListView control is disposed of. The Application object that represents the current ASP.NET AJAX application automatically invokes this method when the current page is about to be disposed of.
Render	Renders the ListView control. You do not need to directly invoke this method because it is automatically invoked under the hood when you bind a data collection to the ListView control.

Since the ListView control derives from the DataConrol base class, it inherits the following members from this base class:

Inherited Member	Description
get_canMoveNext	Gets a Boolean value that specifies whether the ListView control can move to the next data record. It returns false if the data collection bound to the ListView control contains no records or if the current data record is the last record in this collection.
get_canMovePrevious	Gets a Boolean value that specifies whether the ListView control can move to the previous data record. It returns false if the data collection bound to the ListView control contains no records or if the current data record is the first record in this collection.

Inherited Member	Description
get_data	Returns a reference to the data collection bound to the ListView control.
set_data	Binds a data collection to the ListView control. This method automatically invokes the render method of the ListView control to render the control. Therefore, binding the data collection to the ListView control is all it takes to have the control display the data records in the collection.
get_length	Gets the total record count in the data collection bound to the ListView control.
get_dataIndex	Gets the index of the current data record in the data collection bound to the ListView control.
onDataChanged	Simply invokes the render method to render the ListView control.
get_dataItem	Returns a reference to the current data record in the data collection bound to the ListView control.
get_dataContext	Returns a reference to the current data record in the data collection bound to the ListView control.
addItem	Adds an empty record to the data collection bound to the ListView control. (The current implementation of the ListView control does not make use of this method.)
deleteCurrentItem	Deletes the current data record from the data collection bound to the ListView control.
getItem	Returns a reference to the data record in the data collection bound to the ListView control that has the specified index.
moveNext	Moves to the next data record in the data collection bound to the ListView control.
movePrevious	Moves to the previous data record in the data collection bound to the ListView control.
onBubbleEvent	Captures the events raised by those child controls of the ListView control that bubble up their events. (The current implementation of the ListView control catches only the select event. However, you can implement your own custom ListView control in which your implementation of the onBubbleEvent can capture and handle other events, such as update and delete.)

Using ListView

The previous section provided you with an overview of the methods, properties, and events of the ListView control. The examples in this section will show you how to use these methods, properties, and events in your own Web applications.

Listing F-1 presents the first example. If you run this page you'll get the result shown in Figure F-1.

Listing F-1: A Page that Uses the ListView Control

```
<%@ Page Language="C#" %>
<!DOCTYPE html PUBLIC "-//W3C//DTD XHTML 1.0 Transitional//EN"
"http://www.w3.org/TR/xhtml1/DTD/xhtml1-transitional.dtd">
<html xmlns="http://www.w3.org/1999/xhtml">
<head runat="server">
  <title>Untitled Page</title>
  <script language="javascript" type="text/javascript">
    function onSuccess(result, userContext, methodName)
    {
      userContext.set_data(result);
      if (firstTime)
      {
        firstTime = false;
        selectionChangedCallback(userContext);
      }
    }

    function onFailure(result, userContext, methodName)
    {
      var builder = new Sys.StringBuilder();
      builder.append("timedOut: ");
      builder.append(result.get_timedOut());
      builder.appendLine();
      builder.appendLine();
      builder.append("message: ");
      builder.append(result.get_message());
      builder.appendLine();
      builder.appendLine();
      builder.append("stackTrace: ");
      builder.appendLine();
      builder.append(result.get_stackTrace());
      builder.appendLine();
      builder.appendLine();
      builder.append("exceptionType: ");
      builder.append(result.get_exceptionType());
      builder.appendLine();
      builder.appendLine();
      builder.append("statusCode: ");
      builder.append(result.get_statusCode());
      builder.appendLine();
      builder.appendLine();
      builder.append("methodName: ");
      builder.append(methodName);

      alert(builder.toString());
    }
```

```
      function selectionChangedCallback(sender, eventArgs)
      {
        var authorID = sender.get_selectedValue();
        var listView = Sys.Application.findComponent("listView");
        MyWebService.GetBooks(authorID, onSuccess, onFailure, listView);
      }
      var firstTime = true;
      function pageLoad()
      {
        var authorList = Sys.Application.findComponent("authorList");

        if (!authorList.get_data())
          MyWebService.GetAuthors(onSuccess, onFailure, authorList);
      }
    </script>
  </head>
  <body>
    <form id="form1" runat="server">
      <asp:ScriptManager ID="ScriptManager1" runat="server">
        <Services>
          <asp:ServiceReference InlineScript="true" Path="WebService.asmx" />
        </Services>
        <Scripts>
          <asp:ScriptReference Assembly="Microsoft.Web.Preview"
                               Name="PreviewScript.js" />
        </Scripts>
      </asp:ScriptManager>
      <center>
        <b>Select an author: </b>
        <select id="authorList">
        </select>
        <br />
        <br />
      </center>
      <div id="listView" />
      <div style="display: none;">
        <div id="layout">
          <table width="100%">
            <tr>
              <th style="background-color: Tan">
                <b>Title, <i>Publisher</i>, <i>Price</i></b>
              </th>
            </tr>
```

(continued)

Listing F-1 *(continued)*

```
            <tr>
              <td>
                <ul id="itemContainer">
                  <li id="item"><b><span id="title"></span>,</b>
                    <i><span id="publisher"></span></i>,
                    <i><span id="price"></span></i>
                  </li>
                </ul>
              </td>
            </tr>
          </table>
        </div>
      </div>
    </form>
    <script type="text/xml-script">
      <page xmlns="http://schemas.microsoft.com/xml-script/2005">
        <components>
          <selector id="authorList" textProperty="AuthorName"
          valueProperty="AuthorID" selectionChanged="selectionChangedCallback" />

          <listView id="listView" itemTemplateParentElementId="itemContainer">
            <layoutTemplate>
              <template layoutElement="layout"/>
            </layoutTemplate>

            <itemTemplate>
              <template layoutElement="item">

                <label id="title">
                  <bindings>
                    <binding dataPath="Title" property="text" />
                  </bindings>
                </label>

                <label id="publisher">
                  <bindings>
                    <binding dataPath="Publisher" property="text" />
                  </bindings>
                </label>
```

```
                        <label id="price">
                          <bindings>
                            <binding dataPath="Price" property="text" transform="ToString"
                                     transformerArgument="${0}" />
                          </bindings>
                        </label>

                    </template>
                  </itemTemplate>
                </listView>
              </components>
            </page>
          </script>
        </body>
      </html>
```

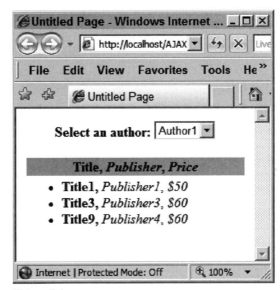

Figure F-1

As you can see, this page consists of two parts. The top part displays a drop-down list of available authors. When you select an author from the list, you get to see the author's books. This part is a <select> DOM element with the id HTML attribute value of authorList, which represents an ASP.NET AJAX Selector client control. In other words, this <select> DOM element is the associated DOM element of the Selector client control:

```
<select id="authorList" />
```

The bottom part is a `<div>` DOM element with the id HTML attribute value of `listView`, which represents an ASP.NET AJAX `ListView` client control. In other words, this `<div>` HTML DOM element is the associated DOM element of the `ListView` client control:

```
<div id="listView" />
```

Recall that the associated DOM element of an ASP.NET AJAX client control normally encapsulates all the other DOM elements that the client control uses to render its user interface. In other words, the associated DOM element of an ASP.NET AJAX client control is normally the outermost or containing DOM element of the control.

This raises the following question: what are the DOM elements that the `ListView` client control uses to render its user interface and to display the data records of the data collection bound to the control? The answer is that the `ListView` client control does *not* use a preset or pre-built set of DOM elements to render its user interface or to display the data records of the bound data collection. This enables you to bind data collections with different numbers of records, different numbers of fields per record, and different types of fields to the `ListView` client control.

All the `ListView` client control expects from you is that you will provide it with a set of DOM elements that it can use as *templates* to build the DOM elements that it needs to render its user interface and to display the data records of the data collection bound to the control. The key word is *templates*. In other words, the `ListView` client control does not directly use these DOM elements to display the data records. Instead it uses them to build the DOM elements that it uses to display the data records.

These template DOM elements provide the `ListView` control with the following information:

- ❏ The type of DOM element that you want the `ListView` control to use to display each data record. For example, you can tell the `ListView` control that you want the control to display each data record in a `<li>` or `<tr>` DOM element.

- ❏ The type of DOM element that you want the `ListView` control to use as the container for the DOM elements used to display the data records. For example, you can tell the `ListView` control that you want the control to use a `<div>` or `<ul>` DOM element as the container for the DOM elements that display the data records. Normally, the type of this container DOM element is determined by the type of DOM elements used to display the data records. For example, if you tell the `ListView` control that you want the control to display each data record in a `<li>` DOM element, the only thing that makes sense is to tell the control to use an `<ul>` DOM element as the container for these `<li>` DOM elements.

- ❏ The type of DOM elements that you want the `ListView` control to use to display different data fields of a data record. For example, you can tell the `ListView` control that you want the control to display a particular data field of a data record in an `<img>` or `<span>` DOM element. This enables you to specify different types of DOM elements for different types of data fields. For example, if the data records have a data field that contains image URL values and another data field that contains Boolean values, you can tell the `ListView` control to display the former data field in an `<img>` DOM element and the latter in an `<input type="checkbox"/>` DOM element.

❑ The type of DOM elements that you want the `ListView` control to use for the overall layout of the control. For example, you can tell the `ListView` control that you want the control to render its user interface in a `<table>` DOM element with a particular header text as the header of this table.

The following excerpt from Listing F-1 shows the template DOM elements that the `ListView` control uses to build the required DOM elements to display the data records:

```
<div style="display: none;">
  <div id="layout">
    <table width="100%">
      <tr>
        <th style="background-color: Tan">
          <b>Title, <i>Publisher</i></b>
        </th>
      </tr>
      <tr>
        <td>
          <ul id="itemContainer">
            <li id="item">
              <b><span id="title"></span>,</b>
              <i><span id="publisher"></span></i>
            </li>
          </ul>
        </td>
      </tr>
    </table>
  </div>
</div>
```

This raises the following question: how do you tell the `ListView` control that you want the control to use the template DOM elements shown in this excerpt? Here is how:

1. Set the `itemTemplateParentElementId` attribute on the `<listView>` element in the xml-script to the `id` HTML attribute value of the DOM element that you want the `ListView` control to use as a template for building the DOM element. This element will act as a container for the DOM elements that display the data records, as shown in the boldface portion of the following excerpt from Listing F-1:

```
<listView id="listView" itemTemplateParentElementId="itemContainer">
    . . .
</listView>
```

2. The boldface portion of this excerpt specifies the DOM element shown in the boldface portion of the following excerpt from Listing F-1 as the template DOM element for building the DOM element that will act as the container for the DOM elements that display the data records:

```
<div style="display: none;">
  <div id="layout">
    <table width="100%">
      <tr>
        <th style="background-color: Tan">
          <b>Title, <i>Publisher</i></b>
        </th>
      </tr>
      <tr>
        <td>
          <ul id="itemContainer">
            <li id="item">
              <b><span id="title"></span>,</b>
              <i><span id="publisher"></span></i>
            </li>
          </ul>
        </td>
      </tr>
    </table>
  </div>
</div>
```

3. First set the `layoutElement` attribute on the `<template>` subelement of the `<layoutTemplate>` subelement of the `<listView>` element in the xml-script. Set it to the `id` HTML attribute value of the DOM element that you want the `ListView` control to use as a template for building the DOM element that determines the overall layout of the constituent DOM elements of the `ListView` control. See the following boldface portion of an excerpt from Listing F-1:

```
<listView id="listView" itemTemplateParentElementId="itemContainer">
  <layoutTemplate>
    <template layoutElement="layout"/>
  </layoutTemplate>
    . . .
</listView>
```

4. The boldface portion of this excerpt specifies the DOM element shown in the boldface portion of the following excerpt from Listing F-1 as the template DOM element for building the DOM element that will determine the overall layout of the constituent DOM elements of the `ListView` control:

```
<div style="display: none;">
  <div id="layout">
    <table width="100%">
      <tr>
        <th style="background-color: Tan">
          <b>Title, <i<Publisher</i></b>
        </th>
      </tr>
```

```
        <tr>
          <td>
            <ul id="itemContainer">
              <li id="item">
                <b><span id="title"></span>,</b>
                <i><span id="publisher"></span></i>
              </li>
            </ul>
          </td>
        </tr>
      </table>
    </div>
  </div>
```

5. Now set the layoutElement attribute on the `<template>` subelement of the `<itemTemplate>` subelement of the `<listView>` element in the xml-script. Set it to the id HTML attribute value of the DOM element that you want the ListView control to use as a template for building the DOM elements that display the data records. See the boldface portion of the following excerpt from Listing F-1:

```
<listView id="listView" itemTemplateParentElementId="itemContainer">
  <layoutTemplate>
    <template layoutElement="layout"/>
  </layoutTemplate>

  <itemTemplate>
    <template layoutElement="item">

      <label id="title">
        <bindings>
          <binding dataPath="Title" property="text" />
        </bindings>
      </label>

      <label id="publisher">
        <bindings>
          <binding dataPath="Publisher" property="text" />
        </bindings>
      </label>
      <label id="price">
        <bindings>
          <binding dataPath="Price" property="text" transform="ToString"
          transformerArgument="${0}" />
        </bindings>
      </label>

    </template>
  </itemTemplate>
</listView>
```

6. The boldface portion of the preceding excerpt specifies the DOM element shown in the boldface portion of the following excerpt from Listing F-1 as the template DOM element for building the DOM elements that display the data records:

```
<div style="display: none;">
  <div id="layout">
    <table width="100%">
      <tr>
        <th style="background-color: Tan">
          <b>Title, <i>Publisher</i></b>
        </th>
      </tr>
      <tr>
        <td>
          <ul id="itemContainer">
            <li id="item">
              <b><span id="title"></span>,</b>
              <i><span id="publisher"></span></i>
            </li>
          </ul>
        </td>
      </tr>
    </table>
  </div>
</div>
```

7. Perform the following tasks for each data field:

❑ Declare the appropriate ASP.NET AJAX control between the opening and closing tags of the template subelement of the itemTemplate subelement of the listView element in the xml-script.

❑ Set the id attribute of this ASP.NET AJAX control to the id HTML attribute value of the DOM element that you want the ListView control to use as a template for building the DOM elements that display the values of this data field, as shown in the boldface portion of the following excerpt from Listing F-1:

```
<listView id="listView" itemTemplateParentElementId="itemContainer">
  <layoutTemplate>
    <template layoutElement="layout"/>
  </layoutTemplate>

  <itemTemplate>
    <template layoutElement="item">

      <label id="title">
        <bindings>
          <binding dataPath="Title" property="text" />
        </bindings>
      </label>
```

```
          <label id="publisher">
            <bindings>
              <binding dataPath="Publisher" property="text" />
            </bindings>
          </label>
          <label id="price">
            <bindings>
              <binding dataPath="Price" property="text" transform="ToString"
              transformerArgument="${0}" />
            </bindings>
          </label>

        </template>
      </itemTemplate>
    </listView>
```

❑   The boldface portion of the preceding excerpt specifies the DOM elements shown in
     the boldface portion of the following excerpt from Listing F-1 as the template DOM
     elements for building the DOM elements that display the values of the title and publisher
     data fields:

```
<div style="display: none;">
  <div id="layout">
    <table width="100%">
      <tr>
        <th style="background-color: Tan">
          <b>Title, <i>Publisher</i></b>
        </th>
      </tr>
      <tr>
        <td>
          <ul id="itemContainer">
            <li id="item">
              <b> <span id="title"></span>,</b>
              <i><span id="publisher"></span></i>,
              <i><span id="price"></span></i>
            </li>
          </ul>
        </td>
      </tr>
    </table>
  </div>
</div>
```

❏ Declare a `bindings` element between the opening and closing tags of this ASP.NET AJAX control, as shown in the boldface portion of the following excerpt from Listing F-1:

```
<listView id="listView" itemTemplateParentElementId="itemContainer">
  <layoutTemplate>
    <template layoutElement="layout"/>
  </layoutTemplate>

  <itemTemplate>
    <template layoutElement="item">

      <label id="title">
        <bindings>
          <binding dataPath="Title" property="text" />
        </bindings>
      </label>

      <label id="publisher">
        <bindings>
          <binding dataPath="Publisher" property="text" />
        </bindings>
      </label>
      <label id="price">
        <bindings>
          <binding dataPath="Price" property="text" transform="ToString"
              transformerArgument="${0}" />
        </bindings>
      </label>

    </template>
  </itemTemplate>
</listView>
```

❏ Declare a `binding` subelement between the opening and closing tags of the `bindings` subelement of this ASP.NET AJAX control, set the `dataPath` attribute on this `binding` subelement to the name of the data field, set the `property` attribute to the name of the appropriate property of the ASP.NET AJAX control, set the `transform` attribute to the name of the appropriate transformer, and set the `transformerArgument` attribute to specify the transformer argument. For example, the boldface portion of the following excerpt from Listing F-1 sets the `dataPath` and `property` attributes on the `binding` subelement of the `bindings` subelement of the label client control to the string value `"Price"`. This specifies that the text property of the associated DOM element of this client control displays the value of the `Price` data field. It also specifies that the transformer named `ToString` will be used to transform the value of the `Price` data field before the value is assigned to the text property of this DOM element. This transformer takes an argument that specifies how the transformer must format the value of this data field.

```
<listView id="listView" itemTemplateParentElementId="itemContainer">
  <layoutTemplate>
    <template layoutElement="layout"/>
  </layoutTemplate>

  <itemTemplate>
    <template layoutElement="item">

      <label id="title">
        <bindings>
          <binding dataPath="Title" property="text" />
        </bindings>
      </label>

      <label id="publisher">
        <bindings>
          <binding dataPath="Publisher" property="text" />
        </bindings>
      </label>
      <label id="price">
        <bindings>
          <binding dataPath="Price" property="text" transform="ToString"
          transformerArgument="${0}" />
        </bindings>
      </label>

    </template>
  </itemTemplate>
</listView>
```

The ListView client control is used to display data records. This raises the following question: where do the data records come from? Obviously they come from the server, but how? The answer is that they come through a Web service. Listing F-1 uses the Web service shown in Listing F-2. As you can see, it exposes the following two Web methods:

1. GetBooks: Returns an array of Book objects of which each object contains the information about a particular book of the specified author. The Book class exposes four properties named Title, AuthorName, Publisher, and Price. This Web method retrieves the information about the books of the specified author from the underlying database. The database consists of two tables named Authors and Books. The Authors table exposes two main data columns named AuthorID and AuthorName. The Books table exposes five main data columns named BookID, AuthorID, Title, Publisher, and Price.

2. GetAuthors: Returns an array of Author objects of which each object contains the information about a particular author. The Author class exposes two properties named AuthorID and AuthorName.

Note that this Web service is annotated with the `ScriptService` metadata attribute to allow the client-side code to use a Web service proxy to interact with the Web service:

```
[WebService(Namespace = "http://tempuri.org/")]
[WebServiceBinding(ConformsTo = WsiProfiles.BasicProfile1_1)]
[ScriptService]
public class MyWebService : System.Web.Services.WebService
```

Technically speaking, it is not necessary for this Web service to derive from the `WebService` base class. In general, deriving from this base class enables you to access typical ASP.NET objects such as `Session`, `Server`, `Response`, and so on. Because this Web service is not accessing any of these objects it does not have to derive from the Web service class. However, Visual Studio 2005 adds this derivation by default. One scenario in which you may have to derive from this base class is when you need to maintain state across two or more requests to the Web service. In general, it is not a good idea to maintain state across different requests to a Web service because it degrades the scalability and performance: Web services are fundamentally designed to be stateless, meaning that each request is on its own and has no recollection of the previous requests. That said, there are times when you have no choice but to maintain state across different requests of the same session. At these times you must derive your Web service from the `WebService` base class so you can use the ASP.NET `Session` object for session state management.

Listing F-2: A Web Service Used by Listing F-1

```
<%@ WebService Language="C#" Class="MyWebService" %>
using System;
using System.Web;
using System.Web.Services;
using System.Web.Services.Protocols;
using System.Data;
using System.Data.SqlClient;
using System.Configuration;
using System.Web.Script.Services;
using System.Web.Script.Serialization;
using System.Collections;
public class Author
{
  private string authorName;
  public string AuthorName
  {
    get { return this.authorName; }
    set { this.authorName = value; }
  }
  private int authorID;
  public int AuthorID
  {
    get { return this.authorID; }
    set { this.authorID = value; }
  }
}
```

```
public class Book
{
  private string title;
  public string Title
  {
    get { return this.title; }
    set { this.title = value; }
  }
  private string authorName;
  public string AuthorName
  {
    get { return this.authorName; }
    set { this.authorName = value; }
  }
  private string publisher;
  public string Publisher
  {
    get { return this.publisher; }
    set { this.publisher = value; }
  }
  private decimal price;
  public decimal Price
  {
    get { return this.price; }
    set { this.price = value; }
  }
}
[WebService(Namespace = "http://tempuri.org/")]
[WebServiceBinding(ConformsTo = WsiProfiles.BasicProfile1_1)]
[ScriptService]
public class MyWebService : System.Web.Services.WebService
{
  [WebMethod]
  public Book[] GetBooks(int authorID)
  {
    ConnectionStringSettings settings =
      ConfigurationManager.ConnectionStrings["MyConnectionString"];
    string connectionString = settings.ConnectionString;

    string commandText = "Select Title, AuthorName, Publisher, Price " +
                         "From Books Inner Join Authors " +
                         "On Books.AuthorID = Authors.AuthorID " +
                         "Where Authors.AuthorID=@AuthorID";
    DataTable dt = new DataTable();
    SqlDataAdapter ad = new SqlDataAdapter(commandText, connectionString);
    SqlParameter parameter = new SqlParameter();
    parameter.ParameterName = "@AuthorID";
    parameter.Value = authorID;
    ad.SelectCommand.Parameters.Add(parameter);
    ad.Fill(dt);
    Book[] books = new Book[dt.Rows.Count];
```

(continued)

Listing F-2 *(continued)*

```
    for (int i=0; i<dt.Rows.Count; i++)
    {
      books[i] = new Book();
      books[i].Title = (string)dt.Rows[i]["Title"];
      books[i].AuthorName = (string)dt.Rows[i]["AuthorName"];
      books[i].Publisher = (string)dt.Rows[i]["Publisher"];
      books[i].Price = (decimal)dt.Rows[i]["Price"];
    }
    return books;
  }
  [WebMethod]
  public Author[] GetAuthors()
  {
    ConnectionStringSettings settings =
      ConfigurationManager.ConnectionStrings["MyConnectionString"];
    string connectionString = settings.ConnectionString;
    string commandText = "Select AuthorID, AuthorName From Authors";
    DataTable dt = new DataTable();
    SqlDataAdapter ad = new SqlDataAdapter(commandText, connectionString);
    ad.Fill(dt);
    Author[] authors = new Author[dt.Rows.Count];
    for (int i = 0; i < dt.Rows.Count; i++)
    {
      authors[i] = new Author();
      authors[i].AuthorID = (int)dt.Rows[i]["AuthorID"];
      authors[i].AuthorName = (string)dt.Rows[i]["AuthorName"];
    }
    return authors;
  }
}
```

Next, I'll walk you through the implementation of those JavaScript functions shown in Listing F-1 that contain the logic that the page shown in this code listing uses to retrieve the required data records from the Web service shown in Listing F-2. I'll begin our discussions with the implementation of the pageLoad method. As the following excerpt from Listing F-1 shows, the pageLoad method first invokes the findComponent method on the Application object that represents the current ASP.NET AJAX application, thereby returning a reference to the Selector client control:

```
    var authorList = Sys.Application.findComponent("authorList");
```

Next, it invokes the get_data method on the Selector client control to check whether the control has already been populated. If not, it invokes the GetAuthors method on the MyWebService proxy to invoke the GetAuthors method on the MyWebService Web service, thereby downloading the list of authors:

```
  MyWebService.GetAuthors(onSuccess, onFailure, authorList);
```

Note that the pageLoad method passes three parameters into the GetAuthors method of the MyWebService proxy. The first parameter references a JavaScript function named onSuccess; the MyWebService proxy invokes this JavaScript function when the server response successfully arrives.

The second parameter references a JavaScript function named `onFailure`; the `MyWebService` proxy invokes this JavaScript function when something goes wrong and the request fails. The third parameter references the `Selector` client control. The `MyWebService` proxy does not do anything with its third parameter. It simply passes it as the second parameter into the `onSuccess` and `onFailure` JavaScript functions when it invokes these functions. This enables you to pass contextual information into these JavaScript functions.

```
function pageLoad()
{
  var authorList = Sys.Application.findComponent("authorList");

  if (!authorList.get_data())
    MyWebService.GetAuthors(onSuccess, onFailure, authorList);
}
```

Next I'll walk you through the implementation of the `onSuccess` JavaScript function, as shown in the following excerpt from Listing F-1:

```
function onSuccess(result, userContext, methodName)
{
  userContext.set_data(result);
  if (firstTime)
  {
    firstTime = false;
    selectionChangedCallback(userContext);
  }
}
```

As you can see, when the `MyWebService` proxy invokes the `onSuccess` method it passes three parameters into the method. The first parameter contains the data received from the Web service, which is the list of authors in this case. The second parameter is the contextual information, which is the reference to the `Selector` client control. The third parameter is the name of the Web method that was invoked, which is the `GetAuthors` Web method. The `onSuccess` method first invokes the `set_data` method on the `context` object, which is the `Selector` client control in this case, to bind the data returned from the Web service to the specified client control, which is the `Selector` client control. Binding the data to the `Selector` client control automatically triggers the re-rendering of the control, which means that the `Selector` client control is automatically populated with the fresh data:

```
userContext.set_data(result);
```

The `onSuccess` function then checks whether this is the first time this function has been invoked, which is true here. If so, it calls a JavaScript function named `selectionChangedCallback`, passing in the reference to the `Selector` client control to populate the `ListView` client control. We'll discuss this procedure shortly.

Listing F-1 registers the `selectionChangedCallback` JavaScript function as an event handler for the `selectionChanged` event of the `Selector` client control. This event handler, like any other ASP.NET AJAX event handler, takes two parameters: the first references the client control that raises the event, which is the `Selector` client control in this case. The following excerpt from Listing F-1 presents the implementation of the `selectionChangedCallback` function:

```
function selectionChangedCallback(sender, eventArgs)
{
  var authorID = sender.get_selectedValue();
  var listView = Sys.Application.findComponent("listView");
  MyWebService.GetBooks(authorID, onSuccess, onFailure, listView);
}
```

As you can see, `selectionChangedCallback` begins by calling the `get_selectedValue` method on the `Selector` client control to return the selected value — that is, the selected author:

```
var authorID = sender.get_selectedValue();
```

Next, it invokes the `findComponent` method on the `Application` object that represents the current ASP.NET AJAX application, to return a reference to the `ListView` client control:

```
var listView = Sys.Application.findComponent("listView");
```

Finally, it invokes the `GetBooks` method on the `MyWebService` proxy to invoke the `GetBooks` method on the `MyWebService` Web service. The `selectionChangedCallback` function passes four parameters into the `GetBooks` method of the proxy. The first is the author ID. The `GetBooks` method of the proxy passes this parameter into the `GetBooks` method of the Web service. The second references the `onSuccess` JavaScript function we discussed earlier. The third references the `onFailure` JavaScript function. Finally, the last parameter is the context object that references the `ListView` client control.

```
MyWebService.GetBooks(authorID, onSuccess, onFailure, listView);
```

When the server response arrives, the `MyWebService` proxy automatically invokes the `onSuccess` function, passing in the data received from the server:

```
function onSuccess(result, userContext, methodName)
{
  userContext.set_data(result);
  if (firstTime)
  {
    firstTime = false;
    selectionChangedCallback(userContext);
  }
}
```

Since this time around the context object references the `ListView` client control, the `onSuccess` function ends up calling the `set_data` method on the `ListView` client control. This automatically binds the data returned from the server to this control and consequently re-renders the control to display this data. The end result is that every time the end user selects an author from the `Selector` client control, the information about the author's books is automatically downloaded from the Web service and displayed in the `ListView` client control.

Applying Styles

Listing F-3 presents a version of the `pageLoad` method that shows how to apply styles in order to customize the appearance of different types of rows in the `ListView` control.

```
function pageLoad()
{
  var listView = Sys.Application.findComponent("listView");
  listView.set_itemCssClass("itemCssClass");
  listView.set_alternatingItemCssClass("alternatingItemCssClass");
  listView.set_selectedItemCssClass("selectedItemCssClass");

  var authorList = Sys.Application.findComponent("authorList");

  if (!authorList.get_data())
    MyWebService.GetAuthors(onSuccess, onFailure, authorList);
}
```

As you can see, this method invokes the `set_itemCssClass`, `set_alternatingItemCssClass`, and `set_selectedItemCssClass` methods on the `ListView` control to specify the CSS style classes named `itemCssClass`, `alternatingItemCssClass`, and `selectedItemCssClass`, respectively, as the style classes for the even-numbered rows, odd-numbered rows, and selected row of the `ListView` control, respectively. Note that the `<style>` HTML subelement of the `<head>` HTML element defines these three CSS style classes:

```
<style type="text/css">
  .itemCssClass { background-color: #eeeeee;}
  .alternatingItemCssClass { background-color: #bbbbbb;}
  .selectedItemCssClass { background-color: #777777;}
</style>
```

If you run the page shown in Listing F-3, you'll see the result shown in Figure F-2.

Listing F-3: A Page that Applies Styles to the ListView Control

```
<%@ Page Language="C#" %>
<!DOCTYPE html PUBLIC "-//W3C//DTD XHTML 1.0 Transitional//EN"
"http://www.w3.org/TR/xhtml1/DTD/xhtml1-transitional.dtd">
<html xmlns="http://www.w3.org/1999/xhtml">
<head runat="server">
  <title>Untitled Page</title>
  <style type="text/css">
    .itemCssClass { background-color: #eeeeee;}
    .alternatingItemCssClass { background-color: #bbbbbb;}
    .selectedItemCssClass { background-color: #777777; color: #ffffff}
  </style>
  <script language="javascript" type="text/javascript">
    function onSuccess(result, userContext, methodName)
    {
      // Same as Listing 1
    }
```

(continued)

Listing F-3 *(continued)*

```
        function onFailure(result, userContext, methodName)
        {
          // Same as Listing 1
        }

        function selectionChangedCallback(sender, eventArgs)
        {
          // Same as Listing 1
        }
        var firstTime = true;
        function pageLoad()
        {
          var listView = Sys.Application.findComponent("listView");
          listView.set_itemCssClass("itemCssClass");
          listView.set_alternatingItemCssClass("alternatingItemCssClass");
          listView.set_selectedItemCssClass("selectedItemCssClass");

          var authorList = Sys.Application.findComponent("authorList");

          if (!authorList.get_data())
            MyWebService.GetAuthors(onSuccess, onFailure, authorList);
        }
      </script>
    </head>
    <body>
      <form id="form1" runat="server">
        <!- Same as Listing 1 ->
      </form>
      <script type="text/xml-script">
        <page xmlns="http://schemas.microsoft.com/xml-script/2005">
          <components>
            <!- Same as Listing 1 ->
          </components>
        </page>
      </script>
    </body>
    </html>
```

Using Table Rows and Columns

The previous examples used the following components:

❑ A `<ul>` DOM element, as the template for building the DOM element that contains the DOM elements that display the data records.

❑ A `<li>` DOM element, as the template for building the DOM elements that display the data records.

❑ `<span>` DOM elements, as the template for building the DOM elements that display the data fields.

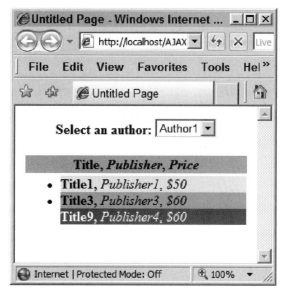

Figure F-2

Listing F-4 presents an example in which:

❑ A `<tbody>` DOM element is the template for building the DOM element that contains the DOM elements that display the data records.

❑ A `<tr>` DOM element is the template for building the DOM elements that display the data records.

❑ `<td>` DOM elements is the template for building the DOM elements that display the data fields.

If you don't use the `<thead>` and `<tbody>` elements, Internet Explorer won't show the table. Internet Explorer expects dynamically generated tables to include `<thead>` and `<tbody>` elements.

If you run Listing F-4, you'll get the result shown in Figure F-3. Note that Listing F-4 registers a JavaScript function named `renderCompleteCallback` as an event handler for the `renderComplete` event of the `ListView` control. The control raises this event when it completes its rendering.

Listing F-4: A Page that Uses <tr> and <td> as Templates

```
<%@ Page Language="C#" %>
<!DOCTYPE html PUBLIC "-//W3C//DTD XHTML 1.0 Transitional//EN"
"http://www.w3.org/TR/xhtml1/DTD/xhtml1-transitional.dtd">
<html xmlns="http://www.w3.org/1999/xhtml">
<head runat="server">
  <title>Untitled Page</title>
  <style type="text/css">
    .itemCssClass { background-color: #eeeeee;}
    .alternatingItemCssClass { background-color: #bbbbbb;}
    .selectedItemCssClass { background-color: #777777; color: #ffffff}
  </style>
```

(continued)

Listing F-4 (continued)

```javascript
<script language="javascript" type="text/javascript">
  function renderCompleteCallback(sender, eventArgs)
  {
    alert("Rendering is completed!");
  }
  function onSuccess(result, userContext, methodName)
  {
    userContext.set_data(result);
    if (firstTime)
    {
      firstTime = false;
      selectionChangedCallback(userContext);
    }
  }

  function onFailure(result, userContext, methodName)
  {
    var builder = new Sys.StringBuilder();
    builder.append("timedOut: ");
    builder.append(result.get_timedOut());
    builder.appendLine();
    builder.appendLine();
    builder.append("message: ");
    builder.append(result.get_message());
    builder.appendLine();
    builder.appendLine();
    builder.append("stackTrace: ");
    builder.appendLine();
    builder.append(result.get_stackTrace());
    builder.appendLine();
    builder.appendLine();
    builder.append("exceptionType: ");
    builder.append(result.get_exceptionType());
    builder.appendLine();
    builder.appendLine();
    builder.append("statusCode: ");
    builder.append(result.get_statusCode());
    builder.appendLine();
    builder.appendLine();
    builder.append("methodName: ");
    builder.append(methodName);

    alert(builder.toString());
  }

  function selectionChangedCallback(sender, eventArgs)
  {
    var authorID = sender.get_selectedValue();
    var listView = Sys.Application.findComponent("listView");
    MyWebService.GetBooks(authorID, onSuccess, onFailure, listView);
  }
```

```
        var firstTime = true;
        function pageLoad()
        {
          var listView = Sys.Application.findComponent("listView");
          listView.set_itemCssClass("itemCssClass");
          listView.set_alternatingItemCssClass("alternatingItemCssClass");
          listView.set_selectedItemCssClass("selectedItemCssClass");

          var authorList = Sys.Application.findComponent("authorList");

          if (!authorList.get_data())
            MyWebService.GetAuthors(onSuccess, onFailure, authorList);
        }
      </script>
  </head>
<body>
    <form id="form1" runat="server">
      <asp:ScriptManager ID="ScriptManager1" runat="server">
        <Services>
          <asp:ServiceReference InlineScript="true" Path="WebService.asmx" />
        </Services>
        <Scripts>
          <asp:ScriptReference Assembly="Microsoft.Web.Preview"
                                               Name="PreviewScript.js" />
        </Scripts>
      </asp:ScriptManager>
      <center>
        <b>Select an author:</b>
        <select id="authorList">
        </select>
        <br />
        <br />
      </center>
      <div id="listView" />
      <div style="display: none;">
        <div id="layout">
          <table width="100%">
            <thead>
              <tr style="background-color: Tan">
                <th>
                  Title</th>
                <th>
                  Publisher</th>
                <th>
                  Price</th>
              </tr>
            </thead>
            <tbody id="itemContainer">
              <tr id="item">
                <td id="title">
                </td>
```

(continued)

Listing F-4 *(continued)*

```
                <td id="publisher">
                </td>
                <td id="price">
                </td>
            </tr>
          </tbody>
        </table>
      </div>
    </div>
  </form>
  <script type="text/xml-script">
    <page xmlns="http://schemas.microsoft.com/xml-script/2005">
      <components>
        <selector id="authorList" textProperty="AuthorName"
            valueProperty="AuthorID" selectionChanged="selectionChangedCallback" />

        <listView id="listView" itemTemplateParentElementId="itemContainer"
        renderComplete="renderCompleteCallback">
          <layoutTemplate>
            <template layoutElement="layout"/>
          </layoutTemplate>

          <itemTemplate>
            <template layoutElement="item">

              <label id="title">
                <bindings>
                  <binding dataPath="Title" property="text" />
                </bindings>
              </label>

              <label id="publisher">
                <bindings>
                  <binding dataPath="Publisher" property="text" />
                </bindings>
              </label>

              <label id="price">
                <bindings>
                  <binding dataPath="Price" property="text" transform="ToString"
                                              transformerArgument="${0}" />
                </bindings>
              </label>

            </template>
          </itemTemplate>
        </listView>
      </components>
    </page>
  </script>
</body>
</html>
```

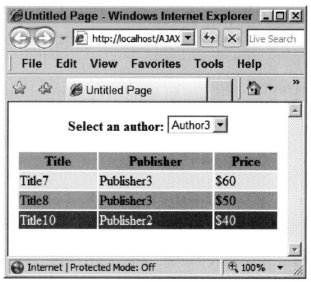

Figure F-3

Surrounding the ASP.NET AJAX Classes and Interface

The previous sections of this appendix showed you how to use the `ListView` control and its members in your own Web applications. The rest of this appendix will dive into the internal implementation of the `ListView` templated client control, where you'll discover how to:

❑ Extend the functionality of the `ListView` client control

❑ Implement templated client controls as complex as the `ListView` client control

This section will discuss the surrounding ASP.NET AJAX classes and interface of the `ListView` client control — that is, those classes and interface that a templated client control such as `ListView` uses internally. I'll begin our discussions with the interface named `ITask`.

ITask

The `ITask` interface defines the API that every ASP.NET AJAX task must implement to execute a task. A task could be anything. For example, as you'll see later, the `ListView` client control uses a rendering task named `ListViewRenderTask` to render its UI. As Listing F-5 shows, this interface exposes a single method named `execute` that each subclass of this interface must override to include the logic that executes its associated task. For example, `ListViewRenderTask` implements this interface and its execute method where it includes the logic that renders the `ListView` templated data control.

Listing F-5: The ITask Interface

```
Sys.Preview.ITask = function Sys$Preview$ITask()
{
  throw Error.notImplemented();
}
function Sys$Preview$ITask$execute()
{
  throw Error.notImplemented();
}
Sys.Preview.ITask.prototype =
{
  execute: Sys$Preview$ITask$execute
}
Sys.Preview.ITask.registerInterface('Sys.Preview.ITask');
```

_TaskManager

The ASP.NET AJAX client-side framework comes with an internal class named _TaskManager that manages all the tasks on the current page. Each ASP.NET AJAX page can contain only a single instance of this class. As the boldface portion of Listing F-6 shows, the ASP.NET AJAX framework automatically instantiates this single instance and assigns it to a global variable named Sys.Preview.TaskManager. Therefore, you must use this global variable to access the current instance of the _TaskManager class as opposed to instantiating a new one:

```
Sys.Preview.TaskManager = new Sys.Preview._TaskManager();
```

I'll discuss the methods and properties of the _TaskManager class in the following sections.

Listing F-6: The _TaskManager Class

```
Sys.Preview._TaskManager = function Sys$Preview$_TaskManager()
{
  Sys.Application.registerDisposableObject(this);
  this._tasks = [];
}
Sys.Preview._TaskManager.prototype =
{
  _timeoutCookie: null,
  _timeoutHandler: null,
  addTask: Sys$Preview$_TaskManager$addTask,
  dispose: Sys$Preview$_TaskManager$dispose,
  _onTimeout: Sys$Preview$_TaskManager$_onTimeout,
  _startTimeout: Sys$Preview$_TaskManager$_startTimeout
}
Sys.Preview._TaskManager.registerClass('Sys.Preview._TaskManager', null,
                                       Sys.IDisposable);
Sys.Preview.TaskManager = new Sys.Preview._TaskManager();
```

Constructor

As Listing F-6 shows, this constructor performs two tasks:

❑ It invokes the `registerDisposableObject` method on the `Application` object that represents the current ASP.NET AJAX application, thereby adding the current `TaskManager` instance to the list of disposable objects that the `Application` object maintains internally.

```
Sys.Application.registerDisposableObject(this);
```

Recall that a disposable object is an object whose type implements the `IDisposable` interface. This interface exposes a method named `dispose`. The `Application` object automatically invokes the `dispose` methods of these disposable objects to allow these objects to perform their final cleanup before they're disposed of.

As Listing F-6 shows, the `_TaskManager` class implements this interface.

```
Sys.Preview._TaskManager.registerClass('Sys.Preview._TaskManager', null,
                        Sys.IDisposable);
```

❑ It instantiates an array named `_tasks`. As you'll see later, the current `TaskManager` instance will store all tasks in this array:

```
this._tasks = [];
```

addTask

Call the `addTask` method on the current `TaskManager` instance to add a new task to the `_tasks` array. As you can see from Listing F-7, this method first invokes the `enqueue` static method on the `Array` class to enqueue the specified task:

```
Array.enqueue(this._tasks, task);
```

Next, it invokes the `_startTimeout` method to schedule the execution of the next task in the `_tasks` array, as we'll discuss in the next section:

```
this._startTimeout();
```

Listing F-7: The addTask Method

```
function Sys$Preview$_TaskManager$addTask(task)
{
    /// <param name="task" type="Sys.Preview.ITask"></param>
    Array.enqueue(this._tasks, task);
    this._startTimeout();
}
```

_startTimeout

As Listing F-8 shows, this method first checks whether the current `TaskManager` instance already has a timeout cookie. If not, it first invokes the `createDelegate` static method on the `Function` class to create a delegate that represents the `_onTimeout` method:

```
this._timeoutHandler = Function.createDelegate(this, this._onTimeout);
```

Then it invokes the `setTimeout` method on the `window` object, passing in the delegate to create a new timeout cookie:

```
this._timeoutCookie = window.setTimeout(this._timeoutHandler,  0);
```

Listing F-8: The _startTimeout Method

```
function Sys$Preview$_TaskManager$_startTimeout()
{
  if (!this._timeoutCookie)
  {
    if (!this._timeoutHandler)
      this._timeoutHandler = Function.createDelegate(this, this._onTimeout);

    this._timeoutCookie = window.setTimeout(this._timeoutHandler,  0);
  }
}
```

_onTimeout

When the `window` object invokes the `_timeoutHandler` delegate, this delegate in turn invokes the `_onTimeout` method. As you can see from Listing F-9, the `_onTimeout` method invokes the `dequeue` static method on the `Array` class to dequeue the next task in the `_tasks` collection. Recall that dequeuing an item from an array removes the item from the array.

```
var task = Array.dequeue(this._tasks);
```

Then it invokes the `execute` method on this task to execute it:

```
task.execute()
```

If the `execute` method returns `false`, the `_onTimeout` method calls the `enqueue` static method on the `Array` class to enqueue the task back in the `_tasks` collection. This allows the task to be executed again:

```
if (!task.execute())
  Array.enqueue(this._tasks, task);
```

Finally, it checks whether the `_tasks` collection contains any more tasks. If so, it invokes the `_startTimeout` method to schedule the execution of the next task:

```
if (this._tasks.length)
  this._startTimeout();
```

As you can see, the current `TaskManager` instance executes the tasks in the order in which they're enqueued in the _tasks collection.

Listing F-9: The _onTimeout Method

```
function Sys$Preview$_TaskManager$_onTimeout()
{
  this._timeoutCookie = 0;
  var task = Array.dequeue(this._tasks);
  if (!task.execute())
    Array.enqueue(this._tasks, task);
  if (this._tasks.length)
    this._startTimeout();
}
```

dispose

As we discussed earlier, the _TaskManager class implements the `IDisposable` interface. Consequently, the class implements the `dispose` method, as shown in Listing F-10. The `dispose` method of the current `TaskManager` instance, like the `dispose` method of any other ASP.NET AJAX object, performs its final cleanup before the instance is disposed of. The method begins by invoking the `clearTimeout` method on the window object to release the timeout cookie:

```
if (this._timeoutCookie)
  window.clearTimeout(this._timeoutCookie);
```

Next, it iterates through the remaining tasks in the _tasks collection and invokes the `dispose` method on each task to allow the task to perform its final cleanup before it is disposed of:

```
if (this._tasks && this._tasks.length)
{
  for (var i = this._tasks.length - 1; i >= 0; i--)
  {
    this._tasks[i].dispose();
  }
}
```

Finally, it invokes the `unregisterDisposableObject` method on the `Application` object that represents the current ASP.NET AJAX application, in order to remove the current `TaskManager` instance from the list of disposable objects. Recall that the constructor of the `TaskManager` class added the current `TaskManager` instance to this list.

```
Sys.Application.unregisterDisposableObject(this);
```

Listing F-10: The dispose Method

```
function Sys$Preview$_TaskManager$dispose()
{
  if (this._timeoutCookie)
    window.clearTimeout(this._timeoutCookie);
  if (this._tasks && this._tasks.length)
  {
    for (var i = this._tasks.length - 1; i >= 0; i--)
    {
      this._tasks[i].dispose();
    }
  }
  this._tasks = null;
  this._timeoutHandler = null;
  Sys.Application.unregisterDisposableObject(this);
}
```

ListViewRenderTask

As you can see from Listing F-11, `ListViewRenderTask`, like any other ASP.NET AJAX task, implements the `ITask` and `IDisposable` interfaces. The main responsibility of `ListViewRenderTask` is to render the specified `ListView` templated data control.

```
Sys.Preview.UI.Data.ListViewRenderTask.registerClass(
                      'Sys.Preview.UI.Data.ListViewRenderTask',
                      null, Sys.Preview.ITask, Sys.IDisposable);
```

I'll discuss the methods and properties of `ListViewRenderTask` in the following sections.

Listing F-11: The ListViewRenderTask Class

```
Sys.Preview.UI.Data.ListViewRenderTask =
function Sys$Preview$UI$Data$ListViewRenderTask(listView, data, itemTemplate,
                                                itemTemplateParent,
                                                separatorTemplate, itemElements,
                                                separatorElements,
                                                itemClass, alternatingItemClass,
                                                separatorClass,
                                                itemFocusHandler, itemClickHandler)
{
  this._listView = listView;
  this._data = data;
  this._itemTemplate = itemTemplate;
  this._itemTemplateParent = itemTemplateParent;
  this._separatorTemplate = separatorTemplate;
  this._itemElements = itemElements;
  this._separatorElements = separatorElements;
  this._itemClass = itemClass;
  this._alternatingItemClass = alternatingItemClass;
  this._separatorClass = separatorClass;
  this._itemFocusHandler = itemFocusHandler;
  this._itemClickHandler = itemClickHandler;
  this._currentIndex = 0;
}
```

```
function Sys$Preview$UI$Data$ListViewRenderTask$dispose()
{
  this._listView = null;
  this._data = null;
  this._itemTemplate = null;
  this._itemTemplateParent = null;
  this._separatorTemplate = null;
  this._itemElements = null;
  this._separatorElements = null;
  this._itemClass = null;
  this._alternatingItemClass = null;
  this._separatorClass = null;
  this._itemFocusHandler = null;
  this._itemClickHandler = null;
}

Sys.Preview.UI.Data.ListViewRenderTask.prototype =
{
  dispose: Sys$Preview$UI$Data$ListViewRenderTask$dispose,
  execute: Sys$Preview$UI$Data$ListViewRenderTask$execute
}
Sys.Preview.UI.Data.ListViewRenderTask.registerClass(
  'Sys.Preview.UI.Data.ListViewRenderTask',
                          null, Sys.Preview.ITask, Sys.IDisposable);
```

Constructor

As Listing F-12 shows, the constructor of the ListViewRenderTask class takes the parameters shown in the following table:

Parameter	Description
listView	References the ListView templated data control that the current ListViewRenderTask is to render.
Data	References the data collection bound to the ListView.
itemTemplate	References the ASP.NET AJAX Template object that represents the itemTemplate subelement of the ListView control.
itemTemplateParent	References the template DOM element for building the DOM element that acts as a container for the DOM elements that display data records.
separatorTemplate	References the ASP.NET AJAX Template object that represents the separatorTemplate subelement of the ListView control.
itemElements	Contains the DOM elements that display data records. (Keep in mind that the ListView control uses the associated DOM element of the item template as a template for building these DOM elements.)

(continued)

(continued)

Parameter	Description
separatorElements	Contains the DOM elements that separate consecutive data DOM elements. A data DOM element is a DOM element that displays a data record.
itemClass	Specifies the name of the CSS style class that the `execute` method of `ListViewRenderTask` must apply to even-numbered data DOM elements.
alternatingItemClass	Specifies the name of the CSS style class that the `execute` method of `ListViewRenderTask` must apply to the odd-numbered data DOM elements.
separatorClass	Specifies the name of the CSS style class that the `execute` method of `ListViewRenderTask` must apply to the DOM elements that separate consecutive data DOM elements.
itemFocusHandler	Specifies the delegate that the `execute` method of `ListViewRenderTask` must register as an event handler for the `focus` event of the data DOM elements.
itemClickHandler	Specifies the delegate that the `execute` method of `ListViewRenderTask` must register as an event handler for the `click` event of the data DOM elements.

Listing F-12: The Constructor of ListViewRenderTask

```
Sys.Preview.UI.Data.ListViewRenderTask =
function Sys$Preview$UI$Data$ListViewRenderTask(listView, data, itemTemplate,
                                    itemTemplateParent,
                                    separatorTemplate, itemElements,
                                    separatorElements,
                                    itemClass, alternatingItemClass,
                                    separatorClass,
                                    itemFocusHandler, itemClickHandler)
{
   this._listView = listView;
   this._data = data;
   this._itemTemplate = itemTemplate;
   this._itemTemplateParent = itemTemplateParent;
   this._separatorTemplate = separatorTemplate;
   this._itemElements = itemElements;
   this._separatorElements = separatorElements;
   this._itemClass = itemClass;
   this._alternatingItemClass = alternatingItemClass;
   this._separatorClass = separatorClass;
   this._itemFocusHandler = itemFocusHandler;
   this._itemClickHandler = itemClickHandler;
   this._currentIndex = 0;
}
```

execute

`ListViewRenderTask`, like any other ASP.NET AJAX task, implements the `execute` method of the `ITask` interface as shown in Listing F-13. This method first takes these steps to determine the total number of records in the data collection:

❑ If the data collection is a JavaScript array, the `execute` method uses the value of the `length` property of the data collection.

❑ If the data collection is not a JavaScript array, but it supports a method named `get_length`, the `execute` method uses the return value of this method. Data collections that implement the `IData` interface support this method.

❑ If the data collection is neither a JavaScript array nor supports the `get_length` method, the `execute` method uses 0 as the total number of records because the `ListView` control supports only these two types of data collections.

```
var isArray = Array.isInstanceOfType(this._data);
var itemLength = isArray ? this._data.length :
        (this._data ? (this._data.get_length ? this._data.get_length() : 0) : 0);
```

Next, the `execute` method determines how many DOM elements are left to render. Keep in mind that the `execute` method renders each data record in the data collection in a separate DOM element:

```
var lastElementToRender = Math.min(itemLength, this._currentIndex + 5);
```

Next, the `execute` method enters a `for` loop in which each iteration takes the following steps to render the next record in the data collection. Each iteration begins by accessing the next data record in the data collection, as follows:

❑ If the data collection is a JavaScript array, it uses the current index as an index into the data collection to return the reference to the current data record.

❑ If the data collection is not a JavaScript array, it assumes that the data collection supports a method named `getItem` and consequently invokes this method, passing in the current index to return a reference to the current data record.

```
var item = isArray? this._data[this._currentIndex] :
        this._data.getItem(this._currentIndex);
```

Next, the `execute` method performs the following tasks if the `itemTemplate` property of the `ListView` templated data control has been set. (Page developers use a declarative approach to set the `itemTemplate` property, adding a `<template>` subelement to the `<itemTemplate>` subelement of the `ListView` control in xml-script and setting the `layoutElement` attribute on this `<template>` subelement to the id HTML attribute of a DOM element on the current page. This tells the `ListView` control that they want the control to use this DOM element as the template for building the DOM elements that display the data records.)

❑ The `execute` method invokes the `createInstance` method on the `itemTemplate`, passing in two parameters: the first references the clone of the parent DOM element of the DOM element whose id HTML attribute is specified in the `layoutElement` attribute of the `<template>` subelement of the `<itemTemplate>` element; the second references the current data record — that is, the data record being displayed.

```
    var itemTemplateInstance =
            this._itemTemplate.createInstance(this._itemTemplateParent, item);
```

❑ The boldface portion of the following excerpt from Listing F-4 shows an example of this parent DOM element, in which the `<tbody>` DOM element with the `id` attribute value of `itemContainer` is the parent DOM element of the `<tr>` DOM element with the `id` attribute value of `item`. As the bottom boldface portion of this excerpt shows, the `layoutElement` attribute on the `<template>` subelement of the `<itemTemplate>` subelement is set to the `id` attribute value of this `<tr>` DOM element — that is, `item`. In this case, the `execute` method passes the clone of the `<tbody>` DOM element with the `id` attribute value of `itemContainer` as the first parameter of the `createInstance` method. You may be wondering who clones this `<tbody>` DOM element. I'll answer that question when we discuss the `render` method of the `ListView` control. For now, suffice it to say that `ListViewRenderTask` receives the clone of the `<tbody>` DOM element from the `render` method of the `ListView` control.

```
<html>
  <body>
  . . .
    <div style="display: none;">
      <div id="layout">
        <table width="100%">
          <thead>
            . . .
          </thead>
          <tbody id="itemContainer">
            <tr id="item">
              <td id="title" />
              <td id="publisher" />
              <td id="price" />
            </tr>
          </tbody>
        </table>
      </div>
    </div>
    . . .
    <script type="text/xml-script">
    <page xmlns="http://schemas.microsoft.com/xml-script/2005">
      <components>
        . . .
        <listView id="listView" renderComplete="renderCompleteCallback"
        itemTemplateParentElementId="itemContainer">
          . . .
          <itemTemplate>
            <template layoutElement="item">
              . . .
            </template>
          </itemTemplate>
        </listView>
      </components>
    </page>
    </script>
  </body>
</html>
```

❑ The `createInstance` method takes these actions under the hood:

    ❑ Clones the DOM element whose `id` HTML attribute value is given by the `layoutElement` attribute on the `<template>` subelement of the `<itemTemplate>` subelement of the `ListView` control. Keep in mind that cloning this DOM element also clones all its descendant DOM elements. For example, in the case of the excerpt from Listing F-4, the `createInstance` method clones the `<tr>` DOM element with the `id` attribute value of `item`, including all its descendant DOM elements — that is, the `<td>` DOM elements with the `id` attribute values of `title`, `publisher`, and `price`. In other words, all the DOM elements shown in the boldface portion of the following excerpt (which repeats that of the one preceding) are cloned:

```html
<html>
  <body>
    . . .
    <div style="display: none;">
      <div id="layout">
        <table width="100%">
          <thead>
            . . .
          </thead>
          <tbody id="itemContainer">
            <tr id="item">
              <td id="title">
              </td>
              <td id="publisher">
              </td>
              <td id="price">
              </td>
            </tr>
          </tbody>
        </table>
      </div>
    </div>
    . . .
  </body>
</html>
```

    ❑ Adds this cloned DOM element, including its descendant elements, as the child element to the cloned DOM element that `ListViewRenderTask` receives from the `render` method of the `ListView` (as mentioned earlier). For example, in the case of this excerpt from Listing F-4, the cloned `<tr>` DOM element with the `id` attribute value of `item`, including its cloned `<td>` child elements, is added to the cloned `<tbody>` element that `ListViewRenderTask` receives from the `render` method.

    ❑ Instantiates a `TemplateInstance` object and stores a reference to this cloned DOM element in the `instanceElement` property of this object, and returns the object to its caller.

❑ Accesses the cloned DOM element that the `createInstance` method has stored in the `instanceElement` property of the `TemplateInstance` object, as we just discussed. For example, in the case of the previous excerpt from Listing F-4, this cloned DOM element is the cloned `<tr>` DOM element with the `id` attribute value of `item`:

```
var element = itemTemplateInstance.instanceElement;
```

❑ If the current row is an even row, createInstance assigns the CSS style class associated with the item template to the className property of the cloned DOM element. For example, in the case of the previous excerpt from Listing F-4, it assigns the CSS style class name to the className property of the cloned <tr> DOM element with an id attribute value of item. If the current row is an alternating row, it assigns the alternating CSS style class name associated with the item template to the className property of the cloned DOM element:

```
if (this._itemClass)
{
  if ((this._currentIndex % 2 === 1) && (this._alternatingItemClass))
    element.className = this._alternatingItemClass;

  else
    element.className = this._itemClass;
}
```

❑ Uses the current index as an index into the _itemsElements collection to add the cloned DOM element to this collection. For example, in the case of the previous excerpt from Listing F-4, it adds the cloned <tr> DOM element with the id attribute value of item to the _itemsElements collection.

```
this._itemElements[this._currentIndex] = element;
```

❑ Sets the dataIndex property of the cloned DOM element to the current index. As you can see, each cloned DOM element in the _itemsElements collection exposes a property named dataIndex that specifies the index of the data record that the cloned DOM element displays. This is the index of the data record in the data collection bound to the ListView control.

```
element.tabIndex = -1;
element.dataIndex = this._currentIndex;
```

❑ Registers the specified handlers as event handlers for the focus and click events of the cloned DOM element.

```
$addHandler(element, "focus", this._itemFocusHandler);
$addHandler(element, "click", this._itemClickHandler);
```

Next, if the page developer has specified the <separatorTemplate> element in the xml-script, the execute method performs the following tasks:

❑ Invokes the createInstance method on the separatorTemplate, passing in the reference to the clone of the parent DOM element of the DOM element whose id HTML attribute is specified in the layoutElement attribute of the <template> subelement of the <separatorTemplate> element. This cloned parent DOM element is the same one that ListViewRenderTask passed into the createInstance method of the itemTemplate.

```
var separatorTemplateInstance =
         this._separatorTemplate.createInstance(this._itemTemplateParent);
```

❑ The `createInstance` method takes these steps under the hood:

 ❑ Clones the DOM element whose `id` HTML attribute value is given by the `layoutElement` attribute on the `<template>` subelement of the `<separatorTemplate>` subelement of the `ListView` control. Keep in mind that cloning this DOM element also clones all its descendant DOM elements.

 ❑ Adds this cloned DOM element as the child element to the cloned DOM element that `ListViewRenderTask` receives from the `render` method of the `ListView`, as mentioned earlier. For example, this cloned DOM element is added to the cloned `<tbody>` element that `ListViewRenderTask` receives from the `render` method.

 ❑ Instantiates a `TemplateInstance` object and stores a reference to this cloned DOM element in the `instanceElement` property of this object, and returns the object to its caller.

❑ Accesses the cloned DOM element that the `createInstance` method has stored in the `instanceElement` property of the `TemplateInstance` object, as just discussed.

```
var sep = separatorTemplateInstance.instanceElement;
```

❑ Assigns the CSS style class associated with the separator template to the `className` property of this cloned DOM element:

```
if (this._separatorClass)
  sep.className = this._separatorClass;
```

❑ Uses the current index as an index into the `_separatorElements` array to store this cloned DOM element into the array.

```
this._separatorElements[this._currentIndex] = sep;
```

As we discussed earlier, the `execute` method returns a Boolean value that specifies whether the method is done with rendering all the data records. Recall from Listing F-9 that if the `execute` method returns `false`, the `_onTimeout` method calls the `enqueue` static method on the `Array` class to enqueue the task back in the `_tasks` collection so that it can be executed again. Note that the `execute` method invokes the `_renderTaskComplete` method on its associated `ListView` templated data control to inform the control that the `execute` method has completed the rendering of all the data records in the data collection bound to the `ListView` control, and `execute` returns `true` to inform the `_onTimeout` method that it has completed its execution:

```
if (this._currentIndex === itemLength)
{
  this._listView._renderTaskComplete(this);
  return true;
}
```

Listing F-13: The execute Method

```
function Sys$Preview$UI$Data$ListViewRenderTask$execute()
{
  var isArray = Array.isInstanceOfType(this._data);
  var itemLength = isArray ? this._data.length :
        (this._data ? (this._data.get_length ? this._data.get_length() : 0) : 0);
  var lengthm1 = itemLength - 1;
  var lastElementToRender = Math.min(itemLength, this._currentIndex + 5);
  for (; this._currentIndex < lastElementToRender; this._currentIndex++)
  {
    var item = isArray? this._data[this._currentIndex] :
              this._data.getItem(this._currentIndex);
    if (this._itemTemplate)
    {
      var itemTemplateInstance =
                this._itemTemplate.createInstance(this._itemTemplateParent, item);
      var element = itemTemplateInstance.instanceElement;
      if (this._itemClass)
      {
        if ((this._currentIndex % 2 === 1) && (this._alternatingItemClass))
          element.className = this._alternatingItemClass;

        else
          element.className = this._itemClass;
      }
      this._itemElements[this._currentIndex] = element;
      element.tabIndex = -1;
      element.dataIndex = this._currentIndex;
      $addHandler(element, "focus", this._itemFocusHandler);
      $addHandler(element, "click", this._itemClickHandler);
    }
    if (this._separatorTemplate && (this._currentIndex !== lengthm1) &&
        this._itemTemplateParent)
    {
      var separatorTemplateInstance =
                this._separatorTemplate.createInstance(this._itemTemplateParent);
      var sep = separatorTemplateInstance.instanceElement;
      if (this._separatorClass)
        sep.className = this._separatorClass;

      this._separatorElements[this._currentIndex] = sep;
    }
  }
  if (this._currentIndex === itemLength)
  {
    this._listView._renderTaskComplete(this);
    return true;
  }

  else
    return false;
}
```

ListView

The `ListView` control, like any other ASP.NET AJAX data control, derives from the `DataControl` base class:

```
Sys.Preview.UI.Data.ListView.registerClass('Sys.Preview.UI.Data.ListView',
                                     Sys.Preview.UI.Data.DataControl);
```

Listing F-14 presents the implementation of the `ListView` control. I'll discuss the members of this control in the following sections.

Listing F-14: The ListView Control

```
Sys.Preview.UI.Data.ListView =
function Sys$Preview$UI$Data$ListView(associatedElement)
{
  Sys.Preview.UI.Data.ListView.initializeBase(this, [associatedElement]);
  this._itemElements = [];
  this._separatorElements = [];
}
Sys.Preview.UI.Data.ListView.registerClass('Sys.Preview.UI.Data.ListView',
                                     Sys.Preview.UI.Data.DataControl);
```

Constructor

As Listing F-15 shows, this constructor, like that of any other ASP.NET AJAX subclass, first invokes the `initializeBase` method to invoke the constructor of its base class — that is, the `DataControl` base class:

```
Sys.Preview.UI.Data.ListView.initializeBase(this, [associatedElement]);
```

Next, it instantiates the following two collections:

❑ `_itemElements`: This array contains all the cloned DOM elements of the DOM element whose id attribute value is given by the `layoutElement` attribute on the `<template>` subelement of the `<itemTemplate>` subelement of the `<listView>` element in the xml-script. As we discussed earlier, each DOM element in this array displays a data record. For example, in the case of the following excerpt from Listing F-4, the `_itemElements` array contains DOM elements that are the clones of the `<tr>` DOM element with an id attribute value of `item`. Each cloned `<tr>` DOM element in this example displays information about a particular book.

```
<html>
  <body>
    . . .
    <div style="display: none;">
      <div id="layout">
        <table width="100%">
          <thead>
            . . .
          </thead>
          <tbody id="itemContainer">
            <tr id="item">
              <td id="title">
              </td>
              <td id="publisher">
              </td>
              <td id="price">
              </td>
            </tr>
          </tbody>
        </table>
      </div>
    </div>
    . . .
  </body>
</html>
```

❑ _separatorElements: This array contains all the cloned DOM elements of the DOM element whose id attribute value is given by the layoutElement attribute on the <template> subelement of the <separatorTemplate> subelement of the <listView> element in the xml-script. As we discussed earlier, each DOM element in this array displays the UI that separates two consecutive data DOM elements. The DOM elements in _itemElements are also known as data DOM elements because they display data records.

Listing F-15: The Constructor of the ListView Control

```
Sys.Preview.UI.Data.ListView =
function Sys$Preview$UI$Data$ListView(associatedElement)
{
  Sys.Preview.UI.Data.ListView.initializeBase(this, [associatedElement]);
  this._itemElements = [];
  this._separatorElements = [];
}
```

Style Properties

In this section I'll present and discuss the implementation of the style properties of the ListView control. These properties specify the CSS style class names for specific types of rows or items of the ListView control.

alternatingItemClass

As Listing F-16 shows, the ListView control exposes a getter named get_alternatingItemCssClass and a setter named set_alternatingItemCssClass that you can use to get and set the alternatingItemClass property of the ListView control. This property contains the CSS style class name that will be applied to the alternating rows of the control — that is, to the alternating, or odd, DOM elements in the _itemElements collection. Recall that the DOM elements in this collection display data records.

The set_alternatingItemCssClass setter takes effect only if the new value is different from the current value. As you can see from Listing F-16, this setter first assigns the new value to the alternatingItemClass property:

```
this._alternatingItemClass = value;
```

Next, it invokes the render method to render the ListView control so this change will take effect immediately:

```
this.render();
```

Finally, it invokes the raisePropertyChanged method to raise the propertyChanged event and consequently to invoke the event handlers registered for this event. The ListView control, like any other, inherits this method from the Component base class.

If you need to run some custom code when the value of the alternatingItemClass property changes, you must wrap your code in a method and register the method as an event handler for the propertyChanged event of the ListView control.

Listing F-16: The Getter and Setter Methods for Getting and Setting the alternatingItemClass Property

```
function Sys$Preview$UI$Data$ListView$get_alternatingItemCssClass()
{
  return this._alternatingItemClass;
}
function Sys$Preview$UI$Data$ListView$set_alternatingItemCssClass(value)
{
  if (value !== this._alternatingItemClass)
  {
    this._alternatingItemClass = value;
    this.render();
    this.raisePropertyChanged('alternatingItemCssClass');
  }
}
```

itemClass

Listing F-17 presents the implementation of the `get_itemCssClass` and `set_itemCssClass` methods of the `ListView` control, which you can use to get and set the value of the `itemCssClass` property of the `ListView` control. This value is applied to the non-alternating, or even, rows of the `ListView` control — that is, the even-numbered DOM elements in the `_itemElements` collection.

Note that `set_itemCssClass` doesn't do anything if the new value is the same as the current value. As you can see, this setter first assigns the new value to the `itemClass` property:

```
this._itemClass = value;
```

Next, it invokes the `render` method to re-render the `ListView` control so this change will take effect immediately:

```
this.render();
```

Finally, it calls the `raisePropertyChanged` method to raise the `propertyChanged` event:

```
this.raisePropertyChanged('itemCssClass');
```

If you need to run some custom code when the value of the `itemClass` property changes, you must wrap your code in a method and register the method as an event handler for the `propertyChanged` event of the `ListView` control.

Listing F-17: The Getter and Setter Methods for Getting and Setting the itemClass Property

```
function Sys$Preview$UI$Data$ListView$get_itemCssClass()
{
  return this._itemClass;
}
function Sys$Preview$UI$Data$ListView$set_itemCssClass(value)
{
  if (value !== this._itemClass)
  {
    this._itemClass = value;
    this.render();
    this.raisePropertyChanged('itemCssClass');
  }
}
```

selectedItemClass

Use the `get_selectedItemCssClass` and `set_selectedItemCssClass` getter and setter methods to get and set the CSS style class name for the selected row or item of the `ListView` control, as shown in Listing F-18.

Listing F-18: Getting and Setting the selectedItemClass Property

```
function Sys$Preview$UI$Data$ListView$get_selectedItemCssClass()
{
  return this._selectedItemClass;
}
function Sys$Preview$UI$Data$ListView$set_selectedItemCssClass(value)
{
  if (value !== this._selectedItemClass)
  {
    this._selectedItemClass = value;
    this.render();
    this.raisePropertyChanged('selectedItemCssClass');
  }
}
```

separatorCssClass

Use the `get_separatorCssClass` and `set_separatorCssClass` getter and setter methods to get and set the CSS style class name for the separator row or item of the `ListView` control, as shown in Listing F-19. A separator row or item is a row or item that separates two consecutive data rows or items. In other words, the `separatorCssClass` is applied to the DOM elements in the `_separatorElements` collection.

Listing F-19: Getting and Setting the separatorClass Property

```
function Sys$Preview$UI$Data$ListView$get_separatorCssClass()
{
  return this._separatorClass;
}
function Sys$Preview$UI$Data$ListView$set_separatorCssClass(value)
{
  if (value !== this._separatorClass)
  {
    this._separatorClass = value;
    this.render();
    this.raisePropertyChanged('separatorCssClass');
  }
}
```

Template Properties

This section will describe the template properties of the `ListView` control.

emptyTemplate

Use the `get_emptyTemplate` and `set_emptyTemplate` getter and setter methods to get and set the empty template. The page developer specifies the required markup text between the opening and closing tags of the `<template>` subelement of the `<emptyTemplate>` element in the xml-script. As you'll see later, the `ListView` control automatically renders this markup if the data collection bound to the `ListView` control does not contain any data records.

As Listing F-20 shows, the `set_emptyTemplate` setter first invokes the `dispose` method on the current `emptyTemplate`. This allows the template to perform its final cleanup before it is disposed of:

```
if (this._emptyTemplate)
  this._emptyTemplate.dispose();
```

Next, it assigns the new template to the empty template:

```
this._emptyTemplate = value;
```

Then it invokes the `render` method to re-render the `ListView` control, if the `ListView` control is not already updating:

```
if (!this.get_isUpdating())
  this.render();
```

Finally, it invokes the `raisePropertyChanged` method to raise the `propertyChanged` event and consequently to inform interested clients that the `emptyTemplate` property has changed its value. Clients express interest in this event by registering an event handler for it.

Listing F-20: Getting and Setting the emptyTemplate Property

```
function Sys$Preview$UI$Data$ListView$get_emptyTemplate()
{
  return this._emptyTemplate;
}
function Sys$Preview$UI$Data$ListView$set_emptyTemplate(value)
{
  if (this._emptyTemplate)
    this._emptyTemplate.dispose();

  this._emptyTemplate = value;
  if (!this.get_isUpdating())
    this.render();

  this.raisePropertyChanged('emptyTemplate');
}
```

itemTemplate

Use the `get_itemTemplate` and `set_itemTemplate` getter and setter methods to get and set the `itemTemplate` property. The implementation of these two methods are very similar to that of the getter and setter methods for the `emptyTemplate` property, as shown in Listing F-21.

Listing F-21: Getting and Setting the itemTemplate Property

```
function Sys$Preview$UI$Data$ListView$get_itemTemplate()
{
  return this._itemTemplate;
}
function Sys$Preview$UI$Data$ListView$set_itemTemplate(value)
{
  if (this._itemTemplate)
    this._itemTemplate.dispose();

  this._itemTemplate = value;
  if (!this.get_isUpdating())
    this.render();

  this.raisePropertyChanged('itemTemplate');
}
```

layoutTemplate

Use the get_layoutTemplate and set_layoutTemplate getter and setter methods to get and set the layoutTemplate property. The implementation of these two methods are very similar to that of the getter and setter methods for the emptyTemplate property, as shown in Listing F-22.

Listing F-22: Getting and Setting the layoutTemplate Property

```
function Sys$Preview$UI$Data$ListView$get_layoutTemplate()
{
  return this._layoutTemplate;
}
function Sys$Preview$UI$Data$ListView$set_layoutTemplate(value)
{
  if (this._layoutTemplate)
    this._layoutTemplate.dispose();

  this._layoutTemplate = value;
  if (!this.get_isUpdating())
    this.render();

  this.raisePropertyChanged('layoutTemplate');
}
```

separatorTemplate

Use the get_separatorTemplate and set_separatorTemplate getter and setter methods to get and set the separator template for the ListView control, as shown in Listing F-23.

Listing F-23: Getting and Setting the separatorTemplate

```
function Sys$Preview$UI$Data$ListView$get_separatorTemplate()
{
  return this._separatorTemplate;
}
function Sys$Preview$UI$Data$ListView$set_separatorTemplate(value)
{
  if (this._separatorTemplate)
    this._separatorTemplate.dispose();

  this._separatorTemplate = value;
  if (!this.get_isUpdating())
    this.render();

  this.raisePropertyChanged('separatorTemplate');
}
```

getItemElement

The get_itemElement method returns the DOM element in the _itemElements collection with the specified index, as shown in Listing F-24.

> *If you can, always use the style and template properties of the ListView control to customize the UI that renders the data records. The problem with using style and template properties is that they are applied to all data rows or items of the ListView control. If you need to customize a specific data row or item, call the getItemElement method to return a reference to the DOM element that contains the UI that renders this row and performs your row-specific customization on this DOM element.*

Listing F-24: The getItemElement Method

```
function Sys$Preview$UI$Data$ListView$getItemElement(index)
{
  return this._itemElements[index];
}
```

set_dataIndex

Listing F-25 contains the implementation of the set_dataIndex method of the ListView control. This method begins by invoking the get_dataIndex method to return the current data index. The ListView control inherits the get_dataIndex method from the DataControl base class. Recall that this method returns the index of the current data record in the data collection bound to the ListView control:

```
var oldIndex = this.get_dataIndex();
```

Next, it calls the getItemElement method to return a reference to the DOM element that contains the UI that renders the data record with the specified data index:

```
var sel = this.getItemElement(oldIndex);
```

Then it removes the current CSS style class name from this DOM element. This is necessary because we're about to change the selected item and we need to deselect the current item:

```
if (sel && this._selectedItemClass)
    Sys.UI.DomElement.removeCssClass(sel, this._selectedItemClass);
```

Next, it invokes the set_dataIndex of its base class — that is, the DataControl class — to specify the new index as the current data index:

```
Sys.Preview.UI.Data.ListView.callBaseMethod(this, 'set_dataIndex', [value]);
```

Then the set_dataIndex method invokes the getItemElement method to return a reference to the DOM element that contains the UI that displays the new data record with the new data index:

```
sel = this.getItemElement(value);
```

Finally, it applies the selected style to this DOM element, because this DOM element is now the selected item or row of the ListView control:

```
if (sel && this._selectedItemClass)
    Sys.UI.DomElement.addCssClass(sel, this._selectedItemClass);
```

Listing F-25: The set_dataIndex Method

```
function Sys$Preview$UI$Data$ListView$set_dataIndex(value)
{
  var oldIndex = this.get_dataIndex();
  if (oldIndex !== value)
  {
    var sel = this.getItemElement(oldIndex);
    if (sel && this._selectedItemClass)
      Sys.UI.DomElement.removeCssClass(sel, this._selectedItemClass);

    Sys.Preview.UI.Data.ListView.callBaseMethod(this, 'set_dataIndex', [value]);
    sel = this.getItemElement(value);
    if (sel && this._selectedItemClass)
      Sys.UI.DomElement.addCssClass(sel, this._selectedItemClass);
  }
}
```

itemTemplateParentElementId

Use the get_itemTemplateParentElementId and set_itemTemplateParentElementId getter and setter methods to get and set the itemTemplateParentElementId property, as shown in Listing F-26.

This property specifies the `id` HTML attribute value of the DOM element whose clone acts as a container for the DOM elements in the `_itemElements` collection.

Listing F-26: Getting and Setting the itemTemplateParentElementId Property

```
function Sys$Preview$UI$Data$ListView$get_itemTemplateParentElementId()
{
  return this._itemTemplateParentElementId;
}
function Sys$Preview$UI$Data$ListView$set_itemTemplateParentElementId(value)
{
  this._itemTemplateParentElementId = value;
  this.raisePropertyChanged('itemTemplateParentElementId');
}
```

renderComplete

The `ListView` control exposes an event named `renderComplete`, as shown in Listing F-27. As the name suggests, the `ListView` control fires this event when it is completely rendered. Use the `add_renderComplete` method to add a new event handler to the list of those registered for the `renderComplete` event. Use the `remove_renderComplete` method to remove an event handler from the list of those registered for this event.

Listing F-27: The renderComplete Event

```
function Sys$Preview$UI$Data$ListView$add_renderComplete(handler)
{
  this.get_events().addHandler("renderComplete", handler);
}
function Sys$Preview$UI$Data$ListView$remove_renderComplete(handler)
{
  this.get_events().removeHandler("renderComplete", handler);
}
```

Initialize

The `ListView` control overrides the `initialize` method that it inherits from its base class, in which it performs several tasks, as can be seen from Listing F-28. First, it invokes the `get_element` method to return a reference to the DOM element on the current page that represents the `ListView` control:

```
var element = this.get_element();
```

Next, it creates a delegate to represent the `_onGotFocus` method, and stores it in a private field named `_focusHandler`:

```
this._focusHandler = Function.createDelegate(this, this._onGotFocus);
```

Then it creates another delegate to represent the `_onKeyDown` method, and stores it in a private field named `_keyDownHandler`:

```
    this._keyDownHandler = Function.createDelegate(this, this._onKeyDown);
```

Next, the `ListView` control creates a third delegate to represent the `_onItemFocus` method, and stores it in a private field named `_itemFocusHandler`:

```
    this._itemFocusHandler = Function.createDelegate(this, this._onItemFocus);
```

Then it creates the fourth delegate to represent the `_onItemClick` method, and stores it in a private field named `_itemClickHandler`:

```
    this._itemClickHandler = Function.createDelegate(this, this._onItemClick);
```

Next, it invokes the `initialize` method of its base class to allow the base class to perform its own initialization:

```
    Sys.Preview.UI.Data.ListView.callBaseMethod(this, 'initialize');
```

Then it registers the `_keyDownHandler` and `_focusHandler` delegates as event handlers for the `keydown` and `focus` events of the DOM element that represents the `ListView` control:

```
    $addHandler(element, "keydown", this._keyDownHandler);
    $addHandler(element, "focus", this._focusHandler);
```

Next, it invokes the `initialize` method on the item template, if the page developer has specified this template in xml-script:

```
    if (this._itemTemplate)
      this._itemTemplate.initialize();
```

Next, `ListView` invokes the `initialize` method on the separator template, if the page developer has specified this template in xml-script:

```
    if (this._separatorTemplate)
      this._separatorTemplate.initialize();
```

Next, it invokes the `initialize` method on the empty template, if the page developer has specified this template in the xml-script:

```
    if (this._emptyTemplate)
      this._emptyTemplate.initialize();
```

Next, it invokes the `initialize` method on the layout template, if this template has been specified:

```
    if (this._layoutTemplate)
      this._layoutTemplate.initialize();
```

Finally, it invokes the `render` method to render the `ListView` control:

```
    this.render();
```

Listing F-28: The initialize Method

```
function Sys$Preview$UI$Data$ListView$initialize()
{
  var element = this.get_element();
  this._focusHandler = Function.createDelegate(this, this._onGotFocus);
  this._keyDownHandler = Function.createDelegate(this, this._onKeyDown);
  this._itemFocusHandler = Function.createDelegate(this, this._onItemFocus);
  this._itemClickHandler = Function.createDelegate(this, this._onItemClick);
  Sys.Preview.UI.Data.ListView.callBaseMethod(this, 'initialize');
  $addHandler(element, "keydown", this._keyDownHandler);
  $addHandler(element, "focus", this._focusHandler);
  if (this._itemTemplate)
    this._itemTemplate.initialize();

  if (this._separatorTemplate)
    this._separatorTemplate.initialize();

  if (this._emptyTemplate)
    this._emptyTemplate.initialize();

  if (this._layoutTemplate)
    this._layoutTemplate.initialize();
  if (!element.tabIndex)
    element.tabIndex = 0;
  this.render();
}
```

_onGotFocus

Recall from Listing F-28 that the initialize method registered the _focusHandler delegate that represents the _onGotFocus method as an event handler for the focus event of the associated DOM element of the ListView control. Recall that the associated DOM element of a control is the DOM element that represents the control on the current page. When the associated DOM element gains the focus, it automatically invokes the _focusHandler delegate, which in turn invokes the _onGotFocus method. Listing F-29 presents the implementation of this method. This method invokes the setFocus method, passing in the references to the ListView control and the DOM element that displays the selected row of the ListView control, thereby setting the focus on the selected row:

```
this.setFocus(this, this.getItemElement(this.get_dataIndex()));
```

Listing F-29: The _onGotFocus Method

```
function Sys$Preview$UI$Data$ListView$_onGotFocus(ev)
{
  if (ev.target === this.get_element())
    this.setFocus(this, this.getItemElement(this.get_dataIndex()));
}
```

setFocus

The setFocus method takes two parameters, as shown in Listing F-30. The main responsibility of this method is to set the focus to the DOM element referenced by its second parameter when the ASP.NET AJAX control referenced by the first parameter gains the focus. The first parameter basically references the owner control of the second parameter.

As you can see, the setFocus method accesses the associated DOM element of the owner ASP.NET AJAX control:

```
var ownerElement = owner.get_element();
```

Next, it calls the setTimeout method, passing in a reference to the focus method and specifying the DOM element referenced by the second parameter of the setFocus as the argument of the focus. This instructs the setTimeout method to invoke the focus method and pass this DOM element into it:

```
setTimeout(Function.createCallback(this.focus, element), 0);
```

Listing F-30: The setFocus Method

```
function Sys$Preview$UI$Data$ListView$setFocus(owner, element)
{
  if (element.focus)
  {
    for(var i = owner.get_length() - 1; i >= 0; i--)
    {
      var sel = owner.getItemElement(i);
      if (sel)
        sel.tabIndex = -1;
    }

    var ownerElement = owner.get_element();
    var t = ownerElement.tabIndex;
    if (t === -1)
      t = ownerElement.__tabIndex;

    element.tabIndex = t;
    setTimeout(Function.createCallback(this.focus, element), 0);
    ownerElement.__tabIndex = t;
    ownerElement.tabIndex = -1;
  }
}
```

focus

The setTimeout method finally invokes the focus method, passing in the DOM element that needs to grab the focus, as shown in Listing F-31. As you can see, the focus method simply invokes the focus method on this DOM element to set the focus on this DOM element.

Listing F-31: The focus Method

```
function Sys$Preview$UI$Data$ListView$focus(element)
{
  try
  {
    element.focus();
  }
  catch(e) {}
}
```

_onKeyDown

Recall from Listing F-28 that the `initialize` method registered the `_keyDownHandler` delegate that represents the `_onKeyDown` method as an event handler for the `keydown` event of the associated DOM element of the `ListView` control. Recall that the associated DOM element of a control is the DOM element that represents the control on the current page. When the end user presses a key while the mouse is over the associated DOM element, the DOM element automatically invokes the `_keyDownHandler` delegate, which in turn invokes the `_onKeyDown` method.

Listing F-32 presents the implementation of this method. When this method is invoked, a `DomEvent` object is passed into it. The method begins by retrieving the key code from this `DomEvent` object:

```
var k = ev.keyCode ? ev.keyCode : ev.rawEvent.keyCode;
```

The value of the key code determines which key was pressed. The various codes are as follows:

❑ The value of `Key.up` or `Key.left` tells the `_onKeyDown` method that the end user wants to move the focus to the previous row or item in the `ListView` control. Recall that each data item or row in the `ListView` control is a DOM element in the `_itemElements` collection of the `ListView` control. Also recall that the `ListView` control maintains in a private field named `_focusIndex` the index of the DOM element (data row or item) that has the focus. This means that the index of the previous DOM element (data row or item) is nothing but `_focusIndex - 1`.

As you can see, the `_onKeyDown` method first invokes the `getItemElement` method, passing in `_focusIndex - 1` to return a reference to the previous DOM element (data row or item):

```
this.getItemElement(this._focusIndex - 1)
```

Next, it invokes the `setFocus` method, passing in the reference to this DOM element to have this method set the focus to it:

```
this.setFocus(this, this.getItemElement(this._focusIndex - 1));
```

If you're wondering who sets the `_focusIndex` field of the `ListView` control, we need to study what happens after the `setFocus` method is invoked. When the previous DOM element gains the focus, it invokes its `focus` event. As you'll see in the following sections, the `render` method of the `ListView` control registers a delegate named `_itemFocusHandler` as an event handler for the `focus` event of all data rows or items. This delegate represents a method named _onItemFocus, which assigns the data index associated with the DOM element that just gained the focus to the _focusIndex field of the ListView control. Therefore, when the previous DOM element raises its focus event, the _itemFocusHandler delegate — and consequently the _onItemFocus method — is automatically invoked, which in turn sets the _focusIndex field to the data index of the data row or item that just gained the focus.

```
ev.preventDefault();
```

❑ The value of Key.down or Key.right tells the _onKeyDown method that the end user wants to move the focus to the next data row or item in the ListView control. The_onKeyDown method first invokes the getItemElement method, passing in the index of the next row or item — that is, _focusIndex + 1 — to return a reference to the next DOM element.

```
this.getItemElement(this._focusIndex + 1)
```

Next, it invokes the setFocus method, passing in the reference to this DOM element to have this method set the focus to this DOM element:

```
this.setFocus(this, this.getItemElement(this._focusIndex + 1));
```

Finally, it invokes the preventDefault method on the DomEvent object to prevent the default behavior of the key from taking effect.

```
ev.preventDefault();
```

Listing F-32: The _onKeyDown Method

```
function Sys$Preview$UI$Data$ListView$_onKeyDown(ev)
{
  if (ev.target === this.getItemElement(this._focusIndex))
  {
    var k = ev.keyCode ? ev.keyCode : ev.rawEvent.keyCode;
    if ((k === Sys.UI.Key.up) || (k === Sys.UI.Key.left))
    {
      if (this._focusIndex > 0)
      {
        this.setFocus(this, this.getItemElement(this._focusIndex - 1));
        ev.preventDefault();
      }
    }

    else if ((k === Sys.UI.Key.down) || (k === Sys.UI.Key.right))
    {
      if (this._focusIndex < (this.get_length() - 1))
      {
        this.setFocus(this, this.getItemElement(this._focusIndex + 1));
        ev.preventDefault();
      }
    }
  }
```

(continued)

Listing F-32 *(continued)*

```
      else if ((k === Sys.UI.Key.enter) || (k === Sys.UI.Key.space))
      {
        if (this._focusIndex !== -1)
        {
          this.set_dataIndex(this._focusIndex);
          ev.preventDefaut();
        }
      }
    }
  }
}
```

render

As the name suggests, the render method is responsible for rendering the ListView control, as shown in Listing F-33.

Listing F-33: The render Method

```
function Sys$Preview$UI$Data$ListView$render()
{
  var associatedElement = this.get_element();
  var i, element;
  for (i = this._itemElements.length - 1; i >= 0; i--)
  {
    element = this._itemElements[i];
    if (element)
      Sys.Preview.UI.ITemplate.disposeInstance(element);
  }

  this._itemElements = [];
  for (i = this._separatorElements.length - 1; i >= 0; i--)
  {
    element = this._separatorElements[i];
    if (element)
      Sys.Preview.UI.ITemplate.disposeInstance(element);
  }
  this._separatorElements = [];
  if (associatedElement.childNodes.length)
  {
    if (this._layoutTemplateElement)
      Sys.Preview.UI.ITemplate.disposeInstance(this._layoutTemplateElement);
  }

  associatedElement.innerHTML = '';
  var tasksPending = false;
  var items = this.get_data();
  var itemLength = items ? (items.get_length ? items.get_length() :
                                                items.length) : (0);
```

```
if (itemLength && itemLength > 0)
{
  var template = this.get_layoutTemplate();
  if (template)
  {
    var itemTemplate = this.get_itemTemplate();
    var separatorTemplate = this.get_separatorTemplate();
    var layoutTemplateInstance = template.createInstance(associatedElement, null,
                                 this.findItemTemplateParentCallback,
                                 this._itemTemplateParentElementId);
    var itemTemplateParent = layoutTemplateInstance.callbackResult;
    this._layoutTemplateElement = layoutTemplateInstance.instanceElement;
    tasksPending = true;
    this._pendingTasks++;
    var renderTask =
        new Sys.Preview.UI.Data.ListViewRenderTask(this, items, itemTemplate,
                                     itemTemplateParent,
                                     separatorTemplate,
                                     this._itemElements,
                                     this._separatorElements,
                                     this._itemClass,
                                     this._alternatingItemClass,
                                     this._separatorClass,
                                     this._itemFocusHandler,
                                     this._itemClickHandler);
    Sys.Preview.TaskManager.addTask(renderTask);
  }
}

else
{
  var emptyTemplate = this.get_emptyTemplate();
  if (emptyTemplate)
    emptyTemplate.createInstance(associatedElement);

  var handler = this.get_events().getHandler('renderComplete');
  if(handler) handler(this, Sys.EventArgs.Empty);
}
}
```

This method begins by invoking the `get_element` method to return a reference to the associated DOM element of the `ListView` control. The `ListView` control, like any other ASP.NET AJAX control, inherits the `get_element` method from the `Control` base class:

```
var associatedElement = this.get_element();
```

Next, the `render` method iterates through the DOM elements in the `_itemElements` collection of the `ListView` control, and invokes the `disposeInstance` static method on the `ITemplate` class for each enumerated DOM element. The `disposeInstance` method allows the template to perform a final cleanup before the DOM element is disposed of:

```
for (i = this._itemElements.length - 1; i >= 0; i--)
{
  element = this._itemElements[i];
  if (element)
    Sys.Preview.UI.ITemplate.disposeInstance(element);
}
```

Next, the `render` method resets the `_itemElements` collection, which means that all DOM elements in this collection are now disposed of. Such disposal is necessary, because we're about to re-render the entire `ListView` control and consequently re-create new data DOM elements:

```
this._itemElements = [];
```

Next, the `render` method iterates through the separator DOM elements in the `_separatorElements` collection, and invokes the `disposeInstance` static method on the `ITemplate` interface for each enumerated separator DOM element in order to perform the final cleanup before the DOM element is disposed of. (Recall that a separator DOM element is a DOM element that separates two consecutive data DOM elements. Also recall that a data DOM element is a DOM element that displays a data record.)

```
for (i = this._separatorElements.length - 1; i >= 0; i--)
{
  element = this._separatorElements[i];
  if (element)
    Sys.Preview.UI.ITemplate.disposeInstance(element);
}
```

Then the `render` method resets the `_separatorElements` collection, which means that all separator DOM elements are now disposed of. Again, such disposal is necessary because we're about to re-render the entire `ListView` control and consequently generate new separator DOM elements:

```
this._separatorElements = [];
if (associatedElement.childNodes.length)
{
  if (this._layoutTemplateElement)
    Sys.Preview.UI.ITemplate.disposeInstance(this._layoutTemplateElement);
}
```

Next, the method resets the inner HTML of the associated DOM element of the `ListView` control, because we're about to regenerate this inner HTML:

```
associatedElement.innerHTML = '';
```

Then it calls the `get_data` method to return a reference to the data collection bound to the `ListView` control:

```
var items = this.get_data();
```

Next, it takes one of the following steps to determine the total number of data records in the data collection:

❑ If the data collection supports a method named `get_length`, it invokes this method to return the total data record count in the collection. Data collections, such as `DataTable`, that implement the `IData` interface support the `get_length` method.

❑ If the data collection does not support the `get_length` method but does support the `length` property, it invokes this property to return the total data record count in the collection. Data collections that are JavaScript arrays support the `length` property.

❑ If the data collection supports neither the `get_length` method nor the `length` property, it returns 0 as the total data record count because the `ListView` control supports only data collections that either implement the `IData` interface or are JavaScript arrays.

```
var itemLength = items ? (items.get_length ? items.get_length() :
                                            items.length) : (0);
```

Next, the `render` method invokes the `get_layoutTemplate`, `get_itemTemplate`, and `get_separatorTemplate` methods to return references to the layout template, item template, and separator template, respectively:

```
var template = this.get_layoutTemplate();
var itemTemplate = this.get_itemTemplate();
var separatorTemplate = this.get_separatorTemplate();
```

Then it invokes the `createInstance` method on the layout template. Recall that this method takes four parameters:

❑ The first parameter references the container DOM element, which is the associated DOM element of the `ListView` control in this case.

❑ The second parameter references the data context — that is, the data record being displayed. Since the layout template is not for displaying data records, the `render` method passes `null` for this parameter.

❑ The third parameter references the JavaScript function or delegate that the `createInstance` method automatically invokes after the call into the `parseNodes` method returns. In this case, the `render` method passes a reference to the `findItemTemplateParentCallback` method, which will be discussed later.

❑ The fourth parameter references the context object, which is the `id` HTML attribute value of the parent DOM element of the layout DOM element. When the `createInstance` method finally invokes the `findItemTemplateParentCallback` method, it passes this parameter as is into this method.

```
var layoutTemplateInstance = template.createInstance(associatedElement, null,
                                    this.findItemTemplateParentCallback,
                                    this._itemTemplateParentElementId);
```

The return value of the `createInstance` method is an instance of the `TemplateInstance` class, which exposes two properties. The first is named `callbackResult`, and contains the return value of the call into the `findItemTemplateParentCallback` method. As mentioned earlier, the `createInstance` method internally invokes the `findItemTemplateParentCallback` method and stores its return value in the `callbackResult` property of the `TemplateInstance` object:

```
var itemTemplateParent = layoutTemplateInstance.callbackResult;
```

The `createInstance` method internally clones the DOM element whose id HTML attribute value is given in xml-script by the `layoutElement` attribute on the `<template>` subelement of the `<layoutTemplate>` subelement of the `<listView>` element. The `createInstance` method assigns this DOM element to the `instanceElement` property of the `TemplateInstance` object. The `render` method uses this property to return the reference to this cloned DOM element.

```
this._layoutTemplateElement = layoutTemplateInstance.instanceElement;
```

Next, the `render` method increments the pending task count, because we're about to create a new rendering task:

```
this._pendingTasks++;
```

Then it creates an instance of `ListViewRenderTask`. The main job of this task is to render the `ListView` control. The `render` method passes all the required information into this task:

```
var renderTask =
    new Sys.Preview.UI.Data.ListViewRenderTask(this, items, itemTemplate,
                                    itemTemplateParent,
                                    separatorTemplate,
                                    this._itemElements,
                                    this._separatorElements,
                                    this._itemClass,
                                    this._alternatingItemClass,
                                    this._separatorClass,
                                    this._itemFocusHandler,
                                    this._itemClickHandler);
```

Next, it calls the `addTask` static method on the current `TaskManager` to add the new task. As you can see, the `render` method does not immediately render the `ListView` control. Instead it schedules a `render` task with the current `TaskManager`. As we discussed earlier, the current `TaskManager` executes each task in the order in which it is scheduled:

```
Sys.Preview.TaskManager.addTask(renderTask);
```

So far we have discussed the case in which the data collection bound to the `ListView` control contains data records. Next, you'll see what the `render` method does if the data collection is empty. The method begins by calling the `get_emptyTemplate` method to return a reference to the empty template:

```
var emptyTemplate = this.get_emptyTemplate();
```

Next, it invokes the `createInstance` method on the empty template to render the markup text that the page developer has specified between the opening and closing tags of the `<template>` subelement of the `<emptyTemplate>` element:

```
if (emptyTemplate)
   emptyTemplate.createInstance(associatedElement);
```

Finally, it calls the `getHandler` method on the `EventHandlerList` object that contains all the event handlers registered for the events of the `ListView` control, in order to return a reference to the JavaScript function whose invocation automatically invokes all the event handlers registered for the `renderComplete` event of the `ListView` control:

```
var handler = this.get_events().getHandler('renderComplete');
if(handler) handler(this, Sys.EventArgs.Empty);
```

_onItemFocus

Recall that Listing F-33 passes the `_itemFocusHandler` delegate that represents the `_onItemFocus` method into the `ListViewRenderTask` constructor. As we discussed earlier, `ListViewRenderTask` registers this delegate as event handler for the `focus` events of the DOM elements that display the data records. When a DOM element raises this event, the `_itemFocusHandler` and consequently the `_onItemFocus` method are automatically invoked. As Listing F-34 shows, this method simply assigns the data index of the data record that the DOM displays to the `_focusIndex` field of the `ListView` control:

```
this._focusIndex = ev.target.dataIndex;
```

This ensures that the `_focusIndex` field is updated when a DOM element gains a focus, so you know which DOM element has the focus.

Listing F-34: The _onItemFocus Method

```
function Sys$Preview$UI$Data$ListView$_onItemFocus(ev)
{
  if (typeof(ev.target.dataIndex) !== "undefined")
     this._focusIndex = ev.target.dataIndex;
}
```

_onItemClick

Recall that Listing F-33 passes the `_itemClickHandler` delegate that represents the `_onItemClick` method into the `ListViewRenderTask` constructor. As we discussed earlier, `ListViewRenderTask` registers this delegate as event handler for the `click` events of the DOM elements that display the data records. When a DOM element raises this event, the `_itemClickHandler` and consequently the `_onItemClick` method are automatically invoked. When this method is invoked, a `DomEvent` object is passed into it. (Recall that this object is an ASP.NET AJAX wrapper around the event object that the browser creates.) As Listing F-35 shows, the `_onItemClick` method first invokes the `target` property on this `DomEvent` to return a reference to the DOM element that raised the `click` event:

```
var s = ev.target;
```

Next, it invokes the `tagName` to return a string that contains the name of the DOM element that raised the event:

```
var srcTag = s.tagName.toUpperCase();
```

Next, it walks up the containment hierarchy of the DOM element, searching for the first DOM element that supports the `dataIndex` property. This property contains the index of the data record that the DOM element displays. It's necessary to walk up the containment hierarchy because the DOM element that raises the `click` event could be the child element of the DOM element that displays the record. For example, the DOM element that displays the record may contain a button DOM element that raises the `click` event. Obviously the button DOM element does not support the `dataIndex`. It is the DOM element that contains the button DOM element that supports the `dataIndex` property.

```
while (s && (typeof(s.dataIndex) === 'undefined'))
    s = s.parentNode;
```

Next, the `_onItemClick` method calls the `dataIndex` property on the DOM element in the containment hierarchy that supports this property, in order to determine the index of the data record that this DOM element displays:

```
var idx = s.dataIndex;
```

Next, it invokes the `getItemElement`, passing in this data index to return a reference to DOM element:

```
sel = this.getItemElement(idx);
```

Then it invokes the `set_dataIndex` method to set the data index of this DOM element to the preceding data index:

```
this.set_dataIndex(idx);`
```

Next, it invokes the `setFocus` method to set the focus to the specified element, if the element is an input, text area, select, button, or link:

```
if ((srcTag !== "INPUT") && (srcTag !== "TEXTAREA") &&
    (srcTag !== "SELECT") && (srcTag !== "BUTTON") && (srcTag !== "A"))
   this.setFocus(this, sel);
```

Listing F-35: The _onItemClick Method

```
function Sys$Preview$UI$Data$ListView$_onItemClick(ev)
{
  var s = ev.target;
  var srcTag = s.tagName.toUpperCase();
  while (s && (typeof(s.dataIndex) === 'undefined'))
    s = s.parentNode;
```

```
    if (s)
    {
      var idx = s.dataIndex;
      sel = this.getItemElement(idx);
      if (sel)
      {
        this.set_dataIndex(idx);
        if ((srcTag !== "INPUT") && (srcTag !== "TEXTAREA") &&
            (srcTag !== "SELECT") && (srcTag !== "BUTTON") && (srcTag !== "A"))
          this.setFocus(this, sel);
      }
    }
}
```

findItemTemplateParentCallback

Recall that Listing F-33 passes the findItemTemplateParentCallback method and the
_itemTemplateParentElementId field into the createInstance method of the layout template.
After invoking the parseNodes method, the createInstance method invokes the
findItemTemplateParentCallback method, passing the value of the _itemTemplateParentElementId
field into it, and stores the return value of this method in the callbackResult property of the
TemplateInstance method that the createInstance method returns to its caller. As Listing F-36
shows, the findItemTemplateParentCallback method invokes the findElement method on the current MarkupContext and passes the value of the _itemTemplateParentElementId field into it to return
a reference to the DOM element whose id HTML attribute is given by this field.

Listing F-36: The findItemTemplateParentCallback Method

```
function Sys$Preview$UI$Data$ListView$findItemTemplateParentCallback(
                                          instanceElement, markupContext, id)
{
  return markupContext.findElement(id);
}
```

The best way to understand the significance of the findItemTemplateParentCallback method is to
revisit the internal implementation of the createInstance method of the Template class. I'll discuss
the implementation of this method in the context of an example — the example presented in Listing F-4.

Recall from Listing F-33 that the render method of the ListView control calls the get_layoutTemplate
method on the ListView control to return a reference to the layout template.

```
        var template = this.get_layoutTemplate();
```

Then it calls the createInstance method on the layout template, passing in four parameters:

```
        var layoutTemplateInstance = template.createInstance(associatedElement, null,
                                          this.findItemTemplateParentCallback,
                                          this._itemTemplateParentElementId);
```

The first parameter references the associated DOM element of the `ListView` control, which is the DOM element shown in the top highlighted portion of the following excerpt from Listing F-4:

```
<%@ Page Language="C#" %>
<html xmlns="http://www.w3.org/1999/xhtml">
 . . .
<body>
  <form id="form1" runat="server">
    . . .

    <div id="listView" />

    <div style="display: none;">
      <div id="layout">
        <table width="100%">
          . . .
          <tbody id="itemContainer">
            <tr id="item">
              <td id="title" />
              <td id="publisher" />
              <td id="price" />
            </tr>
          </tbody>
        </table>
      </div>
    </div>
  </form>
  <script type="text/xml-script">
    <page xmlns="http://schemas.microsoft.com/xml-script/2005">
      <components>
        . . .

        <listView id="listView" itemTemplateParentElementId="itemContainer"

          renderComplete="renderCompleteCallback">
          . . .
        </listView>
      </components>
    </page>
  </script>
</body>
</html>
```

The third parameter passed into the `createInstance` method of the layout template is a reference to the `findItemTemplateParentCallback` method of the `ListView` control. The fourth parameter is the `id` HTML attribute value of the `<tbody>` DOM element, shown in the highlighted portion of the following excerpt from Listing F-4:

```
<%@ Page Language="C#" %>
<html xmlns="http://www.w3.org/1999/xhtml">
. . .
<body>
  <form id="form1" runat="server">
    . . .
 <div id="listView" />
    <div style="display: none;">
      <div id="layout">
        <table width="100%">
          . . .
          <tbody id="itemContainer">
            <tr id="item">
              <td id="title" />
              <td id="publisher" />
              <td id="price" />
            </tr>
          </tbody>
        </table>
      </div>
    </div>
  </form>
  <script type="text/xml-script">
    <page xmlns="http://schemas.microsoft.com/xml-script/2005">
      <components>
        . . .
        <listView id="listView" itemTemplateParentElementId="itemContainer"
        renderComplete="renderCompleteCallback">
          . . .
        </listView>
      </components>
    </page>
  </script>
</body>
</html>
```

Now let's walk through the implementation of the `createInstance` method of the layout template, as shown in Listing F-37.

Listing F-37: The createInstance Method of the Template

```
function Sys$Preview$UI$Template$createInstance(containerElement, dataContext,
                                                instanceElementCreatedCallback,
                                                callbackContext)
{
  var result = new Sys.Preview.UI.TemplateInstance();
  result.instanceElement = this._layoutElement.cloneNode(true);
  var documentFragment = document.createDocumentFragment();
  documentFragment.appendChild(result.instanceElement);
```

(continued)

Listing F-37 *(continued)*

```
    var markupContext =
        Sys.Preview.MarkupContext.createLocalContext(documentFragment,
                                    this._parentMarkupContext, dataContext);
    markupContext.open();
    Sys.Preview.MarkupParser.parseNodes(this._scriptNode.childNodes, markupContext);
    if (instanceElementCreatedCallback)
      result.callbackResult = instanceElementCreatedCallback(result.instanceElement,
                                        markupContext, callbackContext);
    result.instanceElement.markupContext = markupContext;
    containerElement.appendChild(result.instanceElement);
    markupContext.close();
    return result;
}
```

This method begins by creating an instance of the `TemplateInstance` class:

```
    var result = new Sys.Preview.UI.TemplateInstance();
```

Next, it invokes the `cloneNode` method on the DOM element shown in the highlighted portion of the following excerpt from Listing F-4:

```
<%@ Page Language="C#" %>
<html xmlns="http://www.w3.org/1999/xhtml">
. . .
<body>
  <form id="form1" runat="server">
    . . .
    <div id="listView" />
    <div style="display: none;">

      <div id="layout">

        <table width="100%">
          . . .
          <tbody id="itemContainer">
            <tr id="item">
              <td id="title" />
              <td id="publisher" />
              <td id="price" />
            </tr>
          </tbody>
        </table>

      </div>

    </div>
  </form>
```

```
<script type="text/xml-script">
  <page xmlns="http://schemas.microsoft.com/xml-script/2005">
    <components>
      . . .
      <listView id="listView" itemTemplateParentElementId="itemContainer"
      renderComplete="renderCompleteCallback">
        . . .
      </listView>
    </components>
  </page>
</script>
</body>
</html>
```

The `cloneNode` method clones this DOM element and creates the following subtree of DOM elements:

```
<div id="layout">
  <table width="100%">
    <tbody id="itemContainer">
    </tbody>
  </table>
</div>
```

Keep two important things in mind. First, the `cloneNode` method creates a new subtree, which is not part of the current document. This means that you cannot call the `getElementById` method on the document object to return a reference to any of the DOM elements in the new subtree. Second, the `cloneNode` method clones the id attribute values as well. This means that all the DOM elements in the new subtree have the same id attribute values as the DOM elements from which they were cloned.

As Listing F-37 shows, the `createInstance` method stores the root node of this new subtree in the `instanceElement` property of the newly instantiated `TemplateInstance` object:

```
result.instanceElement = this._layoutElement.cloneNode(true);
```

Next, the `createInstance` method creates a new document fragment:

```
var documentFragment = document.createDocumentFragment();
```

Then it adds the new subtree — that is, the cloned subtree — to this document fragment:

```
documentFragment.appendChild(result.instanceElement);
```

Again, keep in mind that this document fragment is not part of the current document. It is sitting in memory on its own. Therefore, if you need to access a DOM element in the new cloned subtree you must search for it in this document fragment, not in the document object.

Next, the `createInstance` method creates a new local `MarkupContext` to represent this document fragment. While the global `MarkupContext` represents the document object, a local `MarkupContext` represents a document fragment, which is not part of the document object.

```
var markupContext =
        Sys.Preview.MarkupContext.createLocalContext(documentFragment,
                                    this._parentMarkupContext, dataContext);
```

Next, the `createInstance` method invokes the `parseNodes` method to parse the nodes within the `<template>` subelement of the `<layoutTemplate>` subelement of the `<listView>` element in xml-script. The `parseNodes` method does not do anything in the case of Listing F-4 because the `<template>` subelement of the `<layoutTemplate>` subelement in this case does not contain any child nodes:

```
Sys.Preview.MarkupParser.parseNodes(this._scriptNode.childNodes, markupContext,
                                this._prefixNamespaceMapping);
```

Next, the `createInstance` method invokes the `findItemTemplateParentCallback` method of the `ListView` control, passing in three parameters. The second parameter references the local `MarkupContext` that represents the document fragment that contains the cloned subtree. The third parameter contains the id HTML attribute value of the `<tbody>` element:

```
result.callbackResult = instanceElementCreatedCallback(result.instanceElement,
                                    markupContext, callbackContext);
```

As you saw from Listing F-36, the `findItemTemplateParentCallback` method invokes the `findElement` method on this local `MarkupContext` to search the cloned subtree for the `<tbody>` DOM element.

```
function Sys$Preview$UI$Data$ListView$findItemTemplateParentCallback(
                                    instanceElement, markupContext, id)
{
    return markupContext.findElement(id);
}
```

The `findElement` method returns a reference to the `<tbody>` DOM element in the cloned subtree. If you were to call the `getElementById` method on the document object instead, you would get a reference to the original `<tbody>` element in the current document, which is the `<tbody>` element shown in the highlighted portion of the following excerpt from Listing F-4:

```
<%@ Page Language="C#" %>
<html xmlns="http://www.w3.org/1999/xhtml">
. . .
<body>
  <form id="form1" runat="server">
    . . .
    <div id="listView" />
    <div style="display: none;">
      <div id="layout">
        <table width="100%">
          . . .

            <tbody id="itemContainer">
```

```
                    <tr id="item">
                      <td id="title" />
                      <td id="publisher" />
                      <td id="price" />
                    </tr>

                  </tbody>
              </table>
            </div>
          </div>
        </form>
        <script type="text/xml-script">
          <page xmlns="http://schemas.microsoft.com/xml-script/2005">
            <components>
              . . .
              <listView id="listView" itemTemplateParentElementId="itemContainer"
              renderComplete="renderCompleteCallback">
                . . .
              </listView>
            </components>
          </page>
        </script>
      </body>
    </html>
```

_renderTaskComplete

Recall from Listing F-10 that the `execute` method of `ListViewRenderTask` invokes the
`_renderTaskComplete` method on the `ListView` control after it renders the control. As Listing F-38
shows, this method first decrements the pending task count, because the current `ListViewRenderTask`
has completed its execution:

```
this._pendingTasks--;
```

If no tasks are pending, the `_renderTaskComplete` method raises the `renderComplete` event and consequently invokes all the event handlers registered for this event:

```
var handler = this.get_events().getHandler('renderComplete');
if(handler)
  handler(this, Sys.EventArgs.Empty);
```

Listing F-38: the _renderTaskComplete Method

```
function Sys$Preview$UI$Data$ListView$_renderTaskComplete(renderTask)
{
  this._pendingTasks--;
  if(this._pendingTasks <= 0)
  {
    this._pendingTasks = 0;
    var handler = this.get_events().getHandler('renderComplete');
    if(handler)
      handler(this, Sys.EventArgs.Empty);
  }
}
```

descriptor

The ListView control, like any other ASP.NET AJAX class, exposes a static property named descriptor, shown in Listing F-39, to enable its clients to inspect its members generically using the ASP.NET AJAX type inspection facilities discussed throughout this book. For example, the ASP.NET AJAX client-side framework uses the ASP.NET AJAX type inspection mechanism to initialize in xml-script the properties and events of the ListView control with the values specified on the attributes and child nodes of the <listView> element.

Listing F-39: The descriptor Property

```
Sys.Preview.UI.Data.ListView.descriptor =
{
  properties: [ { name: 'alternatingItemCssClass', type: String },
                { name: 'layoutTemplate', type:
  Sys.Preview.UI.ITemplate },
                { name: 'itemCssClass', type: String },
                { name: 'itemTemplate', type: Sys.Preview.UI.ITemplate },
                { name: 'itemTemplateParentElementId', type: String },
                { name: 'selectedItemCssClass', type: String },
                { name: 'separatorCssClass', type: String },
                { name: 'separatorTemplate', type: Sys.Preview.UI.ITemplate },
                { name: 'emptyTemplate', type: Sys.Preview.UI.ITemplate } ],
  events: [ {name: 'renderComplete'} ]
}
```

Index

A

abort method
WebRequest class, 506–508
WebRequestExecutor class, 467
XMLHttpExecutor, 485–487
XMLHttpRequest, 7
Action class
example of, 1337–1339
methods, 1334–1335
using SetPropertyAction, 1336–1337
actions
Action class, 1334–1339
descriptor property, 1341–1342
execute method, 1333, 1339–1341
IAction interface, 1333
InvokeMethodAction, 1342–1344
PostBackAction, 1347–1348
setOwner method, 1333
SetPropertyAction, 1345–1346
ActualValue property,
ArgumentOutOfRangeException, 58
add function
instantiating WebServiceProxy, 552–553
local vs. remote implementations of, 597–598
add method
addItem method, 1359
array types, 28
UpdatePanelTriggerCollection, 1003–1004
addAttribute method, TypeDescriptor
class, 403
add_beginRequest method, 1099, 1103
add_click method
Button client control, 328
HyperLink client control, 316–317
add_completed method,
WebRequestExecutor, 461
add_completedRequest method,
WebRequestManager, 471
addComponent method
adding behaviors to applications, 672

_Application class methods, 240–241
IContainer class, 238
MarkupContext class, 1268–1269
parseFromMarkup invoking, 1287
AddComponentProperty method,
ScriptComponentDescriptor, 727
AddContainer method,
BaseMasterDetailControl, 900
addContent method, Mover class methods, 213
addCssClass method
Control class, 288
DomElement class, 166–167
add_disposing method
behaviors, 666–667
INotifyDisposing interface, 224
Monitor class implementing, 226
AddElementProperty method,
ScriptComponentDescriptor, 727–728
addEvent method
ScriptComponentDescriptor, 728
TypeDescriptor, 402–403
_addEventName method, initializeObject
method, 1305–1306
addHandler method
beginRequest event, 1099
DomEvent class, 189–193
implementing pageLoaded event, 1053
Sys.EventHandlerList class, 134
System.ComponentModel.
EventHandlerList, 131
addHandlers method
DomEvent class, 194–197
System.ComponentModel.
EventHandlerList, 131
add_initializeRequest method, 1091, 1096
add_invokingRequest method,
WebRequestManager, 470
addItem method, DataControl, 1358–1360
addMethod method, TypeDescriptor, 401–402
add_pageLoaded method, 1053, 1055–1062
add_pageLoading method, 1235–1244

addProperty method
ScriptComponentDescriptor, 728
TypeDescriptor, 400–401
add_propertyChanged method
behaviors, 667
INotifyPropertyChanged interface, 228, 233
addRange method, array types, 29
addReference method, 1299
Address.js file, CustomTable client control,
396–397
AddScriptProperty method,
ScriptComponentDescriptor, 728–729
AddScriptReferencesForScriptControls method,
ScriptManager, 743–744
addShoppingCartItem method,
ShoppingCartItem, 143–144, 156–157
addTable method, TableProvider, 216–217
addTask method, TaskManager, 1431
add_transform method, BindingBase class, 1326
addUpdatePanel method,
pageLoadedHandler, 1067
ADO.NET, metadata and, 349
AJAX (Asynchronous JavaScript And XML), 1–26
AJAX engine components, 3
AJAX-enabled components, 1–2
framework, 24–25
installing ASP.NET AJAX extensions and ASP.NET
Futures, 25
JavaScript base type extensions. See base types
JSON and, 21–24
overview, 1
summary, 25
XML format and, 16–20
XMLHttpRequest code listing, 6–10
XMLHttpRequest deserialize function, 14–15
XMLHttpRequest instantiation, 4
XMLHttpRequest methods and properties, 5–6
XMLHttpRequest serialize function, 12–14
XMLHttpRequest submitCallback function, 11–12
AjaxControlToolkit namespace, 680
alert function, initializeRequest event, 1099
alt property (alternate text), Image client
controls, 300
alternatingItemClass property, ListView control
styles, 1445
Amazon Web services. See Web services,
Amazon E-commerce
AmazonSearch2.asbx, 819, 838–839, 847–848,
851, 855
AmazonSearchScriptControl server control

code listing, 790–794
GetScriptDescriptors method, 795–796
GetScriptReferences method, 796
overview of, 789
properties, 794–795
RenderContents method, 796–798
AmazonService class, 778–780, 813–817
AmazonService2 class, 829–832
AmazonService3.cs, 844–847
AmazonService4 class, 852–854
AmazonService.cs file, 812
App_Code directory, MasterDetailControl server
control, 916, 925
appearance properties, MasterDetailField data
control, 939–940
append method
StringBuilder, 387
TypeDescriptor, 371–374
AppendScript method,
ScriptComponentDescriptor, 729–730
applendLine method, StringBuilder, 387
Application class
addComponent method, 240–241
application lifecycle, 243–248, 257
constructor, 244–245
disposable objects, 260–263
dispose method, 264–266
_doinitialize method, 246–248
endCreateComponents method, 253–256
events, 258
findComponents method, 242–243
getComponents method, 242
get_events method, 271–272
id method, 269–270
init event, 258–259
initialize method, 246, 267–269
INotifyDisposing interface, 272–280
INotifyPropertyChanged interface, 272
load event, 259
_loadHandler method, 245–246
overview, 239–240
raiseLoad method, 256
raisePropertyChanged method, 270–271
removeComponent method, 241
unload event, 260
application lifecycle
behaviors, 662–663
benefits of ASP.NET, 24
overview, 243–244
summarized, 257

application logic, 564

Application objects, addComponent method, 672

apply method, JavaScript Function type, 79

_applyWatermark method,
        TextBoxWatermarkBehavior, 694–695

App_Themes folder, 918–919

App_Web_amazonsearch.asbx.cdcab7d2.
        rxua8pbv.0.cs, 813–814

argument property
    Button client control, 326
    CommandEventArgs class, 324
    JavaScript Function type, 78

ArgumentException, 53–56

ArgumentNullException, 56–58

ArgumentOutOfRangeException, 58–60

arguments, WSDL, 514–515

ArgumentTypeException, 60–63

ArgumentUndefinedException, 64–66

array types, 28–37
    add, 28
    addRange, 29
    clear, 29
    clone, 30
    contains, 30
    enqueue and dequeue, 31–33
    forEach, 33–34
    indexOf, 34–35
    insert, 35
    overview, 28
    parse, 36
    remove, 36
    removeAt, 37

arrayDeclaration string, 1180

arrayDeclarationNodes array, 1189

arrays, JSON, 21

.asbx files
    AmazonSearch2.asbx, 819
    AmazonSearch3.asbx code listing, 847
    AmazonSearch4.asbx, 851
    AmazonSearch.asbx file, 778
    invoking server side methods from client
        side, 583
    Math custom class described by, 565–567
    ScriptHandlerFactory and, 571
    transformers, 821–823

.asmx files
    invoking server side methods from client
        side, 583
    page method calls and, 561
    ScriptHandlerFactory and, 571

ASP.NET AJAX control toolkit. See control toolkit

ASP.NET AJAX, overview, 24–25

ASP.NET Futures, 25

AspNetAjaxAmazonSearch client control
    code listing, 781–786
    initialize method, 787
    _onNextButtonClick method, 789
    _onPreviousButtonClick method, 788
    _onSearchButtonClick method, 788
    _onSuccess method, 789
    properties, 786–787

.aspx files
    AmazonSearch2.aspx, 838–839
    AmazonSearch3.aspx, 847–848
    AmazonSearch4.aspx, 855
    invoking server side methods from client
        side, 583
    Page class and, 966
    page method calls and, 561

Asynchronous JavaScript And XML. See AJAX
        (Asynchronous JavaScript And XML)

asynchronous partial page rendering. See partial
        page rendering

asyncPostBackControlIDs
    checking type property, 1181
    _getPostBackSettings method, 1074

asyncPostBackTimeout, checking type
        property, 1181

AsyncPostBackTrigger class, 1007–1011

_attachNewDoPostBack method, _
        initializeInternal method, 1043–1044

attributes collection, initializeObject method,
        1298–1299

automatic generation, of proxy classes, 607–608

AWSECommerceService
    adding .asbx file, 778
    AmazonSearch.asbx file, 778
    AmazonSearchScriptControl component. See
        AmazonSearchScriptControl server control
    AmazonService class, 778–780
    AspNetAjaxAmazonSearch component. See
        AspNetAjaxAmazonSearch client control
    creating proxy class for, 777–778
    HtmlGenerator client control. See HtmlGenerator
        client control
    HtmlGeneratorScriptControl. See
        HtmlGeneratorScriptControl server control
    Image class, 775
    ItemAttributes class, 776
    Item/Items classes, 775

AWSECommerceService (continued)
ItemSearch class, 774
ItemSearchRequest class, 774
ItemSearchResponse class, 775
Offer/Offers/OfferListing classes, 776
overview, 773
Price class, 776

B

base classes
behaviors. *See* BehaviorBase class
binding. *See* BindingBase class
components. *See* Component class
controls. *See* Control class
event programming and, 138–141
EventArgs, 324
ExtenderControl, 710–713
ScriptControl, 714–716
base types, 27–52
array types. *See* array types
boolean types, 37
callBaseMethod method, 104–110
date types, 38
error types. *See* error types
getBaseMethod function, 110–113
getBaseType method, 100–102
initializeBase method, 102–103
object types, 38–39
overview, 27–28
string types, 39–41
summary, 41–52
**BaseMasterDetailControl server control,
882–905**
AddContainer method, 900
applying style to container controls, 896
child controls, 883
choosing child controls, 890
choosing layout for child controls, 890
code listing, 883–889
CompositeControl features inherited, 904
container for child controls (TableCell), 891–892
Control collection, overriding, 904–905
ControlStyle method, overriding, 902
CreateChildControls method, 900–902
CreateContainer method, 892–893
CreateContainerChildControls method, 893–896
CreateControlStyle method, overriding, 902
CreateDetail method, 895
deriving from CompositeControl class, 890

detail server control update conditions, 895
exposing properties of child controls, 903–904
INamingContainer interface, 891, 905–906
master server control update conditions, 893
overview of actions in, 883
RenderContainer method, 900
RenderContents method, overriding, 902–903
state management methods, 897–900
summary, 910
TagKey property, overriding, 902
BaseMasterDetailControl2 server control
code listing, 906–908
CreateDetail method, 909
CreateMaster method, 908
properties, 910
RegisterDetailEventHandlers method, 909
beginRequest event
_onFormSubmit method, 1089
PageRequestManager, 1099–1104
beginRequestEventArgs class, 1100
beginRequestHandler function, 1103–1104
beginUpdate method
behaviors, 663
component methods, 250
Behavior class
element methods, 669
id methods, 671–672
instance methods, 672–674
name methods, 669–671
overview, 661–668
properties, 668
static methods, 674–675
BehaviorBase class
ClientState property, 682–683
ClientStatefieldID property, 682
dispose method, 686–687
initialize method, 681–682
overview, 681
_partialUpdateBeginRequest method, 685
_partialUpdateEndRequest method, 685–686
registerPartialUpdateEvents method, 683–684
**BehaviorID property, custom extender
control, 754**
behaviors
Behavior class. *See* Behavior class
BehaviorBase class. *See* BehaviorBase class
overview, 659–661
summary, 706
TextBoxWatermarkBehavior class. *See*
TextBoxWatermarkBehavior class

binding, 1317–1331
Binding class, 1330–1331
BindingBase class, 1319–1325
example of, 1317–1319
execute method, 1340
transformers, 1325–1329
Binding class, 1330–1331
BindingBase class
Binding class, 1330–1331
defined, 1319
descriptor property, 1325
evaluate method, 1321
evaluateIn method, 1321–1323
evaluateOut method, 1324
initialize method, 1324–1325
methods of, 1319–1321
BindingEventArgs
defining custom transformer, 1326–1327
evaluateIn method instantiating, 1322–1323
bindings elements, ListView using, 1416
blur events, _onBlur method, 693–694
body
HTTP messages, 520
SOAP messages, 521
WebRequest class, 459
Boolean types, 37
Boolean values
implementsInterface function, 113–118
inheritsFrom function, 118–120
isImplementedBy function, 121–123
BoundField, MasterDetailField data control, 932
Bounds type, DomElement getBounds method, 175–176
bridge element
example page using, 565–567
XML document elements, 565–567
BridgeBuildProvider, 593, 815
BridgeTransformData class, 820–822
browsers
HttpBrowserCapabilities, 302–303
name=value format, 491
build providers
BridgeBuildProvider, 815
file types and, 593
BuildTemplate method, 992–993
Button client controls, 323–348
add_click method, 328
argument property, 326
command property, 326–327
CommandEventArgs and, 323–324

CommandEventArgs class, 323
constructor, 325
descriptor property, 330
dispose method, 329
event bubbling. *See* event bubbling
features, 325
initialize method, 327
_onClick method, 328–329
overview, 323
prototype property, 325–326
summary, 348
Button server control, 325

C

C#
base syntax, 102
interface implementation patterns, 711
Manager constructors in, 98
virtual methods, 104
call methods
initializeObject method, 1306–1307, 1313
initializeObject method of xml-script, 1301
invoking from client-side code, 561–563
JavaScript Function type, 79
transforming return value of, 817–818
Web service custom page calls, 564–570
callback methods, WebServiceProxy class, 536
callBaseMethod method, JavaScript OOP/type reflection extensions, 104–110
CancelEventArgs class, 132–133
Cascading Style Sheets. *See* CSS (Cascading Style Sheets)
child controls, BaseMasterDetailControl
container for, 891–892
CreateChildControls method, 900–902
CreateContainerChildControls method, 893–896
exposing properties of, 903–904
initializing for Controls collection, 896
layout of, 890
overview, 883, 890
child elements, WSDL documents, 514
ChildrenAsTriggers property, UpdatePanel server controls, 863–864
childUpdatePanelIDs, 1182, 1184
classes
adding new events to, 135–138
inheritance and, 96–100
JavaScript OOP/type reflection extensions, 79–80

clear method
array types, 29
StringBuilder class, 387
**clearHandlers method, DomEvent class
methods, 197**
**clearText method, TextBoxWatermarkBehavior,
692–693**
_clearTimer method, XMLHttpExecutor, 477
click events
Button client control, 328–329
ClickBehavior class, 677
HyperLink client controls, 316–318
ClickBehavior class
click events, 677
descriptor property, 676–677
initialize method, 677–678
overview, 675–676
page example using, 678–680
ClickCallback method, Page_Load method, 1062
client controls, 281–321
AspNetAjaxAmazonSearch. See
AspNetAjaxAmazonSearch client control
base class. See Control class
custom, 290–291
HyperLink. See HyperLink client controls
Image. See Image client controls
Label. See Label client controls
overview, 281
summary, 321
ClientProxyGenerator class
DetermineServiceFullName method, 637
DetermineServiceType method, 636
GenerateConstructor method, 638–639
GenerateNamespace method, 638
GeneratePrototype method, 639
GenerateRegisterClass method, 643
GenerateStaticInstance method, 643–645
GenerateStaticMethods method, 645–647
GenerateWebMethodProxy method, 639–642
GetClientProxyScript, 634–636
PopulateMethodInfos method, 637
PopulateParameterInfos method, 637–638
replica of, 629–634
client-server communication, 457–510
aborting Web requests, 506–508
completedCallback function, 494–495, 498
completion of Web request, 494
DialogResult and MessageBoxStyle
enumerators, 508
invokingRequestCallback function, 503–506

message box and input box methods, 509–510
overview, 457
page using WebRequest, 487–490
page using WebRequestExecutor, 497–498
pageLoad function, 496, 502–503
submitCallback function, 491–492
Web request methods, 492
Web requests. See WebRequest class
WebRequestExecutor class. See
WebRequestExecutor class
WebRequestManager class. See
WebRequestManager class
Window class, 509
XMLDOM class, 474–475
XMLHttpExecutor class. See XMLHttpExecutor
class
XMLHttpRequest, 474
client-side code
client controls and, 290
invoking server side methods from, 570
WSDL documents and, 524
ClientState property
BehaviorBase class, 682–683
custom extender control, 754
ClientStateFieldID property
BehaviorBase class, 682
custom extender control, 754
clone, array types, 30
**cloneNode method, createInstance method,
1377–1378**
close method
createInstance method, 1379
processDocumentScripts, 1276
code reuse, behaviors providing, 660
collections, .NET generics, 733
CollectScripts method, ScriptManager, 742–743
**columns, applying to ListView control,
1424–1429**
Command events, Button server control, 325
**command property, Button client control,
326–327**
CommandArgument, Button server control, 325
**CommandEventArgs, Button client controls,
323–324**
**commandName property, CommandEventArgs
class, 324, 325**
communication patterns, AJAX, 2
**communication protocol, WSDL documents,
516–517, 519**
Compare transformer, 1329

CompareInverted transformer, 1329
CompiledTemplateBuilder class, 989
completed events, WebRequest, 461–462
completed method, WebRequestExecutor, 462
completedCallback function
    client-server communication, 494–495
    parsing strings containing server data, 495
    Web requests and, 492–494
complex properties, control states and, 898
Component class
    beginUpdate method, 250
    Behavior class deriving from, 661–662
    Control and Behavior classes and, 281
    create method, 249–253
    dispose method, 264–266
    get_events method, 271–272
    id method, 269–270
    IDisposable, INotifyDisposing, and
        INotifyPropertyChange interfaces and,
        235–238
    initialize method, 267–269
    INotifyDisposing interface, 272–280
    INotifyPropertyChanged interface, 272
    overview, 235–237, 248–249
    properties, 351–352
    raisePropertyChanged method, 270–271
ComponentModel class, 131
components, 219–280. *See also* **client controls**
    Application class component. *See* Application
        class
    Component class. *See* Component class
    creation phase of application lifecycle,
        257–258
    defined, 219
    IContainer class component, 238–239
    IDisposable interface, 220–224
    INotifyDisposing interface, 224–228
    INotifyPropertyChanged interface, 228–235
    interfaces, 220
    overview, 219
    processDocumentScripts searching for, 1276
    properties, 727
composite controls
    CompositeControl class, 890
    delegation to child controls, 883
composite server controls
    for asynchronous partial page rendering,
        881–882
    BaseMasterDetailControl. *See*
        BaseMasterDetailControl server control

BaseMasterDetailControl2. *See*
    BaseMasterDetailControl2 server control
defined, 882
drop down list examples. *See*
    MasterDetailControl2 server control;
    MasterDetailControl3 server control
grid view example. *See* MasterDetailControl
    server control
list box example. *See* MasterDetailControl3
    server control
CompositeControl class, 890, 904
conditional updates, 860–863, 878–881
constructor
    _Application class, 244–245
    Button client control, 325
    client-side PageRequestManager, 1037–1039
    CommandEventArgs class, 324
    DataColumn class, 453
    DataControl class, 1349–1350
    DomEvent class, 186–187
    GridView control, 331
    GridViewCommandEventArgs class, 342–343
    GridViewRow control, 339
    HyperLink control, 314
    Image client controls, 298, 306–307
    Label client controls, 291
    ListView control, 1442–1444
    ListViewRenderTask class, 1435–1436
    _ScriptLoader class, 1210
    _ScriptLoaderTask class, 1211
    StringBuilder class, 387
    TaskManager class, 1431
    Template class, 1375
    TemplateField custom template, 1381
    TypeDescriptor class, 350
    UpdatePanelTriggerCollection, 1001
    WebRequest class, 457–458
    WebRequestManager class, 468–469
    WebServiceError class, 555–556
    WebServiceProxy class, 535
    XMLHttpExecutor, 475–476
constructor property, JavaScript Function
    type, 78
containers, BaseMasterDetailControl
    applying style to container controls, 896
    for child controls, 891–892
    CreateContainer method, 892–893
    CreateContainerChildControls method, 893–896
ContainerType, BaseMasterDetailControl, 891
contains, array types, 30

containsCssClass method, DomElement methods, 167

content pages
disabling partial page rendering for, 876
UpdatePanel server control and, 871–874

ContentType property, RenderPageCallback method, 1117

Control class, 1350
addCssClass method, 288
Component base class derived from, 352
CreateChildControls method, 900–902
definition of, 281–283
dispose method, 288–289
get_element method, 283
get_id method, 283–284
get_parent method, 285
get_visibility method, 286
get_visible method, 286
GridViewRow class as subclass of, 339
InitRecursive method, 971–972
LoadRecursive method, 995
onBubbleEvent method, 289, 330
overview of, 281
parent property, 336
property types, 898
raiseBubbleEvent method, 290, 329, 330
removeCssClass method, 288
Render method of, 1114
RenderChildren method of, 1114–1115
ScriptManager deriving from, 734
set_id method, 284
set_parent method, 284
set_visibilityMode method, 286–287
set_visible method, 287
themes, 918–919
toggleCssClass method, 288
TypeDescriptor event exposed by, 364
TypeDescriptor methods exposed by, 359

control toolkit, 680

Controls collection
BaseMasterDetailControl overriding, 904–905
initializing child control before adding to, 896

ControlStyle
BaseMasterDetailControl overriding, 902
MasterDetailField data control, 939–940
WebControl class, 896

ControlTemplate property, UpDatePanel, 987

create $ function, JavaScript, 721–722

create function, error types, 41–45

create method, Component base class, 249–253, 662

CreateBaseDataBoundControlMaster method, 913, 923

CreateChildControls method, BaseMasterDetailControl, 900–902

CreateClientStateField property, custom extender control, 754

CreateContainer method, BaseMasterDetailControl, 892–893

CreateContainerChildControls method, BaseMasterDetailControl, 893–896

CreateContents method, UpDatePanel, 984–987

CreateControlStyle method
BaseMasterDetailControl overriding, 902
HtmlGeneratorScriptControl, 808

createDelegate method
JavaScript function, 178–179
_onFormSubmit method, 1087
pageLoadedHandler, 1066–1067

CreateDetail method
BaseMasterDetailControl, 895
BaseMasterDetailControl2, 909

createDocumentFragment method, document objects, 1378

createGlobalContext method
MarkupContext class, 1272
processing xml-script XML document, 1272–1273

CreateHandler method, RestHandler, 590–591

createInstance method
findItemTemplateParentCallback, 1467–1471
ITemplate interface, 1373, 1377–1380
render method, CustomTable control, 1389
TemplateInstance class, 1374

createLocalContext method, MarkupContext class, 1272, 1378

CreateMaster method, BaseMasterDetailControl2, 908

_createPageRequestManagerInstance method, 1034

_createPageRequestManagerParserError method, 1255

_createPageRequestManagerServerError method, 1255

_createPageRequestManagerTimeoutError method, 1254

createParameter method, TypeDescriptor, 402

_createPostBackSettings method, PageRequestManager, 1071–1072, 1079

_createQueryString method, WebRequest, 544–545

_createScriptElement method, _ScriptLoader, 1209

_createUrl method, WebRequest, 543

CSS (Cascading Style Sheets)

addCssClass method of Control class, 288

addCssClass method of DomElement class, 166–167

characteristics of AJAX-enabled components, 1–2

containsCssClass method of DomElement class, 167

removeCssClass method of Control class, 288

removeCssClass method of DomElement class, 167–169

toggleCssClass method of Control class, 288

toggleCssClass method of DomElement class, 169–171

WatermarkCssClass method, 702–703

custom attributes, xml-script not supporting, 1306

custom classes, 607

custom client controls, 290–291

custom exception types

clickCallback function, 75–76

example of, 71–75

implementing, 70–71

validateInput function, 76

CustomErrorHandler, 1256–1264

CustomTable client control, 389–399

Address.js file for Address type, 396–397

controlling display of product records, 397–398

CustomTable.js file, 389–391

dataBind method, 446–447, 450–451

dataSource property, 392

developing custom data control, 1366–1370

methods, 392–394, 1373

pageLoad function, 398–399

Product.js file for Product type, 394–395

revised implementation of, 452–453

StringBuilder class and, 394

CustomTable template data control, 1383–1399

descriptor property, 1391

fields property, 1387

JavaScript file for, 1384–1387

overview, 1383–1384

render method, 1387–1390

style properties, 1387

_toggleCssClass method, 1391

using, 1391–1393

CustomTable.js file, 389–391, 448–449

D

data classes, 407–456

DataColumn, 409–412

DataRow. *See* DataRow class

DataTable. *See* DataTable class

example using DataColumn, DataRow, and DataTable, 446–456

IData, 407–408

overview, 407

data context, 1318

data control fields. *See* MasterDetailField data control

dataBind method, CustomTable client control, 391–393, 446–447, 450–451

DataBinding event, MasterDetailField data control, 938–939

DataColumn class

constructor, 453

example using, 446–456

DataControl class, 1349–1372

addItem method, 1358–1360

constructor, 1349–1350

deleteCurrentItem method, 1360–1361

descriptor property, 1365

developing custom data control, 1366–1372

get_canMoveNext property, 1352

get_canMovePrevious property, 1352–1353

get_data method, 1353

get_dataContext method, 1358

get_dataIndex method, 1356

get_dataItem method, 1357–1358

getItem method, 1362

get_length method, 1355–1356

moveNext method, 1362–1363

movePrevious method, 1363–1364

onBubbleEvent method, 1364–1365

onDataChanged method, 1357

overview of, 1349

prepareChange method, 1350

set_data method, 1353–1355

set_dataIndex method, 1356–1357

triggerChangeEvents method, 1350–1351

data-interchanged formats, XML and JSON, 20

dataItem string, checking type property, 1182

dataItemJsonNodes array, client-side page postbacks, 1182, 1186

_dataItems collection, client-side page postbacks, 1185–1186

DataKeyNames property, MasterDetailControl server control, 916

DataRow class, 412–422

  adding DataRow objects to DataTable, 454

  constructor, 412–413

  descriptor property, 413–414

  example using, 446–456

  getProperty method of ICustomTypeDescriptor, 415–416

  ICustomTypeDescriptor interface implemented by, 414

  INotifyPropertyChange interface implemented by, 420–422

  invokeMethod method of ICustomTypeDescriptor, 419

  overview of, 412

  referencing DataTable object, 419–420

  setProperty method of ICustomTypeDescriptor, 416–419

DataRow type, ICustomTypeDescriptor, 404–405

dataSource property, CustomTable client control, 392

DataTable class

  add method, 425–427

  adding DataRow objects, 454

  clear method, 428–429

  constructor, 422

  createRow method, 439–441

  descriptor property, 432–434

  example using, 446–456

  getChanges method, 441–442

  getColumn method, 442–443

  get_length method, 429

  getRow method, 429–430

  IData interface, 424–425

  INotifyCollectionChanged, 436–439

  INotifyPropertyChange, 434–436

  internal fields, 423–424

  overview of, 422

  parseFromJson method, 443–445

  raiseRowChanged method, 443

  Remove method, 430–432

date types, ASP.NET AJAX, 38

declarative approach, proxy classes, 608–618

default event behavior, preventDefault method, 198–201

default executor type, WebRequestManager, 469

default failed callback methods, WebServiceProxy, 536

default succeeded callback methods, WebServiceProxy, 536

default timeout, WebRequestManager, 469

definition, Control base class, 281–283

<definitions> element, WSDL documents, 514

Delegate class

  AsyncPostBackTrigger class, 1010

  createDelegate method, 178–179

  decoupling callers of methods from methods, 178

  defining delegates with delegate keyword, 178

  Delegates namespace, 183

  isolating Mover class from movable content, 180–183

Delegates.js file

  content of, 1068–1069

  Delegate namespace, 183–184

  ImageProvider class, 185

  Mover class, 184

  TextProvider class, 184–185

deleteCurrentItem method, DataControl class, 1360–1361

dequeue, array types, 31–33

descriptor, GridViewCommandEventArgs class, 343–344

descriptor property

  Action class, 1341–1342

  Binding class, 1331

  BindingBase class, 1325

  Button client control, 330

  ClickBehavior class, 676–677

  CommandEventArgs class, 324

  CustomTable template data control, 1391

  DataControl class, 1365

  GridViewRow control, 341

  HyperLink client controls, 318

  InvokeMethodAction exposing, 1343–1344, 1346

  Label client controls, 294

  ListView control, 1472

  PostBackAction exposing, 1348

  type description and, 371

deserialize function

  XML, 18–20

  XMLHttpRequest, 14–15

_destroyTree method, client-side page postbacks, 1201–1202, 1231–1233

_detachAndStoreOriginalDoPostBack method, 1043

_detachAndStoreOriginalFormOnSubmit method, 1043
detail forms. *See* **master/detail forms**
detail server control
   CreateDetail method, 909
   update conditions, 895
DetailsView control
   as composite control, 328
   in custom composite user control, 946, 956
   deleting a message, 959–960
   displaying details of a message, 958
   MasterDetailControl server control, 918
   MasterDetailField data control, 943–944
   replying to a message, 961–962
   starting new thread, 963–964
   updating a message, 960–961
   XPath and, 959
DetermineServiceFullName method, ClientProxyGenerator, 637
DetermineServiceType method, ClientProxyGenerator, 636
DialogResult enumerators, client-server communication, 508
dictionary, 599
displayEvents, TypeDescriptor, 367–369
displayMethod function, TypeDescriptor, 362–363
displayProperties function, TypeDescriptor, 357
disposable objects, component development, 260–263
_disposableObjects array, component development, 260–263
dispose method
   Behavior class instance methods, 673–674
   BehaviorBase class, 686–687
   behaviors, 667
   Button client control, 329
   component development, 264–266
   Control class, 288–289
   HyperLink client controls, 318
   IDisposable interface and, 220–224
   IHttpModule interface, 584
   Image client controls, extending, 312
   INotifyDisposing interface and, 224–228
   TaskManager class, 1433–1434
   TextBoxWatermarkBehavior class, 700–702
disposeInstance method, ITemplate, 1373
<div> HTML element, attaching ClickBehavior to, 678
document element
   <Envelope> element, 518

XML, 19
xml-script XML document, 1267
Document Object Model. *See* **DOM (Document Object Model)**
document objects, createDocumentFragment method, 1378
_doinitialize method, _Application class, 246–248
DOM (Document Object Model)
   elements. *See* DomElement class
   events. *See* DomEvent class
   overview, 1–2
   overview of, 161
DOM extensions
   delegates, 178–183
   Delegates namespace, 183
   DomElement. *See* DomElement class
   DomEvent. *See* DomEvent class
   ImageProvider, 185
   Key, 176–177
   MouseButton, 176
   Mover. *See* Mover class
   overview of, 161
   summary, 217
   TableProvider class, 216–217
   TextProvider, 184–185
DomElement class
   addCssClass method, 166–167
   behaviors attached to, 659
   client controls and, 290
   containsCssClass method, 167
   Control instances and, 282–283
   _doPostBack method, 1079–1080
   getBounds method, 175
   getElementById method, 161–166
   getLocation method, 171–172
   ListView using template, 1409–1417
   overview of, 161
   removeCssClass method, 167–169
   searching XML documents using MarkupContext, 1267
   setLocation method, 172–175
   toggleCssClass method, 169–171
DomEvent class
   addHandler method, 189–193
   addHandlers method, 194–197
   clearHandlers method, 197
   constructor of, 186–187
   example using, 203–209
   instance methods, 198

DomEvent class (continued)
overview of, 185–186
preventDefault method, 198–201
properties, 187–189
removeHandler method, 193–194
static methods, 189
stopPropagation method, 201–203
_doPostBack function, JavaScript
_initializeInternal method, 1043
page postback via, 1040–1042
PostBackAction invoking, 1347
_doPostBack method
page postbacks via, 1051
PageRequestManager, 1043–1044, 1077–1081
using helper methods, 1071–1076
DropDownList server control
MasterDetailControl2. See MasterDetailControl2
server control
MasterDetailField data control, 943
page containing TextBox and, 1098–1099
DuplicateItemExceptions, 71–75
duration property, Image client controls, 309

E

E-Commerce Web services. See Web services,
Amazon E-commerce
element methods, Behavior class, 669
element parameter, create method of Component
base class, 663
<element> element, WSDL documents, 515–516
elements
DOM. See DomElement class
WSDL documents, 514
elements parameter
Component class, 249, 277
HyperLink client controls, 321
Image client controls, 302, 314
emptyTemplate property, ListView control,
1447–1448
EnablePartialRendering property,
PageRequestManager, 975, 976
EncodeString method
page postbacks server side, 1115–1116,
1156–1161
ProcessFocus method, 1159
ProcessScriptRegistration method, 1157–1158
RenderPageCallback method, 1118–1121,
1155–1156, 1159–1161
server response text on client-side, 1164–1170

UpdatePanel server control, 1156
endCreateComponents method, _Application
class, 253–256
_endPostBack method
client-side page postbacks, 1173, 1216–1222
ending current postback request, 1184
raising endRequest event, 1247–1248
server response text arriving on client-side, 1179
endRequest event
EndRequestEventArgs class, 1248–1249
firing endRequest event. See endRequest event
InvalidOperationException, 1255–1264
PageRequestManagerParserErrorException,
1255
PageRequestManagerServerErrorException,
1254–1255
PageRequestManagerTimeoutException, 1254
using, 1249–1253
EndRequestEventArgs class, 1248–1249
endsWith function, string types, 39
endUpdate method
behaviors, 663–664
components, 253
enqueue, array types, 31–33
_ensureSinglePageRequestManagerInstance
method, 1034
enumeration
isEnum method, 129
isFlags method, 129–130
registerEnum method, 127–128
<Envelope> element, XML, 518
error handling, 978–979
error string, checking type property, 1183
error types, 41–52
create, 41–45
overview, 41
popStackFrame, 45–52
eval JavaScript function, _processNamespaceURI
method, 1283
evaluate method, BindingBase class, 1321
evaluateIn method, BindingBase class,
1321–1323
evaluateOut method, BindingBase class, 1324
_evaluatePath method, TypeDescriptor, 376
_evaluateValue method, TypeDescriptor, 380
event bubbling
GridView control, 330–337, 344–348
GridViewCommandEventArgs, 341–344
GridViewRow control, 334, 339–341
summary, 348

event data classes
 NetworkRequestEventArgs class, 473–474
 ShoppingCartItemAddedEventArgs event,
  153–154
 ShoppingCartItemAdding event, 152
 Sys.CancelEventArgs, 132
 System.EventArgs class, 132
**event handlers. See also Sys.EventHandlerList
  class**
 addHandler method, 134, 189–193
 addHandlers method, 194–197
 adding, 158–159
 clearHandlers method, 197
 _getEvent method, 133–134
 getHandler method, 135–138
 initialization with parseFromMarkup method,
  1284–1287
 overview of, 133
 removeHandler method, 134–135, 193–194
 removing, 158–159
event programming, 131–159
 addHandler method, 134
 addShoppingCartItem, 143–144
 base classes, 138–141
 classes facilitating, 131–132
 DOM. See DomEvent class
 EventHandler list, 133
 _getEvent method, 133–134
 getHandler method, 135–138
 get_shoppingCartItems, 143
 initialize method, 143
 namespaces, 141
 removeHandler method, 134–135
 ShoppingCart class, 142–143
 ShoppingCartItem class, 141–142
 summary, 159
 Sys.CancelEventArgs, 132–133
 Sys.EventArgs class, 132
EventArgs class
 base event data class, 132
 event programming and, 131
 overview, 324
EventHandlerList class
 addHandler method, 134
 _getEvent method, 133–134
 getHandler method, 135–138
 overview of, 133
 removeHandler method, 134–135
events
 adding event handlers, 158–159

 adding new events to classes, 135–138
 addShoppingCartItem method of ShoppingCart
  class, 156–157
 Application class, 258–260
 click events, 677
 DOM. See DomEvent class
 _getEvent method, 133–134
 get_events method of ShoppingCart class, 155
 initialize method of ShoppingCart class, 155
 onShoppingcartInitialized method of
  ShoppingCart class, 155–156
 onShoppingCartItemAdded method of
  ShoppingCart class, 158
 onShoppingCartItemAdding method of
  ShoppingCart class, 158
 overview, 144–152
 propagation of, 201–203
 removing event handlers, 159
 ShoppingCart class, 154
 ShoppingCartItemAddedEventArgs event,
  153–154
 ShoppingCartItemAdding event, 152
 WebRequestManager class, 470–471
_events, TypeDescriptor class, 364–368
events parameter
 create method of Component base class, 249,
  277, 662
 HyperLink client controls, 321
 Image client controls, 301, 314
exception handling, error types and, 41
exception types, 53–76
 ArgumentException, 53–56
 ArgumentNullException, 56–58
 ArgumentOutOfRangeException, 58–60
 ArgumentTypeException, 60–63
 ArgumentUndefinedException, 64–66
 clickCallback function in custom exception,
  75–76
 implementing custom exception type, 70–75
 InvalidOperationException, 66, 1255–1264
 NotImplementedException, 66–68
 overview, 53
 ParameterCountException, 68–70
 summary, 76
 validateInput function in custom exception
  example, 76
execute method
 Action class, 1333, 1339–1341
 ListViewRenderTask class, 1437–1442
 _ScriptLoaderTask class, 1212–1213

executeRequest method
WebRequestExecutor class, 467
WebRequestManager class, 471–473
XMLHttpExecutor, 479–482
executor methods
default executor type, 469
WebRequest class, 460
expando attributes, xml-script not supporting, 1306
expando string, 1180
expandoScript string, 1189
extender control
example using, 761–762
ExtenderControl base class, 710–713
IExtenderControl interface, 709–710
overview, 708, 709
script controls vs., 769–770
summary, 771
why they are needed, 707–709
extender control, custom
BehaviorID property, 754
ClientState property, 754
ClientStateFieldID property, 754
CreateClientStateField property, 754
GetScriptDescriptors method, 755–757
GetScriptReferences method, 755
OnInit method, 757
OnLoad method, 758–759
OnPreRender method, 760–761
overview, 749–754
Page_PreLoad method, 757–758
Render method, 761
WatermarkCssClass method, 754
WatermarkText methods, 754
ExtenderControl base class, 710–713
ExtenderControls collection, ScriptManager class, 740
eXtensible Markup Language. See XML (eXtensible Markup Language)
ExtractValuesFromCell method, MasterDetailField data control, 939

F

false values, JSON, 21–22
fields property, CustomTable template data control, 1387
file types, build providers and, 593
findComponent method
_Application class, 242–243

IContainer class, 238
ListView control, 1422
MarkupContext class, 1269, 1271
findElement method
initializeObject method, 1300–1301
MarkupContext class, 1270
parseFromMarkup, 1286, 1376
TemplateField custom template, 1382
findItemTemplateParentCallback method, ListView control, 1465–1471
_findNearestElement method, PageRequestManager, 1072–1073
_findText method, _onFormSubmitCompleted method, 1177–1178
focus method, ListView control, 1455–1456
focus string, checking type property, 1184
forEach, array types, 33–34
foreign keys, editing, 932
formAction string, checking type property, 1182
formActionNode local variable, 1187
formatting
date types, 38
string types, 41
Function class, JavaScript
getBaseMethod function, 110–113
overview, 78–79
Type class and, 80

G

GenerateConstructor method, ClientProxyGenerator, 638–639
generateDescriptor method, TypeDescriptor, 370–371
generateHtml method
HtmlGenerator client control, 802–803
HtmlGenerator2 client control, 827–828
GenerateNamespace method, ClientProxyGenerator class, 638
GeneratePrototype method, ClientProxyGenerator class, 639
GenerateRegisterClass method, ClientProxyGenerator class, 643
GenerateStaticInstance method, ClientProxyGenerator class, 643–645
GenerateStaticMethods method, ClientProxyGenerator class, 645–647
GenerateWebMethodProxy method, ClientProxyGenerator class, 639–642
get_aborted method

WebRequestExecutor class, 465, 494
XMLHttpExecutor, 479
getAllResponseHeaders method
WebRequestExecutor class, 468
XMLHttpExecutor, 483
XMLHttpRequest, 7
GetAllUpdatePanelIDs method, page postback, 1132–1133
get_alternateText method, Image client controls, 300
get_argument method
Button client control, 326
onBubbleEvent method, 1364
GetAsyncPostBackControlIDs method, PageRequestManager, 1025, 1131
GetAsyncPostBackTimeout method, PageRequestManager, 1026–1027
getAttribute method
CustomTable client control, 394
TypeDescriptor class, 376–377
_get_attributes, TypeDescriptor class, 350
GetAuthors Web method
defined, 1417
displaying data records with ListView, 1421
getBaseMethod function, JavaScript OOP and type reflection extensions, 110–113
getBaseType method, JavaScript OOP and type reflection extensions, 100–102
getBehaviorByName method, Behavior class static methods, 674
getBehaviorByType method, Behavior class static methods, 675
getBehaviors method, Behavior class static methods, 674–675
get_bindings method, 1340
get_body method
beginRequest event, 1103
initializeRequest event, 1099
WebRequest class, 459
GetBooks web method
defined, 1417
displaying data records with ListView, 1422
getBounds method, DomElement methods, 175
get_canMoveNext property, DataControl class, 1352
get_canMovePrevious property, DataControl class, 1352–1353
GetChildUpdatePanelIDs method, page postback, 1133–1134

GetClientProxyScript method, ClientProxyGenerator class, 634–636
get_command method, Button client control, 326–327
get_command source method, GridViewCommandEventArgs class, 343
get_commandName method, 1364
getComponents method
_Application class methods, 242
IContainer class, 238
MarkupContext class, 1270
GetControlIDsFromList method, PageRequestManager, 1025–1026, 1131–1132
GetCurrent method, ScriptManager, 741
get_data method
DataControl class, 1353
developing custom data control, 1366
displaying data records with ListView, 1420
render method, CustomTable control, 1388
get_dataContext method, DataControl class, 1358
get_dataIndex method, DataControl class, 1356
get_dataItem method, DataControl class, 1357–1358
get_default failed callback method, WebServiceProxy class, 536
get_default succeeded callback method, WebServiceProxy class, 536
_getDefaultNamespaces method, 1282, 1283
get_direction method, 1340
get_element method
Behavior class, 669
Control class, 283
CustomTable client control, 394
getElementById method
DomElement, 161–166
_doPostBack method, 1079
getElementsByTagName method, processDocument, 1274
_getEvent method, Sys.EventHandlerList class, 133–134
get_eventHandlerList method
beginRequest event, 1099
implementing pageLoaded event, 1053
initializeRequest event, 1091
_get_eventHandlerList method
_pageLoaded method, 1050–1051
WebRequestManager class, 470

get_eventHandlerList method, page postback, 1186

_get_events, TypeDescriptor class, 364–368

getEvents method, initializeObject method of xml-script, 1298, 1304–1305

get_events method
behaviors, 665–666
component development, 271–272
Monitor class implementing, 226
ShoppingCart class, 155
WebRequestExecutor class, 461

getHandler method
client-side page postbacks, 1186
_onFormSubmit method, 1087, 1089
_pageLoaded method, 1050–1051
ScriptHandlerFactory, 571, 573
Sys.EventHandlerList class, 135–138

get_headers method
initializeRequest event, 1098
WebRequest class, 492
WebRequestExecutor class, 460

get_height method, Image client controls, 299

get_httpVerb method, WebRequest class, 458

get_id method
behaviors, 666, 671
controls, 283–284
INotifyPropertyChanged interface, 233

get_imageURI method, Image client controls, 299

get_imageURL method, Image client controls, 307–308

get_index method, onBubbleEvent method, 1364

getInstance method
beginRequest event, 1103
executing application-specific logic, 1055–1062
initializeRequest event, 1096
PageRequestManager, 1034, 1036–1037
_ScriptLoader class, 1203

getInterfaces method, JavaScript OOP and type reflection extensions, 92–94

get_isUpdating method, behaviors, 666

getItem method
DataControl class, 1362
get_dataItem method, 1357

getItemElement method, ListView control, 1450

get_length method, DataControl class, 1355–1356

_getLoadedScripts method, _ScriptLoader class, 1205

getLocation method, DomElement class, 171–172

_get_methods, TypeDescriptor class, 358–364

get_mouseOverCallback method, Image client controls, 308

get_mouseOverImageURL methods, Image client controls, 308

get_name method, Behavior class, 670–671

getName method, JavaScript OOP and type reflection extensions, 83–84

getNamedItem method
parseFromMarkup, 1286, 1376
TemplateField custom template, 1382

get_navigateURL property, HyperLink client controls, 315

getNodeName method
initializeObject method, 1306
invoking from _getTagType method, 1279

get_object method, WebRequestExecutor class, 466–467

_getPageLoaded method, PageRequestManager, 1246–1247

_getPageLoadedEventArgs method, page load events, 1051, 1054–1055

_getPageLoadingEventArgs method, page postback, 1186–1187, 1233–1234

get_panelsCreated method, pageLoadedHandler, 1062, 1065–1067

get_panelsDeleting method, 1224, 1236, 1241, 1244

get_panelsUpdated method, 1062, 1065–1066

get_panelsUpdating method, 1224, 1236, 1240, 1244

get_parent method, Control class, 285

get_path, WebServiceProxy class, 537

GetPostBackControlIDs method, PageRequestManager, 1026, 1132

get_postBackElement method, 1097

_getPostBackSettings method, 1073–1076, 1079

_get_properties, TypeDescriptor class, 351–358

getProperties method, initializeObject method, 1298

_getProperties method, initializeObject method, 1306

getProperty method
CustomTable client control, 393
TypeDescriptor class, 374–376, 451

getPropertyType method
invoking from evaluateIn method, 1321–1322
TypeDescriptor class, 384–385

GetRefreshingUpdatePanelIDs method, page postback, 1134

GetRender method, RenderChildren method, 1114–1115

get_request method
beginRequest event, 1103
initializeRequest event, 1097

get_responseAvailable method
WebRequestExecutor class, 464–465
XMLHttpExecutor, 479

get_responseData method
client-side page postbacks, 1176
WebRequestExecutor class, 465, 494
XMLHttpExecutor, 483

getResponseHeader method
WebRequestExecutor class, 467–468
XMLHttpExecutor, 482–483
XMLHttpRequest, 7

getRootNamespaces, JavaScript OOP and type reflection extensions, 123–124

get_row method, GridView class, 343

get_rowIndex method, GridViewRow control, 339

GetSchema method, IXmlSerializable interface, 839

GetScript method
ScriptComponentDescriptor class, 720–724
ScriptDescriptor class, 716–717

GetScriptDescriptors method
AmazonSearchScriptControl, 795–796
custom extender control, 755–757
HtmlGeneratorScriptControl, 808–809
IExtenderControl interface, 709
IScriptControl interface, 713

GetScriptReferences method
AmazonSearchScriptControl, 796
custom extender control, 755
HtmlGeneratorScriptControl, 809
IExtenderControl interface, 710
IScriptControl interface, 713–714

get_selectedValue method, displaying data records with ListView, 1422

get_shoppingCartItems, ShoppingCartItem class, 143

_getSourceValue method, 1322

get_started method
WebRequestExecutor class, 464
XMLHttpExecutor, 479

get_statusCode method
client-side page postbacks, 1175
WebRequestExecutor class, 466, 494
XMLHttpExecutor, 484

get_statusText method
WebRequestExecutor class, 466
XMLHttpExecutor, 484

_getTagType method
invoking with parseNode method, 1278
processing xml-script XML document, 1279–1281

get_target method, Action class, 1339

getter/setter methods
AspNetAjaxAmazonSearch client control, 786–787
HtmlGenerator client control, 801–802

get_text method, Label client controls, 292–293

get_timedOut method, XMLHttpExecutor, 478

get_timeOut method
initializeRequest event, 1098
WebRequest class, 459
WebRequestExecutor class, 465, 494
WebServiceProxy class, 535–536

GetType method, object types, 38–39

getTypeDescriptor method
initializeObject method, 1298
TypeDescriptor class, 369–370, 1287

GetUpdatePanelIDsFromList method, PageRequestManager, 1133

get_url method
initializeRequest event, 1098
WebRequest class, 458

get_visibilityMode method, Control class, 286

get_visible method, Control class, 286

get_WatermarkText method, 702

get_webRequest method, WebRequestExecutor class, 463–464

get_width method, Image client controls, 299

get_xml method
WebRequestExecutor class, 466
XMLHttpExecutor, 484–485

global markup context
creating, 1272–1273
defined, 1268
processDocumentScripts invoking open method on, 1276

global namespaces
compared with local, 123
_rootNamespaces array, 87

Google Suggest, 1–2

GridView client control, 344–348
as composite control, 328
constructor, 331
example of page using, 346–347
metadata information and, 349
onBubbleEvent, 332–337
overview, 330–331
GridView server control. *See* MasterDetailControl
server control
GridViewCommandEventArgs class
constructor, 342–343
descriptor for, 343–344
get_command source method, 343
get_row method of, 343
overview, 341–342
GridViewCommandEventArgs.js file, 341–342
GridView.js file, 330, 344–348
GridViewRow control
constructor, 339
descriptor property, 341
onBubbleEvent, 339–340
overview, 334
GridViewRow.js file, 337–338

H

HandlerWrapper, 582–583
headers
HTTP messages, 520
SOAP messages, 521
WebRequest class, 460
headerText property, custom template,
1381–1382
height property, Image client controls, 299–300
HelperMethods class, ScriptComponentDescriptor
class, 725–726
hiddenField string, 1180
hiddenFieldNodes array, 1188
hierarchical path, XPath, 955
HTML
AJAX-enabled components and, 1–2
page postback and, 1099–1100
htmlEncode method, Label client controls,
291–292
HtmlForm server control, 1127–1132
HtmlGenerator client control
code listing, 798–801
generateHtml method, 802–803
properties, 801–802
XmlBridgeTransformer, 826–827

HtmlGeneratorScriptControl server control
code listing, 803–807
CreateControlStyle method, 808
GetScriptDescriptors method, 808–809
GetScriptReferences method, 809
properties, 807
state management methods, 809–811
HTTP handler factories
HandlerWrapper, 582–583
RestHandler replica, 577–582
RestHandlerFactory, 574–577
ScriptHandlerFactory, 571–574
ScriptModule, 583–591
using replicas of, 593–595
WebServiceHandlerFactory, 572–573
HTTP modules
overview, 584
ScriptModule, 583–591
HTTP request messages
client-side code and, 524
SOAP and, 518–521
HTTP response messages
client-side code and, 524
SOAP and, 519–521
HTTP verb, 458–459
HttpApplication object, 24
HttpBrowserCapabilities, 302
HyperLink client controls
add_click method, 316–317
constructor, 314
descriptor property, 318
dispose method, 318
example using, 319–321
initialize method, 315–316
navigateURL property, 315
_onClick method, 317–318
overview, 314
prototype property, 315
remove_click method, 317

I

IAction interface
execute method, 1339–1341
overview, 1333
IBridgeResponseTransformer interface, 819–820
IContainer class component, 238–239
ICustomTypeDescriptor class, 403–405
data row implementing, 451
getProperty method and, 375

methods, 403–404
page using DataRow type, 404–405
ICustomTypeProvider interface, 1288
id methods
behaviors, 671–672
components, 269–270
IData interface, 1360
idHTML attribute, DOM elements, 161
IDisposable interface, 220–224, 235
IE4, event propagation model, 202
IExtenderControl interface, 709–710
IHttpHandlerFactory interface, 571
IHttpModule interface, 584
IIS, ISAPI extension and, 568–569
Image class, AWSECommerceService, 775
Image client controls
alt property (alternate text), 300
constructor, 298
example using, 300–302
height property, 299–300
imageURI, 299
overview of, 297–298
prototype property, 298
width property, 299
Image client controls, extending
constructor, 306–307
dispose method, 312
duration property, 309
example using, 312–314
imageURL methods, 307–308
initialize method, 311–312
mouseOutCallback method, 309
mouseOverCallback method, 308
mouseOverImageURL methods, 308
overview of, 302–306
prototype property, 307
transition property, 310–311
image DOM element, 297
Image server controls, 297
ImageProvider, DOM extensions, 185
imageURI property, Image client controls, 299
imageURL methods, Image client controls, 307–308
imperative approach, proxy classes, 618–620
imperative updates, UpdatePanel, 878–881
implementsInterface function, JavaScript OOP and type reflection extensions, 113–118
INamingContainer interface, 891, 905–906
indexOf, array types, 34–35
inheritance

inheritsFrom function, 118–120
JavaScript OOP and type reflection extensions, 96–100
resolveInheritance method, 103–104
inheritsFrom function, JavaScript OOP and type reflection extensions, 118–120
init events
Application class, 258–259
application lifecycle and, 257
handling, 979–980
Init method
IHttpModule interface, 584
ScriptModule, 586–587
_initHandler method, 1273
initialization phase, application lifecycle, 257
initialize method
Application class, 246
AspNetAjaxAmazonSearch client control, 787
Behavior class, 673
BehaviorBase class, 681–682
behaviors, 664
BindingBase class, 1324–1325
Button client control, 327
ClickBehavior class, 677–678
component development, 267–269
HyperLink client controls, 315–316
Image client controls, 311–312
initializeObject method, 1306
ITemplate interface, 1373
ListView control, 1452–1454
PageRequestManager, 1035–1036
ShoppingCart class, 155
ShoppingCartItem class, 143
TextBoxWatermarkBehavior class, 688–691
UpdatePanel, 998
UpdatePanelTrigger, 1000, 1004–1011
UpdatePanelTriggerCollection, 998–1000
XsltBridgeTransformer, 848
initializeBase method, JavaScript OOP and type reflection extensions, 102–103
InitializeDataCell method, 937–938
_initializeInternal method, PageRequestManager, 1042–1043
initializeObject method, 1287–1315
accessing attributes collection, 1298–1299
accessing properties collection, 1299–1300
_addEventName, 1305
addReference method, 1299
call method, 1301, 1306–1307, 1313
example of implementing, 1288–1293

initializeObject method (continued)
findElement method, 1300–1301
getEvents method, 1298, 1304–1305
getNodeName method, 1306
getProperties method, 1298
_getProperties method, 1306
getTypeDescriptor method, 1298
implementing, 1293–1298
initialize method, 1306
initializing binding object, 1318–1319
myArrayProperty, 1301–1302
myEnumProperty, 1302
overview, 1287
parse method, 1302–1303
parseFromMarkup method invoking,
    1284–1287, 1338–1339
parseNode method, 1312–1313
parseNodes method, 1308, 1313, 1315
set_eventSource method, 1314
setting value of property, 1303
toUpperCase method, 1314
TypeDescriptor class, 1287–1288
**_initializePageRequestManagerInstance
    method, 1034**
initializeRequest event, PageRequestManager
overview, 1090–1092
using, 1092–1099
InitializeRequestEventArgs class
initializeRequest event, 1097–1099
overview, 1091–1092
**initializeRequestHandler JavaScript function,
    1097–1099**
InitRecursive method
life cycle phase, 971–972
page postbacks, 1103–1105
**INotifyDisposing interface, 224–228, 235,
    272–280**
INotifyPropertyChange interface, 235
INotifyPropertyChanged interface, 228–235, 272
**input box methods, in client-server
    communication example, 509–510**
<input> element, WSDL documents, 516
insert, array types, 35
**Insert method, adding new element to tree
    hierarchy, 962**
insertCell method, TypeDescriptor class, 364
**insertRow method, TypeDescriptor class,
    357–358**
instance methods, Behavior class, 672–674
instance methods, DomEvent class

overview, 198
preventDefault method, 198–201
stopPropagation method, 201–203
instantiation
application lifecycle phases, 257
behaviors, 663
interface implementation patterns, C#, 711
interfaces
defining, 90
extender controls, 709–710
getInterfaces method, 92–94
IAction, 1333, 1339–1341
IBridgeResponseTransformer, 819–820
ICustomTypeProvider, 1288
IData, 1360
IDisposable, 220–224
IDisposable interface, 235
IExtenderControl, 709–710
IHttpHandlerFactory, 571
IHttpModule, 584
implementsInterface function, 113–118
INamingContainer, 891, 905–906
INotifyDisposing, 224–228, 272–280
INotifyDisposing interface, 235
INotifyPropertyChange interface, 235
INotifyPropertyChanged, 228–235, 272
IPostBackDataHandler, 1109
IScriptControl, 713–714
isInterface function, 95–96
ITask, 1429–1430
ITemplate, 1373–1374
IXmlSerializable. See IXmlSerializable interface
overview, 220
registerInterface method, 89–92
script controls, 713–714
InvalidOperation method, errors, 1256
**InvalidOperationException, exception types, 66,
    1255–1264**
Invert transformer, 1328–1329
Invoke method, transformers, 819
**invoke method, WebServiceProxy class,
    537–538, 539–542**
invokeMethod method
CustomTable client control, 394
InvokeMethodAction invoking, 1342
TypeDescriptor class, 382–384
InvokeMethodAction, Action class, 1342–1344
invoking Web requests, 462–463
**invokingRequestCallback function, in client-
    server communication example, 503–506**

IPostBackDataHandler, 1109
ISAPI extension, 568–569
isClass method, JavaScript OOP and type reflection extensions, 84–85
IScriptControl interface, 713–714
IsEmpty method, StringBuilder class, 388
isEnum method, JavaScript OOP and type reflection extensions, 129
isFlags method, JavaScript OOP and type reflection extensions, 129–130
isImplementedBy function, JavaScript OOP and type reflection extensions, 121–123
isInterface function, JavaScript OOP and type reflection extensions, 95–96
isNamespace method, JavaScript OOP and type reflection extensions, 88
isScriptLoaded method, ScriptLoader class, 1204
ITask interface, 1429–1430
ItemAttributes class, AWSECommerceService, 776
itemClass property, ListView styles, 1446
Item/Items classes, AWSECommerceService, 775
ITemplate interface, 1373–1374
ItemSearch class, AWSECommerceService, 774
ItemSearch method, AWSECommerceService, 774–781
ItemSearchRequest class, AWSECommerceService, 774
ItemSearchResponse class, AWSECommerceService, 775
itemTemplate property, ListView control, 1448–1449
itemTemplateParentElementId property, ListView control, 1409–1417, 1451–1452
IXmlSerializable interface, 839–848
   AmazonSearch3.asbx code listing, 847
   AmazonSearch3.aspx code listing, 847–848
   AmazonService3.cs code listing, 844–847
   ResultsSchema method, 842–844
   WriteXml method, 842

J

JavaScript
   AJAX-enabled components and, 1–2
   Manager constructors, 98
JSON (JavaScript Object Notification), 21–24
   AJAX-enabled components and, 2
   arrays, 21

   code listing, 22–23
   null, true, and false values, 21–22
   numbers, 21–22
   objects, 21
   REST requests for ScriptHandlerFactory, 573
   REST requests processed by RestHandlerFactory, 574–577
   string specification in, 725
   strings, 21–22
   WebServiceProxy class and, 535
JSON/XML Serializer, AJAX engine components, 3

K

Key, DOM extensions, 176–177
key parameter, getProperty method, 375–376
keyboards, DOM Key enumeration, 176–177
keypress events, _onKeyPress method, 695

L

Label client controls
   constructor, 291
   descriptor property, 294
   example using, 295–297
   htmlEnclode method, 291–292
   overview, 291
   prototype property, 294
   text property, 292–293
layoutTemplate property, ListView control, 1449
leftButton value, MouseButton class, 176
ListBox server control. *See MasterDetailControl3 server control*
ListView control, 1401–1472
   applying styles, 1423–1424
   constructor, 1443–1444
   descriptor property, 1472
   displaying data records, 1417–1422
   DOM template elements and, 1409–1417
   example of, 1405–1409
   findItemTemplateParentCallback method, 1465–1471
   getItemElement method, 1450
   implementing, 1443
   initialize method, 1452–1454
   ITask interface, 1429–1430
   itemTemplateParentElementId property, 1451–1452
   ListView RenderTask class, 1434–1442

ListView control (continued)
  _onGotFocus method, 1454
  _onItemClick method, 1463–1465
  _onItemFocus method, 1463
  _onkeyDown method, 1456–1458
  overview of, 1401–1405
  render method, 1458–1463
  renderComplete event, 1452
  _renderTaskComplete method, 1471
  set_dataIndex method, 1450–1451
  setFocus method, 1455–1456
  style properties, 1444–1447
  table rows and columns used with, 1424–1429
  _TaskManager, 1430–1434
  template properties, 1447–1450
ListView RenderTask class, ListView control, 1434–1442
load event, Application class, 259
load phase, application lifecycle, 258
Load Post Data phase, page postbacks, 1105–1112
_loadHandler method, _Application class, 245–246
LoadPostData method
  PageRequestManager class, 1110–1112
  ScriptManager class, 1109
LoadRecursive method, 995–997
loadScripts method, _ScriptLoader class, 1205–1206
LoadScriptsBeforeUI property, ScriptManager class, 740
_loadScriptsInternal method, _ScriptLoader class, 1207–1209
LoadScrollPosition phase, page postbacks, 1101–1103
LoadViewState method
  BaseMasterDetailControl, 900
  HtmlGeneratorScriptControl, 810
local markup context, 1267–1272
local namespaces, 123
localeFormat method, date types, 38
location path, XPath, 955
logic, code reuse, 660

M

Manager constructors, in JavaScript and C#, 98
MarkupContext class, 1267–1272
  addComponent method of, 1268–1269
  ASP.NET AJAX, 1267–1272

close method, 1271
constructor of, 1268
createGlobalContext method, 1272–1273
createInstance method, 1378
createLocalContext method, 1272, 1378
findComponent method, 1269, 1271
findElement method, 1270
getComponents method, 1270
information contained in, 1267
__initHandler method, 1273
open method, 1272
_pendingReferences collection, 1270–1272
TemplateField custom template, 1382
types of, 1268
MarkupParser class, 1378
master pages, UpdatePanel server control, 871–874
master server control
  CreateMaster method, 908
  GridView as, 911
  update conditions, 893
Master_DataBound method
  MasterDetailControl server control, 915–916
  MasterDetailControl2 server control, 923–924
master/detail forms, 881–882. *See also* **BaseMasterDetailControl server control**
MasterDetailContainer
  ControlStyle method, 896
  derived, from TableCell, 891
MasterDetailControl server control
  code listing, 911–913
  CreateBaseDataBoundControlMaster, overriding, 913
  properties, 916
  RegisterMasterEventHandlers method, 914
  SelectedIndex property, 914–916
  using in Web page, 916–921
MasterDetailControl2 server control
  code listing, 921–923
  CreateBaseDataBoundControlMaster, 923
  example using, 924–927
  Master_DataBound method, 923–924
  Master_SelectedIndexChanged, 923
  properties, 924
  RegisterMasterEventHandlers method, 923
MasterDetailControl3 server control
  code listing, 927–928
  example using, 928–930
MasterDetailControl4 server control, 930–931
MasterDetailField data control

appearance properties, 939–940
BoundField, extending, 932
code listing, 933–937
DataBinding event, handling, 938–939
example using, 940–945
ExtractValuesFromCell method, 939
InitializeDataCell method, overriding, 937–938
overview, 931–932
Master_ResetSelectedValue method, MasterDetailControl server control, 915
Master_SelectedIndexChanged
MasterDetailControl server control, 914–915
MasterDetailControl2 server control, 923
_matchesParentIDInList helper method, PageRequestManage, 1073
Math class, Divide method, 565–567
message box methods, in client-server communication example, 509–510
<message> element
in custom composite user control, 954
WSDL documents, 515–516
MessageBoxStyle enumerators, in client-server communication example, 508
metadata information. See also TypeDescriptor class
dynamic injection with type description, 399–400
exposed by descriptor static property of a type, 371–372
methods for inspecting, 349
methods
calls. See call methods
characteristics of, 178
JavaScript Function type, 79
.NET class, 177
overriding inherited, 699
page methods, 564, 583, 605–607
protected virtual methods, 900
remote method invocation, 600
ways for client-side code to invoke server side methods, 570
WSDL documents, 518
_methods, TypeDescriptor class, 358–364
Microsoft ASP.NET Futures, 297
middleButton value, MouseButton class, 176
Monitor.js file, 220–223
MouseButton class, 176
mousedowncb method, Mover class, 213–214
mousemovecb method, Mover class, 215

mouseOutCallback method, Image client controls, 309
mouseOverCallback method, Image client controls, 308
mouseOverImageURL methods, Image client controls, 308
mouseupcb method, Mover class, 214–215
moveNext method, DataControl class, 1362–1363
movePrevious method, DataControl class, 1363–1364
Mover class
addContent method, 213
defining and registering, 184
enhancements to, 209–213
mousedowncb method, 213–214
mousemovecb method, 215
mouseupcb method, 214–215
myArrayProperty, initializeObject method of xml-script, 1301–1302
myEnumProperty, initializeObject method of xml-script, 1302

N

name methods, Behavior class, 669–671
name property, ArgumentException, 54
name=value format, browsers following, 491
names, custom exception, 71
namespaces
Delegates namespace, 183
event programming, 141
getRootNamespaces method, 123–124
global, 87
isNamespace method, 88
Preview.UI namespace, 291
registerNamespace method, 85–87
navigateURL property, HyperLink client controls, 315
.NET class, 177
.NET Framework
base types, 27
benefits of, 24
component development, 219
delegates, 178
exception types, 53
generics, 733
interfaces, 220
methods for inspecting metadata, 349
programming capabilities, 77

Netscape Navigator 4, 202
NetworkRequestEventArgs class,
        WebRequestManager class, 473–474
new, JavaScript operator, 1286
NotImplementedException, exception types,
        66–68
null values, JSON, 21–22
numbers, JSON, 21–22

O

object composition, 763, 1306
object oriented programming. *See* OOP and type
        reflection extensions
objects
    ASP.NET AJAX, 38–39
    JSON, 21
    Page objects. *See* Page objects
OfferListing class, AWSECommerceService, 776
Offer/Offers classes,
        AWSECommerceService, 776
offsetLeft property, DOM elements, 171
offsetParent property, DOM elements, 171
offsetTop property, DOM elements, 171
_onBlur method, TextBoxWatermarkBehavior
        class, 693–694
onBubbleEvent method
    Control base class, 289
    DataControl class, 1364–1365
    GridView control, 332–337, 345
    GridViewRow control, 339–340
    inherited from Control class, 330
_onClick method
    Button client control, 328–329
    HyperLink client controls, 317–318
onComplete function
    as event handler for completed event of
        WebRequest class, 545–549
    Web service errors and, 553–554
onDataChanged method, DataControl class, 1357
onFailure function, Web service errors and, 553,
        559–560
_onFocus method, TextBoxWatermarkBehavior
        class, 691–692
_onFormSubmit method
    _doPostBack method and, 1081
    overview, 1081–1090
    page postbacks via Submit button, 1043, 1051
    PageRequestManager, 1171
_onFormSubmitCompleted method, 1172–1199

arrayDeclarationNodes array, 1189
calling _findText method, 1177–1178
calling _updateControls method, 1185
checking formActionNode local variable, 1187
checking type property, 1179–1184
client-side page postbacks, 1193–1199
_dataItems collection, 1185–1186
expandoScript string, 1189
get_eventHandlerList method, 1186
getHandler method, 1186
_getPageLoadingEventArgs method, 1186
hiddenFieldNodes array, 1188
invoking _endPostBack method, 1179
iterating through objects in updatePanelNodes
        array, 1187–1188
PageRequestManager, 1172–1176
of PageRequestManager, 1193–1198,
        1219–1222
_registerDisposeScript method, 1187–1188
_ScriptLoader class, 1189–1192
_splitNodeIntoArray method, 1185
updating UpdatePanel server controls, 1184
_onGotFocus method, ListView control, 1454
OnInit method
    extender control, 757
    PageRequestManager, 975–977, 1104–1105
    ScriptManager, 741, 972–975, 1103
    UpDatePanel, 980–982
_onItemClick method, ListView control,
        1463–1465
_onItemFocus method, ListView control, 1463
_onkeyDown method, ListView control,
        1456–1458
_onKeyPress method,
        TextBoxWatermarkBehavior class, 695
OnLoad method
    extender control, 758–759
    page lifecycle and, 995
_onNextButtonClick method,
        AspNetAjaxAmazonSearch client
        control, 789
OnPostAcquireRequestState method,
        ScriptModule, 586
OnPreRender method
    Control class, 712
    extender control, 760–761
    PageRequestManager, 1113–1114
_onPreviousButtonClick method,
        AspNetAjaxAmazonSearch client
        control, 788

**_onPropertyChanged method,
TextBoxWatermarkBehavior class,
696–697**
**_onReadyStateChange method,
XMLHttpExecutor, 476–477**
**onreadystatechange property,
XMLHttpRequest, 6**
**_onSearchButtonClick method,
AspNetAjaxAmazonSearch client control,
788**
**onShoppingcartInitialized method, ShoppingCart
class, 155–156**
**onShoppingCartItemAdded method,
ShoppingCart class, 158**
**onShoppingCartItemAdding method,
ShoppingCart class, 158**
_onsubmit method, postback methods, 1081
**_onSubmit method, TextBoxWatermarkBehavior
class, 700**
onSubmit string, checking type property, 1180
**_onSuccess method, AspNetAjaxAmazonSearch
client control, 789**
_onTimeout method
Task Manager, 1432–1433
XMLHttpExecutor, 477–478
OOP and type reflection extensions, 77–130
callBaseMethod method, 104–110
classes, 79–80
Function type and properties, 78–79
getBaseMethod function, 110–113
getBaseType method, 100–102
getInterfaces method, 92–94
getName method, 83–84
getRootNamespaces, 123–124
implementsInterface function, 113–118
inheritance, 96–100
inheritsFrom function, 118–120
initializeBase method, 102–103
isClass method, 84–85
isEnum method, 129
isFlags method, 129–130
isImplementedBy function, 121–123
isInterface function, 95–96
isNamespace method, 88
overview, 77
parse method, 125–127
registerClass, 81–83
registerEnum method, 127–128
registerInterface method, 89–92
registerNamespace method, 85–87

resolveInheritance method, 103–104
summary, 130
Type class, 80
open method
createInstance method and, 1378
MarkupContext class, 1272
processDocumentScripts invoking, 1276
XMLHttpRequest, 6
**<operation> element, WSDL documents,
516–517**
_originalDoPostBack method, 1081
<output> element, WSDL documents, 516
overrideMimeType property, XMLHttpRequest, 7
overriding, inherited methods, 699
**owner property, UpdatePanelTriggerCollection,
1002–1003**

P

Page class
.aspx files and, 966
Init life cycle phase, 971–972
ProcessRequest method, 969–971
redendering phase, 1019
page lifecycle
benefits of ASP.NET, 24
Init life cycle phase, 971–972
LoadRecursive method, 995
OnLoad method and, 995
partial page rendering, 969–971
redendering phase, 1019
page methods
invoking server side methods from client
side, 583
proxy classes associated with, 605–607
wrapper methods as, 564
Page objects
InitRecursive phase of, 1103
LoadScrollPosition phase of, 1101–1103
ProcessPostData method of, 1105–1108
RetrievePostData phase of, 1097–1101
page postbacks, asynchronous
enabling partial page rendering, 857–859
user controls, 945–955
page postbacks, asynchronous client-side
arrival of server response text, 1171–1192
beginRequest event, 1099–1100
beginRequest event, using, 1101–1104
_createPostBackSettings method, 1071–1072
_destroyTree method, 1201–1202, 1231–1233

page postbacks, asynchronous (continued)
_doPostBack method, 1077–1081
_endPostBack method, 1216–1222
endRequest event, 1247–1265
_findNearestElement method, 1072–1073
_getPageLoadingEventArgs method, 1233–1234
_getPostBackSettings method, 1073–1076
initializeRequest event, 1090–1099
_matchesParentIDInList method, 1073
_onFormSubmit method, 1081–1090
_onFormSubmitCompleted method, 1193–1199
pageLoaded event, 1245–1247
_pageLoaded method, 1215–1216
pageLoading event, 1223–1228
PageRequestManager and, 1071
registerDisposeScript method, 1201
_ScriptLoader class. See _ScriptLoader class
_ScriptLoaderTask class, 1211–1213
_scriptsLoadComplete method, 1213–1215
_updateControls method, 1228–1230
_updatePanel method, 1199–1200,
    1230–1231
using pageLoading event, 1234–1244
page postbacks, asynchronous server side,
    1097–1170
EncodeString method, 1115–1116, 1156–1161
GetAllUpdatePanelIDs method, 1132–1133
GetChildUpdatePanelIDs method, 1133–1134
GetRefreshingUpdatePanelIDs method, 1134
InitRecursive phase, 1103–1105
Load Post Data phase, 1105–1112
LoadScrollPosition phase, 1101–1103
PreRender phase, 1113–1114
ProcessFocus method, 1152–1154
ProcessScriptRegistration method, 1138–1152
ProcessUpatePanels method, 1121–1127
Raise Post Data Changed Event phase,
    1112–1113
Render children method of Control class,
    1114–1115
Render method of Control class, 1114
RenderControl method of HtmlForm,
    1127–1132
RenderDataItems method, 1134–1138, 1157
RenderPageCallback method, 1116–1121,
    1155–1156
RetrievePostData phase, 1097–1101
what text looks like, 1161–1170
page postbacks, synchronous, 1019
PageHandlerFactory, 571

pageLoad function, 502–503
adding DataRow objects to DataTable, 454
beginRequest event, 1102–1103
Button client controls, 336
in client-server communication example, 496
CustomTable client control, 398–399
initializeRequest event, 1091–1099
instantiating instance of Control base
    class, 367
instantiating ShoppingCart objects, 151
overview of, 27–28
pageLoad method
displaying data records with ListView, 1420
using pageLoading event, 1234–1244
Page_Load method, beginRequest event, 1104
pageLoad method, ListView control,
    1423–1424
pageLoaded event, 1055–1071
client-side page postbacks, 1245–1247
Delegates.js JavaScript file, 1068–1070
at end of instantiation/initialization
    process, 1055
executing application-specific logic with,
    1055–1062
invoking createDelegate method, 1055
overview of, 1052–1055
pageLoadedHandler, 1062–1067
Render method of ScriptManager server control,
    1070–1071
_pageLoaded method
client-side page postbacks, 1215–1216
implementing pageLoaded event, 1053
PageRequestManager, 1050–1052, 1245–1246
PageLoadedEventArgs class, 1053–1055
pageLoadedHandler function, 1062–1067
_pageLoadedInitialLoad method,
    PageRequestManager, 1044, 1050
pageLoading event, client-side page postbacks,
    1223–1228, 1234–1244
PageMethods proxy object, 606
Page_PreLoad method, extender control,
    757–758
Page_PreRenderComplete method,
    ScriptManager class, 741–742
pageRedirect string, 1183
PageRequestManager, client-side, 1033–1104
beginRequest event, 1099–1104
constructor, 1037–1039
_createPostBackSettings helper method,
    1071–1072

_createPostBackSettings method,
    1071–1072, 1079
_destroyTree method, 1201–1202
_doPostBack method, 1043–1044, 1077–1081
_endPostBack method, 1173, 1216–1222
_findNearestElement helper method,
    1072–1073
getInstance method, 1036–1037
_getPageLoaded method, 1246–1247
_getPageLoadingEventArgs method, 1233–1234
_getPostBackSettings helper method,
    1073–1076
_initialize method, 1035–1036
_initializeInternal method, 1042–1043
initializeRequest event, 1090–1092
initializeRequest event, using, 1092–1099
making asynchronous page postback, 1071
_matchesParentIDInList helper method, 1073
_onFormSubmit method, 1081–1090, 1172
_onFormSubmitCompleted method, 1193–1199,
    1219–1222
overview of, 1033–1034
page postback via _doPostBack function,
    1040–1042
page postback via Submit button, 1040–1042
pageLoaded event, 1052–1071
_pageLoaded method, 1050–1052, 1245–1246
_pageLoadedInitialLoad method, 1050
registerDisposeScript method, 1201
server response arriving on client-side, 1034
server-side vs. client side partial page
    rendering, 965
_uniqueIDToClientID method, 1049
_updateControls method, 1046–1049
_updatePanel method, 1199–1200
using pageLoading event, 1234–1244
PageRequestManager, server-side
EncodeString method, 1115–1116
focus-related methods, 1152–1153
GetAllUpdatePanelIDs method, 1132–1133
GetAsyncPostBackControlIDs method,
    1025, 1131
GetAsyncPostBackTimeout method, 1026–1027
GetChildUpdatePanelIDs method, 1133–1134
GetControlIDsFromList method, 1025–1026,
    1131–1132
GetPostBackControlIDs method, 1026, 1132
GetRefreshingUpdatePanelIDs method, 1134
GetUpdatePanelIDsFromList method, 1133
IsAsyncPostBackRequest method, 1103–1104

LoadPostData method, 1110–1112
LoadScrollPosition phase, 1101–1103
OnInit method, 975–977, 979, 1104–1105
OnPreRender method, 1113–1114
ProcessFocus method, 1154
ProcessScriptRegistration method, 1138–1152
ProcessUpatePanels method, 1121–1127
RegisterAsyncPostBackControl method,
    1012–1014
RegisterDataItem method, 1137
RegisterUpdatePanel method, 984
Render method, 1020
RenderDataItems method, 1134–1138, 1157
RenderFormCallback method, 1128–1129
RenderPageCallback method, 1116–1121,
    1155–1156
RenderPageRequestManagerScript method,
    1021–1024
RenderUpdatePanelIDsFromList method,
    1024–1025
script block arriving on client-side from,
    1033–1034
server-side vs. client side partial page
    rendering, 965
submitting data to server, 1099–1100
PageRequestManagerParserErrorException,
    1255
PageRequestManagerServerErrorException,
    1254–1255
PageRequestManagerTimeoutException, 1254
PageSize property, MasterDetailControl server
    control, 916
pageTitle string, checking type property, 1183
_panelsToRefreshIDs array, 1184–1185
panelsToRefreshIDs string, 1182
ParameterCountException, exception types,
    68–70
paramName property
ArgumentException, 54
ArgumentOutOfRangeException, 58
parent property, Control class, 336
parent/child pages, proxy classes and, 621–623
parse, array types, 36
parse method
Boolean types, 37
_getTagType method invoking, 1280
initializeObject method of xml-script,
    1302–1303
JavaScript OOP and type reflection extensions,
    125–127

parseFromMarkup method
Action class, 1338–1339
ASP.NET AJAX, 1284–1287
parseNode method invoking, 1278
processing xml-script XML document, 1284–1287
Template class, 1376–1377
TemplateField custom template, 1382–1383

parseNode method, processing xml-script XML document, 1278–1279

parseNodes method
createInstance method, 1378
initializeObject method, 1308, 1313, 1315
processDocumentScripts invoking, 1276
processing xml-script XML document, 1276–1277

partial page rendering
characteristics of, 857
data control. *See* MasterDetailField data control
disabling on content pages, 876
enabling, 857–859
master/detail forms and, 882
server-side vs. client side, 965–966
updates. *See* UpdatePanel
user controls. *See* user controls, partial-rendering enabled

partial page rendering, client-side
arrival of server response text, 1171–1192
beginRequest event, 1099–1100
beginRequest event, using, 1101–1104
compared with server-side, 965–966
_createPostBackSettings method, 1071–1072
_destroyTree method, 1201–1202, 1231–1233
_doPostBack method, 1077–1081
_endPostBack method, 1216–1222
endRequest event, 1247–1265
_findNearestElement method, 1072–1073
_getPageLoadingEventArgs method, 1233–1234
_getPostBackSettings method, 1073–1076
initializeRequest event, 1090–1099
_matchesParentIDInList method, 1073
_onFormSubmit method, 1081–1090
_onFormSubmitCompleted method, 1193–1199
pageLoaded event, 1245–1247
_pageLoaded method, 1215–1216
pageLoading event, 1223–1228
PageRequestManager. *See* PageRequestManager, client-side
PageRequestManager and, 1071
registerDisposeScript method, 1201

_ScriptLoader class. *See* _ScriptLoader class
_ScriptLoaderTask class, 1211–1213
_scriptsLoadComplete method, 1213–1215
_updateControls method, 1228–1230
_updatePanel method, 1199–1200, 1230–1231
using pageLoading event, 1234–1244

partial page rendering, server-side
add method of UpdatePanelTriggerCollection, 1003–1004
BaseMasterDetailControl. *See* BaseMasterDetailControl server control
BaseMasterDetailControl2. *See* BaseMasterDetailControl2 server control
compared with client-side, 965–966
composite server control for, 881–882
constructor of UpdatePanelTriggerCollection, 1001
CreateContents method of UpDatePanel, 984–987
custom UpdatePanelTrigger, 1014–1018
error handling, 978–979
Init event handling, 979–980
Initialize method of UpdatePanel, 998
Initialize method of UpdatePanelTrigger, 1000, 1004–1011
Initialize method of UpdatePanelTriggerCollection, 998–1000
InitRecursive method, 971–972
LoadRecursive method, 995–997
MasterDetailControl. *See* MasterDetailControl server control
MasterDetailControl2. *See* MasterDetailControl2 server control
MasterDetailControl3. *See* MasterDetailControl3 server control
MasterDetailControl4, 930–931
OnInit method of PageRequestManager, 975–977
OnInit method of ScriptManager, 972–975
OnInit method of UpDatePanel, 980–982
owner property of UpdatePanelTriggerCollection, 1002–1003
page lifecycle, 969–971
RegisterAsyncPostBackControl method of PageRequestManager, 1012–1014
RegisterAsyncPostBackControl method of ScriptManager, 1011–1012
RegisterPanel method of UpDatePanel, 982–983

RegisterUpdatePanel method of
PageRequestManager, 984
RegisterUpdatePanel method of
ScriptManager, 983
Render method of ScriptManager, 1020–1027
Render method of UpdatePanel, 1028–1029
rendering, 1019–1020
request processing, 966–969
subclasses of UpdatePanelTrigger, 1001
summary, 1029–1031
templated controls, 987–994
visiting partial-page-rendering enabled Web
page, 971
_partialUpdateBeginRequest method,
BehaviorBase class, 685
_partialUpdateEndRequest method,
BehaviorBase class, 685–686
_partialUpdateEndRequest method,
TextBoxWatermarkBehavior class,
698–700
_parts collection, StringBuilder class, 385,
387–388
path methods, WebServiceProxy class, 537
_pendingReferences collection
initializeObject method of xml-script, 1299
MarkupContext class, 1270–1272
processDocumentScripts invoking, 1276
performAction method
execute method invoking, 1340
InvokeMethodAction invoking, 1342
PostBackAction invoking, 1347
SetPropertyAction invoking, 1345
popStackFrame, error types, 45–52
code listing, 49–51
how it worked, 45–48
properties, 45
PopulateMethodInfos method,
ClientProxyGenerator class, 637
PopulateParameterInfos method,
ClientProxyGenerator class, 637–638
<port> element, WSDL documents, 517
<portType> element, WSDL documents, 516–517
PostAcquireRequestState method, ScriptModule,
586–589
PostBackAction, Action class, 1347–1348
postBackControlIDs, 1181
prepareChange method
DataControl class, 1350
deleteCurrentItem method, 1360
moveNext method, 1362–1363

set_data method, 1353
PreRender method, custom script control,
767–768
PreRender phase, page postbacks, 1113–1114
preventDefault method
DomEvent class instance methods, 198–201
_onFormSubmit method, 1089
PreviewScript.js, 1272
Preview.UI namespace, 291
Price class, AWSECommerceService, 776
processDocument method, processing xml-script
XML document, 1273–1275
processDocumentScripts method, 1274–1276
ProcessFocus method
EncodeString method calls triggered by, 1159
rendering page postbacks server side,
1152–1154
_processNamespaceURI method, 1281–1283
ProcessPostData method, Page objects,
1105–1108
ProcessRequest method, Page class, 969–971
ProcessScriptRegistration method, 1138–1152
EncodeString method triggered by, 1157–1158
internal collections of
ScriptRegistrationManager, 1139–1142
overview of, 1138–1139
script registration methods, 1142–1146
ScriptManager, 1146–1149
script-rendering with ScriptRegistrationManager,
1149–1152
ProcessUpatePanels method, 1121–1127
PageRequestManager, 1123–1124
RenderPageCallback method of, 1116–1117
RequiresUpdate method of UpdatePanel,
1124–1126
SetAsyncPostBackMode method of
UpdatePanel, 1126–1127
Update method of UpdatePanel, 1122
when to update, 1121–1122
Product.js file, 394–395
programming
declarative programming in ASP.NET, 25
.NET Framework programming capabilities, 77
properties
accessing properties collection, 1299–1300
AmazonSearchScriptControl server control,
794–795
appearance properties, 939–940
AspNetAjaxAmazonSearch client control,
786–787

properties (continued)
    BaseMasterDetailControl server control,
        903–904
    BaseMasterDetailControl2 server control, 910
    Behavior class, 668
    Component class, 351–352
    components, 727
    control states and, 898
    DomEvent class, 187–189
    getProperties method, 1298
    _getProperties method, 1306
    HtmlGenerator client control, 801–802
    HtmlGeneratorScriptControl server control, 807
    INotifyPropertyChanged interface, 228–233
    MasterDetailControl server control, 916
    MasterDetailControl2 server controls, 924
    OOP and type reflection extensions, 78–79
    popStackFrame, error types, 45
    Result/Results classes, 833–835
    ShoppingCartItem class, 141–144
    style properties, 1387, 1401–1402,
        1444–1447
    template properties, 1447–1450
    TypeDescriptor class, 351–358
    XMLHttpRequest class, 5–6
properties collection, 1299–1300
properties parameter
    create method of Component base class, 249,
        276–277, 662
    HyperLink client controls, 320
    in Image client control example, 301
    Image client controls, extending, 313–314
PropertyChangedEventArgs, 235
protected virtual methods, 900
prototype property
    Button client control, 325–326
    HyperLink client controls, 315
    Image client controls, 298
    Image client controls, extending, 307
    JavaScript Function type, 78
    Label client controls, 294
    Type class, 80
proxy classes, 597–657
    associated with custom classes, 607
    associated with page methods, 605–607
    associated with Web services, 600–605
    automatic generation of, 607–608
    client proxy REST requests, 576
    ClientProxyGenerator class. *See*
        ClientProxyGenerator class

    declarative approach, 608–618
    deriving from Sys.Net.WebServiceProxy
        class, 602
    EnablePageMethods, 626
    imperative approach, 618–620
    methods for creating, 777
    OnInit method, 626–627
    overview, 597–599
    Page_PreRenderComplete, 627
    parent/child pages, 621–623
    proxy objects acting as a proxy for remote
        objects, 599–600
    RestClientProxyHandler, 647–649
    ScriptManager replica, 624–625
    ServiceReference replica, 627–629
    Services collection replica, 625–626
    types of, 600
    using, 649–657
public methods
    ScriptComponentDescriptor class, 726–728
    wrapper methods as, 564

Q

queueCustomScriptTag method, _ScriptLoader
    class, 1204
queues, enqueue and dequeue array methods,
    31–33
queueScriptBlock method, _ScriptLoader class,
    1204
queueScriptReference method, _ScriptLoader
    class, 1205
QuoteString method, HelperMethods class, 725

R

Raise Post Data Changed Event phase, page
    postbacks, 1112–1113
raiseBubbleEvent method
    Control base class, 290
    in custom client control, 337
    inherited from Control class, 329–330
raiseLoad method, Application class, 256
RaisePostDataChangedEvent method
    Raise Post Data Changed Event phase,
        1112–1113
    ScriptManager class, 1109
raise_propertyChanged method,
    INotifyPropertyChanged interface, 233
raisePropertyChanged method

behaviors, 667–668
component development, 270–271
set_data method, 1354
triggerChangeEvents method, 1351
readLoadedScripts method, _ScriptLoader class, 1202–1203
ReadXml method, IXmlSerializable interface, 839
readyState property, XMLHttpRequest, 6
references parameter
create method of Component base class, 249, 277, 663
HyperLink client controls, 321
in Image client control example, 301–302
Image client controls, extending, 314
RegisterAsyncPostBackControl method
PageRequestManager, 1012–1014
ScriptManager, 1011–1012
registerClass method
defining classes before registering, 90–92
JavaScript OOP and type reflection extensions, 81–83
RegisterDataItem method
PageRequestManager, 1137–1138
ScriptManager, 1136–1137
RegisterDetailEventHandlers method, BaseMasterDetailControl2, 909
RegisterDisposeForDescriptor method, ScriptDescriptor class, 717
registerDisposeScript method, postback methods, 1187–1188, 1201
registerEnum method, JavaScript OOP and type reflection extensions, 127–128
RegisterExtenderControl method, ScriptManager class, 712, 740
_registerHandlerForFormSubmitEvent method, _initializeInternal method, 1043
_registerHandlerFormClickEvent method, _initializeInternal method, 1044
_registerHandlerForWindowLoadEvent method, _initializeInternal method, 1044
_registerHandlerForWindowUnloadEvent method, _initializeInternal method, 1044–1045
registering classes, JavaScript, 81–83
registerInterface method, JavaScript OOP and type reflection extensions, 89–92
RegisterMasterEventHandlers method
MasterDetailControl server control, 914
MasterDetailControl2 server control, 923
registerNamespace method, JavaScript OOP and type reflection extensions, 85–87

RegisterPanel method, UpDatePanel, 982–983
registerPartialUpdateEvents method, BehaviorBase class, 683–684
registerPropertyChanged method, TextBoxWatermarkBehavior class, 695–696
RegisterScriptControl method, ScriptManager class, 740
RegisterScriptDescriptors method, ScriptManager class, 744–746
RegisterUpdatePanel method
PageRequestManager, 984
ScriptManager, 983
ReleaseHandler method, ScriptHandlerFactory, 571
remote objects, proxy objects for, 599–600
remove, array types, 36
remove method, deleteCurrentItem method, 1360–1361
removeAt, array types, 37
remove_beginRequest method, 1099
remove_click method, HyperLink client controls, 317
remove_completed method, WebRequestExecutor class, 461
remove_completedRequest method, 471
removeComponent method
Application class, 241
IContainer class component, 238
removeCssClass method
Control base class, 288
DomElement methods, 167–169
remove_disposing method
behaviors, 667
INotifyDisposing interface, 224
Monitor class implementing, 227
removeHandler method
DomEvent class, 193–194
Sys.EventHandlerList class, 134–135
System.ComponentModel.EventHandlerList class, 131
remove_initializeRequest method, 1091
remove_invokingRequest method, 471
remove_pageLoaded method, 1053
remove_propertyChanged method
behaviors, 667
INotifyPropertyChanged interface, 229, 233
Render children method, page postback, 1114–1115

render method
CustomTable template data control, 1387–1390
developing custom data control, 1366
ListView control, 1458–1463
rendering page postbacks server side, 1114
ScriptManager, 1020–1027
of ScriptManager server control, 1070–1071
set_data method, 1354
UpdatePanel, 1028–1029

Render method
Control class, 1114
extender control, 761
script control, 768

RenderChildren method
Control class, 1114–1115
HtmlForm server control, 1128
UpdatePanel server control, 1130–1131, 1156

renderComplete event, ListView control, 1452

RenderContainer method,
BaseMasterDetailControl, 900

RenderContents method
AmazonSearchScriptControl, 796–798
BaseMasterDetailControl, 902–903

RenderControl method
HtmlForm, 1127–1132
RenderChildren method and, 1114–1115
RenderPageCallback method and, 1118

RenderDataItems method, page postback, 1134–
1138, 1157

Renderer, AJAX engine components, 3

RenderFormCallback method,
PageRequestManager, 1128–1129

rendering aspect, partial page rendering
overview of, 1019–1020
Render method of ScriptManager, 1020–1027
Render method of UpdatePanel, 1028–1029

RenderMethod, RenderPageCallback
method, 1117

RenderPageCallback method
EncodeString method calls triggered by,
1159–1161
OnPreRender method, 1113–1114
page postbacks server response, 1155–1156
rendering page postbacks server side,
1116–1121

_renderTaskComplete method, ListView
control, 1471

RenderUpdatePanelIDsFromList method,
PageRequestManager, 1024–1025

request messages, WSDL documents, 515–516

request processing, partial page rendering,
966–969

request processing pipeline, In ASP.NET,
587–588

RequiresUpdate method, UpdatePanel server,
1124–1126

resolveInheritance method, JavaScript OOP and
type reflection extensions, 103–104

ResolveScriptReference event, ScriptManager
class, 746–748

response messages, WSDL documents,
515–516

responseText property, XMLHttpRequest, 7

responseXML property, XMLHttpRequest, 7

REST method calls, 576

REST requests, JSON
ASP.NET AJAX framework supported, 576
RestHandlerFactory and, 574–576
ScriptHandlerFactory and, 573

RestClientProxyHandler, proxy classes,
647–649

RestHandlerFactory
CreateHandler method, 590–591
implementation of, 574–577
instantiating instances of, 572–573
replica of, 577–582

Result.cs file, 837

Result/Results classes
AmazonSearch2.aspx page code listing,
838–839
code listing, 835–836, 840–841
definition and annotation of, 832–835
implementing IXmlSerializable interface. See
IXmlSerializable interface
properties, 833–835
xsd.exe utility for generating, 837

ResultsSchema method, IXmlSerializable
interface, 842–844

RetrievePostData method, Page object, 1098,
1101

RetrievePostData phase, page postbacks,
1097–1101

return value types, WSDL documents, 515

revealTrans filter
exposing duration property, 309
exposing transition property, 310

rightButton value, MouseButton class, 176

_rootNamespaces array, 87

rowIndex property, GridViewRow control, 339

rows. See DataRow class

S

SaveViewState method
BaseMasterDetailControl, 899
HtmlGeneratorScriptControl, 810
scheduler, AJAX engine components, 3
script controls
AmazonSearchScriptControl server control. *See*
AmazonSearchScriptControl server control
extender controls compared with, 769–770
IScriptControl interface, 713–714
overview of, 708, 713
ScriptBehaviorDescriptor class, 730–732
ScriptComponentDescriptor class. *See*
ScriptComponentDescriptor class
ScriptControl base class, 714–716
ScriptControlDescriptor class, 730
ScriptDescriptor class, 716–717
ScriptManager class. *See* ScriptManager class
ScriptReference class, 732–733
ScriptReferenceCollection class, 733–734
summary, 771
why they are needed, 707–709
script controls, custom, 763–769
example using, 768–769
overview, 763–767
PreRender method, 767–768
Render method, 768
script HTML elements, 1274
ScriptBehaviorDescriptor class, 730–732
scriptBlock string, 1180
ScriptComponentDescriptor class
AppendScript method, 729–730
GetScript method, 720–724
HelperMethods class and, 725–726
public methods, 726–728
replica of, 717–720
ScriptControl base class, 714–716
ScriptControlDescriptor class, 730
ScriptControls collection, 740
ScriptDataItem class, 1137
ScriptDataItemCollection class, 1138
ScriptDescriptor class, 716–717
scriptDispose string, 1183
ScriptHandlerFactory, 571–574
_ScriptLoader class, 1202–1211
constructor, 1210
_createScriptElement method, 1209
getInstance method, 1203
_getLoadedScripts method, 1205

isScriptLoaded method, 1204
loadScripts method, 1205–1206
_loadScriptsInternal method, 1207–1209
queueCustomScriptTag method, 1204
queueScriptBlock method, 1204
queueScriptReference method, 1205
readLoadedScripts method, 1202–1203
_scriptLoaderHandler method, 1210–1211
server response to page postback,
1189–1191
_scriptLoaderHandler method, 1210–1211
_ScriptLoaderTask class
constructor method of, 1211
execute method, 1212–1213
_scriptLoadHandler method, 1213
_scriptsLoadComplete method, 1213–1215
_scriptLoadHandler method, 1213
ScriptManager class
AddScriptReferencesForScriptControls method,
743–744
CollectScripts method, 742–743
declarative approach to adding proxy classes,
608–618
ExtenderControls collection, 740
GetCurrent method, 741
imperative approach to adding proxy classes,
618–620
imperative approach to adding ServiceReference
object to Services collection, 618
implementing IPostBackDataHandler, 1109
LoadScriptsBeforeUI property, 740
OnInit method, 741, 972–975, 1103
OnLoad method, 997
Page_PreRenderComplete method, 741–742
parent/child pages and, 621–623
RegisterAsyncPostBackControl method,
1011–1012
RegisterAsyncPostBackTrigger class, 1009
RegisterDataItem method, 1136–1137
RegisterExtenderControl method, 740
RegisterScriptControl method, 740
RegisterScriptDescriptors method for extender
controls, 744–746
RegisterUpdatePanel method, 983
Render method, 1020–1027
replica, 624–625, 649–657, 734–739
ResolveScriptReference event, 746–748
ScriptControls collection, 740
Scripts collection property, 740
server control, 27–28

ScriptManager class (continued)
ServiceReference object added to Services collection, 608

ScriptManager server controls
BaseMasterDetailControl server control example. *See* BaseMasterDetailControl server control
master pages and content pages and, 874
partial page rendering and, 857
public registration methods of, 1146–1149
Render method of, 1070–1071
SetFocus method overloads of, 1152

ScriptManagerProxy server control, 621–623

ScriptModule, 583–591
.aspx file requests and, 583–584
bypassing ASP.NET request processing pipeline, 587–589
IHttpModule interface and, 584
Init method, 586–587
OnPostAcquireRequestState method, 586

ScriptReference class, 732–733

ScriptReferenceCollection class, 733–734

ScriptRegistrationManager class, 1142–1146
internal collections of current, 1139–1142
script registration methods, 1142–1146
script-rendering methods of, 1149–1152

Scripts collection property, ScriptManager class, 740

_scriptsLoadComplete method, page postback, 1213–1215

SelectedIndex property, MasterDetailControl server control, 914–916

selectedItemClass property, ListView control, 1446–1447

selectionChangedCallback function, ListView control, 1421–1422

send method, XMLHttpRequest, 7

separatorCssClass property, ListView control, 1447

separatorTemplate property, ListView control, 1449–1450

<sequences> element, WSDL documents, 515

serialize function
XML, 16
XMLHttpRequest, 12–14

server controls
AmazonSearchScriptControl server control. *See* AmazonSearchScriptControl server control
benefits of ASP.NET, 24–25
Button server control, 325
client controls emulating, 290–291
composite. *See* composite server controls
extender controls. *See* extender control
GridView, 349
HyperLink, 315
master/detail forms, 881–882
script controls. *See* script controls
TypeDescriptor, 350
UpdatePanel. *See* UpdatePanel server controls
Web service bridges. *See* AmazonSearchScriptControl server control

server response text, arriving on client-side, 1171–1192. *See also* **_onFormSubmitCompleted method**
appearance of, 1161–1170
checking type property, 1179–1184
completed method, 1172–1176
example of, 1176
_onFormSubmit method, 1171–1172
_onReadyStateChange method, 1172
parsing substrings, 1177–1179

server side methods
client-side code for invoking, 570
static limitation of, 589

<service> element, WSDL documents, 518

ServiceReference class
automatic generation of proxy classes, 608
declarative approach to adding proxy classes, 608–618
imperative approach to adding proxy classes, 618–620
parent/child pages and, 621–623
replica of, 627–629
using Service Reference replica, 649–657

Services collection
adding ServiceReference object to, 608, 621–623
imperative approach to adding ServiceReference object to, 618
parent/child pages and, 621
replica of, 625–626

set_alternateText method, Image client controls, 300

set_argument method, Button client control, 326

set_body method
beginRequest event, 1104
WebRequest class, 459

set_command method, Button client control, 326–327

set_data method, DataControl class, 1353–1355

set_dataIndex method
  DataControl class, 1356–1357
  ListView control, 1450–1451
  onBubbleEvent method, 1364–1365
set_default failed callback method,
    WebServiceProxy class, 536
set_default succeeded callback method,
    WebServiceProxy class, 536
set_element method, Behavior class, 669
set_events method, WebRequestExecutor
    class, 461
set_eventSource method, initializeObject
    method, 1314
setFocus method, ListView control, 1455–1456
SetFocus method, PageRequestManager,
    1152–1154
set_headers method, WebRequestExecutor
    class, 460
set_height method, Image client controls,
    299–300
set_httpVerb method, WebRequest class, 458
set_id method
  Behavior class, 671
  Control base class, 284
  INotifyPropertyChanged interface, 233–234
set_imageURI method, Image client controls,
    299
set_imageURL method, Image client
    controls, 307–308
setLocation method, DomElement, 172–175
set_mouseOverImageURL methods, Image client
    controls, 308
set_name method, Behavior class, 669–670
set_navigateURL property, HyperLink client
    controls, 315
SetNoServerCaching method,
    RenderPageCallback method, 1117
setOwner method, actions, 1333
set_parent method, Control base class, 284
set_path, WebServiceProxy class, 537
_setPath method, TypeDescriptor class, 379–380
setProperty method
  SetPropertyAction, 1345
  TypeDescriptor class, 377–382
SetPropertyAction
  Action class, 1345–1346
  example using, 1336–1339
SetRenderMethodDelegate method, 1117
setRequestHeader method, XMLHttpRequest, 7
set_rowIndex method, GridViewRow control, 339

set_target method, Action class, 1339
set_text method, Label client controls,
    292–293
set_Text method, TextBoxWatermarkBehavior
    class, 697–698
setTimeout method, 1455–1456
set_timeout method
  WebRequest class, 459, 492
  WebServiceProxy class, 535–536
set_url method, WebRequest class, 458, 492
set_visibilityMode method, Control base class,
    286–287
set_visible method, Control base class, 287
set_WatermarkText method, 702
set_webRequest method, WebRequestExecutor
    class, 464
set_width method, Image client controls, 299
ShoppingCart class, 142–143
  adding event handlers, 158–159
  addShoppingCartItem method, 156–157
  event programming base classes, 138
  get_events method, 155
  implementation of, 142–143
  initialize method of ShoppingCart class, 155
  methods, 154
  onShoppingcartInitialized method, 155–156
  onShoppingCartItemAdded method, 158
  onShoppingCartItemAdding method, 158
  removing event handlers, 159
  supporting events, 144–152
ShoppingCartItem class, 141–142
  event programming base classes, 138
  properties and methods, 141–144
ShoppingCartItemAddedEventArgs event, event
    data class, 153–154
ShoppingCartItemAdding event, event data
    class, 152
simple properties, control states and, 898
SkinID property, MasterDetailField data control,
    940
SOAP messages, 518–533
  client-side code and, 518
  example of page exchanging SOAP messages
    with Web service, 525–528
  HTTP request message, 518–521
  HTTP response message, 519–521
  overview, 518
  submitCallback function and, 528–533
  WSDL documents determining methods,
    parameters, and return value of, 522–525

<span> HTML element
example page containing, 660–661
Label client controls and, 291
_splitNodeIntoArray method, page postback, 1185
startsWith, string types, 40
_startTimeout method, TaskManager class,
1432–1433
state management methods
BaseMasterDetailControl, 897–900
HtmlGeneratorScriptControl, 809–811
static methods
array types, 28
Behavior class, 674–675
Component base class, 661–662
server side and, 589
static methods, DomEvent class, 189
addHandler method, 189–193
addHandlers method, 194–197
clearHandlers method, 197
removeHandler method, 193–194
status property, XMLHttpRequest, 6
statusText property, XMLHttpRequest, 7
stopPropagation method, DomEvent class,
201–203
_storeOriginalFormAction method, 1045
string types, 39–41
& symbol separating, 492
creating custom exceptions, 71
endsWith, 39
formatting, 41
overview, 39
startsWith, 40
trim, 40–41
StringBuilder class
append method, 387
applendLine method, 387
clear method, 387
constructor, 387
CustomTable client control, 394
CustomTable client control and, 394
example of page using, 388–389
IsEmpty method, 388
overview, 385–387
pageLoadedHandler, 1063
toString method, 388–389
strings, JSON, 21–22
style
applying to container controls, 896
ControlStyle property, 939–940
CustomTable template data control, 1387

styles, BaseMasterDetailControl
overriding ControlStyle method, 902
overriding CreateControlStyle method, 902
styles, ListView control, 1401–1402, 1423–
1424, 1444–1447
subclasses, UpdatePane, 1001
Submit button, page postback via, 1040–1041
submit method, _doPostBack function
invoking, 1041
submitCallback function
in client-server communication example,
491–492
HTTP request message and, 528–533
Web requests using, 491–492
XMLHttpRequest, 11–12
Sys.CancelEventArgs class, 132–133
Sys.EventHandlerList class. *See* **EventHandlerList**
class
Sys.IDisposable interface. *See* **IDisposable**
interface
Sys.INotifyDisposing interface. *See*
INotifyDisposing interface
Sys.INotifyPropertyChange interface. *See*
INotifyPropertyChanged interface
Sys.Net.WebServiceProxy class. *See*
WebServiceProxy class
Sys.Preview.UI namespace. *See* **Preview.UI**
namespace
System.ComponentModel.CancelEventArgs
class. *See* **ComponentModel class**
System.EventArgs class. *See* **EventArgs class**
Sys.UI.Behavior, 281
Sys.UI.Control, 281

T

table rows
applying to ListView control, 1424–1429
GridViewRow control, 337
TableCell, MasterDetailContainer derived
from, 891
TableProvider class, DOM extensions, 216–217
tables
custom control. *See* CustomTable client control
data tables. *See* DataTable class
TagKey property, BaseMasterDetailControl
overriding, 902
target server control, of extender control,
711, 740
target URL, WebRequest class, 458

_TaskManager, ListView control, **1430–1434**
<tbody> DOM element, **1425**
<td> DOM element, **1425–1429**
Template class
    constructor, 1375
    ITemplate interface, 1375
template containers, 987
template properties, ListView control, 1402–1403, 1447–1450
templated controls, 1373–1399
    constructor, 1375
    createInstance method, 1377–1380
    developing custom template, 1380–1383
    developing custom templated data control, 1383–1393
    ITemplate interface, 1373–1374
    methods, 1373
    parseFromMarkup method, 1376–1377
    partial page rendering, 987–994
    Template type, 1375
    TemplateInstance class, 1374
TemplateField custom template, 1380–1383
    constructor, 1381
    headerText property, 1381–1382
    JavaScript file for, 1380–1381
    parseFromMarkup method, 1382–1383
    using, 1391–1393
TemplateInstance class, ITemplate interface, 1374
text
    Label client controls, 292–293
    server response, 1161–1170
    set_Text method, 697–698
    WatermarkText methods, 702
TextBox control
    editing foreign key fields, 932
    page containing DropDownList server control and, 1098–1099
TextBoxWatermarkBehavior class
    _applyWatermark method, 694–695
    clearText method, 692–693
    dispose method, 700–702
    example page using, 703–706
    initialize method, 688–691
    _onBlur method, 693–694
    _onFocus method, 691–692
    _onKeyPress method, 695
    _onPropertyChanged method, 696–697
    _onSubmit method, 700
    overview, 687–688
    _partialUpdateEndRequest method, 698–700
    registerPropertyChanged method, 695–696
    set_Text method, 697–698
    WatermarkCssClass method, 702–703
    WatermarkText method, 702
TextBoxWatermarkExtenderControl. See extender control, custom
TextBoxWatermarkScriptControl. See script controls, custom
TextProvider, DOM extensions, 184–185
themes
    applying to controls, 918–919
    MasterDetailField data control, 940
timeout methods
    default timeout in WebRequestManager class, 469
    WebRequest class, 459
    WebServiceProxy class, 535–536
toggleCssClass method
    Control class, 288
    CustomTable template data control, 1391
    DomElement methods, 169–171
    InvokeMethodAction, 1343–1344
    render method, 1388–1389
toolkit. See control toolkit
toString method, StringBuilder class, 388–389
ToString transformer, 1327–1328
toUpperCase method
    _getTagType method using, 1280
    initializeObject method, 1314
<tr> DOM element, 1425–1429
TrackViewState method
    BaseMasterDetailControl, 899
    HtmlGeneratorScriptControl, 810–811
Transform method, XmlBridgeTransformer, 824–825
Transform method, XsltBridgeTransformer, 848–849
transformers, 1325–1326
    BridgeTransformData class, 820–822
    code listing, 813–814
    Compare transformer, 1329
    CompareInverted transformer, 1329
    IBridgeResponseTransformer interface, 819–820
    Invert transformer, 1328–1329
    Invoke method instantiating, 819
    steps in adding for specific method, 818–819
    summary, 855

transformers (continued)
 tasks performed for each transform element in .
  asbx files, 821–823
 ToString transformer, 1327–1328
 transformation of return value of method calls,
  817–818
 XmlBridgeTransformer. See
  XmlBridgeTransformer
 XsltBridgeTransformer. See
  XsltBridgeTransformer
transition property, Image client controls,
 310–311
TreeView server control
 in custom composite user control,
  946, 956
 displaying all messages, 957
triggerChangeEvents method
 addItem method, 1359
 DataControl class, 1350–1351
 deleteCurrentItem method, 1361
 moveNext method, 1363
 movePrevious method, 1363–1364
 set_data method, 1354
triggers, UpdatePanel
 ChildrenAsTriggers property, 863–864
 triggers causing asynchronous page postback,
  877–878
 UpdatePanelTrigger, 1000, 1004–1011,
  1014–1018
 UpdatePanelTriggerCollection, 998–1000
trim, string types, 40–41
true values, JSON, 21–22
try-catch-finally blocks, 41
Type class
 isClass method, 84
 JavaScript OOP and type reflection
  extensions, 80
 parse method, 125
type description
 dynamic injection of metadata information with,
  399–400
 ICustomTypeDescriptor class, 403–405
 StringBuilder class in implementation of, 385
 TypeDescriptor. See TypeDescriptor class
type parameter
 create method of Component base class, 249,
  276, 662
 HyperLink client controls, 320
 Image client control, 301, 313
type property, 1179–1184

type reflection extensions, JavaScript. *See* **OOP**
 and type reflection extensions
TypeDescriptor class
 addAttribute method, 403
 addEvent method, 402–403
 addMethod method, 401–402
 addProperty method, 400–401
 append method, 371–374
 constructor, 350
 CustomTable client control, 389–399
 _events, 364–368
 generateDescriptor method, 370–371
 getAttributed method, 376–377
 getProperty method, 374–376
 getPropertyType method, 384–385
 getTypeDescriptor method, 369–370
 initializeObject method, 1287–1288, 1298
 invokeMethod method, 382–384
 InvokeMethodAction invoking, 1342–1343
 _methods, 358–364
 overview, 349
 _properties, 351–358
 setProperty method, 377–382
 SetPropertyAction invoking, 1345
<types> element, WSDL documents, 514–515

U

UI.Behavior, Component class, 281
UI.Control, Component class, 281
UniqueID properties, server controls, 1098
_uniqueIDToClientID method
 _doPostBack method, 1079
 PageRequestManager, 1049
unload event, Application class, 260
Update method, Update Panel server, 1122
_updateControls method
 page postbacks, 1185, 1228–1230
 PageRequestManager, 1046–1049
updated method, behaviors, 664
UpdatePanel
 add method for UpdatePanelTriggerCollection,
  1003–1004
 constructor of UpdatePanelTriggerCollection,
  1001
 ControlTemplate property, 987
 CreateContents method, 984–987
 Initialize method, 998
 Initialize method of UpdatePanelTrigger, 1000,
  1004–1011

Initialize method of
UpdatePanelTriggerCollection, 998–1000
OnInit method, 980–982
OnLoad method, 996–997
owner property of UpdatePanelTriggerCollection,
1002–1003
RegisterPanel method, 982–983
Render method, 1028–1029
subclasses of UpdatePanelTrigger, 1001
TreeView and DetailView as children of, 946
UpdatePanelControlTrigger class, 1004
_updatePanel method
page postbacks, 1199–1200, 1230–1231
server response text arriving on
client-side, 1187
UpdatePanel server controls
attaching movers to, 1066–1067
BaseMasterDetailControl2. See
BaseMasterDetailControl2 server control
checking type property, 1179–1184
children as triggers, 863–864
code listing for page using conditional updates,
862–863
code listing for page using two UpdatePanel
server controls, 860–861
direct inclusion of one UpdatePanels in another
UpdatePanel, 864–867
EncodeString method call triggered by, 1156
imperative updates, 878–881
implementing IPostBackDataHandler, 1109
indirect inclusion of one UpdatePanels in
another UpdatePanel via content page,
871–876
indirect inclusion of one UpdatePanels in
another UpdatePanel via user control,
868–871
master server control contained in, 893
partial page rendering and, 857
RenderControl method of, 1129–1131
triggers causing asynchronous page postback,
877–878
_updatePanel method, 1199–1200
updating, 1184
UpdatePanelControlTrigger class, 1004
updatePanelIDs, 1181
updatePanelNodes array, 1187
UpdatePanelTrigger
custom, 1014–1018
Initialize method, 1000, 1004–1011
subclasses, 1001

UpdatePanelTriggerCollection
add method, 1003–1004
constructor, 1001
Initialize method, 998–1000
owner property, 1002–1003
triggers causing asynchronous page
postback, 877
updates. See UpdatePanel
URLs
<port> element for specifying, 517
target URL for Web requests, 537
user controls
UpdatePanel server control as parent of,
869–871
UpdatePanel server control encapsulated
in, 868
user controls, partial-rendering enabled, 945
code listing, 947–952
deleting a message, 959–960
displaying all messages, 957–958
displaying details of a message, 958–959
overview, 945–946
replying to a message, 961–962
starting new thread, 963–964
updating a message, 960–961
XML document that stores message, 953–957

V

_value collection, StringBuilder class, 385,
387–388
virtual methods, C#, 104
VisibilityMode properties, Control class,
286–287

W

W3C, event propagation model, 202
WatermarkCssClass method
custom extender control, 754
TextBoxWatermarkBehavior class, 702–703
watermarks. See TextBoxWatermarkBehavior
class
WatermarkText methods
custom extender control, 754
TextBoxWatermarkBehavior class, 702
Web methods
.asmx file extension for, 564
invoking, 537–538
wrapper methods as, 564

Web pages
  MasterDetailControl server control used in, 916–921
  visiting partial-page-rendering enabled Web page, 971
Web service bridges
  client control component. *See* AspNetAjaxAmazonSearch client control
  defined, 564
  demystified, 591–593
  HtmlGenerator client component. *See* HtmlGenerator client control
  HtmlGenerator server component. *See* HtmlGeneratorScriptControl server control
  overview of, 781
  server control component. *See* AmazonSearchScriptControl server control
  steps in using, 564–565
  using bridge-enabled script server components, 811–812
  wrapper methods and, 570
Web services
  building, 511–512
  calling custom methods, 564–570
  calling page methods, 561–563
  client-side code for invoking server side methods, 570
  consuming via JSON messages, 535
  example of page exchanging SOAP messages with Web service, 525–528
  example page using WebServiceError class, 557–561
  HandlerWrapper, 582–583
  obtaining data records from, 1417–1422
  overview, 511
  proxy classes associated with, 600–605
  RestHandler, 577–582
  RestHandlerFactory, 574–577
  ScriptHandlerFactory, 571–574
  ScriptModule, 583–591
  SOAP messages. *See* SOAP messages
  transformers. *See* transformers
  using replicas of HTTP handler factories, 593–595
  WebServiceError class, 553–556
  WebServiceProxy class. *See* WebServiceProxy class
  wrapping a custom class, 591–592
  WSDL documents. *See* WSDL documents
Web services, Amazon E-commerce
  ItemSearch, 774–781
  overview of, 773–774
web.config file, 573–574, 583–584
WebControl class, 896
WebRequest class
  abort method, 506–508
  body of request, 459
  in client-server communication example, 492
  client-side code for downloading WSDL documents and loading into XMLDOM documents, 524
  completed event, 461–462
  completion of Web request, 494
  constructor, 457–458
  example page using, 487–490
  executor methods, 460
  headers, 460
  HTTP verb, 458–459
  invoking Web requests, 462–463
  overview, 457
  submitCallback function instantiating, 492
  target URL, 458
  timeout methods, 459
  WebServiceProxy class encapsulating logic of, 535
WebRequest object, 1172–1176
WebRequestExecutor class
  abort method, 467
  client-side code for downloading WSDL documents and loading into XMLDOM documents, 524
  completion of Web requests, 494
  constructor, 463
  example page using, 497–498
  executeRequest method, 467
  get_aborted method, 465
  getAllResponseHeaders method, 468
  get_object method, 466–467
  get_responseAvailable method, 464–465
  get_responseData method, 465
  getResponseHeader method, 467–468
  get_started method, 464
  get_statusCode method, 466
  get_statusText method, 466
  get_timeOut method, 465
  get_xml method, 466
  overview, 463
  referencing WebRequest object, 463–464
  requestCompleted event, 493

WebRequestExecutor object, 1172–1176
WebRequestManager class, 498–502
    client-side code for downloading WSDL
        documents and loading into XMLDOM
        documents, 524
    constructor, 468–469
    default executor type, 469
    default timeout, 469
    events, 470–471
    executing Web request, 471–473
    NetworkRequestEventArgs class, 473–474
    overview, 468
    single instance of, 498–502
    WebServiceProxy class encapsulating logic
        of, 535
WebServiceError class
    code listing, 555
    constructor, 555–556
    example page using, 557–561
    onComplete method and, 553–554
WebServiceHandlerFactory, 572–573
WebServiceProxy class
    add function for instantiating, 552–553
    constructor, 535
    _createQueryString method of WebRequest
        class, 544–545
    _createUrl method of WebRequest class, 543
    default failed callback methods, 536
    default succeeded callback methods, 536
    example page using, 549–551
    _invoke method, 537–538
    invoke method, 539–542
    onComplete method, 545–549
    overview, 535
    path methods, 537
    proxy classes deriving from, 602
    timeout methods, 535–536
    Web service used by example page, 551–552
width property, Image client controls, 299
Window class, client-server communication, 509
wrapper methods
    choices for placing, 564
    Web service bridges and, 570
    Web service wrapping a custom class, 591–592
**WriteXml method, IXmlSerializable interface,
    839, 842**
WSDL documents, 512–518. *See also* **SOAP
    messages**
    argument names, types, and order, 514–515
    client-side code and, 524

    communication protocol determined by, 519
    communication protocol used by method,
        516–517
    <definitions> element, 514
    describing XML Web service, 513–514
    information about XML Web service methods,
        512–513
    method, parameters, and return value of SOAP
        messages determined by, 522
    request and response messages in method,
        515–516
    return value types and order, 515
    site for method access, 517–518
    specifying method class, 518

X

x and y coordinates
    DomElement getBounds method, 175–176
    DomElement getLocation method, 171
    DomElement setLocation method, 172–175
XHTML, 1–2
XML (eXtensible Markup Language)
    AJAX-enabled components and, 2
    code listing, 16–18
    deserialize function, 18–20
    serialize and deserialize functions in, 16
    transformer. *See* XmlBridgeTransformer
XML documents
    bridge element, 565–567
    SOAP messages and, 518
    user controls, partial-rendering enabled,
        953–957
XML namespace
    _getTagType method, 1279–1281
    _processNamespaceURI method, 1281–1283
XML Schema, serializing. *See* **XmlSerializer**
XML Web services
    SOAP messages. *See* SOAP messages
    WSDL documents. *See* WSDL documents
XmlAttribute, metadata attribute, 833
XmlBridgeTransformer, 823–848
    code listing, 823–824
    example (HtmlGenerator2 client control),
        826–827
    overview of, 823
    provided by ASP.NET AJAX framework, 818
    serializing XML Schema correctly. *See*
        XmlSerializer
    Transform method, 824–825

XmlDataSource control, 954–957
XMLDOM class, 474–475, 524
XMLDOM document, 1274
XMLHttpExecutor class, 475–487
    abort method, 485–487
    _clearTimer method, 477
    constructor, 475–476
    default executor type, 469
    executeRequest method, 479–482
    get_aborted method, 479
    getAllResponseHeaders method, 483
    get_responseAvailable method, 479
    get_responseData method, 483
    getResponseHeader method, 482–483
    get_started method, 479
    get_statusCode method, 484
    get_statusText method, 484
    get_timeOut method, 478
    get_xml method, 484–485
    _onReadyStateChange method, 476–477
    _onTimeout method, 477–478
    overview, 475
    page using WebRequestExecutor, 497–498
    WebServiceProxy class encapsulating logic
        of, 535
XMLHttpRequest class, 4–15
    characteristics of AJAX-enabled
        components, 2
    in client-server communication, 474
    code listing, 6–10
    deserialize function, 14–15
    instantiation process, 4
    methods and properties, 5–6
    serialize function, 12–14
    submitCallback function, 11–12
XMLHttpRequest methods and properties,
    AJAX, 5–6
XmlSchemaProvider, 839

xml-script, 1272–1315
    binding in. See binding
    _getDefaultNamespaces method, 1283
    _getTagType method, 1279–1281
    __initHandler method, 1273
    initializeObject method, 1287–1315
    MarkupContext class, 1267–1272
    overview of, 1267
    parseFromMarkup method, 1284–1287
    parseNode method, 1278–1279
    parseNodes method, 1276–1277
    processDocument method, 1273–1275
    processDocumentScripts method, 1275–1276
    _processNamespaceURI method, 1281–1283
    starting script, 1272–1273
XmlSerializer, 828–848
    code listing for AmazonService2 class,
        829–832
    IXmlSerializable interface as approach to
        communication with, 839–848
    methods for communicating with, 828
    Results and Result classes as approach to
        communication with, 832–839
XPath
    DetailsView control and, 959
    hierarchical or location path for identifying tree
        nodes, 955
xsd.exe utility, 837
XsltBridgeTransformer, 848–855
    AmazonSearch4.asbx code listing, 851
    AmazonSearch4.aspx code listing, 855
    AmazonService4 class, 852–854
    code listing, 850–851
    overview of, 840

Y

y coordinates. See x and y coordinates